Borland®
C++Builder™ 4

Kent Reisdorph, et al.

SAMS

Unleashed

Borland® C++Builder™ 4 Unleashed

Copyright © 1999 by Sams Publishing

International Standard Book Number: 0-672-31510-6

Library of Congress Catalog Card Number: 98-87917

Printed in the United States of America

First Printing: June 1999

01   00   99   4   3   2   1

Trademarks

Warning and Disclaimer

EXECUTIVE EDITORS
Brian Gill
Don Roche

ACQUISITIONS EDITOR
Carol Ackerman

DEVELOPMENT EDITORS
Gus Miklos
Heather Goodell

MANAGING EDITOR
Lisa Wilson

PROJECT EDITOR
Rebecca M. Mounts

COPY EDITORS
Tonya Maddox
Kelli M. Brooks
Charles Hutchinson
Sean Medlock

INDEXER
Kevin Fulcher

PROOFREADER
Maryann Steinhart

TECHNICAL EDITORS
Ellie Peters
Robert West

SOFTWARE DEVELOPMENT SPECIALIST
Dan Scherf

INTERIOR DESIGNER
Gary Adair

COVER DESIGNER
Aren Howell

COPY WRITER
Eric Borgert

LAYOUT TECHNICIANS
Brian Borders
Susan Geiselman
Eric S. Miller
Heather Hiatt Miller

Overview

Contents

4 C++ TEMPLATES 123

5 THREADS 179

About the Authors

Kent Reisdorph is the author of *Sams Teach Yourself Borland C++Builder 4 in 24 Hours* and *Sams Teach Yourself Borland Delphi 4 in 21 Days*. Kent is a Senior Engineer at TurboPower Software, a leading borland.com product-based development company. He is also one of several independent programmers and consultants on borland.com's TeamB, an outside group that works closely with borland.com on product development and provides online support to borland.com developers and programmers.

Bruneau Babet joined Borland in 1990. He currently works on the C++Builder and Delphi projects focusing on Type Libraries and ActiveX.

Charlie Calvert is a best-selling author and well-respected programming guru. He is the author of *Charlie Calvert's Delphi 4 Unleashed, C++Builder 3 Unleashed, Delphi 2 Unleashed*, and *Sams Teach Yourself Windows 95 Programming in 21 Days*. His day job is at Inprise International, where he works as a manager in Developer Relations.

Jeff Cottingham is currently working as a Developer in Santa Cruz, California. He spent many years prior to this working in Developer Support at Borland.

Jody Hagins is a software engineer for Automated Trading Desk, in Mt. Pleasant, South Carolina. He earned a B.S. in Mathematics and Computer Science from the University of South Carolina, and an M.S. in Computer Science from Vanderbilt University. He has been using Borland tools since 1986, and has been programming professionally in C/C++ for more than 10 years on projects ranging from Unix kernel internals to telephony switching systems to real-time financial models. As a member of Borland's TeamB, he can be found in the C++Builder newsgroups.

Harold Howe lives in Des Moines, Iowa, and received a B.S. in Electrical Engineering from Iowa State in 1994. He began using Borland C++Builder in 1996, after using Turbovision and OWL with Borland C++ 4.5 and C++ 5. Harold co-authored *C++Builder How-To*, and he maintains bcbdev.com, a C++Builder Web site.

Dana S. Kaufman is a principal consultant for the Inprise Professional Services Organization and the former Chief Technology Officer of Apogee Information Systems, an Inprise Premier Integrator Partner. Dana specializes in the design and development of multitier solutions using the Inprise suite of products. He has delivered presentations on Borland tools development at conferences in the USA, Canada, U.K., and the Netherlands and has been published in several industry journals. Dana has a BSEE from Clarkson University.

Bob Swart (aka Dr. Bob—www.drbob42.com) is a professional knowledge engineer and technical consultant using Delphi, JBuilder and C++Builder for Bolesian (www.bolesian.com). Bob is a freelance technical author for *The Delphi Magazine* and the *UK-BUG* newsletter, and co-author of *The Revolutionary Guide to Delphi 2* and *Delphi 4 Unleashed*.

About the Technical Editors

Ellie M. Peters is a Senior Quality Assurance engineer at Portera Systems. She was formerly with Borland/Inprise Corporation, where she was a quality assurance engineer for Borland C++Builder and Delphi products. She holds a computer science degree from the University of California, Santa Cruz.

Robert West is a Quality Assurance engineer for Borland/Inprise Corporation and specializes in ActiveX and DCOM enabling technologies. A graduate of the University of California, Santa Cruz, he holds a degree in political science.

Dedication

As always, I dedicate this book to my wife, Jennifer. It is only through her support that my books exist. There is no other person I would consider dedicating a book to. It has always been her love and support that keep me going when things get hectic. Thanks, Jen, one more time, for all you do for me.—Kent Reisdorph

Acknowledgments

People at Macmillan I'd like to thank include Brian Gill, Carol Ackerman, and Don Roche. These three individuals shared in the always-interesting job of making sure that work on the book stayed on course. I'd also like to thank Gus Miklos of Macmillan. As the development editor for the book, it was Gus's job to take our ramblings and mold them into a complete book. This is the second book I've worked on with Gus and I have enjoyed every minute of it (well, *almost* every minute). Gus really knows how to take raw author material and turn it into an end product to be proud of. I'd also like to thank Heather Goodell, who stepped in to help us out with development editing so that we could meet our deadlines.

The technical editors of this book were Ellie Peters and Robert West. Ellie is easily the best technical editor I've ever dealt with. I've come to think of Ellie as *my* technical editor and I would hesitate to do a book without her involvement. In addition, she's one of the nicest people I know and I am thankful to have her as a friend. Robert West also did a great job on this book. I've known Robert just about as long as I've known Ellie and I'm glad he was available to help out with some of the book's technical editing.

The list of contributing authors for this book is substantial. Some of the book's more difficult subjects were handled by Bruneau Babet of Borland. I'm not sure Bruneau knew what he was getting into when he agreed to do the COM and ActiveX chapters, but I'm very thankful for his help. Bob Swart also wrote more than one of the book's more difficult chapters. Thanks to Bob for his willingness to take on additional work when it became necessary. Dana Kaufman helped on the chapters dealing with CORBA. Dana stepped in when we needed some fast help on the CORBA chapters and for that I'm in his debt. Dana, the next time we're in Toronto the festivities are on me. Jeff Cottingham (aka Goldilocks) was also instrumental in writing portions of the book. Last, but certainly not least, I want to thank my fellow TeamB members, Harold Howe and Jody Hagins. Harold and Jody coauthored the chapter on C++ templates—an important subject due to C++Builder 4's new template support.

As always, I have to give my most sincere thanks to my wife, Jennifer. I cannot understate the importance of Jennifer's contribution to my writing efforts. Without her support it would not be possible for me to continue writing these books. I keep promising her that someday I will give her and our children the proper amount of attention. It will happen some day, Jen!

Finally, I want to thank Charlie Calvert for providing the material that makes up the bulk of this book. Charlie wasn't directly involved in the manual process of putting this book together this time around. However, much of the book is his creation and as such he deserves credit for a good part of the book in its final form.—*Kent Reisdorph*

I would like to thank Gus A. Miklos of Macmillan Computer Publishing for being one of the best development editors I've ever worked with. I would also like to thank Nan Borreson, the former Borland/Inprise publishing relations manager, without whom I would've never known the excitement of reviewing technical books. I'm honored to have had this as my fourth opportunity to work with the best author I've ever known, Kent Reisdorph. Kent's also become a great friend over the past few years. Last but not least, I would like to thank my husband, Jeff, who's always there for me.—*Ellie Peters*

Tell Us What You Think!

As the reader of this book, *you* are our most important critic and commentator. We value your opinion and want to know what we're doing right, what we could do better, what areas you'd like to see us publish in, and any other words of wisdom you're willing to pass our way.

As an Executive Editor for Sams, I welcome your comments. You can fax, email, or write me directly to let me know what you did or didn't like about this book—as well as what we can do to make our books stronger.

Please note that I cannot help you with technical problems related to the topic of this book, and that due to the high volume of mail I receive, I might not be able to reply to every message.

When you write, please be sure to include this book's title and author as well as your name and phone or fax number. I will carefully review your comments and share them with the author and editors who worked on the book.

Fax: (317) 581-4770

Email: droche@mcp.com

Mail: Don Roche
            Executive Editor
            Sams Publishing
            201 West 103rd Street
            Indianapolis, IN 46290 USA

Introduction to C++Builder 4 Unleashed

Welcome to *C++Builder 4 Unleashed*! Our goal for this incarnation of the book is twofold. First, we want this book to contain information on C++Builder programming that is not otherwise readily available in print. Second, we want this book to live up to its name. We removed material that was of an introductory nature and replaced it with more advanced material. We trust that you will find the changes favorable ones.

The chapters attributed to Charlie Calvert and myself (or other contributing authors) were written primarily by Charlie. We began with Charlie's text (from the previous edition) and updated it for C++Builder 4, ensured that the examples work properly, and made other revisions relevant to this latest release of the C++Builder software.

Additional C++Builder 4 Resources

The Internet is obviously a great place for obtaining information on C++Builder programming. Three C++Builder Web sites come immediately to mind. The first is The Bits at `http://www.cbuilder.dthomas.co.uk`. This is one of the premier destinations for C++Builder programmers on the Internet. The second Web site that comes to mind is fellow TeamB member Harold Howe's BCBDEV.COM at `http://www.bcbdev.com`. Third, but certainly not least, is Bob Swart's Dr. Bob's C++Builder Gate at `http://www.drbob42.com/cbuilder`. These Web sites contain links to other C++Builder sites.

You can also check my Web site, `http://www.reisdorph.com/bcb`, for updates on this book. The site contains errata for all my books and links to articles I have written. You will also want to check out the Borland Web site at `http://www.borland.com` and the Inprise Web site at `http://www.inprise.com`.

You can never have too many books on C++Builder programming. I recommend the following C++Builder books:

> *Sams Teach Yourself C++Builder 3 in 21 Days* by Kent Reisdorph; Sams Publishing
>
> *C++Builder How-To* by Miano, Howe, and Cabanski; Waite Group Press

It shouldn't come as any surprise that I recommend my own book. The reason I do, however, is not because of ego, but because literally hundreds of people have told me how much it has helped them. Don't let the book's title fool you. It has a fair amount of information in the intermediate-level category. I'll add that while this book was written for C++Builder 3, 90% of it or more is applicable to C++Builder 4.

C++Builder How-To is another good book that every C++Builder programmer should have. This book was originally written for C++Builder 1, but the material presented is not version-specific so you won't have any trouble using it with C++Builder 4.

If you are interested in more information on component writing, I suggest these books:

> *Developing Custom Delphi Components*, by Ray Konopka; The Coriolis Group
>
> *Delphi Component Design*, by Danny Thorpe; Addison Wesley

You may have noticed that both of these books have *Delphi* in their titles. True enough, they are books on writing components in Delphi, but don't let that put you off. These books have great information on writing components and that information applies to writing components in both Delphi and C++Builder.

I also want to encourage you to investigate the *C++Builder Developer's Journal*. This journal is a great source of information on C++Builder programming. I have written a large portion of the journal for the past two years. The journal has many other highly qualified contributing authors and every serious C++Builder programmer should check it out. As I write this, the journal is in the process of being transitioned from Ziff-Davis Education to another publishing company. For that reason it is difficult for me to point you to a specific Web site for information on the journal. You can always find the latest contact information for the journal on my Web site at http://www.reisdorph.com/bcb.

Differences in C++Builder 4 Versions

This book focuses on the features found in the Professional and Enterprise versions of C++Builder. Some of the topics covered apply to all versions of C++Builder, some to the Professional and Enterprise versions, and some topics apply only to the Enterprise version. We don't specifically identify the versions of C++Builder that a particular chapter applies to, but a quick look at the C++Builder feature matrix on the Borland Web site will make this readily apparent.

C++Builder 4 is a great C++ Windows compiler and I'm sure you'll find writing programs with it both very enjoyable and profitable. I trust you will find this book entertaining to read as well as highly informative.

Special Conventions Used in the Book

There are several special conventions used in this book to make it easier to read and understand. Look for these special conventions throughout the book to enhance your learning experience.

Shortcut Key Combinations. In this book, shortcut key combinations are joined with plus signs. For example, Ctrl+V means hold down the Ctrl key while pressing the V key.

Typefaces. This book also has the following typeface enhancements to indicate special text, as shown in the following table:

Typeface	Description
Italic	Italics are used to indicate new terms.
Boldface	This bold typeface is used to indicate text you type.
`Computer Type`	This typeface is used for onscreen messages, commands, and code.
`Computer Italic Type`	This typeface is used to indicate placeholders in code and commands.

Code Continuation Characters. There are many C++Builder program listings in this book. Because of space limitations, some of the code lines had to be wrapped (continued on the next line). However, in actual use, you would enter this code as one extended line without a line break. To indicate such lines, a special code continuation character (➡) has been used. When you see this character at the beginning of a line, it means that line should be added, as one line, to the line that precedes it.

CHAPTER 1

Program Design Basics

by Charlie Calvert

Welcome to *C++Builder 4 Unleashed*. This book is about Rapid Application Development (RAD) Windows programming in C++ using C++Builder, the world's greatest C++ programming tool.

I doubt that this book lives up to its subject matter, but I will try to make it as entertaining, lively, and informative as possible. The text covers intermediate and advanced programming topics, including discussions of the following:

- Component creation
- COM and distributed computing
- Database programming
- Internet programming
- General programming issues
- Graphics and DirectX programming

As always, my goal is to talk about these subjects in clear, easy-to-understand language that makes difficult topics accessible. Whenever possible, I try to use a friendly, conversational tone so that you will feel comfortable and at ease while exploring a wide range of technical subjects.

This chapter features introductory material describing the subject matter of this book. I also talk briefly about designing applications. These latter, more theoretical portions of the chapter focus on the proper use of object-oriented technologies.

The Structure of This Book

C++Builder comes equipped with an excellent online reference featuring context-sensitive help. This book is therefore not necessarily a reference. It is also not a tutorial, although occasionally I use short tutorial-like sections to walk you through the steps of a wizard or some relatively mundane but essential procedure.

Thus, throughout this book, I use a more narrative style that is meant to be read quietly while sitting in a comfortable chair, lying on a bed, soaking in a bath or hot tub, or even while catching rays at the beach. I don't expect you to read the book from cover to cover because that is not the approach technical people, including myself, take with this kind of documentation. Instead, I wrote this book so that you can read it one chapter—or one portion of a chapter—at a time.

Without first reading the chapters, you will probably find them frustrating for immediate use as a simple reference. I recommend taking this book to some quiet place and reading a chapter through from the beginning, going back to the computer and playing with the sample programs, and finally, creating your own programs based on the things you have learned.

This book takes a conceptual view of the material under discussion. I want to show you how something works and why it works that way. I believe that you can always figure out how things work after understanding the theory behind the technology. For instance, in one section of this book, I explain how and when to use something called a *type library*. If I were creating a pure reference, I would just give you a list of when to use and when not to use type libraries. I don't take that approach. Instead, I explain what a type library is, why it exists, and how it helps with core tasks such as marshaling data. After you understand all these things, you don't need a list of when to use a type library; all you have to do is apply the theoretical knowledge I have given you. From there you can figure out when a type library is needed and when it is not needed.

Readers who are desperate to get past the theoretical portions of the chapters will find that I usually start a chapter with two to six pages of introduction, overview, and theory. After that, I illustrate my points with specific examples. This means you can almost always skip ahead a few pages to find code listings and demonstrations illustrating the points I make in a chapter's more prosaic opening passages.

Because this is a book about programming, I include a great deal of code. You should take the time to run these programs and to see how they relate to the material discussed in the pages of this book. As said earlier, the best way to use this book is through a combination of reading the text and running the programs.

The programs I created can be pillaged for your own uses to whatever degree you want, as long as you don't simply recycle them as training materials without first asking for my permission. Teachers in accredited schools and colleges can, of course, use this material as they want, as long as their students buy copies of the book. Programmers can reuse the code anywhere they want to whatever degree they want, as long as they are not simply taking one of my programs and reselling it with few or no modifications.

By all means, use the code I write in your own programs. I don't mind if you lift entire units or forms from my code, as long as you are not basing an entire program solely on what you find on this book's CD-ROM.

If you read a chapter in this book and then run the code from that chapter, you should have all the knowledge you need to begin doing serious work in a particular subject. Creating the programs for a chapter usually takes me as long as creating the chapter itself. Spend time with the code, study it, and use it in your own programs. The words in this book are only part of the story; the rest is on the CD-ROM that comes with the book.

Creating Well-Designed Programs

The next few sections discuss creating programs that work. This passage isn't particularly technical, unlike the subject matter of the remaining chapters. However, this text is important in that it lays out a series of themes that are referenced again and again.

Let me be specific about the three things that are important to every programmer:

- Creating a good design for your program before you write it. While writing the program, you should iteratively refine that design so that it incorporates the things you learned from your own experience and from the experience of your testers.

- Understanding the basics of object-oriented programming (OOP); encapsulation, interface design, and information hiding in particular.

- Knowing how to write and use components.

In abbreviated form, the list of important items is design, OOP, and components. I cover each of these subjects over the next few pages.

Writing Simple Code

This book's theme is based on a quote from George Sand that I keep pinned above my desk: "Simplicity is the most difficult thing to secure in this world; it is the last limit of experience, and the last effort of genius." This book was written for intermediate to advanced programmers, but my overall theme is this: "Do everything you can to keep your programs as simple as possible."

Almost every step you take in the programming world is simple. Programming appears difficult because it involves layering many simple processes on top of each other. Two simple things are a bit more complex than one simple thing. Twenty simple things are noticeably more complex than one simple thing. Ten thousand simple things placed together in one heap will seem complex to all but a handful of people. Even a simple C++Builder form consists, when you look at it deeply enough, of thousands of complicated pieces. Your goal as a programmer is to harmonize all these pieces.

This book is about finding ways to make it easy for you to create powerful programs using C++Builder 4. I strive to be modest in my goals, sparing in my use of resources, and spare in my choice of aesthetics. I strive to create programs that are simple to use and easy to understand. A good application's architecture ought to have the same simple structure as its menu system. The Parthenon is beautiful to look at, but easy to understand. That is one of the reasons it is standing after so many years and why it is universally admired. The Parthenon's architecture is based on simple architectural principles,

and I believe that C++Builder programs should be based on the same model. This book may occasionally focus on digging to the deepest and darkest parts of the machine, but I always promote doing so in a way that is simple, natural, and powerful. The goal is to achieve success gracefully and easily.

It should be obvious that the design phase is the time to determine the features of a program. It is important that, from the start, the design takes into account those features that can make a simple project more complicated than it might at first appear. For instance, I do myself a disservice if I jump in and start coding without a solid design. I might not have initially considered the need for reports, for saving state, or for creating certain kinds of graphs. If I can recognize these features as vital to the design from the start, I save myself time and effort.

I can often design something in 15 minutes or an hour, but executing it takes me an entire day—or even several days. The trap to avoid is spending several days coding something that is fundamentally flawed. If 15 or 20 minutes of careful consideration can save me two days of coding, then taking the time is well worthwhile.

Part of the design phase may mean creating a quick prototype of an application. Prototypes are very easy to create with C++Builder. A prototype allows you to design an application's look and feel without writing any code (or very little code). As you work with the prototype, you will almost certainly discover additional features your program should implement. Again, taking some time to create a prototype before actual coding begins will save you time and effort in the long run.

Following a Design Process

Sometimes I can't proceed with a design process without writing some test code. In such cases, I try a few experiments to test the validity of my theories. When I begin to see an algorithm's shape, I often stop and finalize the design. I might then write more code and once again study the design of the project.

The process ends up being iterative. Write some code, step back and look for objects, and then step back and work on design issues. Write more code; come back and work on design.

The process should ultimately end up being a spiral. You start at the bottom with a broad cycle and work in successively smaller cycles that iterate between coding and design. Each revolution should be smaller than the last, until you finally reach the top. At the peak, the cycle should narrow to a fine point that defines the correct implementation for your program.

Programming with Objects

I have made it abundantly clear that my goal is simplicity. I want my programs to be easy to use and to be based on a clear, simple architecture. The question, then, is how to achieve simplicity of design. For me, the answer is object-oriented programming (OOP), but I believe that you have to be very careful about the way this powerful technology is used.

OOP is a double-edged sword. The basic idea behind it is very valuable. (Unfortunately, many OOP programs are classic examples of how not to write code.)

Consider the following lines of code:

```
printf("Foo");
WriteLn("Foo");
```

Both statements exhibit all the features of good code. Even a nonprogrammer can understand what they do, and everyone in the programming world understands how they work and why they work that way.

Consider the following declaration:

```
class TBird {
  private:
    String FName;
    int FWeight;
    TColor FColor;
  public:
    void Fly();
    void Walk();
};
```

Everything about a declaration of this type is elegant and worthy of reverence. It is simple, clean, easy to understand, and very powerful. It ties up a set of specific features into one abstract whole that can be easily manipulated.

To understand how to work with objects, you must understand encapsulation and inheritance, and it is best if you also understand polymorphism. The most important thing you can learn is how to structure your objects properly.

An object-oriented programmer's main task is to discover objects. When I sit down to write code, my goal is to find the objects in my project and surface them. If I can find the objects in a project, I can usually complete the program in a robust manner in a short order. If I can't find the objects in a program, I usually end up writing a lot of unreliable code that needs to be rewritten.

Sometimes finding the objects in a program is easy. For instance, it was obvious that there needed to be objects in the VCL that would wrap the basic Windows components

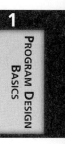

such as TEdit and TButton. Less obvious were some of the core VCL classes such as TApplication, TControl, TWinControl, TDataSet, and TPersistent.

Sometimes when you discover an object, its existence seems obvious. The need for its existence is completely beyond debate. For instance, TApplication and TDataSet strike me as inevitable objects that were simply waiting to be discovered. This does not mean that understanding that TApplication and TDataSet had to exist was easy. They had the ring of inevitability after they were discovered.

Using Event Handlers Wisely

Nothing can lead an OOP programmer down the path to destruction more quickly than the indiscriminate use of event handlers. The quest to discover objects is frustrated at every turn by the ease with which C++Builder allows you to fold code into the main form by using event handlers.

In most cases, keeping complex, low-level code out of the file in which your form is defined is a good idea. Complex, low-level code belongs in separate objects, not inside your main form.

The *source file* (a file with a CPP extension) for the main form is a good place to keep user-interface code. If you find yourself writing a lot of complex logic inside one of these source files, chances are good that you are sitting on top of an object that needs to be identified and moved into its own module.

For instance, I was recently working on a form that had a lot of complex logic regarding the reading of strings from several different resources. The code read the strings from the resources, stored them in lists, and then displayed the lists to the user. After looking at my program for a while, I came to the conclusion that the code for reading the resources and converting them into lists was really part of a separate object that had nothing to do with main form. I removed it from the form, stuck it in its own module, and then called it with code that looked like this:

```
TResourceObject* ResourceObject = new TResourceObject;
ComboBox1->Items = ResourceObject->GetItemList();
delete ResourceObject;
```

These few lines have no complicated logic in them at all. They are trouble free. All the tricky code in ResourceObject gets called from the constructor or GetItemList() method. (The exact nature of the code is not important to the current case; you just need to know that it had 40 or 50 lines of string parsing and list creation inside it.) The goal here is to use the TResourceObject to *encapsulate* that complexity in a separate object so that my form code stays clean and easy to use.

Once again, my point is not that writing tricky code is wrong, but that you should encapsulate that tricky code inside an object. That way, you can call it with little risk of making a careless error.

Another good reason to structure your programs this way is to promote reuse. Two problems would arise if I wrapped up my code for reading and parsing the resources inside a single form:

1. That form would also likely contain logic involving other processes specific to the current program. I would have no way of isolating the code that had to do with resources, but would instead mix it in with a lot of other code needed to run the form.

2. Even if I decided I could reuse the code, the only good way to reuse it would be to copy the entire form into the new project. In fact, the act of copying the form into the new project is not in itself flawed because that form would then encapsulate the logic in a convenient package. The trouble would come, however, if I needed to tweak the code in the form. In such a case, something like the following scenario would almost certainly occur:

   I might tweak the form code in such a way that it would make the form unusable in the first project. In such a case, I would need to have two copies of the code: one in the new project and one in the old. If I made fixes to one copy of the code, I would have to go back and make fixes to the same code in its other incarnation. As you well know, almost no one can be counted on to actually fix a single bug in two places, so trouble would soon arise. Conversely, I might decide to keep one copy of the code in both projects, but I would never dare customize it for use in either program on the grounds that it might compromise the other partner in the deal. As a result, I would feel artificially constrained not to fix minor interface problems for which I could easily see a remedy.

In short, encapsulating certain kinds of code inside a form is often not a good idea. Instead, you should keep the code in a separate, easy-to-access object. You can then write interface code that accesses that object from any form that you might create. You would have interface code in the form. You would have low-level code in the object. Doing things this way might force you to write a few extra lines of code one time, but it would be likely to save you a great deal of time later, when you had to customize interfaces or perform basic maintenance on the object. It also makes it easier to reuse your code.

Combing the Kinks Out of a Program

The act of discovering objects is sometimes iterative. For instance, I might be working on a form for a while and find that things are finally starting to work correctly. When I was new to programming, I used to think that meant I was nearly finished with the form. Now I tend to comb through the form looking for objects that need to be discovered and given their own scope.

Laziness often leads me astray at this point. Leaving an object buried inside another chunk of code is often simpler—at first. Only later does this laziness catch up and cause trouble.

When I have a portion of a form working correctly, most often the correct thing to do is take the code from that portion of the program out of the form and place it in its own object. This operation takes work, but it saves more work later on. I can go back and work on the form some more. Over time, I will once again have to comb through the form looking for hidden objects.

I was recently performing a lot of relatively complex calculations on an array. After a time, I discovered that the array really needed to be in a separate object so that I could write code that looked like this:

```
TGridArray* GridArray = new TGridArray;
AResult = GridArray->PerformCalculations(Data1, Data2, Data3);
delete GridArray;
```

Now a portion of the work that was embedded in my form was encapsulated inside the `TGridArray` object.

When I first performed this operation, it seemed like a lot of painful work that wasn't yielding many results. Later, however, I found that I needed to create a series of `TDailyTotal` objects in my main form, each of which needed to perform calculations on the array. Because I had the right architecture, all I needed to do was pass the `GridArray` object to my `TDailyTotal` objects and have them call the `PerformCalculations()` method with their own sets of data. In short, the architecture for my program fell in place with little on my part.

Had I not created the `TDailyTotal` and the `TGridArray` objects, I would have had a hard time writing code that was easy to maintain and understand. I would have had three or four methods in my main form that performed calculations on an array and three or four more methods that created a daily total. At one point, the daily total method would call the grid methods—but how could I designate that one set of methods belonged to one task and one to the other task? How could I define the relationship between the two sets of methods? There are no good answers to these questions because the architecture of my program demanded the presence of the `TDailyTotal` and `TGridArray` objects. They were inevitable objects, just as `TApplication` and `TDataSet` are inevitable parts of the VCL architecture.

When I found the `TDailyTotal` and `TGridArray` objects, my program came together simply and easily. I'm sure I will understand its architecture almost immediately if I have to return to the program months or years from now. Without these objects, sorting through the spaghetti code that wound back and forth through my form might take me hours.

The key point is that I must iteratively comb through my code looking for objects. When I discover them, I have to overcome inertia and force myself to separate them from the form or module I'm creating. It seems like a waste of effort at the time, but it is usually worth the effort many times over in the long haul.

Encapsulating Objects by Design

Good OOP programmers never allow objects to share private data. They always design objects that stand on their own, which allows others to use their data only through designated interfaces.

These rules are important for two reasons:

- They help promote reuse. If you have two or more objects bound tightly together via their data, reusing one of the objects in a separate project is difficult. The objects are bound to one another and you cannot easily separate them.

- A primary object-oriented programming goal is to encapsulate tasks in a single object. One of the main reasons for doing so is that it limits the scope of the problems that can arise. If you build a discreet object with no reliance on other objects, then the domain of possible problems for that object is restricted. The moment you let two objects intimately bind their data together, you are immediately widening the scope of your potential problems from one object to two objects. Your problem domain has doubled in size, thereby making maintenance at least twice as difficult.

A strict adherence to the principle of encapsulation can do a tremendous amount toward helping you create small, simple programs. Breaking encapsulation by sharing data indiscriminately between objects can add unneeded complexity to your programs and destroy the purity of your architecture.

For instance, if I tied the `TDailyTotal` and `TGridArray` objects from the preceding section together by sharing their data, I could not easily reuse the `TGridArray` object. If I found the need to build a `TMonthlyTotal` object, then I would want to pass it the `TGridArray` object so that it could be reused. Reuse might be difficult if `TGridArray` were bound to the data of the `TDailyTotal` object. In fact, I might be forced to rewrite the `TGridArray` object so that it could be reused. In the process I might end up with both `TDailyGridArray` and `TMonthlyGridArray` objects. This arrangement, although probably effective, would nonetheless likely herald the creation of a redundant and overly complex architecture.

Creating Short Methods

In the interest of keeping things simple, I like to create short methods. Not all methods need be short, but most of them should be short. In particular, I think about four out of five methods that I write should be short. (I define short as 25 lines or fewer.)

Just as it is important to see that a program's Form1 object can contain multiple objects, so is it important to see that a single method can contain multiple methods that need to be broken out. I try to discover the methods buried in my code, just as I seek to find the objects buried in my code.

The most obvious sign that a method is too large appears when it contains chunks of logic that need to be called from two different methods. For instance, I have often written code that extracts the path to my application's root directory. Sometimes I need to reuse this logic in several different places in my program. Rewriting this logic inside each method that requires the information makes no sense. Instead, the simplest course of action is to separate the logic out of these methods and encapsulate it inside a single method that can be called from various sources. This means that each method used to contain this logic grows smaller because it can now delegate the task to another method.

Creating short methods that are easy to understand and easy to debug is generally a useful idea. Long methods, though sometimes necessary or sensible, can be the source of innumerable bugs.

Naming Variables, Methods, and Procedures

I find it best to give variables, methods, and procedures clear, easy-to-understand names. Using abbreviations and generic, nondescriptive names can be a source of trouble.

You will often find that I give the short objects examples in this book generic names such as TMyGrid or TMyEdit. However, I try to come up with descriptive names for objects in complex programs. For instance, TMyGrid might become TDailyEarningsGrid or TMilesTraveledGrid. Typing out these longer names takes a little extra work, but it tends to save me trouble in the long run.

C++Builder is smart enough to use short tokens in place of these long names. You will not waste space in your final executable just because you give an object a descriptive name.

C++Builder programmers tend to support certain naming conventions. For instance, private data in an object usually has the letter *F* added as a prefix, as in FWidth or FHeight. This letter designates the variable as a private field of an object. Types that you declare in a program should prefaced with the letter *T*, for type. For instance, key VCL objects have names like `TObject`, `TComponent`, and `TEdit`. I follow this convention in all the programs used in this book.

Avoiding Feature Creep

The process of continually changing the spec to accommodate new ideas is called *feature creep*. This particular malady has probably been the single biggest source of trouble in my own programming projects. If I try to design and code at the same time, I get tempted to follow each new idea as it arises. Working this way can lead to a process in which projects never seem to come to a finish. One more thing always has to be done, and old code continually has to be rewritten to conform to the new paradigm.

Having a clean design for a project is much better. If I come up with a new idea mid-project, or if someone involved in the project comes up with the idea, I can discard it on the grounds that it doesn't fit into the current design. "That's great," I might say. "I like it. Let's get it into a notebook as a feature for the next version of the product!"

The middle of a project is not the right time to adopt new programming techniques or to change a product's design. The proper place for these is in between projects or during the design phase.

Creating Components

Perhaps the single most powerful technique I know for creating robust programs is developing components. A component has the following virtues:

- By its very nature, each component I create must stand alone, independent of any other object. This way, I can easily test my object and reuse it.

- Each component I create must be manipulated through the Object Inspector. This restriction forces me to create a simple, easy-to-use interface for an object.

- Components help design programs by allowing me to quickly put together demos that test the strength of my ideas.

Using Third-Party Tools

I am, at last, at the end of this section on designing programs. As a footnote to this subject, I am going to spend a few paragraphs recommending products that I believe can help you create better programs. My main purpose here is to promote the idea of using third-party products. If I mention particular names, I do so only because I want to give you a place at which to start your search for useful tools.

If you are a serious C++Builder programmer, you should spend a considerable amount of time exploring third-party libraries. In particular, you can find companies such as

TurboPower Software or Raize Software that sell libraries of components, objects, and routines that ship with source. You would do well to explore these tools.

Consider, for instance, these excerpts from the SysTools2 User's Manual:

Chapter 5, "Date/Time Routines"

Chapter 6, "High-Precision Floating Point Math"

Chapter 7, "Real Business Finance/Statistics"

Chapter 8, "Operating Systems and Low Level Data Manipulation"

Chapter 9, "System Components"

- TStShellAbout
- TStTrayIcon
- TStShortcut
- TStVersionInfo
- And So On

Chapter 10, "Bar Codes"

Chapter 11, "CRC Routines"

Chapter 12, "Internet Data Conversion Kit (Mime)"

Chapter 13, "Container Classes"

- TStDQue
- TStLMatrix
- TStDictionary
- TStHashTable
- StTree Unit: Balanced Binary Search Tree
- And So On

Chapter 14, "Sort Engine"

Chapter 15, "Registry and Ini Files"

Chapter 16, "Astronomical Routines"

I'm not going to discuss the significance of this listing but instead leave it up to you to pursue and judge it on its own merits. TurboPower makes eight different products, and this is just a brief excerpt from the manual for one of those. Can any serious C++Builder programmer afford not to dig into resources of this type? How about the fact that versions of all these routines are available not only for C++Builder, but also for Delphi?

Evaluation copies of all of TurboPower's tools are available on its Web site at www.turbopower.com. Classic TurboPower tools such as Orpheus, SysTools, and Async

Professional have powered innumerable successful Delphi and C++Builder programs. If you have the desire to expand your knowledge of C++Builder, TurboPower Software is one resource you should definitely know about.

TurboPower, however, is just the tip of the iceberg. The Internet tools from HRef Software (`www.href.com`) are not a bit less miraculous. You can use these tools to develop powerful commercial Web sites, and you can find whole libraries of routines that every developer should explore.

I always stand in awe of the fine-tuned precision of Ray Konopka's components from `www.raize.com`. Ray is a perfectionist, and every single one of his components is a little jewel that elegantly fulfills its task in life. Woll2Woll Software is yet another company that consistently earns top honors from developers. You should check out the powerful InfoPower grid at `www.woll2woll.com`.

Other companies that build valuable tools include Apiary, Dart, Distinct, Eagle Software, Attachmate, Logic Works, Luxent Software, Rational Software, Software Science, Sylvan Faust, Eagle Research, Regatta, NuMega, Nevrona, Starbase, Ryle Design, MicroEdge, Premia, American Cybernetics, Skyline Tools, Ted Gruber Software, Opaque Software, Blue Sky Software, Pegasus Imaging, Bill White Software, InstallShield, SAGE Inc, 20/20 Software, Ensemble, Cayenne, and many, many more.

I mention these companies not because I want to promote their products above others, but because I want to make you a better C++Builder programmer. These tools are incredibly powerful, and your code will be the better for it if you leverage them. No C++Builder programmer ever has to look at the resources of C++ programmers and think that it would be nice to get at some of those goodies. The C++Builder world is rife with more resources than any one programmer could ever use, and it is madness not to take advantage of it. For more information, check the Inprise Web site at `http://www.inprise.com`. You will find a relatively complete list of tool vendors, including links to their home pages.

I have listed many other resources on my Web site (`http://users.aol.com/charliecal`). Among the links there is `http://www.drbob42.com/`, which is maintained by Bob Swart, one of this book's contributing authors.

Finally, I want to remind you to visit `www.turbopower.com` and to also check my home page at `http://users.aol.com/charliecal` or `http://members.aol.com/charliecal` for news and updates to this book. Setting a day or so aside each month to just explore C++Builder resources is a worthwhile endeavor.

Notes on the Text of This Book

In most of the remainder of this chapter, I will add a few general notes about this book's text. These comments apply not to any one particular chapter, but to the book as a whole.

Setting Up a Network

Many of the programs in this book are network based. At work, I can tap into the very sophisticated Inprise network. However, most of the testing I did for this book was carried out at home. My home network consists of a couple run-of-the-mill PCs (one for me and one for my wife) and an NT-based laptop that I use at work and usually carry home in the evenings. For a long while I had a 486 as part of this network, but that machine has been retired.

When talking to developers, I have sometimes mentioned my home network and found that it generated a certain amount of interest. Although many people already have home networks, others asked, how I did it. The answer is that it is not very difficult.

You can learn a lot about networks just by buying a couple $20 network cards and hooking up two machines in your home. You might want to spend up to $100 on a network card if you have extra cash, which is what I usually do. For years I had good luck with a simple $20 no-name card.

Windows 95/98 and NT machines come with built-in peer-to-peer and TCP/IP networks. Setting them up is simple. The peer-to-peer network requires almost no configuration. For help with TCP/IP, see the "Installing TCP/IP" section in Chapter 16, "Internet Connection with C++Builder."

I can't emphasize enough the value of having a home network to play with and to test your code on. I end up using both machines quite often for testing.

The Borland/Inprise Name Change

As readers of this book no doubt know, Borland recently changed its name to Inprise. However, C++Builder 4 ships under the name *Borland C++Builder*, and the brand name is still associated with the company. To further complicate the issue, Inprise was recently split into two divisions: Inprise and borland.com. As a result, I tend to refer to the company as *Borland* throughout most of this book, though I may occasionally use *Inprise* or even *Borland/Inprise*.

I think it's only fair that you should know that I have been working for Borland since March 2, 1992. This is an unusually long time for anyone to work for any one company in this industry. I have a rather strong loyalty to the company after all these years, much of it based on my admiration for the company's C++, Java, and Pascal compilers.

I want to make it clear, however, that my primary loyalty is to the field of computer science. I like working at Borland because its products contribute to computer science and to the sum of knowledge that we have about computers. I get paid for doing what I love, which is a great thing, and I am grateful to Borland for providing me with a good job.

Borland does not, however, own my mind, and this book is written under a contract between Macmillan Computer Publishing and me, not between Borland and me. Therefore, I will generally say what I believe to be true, and not necessarily what I think is best for Borland. Still, as the reader you need to be conscious of how long I have worked for this company and that no one can remain entirely objective after such a long tenure.

Commenting My Code

Readers who have seen my other books might be surprised to find that I have had a change of heart about documenting my code. After using comments for a while, I began to find them extremely helpful, perhaps in part because I no longer remember things as well as I did when I was younger. A more significant reason? We are now facing a time in computing where one of the primary difficulties is managing the complexity of our systems. We all write huge amounts of code and deal with very large APIs. To manage this degree of complexity, I have to use every tool at my disposal; writing extensive comments seems to help.

At any rate, I comment my code fairly heavily now, though I still can't bring myself to mix code and comments. My comments are nearly all placed before a method, or at the top of a unit. One further note on this matter: I found that the default italic font for comments was annoying. I tend to turn the italics off by choosing Tools, Environment Options, Colors, Text Attribute. For some reason, it is easier on my eyes if I have the comments appear in a different color, without the italics. I realize that this use of color versus italics is subjective, but it makes a significant difference to me.

Closing Thoughts

As a programmer, the future of our society rests partially in your hands. You have the ability to decide what shape parts of our society will take, and in particular, you have the power to influence the young, who are enamored of computers. Only cowardice or lack of foresight would allow you to trade that power for the dubious blessings bestowed on you by people who neither comprehend the nature of your talents nor the importance of the technology that you have mastered.

When you program, think about your wife or husband; think about your children; think about your neighbors, the members of your church, synagogue, or sangha. When you program, think about the poor people in your town, think about the talented children in your schools, think about that beautiful man or woman you passed in the street. Think about your pets, about animals that live in the forest, trees that grow on mountainsides, and the stars that you see in pictures returned from the Hubble telescope. Think about a beautiful painting you saw in a museum, about a piece of music that moved you, or a book that touched your heart. Programmers are part of a larger world to which they owe allegiance. Study that world and strive to serve it.

Whether you live in Washington, D.C., or Bangkok, Thailand, your society is under attack by small-minded people who value money or power more than their own family or the members of their community. They live off the effluvium sparked by seesawing exchanges of power the same way normal people live off love, laughter, and the wonder of the natural world. Don't fall prey to their folly. Practice your profession for the sake of those you love and for the good of others. In the long run, your only heritage will be the one you create with your own hands. Make sure it is worthy of you and that you are worthy of it.

I believe that programming is among the most fascinating of all human endeavors. I think we all are wonderfully privileged to be alive at a time when it is possible to pursue this discipline. For those of us with an inward and studious turn of mind, it is hard to imagine any more worthy subject of intellectual pursuit.

When I first started working with computers in the mid-1980s, I found them to be magical machines. My study of them was motivated as much by the mystery of their operation as by my desire to truly understand them. The first computers I played with seemed inexplicable, and I have to confess that I was drawn strongly to the sense of wonder they invoked in my perhaps too credulous soul.

Over time, I came to understand computers all too well, and I lost my sense of wonder. I now know the answers to the questions that used to mystify me. Yet strangely enough, in recent months I've found myself coming around full cycle, back to the point where I am intrigued by the fundamental mystery. At the heart of these machines is the capability to carefully and precisely control the flow of electrons whirling through silicon. What is electricity? What is an electron? Scientists aren't even sure whether electrons are solid particles or simply tiny flows of raw energy in a constant state of flux.

If there were true magicians walking the world today, would their art really be any more mysterious than our ability to manipulate words, sounds, pictures, and mathematical expressions with a computer? They say that any technology that is sufficiently advanced appears magical to the user. What is miraculous about computers is that they allow us to manipulate the formless particles such as electrons and light that lie near the outer edges of our understanding of the world. It is as if we can take the formless raw energy out of which the universe is made and tap into that wellspring of incomprehensible intelligence.

Computers are logic machines, and science is a rigorous discipline that leaves little room for sentiment or superstition. Yet science itself is wonderful, particularly on its subtlest, most rarified levels. Quantum physics, chaos theory, and computer science have turned out to be as miraculous and mysterious as the superstitions that science has displaced.

Summary

Writing good programs, as much as anything else, revolves around solid design. A few hours spent on design may very well save you days or weeks of coding time. Writing code is the fun part of creating applications. In your haste to begin programming you will almost certainly cost yourself time if you don't first have a solid design. Get in the habit of writing design documents. If you are doing contract programming, demand a design document from your customer. Having a design document greatly reduces feature creep, the bane of all programmers.

Whenever and wherever possible, strive to write simple code. Writing simple code does not refer to the technical complexity of your code as much as it refers to the way you approach that code. You can make complex code appear simple by creating well-designed objects (components or classes).

Finally, don't overlook the importance of third-party component libraries and tools. There is no point in spending days, weeks, or months writing a component to perform a complex task if a component that performs that task is readily available. In most cases the cost of third-party components is trivial when compared to the cost of your time.

This book is about computer science. As such, it should invoke not just the smell of dusty schoolrooms and powdered chalk, but a sense of mystery and wonder. It does as such in my mind, and I hope that you will share that sense of wonder when you travel with me on this exploration of C++Builder programming and the C++ language.

Creating
Components

by Kent Reisdorph

CHAPTER 2

In this chapter I discuss component creation and design. I started out writing this chapter not wanting to cover the basics of creating components. The further I got, however, I realized that I couldn't easily ignore the fundamentals of component writing. Having said that, I'll add that the purpose of this and the next chapter is not to introduce you to the basics of component writing. Instead, I focus on the more challenging and troublesome aspects of component writing.

The components I have created for this chapter are not in any way complex. I thought it better to create simple components that clearly illustrate concepts I want to present rather than create complex components that might impress you. After reading this chapter you will know how to do the following:

- Create components with C++Builder
- Use aggregation to create complex components
- Add events to components
- Override the `CreateWnd()` and `WndProc()` methods
- Create packages for your components
- Use the `ComponentState` property to control component behavior
- Paint custom components using the `Paint()` method

Why Write Components?

C++Builder comes with a wide assortment of components. Part of the beauty of programming with C++Builder is that you can drop any of the standard components on a form and create a prototype of an application in a very short period of time. Naturally, C++Builder doesn't include components for every possible programming requirement. Third-party component vendors fill the gap by providing components that perform services not found in the standard Visual Component Library (VCL). My employer, TurboPower Software Company, sells a number of component libraries that contain literally hundreds of components. TurboPower is just one such component vendor. There are many other commercial third-party component vendors out there. The number of commercially available components for C++Builder is impressive. In addition to commercial components, you can find hundreds of freeware and shareware components on the Web.

> **NOTE**
>
> Most third-party components available for use in C++Builder are written in Object Pascal. That shouldn't concern you any more than the fact that the VCL itself is written in Object Pascal. By writing components in Object Pascal,

component vendors can reach the widest possible audience. Object Pascal components can be used in either Delphi or C++Builder. At the current time C++Builder components can only be used in C++Builder. You may see more commercial components written entirely in C++Builder if and when components written in C++Builder and Delphi become truly interchangeable.

With the vast number of components available, why would you consider writing your own components? You may write components for any of the following reasons:

- You want to learn how to write components.
- You have a programming need that is not addressed by any existing components.
- You want to write components to sell commercially.
- You work for a company that believes in keeping everything in-house to maintain independence.
- You feel you cannot afford to buy commercial components.

These are all valid reasons, but the last one is a bit suspect, particularly for professional programmers. Consider TurboPower's Async Professional, for example. Async Professional is a complete serial communications library. It includes components for talking to serial ports, dialing modems, doing file transfers (XModem, ZModem, Kermit, and so on), a terminal window, faxing, and much, much more. It even includes a fax printer driver so that you can "print" a fax file from any Windows program. I'm convinced it would take a single programmer close to a year to duplicate all the features found in Async Professional. The list price of Async Professional is around $279.00 as of this writing. Obviously, it would be foolish to spend a year writing a component library that you can buy for that price. For most professional programmers it would be foolish to spend even a *day* writing a component that could be purchased for a reasonable amount of money.

For whatever reason, at some time during your C++Builder programming career you will probably find yourself in a position where you must write your own components.

Overview of Component Writing

This section is an overview of component writing. I won't spend much time on the basics because I want to devote more time to complex issues involved in component writing. The example component for this section is a simple component called `TUnlURLLabel`. This component, as its name indicates, is a label that displays an URL. When you click the label, your default Web browser is invoked and the page defined by the URL property is loaded. This is the simplest component that I could think of to write, and yet one that has some practical use.

Writing components is challenging. Maybe I should say that writing components that *work correctly* is challenging. It's easy to write bad components. It's much more difficult to write components that work as well as the VCL components or as well as the components written by proven third-party commercial component vendors. Even if you are an experienced C++Builder programmer, you should be aware that writing components is a completely different ballgame. You'll encounter aspects of the VCL that you never knew existed as you write them.

It's important to understand that your components need to work correctly in many different situations. For example, you might write a component that works fine when placed on a form at design time, but fails miserably when the user creates the component dynamically at run time; you may have failed to consider that your component might be used in a DLL. Thinking about these possibilities before you start writing a component will help you write robust components that work wherever and whenever needed.

Getting Started

To create a new component, start with a blank project. This project will be the test bed for your new component. Now choose File, New from the main menu and double-click the Component icon in the Object Repository. In the New Component dialog, choose a base class and give your component a name. Figure 2.1 shows the New Component dialog as it appeared when I created the `TUnlURLLabel` component.

FIGURE 2.1

The New Component dialog is used to set a new component's characteristics.

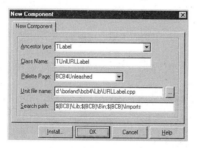

The first step in creating a new component is selecting the ancestor type for your component. This is an important step, so let me digress for a moment and talk about base classes for components.

Before selecting the ancestor type (the base class) for your component, you need to spend some time thinking about what the component does and how it will be used. I had two choices in the case of TUnlURLLabel. (I had more than two choices, actually, but only two made sense.) I could derive from either TLabel or TCustomLabel.

Most VCL components are derived from a custom class. These classes serve as a base class from which other components can be derived. In the case of label components, the base class is TCustomLabel. The important thing to realize about the custom classes is that nearly all of the class properties are declared as protected. It's important because this scenario allows you to promote a property's visibility in derived classes. Take the Transparent property of TLabel, for example. Let's say you were tasked with creating a label that, by definition, should never be transparent. In this case you wouldn't want the Transparent property published. In fact, you wouldn't even want it public. Given that, you would derive your component from TCustomLabel and publish all the properties except the Transparent property.

You should derive from one of the custom classes if you need to change the visibility of one or more properties or methods found in the base class. If you are simply adding one or more properties to a functioning component, you will derive from that component rather from a custom class.

Now that you have selected the ancestor type, you must provide a class name for the new component. Enter any class name you like, but keep in mind that most components begin with the letter T.

TIP

You would be wise to adopt a specific naming convention for your components. Doing so will help avoid conflicts between your components and other third-party components. For example, you might create a component called TCoolLabel. Later you find a freeware component library on the Web and install it. Lo and behold, this component library also has a TCoolLabel component. C++Builder won't allow you to install the library because a component with the name TCoolLabel already exists.

At TurboPower we use a product name code in the component class name. Our Orpheus components start with TOvc, our Abbrevia components start with TAb, our Async Professional components start with TApd, and so on. A naming convention won't completely eliminate the possibility of two components with the same name, but it will drastically reduce it.

Now you can enter the name of the Component Palette page where you want the new component to appear. You can type any name in the `Palette Page` field. If the page does not exist on the Component Palette, it is created when you install the component. The `Unit File Name` field is automatically set for you based on the class name you gave the component. You can modify the path or accept the defaults.

The New Component dialog has a button labeled Install. It allows you to immediately add the new component to a package and install it on the Component Palette. I can't see any reason to install the component at this time, however. The new component needs testing before it can be used on the Component Palette. I would never advocate installing a new component to the Component Palette until after it has undergone extensive testing.

Finally, you are ready to click OK on the New Component dialog. When you click OK, C++Builder creates a new unit for your component. At this point you should save the component to disk. Click the Add to Project button on the IDE's toolbar to add the component's unit to the test application and then save the test application. This is necessary because you are first going to test your component by creating the component dynamically in the test application. The component source must be part of the test application project so that it will be recompiled when you make changes to the component.

All of this might sound like basic information; it is. On the other hand, it is important to get started right when creating a new component. Many component writers get in a hurry to see their new component on the Component Palette and neglect to properly test the component first. This is a time-wasting way to approach component writing. Test your component as thoroughly as you can before adding it to the Component Palette. I cannot stress this point enough.

The `TUnlURLLabel` Component

Before going further, let me show you the source for the `TUnlURLLabel` component. I'll discuss the pertinent aspects of this component in the following sections. Listings 2.1 and 2.2 show the header and the source for this component.

LISTING 2.1   THE HEADER FOR THE `TUnlURLLabel` COMPONENT

```
#ifndef URLLabelH
#define URLLabelH

#include <SysUtils.hpp>
#include <Controls.hpp>
#include <Classes.hpp>
#include <Forms.hpp>
#include <StdCtrls.hpp>

class PACKAGE TUnlURLLabel : public TLabel
{
```

```
private:
  String FURL;
protected:
  void __fastcall Click();
  DYNAMIC void __fastcall SetURL(String Value);
public:
  __fastcall TUnlURLLabel(TComponent* Owner);
__published:
  __property String URL  = { read = FURL, write = SetURL };
};

#endif
```

LISTING 2.2   THE SOURCE CODE FOR THE TUnlURLLable COMPONENT

```
#include <vcl.h>
#include <shellapi.h>
#pragma hdrstop

#include "URLLabel.h"
#pragma package(smart_init)
#pragma resource "urllabel.res"

// ValidCtrCheck is used to assure that the components created do not have
// any pure virtual functions.
//

static inline void ValidCtrCheck(TUnlURLLabel *)
{
  new TUnlURLLabel(NULL);
}

__fastcall TUnlURLLabel::TUnlURLLabel(TComponent* Owner)
  : TLabel(Owner)
{
  Font->Color = clBlue;
  Font->Style = TFontStyles() << fsUnderline;
  Cursor = crHandPoint;
}

void __fastcall TUnlURLLabel::Click()
{
  TLabel::Click();
  ShellExecute(Parent->Handle, "open", URL.c_str(), 0, 0, SW_NORMAL);
}

void __fastcall TUnlURLLabel::SetURL(String value)
{
  FURL = value;
  Caption = value;
}
```

continues

LISTING 2.2 CONTINUED

```
namespace Urllabel
{
  void __fastcall PACKAGE Register()
  {
    TComponentClass classes[1] = {__classid(TUnlURLLabel)};
    RegisterComponents("BCB4Unleashed", classes, 0);
  }
}
```

In this example, `TUnlURLLabel` is derived from `TLabel`. I derived from `TLabel` because I simply want to take everything found in a standard Label component and add a property of my own. I could have derived from `TCustomLabel`, but then I would have to redeclare a bunch of properties in my derived class. (I discuss redeclaring properties later in the section "Publishing Base Class Properties.") I've already talked about when you should derive from the custom classes.

Notice the `Register()` function in Listing 2.2:

```
namespace Urllabel
{
  void __fastcall PACKAGE Register()
  {
    TComponentClass classes[1] = {__classid(TUnlURLLabel)};
    RegisterComponents("BCB4Unleashed", classes, 0);
  }
}
```

Every component contains a `Register()` function. This function is automatically called by the IDE when the package in which the component resides is loaded by the IDE. The call to `RegisterComponents()` passes the name of the Component Palette tab where the component will reside, an array of __classids, and the index of the last pointer in the array. This function is generated by C++Builder, so you normally don't have to modify it.

Another function that C++Builder generates is called `ValidCtrCheck()`. This function is used by the IDE to ensure that the component doesn't contain any pure virtual functions. A class that has pure virtual functions is an abstract base class and cannot be instantiated directly. As such, it cannot be used as a component. If you accidentally add a pure virtual function to a component when you compile the component's source code, you get an error that reads

```
Cannot create instance of abstract class 'TMyComponent'
```

You should understand that `ValidCtrCheck()` is never called by your component nor by the IDE. It is simply there so that at compile time the compiler can warn you that a pure virtual function exists in your component. You can delete this function from your component source code altogether if you are sure you don't have any pure virtual functions in your code.

Adding Setup Code to the Constructor

A label that represents an URL should probably be underlined and colored blue. In addition, the mouse cursor should change to a pointing hand when it passes over the URL label. The code to set up these parameters is placed in the constructor:

```
__fastcall TUnlURLLabel::TUnlURLLabel(TComponent* Owner)
  : TLabel(Owner)
{
  Font->Color = clBlue;
  Font->Style = TFontStyles() << fsUnderline;
  Cursor = crHandPoint;
}
```

Here I simply set the font color to `clBlue`, the font style to a set containing the `fsUnderline` style, and the `Cursor` property to the VCL's built-in pointing hand cursor (`crHandPoint`). Any initialization code for a component will usually be placed in the constructor. This includes allocating memory for classes or other components that the component uses internally. Naturally, any cleanup is done in the component's destructor. There isn't any cleanup required in the case of `TUnlURLLabel`, so it does not have a destructor.

Adding a Property with the Class Explorer

The `TUnlURLLabel` component adds just one property to those found in the `TLabel` component. This property, called `URL`, is the name of the URL that will be used to display a Web page. Without question, the easiest way to add a property or method to a new component is by using the Class Explorer. The Class Explorer is included in the Professional and Enterprise versions of C++Builder. If you have the Standard version of C++Builder, you will have to enter the property's code by hand. To add a property using the Class Explorer, right-click the class name of your component in the Class Explorer window and choose New Property. Figure 2.2 shows the Code Editor and Add Property dialog when adding the `URL` property.

When you click OK, the Class Explorer adds the following declarations to the `TUnlURLLabel` class:

```
private:
  String FURL;
  void SetURL(String value);
__published:
  __property String URL  = { read = FURL, write = SetURL };
```

2

CREATING
COMPONENTS

FIGURE 2.2

The Class Explorer's Add Property dialog as it appears when adding the URL property.

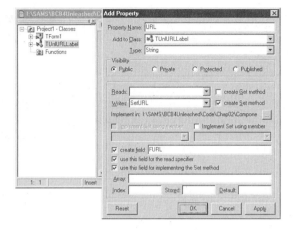

Most properties have an underlying data member associated with them. By tradition, the data member is the name of the property with an F tacked to the front. The Class Explorer automatically adds an F to the front of the property name if you check the create field check box on the Add Property dialog. You can change the name of the data member, but most of the time you will accept the name that the Class Explorer generates. In this case I am using direct access when the property is read, and a write method when the property is written to. Refer to Figure 2.2 to see the options I selected on the Add Property dialog to get this behavior.

The Class Explorer also adds the SetURL() method to the component's source code:

```
void __fastcall TUnlURLLabel::SetURL(String value)
{
  FURL = value;
}
```

This is a stub that fulfills the basic requirements of the write method for a property. I filled out the stub with this code:

```
void __fastcall TUnlURLLabel::SetURL(String value)
{
  FURL = value;
  Caption = value;
}
```

I'm anticipating that the URL provided will also be used as the component's caption. As such, I set the Caption property to the same value as the URL property. I could have provided a custom SetCaption() method for this component that would set the URL property when the caption changes. I didn't do that because I want to keep this example component as simple as possible.

> **CAUTION**
>
> You have to be careful when you have two properties that contain `write` methods that set each other's value. You could easily end up with an infinite loop where one property is setting another property that turns right around and sets the first property, and on and on. Writing code to avoid this situation is not hard, but you should be aware that without some sort of guard code you could end up with a stack overflow the first time you try to set one of the property's values.

Handling the Mouse Click

The `TUnlURLLabel` component invokes the user's default Web browser when the label is clicked. Obviously, I need to determine when the label is clicked before I can invoke the Web browser. It's fairly obvious that the standard `Label` component has an `OnClick` event. What may not be obvious, however, is that the `TCustomLabel` class has a virtual function called `Click()` that fires the `OnClick` event. The correct way to intercept a mouse click, then, is to override the `Click()` method. Some might argue that `TUnlURLLabel` should have a separate event that fires when the label is clicked. I think a separate event would be overkill in this case.

Once again, I used the Class Explorer to create the overridden `Click()` method. Figure 2.3 shows the Class Explorer's Add Method dialog as it appeared when I added the `Click()` method.

FIGURE 2.3

The Class Explorer makes adding methods to a component easy.

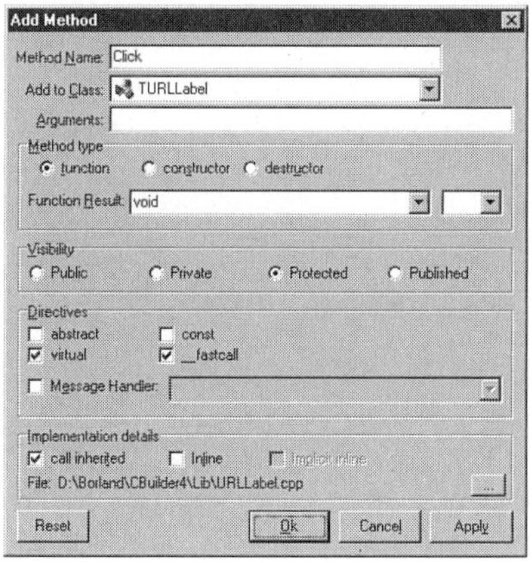

The Class Explorer generated this declaration for the `Click()` method:

```
protected:
  virtual void __fastcall Click();
```

Believe it or not, this code won't compile. The compiler generates an error message that reads as follows:

```
Cannot override a dynamic with a virtual function.
```

It's not the fault of the Class Explorer, exactly. Let me explain.

As you probably know, the VCL is written in Object Pascal. Object Pascal has two ways of declaring what are known in C++ as *virtual functions*. One way is with the `dynamic` keyword, and the other is with the `virtual` keyword. The difference in these keywords is the manner in which the *vtable* (the virtual method table) is handled. The exact difference isn't germane to this discussion, but you need to know that these two keywords exist. In the case of the `Click()` method, it is declared as `dynamic` and not `virtual`. To get this code to compile, I need to change the declaration as follows:

```
DYNAMIC void __fastcall Click();
```

DYNAMIC is a macro declared in `SYSMAC.H`:

```
#define DYNAMIC __declspec(dynamic)
```

You'll know when the DYNAMIC macro is needed because the compiler will tell you. From this point on I'll refer to both dynamic and virtual functions as virtual functions because that is the correct terminology for C++.

By the way, I wouldn't have had to make the `Click()` method virtual at all. I made it virtual in case I someday found the need to derive a component from `TUnlURLLabel`. This is a seemingly small point, but one that I need to stress. You should make any component methods virtual in the event that you need to extend that component in the future. Failure to provide virtual methods where they are needed has caused many a programmer to pull out hair in frustration. A lack of virtual methods in the VCL has been a big problem in the past. Fortunately, Inprise has gotten better at making more methods virtual as the VCL matures.

Now let's look at the completed `Click()` method:

```
void __fastcall TUnlURLLabel::Click()
{
  TLabel::Click();
  ShellExecute(Parent->Handle, "open", URL.c_str(), 0, 0, SW_NORMAL);
}
```

The first line of code here calls the base class `Click()` method. This is required so that the default behavior of the click action is preserved. This ensures that the `OnClick` event works as it does with a standard `Label` component. I cannot be sure that my users won't want to respond to the `OnClick` event, so I want to be sure they are able to do that if they prefer. You can place the call to the base class `Click()` function either before or after your code. It depends on whether you want the default behavior for an event to occur before or after your code executes. In this case it doesn't much matter where the call to `TLabel::Click()` falls.

The second line of code in the `Click()` method calls `ShellExecute()` to invoke the user's default browser. `ShellExecute()` knows how to handle an URL automatically. I don't have to do anything more than pass the `open` command and the value of the `URL` property to `ShellExecute()`. Windows does the rest.

NOTE

Writing even the most simplistic of components can lead to all sorts of interesting design questions. In this case I passed `Parent->Handle` to the `ShellExecute()` function. When placed on a form itself, the component parent is the form. If the component is placed on a `Panel`, a `GroupBox`, or other container component, that component will be the parent. In this case, the code will probably work the same regardless of who the component's parent is. However, in a real-world component I would probably write the call to `ShellExecute()` like this:

```
TForm* form = dynamic_cast<TForm*>(Owner);
HWND theHandle;
if (form)
  theHandle = form->Handle;
else
  theHandle = Application->Handle;
ShellExecute(theHandle,
  "open", URL.c_str(), 0, 0, SW_NORMAL);
```

This code ensures that the form's handle is used in the first parameter to `ShellExecute()` if the component's owner is a form. I have to cast the `Owner` property to a `TForm*` because `Owner` is a `TComponent*` and the `TComponent` class does not have a `Handle` property. I use the `Application` object's handle if the `Owner` of the component is not a form.

Why bother with all of this? Remember that any component can be created dynamically at run time. The user may elect to pass 0 for the owner when the component is created. In other words, I can't assume that my component's `Owner` property will be valid. For that reason I need to take steps to ensure that my component works, even if the user doesn't play by the rules. From this one simple example you can see that there are a lot of details to consider when writing components.

This section touched briefly on dealing with events from the component writer's perspective. I discuss events in more detail later in the section "Adding Events to a Component."

Testing the Component

The code for the component is now complete, but it must be tested before being added to the Component Palette. Testing a component before it is on the Component Palette means creating an instance of the component dynamically. First I included the UnlURLLabel's header in the source file for my test program's main form. Next I placed this code in my test application's OnCreate event handler:

```
void __fastcall TForm1::FormCreate(TObject *Sender)
{
  TUnlURLLabel* urlLabel = new TUnlURLLabel(this);
  urlLabel->Parent = this;
  urlLabel->Top = 20;
  urlLabel->Left = 20;
  urlLabel->URL = "http://www.turbopower.com";
}
```

The key line of code here is the line that sets the Parent property to this. Omitting this one line of code has caused many C++Builder programmers fits. Without setting the Parent property, the component will never be visible on the form. Remember that the write method for the URL property sets the Caption property, so there's no need to set the Caption property in the code. Figure 2.4 shows the test application at run time. Note

FIGURE 2.4

The test application with the UnlURLLabel *component visible at run time.*

the pointing hand cursor.

In this case testing the component is a trivial exercise. With more complex components you may need to assign event handlers in code and put the component through its paces to ensure that it operates correctly. Once you are satisfied that the component is working the way you expect, you can to install the component to the Component Palette.

Creating a Glyph for the Component

In most cases you will want to create a distinctive glyph for your component that appears on the Component Palette. A default glyph will be applied automatically if you don't provide your own. If your component is derived from one of the standard components, then that component's glyph will be used by default. In the case of TUnlURLLabel, for example, the normal Label component's glyph will be used. If your component is derived from one of the custom classes, from TComponent, or from TWinControl, then the default glyph is the Inprise cube, pyramid, and circle bitmap.

Use the Image Editor to create your component's glyph. Start a new resource project and add a bitmap resource. Make the bitmap 24×24 pixels. The lower-left pixel in the bitmap is used as the transparent color. I usually start by filling the bitmap with either olive or purple (colors I don't typically use in the image itself). I then go to work creating a design that attempts to represent the component's purpose.

> **NOTE**
>
> If you are writing components for commercial sale, consider hiring a graphic artist to create your glyphs. Professional component packages should not only operate well, but should look good on the Component Palette.

The bitmap resource must have the same name as the component in all uppercase letters. For example, I gave the bitmap for the TUnlURLLabel component the name TUNLURLLABEL. Save the resource file in the same directory as the component. You will typically use the same name as the component's source file, but with a .RES extension. The extension is automatically added by the Image Editor.

The final step in implementing the glyph is to add a line of code to the component's source to link in the resource file:

```
#pragma resource "urllabel.res"
```

This causes the resource file to be linked to the package when the package is built. I talk about packages next.

Creating and Using Packages

Every component must reside in a package. A *package* is a specialized DLL that the C++Builder IDE understands. Packages give many C++Builder users more trouble than they should, primarily because those users don't take the time to understand how packages work. In this section I detour from the subject of creating components and discuss packages.

Types of Packages

Packages come in three forms:

1. Runtime packages
2. Designtime packages
3. Both runtime and designtime packages

Other books have covered these package types in detail, so I will only give you an overview of each.

Designtime packages contain code and forms that components need to be manipulated at design time. Usually this means that the designtime package contains the components' component and property editors. If your components don't have component or property editors, then you don't specifically need to create a designtime package. Designtime packages exist because they contain forms and code only used by the IDE at design time. They don't contain any code needed at run time. You keep the size of your executables to a minimum by placing these forms and their associated code in a designtime package. There's no point in lugging around extra forms and code when they are useless to the finished application.

Runtime packages, on the other hand, contain all the code the component needs to function. The IDE creates three files when a runtime package is compiled: .BPL file, .BPI file, and .LIB file. The .BPL file is the code for the component when the application is deployed using runtime packages. As I have said, the runtime package is a form of DLL and, as far as your application is concerned, operates just like a DLL. The .BPI file is the package import library file. The IDE automatically adds the .BPI to your project when you build an application using runtime packages. The .BPI file is equivalent to a standard DLL's import library (.LIB) file. The package's .LIB file is the static library for the package. This file is used when you build an application without using runtime packages. The code for the component is pulled from the .LIB file when you build your application and is linked into the executable.

Designtime/runtime packages are referred to here as *dual packages*. You can get by with creating a dual package if your components don't use any property or component editors.

> **NOTE**
>
> C++Builder users on the Inprise newsgroups are constantly asking, "How do I build my application so that it operates as a standalone application?" I wouldn't normally put a note like this in an advanced programming book, but this issue

comes up so often that I thought it couldn't hurt to address it here. To create a standalone application you should do the following:

1. Open the Project Options dialog.
2. On the Linker page, turn off the Dynamic RTL option.
3. On the Packages page, turn off the Build with Runtime Packages option.

All the code your application needs is now linked into the EXE. Keep in mind that applications that use the Borland Database Engine (BDE) or any ActiveX controls cannot be statically linked.

As explained at the beginning of this section, all components must reside in a package. C++Builder provides a default user package for miscellaneous components that you install, whether they are components of your own creation or components you have downloaded from the Internet. The default user package is called DCLUSR40.BPK. Although this package is fine for occasional components, I wouldn't use it for any components that I create. I prefer to have my components grouped in specific packages. For the components presented in this chapter and the one that follows, I have created two packages. The designtime package is called BCB4Un1D.BPK and the runtime package is called BCB4Un1R.BPK. You can find these packages in the Code\Packages subdirectory of the book's CD-ROM.

As with components, you should adopt a naming convention for your packages. Inprise recommends that you use the VCL version number somewhere in your package names. At TurboPower we use a product code, product version, designtime or runtime code, and the VCL version to make up our package names. Our primary Orpheus 3 designtime package, for example, is named 0300_D40.BPL and its corresponding runtime package is named 0300_R40.BPL. Our users can, at a glance, identify the version of our product and the VCL version for which the package was built. The exact naming convention is unimportant. What is important is that you have some way of identifying your packages by package filename.

Using the Package Manager

To create a new package, choose File, New from the C++Builder main menu and double-click the Package icon in the Object Repository. A new package is created and the Package Manager window is displayed as shown in Figure 2.5.

2

CREATING
COMPONENTS

FIGURE 2.5

The Package Manger aids in creating packages.

The Package Manager is new in C++Builder 4. As you can see, the Package Manager tree contains two nodes. The `Contains` node is a list of source files that the package contains. A package can, and usually does, contain the source for more than one component. To add a component's source to the package, right-click the `Contains` node, and choose Add. You can then browse to the file you want and add it to the package.

The Package Manager's `Requires` node is a list of packages that this package needs in order to operate. It's important to understand that the IDE doesn't know what packages your package requires. In Figure 2.5 you'll see that the IDE added the `VCL40`, `VCLDB40`, `VCLMID40`, and `VCLX40` packages to the Requires list. You always need at least the `VCL40` package for all packages you create. Packages not specifically required by your package should be removed from the Requires list. In this case I certainly don't want the database (`VCLDB40`) and MIDAS (`VCLMID40`) packages in the Requires list. I don't need the `VCLX40` package, either. To remove required packages, right-click the `Requires` node and choose Remove File. The Remove From Project dialog comes up, allowing you to select files to be removed from the package. Simply choose one or more files from the dialog and click OK. The selected files are removed from the package.

The C++Builder linker is smart enough not to link packages that are in the Requires list but are not used. On the other hand, you don't necessarily know what version of C++Builder your users have. For example, the `VCLMID40` package is for the MIDAS components and only ships with the Enterprise version of C++Builder. If you leave this package in the Requires list, users of C++Builder Professional won't be able to build your packages unless they remove the unwanted packages from the Requires list.

If you are creating a designtime package, then its corresponding runtime package must be in the Requires list. The designtime package can be thought of as simply a support package for the runtime package that contains the real code. It should be fairly obvious that you need to create the runtime package first if you are using separate designtime and runtime packages. Since the designtime package requires the runtime package, you must first have built the runtime package in order for the IDE to find the files it needs to build the designtime package.

Earlier I talked about the different types of packages, but I haven't yet told you how to set the package type. Click the Options button on the Package Manager's toolbar. The Project Options dialog is displayed as shown in Figure 2.6.

FIGURE 2.6

The Project Options dialog for a package project contains a page called Description.

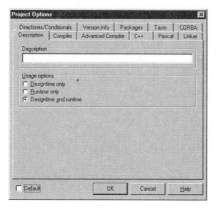

This is the same Project Options dialog you see for a regular application except that this one contains an additional page called Description. This page allows you to select the package type in the Usage options section. It also contains a field called Description in which you enter a description of the package. This is the description that is displayed on the Packages page of the Project Options dialog. The path and filename of the package are displayed on the Packages page if you don't provide a description. As long as you are working with the Project Options dialog you will probably want to provide the version information for your package. This is particularly important if you plan on distributing your components to the general public.

Once you have added all the contained and required files to the package, you can click the Compile button on the Package Manager to build the package. If you have forgotten to add a needed unit or package, the IDE is sometimes helpful enough to prompt you and add the missing file automatically. This mechanism is not necessarily foolproof, so be sure to be diligent when adding files to your packages.

After the package has been compiled, click the Install button on the Package Manager toolbar to install the package to the C++Builder Component Palette. Your new component will show up on the Component Palette if you have done everything right.

Creating a Registration Unit

Earlier I talked about using #pragma resource as the method by which you link the component's bitmap glyph to the package. I also discussed the Register() function and how it is used to register components with C++Builder. If you prefer, both the resource linking code and the registration code can be moved to a single unit that will serve as a registration unit. Listing 2.3 shows an example registration unit.

LISTING 2.3 A REGISTRATION UNIT FOR MULTIPLE COMPONENTS

```cpp
#include <vcl.h>
#pragma hdrstop

#include "urllabel.h"
#include "pictureselector.h"
#include "unlclock.h"

#pragma resource "urllabel.res"
#pragma resource "unlclock.res"
#pragma resource "pictureselector.res"

#pragma package(smart_init)

namespace Pictureselector
{
  void __fastcall PACKAGE Register()
  {
    TComponentClass classes[1] = {__classid(TUnlPictureSelector)};
    RegisterComponents("BCB4Unleashed", classes, 0);
  }
}

namespace Unlclock
{
  void __fastcall PACKAGE Register()
  {
    TComponentClass classes[1] = {__classid(TUnlClock)};
    RegisterComponents("BCB4Unleashed", classes, 0);
  }
}

namespace Urllabel
{
  void __fastcall PACKAGE Register()
  {
    TComponentClass classes[1] = {__classid(TUnlURLLabel)};
    RegisterComponents("BCB4Unleashed", classes, 0);
  }
}
```

I removed the code you see here from each of the component source code units because it was no longer needed there.

Creating a registration unit allows you to move unwanted code out of your component source files. It also gives you a central place to put your registration code, including property editor and component editor registration. I discuss component and property editors in Chapter 3, "Advanced Component Creation."

Creating Components Using Aggregation

Components writers commonly use aggregation to build a single component by implementing one or more existing components. The example component for this section is called TUnlPictureSelector. This component will combine a ComboBox component and an Image component into a single component. The combo box will contain a list of bitmap files. When a bitmap file in the ComboBox is selected, it will be shown in the Image component. Figure 2.7 shows this component on a form at run time.

FIGURE 2.7

The PictureSelector *component combines the* ComboBox *and* Image *components into a single component.*

TUnlPictureSelector is derived from TWinControl. TWinControl is the base class for all windowed controls. Listings 2.4 and 2.5 show the header and source for TUnlPictureSelector.

LISTING 2.4   THE HEADER FOR THE PictureSelector COMPONENT

```
#ifndef PictureSelectorH
#define PictureSelectorH

#include <SysUtils.hpp>
#include <Controls.hpp>
#include <Classes.hpp>
#include <Forms.hpp>

const String Strings[] = {
  "handshak.bmp",
  "factory.bmp",
```

continues

LISTING 2.4   CONTINUED

```
  "chemical.bmp",
  "shipping.bmp",
  "finance.bmp"
};

class PACKAGE TUnlPictureSelector : public TWinControl
{
private:
  TComboBox* FComboBox;
  TImage* FImage;
protected:
  void __fastcall ComboBoxClick(TObject* Sender);
  virtual void __fastcall CreateWnd();
public:
  __fastcall TUnlPictureSelector(TComponent* Owner);
};

#endif
```

LISTING 2.5   THE SOURCE CODE FOR THE PictureSelector COMPONENT

```
#include <vcl.h>
#pragma hdrstop

#include "PictureSelector.h"
#pragma resource "PictureSelector.res"
#pragma package(smart_init)

// ValidCtrCheck is used to assure that the components created do not have
// any pure virtual functions.
//

static inline void ValidCtrCheck(TUnlPictureSelector *)
{
  new TUnlPictureSelector(NULL);
}

__fastcall TUnlPictureSelector::TUnlPictureSelector(TComponent* Owner)
  : TWinControl(Owner)
{
  Width = 240;
  Height = 205;
  FComboBox = new TComboBox(this);
  FComboBox->Left = 0;
  FComboBox->Top = 0;
  FComboBox->Width = 150;
  FComboBox->Style = csDropDownList;
  FComboBox->OnClick = ComboBoxClick;
```

```
  FComboBox->Parent = this;
  FImage = new TImage(this);
  FImage->Left = 0;
  FImage->Top = FComboBox->Height;
  FImage->Width = Width;
  FImage->Height = Height - FComboBox->Height;
  FImage->Parent = this;
}

void __fastcall TUnlPictureSelector::CreateWnd()
{
  TWinControl::CreateWnd();
  for (int i=0;i<6;i++)
    FComboBox->Items->Add(Strings[i]);
  FComboBox->ItemIndex = 0;
  ComboBoxClick(0);
}

void __fastcall TUnlPictureSelector::ComboBoxClick(TObject* Sender)
{
  int index = FComboBox->Items->IndexOf(FComboBox->Text);
  FImage->Picture->LoadFromFile(Strings[index]);
}

namespace Pictureselector
{
  void __fastcall PACKAGE Register()
  {
    TComponentClass classes[1] = {__classid(TUnlPictureSelector)};
    RegisterComponents("BCB4Unleashed", classes, 0);
  }
}
```

The first draft of this component doesn't contain a lot of code. The component is not what I would call finished, but it does what it is advertised to do and that's all that counts for now. In order for this component to be finished, I should (at a minimum) resurface some of the TComboBox and TImage events. For example, I should have an OnSelectionChanged event that simply passes on the combo box's OnClick event. I talk about adding events later in the chapter in the section "Adding Events to a Component."

Creating the `ComboBox` and `Image` Components

This component declares two variables in the `private` section:

```
private:
  TComboBox* FComboBox;
  TImage* FImage;
```

These two controls are dynamically created, given some default values, and positioned in the component's constructor:

```
__fastcall TUnlPictureSelector::TUnlPictureSelector(TComponent* Owner)
  : TWinControl(Owner)
{
  Width = 240;
  Height = 205;
  FComboBox = new TComboBox(this);
  FComboBox->Left = 0;
  FComboBox->Top = 0;
  FComboBox->Width = 150;
  FComboBox->Style = csDropDownList;
  FComboBox->OnClick = ComboBoxClick;
  FComboBox->Parent = this;
  FImage = new TImage(this);
  FImage->Left = 0;
  FImage->Top = FComboBox->Height + 1;
  FImage->Width = Width;
  FImage->Height = Height - FComboBox->Height + 1;
  FImage->Parent = this;
}
```

First the component itself is set to a default size of 240 pixels wide and 205 pixels high. These are somewhat arbitrary values. I knew I would be using the splash images installed with C++Builder and that the images were 180×240 pixels. You can find the images in \Program Files\Common Files\Borland Shared\Images\Splash\256Color.

Every component has a default size and this code shows how to set the default size for a component.

Next I create the ComboBox dynamically and set some of its properties:

```
FComboBox = new TComboBox(this);
FComboBox->Left = 0;
FComboBox->Top = 0;
FComboBox->Width = 150;
FComboBox->Style = csDropDownList;
FComboBox->OnClick = ComboBoxClick;
FComboBox->Parent = this;
```

Notice that I set the Top and Left properties to 0. The TUnlPictureSelector will be the parent of the ComboBox and, as such, the position (0,0) is the top-left corner of the component. I set the Width property to an arbitrary value of 150 pixels. I thought the component looked better this way rather than having the combo box extend across the width of the component.

Now turn your attention to the line of code that assigns the OnClick event:

```
FComboBox->OnClick = ComboBoxClick;
```

This code assigns the combo box's OnClick event to a function called ComboBoxClick(). Here is the ComboBoxClick() function:

```
void __fastcall TUnlPictureSelector::ComboBoxClick(TObject* Sender)
{
  int index = FComboBox->Items->IndexOf(FComboBox->Text);
  FImage->Picture->LoadFromFile(Strings[index]);
}
```

When the combo box is clicked, the ComboBoxClick() function is called and the bitmap associated with the selected combo box item is loaded into the Image component. Without providing an internal handler for the combo box's OnClick event, I would have no way of knowing when the combo box selection changed.

Finally, notice the line of code that assigns the TUnlPictureSelector as the combo box's parent:

```
FComboBox->Parent = this;
```

As I said earlier, the combo box would never show itself without this line of code. Forgetting this one line of code has left many new component writers scratching their heads, wondering why the aggregate component isn't visible.

The rest of the code in the constructor creates the Image component and gives its properties default values. The bulk of the code is positioning and sizing code. I position the Image component on the left edge and just below the combo box. I size the Image so that it fills the remainder of the TUnlPictureSelector component.

> **NOTE**
>
> You may have noticed that the TUnlPictureSelector component does not have a destructor. If you are new to the VCL, you might think that I have violated the rules of object-oriented programming by not deleting the objects I allocated with operator new. I don't need to delete the objects because the VCL will do it for me. When the TUnlPictureSelector component is destroyed, the VCL automatically destroys the FComboBox and FImage objects.

Window Handles and Aggregate Components

A situation often arises when using aggregate components. In this component I am filling the combo box with a list of strings contained in a const variable called Strings. Most component writers' first thought is to fill the combo box with strings in the component's constructor. The problem with this approach is that the combo box doesn't have a window handle at this point in the creation process. Attempting to call any methods of the combo box that require a window handle will result in an exception at run time that reads as follows:

```
Control has no parent window.
```

This somewhat cryptic message is telling you that you are attempting to access some portion of the combo box that requires a window handle and that the window handle has not yet been created. The solution is to override the `CreateWnd()` method. When the base class `CreateWnd()` returns, all of the components have been created and the window handle is valid. Here's my overridden `CreateWnd()`:

```
void __fastcall TUnlPictureSelector::CreateWnd()
{
  TWinControl::CreateWnd();
  for (int i=0;i<6;i++)
    FComboBox->Items->Add(Strings[i]);
  FComboBox->ItemIndex = 0;
  ComboBoxClick(0);
}
```

First I call the base class's `CreateWnd()` function. After the base class's `CreateWnd()` function returns, I know that I have a valid window handle for the combo box and that I can add the strings to it. I also set the `ItemIndex` property to `0` so that the combo box displays the first item when the program runs. The combo box selection would be blank on program startup without this step. The last line of code calls the `ComboBoxClick()` function to display the bitmap in the `Image` component.

NOTE

In the last line of code in the preceding code example I call the `ComboBoxClick()` function like this:

```
ComboBoxClick(0);
```

I pass `0` for the `Sender` parameter because I'm not doing anything with `Sender` in the `ComboBoxClick()` function. In other words, it doesn't matter one bit what I pass in the `Sender` parameter because `ComboBoxClick()` doesn't use the parameter. Some folks would be more comfortable if I had called the function like this:

```
ComboBoxClick(this);
```

`Sender` is a `TObject` pointer, so passing `0` is just as good as passing `this` as long as I know that I'm not using the parameter in the `ComboBoxClick()` function.

File what I have said in this section away for future reference. I can almost guarantee that you'll get the "Component has no parent window" exception at some point. Remembering this one tidbit regarding `CreateWnd()` will save you hours of frustration when that time comes.

Using the `ComponentState` Property

Every component has a set property called `ComponentState`. Table 2.1 shows the possible values for the `ComponentState` property.

TABLE 2.1 `ComponentState` VALUES

Value	Description
csAncestor	The component was introduced in an ancestor form.
csDesigning	The component is being used at design time.
csDestroying	The component is about to be destroyed.
csFixups	The component is linked to a component on another form and that form hasn't yet been created. This flag is cleared when all fixes are completed.
csLoading	The form is being streamed in and the component is being loaded.
csReading	The component's property values are being loaded from a stream.
csUpdating	The component is updating its property values because an ancestor form is being modified.
csWriting	The form is being saved and the component's property values are being streamed out.

As a component writer, the `ComponentState` values you are most often concerned with are `csDesigning` and `csLoading`. By far, the `csDesigning` state is most widely used in component writing. Curious about this myself, I used C++Builder's Find in Files to search the VCL source code for the various component state values. Table 2.2 shows the results of the search.

TABLE 2.2 `ComponentState` VALUES FOUND IN THE VCL SOURCE CODE

Value	Count
csDesigning	254
csLoading	120

continues

TABLE 2.2 CONTINUED

Value	Count
csReading	50
csDestroying	35
csFixups	16
csUpdating	9
csWriting	6
csAncestor	3

I'm probably not going too far out on a limb by suggesting that you won't likely use ComponentState values other than csDesigning and csLoading.

Querying Design Time Use with csDesigning

One of the great aspects of components in C++Builder is that you often see at design time what the component will look like at run time. This is due to the fact that all of the code available to the component at run time is also available at design time. For example, setting a Label component's Caption property results in the label's text being updated on the form. Sometimes, however, you don't want all possible code executing at design time. Take the TUnlPictureSelector component, for example. As it was presented earlier in the chapter, this component will show the bitmap at design time as well as at run time. If you recall, the code that performs this step was in the CreateWnd() and ComboBoxClick() methods:

```
void __fastcall TUnlPictureSelector::CreateWnd()
{
  TWinControl::CreateWnd();
  for (int i=0;i<6;i++)
    FComboBox->Items->Add(Strings[i]);
  FComboBox->ItemIndex = 0;
  ComboBoxClick(0);
}

void __fastcall TUnlPictureSelector::ComboBoxClick(TObject* Sender)
{
  int index = FComboBox->Items->IndexOf(FComboBox->Text);
  FImage->Picture->LoadFromFile(Strings[index]);
}
```

Now suppose that you don't want the combo box's strings set at design time, nor do you want the bitmap displayed. In that case you would write the CreateWnd() method like this:

```
void __fastcall TUnlPictureSelector::CreateWnd()
{
  TWinControl::CreateWnd();
  if (!ComponentState.Contains(csDesigning)) {
    for (int i=0;i<6;i++)
      FComboBox->Items->Add(Strings[i]);
    FComboBox->ItemIndex = 0;
    ComboBoxClick(0);
  }
}
```

Now the code that loads the combo box and calls ComboBoxClick() is only executed at run time. The key line of code, of course, is this line:

```
if (!ComponentState.Contains(csDesigning)) {
```

This line effectively says, "If csDesiging is not in the ComponentState set, then perform the following code." Figure 2.8 shows the TUnlPictureSelector component on the form at design time when this code is implemented.

FIGURE 2.8

The PictureSelector *on a form at design time with the* csDesigning *check in place.*

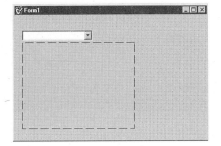

Earlier I encouraged you to test your components before installing them to the Component Palette. No matter how well you test your components, you will find that you need to modify the code after the component is installed. In particular, you won't be able to query the ComponentState property until the component is installed and used on a form at design time.

> **TIP**
>
> Once I have installed a component, I like to have the Package Manager handy so that I can quickly recompile it in order to see the changes I made to a component. I have found that docking the Package Manager to the bottom of the Code Editor is the best way to keep it where I can always get to it. I don't have to see the entire Package Manager window, just the toolbar. That way the Compile button is always within easy reach. Each time you recompile a package, any components in the package that are currently on a form are immediately updated with the new code changes.

Using `csLoading` to Determine a Component's Load State

Explaining a good use for the `csLoading` flag is more difficult than the case of the `csDesigning` flag. An explanation requires me to sidetrack for a moment and describe how the VCL form streaming mechanism works.

As you may or may not be aware, a VCL form is stored in the EXE as an `RCDATA` resource. In other words, a VCL form is not stored in the EXE as a window, nor is it a dialog resource. All C++Builder applications have a line in the project source code similar to this:

```
Application->CreateForm(__classid(TForm1), &Form1);
```

When this code executes, the VCL "unpacks" the `RCDATA` resource and creates a traditional window that can be displayed on the screen. It does the same for each of the components on the form. Part of that process means setting property values that were assigned at design time. This is typically referred to as *streaming the form in*. If any of the form's properties has a `write` method, then the `write` method is called during the streaming process. (This does not happen for properties that have an unaltered default value, but that's a discussion for a later time.) There are certain times when you don't want a property's `write` method to execute during the streaming process. The reasons are as varied as the wind, but you'll eventually run into this situation. You can prevent the code in a `write` method from executing if `csLoading` is found in the `ComponentState` property. Here's an example:

```
void __fastcall TStCustomTrayIcon::SetImages(TImageList* Value)
{
  FImages = Value;
  if (!ComponentState.Contains(csDesigning)
      && !ComponentState.Contains(csLoading))
```

```
    if (FIcon->Handle == 0 && Value != 0)
    {
      FImages->GetIcon(FImageIndex, ActiveIcon);
      ResetIcon();
    }
}
```

I originally wrote this code for the TStTrayIcon component in TurboPower's SysTools library. This code is meant to reload a system tray icon if the ImageList component used to store the icon is modified. I only want this code to execute if the user changes the component's Images property at run time. I do not want it to execute at design time, nor do I want it to execute during the form streaming process. By checking for both csDesigning and csLoading in the ComponentState, I am assured that the component functions as I expect.

Publishing Base Class Properties

Regardless of what class you derive your component from, you will almost certainly need to promote some of the base class's properties to published. Let me take a moment to discuss class visibility and how it pertains to properties.

The most restrictive form of class visibility is private visibility. *Private properties* are essentially for the component's internal use and are never available to the outside world. They aren't available to class or component users, and they aren't visible in derived classes. Once a property is declared private you can't get to it no matter what you do.

The next level of class visibility is protected. *Protected properties* cannot be accessed by class or component users. They can, however, be accessed from derived classes. In addition, they can be promoted to public or published by redeclaring them in derived classes.

Public properties can be accessed at run time via code. The Parent property is a perfect example. This property is not displayed in the Object Inspector, but is accessible at run time.

Published properties are those that are displayed in the Object Inspector when you drop a component on a form.

In order to promote a property's visibility, you simply redeclare the property in either the public or published section of your component. Earlier in the chapter I talked about the custom classes that VCL provides when I introduced the TUnlURLLabel component. Remember, TUnlURLLabel is derived from TLabel. I could have derived TUnlURLLabel from TCustomLabel instead. Had I derived from TCustomLabel, I would have had to publish all of the TCustomLabel properties. In that case, the declaration of TUnlURLLabel would look like the one shown in Listing 2.6.

LISTING 2.6   THE TUnlURLLabel DECLARATION IF THE COMPONENT WERE DERIVED FROM
`TCustomLabel`

```
class PACKAGE TUnlURLLabel : public TCustomLabel
{
private:
  String FURL;
protected:
  void __fastcall Click();
  DYNAMIC void __fastcall SetURL(String value);
public:
  __fastcall TUnlURLLabel(TComponent* Owner);
__published:
  // My new property
  __property String URL  = { read = FURL, write = SetURL };

  // The published properties of TLabel
  __property Align ;
  __property Alignment ;
  __property Anchors ;
  __property AutoSize ;
  __property BiDiMode ;
  __property Caption ;
  __property Color ;
  __property Constraints ;
  __property DragCursor ;
  __property DragKind ;
  __property DragMode ;
  __property Enabled ;
  __property FocusControl ;
  __property Font ;
  __property ParentBiDiMode ;
  __property ParentColor ;
  __property ParentFont ;
  __property ParentShowHint ;
  __property PopupMenu ;
  __property ShowAccelChar ;
  __property ShowHint ;
  __property Transparent ;
  __property Layout ;
  __property Visible ;
  __property WordWrap ;
  __property OnClick ;
  __property OnDblClick ;
  __property OnDragDrop ;
  __property OnDragOver ;
  __property OnEndDock ;
  __property OnEndDrag ;
  __property OnMouseDown ;
  __property OnMouseMove ;
  __property OnMouseUp ;
  __property OnStartDock ;
  __property OnStartDrag ;
};
```

That's all there is to promoting a property's visibility. All published components found in TLabel are redeclared in the __published section of the TUnlURLLabel class.

> **TIP**
>
> The list of redeclared properties in Listing 2.6 is significant. I didn't type them all in by hand. Instead, I knew that the list of properties I had to redeclare was precisely the same list of properties redeclared by the TLabel class. I simply opened STDCTRLS.HPP, located the declaration for the TLabel class, copied the list of properties from the published section of that class, and pasted it into my code.

It's important to understand that you can promote a property's visibility, but that you cannot reduce the visibility. In other words, once a property is published you cannot make it protected or private in a base class. That is precisely why the custom classes exist in the VCL, and why their properties are declared as protected. This gives you the option of deriving from one of the custom classes and promoting only those properties that you want in your new component.

The issue of redeclaring properties brings up an important question. Should you create a custom class for every component you write? I don't believe it's necessary in every situation. It's simply overkill in many cases. If, however, you are writing components for resale or for use by a large number of other programmers, then you should consider writing custom classes and deriving your actual component from the custom class. It will make your component more valuable to programmers wanting to extend the component.

Before leaving this discussion of redeclaring properties, let's go back for a moment to the TUnlPictureSelector component. You may have noticed that I didn't redeclare any properties when I created that component. As such, the component will only display a few properties in the Object Inspector. Figure 2.9 shows the Object Inspector when a TUnlPictureSelector is placed on the form.

FIGURE 2.9

The Object Inspector shows the published properties of the PictureSelector *component.*

Why are the properties shown in Figure 2.9 published for a component derived from TWinControl? It is because they are declared as published in either TWinControl or its ancestors TControl and TComponent. This list of properties will automatically be published for any component derived from TWinControl.

Once you have created your component you need to decide which of the base class's properties to promote to published. I can't give much advice regarding which properties to publish. Many component writers republish all of the base class properties. Some only republish those that make sense for the type of component they are writing. Certainly the latter approach is preferable, but it takes some understanding of the VCL to determine which properties to publish and which to leave protected.

The **TUnlClock** Component

The remainder of the topics covered in this chapter are illustrated by a clock component called TUnlClock. TUnlClock is derived from TCustomControl. I derived from TCustomControl because I needed both a window handle (for the timer messages) and a canvas on which to paint the control. TCustomControl provides both so it makes a perfect base class for my component. Table 2.3 lists the primary properties and events of TUnlClock.

TABLE 2.3   PRIMARY PROPERTIES AND EVENTS OF TUnlClock

Property or Event	*Description*
AutoSize property	When true, the component sizes itself based on the current font.
Color property	Sets the background color of the component.
Font property	Sets the font for the component.
Style property	Determines whether the time is displayed in 12- or 24-hour format.
Time property	Returns the current time. Time is a read-only public (run-time) property.
OnHourChange event	Generated each time the hour changes.
OnMinuteChange event	Generated each time the minute changes.
OnSecondChange event	Generated each time the second changes.

In addition to the properties listed in Table 2.3, TUnlClock also contains the published properties of its ancestor classes. Figure 2.10 shows the TUnlClock component on a form at run time.

Listings 2.7 and 2.8 show the header and source code for this component.

FIGURE 2.10

The TUnlClock *component displays a digital clock.*

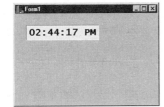

LISTING 2.7   THE HEADER FOR THE TUnlClock COMPONENT

```
#ifndef UnlClockH
#define UnlClockH

// enum for the Style property
enum TUnlClockStyle { cs24Hour, cs12Hour };

// event handler typedefs
typedef void __fastcall(__closure *TUnlClockMinuteChangeEvent)
  (TObject* Sender, int Minute);

typedef void __fastcall(__closure *TUnlClockHourChangeEvent)
  (TObject* Sender, int Hour);

class PACKAGE TUnlClock : public TCustomControl
{
private:
  // property data storage variables
  bool FAutoSize;
  TUnlClockStyle FStyle;

  // event data storage variables
  TNotifyEvent FOnSecondChange;
  TUnlClockMinuteChangeEvent FOnMinuteChange;
  TUnlClockHourChangeEvent FOnHourChange;

  // property read and write methods
  TDateTime __fastcall GetTime();
  void __fastcall SetAutoSize(bool value);

  // internal private variables
  int oldHour;
  int oldMinute;

protected:
  // overridden base class virtual methods
  virtual void __fastcall WndProc(TMessage& Message);
  virtual void __fastcall Paint();
  virtual void __fastcall CreateWnd();
```

continues

LISTING 2.7   CONTINUED

```cpp
  // virtual methods
  virtual void DoSecondChange();
  virtual void DoMinuteChange(int minute);
  virtual void DoHourChange(int hour);
  virtual void SetSize();
public:
  __fastcall TUnlClock(TComponent* Owner);
  __fastcall ~TUnlClock();

  // public property
  __property TDateTime Time  = { read = GetTime };

__published:

  // published properties
  __property bool AutoSize  =
     { read = FAutoSize, write = SetAutoSize, default = true };
  __property TUnlClockStyle Style  =
     { read = FStyle, write = FStyle };

  // published events
  __property TNotifyEvent OnSecondChange  =
     { read = FOnSecondChange, write = FOnSecondChange };
  __property TUnlClockMinuteChangeEvent OnMinuteChange  =
     { read = FOnMinuteChange, write = FOnMinuteChange };
  __property TUnlClockHourChangeEvent OnHourChange  =
     { read = FOnHourChange, write = FOnHourChange };

  // base class properties redeclared
  __property Color;
  __property Font;
};

#endif
```

LISTING 2.8   THE SOURCE CODE FOR THE TUnlClock COMPONENT

```cpp
#include <vcl.h>
#pragma hdrstop

#include "UnlClock.h"
#pragma package(smart_init)
#pragma resource "unlclock.res"

__fastcall TUnlClock::TUnlClock(TComponent* Owner)
        : TCustomControl(Owner)
{
  Width = 75;
```

```
    Height = 25;
    FStyle = cs12Hour;
    FAutoSize = true;
    Canvas->Brush->Style = bsClear;
    Word h, m, s, ms;
    Now().DecodeTime(&h, &m, &s, &ms);
    oldHour = h;
    oldMinute = m;
}


__fastcall TUnlClock::~TUnlClock()
{
    KillTimer(Handle, 1);
}

void __fastcall TUnlClock::CreateWnd()
{
    if (ComponentState.Contains(csDestroying))
        return;
    TCustomControl::CreateWnd();
    if (ComponentState.Contains(csDesigning))
        SetSize();
    SetTimer(Handle, 1, 1000, 0);
    ControlStyle = ControlStyle << csFramed << csOpaque;
}


TDateTime __fastcall TUnlClock::GetTime()
{
    return Now();
}

void __fastcall TUnlClock::WndProc(TMessage& Message)
{
    TCustomControl::WndProc(Message);
    if (Message.Msg == WM_TIMER) {
        Repaint();
        DoSecondChange();
        Word h, m, s, ms;
        Now().DecodeTime(&h, &m, &s, &ms);
        if (h != oldHour) {
            oldHour = h;
            DoHourChange(h);
        }
        if (m != oldMinute) {
            oldMinute = m;
            DoMinuteChange(m);
        }
    }
    if (Message.Msg == CM_FONTCHANGED)
        SetSize();
}
```

continues

LISTING 2.8   CONTINUED

```
void __fastcall TUnlClock::Paint()
{
  String S;
  Canvas->Font = Font;
  if (FStyle == cs24Hour)
    S = FormatDateTime("hh:mm:ss", Now());
  else
    S = FormatDateTime("hh:mm:ss ampm", Now());
  TRect rect = ClientRect;
  Canvas->Pen->Color = Color;
  Canvas->Brush->Color = Color;
  Canvas->Rectangle(0, 0, Width, Height);
  DrawText(Canvas->Handle, S.c_str(), S.Length(),
    &rect, DT_SINGLELINE | DT_VCENTER | DT_CENTER);
}

void TUnlClock::DoSecondChange()
{
  if (FOnSecondChange)
    FOnSecondChange(this);
}

void TUnlClock::DoMinuteChange(int Minute)
{
  if (FOnMinuteChange)
    FOnMinuteChange(this, Minute);
}

void TUnlClock::DoHourChange(int Hour)
{
  if (FOnHourChange)
    FOnHourChange(this, Hour);
}

void TUnlClock::SetSize()
{
  if (FAutoSize) {
    Canvas->Font = Font;
    Width = Canvas->TextWidth("00:00:00 AM") + 10;
    Height = Canvas->TextHeight("0") + 10;
  }
}

void __fastcall TUnlClock::SetAutoSize(bool value)
{
  FAutoSize = value;
  if (FAutoSize) {
    SetSize();
    Repaint();
```

```
  }
}

namespace Unlclock
{
  void __fastcall PACKAGE Register()
  {
    TComponentClass classes[1] = {__classid(TUnlClock)};
    RegisterComponents("BCB4Unleashed", classes, 0);
  }
}
```

The following sections describe the TUnlClock component code as I introduce you to additional component creation strategies.

Adding Events to a Component

Adding an event to a component is not particularly difficult, but it requires some forethought. Specifically, adding an event to a component requires these steps:

1. Carefully consider what the event does and what parameters the event handler should have.
2. Create an event handler function pointer.
3. Create a virtual method that will fire the event at the appropriate time.
4. Declare a data member for the event in the private section of the component's class.
5. Declare the event in the component's class.
6. Implement the code that fires the event.

I'll discuss the more complex of these steps in the following sections.

Defining an Event Handler

The most basic form of event is an event that simply provides notification that the event has occurred. An example is the OnClick event, which is found in most visual components. This event has a single parameter called Sender:

```
void __fastcall TForm1::FormClick(TObject *Sender)
{
}
```

This event type is defined in the VCL as TNotifyEvent. Here's the typedef for TNotifyEvent:

```
typedef void __fastcall
  (__closure *TNotifyEvent)(System::TObject* Sender);
```

This is a typedef for a closure, which is a special kind of function pointer used by the VCL. I won't explain closures here, but you can look it up in the C++Builder online help if you want more information.

When creating an event that provides simple notification, you declare the event of type TNotifyEvent. The OnSecondChange event of TUnlClock is a simple notification event. It is declared as follows:

```
__property TNotifyEvent OnSecondChange =
  { read = FOnSecondChange, write = FOnSecondChange };
```

The data storage member for the OnSecondChange event is called FOnSecondChange. It is declared in the private section of the TUnlClock class:

```
TNotifyEvent FOnSecondChange;
```

Writing a Virtual Method to Fire the Event

Each event should have a virtual method that is used within the component to fire the event. The method is virtual so that descendent classes can gain access to the method. It is declared in the protected section of the component's class for obvious OOP reasons. The virtual method that fires the OnSecondChange event is called DoSecondChange():

```
void TUnlClock::DoSecondChange()
{
  if (FOnSecondChange)
    FOnSecondChange(this);
}
```

This is standard event-generation code and illustrates the proper way to fire events. First I check to see if an event handler has been assigned to the event. I call FOnSecondChange if an event handler has been assigned, passing a pointer to the component (this) as a parameter. It is important that you write your event-firing code in this manner because, as you know, not all events must be handled. The user is free to handle any events he or she wants, and let any other events be handled in a default way. Writing your event-firing code following this formula will ensure that your component users can either handle the event or not handle the event as they choose.

I obviously need to call DoSecondChange() somewhere in my code or the event will never be fired. In the case of the TUnlClock component I do that in the WndProc() method:

```
void __fastcall TUnlClock::WndProc(TMessage& Message)
{
  TCustomControl::WndProc(Message);
  if (Message.Msg == WM_TIMER) {
    Repaint();
    DoSecondChange();
    Word h, m, s, ms;
    Now().DecodeTime(&h, &m, &s, &ms);
    if (h != oldHour) {
      oldHour = h;
      DoHourChange(h);
    }
    if (m != oldMinute) {
      oldMinute = m;
      DoMinuteChange(m);
    }
  }
  if (Message.Msg == CM_FONTCHANGED)
    SetSize();
}
```

I discuss this method in detail in the section, "Overriding WndProc()." For now you only need to know that this method will be called every time a WM_TIMER message is received (once per second in this case). Note that I call DoSecondChange() in response to the WM_TIMER message. DoSecondChange() will in turn call the user's OnSecondChange event handler if one has been provided.

As I have said, the OnSecondChange event is a TNotify event. TNotify is provided by the VCL, so you can use it anytime you need a notification event. Further, you can use any of the VCL event handler types in your components. If you have an event whose parameters correspond to an existing VCL event, then you can use that event type to declare your event.

Creating User-Defined Events

You can use any of the VCL event types when declaring an event. Eventually, though, you will encounter a situation where no VCL event type matches the event you are creating. In that case, you need to declare your own event type. TUnlClock has two events that fall into this category: OnMinuteChange and OnHourChange. These two events each pass the current minute or hour to the event handler. A blank event handler for OnMinuteChange, for example, looks like this:

```
void __fastcall
TForm1::UnlClock1MinuteChange(TObject *Sender, int Minute)
{
}
```

As you can see, this event handler has the usual `Sender` parameter. In addition, it has an integer parameter called `Minute`. Look at the declaration for the `OnHourChange` and `OnMinuteChange` events:

```
__property TUnlClockMinuteChangeEvent OnMinuteChange  =
   { read = FOnMinuteChange, write = FOnMinuteChange };
__property TUnlClockHourChangeEvent OnHourChange  =
   { read = FOnHourChange, write = FOnHourChange };
```

Note that the `OnMinuteChange` event is of type `TUnlClockMinuteChangeEvent` and that the `OnHourChange` event is of type `TUnlClockHourChange`. These two event types are declared as follows:

```
typedef void __fastcall(__closure *TUnlClockMinuteChangeEvent)
   (TObject* Sender, int Minute);
typedef void __fastcall(__closure *TUnlClockHourChangeEvent)
   (TObject* Sender, int Hour);
```

Granted, these type names are rather long and unwieldy. The type names themselves are never seen by the user of the component, so it's not really a factor. I'd rather see long type names for event handlers than short, cryptic names.

The `OnHourChange` and `OnMinuteChange` events work exactly the same, so I'll finish this section by describing just the `OnMinuteChange` event. `OnMinuteChange`, like `OnSecondChange` discussed earlier,.is fired from the `WndProc()` method. Here's the pertinent code:

```
Word h, m, s, ms;
Now().DecodeTime(&h, &m, &s, &ms);
if (m != oldMinute) {
  oldMinute = m;
  DoMinuteChange(m);
}
```

I use the `DecodeTime()` method of the `TDateTime` class to break the current time into hours, minutes, seconds, and milliseconds. I then check the current minute against a class variable called `oldMinute`. If the two values are the same, it means that the minute hasn't changed since the last time I fired the `OnMinuteChange` event; I don't do anything further. If the current minute is not the same as the value stored in `oldMinute`, then I need to fire the event. I set `oldMinute` to the current minute and then call `DoMinuteChange()`, passing the current minute as a parameter. `DoMinuteChange()` looks like this:

```
void TUnlClock::DoMinuteChange(int Minute)
{
  if (FOnMinuteChange)
    FOnMinuteChange(this, Minute);
}
```

This should look familiar to you, as it is nearly identical to the DoSecondChange() method discussed earlier. The only difference is that I pass the current minute to the user's OnMinuteChange event handler, if it has been assigned. The user can then do something in his or her event handler based on the new minute value.

> **NOTE**
>
> C++Builder has a quirk when it comes to events such as OnMinuteChange and OnHourChange. Note that the event types for these two events have identical parameters; they both have a TObject* parameter and an int parameter. C++Builder generates this event handler when you generate an event handler for the OnHourChange event at design time:
>
> ```
> void __fastcall
> TForm1::UnlClock1HourChange(TObject *Sender, int Minute)
> {
> }
> ```
>
> Do you see the problem? The event handler has a parameter called Minute, rather than Hour, as it should be. This is because the IDE searches for the first event type in the component's header that matches the required type. In this case the IDE finds the TUnlMinuteChangeEvent declaration, sees that it has the correct parameter list, and uses it to generate the event handler. There's nothing wrong with the code as far as the compiler is concerned. The program will compile and run just fine. The problem is that the name of the second parameter is not what you expect. In my opinion this is a bug in the IDE's code generation logic, but I'm sure that others would disagree.
>
> In the real world I would have created a single event type that had a parameter named Value. That way the event handler could be used with both the OnMinuteChange event and the OnHourChanged event. I actually coded this component as I did so I could point out this quirk in C++Builder.

Returning Values from Event Handlers

The events discussed thus far don't require, nor do they accept, feedback from the component user. Sometimes, however, you want to get input from the user in an event handler. Event handlers should not return a value. That is, an event handler's return type should always be void.

> **NOTE**
>
> The compiler won't prevent you from declaring an event handler that has a
> return type other than void. It is generally understood by component writers,
> however, that return types other than void may not be supported in future ver-
> sions of Delphi and C++Builder. For that reason you should always create event
> types that return void.

If an event handler cannot (or should not) return a value, how do you get input from the
user? The answer is that you declare an event type that has one or more parameters
passed by reference or by pointer. Let's take the case of a component that performs a
lengthy process. Such a component could have an event called OnProgress. The
OnProgress event handler might contain a parameter called Abort. The event type would
be declared as follows:

```
typedef void __fastcall(__closure *TMyProgressEvent)
  (TObject* Sender, bool& Abort);
```

The code that does your processing will look something like this:

```
void TMyComponent::StartProcessing()
{
  bool done = false;
  while (!done) {
    // code that does some processing
    done = DoProgress();
  }
}

bool TMyComponent::DoProgress()
{
  bool abort = false; // false by default
  if (FOnDoProgress)
    FOnDoProgress(this, abort)
  return abort;
}
```

Note that the processing loop calls the DoProgress() method to periodically fire the
OnProgress event. It also sets the done variable to the return value of DoProgress(). A
local variable called abort in the DoProgress() method is declared and set to false.
This is the default for the event's Abort parameter. Processing will continue if the user
doesn't specifically set the Abort parameter to true. Additionally, if the user doesn't
define an event handler for the OnProgress event, the DoProgress() method returns
false and processing continues uninterrupted. Processing will stop, however, if the user

has an event handler for the `OnProgress` event and sets `Abort` to `true`. An example follows:

```
void __fastcall TForm1::MyComponentProgress(TObject *Sender, bool &Abort)
{
  // do some checking on the progress and then...
  if (SomeCondition)
    Abort = true;
}
```

When the `Abort` parameter is set to `true`, processing in the component stops. Naturally, this fictitious event handler should probably have an additional parameter to provide a percentage complete value to the user. I didn't add that parameter to the event because I wanted to keep the example to a minimum.

Overriding the `WndProc()` Method

Every windowed component has a virtual method called `WndProc()`. This method is called every time Windows or the VCL sends a message to the component's window handle. In the case of `TUnlClock`, I am looking for two messages: `WM_TIMER` and `CM_FONTCHANGED`.

Before I get into the specifics of how I use `WndProc()`, let me explain how I am using the timer in the `TUnlClock` component. I chose to use the Windows API to implement the timer rather than using a VCL `TTimer` within my class. I did this so I could show you that you can use the API just as easily as you can use the VCL within a component. I start the timer in my `CreateWnd()` method:

```
SetTimer(Handle, 1, 1000, 0);
```

I pass the window handle of my component, 1 for the timer ID, `1000` for the timer interval (1 second), and `0` for the final parameter. The final parameter is used only if you have a timer callback function. In this case I am telling Windows to send the `WM_TIMER` message to my window procedure and am not using a timer callback. The timer starts when this code executes.

I remove the timer in my destructor:

```
KillTimer(Handle, 1);
```

I call `KillTimer()`, again passing my window handle and the timer ID I used when I started the timer. That's all there is to creating and destroying a timer via the Windows API.

Once the timer has started, my window procedure will get a `WM_TIMER` message every 1,000 milliseconds. VCL surfaces the window procedure through the `WndProc()` method.

I perform the appropriate processing in my `WndProc()` that I do when I get a `WM_TIMER` message:

```
void __fastcall TUnlClock::WndProc(TMessage& Message)
{
  TCustomControl::WndProc(Message);
  if (Message.Msg == WM_TIMER) {
    Repaint();
    DoSecondChange();
    Word h, m, s, ms;
    Now().DecodeTime(&h, &m, &s, &ms);
    if (h != oldHour) {
      oldHour = h;
      DoHourChange(h);
    }
    if (m != oldMinute) {
      oldMinute = m;
      DoMinuteChange(m);
    }
  }
  if (Message.Msg == CM_FONTCHANGED)
    SetSize();
}
```

I've already explained most of the processing I do in response to a `WM_TIMER` message. The first line of code following the `if` statement calls `Repaint()` to force my `Paint()` method to be called. After that comes the code that fires the various events.

Notice that I am also responding to the `CM_FONTCHANGED` message. The VCL sends this message when any of the font's properties are changed. I need this message so that I can determine whether the font changed, both at run time and design time. This allows the component to be immediately updated if any aspect of the font changes. In this case I call a private method called `SetSize()` to update the component's size. Here's the `SetSize()` method:

```
void TUnlClock::SetSize()
{
  if (FAutoSize) {
    Canvas->Font = Font;
    Width = Canvas->TextWidth("00:00:00 AM") + 10;
    Height = Canvas->TextHeight("0") + 10;
  }
}
```

This method sets the size of the component, but only if the `AutoSize` property is `true`. I pass the widest string my clock can display to the `TextWidth()` method of the canvas and add a little extra for the border. I assign the return value from `TextWidth()` to the `Width` property. The call to `TextHeight()` does the equivalent to set the height of the component. If `AutoSize` is `false`, nothing happens when this method is called.

I could have used a message map to respond to the WM_TIMER and CM_FONTCHANGED messages rather than overriding WndProc(). Had I done that, the message map and its corresponding message handlers would look like this:

```
BEGIN_MESSAGE_MAP
  VCL_MESSAGE_HANDLER(WM_TIMER, TMessage, WmTimer);
  VCL_MESSAGE_HANDLER(CM_FONTCHANGED, TMessage, CmFontChanged);
END_MESSAGE_MAP(TCustomControl)

void __fastcall TUnlClock::WmTimer(TMessage& Message)
{
  Repaint();
  DoSecondChange();
  Word h, m, s, ms;
  Now().DecodeTime(&h, &m, &s, &ms);
  if (h != oldHour) {
    oldHour = h;
    DoHourChange(h);
  }
  if (m != oldMinute) {
    oldMinute = m;
    DoMinuteChange(m);
  }
}

void __fastcall TUnlClock::CmFontChanged(TMessage& Message)
{
  SetSize();
}
```

In the end, it probably doesn't matter whether you override WndProc() or whether you use a message map. I must confess that I initially chose to override WndProc() because I don't like typing those message map macros!

Painting the Component

Custom components often involve a fair amount of painting code. The TCustomControl class has a Paint() method and this is where you place your painting code. As I said earlier, I chose TCustomControl as a base class because I knew I could override Paint() and paint my component there. Here's the Paint() method for TUnlClock:

```
void __fastcall TUnlClock::Paint()
{
  String S;
  Canvas->Font = Font;
  if (FStyle == cs24Hour)
    S = FormatDateTime("hh:mm:ss", Now());
  else
```

```
    S = FormatDateTime("hh:mm:ss ampm", Now());
  TRect rect = ClientRect;
  Canvas->Pen->Color = Color;
  Canvas->Brush->Color = Color;
  Canvas->Rectangle(0, 0, Width, Height);
  DrawText(Canvas->Handle, S.c_str(), S.Length(),
     &rect, DT_SINGLELINE | DT_VCENTER | DT_CENTER);
}
```

The second line in the Paint() method assigns the component's font to the Font property of the component's Canvas. The Canvas property is a member of TCustomControl, so you won't find it declared anywhere in the TUnlClock class declaration. It's already there, so I can use it without doing anything special. After that I use the Style property's value to format a string for display. I use the FormatDateTime() function to set the display type I want. Notice that I pass the global function Now() to get the current system time.

The rest of the code is typical painting code. I set canvas's pen and brush colors to the value of the Color property. After that I call Rectangle() to fill the client area of the component with the specified color. This gives me a clean slate on which to draw the text. Finally, I call DrawText() to paint the formatted display string on the component. I admit a personal fondness for the DrawText() function. This function allows you to display text in a rectangle in many different ways. In this case I am centering the text both horizontally and vertically. Why the TCanvas class doesn't have its own DrawText() method is something I can't fully comprehend. It's a very useful function to have in your component painting arsenal.

You may have noticed in Figure 2.10 that TUnlClock has a 3D border. The Paint() method obviously doesn't contain any code to draw the border. The border is automatically drawn when the ComponentStyle property contains the csFramed style. I set that style in the CreateWnd() method:

```
ControlStyle = ControlStyle << csFramed << csOpaque;
```

I added the csFramed style simply because I like the look. If I were creating this component for public consumption, I would have either added a BorderStyle property that turned the frame on and off or provided additional border styles. In that case I would have to manually draw the border. I might use a series of MoveTo()/LineTo() function calls to draw the border. That's tedious business, though, so I would likely save myself some time and use the little-known Frame3D() function. An example follows:

```
Frame3D(Canvas, rect, clBtnShadow, clBtnHighlight, 1);
```

This call draws the component's border with a recessed look. The third parameter specifies the top color and the fourth parameter specifies the bottom color. The fifth parameter specifies the border width. To get a raised look, reverse the third and fourth parameters:

```
Frame3D(Canvas, rect, clBtnHighlight, clBtnShadow, 1);
```

Further, you can draw a bevel by drawing one frame inside another with the colors reversed. This is an example:

```
Frame3D(Canvas, rect, clBtnShadow, clBtnHighlight, 1);
rect.Left = 1;
rect.Top = 1;
rect.Bottom - rect.Bottom - 1;
rect.Left - rect.Left - 1;
Frame3D(Canvas, rect, clBtnHighlight, clBtnShadow, 1);
```

The VCL uses `Frame3D()` to draw the `Panel` component's border based on the values of the `BevelInner`, `BevelOuter`, and `BevelWidth` properties. Don't forget about this function and its cousin, `DrawButtonFace()`. They will come in handy when drawing custom components.

Summary

After reading this chapter you should have a good understanding of how to write basic components. I introduced you to component writing and gave you some important information for writing robust components. At the risk of repeating myself, I'll say that writing robust components means carefully considering all situations in which your components might be used. This chapter described some of the obstacles that can cause the beginning component writer to give up in frustration and provided solutions for those obstacles. Personally, I think writing good components is a challenging and satisfying experience. The best way to learn how to write components is to simply write a lot of components. There are many design issues that you are likely to encounter when you start writing components in earnest. The only sure way to solve those issues is through experience.

CHAPTER 3

Advanced Component Creation

by Kent Reisdorph

This chapter covers some of the more advanced component creation topics. I start with a discussion of property and component editors. At the end of those sections, I revisit the question of packages and talk a bit more about how to separate your components into runtime and designtime packages. After that I spend some time explaining a few of the VCL virtual methods you may have to override in your components. I also explain how to create exception classes for your components and how to use exceptions to write robust components. I end this chapter explaining some of the techniques you may need to implement when writing non-visual components.

After reading this chapter you will know how to

- Create component and property editors
- Create a property editor for an `AnsiString` property
- Debug component and property editors
- Create exception classes for your components
- Create a hidden window for non-visual components

Writing Property Editors

Simply put, *property editors* provide a mechanism that allows you to modify property values in the Object Inspector. All published properties use a property editor. You might not have given it much thought, but all property values in the Object Inspector are displayed as strings. That means that the property's actual value must be converted to a string so that it can be displayed. You don't have to often worry about property editors because the VCL has built-in property editors that are automatically applied based on the property type. For example, say you write a component that has the properties shown in Table 3.1.

TABLE 3.1 Properties of a Sample Component

Property	Type
Options	set
Style	enumeration
Size	integer
Helper	THelper class
Caption	string
Active	Boolean

You don't have to write any property editors for these properties because the VCL automatically applies a built-in property editor in each case. As component writers, we take this service for granted. The VCL does a tremendous amount of work behind the scenes to assist component writers.

When do you need a property editor? You need a property editor when one of your properties has special requirements for presenting the property value to the user in the Object Inspector or special rules for setting the property value.

It's easy to confuse property editors with the services your read and write methods can provide. Say, for example, that you have written a meter component and that it has a `Position` property. Further, say you only allow the `Position` property to have a range of 0 to 100. In this case you don't need a property editor to enforce the 0 to 100 range. All you need is a properly implemented write method:

```
void __fastcall TMyMeter::SetPosition(int value)
{
  if (value < 0 || value> 100)
    value = 0;
  FPosition = value;
}
```

This code simply changes the `Position` property to 0 if a value outside the range of 0 to 100 is entered. The use of a property editor would be overkill in this case. Don't go looking for extra work when it may not be necessary!

All of the proceeding aside, there are still times when you must create a property editor for your properties. Creating a property editor requires these steps:

1. Choose a base class for your property editor.

2. Create a property editor class by deriving from one of the VCL property editor classes and override methods of the base class to provide specialized editing of the property.

3. Register the property editor.

The following sections explain how to create a property editor. The next few sections are theoretical in nature; later sections get to some concrete examples of property editors.

Choosing a Base Class

You must create a property editor class for each property that requires specialized editing. First you must decide on the base class from which you will derive your new class. As I said earlier, the VCL provides built-in property editors for the basic data types found in the VCL. Table 3.2 shows the VCL classes that can be used as base classes for your property editors, and has a description of each.

3

ADVANCED
COMPONENT
CREATION

TABLE 3.2   VCL PROPERTY EDITOR BASE CLASSES

Class Name	*Description*
TCharProperty	For properties of type char. The Password property of the TEdit component is this type of property editor. The editor allows you to enter a single character or a decimal value preceded by a pound sign. For example, to make the password character an asterisk you can enter either * or #42 for the property's value.
TClassProperty	For properties that are instances of a class. The Object Inspector displays each published property of the class when the property node is expanded. The Font property found in most windowed components provides an example.
TColorProperty	For properties of type TColor. The user can choose a value from the drop-down list or can type a hexadecimal value directly. Additionally, the Color dialog is displayed when you double-click the value.
TComponentProperty	For properties that are other components. The Images property of the ToolBar component provides an example. When you drop down the property editor in the Object Inspector, a list of ImageList components on the form is displayed.
TEnumProperty	For properties that are enumerations. Each item in the enumeration is shown in the drop-down list.
TFloatProperty	For floating-point properties.
TFontNameProperty	A list of all installed fonts on the system is displayed in the drop-down list. The Name property of the TFont class has this type of property editor.
TFontProperty	For properties of type TFont. The Font dialog is displayed when you click the ellipses button in the Object Inspector.
TIntegerProperty	For properties of type int.
TMethodProperty	Used to choose a method. This property editor is used by the VCL to display event handlers available for a particular event.
TOrdinalProperty	The base class for all the integral data type property editors (TCharProperty, TIntegerProperty, TEnumProperty, and so on).
TPropertyEditor	The base class for all property editors.
TSetElementProperty	The property editor for set elements. The set element can be toggled to true or false to include or exclude the element from the set. The individual styles found in the Style property of the TFont class use this type of property editor. The base class for this property editor is TNestedProperty.

Class Name	Description
TSetProperty	For set properties. The set elements are displayed when the property name is double-clicked in the Object Inspector. The Style property of the TFont class uses this type of property editor.
TStringProperty	For properties of type AnsiString.

The property editor classes listed in Table 3.2 are not by any means the only property editors that VCL provides. Instead, Table 3.2 lists those property editors that you are most likely to use as base classes for your own property editors. Other property editor classes found in the VCL include:

TBoolProperty	TImeNameProperty
TCaptionProperty	TModalResultProperty
TComponentNameProperty	TMPFilenameProperty
TCursorProperty	TShortCutProperty
TDateProperty	TTabOrderProperty
TDateTimeProperty	TTimeProperty
TFontCharsetProperty	

Without question, the TStringProperty class is used most often to create custom property editors. The TComponentProperty and TClassProperty editor classes also get some work. You'll have to derive from the ultimate base class of all property editors—TPropertyEditor—for true custom property editors.

It's fairly obvious where some of these component editors might be used. There are others, however, whose use might not be immediately apparent. A few examples could help you understand how you could use some of the lesser-used property editors. Assume you are writing a component that encapsulates serial communications. You would likely have a communications port component that has a BaudRate property. The property editor for the BaudRate property allows you to select from a list of typical baud rates. Your property editor likely displays the values 150, 300, 600, 1200, 2400, and so on, up to a baud rate of 115200.

Next consider the case of an enumeration property. In some cases the user might be allowed to select an item from the list, or elect not to select anything at all. A property

3

ADVANCED
COMPONENT
CREATION

editor for this type of property might show the list of possible values, as well as an item at the top of the list labeled (None).

Choose the base class for your property editor based on the property type and on the property editor's purpose. It may take some experience writing property editors before you know exactly which base class to use for a particular type of property editor.

Creating a Property Editor Class

After you have decided on a base class for your property editor, you must derive a class from the base class. This step is so simple as to not warrant further explanation. (I'll show you an example in just a bit.) The real work comes when you begin overriding the base class's virtual methods. Table 3.3 lists some of the virtual methods that you may have to override depending on the type of property editor you are creating.

TABLE 3.3 PROPERTY EDITOR VIRTUAL METHODS

Value	*Description*
AllEqual	This method is called when multiple properties are selected on a form. If AllEqual() returns true, the property value is shown in the Object Inspector. If AllEqual() returns false, the property is blank in the Object Inspector.
Edit	This method is called when the property editor's ellipses button is clicked or when the property is double-clicked. Generally used when the property editor displays a dialog.
GetAttributes	Sets the property editor attributes.
GetEditLimit	Sets the number of characters the user is allowed to enter for the property. If no edit limit is specified, the default of 255 is used.
GetValue	Returns the string value of the property.
GetValues	Used to specify a list of values to display in the property editor. Usually used for enumerated properties but can be used for other property types as well.
SetValue	Sets the string value for the property.

Once again, this is not an all-inclusive list. These are simply the methods that you are most likely to override when writing property editors.

Before I go on, let me show you a complete property editor class. The class, shown in Listing 3.1, is the property editor for a property called FileName. It simply pops up an Open dialog so the user can choose a filename. First look at the listing; I explain later what it does.

LISTING 3.1 A PROPERTY EDITOR FOR THE *FileName* PROPERTY

```
class TUnlFileNameProperty : public TStringProperty {
  public:
    TPropertyAttributes __fastcall GetAttributes()
    {
      return TPropertyAttributes() << paDialog;
    }
    void __fastcall Edit()
    {
      TOpenDialog* dlg = new TOpenDialog(Application);
      dlg->FileName = GetValue();
      if (dlg->Execute())
        Value = dlg->FileName;
    }
};
```

Notice that this class is derived from `TStringProperty` and that it overrides the `GetAttributes()` and `Edit()` methods.

In this property editor I used inline functions for the `GetAttributes()` and `Edit()` functions. I did this for two primary reasons. First, the code is easier to read if you keep it all in one place. Second, I know that only one instance of this class will appear in the designtime package so there's no penalty for using inline functions in this case.

Overriding the `GetAttributes()` Method

The first function you see in Listing 3.1 is `GetAttributes()`. You should always override `GetAttributes()` in your property editors. This function is used to tell the VCL what parameters the property editor will operate under. As you can see, `GetAttributes()` returns a `TPropertyAttributes` set. Table 3.4 lists the possible values for `TPropertyAttributes`.

TABLE 3.4 ELEMENTS IN THE TPropertyAttributes SET

Value	Description
paAutoUpdate	The property should be immediately updated on any change to the property. The `Caption` property of most components has this attribute.
paDialog	The property editor displays a form to the user. When this value is set, an ellipses button appears in the Object Inspector when the property is selected. The property editor's `Edit()` method is called when the ellipses button is clicked. Override the `Edit()` method to display a form to the user.
paMultiSelect	The property editor is available when the user selects multiple components on a form.

continues

TABLE 3.4   CONTINUED

Value	Description
paReadOnly	The property is forced to read-only.
paRevertable	Indicates that the Revert to Inherited Item on the Menu Designer context menu should be enabled.
paSortList	The property editor sorts the list of values.
paSubProperties	The property editor has subproperties. Override the `GetProperties()` method to provide the property values.
paValueList	The property editor displays a list of possible values. Override the `GetValues()` method to provide the values the Object Inspector will display.

A couple more examples will help drive home my point about `GetAttributes()`. Say you have a `Version` property that shows the current version of your product. Further, say that the property editor for this property displays an About dialog to the user proclaiming the greatness of your company. Your overridden `GetAttributes()` method will look like this:

```
PropertyAttributes __fastcall GetAttributes()
{
  return TPropertyAttributes() << paDialog << paReadOnly;
}
```

In the case of a property editor that displays a list of values to the user, the `GetAttributes()` method would be overridden as follows:

```
PropertyAttributes __fastcall GetAttributes()
{
  return TPropertyAttributes() << paValueList;
}
```

Overriding `GetAtributes()` is a simple step, but one you don't want to forget.

Overriding the `Edit()` Method

The `Edit()` method is the only remaining code in the property editor shown in Listing 3.1:

```
void __fastcall Edit()
{
  TOpenDialog* dlg = new TOpenDialog(Application);
  dlg->FileName = GetValue();
  if (dlg->Execute())
    Value = dlg->FileName;
  delete dlg;
}
```

This code first creates a `TOpenDialog` component dynamically. Next, the `FileName` property of the Open dialog is set to the current value of the component's `FileName` property. This is done by calling `GetValue()`, which returns the value of the property for which this property editor has been registered. After that, the `Execute()` method is called to show the Open dialog. If the user clicks OK, the value of the Open dialog's `FileName` property is assigned to the `Value` property of the property editor. This updates the property's value in the Object Inspector. Finally, I delete the `TOpenDialog` pointer to free the memory allocated for the dialog.

The `Value` property is mentioned in the previous paragraph. This property contains the string value of the property. Look at the second line of code again:

```
dlg->FileName = GetValue();
```

I could have used the `Value` property here instead of calling `GetValue()`:

```
dlg->FileName = Value;
```

The `SetValue()` and `GetValue()` methods and the `Value` property work together; you can use them almost interchangeably. I used both the `GetValue()` method and the `Value` property in the `TUnlFileNameProperty` class to illustrate use of both.

Other `TPropertyEditor` Properties and Methods

As you might have guessed from the previous discussion of the `Value` property, the `TPropertyEditor` class has several properties that you can use when writing property editors. Those properties are listed in Table 3.5.

TABLE 3.5 `TPropertyEditor` PROPERTIES

Property	Description
Designer	A pointer to the IDE's `IFormDesigner` interface.
PrivateDirectory	A string that contains a working directory as specified by the IDE. If your component uses temporary files, they should be stored in this directory.
PropCount	The count of the components selected that have this property. Only valid when the `paMultiSelect` attribute is set.
Value	The string representation of the property's value.

Earlier I presented a list of virtual functions found in the `TPropertyEditor` class. In addition to those methods, there are other `TPropertyEditor` methods you can call within your property editors. The only two methods of significance are `GetComponent()` and `GetName()`. The `GetComponent()` method returns a pointer to the Nth component being edited. If the property editor doesn't support multiple selection, then only the 0th component can be retrieved. The pointer returned is of type `TPersistent`, so you must cast the pointer to the type of your component to gain access to the component. An example follows:

```
TMyComponent* myComponent =
  dynamic_cast<TMyComponent*>(GetComponent(0));
```

The `GetName()` method, as its name implies, returns the name of the property being edited.

Registering the Property Editor

Once you have your property editor written, you need to register it with the C++Builder IDE. Registering a property editor is accomplished with a call to `RegisterPropertyEditor()`. Here is the declaration for `RegisterPropertyEditor()`:

```
extern PACKAGE void __fastcall RegisterPropertyEditor(
  PTypeInfo PropertyType,
  TMetaClass* ComponentClass,
  const AnsiString PropertyName,
  TMetaClass* EditorClass);
```

An example call to `RegisterPropertyEditor()` looks like this:

```
RegisterPropertyEditor(__typeinfo(TMyOptions),
  __classid(TTestLabel), "Options",
  __classid(TMyOptionsProperty));
```

The `PropertyType` parameter is used to specify the data type of the property for which this property editor applies. You obtain the property type via the `__typeinfo` keyword. Unfortunately, `__typeinfo` is designed for use with VCL classes only. This limitation immediately puts the C++Builder component writer at a disadvantage. It effectively means that you cannot register property editors for intrinsic types such as `int` or `char`. It also means you can't register property editors for properties of the `AnsiString` and `Set` classes. As you might guess, that excludes nearly all properties your component might contain! Fortunately, there is a workaround, which is discussed in the next section, "Registering `AnsiString` Property Editors."

The `ComponentClass` parameter is used to specify which components use this property editor. In most cases you will pass the class name of your component for this parameter. In some cases, you may want the property editor to be registered for every component of yours that is derived from a common base class. In that case you will pass the name of your base class in this parameter. In rare cases you will want the property editor to be registered for all properties with the given name. In that case you would pass 0 for the

ComponentClass parameter. Obviously, you need to take great care in using this technique; you may affect components other than your own. The class name is passed via the __classid keyword.

The PropertyName parameter is the name of the property for which this property editor will be registered. If you pass an empty string for the PropertyName parameter, the property editor is registered for all properties of the type specified in the PropertyType parameter. Here again, you need to be careful if you choose to register a property editor for all properties of a given type.

The EditorClass property is the name of your property editor class. Like the ComponentClass parameter, this parameter is passed using the __classid keyword.

The call to RegisterPropertyEditor() must be located in the component's Register() function. It is usually placed just above the call to RegisterComponents() in your component source code. An example follows:

```
namespace Filememo
{
  void __fastcall PACKAGE Register()
  {
    RegisterPropertyEditor(__typeinfo(TMyOptions),
      __classid(TTestLabel), "Options",
      __classid(TMyOptionsProperty));
    TComponentClass classes[1] = {__classid(TUnlFileMemo)};
    RegisterComponents("BCB4Unleashed", classes, 0);
  }
}
```

If all of the parameters are correct, your property editor will be registered when your component's package is installed to the Component Palette. If one or more parameters are incorrect, you may get a compiler error; alternatively, the package will compile but the component editor won't be installed. If that happens, be sure to double check your RegisterPropertyEditor() function and make any necessary adjustments.

Registering AnsiString Property Editors

As I said earlier, most of the property editors you write will be for string properties. This immediately raises a problem. If you recall, the first parameter for the RegisterPropertyEditor() function takes a __typeinfo keyword. Unfortunately, __typeinfo only works with classes derived from VCL classes. The C++Builder string class, AnsiString, isn't derived from a VCL class. As such, the following code will generate a compiler error:

```
RegisterPropertyEditor(__typeinfo(String),
  __classid(TMyFileMemo), "FileName",
  __classid(TMyFileNameProperty));
```

When this code is compiled, the compiler will issue a compiler error that says the following:

```
__classid requires VCL style class type.
```

At this point the game is up for many C++Builder component writers. This is not the type of compiler error to which you can say, "Oh, I know what the problem is," fix it, and go on. This is a compiler error that leaves you staring at the monitor, wondering what your next step should be.

Fortunately, there is a solution to the problem. Actually, there are two solutions, but one is terribly unwieldy. Until fairly recently, the prescribed solution to this problem was to derive a class from TPersistent, add an AnsiString as a class member, and then register this class as the property type in the call to RegisterPropertyEditor(). This also meant that the property itself would have to be of this type rather than just a plain AnsiString. This meant writing code like this:

```
FileName->String = "c:\\test.dat";
```

You could have just written this:

```
FileName = "c:\\test.dat";
```

This class you create could contain a lot of constructors and overloaded operators to make the code more readable, but writing code like that starts to get pretty deep pretty fast for many C++ programmers. Clearly, implementing an AnsiString property editor using this technique takes some work.

> **NOTE**
>
> If you want to know more about this method of writing an AnsiString property editor, I suggest you check out Mark Cashman's Web site at
> http://www.geocities.com/~mcashman/workshop/cbuilder/propedit.htm.

Fortunately, a simpler solution was posted recently on the Inprise newsgroups by Mark Van Ditta. Mark dug around in the VCL source code and decided that there had to be a way to solve this problem without going to so much trouble. What he discovered what that C++Builder's __typeinfo keyword was simply emulating what Object Pascal's TypeInfo() function does. Specifically, it returns a pointer to a TTypeInfo structure. TTypeInfo and a related enumeration, TTypeKind, are declared like this in TYPINFO.HPP:

```
enum TTypeKind { tkUnknown, tkInteger, tkChar, tkEnumeration,
  tkFloat, tkString, tkSet, tkClass, tkMethod, tkWChar,
  tkLString, tkWString, tkVariant, tkArray, tkRecord,
  tkInterface, tkInt64, tkDynArray };

struct TTypeInfo
{
  TTypeKind Kind;
  System::ShortString Name;
} ;
```

Armed with that information, Mark created this function:

```
PTypeInfo AnsiStringTypeInfo(void)
{
  PTypeInfo typeInfo = new TTypeInfo;

  typeInfo->Name = "AnsiString";
  typeInfo->Kind =  tkLString;

  return typeInfo;
}
```

This function can be used in a call to `RegisterPropertyEditor()` as follows:

```
RegisterPropertyEditor(AnsiStringTypeInfo(),
  __classid(TMyFileMemo), "FileName",
  __classid(TMyFileNameProperty));
```

This solution is a lifesaver for C++Builder programmers writing components. Gone are the headaches of the `TPersistent`-derived class technique for solving the problem of `AnsiString` property editors. This solution appears simple and I must admit that after reading about it I thought it made sense. Still, this problem vexed C++Builder programmers for almost two years before Mark Van Ditta solved the riddle.

There's more to this story. Not only does `__typeinfo` not work for classes such as `AnsiString`, but it also does not work for the C++ integral data types such as `int`, `char`, `long`, and so on. It doesn't take much, though, to modify the `AnsiStringTypeInfo()` function to work with other data types. Here's a modified version of the function, called `IntTypeInfo()`, that allows you to register a property editor of type `int`:

```
PTypeInfo IntTypeInfo(void)
{
  PTypeInfo typeInfo = new TTypeInfo;
  typeInfo->Name = "int";
  typeInfo->Kind =  tkInteger;
  return typeInfo;
}
```

From here it's a simple matter to write an *xxx*TypeInfo() function for any of the integral data types for which you need a property editor (where *xxx* is the data type).

Why functions like this are not part of C++Builder 4, I do not know; probably it's nothing more than an oversight. Expect this type of function to appear in future versions of C++Builder.

Property Editor Examples

After that long-winded discussion of property editor theory, it's finally time for some working examples. I'll give you examples of creating different types of property editors. Additional examples can be found in the sample components that ship with C++Builder. Look in the CBuilder4\Examples\Controls\Source directory for the source of the example components' property editors.

The first property editor I present is used with a component called TUnlFileMemo. The remaining property editors discussed in this section can be tested through a component I created just for this purpose. The component is called TPropertyEditorExample and its source file, PropertyEditorExample.cpp, can be found in the book's accompanying CD-ROM in Chap03\Components directory. The component doesn't do anything, it just allows you to test the property editors.

An `AnsiString` Property Editor for a `FileName` Property

The first property editor example is used in a component called TUnlFileMemo, which is derived from TMemo. This component simply adds a FileName property to the standard Memo component and adds methods called Load() and Save(). Its property editor is the FileName property editor shown in Listing 3.1. Listings 3.2 and 3.3 show the component's header and its source code.

LISTING 3.2 THE HEADER FOR THE TUnlFileMemo COMPONENT AND ITS PROPERTY EDITOR

```
#ifndef FileMemoH
#define FileMemoH

#include <SysUtils.hpp>
#include <Controls.hpp>
#include <Classes.hpp>
#include <Forms.hpp>
#include <StdCtrls.hpp>
#include <DsgnIntf.hpp>

// The property editor for the FileName property.
class TUnlFileNameProperty : public TStringProperty {
  public:
```

```
    TPropertyAttributes __fastcall GetAttributes()
    {
      return TPropertyAttributes() << paDialog;
    }
    void __fastcall Edit()
    {
      TOpenDialog* dlg = new TOpenDialog(Application);
      dlg->FileName = GetValue();
      if (dlg->Execute())
        Value = dlg->FileName;
      delete dlg;
    }
};

class PACKAGE TUnlFileMemo : public TMemo
{
private:
  String FFileName;
  void __fastcall SetFileName(String value);
protected:
    void __fastcall Loaded();
public:
  __fastcall TUnlFileMemo(TComponent* Owner);
  void Load();
  void Save();
__published:
  __property String FileName  = { read = FFileName, write = SetFileName };
};

#endif
```

LISTING 3.3   THE SOURCE CODE FOR THE TUnlFileMemo COMPONENT

```
#include <vcl.h>
#pragma hdrstop

#include "FileMemo.h"
#pragma package(smart_init)

__fastcall TUnlFileMemo::TUnlFileMemo(TComponent* Owner)
        : TMemo(Owner)
{
}

void __fastcall TUnlFileMemo::Loaded()
{
  TMemo::Loaded();
  if (FileName != "" && !ComponentState.Contains(csDesigning))
    if (FileExists(FileName))
```

continues

LISTING 3.3   CONTINUED

```
      Load();
}

void __fastcall TUnlFileMemo::SetFileName(String value)
{
  FFileName = value;
}

void TUnlFileMemo::Load()
{
  if (FileName != "")
    Lines->LoadFromFile(FileName);
}

void TUnlFileMemo::Save()
{
  if (FileName != "")
    Lines->SaveToFile(FileName);
}

// AnsiStringTypeInfo function courtesy of Mark Van Ditta
TTypeInfo* AnsiStringTypeInfo(void)
{
    TTypeInfo* typeInfo = new TTypeInfo;
    typeInfo->Name = "AnsiString";
    typeInfo->Kind =  tkLString;
    return typeInfo;
}

namespace Filememo
{
  void __fastcall PACKAGE Register()
  {
    RegisterPropertyEditor(AnsiStringTypeInfo(),
      __classid(TUnlFileMemo), "FileName",
      __classid(TUnlFileNameProperty));
     TComponentClass classes[1] = {__classid(TUnlFileMemo)};
     RegisterComponents("BCB4Unleashed", classes, 0);
  }
}
```

I've already explained what the property editor does; it's not examined again here. There isn't a lot of code to the component itself, and the existing code is self-explanatory. Figure 3.1 shows the component on a form at run time with the property editor displayed.

FIGURE 3.1

The property editor for the FileName *property displays the Open dialog so that the user can select a filename.*

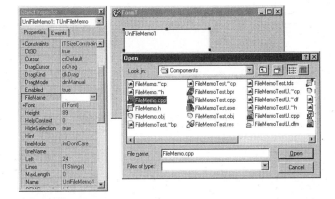

> **NOTE**
>
> I am violating the rule that says property editors should go into their own units and that they should be placed in designtime packages. I did this simply so I could show you the component and property editor together in one place. The property editor in this particular example generates very little code so it doesn't hurt to put it into a dual designtime/runtime package.

An Integer Property Editor

Earlier in the chapter I mentioned a property editor for a serial communications port component that has a BaudRate property. In that discussion I said that you might have a property editor that displays common baud rates and allows the user to select a baud rate from the list. Figure 3.2 shows the Object Inspector displaying the list of baud rate values for the TPropertEditorExample component's BaudRate property. Listing 3.4 shows the source code for this type of property editor.

FIGURE 3.2

The BaudRate *property editor displays a list of possible baud rates to the user.*

3

ADVANCED
COMPONENT
CREATION

Listing 3.4 A Property Editor that Presents a List of Baud Rates to the User

```
class TBaudRateProperty : public TIntegerProperty {
  public:
    TPropertyAttributes __fastcall GetAttributes(void)
    {
      return TPropertyAttributes() << paValueList;
    }
    void __fastcall GetValues(TGetStrProc Proc)
    {
      Proc("150");
      Proc("300");
      Proc("600");
      Proc("1200");
      Proc("2400");
      Proc("4800");
      Proc("9600");
      Proc("19200");
      Proc("38400");
      Proc("57600");
      Proc("115200");
    }
};
```

Notice that the TBaudRateProperty class is derived from TIntegerProperty. Notice also that the GetAttributes() function returns a set containing just the paValueList attribute. This is the attribute used for a property editor that presents a list of values to the user.

Now look at the GetValues() method. This function is called automatically when the attributes include paValueList. The single parameter for GetValues() is the address of a VCL procedure that adds the values to the display list. You call Proc() for each value you want added to the list. That's all there is to this type of property editor. You simply pass the strings to the Proc() function and the VCL does the rest.

Listing 3.5 shows the code for registering the TBaudRateProperty editor.

Listing 3.5 The Registration Code for the BaudRate Property Editor

```
TTypeInfo* IntTypeInfo(void)
{
  TTypeInfo* typeInfo = new TTypeInfo;
  typeInfo->Name = "int";
  typeInfo->Kind = tkInteger;
  return typeInfo;
}

namespace Testcomponent
```

```
{
  void __fastcall PACKAGE Register()
  {
    RegisterPropertyEditor(IntTypeInfo(),
      __classid(TTestComponent), "BaudRate",
      __classid(TBaudRateProperty));
    TComponentClass classes[1] = {__classid(TTestComponent)};
    RegisterComponents("Samples", classes, 0);
  }
}
```

Note that I have implemented the `IntTypeInfo()` function as I described in the section, "Registering `AnsiString` Property Editors." (I changed `PTypeInfo` to `TTypeInfo*` because I prefer the syntax, but otherwise it's the same function.)

A Directory Selector Property Editor

For components that have a `Directory` property, a directory selector dialog is great for quickly choosing a directory rather than forcing the user to type the directory in by hand. Figure 3.3 shows the dialog produced by this type of property editor.

3

ADVANCED
COMPONENT
CREATION

FIGURE 3.3

A directory property editor allows the user to select a directory.

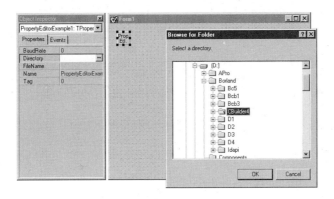

This property editor is a string property editor and has the `paDialog` attribute. Listing 3.6 shows the source code for the directory property editor.

LISTING 3.6   THE SOURCE CODE FOR THE DIRECTORY PROPERTY EDITOR

```
class TDirectoryProperty : public TStringProperty {
  public:
    TPropertyAttributes __fastcall GetAttributes(void)
    {
      return TPropertyAttributes() << paDialog;
    }
```

continues

LISTING 3.6   CONTINUED

```
void __fastcall Edit()
{
  BROWSEINFO bi;
  char buff[MAX_PATH];
  memset(&bi, 0, sizeof(bi));
  memset(buff, 0, sizeof(buff));
  bi.hwndOwner = Application->Handle;
  bi.lpszTitle = "Select a directory.";
  LPITEMIDLIST pidl = SHBrowseForFolder(&bi);
  if (pidl) {
    SHGetPathFromIDList(pidl, buff);
    Value = buff;
    LPMALLOC malloc;
    if (SHGetMalloc(&malloc) == NOERROR)
      malloc->Free(pidl);
  }
}
};
```

The `Edit()` method uses the `SHBrowseForFolder()` API function to display the shell's browser dialog. Although there is a fair amount of code here, it isn't germane to this discussion on property editors; not every detail of the code is explained here. Look up `SHBrowseForFolder()` in the Win32 API Help if you want to understand more about how this code works. In any case, feel free to use this code in your own property editors.

There is one aspect of this code that I want to talk about. Notice this line:

`bi.hwndOwner = Application->Handle;`

The `hwndOwner` member of the `BROWSEINFO` structure is used to specify the window that will act as the owner of the Browse dialog. As you can see, I set this member to the `Handle` property of the `Application` object, with which you are almost certainly familiar. In a VCL application, the `Application` object manages the application's message loop, Help file system, and a few other mundane tasks. In a property editor, however, the `Application` object refers to the IDE itself. This code, then, sets the IDE as the owner for the Browse dialog. This is important so the Browse dialog doesn't get lost behind a form or another IDE window. With this code in place, the Browse dialog acts like any other modal dialog in the IDE.

An About Property Editor

As mentioned earlier in the chapter, some component vendors provide an `About` or `Version` property that shows the version number of the component library in the Object Inspector. The property is almost always a read-only property. When the property is double-clicked in the Object Inspector, a dialog showing company and product information is displayed. Figure 3.4 shows this type of property editor at design time.

FIGURE 3.4

This About *property editor displays a standard VCL form.*

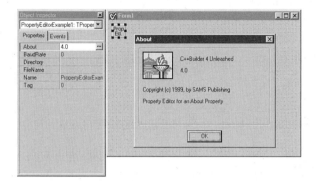

This type of property editor is not complicated at all, but it and the property it represents bear some explanation. To create the dialog itself, I simply created a stock About dialog from the Object Repository; I then made a few changes to the form and saved the unit. This is a standard C++Builder form and is no different than any other VCL form.

Writing the component for this type of property requires a small trick. This property is read-only. The IDE, however, doesn't like property editors applied to read-only properties. After all, if the property is read-only, what's the point of the property editor? You have to jump through a couple of hoops to create a read-only property that uses a property editor. What you must do is create a regular read/write property that doesn't have an underlying data member. You need both a read and a write method for the property. Here's the property declaration:

```
__property String About  = { read = GetAbout, write = SetAbout };
```

The read and write methods look like this:

```
String __fastcall TMyComponent::GetAbout()
{
  return "4.0";
}

void __fastcall TMyComponent::SetAbout(String Value)
{
}
```

The read method, GetAbout(), simply returns the text you want displayed in the Object Inspector. The write method, SetAbout(), does nothing at all. This prevents the property value from being modified in the Object Inspector, but allows you to register a property editor for the About property.

The source code for the About property's property editor is shown in Listing 3.7. It is a typical string property editor. The edit method dynamically creates an instance of the TAboutBox form, shows it, and deletes the instance.

LISTING 3.7 THE SOURCE CODE FOR THE About PROPERTY'S EDITOR

```
class TAboutProperty : public TStringProperty {
  public:
    TPropertyAttributes __fastcall GetAttributes(void)
    {
      return TPropertyAttributes() << paDialog <<paReadOnly;
    }
    void __fastcall Edit()
    {
      TAboutBoxPE* about = new TAboutBoxPE(Application);
      about->ShowModal();
      delete about;
      Value = "4.0";
    }
};
```

Notice that the GetAttributes() function returns a set containing both paDialog and paReadOnly. The rest of the property editor contains a variation on code that you saw earlier in the chapter.

Writing Component Editors

A *component editor* is used when you want your users to be able to edit one or more properties at a time. Put another way, a component editor is a way for the user to modify the entire component rather than a single property. Most component editors display a dialog to the user. A perfect example is the component editor for the TChart component. Figure 3.5 shows the component editor for TChart.

FIGURE 3.5

The component editor for the TChart *component allows you to set the component's properties via a dialog.*

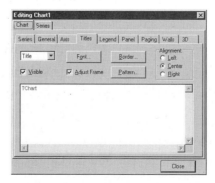

The TChart property editor is one of the more complex property editors that I can think of. It is a tabbed dialog with at least 10 pages. Each page represents a particular aspect of a chart such as the chart titles, legends, axis settings, chart style, and so on. Most of your component editors will not likely be this complex. Still, the TChart component editor gives you some indication of what is possible with component editors.

In many ways, component editors are easier to implement than property editors. There are a limited number of methods that you must override in order to provide functionality for your component editor. I'll discuss those methods later in the section "TComponentEditor Properties and Methods."

A component editor can do one or more of the following:

- Add menu items to the code editor's context menu and perform some action when the menu items are clicked
- Display a dialog to the user when the component is double-clicked at design time
- Generate a specific event handler when the component is double-clicked at design time

Component Editor Base Classes

As with property editors, you create a component editor by deriving a class from one of the VCL's component editor base classes. In the case of component editors, there are only two base classes to choose from:

- TDefaultEditor
- TComponentEditor

The base class you choose depends on how you are implementing the component editor. If, for example, you want the component editor invoked when the user double-clicks the component on a form, then you will derive from TComponentEditor. If you want the component editor invoked only when the user selects an item from the Menu Designer context menu, you will derive from TDefaultEditor. I'll give some examples of each in the following sections. I should add that TDefaultEditor is itself derived from TComponentEditor.

There is one other situation where you will derive from TDefaultEditor. You have almost certainly noticed that when you double-click a Button component at design time, C++Builder generates an OnClick event handler for the button. Why does C++Builder generate an event handler for the OnClick event and not for some other event? It is simply because OnClick is the first event handler in the Button component's list of events. This behavior applies to all components. When you double-click the component at design time, C++Builder searches the list of published events and generates an event handler for the first event it finds. Suppose you want C++Builder to generate an event handler for a specific event when your component is double-clicked rather than for the first component in the list. You must derive from TDefaultEditor in order to get this behavior. I'll explain exactly how to do that in the section, "Specifying an Event Handler."

TComponentEditor Properties and Methods

The TComponentEditor class has several virtual methods that you can override in order to define your component editor's behavior. Table 3.6 lists the TComponentEditor virtual methods and gives a description of each.

TABLE 3.6 TComponentEditor VIRTUAL METHODS

Method	Description
Copy	Called when the user chooses Edit, Copy from the IDE main menu when your component is selected on a form. Used to copy data to the Clipboard in a format specific to your component.
Edit	Called when the user double-clicks the component at design time. You can use this method to display a dialog to the user.
ExecuteVerb	Called when the user clicks one of the component editor's menu items on the Menu Designer context menu.
GetVerb	Called for each menu item your component editor adds to the Menu Designer context menu.
GetVerbCount	Called when the IDE wants a count of the menu items you are adding to the Menu Designer context menu.

The TDefaultEditor class, being derived from TComponentEditor, contains all of the virtual methods found in Table 3.6 and adds one more: EditProperty(). The EditProperty() method is called by the IDE when the user double-clicks the component at design time. You can use this method to instruct the IDE to generate an event handler for a specific event.

The TComponentEditor class has two public properties. The Component property returns a pointer to the component being edited. You can use this pointer to set any of the component's properties as needed. Of course, you'll have to cast the Component property to a pointer of your component's type in order to gain full access to the component. You'll see an example of this in the "Modifying a Component via the Component Editor" section. The Designer property returns an interface to the IDE's form designer. You need this property to notify the IDE of changes that the component editor makes to the component.

A Simple Component Editor

Assume you simply want to display an About box with your company information when your component is double-clicked at design time. In that case the component editor would be relatively simple to write. Listing 3.8 shows the code for this type of property editor.

LISTING 3.8   A PROPERTY EDITOR THAT DISPLAYS AN ABOUT BOX

```
class TAboutEditor : public TComponentEditor {
  public:
    void __fastcall Edit()
    {
      TAboutBoxPE* about = new TAboutBoxPE(Application);
      about->ShowModal();
      delete about;
    }
};
```

This code is nearly identical to the code for the property editors shown earlier. The overridden `Edit()` method simply creates an instance of the `TAboutBoxPE` form, shows it, and then destroys it. The `Edit()` method is called automatically when the component is double-clicked. As you can see from this example, a component editor that displays an About box to the user is very simple to write.

Registering the Component Editor

Component editors, like property editors, must be registered before they will function in the IDE at design time. The function used to register component editors is called `RegisterComponentEditor()`. Earlier in the chapter I mentioned a component that I wrote to illustrate property editors; that component is called `TPropertyEditorExample`. Use this code to register the component editor shown in Listing 3.8 as belonging to the `TPropertyEditorExample` component:

```
RegisterComponentEditor(
  __classid(TPropertyEditorExample),
  __classid(TAboutEditor));
```

As you can see, registering component editors with `RegisterComponentEditor()` is simpler than registering property editors. You pass the component's class name in the first parameter and the class name of the component editor in the second parameter. This code

3

ADVANCED
COMPONENT
CREATION

should be placed either in the component's `Register()` function or in the `Register()` function of a dedicated registration unit.

Adding Menu Items to the Menu Designer Context Menu

Some component editors use the Menu Designer context menu to invoke the component editor rather than allowing the user to double-click the component to invoke the editor (and some do both). For example, you may want a double-click on the component to create a specific event handler rather than showing the component editor. In that case you would use a menu item to invoke the component editor. Writing this type of component editor takes a little more work than the simple component editor shown previously, but not much more. Listing 3.9 shows the code for a property editor that adds a single menu item to the Menu Designer context menu. The component editor is displayed when that menu item is selected.

LISTING 3.9   A COMPONENT EDITOR THAT PLACES A MENU ITEM ON THE MENU DESIGNER CONTEXT MENU

```
class TMenuAboutEditor : public TDefaultEditor {
  public:
    int __fastcall GetVerbCount()
    {
      return 1;
    }
    String __fastcall GetVerb(int Index)
    {
      return "&About My Company";
    }
    void __fastcall ExecuteVerb(int Index)
    {
      if (Index == 0) {
        TAboutBoxPE* about = new TAboutBoxPE(Application);
        about->ShowModal();
        delete about;
      }
    }
};
```

The `GetVerbCount()` method returns 1 to tell the IDE that one menu item should be added to the Menu Designer context menu. The `GetVerb()` method returns the text for the menu item (see Figure 3.6).

The `ExecuteVerb()` method shows the About dialog when the user clicks the menu item. Other than the check for `Index == 0`, the code is identical to the simple component editor shown in Listing 3.8. Figure 3.6 shows the form designer and Menu Designer context menu when this component editor is registered.

FIGURE 3.6

The component editor in Listing 3.9 adds a menu item to the Menu Designer context menu.

This component editor adds a single menu item to the Menu Designer context menu. Adding multiple menu items means writing a little extra code but is otherwise the same. Listing 3.10 shows a component editor that adds three menu items to the context menu and handles the click of each menu item.

LISTING 3.10 A COMPONENT EDITOR THAT IMPLEMENTS THREE MENU ITEMS

```
class TMyComponentEditor : public TDefaultEditor {
  public:
    int __fastcall GetVerbCount()
    {
      return 3;
    }
    String __fastcall GetVerb(int Index)
    {
      String S;
      switch (Index) {
        case 0 : S = "&About TurboPower"; break;
        case 1 : S = "&TurboPower on the Web"; break;
        case 2 : S = "&Designer";
      }
      return S;
    }
    void __fastcall ExecuteVerb(int Index)
    {
      switch (Index) {
        case 0 : {
          TAboutBoxPE* about = new TAboutBoxPE(Application);
          about->ShowModal();
          delete about;
          break;
        }
```

continues

3

ADVANCED COMPONENT CREATION

Listing 3.10   CONTINUED

```
    case 1 : {
      ShellExecute(Application->Handle, "open",
        "http://www.turbopower.com", 0, 0, SW_NORMAL);
      break;
    }
    case 2 : {
      TDesignerForm* designer = new TDesignerForm(Application);
      if (designer->ShowModal() == mrOk) {
        // do some stuff here
        Designer->Modified();
      }
      delete designer;
    }
    }
  }
};
```

This code is basically self-explanatory. Note that the GetVerb() method is called once for each menu item (three in this case). The Index parameter contains the index of the menu item for which the menu text is being requested. The switch statement uses the Index parameter to determine which string to return. Similarly, the ExecuteVerb() method uses the Index parameter to determine which of the three menu items was clicked. It performs some action depending on the menu item clicked. Note that if the Index parameter is 2, a form is displayed to allow the user to edit the component's properties. That type of operation is explained next.

Modifying a Component via the Component Editor

Up to this point, the component editor examples don't actually have any effect on the component itself. In this section I'll show you a component editor that modifies the component for which the editor is registered.

The whole idea behind component editors is that they offer the user a convenient way of modifying the component's properties. Usually this means a dialog is displayed, allowing the user to visually set the component's properties.

Return for a moment to the component that was used to explain property editors. That component has three properties: BaudRate, Directory, and FileName. Now say that you want a component editor that would allow the user to set all three of these properties via a single dialog. In that case, the component editor's Edit() method would look like this:

```
void __fastcall Edit()
{
  TDesignerForm* form = new TDesignerForm(Application);
  TPropertyEditorExample* component =
    dynamic_cast<TPropertyEditorExample*>(Component);
  form->BaudRateCombo->Text = String(component->BaudRate);
  form->DirEdit->Text = component->Directory;
  form->FileNameEdit->Text = component->FileName;
  if (form->ShowModal() == mrOk) {
    component->BaudRate = form->BaudRateCombo->Text.ToIntDef(0);
    component->Directory = form->DirEdit->Text;
    component->FileName = form->FileNameEdit->Text;
    Designer->Modified();
  }
  delete form;
}
```

The first line of code creates an instance of the form that will be used as the component editor's visual interface:

```
TDesignerForm* form = new TDesignerForm(Application);
```

I then cast the Component property to a type of the component being edited:

```
TPropertyEditorExample* component =
  dynamic_cast<TPropertyEditorExample*>(Component);
```

This allows me to get at the individual properties of the component being edited. After that I set the components on the form to their corresponding properties in the component being edited:

```
form->BaudRateCombo->Text = String(component->BaudRate);
form->DirEdit->Text = component->Directory;
form->FileNameEdit->Text = component->FileName;
```

This code ensures that when the form is displayed, the fields on the form contain the current properties' values of the component for which the editor is registered.

Now I show the form. If the OK button on the form was pressed, I copy the appropriate values from the form to the corresponding properties of the edited component:

```
if (form->ShowModal() == mrOk) {
  component->BaudRate = form->BaudRateCombo->Text.ToIntDef(0);
  component->Directory = form->DirEdit->Text;
  component->FileName = form->FileNameEdit->Text;
  Designer->Modified();
}
```

Notice that at the end of this process I call the following to inform the IDE that I have made changes to the properties of the component I am editing:

```
Designer->Modified();
```

This step is required any time you programmatically change a property value from a component editor.

Specifying an Event Handler

As explained earlier, when a component on a form is double-clicked, the IDE generates an event handler for the first event it finds for that component. This usually means an event handler is generated for the OnClick event. For some components you want the IDE to generate an event handler not for the first event in the list, but for a specific event you choose. Gaining this behavior requires that you write a component editor for the component.

The IDE enumerates all property editors for any double-clicked component. Remember that even though you may not have specifically created a property editor for your component, the IDE has applied default property editors on your behalf. The IDE calls the EditProperty() method for each property editor registered. In your component editor, you override the EditProperty() method as shown in Listing 3.11.

LISTING 3.11 A COMPONENT EDITOR THAT SPECIFIES THE EVENT HANDLER GENERATED WHEN THE COMPONENT IS DOUBLE-CLICKED

```
class TClockEditor : public TDefaultEditor {
  public:
    void __fastcall EditProperty(TPropertyEditor* PropertyEditor,
      bool& Continue, bool& FreeEditor)
    {
      if (PropertyEditor->ClassNameIs("TMethodProperty") &&
        CompareText(PropertyEditor->GetName(), "OnSecondChange") == 0)
        TDefaultEditor::EditProperty(
          PropertyEditor, Continue, FreeEditor);
    }
};
```

Do you remember the TUnlClock component from Chapter 2, "Creating Components"? It had three events: OnHourChange, OnMinuteChange, and OnSecondChange. I assume that users are going to want to use the OnSecondChange event most often, so the property editor in Listing 3.11 forces the IDE to create an event handler for OnSecondChange when the component is double-clicked. Again, the IDE calls EditProperty() for each property editor. The default property editor class for events is TMethodProperty. The code in the EditProperty() method of Listing 3.11 checks for a property editor class name of TMethodProperty and a property name of OnSecondChange. If it finds a match, it calls the base class's EditProperty() method, causing the IDE to generate an event handler for the OnSecondChange event.

This type of component editor is simple, but its implementation is not necessarily straightforward so I thought it a good idea to explain how to perform this particular task.

Debugging Component and Property Editors

I'd be lying if I said that debugging component and property editors is easy. Because property and component editors operate within the C++Builder IDE, you are immediately faced with a challenge that you don't face when debugging applications. Specifically, you can't just set breakpoints and run the program because the IDE is already running.

There are essentially two techniques you can use to debug component and property editors:

1. Temporarily place MessageBox() or ShowMessage() calls in your component and property editor code.
2. Invoke a second instance of the IDE running under the debugger.

I'll admit that the first technique listed here is a bit of a hack. I'll also admit that I use this technique with some regularity. Using a message box to see what is going on within an editor is a quick and easy solution.

Using a message box, however, also has some major drawbacks. For example, say you placed a call to ShowMessage() at the top of the EditProperty() method shown in Listing 3.11. It might look like this:

```
void __fastcall EditProperty(TPropertyEditor* PropertyEditor,
  bool& Continue, bool& FreeEditor)
{

  ShowMessage(PropertyEditor->ClassName()
    + "::" + PropertyEditor->GetProperty());

  if (PropertyEditor->ClassNameIs("TMethodProperty") &&
      CompareText(PropertyEditor->GetName(), "OnSecondChange") == 0)
    TDefaultEditor::EditProperty(
      PropertyEditor, Continue, FreeEditor);
}
```

Depending on the component attached to this component editor, the EditProperty() method might be called dozens of times. That means that you'll have to dismiss the message boxes repeatedly until the IDE is done enumerating the property editors. This technique is not exactly elegant, but it gets the job done.

The second way of debugging component and property editors is probably more professional. In fact, I found this technique fairly easy to use once I figured out how to do it. Here are the steps you need to perform:

1. Choose Run, Parameters from the IDE context menu. In the Run Parameters dialog, enter the full path to the C++Builder IDE. For example

   ```
   c:\program files\borland\cbuilder4\bin\bcb.exe
   ```

2. Click the Load button to start a second instance of the IDE running.

3. As the second instance of the IDE is loading, the debugger stops at an internal breakpoint and the CPU window is displayed. This is normal, but can be confusing the first time you see it. The second instance of the IDE is not yet visible at this point. Click the Run button to continue loading the second IDE instance. The second instance of the IDE now loads and you have two copies of C++Builder running.

4. Switch to the original instance of the IDE and set a breakpoint on a line of code in your component or property editor.

5. Switch to the second instance of C++Builder and drop the component you want to debug on a form. Do whatever it takes to invoke your component or property editor. For example, for a component editor you will likely double-click the component. For a property editor you will modify the property value.

6. When the breakpoint you set is hit, the first instance of the IDE comes to the top and you can debug as you normally would.

7. When you are done debugging, close the second instance of the IDE.

This technique, while seemingly complex, works remarkably well. There is one thing, however, that you must know about it. In this chapter I have been using inline functions for my component and property editor methods. I've done this because it's easy, because it's an efficient use of code, and because that way I can show you a single listing instead of two for each editor. In order to stop at a breakpoint, however, you must change your component and property editor methods from inline to regular member functions. This means moving the methods from the header to the source (CPP) file for your component and property editors. It's a small price to pay to be able to debug your editors.

The C++Builder Event Log is another debugging tool you can use if you invoke a second instance of the IDE. Simply sprinkle calls to OutputDebugString() throughout your component or property editor's code. Work with your component in the second instance of the IDE, switch to the first instance, and view the Event Log (Ctrl+Alt+E or View, Debug Windows, Event log from the menu). The text from your OutputDebugString() calls is shown in the Event Log. Browse the Event Log entries to see what is happening within your component or property editors.

Using Components with Packages

Chapter 2 discusses runtime versus designtime packages. Now that I have discussed component and property editors, I want to revisit the topic of packages.

The designtime package should contain your component and property editors. The reason, of course, is that the code for your component and property editors should not be included in the runtime package. Figure 3.7 shows the Package Editor for the runtime package I created for these two chapters on component writing. Figure 3.8 shows the Package Editor for the designtime package.

FIGURE 3.7

The Package Editor for the BCB4UnlR runtime package shows the files contained in the package.

FIGURE 3.8

The Package Editor for the BCB4UnlD designtime package shows the files contained in the package.

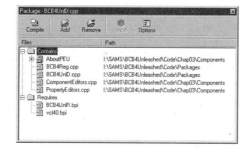

Take a look at the files contained in the runtime package in Figure 3.7. What you see is simply the files for the individual components included in the package. What you do not see is the source code for any component or property editors. The runtime package is the easier package to create.

Now look at the files contained in the designtime package in Figure 3.8. Look at the files in the Requires list. Note that the runtime package's import library file, `BCB4UnlR.bpi`, is in the Requires list. The designtime package links to the runtime package and needs the code from that package in order to operate in the IDE.

Now look at the files in the Contains list. The files you see are the individual files that make up the property and component editors. Notice that the Contains list has no units for the individual components themselves, only for the supporting units. Another important file in the designtime package's Contains list is the file called BCB4Reg.cpp. This file contains all the registration code for the components themselves, as well as for the component and property editors. Listing 3.12 shows the registration unit.

LISTING 3.12   THE SOURCE CODE FOR THE REGISTRATION UNIT

```
#include <vcl.h>
#pragma hdrstop

#include "BCB4Reg.h"
#include "../Chap02/Components/URLLabel.h"
#include "../Chap02/Components/PictureSelector.h"
#include "../Chap02/Components/UnlClock.h"
#include "../Chap03/Components/FileMemo.h"
#include "../Chap03/Components/PropertyEditorExample.h"
#include "../Chap03/Components/PropertyEditors.h"
#include "../Chap03/Components/ComponentEditors.h"

#pragma resource "../Chap02/Components/urllabel.res"
#pragma resource "../Chap02/Components/PictureSelector.res"
#pragma resource "../Chap02/Components/Unlclock.res"
#pragma resource "../Chap03/Components/FileMemo.res"
#pragma resource "../Chap03/Components/PropertyEditorExample.res"

#pragma package(smart_init)

// AnsiStringTypeInfo function courtesy of Mark Van Ditta
TTypeInfo* AnsiStringTypeInfo(void)
{
    TTypeInfo* typeInfo = new TTypeInfo;
    typeInfo->Name = "AnsiString";
    typeInfo->Kind =  tkLString;
    return typeInfo;
}

TTypeInfo* IntTypeInfo(void)
{
    TTypeInfo* typeInfo = new TTypeInfo;
    typeInfo->Name = "int";
    typeInfo->Kind =  tkInteger;
    return typeInfo;
}

namespace Bcb4reg
{
  void __fastcall PACKAGE Register()
```

```
  {
    RegisterPropertyEditor(AnsiStringTypeInfo(),
      __classid(TUnlFileMemo), "FileName",
      __classid(TUnlFileNameProperty));
    RegisterPropertyEditor(AnsiStringTypeInfo(),
      __classid(TPropertyEditorExample), "FileName",
      __classid(TUnlFileNameProperty));
    RegisterPropertyEditor(AnsiStringTypeInfo(),
      __classid(TPropertyEditorExample), "Directory",
      __classid(TDirectoryProperty));
    RegisterPropertyEditor(IntTypeInfo(),
      __classid(TPropertyEditorExample), "BaudRate",
      __classid(TBaudRateProperty));
    RegisterPropertyEditor(AnsiStringTypeInfo(),
      __classid(TPropertyEditorExample), "About",
      __classid(TAboutProperty));

    RegisterComponentEditor(__classid(TPropertyEditorExample),
      __classid(TMyComponentEditor));

    RegisterComponentEditor(__classid(TUnlClock),
      __classid(TClockEditor));

    TComponentClass classes[] = {
      __classid(TUnlFileMemo),
      __classid(TUnlClock),
      __classid(TUnlPictureSelector),
      __classid(TUnlURLLabel),
      __classid(TPropertyEditorExample)
    };

    RegisterComponents("BCB4Unleashed", classes, 4);
  }
}
```

Notice that I have moved all of the registration code from the individual components into this one unit. Notice also that I wrapped the registration code inside a namespace:

```
namespace Bcb4reg
{
  void __fastcall PACKAGE Register()
  {
    // registration code here
  }
}
```

This is required so that C++Builder can locate the registration code. The designtime package must contain the component registration code because it is the package that is installed into the IDE. The runtime package is never installed and must not contain any registration code.

The issue of runtime and designtime packages can be difficult to sort out the first couple of times. Many component writers give up in frustration and opt for a dual runtime/designtime package. That solution is fine as long as you don't have component or property editors. If you do have component and property editors, you need to take the time to create both runtime and designtime packages.

> **NOTE**
>
> I created individual resource files for my components' bitmaps because I created them as I wrote each component. I could just as easily have created one resource file containing all the bitmaps. In that case I would have only one #pragma resource line in the registration file.

Overriding Component Virtual Methods

The VCL base components offer a host of methods that you can override in components you write. Chapter 2 gives examples of overriding the CreateWnd() and WndProc() methods. This section touches on other virtual methods that you might need to override when writing components.

Detecting Form Loading with the Loaded() Method

The Loaded() method is called after the form and all its components have been streamed. Override the Loaded() method when you want to perform some processing after all the components on a form have been streamed, and before the form is shown. For example, I overrode Loaded() as follows in the TUnlFileMemo component:

```
void __fastcall TUnlFileMemo::Loaded()
{
  TMemo::Loaded();
  if (FileName != "" && !ComponentState.Contains(csDesigning))
    if (FileExists(FileName))
      Load();
}
```

First I call the base class Loaded() method to ensure that the base class behavior is preserved. Next I check the FileName property to see if it contains something other than an empty string. I also determine whether the component is being used in design mode. If the filename is not empty and is not in design mode, I check to see if the file specified in the `FileName` property exists. If so, I call the component's `Load()` method to load the file in the memo. The net result is fairly easy to comprehend—when the program runs, the file is loaded into the memo.

Detecting Components Added or Removed from a Form with the `Notification()` Method

The `Notification()` method is called anytime a component is added to the form or removed from a form. Use of the `Notification()` method is not quite as common as that of the `Loaded()` method. Here's the declaration:

```
virtual void __fastcall Notification(
  TComponent* AComponent, TOperation Operation);
```

The `AComponent` parameter is a pointer to the component being added or removed from the form. The `Operation` parameter indicates whether the component is being added to the form or removed from the form. `TOperation` is defined as follows:

```
enum TOperation { opInsert, opRemove };
```

`Notification()` is commonly used for components that have properties that hook to other components on a form. For example, say that you are writing a file most-recently-used (MRU) component. In that case you might have a `Menu` property that is hooked up to a `TMainMenu` on the form. You can use `Notification()` to automatically hook up the `Menu` property to the main menu as follows:

```
void __fastcall
TMRU::Notification(TComponent* AComponent, TOperation Operation)
{
  TComponent::Notification(AComponent, Operation);
  if (ComponentState.Contains(csDesigning)) {
    TMainMenu* menu = dynamic_cast<TMainMenu*>(AComponent);
    if (menu)
      if (Operation == opInsert)
        FMenu = menu;
      else
        FMenu = 0;
  }
}
```

Here I first call the base class `Notification()` method. After that I check to see if the component is being used in design mode. Understand that `Notification()` gets called both at design time and at runtime when the form is being streamed or destroyed. You need to account for that fact. In this case I am only executing code if the component is being used in design mode. If that's the case, I cast the component being added or

3

ADVANCED COMPONENT CREATION

removed to a `TMainMenu` pointer. I know that a `MainMenu` component was just added to the form if the component is a `MainMenu` component and the `Operation` parameter is `opInsert`. In that case I assign the `MainMenu` component to the `FMenu` data member, setting my component's `Menu` property as a result. If a `MainMenu` component is being removed from the form, I set the `FMenu` variable to `0`. This code is fairly simplistic in that it assumes you'll only have one `MainMenu` component on the form at a given time. In a working component I would add code to account for the fact that multiple `MainMenu` components may exist on a given form.

Controlling Creation Parameters with the `CreateParams()` Method

The `CreateParams()` method is called just before the VCL constructs the `Window` class for a particular component. Here's the `CreateParams()` declaration:

```
virtual void __fastcall CreateParams(TCreateParams &Params);
```

The single parameter is a reference to a `TCreateParams` structure. Here is how `TCreateParams` is declared:

```
struct TCreateParams
{
  char *Caption;
  int Style;
  int ExStyle;
  int X;
  int Y;
  int Width;
  int Height;
  HWND WndParent;
  void *Param;
  tagWNDCLASSA WindowClass;
  char WinClassName[64];
} ;
```

Most of the time you override `CreateParams()` in order to change a component's window style. Take the case of a `Button` component that can display multiple lines of text. To create a multiline `Button` component, you could derive a class from `TButton` and then override `CreateParams()`:

```
void __fastcall TMultilineButton::CreateParams(TCreateParams& Params)
{
  TButton::CreateParams(Params);
  Params.Style |= BS_MULTILINE;
}
```

This code first calls the base class `CreateParams()` method. This step retrieves the default creation parameters for the button. After that I simply `OR` the `BS_MULTILINE` style in with the existing styles.

Creating Exception Classes for Components

Component users deal with exceptions on a regular basis. Usually this comes in the form of placing `try/catch` blocks around a particular section of code. The component writer, however, must deal with exceptions on a different level. Specifically, the component writer must throw exceptions when an error condition occurs within the component. To this end, the component writer must create exception classes that describe what went wrong.

The first step in this process is deriving a class from the VCL's standard exception class, `Exception`. Go back to the earlier example of a component that contains a `BaudRate` property. The maximum baud rate that Windows supports is 115,200. If the user attempts to set the `BaudRate` property to a baud rate greater than 115,200, you should throw an exception alerting the user to the fact that the baud rate is invalid. You would first create an exception class called `EInvalidBaudRate`. The exception class you create contains no code at all:

```
class EInvalidBaudRate : public Exception {
  public:
    EInvalidBaudRate(const String Msg) :
      Exception(Msg) {}
};
```

The purpose of creating an exception class is to allow component users to catch a specific exception type. An example follows:

```
try {
  TheComponent->BaudRate = Edit1->Text.ToInt();
}
catch (EInvalidBaudRate&) {
  ShowMessage("The baud rate you have entered is not valid.");
}
```

Naturally, you must throw the exception from within your component if an invalid baud rate is entered. The write method for the `BaudRate` property would be a good place to do that:

```
void __fastcall TMyComponent::SetBaudRate(int Value)
{
  if (Value> 115200)
```

```
      throw EInvalidBaudRate("Baud rate must not be over 115200");
    FBaudRate = Value;
}
```

Figure 3.9 shows the C++Builder Object Inspector and Form Designer when this exception is thrown.

FIGURE 3.9

The
EInvalidBaudRate
exception is
thrown if the user
enters a baud rate
greater than
115,200.

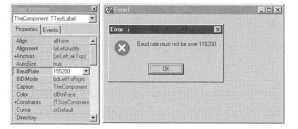

I used this code to throw the EInvalidBaudRate exception:

```
throw EInvalidBaudRate("Baud rate must not be over 115200");
```

The problem with this approach is that I am using a literal string for the exception text. This is not a particularly internationally-friendly way of displaying exception text. A better approach is to create a string table in a resource script file. Users of my component around the world could then translate the string table to other languages, thereby presenting the exception text in any language they choose.

You don't have to create an exception class for every conceivable error condition. You can, for example, reuse the VCL exception classes where it makes sense. Take the TUnlFileMemo component, for example. If you recall, this component has a FileName property and a Load() method. When you call the Load() method, the file specified in the FileName property is loaded into the memo. If the filename is not valid, you will probably want to throw an exception when the Load() method is called. The VCL already has an exception class for this type of exception: EFOpenError. Rather than creating your own exception class in this case, you can just throw an exception of type EFOpenError.

You should create an exception class for each unique type of exception that might occur within your component. Throw exceptions from your components for any conditions that will cause the component to stop working properly. This includes invalid property values, missing property values, invalid parameters in methods, and so on. Judicious use of exceptions is one of the things that separates the good components from the bad components.

Special Considerations for Non-Visual Components

A *non-visual component* is one that appears on the form at design time but is not visible at run time. Derive your component from TComponent to create a non-visual component. Add properties, methods, and events, just as you would for a visual component. For the most part, non-visual components operate just like visual components do. The obvious exception is that non-visual components don't have any painting code.

The rest of this section addresses aspects of component creation that deal specifically with non-visual components.

Message Handling for Non-Visual Components

Non-visual components, by definition, don't have a window handle. Sometimes, though, you need a window handle in order to receive Windows messages, even within a non-visual component. Component writers often use non-visual components to wrap a particular Windows API. Examples that come immediately to mind are the Windows Telephony API (TAPI), the Winsock API, and the low-level multimedia APIs. These APIs receive messages from Windows based on state changes or other events occurring that the API needs to know about. Your component must have a window procedure in order to receive messages; your component must have a window in order to have a window procedure. The prescribed way of handling this situation is to create a hidden window for your component so that your component can receive messages.

Creating a hidden window for non-visual components requires these steps:

1. Declare a private variable to hold the window handle.
2. Declare a private method to act as a window procedure. This method will receive Windows messages.
3. Create a hidden window with the AllocateHWnd() function.
4. Handle any incoming messages in your window procedure method.
5. Deallocate the window handle when the component is destroyed.

Let me lay some groundwork before I get to the specifics of how to create a hidden window.

As said earlier, you must have a window handle in order to receive Windows messages. The AllocateHWnd() method provides a way of creating an invisible window within a non-visual component. The declaration of AllocateHWnd() looks like this:

```
HWND __fastcall AllocateHWnd(TWndMethod Method);
```

The single parameter for AllocateHWnd() is a pointer to a function that will receive Windows messages. This parameter is of type TWndMethod. TWndMethod is declared as follows:

```
typedef void __fastcall
  (__closure *TWndMethod)(Messages::TMessage &Message);
```

If you are like me, you don't necessarily enjoy looking at a typedef for closures. To put it a bit more clearly, here's how you declare a method that serves as your window procedure:

```
void __fastcall WndProc(TMessage& Message);
```

You should recognize that this function declaration is identical to the WndProc() function discussed in Chapter 2.

With that bit of theory behind us, look at a component that implements a hidden window. Listings 3.13 and 3.14 show the header and source file for this type of component. The component has a single method called Test(), which sends the component a user-defined message.

LISTING 3.13 THE HEADER FOR A COMPONENT THAT IMPLEMENTS A HIDDEN WINDOW

```
#ifndef HwndComponentH
#define HwndComponentH

#include <SysUtils.hpp>
#include <Controls.hpp>
#include <Classes.hpp>
#include <Forms.hpp>

class PACKAGE THwndComponent : public TComponent
{
private:
  HWND FHandle;
  void __fastcall WndProc(TMessage& Message);
protected:
public:
  __fastcall THwndComponent(TComponent* Owner);
  __fastcall ~THwndComponent();
  void Test();
__published:
};

#endif
```

LISTING 3.14 THE COMPONENT'S SOURCE CODE

```cpp
#include <vcl.h>
#pragma hdrstop

#include "HwndComponent.h"
#pragma package(smart_init)

#define MSG_MYMESSAGE WM_USER + 1

__fastcall THwndComponent::THwndComponent(TComponent* Owner)
  : TComponent(Owner)
{
  FHandle = AllocateHWnd(WndProc);
}


__fastcall THwndComponent::~THwndComponent()
{
  DeallocateHWnd(FHandle);
}

void __fastcall THwndComponent::WndProc(TMessage& Message)
{
  if (Message.Msg == MSG_MYMESSAGE)
    MessageBeep(0);
  try {
    Dispatch(&Message);
    if (Message.Msg == WM_QUERYENDSESSION)
      Message.Result = 1;
  }
  catch (...) {
    Application->HandleException(this);
  }
}

void THwndComponent::Test()
{
  PostMessage(FHandle, MSG_MYMESSAGE, 0, 0);
}

namespace Hwndcomponent
{
  void __fastcall PACKAGE Register()
  {
    TComponentClass classes[1] = {__classid(THwndComponent)};
    RegisterComponents("Samples", classes, 0);
  }
}
```

The `private` section of the component's class declaration contains these two declarations:

```
private:
  HWND FHandle;
  void __fastcall WndProc(TMessage& Message);
```

The `FHandle` data member holds the window handle for the component's hidden window when obtained. The `WndProc()` method is the window procedure that receives messages sent to the hidden window.

The component's constructor allocates the window handle:

```
__fastcall THwndComponent::THwndComponent(TComponent* Owner)
  : TComponent(Owner)
{
  FHandle = AllocateHWnd(WndProc);
}
```

I call `AllocateHWnd()`, passing the address of my window procedure as the single parameter. This tells Windows to send any messages destined for my hidden window to my `WndProc()` method. The return value from `AllocateHWnd()` is the window handle for the hidden window. I store this value in the `FHandle` variable for future use.

The `Test()` method of the component simply posts a message to the component's hidden window:

```
void THwndComponent::Test()
{
  PostMessage(FHandle, MSG_MYMESSAGE, 0, 0);
}
```

I declared the `MSG_MYMESSAGE` message identifier at the top of the source file. The code in this method simply posts a message to the hidden window by passing `FHandle` in the first parameter. When this code executes, Windows passes the message on to the component's window procedure. The window procedure looks like this:

```
void __fastcall THwndComponent::WndProc(TMessage& Message)
{
  if (Message.Msg == MSG_MYMESSAGE)
    MessageBeep(0);
  try {
    Dispatch(&Message);
    if (Message.Msg == WM_QUERYENDSESSION)
      Message.Result = 1;
  }
  catch (...) {
    Application->HandleException(this);
  }
}
```

If the message received was my user-defined message, I beep the PC speaker as an indication that the message was received. Any other messages get passed on to Windows for default processing. This is accomplished by calling the `Dispatch()` method.

Notice the check for the `WM_QUERYENDSESSION` message. This message is sent to all window procedures when Windows is shutting down. The VCL has a bug in that this message is not handled correctly by the default VCL processing. The code you see here ensures that the little component won't hang Windows if an application using the component is running when Windows shuts down. I set the message's `Result` to `1`, telling Windows that it's okay to shut down.

The component's destructor cleans up by disposing of the hidden window when the component is destroyed:

```
__fastcall THwndComponent::~THwndComponent()
{
  DeallocateHWnd(FHandle);
}
```

Granted, this simple component doesn't do anything useful, but it does illustrate the use of a hidden window in a non-visual component.

Hooking the Application Window Procedure in Non-Visual Components

Some non-visual components must monitor the messages sent to either the application's main form or to the `Application` object itself. An example that comes immediately to mind is a tray icon component. This type of component will need to know when the main form is minimized or when the close box is clicked. For this section I'll isolate the form's minimize action. Detecting the form close is simply a variation on the same theme.

There are two ways to detect when the form on which a non-visual component resides is being minimized—the right way and the wrong way.

The wrong way is to assign your own event handler to the `Application` object's `OnMinimize` event. Unfortunately, this is exactly what many novice component writers do. Consider what happens if I place two such components on my form at the same time. Each of the components will assign an event handler to the `OnMimimize` event of the `Application` object. Because there is only one `OnMinimize` event, one of the components simply won't function properly. Worse yet, if I have my own `OnMinimize` event handler for the `Application` object, then neither component will work properly. Events are not chainable, so there can only be one event handler for the `OnMinimize` event active at any one time.

When a form is minimized, Windows sends a WM_SYSCOMMAND message to the form with a wParam of SC_MINIMIZE. The right way to trap the WM_SYSCOMMAND message from a component is to hook the window procedure for the main form. Because window procedures are chainable, I can insert my component's window procedure into the chain, examine all messages coming in, and then pass each message on to the next window procedure in the chain. This gives me the opportunity to spy on messages destined for the main form without interrupting the flow of messages.

Setting up a window procedure hook is a bit complicated. First look at the source code for a component that hooks the window procedure of the main form; then I'll explain how the code works. Listings 3.15 and 3.16 show the header and main form for a component that hooks the main form's window procedure.

LISTING 3.15 THE HEADER FOR A COMPONENT THAT HOOKS THE MAIN FORM'S WINDOW PROCEDURE

```
#ifndef HookComponentH
#define HookComponentH

#include <SysUtils.hpp>
#include <Controls.hpp>
#include <Classes.hpp>
#include <Forms.hpp>

class PACKAGE THookComponent : public TComponent
{
private:
  void __fastcall FormWndProc(TMessage& Message);
  TFarProc NewWndProc;
  TFarProc PrevWndProc;
protected:
  void __fastcall Loaded();
public:
  __fastcall THookComponent(TComponent* Owner);
    __fastcall ~THookComponent();
__published:
};

#endif
```

LISTING 3.16 THE COMPONENT'S SOURCE CODE

```
#include <vcl.h>
#pragma hdrstop

#include "HookComponent.h"
#pragma package(smart_init)
```

```
__fastcall THookComponent::THookComponent(TComponent* Owner)
          : TComponent(Owner)
{
  NewWndProc = 0;
  PrevWndProc = 0;
  if (!ComponentState.Contains(csDesigning))
    NewWndProc = MakeObjectInstance(FormWndProc);
}

__fastcall THookComponent::~THookComponent()
{
  if (NewWndProc) {
    TForm* ownerForm = dynamic_cast<TForm*>(Owner);
    if (!ownerForm)
      return;
    SetWindowLong(ownerForm->Handle, GWL_WNDPROC, (long)PrevWndProc);
    PrevWndProc = 0;
    FreeObjectInstance(NewWndProc);
  }
}

void __fastcall THookComponent::Loaded()
{
  TComponent::Loaded();
  if (!ComponentState.Contains(csDesigning)) {
    TForm* ownerForm = dynamic_cast<TForm*>(Owner);
    if (!ownerForm)
      return;
    PrevWndProc = (void*)SetWindowLong(
      ownerForm->Handle, GWL_WNDPROC, (long)NewWndProc);
  }
}

void __fastcall THookComponent::FormWndProc(TMessage& Message)
{
  if (Message.Msg == WM_SYSCOMMAND)
    if (Message.WParam == SC_MINIMIZE)
      ShowMessage("Main Form Minimized");
  if (PrevWndProc) {
    TForm* ownerForm = dynamic_cast<TForm*>(Owner);
    Message.Result = CallWindowProc((FARPROC)PrevWndProc,
      ownerForm->Handle, Message.Msg, Message.WParam, Message.LParam);
  }
}
```

The private section of the component's declaration includes these declarations:

```
private:
  void __fastcall FormWndProc(TMessage& Message);
  TFarProc NewWndProc;
  TFarProc PrevWndProc;
```

The `FormWndProc()` method is the window procedure that I will insert into the form's window procedure chain. The `NewWndProc` variable is a pointer to the `FormWndProc()` method. The `PrevWndProc` variable is a pointer to the form's original window procedure. I'll explain how these variables are used in just a bit.

The component's constructor initializes the `NewWndProc` variable as follows:

```
if (!ComponentState.Contains(csDesigning))
  NewWndProc = MakeObjectInstance(FormWndProc);
```

This code calls the `MakeObjectInstance()` function to create a window procedure pointer from a class member function. A window procedure must normally be a standalone function (not a class member function). `MakeObjectInstance()` performs some magic to allow a class member function to be used as a window procedure; it returns a pointer to the class member function as a result. I save this pointer in the `NewWndProc` variable. The rest of the window hook code is performed in my overridden `Loaded()` method:

```
void __fastcall THookComponent::Loaded()
{
  TComponent::Loaded();
  if (!ComponentState.Contains(csDesigning)) {
    TForm* ownerForm = dynamic_cast<TForm*>(Owner);
    if (!ownerForm)
      return;
    PrevWndProc = (void*)SetWindowLong(
      ownerForm->Handle, GWL_WNDPROC, (long)NewWndProc);
  }
}
```

The first few lines of code in the `Loaded()` method check to ensure that the component is being used at run time and that the owner of the component is a form. This line does the important stuff:

```
PrevWndProc = (void*)SetWindowLong(
  ownerForm->Handle, GWL_WNDPROC, (long)NewWndProc);
```

This code calls `SetWindowLong()` to install my new window procedure for the form. When `SetWindowLong()` is called with the `GWL_WNDPROC` flag, it returns a pointer to the form's original window procedure. I save this pointer in the `PrevWndProc` variable because I'll need it later to keep the window procedure chain intact. After this code executes, all messages destined for the form will now come to my `FormWndProc()` method. Here's what that method looks like:

```
void __fastcall THookComponent::FormWndProc(TMessage& Message)
{
  if (Message.Msg == WM_SYSCOMMAND)
    if (Message.WParam == SC_MINIMIZE)
      ShowMessage("Main Form Minimized");
```

```
  if (PrevWndProc) {
    TForm* ownerForm = dynamic_cast<TForm*>(Owner);
    Message.Result = CallWindowProc((FARPROC)PrevWndProc,
      ownerForm->Handle, Message.Msg, Message.WParam, Message.LParam);
  }
}
```

The first few lines of code check to see if the form is being minimized. If so, a message is displayed as a way of proving that the component has successfully hooked the form's window procedure. The next few lines are vital:

```
if (PrevWndProc) {
  TForm* ownerForm = dynamic_cast<TForm*>(Owner);
  Message.Result = CallWindowProc((FARPROC)PrevWndProc,
    ownerForm->Handle, Message.Msg, Message.WParam, Message.LParam);
}
```

This code passes any and all messages on to the form's original window procedure. This is accomplished with a call to `CallWindowProc()`. The first parameter to `CallWindowProc()` is a pointer to the window procedure that is being called. Remember, I saved the pointer to the form's original window procedure in my `PrevWndProc` variable in the `Loaded()` method. The rest of the parameters to `CallWindowProc()` are the window handle of the main form, the incoming message, and its parameters. It is important that you call the next window procedure in the chain; otherwise, the form won't get any messages destined for it. An unloadable application is the result.

Finally, my component's destructor uninstalls my `FormWndProc()` method as the current window procedure and reinstates the form's original window procedure:

```
__fastcall THookComponent::~THookComponent()
{
  if (NewWndProc) {
    TForm* ownerForm = dynamic_cast<TForm*>(Owner);
    if (!ownerForm)
      return;
    SetWindowLong(ownerForm->Handle, GWL_WNDPROC, (long)PrevWndProc);
    PrevWndProc = 0;
    FreeObjectInstance(NewWndProc);
  }
}
```

The call to `SetWindowLong()` is identical to the one shown earlier, with the obvious exception that this time I pass `PrevWndProc` in the last parameter. Finally, I call `FreeObjectInstance()` to free the memory allocated in the earlier call to `MakeObjectInstance()`.

This code might appear a bit convoluted, but you need to know how to properly hook the main form's window procedure if you want to write robust components.

Summary

In this chapter you found out how to write component and property editors. Component and property editors are not difficult to write, but there has been so little information available on how to write them that many C++Builder programmers have simply avoided the subject. I also talked a bit more about packages in this chapter. Specifically, I told you what units should go into the runtime package and what units should go into the designtime package. I also showed you how to write a registration unit for the design-time package. Following that, I discussed exceptions and exception classes as they pertain to component writing. I ended the chapter with some techniques commonly used when writing non-visual components.

As I've said, I find component writing challenging. There are so many variables that there is always some new aspect to discover. There's no doubt that component writing is rewarding. It's also a bit harrowing if you are writing components for use by the general public. Component users will find ways of using (and abusing) your components that you never dreamed of. Writing good components takes lots of practice. With time and patience, you can write components with the best of them.

C++ Templates

by Harold Howe and Jody Hagins

CHAPTER **4**

In this chapter you learn how to write robust, reusable programs using C++ templates. Most C++ programmers consider programming with templates a black art. This misconception is quite unfortunate, as templates provide a solid backbone for code reusability. However, with an ever-changing C++ standard (until recently), and the sometimes difficult syntax of templates, this misconception is entirely understandable. This chapter's goal is to teach you how to write solid, reusable code with templates, and to dispel some of black art myths surrounding templates.

Note, however, that this chapter does not even begin to cover every aspect of C++ templates. The ISO ANSI standard contains a 55-page chapter on templates. Those 55 pages are, to put it kindly, a tad on the dry side. They contain legalistic specifications and very little annotation. We would need an entire book in order to adequately cover every aspect of templates, while maintaining a form that can be read by humans. It would be impossible to cover everything about templates in this single chapter.

After reading this chapter you will know how to

- Read and understand the syntax of C++ templates
- Write your own template classes and functions
- Use the new C++Builder 4 template features
- Harness the power of the STL

> **NOTE**
>
> Some of the techniques discussed in this chapter are relatively new additions to the ISO ANSI standard. C++Builder 4 is one of the few compilers that will correctly compile the example code from this chapter.

New Template Support in C++Builder 4

With respect to template support, C++Builder 4 is nearly 100% ANSI compliant. This chapter discusses some of the new C++Builder 4 template features.

It is beneficial to know which template features are new to C++Builder 4, and what features were supported in older versions. The following list summarizes some of the template features that are new to C++Builder 4:

- Template member functions and template member classes
- Partial specialization for class templates

- The typename template qualifier keyword
- Explicit instantiation of individual members
- Friend templates
- Template parameters

This not a complete list by any means, but it does highlight the new template features that you are most likely to utilize. For a more complete list, see the "What's New in C++Builder?" help file that comes with C++Builder 4.

Template Basics

If you are new to templates, you may be wondering what all the fuss is about. What is a template? Why do templates foster code reuse?

A *template* defines a family of functions or classes. In order to create a template, you must declare a function or class using the keyword `template`. For example, both of the following are templates:

```
template <class T>
void foo(T t)
{
}

template <class T>
class Foo
{
};
```

The first example defines a family of functions, each called `foo()`. Each function in the family takes an argument of some type. The second example specifies an almost infinite set of classes, typed by the template argument `T`.

A template supplies a generic set of code that can be applied to almost any type. When the compiler recognizes that a template is being used, it creates an instance of that code with the specific parameterized type. Think of it as an automatic copy-and-paste operation. The following code will cause the compiler to generate two different functions, each named `foo()`. One function will take an `int` and the other will take a user-defined type of `Bar`.

```
foo(10);
Bar b;
foo(b);
```

4

C++ TEMPLATES

The next example generates three separate classes, based on the class template `Foo`:

```
Foo<int> aFooInt;
Foo<Bar> aFooBar;
Foo< Foo<Bar> > aFooFooBar;
```

Some of this syntax may seem foreign to you at this point. That's okay. It will make more sense as you continue through the chapter. For now, just remember that a template defines a generic piece of code that works with different types of variables.

Function Templates

Imagine, for a second, that one of your co-workers has written a function that takes two integer arguments and returns the maximum of the two values. The code might look like this:

```
int Max( int arg1, int arg2)
{
  if(arg2 > arg1)
    return arg2;
  else
    return arg1;
}
```

The function does one thing, and does it well. What more could you ask? What happens if you need to find the maximum of two double precision floating-point numbers? You certainly don't want to use the integer version of `Max()` for floating-point values because truncation could cause erroneous results. You need a version of `Max()` that works correctly for floats.

To create a version of `Max()` that works correctly for floats, you could copy the integer version of `Max()`, paste it into the source file just below the integer version, and replace `int` with `double`. You would end up with a new version of `Max()` that looks like this:

```
double Max( double arg1, double arg2)
{
  if(arg2 > arg1)
    return arg2;
  else
    return arg1;
}
```

Now you have two versions of `Max()`, one for `doubles`, and one for `ints`. You realize that having two versions of the same function might create code maintenance headaches, but you reassure yourself that there was simply no other way to solve the problem. Plus, you can always tell your boss that you just "wrote a highly optimized maximization routine using the native IEEE 64-bit floating-point format." Then you can take the afternoon off and play ice hockey while your boss basks in your greatness. Life is good until you realize that you also need a version of Max() that works with AnsiString, Currency objects, and complex numbers.

You are faced with a decision. You can rely on those trusted allies, copy and paste, to create three more versions of the Max() function, or you can find a new way of solving the problem. Wouldn't it be great if the compiler could handle the chore of cutting and pasting the code for you? With templates, C++Builder can do exactly that.

A Function Template Example

The C++ template mechanism allows you to create a generic Max() function that can be used for any type of argument. Whether the arguments are integers, doubles, foobars, or AnsiStrings doesn't matter. The following demonstrates how to create a template version of the Max() function:

```
template <class T>
T Max (T arg1, T arg2)
{
  if(arg2 > arg1)
    return arg2;
  else
    return arg1;
}
```

Compare the template version of Max() with the initial version of Max() that worked with integer types. If you throw out the first line—the line that contains template <class T>—you should see that the two functions are identical, except that int has been replaced with T. When you use the template version of Max(), the compiler replaces T with the type of arguments that you are using. If you pass integers, T will be replaced with int. If you pass doubles, T is replaced with double.

> **NOTE**
>
> The template parameter does not have to be T. It can be U, type, or the like. Most people seem to use T out of habit.

Our original goal was to create a version of Max() that works with multiple types of arguments. The template version of Max() works with objects, such as AnsiString and Currency, as well as integral types like double and int. However, the template version might be used with objects; it is therefore wise to pass and return objects by reference to

4

C++ TEMPLATES

prevent construction and destruction of temporary objects. The next snippet shows an improved version of Max() that does not generate temporary objects:

```
template <class T>
const T& Max (const T& arg1, const T& arg2)
{
  if(arg2 > arg1)
    return arg2;
  else
    return arg1;
}
```

Now all we need is some code that uses the template function. Listing 4.1 shows a complete code example. The program is a console mode project that was generated using the Console Wizard from the C++Builder Object Repository.

LISTING 4.1 USING THE Max() TEMPLATE IN A PROGRAM

```
#include <condefs.h>
#include <iostream>

// cout and endl are in the std namespace.
using std::cout;
using std::endl;

template <class T>
const T& Max (const T& arg1, const T& arg2)
{
  if(arg2 > arg1)
    return arg2;
  else
    return arg1;
}

int main()
{
  cout << Max(15,5)     << endl;    // calls Max(int,int)
  cout << Max('a','b') << endl;     // calls Max(char,char)
  //cout << Max(29,'b') << endl;    // Error Max(int,char) does not exist
  cout << Max<int>(15,'b') << endl; // OK. converts 'b' to int

  return 0;
}
```

Now we have one version of the Max() function to maintain, instead of three or four copies. The burden of generating new versions of Max() for new types of arguments has been shifted to the compiler. This is an important concept to understand. Templates allow the compiler to do more of your work.

Macros Versus Templates

You may be thinking to yourself, "Why not just create a `Max()` macro?" Yes, our original version of the `Max()` function could have been converted to a macro. The macro would have looked like this:

```
#define Max(a,b) (((a) > (b)) ? (a) : (b))
```

However, by their very nature, macros do not promote predictable and maintainable code. One of the subtle dangers of macros is that they do not behave like real functions. Can you spot the bug in the following code?

```
#define Max(a,b) (((a) > (b)) ? (a) : (b))

int main()
{
  int i = 0;
  int j = 0;

  cout << Max(i,++j) << endl;
  cout << i << endl
       << j << endl;
  return 0;
}
```

In this code, j is incremented twice by the macro. After executing the macro, j has a value of 2, not 1 as you might expect. Macros have several other downfalls:

- Macros require special preprocessor syntax, which is unwieldy and error prone.
- Macros can have undesirable and unnoticed side effects because parameters may be expanded multiple times. (This is why j was incremented twice in the previous example.)
- Macros provide very little type safety.
- Debugging macros can be difficult because you cannot step into the macro code itself.

Templates address each of these downfalls. The syntax of templates is similar to the syntax of normal functions and classes. Templates behave like real functions and classes, so you don't have the problem of undesirable side effects. Templates provide very strong type safety. Lastly, you can debug template code much more easily than you can debug macro code. You can step into a template function, trace execution, and inspect variables.

> **TIP**
>
> Programmers often use macros because they don't incur the overhead of a function call. However, you can achieve the same effect by creating a template function that is declared as inline.
>
> ```
> template <class T>
> inline T Max (T arg1, T arg2)
> {
>   if(arg2 > arg1)
>     return arg2;
>   else
>     return arg1;
> }
> ```

Instantiating Function Templates

As you saw in Listing 4.1, the compiler will try to figure out which function template to call. If you pass integer arguments to the Max() function, the compiler instantiates a version of Max() that takes integer parameters. If you pass double precision arguments, the compiler instantiates a double precision version of Max(). The compiler only instantiates the versions of Max() that your code needs.

The compiler instantiates a function template when you call the function or when you take the address of the function—whichever occurs first. *Instantiation* of a function template means that the compiler takes the function skeleton, replaces the parameter types with the types of arguments that you are passing, and pastes the object code for that function into your executable. Think of template instantiation as a glorified copy-and-paste operation.

What happens when two source files use the same version of a template function? Say that you have two source files, unit1 and unit2, and they both call the integer version of Max(). Each unit instantiates its own copy of Max(), but the compiler and linker work together to ensure that the units share the same copy of Max() in the final executable. Only one copy of Max<int>() will exist in the program.

When discussing templates, it is often beneficial to refer to a specific instance of a template. For example, we may need to refer to the integer version of Max(). To do so, we use the syntax Max<int>(). You refer to Max<int>() as "Max of int."

You can tell the compiler to not instantiate function templates automatically. To do so, select Projects, Options, C++, and check the External box in the Templates group. If you check this box, you need to explicitly instantiate your templates. Explicit template instantiation is covered in the "Advanced Template Concepts" section.

It is interesting to take a peek at what code actually ends up in the executable when you use a template function in your program. You can do this by telling the C++Builder linker to generate a map file. To generate a map file, select Project, Options, Linker and check the Detailed radio button in the Map File group.

The map file for the program in Listing 4.1 reveals two occurrences of the `Max()` function, which we expected:

```
Address           Publics by Name
0001:00000244     const char& Max<char>(const char&, const char&)
0001:00000208     const int& Max<int>(const int&, const int&)
```

Class Templates

The C++ template mechanism supports class templates as well as function templates. In fact, class templates pack more power than function templates because class templates combine the object-oriented benefits of classes with the generality of templates.

You can solve many problems by using class templates. You can create container classes such as stacks, queues, and lists without specifying the type of objects that are stored in the container. You can also create smart pointers and auto pointers that simplify the creation, management, and deletion of pointers. Here is a simple template class:

```cpp
template <class T>
class Container
{
  private:
    T m_t;
  public:
    Container(const T& t)
      :m_t(t)
    {}

    void DoSomething() { cout << "doing something: " << m_t << endl; }
};

int main()
{
  Container<int>    c1(15);
  Container<char *> c2("Hello Dr Crane");
  c1.DoSomething();
  c2.DoSomething();
  return 0;
}
```

The `Container` class is a simple template class. It stores a member variable called `m_t` whose type is not known until the template is instantiated. The `main()` function uses two versions of the `Container` class: one version for integers and one version for character strings. In the integer version, m_t becomes an `int`; in the string version, m_t becomes a `char *`.

Notice that the code defines the member functions of the `Container` class directly inside the class declaration. This means that the member functions will be inline functions. You can also define member functions outside the class. The next example shows the syntax for doing so:

```
template <class T>
class Container
{
  private:
    T m_t;
  public:
    Container(const T& t);
    void DoSomething();
};

template <class T>
Container<T>::Container(const T& t)
  :m_t(t)
{
}

template <class T>
void Container<T>::DoSomething()
{
  cout << "doing something: " << m_t << endl;
}
```

The class declaration hasn't really changed, other than the fact that the function bodies for the constructor and the `DoSomething()` method have been removed. The syntax for a member function of a template class is almost no different than the syntax for a template function. There is a `template` keyword and some template parameters, followed by the body of the function.

Notice that the class name preceding the member function name is `Container<T>`, rather than just `Container`. The presence of the template parameter in the class name is critical. If you omit it, the compiler will generate an error. The template parameter in the class name tells the compiler which template class the function is a member of.

Instantiating Class Templates

Unlike function templates, the compiler will not try to figure out which class template you need for a particular situation. When you need to use a class template, you must tell the compiler which version of the template you want. You do this by listing the template's class name followed by your template arguments enclosed in angle brackets.

The code example in the preceding section used the template `Container` class in two ways—once with integer types and once with `char *` types:

```
Container<int>    c1(15);
Container<char *> c2("Hello Dr Crane");
```

`Container<int>` tells the compiler that you want to work with the `int` version of the `Container` template. Think of `Container<int>` as a class name equivalent to `TComponent` or `TForm`.

Static Members of a Template Class

A template class can contain static methods and static data members. The syntax for static members is worth taking a look at. Listing 4.2 shows how to add static methods and data members to the `Container` template class.

LISTING 4.2   STATIC MEMBERS OF A TEMPLATE CLASS

```cpp
template <class T>
class Container
{
  public:
    Container() {}

    static int ref_count;
    static T   some_object;
    static int GetRefCount();
    static T   GetObject();
};

template <class T>
int Container<T>::ref_count = 5;

template <class T>
T Container<T>::some_object;

template <class T>
int Container<T>::GetRefCount()
{
    return Container<T>::ref_count;
}

template <class T>
T Container<T>::GetObject()
{
    return Container<T>::some_object;
}
```

continues

LISTING 4.2   CONTINUED

```
int main()
{
  Container<char>::ref_count      = 29;
  Container<char>::some_object    = 'x';
  Container<double>::ref_count    = 700;
  Container<double>::some_object = 3.14159;

  cout << Container<char>::GetRefCount()   << endl;
  cout << Container<char>::GetObject()     << endl;
  cout << Container<double>::GetRefCount()<< endl;
  cout << Container<double>::GetObject()   << endl;
  return 0;
}
```

This is the output from this program:

```
29
x
700
3.14159
```

Each instance of a template class gets its own copy of static members. In this example, the static members of Container<char> are separate from the static members of Container<double>. The static variables are not static across all instances of the template. The output from the example code proves this. The ref_count member of Container<char> had a value of 29, while the ref_count member of Container<double> was 700.

> **TIP**
>
> You can create static variables that are shared by every instance of a template class by creating a base class that contains the static variables. The template class derives from the base class.

Inheritance

Template and non-template classes follow the same inheritance rules. You can create a new template class that derives from a non-template base class. You can also create a class that derives from an instantiated template class. Yet another option is to create a new template class that derives from an existing template class.

Listing 4.3 demonstrates how to derive a template class from a normal base class.

LISTING 4.3 DERIVING A TEMPLATE CLASS FROM A NON-TEMPLATE BASE

```
// create a non-template base class
class Base
{
  public:
    Base() {}
    virtual void DoSomething(){ cout << "base DoSomething" << endl; }
};

// derive a template class from the base class.
template <class T>
class Derived : public Base
{
  private:
    T m_t;
  public:
    Derived(const T& t): Base(), m_t(t) {}
    virtual void DoSomething();
};

template <class T>
void Derived<T>::DoSomething()
{
  cout << "derived DoSomething: " << m_t << endl;
  Base::DoSomething();
}

int main()
{
  Base           base;
  Derived<int>    d1(15);
  Derived<char *> d2("Hello Dr Crane");
  base.DoSomething();
  d1.DoSomething();
  d2.DoSomething();
  return 0;
}
```

Listing 4.4 reverses the scenario by deriving a non-template class from a template base class. In doing so, the derived class must pick a version of the base class to derive from. In this example, the derived class inherits from Base<int>.

LISTING 4.4 DERIVING A NON-TEMPLATE CLASS FROM A TEMPLATE BASE

```
// create a template base class
template <class T>
class Base
```

continues

LISTING 4.4   CONTINUED

```cpp
{
  private:
    T m_t;
  public:
    Base(const T& t): m_t(t) {}
    virtual void DoSomething()
    { cout << "base DoSomething: " << m_t << endl; }
};

class Derived : public Base<int>
{
  public:
    Derived(int arg) {}
    virtual void DoSomething();
};

void Derived::DoSomething()
{
  cout << "Derived DoSomething, calling base class." << endl;
  Base<int>::DoSomething();
}

int main()
{
  Base<int>    b1(29);
  Base<char *> b2("Hello Dr Crane");
  Derived      derived(15);

  b1.DoSomething();
  b2.DoSomething();
  derived.DoSomething();
  return 0;
}
```

Notice that whenever the derived class refers to the base class, it must do so by referencing Base<int>. It is not sufficient to simply refer to the base class as Base. Coding the DoSomething() method of Derived like this generates a syntax error:

```cpp
void Derived::DoSomething()
{
  Base::DoSomething();  // Error: which version of Base?
}
```

Furthermore, when the derived class is a non-template class, it must derive from a specific instance of the base class, whether it be Base<int>, Base<double>, or some other instance of Base. The derived class cannot derive from the generic Base<T>, unless you turn the derived class into a template class as well. Listing 4.5 demonstrates this.

LISTING 4.5 DERIVING A TEMPLATE CLASS FROM A TEMPLATE BASE

```cpp
// create a template base class
template <class T>
class Base
{
    protected:
        T m_t;
    public:
        Base(const T& t): m_t(t) {}
        virtual void DoSomething()
        { cout << "base DoSomething: " << m_t << endl;}
};

template <class T>
class Derived : public Base<T>
{
    public:
        Derived(const T& t): Base<t>(t) {}
        virtual void DoSomething();
};

template <class T>
void Derived<T>::DoSomething()
{
    cout << "Derived: protected member is visible: " << m_t << endl;
    Base<T>::DoSomething();
}

int main()
{
    Base<int>       b1(29);
    Base<char *>    b2("Hello Dr Crane");
    Derived<int>    d1(15);
    Derived<char *> d2("Hello Mr. Derived");
    b1.DoSomething();
    b2.DoSomething();
    d1.DoSomething();
    d2.DoSomething();
    return 0;
}
```

4

C++ TEMPLATES

There are a couple of things worth mentioning about this code. First, look at how the derived class references the base class. The syntax for referencing the base class is Base<T> instead of Base<int>, as in the previous example. Second, derived template classes can see variables and functions that are declared as protected in the base class. The base class in this example has a protected member variable called m_t. The derived class can read and write this variable.

All of the template classes thus far have contained a member variable of type T. To demonstrate the flexibility of C++ templates, the next code example breaks from this tradition. Instead of containing a member variable of type T, the code in Listing 4.6 derives from the template parameter T.

LISTING 4.6 DERIVING A TEMPLATE CLASS FROM AN UNKNOWN BASE

```
// create two non-template base classes
class Base1
{
  public:
    Base1() { cout << "Base1 constructed" << endl; }
};

class Base2
{
  public:
    Base2() { cout << "Base2 constructed" << endl; }
};

// create a template class derived from some
// unknown base class.
template <class T>
class Derived : public T
{
  public:
    Derived();
};

template <class T>
Derived<T>::Derived()
  :T()
{  cout << "created a Derived of some kind " << endl; }

int main()
{
  Derived<Base1>  d1;
  Derived<Base2>  d2;
  return 0;
}
```

NOTE

C++Builder uses Microsoft's Active Template Library (ATL) for its COM and ActiveX support. The ATL, as its name implies, relies heavily on templates. The ATL class `CComObject` uses a technique similar to the code in Listing 4.6.

CComObject is a template class that derives from an unknown type. You specify the base class when you use the CComObject class. The class TATLModule also uses this technique.

Understanding Template Syntax

Probably the most difficult aspect of writing and using templates is understanding the syntax. The previous sections of this chapter contain examples of template functions and template classes, but each of the examples is pretty simple. Now that you have been introduced to templates, it's time to dig a little deeper. This section of the chapter explores the rich syntax of C++ templates and helps clarify what you can and cannot do with templates.

The C++ template mechanism relies heavily on the template keyword. All template declarations, definitions, and explicit instantiations must begin with template. Recall that a *declaration* equates to a function prototype or a class declaration. A *definition* equates to function body. An explicit instantiation is something that we haven't covered yet. For now, just remember that whatever an explicit instantiation is, it will involve the template keyword.

Every template has one or more parameters. The template parameters are the parts of the template that are not yet known. The compiler fills in the template parameters when you instantiate the template. Parameters appear between angle brackets (< >) and are separated by commas. In the following example, class T and class U are template parameters:

```
template <class T, class U>
U Foo(T arg) {}
```

> **NOTE**
>
> It is crucial that you understand the difference between a template parameter and a template argument. The declaration of a template contains template parameters. A template is instantiated by passing template arguments to it. In the following code, class X is the template parameter and int is the template argument:
>
> ```
> template <class X> class Z { /* … */ };
> ```
>
> ```
> Z<int> z;
> ```
>
> This difference in terminology is subtle, but it is important to remember—especially if you ever decide to read the ISO ANSI C++ specification. Fortunately, this usage of the terms *parameter* and *argument* coincides with how they are used when dealing with traditional C functions. A function has parameters, but you pass it arguments.

4

C++ TEMPLATES

Template parameters can have default values. The syntax resembles the syntax for default function parameters. The following template class has two template parameters. The second parameter has a default value of AnsiString.

```
template <typename X, typename Y = AnsiString> myclass { /* … */ };

myclass<int>            m1; // myclass<int, AnsiString>
myclass<int, AnsiString> m2; // myclass<int, AnsiString>
myclass<int, double>    m3; // myclass<int, double>
```

In this case, both X and Y are type parameters for the template. The Y parameter defaults to AnsiString if only one argument is supplied when the template is instantiated. Once a parameter has been declared as having a default value, all subsequent parameters must also have default values:

```
template <typename X = int, typename Y> myclass{};               // Error!
template <typename X, typename Y = int, typename Z> myclass{};   // Error!
template <typename X = int, typename Y=double> myclass{};        // OK
template <typename X, typename Y=int, typename Z=int> myclass{}; // OK
```

The first line is incorrect because the first template parameter has a default argument, but the second parameter does not. The second line is incorrect for the same reason. If Y has a default argument, Z must also have a default.

Template Parameters

Templates are also known as *parameterized types* because you can generate code using data types as the parameters. A template parameter may take one of three forms: a type, a non-type, or another template.

Type Template Parameters

A *type parameter* is declared by using one of two keywords: class or typename. There is no semantic difference between the two when used as template parameters, so you can use whichever you like. Most template code uses the class keyword instead of the typename keyword. One reason for this is that many compilers still do not support the typename keyword. Although the class keyword is more prevalent, it is recommended that you consider using the typename keyword because it is more descriptive.

A type parameter is just what it sounds like. It is a parameter that represents some data type. You provide the data type when you instantiate the template. The Max() template function and the Container template class used type template parameters.

Non-Type Template Parameters

A non-type template parameter can be

• An integral type or enumeration

• A pointer or reference to an object

• A pointer or reference to a function

• A pointer to a member

Non-type parameters that are not references cannot be assigned a new value, nor can their address be taken. In fact, a temporary object is used in these cases. Also note that float, double, class, and void cannot be used as non-type template parameters.

The following example demonstrates non-type template parameters. Notice that the second line does not compile because double cannot be used as a template parameter. The assignment to tmp does not compile because tmp is not a reference.

```
template <int N> class xyz { /* … */ };
template <double D> class abc { /* … */ }; // Error!
template <SomeClass & ref, SomeClass tmp> void foo()
{
  ref = tmp;  // OK - ref is a reference, so you can assign it a value
  tmp = ref;  // Error-tmp is not a reference
}
```

Templates as Parameters

A template parameter may be a template itself. For example, the following code is a valid template specification:

```
template <template <typename Y> class Z>
class Foo { /* … */ };
```

This declaration states that Foo is a class template with one parameter. The parameter, Z, is a template parameter. The template parameter Z is a template that has one parameter, Y. If this seems confusing, don't worry—you will see examples of template parameters in the following section on template arguments.

Template Arguments

Template arguments are used to instantiate a class or function template. Because the compiler actually generates code for templates, template arguments are limited to compile time. You can't instantiate a template at run time. Note that template arguments closely mirror template parameters.

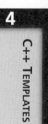

> **NOTE**
>
> It's quite unfortunate that the term *instantiate* is overloaded. Objects are instantiated at run time, when they are created. Templates are instantiated at build time, when the compiler recognizes the need for a certain piece of template code.

Type Template Arguments

Valid arguments to a type template parameter are any valid data type. This is an example:

```
template <typename X, typename Y, typename Z> class XYZ { /* … */ };
XYZ<int, double, char *> xyz;      // ok
XYZ<int, SomeClass, void *&> abc; // ok too
XYZ<7, SomeClass, void *&> notOk; // error, 7 is not a type
```

Non-Type Template Arguments

Non-type template arguments must match non-type template parameters in the template declaration. Since they are built at compile time, non-type template arguments must be constant expressions. Variables are not allowed. This is an example:

```
template <size_t N>
class FixedString
{
public:
  FixedString() : { str_[0] = '\0'; }
  char const * c_str() const { return str_; }
  size_t length() const { return strlen(str_); }
  size_t capacity() const { return N; }
private:
  char str_ [ N + 1 ];
};

typedef FixedString<80> String80;
```

Templates as Arguments

A template may also be passed as an argument:

```
template <template <typename Y> class Z>
class Foo { Z<int> collection_; /* … */ };

Foo<std::list> fooList;
Foo<std::vector> fooVector;
```

In this example, Foo has a member variable, which is a collection of ints. It doesn't matter how the collection is implemented, so long as the implementation supports the interface assumed by the class Foo. The Standard Template Library (STL) comes with several collection class templates. Both list and vector support the same minimal insertion, deletion, and access methods, so either one could be used here.

This is an example of strategizing a class, by using templates to provide a specific implementation of a common interface.

Advanced Template Concepts

This section of the chapter covers advanced template concepts. We will discuss template members, template specialization, explicit template instantiation, and a handful of other topics. Many of the topics in this section rely on new template features in C++Builder 4.

Template Member Functions and Classes

C++Builder 4 allows you to write classes that have members that are templates. The members can be function templates or class templates. The parent class itself can be a template class or a normal, non-template class. Shown here is an example of a regular C++ class that contains a member function that is a template:

```cpp
class MyClass
{
  private:
    template <class T>
    void DoSomething(T t)
    { cout << "doing something: " << t << endl; }
  public:
    MyClass()
    {
      DoSomething(5);
      DoSomething("hello");
      DoSomething(3.14159);
    }
};

int main()
{
  MyClass foo;
  return 0;
}
```

MyClass contains a generic DoSomething() method. This method is a template member function. The constructor for MyClass calls three versions of the template member: one for ints, one for character strings, and one for floats. The result is a class with three

instantiations of the `DoSomething()` member function. You can see these instantiations in the map file for the project:

```
Address              Publics by Name
0001:000001EC        void MyClass::DoSomething<char *>(char *)
0001:00000220        void MyClass::DoSomething<double>(double)
0001:000001B8        void MyClass::DoSomething<int>(int)
```

A template class can also have member templates. The next code example demonstrates a template class that has two member functions. One is a template member and one is not.

```cpp
template <class T>
class MyClass
{
  private:
    T m_t;
  public:
    MyClass(const T &t): m_t(t) {}

    template <class type>
    void DoSomething(type t);

    void DoSomethingElse();
};

template <class T>
template <class type>
void MyClass<T>::DoSomething(type t)
{
  cout << "doing something with type: " << t << endl;
  cout << "but I can still see m_t: "   << m_t << endl;
}

template <class T>
void MyClass<T>::DoSomethingElse()
{
  cout << "doing something else: " << m_t << endl;
}

int main()
{
  MyClass<int>    foo(29);
  MyClass<char>  bar('x');
  foo.DoSomething("hello there");
  foo.DoSomething(65);
  foo.DoSomething('v');
  bar.DoSomethingElse();
  return 0;
}
```

A template class called `MyClass` is created in this example. In the `main()` function of the program, there are two forms of `MyClass` instantiated: one for integers and one for `char`s. The `foo` variable is of the type `MyClass<int>`, and the `bar` variable is a `MyClass<char>`.

After constructing the two objects, the template member function `DoSomething()` is called three times for the `MyClass<int>` object. `DoSomething()` is a template member of the class. Each call to `DoSomething()` passes a different type of argument, so the compiler instantiates three versions of `DoSomething()`.

Notice that the `DoSomethingElse()` member function is not called for the `MyClass<int>` object. Additionally, the `DoSomething` template method is never called for the `bar` object. Because these methods are not called, they do not get instantiated. This can be verified by looking at the map file:

```
Address             Publics by Name
0001:000001EC       MyClass<char>::MyClass<char>(const char&)
0001:000001C0       MyClass<int>::MyClass<int>(const int&)
0001:00000338       MyClass<char>::DoSomethingElse()
0001:00000218       void MyClass<int>::DoSomething<char *>(char *)
0001:000002D8       void MyClass<int>::DoSomething<char>(char)
0001:00000278       void MyClass<int>::DoSomething<int>(int)
```

You can see two `MyClass` constructors. You also see a copy of `MyClass<char>::DoSomethingElse()`, but no copy of `DoSomethingElse()` exists for the `MyChar<int>` class. This makes sense because `DoSomethingElse()` was called for the `char` version of `MyClass`, but not for the `int` version.

In addition to template member functions, you can also create template member classes. The next example demonstrates this concept:

```cpp
class MyClass
{
  template <class T>
  class InternalClass
  {
    private:
      T m_t;
    public:
      InternalClass(const T& t)
        :m_t(t) {}
      void DoSomething() { cout << m_t << endl; }
  };

  public:
    MyClass()
      :ic1(3.14159),ic2(22)
    {}
```

```
    void DoSomething()
    {
      ic1.DoSomething();
      ic2.DoSomething();
    }

  private:
    InternalClass<float> ic1;
    InternalClass<int>   ic2;
};
```

MyClass contains an internal class called InternalClass, which is a template class. MyClass instantiates two versions of the template class: one for floats and one for ints.

Template Specialization

C++Builder 4 allows you to specialize template functions and classes. Begin your study of specialization with an example. For that, return to your trusted friend, the Max() template function:

```
template <class T>
T Max (T arg1, T arg2)
{
  if(arg2 > arg1)
    return arg2;
  else
    return arg1;
}
```

As you have already seen, this function works well for integers, chars, and double-precision floats. It also works for char pointers, but it doesn't work as you might expect. Imagine that you execute this line of code:

```
cout << Max ("hello", "bob") << endl;
```

The compiler will flesh out a Max() function that takes two char * arguments. The char * version of Max() would be equivalent to this:

```
char* Max (char * arg1, char* arg2)
{
  if(arg2 > arg1)
    return arg2;
  else
    return arg1;
}
```

The if statement compares one pointer to see it if is greater than the other. This is equivalent to comparing machine addresses. Which is greater, "hello" or "bob"? That depends on where the compiler puts each string in memory.

Comparing machine addresses is not the correct way to compare strings. You need a version of Max() that compares the strings, not the addresses where the strings reside. What you really need is for Max() to call the strcmp() function from the C Runtime Library (RTL).

Template specialization allows you to create a custom version of Max() that works correctly for character strings. When you specialize a template, you create a special version of the template for a specific type. The next code segment demonstrates how to specialize the Max() function for char pointer arguments:

```
template <> char * Max<char *>( char* arg1, char* arg2)
{
  if(strcmp(arg1, arg2) < 0)
    return arg2;
  else
    return arg1;
}
```

Notice the empty angle brackets. The empty brackets tell the compiler that this is a specialization of an existing template. Also notice the angle brackets that follow the Max() function name. The <char *> in Max<char *> tells the compiler which version of Max() is being specialized. In this case, you want to specialize the char * version of Max().

This form of specialization is called *explicit specialization*, which means that there are no unknowns in the specialized function—there are no template parameters. In addition to explicit specialization, C++ also supports partial specialization. With *partial specialization*, there is still something unknown about the template.

> **NOTE**
>
> You can also create a custom version of Max() for char pointers by using function overloading instead of using the explicit specialization syntax:
>
> ```
> char * Max( char* arg1, char* arg2)
> {
>   if(strcmp(arg1, arg2) < 0)
>       return arg2;
>   else
>       return arg1;
> }
> ```
>
> You can use function overloading when the template parameters of the function are passed as arguments.

Partially Specializing Template Functions

In the explicit specialization of `Max()`, you create a special version of the template that works correctly for `char *` arguments. What about other pointer types, such as pointers to `integers`, or pointers to `doubles`? They will utilize the generic version of `Max()`, which means that their addresses will be compared with one another. With partial specialization, you can create a special version of `Max()` that works with all pointers (except `char` pointers, of course). Here is a partially specialized version of `Max()` for pointers:

```
template <class T>
T* Max(T* arg1, T* arg2)
{
  if(*arg2 > *arg1)
    return arg2;
  else
    return arg1;
}
```

The compiler will use this version of the `Max()` template if the arguments to `Max()` are pointers or addresses of existing variables. If the arguments are not pointers, the compiler uses the original `Max()` template.

The syntax of a partial specialization differs slightly from the syntax of an explicit specialization. Notice that the angle brackets are not empty. With partial specialization, something about the template is still unknown; the template still needs parameters.

Partially Specializing Template Classes

Everything discussed regarding specialization was already supported in C++Builder 3. C++Builder 4 adds support for partial specialization of a class template. Examples thus far have specialized the template function `Max()`. Listing 4.7 demonstrates a class template that is partially specialized.

Listing 4.7   Partially Specializing a Template Class

```
// Generic template
template <class T>
class Container
{
  private:
    T m_t;
  public:
    Container(T t)
      :m_t(t) {}
    void DoSomething()
    {
        cout << "Generic DoSomething: " << m_t << endl;
```

```
    }
};

// specialized version for pointers
template <class T>
class Container<T *>
{
  private:
    T* m_t;
  public:
    Container(T *t)
    :m_t(t) {}

    void DoSomething()
    {
      cout << "Special DoSomething for pointers: " << *m_t << endl;
    }
};

int main()
{
  int j = 29;
  int *ptr = &j;
  Container<int> con1(j);      // use generic template
  Container<int*>con2(ptr);    // use special template for pointers
  con1.DoSomething();
  con2.DoSomething();
  return 0;
}
```

This is the output when this project is executed:

```
Generic DoSomething: 29
Special DoSomething for pointers: 29
```

The compiler instantiates the generic version of the template for `Container<int>`, but it uses the special version of the template for `Container<int *>`.

Controlling Template Instantiation

Under normal circumstances, the compiler decides when to instantiate a template. In the case of template classes, the compiler decides which parts of the template class to instantiate and which parts are not needed by the program. There are times, however, when it is advantageous to take control of template instantiation yourself. This process is known as *explicit template instantiation*.

With explicit instantiation, you can tell the compiler to flesh out a version of a template at a specific point in your code. It doesn't matter whether that version of the template is needed in the source file where you instantiate it. The syntax for explicit instantiation is as follows:

```
template int Max<int>(int, int); // instantiate Max<int>
template class FooBar<int>;       // instantiate FooBar<int>
```

The first line instantiates a template function and the second line instantiates a template class. When you instantiate a template class explicitly, the compiler generates every member function of the class, regardless of whether they are needed.

In order to avoid generating unused class members, you can explicitly instantiate individual class members. This support is new to C++Builder 4. Assume that the FooBar template class from the previous code segment contains a constructor and two member functions, Foo1() and Foo2(). The following code demonstrates how to explicitly instantiate just the constructor and one of the member functions:

```
template <class T>
class FooBar
{
  private:
    T m_t;
  public:
    FooBar(const T& t)
      :m_t(t){}
    void Foo1(int x, double y)
    { cout << "Foo1: " << m_t << " " << x * y <<endl; }
    void Foo2()
    { cout << "Foo2" <<endl; }
};

// instantiate constructor and Foo1 here
template FooBar<int>::FooBar(const int &);
template void FooBar<int>::Foo1(int, double);
```

An explicit instantiation behaves as if the code for the template were pasted into the source code at the point where the instantiation is located. The explicit instantiations of the FooBar() constructor and the Foo1() method behave as if the following code were pasted into the source file:

```
// results of explicit instantiation of FooBar's members
// Functions are inline because the template skeleton defined
// the functions inside the body of the class
inline FooBar<int>::FooBar(const int &t)
  m_t(t)
{}
inline void FooBar<int>::Foo1(int x, double y)
{  cout << "Foo1: " << m_t << " " << x * y <<endl; }
```

> **NOTE**
>
> An explicit instantiation equates to pasting real code into a source file. For this reason, you usually place explicit instantiations in C++ source files—not in header files.

Partial Template Argument Lists

As you saw in the `Max()` template function, the compiler will try to figure out which version of a template function to instantiate based on the arguments you pass to the function and the return type of the function. What happens when the function's parameters and return value do not involve the template parameter, as shown in the following example?

```
template <class T>
int WorthlessFunction (int arg)
{
    T t(arg);
    cout << "This didn't accomplish much: " << t << endl;
    return arg;
}
```

In this example, the template parameter `T` is not an argument or a return value from the function. As a result, the compiler cannot automatically deduce how it should replace the template parameter `T` when you call the function. In order to call this function, you must specify which version of the function you want by enclosing the type argument in angle brackets:

```
int main()
{
  cout << WorthlessFunction<float>(29)<< endl;
  cout << WorthlessFunction<char> (74)<< endl;
  return 0;
}
```

`WorthlessFunction<float>` tells the compiler that you want to instantiate and call the `float` version of the template function. `WorthlessFunction<char>` works the same way, but for `char` types. Without the `<float>` and `<char>` qualifiers, the main function would not compile because the template parameter would be undetermined.

Now consider a template function that has two template parameters. One of the template parameters is also a parameter for the function. The other template parameter is used internally by the function, but is not a parameter to the function.

```
template <class U, class T>
void FooFunction(T arg)
```

```
{
    U u(arg);
    cout << "This didn't accomplish much either: "
        << arg << " " << u << endl;
}
```

The T template parameter is a parameter to the function, but the U parameter is not. Because the U template parameter is not a parameter to the function, you must provide a template argument for U when you call the function. This raises a potential problem. When you list the template arguments, should you specify one argument or two?

Although the template has two parameters and neither parameter has a default value, you only have to pass a template argument for the template parameter that cannot be deduced from context. In other words, you must pass a template argument for the U type, but not for the T type because the compiler can calculate the T argument based on the type of argument that you pass to the function. The act of passing only the template arguments that are needed is called passing a *partial argument list*. The following code demonstrates this concept:

```
template <class U, class T>
void FooFunction(T arg)
{
    U u(arg);
    cout << "This didn't accomplish much either: "
        << arg << " " << u << endl;
}

int main()
{
    FooFunction<int>('x');          // calls FooFunction<int, char>('x');
    FooFunction<int>(42.15);        // calls FooFunction<int, double>(42.15);
    FooFunction(12);                // Error! U template arg is unknown
    FooFunction<int, char>('b');    // OK, but superfluous
    return 0;
}
```

In the first call to FooFunction(), the <int> template argument specifies a value for the U template parameter. The compiler calculates the T template parameter from the argument to the function, which is the char value 'x' in this case.

The compiler imposes a restriction on your use of partial argument lists. The template parameters that cannot be deduced from context must be the leftmost parameters in the template declaration. This rule works similarly to the rule for default arguments to a function. The following code does not compile:

```
template <class T, class U>
void FooFunction(T arg) { /* ... */}
```

```cpp
int main()
{
    FooFunction<int>('x');        // Error! U still not known
    FooFunction<char, int>('x');  // Ok. Now we know what U is
    return 0;
}
```

Template Friends

Template classes can have friend classes and friend functions in the same way that normal, non-template classes can have friends. The friend of a template class can be a regular, non-template class or a non-template function. The following example shows this scenario:

```cpp
template <class T>
class Foo
{
    private:
        // declare the class BuddyClass and
        // the function BuddyFunction to be friends
        friend class BuddyClass;
        friend void BuddyFunction();

        T m_t;
        void DoSomething() { cout << "doing something: " << m_t << endl; }
    public:
        Foo(const T& t)
            : m_t(t){}
};

// Some global Foo's
Foo<int>  Foo1(24);
Foo<Char> Foo2('c');

void BuddyFunction()
{
    // since we are a friend of the Foo<> family of classes
    // let's mess with their internal data.
    cout << "Foo1's private data: " << Foo1.m_t << endl;
    cout << "Foo2's private data: " << Foo2.m_t << endl;
    cout << "Foo1's private method: " << endl;
    Foo1.DoSomething();
}

class BuddyClass
{
    public:
        void BuddyMethod()
        {
            cout << "Foo2's private method: " << endl;
```

```
      Foo2.DoSomething();
   }
};
```

This code example contains a template class called Foo, a non-template function called BuddyFunction(), and a non-template class called BuddyClass. The template class Foo declares that BuddyFunction() and BuddyClass are its friends. What does this mean when Foo is a template class? It means that BuddyFunction() and BuddyClass are friends of every instantiation of the template class Foo. The code example instantiates two forms of the Foo template class. One version is for integers and the other is for characters. BuddyFunction() and BuddyClass are friends of both, and they will be friends of any other instance of the Foo template that you create.

The friend of a template class can also be a specific instance of a template class or function. The following illustrates this scenario:

```
template <class T>
class Buddy;

template <class T>
class Foo
{
   private:
     friend class Buddy<int>;

     T m_t;
   public:
     Foo(const T& t)
        : m_t(t){}
};

Foo<int>  Foo1(24);
Foo<Char> Foo2('c');

template <class T>
class Buddy
{};

template <>
class Buddy<int>
{
   public:
     void DoSomething()
     {
        cout << "Foo1's private data: " << Foo1.m_t << endl;
        cout << "Foo2's private data: " << Foo2.m_t << endl;
     }
};
```

```
int main()
{
    Buddy<int> buddy;
    buddy.DoSomething();
    return 0;
}
```

Template class `Foo` desperately wants `Buddy<int>` to be its friend. Every instance of `Foo`—whether it be `Foo<char>`, `Foo<int>`, or some other instance—will behave as if `Buddy<int>` were a friend class. The `Foo` template class does not state that `Buddy<char>`, `Buddy<double>`, or any other instance of `Buddy` is a friend class.

There are a couple of interesting points in the code example. First, notice that a forward declaration is added for the `Buddy` class just above the declaration of the `Foo` template class. If `Buddy` were not a template class, the forward declaration would not be necessary. It is required because of the `<int>` template parameter in the friend declaration. If you omit the forward declaration, the compiler doesn't know that `Buddy` is a template class; the `<int>` template argument therefore seems out of place. The forward declaration tells the compiler that there is a `Buddy` class out there somewhere, and that it is a template class with one parameter. Once the compiler knows that `Buddy` is a template class, the `<int>` template argument in the friend declaration makes perfect sense.

The second thing to notice is that the integer version of `Buddy` is coded using an explicit specialization. If `Foo` wants `Buddy<int>` to be its friend, then the integer version of `Buddy` has to contain different code than the generic `Buddy` template class. Think of it this way: `Buddy<int>` has access to the private parts of `Foo`. None of the other instantiations of `Buddy` has this level access. The only way to allow `Buddy<int>` to take advantage of his access rights is to specialize the integer version of the `Buddy` template.

A more useful scenario is to declare that `Buddy<char>` is a friend of `Foo<char>`, and that `Buddy<int>` is a friend of `Foo<int>`. This can be done by changing the friend declaration within the `Foo` class. Instead of making `Buddy<int>` a friend of the template class, `Buddy<T>` is made a friend as shown here:

```
template <class T>
class Buddy;

template <class T>
class Foo
{
  private:
    friend class Buddy<T>;
    T m_t;
  public:
    Foo(const T& t)
      : m_t(t){}
};
```

4

C++ TEMPLATES

```
template <class T>
class Buddy
{
  public:
    void DoSomething(const Foo<T> &foo)
    { cout << "foo's private data: " << foo.m_t << endl; }
};

int main()
{
  Foo<int>    foo1(29);
  Foo<double> foo2(3.14159);

  Buddy<int>    buddy1;
  Buddy<double> buddy2;
  buddy1.DoSomething(foo1);
  buddy2.DoSomething(foo2);

  return 0;
}
```

Each instantiation of Foo has one corresponding instantiation of the Buddy class as a friend. For example, Buddy<int> is a friend of Foo<int>. Buddy<int> will have access to the private and protected members of Foo<int>. Likewise, Buddy<char> is a friend of Foo<char>. However, Buddy<int> is not a friend of Foo<char>. The friendship only exists between instantiations of the same type. The relationship is one to one.

Thus far, three friendship scenarios have been described. All of these scenarios were supported by C++Builder 3. C++Builder 4 supports a new friendship scenario. C++Builder 4 allows you to declare that every instance of a template is a friend of every instance of a template class. That's a mouthful to swallow. The code example clarifies:

```
template <class T>
class Buddy
{
  private:
    T m_t;
  public:
    Buddy(const T&t)
      :m_t(t){}
};

template <class T>
class Foo
{
  private:
    template <class U>
    friend class Buddy;
```

```
      T m_t;

   public:
      Foo(const T& t)
         : m_t(t){}
};
```

There are two template classes involved. The template class Foo declares the template class Buddy is its friend. Notice that the template parameter in the friend declaration of Foo is a new template parameter, U. This syntax declares that for a given instance of Foo, every instance of Buddy is a friend. For example, say you instantiate the integer version of Foo. Buddy<int> will be a friend of the integer Foo class, as will Buddy<char>, Buddy<double>, and every other instance of the Buddy template. This type of friendship sets up a many-to-many relationship. The next code example describes how the Buddy template class can utilize, or abuse, its friendship rights:

```
template <class T>
class Buddy;

template <class T>
class Foo
{
   private:
      template <class U>
      friend class Buddy;

      T m_t;
      void DoSomething()
      { cout << "doing something: " << m_t << endl; }
   public:
      Foo(const T& t)
         : m_t(t){}
};

template <class T>
class Buddy
{
   private:
      T m_t;
   public:
      Buddy(const T&t)
         :m_t(t){}

      template <class U>
      void AbuseAFoo(Foo<U> &foo, U newValue)
      {
         cout << "Foo thinks I'm his friend." << endl
              << "Let's strain the relationship." << endl
```

```
            << "Want to see Foo's private data? " << foo.m_t << endl
            << "Now let's call Foo's private method: " << endl;
        foo.DoSomething();

        cout << "Change Foo's private data to : " <<  newValue <<endl;
        foo.m_t = newValue;
        cout << "Now execute that private method of foo again." << endl;
        foo.DoSomething();

        cout << "In case you wanted to know, my data is: "
            << m_t << endl << endl;
    }
};

int main()
{
  Foo<int>    foo1(15);
  Foo<double> foo2(3.14159);

  Buddy<char *> buddy1("A good buddy");
  Buddy<int>    buddy2(100);
  buddy1.AbuseAFoo(foo1, 29);
  buddy1.AbuseAFoo(foo2, 2 * 3.14159);
  buddy2.AbuseAFoo(foo2, 180.25);

  return 0;
}
```

The Foo template class declared that every instance of the Buddy template would be a friend. Foo<int> has two friends in the previous example; they are Buddy<int> and Buddy<char *>. Foo<double> has the same two friends. This means that both of the Buddy objects can access the private data of either Foo object. You can see this access in the AbuseAFoo() function calls.

Notice that the AbuseAFoo() member of the Buddy class is a template member function. This turns out to be for a very good reason. The Buddy class wants to abuse its friendship with Foo. Buddy isn't satisfied by simply abusing the integer version of Foo or the char version of Foo. It wants to abuse all types of Foo. In order to abuse all Foo types, the AbuseAFoo() member must adapt to the type of parameter that you pass it. In order to adapt, the AbuseAFoo() method must be a template member.

Because the AbuseAFoo() function is a member template, the compiler will instantiate a version of AbuseAFoo() for every type of Foo that you pass it. In the preceding example, the Buddy<char *> object abused two types of Foos: Foo<int> and Foo<double>. The map file for the project reveals that indeed, two AbuseAFoo() members of Buddy<char *> went into the executable:

```
Address        Publics by Name
0001:000003D0 void Buddy<char *>::AbuseAFoo<double>(Foo<double>&, double)
0001:000002BC void Buddy<char *>::AbuseAFoo<int>(Foo<int>&, int)
```

Header File Organization

Thus far, the code examples in this chapter have been short and simple. The examples have consisted of only one source file. That source file has contained both the main() function of the program and the code for a template function or class.

This organization is not practical in a large-scale project. You will undoubtedly have multiple source files in your projects. If you create a template function or class, you will want to use that template from more than one source file. This brings up an interesting dilemma. How do you organize your header files and source files when dealing with templates?

Recall that a template is not a real section of code; it is a skeleton. Something within the template is not yet known. That unknown is usually a variable type. When you use a template, the compiler has to flesh out the template skeleton using concrete types.

The process of fleshing out a template imposes some restrictions on you and the compiler. Analyze your original template function, Max(). Imagine that you have two different source files that need to utilize the Max() routine. If the Max() function were not a template function, you would probably place a prototype for Max() in a header file and place the function body for Max() in a C++ source file. You would then include the header file in any source file that needs to call the Max() function.

When the Max() function is a template function, this structure is inadequate. If a source file calls the integer version of Max(), the compiler has to instantiate the template. In other words, the compiler has to copy the code from the Max() template and replace each occurrence of the template parameter T with int. Herein lies the problem. If the header file for Max() contains only a function prototype, the compiler cannot flesh out the body of the template.

The compiler can't instantiate what it can't see. Therefore, it is necessary to place the entire function body for the Max() template in a place where multiple source files can see the definition. When you include the header file for the template, you must include the entire definition of the template, not just the prototype. Here is how to create a header file for the Max() template function:

```
//————————————————————————————
#ifndef maxH
#define maxH
//————————————————————————————
```

```
template <class T>
const T& Max (const T& arg1, const T& arg2)
{
  if(arg2 > arg1)
    return arg2;
  else
    return arg1;
}
#endif
```

Notice that the entire body of the Max() template function resides in the header file. This seems to violate the rule against defining functions and variables in a header file. In reality, we haven't defined a function in a header file. The template function does not generate any real code until you instantiate the function.

Templates are similar to inline functions with respect to header file organization. As a general rule, you define both inline functions and templates in a header file. No code is generated until you use the inline function or the template function.

> **NOTE**
>
> The ANSI committee recently accepted a proposal to allow separate compilation of templates. Under the new system, you can declare a template using a new keyword, export. You would then define the template in a C++ source file. At the time of this writing, C++Builder 4 did not support the separate compilation model, nor did it support the export keyword.

Templates and the STL

The *Standard Template Library* (*STL*) is a collection of template classes and algorithms used for generic programming. Since you will probably get far more use out of the STL than your own template classes, a brief overview is appropriate. Note, however, that this is a very brief overview. The STL is a huge subject, which deserves a book all its own.

Working with Containers

The STL includes many different container classes. Each container belongs to a classification, depending on the container's attributes. For example, there are ordered containers (set, map) and unordered containers (list, vector). Although there are different container classifications, all containers share a common subset of methods, such as begin(), end(), size(), and empty().

Containers hold objects. The type of object that a container holds depends on the template argument that you specify when you instantiate the container. For example, the following code shows how to create a linked list of AnsiString objects:

```
#include <list>
std::list<AnsiString> string_list;
```

STL containers are discussed in more detail later; first, iterators.

Working with Iterators

Iterators allow you to move through the objects in a container. An iterator behaves like a pointer to an object in a container. All of the containers in the STL support iteration. Note, however, that iterators are class specific. Each container sports its own special brand of iterator. When you need an iterator for a container, you obtain it from the container itself.

There are several categories of iterators. There are forward iterators and reverse iterators. A *forward iterator* allows you to iterate from the front of a container to the back. *Reverse iterators* allow you to iterate a container from back to front. There are also const iterators and non-const iterators. *Const* iterators do not modify the contents of the container.

The containers in the STL provide methods for retrieving an iterator to the container. The begin() method returns an iterator for the start of the container. The end() method returns an iterator for one past the last element in the container. The rbegin() and rend() methods work the same way, but they return reverse iterators.

The syntax for iterating a container is similar for all types of containers. Here is how you would iterate a list of AnsiString objects:

```
#include <list>
...
std::list<AnsiString> string_list;
std::list<AnsiString>::iterator iter = string_list.begin();
for(; iter != string_list.end(); ++iter)
  ListBox1->Items->Add( *iter );
```

The begin() method returns an iterator that points to the first element in the list. The for loop executes until the iterator points to the end of the list. Notice that the iterator is incremented using the ++ operator and that you can extract the contents of the iterator using the * operator. The syntax for iterators resembles the syntax for pointers.

Using the vector Container

The vector container implements an array whose size can change dynamically. Adding elements to and removing elements from the end of a vector is very fast. Inserting

4

C++ TEMPLATES

elements in the middle is supported, but the insertion is much slower than adding elements at the end.

You add elements to a vector by calling the push_back() member function. To remove the last element, call the pop_back() method. Listing 4.8 demonstrates how to use a vector of strings.

LISTING 4.8   CREATING A VECTOR OF STRINGS

```
#include <iostream>
#include <vector>
using std::cout;
using std::endl;

int main()
{
  std::vector<std::string> strings;
  strings.push_back("Hello");
  strings.push_back("Dr.");
  strings.push_back("Craven");

  cout << "The second element in the vector is: "
       << strings[1] << endl;
  return 0;
}
```

The vector container resides in the std namespace, which is why the code refers to it as std::vector. You could omit the std namespace qualifier by adding a using statement to your source file, similar to how it is done for cout and endl. Because the code refers to several items from the std namespace, you can cover all your bases by using the entire namespace as this example shows:

```
#include <condefs.h>
#include <iostream>
#include <vector>

using namespace std;
```

> **CAUTION**
>
> In general, you don't want to place a using statement for the entire std namespace in a header file. If you place a using statement in a header file, it affects every C++ source file that includes the header.

Now look at a `vector` example that utilizes `iterators`. Listing 4.9 implements a `vector` of integers and iterates through them forward and backward.

LISTING 4.9 ITERATING THROUGH A VECTOR

```
#include <condefs.h>
#include <iostream>
#include <vector>
using std::cout;
using std::endl;

int main()
{
  std::vector<int> arr;
  for (int i = 0; i < 10; ++i)
    arr.push_back(i);

  for (int i = 0; i < 10; ++i)
    cout << "arr[" << i << "] = " << arr[i] << endl;

  std::vector<int>::iterator iter = arr.begin();
  for (; iter != arr.end(); ++iter)
    cout << " " << *iter;

  cout << endl;
  std::vector<int>::reverse_iterator riter = arr.rbegin();
  for (; riter != arr.rend(); ++riter)
    cout << " " << *riter;

  cout << endl;
  return 0;
}
```

The first `for` loop adds 10 integers to the vector. The second `for` loop demonstrates how to access the integers with the `[]` operator of `vector`. This is similar to how you access the string objects in the first `vector` example. The last two `for` loops show something new. They iterate through the `vector` using iterators, rather then relying on the `[]` operator.

The `vector` container has `insert()` and `erase()` methods for adding and removing elements in the middle of the container, although such operations are slower than they are for the `list` container. Both of these methods rely on iterators. The `vector` container also has a `clear()` method for removing every item from the container.

```
arr.erase(arr.begin() + 5);          // erase the sixth item
arr.insert(arr.end() - 2, 29);       // insert 29 before second to last item
arr.erase(arr.begin() + 2, arr.begin() + 4); // erase 3rd and 4th items
arr.clear();                          // remove all items
```

4

C++ TEMPLATES

The `insert()` method inserts a new element just before the position of the iterator. The `erase()` method has two forms. One form takes a single iterator argument. This version of `erase()` removes the item that the iterator points to. The second version of `erase()` takes two iterators as arguments. The syntax of the second version is `erase(iter1, iter2)`. This version deletes items starting at `iter1` and up to, but not including, `iter2`.

> **TIP**
>
> You can advance a `vector` iterator by simply adding a number to it:
>
> ```
> std::vector<int>::iterator iter = arr.begin();
> iter += 5;
> ```
>
> You cannot do this with `list` or `map` iterators. If you take advantage of this feature of `vector`, make sure that you don't advance the iterator past the last element in the container.

The `vector` container has a few more functions worth mentioning. The `size()` method returns the number of items in the container. The `empty()` method returns `bool` `true` or `false` to indicate whether the container is empty. The `reserve()` method allows you to reserve memory for new additions to the container. Normally, the `vector` allocates memory as it sees fit. You can tell the container to reserve some memory ahead of time, so it doesn't have to allocate memory along the way. The `capacity()` function returns how much memory has been reserved.

Now analyze how the `vector` container reserves memory, and how you can take control of it as shown in this example:

```cpp
int main()
{
  std::vector<int> arr;
  cout << "Initial size is: " << arr.size() << endl;
  cout << "Initial capacity is: " << arr.capacity() << endl;

  arr.push_back(4); // add one item;
  cout << "After one push_back, size is: " << arr.size() << endl;
  cout << "After one push_back, capacity is: " << arr.capacity() << endl;

  arr.clear();
  cout << "After clear, size is: " << arr.size() << endl;
  cout << "After clear, capacity is: " << arr.capacity() << endl;
  return 0;
}
```

This code explores `vector`'s default memory allocation scheme. The output from the program is as follows:

```
Initial size is: 0
Initial capacity is: 0
After one push_back, size is: 1
After one push_back, capacity is: 256
After clear, size is: 0
After clear, capacity is: 256
```

The capacity of the container is `0` before you add items to a `vector`. This makes sense; why allocate memory until you actually need it? Notice what the `vector` does after you insert one item. Instead of allocating space for just one item, the `vector` allocates space for 256 items. The `vector` holds on to this memory until it needs more memory, or until the `vector` is destroyed. The `vector` retains space for 256 items even after you call the `clear()` method.

If you are going to fill a `vector` with more than 256 elements, you may want to take control of the container's capacity as shown here:

```
int main()
{
  std::vector<int> arr;
  arr.reserve(100000);  // reserve space for 100000 items.
  cout << "Initial size is: " << arr.size() << endl;
  cout << "Initial capacity is: " << arr.capacity() << endl;

  for (int i = 0; i < 100000; ++i)
  {
    arr.push_back(i);
  }

  cout << "Current size is: "    << arr.size() << endl;
  cout << "Current capacity is: " << arr.capacity() << endl;

  arr.push_back(29); // add one more item
  cout << "Final size is: " << arr.size() << endl;
  cout << "Final capacity is: " << arr.capacity() << endl;
  return 0;
}
```

The output of this program is as follows:

```
Initial size is: 0
Initial capacity is: 100000
Current size is: 100000
Current capacity is: 100000
Final size is: 100001
Final capacity is: 200000
```

As long as you add fewer items than the current capacity, the `vector` does not allocate any additional memory. If you do exceed the capacity, the `vector` allocates additional memory. The `vector` class allocates in increments of whatever value you specify as the capacity. In this example, the capacity is set to `100,000` by using the `reserve()` method; the `vector` therefore increments the capacity in multiples of 100,000.

Using the `list` Container

From a syntax standpoint, the `list` container looks very much like the `vector` container, with some exceptions. The `list` container does not support the `[]` array operator. You cannot add and subtract offsets to a `list` iterator, and you cannot control the capacity of a `list`.

Despite the similarities in their appearance, the `list` container and the `vector` container are internally very different. The `list` container is very fast at inserting and deleting elements in the middle of the container, whereas the `vector` is much slower. Furthermore, you can move elements around in a `list` with greater efficiency than you can in a `vector`. Listing 4.10 demonstrates some of the ways that you can manipulate a `list`.

LISTING 4.10   USING THE `list` CONTAINER

```
#include <iostream>
#include <list>
using std::cout;
using std::endl;

int main()
{
  std::list<int> list1;
  std::list<int> list2;
  list1.push_back(4);
  list1.push_back(7);
  list1.push_back(4);

  for(int j=-5; j<15; j+=3)
    list2.push_front(j);

  // sort the lists
  list1.sort();
  list2.sort();

  // merge list2 with list1
  list1.merge(list2);

  std::list<int>::const_iterator iter = list1.begin();
  for(; iter != list1.end(); ++iter)
    cout << *iter << endl;
  return 0;
}
```

A list can insert an item anywhere in the container with ease. The list container provides member functions that allow you to take advantage of that speed. One such method is the push_front() function, which allows you to insert elements at the beginning of the list. Another example is the sort() method, which can sort all of the elements in the container.

Using the map Container

A map is a sorted collection of ordered pairs. The ordered pairs consist of a key and a value. The map container works like a lookup table that returns a value for a given key. The next example creates a map that returns a double when given an AnsiString:

```
#include <map>
std::map<AnsiString, double> mymap;
mymap["pi"] = 3.14159;
mymap["e"] = 2.718;
mymap["speed of light"] = 2.998E8;

double radius = 10;
double area = radius * radious * mymap["pi"];
```

When you declare a map, the first template argument is the key, and the second argument is the value. In this example, the map's key is AnsiString and the value is double. The map will look up and return a double given an AnsiString key. The map container provides an optional third parameter that allows you to control how elements in the map are sorted.

Like the vector container, the map container provides an overloaded [] array operator. However, the array operator works differently for the map container. Arguments to the [] function are key values instead of integer index values.

map sorts elements in the container by key. By default, the container uses the less template to perform the comparison between objects. You can override this behavior to change how the map performs the sort. The following code shows how to customize the sorting mechanism of a map and how to iterate a map:

```
#include <map>

struct CharPtrLess
{
  bool operator() (char const * lhs, char const * rhs)
    { return strcmp(lhs, rhs) < 0; }
};

int main()
{
  typedef std::map<char const *, int, CharPtrLess> Map;
```

```
Map mymap;
for (int i = 0; i < 10; ++i)
  mymap[createRandomString()] = i;

Map::iterator iter = mymap.begin();
for (; iter != mymap.end(); ++iter)
  cout << " " << (*iter).first << " " << (*iter).second;

cout << endl;
Map::reverse_iterator riter = mymap.rbegin();
for (; riter != mymap.rend(); ++riter)
  cout << " " << riter->first << " " << riter->second;

cout << endl;
return 0;
}
```

If you did not specify a comparison class, `map` would sort the ordered pairs based on the machine addresses of the strings in the `map`. By using the `CharPtrLess` structure to perform the comparison, you can sort the items correctly by calling `strcmp()`.

A `map` iterator contains a `pair` object. The `pair` structure from the STL has two members, `first` and `second`. The `first` member contains the key of the `map`, the `second` member contains the value. Also notice how the iterator is accessed. In C++Builder 3, you had to dereference map iterators using the syntax `(*iter).first`. Now that C++Builder supports member templates, you can use the much more readable `iter->first`.

Working with Algorithms

Probably one of the coolest things about the STL is that it supplies a large number of algorithms. There are algorithms for sorting, searching, comparing, permuting, generating random numbers, counting elements, removing elements, and more. Of course, the algorithms rely on templates, which means that they are generic. You can use them with almost any type of variable.

The `find` Algorithm

The `find` algorithm allows you to find an element in a container. `find` takes two iterator arguments and a value argument. It searches between the two iterators for the value that you specified. It returns an iterator for the position where the item was found. If the value is not found, `find` returns the second iterator argument as shown here:

```
#include <iostream>
#include <vector>
#include <algorithm>
using namespace std;
```

```
int main()
{
  vector<int> my_vector;
  for (int i = -50; i <= 50 ; ++i)
    my_vector.push_back(i);

  // find the value 29
  vector<int>::iterator iter;
  iter = find(my_vector.begin(), my_vector.end(), 29);
  if(iter != my_vector.end())
    cout << "29 was found" << endl;
  else
    cout << "29 not found" << endl;

  return 0;
}
```

iter1 is included in the call to find(iter1, iter2, val), but iter2 is not. find
returns iter2 if val is not found.

The min() and max() Algorithms

The Max() template function has been touted as an exquisite work of art throughout this
chapter. It turns out that creating a Max() template function was unneccessary. The STL
already provides a function called max() (in addition to min()), as shown in this example:

```
#include <iostream>
#include <algorithm>
using std::cout;
using std::endl;

int main()
{
  cout << std::max(15,5)    << endl;
  cout << std::max('a','b') << endl;
  cout << std::min(3.14,24.5) << endl;
  return 0;
}
```

The random_shuffle() and sort() Algorithms

The random_shuffle() algorithm randomly mixes the elements in a container. You pass
random_shuffle() two iterators. The function randomly mixes the order of the elements
between the two iterators. The sort() algorithm does the opposite of random_shuffle().
It sorts the items in a container. Listing 4.11 uses random_shuffle() to shuffle the elements in a vector and then calls sort() to arrange them again.

4

C++ TEMPLATES

LISTING 4.11 USING THE sort ALGORITHM

```cpp
#include <iostream>
#include <vector>
#include <algorithm>
#include <functional>
using std::cout;
using std::endl;

int main()
{
  std::vector<int> card_deck;
  for (int i = 1; i <= 52; ++i)
    card_deck.push_back(i);

  // shuffle the deck and display the values
  std::random_shuffle(card_deck.begin(), card_deck.end());
  std::vector<int>::const_iterator iter = card_deck.begin();
  for (; iter!= card_deck.end(); ++iter)
    cout << " " << *iter;
  cout << endl << endl;

  // sort the deck again, from lowest to highest
  std::sort(card_deck.begin(), card_deck.end());
  iter = card_deck.begin();
  for (; iter!= card_deck.end(); ++iter)
    cout << " " << *iter;
  cout << endl << endl;

  // sort the deck, this time from highest to lowest
  std::sort(card_deck.begin(), card_deck.end(), std::greater<int>());
  iter = card_deck.begin();
  for (; iter!= card_deck.end(); ++iter)
    cout << " " << *iter;
  cout << endl;
}
```

Putting It All Together

You create a smart pointer class in this section. You will use C++ templates to create a smart pointer that works with any type of object. The smart pointer will use new template features in C++Builder 4 to support implicit upcasting of a derived class to its base class. (Implicit upcasting is explained later.)

Understanding Smart Pointers

The burden of managing memory in C++ lies mostly on the programmer. Memory management can be a tedious and error-prone process. Wouldn't it be nice if you could

simply allocate an object and let the program automatically delete the object when it was
no longer needed? You can do just that with a reference-counted smart pointer.

A *smart pointer* is an object that acts like a pointer. The following code implements a
smart pointer:

```
class SomeClass
{
public:
  void doSomething(){}
};

class SmartPointer
{
public:
  SmartPointer(SomeClass * p) : ptr_(p) { }
  ~SmartPointer() { delete ptr_; }
  SomeClass * operator -> () { return ptr_; }
private:
  SomeClass * ptr_;
};

int main()
{
  SmartPointer sp(new SomeClass);
  sp->doSomething();
}
```

While this smart pointer isn't very interesting, it does form the basis for what a smart
pointer should do. The smart pointer provides a constructor that takes a pointer as an
argument. That pointer is stored in a member variable. When the smart pointer is
destroyed, its destructor cleans up the pointer. The overloaded -> operator provides
access to the SomeClass pointer.

The smart pointer class in the example only works with SomeClass pointers. What if you
want to use the smart pointer to maintain pointers to other types? You could employ a
strategic cut-and-paste bombing campaign, or you could turn the smart pointer into a
template class and be done with it. The next example shows how to convert the smart
pointer class into a template class:

```
template <class T>
class SmartPtr
{
public:
  SmartPtr(T * p = 0) : ptr_(p) { }
  ~SmartPtr() { delete ptr_;}
  T const * ptr() const { return ptr_; }
  T * ptr() { return ptr_; }
  T const * operator -> () const { return ptr_; }
```

```
  T * operator -> () { return ptr_; }
  T const & operator * () const { return *ptr_; }
  T & operator * () { return *ptr_; }

private:
  T * ptr_;
};

class Foo
{
  public:
    void someFunction() {}
};

int main()
{
  SmartPtr<Foo> fooPtr = new Foo;
  SmartPtr<int> intPtr = new int;
  FooPtr->someFunction();
  *intPtr = 12;
}
```

The new version of the smart pointer contains a member function called `ptr()` that provides access to the internal pointer. In addition to the `ptr()` member function, the smart pointer class overloads the `->` and `*` operators. This allows you to treat a smart pointer object as if it were an actual pointer.

The template version of the smart pointer class automatically deletes the underlying pointer when the smart pointer itself is destroyed. However, the way it deletes the pointer could be improved. The following code highlights a downfall of the current smart pointer implementation:

```
int main()
{
  SmartPtr<Foo> fooPtr1 = new Foo;
  SmartPtr<Foo> fooPtr2 = fooPtr1.ptr();
}
```

Both smart pointers reference the same `Foo` pointer. When the smart pointers are destroyed, they will both attempt to delete the `Foo` pointer. Deleting the same pointer twice is a bad thing. What you need is a smart pointer that can maintain a reference count. In order to support reference counting, you need to implement a mechanism for counting objects.

Counted Objects

Counted objects are objects that manage a reference count, and they destroy themselves when the reference count goes to 0. Such a counted object could be implemented as follows:

```
class CountedObject
{
public:
  virtual ~CountedObject() { }
  CountedObject & operator = (CountedObject const &) { return *this; }
  void obtainReference() { ++refCount_; }
  void releaseReference() { if (--refCount_ == 0) delete this; }
protected:
  CountedObject() : refCount_(0) { }
  CountedObject(CountedObject const &) : refCount_(0) { }
private:
  unsigned long refCount_;
};
```

The constructor initializes the reference count to 0. The copy constructor does not copy the refCount_ from the source because the new CountedObject is being constructed; no other object holds a reference to it as of yet. The assignment operator does nothing because the object still has the same references. The only real meat is in the releaseReference() method. If this method is called and there are no more references to the object, then the object deletes itself.

Counted Pointers

You can build a smart pointer that can maintain a reference count on the underlying pointer by combining the smart pointer class with the counted objects class:

```
template <class T>
class CountedPtr
{
public:
  CountedPtr(T * p = 0) : ptr_(p) { init(); }
  ~CountedPtr() { fini(); }
  CountedPtr(CountedPtr const & rhs) : ptr_(rhs.ptr_) { init(); }
  CountedPtr & operator = (CountedPtr<T> const & rhs)
  {
    if (ptr_ != rhs.ptr_)
    {
      fini();
      ptr_ = rhs.ptr_;
      init();
    }
    return *this;
```

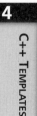

```
    }
    T const * ptr() const { return ptr_; }
    T * ptr() { return ptr_; }
    T const * operator -> () const { return ptr_; }
    T * operator -> () { return ptr_; }
    T const & operator * () const { return *ptr_; }
    T & operator * () { return *ptr_; }

private:
    T * ptr_;

    void init()
    {
        if (ptr_)
            ptr_->obtainReference();
    }
    void fini()
    {
        if (ptr_)
            ptr_->releaseReference();
    }
};
```

The complete class, with proper comparison operators and so on, is provided on this book's CD-ROM. There's not much left to this class that relates to templates, so it's skimmed here. Notice how the assignment operator is implemented. When you assign one counted pointer to another, the class releases the reference to the old object and obtains a reference to the new object. This ensures that the underlying object is destroyed as soon as it is no longer being referenced.

For example, consider the following code:

```
Class Foo : public CountedObject { }
CountedPtr<Foo> foo = new Foo; // one reference
CountedPtr<Foo> foo2 = foo; // two references
```

When foo and foo2 go out of scope, the destructor for each object gets called. After the first destructor runs, the reference count will be decremented by 1. After the second object is destroyed, the reference count reaches 0. At this point the object is destroyed. Note that since the reference is handled in the destructor, the CountedPtr class is exception safe.

This implementation of CountedPtr gives you a smart pointer that you can use with any data type that implements the obtainReference() and releaseReference() functions. However, any type that does not implement these methods will not work with the CountedPtr class.

Counting Uncountable Objects

The `CountedPtr` class template does not support classes that do not implement the reference count methods. Thus, it seems totally useless when dealing with built-in data types and class libraries such as the VCL. Fortunately, there is a workaround.

You can create a proxy class that inherits from `CountedObject`. The proxy class contains a pointer to an uncountable object. This technique is known as the *adapter design pattern*. It is a popular method for converting one data type into another. Listing 4.12 shows how to create a proxy class.

LISTING 4.12 COUNTING OBJECTS WITH A PROXY CLASS

```
template <class T>
struct CountedProxyObject : public CountedObject
{
  CountedProxyObject(T * p) : ptr_(p) { }
  ~CountedProxyObject() { delete ptr_; }
  T * ptr_;
};

template <class T>
class CountedProxyPtr
{
public:
  CountedProxyPtr(T * p = 0) : proxy_(new CountedProxyObject<T>(p))
    { init(); }
  ~CountedProxyPtr() { fini(); }
  CountedProxyPtr(CountedProxyPtr const & rhs) : proxy_(rhs.proxy_)
    { init(); }
  CountedProxyPtr & operator = (CountedProxyPtr<T> const & rhs)
  {
    if (proxy_ != rhs.proxy_)
    {
      fini();
      proxy_ = rhs.proxy_;
      init();
    }
    return *this;
  }
  T const * ptr() const { return proxy_->ptr_; }
  T * ptr() { return proxy_->ptr_; }
  T const * operator -> () const { return ptr(); }
  T * operator -> () { return ptr(); }
  T const & operator * () const { return *ptr(); }
  T & operator * () { return *ptr(); }
  CountedProxyObject<T> * proxy() { return proxy_; }
```

continues

LISTING 4.12   CONTINUED

```
template <class Y>
CountedProxyPtr(CountedProxyPtr<Y> const & rhs)
  : proxy_(new CountedProxyObject<T>(const_cast<Y*>(rhs.ptr())))
{ init(); }
template <class Y>
CountedProxyPtr<T> & operator = (CountedProxyPtr<Y> const & rhs)
{
  if (ptr() != const_cast<Y*>(rhs.ptr()))
  {
    fini();
    proxy_ = new CountedProxyObject<T>(const_cast<Y*>(rhs.ptr()));
    init();
  }
  return *this;
}
private:
  CountedProxyObject<T> * proxy_;

  void init()
  {
    if (proxy_)
      proxy_->obtainReference();
  }
  void fini()
  {
    if (proxy_)
      proxy_->releaseReference();
  }
};
```

You can use this class to simulate the creation of VCL objects on the stack:

```
CountedProxyPtr<TfileStream> fileStream =
  new TfileStream(fileName, fmOpenRead¦fmShareCompat);
```

In fact, you can use this class to implement a pure VCL object that is a counted pointer
to a TObject:

```
class TVclPtr : public TObject
{
public:
  TVclPtr(TObject * p = 0) : ptr_(p) { }
  TObject * ptr() { return ptr_.ptr(); }
  TObject const * ptr() const { return ptr_.ptr(); }
  TObject * operator -> () { return ptr(); }
  TObject const * operator -> () const { return ptr(); }
  TObject & operator * () { return *ptr(); }
  TObject const & operator * () const { return *ptr(); }
private:
  CountedProxyPtr<TObject> ptr_;
};
```

Improving the `CountedPtr` Class

Imagine that you have a class `Bar` that derives from `Foo`. Through polymorphism, any pointer to a `Bar` object can be treated as a pointer to a `Foo` object. The `CountedPtr` class template, as shown here, supports this form of polymorphism:

```
class Foo : public CountedObject { };
class Bar : public Foo { }

Foo * foop = new Foo;
CountedPtr<Foo> foo = foop;
Bar * barp = new Bar;
CountedPtr<Foo> bar = barp; // OK Bar * can be treated as Foo *
```

However, the following code does not compile:

```
CountedPtr<Bar> bar = new Bar;
CountedPtr<Foo> foo = bar;
```

This code does not compile because you cannot assign a `CountedPtr<Bar>` to a `CountedPtr<Foo>`. You would like to provide a way to assign `CountedPtr`s of one type to `CountedPtr`s of a different type if the two represent compatible types. You can add this support by using member templates:

```
template <class T>
class CountedPtr
{
  …

template <class Y>
  CountedPtr(CountedPtr<Y> const & rhs)
    : ptr_(const_cast<Y*>(rhs.ptr())) { init(); }

  template <class Y>
  CountedPtr<T> & operator = (CountedPtr<Y> const & rhs)
  {
    if (ptr_ != const_cast<Y*>(rhs.ptr()))
    {
      fini();
      ptr_ = const_cast<Y*>(rhs.ptr());
      init();
    }
    return *this;
  }

  …
};
```

The first template member is a constructor. This constructor allows you to initialize a `CountedPtr<T>` given a `CountedPtr<Y>`. The `const_cast` call ensures that there is a logical way to get from a `Y*` to a `T*`. The second template member is an assignment operator and it allows you to assign a `CountedPtr<Y>` to a `CountedPtr<T>` after the `CountedPtr<T>` has already been constructed.

Summary

In this chapter you learned the basics of programming with templates. The fundamental syntax involved with creating template functions and classes is covered. This chapter also discussed advanced features, such as template specialization and member templates, and touched on the powerful features of the STL.

This chapter was unable to cover every aspect of C++ templates. The goal, however, was not to bore you into submission by discussing every little detail of template programming. Instead, it was to show you that templates are cool; to show you that templates allow you to write less code, not more; to demonstrate that there is a way to write generic, reusable routines that can be applied to many different types of variables; finally, to show you that a wealth of code has already been written for you in the STL.

If there is one single point that you should take from this chapter, it is this: Use the STL. The STL does for non-visual programming what the VCL does for GUI development. Combine the two and you have one powerful development environment. Before you set out to write a "highly optimized maximization routine using the native IEEE 64 bit floating-point format," check the STL first. Someone else may have already written the algorithm for you.

To further your knowledge of templates, the following books are recommended:

- Stroustroup, Bjarne: *The C++ Programming Language*, 3rd edition. 1997, Addison Wesley.

- Lippman, Stanly B. and Josee Lajoie: *C++ Primer*, 3rd edition. 1998, Addison Wesley.

- Musser, David R. and Atul Saini: *STL Tutorial and Reference Guide*. 1996, Addison Wesley.

Threads

*by Charlie Calvert
and Kent Reisdorph*

IN THIS CHAPTER

CHAPTER 5

This chapter is about advanced programming with threads. It is a gateway to the upper echelons of Windows programming and introduces you to some of the most powerful capabilities of Win32.

This chapter covers the following subjects in particular:

- The basics of the Win32 architecture
- Processes
- Threads
- Critical sections
- Mutexes
- The VCL TThread object
- Thread priorities
- Open queries inside a thread
- VCL threadsafe objects

The goal for this chapter is to isolate some of the most important aspects of advanced Windows programming and introduce them in a way that makes it easy for you to use them in your applications. Five different programs are presented in this chapter, each designed to show off a key feature related to threads and multitasking.

The word *advanced* is used in this overview several times, but you will find that most of the code in this chapter is easy to use. I have sought to show you simple ways to get at some of the most powerful features in the Windows operating system. I would need another 500 or 600 pages to cover these subjects in depth, but the material you find here will get you started with these invaluable technologies. In fact, you will find plenty of information in this chapter that enables you to incorporate threading into your own programs.

I want to thank Jeff Cottingham, who added valuable sections to this chapter on using databases and threads and on executing graphics code in threads. All the sections of this chapter that apply to those subjects were written by him.

Processes and Memory

A *process* is the hip Win32 term for a program that is currently loaded. An *executable file* on disk is just a file. If it has been started, it's a process.

> **NOTE**
>
> If you want to create a process, call CreateProcess(). This function does what the WinExec() function did in Windows 3.1. WinExec() is now obsolete, so you should use CreateProcess() instead.

Processes don't do anything; they just exist. The entity that does something inside a program is called a *thread*. Each program has at least one thread. All Windows 3.1 programs, by definition, have only one thread. The idea that each program can have its own thread or that a program can have multiple threads is specific to fancy operating systems such as UNIX, OS/2, Windows NT, and Windows 9x. The key point to understand here is that a process is a loaded program. It's not running; it's not executing. Remember that processes don't run—threads run. Threads are the doers.

When Windows loads a process, it simply opens a memory-mapped file and sucks the contents of an executable file or DLL into memory.

All processes have an HInstance associated with them. This parameter is declared globally inside all C++Builder programs. You don't have to do anything to get hold of this variable. It's there automatically at program startup.

An application's HInstance is the base memory address where it is loaded. In Windows 9x, this value is typically 10×00400000, or 4,194,304. In other words, the program is usually loaded in at the 4MB mark. It then ranges from that point up to the 2GB mark. This means a Win32 program has 2GB minus 4MB worth of room in which to stretch out. Both the program's code and its data are loaded into this 2GB address space. As a result, the operating system gives you virtually unlimited resources in which to run your program. (Your hardware, however, might not share the operating system's largesse.)

The specific value at which your program is loaded is under your control. If you select the Project, Options, Linker page from the menu, you will see that this value is accessible to you as the Image base.

What does it mean to say that a program is loaded into a 4GB address space? If you have only a few megabytes of memory on your machine, what sense does it make to talk about such huge amounts of memory?

The answer is that each program is assigned not an actual area in physical RAM, but a virtual address space; it's assigned a range of addresses. When you need to access that memory, physical addresses are assigned to it. The act of assigning physical addresses to virtual memory is called *mapping*.

Windows is constantly mapping virtual memory into physical address spaces. That is, it's assigning physical addresses to virtual memory. Because of this system, people who have only 8MB of memory on their systems can have variables or even entire processes that have addresses in the 3–4GB range. Every program thinks it's running in its own private 4GB address space and that it can use 2GB of this space as it pleases. What's really happening in some cases is that pages of that virtual 4GB space are being mapped into the actual memory available on your system.

> **NOTE**
>
> Because each process runs in its own 4GB address space, the global `hPrevInstance` variable from Windows 3.1 is meaningless in Win32. There can't be a previous instance of a program because each program is running in its own virtual world, and there is only one virtual world in all the universe. (Actually, more than one world exists inside a computer, but each process is convinced that it is alone. Its world is 4GB, guaranteed, and the inhabitants of that world are prepared to prove it to you; and it's the only one there is. Any science fiction writers want to pick up this ball and run with it?)

A page of memory is typically 4KB. Windows is always mapping pages of virtual memory into physical address spaces. When this happens, the address that your program sees does not change. Windows maintains another table that translates these virtual addresses into physical addresses. This process is called *indirection*, or perhaps more accurately, *double indirection*. (The pointer itself is one level of indirection; the virtual address, a second level.) The addresses that you see in your program are never direct references to real memory. Instead, they are indirect references. You see one address in your program; Windows maintains a table that enables the virtual addresses you see to be mapped into physical memory that resides in RAM. RAM is physical memory; the addresses you see are virtual memory. Virtual memory is not real memory any more than virtual reality is real reality.

Why does Windows maintain this elaborate fiction of virtual addresses? The main reason is to protect one process from another. Each process is running in its own 4GB address space. It thinks it owns the whole computer. It has no idea that other processes exist on the computer.

Because each process is totally separated from the other processes on the computer, there is much less chance that they will overwrite one another. It is therefore unlikely that an invalid memory access by one program will overwrite another program or overwrite some part of the operating system. Each process is boxed away in a virtual world, where it can't get at any other programs. This process is very different than it was in Windows 3.1 and makes it much less likely that your computer will crash when a particular program misbehaves.

Furthermore, when you close a Win32 program, all the resources allocated to it are automatically closed. By definition, they can reside only inside that program's one virtual world. All the resources associated with the virtual world are also closed. If you forget to deallocate memory, or if you forget to deallocate resources, all your mistakes are covered up the moment you close your program. (This is not, however, a theory on which to base program memory management! You should at least try to handle memory correctly. However, if you make a mistake, you are not permanently sullying the operating system's environment the way you did in Windows 3.1.)

> **NOTE**
>
> All 16-bit Windows programs that run on Windows 9x share the same address space by default. It's as if they are all running on their own miniature versions of Windows 3.1. Errors made by one 16-bit process can affect other 16-bit processes. However, when you close out all the 16-bit applications, their virtual world disappears, and all the resources dedicated to it are reclaimed. If one 16-bit program is giving you trouble, don't just close it. Close all the 16-bit programs in your Windows 9x session; then reopen the ones that you feel are running properly. That one program dirtied the water that all the other 16-bit programs used. The only thing to do in that case is close all the 16-bit programs and create a new, pristine virtual 16-bit world by reopening one of them. Remember that I'm talking about Windows 9x here, not Windows NT.

Threads and Multitasking

Each process has one or more threads assigned to it. Threads are the part of a program that executes.

Windows 9x and Windows NT are true multitasking operating systems. At any one time, they have x number of threads running. (*Multitasking* is simply the term used to describe the operating system feature that allows it to run multiple threads concurrently.) Windows assigns a time slice to each of these threads. The technical name for a time slice is a *quantum*, but don't worry: I'm not going to call them that.

Each thread on the system has something called a *context*. The API's _CONTEXT structure is a data structure that contains information about the state of a thread. More specifically,

5

THREADS

it contains information about the state of the registers in the CPU when that thread is running. If you want to see the declaration for _CONTEXT, look in WINNT.H:

```
typedef struct _CONTEXT {
    DWORD ContextFlags;
    DWORD   Dr0;
    DWORD   Dr1;
    DWORD   Dr2;
    DWORD   Dr3;
    DWORD   Dr6;
    DWORD   Dr7;
    DWORD   SegGs;
    DWORD   SegFs;
    DWORD   SegEs;
    DWORD   SegDs;
    DWORD   Edi;
    DWORD   Esi;
    DWORD   Ebx;
    DWORD   Edx;
    DWORD   Ecx;
    DWORD   Eax;
    DWORD   Ebp;
    DWORD   Eip;
    DWORD   SegCs;
    DWORD   EFlags;
    DWORD   Esp;
    DWORD   SegSs;
} CONTEXT;
```

The structure quoted here is stripped of all its comments, which are by far the most enlightening part of the declaration. The comments are extensive, however, and of true interest to only a small number of readers. The rest of us can get by with only a quick glance at the structure's general lineaments. I should add that the _CONTEXT structure is typedef as TContext in the VCL headers. Because you don't use _CONTEXT directly, it's unlikely that you'll ever find the need to use the TContext type.

For the moment, think of all the threads in a computer as if they were placed on a big wheel similar to those that spin around at a gambling casino. As the wheel spins, at some time each of the threads appears near the top of the wheel. Starting a few degrees before it reaches the top of the wheel, and extending a few degrees after, is the period of time when a thread is actually executing. The thread's context is loaded the moment it comes into that range. That is, the CPU register values that it stores in its _CONTEXT structure are loaded into the physical CPU found on the computer. That thread then begins executing at the point where its instruction pointer is currently located. It executes for a few cycles, until the wheel that owns it spins out of range. Just before it goes out of range, its _CONTEXT structure is updated with the current state of the CPU.

The preceding description is one way to think of how multitasking works. The key point is that each thread is given a time slice. It executes during the duration of its time slice, and then another thread gets a chance. While it is running, the thread has its own unique set of register values. When its time slice is over, the values are stored in a _CONTEXT structure, and the next thread's CPU values are loaded into memory.

No two threads are ever running at the same time, although it may seem like they are. That's because computers are fast. Like most sleight-of-hand tricks, the operating system's multitasking capability is based on speed and dexterity. Computers don't really do the impossible; they just give the illusion of doing so.

> **NOTE**
>
> Threads can be assigned priorities. A thread with a high priority gets called more frequently than a thread with a low priority. You can theoretically start a thread that performs a task entirely in the background. It never takes up any of the system's time unless all the other threads are idle.

The 32-bit programs that run on Windows 9x are really multitasked. (The 16-bit programs in their single address space are not really multitasked, but you don't have to run them if you don't want to. Also, they can't steal the show entirely from 32-bit applications—only from each other. Therefore, you are not in bad shape if you run only one 16-bit process at a time.)

Preemptive and Nonpreemptive Multitasking

Windows 9x has what is called *preemptive multitasking*. Preemptive multitasking is the process described earlier. When a task's time slice is up, it is preempted. It's cut off and it can't do any more damage until it gets another time slice. This means that no one program can hog the CPU.

Windows 3.1 has what is called *nonpreemptive multitasking*, which enables a program to take over control of the CPU and return it only when it is good and ready. In truth, most good Windows 3.1 programmers tried hard not to hog the CPU. They used timers, `PeekMessage()`/`TranslateMessage()` loops, and other tools to ensure that the system could get the CPU back if necessary. However, sometimes a program would not give the CPU back to the system. For instance, it might get stuck in an infinite loop. When the program started looping, it would not give you a chance to preempt it. Therefore, you could not even switch to another program long enough to save your data before the system crashed. You just sat there helplessly, while everything went to pieces.

Preemptive multitasking puts an end to this nightmare. If a program is stuck in an infinite loop, or if it is just busy doing something that takes a long time, the user can usually switch away to another program. That new program keeps getting time slices, as regular as clockwork, right on schedule, despite what might be going on in the first program. This way, you often can save your work in one program and then press Ctrl+Alt+Delete so that you can shut down an ill-behaved program. If all goes well, you can just continue your Windows session. If the ill-behaved program won't give up the ghost, at least you had a chance to save your work before rebooting.

Programming Simple Threads

Something about the topic of threads is innately intimidating. Somehow it sounds as if it must be part of the guru's bag of tricks. Thread synchronization, thread local storage (TLS), and related topics do have their complex sides. However, I think you will be surprised at how easily you can add threads to your programs. Even some of the more advanced thread synchronization-related topics such as critical sections and mutexes are fairly simple, at least in principle.

As usual, getting specific is hard without having a sample program to examine. Listings 5.1 and 5.2 show the header and main unit for the Thread1 program. This example shows how to create a simple thread. Go ahead and run the program; then come back and read about how it works.

LISTING 5.1   THE HEADER FOR THE THREAD1 PROGRAM'S MAIN UNIT

```
#ifndef MainH
#define MainH

#include <Classes.hpp>
#include <Controls.hpp>
#include <StdCtrls.hpp>
#include <Forms.hpp>

class TForm1 : public TForm
{
__published:    // IDE-managed Components
  TButton *bUseThread;
  TButton *bNoThread;
  void __fastcall bUseThreadClick(TObject *Sender);
  void __fastcall bNoThreadClick(TObject *Sender);
private:        // User declarations
public:         // User declarations
  __fastcall TForm1(TComponent* Owner);
};

extern PACKAGE TForm1 *Form1;

#endif
```

LISTING 5.2   THE THREAD1 PROGRAM'S MAIN UNIT

```
#include <vcl.h>
#pragma hdrstop

#include "Main.h"


/*  This program has two buttons, one called Use
    Threads and the other called No Thread. Pressing
    the Use Thread button shows the advantage of using
    threads in a Delphi application.

    When you are using threads, you can grab the
    form and move the main window around even while
    the program is iterating through a loop. When you
    aren't using threads, you will not be able to
    move the main window of this app while the
    CPU is employed iterating through a loop.
    You can tell you are inside the loop by watching
    the counter painted on the main form. */

#pragma package(smart_init)
#pragma resource "*.dfm"
TForm1 *Form1;

__fastcall TForm1::TForm1(TComponent* Owner)
        : TForm(Owner)
{
}

DWORD CALLBACK ThreadFunc(void* P)
{
  HDC DC = GetDC(Form1->Handle);
  for (int i = 0;i<=100000;i++) {
    String S = i;
    TextOut(DC, 10, 10, S.c_str(), S.Length());
  }
  ReleaseDC(Form1->Handle, DC);
  return 0;
}

void __fastcall TForm1::bUseThreadClick(TObject *Sender)
{
  DWORD ThreadID;
  HANDLE hthread = CreateThread(
    0,            //Security attribute
    0,            //Initial Stack
    ThreadFunc,   //Starting address of thread
    0,            // argument of thread
    0,            // Create flags
    &ThreadID);   // thread ID
```

continues

LISTING 5.2   CONTINUED

```
  if (hthread == 0)
    MessageBox(Handle, "No Thread", 0, MB_OK);
}

void __fastcall TForm1::bNoThreadClick(TObject *Sender)
{
  ThreadFunc(0);
}
```

When this program begins, it displays the simple window shown in Figure 5.1. The main window contains two buttons. If you select the one labeled Use Thread, the program counts from 0 to 100,000 using a thread. You can use the mouse to move or resize the main window while this is going on. If you click the second button, the program also counts from 0 to 100,000. However, this second counting process is not run in a separate thread, so you cannot move or resize the window until the loop that performs the counting is finished.

FIGURE 5.1

The Thread1 program counts from 0 to 100,000 when the user selects either button on its main form.

The structure of the Thread1 program is very simple. It has two button response methods. The first runs a function called `ThreadFunc()` as a separate thread, and the second runs the same function as part of the main thread of the program. If you click the first button, the program has two threads running simultaneously; if you click the second button, the program has only its main thread running. If you try to move the form on which the program is built immediately after the single-threaded button is clicked, you will have no luck because the program is always busy. If you click the threaded button, you will be able to move the window because the program is given cycles on a separate thread.

You have two main tasks when working with threads:

1. Create the thread.
2. Create a function that serves as the thread entry point.

As you learned earlier, each program has one thread by default. In a sense, this thread is started at the moment your program is launched. Just as the `WinMain()` function in a project's BPR file is the entry point for a program, so is the thread function the entry point for a thread. Unlike the code in the project source file, the thread function(s) you create can be located anywhere in your program.

The Windows API call to create a thread is known (naturally enough) as CreateThread(). The thread function itself can have any name. However, it always takes one void* variable as a parameter and always returns a DWORD (an unsigned long). Because the function's single parameter is a void pointer, you can pass in a pointer to almost any data in this variable (an integer, a pointer to a class or structure, a string, and so on). You can also pass in a 32-bit integer value in this parameter. I'll give you more details on this issue later.

The following code creates the thread:

```
DWORD ThreadID;
HANDLE hthread = CreateThread(
   0,            //Security attribute
   0,            //Initial Stack
   ThreadFunc,   //Starting address of thread
   0,            // argument of thread
   0,            // Create flags
   &ThreadID);   // thread ID

if (!hthread)
   MessageBox(Handle, "No Thread", 0, MB_OK);
```

This code does nothing more than attempt to create a thread. If something goes wrong, it brings up a message box informing the user that an error has occurred.

The following is the declaration for the CreateThread() function:

```
HANDLE CreateThread(
   LPSECURITY_ATTRIBUTES lpThreadAttributes,
       // pointer to thread security attributes
   DWORD dwStackSize,  // initial thread stack size, in bytes
   LPTHREAD_START_ROUTINE lpStartAddress, // pointer to thread function
   LPVOID lpParameter,                     // argument for new thread
   DWORD dwCreationFlags,                  // creation flags
   LPDWORD lpThreadId  // pointer to returned thread identifier
);
```

The first parameter takes a series of security attributes. If this parameter is 0, the default security attributes are used. On Windows 9x, it is standard to set this parameter to 0. The only time you might want to vary from this pattern is if you want child processes to inherit the thread. (For more information, look up SECURITY_ATTRIBUTES in the Win32 Help file.)

5

THREADS

If the second parameter for the thread is 0, the stack size for the thread is the same as the stack size for the application. In other words, the primary thread and the thread you are starting have stacks that are the same size. The stack automatically grows, if necessary. In short, you can usually set this parameter to 0.

The lpStartAddress parameter is the most important portion of the function call. It is the place where you specify the name of the thread function that is called when the thread begins execution. Just enter the name of the function in this parameter. The thread function must have the following signature:

```
DWORD CALLBACK ThreadFunc(void*);
```

If you want to pass additional data to your function, you specify that data in lpParameter. Typically, you create a structure and pass in its address in this parameter. The variable you use does not have to be a structure; it could be a string or some other type of variable.

The dwCreationFlags parameter enables you to pass in certain flags that are associated with your thread. The only flag used in this parameter is called CREATE_SUSPENDED. If you create a suspended thread, the thread itself is created, its stack is created, and its _CONTEXT structure is filled with CPU values—but the thread is never assigned any CPU time. It's all set to go, but it won't execute until you call ResumeThread(). You can then suspend the thread again by calling SuspendThread(). The whole subject of suspended threads is really an advanced topic relating to thread synchronization. For now, you should just pass in 0 in this parameter.

The final parameter, lpThreadID, is a pointer to a DWORD. This variable is assigned a unique ID by the system if the call to CreateThread() is successful. On Windows 9x, this parameter can be 0, and indeed most of the time you won't use the thread ID, so you might have an inclination to set it to 0. On Windows NT, however, this parameter cannot be 0; if you are interested in portability between Windows 9x and Windows NT, you should not set this value to 0. In other words, if your application goes into general release, you should pass in the address of a DWORD variable and should avoid setting this value to 0. Remember: You are not passing anything to Windows in this parameter. Rather, you are passing in a variable that is assigned a value by Windows.

> **NOTE**
>
> All the programs used in this book are tested on both Windows 9x and Windows NT machines.

After you have created a non-suspended thread, the function you passed to it is automatically called. In other words, after you create a thread, the function representing the entry point for that thread is called almost immediately.

The following is the thread function for the Thread1 program:

```
DWORD CALLBACK ThreadFunc(void* P)
{
  HDC DC = GetDC(Form1->Handle);
  for (int i = 0;i<=100000;i++) {
    String S = i;
    TextOut(DC, 10, 10, S.c_str(), S.Length());
  }
  ReleaseDC(Form1->Handle, DC);
  return 0;
}
```

Prior to the release of C++Builder 3, using the Canvas object for Form1 in this routine was not safe because most of the visual objects in the Visual Component Library (VCL) were not threadsafe. The C++Builder 3 VCL introduced the Lock() and Unlock() methods for graphics objects and all their descendents, thus making these objects threadsafe. You can now "lock" a canvas while you are drawing on it from a nonmain thread and then "unlock" it when you are done with the drawing. For this example, this property is not the best solution; it will lock the entire canvas of the form. (I'll give you more details on this issue later.) Also, during the TThread object discussion, you will see a way to safely use the other VCL objects inside threads. However, as a general rule, you should consider using the Windows API exclusively in your thread function. I'm not saying that your program cannot be VCL-based. In fact, there is no restriction on the number or kind of VCL objects you use in multithreaded programs. However, if the code in one of your threads wants to talk to a VCL object, it should use the Windows API. In particular, it should use SendMessage(); occasionally, it should use PostMessage()—or else you should use the TThread object.

> **NOTE**
>
> I want to emphasize that the VCL TThread object provides a way to call the VCL from inside threads. That object is explored later in this chapter in the sections "Threads and the VCL" and "Using the TThread Object." Furthermore, certain key commands, such as TQuery::Open, are safe to perform inside threads.
>
> I need to make one last comment in this context. You can use many parts of the VCL inside a thread. You mostly just need to watch out for TComponent descendants, and then only within certain parameters. This topic is addressed in more depth in the section on the TThread object.

5

THREADS

The ThreadFunc() routine first gets the device context from the system and then uses the device context to write 100,001 strings to the surface of the form. The device context is returned to the system when the loop is finished.

Two threads are running simultaneously in the Thread1 program while this function is operating. If you resize or move the main window, then you are using the main thread for your program. The code that increments and paints numbers to the screen is part of the second thread. You can switch between the two threads just by moving or resizing the form.

If you call the ThreadFunc() routine directly, rather than as a thread, you cannot move or resize the main window until the loop is finished because the program is entirely occupied with the loop and has no second thread available to handle other tasks. This sample program shows how you can get one program to do two things at the same time. Part of the program is painting numbers to the screen, but the other part is free to handle resizing or any other task you might give it.

As you can see, nothing is very complicated about threads when you are looking at them from the most elemental level. Complications occur when you have multiple threads trying to access the same data at the same time. When that happens, you need to find a way to get the threads to synchronize with one another so that they are not working at cross purposes.

Programming Multiple Threads

Now that you know the basics about threads, the next step is to see how to run multiple threads from inside the same program. This is a bit like multitasking inside a single program—although, of course, the operating system doesn't necessarily treat two threads inside one program any differently than it would treat two threads from separate executables.

The sample program in Listings 5.3 through 5.5 shows how a program can have four separate threads running at the same time. Three of the threads are painting graphics to the screen. The fourth thread, which performs some simple math, is the main thread for the program. It continues functioning normally even when the other threads are active.

LISTING 5.3 THE HEADER FOR THE THREAD2 PROGRAM'S MAIN UNIT

```
#ifndef MainH
#define MainH

#include <Classes.hpp>
#include <Controls.hpp>
```

```
#include <StdCtrls.hpp>
#include <Forms.hpp>
#include <Menus.hpp>

const int Margin = 20;

struct TData {
  int XPos;
  int YPos;
};

class TForm1 : public TForm
{
__published:    // IDE-managed Components
  TEdit *Edit1;
  TButton *bSquare;
  TMainMenu *MainMenu1;
  TMenuItem *Start1;
  void __fastcall FormPaint(TObject *Sender);
  void __fastcall FormCreate(TObject *Sender);
  void __fastcall Start1Click(TObject *Sender);
  void __fastcall bSquareClick(TObject *Sender);
  void __fastcall FormResize(TObject *Sender);
private:         // User declarations
  HBITMAP EarthMap;
  void DrawBitmap(HDC PaintDC, HBITMAP Bitmap, int XVal, int YVal);
public:          // User declarations
  __fastcall TForm1(TComponent* Owner);
};

extern PACKAGE TForm1 *Form1;

#endif
```

LISTING 5.4   THE MAIN UNIT FOR THE THREAD2 PROGRAM

```
#include <vcl.h>
#include <math.h>
#pragma hdrstop

#include "Main.h"

#pragma package(smart_init)
#pragma resource "*.dfm"
TForm1 *Form1;
int AWidth, AHeight;

__fastcall TForm1::TForm1(TComponent* Owner)
  : TForm(Owner)
```

5

THREADS

continues

LISTING 5.4   CONTINUED

```
{
}

void TForm1::DrawBitmap(HDC PaintDC, HBITMAP Bitmap, int XVal, int YVal)
{
  HDC MemDC = CreateCompatibleDC(PaintDC);
  HBITMAP OldBitmap = SelectObject(MemDC, Bitmap);
  BitBlt(PaintDC, XVal, YVal, AWidth,
         AHeight, MemDC, 0, 0, SRCCOPY);
  SelectObject(MemDC, OldBitmap);
  DeleteObject(MemDC);
}

void __fastcall TForm1::FormPaint(TObject *Sender)
{
  if (EarthMap)
    DrawBitmap(GetDC(Handle), EarthMap, Margin, 0);
}

void __fastcall TForm1::FormCreate(TObject *Sender)
{
  BITMAP BStruct;
  EarthMap = LoadBitmap(HInstance, "Earth");
  GetObject(EarthMap, sizeof(BITMAP), &BStruct);
  AWidth = BStruct.bmWidth;
  AHeight = BStruct.bmHeight;
  PostMessage(Handle, WM_SIZE, 0, 0);
}

DWORD CALLBACK ThreadFunc(void* Ptr)
{
  TData* Data = static_cast<TData*>(Ptr);
  HDC DC = GetDC(Form1->Handle);
  for (int j = 0;j<AHeight;j++)
    for (int i = Margin;i<AWidth + Margin;i++) {
      TColorRef P = GetPixel(DC, i, j);
      SetPixel(DC, i + Data->XPos, Data->YPos + j, P);
    }
  ReleaseDC(Form1->Handle, DC);
  delete Data;
  return 0;
}

void __fastcall TForm1::StartMenu(TObject *Sender)
{
  DWORD ThreadID;
  TData* Data = new TData;
  Data->XPos = AWidth;
  Data->YPos = 0;
```

```
  HANDLE hThread1 = CreateThread(
    0, 0, ThreadFunc, Data, 0, &ThreadID);

  Data = new TData;
  Data->XPos = 0;
  Data->YPos = AHeight;
  HANDLE hThread2 = CreateThread(
    0, 0, ThreadFunc, Data, 0, &ThreadID);

  Data = new TData;
  Data->XPos = AWidth;
  Data->YPos = AHeight;
  HANDLE hThread3 = CreateThread(
    0, 0, ThreadFunc, Data, 0, &ThreadID);

  if (!hThread1 ¦¦ !hThread2 ¦¦ !hThread3)
    MessageBox(Handle, "No Thread!", 0, MB_OK);
}

void __fastcall TForm1::bSquareClick(TObject *Sender)
{
  double r = Edit1->Text.ToDouble();
  String S;
  Edit1->Text = S.sprintf("%f", sqrt(r));
}

void __fastcall TForm1::FormResize(TObject *Sender)
{
  Edit1->Left = ClientWidth - (Edit1->Width + Margin);
  bSquare->Left = ClientWidth - (bSquare->Width + Margin);
}
```

Listing 5.5 references a bitmap file called EARTH.BMP. This file is included with the code on the book's CD-ROM. If you performed a default C++Builder installation, you can also find this file in your \Program Files\Common Files\Borland Shared\Images \Splash\16Color directory.

LISTING 5.5 THE RESOURCE FILE FOR THE THREAD2 PROGRAM

```
//////////////////////////////////////////////////////////
// EARTH.RC
//////////////////////////////////////////////////////////

Earth BITMAP "earth.bmp"
```

When you first run this program, a bitmap appears in the upper-left corner of the screen. If you select the program's sole menu item, three other copies of this bitmap are slowly painted in, as shown in Figure 5.2. A button and an edit control appear in the upper-right corner of the screen. You can enter data in this edit control and then press the button to find its square root.

FIGURE 5.2

The Thread2 program after three copies of the original bitmap were made by three separate threads.

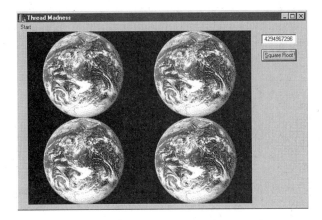

What's interesting about the program is that you can perform mathematical calculations at the same time that the program is very busy painting three bitmaps to the screen. The program appears to be doing four things at once, which would have been impossible under Windows 3.1. (You could have faked this same kind of capability in Windows 3.1 by using a series of `PostMessage()` commands, but that kind of code is awkward to implement and difficult to maintain.)

Using Threads in the Thread2 Program

The core of the Thread2 program is very simple. A bitmap is blitted to the screen; three threads are started; each of the threads laboriously copies the original bitmap to the screen, one pixel at a time.

> **NOTE**
>
> The Windows API function that performs the copying of bitmap bits from one device context to another is called `BitBlt()`; that is short for "bit block transfer." Windows API programmers adopted the term *blit* to refer to the process of copying a bitmap from one device context to another.

I could have made additional copies of the bitmap by blitting it to the screen multiple times in different locations. However, in this case I didn't want to do things the fast way. Instead, I wanted things to go slowly so you could watch a thread at work. In other words, I didn't want the thread to be over before it had seemingly begun, which is what would have happened if I had called BitBlt() from inside each of the three secondary threads in the program.

Instead of BitBlt(), I had each of the secondary threads read the original bitmap, one pixel at a time, and then copy it, again one pixel at a time, to another portion of the screen:

```
for (int j = 0;j<AHeight;j++)
  for (int i = Margin;i<AWidth + Margin;i++) {
    TColorRef P = GetPixel(DC, i, j);
    SetPixel(DC, i + Data->XPos, Data->YPos + j, P);
  }
```

This time-consuming process has the side benefit of being fun to watch.

You probably noticed that the Thread2 program also contains a button and an edit control. If you enter a number in the edit control, you will find that clicking the program's button gives you its square root. In fact, the program starts out with an outrageously high number (4GB) in the edit control. If you click the button several times, this number has its square root taken multiple times, until you start approaching the number 1.

What's interesting about the Thread2 program is not that it knows how to get a square root. (It's a given that a computer can do that math for you.) What's amazing is that you can ask it to calculate square roots at the same time that all three threads are busy copying the original bitmap.

The point here is that there is no apparent degradation in the way the button and edit control respond. The computer is obviously very busy copying pixels, yet it always lets you type in numbers and calculate square roots almost exactly as it would if you had the entire CPU to yourself. This is what preemptive multitasking is all about. When the time slices for the secondary threads are up, the processor is given over to the other threads on the system. No delay or degradation of performance is apparent to the user. The computer appears to be doing at least four things at the same time. In fact, for all practical purposes, it is doing four things at the same time.

Passing a Parameter to a Thread Function

The Thread2 program takes advantage of the lpParameter parameter of CreateThread(), as shown by the Data variable in the following code sample:

```
HANDLE hThread1 = CreateThread(
  0, 0, ThreadFunc, Data, 0, &ThreadID);
```

The thread function is called ThreadFunc(), and the parameter passed to it is a TData pointer. (See Listing 5.3 for the declaration of the TData structure.)

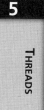

5

THREADS

The XPos and YPos members of this structure designate the point at which each thread should start its copy of the picture.

Now here's the interesting part: Suppose you declared Data as a global variable. Then suppose you assigned this global variable a starting x and y location for a picture and passed it to a thread. You assigned this same variable a new value and started a new thread. When you assigned the global variable a new value, it automatically changed the value passed to the first thread. This means that the first thread would now start painting at the place where the second picture should be rather than in the place you originally asked it to paint. (One way around this type of problem is to use something called *thread local storage*, which is a subject beyond the scope of this book.)

As you saw in the preceding paragraph, simply declaring a global variable is not a solution to the problem presented by these three threads. A second possible idea is to declare the Data variable as local to the StartMenu() method, which is the method called when the Start menu item is selected. However, if you took this approach, you would get into even deeper trouble. Specifically, you would assign the variable a value and then pass it to the thread. At that point, the StartMenu() method would go out of scope, and the value that the thread was trying to use would suddenly disappear from underneath it. This alternative won't work either.

A third alternative, and the one used in this program, involves using pointers. Allocate memory for a variable; then pass it to the first thread. Next, allocate memory for a second variable and pass it to the second thread. Finally, you could allocate memory for a third variable and pass it in to the third thread. Each thread is responsible for deleting the memory passed in to it. Each variable would, of course, contain a different set of coordinates:

```
void __fastcall TForm1::StartMenu(TObject *Sender)
{
  DWORD ThreadID;
  TData* Data = new TData;
  Data->XPos = AWidth;
  Data->YPos = 0;
  HANDLE hThread1 = CreateThread(
    0, 0, ThreadFunc, Data, 0, &ThreadID);

  Data = new TData;
  Data->XPos = 0;
  Data->YPos = AHeight;
  HANDLE hThread2 = CreateThread(
    0, 0, ThreadFunc, Data, 0, &ThreadID);

  Data = new TData;
  Data->XPos = AWidth;
```

```
    Data->YPos = AHeight;
    HANDLE hThread3 = CreateThread(
      0, 0, ThreadFunc, Data, 0, &ThreadID);

    if (!hThread1 || !hThread2 || !hThread3)
      MessageBox(Handle, "No Thread!", 0, MB_OK);
}
```

The preceding code calls new three times, once for each copy of the TData structure. The calls to new allocate memory for the TData structure. The code assigns values to the structure's members and then passes them in to the appropriate thread.

Given the scenario outlined earlier, each thread is then responsible for deallocating the structure passed in to it:

```
DWORD CALLBACK ThreadFunc(void* Ptr)
{
  TData* Data = static_cast<TData*>(Ptr);
  HDC DC = GetDC(Form1->Handle);
  for (int j = 0;j<AHeight;j++)
    for (int i = Margin;i<AWidth + Margin;i++) {
      TColorRef P = GetPixel(DC, i, j);
      SetPixel(DC, i + Data->XPos, Data->YPos + j, P);
    }
  ReleaseDC(Form1->Handle, DC);
  delete Data;
  return 0;
}
```

The relevant call in this case is the call to delete where the Data variable is disposed of.

The process described here shows one way of handling data that is passed to a thread. You have three threads, so you have to create three separate instances of the data.

As it turns out, the basic problem of how a thread handles data is one that has many implications. As a rule, the issues surrounding this subject are categorized under a topic called *thread synchronization*. The reason they are given this name becomes clear in just a moment.

Critical Sections: Getting Threads to Work Together

The classic problem encountered when using threads involves a piece of global data that is being accessed by more than one thread. Variations on this theme involve a series of threads, all of which have to access the same file, the same DLL, the same communications resource, or any of a number of different objects.

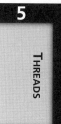

To take a classic database-related problem, imagine what would happen if two threads were accessing the same database. Suppose one of them opened a record and made some changes to the record's data. Then suppose a second program came along and made some changes to a different part of the same record and wrote them to the database. Now the first program writes its changes to the database and in the process effectively undoes the changes made by the second program.

This is a classic problem as it would apply to thread synchronization. You will find many variations on this type of problem and many solutions to them. The programs you are about to see use critical sections and mutexes to resolve this problem.

Critical sections solve the problem by effectively blocking the second thread from accessing the sensitive data when it is being used by the first thread. In particular, it stops the second thread from executing by ensuring that it doesn't get any time slices. The parallel in the database world would be locking a record, but the analogy is not exact.

The mechanisms involved in this process are not hard to understand. Critical sections are a simple solution to what sounds like a fairly complex problem. Go ahead and get the CritSect program, shown in Listings 5.6 and 5.7, up and running. After you read the description of how it works, you'll see that this whole issue is easy to resolve.

LISTING 5.6   THE HEADER FOR THE CRITSECT PROGRAM'S MAIN UNIT

```
#ifndef mainH
#define mainH

#include <Classes.hpp>
#include <Controls.hpp>
#include <StdCtrls.hpp>
#include <Forms.hpp>
#include <Menus.hpp>

const int TotalCount = 20;

class TForm1 : public TForm
{
__published:    // IDE-managed Components
  TListBox *ListBox1;
  TListBox *ListBox2;
  TMainMenu *MainMenu1;
  TMenuItem *Options1;
  TMenuItem *RunThread1;
  TMenuItem *CritSects1;
  void __fastcall FormCreate(TObject *Sender);
  void __fastcall FormDestroy(TObject *Sender);
```

```
  void __fastcall RunThread1Click(TObject *Sender);
  void __fastcall CritSects1Click(TObject *Sender);
private:        // User declarations
public:         // User declarations
  __fastcall TForm1(TComponent* Owner);
};

extern PACKAGE TForm1 *Form1;

#endif
```

LISTING 5.7   THE MAIN UNIT OF THE CRITSECT PROGRAM

```
#include <vcl.h>
#pragma hdrstop

#include "main.h"

#pragma package(smart_init)
#pragma resource "*.dfm"
TForm1 *Form1;

bool CritSects;
TRTLCriticalSection Sect1;
int GlobalData;

__fastcall TForm1::TForm1(TComponent* Owner)
  : TForm(Owner)
{
}

//////////////////////////////////////////////////////////
// The thread routine
//////////////////////////////////////////////////////////
DWORD CALLBACK ThreadFunc1(void* P)
{
  Form1->ListBox1->Items->Clear();
  int i;
  for (int j = 0;j<TotalCount;j++) {
    if (CritSects)
      EnterCriticalSection(&Sect1);
    Sleep(3);
    GlobalData += 3;
    i = GlobalData - 3;
    String S;
    S.sprintf("Information: %d", i);
    SendMessage(Form1->ListBox1->Handle, LB_ADDSTRING, 0,
(long)S.c_str());
    GlobalData -= 3;
    if (CritSects)
```

continues

LISTING 5.7   CONTINUED

```cpp
      LeaveCriticalSection(&Sect1);
  }
  return 0;
}

///////////////////////////////////////////////////////
// The thread routine
///////////////////////////////////////////////////////
DWORD CALLBACK ThreadFunc2(void* P)
{
  Form1->ListBox2->Clear();
  int i;
  for (int j = 0;j<TotalCount;j++) {
    if (CritSects)
      EnterCriticalSection(&Sect1);
    Sleep(3);
    GlobalData -= 3;
    i = GlobalData + 3;
    String S;
    S.sprintf("Information: %d", i);
    SendMessage(Form1->ListBox2->Handle, LB_ADDSTRING, 0,
➥(long)S.c_str());
    GlobalData += 3;
    if (CritSects)
      LeaveCriticalSection(&Sect1);
  }
  return 0;
}

void __fastcall TForm1::FormCreate(TObject *Sender)
{
  InitializeCriticalSection(&Sect1);
  CritSects = false;
}

void __fastcall TForm1::FormDestroy(TObject *Sender)
{
  DeleteCriticalSection(&Sect1);
}

void __fastcall TForm1::RunThread1Click(TObject *Sender)
{
  DWORD ThreadID1;
  DWORD ThreadID2;
  HANDLE ThreadHandles[2];
  GlobalData = 100;

  ThreadHandles[0] = CreateThread(
    0, 0, ThreadFunc1, 0, 0, &ThreadID1);
```

```
    ThreadHandles[1] = CreateThread(
      0, 0, ThreadFunc2, 0, 0, &ThreadID2);

    if (!ThreadHandles[0] || !ThreadHandles[1])
      MessageBox(Handle, "No Thread", 0, MB_OK);
}

void __fastcall TForm1::CritSects1Click(TObject *Sender)
{
  CritSects1->Checked = !CritSects1->Checked;
  CritSects = CritSects1->Checked;
}
```

The CritSect program has a single window with two list boxes and a menu. If you select the Run Thread menu item, the list boxes are filled with numbers, as shown in Figure 5.3.

FIGURE 5.3

The CritSect program as it appears when its threads are not synchronized.

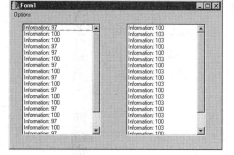

As you can see, the two columns of numbers are not identical. For reasons that are explained in just a moment, the program appears this way when its threads are not synchronized. If you select the CritSects menu item and then choose Run Thread a second time, you see that the two columns are now identical, as shown in Figure 5.4. For reasons that are explained shortly, the program looks this way when its threads are synchronized.

FIGURE 5.4

The CritSect program as it appears when its threads are synchronized.

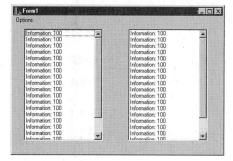

The CritSect program has a single global variable called `GlobalData`, which is of type `int`. Each thread in the program manipulates this global data and then restores it to its original value. For instance, the first thread adds 3 to this number, sets a second variable called `i` to the new value `GlobalData` - 3, and then shows the number in the first list box:

```
GlobalData += 3;
i = GlobalData - 3;
String S;
S.sprintf("Information: %d", i);
SendMessage(Form1->ListBox1->Handle, LB_ADDSTRING, 0, (long)S.c_str());
GlobalData -= 3;
```

If you add 3 to a number and then subtract 3 from that same number, it should be restored to its original value. In fact, you would have to be living in a very non-Euclidean, nonlinear world if adding 3 to a number and then subtracting it did not take you back to the original number. For example, 100 plus 3 equals 103, and 103 minus 3 equals 100. That's all there is to it, and there's no point in talking about the matter any further—except for the fact that when the CritSect program tries to do this math, sometimes it gets 100, and sometimes it gets 97.

The other thread in the program, the one that writes to the second list box, does the exact opposite. It subtracts 3 from 100 and then adds 3 to the new number. Obviously, this process would have to yield 100 as a result each and every time. That's the way the universe is put together, and that's the way things have to be—but it doesn't turn out that way. Instead of getting the result you would expect, sometimes you get 103. Something is clearly very wrong here.

What's going on is not some metaphysical curiosity, but the kind of complication that ensues when two threads are accessing and manipulating the same data. Specifically, one thread adds 3 to the global data, thereby setting it equal to 103. The second thread accesses the data and subtracts 3 from it, thereby setting it equal to 100. When the second thread adds the 3 that it took away, the result is not 100, but 103. Conversely, when the first thread subtracts 3, it gets not 100, but 97. It's all a matter of timing.

As you can see, what's happening here is the same type of problem that I described when talking about two threads simultaneously accessing the same record. The problem is one of synchronization. One thread needs to be able to tell the other that the global data is in a sensitive or critical state and that it shouldn't be touched.

Clearly, this is what critical sections are all about. They are a way of designating that a particular piece of data is currently off limits and can't be touched.

The solution implementation is extremely literal. You mark the blocks of code that manipulate the data as "critical sections." Before the code in these sections can be executed, the computer has to check a global structure that indicates whether another thread is currently in the middle of a critical section. (Furthermore, it checks to see whether this critical section is related to the first critical section. You could have different sets of critical sections in the same program.)

Here's how it works. The CritSect program initializes a variable of type TRTLCriticalSection in the OnCreate handler:

```
InitializeCriticalSection(&Sect1);
CritSects = false;
```

NOTE

TRTLCriticalSection is a typedef for the Windows structure called _RTL_CRITICAL_SECTION. What _RTL_CRITICAL_SECTION looks like is unimportant, but you can find the structure declaration in WINNT.H:

```
typedef struct _RTL_CRITICAL_SECTION {
    PRTL_CRITICAL_SECTION_DEBUG DebugInfo;
    LONG LockCount;
    LONG RecursionCount;
    HANDLE OwningThread;
    HANDLE LockSemaphore;
    DWORD SpinCount;
} RTL_CRITICAL_SECTION, *PRTL_CRITICAL_SECTION;
```

You can mark a section of code as a critical section:

```
EnterCriticalSection(&Sect1);
...
// First swatch of Critical code appears here...
...
LeaveCriticalSection(&Sect1);
```

The moment EnterCriticalSection() is passed Sect1, it sets one or more of its data members to reflect the fact that a critical section is active. If a second critical section is called by another thread, EnterCriticalSection() can now see that a critical section is active. It puts the second thread to sleep:

```
EnterCriticalSection(&Sect1);
...
// Second swatch of Critical code appears here...
...
LeaveCriticalSection(&Sect1);
```

The second thread does not get any time slices while it is asleep. It's marked as inactive; the CPU wastes no time trying to call it. This system is extremely efficient, and very few clock cycles are wasted by a process that has been put to sleep.

When the first critical section exits, `LeaveCriticalSection()` is called. The variables in `Sect1` are then changed and the second thread is free to execute. The second thread immediately enters its own critical section, thereby preventing the first thread from executing the offending code. At this stage, the two critical sections in this program end up swapping, with each given a chance to execute while the other waits.

By using the process described earlier, you can mark the areas where a thread accesses the `GlobalData` variable as critical. Therefore, only one thread is able to access the data at a time. This approach effectively solves the problem. When the critical sections are active, the program always produces the results you would expect, as shown in Figure 5.4.

You should always delete a variable of type `TRTLCriticalSection` when you are through using it:

```
DeleteCriticalSection(&Sect1);
```

This step is important because it frees system resources. However, you should be sure that you do not call `EnterCriticalSection()` or `LeaveCriticalSection()` with an invalid variable. Doing so causes an exception.

As mentioned, synchronization seems like a fairly complex problem. However, the solution to the problem is very simple. Critical sections are easy to use.

Working with Mutexes

Mutexes are similar to critical sections, except that they work not only in one process, but in multiple processes at the same time. In other words, they can help synchronize not only two or more threads in a single application, but two or more threads that reside in separate applications.

Mutexes get their name from the words *mutually exclusive*. Only one thread can own a mutex at a time. If a thread owns that mutex, the mutex is said to be *signaled*. If no thread owns the mutex, the mutex is said to be *nonsignaled*. (This terminology is confusing for a very simple concept. You can just think of the mutex as being owned or free. An owned mutex is signaled, and an unowned mutex is nonsignaled.)

Call `CreateMutex()` in order to create a mutex. Here is the `CreateMutex()` declaration:

```
HANDLE CreateMutex(
  LPSECURITY_ATTRIBUTES lpMutexAttributes, // point to security attributes
  BOOL bInitialOwner,                       // flag initial ownership
  LPCTSTR lpName                            // point to mutex-object name
);
```

The first parameter is a structure that defines the security attributes for the mutex. If you set this parameter to `0`, the mutex is assigned a default set of security attributes. (For more information on this parameter, see the Win32 online help.)

The second parameter specifies whether the mutex is owned by the calling thread. You can use this parameter to specify whether the mutex should go immediately into the signaled state.

The final parameter gives the mutex a name. If one process creates a mutex and gives it a name, and a second process then attempts to create or open a mutex of the same name, the process gets the same mutex back in return. The two processes can then use the mutex to synchronize their actions. You can pass 0 in this parameter if you like. Doing so produces an unnamed mutex:

```
hMutex = CreateMutex(0, false, 0);
```

Listings 5.8 and 5.9 show the Mutex1 program, which is nearly identical to the CritSect program. The only difference is that the Mutex1 program uses mutexes rather than critical sections.

LISTING 5.8   THE HEADER FOR THE MUTEX1 PROGRAM'S MAIN FORM

```
#ifndef MainH
#define MainH

#include <Classes.hpp>
#include <Controls.hpp>
#include <StdCtrls.hpp>
#include <Forms.hpp>
#include <Menus.hpp>

const int TotalCount = 20;

class TForm1 : public TForm
{
__published:    // IDE-managed Components
  TListBox *ListBox1;
  TListBox *ListBox2;
  TMainMenu *MainMenu1;
  TMenuItem *Options1;
  TMenuItem *RunThread1;
  TMenuItem *UseMutex1;
  void __fastcall FormCreate(TObject *Sender);
  void __fastcall FormDestroy(TObject *Sender);
  void __fastcall RunThread1Click(TObject *Sender);
  void __fastcall UseMutex1Click(TObject *Sender);
private:        // User declarations
public:         // User declarations
  __fastcall TForm1(TComponent* Owner);
};

extern PACKAGE TForm1 *Form1;

#endif
```

5

THREADS

LISTING 5.9   THE MAIN UNIT OF THE MUTEX1 PROGRAM

```cpp
#include <vcl.h>
#pragma hdrstop

#include "Main.h"

bool UseMutex;
HANDLE hMutex;
int GlobalData;

#pragma package(smart_init)
#pragma resource "*.dfm"
TForm1 *Form1;

__fastcall TForm1::TForm1(TComponent* Owner)
  : TForm(Owner)
{
}

//////////////////////////////////////////////////////
// The thread routine
//////////////////////////////////////////////////////
DWORD CALLBACK ThreadFunc1(void* P)
{
  Form1->ListBox1->Items->Clear();
  int i;
  for (int j = 0;j<TotalCount;j++) {
    if (UseMutex)
      WaitForSingleObject(hMutex, INFINITE);
    Sleep(3);
    GlobalData += 3;
    i = GlobalData - 3;
    String S;
    S.sprintf("Information: %d", i);
    SendMessage(Form1->ListBox1->Handle, LB_ADDSTRING, 0, (int)S.c_str());
    GlobalData -= 3;
    if (UseMutex)
      ReleaseMutex(hMutex);
  }
  return 0;
}

//////////////////////////////////////////////////////
// The thread routine
//////////////////////////////////////////////////////
DWORD CALLBACK ThreadFunc2(void* P)
{
  Form1->ListBox2->Items->Clear();
  int i;
  for (int j = 0;j<TotalCount;j++) {
```

```
    if (UseMutex)
      WaitForSingleObject(hMutex, INFINITE);
    Sleep(3);
    GlobalData -= 3;
    i = GlobalData + 3;
    String S;
    S.sprintf("Information: %d", i);
    SendMessage(Form1->ListBox2->Handle, LB_ADDSTRING, 0, (int)S.c_str());
    GlobalData += 3;
    if (UseMutex)
      ReleaseMutex(hMutex);
  }
  return 0;
}

void __fastcall TForm1::FormCreate(TObject *Sender)
{
  hMutex = CreateMutex(0, false, 0);
  UseMutex = false;
}

void __fastcall TForm1::FormDestroy(TObject *Sender)
{
  CloseHandle(hMutex);
}

void __fastcall TForm1::RunThread1Click(TObject *Sender)
{
  DWORD ThreadID1;
  DWORD ThreadID2;
  HANDLE ThreadHandles[3];
  GlobalData = 100;

  ThreadHandles[0] = CreateThread(
    0, 0, ThreadFunc1, 0, 0, &ThreadID1);

  ThreadHandles[1] = CreateThread(
    0, 0, ThreadFunc2, 0, 0, &ThreadID2);

  if (!ThreadHandles[0] || !ThreadHandles[1])
    MessageBox(Handle, "No Thread", 0, MB_OK);
}

void __fastcall TForm1::UseMutex1Click(TObject *Sender)
{
  UseMutex1->Checked = !UseMutex1->Checked;
  UseMutex = UseMutex1->Checked;
}
```

As stated earlier, the Mutex1 and CritSect programs are nearly identical. In fact, from the user's point of view, their behavior is indistinguishable.

The Mutex1 program calls `CreateMutex()` in the part of the `OnCreate` handler where `CritSect` called `InitializeCriticalSection()`. Instead of calling `EnterCriticalSection()`, the Mutex1 program calls `WaitForSingleObject()`. Instead of calling `LeaveCriticalSection()`, the Mutex1 program calls `ReleaseMutex()`:

```
if (UseMutex)
  WaitForSingleObject(hMutex, INFINITE);
Sleep(3);
GlobalData += 3;
i = GlobalData - 3;
String S;
S.sprintf("Information: %d", i);
SendMessage(Form1->ListBox1->Handle, LB_ADDSTRING, 0, (int)S.c_str());
GlobalData -= 3;
if (UseMutex)
  ReleaseMutex(hMutex);
```

`WaitForSingleObject()` takes two parameters. The first is the handle to a mutex and the second is the number of milliseconds the function should wait before returning. `WaitForSingleObject()` returns only if the mutex becomes signaled or if the time specified has elapsed. That is, it returns when it owns the mutex or when the time interval specified in the second parameter elapses. If you pass in the `INFINITE` flag in this parameter, the routine returns only when the mutex is signaled. (There is also a function called `WaitForMultipleObjects()`. The name says it all, although you can look up the particulars in the Win32 online help.)

When a thread is finished with a mutex, it should call `ReleaseMutex()`, which takes a handle to a mutex as a parameter. The mutex is free after the call to `ReleaseMutex()`, and other code that has been waiting to own the handle can now execute. This process is a bit like passing a baton between teams of runners. The ones that own the mutex run, and the others wait for it to be passed to them.

You should close a mutex when you are completely done with and don't need it any more:

```
CloseHandle(hMutex);
```

> **NOTE**
>
> Both the Mutex1 and the CritSect program call the `Sleep()` function. `Sleep()` suspends the execution of a thread for a specified number of milliseconds. A value of `INIFINITE` causes the thread to sleep for an indefinite period of time.

I call `Sleep()` in the Mutex1 and CritSect programs because I want to exaggerate the two threads' innate lack of synchronicity. In other words, I use this call to force the two threads out of sync so that it is almost certain that they will not both normally print out 100 each time. Because I use the function, the chance of coincidental synchronicity between the two threads is low. Therefore, I have to use critical sections or mutexes to get them in line.

Threads and the VCL

With a few crucial exceptions, the VCL in C++Builder 4 is not threadsafe. The reason for this is simply that making it threadsafe would make it both bigger and slower. In particular, critical sections or mutexes would have to be wrapped around certain portions of the VCL code. The sheer number of these sections would be so great that the VCL would end up being noticeably bigger and slower. To avoid this situation, the Inprise engineers had to reach a compromise of some kind; that compromise is called the TThread object.

NOTE

If you try to call the visual elements of VCL from inside a thread, you will almost certainly end up crashing your program. The crash will not, however, necessarily occur right away.

The TThread object gives you an advantage: It provides a Synchronize() function that enables you to make calls to the VCL from inside a thread.

Synchronize() is a method of the TThread object. You wrap it around the call to a method that is going to call the VCL. For instance, if you access the VCL from inside a function called ShowData(), you should call ShowData() like this:

```
Synchronize(ShowData);
```

The function declaration for a function called via Synchronize() must have the following declaration:

```
void __fastcall Function();
```

Any other function declaration will result in a compiler error.

As a rule, the only way you can call the VCL inside a thread is to use the `Synchronize()` method. In particular, `Synchronize()` performs some hand waving that essentially makes your thread a temporary part of the application's main thread. You can access the VCL during this time. You should break out of the synchronized section of your code the moment you don't need the VCL. Your program will then once again have multiple threads.

The point is that most of the VCL is not threadsafe, so you can't access it while you are in a thread. Period. That's it. The solution is to call `Synchronize()`, which in effect puts a temporary end to your thread and makes it part of the main thread for the application. You can call the VCL during this time. The function gets its name because it synchronizes your thread with the application's main thread.

Now that I have made such a big point of saying that you can't call the VCL while inside a thread, I want to qualify the statement a little by pointing out some exceptions to this rule.

In general, descendants of `TComponent` are not threadsafe. Some big parts of the VCL, however, do not descend from `TComponent`. For instance, no `TComponent` descendants appear anywhere in the VCL's `CLASSES` unit.

> **NOTE**
>
> This note is one of the early occasions in this book when I am going to remind you of the importance of having the source to the VCL. I return to this theme a number of times, but the key point is that really good C++Builder programmers almost all have a copy of the VCL. The VCL ships with the Professional and Enterprise versions of C++Builder. Although the VCL is in Object Pascal, it remains an invaluable source of information for the serious programmer. Even if you are not a Pascal programmer, you can easily learn to read the VCL source and understand what it is doing.

The following are some of the objects declared in the `CLASSES` unit:

- `TList`
- `TStrings`
- `TStringList`
- `TStream`
- `TFileStream`
- `TMemoryStream`
- `TFiler`
- `TReader`
- `TWriter`
- `TBits`
- `TParser`
- `TComponent`

You can safely use these classes, as well as TObject or the exception classes, in a thread. You can even design your own threadsafe TComponent descendants if you are very careful and know exactly what you are doing.

> **NOTE**
>
> The key to creating a threadsafe TComponent descendant would be judicious use of critical sections or mutexes. In other words, if you wrapped all the dangerous sections of your TComponent object in a critical section, you could access it in a thread. Clearly, this is a big opportunity for some third parties to come along and make some hay while the sun shines. You need to work quickly, however, because the VCL might well be threadsafe in future versions.

If you think about this situation for a moment, it becomes obvious that at least part of the VCL has to be threadsafe. For instance, the TThread object itself is part of the VCL, and it is obviously threadsafe. It's just a question of learning what you can and can't do.

Threadsafe Database Access

Most of the rest of the VCL is out of bounds, with yet a few more exceptions. One of the most important exceptions is calling the Open() methods of TQuery, TDatabase, and TTable objects.

The Borland Database Engine itself is not multithreaded. It can, however, be made threadsafe with the use of sessions or the TSession component. You should keep two ideas in mind when running a threaded query in the background:

1. Let each Query object run in its own session. Each background query needs to have a separate Session object associated with it. The SessionName property of the thread's Query object needs to be set to the name of the TSession component. If you are using a TDatabase object, you need to have a separate TDatabase associated with each Session.

2. A threaded TQuery component cannot be connected to a TDataSource in the context of the thread that it will be used. You should connect to a TDataSource only in the context of the main VCL thread or in a Synchronize() method. You therefore need to make the connection not at design time, but at run time.

You can compose a complex query, put it in the SQL property of a TQuery object that is part of a thread and then call Open(). While all those calculations are going on in the background, you could use the main thread of your program, or other threads of your program, to interact with the user. The moment the SQL statement is finished executing, you could pop the results into a grid or other data-aware control and show them to the user.

Once again, let me emphasize that you can execute SQL statements in the background by giving them their own threads. You need to be to be sure, however, that each thread has its own TSession object and that the TQuery object is not hooked up to anything else, including a TDataSource object. After the SQL statement executes, you can use the Synchronize() method to hook the SQL object up to a TDataSource so that the user can view the results.

The following example in Listings 5.10 and 5.11 shows how to run background queries. In the example, I run two background queries against a local table. From the user's point of view, the queries seem to be executing at the same time.

LISTING 5.10 THE HEADER FOR THE QUERY PROGRAM'S MAIN UNIT

```
#ifndef MainH
#define MainH

#include <Classes.hpp>
#include <Controls.hpp>
#include <StdCtrls.hpp>
#include <Forms.hpp>
#include <Db.hpp>
#include <DBGrids.hpp>
#include <DBTables.hpp>
#include <Grids.hpp>

class TQueryThread : public TThread {
  private:
    TSession* FSession;
    TQuery* FQuery;
    TDataSource* FDataSource;
    Exception* FQueryException;
    void __fastcall ConnectDataSource();
    void __fastcall ShowQryError();
  protected:
    virtual void __fastcall Execute();
  public:
    __fastcall TQueryThread(TSession* Session,
      TQuery* Query, TDataSource* DataSource);
};

class TForm1 : public TForm
{
__published:    // IDE-managed Components
  TDBGrid *DBGrid1;
```

```
   TDBGrid *DBGrid2;
   TQuery *Query1;
   TQuery *Query2;
   TDataSource *DataSource1;
   TDataSource *DataSource2;
   TTable *Table1;
   TTable *Table2;
   TButton *Button1;
   TSession *Session1;
   TSession *Session2;
   void __fastcall Button1Click(TObject *Sender);
private:        // User declarations
public:         // User declarations
   __fastcall TForm1(TComponent* Owner);
};

extern PACKAGE TForm1 *Form1;

#endif
```

LISTING 5.11 THE QUERY PROGRAM SHOWING HOW TO RUN QUERIES IN THE
BACKGROUND

```
#include <vcl.h>
#pragma hdrstop

#include "Main.h"

#pragma package(smart_init)
#pragma resource "*.dfm"
TForm1 *Form1;

__fastcall TForm1::TForm1(TComponent* Owner)
   : TForm(Owner)
{
}

__fastcall TQueryThread::TQueryThread(TSession* Session,
   TQuery* Query, TDataSource* DataSource) : TThread(true)
{
   FSession = Session;
   FQuery = Query;
   FDataSource = DataSource;
   FreeOnTerminate = true;
   Resume();
}

void __fastcall TQueryThread::Execute()
{
```

LISTING 5.11 CONTINUED

```
  try {
    FQuery->Open();
    Synchronize(ConnectDataSource);
  }
  catch (Exception* E) {
    FQueryException = E;
    Synchronize(ShowQryError);
  }
}

void __fastcall TQueryThread::ConnectDataSource()
{
  FDataSource->DataSet = FQuery;
}

void __fastcall TQueryThread::ShowQryError()
{
  Application->ShowException(FQueryException);
}

void RunBackgroundQuery(TSession* Session,
  TQuery* Query, TDataSource* DataSource)
{
  new TQueryThread(Session,  Query, DataSource);
}

void __fastcall TForm1::Button1Click(TObject *Sender)
{
  RunBackgroundQuery(Session1, Query1, DataSource1);
  RunBackgroundQuery(Session2, Query2, DataSource2);
}
```

The code from the Query program uses the VCL TThread object. This program opens up two queries when you click Button1. Each query is opened in a thread that runs in the background. The user is therefore free to use other parts of the program while the queries are being opened.

The queries aren't opened in the confines of the Synchronize() method. However, any messages that must be shown to the user are ferried through the Synchronize() method. Judicious use of the Synchronize() method ensures that the smallest possible amount of time is spent with the threads effectively shut down, to accommodate the limits of the VCL.

VCL Threadsafe Objects

As you learned earlier in this chapter, VCL objects are not threadsafe, and their properties and methods have to be accessed or executed from the main VCL thread. However, two VCL objects are the exception and are threadsafe. The first is any graphic object, and the second is a TThreadList.

What this means is that you do not need to be in the main VCL thread to set the color of a canvas's pen or to change the style of a brush; you can do it from within the context of a secondary thread. You also learned about using the thread's Synchronize() method. It, too, is unnecessary, as both of these objects have locking and unlocking methods. For the graphics objects, they are Lock() and Unlock(); for the ThreadList class, they are LockList() and UnlockList(). These methods act like critical sections and, when called, prevent the execution of other threads. One thing to remember is that they do work in pairs; calls to Lock() and Unlock() can be nested so that the lock will not be released until the last lock is released with the matching call to Unlock(). You can always find the number of locks that are active by examining the LockCount property. One other thing to keep in mind is that because Lock() does suspend all other threads from executing, your application's performance could suffer if it is used unwisely. If you look at the first thread example in this chapter (Thread1), you could modify the code in the ThreadFunc() function as follows:

```
DWORD CALLBACK ThreadFunc(void* P)
{
  Form1->Canvas->Lock();
  for (int i = 0;i<=100000;i++) {
    String S = i;
    Form1->Canvas->TextOut(10, 10, S);
  }
  Form1->Canvas->Unlock();
  return 0;
}
```

You would then see less responsiveness to window resizing and movement when the Use Thread button is clicked. The delay is mostly due to the fact that this loop construct is very tight.

Using the TThread Object

The short example found in Listings 5.12 and 5.13 shows how to use the TThread object. It is based on the Thread1 example shown earlier. The program has two threads. One thread is designed correctly; the other is designed incorrectly. By studying the difference between the two, you will see how to use the TThread object.

5

THREADS

LISTING 5.12   THE HEADER FOR THE THREAD1A PROGRAM'S MAIN UNIT

```cpp
#ifndef MainH
#define MainH

#include <Classes.hpp>
#include <Controls.hpp>
#include <StdCtrls.hpp>
#include <Forms.hpp>
#include <Buttons.hpp>
#include <ExtCtrls.hpp>

#define wm_ThreadDone WM_USER + 1

class TBadThread : public TThread {
  private:
    void __fastcall RunUpdate();
  protected:
    void __fastcall Execute();
  public:
    __fastcall TBadThread(bool CreateSuspended)
      : TThread(CreateSuspended) {}
};

class TMyThread2 : public TThread {
  private:
    int FCount;
    void __fastcall RunUpdate();
  protected:
    void __fastcall Execute();
  public:
    __fastcall TMyThread2(bool CreateSuspended)
      : TThread(CreateSuspended) {}
};

class TForm1 : public TForm
{
__published:    // IDE-managed Components
  TButton *bGoodThread;
  TBitBtn *bBadThread;
  TMemo *Memo1;
  TPanel *Panel1;
  void __fastcall bBadThreadClick(TObject *Sender);
  void __fastcall bGoodThreadClick(TObject *Sender);
  void __fastcall FormCreate(TObject *Sender);
private:        // User declarations
  TBadThread* BadThread;
  TMyThread2* T2;
  void ButtonsOff(bool Setting);
  void __fastcall GoodThreadDone(TObject* Sender);
  void __fastcall BadThreadDone(TObject* Sender);
```

```
public:          // User declarations
  __fastcall TForm1(TComponent* Owner);
};

extern PACKAGE TForm1 *Form1;

#endif
```

LISTING 5.13   THE THREAD1A PROGRAM'S MAIN UNIT

```
#include <vcl.h>
#pragma hdrstop

//  Example program shows how to use TThread object
//  that ships with C++Builder.

//  Using the TThread object makes the VCL threadsafe.

#include "Main.h"

#pragma package(smart_init)
#pragma resource "*.dfm"
TForm1 *Form1;

void __fastcall TBadThread::RunUpdate()
{
  for (int i = 1;i<=100000;i++) {
    Form1->Panel1->Caption = i;
    Form1->Panel1->Update(); // Wouldn't have to do this in good thread
  }
}

void __fastcall TBadThread::Execute()
{
  InvalidateRect(Form1->Handle, 0, true);
  Synchronize(RunUpdate);
  PostMessage(Form1->Handle, wm_ThreadDone, 1, 0);
}

void __fastcall TMyThread2::RunUpdate()
{
  Form1->Panel1->Caption = FCount;
}

void __fastcall TMyThread2::Execute()
{
  InvalidateRect(Form1->Handle, 0, true);
  for (int i = 1;i<=100000;i++)
    if (i % 10 == 0) {
```

continues

5

THREADS

LISTING 5.13   CONTINUED

```cpp
      FCount = i;
      Synchronize(RunUpdate);
    }
  PostMessage(Form1->Handle, wm_ThreadDone, 2, 0);
}


__fastcall TForm1::TForm1(TComponent* Owner)
  : TForm(Owner)
{
}

void TForm1::ButtonsOff(bool Setting)
{
  for (int i = 0;i<ComponentCount;i++) {
    TButton* button = dynamic_cast<TButton*>(Components[i]);
    if (button)
      button->Enabled = !Setting;
  }
}

void __fastcall TForm1::bBadThreadClick(TObject *Sender)
{
  ButtonsOff(true);
  BadThread = new TBadThread(false);
  BadThread->OnTerminate = BadThreadDone;
}

void __fastcall TForm1::bGoodThreadClick(TObject *Sender)
{
  ButtonsOff(true);
  T2 = new TMyThread2(false);
  T2->OnTerminate = GoodThreadDone;
}

void __fastcall TForm1::GoodThreadDone(TObject* Sender)
{
  delete T2;
  ButtonsOff(false);
  ShowMessage("On Terminate for Thread 2 received");
}

void __fastcall TForm1::BadThreadDone(TObject* Sender)
{
  delete BadThread;
  ShowMessage("On Terminate for Bad Thread received");
}

void __fastcall TForm1::FormCreate(TObject *Sender)
{
```

```
    Memo1->Text =
      "Press the Good Thread button and you will find that you can "
      "move the window around, or resize it, while the thread is "
      "running. Press the Bad Thread button and you will find that "
      "the window is inert while the thread is running.";
}
```

This program has two buttons on it. If you click the button labeled Bad Thread, you start a thread that is poorly designed. While it is running, you will find that it takes up all the cycles allocated to the program. You can't do anything else in the program while this thread is running. The second button in the program, Good Thread, enables you to move or resize the program window while it is running. It is a well-behaved thread.

The key methods for the TThread class are as follows:

- The constructor
- Execute()
- Synchronize()

The TThread constructor is meant to start and run the thread. It doesn't just allocate memory for the thread; it actually creates and calls the thread. The thread is actually running by the time the constructor has ended. TThread's internal thread function does little more than call the Execute() method.

The Execute() method is declared as a pure virtual function. This makes TThread an abstract base class. As such, you cannot use the TThread class directly. Instead, you must create a descendent of TThread and override the Execute() method. An example follows:

```
class TMyThread2 : public TThread {
  private:
    int FCount;
    void __fastcall RunUpdate();
  protected:
    void __fastcall Execute();
  public:
    __fastcall TMyThread2(bool CreateSuspended);
};
```

Every time you create a descendent of a TThread object, you override the Execute() method. That's a given. In essence, the Execute() method becomes the thread function itself. In the case shown here, I have also included an FCount variable and a method called RunUpdate().

The following implementation of TMyThread2 is the "good" thread in the Thread1a example:

```
void __fastcall TMyThread2::RunUpdate()
{
  Form1->Panel1->Caption = FCount;
}

void __fastcall TMyThread2::Execute()
{
  InvalidateRect(Form1->Handle, 0, true);
  for (int i = 1;i<=100000;i++)
    if (i % 10 == 0) {
      FCount = i;
      Synchronize(RunUpdate);
    }
  PostMessage(Form1->Handle, wm_ThreadDone, 2, 0);
}
```

This code simply counts from 1 to 100,000 while regularly updating the user as to the status of the operation.

The thread begins by clearing the screen. It doesn't do so by calling the internal VCL function called Invalidate(). Instead, it calls the Windows API function called InvalidateRect(). The reason for this is simple: Invalidate() is a method of TForm, and as such is out of bounds to call inside a thread. That's no big deal; you can just call InvalidateRect() instead.

After clearing the screen, the code iterates through a loop 100,000 times. Each time it completes 10 cycles, it prints out the current iteration to the screen with a standard VCL function:

```
Form1->Panel1->Caption = FCount;
```

It does not, however, call this function directly. Instead, it wraps the function inside a method called RunUpdate(), and it wraps the call to that function inside a method called Synchronize():

```
Synchronize(RunUpdate);
```

Your thread temporarily becomes part of the main thread for the executable while Synchronize() is executing. This means that the main thread for the program is temporarily halted—it is not running. Instead, your thread is running. As soon as the Synchronize() method is finished, the thread resumes.

The point is that the main thread is not running when Synchronize() is called; therefore, the VCL cannot receive any other messages. It is safe for you to call the VCL during the time that Synchronize() is executing.

The key point is that you should get out of the Synchronize() procedure as quickly as possible. The following code is an example of the wrong way to call Synchronize() as a secondary thread:

```
void __fastcall TBadThread::RunUpdate()
{
  for (int i = 1;i<=100000;i++) {
    Form1->Panel1->Caption = i;
    Form1->Panel1->Update(); // Wouldn't have to do this in good thread
  }
}

void __fastcall TBadThread::Execute()
{
  InvalidateRect(Form1->Handle, 0, true);
  Synchronize(RunUpdate);
  PostMessage(Form1->Handle, wm_ThreadDone, 1, 0);
}
```

In this case, the entire loop executes inside the call to Synchronize(). Taking this approach might seem like the right thing to do because most of the time spent in the loop is dedicated to updating the main screen of the program. The flaw in this theory, however, is that the application's main thread never gets a chance to execute while Synchronize() is being called. As a result, the program doesn't really have two threads running; it has just one. The secondary thread has taken over the main thread, thereby rendering the whole enterprise worthless. It isn't really a bug, and it doesn't threaten the stability of the program, but it's a classic case of poor design. (Not that you should feel bad if you have done this. I wouldn't have the example here to present if I hadn't fallen in this trap once myself.)

I ought to say a couple of other things about the TThread object before closing this section. An event called OnTerminate can be sent to your program at the appropriate time:

```
void __fastcall TForm1::bGoodThreadClick(TObject *Sender)
{
  ButtonsOff(true);
  T2 = new TMyThread2(false);
  T2->OnTerminate = GoodThreadDone;
}

void __fastcall TForm1::GoodThreadDone(TObject* Sender)
{
  delete T2;
  ButtonsOff(false);
  ShowMessage("On Terminate for Thread 2 received");
}
```

You can see that I have set up the GoodThreadDone() method so that it will be called when the TMyThread2 object has completed its run.

5

THREADS

A trap that you need to avoid involves the WaitFor() method of TThread. This method enables the main program to wait until the thread finishes executing. Calling WaitFor() if the thread is going to call Synchronize() is a serious error. You then end up with a deadlock in which the thread waits for the main program and the main program waits for the thread. In the meantime, nothing happens, and you are forced to shut the program down through the IDE or by pressing Ctrl+Alt+Delete. A call to WaitFor() under these circumstances should raise an exception.

In this section, you have seen how to use the TThread object to run a thread. The two key points to remember about the TThread object are that it gives you a safe way to call the VCL while a thread is running, and it gives you a way to create local variables that are used only by the thread. These variables are the data members of your TThread descendant. Windows also provides a technique for doing this called *thread local storage*. TLS is a powerful technique, but can be slower than using a TThread object to obtain the same end.

Setting a Thread's Priority

Not all threads need to be created equal. You can set a thread's priority level so that it gets more or fewer CPU cycles than other threads. The function used to set a thread's priority level is called SetThreadPriority().

The actual number of cycles a thread gets depends on its priority level and the priority class of its process. You can call GetPriorityClass() to get the priority of your process and you can call SetPriorityClass() to set the priority of your process. All the functions mentioned in this paragraph are Windows API functions.

The program shown in Listings 5.14 and 5.15 is the C++Builder version of a Delphi program written by David Intersimone, a fellow Inprise employee. You can find the program in the ThSorts directory for this chapter's code. It uses two blank forms saved in units called SecForm and ThForm. (The code has some historical significance, as it was written on the flight to the Windows 95 launch in Seattle and then updated during a flight to a recent Inprise conference in Germany.)

LISTING **5.14**   THE HEADER FOR DAVID INTERSIMONE'S DREADED SORTS PROGRAM, C++BUILDER VERSION

```
#ifndef MainH
#define MainH

#include <Classes.hpp>
#include <Controls.hpp>
```

```cpp
#include <StdCtrls.hpp>
#include <Forms.hpp>
#include <Buttons.hpp>
#include <ComCtrls.hpp>

const int pixeloffset = 5;   // pixeloffset provides a border area
                             // inside the window
const int formgap = 10;      // # of pixel gap between main form and
                             // sorting windows
const TColor formcolor = clBlack;  // background color for the sort
                                   // form windows
const TColor pixelcolor = clWhite; // pixel color for the sort
                                   // data items

class TForm1 : public TForm
{
__published:    // IDE-managed Components
  TLabel *Label2;
  TLabel *Label1;
  TLabel *Label3;
  TLabel *Label4;
  TLabel *Label5;
  TEdit *Edit1;
  TTrackBar *BubbleTrackBar;
  TTrackBar *QuickTrackBar;
  TButton *Button1;
  void __fastcall Button1Click(TObject *Sender);
  void __fastcall FormDestroy(TObject *Sender);
  void __fastcall FormCreate(TObject *Sender);
private:        // User declarations
  HANDLE T1;
  HANDLE T2;
  int ScreenWidth, ScreenHeight, SortWindowClientArea;
  int FrameSize, CaptionSizem, SortWindowSize;
public:         // User declarations
  int* a;
  int* b;
  int NumItems;
  __fastcall TForm1(TComponent* Owner);
};

extern PACKAGE TForm1 *Form1;

#endif
```

LISTING 5.15   MAIN UNIT FOR DAVID INTERSIMONE'S DREADED SORTS PROGRAM,
C++BUILDER VERSION

```cpp
#include <vcl.h>
#include <math.h>
#include <stdlib.h>
#pragma hdrstop

#include "Main.h"
#include "SecForm.h"
#include "ThForm.h"

#pragma package(smart_init)
#pragma resource "*.dfm"
TForm1 *Form1;

__fastcall TForm1::TForm1(TComponent* Owner)
  : TForm(Owner), a(0), b(0)
{
}

// bubble sort procedure - called by BubbleThread function
void BubbleSort(int* ia, int items)
{
  HDC DC = GetDC(Form2->Handle);
  int t;
  for (int i = items;i>0;i—)
  {
    for (int j = 0;j<items;j++)
      if (ia[j] < ia[j+1])
      {
        t = ia[j];
        // use the value from the array for x, use the index
        SetPixel(DC, ia[j+1]+pixeloffset, j+1+pixeloffset, formcolor);
        SetPixel(DC, ia[j]+pixeloffset, j+pixeloffset, formcolor);
        ia[j] = ia[j+1];
        ia[j+1] = t;
        SetPixel(DC, ia[j+1]+pixeloffset,j+1+pixeloffset, pixelcolor);
        SetPixel(DC, ia[j]+pixeloffset,j+pixeloffset, pixelcolor);
      }
  }
  ReleaseDC(Form2->Handle, DC);
}

// quick sort void - called by QuickThread function
void QuickSort(int* ia, int iLo, int iHi)
{
  int T;
  int Lo = iLo;
  int Hi = iHi;
  int mid = ia[(Lo+Hi) / 2];
```

```
   HDC DC;
   do {
     DC = GetDC(Form3->Handle);
     while (ia[Lo] < mid)
       Lo++;
     while (ia[Hi]> mid)
       Hi—;
     if (Lo <= Hi)
     {
       T = ia[Lo];
       SetPixel(DC, ia[Lo]+pixeloffset,Lo+pixeloffset, formcolor);
       SetPixel(DC, ia[Hi]+pixeloffset,Hi+pixeloffset, formcolor);
       ia[Lo] = ia[Hi];
       ia[Hi] = T;
       SetPixel(DC, ia[Lo]+pixeloffset,Lo+pixeloffset, pixelcolor);
       SetPixel(DC, ia[Hi]+pixeloffset,Hi+pixeloffset, pixelcolor);
       Lo++;
       Hi—;
       // sleep(5);
     }
   } while (Lo <= Hi);
   if (Hi> iLo) QuickSort(ia,iLo,Hi);
   if (Lo < iHi) QuickSort(ia,Lo,iHi);
   ReleaseDC(Form3->Handle, DC);
}

// bubble sort thread function
DWORD CALLBACK BubbleThread(void* parms)
{
  BubbleSort(Form1->a,Form1->NumItems-1);
  return 0;
}

// quick sort thread function
DWORD CALLBACK QuickThread(void* parms)
{
  QuickSort(Form1->b,0,Form1->NumItems-1);
  return 0;
}

void __fastcall TForm1::Button1Click(TObject *Sender)
{
  DWORD ThreadID;
  // place bubblesort form on desktop
  delete Form2;
  Form2 = new TForm2(this);
  Form2->Top = Form1->Top+Form1->Height+formgap;
  Form2->Left = (ScreenWidth-(SortWindowSize*2)) / 2;
  // place bubblesort window on left half of screen
  Form2->Width = SortWindowSize;
  Form2->Height = SortWindowSize;
```

continues

5

THREADS

LISTING 5.15   CONTINUED

```
Form2->Color = formcolor;
Form2->Caption = "Bubble Sort";
Form2->Show();

// place quicksort form on desktop
delete Form3;
Form3 = new TForm3(this);
Form3->Top = Form1->Top+Form1->Height+formgap;
Form3->Left = Form2->Left+Form2->Width;   // place quicksort window
                                          // on right half of screen
Form3->Width = SortWindowSize;
Form3->Height = SortWindowSize;
Form3->Color = formcolor;
Form3->Caption = "Quick Sort";
Form3->Show();

// set # of items to sort equal to the form
// clientwidth - pixeloffset border
NumItems = Form2->ClientHeight - pixeloffset*2;

// allocate arrays to hold sort data
delete[] a;
a = new int[NumItems];
delete[] b;
b = new int[NumItems];

// generate random numbers to sort
randomize();
for (int i = 0;i<NumItems;i++)
{
  a[i] = random(NumItems);
  b[i] = a[i];
  Form2->Canvas->Pixels[a[i]+pixeloffset][i+pixeloffset] = pixelcolor;
  Form3->Canvas->Pixels[b[i]+pixeloffset][i+pixeloffset] = pixelcolor;
}
// start bubblesort thread
T1 = CreateThread(0,0,BubbleThread,0,0,&ThreadID);
// set bubblesort thread to the track bar position value
SetThreadPriority(T1, BubbleTrackBar->Position);

// start quicksort thread
T2 = CreateThread(0,0,QuickThread,0,0,&ThreadID);
// set quicksort thread to the track bar position value
SetThreadPriority(T2, QuickTrackBar->Position);
// note:  to see the recursive quick sort in action - set its
//        thread priority to -1 || -2
//        to see if bubble sort can beat quick sort, set its
//        thread priority to +2 && quick sort to -2

}
```

```
void __fastcall TForm1::FormDestroy(TObject *Sender)
{
  delete[] a;
  delete[] b;
}

void __fastcall TForm1::FormCreate(TObject *Sender)
{
  // get size of desktop
  ScreenWidth = GetSystemMetrics(SM_CXSCREEN);
  ScreenHeight = GetSystemMetrics(SM_CYSCREEN);

  // move the main form to the top center of the desktop
  Form1->Top = 0;
  Form1->Left = (ScreenWidth - Form1->Width) / 2;

  // determine how many items can be displayed in the 2 windows
  SortWindowSize = ScreenHeight-Form1->Height;
  if (SortWindowSize> (ScreenWidth / 2))
    SortWindowSize = ScreenWidth / 2;
}
```

The Dreaded Sorts program creates two threads. One thread runs a bubble sort and the second runs a quick sort. You can use trackbars to adjust the priority of the bubble sort upward, so that it gets lots of clock cycles, while simultaneously lowering the priority of the quick sort. The end result is that the bubble sort finishes in about the same time as the quick sort, even though it is a much slower algorithm. The two extra blank forms used by the project visually depict the progress of the sorts, as shown in Figure 5.5.

FIGURE 5.5

The bubble sort, shown on the left, is naturally slower than the quick sort, shown on the right.

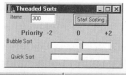
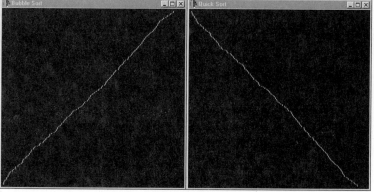

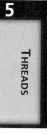

Code that sets a thread's priority looks like this:

```
T1 = CreateThread(0,0,BubbleThread,0,0,&ThreadID);
SetThreadPriority(T1, BubbleTrackBar->Position);
T2 = CreateThread(0,0,QuickThread,nil,0,&ThreadID);
SetThreadPriority(T2, QuickTrackBar->Position);
```

You can see two threads being created. Each thread is assigned a priority by the
`SetThreadPriority()` function. Here's the declaration for `SetThreadPriority()`:

```
BOOL SetThreadPriority(
  HANDLE hThread,     // handle to the thread
  int nPriority       // thread priority level
);
```

The following constants can be passed in the second parameter of
`SetThreadPriority()`:

```
THREAD_PRIORITY_LOWEST = THREAD_BASE_PRIORITY_MIN;
THREAD_PRIORITY_BELOW_NORMAL = THREAD_PRIORITY_LOWEST + 1;
THREAD_PRIORITY_NORMAL = 0;
THREAD_PRIORITY_HIGHEST = THREAD_BASE_PRIORITY_MAX;
THREAD_PRIORITY_ABOVE_NORMAL = THREAD_PRIORITY_HIGHEST - 1;
THREAD_PRIORITY_ERROR_RETURN = MAXLONG;
THREAD_PRIORITY_TIME_CRITICAL = THREAD_BASE_PRIORITY_LOWRT;
THREAD_PRIORITY_IDLE = THREAD_BASE_PRIORITY_IDLE;
```

You can use the following constants to help make sense of the values shown earlier:

```
THREAD_BASE_PRIORITY_LOWRT = 15; // gets a thread to LowRealtime-1
THREAD_BASE_PRIORITY_MAX = 2;    // maximum thread base priority boost
THREAD_BASE_PRIORITY_MIN = -2;   // minimum thread base priority boost
THREAD_BASE_PRIORITY_IDLE = -15; // value that gets a thread to idle
```

Related functions that you should look up in the Win32 online help include
`SetPriorityClass()` and `GetPriorityClass()`.

The Dreaded Sorts program is interesting to study; you should spend some time with it
if you are interested in this subject, or if you just need a chance to sit back and have
some fun.

C++Builder Threads Revisited

You have seen that even fairly sophisticated manipulation of threads is not difficult.
Using the information presented in this book, you can add a great deal of powerful
thread technology to your programs. However, be careful not to make your program
nothing but a series of threads. If you get carried away, you are likely to get into some
very complicated design problems. Use threads when you need them and when you can

see how they fit into your program from beginning to end. Try to avoid creating programs that become a mangled tangle of threads. The result could become a new form of spaghetti code called mangled tangled code. Avoid it.

On multiprocessor systems, different threads can end up executing on different processors, which is an enormously powerful concept. Just imagine one Pentium executing your graphics code, while the second parses a spreadsheet, and the third opens an SQL query. In the multitier world of C++Builder 4 programming, you can even have threads executing on separate machines, with one machine working on one part of your program, while a second machine works on another part.

The information presented here is complete, and it can serve as a reliable basis for using threads in an application. However, it is not the whole story, and you should pursue the matter further if you are interested in the subject and its possibilities. In particular, the major subject I did not have time to cover here was thread local storage, though I did mention that the TThread object serves as a more than adequate substitute for this technology. You can find out more about thread local storage in Jeffrey Richter's excellent book, *Advanced Windows* (Microsoft Press).

If you elect to use TLS, you can use the C++Builder __thread keyword instead of actually calling the Win32 TLS API routines to allocate storage local to each thread. This keyword tells the compiler that the variable is a TLS variable and that the compiler should handle making any needed Win32 API calls in order for it to be accessed. The __thread keyword is applicable to global and static local variables only. An example follows:

```
int __thread ThreadVar;
```

C++Builder also supports the Microsoft Visual C++ syntax for this keyword. An example follows:

```
__declspec(thread) int ThreadVar;
```

Summary

In this chapter you explored multitasking and threads. When working with threads, you saw how to create single threads. You also saw how to allocate memory so that you can pass in data to a single thread that has multiple copies of itself running at one time. You also saw the reverse of this process: how to synchronize multiple threads so that they can all share access to a single block of data. In particular, you studied critical sections and mutexes.

5

THREADS

You also got a good look at the TThread object that is part of the C++Builder VCL. The TThread object enables you to use both the VCL and threads at the same time. This statement is somewhat misleading in that there are no inherent conflicts between the VCL and threads, and indeed, the TThread object is very much a part of the VCL. However, most of the TComponent descendants are incompatible with threads. You will find some exceptions, such as the TOpenDialog component, which works properly as long as it is created in code. The TQuery and TTable objects also work inside threads, as long as you handle them properly. However, most visual VCL objects won't work inside threads unless you use the TThread object.

Writing NT Services

by Kent Reisdorph

IN THIS CHAPTER

CHAPTER 6

C++Builder 4 introduces a new application type to make writing Windows NT services easier than it's ever been before. In this chapter I'll explain how to create NT services using C++Builder. I'll start with a description of services and how they work under NT. After that I'll get into the specifics of writing services with C++Builder.

> **NOTE**
>
> The NT Service Wizard is available in the Professional and Enterprise versions of C++Builder. The Enterprise version shipped with the NT Service Wizard, but the Professional version did not initially ship with this wizard. Professional owners can download the NT Service Wizard from the borland.com Web site at
> http://www.borland.com/devsupport/bcppbuilder/file_supplements.html.

Understanding NT Services

An NT service is a specialized application that can be automatically started when the operating system starts. As its name implies, an NT service is designed to be used on machines running Windows NT server or workstation. NT services have the following features:

- They can be configured to start automatically, even when no user is logged on.
- They can control access through user access rights.
- They can be configured remotely by a network administrator.
- They can operate independently or can be dependant on another service.

A common use of an NT service is as a server of one form or another. For example, Microsoft's primary Web server, Internet Information Server (IIS), is implemented as a service, as are the Microsoft FTP, news, and Exchange servers. Borland's InterBase is implemented as a service as well. (InterBase is discussed in detail in Chapter 11, "Working with the Local InterBase Server.") Other services perform system functions such as the Spooler (for spooling print jobs), Directory Replicator, Event Log, and Messenger services.

Many NT services run invisibly with no user intervention required or desired. Other services, called *interactive services*, allow some user interaction. Interactive services often display an icon in the system tray and usually display a configuration dialog to the user so he or she can set service parameters. An example of this type of service is the Borland Socket Server, which can be run as either an external application or as a service. (The Borland Socket Server is described in Chapter 21, "ActiveForms," in the section

"Creating the MIDAS-Based ActiveForm"). The Borland Socket Server displays an icon in the system tray. Double-clicking the icon in the tray displays a configuration dialog as shown in Figure 6.1.

FIGURE 6.1

The Borland Socket Server service displays a configuration dialog that allows the user to set server parameters.

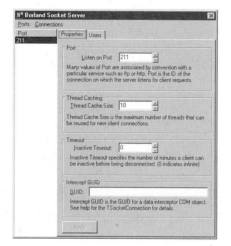

Services can be configured to operate in one of the following startup modes:

- Automatic—The service starts automatically when the operating system loads.
- Manual—The service isn't initially started but can be started manually by the user. (I'll describe how to start a service later in the section, "Controlling Services.")
- Disabled—The service is installed but is disabled. Disabled services can be started manually by changing the startup mode.

The startup mode you select depends on what your service does. Most services are configured to start automatically. The important thing to understand about services configured to start automatically is that they will begin when the operating system starts, even if no user is logged on. In other words, automatic services start as soon as the operating system loads. This means that by the time the Windows NT logon screen appears, NT has already started to load all the automatic services. It may take a while for all the services to start but they will all eventually start (assuming no errors occur within the services). This is important because many services run on NT servers that don't typically require any user interaction. A server may be started and then not be looked at again for days or weeks unless something goes wrong or until some maintenance is required. If you are writing an interactive service, be sure that the service can start without requiring any input from the user.

Services configured to start manually can be started in one of two ways:

1. By another service
2. By human intervention

An example of a service that is started by another service is the InterBase Server. Assuming you have installed the InterBase Guardian, the guardian will keep an eye on the InterBase Server and will restart the server if for some reason it goes down. InterBase Guardian is configured to start automatically. InterBase Server, on the other hand, is configured to start manually. When the operating system loads, InterBase Guardian is automatically started and it, in turn, starts the InterBase Server service.

Very few services are configured to start disabled. I can think of at least one service that, at least on some NT systems, may be configured to start disabled. Before I explain this scenario, let me first sidetrack a minute and describe how service applications work.

A service lives in a binary file called a *service program*. A service program may contain a single service or it may contain multiple services. Windows NT places several services in the service program called SERVICES.EXE. Among the services in this service application are the Alerter, Computer Browser, DHCP Client, Event Log, Messenger, Server, and Workstation services. When SERVICES.EXE is installed, all services that reside in it are installed. Depending on your NT system configuration, not all of these services are required. That leads us back to the issue of services that are configured to start disabled.

The DHCP Client service is one of several services found in SERVICES.EXE. (Exactly what a DHCP server does is not important. Essentially, it takes care of managing IP addresses on a network.) Depending on how NT was installed, the DHCP Client service may or may not be required. Because the DHCP Client service is part of SERVICES.EXE it is installed by default; it is installed as disabled, however, for those NT configurations that don't require a DHCP client. It is unlikely that you will write a service that is installed in disabled mode.

Services are managed by the operating system's Service Control Manager (SCM). The SCM maintains a database of installed services and their configurations. This information is stored in the Registry. You can see the list of installed services by running Regedit and examining this key:

```
HKEY_LOCAL_MACHINE\SYSTEM\CurrentControlSet\Services
```

You will unlikely modify this Registry key directly. Instead, you will use one of several utilities to modify a service's configuration parameters. Those utilities are discussed in the next section, "Controlling Services."

A service can be created as one of three types: Win32, device driver, or file system driver. A Win32 service is a generic type of service. Win32 services can perform a wide variety of functions. As you might guess, device driver and file system driver services are low-level services that require specialized programming skills to write. The rest of this chapter will focus solely on Win32 services as driver services are beyond the scope of this book.

As I said earlier, some services are dependant on other services in order to operate. Naturally, this type of service should not be started until all the other services it relies on have been started. Windows allows you to specify a service's dependencies when you create the service. Windows won't attempt to start your service until all the services on which it depends have started.

You can also specify the security attributes for your service. You can specify that the service should use the built-in LocalSystem account or you can specify a username and password for the service. All services using the LocalSystem account inherit the security context of the SCM. This has several implications for services. Rather than attempt to describe those implications, I'll instead suggest that you read the Win32 API help topic, "The LocalSystem Account." To find this help topic, search the help index for the "Services" topic and hit the Next Topic browse button until you find the LocalSystem account topic. Most services use the LocalSystem account.

> **NOTE**
>
> If you have a service application that contains more than one service, then all services in the service application must use the LocalSystem account. If you are writing an interactive service (one that displays a dialog to the user), then that service must use the LocalSystem account as well.

Controlling Services

Services are managed by the operating system's SCM. The SCM keeps track of the installed services and each service's current state. The SCM can be accessed by one of several Windows NT utilities, including the following:

- The NET.EXE command-line utility
- The Services Control Panel (SCP) applet
- The Win32 SDK command-line utility, SC.EXE
- The Server Manager

These utilities allow you to perform some or all of the following:

- View all installed services
- Start a service
- Stop a service
- Pause a service
- Continue running a paused service
- Specify command-line arguments for a service
- Set the hardware profile in which a service will operate
- Set a service's startup mode

I'll address these utilities from the simplest to the most complex.

Controlling Services with NET.EXE

The NET.EXE utility is a workhorse in NT. You are probably most familiar with this utility as a way to map a network drive from the command line. NET.EXE's service control features are somewhat limited; it only allows you to start, stop, pause, and continue a paused service. The NET.EXE commands specific to services are, not surprisingly, START, STOP, PAUSE, and CONTINUE. You pass the service control command you want to issue followed by the name of the service you want to control. To stop a service, for example, you would enter something like this at the command line:

```
net stop myservice
```

NET.EXE will respond with a message indicating the result of the service control command. For example, NET.EXE reports the following if the service is successfully stopped:

```
The MyService service was stopped successfully.
```

The rest of the service control commands are simple enough that they don't warrant additional attention. I should mention, however, that NET.EXE can also list the services that are currently started on your system. To list all started services, run NET.EXE with the START command and without supplying a service name:

```
net start
```

On my system, running NET.EXE in this manner produced the following output:

```
These Windows NT services are started:

   Alerter
   Borland Socket Server
   Computer Browser
   EventLog
```

```
IIS Admin Service
InterBase Guardian
InterBase Server
License Logging Service
Messenger
MSDTC
NT LM Security Support Provider
Plug and Play
Protected Storage
Remote Access Connection Manager
Remote Procedure Call (RPC) Service
Server
Spooler
TCP/IP NetBIOS Helper
Telephony Service
Workstation
World Wide Web Publishing Service
```

```
The command completed successfully.
```

NET.EXE doesn't provide much control over services, but if you are a command line fan and want to simply start, stop, pause, or continue a service, you might find this utility preferable to the others discussed.

Controlling Services with the Service Control Panel Applet

Without question, the easiest way to control services is using the Services Control Panel (SCP) applet. To start the SCP, open the Control Panel and double-click the Services icon. Figure 6.2 shows the SCP as it looks on my system.

FIGURE 6.2

The Services Control Panel applet allows you to manipulate services.

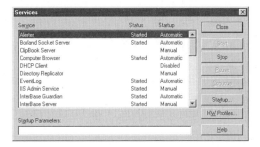

The SCP allows you to stop, start, pause, and continue services with the click of a button. Depending on how the service is written, the Stop and Pause buttons for a particular service may be disabled. Some services simply don't take kindly to being stopped or paused. For example, the Remote Procedure Call (RPC) service is vital to the way NT operates and stopping this service would likely bring the entire system to its knees. As such, the authors of the RPC service stipulated that it can't be stopped or paused. Later I'll show you how to specify whether your service allows stopping and pausing.

The SCP also allows you to change the startup mode of a service. A dialog like that shown in Figure 6.3 is displayed when you click the Startup button. The Startup Type section of this dialog allows you to select Automatic, Manual, or Disabled. Obviously, you don't want to change these settings for system services unless you know exactly what you are doing. The Log On As section allows you to set the startup security for the service. Note the checkbox labeled Allow Service to Interact with Desktop. This checkbox is checked when a service has the ability to display a dialog to the user. I'll show you how to display a form from a service in the "Writing Interactive Services" section.

FIGURE 6.3

The Startup dialog of the Service Control Panel applet allows you to modify the startup mode for a service.

The SCP is good for quickly testing your service's capability to start, stop, pause, and continue. This is beneficial when you are developing a service. All you have to do is click the appropriate button and see how the service responds (or doesn't respond, as the case may be).

One problem with the SCP is that it has no capability to refresh its display. This means that you will have to close the SCP and reopen it to see any changes to installed services. Say, for example, that you have the SCP open and you install a service you are writing. The service won't be displayed in the list of installed services until you close the SCP and open it again from the Control Panel.

NOTE

Earlier I said that services can be controlled from NT's Server Manager utility. When you choose Computer, Services from the Server Manager menu, NT will display the Service Control Panel applet just as you see it when you run it from the Control Panel.

It's easy to think of the Service Control Panel applet as the system's Service Control Manager. It is simply an interface to the SCM, though—not the SCM itself.

Controlling Services with SC.EXE

The SC.EXE utility ships with the Win32 SDK and with the Microsoft Development Network (MSDN) CD-ROM. If you have the SDK or MSDN, you can use this utility to control services from the command line. SC.EXE provides much more control over services than do either the NET.EXE utility or the SCM. In particular, SC.EXE allows you to control a service on a remote machine and to get detailed status information from a service. Explaining how to use SC.EXE is beyond the scope of this book. If you want to know more about this utility, see the article "Using SC.EXE to Develop Windows NT Services" either on the MSDN CD-ROM or on Microsoft's Web site.

Writing Services with C++Builder

Writing a service with the Windows API can be a daunting task. There are a lot of rules to follow to ensure that your service works and plays well with both the operating system and with the SCM. Fortunately, C++Builder provides an application type called a *service application* that greatly simplifies writing services. In fact, writing services with C++Builder using the service application is relatively easy. To create a new service application, choose File, New from the C++Builder main menu and double-click the service application icon. C++Builder will create a service application. Again, a service application may contain a single service or multiple services. When C++Builder creates a service application, it creates a new service at the same time. Figure 6.4 shows the C++Builder IDE after creating a new service application.

FIGURE 6.4

The C++Builder IDE as it looks after creating a new service application.

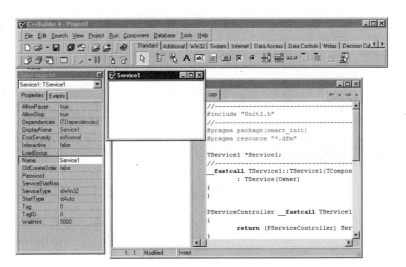

The service application itself is an instance of the TServiceApplication class and is more or less invisible, just as a regular GUI program's Application object is invisible. The form you see in Figure 6.4 is actually the service itself, not the service application. You may have noticed that the service looks much like a data module. This is no coincidence; the class that represents a service, TService, is in fact derived from TDataModule. (Data modules are discussed in Chapters 8 through 10.) The following sections describe the TServiceApplication and TService classes. These classes, along with supporting classes, are defined in the VCL unit called SvcMgr.pas. The declarations, naturally, can be found in SvcMgr.hpp.

The TServiceApplication Class

As I have said, a service's main application is an instance of the TServiceApplication class. TServiceApplication has only two properties and no methods beyond what its base classes provide. The ServiceCount property returns the count of the services within the service application. The Title property can be used to specify a title for the service application. The text in the Title property is used when the service application is minimized. To be honest, I find the existence of the Title property a bit strange for a service application; a service application doesn't have a main form that can be minimized. Nonetheless, the Title property is there should you ever need to use it.

On the surface, TServiceApplication appears to be extremely simple. It does a great deal of work behind the scenes, though. Specifically, it performs much of the work you would have to do if you were writing a service using the API. This includes installing and uninstalling services, handling exceptions, and managing the service's main thread. (I'll discuss the service's main thread in the next section.) The TServiceApplication class handles service application chores behind the scenes and, as such, you won't have much interaction with this class when writing services.

The TService Class

The TService class represents a service in C++Builder. This is the class by which you will control your service, determine its type, its configuration, and its security attributes. In this section I give you an overview of the TService class. In the next section, "Writing a Simple Service," I apply the information provided in this section to practical use.

As I have said, when you create a service application, C++Builder automatically creates a service for that application. You can add additional services to a service application by choosing File, New, and then double-clicking the service icon in the Object Repository.

Almost all of a service's parameters are controlled by the TService properties. Table 6.1 lists the primary TService properties and provides a description of each.

TABLE 6.1 THE PRIMARY TService PROPERTIES

Property	Description
AllowPause	Indicates whether the service can be paused. When this property is true, the Pause button in the SCP is enabled when the service is selected. When false, the Pause button is disabled.
AllowStop	Indicates whether the service can be stopped. When this property is true, the Stop button in the SCP is enabled when the service is selected. When false, the Stop button is always disabled.
Dependencies	A list of service names that this service depends on in order to run.
DisplayName	The display name of the service as shown in the SCP.
ErrCode	The server-specific error code returned in case of an error or to provide status information. Use of this property is optional. You can set it to any error codes your service defines. If ErrCode is 0, then the Win32ErrCode property is used.
ErrorSeverity	Indicates how the service should be handled by the SCM if an error occurs when starting the service.
Interactive	Indicates whether this service can show a dialog to the user. Only applies to Win32 service types.
Name	The name of the service. The Name property has implications beyond how the Name property is used for most VCL components. The Name property identifies the name of the service as used by the SCM. If you use SC.EXE or NET.EXE to control a service, you must pass the value of the Name property, not the DisplayName property.
Param	A list of parameters passed to the service at startup. Parameters can be specified in the SCP or from the command line when using the SC.EXE utility to start the service. This property is primarily used as a development tool as most services don't use parameters.
ParamCount	The number of parameters passed to the service.
Password	The password for the service. The password is only used for services not using the LocalSystem account.
ServiceStartName	The account name to which this service applies, in domain/username format.
ServiceThread	The internal thread for the service. This thread handles service commands and requests. The internal thread can be used for the service's processing or a separate thread can be spawned to perform service processing.
ServiceType	The service type. Can be stWin32 (for a Win32 service), stDevice (for device driver services), or stFileSystem (for file system services).

continues

TABLE 6.1   CONTINUED

Property	Description
Status	Reports the current status of the service (running, stopped, paused, stop pending, and so on).
Terminated	Indicates whether the internal service thread has terminated.
WaitHint	The estimated amount of time the service is expected to respond to control commands or status requests. If the service does not respond within the time specified by WaitHint, the SCM will assume an error occurred in the service.
Win32ErrCode	Contains the system-defined error code when an error occurs (starting or stopping the service) and if the ErrCode property is 0.

The TService events are used to detect when a service is installed and when it is sent a stop, start, pause, or continue request. Table 6.2 shows the TService events and their descriptions.

TABLE 6.2   TService EVENTS

Event	Description
AfterInstall	Generated after the service is installed.
AfterUninstall	Generated when the service is uninstalled.
BeforeInstall	Generated when the service is about to be installed.
BeforeUninstall	Generated when the service is about to be uninstalled.
OnContinue	Generated when the SCM continues a paused service.
OnExecute	Generated after the service starts. Services using a user-defined thread will implement the thread in this event handler.
OnPause	Generated when the SCM pauses the service.
OnShutdown	Generated when the operating system is shutting down. Use this event to save any service-specific data.
OnStart	Generated when the SCM starts the service.
OnStop	Generated when the SCM stops the service.

TService only has two methods aside from what its base classes provide. The LogMessage() method sends a message to the NT event log. Messages can be viewed using NT's Event Viewer utility. I'll discuss the LogMessage() method later in the section, "Sending Messages to the Event Log." The ReportStatus() method sends a service's status information to the SCM. You probably won't use `ReportStatus()` very often, as these chores are handled for you automatically by the service application.

With this bit of information behind us, we can now move on to the more interesting topic of writing a simple service.

Writing a Simple Service

The example program for this section is called BeepSrvc. This service does nothing more than beep the PC speaker once each second. A service that beeps every second (or some other interval) is sort of the "Hello World" of NT services. It's not exactly exciting, but it will show you how services work. The service's name is BeepService. The header and source for the `BeepService` unit is shown in Listings 6.1 and 6.2.

LISTING 6.1 THE HEADER FOR THE BeepService UNIT

```
#ifndef BeepSrvcUH
#define BeepSrvcUH

#include <SysUtils.hpp>
#include <Classes.hpp>
#include <SvcMgr.hpp>

class TBeepService : public TService
{
__published:    // IDE-managed Components
  void __fastcall Service1Execute(TService *Sender);
private:          // User declarations
public:           // User declarations
  __fastcall TBeepService(TComponent* Owner);
  PServiceController __fastcall GetServiceController(void);
  friend void __stdcall ServiceController(unsigned CtrlCode);
};

extern PACKAGE TBeepService *BeepService;

#endif
```

LISTING 6.2 THE SOURCE CODE FOR THE BeepService UNIT

```
#include "BeepSrvcU.h"

#pragma package(smart_init)
#pragma resource "*.dfm"

TBeepService *BeepService;
```

continues

LISTING 6.2   CONTINUED

```
__fastcall TBeepService::TBeepService(TComponent* Owner)
        : TService(Owner)
{
}

PServiceController __fastcall TBeepService::GetServiceController(void)
{
  return (PServiceController) ServiceController;
}

void __stdcall ServiceController(unsigned CtrlCode)
{
  BeepService->Controller(CtrlCode);
}

void __fastcall TBeepService::Service1Execute(TService *Sender)
{
  while (!Terminated)
  {
    MessageBeep(0);
    Sleep(1000);
    ServiceThread->ProcessRequests(false);
  }
}
```

As you can see from these listings, this simple service contains very little code. Most of the hard stuff is handled behind the scenes by the TService and TServiceApplication classes. In fact, I wrote only four lines of code for this service. The rest of the code was generated by C++Builder. I'll address the code generated by C++Builder in the following section.

This service uses default values for all of the service's properties except for the Name and DisplayName properties, both of which I have set to BeepService.

> **TIP**
>
> You will save yourself some headaches if you set the Name and DisplayName properties to the same value. In fact, you'll notice that when you set the Name property in the Object Inspector, the DisplayName property changes to match. It's easier to manage your service during development when both the DisplayName and Name have the same value.
>
> When I first wrote this service I set the DisplayName property to BeepService and the Name property to BeepSrvc. I then used the SC.EXE utility to start and stop the service. I typed the following from the command line:
>
>   sc stop BeepService

> I kept getting an error from SC.EXE when using this syntax. It took me a couple of minutes to realize that I was passing the service's display name to SC.EXE when I should have been passing the service's actual name. The display name is simply the text that is displayed in the SCP for the service. The service name is the text that the SCM uses to refer to the service. The proper command-line syntax for stopping the service should have been the following:
>
> ```
> sc stop BeepSrvc
> ```
>
> By setting the Name and DisplayName properties to the same value, I eliminated the confusion caused by using two different values for these properties.

This service uses the default values for all other properties, allowing the service to be stopped, paused, and continued from the SCP or by using one of the service command-line utilities discussed earlier. The defaults also specify that this is a Win32 service, that it is not interactive (it cannot display a dialog to the user), and that it is set to auto-start when NT boots.

Understanding the C++Builder–Generated Code for Services

Before we get into what little code this service contains, I want to spend a moment discussing the code that C++Builder generates. You will find this code near the top of the main source unit:

```
PServiceController __fastcall TBeepService::GetServiceController(void)
{
  return (PServiceController) ServiceController;
}

void __stdcall ServiceController(unsigned CtrlCode)
{
  BeepService->Controller(CtrlCode);
}
```

Each service must have a function that processes service control requests. This function is commonly called the *service handler*. The service handler is registered with Windows by the TService class. As with many Windows callbacks, the service handler must be a standalone function. (It can't be a class member function.) The code you see here is the mechanism the VCL uses to implement the service handler. The implementation in SvcMgr.pas looks like this:

```
FStatusHandle :=
  RegisterServiceCtrlHandler(PChar(Name), GetServiceController);
```

Granted, this is Object Pascal code, but it's easy enough to understand even if you aren't a Pascal programmer. This code calls the Windows `RegisterServiceCtrlHandler()` function, passing the service name in the first parameter. The second parameter is a call to the service's `GetServiceController()` method. As you can see from the earlier code snippet, this method returns a pointer to the standalone `ServiceController()` function. Once registered, the `ServiceController()` function will be called each time the service receives a control request from the SCM. It's not vital that you understand service control requests at this time, but I wanted to explain the meaning of these two functions.

You may have noticed that the `ServiceController()` function calls the service's `Controller()` method. The `Controller()` method is declared as protected in the `TService` class. How does the standalone `ServiceController()` function gain access to the `Controller()` method? If you look at the service's class declaration in Listing 6.1, you will notice that the `ServiceController()` function is declared as a friend of the service class:

```
friend void __stdcall ServiceController(unsigned CtrlCode);
```

This makes it possible for the `ServiceController()` function to call the protected `Controller()` method.

> **NOTE**
>
> There is a minor bug in the code generation for service applications. When you create a new service, C++Builder gives the service a default name of `Service1`. It then generates a `ServiceController()` function that looks like this:
>
> ```
> void __stdcall ServiceController(unsigned CtrlCode)
> {
>   Service1->Controller(CtrlCode);
> }
> ```
>
> Now let's say you change the service's `Name` property to `MyService`. C++Builder will change all of the references to `Service1` with `MyService`, *except* the reference in the `ServiceController()` function. Before your code will compile, you will have to manually change the code in the `ServiceController()` function so that it uses the correct class name. In this case you would have to modify the code as follows:
>
> ```
> void __stdcall ServiceController(unsigned CtrlCode)
> {
>   MyService->Controller(CtrlCode);
> }
> ```

Service Threads and the OnExecute Event

Each service has its own thread. The ServiceThread property is a pointer to the service's internal thread. ServiceThread is an instance of the TServiceThread class. TServiceThread is derived from TThread. TServiceThread only provides one method beyond the usual methods of TThread. That method is ProcessRequests() and its purpose is to process service requests sent to the service by the SCM.

For simple services, you can use the service's built-in thread. That's what the BeepService example does. All of the code for the BeepService is in the service's OnExecute event handler:

```
void __fastcall TBeepService::Service1Execute(TService *Sender)
{
  while (!Terminated)
  {
    MessageBeep(0);
    Sleep(1000);
    ServiceThread->ProcessRequests(false);
  }
}
```

This code is fairly straightforward. It simply executes a loop as long as the service thread is still running. The code within the loop beeps the PC speaker, sleeps for one second, and then calls the service thread's ProcessRequests() method. The call to ProcessRequests() is vital. If you don't call ProcessRequests(), your service will execute the loop once and then stop.

This service is not very exciting. In fact, it's downright annoying when it's running. Still, it's a perfectly valid service and shows the simplest type of service you can write. What may not be obvious, though, is all the work being done behind the scenes by the VCL. You can find the code for this service on the book's CD-ROM. Load the project in C++Builder and build it. You can then proceed to the next step, installing the service.

Installing the Service

A service must be installed after it is built. Installing a service registers the service with the SCM. The SCM, in turn, adds the service's configuration information to the Registry. Figure 6.5 shows the Registry key for BeepService.

To install a service, run the service application from the command line using the INSTALL switch:

```
beepsrvc /install
```

FIGURE 6.5

*The Registry key
created by the
SCM when it
registered the
BeepService.*

After a second or so, you will see a message box that reads as follows:

```
Service installed successfully
```

If the service didn't install successfully, you'll need to check your code to see if you've missed anything. If you have loaded BeepService from the book's CD-ROM, it will install without error.

> **NOTE**
>
> NT services are, naturally, for use with the NT operating system. If you attempt to run a stock service application from Win9x, it will return without doing anything at all. Technically speaking, it is possible to run services in Win9x using various tricks and utilities. On the other hand, the Win9x operating systems certainly do not have full support for services and I do not attempt to cover the use of services on those platforms in this chapter.

To uninstall a service, first stop the service if it is started. (I discuss controlling services in the next section.) Run the service application again, this time with the UNINSTALL switch:

```
beepsrvc /uninstall
```

A message box will tell you that the service was successfully uninstalled. Understand that uninstalling a running service does not terminate the service; it only removes the service from the Registry. For that reason you should stop the service before uninstalling the service.

> **NOTE**
>
> While developing a service you will continually be in a cycle of changing code, compiling, and running the service to test the results of your code changes. It is not necessary to uninstall the service each time you build the service application from C++Builder. It is, however, necessary for you to stop the service before building the service application. Failure to stop the service prior to building the service application will result in a C++Builder linker error message that reads as follows:
>
> ```
> Could not open D:\Services\BeepSrvc.exe (program still running?).
> ```
>
> You will know that you need to stop the service before continuing if you get this error message when building the service application.

I usually keep a command prompt box open when developing a service. Once I have typed the install or uninstall command, I can easily install or uninstall a service by taking advantage of NT's capability to recall commands typed at the command prompt (using the up and down arrows on the keyboard).

Testing the Service

If the service installed successfully, open the SCP from the Control Panel and you will see the service listed among the other installed services. You will see the service name, BeepService, and the Startup type listed as Automatic. The `Status` column will be blank, indicating that the service is stopped. Even though the service is configured to start automatically, this doesn't happen until the system is restarted. You will have to reboot NT to test your service's auto-start capability.

To start BeepService, click the Start button on the SCP. NT will start the service and you will hear the PC speaker beep every second. Figure 6.6 shows the SCP when starting BeepService.

FIGURE 6.6

The SCP will start BeepService when you click the Start button.

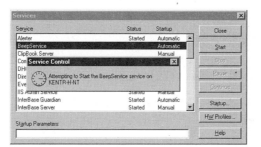

After the service has started, the Status column in the SCP will show Started. Test the service's capability to pause by clicking the Pause button. Restart the service by clicking the Continue button. Stop the service and restart it. You will notice that the service responds correctly to your control requests. The VCL takes care of handling the service control requests automatically. It's impossible to overstate the benefits of writing services with C++Builder. If you've ever had to write a service using the API, you can appreciate all the work that the VCL is doing in the background.

Most of the time it's convenient to simply use the SCP to start, stop, pause, continue, or configure your service. One annoyance of the SCP is that it has no associated taskbar button. This means that you can't easily find the SCP when it gets lost behind other windows. Further, the SCP has no capability to refresh its display. If the SCP is already running and you double-click its icon in the Control Panel, NT simply brings the SCP to the top—it won't update its display. Say, for example, that you have the SCP open and you install your service from a command prompt box. If you switch back to the SCP, your service won't show up in the list of installed services. You have to close the SCP and then reopen it by double-clicking the services icon in the Control Panel. If for some reason your service doesn't show up when installed or doesn't disappear when uninstalled, remember to close the SCP and reopen it.

Using a Separate Thread for the Service

You can use the service's built-in service thread for simple services. For other types of services, you probably want to spawn a separate thread to execute the service's code. Whether or not you do this depends largely on what the service does. If, for example, the service is expected to handle multiple client requests, then you may want a separate thread for each client request.

You should also use a separate thread for your service if your service performs lengthy startup tasks. The SCM allows two minutes for a service to start. The SCM instructs the service to start and then waits for a response from the service. If the response doesn't come back within two minutes, NT assumes that the service is hung and kills the service process. If your startup tasks will take longer than two minutes, you should spawn a separate thread to perform the startup tasks. This frees the service thread to handle service requests from the SCM.

Listings 6.3 and 6.4 show a modified beep service called BeepSrvcThread. This version of the beep services uses a separate thread to handle the service's code.

LISTING 6.3   THE HEADER FOR THE BEEPSRVCTHREAD PROGRAM

```
#ifndef BeepServiceThreadUH
#define BeepServiceThreadUH

#include <SysUtils.hpp>
#include <Classes.hpp>
#include <SvcMgr.hpp>

class TBeepThread : public TThread {
  public:
    virtual __fastcall void Execute();
    __fastcall TBeepThread(bool CreateSuspended);
};

class TBeepServiceThread : public TService
{
__published:     // IDE-managed Components
  void __fastcall BeepServiceThreadStart(
    TService *Sender, bool &Started);
  void __fastcall BeepServiceThreadStop(
    TService *Sender, bool &Stopped);
  void __fastcall BeepServiceThreadPause(
    TService *Sender, bool &Paused);
  void __fastcall BeepServiceThreadContinue(
    TService *Sender, bool &Continued);
private:          // User declarations
  TBeepThread* BeepThread;
public:           // User declarations
  __fastcall TBeepServiceThread(TComponent* Owner);
  PServiceController __fastcall GetServiceController(void);
  friend void __stdcall ServiceController(unsigned CtrlCode);
};

extern PACKAGE TBeepServiceThread *BeepServiceThread;

#endif
```

LISTING 6.4   THE SOURCE CODE FOR THE BEEPSRVCTHREAD PROGRAM

```
#include "BeepServiceThreadU.h"

#pragma package(smart_init)
#pragma resource "*.dfm"

TBeepServiceThread *BeepServiceThread;

// TBeepThread implementation
__fastcall TBeepThread::TBeepThread(bool CreateSuspended)
 : TThread(CreateSuspended)
```

continues

Listing 6.4   CONTINUED

```
{
}

void __fastcall TBeepThread::Execute()
{
  while (!Terminated) {
    MessageBeep(0);
    Sleep(1000);
  }
}

// TBeepServiceThread implementation
__fastcall TBeepServiceThread::TBeepServiceThread(TComponent* Owner)
        : TService(Owner)
{
}

PServiceController __fastcall
  TBeepServiceThread::GetServiceController(void)
{
        return (PServiceController) ServiceController;
}

void __stdcall ServiceController(unsigned CtrlCode)
{
        BeepServiceThread->Controller(CtrlCode);
}

void __fastcall TBeepServiceThread::BeepServiceThreadStart(
      TService *Sender, bool &Started)
{
  BeepThread = new TBeepThread(false);
  Started = true;
}

void __fastcall TBeepServiceThread::BeepServiceThreadStop(
  TService *Sender, bool &Stopped)
{
  BeepThread->Terminate();
  Stopped = true;
}

void __fastcall TBeepServiceThread::BeepServiceThreadPause(
  TService *Sender, bool &Paused)
{
  BeepThread->Suspend();
  Paused = true;
}
```

6

```
void __fastcall TBeepServiceThread::BeepServiceThreadContinue(
  TService *Sender, bool &Continued)
{
  BeepThread->Resume();
  Continued = true;
}
```

There are two important differences between this service and the BeepService program presented earlier:

1. This service does not use the service's OnExecute event.

2. This service provides event handlers for the OnStart, OnStop, OnPause, and OnContinue events.

Since I am not using the service's built-in service thread, I must take responsibility for specifically starting, stopping, suspending, and resuming my thread when the SCM sends the start, stop, pause, or continue requests. For example, the OnPause and OnContinue event handlers look like this:

```
void __fastcall TBeepServiceThread::BeepServiceThreadPause(
  TService *Sender, bool &Paused)
{
  BeepThread->Suspend();
  Paused = true;
}

void __fastcall TBeepServiceThread::BeepServiceThreadContinue(
  TService *Sender, bool &Continued)
{
  BeepThread->Resume();
  Continued = true;
}
```

Notice that I set the Paused parameter to true in the OnPause event handler after I suspended the thread. If I don't set Paused to true, Windows can't pause the thread. You may want to set Paused to false if your service is in a state where pausing the service will cause catastrophic results. Be aware, though, that if you do this, Windows will report an error if it cannot pause the service within three seconds. This same discussion applies to stopping a service or to continuing a paused service.

There isn't much more to say on the subject of using separate threads for your services. Actually, that statement is a bit misleading. The reality is that there is so much more to say on this subject that it would take dozens of pages to adequately cover it. I realize that this short example doesn't give you much information on the nitty-gritty details of dealing with threads in services. The reason is simply that services are so varied that I really can't anticipate what issues you might encounter with a particular service you might write.

Writing Interactive Services

An *interactive service* is one that can interact with the Windows desktop. Generally this means that the service can display a dialog to the user. Often the dialog allows the user to configure some aspect of how the service operates. The example program for the remainder of the subjects discussed in this chapter is called PingService. You can find the complete project on the book's CD-ROM. The service has the following functionality and features:

- Pings a remote machine at periodic intervals.
- If the remote machine doesn't respond to the ping, the service takes one of two actions depending on the service's configuration:
  - Logs the failure to the system Event Log.
  - Sends email to a specified address notifying you of the failure.
- When the remote machine comes back up, the event is logged (or email sent).
- A configuration dialog allows you to set the remote machine name, the ping interval, the notification type, the email address, and the email host to use for email notification.
- Configuration data is stored in the Registry to be reloaded the next time the service starts.
- Displays an icon representing the service in the system tray.
- Displays a pop-up menu for the tray icon.

The service has three units: The first is the service's main unit, the second is the thread that performs the ping, and the third is the service's configuration form. Listings 6.5 through 6.10 show each of the units and their headers.

LISTING 6.5   THE HEADER FOR THE PingService UNIT

```
#ifndef PingServiceUH
#define PingServiceUH

#include <SysUtils.hpp>
#include <Classes.hpp>
#include <SvcMgr.hpp>
#include <Controls.hpp>
#include <Menus.hpp>
#include <ExtCtrls.hpp>
#include "PingThreadU.h"

class TBCB4UnlPing : public TService
```

```
{
__published:     // IDE-managed Components
  void __fastcall BCB4UnlPingStart(TService *Sender, bool &Started);
  void __fastcall BCB4UnlPingStop(TService *Sender, bool &Stopped);
  void __fastcall BCB4UnlPingExecute(TService *Sender);
private:          // User declarations
public:           // User declarations
  TPingThread* PingThread;
  __fastcall TBCB4UnlPing(TComponent* Owner);
  PServiceController __fastcall GetServiceController(void);
protected:
  friend void __stdcall ServiceController(unsigned CtrlCode);
};

extern PACKAGE TBCB4UnlPing *BCB4UnlPing;

#endif
```

LISTING 6.6   THE SOURCE CODE FOR THE PingService UNIT

```
#include "PingServiceU.h"
#include "ConfigU.h"
#include "PingThreadU.h"

#pragma package(smart_init)
#pragma resource "*.dfm"

TBCB4UnlPing *BCB4UnlPing;

__fastcall TBCB4UnlPing::TBCB4UnlPing(TComponent* Owner)
        : TService(Owner)
{
}

PServiceController __fastcall TBCB4UnlPing::GetServiceController(void)
{
        return (PServiceController) ServiceController;
}

void __stdcall ServiceController(unsigned CtrlCode)
{
        BCB4UnlPing->Controller(CtrlCode);
}

void __fastcall TBCB4UnlPing::BCB4UnlPingStart(TService *Sender,
      bool &Started)
{
  PingThread = new TPingThread(false);
  ConfigForm->LoadConfiguration();
```

continues

LISTING 6.6   CONTINUED

```
  Started = true;
}

void __fastcall TBCB4UnlPing::BCB4UnlPingStop(TService *Sender,
      bool &Stopped)
{
  PingThread->Terminate();
  Stopped = true;
}

void __fastcall TBCB4UnlPing::BCB4UnlPingExecute(TService *Sender)
{
  while (!Terminated)
    ServiceThread->ProcessRequests(false);
}
```

LISTING 6.7   THE HEADER FOR THE TPingThread CLASS

```
#ifndef PingThreadUH
#define PingThreadUH
#include <NMsmtp.hpp>
#include <Psock.hpp>

class TPingThread : public TThread {
  private:
    bool ServerDownReported;
    int IPAddress;
    bool Ping();
    void SendMail(bool ServerUp);
  public:
    String IPString;
    String EMailToAddress;
    String EMailFromAddress;
    String EMailHostAddress;
    bool LogError;
    int PingInterval;
    void MakeIPAddress();
    virtual __fastcall void Execute();
    __fastcall TPingThread(bool CreateSuspended);
};

#endif
```

LISTING 6.8 THE SOURCE CODE FOR THE TPingThread CLASS

```cpp
#include <vcl.h>
#pragma hdrstop

extern "C" {
#include "ipexport.h""
#include "icmpapi.h"
}
#include "PingThreadU.h"
#include "PingServiceU.h"

#pragma package(smart_init)

const char* statusMsg = "The server at %s is %s";

__fastcall TPingThread::TPingThread(bool CreateSuspended)
 : TThread(CreateSuspended)
{
  LogError = true;
  PingInterval = 5000;
  IPAddress = -1;
  ServerDownReported = false;
  FreeOnTerminate = true;
}

void __fastcall TPingThread::Execute()
{
  while (!Terminated) {
    Sleep(PingInterval);
    if (IPString != "") {
      bool goodPing = Ping();
      if (!goodPing && !ServerDownReported) {
        if (LogError) {
          String Msg = String().sprintf(
            statusMsg, IPString.c_str(), "down.");
          BCB4UnlPing->LogMessage(
            Msg, EVENTLOG_INFORMATION_TYPE, 0, 0);
        }
        else
          SendMail(false);
        ServerDownReported = true;
      }
      if (goodPing && ServerDownReported) {
        ServerDownReported = false;
        if (LogError) {
          String Msg = String().sprintf(
            statusMsg, IPString.c_str(), "up.");
          BCB4UnlPing->LogMessage(
            Msg, EVENTLOG_INFORMATION_TYPE, 0, 0);
        }
```

continues

LISTING 6.8   CONTINUED

```
          else
            SendMail(true);
        }
      }
    }
}

bool TPingThread::Ping()
{
  bool result = true;
  HANDLE hIcmp = IcmpCreateFile();
  if (!hIcmp) {
    BCB4UnlPing->LogMessage("Unable to load ICMP.DLL. The "
      "service is terminating.", EVENTLOG_ERROR_TYPE, 0, 0);
    Terminate();
    return false;
  }
  int size = sizeof(icmp_echo_reply) + 8;
  char* buff = new char[size];
  DWORD res = IcmpSendEcho(
    hIcmp, IPAddress, 0, 0, 0, buff, size, 1000);
  if (!res)
    // timed out
    result = false;
  else {
    icmp_echo_reply reply;
    memcpy(&reply, buff, sizeof(reply));
    delete[] buff;
    if (reply.Status> 0)
      // error
      result = false;
  }
  IcmpCloseHandle(hIcmp);
  return result;
}

void TPingThread::SendMail(bool ServerUp)
{
  TNMSMTP* SMTP = new TNMSMTP(0);
  try {
    SMTP->PostMessage->FromName = "BCB 4 Unleashed Ping Service";
    SMTP->PostMessage->ToAddress->Add(EMailToAddress);
    SMTP->PostMessage->FromAddress = EMailFromAddress;
    SMTP->Host = EMailHostAddress;
    SMTP->PostMessage->Subject = "Server Alert";
    String Msg;
    if (ServerUp)
      Msg.sprintf(statusMsg, IPString.c_str(), "up.");
    else
      Msg.sprintf(statusMsg, IPString.c_str(), "down.");
```

```
      SMTP->PostMessage->Body->Add(Msg);
      SMTP->Connect();
      SMTP->SendMail();
    }
    catch (Exception& E) {
      BCB4UnlPing->LogMessage("Unable to send e-mail: " +
        E.Message, EVENTLOG_ERROR_TYPE, 0, 0);
      delete SMTP;
      return;
    }
    delete SMTP;
}

void TPingThread::MakeIPAddress()
{
  // Intialize Winsock.dll
  WSADATA wsaData;
  memset(&wsaData, 0, sizeof(WSADATA));
  #pragma warn -prc
  Word lowVersion = MAKEWORD(2, 0);
  int res = WSAStartup(lowVersion, &wsaData);
  if (res) {
    BCB4UnlPing->LogMessage("Unable to load Winsock. The "
      "service is terminating.", EVENTLOG_ERROR_TYPE, 0, 0);
    Terminate();
    return;
  }
  // Strip spaces from the IPString text
  for (int i=IPString.Length();i>0;i—) {
    if (IPString[i] == ' ')
      IPString.Delete(i, 1);
  }
  // Is the address in IP format?
  IPAddress = inet_addr(IPString.c_str());
  if (IPAddress == -1) {
    // Is the address a host name?
    hostent* he =
      gethostbyname(IPString.c_str());
    if (!he) {
      int error = WSAGetLastError();
      BCB4UnlPing->LogMessage("Winsock error: " + String(error),
        EVENTLOG_ERROR_TYPE, 0, 0);
      Terminate();
      return;
    }
    else
      memcpy(&IPAddress,
        he->h_addr_list[0], sizeof(int));
  }
  WSACleanup();
}
```

LISTING 6.9 THE HEADER FOR THE CONFIGURATION FORM

```cpp
#ifndef ConfigUH
#define ConfigUH

#include <Classes.hpp>
#include <Controls.hpp>
#include <StdCtrls.hpp>
#include <Forms.hpp>
#include <Registry.hpp>
#include <Menus.hpp>
#include <ExtCtrls.hpp>
#include <shellapi.h>

#define WM_PINGICONMESSAGE WM_USER + 1


class TConfigForm : public TForm
{
__published:    // IDE-managed Components
  TLabel *Label1;
  TLabel *Label2;
  TEdit *ServerEdit;
  TEdit *FrequencyEdit;
  TGroupBox *GroupBox1;
  TRadioButton *LogRadioBtn;
  TRadioButton *EmailRadioBtn;
  TEdit *EmailToEdit;
  TLabel *Label3;
  TButton *OKBtn;
  TLabel *Label4;
  TLabel *Label5;
  TEdit *EmailFromEdit;
  TEdit *EmailHostEdit;
  TPopupMenu *PopupMenu;
  TMenuItem *Configure;
  TTimer *Timer;
  void __fastcall OKBtnClick(TObject *Sender);
  void __fastcall FormShow(TObject *Sender);
  void __fastcall RadioButtonClick(TObject *Sender);
  void __fastcall FormDestroy(TObject *Sender);
  void __fastcall ConfigureClick(TObject *Sender);
  void __fastcall TimerTimer(TObject *Sender);
private:        // User declarations
  NOTIFYICONDATA IconData;
  void SaveConfiguration();
  void __fastcall PingIconMessage(TMessage& Msg);
    void AddIcon();
public:         // User declarations
  __fastcall TConfigForm(TComponent* Owner);
  void LoadConfiguration();
```

```
  BEGIN_MESSAGE_MAP
    VCL_MESSAGE_HANDLER(WM_PINGICONMESSAGE, TMessage, PingIconMessage)
  END_MESSAGE_MAP(TForm)
};

extern PACKAGE TConfigForm *ConfigForm;

#endif
```

LISTING 6.10   THE SOURCE CODE FOR THE CONFIGURATION FORM

```
#include <vcl.h>
#pragma hdrstop

#include "ConfigU.h"
#include "PingServiceU.h"

#pragma package(smart_init)
#pragma resource "*.dfm"
const char* regKey =
  "System\\CurrentControlSet\\Services\\BCB4UnlPing\\Parameters";
TConfigForm *ConfigForm;

__fastcall TConfigForm::TConfigForm(TComponent* Owner)
  : TForm(Owner)
{
}

void __fastcall TConfigForm::OKBtnClick(TObject *Sender)
{
  BCB4UnlPing->PingThread->IPString = ServerEdit->Text;
  if (BCB4UnlPing->PingThread->IPString != "")
    BCB4UnlPing->PingThread->MakeIPAddress();
  BCB4UnlPing->PingThread->PingInterval =
    FrequencyEdit->Text.ToIntDef(5000);
  BCB4UnlPing->PingThread->EMailFromAddress = EmailFromEdit->Text;
  BCB4UnlPing->PingThread->EMailToAddress = EmailToEdit->Text;
  BCB4UnlPing->PingThread->EMailHostAddress = EmailHostEdit->Text;
  BCB4UnlPing->PingThread->LogError = LogRadioBtn->Checked;
  SaveConfiguration();
  Close();
}

void __fastcall TConfigForm::FormShow(TObject *Sender)
{
  SetForegroundWindow(Handle);
  RadioButtonClick(0);
  ServerEdit->Text = BCB4UnlPing->PingThread->IPString;
  FrequencyEdit->Text = BCB4UnlPing->PingThread->PingInterval;
```

continues

LISTING 6.10 CONTINUED

```
  EmailFromEdit->Text = BCB4UnlPing->PingThread->EMailFromAddress;
  EmailToEdit->Text = BCB4UnlPing->PingThread->EMailToAddress;
  EmailHostEdit->Text = BCB4UnlPing->PingThread->EMailHostAddress;
  LogRadioBtn->Checked = BCB4UnlPing->PingThread->LogError;
  EmailRadioBtn->Checked = !BCB4UnlPing->PingThread->LogError;
}

void __fastcall TConfigForm::RadioButtonClick(TObject *Sender)
{
  if (LogRadioBtn->Checked) {
    EmailFromEdit->Enabled = false;
    EmailToEdit->Enabled = false;
    EmailHostEdit->Enabled = false;
    EmailFromEdit->Color = clBtnFace;
    EmailToEdit->Color = clBtnFace;
    EmailHostEdit->Color = clBtnFace;
  }
  else {
    EmailFromEdit->Enabled = true;
    EmailToEdit->Enabled = true;
    EmailHostEdit->Enabled = true;
    EmailFromEdit->Color = clWindow;
    EmailToEdit->Color = clWindow;
    EmailHostEdit->Color = clWindow;
  }
}

void TConfigForm::LoadConfiguration()
{
  TRegistry* reg = new TRegistry;
  reg->RootKey = HKEY_LOCAL_MACHINE;
  reg->OpenKey(regKey, true);
  if (reg->ValueExists("IPAddress")) {
    BCB4UnlPing->PingThread->IPString = reg->ReadString("IPAddress");
    BCB4UnlPing->PingThread->MakeIPAddress();
    BCB4UnlPing->PingThread->EMailToAddress =
      reg->ReadString("EMailTo");
    BCB4UnlPing->PingThread->EMailFromAddress =
      reg->ReadString("EMailFrom");
    BCB4UnlPing->PingThread->EMailHostAddress =
      reg->ReadString("EMailHost");
    BCB4UnlPing->PingThread->PingInterval =
      reg->ReadInteger("Interval");
    BCB4UnlPing->PingThread->LogError = reg->ReadBool("LogError");
  }
  delete reg;
}

void TConfigForm::SaveConfiguration()
```

```
{
  TRegistry* reg = new TRegistry;
  reg->RootKey = HKEY_LOCAL_MACHINE;
  reg->OpenKey(regKey, true);
  reg->WriteString("IPAddress", BCB4UnlPing->PingThread->IPString);
  reg->WriteString("EMailTo", BCB4UnlPing->PingThread->EMailToAddress);
  reg->WriteString("EMailFrom",
    BCB4UnlPing->PingThread->EMailFromAddress);
  reg->WriteString("EMailHost",
    BCB4UnlPing->PingThread->EMailHostAddress);
  reg->WriteInteger("Interval", BCB4UnlPing->PingThread->PingInterval);
  reg->WriteBool("LogError", BCB4UnlPing->PingThread->LogError);
  delete reg;
}

void __fastcall TConfigForm::PingIconMessage(TMessage& Msg)
{
  if (Msg.LParam == WM_RBUTTONDOWN) {
    POINT p;
    GetCursorPos(&p);
    SetForegroundWindow(Handle);
    PopupMenu->Popup(p.x, p.y);
  }
  if (Msg.LParam == WM_LBUTTONDBLCLK) {
    BCB4UnlPing->PingThread->Suspend();
    ShowModal();
    BCB4UnlPing->PingThread->Resume();
  }
}

void __fastcall TConfigForm::FormDestroy(TObject *Sender)
{
  Shell_NotifyIcon(NIM_DELETE, &IconData);
}

void __fastcall TConfigForm::ConfigureClick(TObject *Sender)
{
  BCB4UnlPing->PingThread->Suspend();
  ShowModal();
  BCB4UnlPing->PingThread->Resume();
}

void __fastcall TConfigForm::TimerTimer(TObject *Sender)
{
  if (FindWindow("Progman", 0)) {
    AddIcon();
    Timer->Enabled = false;
  }
}

void TConfigForm::AddIcon()
```

continues

LISTING 6.10   CONTINUED

```
{
  IconData.cbSize = sizeof(NOTIFYICONDATA);
  IconData.hWnd = Handle;
  IconData.uID = 1;
  IconData.uFlags = NIF_MESSAGE | NIF_ICON | NIF_TIP;
  IconData.uCallbackMessage = WM_PINGICONMESSAGE;
  IconData.hIcon = LoadIcon(HInstance, "SERVICEICON1");
  strcpy(IconData.szTip, "Unleashed Ping");
  Shell_NotifyIcon(NIM_ADD, &IconData);
}
```

I won't discuss the code that performs the ping and the code that converts the server host name or IP address string to a 32-bit IP address. I will cover those topics in Chapter 16, "Internet Connection with C++Builder." I also won't explain the code that sends the notification emails, as that code is simple enough to understand without further explanation.

The design of the PingService is as follows: The service unit contains very little code. It contains the minimum amount of code needed to spawn the service's secondary thread, and to handle the service's stop and start commands. Because this is an interactive service, the Interactive property is set to true at design time. I have also set the AllowPause property to false in order to avoid the complications that come with a paused service that displays a tray icon. There's not much benefit in pausing the PingService.

The main processing for the service is done by the TPingThread class. This thread sits in a loop and pings a remote machine at an interval determined by the configuration parameters. The default ping interval is five seconds (5,000 milliseconds). If the ping fails, the thread either logs the failure in the system Event Log or sends a notification email, depending on the service's configuration parameters. When the remote machine comes back up, the thread either logs the event or sends a notification email. Note that the service's email feature assumes the service is being run on a network server that has email access. No attempt is made to connect to the network via Dial-Up Networking.

The configuration form unit contains a fair amount of code. The code in this unit manages the service's configuration settings, the service's icon in the system tray, and the pop-up menu for the tray icon. The form's Visible property is set to false at design time and the form is only shown when needed. The form is auto-created and is not destroyed until the service terminates. I explain later why it is important to keep the form around, even when not directly being used.

> **NOTE**
>
> This service is intended to be used as the basis for a network monitoring system. In its present incarnation, the service only pings a single remote machine. In a real-world implementation you would likely provide a list of IP addresses that the service could ping. In addition, PingService only pings the remote machine's IP address to ensure that the machine is running. It doesn't attempt to ping a particular server on the machine (such as a Web server or an FTP server). If you want to extend this service to add those features, you need to spend some time experimenting with the technologies involved. I encourage you to check the Borland C++Builder newsgroups for information on this subject (see the cppbuilder.internet newsgroup in particular).

Understanding the Service's Ping Thread

There a few aspects of the ping thread that I want to discuss before getting on to items specific to interactive services. Most of the code I discuss is found in the thread's Execute() method. The Internet-related code is addressed in Chapter 16. All of the service's configuration parameters are reflected in the TPingThread class's public data members:

```
public:
  String IPString;
  String EMailToAddress;
  String EMailFromAddress;
  String EMailHostAddress;
  bool LogError;
  int PingInterval;
```

These data members correspond directly to the fields on the configuration dialog. I probably should have made these variables properties rather than public data members, but I wanted to keep things simple. These data members are public so the configuration form can update their values when the configuration changes.

The PingThread's Execute() method sleeps the designated amount of time and then attempts to ping the remote machine:

```
while (!Terminated) {
  Sleep(PingInterval);
  if (IPString != "") {
    bool goodPing = Ping();
    // code omitted
  }
}
```

Notice that the thread first ensures that the IPString data member is not empty. This check is necessary for obvious reasons. When the service is first installed, for example, the IP address and other parameters have not yet been set. If IPString contains text, then the Ping() function is called to ping the remote machine.

The next few lines of code in the Execute() function check to see if the ping succeeded and, if not, whether the failure has already been reported:

```
if (!goodPing && !ServerDownReported) {
  if (LogError) {
    String Msg = String().sprintf(
      statusMsg, IPString.c_str(), "down.");
    BCB4UnlPing->LogMessage(
      Msg, EVENTLOG_INFORMATION_TYPE, 0, 0);
  }
  else
    SendMail(false);
    ServerDownReported = true;
  }
}
```

A private variable called ServerDownReported is used internally to determine whether the failure has been reported. Had I not written the service this way, the failure would be continuously reported every five seconds (the default ping interval). I only want the failure to be reported once. The LogError data member indicates whether the user has configured the service to log the error or to send email. If LogError is true, the failure is written to the NT Event Log by calling the service's LogMessage() method. (I discuss event logging in more detail later in the section, "Sending Messages to the Event Log.") If LogError is false, I call the SendMail() function of the ping thread to send email notification of the failure.

A network administrator will naturally want to know if the server comes back up again. The remaining code in the Execute() method reports the server's up status:

```
if (goodPing && ServerDownReported) {
  ServerDownReported = false;
  if (LogError) {
    String Msg = String().sprintf(
```

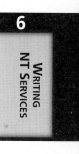

```
      statusMsg, IPString.c_str(), "up.");
    BCB4UnlPing->LogMessage(
      Msg, EVENTLOG_INFORMATION_TYPE, 0, 0);
  }
  else
    SendMail(true);
}
```

As with reporting the failure, the server's coming back online will only be reported once.

Displaying a Form from a Service

PingService displays a configuration form to the user so that he or she can set the IP address of the server and other configuration parameters. You don't have to do anything special to add a form to a service application. Just click the New Form button like you would for a regular GUI application. The configuration form is shown in Figure 6.7.

FIGURE 6.7

The PingService configuration dialog allows the user to set the service's parameters.

The IP address can be specified in either IP address dot notation format or by server name. (The MakeIPAddress() function in the TPingThread class converts the IP address string to an integer value.) The rest of the fields on the configuration dialog are self-explanatory. Note, though, that each field on the form maps directly to one of the public data members you saw in the TPingThread class earlier.

The configuration form is auto-created when the service starts. Granted, this means that the service uses more memory than it would if the configuration form were created on demand and then deleted. The reasons for the form being auto-created are almost exclusively related to the handling of the service's tray icon. These two subjects (the configuration form and the tray icon) are related, so I'll give you just enough information in this section to understand how the configuration form works. The specifics of the tray icon implementation are discussed in the next section.

A tray icon without mouse support isn't much good. In the case of PingService, double-clicking the tray icon invokes the configuration dialog and right-clicking displays the service's pop-up menu. Further, moving the mouse cursor over the tray icon will display a pop-up hint describing the service. In order to facilitate all of this, the service must be able to receive tray icon mouse notification messages. You must have a window handle in order to receive messages. Neither the `TServiceApplication` nor the `TService` classes has a window handle. This is where the configuration form comes into play.

Obviously, a form has a window handle. For this reason, the form's unit is a good place to put the code that handles the tray icon's mouse messages. It doesn't matter that the form is hidden—it still gets the mouse messages and that's what is important. In addition, the form offers a repository for the `PopupMenu` component that defines the service's pop-up menu.

> **NOTE**
>
> I could have used the `AllocateHWnd()` function to create a hidden window for the service unit. In fact, that's what I originally had in mind as a way to handle the tray icon's mouse messages. I ran into several problems with this approach, though. One problem was that I could not get the pop-up menu to work reliably. Another problem was that the service would not shut down properly when the operating system was restarted. The service would hang during shutdown, which resulted in NT's "not responding" dialog. For these reasons I decided to use the configuration form for handling the tray icon and the pop-up menu. This approach proved to be much more reliable and much more robust than my first attempt.

The configuration form is displayed in response to a double-click on the tray icon, or in response to the user selecting the Configure item on the pop-up menu. Here's the event handler for the pop-up menu's `click` event:

```
void __fastcall TConfigForm::ConfigureClick(TObject *Sender)
{
  BCB4UnlPing->PingThread->Suspend();
  ShowModal();
  BCB4UnlPing->PingThread->Resume();
}
```

I first suspend the ping thread. Since the user is configuring the service, it makes sense that the thread would be suspended during this time. Next, I call `ShowModal()` to display the form. Finally, I restart the ping thread when the user dismisses the form.

The configuration form's `OnShow` event handler loads the configuration from the `PingThread` unit into the form's components:

```
void __fastcall TConfigForm::FormShow(TObject *Sender)
{
  SetForegroundWindow(Handle);
  RadioButtonClick(0);
  ServerEdit->Text = BCB4UnlPing->PingThread->IPString;
  FrequencyEdit->Text = BCB4UnlPing->PingThread->PingInterval;
  EmailFromEdit->Text = BCB4UnlPing->PingThread->EMailFromAddress;
  EmailToEdit->Text = BCB4UnlPing->PingThread->EMailToAddress;
  EmailHostEdit->Text = BCB4UnlPing->PingThread->EMailHostAddress;
  LogRadioBtn->Checked = BCB4UnlPing->PingThread->LogError;
  EmailRadioBtn->Checked = !BCB4UnlPing->PingThread->LogError;
}
```

The first line in this method ensures that the form comes to the top when displayed. The second line calls the form's `RadioButtonClick()` method to enable or disable the email fields depending on whether the user has selected the email notification option. The remaining code simply copies the values of the ping thread's data members to the corresponding fields on the form.

Similarly, when the OK button is clicked, the data in the form's fields are copied back to the ping thread's data members:

```
void __fastcall TConfigForm::OKBtnClick(TObject *Sender)
{
  BCB4UnlPing->PingThread->IPString = ServerEdit->Text;
  if (BCB4UnlPing->PingThread->IPString != "")
    BCB4UnlPing->PingThread->MakeIPAddress();
  BCB4UnlPing->PingThread->PingInterval =
    FrequencyEdit->Text.ToIntDef(5000);
  BCB4UnlPing->PingThread->EMailFromAddress = EmailFromEdit->Text;
  BCB4UnlPing->PingThread->EMailToAddress = EmailToEdit->Text;
  BCB4UnlPing->PingThread->EMailHostAddress = EmailHostEdit->Text;
  BCB4UnlPing->PingThread->LogError = LogRadioBtn->Checked;
  SaveConfiguration();
  Close();
}
```

In the third line of this function I call the thread's `MakeIPAddress()` function. This function converts a text string containing either an IP address or a server name into a 32-bit value. (The ping thread's `Ping()` function requires a 32-bit IP address value, not a string value.) Had I used a property for the ping thread's `IPString` data member, this step could have been automated by the property's `write` method. To be honest, I was feeling a bit lazy by this point in the process and opted to leave things as I had them. After the form's field values are copied to the ping thread variables, I call the `SaveConfiguration()` method to write the new values to the Registry and then close the form. I'll discuss saving the service's configuration parameters to the Registry in the section, "Saving Service Configuration Parameters."

The rest of the code in the configuration form's unit is specific to the tray icon support and to saving the service's configuration parameters. I'll discuss those topics in the next few sections, starting with the tray icon.

Dealing with Tray Icons in an Interactive Service

The act of adding an icon to the system tray is almost trivial. You add or remove an icon from the tray by calling the Shell_NotifyIcon() API function. This function is declared in shellapi.h so you'll have to include that header in any of your services that implement a tray icon.

There are certain considerations you must take into account when implementing a tray icon in a service. For example, remember that a service will be started when the operating system loads, even if no user has logged on. The Windows shell doesn't load until the user logs on. As such, the system tray may not exist when the service starts. I'll get back to that issue in just a minute. First let me show you the code that adds an icon to the system tray. The code is placed in the configuration form's AddIcon() method:

```
void TConfigForm::AddIcon()
{
  IconData.cbSize = sizeof(NOTIFYICONDATA);
  IconData.hWnd = Handle;
  IconData.uID = 1;
  IconData.uFlags = NIF_MESSAGE ¦ NIF_ICON ¦ NIF_TIP;
  IconData.uCallbackMessage = WM_PINGICONMESSAGE;
  IconData.hIcon = LoadIcon(HInstance, "SERVICEICON1");
  strcpy(IconData.szTip, "Unleashed Ping");
  Shell_NotifyIcon(NIM_ADD, &IconData);
}
```

The first several lines of code fill in the IconData structure. IconData is declared in the configuration form's private section:

```
NOTIFYICONDATA IconData;
```

The hWnd member of the NOTIFYICONDATA structure is used to specify the window handle that will receive the tray icon's mouse messages. I assign the Handle property of the form to this member. The uID member is only significant if your service has more than one tray icon. I set this member to 1, but any value would do because there is only one tray icon for PingService. I set the uFlags member to indicate that I want mouse messages, that I will provide an icon, and that the tray icon will display a ToolTip when the mouse passes over the icon. The `szTip` member is a character array that holds the tray icon's tip text. I use the `strcpy()` function to copy my ToolTip text to this member. The `uCallbackMessage` data member is used to specify the ID of the message that Windows sends to your window procedure (more on that in the next section). The `hIcon` member is used to specify the handle to the icon that will be displayed in the system tray. I created a one-line resource script file in order to bind the icon resource to the service application. The resource script file, `PingServiceRes.rc`, looks like this:

```
SERVICEICON1 ICON "ping2.ico"
```

I load the icon for the service application using the `LoadIcon()` API function.

After setting the members of the `NOTIFYICONDATA` structure, I call `Shell_NotifyIcon()`, passing the `NIM_ADD` constant and the address of the `NOTIFYICONDATA` structure. As you might guess, the `NIM_ADD` constant tells Windows to add the icon to the system tray.

Handling Tray Icon Mouse Messages

The `uCallbackMessage` member contains the value of the message identifier that Windows will use to send mouse messages to the form. This message identifier can be thought of exactly like a user-defined message identifier. In effect, that's what it is. I declared the message ID near the top of the configuration form's header file:

```
#define WM_PINGICONMESSAGE WM_USER + 1
```

A mouse message will be generated any time a mouse event occurs in the tray icon's bounding rectangle in the tray. When a mouse message is generated, Windows will send the `WM_PINGICONMESSAGE` message to the form's window procedure, passing the specific mouse message in the `LPARAM`. The way to handle messages in a C++Builder form is by implementing a message map. The message map is declared in the configuration form's class declaration:

```
BEGIN_MESSAGE_MAP
  VCL_MESSAGE_HANDLER(WM_PINGICONMESSAGE, TMessage, PingIconMessage)
END_MESSAGE_MAP(TForm)
```

The VCL_MESSAGE_HANDLER macro tells the VCL to send all `WM_PINGICONMESSAGE` messages to the form's `PingIconMessage()` method. The `PingIconMessage()` method looks like this:

```
void __fastcall  TConfigForm::PingIconMessage(TMessage& Msg)
{
  if (Msg.LParam == WM_RBUTTONDOWN) {
    POINT p;
    GetCursorPos(&p);
    SetForegroundWindow(Handle);
    PopupMenu->Popup(p.x, p.y);
```

```
    }
    if (Msg.LParam == WM_LBUTTONDBLCLK) {
      BCB4UnlPing->PingThread->Suspend();
      ShowModal();
      BCB4UnlPing->PingThread->Resume();
    }
}
```

The WParam of the WM_PINGICONMESSAGE message is the value passed in the uID member of the NOTIFYICONDATA structure. I ignore the WParam in the PingIconMessage() method because I know I am dealing with only one tray icon. The LParam contains the mouse message that was generated as the result of user interaction with the tray icon.

If the message is WM_RBUTTONDOWN, the user has right-clicked the tray icon so I display the pop-up menu at the current mouse position. The PopupMenu component on the configuration form has its AutoPopup property set to false, so I must call the Popup() method to display the pop-up menu. Notice that I call SetForegroundWindow() before I show the pop-up menu. Without this call, the pop-up menu would appear behind the system tray. If the users clicks the Configure item on the pop-up menu (the only item on this particular menu), then the ConfigureClick() method is called and the configuration form is displayed.

The other mouse message I check for is the WM_LBUTTONDBLCLK message, indicating the user has double-clicked the tray icon. I show the configuration form when this message is received. The code used to display the form is identical to the code you saw earlier when I discussed the ConfigureClick() method.

> **NOTE**
>
> I specified the tray icon's ToolTip text in the AddIcon() function discussed earlier. Here's the line of code that sets the ToolTip text:
>
> ```
>     strcpy(IconData.szTip, "Unleashed Ping");
> ```
>
> I don't have to handle any mouse messages to display the tray icon's ToolTip. The ToolTip is displayed automatically by Windows.

Displaying the Tray Icon After User Logon

A service will start when the operating system loads (provided it is set to auto-start, of course). You can't add the tray icon to the system tray until after the user has logged on. Windows starts the system shell (Explorer.exe) when the user logs on. After the shell starts, you can add your icon to the system tray.

There are probably several ways to detect when the user has logged on. I chose to implement a timer that checks for the existence of Explorer.exe once per second. PingService's configuration form contains a Timer component. The Timer component's OnTimer event handler looks like this:

```
void __fastcall TConfigForm::TimerTimer(TObject *Sender)
{
  if (FindWindow("Progman", 0)) {
    AddIcon();
    Timer->Enabled = false;
  }
}
```

This code uses the FindWindow() API function to look for the Explorer.exe window. (The window is hidden but that doesn't matter, FindWindow() still works.) To use FindWindow(), you supply either the window's class name, the window's title text, or both. In the case of Explorer.exe, the window class name is Progman. If Explorer.exe isn't found, the timer keeps running. Once it is located, I call AddIcon() to add the service's icon to the system tray and then disable the timer.

This code isn't particularly complex or impressive, but it provides a ready-made solution that you can use in your interactive services.

Saving Service Configuration Parameters

Among its other duties, the configuration form is responsible for saving the service's configuration parameters between instances of the service. This is not only important when the system shuts down and restarts, but it is equally important when the service is stopped and restarted by human intervention. When the user stops a service, the service is unloaded from memory. When the service is restarted, the service is loaded into memory and executed. The end result is that your service won't be able to retain any configuration or state information even during the same Windows session.

There are two primary ways to save and restore a service's configuration parameters. One way is to use a file on disk. I don't like this method because it means keeping a file on disk that the user might find and modify, or even delete. A better way to save a service's configuration parameters is in the Registry. Microsoft recommends that you store the configuration parameters for a service in a key called Parameters under the following:

```
HKEY_LOCAL_MACHINE\SYSTEM\CurrentControlSet\Services\ServiceName
```

ServiceName is the name of your service. I have declared this constant at the top of the configuration form's unit:

```
const char* regKey =
  "System\\CurrentControlSet\\Services\\BCB4UnlPing\\Parameters";
```

I use this key to store the service's configuration parameters. The methods that load and save the configuration information are called, surprisingly enough, LoadConfiguration() and SaveConfiguration(). Here are those methods:

```
void TConfigForm::LoadConfiguration()
{
  TRegistry* reg = new TRegistry;
  reg->RootKey = HKEY_LOCAL_MACHINE;
  reg->OpenKey(regKey, true);
  if (reg->ValueExists("IPAddress")) {
    BCB4UnlPing->PingThread->IPString = reg->ReadString("IPAddress");
    BCB4UnlPing->PingThread->MakeIPAddress();
    BCB4UnlPing->PingThread->EMailToAddress =
      reg->ReadString("EMailTo");
    BCB4UnlPing->PingThread->EMailFromAddress =
      reg->ReadString("EMailFrom");
    BCB4UnlPing->PingThread->EMailHostAddress =
      reg->ReadString("EMailHost");
    BCB4UnlPing->PingThread->PingInterval =
      reg->ReadInteger("Interval");
    BCB4UnlPing->PingThread->LogError = reg->ReadBool("LogError");
  }
  delete reg;
}

void TConfigForm::SaveConfiguration()
{
  TRegistry* reg = new TRegistry;
  reg->RootKey = HKEY_LOCAL_MACHINE;
  reg->OpenKey(regKey, true);
  reg->WriteString("IPAddress", BCB4UnlPing->PingThread->IPString);
  reg->WriteString("EMailTo", BCB4UnlPing->PingThread->EMailToAddress);
  reg->WriteString("EMailFrom",
    BCB4UnlPing->PingThread->EMailFromAddress);
  reg->WriteString("EMailHost",
    BCB4UnlPing->PingThread->EMailHostAddress);
  reg->WriteInteger("Interval", BCB4UnlPing->PingThread->PingInterval);
  reg->WriteBool("LogError", BCB4UnlPing->PingThread->LogError);
  delete reg;
}
```

These methods contain basic TRegistry code, so I don't need to go over every detail of the code. You should note that I set the RootKey property to HKEY_LOCAL_MACHINE, the root key where all the services registry entries reside.

The call to LoadConfiguration() is in the service's OnStart event handler:

```
void __fastcall TBCB4UnlPing::BCB4UnlPingStart(TService *Sender,
    bool &Started)
{
```

```
PingThread = new TPingThread(false);
ConfigForm->LoadConfiguration();
Started = true;
}
```

By placing the code here, the configuration is loaded each time the service starts. It is unnecessary to place the code anywhere else in the service, as the `PingThread` unit maintains the current configuration internally. Because the `LoadConfiguration()` method is called from the service's main unit, it is declared in the public section of the form's class declaration.

The call to `SaveConfiguration()` is in the form's `OKBtnClick()` method as you saw earlier:

```
void __fastcall TConfigForm::OKBtnClick(TObject *Sender)
{
  // code removed for brevity
  SaveConfiguration();
  Close();
}
```

The configuration information is saved to the Registry each time the user displays the configuration form and clicks the OK button.

It could be argued that the code to load and save the service's configuration parameters should have been placed in the `TPingThread` class rather than in the configuration form's class. I could be convinced of that fact without much argument, but the form's class is the place I chose to implement this code.

Sending Messages to the Event Log

NT's Event Log is where system messages are logged. The Event Log is managed and viewed through NT's `Event Viewer` utility. You can add messages to the Event Log by calling the `LogMessage()` method of the `TService` class. PingService uses the `LogMessage()` method to log server failures and when the server comes back up again if the user has configured the service to log messages rather than sending email. You will find this code in PingThread's `Execute()` method:

```
if (!goodPing && !ServerDownReported) {
  if (LogError) {
    String Msg = String().sprintf(
      statusMsg, IPString.c_str(), "down.");
    BCB4UnlPing->LogMessage(
      Msg, EVENTLOG_INFORMATION_TYPE, 0, 0);
  }
  // code omitted
}
```

If the `LogError` data member is `true`, I call the service's `LogMessage()` method to log the message. You can view the message by opening the Event Viewer and choosing Log, Application from the Event Viewer's menu. A list of events is presented. Double-click the event you want to view and the Event Viewer will display the details of the event in a dialog box. Figure 6.8 shows the Event Viewer displaying the details of a message from PingService.

FIGURE 6.8

The Event Viewer can be used to examine the messages from PingService.

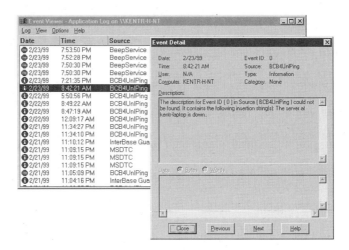

In this case I am using `LogMessage()` to report a server condition (up or down) to the Event Log. Typically, the Event Log is used to report error conditions that occur within a service. You should log any errors that occur within your service. This gives system administrators a way of understanding what went wrong with your service if an error occurs.

The `LogMessage()` function is used internally by the `TService` and `TServiceApplication` classes. Any VCL exceptions that your application doesn't handle will be reported in the Event Log, but only if the service is not interactive. If the service is interactive, the standard VCL exception message box will be displayed. Obviously, an error message popping up on the screen is not something you want in a service. You should strive to handle all exceptions that the VCL might throw.

Now that you are at the end of this section on interactive services, I want to present you with an alternative to interactive services. As you have seen, interactive services add a degree of complexity to the already complex world of NT services. Another way to accomplish the same benefits as an interactive service is to create a client application that gathers configuration information from the user. The client application then sends the configuration information to the service. The client application and service can communicate with one another through one of several of Windows interprocess communications methods including named pipes, I/O completion ports, sockets, and so on. Overall, this strategy might be a better solution than interactive services. You can read more about interprocess communications on the Microsoft Web site, on MSDN, or in the Win32 API help file.

Debugging Services

Chapter 3, "Advanced Component Creation," discusses the fact that component and property editors can be difficult to debug. Services are a magnitude of order more difficult to debug than property editors. Probably by this point in the chapter you have an appreciation for the issues involved. Naturally, you won't be able to use the C++Builder debugger to test your service's ability to start properly when the operating system loads. In addition, services are difficult to debug even after the operating system is up and running.

You can use the C++Builder debugger to debug your services, but only up to a point. With a service application loaded in the IDE, you can set a breakpoint and hit the Run button. Nothing will appear to happen, however. You must then switch to the Control Panel and start the service from the SCP. When your breakpoint is hit, the C++Builder debugger will come to the top and stop at your breakpoint. At this point you can step through your code like you would a regular application. Unfortunately, the SCM will stop your service as soon as your breakpoint is hit. The service is running as far as the debugger is concerned, but not as far as the SCM is concerned. Considering that, a debugging session for a service ends up being a cycle of the following steps:

1. Modify your code.
2. If it's running, stop the service with the SCP.
3. Place a breakpoint on a line of code and press the Run button in the IDE.
4. Start the service with the SCP.
5. When the breakpoint is hit, step through code in the usual ways.
6. Use Run, Program Reset to terminate the process in the debugger.

I won't say that debugging services with the IDE debugger is impossible, but it certainly is not as straightforward as debugging a regular application.

Chapter 3 mentions using `MessageBox()` or `ShowMesage()` as an aid to debugging component and property editors. This method will only work with interactive services and is not something I would recommended for services in any case.

One debugging technique that has merit is to log tracing and debugging messages to the system Event Log as discussed in the previous section. You can then use the Event

Viewer to examine any messages your service logged. You could also use a log file on disk to log messages or use a memory mapped file. Use of a memory mapped file assumes that your service has some way of extracting the info from the memory mapped file at some point in the debug process.

Deploying Services

Once you have your service built and debugged, you need to deploy the service on your users' machines. There are essentially three ways to deploy services:

1. Ask your users to install the service from the command line.
2. Write a utility that installs your service using the API's service control functions.
3. Use a good install program.

The first method is relatively simple to implement, but might not impress your users. I've already explained how to install a service from the command line—simply have your users run the service using the INSTALL command-line switch. I don't like this way of installing services for one primary reason: I think it is not the most professional way of installing services. I don't like asking users to manually perform any installation process that I can perform for them. I also dislike the confirmation dialog that a VCL service application brings up when a service is installed or uninstalled. Although this is fine for testing services, I wouldn't want users to see this dialog in a real-world situation. Further, the presence of the confirmation dialog makes it impossible to silently run the service application from another application.

Using the API's service control functions is certainly an option, albeit one that requires a bit of perseverance to get right. I won't attempt to describe all that is required, but I can tell you that the functions you need to use include OpenSCManager() and CreateService().

Finally, we come to the method that I prefer: using a good install program to deploy your services. I like this solution because it is professional, it is easy, and it is a tested solution. I have used Wise Install a fair amount, so I am comfortable recommending Wise Solutions products for your installations. Check the Wise Solutions Web site (www.wisesolutions.com) for their various installation offerings.

> **NOTE**
>
> The Wise for C++Builder found on the C++Builder 4 companion CD-ROM does not support installation for services.

The deployment option you choose depends largely on who your users are. If you are creating a service for your own use, then you will almost certainly just install the service from the command line. Similarly, if your service will be used in-house at your company, then it probably doesn't much matter if the install is pretty. If you are writing services for the general public's use, you should opt for a professional installation option.

A Few Final Thoughts on Services

Besides what I have already said, there are a few things to keep in mind when writing services:

- Services run invisibly.
- Services are meant to run 24/7 (24 hours a day, 7 days a week).
- Services must reside in a service application.
- Services can only contain non-visual components.

The fact that services run invisibly has implications beyond what you have to consider when writing a typical GUI application. Specifically, services do not display dialogs or message boxes to the user by default. (The exception is an interactive service, as is previously discussed at length.) You can call MessageBox() from a non-interactive service, but Windows will simply ignore the call to MessageBox(). As I said earlier, many services are meant to run on NT servers tucked away in a back room somewhere. Don't write interactive services that require human intervention (such as dismissing a dialog) unless you know the service will run on a machine with a human operator.

The fact that services are meant to run 24/7 means that you must be very conscious of writing robust code. In particular, you need to be aware that throwing an exception from the wrong place in a service may cause the service to stop. This means not only exceptions that you might throw, but exceptions that the VCL might throw. Try to anticipate any possible exceptions and be prepared to handle those exceptions efficiently and completely.

It is probably obvious that services should only be placed in a service application project. For some odd reason, C++Builder allows you to add a service to a regular GUI application. The service won't function properly, though (and will likely not function at all), because the service application code is not present to properly handle service requests.

Finally, the service form itself can only contain non-visual components (although a support form in an interactive service can contain any type of component). This makes sense because services are intended to run invisibly. The number and type of non-visual components you can place on a service form, however, is virtually unlimited. You will get an exception from the C++Builder IDE if you attempt to place a visual component on a service form.

If you want to learn more about services, I recommend the following MSDN articles:

- "Design a Windows NT Service to Exploit Special Operating System Facilities"
- "Creating a Simple Windows NT Service in C++"
- "Using SC.EXE to Develop Windows NT Services"
- "HOWTO: Debugging a Service"

None of these articles is specific to writing services with C++Builder. Fortunately, most of the hard stuff mentioned in these articles is handled for you by the VCL service classes. Still, these articles include general information on writing NT services and each has tidbits you can use. These articles are probably available on Microsoft's Web site as well as on MSDN.

Summary

There is no question that writing services requires a lot of forethought. Once you have the service designed and the code written, you still have a lot of work to do when ensuring that your service works in all circumstances. This includes your service's capability to auto-start and to properly terminate when NT shuts down. It also includes your service's capability to start, stop, pause, and continue if the service is written to allow those options. Interactive services add a level of complexity to writing services. You may find yourself in the position of having to write a client application that communicates with your service in order to allow your users to set the service's configuration parameters. Last but not least, for services that are servers, you may have to ensure that your service handles multiple connections gracefully.

Writing services with C++Builder is much easier than it is with other C++ compilers available on the market today. Writing robust services is still the burden of the programmer, but at least C++Builder handles the tedious aspects of writing services for you.

Using the RichEdit Component

by Kent Reisdorph

IN THIS CHAPTER

CHAPTER 7

The VCL's `TRichEdit` component allows you to view, edit, save, and print rich text format (RTF) files. RTF files have the following features and characteristics in addition to what the standard Windows edit control provides:

- Text formatting at the character level
- Paragraph formatting
- Better control over character positions and text selection
- Better control over printing operations
- Control over word and line breaks
- Embedding of OLE objects

For most users, the ability to format text at the character level is the most compelling reason to use a rich edit control. For example, you can intermix different fonts and font styles (bold, italic, underlined, and so on) all on the same line. Contrast this with the VCL `TMemo` component which only allows you to set the font attributes for the entire component.

Another compelling reason to use a rich edit control is the concept of paragraphs. Paragraph attributes include right and left indents, alignment (right, left, and centered), tabs, and bullets.

Most of the preceding features are included in the VCL's `TRichEdit` class as it exists right out of the box. Implementing other rich edit features (most notably support for OLE objects) requires you to go to the API level and do the work yourself.

In this chapter, I cover some of the aspects of using `RichEdit` that give users the most trouble. I never cease to be amazed at the number of questions I see on the borland.com newsgroups regarding the `RichEdit` component. In this chapter, you will find information on dealing with font and paragraph attributes, implementing style sheets, and printing a `RichEdit` component.

As is often the case, I wrote this chapter with a little help from my C++Builder friends. Specifically, I made use of Robert Dunn's Web site at `http://home.att.net/ ~robertdunn/Yacs.html`.

I primarily used Robert's site as a barometer to determine the types of issues C++Builder programmers run into when dealing with `TRichEdit`. I don't know of a single C++Builder developer who has spent more time with the `RichEdit` control than Robert has (both at the VCL level and at the API level). My thanks to Robert on behalf of the entire C++Builder community for sharing his considerable knowledge of the rich edit control. I would also like to add my personal thanks to Robert for helping me with this chapter.

This chapter starts with a short description of the RichEdit control and its various versions. The rest of the chapter is devoted to specific RichEdit functionality. I begin with some of the more elementary aspects of using the RichEdit control and progress to more complex issues.

The Basics of RichEdit

Like all of the controls on the C++Builder Component Palette's Win32 page, the TRichEdit component is a wrapper around a Windows common control. In this case, the control is Windows' RichEdit control. That simple statement is rife with complexity right from the start. At the time of this writing, there are at least two versions of rich edit. The original rich edit, version 1.0, ships with all versions of Windows 9x and Windows NT. Some systems have rich edit version 2.0 in addition to version 1.0. Rich edit 2.0 is installed with certain Microsoft products, such as Microsoft Office. Further, Windows 2000 will introduce version 3.0 of the RichEdit control. Table 7.1 lists the known rich edit versions and the name of the DLL that corresponds to each. Note that the filename for the rich edit 3.0 DLL is the same as for rich edit 2.0.

TABLE 7.1   RICH EDIT VERSIONS AND THEIR CORRESPONDING DLLS

Version	DLL Name
1.0	RICHED32.DLL
2.0	RICHED20.DLL
3.0	RICHED20.DLL

The VCL's TRichEdit component uses rich edit version 1.0. As such, it cannot take advantage of rich edit 2.0 features without some tweaking. Some of the features of rich edit 2.0 not found in version 1.0 are

- Automatic URL detection
- Support for multiple undo/redo operations
- Support for additional RTF codes
- Enhanced character and paragraph formatting

Rich edit 3.0 promises some interesting new features including zoom, simple tables, built-in styles, more underline types, hidden text, underline coloring, smart quotes, better performance, and much more. You can read more about rich edit 3.0 on Microsoft's Web site. At the time of this writing, the URL for the rich edit 3.0 feature additions is at http://msdn.microsoft.com/library/sdkdoc/winui/richedit_58qb.htm.

If this URL is no longer valid, search the Microsoft Web site for the topic "Rich Edit 3.0 Feature Additions" or see Robert Dunn's Web site.

Because C++Builder 4 uses rich edit 1.0, I won't cover the rich edit 2.0 features in this chapter. At the time of this writing, Windows 2000 is still in beta so I won't attempt to cover rich edit 3.0 features either.

Retrieving and Setting Selection Attributes

The RichEdit component's SelAttributes property returns the font attributes of the currently selected text. This includes the character set, font size, typeface name, character style (bold, italic, underline, or strikethrough), whether or not the text is protected, and so on. If no text is selected, SelAttributes returns the attributes of the character before the editing caret. Using SelAttributes, you can easily implement a character formatting toolbar, allowing the user to set the current selection to bold, italic, underline, and so on.

SelAttributes is an instance of the TTextAttributes class. Table 7.2 shows the properties of TTextAttributes.

TABLE 7.2 TTextAttributes PROPERTIES

Property	Description
CharSet	The font's character set.
Color	The font's color.
ConsistentAttributes	Indicates whether text attributes are consistently applied across the current selection.
Height	The font's height, in pixels.
Name	The font's typeface name (Arial, Courier New, Times New Roman, and so on).
Pitch	The font's pitch (default, variable, or fixed).
Protected	Indicates whether or not the text is protected. Protected text is read-only unless the RichEdit's OnProtectChange event allows the text to be edited.
Size	The font's size, in points.
Style	The font's style attributes (bold, italic, underline, or strikethrough).

TTextAttributes has only one method of interest: the Assign() method. This method allows you to assign a TFont object to an instance of TTextAttributes, thereby setting all of the object's properties at one time (rather than having to set them all individually).

The example program for this section is called FontStyles. The program allows you to open an RTF file and change the text attributes by clicking a button on the program's toolbar. Additionally, you can change all text attributes for the selected text at one time by invoking the Font dialog. Figure 7.1 shows the FontStyles program at run time. Listing 7.1 shows the source code for the FontStyles program's main unit. I don't show the header for the main unit as it contains only C++Builder-generated code.

FIGURE 7.1

The FontStyles program allows you to change the selected text's font attributes by clicking a button on the toolbar.

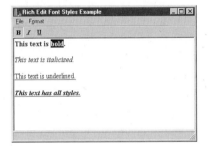

LISTING 7.1   THE SOURCE CODE FOR THE FONTSTYLES PROGRAM

```cpp
#include <vcl.h>
#pragma hdrstop

#include "FontStylesU.h"

#pragma package(smart_init)
#pragma resource "*.dfm"
TMainForm *MainForm;

__fastcall TMainForm::TMainForm(TComponent* Owner)
  : TForm(Owner)
{
}

void __fastcall TMainForm::StyleButtonClick(TObject *Sender)
{
  TFontStyles fs = RichEdit->SelAttributes->Style;
  if (Sender == BoldBtn)
    if (fs.Contains(fsBold))
      fs>> fsBold;
    else
```

continues

LISTING 7.1 CONTINUED

```
      fs << fsBold;
  if (Sender == ItalicsBtn)
    if (fs.Contains(fsItalic))
      fs>> fsItalic;
    else
      fs << fsItalic;
  if (Sender == UnderlineBtn)
    if (fs.Contains(fsUnderline))
      fs>> fsUnderline;
    else
      fs << fsUnderline;
  RichEdit->SelAttributes->Style = fs;
}

void __fastcall TMainForm::OnIdle(TObject* Sender, bool& Done)
{
  TFontStyles fs = RichEdit->SelAttributes->Style;
  BoldBtn->Down = fs.Contains(fsBold);
  ItalicsBtn->Down = fs.Contains(fsItalic);
  UnderlineBtn->Down = fs.Contains(fsUnderline);
}

void __fastcall TMainForm::FormCreate(TObject *Sender)
{
  Application->OnIdle = OnIdle;
}

void __fastcall TMainForm::Open1Click(TObject *Sender)
{
  if (OpenDialog->Execute())
    RichEdit->Lines->LoadFromFile(OpenDialog->FileName);
}

void __fastcall TMainForm::Exit1Click(TObject *Sender)
{
  Close();
}

void __fastcall TMainForm::OptionsFontClick(TObject *Sender)
{
  if (FontDialog->Execute())
    RichEdit->SelAttributes->Assign(FontDialog->Font);
}
```

I discuss the features of the FontStyles program in the following sections.

Toggling a Character Style

The FontStyles program has a single `OnClick` event handler for all of the toolbar's buttons. The event handler checks to see which button was clicked and then either sets or clears a particular style based on the button that was clicked. Here is the portion of the code that handles the click of the Bold button:

```
TFontStyles fs = RichEdit->SelAttributes->Style;
if (Sender == BoldBtn)
  if (fs.Contains(fsBold))
    fs>> fsBold;
  else
    fs << fsBold;
```

Note that I first get the current style attributes by declaring an instance of the `TFontStyles` set and assigning the `RichEdit`'s `SelAttributes::Style` property to it. This retrieves the current style setting for the selected text. Next, I check to see if the Bold button on the toolbar was clicked. If the selected text includes bold text, I remove `fsBold` from the set. Likewise, if the selection does not include bold text, I add the `fsBold` element to the set. The effect is that the bold style is toggled on or off each time the user clicks the Bold button on the toolbar.

At the end of the event handler, I set the selection attribute's `Style` property to the value of the `fs` variable:

```
RichEdit->SelAttributes->Style = fs;
```

Because of the way C++Builder handles sets, you must specifically assign a value to the `Style` property for the style to be properly updated. That is why I declared a `TFontStyles` variable at the top of the function, added or removed elements to the set, and then assigned the variable to the `Style` property at the end of the function.

Detecting the Presence of a Character Style

Another feature of the FontStyles program can be seen when you select text. The toolbar buttons show the current style settings. If, for example, you select bold text in `RichEdit`, the Bold button on the toolbar will be down. Likewise, if the selected text is italic and underlined, both the Italic and Underline buttons on the toolbar will be down. This feature allows you to look at the toolbar to see what styles are applied to the selected text. I accomplish this effect by checking the `SelAttributes` property in the application's `OnIdle` event handler. The form's `OnCreate` event handler contains this code:

```
Application->OnIdle = OnIdle;
```

This code ensures that my `OnIdle()` method is called whenever the application is idle. In my `OnIdle()` method, I check the selection attributes and set the appropriate toolbar button's `Down` property according to the style:

```
void __fastcall TMainForm::OnIdle(TObject* Sender, bool& Done)
{
  TFontStyles fs = RichEdit->SelAttributes->Style;
  BoldBtn->Down = fs.Contains(fsBold);
  ItalicsBtn->Down = fs.Contains(fsItalic);
  UnderlineBtn->Down = fs.Contains(fsUnderline);
}
```

In this case, I use a local `TFontStyles` variable for a different reason than that mentioned earlier. The `Style` property has a read method called `GetStyle()`. By using a local variable, the compiler only has to call the `GetStyle()` method once, thereby making the code more efficient. In many cases, it doesn't matter, but any code in an `OnIdle` event handler should be as efficient as possible because the event handler will be called very frequently.

The form's `OptionsFontClick()` method is called when the user selects Format, Font from the FontStyles program's main menu. Here is that method:

```
void __fastcall TMainForm::OptionsFontClick(TObject *Sender)
{
  if (FontDialog->Execute())
    RichEdit->SelAttributes->Assign(FontDialog->Font);
}
```

I show the Font dialog, and, if the user clicks the OK button on the Font dialog, I call the `Assign()` method of `TTextAttributes` to set the selection attributes in one fell swoop. The `Assign()` method allows you to easily set `RichEdit`'s font attributes with the contents of any `TFont` object.

It is important to understand that the `SelAttributes` property only looks at the first character in the selection. Take this text, for example:

This *is a* **test**.

If you select this text in its entirety, `SelAttributes->Style` reports that the text contains no formatting. In other words, the `Style` set will be any empty set and will not contain `fsBold` or `fsItalic`. This is where the `ConsistentAttributes` property comes into play.

Understanding the `ConsistentAttributes` Property

If you want to detect whether a given style is in a selection, you can use the `ConsistentAttributes` property in conjunction with the `Style` property. `ConsistentAttributes` is a set that indicates the styles that are consistent throughout the current selection. For example, if you select only bold text, then the `ConsistentAttributes` property will contain the `caBold` element. If your selection includes both bold and non-bold characters, `ConsistentAttributes` will not contain `caBold` because not all characters in the selection have the same (consistent) attributes. Here is a modified version of the FontStyles program's `OnIdle()` method that illustrates the `ConsistentAttributes` property:

```
void __fastcall TMainForm::OnIdle(TObject* Sender, bool& Done)
{
  TFontStyles fs = RichEdit->SelAttributes->Style;
  TConsistentAttributes ca =
    RichEdit->SelAttributes->ConsistentAttributes;
  if (ca.Contains(caBold))
    BoldBtn->Down = fs.Contains(fsBold);
  else
    BoldBtn->Down = true;
  if (ca.Contains(caItalic))
    ItalicsBtn->Down = fs.Contains(fsItalic);
  else
    ItalicsBtn->Down = true;
  if (ca.Contains(caUnderline))
    UnderlineBtn->Down = fs.Contains(fsUnderline);
  else
    UnderlineBtn->Down = true;
}
```

The first `if` statement checks to see whether `ConsistentAttributes` contains `caBold`. If it does, I read the `Style` property and set the Bold button's `Down` property based on whether the selection contains bold (and only bold) text. If not, I set the Bold button's `Down` property to `true` because at least part of the selection must contain bold text.

To be honest, when I first looked at `ConsistentAttributes`, I was confused as to how it worked. It's important to understand that `ConsistentAttributes` does not indicate an On state for a style, only whether that style is applied consistently across the selection. For example, if you select plain text (no bold text), `ConsistentAttributes` will contain `caBold`. Why? Because it is true that the bold style is consistently applied throughout the selection. In this case, the bold style is consistently off, but is consistent nonetheless.

This is why you must use `ConsistentAttributes` in conjunction with the `Style` property. `ConsistentAttributes` only tells you whether or not the style is consistently applied across the section; the `Style` property then tells you whether the style is on or off.

`ConsistentAttributes` has implications beyond character styles. It can also tell you whether the selection contains consistency of the font color, typeface name, size, or protection mode.

Working with text attributes in a `RichEdit` component is not terribly complex, but it does take some knowledge of the `SelAttributes` property to get it right.

Working with Paragraphs

The `RichEdit` control supports paragraphs and paragraph formatting. Paragraph formatting includes

- Text alignment (left, centered, or right)
- Paragraph indententation (first line, left, and right)
- Bullet lists
- Tabs

It is important to understand that a paragraph does not contain any font information. It only contains information about the layout of the paragraph.

The `RichEdit` component has a property called `Paragraph`, which is of type `TParaAttributes`. `Paragraph` is a pointer to the `TParaAttributes` object describing the current paragraph (the paragraph containing the editing cursor). If multiple paragraphs are selected, `Paragraph` is a pointer to the `TParaAttributes` object representing the first paragraph in the selection. `Paragraph` is a read-only property so you can't modify it directly. By that, I mean that you can't set up several `TParaAttributes` objects and simply assign one of them to the `Paragraph` property when you want to change paragraph attributes. Instead, you must modify the individual `TParaAttributes` properties when you want to change the attributes of a paragraph. Table 7.3 lists the properties of `TParaAttributes` along with a description of each.

TABLE 7.3   `TParaAttributes` PROPERTIES

Property	Description
Alignment	The paragraph alignment (right, left, or centered).
FirstIndent	The indentation, in pixels, of the paragraph's first line.
LeftIndent	The indentation, in pixels, of the paragraph's left edge.

Property	Description
Numbering	Indicates whether the paragraph acts as a bullet list. Despite this property's name, the only available choices are to have a bullet or no bullet. Numbered paragraphs are not supported.
RightIndent	The indentation, in pixels, of the paragraph's right edge.
Tab	An array of the paragraph's tab stops, with each tab stop expressed in pixels.
TabCount	The number of tab stops in the Tab array.

TParaAttributes has an Assign() method, but it cannot be used to assign an instance of TParaAttributes to the Paragraph property. This is due to the fact that the TParaAttributes constructor takes a pointer to a RichEdit component. As soon as you create a new instance of TParaAttributes, it is automatically assigned to the Paragraph property of the owning RichEdit component by the VCL. Take this code, for example:

```
TParaAttributes* attr = new TParaAttributes(RichEdit1);
attr->Alignment = taCenter;
```

As soon as the first line executes, the newly-created TParaAttributes instance is assigned to the RichEdit component's Paragraph property. As a result, the paragraph attributes of the current paragraph are immediately changed. This is almost certainly not the desired effect.

The example program for this section is called ParagraphStyles. The user interface of this program is nearly identical to the FontStyles program discussed earlier. The program's toolbar contains buttons allowing you to set the paragraph alignment. In addition, the program displays a second form that allows you to set all paragraph options at one time. Figure 7.2 shows the ParagraphStyles program's main form, and Figure 7.3 shows the Paragraph Options dialog.

FIGURE 7.2

The ParagraphStyles program allows you to change a paragraph's attributes.

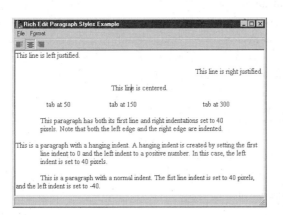

7

USING THE RICHEDIT COMPONENT

Figure 7.3

The Paragraph Options dialog lets you set all the attributes of a paragraph.

The code for the program's two units is shown in Listings 7.2 and 7.3. I don't show the headers for either unit as they don't contain any valuable information.

Listing 7.2 The Source for the ParagraphStyles Program's Main Unit

```
#include <vcl.h>
#pragma hdrstop

#include "ParagraphStylesU.h"
#include "ParaOptionsU.h"

#pragma package(smart_init)
#pragma resource "*.dfm"
TMainForm *MainForm;

__fastcall TMainForm::TMainForm(TComponent* Owner)
  : TForm(Owner)
{
}

void __fastcall TMainForm::StyleButtonClick(TObject *Sender)
{
  if (Sender == LeftBtn)
    RichEdit->Paragraph->Alignment = taLeftJustify;
  if (Sender == CenterBtn)
    RichEdit->Paragraph->Alignment = taCenter;
  if (Sender == RightBtn)
    RichEdit->Paragraph->Alignment = taRightJustify;
}

void __fastcall TMainForm::OnIdle(TObject* Sender, bool& Done)
{
  LeftBtn->Down = RichEdit->Paragraph->Alignment == taLeftJustify;
  CenterBtn->Down = RichEdit->Paragraph->Alignment == taCenter;
  RightBtn->Down = RichEdit->Paragraph->Alignment == taRightJustify;
}
```

```
void __fastcall TMainForm::FormCreate(TObject *Sender)
{
  Application->OnIdle = OnIdle;
}

void __fastcall TMainForm::Open1Click(TObject *Sender)
{
  if (OpenDialog->Execute())
    RichEdit->Lines->LoadFromFile(OpenDialog->FileName);
}

void __fastcall TMainForm::Exit1Click(TObject *Sender)
{
  Close();
}

void __fastcall TMainForm::OptionsParagraphClick(TObject *Sender)
{
  TParaOptionsForm* form = new TParaOptionsForm(this);
  form->Execute(RichEdit->Paragraph);
  delete form;
}
```

LISTING 7.3   THE SOURCE CODE FOR THE PARAGRAPHSTYLES PROGRAM'S ParaOptions
UNIT

```
#include <vcl.h>
#pragma hdrstop

#include "ParaOptionsU.h"

#pragma package(smart_init)
#pragma resource "*.dfm"
TParaOptionsForm *ParaOptionsForm;

__fastcall TParaOptionsForm::TParaOptionsForm(TComponent* Owner)
        : TForm(Owner)
{
}

void TParaOptionsForm::Execute(TParaAttributes* Attr)
{
  Attributes = Attr;
  AlignmentGroup->ItemIndex = (int)Attributes->Alignment;
  FirstIndentEdit->Text = Attributes->FirstIndent;
  LeftIndentEdit->Text = Attributes->LeftIndent;
  RightIndentEdit->Text = Attributes->RightIndent;
  BulletCheckBox->Checked = Attributes->Numbering == nsBullet;
```

continues

LISTING 7.3   CONTINUED

```
  for (char i=0;i<Attributes->TabCount;i++)
    TabsMemo->Lines->Add(Attributes->Tab[i]);
  ShowModal();
}

void __fastcall TParaOptionsForm::OKBtnClick(TObject *Sender)
{
  Attributes->Alignment = (TAlignment)AlignmentGroup->ItemIndex;
  Attributes->FirstIndent = FirstIndentEdit->Text.ToIntDef(0);
  Attributes->LeftIndent = LeftIndentEdit->Text.ToIntDef(0);
  Attributes->RightIndent = RightIndentEdit->Text.ToIntDef(0);
  Attributes->Numbering = (TNumberingStyle)BulletCheckBox->Checked;
  char tabCount = 0;
  for (int i=0;i<TabsMemo->Lines->Count;i++) {
    int tab;
    try {
      tab = TabsMemo->Lines->Strings[i].ToInt();
    }
    catch (EConvertError&) {
      continue;
    }
    Attributes->Tab[tabCount] = tab;
    tabCount++;
  }
  Attributes->TabCount = tabCount;
  Close();
}
```

Changing Paragraph Alignment

Changing the paragraph alignment is ridiculously simple. This is done in the
ParagraphStyles program's StyleButtonClick() method:

```
void __fastcall TMainForm::StyleButtonClick(TObject *Sender)
{
  if (Sender == LeftBtn)
    RichEdit->Paragraph->Alignment = taLeftJustify;
  if (Sender == CenterBtn)
    RichEdit->Paragraph->Alignment = taCenter;
  if (Sender == RightBtn)
    RichEdit->Paragraph->Alignment = taRightJustify;
}
```

As you can see, I simply assign one of the TAlignment enumeration's values to the paragraph's Alignment property based on the toolbar button that was clicked. As I have said,
the Paragraph property refers to the paragraph containing the editing cursor. When an
alignment button is clicked, the current paragraph's alignment is updated. If multiple
paragraphs are selected, then each paragraph's alignment changes.

As with the FontStyles program, the ParagraphStyles program uses the Application object's OnIdle event to toggle the toolbar buttons' states when a paragraph is selected:

```
void __fastcall TMainForm::OnIdle(TObject* Sender, bool& Done)
{
  LeftBtn->Down = RichEdit->Paragraph->Alignment == taLeftJustify;
  CenterBtn->Down = RichEdit->Paragraph->Alignment == taCenter;
  RightBtn->Down = RichEdit->Paragraph->Alignment == taRightJustify;
}
```

In this case, the code is much simpler than it is when checking character styles. A paragraph's Alignment property can only contain one of the alignment values, so I simply set each toolbar button's up or down state based on whether or not a particular alignment value is in effect.

Using a Dialog to Set Paragraph Options

One of the major features of the ParagraphStyles program is that it allows the user to set all paragraph styles from a single dialog (refer to Figure 7.3). The dialog is invoked by choosing Format, Paragraph from the ParagraphStyles program's main menu.

The Paragraph Options form is contained in the ParaOptionsU unit. The form's class has a public method called Execute() that is used to show the form. It also has a private data member called Attributes. This variable holds a pointer to the RichEdit's Paragraph property when the form is invoked. Here are the declarations for the Attributes data member and the Execute() method:

```
private:
  TParaAttributes* Attributes;
public:
  void Execute(TParaAttributes* Attr);
```

I call the ParaOptions form from the main form's OptionsParagraphClick() method:

```
void __fastcall TMainForm::OptionsParagraphClick(TObject *Sender)
{
  TParaOptionsForm* form = new TParaOptionsForm(this);
  form->Execute(RichEdit->Paragraph);
  delete form;
}
```

Note that I pass the RichEdit's Paragraph property to the Execute() method. That's all I have to do in the main form because the ParaOptions form handles everything from there. The first thing the ParaOptions form does is populate the fields on the form based on the current paragraph attributes. This is done in the Execute() method:

```
void TParaOptionsForm::Execute(TParaAttributes* Attr)
{
  Attributes = Attr;
  AlignmentGroup->ItemIndex = (int)Attributes->Alignment;
  FirstIndentEdit->Text = Attributes->FirstIndent;
  LeftIndentEdit->Text = Attributes->LeftIndent;
  RightIndentEdit->Text = Attributes->RightIndent;
  BulletCheckBox->Checked = Attributes->Numbering == nsBullet;
  for (char i=0;i<Attributes->TabCount;i++)
    TabsMemo->Lines->Add(Attributes->Tab[i]);
  ShowModal();
}
```

I first assign the private Attributes variable to the TParaAttributes pointer passed to the function. I use this variable later if the user presses the OK button on the form. After that, I simply fill in each of the form's fields with the corresponding properties of the Attributes variable. After I have populated the fields on the form, I call the ShowModal() method to display the form.

If the user clicks the Cancel button, I simply allow the form to close without doing anything further. If the user clicks the OK button, however, I need to extract all of the information from the form's fields and copy that information back to the Attributes variable's properties. I do that from within the ParaOptions form's OKBtnClick() method. The first part of this process is relatively simple in that it simply copies data from the form's fields to the corresponding TParaAttributes property:

```
Attributes->Alignment = (TAlignment)AlignmentGroup->ItemIndex;
Attributes->FirstIndent = FirstIndentEdit->Text.ToIntDef(0);
Attributes->LeftIndent = LeftIndentEdit->Text.ToIntDef(0);
Attributes->RightIndent = RightIndentEdit->Text.ToIntDef(0);
Attributes->Numbering = (TNumberingStyle)BulletCheckBox->Checked;
```

In the Execute() method, I saved the pointer to the current RichEdit paragraph in the Attributes variable. In the OKBtnClick() method I use that pointer to update the paragraph attributes. Note that I use the ToIntDef() method of the AnsiString class when converting the text in the edit controls to an integer value. If the user enters something other than an integer in any of the edit fields, a default value of 0 is used instead.

I'll take just a moment to explain the first line in the preceding code snippet. Here's that line again:

```
Attributes->Alignment = (TAlignment)AlignmentGroup->ItemIndex;
```

This code sets the paragraph alignment based on which radio button was selected in the Alignment section of the form. The Alignment property is of type TAlignment, which is an enumeration. The radio group's ItemIndex property, however, is an integer. By casting the ItemIndex to a TAlignment enumeration, I can set the Alignment property with a single statement. This eliminates the need for a switch statement or a series of if/else statements. This technique works because the labels on the alignment radio buttons appear in exactly the same order as their corresponding values in the TAlignment enumeration. The code that sets the Numbering property (a Boolean value) works in exactly the same way.

The code that sets the paragraph's tab stops requires some explanation. Because the tab stops are entered into a Memo component, I have to do some work to ensure that correct values are entered. First, I declare a variable called tabCount and set its value to 0:

```
char tabCount = 0;
```

The variable is declared as a char because the TParaAttributes TabCount property is of type char (declared as a Byte in the underlying VCL code). Using a char rather than an int (as I would typically use) prevents the following compiler warning when I assign the number of tab stops to the TabCount property (which I explain in just a bit):

```
Conversion may lose significant digits
```

After that, I enter a loop that runs through each line of the memo:

```
for (int i=0;i<TabsMemo->Lines->Count;i++) {
```

The body of the loop attempts to convert each line in the Memo component to an integer value. If the value cannot be converted, I catch the resulting EConvertError exception and continue looping:

```
int tab;
try {
  tab = TabsMemo->Lines->Strings[i].ToInt();
}
catch (EConvertError&) {
  continue;
}
```

If the value in the Memo line was successfully converted to an integer, I assign the value to the Tab array and increment the tabCount variable:

```
Attributes->Tab[tabCount] = tab;
tabCount++;
```

The effect of the code in the loop is to check the validity of each value in the memo and to keep a running count of the valid tab stop numbers.

After the loop exits, I assign the value of the tabCount variable (which now contains the exact number of valid tab stops entered into the Memo) to the TabCount property of the TParaAttributes object:

```
Attributes->TabCount = tabCount;
```

7

USING THE
RICHEDIT
COMPONENT

Certainly, there are other ways to allow the user to set tab stops. In a real-world application, you would probably opt for a technique that more tightly controls the values the user is allowed to enter for the tab stops.

> **NOTE**
>
> The `RichEdit` control supports a maximum of 32 tab stops as defined by the MAX_TAB_STOPS macro in `RICHEDIT.H`.

Finally, after all the data has been copied from the form's fields to the paragraph attributes, I close the form:

```
Close();
```

After the `OKBtnClick()` method returns, the current paragraph (or paragraphs, in the case of multiple selection) are updated with the new paragraph attributes.

Dealing with paragraph attributes is a bit more straightforward than dealing with text attributes. For the most part, implementing paragraph attributes is fairly trivial.

Using Style Sheets

Most commercial word processors implement style sheets. A style sheet allows the user to apply preselected font and paragraph attributes with a few mouse clicks. For example, Microsoft Word has predefined styles called Normal, Heading 1, Heading 2, and so on. By this point in the chapter, you have probably surmised that, with a bit of work, you can implement style sheets in your C++Builder programs that use the `RichEdit` component. Implementing a style sheet means combining the paragraph attributes and the character attributes and applying them to the current selection. The previous statement is an oversimplification of the process involved. In reality, a program that uses style sheets should provide features that

- Create new style sheets, including the ability to inherit styles
- Delete existing style sheets
- Edit existing style sheets
- Apply style sheets to the current selection
- Apply style sheets to the entire paragraph the editing cursor is in when no text is selected
- Save style sheets to the Registry
- Reload style sheets when the application starts

Granted, implementing style sheets to this degree takes a fair amount of work. The example program for this section is called StyleSheets. It provides all of the features outlined in the preceding list. I must admit, writing this example took much longer than I originally thought it would. Properly implementing and applying styles consistent with how I thought styles should work was a challenge. The entire program is much too long to list here, so I explain only the more interesting portions of the program. You can load the program from the book's code on the CD-ROM. Figure 7.4 shows the StyleSheets program's main unit at run time.

FIGURE 7.4

The StyleSheets example allows you to apply, create, edit, and delete style sheets in a `RichEdit` *control.*

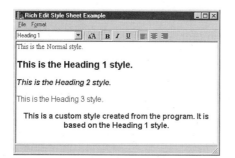

In addition to the main form, the StyleSheets example program has three additional forms. One form allows you to set paragraph options. This form is identical in appearance to the Paragraph Options form shown in Figure 7.3. The remaining two forms are used to create, edit, and delete style sheets. Figure 7.5 shows these two forms when creating a new style sheet.

FIGURE 7.5

The Styles form allows you to edit, create, and delete style sheets and to view the current styles and the New Style form allows you to set the style sheet's properties.

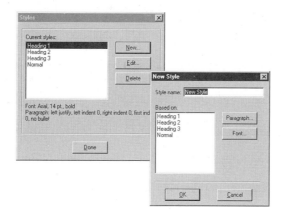

Writing a Style Sheet Class

Much of the work done by the StyleSheets example revolves around a class I wrote to handle style sheets. The class, `TUnlStyle`, mimics most of the properties of the `TParaAttributes` and `TTextAttributes` classes. The `TUnlStyle` class's properties are shown in Table 7.4 and its methods in Table 7.5.

TABLE 7.4 THE `TUnlStyle` PROPERTIES

Property	Description
Alignment	Same as `TParaAttributes::Alignment`
Color	Same as `TTextAttributes::Color`
FirstIndent	Same as `TParaAttributes::FirstIndent`
FontName	Same as `TTextAttributes::Name`
FontStyle	Same as `TTextAttributes::Style`
LeftIndent	Same as `TParaAttributes::LeftIndent`
Numbering	Same as `TParaAttributes::Numbering`
RightIndent	Same as `TParaAttributes::RightIndent`
StyleName	The name of the style (Normal, Heading 1, Heading 2, and so on)
Size	Same as `TTextAttributes::Size`
Tab	Same as `TParaAttributes::Tab`
TabCount	Same as `TParaAttributes::TabCount`

TABLE 7.5 THE `TUnlStyle` METHODS

Method	Description
Apply	Applies the style to the current paragraph of the given `RichEdit` component.
Assign	Copies the properties of an existing `TUnlStyle` object to this object.
AssignFont	Copies the properties of a `TFont` object to this object.
AssignParagraph	Copies the properties of a `TParaAttributes` object to this object.
AssignSelAttr	Copies the properties of a `TTextAttributes` object to this object.
FindStyle	Returns a pointer to the `TUnlStyle` instance if the style matches the `RichEdit`'s `Paragraph` and `SelAttribute` properties, or 0 if the styles do not match.
LoadFromRegistry	Loads the style from the Registry.
SaveToRegistry	Saves the style to the given Registry key.
TUnlStyle	The constructor. Allows you to create a new style with default attributes or to create a style based on an existing `TUnlStyle` object.

Using the RichEdit *Component*

CHAPTER 7

303

7

USING THE
RICHEDIT
COMPONENT

When I set out to create the TUnlStyle class, I originally thought to inherit from either TParaAttributes or TTextAttributes. Neither would work, though, because both classes require an existing RichEdit component in their constructors (and, in fact, cannot be created without modifying the attached RichEdit). Instead, I mimicked the properties of each class in the TUnlStyle class. I explain how the TUnlStyle class is used in the following sections.

> **NOTE**
>
> The terms *style sheet* and *style* are used more or less interchangeably. It gets a bit cumbersome to say *style sheet* over and over again, so I'll use the term *style* for the remainder of this section on style sheets.

Using a Style List

The StyleSheet program uses a VCL TList object, called StyleList, to store the list of styles. Each style is a separate instance of the TUnlStyles class. (It occurred to me later that I could have implemented a second class that maintained the list of styles. It certainly would have made the code in the StyleSheet program simpler.) The style list is, naturally enough, created in the main form's OnCreate event handler:

```
StyleList = new TList;
```

This is basic VCL code and doesn't require further explanation.

Loading the Style List

The main form's OnCreate event handler checks the Registry to see if a list of styles is available. Figure 7.6 shows the Registry key created by the StyleSheet program.

FIGURE 7.6

The StyleSheet program creates a Registry key for each style.

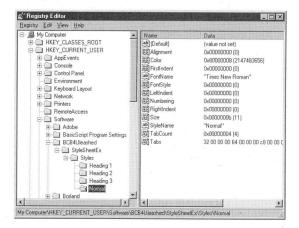

If the Registry key containing the styles exists, each style is loaded into the style list:

```
TRegistry* reg = new TRegistry;
reg->OpenKey(RegKey, true);
TUnlStyle* style;
if (reg->KeyExists("Normal")) {
  TStringList* list = new TStringList;
  reg->GetKeyNames(list);
  delete reg;
  reg = 0;
  for (int i=0;i<list->Count;i++) {
    style = new TUnlStyle;
    style->LoadFromRegistry(RegKey, list->Strings[i]);
    StyleList->Add(style);
    if (style->StyleName == "Normal")
      style->Apply(RichEdit);
  }
  delete list;
}
```

I load the list of style key names from the Registry into a `TStringList` object using `TRegistry`'s `GetKeyNames()` method. (The StyleSheet program includes code to prevent the user from deleting the Normal style so this code will survive any potential user intervention.) I then run through the list of key names, create an instance of the `TUnlStyle` class for each key name, and call the `TUnlStyle` class's `LoadFromRegistry()` method to load each style. I'll explain how the `LoadFromRegistry()` and `SaveToRegistry()` methods work in the section, "Using the Registry to Store Styles." As each style is loaded, I add it to the style list using the `Add()` method of `TList`. Notice that when the Normal style is loaded, I apply the style by calling the style's `Apply()` method. This sets the Normal style as the default when the program starts. I discuss the `Apply()` method in detail in the section, "Applying Styles."

If the Registry key containing the styles does not yet exist (as is the case the first time the program is run), I create four styles called Normal, Heading 1, Heading 2, and Heading 3. I add each style to the list as it is created. Here is the code that creates the new styles and adds them to the styles list:

```
else {
  style = new TUnlStyle;
  style->StyleName = "Normal";
  style->FontName = "Times New Roman";
  style->Size = 11;
  StyleList->Add(style);
  style->Apply(RichEdit);
  style = new TUnlStyle;
  style->StyleName = "Heading 1";
  style->FontName = "Arial";
  style->Size = 14;
```

Using the RichEdit *Component*

CHAPTER 7

305

7

USING THE
RICHEDIT
COMPONENT

```
    style->FontStyle = TFontStyles() << fsBold;
    StyleList->Add(style);
    style = new TUnlStyle;
    style->StyleName = "Heading 2";
    style->FontName = "Arial";
    style->Size = 12;
    style->FontStyle = TFontStyles() << fsBold << fsItalic;
    StyleList->Add(style);
    style = new TUnlStyle;
    style->StyleName = "Heading 3";
    style->FontName = "Arial";
    style->Size = 12;
    StyleList->Add(style);
}
```

Notice that I don't need to set each and every property for the styles. This is because the TUnlStyle class's constructor assigns default values to each of the class's properties. Therefore, I only need to assign values to the styles I want to specifically set. After I load the styles into the style list, I call a method of the main form called UpdateStylesCombo(). This method simply adds each style name to a combo box on the main form's toolbar:

```
void TMainForm::UpdateStylesCombo()
{
    StylesCombo->Items->Clear();
    for (int i=0;i<StyleList->Count;i++) {
        TUnlStyle* style = (TUnlStyle*)StyleList->Items[i];
        StylesCombo->Items->Add(style->StyleName);
    }
    StylesCombo->ItemIndex = StylesCombo->Items->IndexOf("Normal");
}
```

Note the for loop that iterates the style list. It is important to understand that TList simply stores a list of 32-bit values. In this case, I am storing a list of TUnlStyle pointers. Because TList has no knowledge of the type of pointer it contains, I must cast each pointer to a TUnlStyle pointer to access properties and methods of the TUnlStyle class. In this case, I add the value of each style's StyleName property to the items in the StylesCombo combo box. You will see several occurrences of this code (the code that iterates the styles list) in the following sections.

Let me digress a moment from the subject of creating a style list and discuss the TUnlStyle constructor.

Understanding the TUnlStyle Constructor

Here is the declaration for the TUnlStyle constructor:

```
TUnlStyle(TUnlStyle* PrevStyle = 0);
```

As I said earlier, an instance of the TUnlStyle class can be created by using an existing style. Take this code, for example:

```
TUnlStyle* Normal = new TUnlStyle;
Normal->StyleName = "Normal";
TUnlStyle* NormalBold = new TUnlStyle(Normal);
Normal->StyleName = "Normal Bold";
Normal->FontStyle = Normal->FontStyle << fsBold;
```

The first instance of the TUnlStyle class, called Normal, is created using the class defaults. I don't need to pass a parameter to the constructor because its single parameter has a default value of 0. The second instance is created using the first instance as a pattern. You can see how this is implemented by looking at the code for the TUnlStyle constructor:

```
TUnlStyle::TUnlStyle(TUnlStyle* PrevStyle)
{
  if (PrevStyle)
    Assign(PrevStyle);
  else {
    Alignment = taLeftJustify;
    FirstIndent = 0;
    LeftIndent = 0;
    RightIndent = 0;
    Numbering = nsNone;
    for (char i=0;i<32;i++)
      Tab[i] = 0;
    TabCount = 0;
    Color = clWindowText;
    FontName = "Times New Roman";
    Size = 11;
    FontStyle = TFontStyles();
    StyleName = "New Style";
  }
}
```

If no existing object is passed to the TUnlStyle constructor, I assign defaults to each property. If an existing object is passed to the constructor, I call the Assign() method of TUnlStyle. Here is that method:

```
void TUnlStyle::Assign(TUnlStyle* PrevStyle)
{
  Alignment = PrevStyle->Alignment;
  FirstIndent = PrevStyle->FirstIndent;
  LeftIndent = PrevStyle->LeftIndent;
  RightIndent = PrevStyle->RightIndent;
  Numbering = PrevStyle->Numbering;
  for (char i=0;i<32;i++)
    Tab[i] = PrevStyle->Tab[i];
  TabCount = PrevStyle->TabCount;
```

```
    Color = PrevStyle->Color;
    FontName = PrevStyle->FontName;
    Size = PrevStyle->Size;
    FontStyle = PrevStyle->FontStyle;
    StyleName = PrevStyle->StyleName;
}
```

I'll admit that the `Assign()` method has a Pascal-like look to it. Given that this is a C++ class, I probably should have overridden the = operator or provided a copy constructor to do the work that the `Assign()` method does.

> **NOTE**
>
> As I work more with the `TUnlStyle` class, I see literally dozens of places where the class can be improved. My goal in writing this class was not to provide an all-encompassing solution, but rather to give you a place to start when implementing `RichEdit` style sheets.

Adding and Removing Styles from the Style List

Styles are added to and removed from the list at various times throughout the StyleSheet program. You already saw how the styles are initially added to the style list when I showed you the code for the main form's `OnCreate` event handler. Styles are also added to the list when the user creates a new style. This is done in the `EditStyleU.cpp` unit when the user clicks the OK button:

```cpp
void __fastcall TEditStyleForm::OKBtnClick(TObject *Sender)
{
  String styleName = NewStyleNameEdit->Text;
  NewStyle->StyleName = styleName;
  if (!Editing)
    if (FindStyle(styleName) == -1)
      StyleList->Add(NewStyle);
  else {
    String Msg = String().sprintf(
      "A style called '%s' already exists", styleName.c_str());
    MessageBox(Handle, Msg.c_str(),
      "StyleSheet Error", MB_OK | MB_ICONWARNING);
    ModalResult = mrNone;
    NewStyleNameEdit->SetFocus();
    return;
  }
  ModalResult = mrOk;
}
```

The `EditStyleForm` doubles both as a mechanism for adding new styles and for editing existing styles. That is why you see code that checks to see whether the `Editing` variable is `false`. The `NewStyle` variable in this code is a `TUnlStyle` pointer that was created in the form's `Execute()` method. This code also checks to see whether the style being added already exists in the style list. If so, a message is displayed to the user and the form remains open. The actual act of adding a style to the style list is trivial:

```
StyleList->Add(NewStyle);
```

> **NOTE**
>
> Depending on how much experience you have with the `TList` class, you might be wondering if the code I've shown you thus far is in error. Let's go back to the main form's `OnCreate` event handler for just a moment. Here's some abbreviated code from that method:
>
> ```
> style = new TUnlStyle;
> style->StyleName = "Normal";
> style->FontName = "Times New Roman";
> style->Size = 11;
> StyleList->Add(style);
> style = new TUnlStyle;
> style->StyleName = "Heading 1";
> ```
>
> Note that I do not call `delete` on the `style` variable after I add the variable to the style list. This is how `TList` works. It "owns" the pointers passed to it. I do actually free the pointers stored in the list, but not until later (either when a style is deleted or when the application terminates).

Deleting a style from the style list requires a bit more work, but not much. The StyleSheet program allows the user to delete a style by selecting the style from a list box and clicking the Delete button. This is done from the `FormatStylesForm` unit in response to the `DeleteBtnClick()` method:

```
for (int i=0;i<StyleList->Count;i++) {
  TUnlStyle* style = (TUnlStyle*)StyleList->Items[i];
  if (styleName == style->StyleName) {
    delete style;
    StyleList->Delete(i);
    UpdateStylesListBox();
  }
}
```

This code first finds the style in the style list by matching its `StyleName` property with the style name selected in the form's list box. It casts each style in the list to a `TUnlStyle` pointer, checks the `StyleName` property, and, if the style is found, deletes the pointer. It then calls the TList class's Delete() method to remove the style from the style list. It is important that I both delete the pointer returned from the style list and call TList::Delete() to remove the now invalid pointer from the list.

The other place that I delete styles from the list is in the StyleSheet program's OnDestroy event handler. Here is the relevant code from the FormDestroy() method:

```
for (int i=0;i<StyleList->Count;i++) {
  TUnlStyle* style = (TUnlStyle*)StyleList->Items[i];
  delete style;
}
delete StyleList;
```

The principle here is the same as I described just a few paragraphs earlier; I must call delete on each of the pointers in the style list and then delete the style list itself.

Applying Styles

Having a style list is not much good if it is never put to use. The StyleSheet program uses the style list in several different places. I don't explain each use of the style list, but I do show you the most obvious. First, let me explain how I implemented style sheets in this program.

For the most part, I attempted to emulate how Microsoft Word handles styles. The simplest use of styles is to position the editing cursor on a line of text and choose a style name from a combo box containing the list of styles. Another way to apply a style is to select multiple paragraphs and apply a single style to all the selected paragraphs, again by selecting the style from a style list combo box. Finally, Word has a feature that Microsoft calls the Format Painter. This feature allows you to click one paragraph to pick up a style and then click a second paragraph to apply the style. The StyleSheet program implements each of these methods of applying a style. Let's take the simplest method first: selecting a style from a combo box.

The StyleSheet program applies a style when the user selects a style from the style combo box. The combo box's OnChange event handler provides a good place to implement the change of styles:

```
void __fastcall TMainForm::StylesComboChange(TObject *Sender)
{
  for (int i=0;i<StyleList->Count;i++) {
    TUnlStyle* style = (TUnlStyle*)StyleList->Items[i];
    if (style->StyleName == StylesCombo->Text)
      style->Apply(RichEdit);
  }
  RichEdit->SetFocus();
}
```

First, I find the style whose `StyleName` property matches the combo box selection. After that, I simply call the `TUnlStyle` class's `Apply()` method. That sounds simple, but the `Apply()` method contains a fair amount of code to ensure that applying a style works in a wide variety of circumstances. Here is the `Apply()` method:

```cpp
void TUnlStyle::Apply(TRichEdit* RichEdit)
{
  int selStart = RichEdit->SelStart;
  int selLength = RichEdit->SelLength;
  char c;
  LockWindowUpdate(RichEdit->Handle);
  if (!selLength) {
    bool found = false;
    for (int i=selStart;i>0;i—) {
      try {
        c = RichEdit->Text[i+1];
      }
      catch (ERangeError&) {
        continue;
      }
      if (c == '\n') {
        RichEdit->SelStart = i + 1;
        found = true;
        break;
      }
    }
    if (!found)
      RichEdit->SelStart = 0;
    int length = RichEdit->Text.Length();
    for (int i=selStart;i<length + 1;i++) {
      try {
        c = RichEdit->Text[i+1];
      }
      catch (ERangeError&) {
        RichEdit->SelLength = RichEdit->Text.Length();
        break;
      }
      if (c == '\n' || i == length - 1) {
        RichEdit->SelLength = i - RichEdit->SelStart;
        break;
      }
    }
  }
  RichEdit->Paragraph->Alignment = Alignment;
  RichEdit->Paragraph->FirstIndent = FirstIndent;
  RichEdit->Paragraph->Numbering = Numbering;
  RichEdit->Paragraph->RightIndent = RightIndent;
  for (char i=0;i<TabCount;i++)
    RichEdit->Paragraph->Tab[i] = Tab[i];
  RichEdit->Paragraph->TabCount = TabCount;
}
```

```
char start = 0;
char end = 0;
try {
  start = RichEdit->Text[selStart];
  end = RichEdit->Text[selStart + 1 + selLength];
}
catch (ERangeError&) {
}
if ((start == '\n' ¦¦ selStart == 0) && (end == '\n' ¦¦ end == 0)) {
  RichEdit->Paragraph->Alignment = Alignment;
  RichEdit->Paragraph->FirstIndent = FirstIndent;
  RichEdit->Paragraph->Numbering = Numbering;
  RichEdit->Paragraph->RightIndent = RightIndent;
  for (char i=0;i<TabCount;i++)
    RichEdit->Paragraph->Tab[i] = Tab[i];
  RichEdit->Paragraph->TabCount = TabCount;
}
RichEdit->SelAttributes->Color = Color;
RichEdit->SelAttributes->Name = FontName;
RichEdit->SelAttributes->Size = Size;
RichEdit->SelAttributes->Style = FontStyle;
RichEdit->SelStart = selStart;
RichEdit->SelLength = selLength;
LockWindowUpdate(0);
}
```

The bulk of the code in this method has to do with selecting a paragraph. The RichEdit's SelAttributes property only works on selected text. Therefore, I must select the entire paragraph before I can attempt to set the font attributes. Further complicating the issue is the fact that the user might have selected multiple paragraphs and wants to format them all with a given style. I won't attempt to explain all the code that selects a paragraph. Suffice it to say that I first move forward from the cursor position looking for a carriage return character ('\n') to determine the end of the paragraph. When I find a carriage return, I then search backward from the cursor position looking for another carriage return (marking the end of the preceding paragraph). All of this is complicated by two factors:

1. There might not be a trailing carriage return for a paragraph if that paragraph is the final paragraph in the file. Similarly, there might not be a preceding paragraph if the paragraph containing the cursor is the first paragraph in the file.

2. The RichEdit's Text property is an instance of the AnsiString class. AnsiString's index operator is 1-based, whereas the SelStart property is 0-based. This is why you see several try/catch blocks which attempt to handle AnsiString's ERangeError exception.

During this process, I am physically changing the selection in the RichEdit component. After I have selected the paragraph (or paragraphs, in the case of multiple selection), I apply the paragraph attributes:

```
RichEdit->Paragraph->Alignment = Alignment;
RichEdit->Paragraph->FirstIndent = FirstIndent;
RichEdit->Paragraph->Numbering = Numbering;
RichEdit->Paragraph->RightIndent = RightIndent;
for (char i=0;i<TabCount;i++)
  RichEdit->Paragraph->Tab[i] = Tab[i];
RichEdit->Paragraph->TabCount = TabCount;
```

I do the same for the character attributes:

```
RichEdit->SelAttributes->Color = Color;
RichEdit->SelAttributes->Name = FontName;
RichEdit->SelAttributes->Size = Size;
RichEdit->SelAttributes->Style = FontStyle;
```

After I have set the paragraph and character attributes, I reset the selection to the text the user originally had selected:

```
RichEdit->SelStart = selStart;
RichEdit->SelLength = selLength;
```

The result is that the entire paragraph containing the cursor is selected, the paragraph and font attributes are set, and the original selection is restored—all without the user ever being aware of it. That leads us to one other aspect of the Apply() method that I have refrained from explaining until now. Consider this code:

```
LockWindowUpdate(RichEdit->Handle);
// bulk of the function's code omitted
LockWindowUpdate(0);
```

LockWindowUpdate() is a Windows API function that prevents a particular window from being repainted. In this case, I pass the window handle of the RichEdit component to LockWindowUpdate(). Any painting is suppressed until I call LockWindowUpdate() again, this time passing 0 as a parameter. Without this code, the user would see the RichEdit component flash while I am selecting text and changing the paragraph and font attributes.

> **NOTE**
>
> Windows only allows one window lock for the system at any given time. For this reason, you should check the return value from your initial call to LockWindowUpdate() to see if your lock succeeded. If the lock fails, don't call LockWindowUpdate(0) to release the lock or you will release a lock some other application placed.

Using the Registry to Store Styles

As I have said, the TUnlStyle class has methods for saving a style to the Registry and
for loading the style from the Registry. You have already seen the code in the StyleSheet
program's main form that calls the LoadFromRegistry() method for each style. The
styles are saved to the Registry in the form's OnDestroy event handler. This happens as
each style is being deleted from the style list:

```
TRegistry* reg = new TRegistry;
reg->DeleteKey(RegKey);
delete reg;
for (int i=0;i<StyleList->Count;i++) {
  TUnlStyle* style = (TUnlStyle*)StyleList->Items[i];
  style->SaveToRegistry(RegKey);
  delete style;
}
```

First, I delete the Registry key containing the style sheet entries. I do this because the
user might have deleted one or more styles, and I want to make sure that the values contained in the Registry exactly match the contents of the style list. After that, I run
through the list of styles. Just before I delete a style, I call its SaveToRegistry()
method. Here is the TUnlStyle class's SaveToRegistry() method:

```
void TUnlStyle::SaveToRegistry(String Key)
{
  TRegistry* reg = new TRegistry;
  reg->OpenKey(Key + "\\" + StyleName, true);
  reg->WriteInteger("Alignment", (int)Alignment);
  reg->WriteInteger("FirstIndent", FirstIndent);
  reg->WriteInteger("LeftIndent", LeftIndent);
  reg->WriteInteger("RightIndent", RightIndent);
  reg->WriteInteger("Numbering", (int)Numbering);
  int* tabArray = new int[TabCount];
  for (char i=0;i<TabCount;i++)
    tabArray[i] = Tab[i];
  reg->WriteBinaryData("Tabs", tabArray, sizeof(int) * TabCount);
  delete[] tabArray;
  reg->WriteInteger("TabCount", TabCount);
  reg->WriteInteger("Color", (int)Color);
  reg->WriteString("FontName", FontName);
  reg->WriteInteger("Size", Size);
  int styleBits = 0;
  if (FontStyle.Contains(fsBold))
    styleBits |= 1;
  if (FontStyle.Contains(fsItalic))
    styleBits |= 2;
  if (FontStyle.Contains(fsUnderline))
    styleBits |= 4;
  if (FontStyle.Contains(fsStrikeOut))
```

```
    styleBits |= 8;
  reg->WriteInteger("FontStyle", styleBits);
  reg->WriteString("StyleName", StyleName);
  delete reg;
}
```

Most of this code is standard `TRegistry` code and I don't need to explain it line by line. I will, however, explain some parts of this code. For example, here is the code that saves the `Tab` property (an array of tab stops) to the Registry:

```
int* tabArray = new int[TabCount];
for (char i=0;i<TabCount;i++)
  tabArray[i] = Tab[i];
reg->WriteBinaryData("Tabs", tabArray, sizeof(int) * TabCount);
delete[] tabArray;
```

I first create a dynamically allocated array of integers whose size is based on the value of the `TabCount` property. Next, I copy each of the tab values from the `Tab` property to the integer array. After that I write the integer array to the Registry using the `WriteBinaryData()` method of the `TRegistry` class. Finally, I delete the integer array. I should explain that the `Tab` property has an underlying data member called `FTab`. This data member is an array of 32 integers. I could have saved myself some trouble by writing the entire array of integers to the Registry directly from the `FTab` data member. That would have resulted in wasted space in the Registry, however, so I opted for this method instead.

Another aspect of saving a style to the Registry that deserves mention is the way I save the font styles. Here is that code:

```
int styleBits = 0;
if (FontStyle.Contains(fsBold))
  styleBits |= 1;
if (FontStyle.Contains(fsItalic))
  styleBits |= 2;
if (FontStyle.Contains(fsUnderline))
  styleBits |= 4;
if (FontStyle.Contains(fsStrikeOut))
  styleBits |= 8;
reg->WriteInteger("FontStyle", styleBits);
```

This code builds a bit set based on the styles that are found in the `FontStyles` property. After I have built the bit set, I write it to the Registry using the `WriteInteger()` method. There are several ways to approach saving a set to the Registry, but this is the one I settled on.

Loading the styles from the Registry requires nothing more than reversing the process shown in the `SaveToRegistry()` method. Here is how the `TUnlStyle` class's `LoadFromRegistry()` method looks:

```
void TUnlStyle::LoadFromRegistry(String Key, String Style)
{
  TRegistry* reg = new TRegistry;
  bool exists = reg->OpenKey(Key + "\\" + Style, false);
  if (!exists) {
    delete reg;
    return;
  }
  Alignment = (TAlignment)reg->ReadInteger("Alignment");
  FirstIndent = reg->ReadInteger("FirstIndent");
  LeftIndent = reg->ReadInteger("LeftIndent");
  RightIndent = reg->ReadInteger("RightIndent");
  Numbering = (TNumberingStyle)reg->ReadInteger("Numbering");
  TabCount = reg->ReadInteger("TabCount");
  int* tabArray = new int[TabCount];
  reg->ReadBinaryData("Tabs", tabArray, sizeof(int) * TabCount);
  for (char i=0;i<TabCount;i++)
    Tab[i] = tabArray[i];
  delete[] tabArray;
  Color = (TColor)reg->ReadInteger("Color");
  FontName = reg->ReadString("FontName");
  Size = reg->ReadInteger("Size");
  int styleBits = reg->ReadInteger("FontStyle");
  TFontStyles fs;
  if ((styleBits & 1) == 1)
    fs << fsBold;
  if ((styleBits & 2) == 2)
    fs << fsItalic;
  if ((styleBits & 4) == 4)
    fs << fsUnderline;
  if ((styleBits & 8) == 8)
    fs << fsStrikeOut;
  FontStyle = fs;
  StyleName = Style;
  delete reg;
}
```

Because you understand how the SaveToRegistry() method works, you won't have any trouble understanding what LoadFromRegistry() does.

Adding, Deleting, and Editing Styles

The code for adding, deleting, and editing styles is a variation on the code discussed up to this point. These tasks are performed in the FormatStylesU.cpp and EditStyleU.cpp units. I don't discuss the code here, but instead refer you to the StyleSheet program on the book's CD-ROM.

Showing the User the Current Style

After a user has applied one or more styles to a document, he or she might want to know what style a particular paragraph contains. Clicking a paragraph should update the styles combo box on the toolbar with the name of the current style. The `RichEdit` control does not natively have support for styles. What this means is that you cannot immediately tell what style a particular paragraph contains by reading a property or by any other high-level means. The best you can do is compare the attributes of the current paragraph to see if they match a known style. This is done in the StyleSheet program in the `RichEdit`'s `OnSelectionChanged` event handler:

```
void __fastcall TMainForm::RichEditSelectionChange(TObject *Sender)
{
  // some code removed for brevity
  // See if the current selection matches one of our styles.
  bool found = false;
  for (int i=0;i<StyleList->Count;i++) {
    TUnlStyle* style = (TUnlStyle*)StyleList->Items[i];
    if (style->FindStyle(
        RichEdit->Paragraph, RichEdit->SelAttributes)) {
      // Found a match so update the styles combo to show
      // the selected style.
      StylesCombo->ItemIndex =
        StylesCombo->Items->IndexOf(style->StyleName);
      StylesCombo->Font->Color = clWindowText;
      found = true;
      break;
    }
  }
  if (!found)
    // Can't find an exact match so blank the styles combo.
    StylesCombo->Font->Color = StylesCombo->Color;
}
```

The pertinent line of code is the line that calls the `TUnlStyle` class's `FindStyle()` method:

```
if (style->FindStyle(
  RichEdit->Paragraph, RichEdit->SelAttributes)) {
```

The `FindStyle()` method compares the paragraph and selection attributes passed to it and returns a pointer to the style if the style matches, or `0` if it does not:

```
TUnlStyle* TUnlStyle::FindStyle(
  TParaAttributes* ParaAttr, TTextAttributes* TextAttr)
{
  bool paraMatch =
    Alignment == ParaAttr->Alignment &&
    FirstIndent == ParaAttr->FirstIndent &&
```

```
      LeftIndent == ParaAttr->LeftIndent &&
      Numbering == ParaAttr->Numbering &&
      RightIndent == ParaAttr->RightIndent &&
      TabCount == ParaAttr->TabCount;
  bool fontMatch = false;
  if (TextAttr)
    fontMatch =
      Color == TextAttr->Color &&
      FontName == TextAttr->Name &&
      Size == TextAttr->Size &&
      FontStyle == TextAttr->Style;
  if (TextAttr && paraMatch && fontMatch)
    return this;
  else if (!TextAttr && paraMatch)
    return this;
  else
    return 0;
}
```

This function is somewhat more complicated than it needs to be due to the fact that it can be used to find only paragraph attributes, or both paragraph and font attributes.

If a style was found that matches the current paragraph and font attributes, I set the style combo box's `ItemIndex` property to show the selected style:

```
StylesCombo->ItemIndex =
  StylesCombo->Items->IndexOf(style->StyleName);
```

If a match could not be found, I use a trick to blank out the style combo box's text. I simply set the text color of the combo box to the same color as the background color, thereby making the combo box appear to be blank:

```
if (!found)
  StylesCombo->Font->Color = StylesCombo->Color;
```

There could be any number of reasons that a matching style could not be found. The primary reason is that the user has applied a style and then modified the characteristics of the paragraph or font in some way. Let's say, for example, that the user chooses a style of Heading 1. This style has left alignment by default. Now let's say the user chooses to center the text by clicking the toolbar's Center button. At this point, the style does not exactly match the Heading 1 style because the paragraph alignment has been changed to centered.

As you can see, implementing styles for a rich edit takes a fair amount of work. If you are writing an application that needs to use style sheets, however, you must make the effort. After you have written a class or component that handles style sheets, you can use that object in any application requiring style sheets.

Printing the Contents of a Rich Edit

Printing from the `RichEdit` component can be as simple or as complicated as you like. For example, if you simply want to print the contents of a rich edit without any fuss, you can simply call the `Print()` method:

```
RichEdit->Print("MyProgram - " + FileName);
```

The `Print()` method has a single parameter called `Caption`. This parameter is used to specify the string that is displayed in Windows' print manager when the document is printing. Many users incorrectly assume that the `Caption` parameter is text that will be printed as the header for each page. Where they get this notion, I don't know, but it is a common source of confusion for beginning rich edit programmers.

It won't be long, however, before you realize that the `Print()` method just isn't good enough for any but the most simple applications. There are two primary problems with the `Print()` method:

1. It prints the entire contents of the `RichEdit` component.
2. It has no capability for specifying print margins.

> **NOTE**
>
> The `RichEdit` component has a property called `PageRect` that can, at least in theory, allow you to specify the rectangle on which to print (thereby specifying printing margins). By looking at the VCL source, however, it appears that the `PageRect` property is not properly implemented, and my initial attempts at using this property produced undesirable results.

To do serious printing with the `RichEdit` component, you have to get down to the API level. Before I get into the code for this section, I need to give you some background information on printing with the `RichEdit` component.

Understanding `RichEdit` Printing Capabilities

Printing the contents of a `RichEdit` control is not necessarily an exact science. This is partly due to inconsistencies in the common control itself and partly due to the complexity of dealing with the vast array of printers available today. To oversimplify, printing the contents of a rich edit involves sending the component an `EM_FORMATRANGE` message. The Win32 API help for `EM_FORMATRANGE` is so sparse as to be practically useless. It takes a certain degree of perseverance and a mind-numbing amount of experimentation to figure out how to use EM_FORMATRANGE (not to mention a lot of paper!). I explain how to use EM_FORMATRANGE in this section.

The EM_FORMATRANGE message provides services that can be defined in two broad categories:

1. Measuring the text in the control
2. Rendering the text in the control

As I said, these are broad categories. For example, measuring the text aids in accomplishing several tasks, not the least of which is getting a page count of the number of pages you will be printing. Another important service that measuring the text provides is in preparing one or more pages for actual printing. If you plan to do serious printing, then you will always measure the text before you print.

You might think of rendering the text as the act of printing. That's partially true, but rendering really means sending the formatted text to a device context. Think about that for a moment. If you render to a printer device context, then the text will indeed be printed. But consider the bigger picture. What if you were to render to a window device context, a memory device context, or to a metafile? By now you may have figured out that rendering is also used when you want to create a print preview window for a rich edit.

> **NOTE**
>
> In this section, I talk about printing the text in a RichEdit component. The Windows RichEdit control is capable of containing embedded OLE objects as well as text. You can, for example, add images (bitmaps or metafiles) to your rich edit documents. Unfortunately, the VCL's RichEdit component does not directly support inserting OLE objects in a document, and I do not have the space to adequately cover that subject. See Robert Dunn's Web site at http://home.att.net/~robertdunn/Yacs.html for information on using OLE objects with TRichEdit.

When you send the RichEdit an EM_FORMATRANGEmessage, you specify whether you are rendering the text or measuring the text by setting the WPARAM of the message to either 0 or a non-zero value. If the WPARAM is 0, the text is measured. If the WPARAM is non-zero, the text is rendered.

All of the information Windows needs to render or measure the contents of the document is provided by way of a FORMATRANGE structure. (You could also use the VCL's

TFormatRange structure. In the end, it doesn't matter which you use.) FORMATRANGE is declared in RICHEDIT.H as follows:

```
typedef struct _formatrange
{
  HDC hdc;
  HDC hdcTarget;
  RECT rc;
  RECT rcPage;
  CHARRANGE chrg;
} FORMATRANGE;
```

The hdc member is used to specify the device context on which the text will be rendered. The hdcTarget member is the target device for which formatting will be performed. In most cases, the hdc and hdcTarget members will be set to the same DC. When printing, for example, both members will be set to the device context of the particular printer on which you are printing. When creating a print preview window, you set the hdc member to the device context of a preview window you create, and the hdcTarget member to the printer's device context. Put another way, the contents of the RichEdit are formatted for the device specified in hdcTarget and sent to the device context specified in hdc.

The rcPage member is used to specify the size (the page rectangle) of a full page on the target device. The rc member is used to specify the portion of the page that will actually be printed on—the rendering rectangle. For example, let's say that you are formatting output for a printer and that you want to use one inch margins all around. Figure 7.7 illustrates the difference between the page rectangle and the rendering rectangle given that scenario.

Notice in Figure 7.7 that the page rectangle does not entirely cover the physical page. This is due to the fact that nearly all printers have a non-printable margin—the portion of the page that they are unable to print on. This margin varies on every printer and is something that you must account for when printing. I explain how to account for a printer's non-printable area in the next section. By modifying the rendering rectangle, you can specify print margins, print on half pages, or even print columns.

The chrg member of the FORMATRANGE structure is used to specify the starting and ending positions of the text that makes up a page. More accurately, the chrg member specifies the starting and ending positions of the text that will fit in the rendering rectangle (whether it be a full page or a portion of a page). Windows gives you these values when you measure the text prior to printing. The chrg member is an instance of the CHARRANGE structure:

FIGURE 7.7

The page rectangle represents the largest printable area and the rendering rectangle specifies the portion of the page rectangle that will be used for rendering.

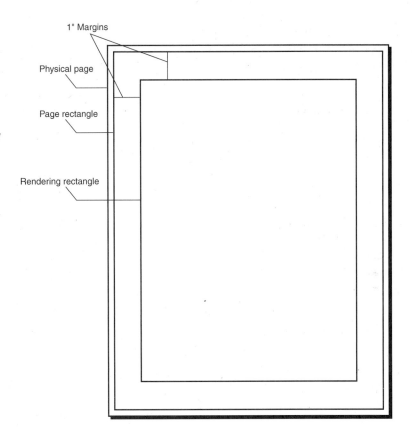

1" Margins

Physical page

Page rectangle

Rendering rectangle

7

USING THE
RICHEDIT
COMPONENT

```
typedef struct _charrange
{
  LONG cpMin;
  LONG cpMax;
} CHARRANGE;
```

The `cpMin` member of this structure identifies the starting character, and the `cpMax` member identifies the end character.

I explain how to use the `EM_FORMATRANGE` message and the `FORMATRANGE` structure in the next section when I begin detailing the code needed to print a `RichEdit` control.

As you no doubt know, Windows device contexts use a grid of pixels to determine where text or graphics will be drawn. The `RichEdit` control uses twips, rather than pixels, to determine where text and graphics will be drawn. *Twip* is one of those odd terms inherited from the world of typography. A twip is 1/20 of a printer's point, hence the acronym (*twen*t*i*eth of a *p*oint). There are 1,440 twips in an inch (567 twips in a centimeter). To properly render the contents of a rich edit, you must specify the page and rendering rectangles in twips. I show you how to convert from pixels to twips in the next section where I begin to show you rich edit printing code.

Printing with Margins

At a minimum, you probably want to allow your users to set the print margins. Printing a rich edit document that implements margins involves these steps:

1. Get the requested margins from the user.
2. Determine the printer resolution.
3. Determine the number of logical units per inch for the printer.
4. Determine the non-printable area for the printer.
5. Set up the page and rendering rectangles, converting logical units to twips.
6. Create a loop that does the actual printing.

I explain each of these steps in the following pages. First, let me show you the code for a sample method that prints an entire rich edit document. In just a bit, I'll show you a working program that performs more complex printing. Here's the code for printing all the text in a rich edit using margins:

```
void __fastcall TMainForm::Print1Click(TObject *Sender)
{
  int width = GetDeviceCaps(Printer()->Handle, PHYSICALWIDTH);
  int height = GetDeviceCaps(Printer()->Handle, PHYSICALHEIGHT);
  int logPixelsX = GetDeviceCaps(Printer()->Handle, LOGPIXELSX);
  int logPixelsY = GetDeviceCaps(Printer()->Handle, LOGPIXELSY);
  int xOffset = GetDeviceCaps(Printer()->Handle, PHYSICALOFFSETX);
  int yOffset = GetDeviceCaps(Printer()->Handle, PHYSICALOFFSETY);

  if (!PrintDialog->Execute())
    return;
  Printer()->Title = "Rich Edit Printing Example " +
    ExtractFileName(OpenDialog->FileName);

  Printer()->BeginDoc();
  SetMapMode(Printer()->Handle, MM_TEXT);

  FORMATRANGE fr;
  memset(&fr, 0, sizeof(fr));
  fr.hdc = Printer()->Handle;
  fr.hdcTarget = Printer()->Handle;

  fr.rcPage.left = 0;
  fr.rcPage.top = 0;
```

```
    fr.rcPage.right  =  MulDiv(width - xOffset, 1440, logPixelsX);
    fr.rcPage.bottom = MulDiv(height - yOffset, 1440, logPixelsY);

    fr.rc.left = fr.rcPage.left + (LeftMargin * 1440) - xOffset;
    fr.rc.top = fr.rcPage.top + (TopMargin * 1440) - yOffset;;
    fr.rc.right = fr.rcPage.right - (RightMargin * 1440);
    fr.rc.bottom = fr.rcPage.bottom - (BottomMargin * 1440);

    fr.chrg.cpMin = 0;
    fr.chrg.cpMax = -1;

    int textLen = RichEdit->Text.Length();
    int textPrinted;

    do {
      Printer()->NewPage();
      textPrinted = SendMessage(
        RichEdit->Handle, EM_FORMATRANGE, true, (int)&fr);
      if (textPrinted < textLen) {
        fr.chrg.cpMin = textPrinted;
        fr.chrg.cpMax = -1;
      }
    } while (textPrinted < textLen);

    SendMessage(RichEdit->Handle, EM_FORMATRANGE, 0, 0);
    Printer()->EndDoc();
}
```

The first thing I do in this code is determine the printer capabilities. This is done with the API function, GetDeviceCaps():

```
int width = GetDeviceCaps(Printer()->Handle, PHYSICALWIDTH);
int height = GetDeviceCaps(Printer()->Handle, PHYSICALHEIGHT);
int logPixelsX = GetDeviceCaps(Printer()->Handle, LOGPIXELSX);
int logPixelsY = GetDeviceCaps(Printer()->Handle, LOGPIXELSY);
```

The first two lines get the printer's physical width and physical height, in pixels. The next two lines get the vertical and horizontal number of pixels per inch for the printer. On my printer (a 600-dpi laser) set to print on regular paper (8.5×11 inches), I get the following values:

```
width     5100
height    6600
logPixelsX    600
logPixelsY    600
```

If you examine these values closely, you can see that there is a direct correlation; 600 pixels per inch times 8.5 inches equals 5,100, and 600×11 inches equals 6,600 pixels. If my printer were set to print legal size (8.5×14 inches), then the height value would be 8,400. I will use these values later when I set up the page rectangle.

Next, you need to get the non-printable area of the printer. These two lines do the job:

```
int xOffset = GetDeviceCaps(Printer()->Handle, PHYSICALOFFSETX);
int yOffset = GetDeviceCaps(Printer()->Handle, PHYSICALOFFSETY);
```

My printer returns 100 and 102, respectively, for these values. That means that my printer cannot print on the topmost 100 pixels nor on the leftmost 102 pixels. Translated to inches, this means that just under 1/8" of the top and left sides of the page are unprintable.

CAUTION

It's important to understand how the `Handle` property of the VCL's `TPrinter` object works. Before you call `BeginDoc()`, `TPrinter::Handle` returns a handle to an information context, not a device context. The information context is fine for obtaining printer device capabilities, as you see in the preceding code examples, but cannot be used for the actual printing.

After you call the `BeginDoc()` method, the `Handle` property returns a device context which you can use for the actual printing. However, that device context is destroyed when you call `EndDoc()`. This means that each time you call `BeginDoc()`, the `Handle` property might return a different device context handle. For these reasons, you should never attempt to save the value of the `Handle` property in an attempt to reuse it for later operations that require a printer device context.

After I have the printer capabilities, I show the Print dialog:

```
if (!PrintDialog->Execute())
  return;
Printer()->Title = "Rich Edit Printing Example " +
  ExtractFileName(OpenDialog->FileName);
```

If the user clicks the Cancel button, I return without doing anything further. If the user clicks the OK button, I set the printer's `Title` property to the name of the file I am printing. The string specified in the `Title` property is displayed in Windows print manager while printing is taking place. Notice that I use the VCL function, `Printer()`, to get a pointer to the global `TPrinter` object. This function returns a `TPrinter` pointer that provides access to the user's currently-selected printer. Before you can call the `Printer()` function, you must first include the `Printers.hpp` header:

```
#include <Printers.hpp>
```

Now I can begin printing. First, I call the printer's `BeginDoc()` method:

```
Printer()->BeginDoc();
```

This tells Windows that we are about to start printing. As soon as `BeginDoc()` returns, the Windows print manager icon is displayed in the system tray.

After that, I set the map mode to `MM_TEXT`:

```
SetMapMode(Printer()->Handle, MM_TEXT);
```

This sets the printer to the proper mapping mode for printing. The `MM_TEXT` mode specifies that one logical unit is mapped to one device pixel and that standard Windows x,y coordinates (positive x is to the right, positive y is down) are to be used.

Now we get to the part of the code that specifically deals with printing a `RichEdit`. Here's the first part of this code:

```
FORMATRANGE fr;
memset(&fr, 0, sizeof(fr));
fr.hdc = Printer()->Handle;
fr.hdcTarget = Printer()->Handle;
```

I declare an instance of the `FORMATRANGE` structure, zero its memory, and assign the value of the printer's device context to its `hdc` and `hdcTarget` members. Because I have already called `BeginDoc()`, the `Handle` property of `TPrinter` returns the printer's device context handle. Earlier I said that, when printing, the `hdc` and `hdcTarget` members of the `FORMATRANGE` structure are set to the same value.

Now I need to set up the page rectangle. Here is the code that sets up the page rectangle:

```
fr.rcPage.left = 0;
fr.rcPage.top = 0;
fr.rcPage.right =  MulDiv(width - xOffset, 1440, logPixelsX);
fr.rcPage.bottom = MulDiv(height - yOffset, 1440, logPixelsY);
```

The `rcPage` member is an instance of Windows' `RECT` structure. I set the `top` and `left` members to `0` to set the top-left corner of the page. The code that sets the `right` and `bottom` members of the page rectangle requires a bit of explanation. The `MulDiv()` function multiplies two values and then divides by a third value. The code that sets the `right` member of the structure takes the physical width, subtracts the non-printable area of the printer, multiplies that value by 1440, and divides by the number of pixels in a logical inch. On my printer, this translates to:

```
((5100 - 100) * 1440)) / 600
```

In this case, the result is 12,000 twips. The last line of code in the preceding code example sets the `bottom` member of the page rectangle using the same logic.

Next, I need to set the rendering rectangle. I take the page rectangle and adjust it based on the margins specified by the user. The following code assumes that I have obtained

the page margins (in inches) from the user and have stored them in variables called
`LeftMargin`, `RightMargin`, `TopMargin`, and `BottomMargin`. Here's the code:

```
fr.rc.left = fr.rcPage.left + (LeftMargin * 1440) - xOffset;
fr.rc.top = fr.rcPage.top + (TopMargin * 1440) - yOffset;;
fr.rc.right = fr.rcPage.right - (RightMargin * 1440);
fr.rc.bottom = fr.rcPage.bottom - (BottomMargin * 1440);
```

Note that I multiply each margin by the value of one inch in twips. Note that, in the case
of the left and top margins, I subtract the amount of the printer's non-printable area. The
result of this code is that the rendering rectangle is the page rectangle reduced by the
amount of the user-specified margins.

> **NOTE**
>
> Earlier, I said that printing the contents of a `RichEdit` control is not an exact science. The code I have shown that sets the page and rendering rectangles is based on experimentation and, at least in my testing, comes the closest to getting the correct margins. There are no doubt many different ways to calculate the page and rendering rectangles, but this is code that works for me. In your applications, you should check the margins that the user has specified against the non-printable area for the printer and take appropriate action if the user has asked for margins that are less than the non-printable area.

Now I need to tell Windows the range of characters to print. This is done by setting the
`FORMATRANGE` structure's `chrg` member to starting and ending values:

```
fr.chrg.cpMin = 0;
fr.chrg.cpMax = -1;
```

I set the `cpMin` member of the `chrg` structure to `0` (the beginning of the document) and
the `cpMax` member to `-1`. Setting the `cpMax` member to `-1` tells Windows to print the
entire document. At this point, we are ready to start a loop that prints the document.
Here's the code:

```
int textLen = RichEdit->Text.Length();
int textPrinted;
do {
  Printer()->NewPage();
  textPrinted = SendMessage(
    RichEdit->Handle, EM_FORMATRANGE, true, (int)&fr);
  if (textPrinted < textLen) {
    fr.chrg.cpMin = textPrinted;
    fr.chrg.cpMax = -1;
  }
} while (textPrinted < textLen);
```

Using the RichEdit *Component*
CHAPTER 7

327

7

USING THE
RICHEDIT
COMPONENT

I get the length of the RichEdit's text and store it in a variable called textLen. I also declare a variable called textPrinted that will hold the number of characters printed to this point. Note that I use these two variables as the while loop's condition to determine when printing has finished.

The call to the NewPage() method of the TPrinter class ejects a page and starts a new page. The first time through, the call is ignored because no information has been sent to the printer. Finally, we get to the line of code that actually sends a page of printed text to the printer:

```
textPrinted = SendMessage(
  RichEdit->Handle, EM_FORMATRANGE, true, (int)&fr);
```

I send the RichEdit an EM_FORMATRANGE message, passing true for the WPARAM, and the address of the FORMATRANGE structure in the LPARAM. The EM_FORMATRANGE message returns the position of the last character that fits on this page, plus one. I use that value to update the cpMin member for the next pass through the loop:

```
if (textPrinted < textLen) {
  fr.chrg.cpMin = textPrinted;
  fr.chrg.cpMax = -1;
}
```

Let me explain how the loop works. Each time the EM_FORMATRANGE message is sent, Windows formats a page, placing as much text as it can fit into the rendering rectangle. Next, it sends the page to the printer. It then returns the position of the next character to be printed. I update the starting position of the text to be printed with the return value, and loop. Each time through the loop, Windows formats the next block of text and sends it to the printer. This process continues until all the text has been printed.

After all the text has been printed, I send another EM_FORMATRANGE message, this time passing 0 for both the WPARAM and the LPARAM. This clears any cached printing information and is something you must do when you are done printing. After that, I call the EndDoc() method of the printer object to close the print session:

```
SendMessage(RichEdit->Handle, EM_FORMATRANGE, 0, 0);
Printer()->EndDoc();
```

Granted, the code to print the contents of a RichEdit control with user-specified margins is not trivial. Still, for any serious application, you have to implement code like this if you want professional-looking printed output.

Printing Single Pages or a Range of Pages

The code in the previous section explained how to print an entire rich edit document with user-specified margins. The next logical step is to allow the user to print all pages, a single page, or a range of pages. The program for this section is called Printing and can be found on the book's CD-ROM. The Printing program uses the standard VCL `PrintDialog` component to get the pages to print from the user. It also allows the user to set the page margins from a dialog as shown in Figure 7.8.

FIGURE 7.8

The Printing program gets the margins from the user via the Page Setup dialog.

The bulk of the program's code is in its `Print1Click()` method. This method is called in response to the user selecting the File, Print item from the program's menu. Listing 7.4 shows the Printing program's `Print1Click()` method. I show only this method because the rest of the program's code contains basic file open/file save code that isn't particularly interesting. The code that extracts the printer margins from the Page Setup form is trivial and doesn't require explanation.

LISTING 7.4   THE PRINTING PROGRAM'S `Print1Click()` METHOD

```
void __fastcall TMainForm::Print1Click(TObject *Sender)
{
  Screen->Cursor = crHourGlass;
  Application->ProcessMessages();

  TList* pageList = new TList;
  int width = GetDeviceCaps(Printer()->Handle, PHYSICALWIDTH);
  int height = GetDeviceCaps(Printer()->Handle, PHYSICALHEIGHT);
  int logPixelsX = GetDeviceCaps(Printer()->Handle, LOGPIXELSX);
  int logPixelsY = GetDeviceCaps(Printer()->Handle, LOGPIXELSY);
  int xOffset = GetDeviceCaps(Printer()->Handle, PHYSICALOFFSETX);
  int yOffset = GetDeviceCaps(Printer()->Handle, PHYSICALOFFSETY);

  SendMessage(RichEdit->Handle, EM_FORMATRANGE, 0, 0);
  FORMATRANGE fr;
  memset(&fr, 0, sizeof(fr));
  fr.hdc = Printer()->Handle;
  fr.hdcTarget = Printer()->Handle;
  SetMapMode(fr.hdc, MM_TEXT);

  TRect pageRect;
  pageRect.left = 0;
  pageRect.top = 0;
```

```
pageRect.right = MulDiv(width - xOffset, 1440, logPixelsX);
pageRect.bottom = MulDiv(height - yOffset, 1440, logPixelsY);

TRect rendRect;
rendRect.left = pageRect.left + (Margins->Left * 1440) - xOffset;
rendRect.top = pageRect.top + (Margins->Top * 1440) - yOffset;
rendRect.right = pageRect.right - (Margins->Right * 1440);
rendRect.bottom = pageRect.bottom - (Margins->Bottom * 1440);

fr.chrg.cpMin = 0;
fr.chrg.cpMax = -1;
int textLen = RichEdit->Text.Length();
do {
  fr.rc = rendRect;
  fr.rcPage = pageRect;
  TPrinterPage* page = new TPrinterPage;
  page->StartPos = fr.chrg.cpMin;
  fr.chrg.cpMin = SendMessage(
    RichEdit->Handle, EM_FORMATRANGE, false, (int)&fr);
  page->EndPos = fr.chrg.cpMin - 1;
  pageList->Add(page);
} while (fr.chrg.cpMin != -1 && fr.chrg.cpMin < textLen);

SendMessage(RichEdit->Handle, EM_FORMATRANGE, 0, 0);

PrintDialog->MaxPage = pageList->Count;
if (!PrintDialog->Execute()) {
  Screen->Cursor = crDefault;
  return;
}
Printer()->Title = "Rich Edit Printing Example " +
  ExtractFileName(OpenDialog->FileName);
int startPage, endPage;
if (PrintDialog->PrintRange == prPageNums) {
  startPage = PrintDialog->FromPage - 1;
  endPage = PrintDialog->ToPage - 1;
}
else {
  startPage = 0;
  endPage = pageList->Count - 1;
}

Screen->Cursor = crHourGlass;
Application->ProcessMessages();

textLen = RichEdit->Text.Length();
Printer()->BeginDoc();
SetMapMode(Printer()->Handle, MM_TEXT);
fr.hdc = Printer()->Handle;
fr.hdcTarget = Printer()->Handle;
int pageCount = startPage;
```

continues

LISTING 7.4   CONTINUED

```
do {
  fr.rc = rendRect;
  fr.rcPage = pageRect;
  TPrinterPage* pp = (TPrinterPage*)pageList->Items[pageCount];
  fr.chrg.cpMin = pp->StartPos;
  fr.chrg.cpMax = pp->EndPos;
  Printer()->NewPage();
  SendMessage(RichEdit->Handle, EM_FORMATRANGE, true, (int)&fr);
} while (++pageCount < endPage + 1);

SendMessage(RichEdit->Handle, EM_FORMATRANGE, 0, 0);
Printer()->EndDoc();

for (int i=0;i<pageList->Count;i++)
  delete (TPrinterPage*)pageList->Items[i];
delete pageList;
Screen->Cursor = crDefault;
}
```

Much of the code in Listing 7.4 is identical or very similar to the code presented in the previous section. I only discuss the code that is specific to printing selected pages in this section.

Let me lay some groundwork. First, the code relies on a class declared in the page setup form's header and a pointer to that class declared in the main form's class. The class, called TPrinterMargins, simply contains members representing the top, left, bottom, and right margins, in inches. It also contains a constructor to initialize all margins to the default of one inch. Here's TPrinterMargins' declaration:

```
class TPrinterMargins {
  public:
    float Top;
    float Bottom;
    float Left;
    float Right;
    TPrinterMargins()
    {
      Top = 1;
      Bottom = 1;
      Left = 1;
      Right = 1;
    }
};

private:
  TPrinterMargins* Margins;
```

Using the `RichEdit` *Component*

CHAPTER 7

331

7

USING THE
RICHEDIT
COMPONENT

Second, I want to explain in very general terms how the code in the `PrintClick1()` method works. Naturally, it sets up the page and rendering rectangles. After the rectangles are set up, it uses a two-pass design to prepare the text in the component for printing and then to print. The first pass is a formatting pass. The text is measured, but is not actually printed on the first pass. In the measuring pass, I save each page's starting and ending text position in a structure. Here's the declaration of the structure:

```
struct TPrinterPage {
  int StartPos;
  int EndPos;
};
```

Each time through the formatting loop, I create an instance of the `TPrinterPage` structure, assign values to its `StartPos` and `EndPos` members based on the values returned from the `EM_FORMATRANGE` message, and then add the instance to a `TList`. This process gives me a list of pages that can be printed.

On the second pass, I actually perform the printing. I print the pages the user has asked for by pulling the appropriate values from the page list.

With that quick overview, let me get on to explaining the code. I should add that the code in the `Print1Click()` method contains some niceties like setting the cursor to an hourglass while the formatting and printing are taking place. That code is simple enough so I won't spend any time explaining it.

Near the top of the `Print1Click()` method, I create an instance of the `TList` class:

```
TList* pageList = new TList;
```

I've already explained what this list contains so I'll move on to more interesting things.

In this case, I used a slightly different technique to supply the page and rendering rectangles. I created two instances of the `TRect` class called `pageRect` and `rendRect`. The code used to set the rectangles is identical to the code you saw earlier. Only the use of the two `TRect` variables is different:

```
TRect pageRect;
pageRect.left = 0;
pageRect.top = 0;
pageRect.right = MulDiv(width - xOffset, 1440, logPixelsX);
pageRect.bottom = MulDiv(height - yOffset, 1440, logPixelsY);

TRect rendRect;
rendRect.left = pageRect.left + (Margins->Left * 1440) - xOffset;
rendRect.top = pageRect.top + (Margins->Top * 1440) - yOffset;
rendRect.right = pageRect.right - (Margins->Right * 1440);
rendRect.bottom = pageRect.bottom - (Margins->Bottom * 1440);
```

After the page and rendering rectangles are set up, I perform the formatting pass:

```
fr.chrg.cpMin = 0;
fr.chrg.cpMax = -1;
int textLen = RichEdit->Text.Length();
do {
  fr.rc = rendRect;
  fr.rcPage = pageRect;
  TPrinterPage* page = new TPrinterPage;
  page->StartPos = fr.chrg.cpMin;
  fr.chrg.cpMin = SendMessage(
    RichEdit->Handle, EM_FORMATRANGE, false, (int)&fr);
  page->EndPos = fr.chrg.cpMin - 1;
  pageList->Add(page);
} while (fr.chrg.cpMin != -1 && fr.chrg.cpMin < textLen);
```

This is nearly identical to the code you saw earlier. Each time through the loop, I set the `rc` and `rcPage` members of the `FORMATRANGE` structure to the `rendRect` and `pageRect` variables, respectively. I do this as a precaution because when I send the `EM_FORMATRANGE` message, Windows might modify the rendering rectangle. By setting the page and rendering rectangles each time, I am assured that they remain consistent each time through the loop. Before I send the `EM_FORMATRANGE` message, I create an instance of the `TPrinterPage` structure and assign the starting text position to its `StartPos` member. I then send the `EM_FORMATRANGE` message specifying `false` in the `WPARAM`. Passing `false` for the `WPARAM` tells Windows to format the text but not print it.

After the `EM_FORMATRANGE` message has been sent, I assign its return value to the `EndPos` member of the `TPrinterPage` instance. I subtract one from the return value because the value returned from the `EM_FORMATRANGE` message is the value of the next character to be formatted. After the call to `SendMessage()` returns, I have a structure that contains the starting and ending positions of a formatted page of text. I add the instance of the structure to the page list by calling `TList`'s `Add()` method:

```
pageList->Add(page);
```

When the formatting loop finishes, I have a list of pages in the page list. At the end of the formatting loop, I have to clear the printer cache by sending another `EM_FORMATRANGE` message with an `LPARAM` of `0`:

```
SendMessage(RichEdit->Handle, EM_FORMATRANGE, 0, 0);
```

The next block of code sets up the `PrintDialog` component, shows it to the user, and extracts the starting and ending page numbers:

```
Printer()->Title = "Rich Edit Printing Example " +
  ExtractFileName(OpenDialog->FileName);
int startPage, endPage;
```

Using the RichEdit *Component*

CHAPTER 7

333

7

USING THE
RICHEDIT
COMPONENT

```
if (PrintDialog->PrintRange == prPageNums) {
  startPage = PrintDialog->FromPage - 1;
  endPage = PrintDialog->ToPage - 1;
}
else {
  startPage = 0;
  endPage = pageList->Count - 1;
}
```

If the user specified a range of pages, then I assign the start and end page to variables called `startPage` and `endPage`. I subtract one from each value because the list of pages is zero-based (page 1 corresponds to index 0 in the list).

The printing loop is only marginally different from the printing loop I discussed in the previous section. Here is the printing loop:

```
int pageCount = startPage;
do {
  fr.rc = rendRect;
  fr.rcPage = pageRect;
  TPrinterPage* pp = (TPrinterPage*)pageList->Items[pageCount];
  fr.chrg.cpMin = pp->StartPos;
  fr.chrg.cpMax = pp->EndPos;
  Printer()->NewPage();
  SendMessage(RichEdit->Handle, EM_FORMATRANGE, true, (int)&fr);
} while (++pageCount < endPage + 1);
```

Note that before entering the loop, I declare a variable called `pageCount` and assign it to the value of `startPage`. This variable is used to count the pages printed and to retrieve a specific page's parameters from the page list. In the first couple of lines of the printing loop, I assign the `rendRect` and `pageRect` rectangles to their corresponding members in the `FORMATRANGE` structure.

I then declare a local variable of type `TPrinterPage*` and assign an item from the page list to it:

```
TPrinterPage* pp = (TPrinterPage*)pageList->Items[pageCount];
```

This gives me the parameters (the starting and ending character offsets) of a particular page in the list. I then assign those values to the `cpMin` and `cpMax` members of the `FORMATRANGE` structure's `chrg` member:

```
fr.chrg.cpMin = pp->StartPos;
fr.chrg.cpMax = pp->EndPos;
```

After that I send an `EM_FORMATRANGE` message to send the text to the printer. When the printing loop terminates, I send a final `EM_FORMATRANGE` message to clear the cache, call `EndDoc()` to end the print job, and free up the memory used for the page list and its contents.

Formatting text with margins and printing selected pages is tricky the first few times around. After you know what you need to do, however, you have a piece of code that you can use in all of your applications that use the RichEdit component.

Before I leave this subject, I'll say one more thing about the formatting loop. It's fairly obvious that you can use the formatting loop to count the number of pages in the document. You might consider calling a formatting loop periodically to perform pagination of the document. This would allow you to display the number of pages in the document in your application's status bar. For efficiency, you could spawn a separate thread to perform the pagination while the user continues typing text in the document.

Printing Headers and Footers

Printing headers and footers is simply a variation on what you know about printing thus far. You can print headers and footers in one of two ways:

1. Write directly to the printer canvas using standard TCanvas calls.
2. Use separate RichEdit components for the header and footer and use the RichEdit printing methods discussed earlier.

I focus on the latter of these two methods in this section. The example program for this section is called HeaderFooter and can be found on the book's CD-ROM. The program allows the user to specify the header and/or footer in a form as shown in Figure 7.9. This form contains two RichEdit components called HeaderRichEdit and FooterRichEdit. This example is intended to illustrate the basics of printing headers and footers and, as such, doesn't contain a lot of features. For example, it doesn't provide a formatting toolbar on the Header and Footer form, nor does it allow the user to specify the position of the header and footer. It's easy enough to add those features to your applications, though. One additional feature of the program is that it prints a default header and footer if the user hasn't specifically set the header and footer text.

FIGURE 7.9

The Header and Footer form allows you to specify the header and footer used when printing.

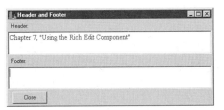

I don't show all the code for the HeaderFooter program because the bulk of it is code that you have seen already.

Printing headers and footers consist of nothing more than creating rendering rectangles for the header and footer and sending additional EM_FORMATRANGE messages before calling the NewPage() method of TPrinter. That might sound like an oversimplification, but it really is that easy. Like the Printing example discussed earlier, the main form of the HeaderFooter example contains a method called Print1Click() that does all the work of printing. Listing 7.5 shows the Print1Click() method.

LISTING 7.5   THE Print1Click() METHOD OF THE HEADERFOOTER PROGRAM

```
void __fastcall TMainForm::Print1Click(TObject *Sender)
{
Screen->Cursor = crHourGlass;
  Application->ProcessMessages();

  TList* pageList = new TList;
  int width = GetDeviceCaps(Printer()->Handle, PHYSICALWIDTH);
  int height = GetDeviceCaps(Printer()->Handle, PHYSICALHEIGHT);
  int logPixelsX = GetDeviceCaps(Printer()->Handle, LOGPIXELSX);
  int logPixelsY = GetDeviceCaps(Printer()->Handle, LOGPIXELSY);
  int xOffset = GetDeviceCaps(Printer()->Handle, PHYSICALOFFSETX);
  int yOffset = GetDeviceCaps(Printer()->Handle, PHYSICALOFFSETY);

  SendMessage(RichEdit->Handle, EM_FORMATRANGE, 0, 0);
  FORMATRANGE fr;
  memset(&fr, 0, sizeof(fr));
  fr.hdc = Printer()->Handle;
  fr.hdcTarget = Printer()->Handle;
  SetMapMode(fr.hdc, MM_TEXT);

  TRect pageRect;
  pageRect.left = 0;
  pageRect.top = 0;
  pageRect.right = MulDiv(width - xOffset, 1440, logPixelsX);
  pageRect.bottom = MulDiv(height - yOffset, 1440, logPixelsY);

  TRect rendRect;
  rendRect.left = pageRect.left + (Margins->Left * 1440) - xOffset;
  rendRect.top = pageRect.top + (Margins->Top * 1440) - yOffset;
  rendRect.right = pageRect.right - (Margins->Right * 1440);
  rendRect.bottom = pageRect.bottom - (Margins->Bottom * 1440);

  TRect headerRect;
  headerRect.left = pageRect.left + (Margins->Left * 1440) - xOffset;
  headerRect.top = pageRect.top + (.5 * 1440) - yOffset;
  headerRect.right = pageRect.right - (Margins->Right * 1440);
  headerRect.bottom = (.75 * 1440);

  TRect footerRect;
  footerRect.left = pageRect.left + (Margins->Left * 1440) - xOffset;
```

continues

7

USING THE
RICHEDIT
COMPONENT

LISTING 7.5   CONTINUED

```cpp
footerRect.top = pageRect.bottom - (.5 * 1440) - yOffset;
footerRect.right = pageRect.right - (Margins->Right * 1440);
footerRect.bottom = pageRect.bottom;

fr.chrg.cpMin = 0;
fr.chrg.cpMax = -1;
int textLen = RichEdit->Text.Length();
do {
  fr.rc = rendRect;
  fr.rcPage = pageRect;
  TPrinterPage* page = new TPrinterPage;
  page->StartPos = fr.chrg.cpMin;
  fr.chrg.cpMin = SendMessage(
    RichEdit->Handle, EM_FORMATRANGE, false, (int)&fr);
  page->EndPos = fr.chrg.cpMin - 1;
  pageList->Add(page);
} while (fr.chrg.cpMin != -1 && fr.chrg.cpMin < textLen);

SendMessage(RichEdit->Handle, EM_FORMATRANGE, 0, 0);

PrintDialog->MaxPage = pageList->Count;
if (!PrintDialog->Execute()) {
  Screen->Cursor = crDefault;
  return;
}
Printer()->Title = "Rich Edit Printing Example " +
  ExtractFileName(OpenDialog->FileName);
int startPage, endPage;
if (PrintDialog->PrintRange == prPageNums) {
  startPage = PrintDialog->FromPage - 1;
  endPage = PrintDialog->ToPage - 1;
}
else {
  startPage = 0;
  endPage = pageList->Count - 1;
}

Screen->Cursor = crHourGlass;
Application->ProcessMessages();

textLen = RichEdit->Text.Length();
Printer()->BeginDoc();
SetMapMode(Printer()->Handle, MM_TEXT);
fr.hdc = Printer()->Handle;
fr.hdcTarget = Printer()->Handle;
int pageCount = startPage;

bool autoFooter = false;
if (HeaderFooterForm->HeaderRichEdit->Text == "")
```

```
      HeaderFooterForm->HeaderRichEdit->Text = OpenDialog->FileName;
  if (HeaderFooterForm->FooterRichEdit->Text == "")
    autoFooter = true;

  do {
    fr.rc = rendRect;
    fr.rcPage = pageRect;
    TPrinterPage* pp = (TPrinterPage*)pageList->Items[pageCount];
    fr.chrg.cpMin = pp->StartPos;
    fr.chrg.cpMax = pp->EndPos;
    Printer()->NewPage();
    SendMessage(RichEdit->Handle, EM_FORMATRANGE, true, (int)&fr);

    fr.rc = headerRect;
    fr.rcPage = pageRect;
    fr.chrg.cpMin = 0;
    fr.chrg.cpMax = -1;
    SendMessage(HeaderFooterForm->HeaderRichEdit->Handle,
      EM_FORMATRANGE, true, (int)&fr);

    fr.rc = footerRect;
    fr.rcPage = pageRect;
    fr.chrg.cpMin = 0;
    fr.chrg.cpMax = -1;
    if (autoFooter)
      HeaderFooterForm->FooterRichEdit->Text = "Page " +
        String(pageCount + 1) + " of " + String(pageList->Count);
    SendMessage(HeaderFooterForm->FooterRichEdit->Handle,
      EM_FORMATRANGE, true, (int)&fr);
  } while (++pageCount < endPage + 1);

  SendMessage(RichEdit->Handle, EM_FORMATRANGE, 0, 0);
  Printer()->EndDoc();

  for (int i=0;i<pageList->Count;i++)
    delete (TPrinterPage*)pageList->Items[i];
  delete pageList;
  Screen->Cursor = crDefault;
}
```

First, notice that I declare two rendering rectangles for the header and footer areas:

```
TRect headerRect;
headerRect.left = pageRect.left + (Margins->Left * 1440) - xOffset;
headerRect.top = pageRect.top + (.5 * 1440) - yOffset;
headerRect.right = pageRect.right - (Margins->Right * 1440);
headerRect.bottom = (.75 * 1440);

TRect footerRect;
footerRect.left = pageRect.left + (Margins->Left * 1440) - xOffset;
```

```
footerRect.top = pageRect.bottom - (.5 * 1440) - yOffset;
footerRect.right = pageRect.right - (Margins->Right * 1440);
footerRect.bottom = pageRect.bottom;
```

From this code, you can deduce that the header prints 1/2" from the top of the printable area and is only 1/4" in height. The footer prints 1/2" from the bottom of the page and extends to the bottom of the page rectangle.

As I said earlier, the HeaderFooter program generates a default header and footer if the user hasn't specified the header or footer text. This feature is provided primarily so that you can run the program, load a file, print, and see immediate results. The default header prints the path and filename of the file in the RichEdit component. The default footer prints the page number and the total pages in traditional format. For example:

```
Page 1 of 5
```

Here is the code that sets the default header and sets a flag indicating that a default footer should be generated later in the printing loop:

```
bool autoFooter = false;
if (HeaderFooterForm->HeaderRichEdit->Text == "")
  HeaderFooterForm->HeaderRichEdit->Text = OpenDialog->FileName;
if (HeaderFooterForm->FooterRichEdit->Text == "")
  autoFooter = true;
```

The only other code of significance is the code in the printing loop. First, I print the actual page using the exact code I showed you earlier. I then set up the FORMATRANGE structure to print the header and send a second EM_FORMATRANGE message, this time to the HeaderRichEdit component:

```
fr.rc = headerRect;
fr.rcPage = pageRect;
fr.chrg.cpMin = 0;
fr.chrg.cpMax = -1;
SendMessage(HeaderFooterForm->HeaderRichEdit->Handle,
  EM_FORMATRANGE, true, (int)&fr);
```

Notice that I have set the rc member of the FORMATRANGE structure to the headerRect variable. Notice also that I set cpMin to 0 and cpMax to -1 to print the entire contents of the RichEdit component that contains the header text. The text is sent to the printer by sending the HeaderRichEdit component an EM_FORMATRANGE message.

The code to send the footer to the printer is identical in purpose with the obvious exception that I set up the FORMATRANGE structure to use the footer rectangle and that I send the EM_FORMATRANGE message to the FooterRichEdit component:

```
fr.rc = footerRect;
fr.rcPage = pageRect;
```

```
fr.chrg.cpMin = 0;
fr.chrg.cpMax = -1;
if (autoFooter)
  HeaderFooterForm->FooterRichEdit->Text = "Page " +
    String(pageCount + 1) + " of " + String(pageList->Count);
SendMessage(HeaderFooterForm->FooterRichEdit->Handle,
  EM_FORMATRANGE, true, (int)&fr);
```

This code also sets up the default text for the footer if the `auotFooter` variable (defined earlier) is `true`.

At this point in the process, the printer's device context is set up with the body of the page, the header text, and the footer text. The next time the `NewPage()` method is called, the page is sent to the printer, complete with header and footer.

Summary

This chapter presented some of the issues you are likely to encounter when dealing with the `RichEdit` component. There are many rich edit operations that I wanted to discuss in this chapter but simply didn't have the room to cover. Those operations include creating a print preview window, using rich edit 2.0 in your applications, and embedding OLE objects (such as graphics) in your rich edit documents. Fortunately, you can find out more information on these subjects on Robert Dunn's Web site at `http://home.att.net/~robertdunn/Yacs.html`. Robert's site is called *Just Another Code Site*, but I can assure you that it is anything but that. It is the premier site for C++Builder users who are doing serious work with the `RichEdit` component.

As you have seen, the `RichEdit` component does not completely wrap the capabilities of the underlying `RichEdit` control. Still, with a little help from the Windows API, you can create professional applications that require an edit control complete with formatted text.

7

USING THE RICHEDIT COMPONENT

Fields and Database Tools

*by Charlie Calvert
and Kent Reisdorph*

IN THIS CHAPTER

This chapter covers a set of visual tools you can use to simplify database development. The major areas of concentration are as follows:

- Relational databases
- The Fields Editor
- `TField` descendant objects
- Calculated fields
- The `TDBGrid` component
- Lookup fields
- The SQL Explorer
- The Database Desktop (DBD)
- Query by Example (QBE)
- Multirecord objects—`TDBCtrlGrid`

Using C++Builder's visual and programmatic tools to manage relational databases is the theme binding these subjects together. C++Builder has become a very sophisticated database tool, so getting a feeling for the breadth of the tools available to client/server developers takes time. One of this chapter's goals is to give you some sense of the key components used when designing database applications.

One of the most frequently mentioned tools in this chapter is the Fields Editor. By using the Fields Editor, you can create objects that you can use to influence the manner and types of data that appear in visual controls such as `TDBEdit` and `TDBGrid`. For instance, you can use the objects made in the Fields Editor to format data so that it appears as currency or as a floating-point number with a defined precision. These same changes can be accomplished through the Data Dictionary in the SQL Explorer or through the Database Desktop. These latter tools, however, have a global impact on the field's potential values, whereas the changes made in the Object Inspector affect only the current application.

The `TDBGrid` control's `Columns` property can be used to change the appearance of a grid so that its columns are arranged in a new order or are hidden. You can also use the `Columns` property to change the color of columns in a grid, or to insert drop-down combo boxes into a grid.

The lessons you learn in this chapter demonstrate techniques used by most programmers when they present database tables to their users. Much of the material involves manipulating visual tools, but the basic subject matter is fairly technical and assumes an understanding of the C++Builder environment and language.

Getting Started with Relational Databases

Many different kinds of databases are possible, but only two kinds have any significant market share for the PC in today's world:

- Flat-file databases
- Relational databases

> **NOTE**
>
> A new system, *object-oriented databases*, has emerged in recent years. These databases represent an interesting form of technology, but I will omit discussion of them here because they have a small user base at this time.
>
> Oracle has also made significant improvements to its database model, many of which are supported by C++Builder 4. That topic is not covered in this book because its appeal is limited to users of a specific third-party product rather than to C++ programmers as a whole.

A *flat-file database* consists of a single file. The classic example is an address book that contains a single table with six fields in it: Name, Address, City, State, Zip, and Phone. If that is your entire database, what you have is a flat-file database. In a flat-file database, the words *table* and *database* are synonymous.

In general, relational databases consist of a series of tables related to each other by one or more fields in each table. The Address program shown in Chapter 9, "Flat-File Real-World Databases," is an example of a flat-file database. Chapter 10, "Relational Databases," holds a program called KdAdd; it is a relational database.

Consider these three key differences between relational and flat-file databases:

1. A flat-file database, like the address book example outlined previously, consists of one single table. That's the whole database. There is nothing more to say about it. Each table stands alone, isolated in its own solipsistic world.
2. Relational databases always contain multiple tables. For instance, the Customer and Orders tables are both part of the BCDEMOS database that ships with C++Builder. As you will see, many other tables are included in that database, but for now concentrate on the Customer and Orders tables.

3. Tables in relational databases are tied together on special fields. These fields are called *primary* and *foreign keys*. These keys usually have indices, and they usually— but by no means always—consist of a simple integer value. For instance, the CustNo field relates the Customer and Orders tables to one another. The CustNo field is a primary key in the Customer table and a foreign key in the Orders table. Both fields also have indices.

NOTE

Indices are about searching and sorting. *Keys*, on the other hand, are about relating tables, and particularly about something called referential integrity. *Referential integrity* applies specifically to relational databases and refers to the fact that the database architecture itself enforces rules about how the database can be modified.

In practice, these concepts get mixed together in some pretty ugly ways, but the underlying theory relies on the kinds of distinctions I am drawing in this note. For instance, keys are usually indexed, and so people often talk about keys and indices as if they were the same. They are, however, distinct concepts.

One way to start drawing the distinction is to understand that keys are part of the *theory* of relational databases, whereas indices are part of the *implementation* of relational databases. You learn more on this subject as the chapter evolves.

Clearly, relational databases are radically different from flat-file databases. Relational databases typically consist of multiple tables, at least some of which are related by one or more fields. Flat-file databases, on the other hand, consist of only a single table, which is unrelated to any other table.

Advantages of Relational Databases

What advantages do relational databases have over flat-file databases? This system has many strengths. The following are a few of the highlights:

- Relational databases enforce referential integrity. These constraints help you enter data in a logical, systematic, and error-free manner.
- Relational databases save disk space.

  For instance, the Customer table holds information about customers, including their addresses, phone numbers, and other contact information. The Orders table holds information about orders, including their dates, cost, and payment method. If you were forced to keep all this information in a single table, each order would also have to list the customer information, which would mean that some customers' addresses would be repeated dozens of times in the database. That kind of duplication in a big database can easily burn up megabytes of disk space. Using a relational database is better because each customer's address is entered only once. You could also have two flat-file databases, one holding the customer information and the other holding the order information. The problem with this second scenario is that flat-file databases provide no means of relating the two tables.

- Relational databases enable you to create one-to-many relationships.

  For instance, you can have one name that is related to multiple addresses. You cannot capture that kind of relationship in a simple way in a flat-file database. You will see in the KdAdd program that you can easily relate multiple addresses, phone numbers, and so on, with each name. The flexible structure of relational databases enables programmers to adapt to these kinds of real-world situations. For many entries in a database, you will want to keep track of two addresses: one for a person's home and the other for his or her work. If someone you know has a summer home or an apartment in the city, you need to add yet more addresses to the listing. You cannot add these addresses conveniently in flat-file databases. Relational databases handle this kind of thing with ease. In the preceding point, I emphasized that this kind of feature saves space; here, I'm emphasizing that it allows for a more logical, flexible, and easy-to-use arrangement of your data.

A relational database offers these possibilities:

1. You can view the Customer table alone, or you can view the Orders table alone.

2. You can place the two tables in a one-to-many relationship so that you can see them side by side but see only the orders relating to the currently highlighted customer.

3. You can perform a join between the two tables so that you can see them as one combined table, much like the combined table you would be forced to use if you wanted to "join" the Customer and Orders table in a single flat-file database. However, you can decide which fields from both tables will be part of the join, leaving out any you don't want to view. The joined table is also temporary and does not permanently take up unnecessary disk space. In short, relational databases can use joins to provide some of the benefits of flat-file databases, whereas flat-file databases cannot emulate the virtues of relational databases.

As you can see, the three concepts that stand out when talking about relational databases are referential integrity, flexibility, and conservation of disk space. In this case, the word *flexibility* covers a wide range of broad features that can only be fully appreciated over time.

8

FIELDS AND DATABASE TOOLS

The one disadvantage that relational databases have when compared to flat-file databases is that they are more complicated to use. This disadvantage is not just a minor sticking point. Neophytes are often completely baffled by relational databases. They don't have a clue as to what to do with them. Even if you have a relative degree of expertise, you can still become overwhelmed by a relational database that consists of three dozen tables related to one another in some hundred different ways (and yes, complexity on that scale is not uncommon in corporate America).

The Basis of Relational Databases

The basis for relational databases is a simple form of mathematics. In its simplest case, each table represents a set that can be related to other tables through fundamental mathematics. Because computers are so good at math, particularly integer math, they find relational databases easy to manipulate.

One common relational databases feature is that most records will have a unique number associated with them. These numbers are used as the keys that relate one table to another. These keys enable you to group tables together using simple mathematical relationships. In particular, you can group them using simple integer-based set arithmetic. I should add, however, that there is no reason why you can't use a nonnumeric field as a key. In fact, using such a field this way is common practice in many corporate databases. Evidence of this practice can be seen in the strange combination of letters and numbers you find in the serial numbers or account numbers on products and services you might use in your own home. However, you will find an admirable purity in the way tables relate when they are keyed on integer fields.

In the Customer table from BCDEMOS, each record has a unique CustNo field. This CustNo field serves as a key. Furthermore, the Orders table has a unique OrderNo field associated with it. This field is also a key field. The Orders table also has a CustNo field that will relate it to the Customer table. The terminology of relational databases expresses these ideas by saying that the Customer table has a primary key called CustNo and that the Orders table has a primary key called OrderNo as well as a foreign key called CustNo. This is shown in the following minitable:

Table Name	Primary Key	Foreign Key (Secondary Index)
Customer	CustNo	N/A
Orders	OrderNo	CustNo

Given this scenario, you can say, "Show me the set of all orders such that their CustNo field is equal to X or within the range of X–Y." Computers love these kinds of simple mathematical relationships. They are their bread and butter. In essence, you are just asking for the intersection of two sets: Show me the intersection of this record from the

Customer table with all the records from the Orders table. This intersection will consist of one record from the Customer table with a particular CustNo, plus all the records from the Orders table that have the same CustNo in their foreign keys.

These CustNo, OrderNo, AuthorNo, BookNo, and similar fields might also be used in flat-file databases as indices, but they play a unique role in relational databases because they are the keys used to relate different tables. They make it possible to reduce the relationship between tables to nothing more than a simple series of mathematical formulas. These formulas are based on keys rather than on indices. It is merely a coincidence that in most tables the keys also happen to be indexed.

Viewing Indices and Keys in DBD or the SQL Explorer

In the next few sections, I define primary and secondary keys and describe how to use them. Prefacing this discussion with a brief description of how to view keys using some of the tools that ship with C++Builder might be helpful. Keep in mind that this information provides just a preliminary look at this material. I cover it again in greater depth later in this chapter in a section called "Exploring Keys and Indices: The BCDEMOS Database."

You can view the indices and keys on a table in two ways. The best way is to use the SQL Explorer. Open the Explorer and view the BCDEMOS database, as shown in Figure 8.1.

FIGURE 8.1

Viewing the BCDEMOS database in the SQL Explorer.

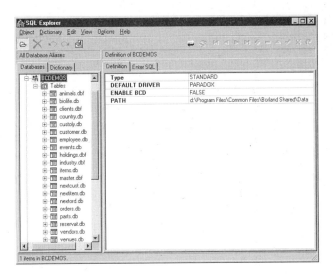

Click the Orders table and open the Referential Constraints branch, as shown in Figure 8.2. Notice the two constraints on this table: RefCustinOrders and RefOrders. The RefCustinOrders field defines CustNo as a foreign key that relates to the CustNo field in the Customer table.

FIGURE 8.2

The primary and foreign fields of the Orders table.

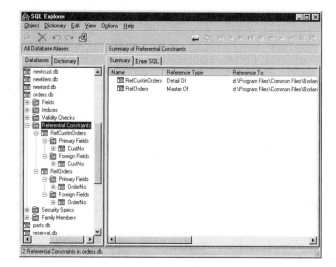

A second way to view this key is to use the Database Desktop. Set the Working Directory from the File menu to BCDEMOS alias. Open the Orders table in the Database Desktop and select Table, Info Structure. Drop down Table properties and select Referential Integrity, as shown in Figure 8.3.

FIGURE 8.3

Selecting Referential Integrity in the Database Desktop.

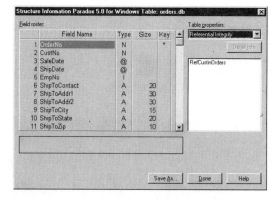

Double-click `RefCustinOrders` to bring up the Referential Integrity dialog, shown in Figure 8.4.

FIGURE 8.4

The CustNo *field in the* Orders *table relates to the* CustNo *field in the* Customer *table.*

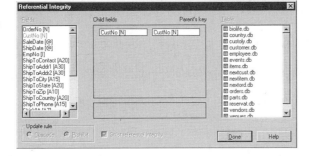

The fields on the left side of this dialog belong to the `Orders` table. On the right is a list of all the tables in the database. In the center you can see that the `CustNo` field has been selected from the `Orders` table and that the `CustNo` field has been selected from the `Customer` table. The `Customer` table's primary key is related to the foreign key of the `Orders` table.

Now go back to the SQL Explorer and open the Indices branch of the `Orders` table, as shown in Figure 8.5.

FIGURE 8.5

The primary and CustNo *indices on the* Orders *table.*

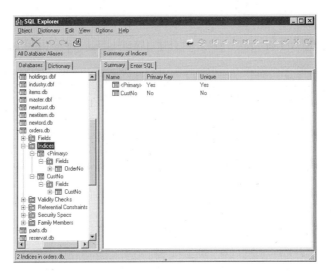

Note that you can see the names of the indices, here labeled as `<primary>` and `CustNo`. The fields found in the indices are also displayed. For instance, you can see that the primary index consists of the OrderNo field and that the secondary index consists of the CustNo field.

I am showing these figures to you so that you will begin to see the distinction between keys and indices. The concepts are distinct. For further proof, open the IBLOCAL database in the SQL Explorer. (This assumes that you installed Local Interbase when you installed C++Builder.) Use SYSDBA as the username and masterkey as the password. Now open the EMPLOYEE PROJECT table, as shown in Figure 8.6. Note the separate listings for the index, primary key, and foreign key.

FIGURE 8.6

The
EMPLOYEE_PROJECT
table has three indices, one primary key, and two foreign keys.

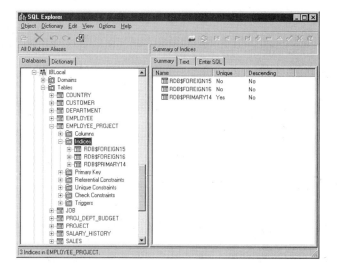

You can also see the indices for a table inside the Database Desktop. To get started, open the Orders table and select Table, Info Structure. The fields with the stars beside them are part of the primary index. Bring down the Table Properties combo box to view the secondary indices. Double-click the indices you see to view the details of their design. If you want to change the structure of a table, choose Table, Restructure rather than Table, Info Structure.

The Database Desktop is most often the right tool when I want to create or modify a table, and SQL Explorer is most often the right tool to use when I want to view the structure of a table. The SQL Explorer loads faster than the Database Desktop. However, I often find myself jumping back and forth between the tools to get the best features of each. Third-party Computer-Aided Software Engineering (CASE) tools are generally superior to either of the products discussed in this section. However, no CASE tools ship with C++Builder, so I emphasize the universally available tools in this text.

Throughout the ensuing discussion, you might have occasion to use the SQL Explorer to examine the structure of the `Customer`, `Orders`, `Items`, and `Parts` tables. I use these tables when defining what relational databases are all about.

Creating a Primary Key Is the Key

The preceding sections introduce you to some of the key concepts in relational databases. Based on this information, you should begin to see the importance of creating a unique key in the first field of most tables you create. This field is called a *primary key*. In both Paradox and InterBase, creating a primary key without also simultaneously creating an index is impossible.

If you want to have a list of addresses in a table, don't just list `Address`, `City`, `State` and `Zip` fields. Be sure to also include a `CustNo`, `AddressNo`, or `Code` field. This field will usually be both an index and the first field of the database. It is the primary key for your table and must be, by definition, unique. That is, each record should have a unique `Code` field associated with it. This field need not be an integer value, but an integer is a logical choice for this kind of field.

The primary key does the following:

- It serves as the means of differentiating one record from another.
- It is used in referential integrity.
- Because it is usually indexed, it can also help with fast searches and sorts.

As said earlier, the distinction between indices and keys becomes blurred at times. Nevertheless, they are distinct concepts. Just to make sure this information is clear, I'll list the right and wrong ways to create a table:

Right Method

CustNo: Integer

LastName, FirstName, Address, City, State, Zip: String

Wrong Method

LastName, FirstName, Address, City, State, Zip: String

The first example is "correct" because it has a primary index called `CustNo`. It is declared as a unique `Integer` value. The second example is "wrong" because it omits a primary index. In this case the primary index is an integer field. The primary index can be of any data type so long as the values stored in that field will be unique.

I put the words *correct* and *wrong* in quotation marks because this discipline really doesn't have any hard and fast rules. On some occasions, you might not want to create a table that has a primary index. However, that's exactly what you want to do 99 percent of the time.

Even if you don't yet understand how relational databases work, for now I suggest that you automatically add a simple numerical value in a primary index to all your tables. Do so even if you are not using the field at this time. After you get a better feeling for relational databases, you will understand intuitively when the field is needed and when you are encountering one of those rare occasions when it is going to be useless.

When people first work with relational databases, they may get a little hung up about the overhead involved in creating all these extra key fields. The point to remember is that these fields allow the database to be treated as nothing more than sets related in various combinations. Computers don't feel weighed down by the extra field any more than a car feels weighed down by a steering wheel, people feel weighed down by their hands, or a rosebush feels weighed down by a rose. Computers like logic; they like numbers; they like nice, clean, easily defined relationships. They like primary keys in the first field of a table.

The Data and the Index

One good way to begin understanding relational databases is by working with the Customer, Orders, Items, and Parts tables from the BCDEMOS database. All four of these tables are related in one-to-many relationships, each-to-each. That is, the Customer table is related to the Orders table, the Orders table to the Items table, and the Items table to the Parts table. (The relationship also works in the opposite direction, but it may be simpler at first to think of it as going in only one direction.)

Master	Detail	Connector (Primary Key and Foreign Key)
Customer	Orders	CustNo
Orders	Items	OrderNo
Items	Parts	PartNo

Read the preceding minitable as a series of rows, starting left and moving to the right, as if they were sentences. The list shows that the Customer and Orders tables are related in a one-to-many relationship, with Customer being the master table and Orders being the detail table. The connector between them is the CustNo field; they both have a CustNo field.

The CustNo field is the primary key of the Customer table and the foreign key of the Orders table. The OrderNo field is the primary key of the Orders table and a foreign key of the Items table. The PartNo field is the primary key of the Parts table and a foreign key of the Items table. Figure 8.7 shows the relationships between these tables.

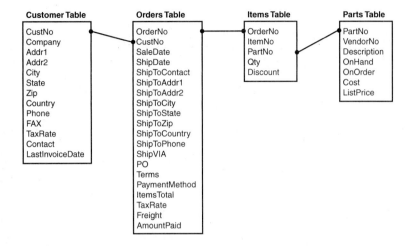

FIGURE 8.7

The table relationship.

The `Customer`, `Orders`, `Items`, and `Parts` tables are joined by a sequence of primary and foreign keys. You can see all these relationships in action by running the Relate program from the CD-ROM that accompanies this book.

The relationship between these tables can be reversed. For instance, the `Parts` table could become the master table and the `Items` table the detail table, and so on, back down the line. The reason you can reverse the relationship becomes clear when you think in purely mathematical terms. The `Customer` table has a series of `CustNo` fields. Say the `CustNo` for the first record is `1000`. To get the orders associated with that customer, you ask this question: "What are all the rows from the `Orders` table that have a `CustNo` of `1000`?" This is the SQL statement that performs the query:

```
Select * from Orders where CustNo = 1000
```

Clearly, you could reverse this question. If you select a particular row from the `Orders` table, you could find which item from the `Customer` table it is related to by asking for the set of all `Customer` records with a `CustNo` of `1000`. Because the `CustNo` field for the `Customer` table is a unique index, you will get only one record back. However, the way you relate the tables is still the same:

```
Select * from Customer where CustNo = 1000
```

Primary Keys and Primary Indices

The `Parts`, `Orders`, `Items`, and `Customer` tables have various keys. As it happens, these keys are also indices. An *index* enables you sort tables on a particular field. A *key* helps you define the relationship between two tables or otherwise group related bits of information by a set of predefined and automatically enforced rules.

Unfortunately, you can still relate tables without the presence of any keys or indices. For instance, if no `CustNo` primary and foreign keys appeared in the `Customer` and `Orders` tables, Paradox would still let you use SQL to relate the tables in a one-to-many relationship. However, performance in this scenario would be slow because you have no index; you also have no constraints on the data you could enter in the two tables because no primary and foreign keys define referential integrity. The tables are still part of a relational database, but they lack the features that make a relational database appealing. You need both the keys and the indices to make a relational database appealing.

I'll draw a distinction between only two different kinds of keys. The first kind I will discuss is called a primary key. The second is called a foreign key.

- A *primary key* is a unique value used to identify a record in a table. It is usually numerical and it is usually indexed. It can be combined with a foreign key to define referential integrity. I will talk more about referential integrity later in this chapter.

- Because the primary key is indexed, it defines the default sort order for the table. When you first open a table, it is automatically sorted on this field. If a table does not have a primary index, records will appear in the order in which they were added to the table. For all practical purposes, a table without an index has no defined order in which records will appear.

- With Paradox tables, each entry in the primary index must be unique. You can't have two `CustNos` in the `Customer` table that are the same. You can, however, have multiple foreign keys that are not unique.

- Having multiple fields in the primary index of a Paradox table is legal. This type is called a *composite index*. These fields must be sequential, starting with the first field in the table. You can't have the primary index consist of a table's first, third, and fourth fields. A *composite index* with three fields must consist of the first, second, and third fields. If you have `FirstName` and `LastName` fields in your database, they can both be part of the primary index. You should, however, declare the `LastName` before the `FirstName` so that your index will list people alphabetically by last name: `CustNo, LastName, FirstName`. To get a good sort on these fields, you should define a secondary index on the `LastName` and `FirstName` fields.

- Unlike an index, the primary and foreign keys are never composite. They always consist of one field.

Creating a primary key enables you to list two people with the same name but with different addresses. For instance, you can list a John Doe on Maple Street who has a `CustNo` of 25 and a John Doe on Henry Street who has a `CustNo` of 2000. The names may be the same, but the database can distinguish them by their `CustNos`.

Secondary Indices and Foreign Keys

You're now ready to move on to a consideration of foreign keys. The CustNo field of the Orders table is a foreign key because it relates the Orders table to the primary key of the Customer table. It is also a secondary index that aids in sorting and searching through data. Indices also speed operations such as joins and other master-detail relationships.

When writing this section, I found it difficult to totally divorce the idea of foreign key and secondary index. However, I will try to split them up into two categories, taking foreign keys first:

- A *foreign key* provides a means for relating two tables according to a set of predefined rules called *referential integrity*.

- With Paradox tables, you use the referential integrity tools from the Database Desktop to define foreign keys. There is no such thing as a composite foreign key.

- Using SQL, you can relate two tables in a one-to-many relationship even if no index or key appears in either table. Your performance will be better if you have indices. You will have no way to enforce referential integrity if you don't define foreign and primary keys.

- Using the TTable object, you cannot relate two tables in a one-to-many relationship without indices. (This point doesn't clearly belong in either the section on keys or the one on indices. It relates to both subjects.)

Here are some facts about secondary indices:

- A *secondary index* provides an alternative sort order to the one provided by the primary key.

- You need to explicitly change the index if you want to switch from the primary index to a secondary index. Remember that the default sort order for a Paradox table is provided by the primary index. If you want to switch from the primary index to a secondary index, you need to change your table's IndexName or IndexFieldName property. You don't have to do anything if you want to use the primary index; the table will sort on that field automatically.

- An index that contains more than one field is called a *composite index*. You can create composite secondary indices, which means the indices will contain multiple fields. In practice, fields such as FirstName and LastName can often be part of a secondary index because your primary index is usually a unique numerical value.

- All primary and foreign keys in Paradox tables must be indexed. You can't define referential integrity without indices, and in particular, you must have a primary key. Furthermore, in InterBase tables, the act of defining a primary or foreign key will automatically generate an index. (Once again, this item doesn't clearly belong in either the discussion of keys or of indices, but relates to both. Sometimes the distinctions between the two subjects become blurred.)

If you are new to databases, you will undoubtedly be frustrated to discover that different databases have varying rules for setting up indices, keys, and so on. In this book, I tend to use Paradox tables as the default, but I also spend considerable time describing InterBase tables. If you use some other database, such as dBASE, Oracle, or Sybase, be sure to read up on the basic rules for using those tools. For instance, some databases let you set up a foreign key that is not an index. In the Paradox and InterBase world, however, foreign keys are always accompanied by an index, so the two words become synonymous—particularly in the hands of people who don't really understand how relational databases work.

The good news is that you will find that, overall, certain basic principles define how databases work. The details may vary from implementation to implementation, but the fundamental ideas stay the same.

Relating Information with Keys

Let me take this whole paradigm even one step further. When I first looked at a database, I thought of it as a place to *store* information. After spending a lot of time with relational databases, I now think of them primarily as a way to *relate* bits of information through keys and indices.

I know this is putting the cart before the horse, but what really interests me about databases now is not the fact that they contain information per se, but that I can query them to retrieve related bits of information. In other words, I'm more interested in the logic that defines how tables relate to one another than I am in the information itself.

No one can get excited about a list of addresses or a list of books. The lists themselves are very boring. What's interesting is the system of keys and indices that relates tables and the various SQL statements you can use to ask questions against various sets of tables.

When I picture a table, I see its primary and foreign keys as great big pillars, and I envision all the rest of the data as a little stone altar that is dwarfed by the pillars. Like a pagan temple, it's the pillars that you notice first; the altar is just a small stone structure you might overlook until someone points it out. Of course, the temple is built around the altar, and databases are built around their data. In practice, it is easy to overlook the data. You care about the pillars; you care about the primary and foreign keys. The rest tends to fade into the background.

Give me a well-designed database with lots of related tables, and I can have fun asking it all sorts of interesting questions. It's not the data itself that is important, but the way the data is related!

The act of properly relating a set of tables in a database is called, tragically enough, *normalizing* the data. Normalizing a database is the fun part of creating a database application.

This ends the portion of this chapter that deals entirely with theoretical issues. The remainder of the chapter shows you how to use some of the database tools that ship with C++Builder, as well as how to write code that demonstrates some of the key features of C++Builder database programming.

Using Database Tools

In the next few sections, I describe how to use the SQL Explorer, Database Desktop, and other tools. The programs provide core functionality needed by C++Builder database programmers. The Database Desktop is particularly important to developers using local databases such as Paradox or dBASE. However, it provides services that are useful to all programmers.

The SQL Explorer is one of the most important tools in C++Builder, and every database programmer should be familiar with how it works. Depending on the version of C++Builder that you have, this tool may be called either the *SQL Explorer* or the *Database Explorer*. With some versions of the product, you can access it from the Database menu in the IDE; you can access it from the Start menu with other versions.

Exploring Keys and Indices: The BCDEMOS Database

The following is a list of the indices on the Customer, Orders, Items, and Parts tables:

Table Name	Fields in Primary Index	Secondary Indices
Customer	CustNo	Company
Orders	OrderNo	CustNo
Items	OrderNo, ItemNo	OrderNo, PartNo
Parts	PartNo	VendorNo, Description

Notice that the Items table has a composite primary index consisting of the OrderNo and ItemNo fields. It also has two secondary indices, one on the OrderNo field and one on the PartNo field. The Parts table has two secondary indices, one on the VendorNo and one on the Description field.

If you do not have a list like this one already made, you can find this information in at least four ways:

- Using the Object Inspector
- Using the SQL Explorer
- Using the Database Desktop
- Creating a program that leverages the methods of the `TSession` object (such a program is shown in Chapter 10, "Relational Databases").

I will explain all these methods and then discuss some possible alternative techniques.

If you drag the `Customer` table off the SQL Explorer and onto a form, you can view its indices in the Object Inspector. If you bring down the `IndexName` Property Editor, you will see that one index is listed there. It is the secondary index, called `ByCompany`. If you select this index, the table will sort on the `Company` field.

If you set the `IndexName` property back to blank, the table sorts automatically on the primary index, which is the `CustNo` field. In other words, C++Builder never explicitly lists the primary index in the `IndexName` Property Editor. I suppose that the VCL architects assumed that all tables have a primary index and that if you don't specify a particular index name, you want to sort on that index. Of course, creating a table that has no primary index is not an error, and C++Builder can still work with that kind of table.

You can also bring down the `IndexFieldNames` property, which gives you a list of the fields that are indexed—in this case, the `CustNo` and `Company` fields. Here you can see the fields included in the primary index, but they are not marked as belonging to any particular index.

> **NOTE**
>
> To study an interesting case, place a `TTable` on a form and set the `Table` property to `items.db`. Recall that this table has a primary index on the `OrderNo` and `ItemNo` fields and secondary indices on the `OrderNo` and `PartNo` fields. If you bring down the `IndexFieldNames` property in the Object Inspector, you see the following list:
>
> ```
> OrderNo
> OrderNo;ItemNo
> PartNo
> ```
>
> The first item is the `OrderNo` index; the second, the primary index; and the third, the `PartNo` index.

The IndexName and IndexFieldNames properties give you a handy way of tracking indices at design time. They don't, however, give you all the information you might need, such as exactly what fields make up which parts of the primary and secondary indices. You could probably guess in this case, but it would be nice to get a more definitive answer.

If you open the SQL Explorer, expand the BCDEMOS, Tables, Customer, and Indices nodes, you get (naturally enough) a list of the indices on the Customer table. This feature is great, and you should use it whenever possible. Figure 8.8 shows the expanded nodes of the Indices for the Customer table. (The KdAddExplore program from Chapter 10 also uses the TSession object to do the same thing in a C++Builder program.)

FIGURE 8.8

The indices of the Customer *table viewed in the SQL Explorer.*

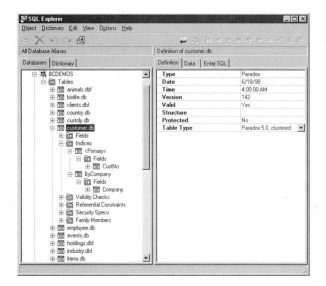

While you have the SQL Explorer open, you should also expand the Fields node, as shown in Figure 8.9. This way, you get a list of all the fields and their types. Notice that you can drag and drop individual fields onto a form.

A third way to get a look at the structure of a table is through the Database Desktop (DBD). You can open this program from the Tools menu in C++Builder. Use the File menu in the DBD to set the Working Directory to the BCDEMOS Alias. Open the Customer table and choose Table, Info Structure. Drop down the Table Properties combo box and look up the secondary indices, as shown in Figure 8.10. The primary index is designated by the asterisks after the keyed fields in the Field Roster. In this case, only the CustNo field is starred because it is the sole keyed field.

8

FIELDS AND
DATABASE TOOLS

FIGURE 8.9

The Fields view of the Customer *table from the SQL Explorer.*

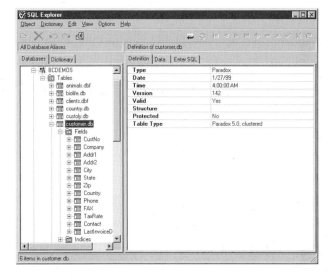

FIGURE 8.10

The Database Desktop struts its venerable features by displaying the indices on the Customer *table.*

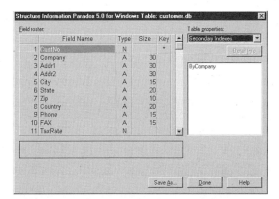

NOTE

Over time, the Database Desktop will probably be replaced entirely by the SQL Explorer. However, the DBD still does some things better than the SQL Explorer, so both products ship with C++Builder.

Notice the Save As button on the Info Structure dialog. You can use this button to save a table that contains the structure of the Customer table. You can then print this table on a printer using TQuickReports. Be sure to use a fixed-size font, not a proportional font:

```
Field Name          Type    Size Key
CustNo              N              *
Company             A       30
Addr1               A       30
Addr2               A       30
City                A       15
State               A       20
Zip                 A       10
Country             A       20
Phone               A       15
FAX                 A       15
TaxRate             N
Contact             A       20
LastInvoiceDate     &
```

In the example shown here, I have printed only the first four elements of the table because of space considerations. (The fields are `Field Name`, `Type`, `Size`, and `Key`.) If I then recursively print the structure of the table used to house the structure of the `Customer` table, I get the following report:

```
Field Name          Type    Size   Key
Field Name          A       25
Type                A       1
Size                S
Key                 A       1
_Invariant Field ID S
_Required Value     A       1
_Min Value          A       255
_Max Value          A       255
_Default Value      A       255
_Picture Value      A       176
_Table Lookup       A       255
_Table Lookup Type  A       1
```

This information is the same as found in the Data Dictionary; it should prove sufficient under most circumstances.

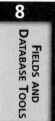

Using the Database Desktop to Create Indices

To create a unique primary key in a Paradox table, open the Database Desktop and create a table with the first field declared as a `Number` or autoincrement value. Place a star next to the first field, which tells Paradox to create a primary index on it, as shown in Figure 8.11.

To create a secondary index, drop down the Table Properties list and choose Secondary Indexes; click the Define button. Select the fields from your table that you want to be part of your index, as shown in Figure 8.12; click OK. A simple dialog comes up, asking you to name the index. I usually name an index based on the fields being indexed. For instance, if I want to create an index on the `CustNo` field, I would call the index

CustNoIndex or ByCustNo. If I wanted to create one on a field called Name, I would call the index NameIndex or ByName.

FIGURE 8.11

Place stars next to the first field or fields of a table to designate the primary index.

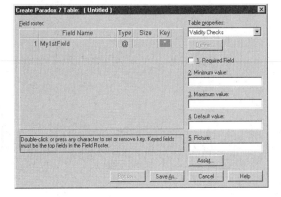

FIGURE 8.12

Creating a secondary index in a Paradox table.

Creating an Alias

On the CD-ROM that ships with this book, you will find two tables called MasterTable and DetailTable. A program called MasterDetail uses these tables. To run this program, you must define an alias in the SQL Explorer.

To create an alias, start the SQL Explorer and choose Object, New. Select STANDARD as your Database Driver Name. Click OK and type the name of your alias; in this case, enter **BCB4UNLEASHED**. Set the path for the alias to point to the directory on your hard drive where the data files from the CD-ROM that accompanies this book are stored. By default, this directory is called Data; you will recognize it because MasterTable.db and DetailTable.db are located inside this directory. (Other files associated with these tables have extensions such as .xg0, .x02, and so on.) Note that you can click a button in the editor for the pathname to browse for the file. When you are done, choose Object, Apply to save your work.

You can test the alias by clicking the + (plus) sign to the left of your alias name. A tree with a branch called Tables will open. Open this branch, click one of the table names, and select the Data tab. Everything has been set up correctly if you can see the data from the table. If you cannot complete these steps, the most likely problem is that you are not pointing the path in the correct location.

That's all there is to setting up the alias. Most of the database programs in this book will use either the BCB4UNLEASHED alias or BCDEMOS, which is created automatically when you install C++Builder.

Using the Database Desktop to Create Primary and Foreign Keys

To create a primary or foreign key on a Paradox table, you need to define referential integrity. You cannot define referential integrity without first defining primary keys on both tables involved. An index also must be located on the foreign key, but this index is created automatically for you when you create the foreign key.

In InterBase, the situation is somewhat different. The act of creating primary or foreign keys automatically defines indices. As said earlier, you will find little variation on the main themes of relational databases, depending on what kind of database you use.

Figure 8.13 shows how to use the Database Desktop to create the MasterTable. The tables look like this, with the MasterTable listed first and the DetailTable listed second:

Field Name	Type	Size	Primary Index?
Code	+		*
Name	A	25	

Field Name	Type	Size	Primary Index?
Code	+		*
MasterCode	I		
SubName	A	25	

To create referential integrity between these two tables, you should open DetailTable in the Database Desktop; choose Table, Restructure. Select Referential Integrity from the Table Properties combo box. Click the Define button and set up the elements so that they look like Figure 8.13. Click the OK button and give this relationship a name, such as RefMasterDetail.

FIGURE 8.13

Defining referential integrity between DetailTable *and* MasterTable.

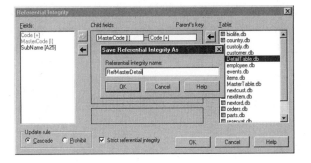

When you are done, you will have created primary keys and foreign keys on MasterTable and DetailTable. The best way to see these keys is to use the SQL Explorer. On my system, I used the BDE Administrator to create an alias called BCB4Unleashed that points to the Data subdirectory. If you open this alias in the SQL Explorer and go to MasterTable, you can see the primary and foreign keys, which Paradox calls *primary* and *foreign fields*.

Exploring Referential Integrity

Referential integrity is one of the most valuable tools in a database programmer's bag of tricks. In particular, referential integrity will help guide the users so that they do not accidentally enter invalid data or accidentally delete needed records.

To see referential integrity in action, use the Database Desktop to enter two records in MasterTable. The first should have the word Days in the Name field, and the second should have the word Months in the Name field. You do not have to fill in the Code field because it is an autoincrement field (+) and is updated automatically:

Code	Name
1	Days
2	Months

In the DetailTable, enter a few names of days of the week or months of the year in the SubName field. Give the MasterCode field a 1 if you are entering a day; give it a 2 if you are entering a month.

Code	Master Code	Subname
1	1	Monday
2	1	Tuesday
3	2	January
4	2	February
5	2	March

You can define a one-to-many relationship with this data in the tables such that, if you viewed the `MasterTable` record with `Days` in the `Name` field, you would see only the days in `DetailTable`. If you selected `Months`, you would see only the month names from the `DetailTable`.

Referential integrity will do two things to help make sure that these tables stay in good shape:

- It prevents you from deleting a record in `MasterTable` that has detail records associated with it in `DetailTable`. For instance, if you select `MasterTable`, set the Database Desktop in Edit mode, and press Ctrl+Delete, you will be unable to delete a record from `MasterTable`.

- Referential integrity prevents you from entering a value in the `MasterCode` field of `DetailTable` that is not in the primary key of `MasterTable`. For instance, if you tried to enter the number 3 in `DetailTable`'s `MasterCode` field, you would get the error message `"Master record missing"` because no record in `MasterTable` with a `Code` field of 3 even exists. Of course, if you added a record to `MasterTable` with a `Code` field that had 3 in it, the database would let you enter the data.

These rules are also enforced inside C++Builder. You might want to create exception handlers for your own programs that bring up messages that explain to the users exactly what was wrong and why they could not perform a particular operation. Most users would not respond well to an exception that said no more than `Master field missing`!

The MasterDetail sample program on the CD-ROM that accompanies this book shows how to use the `MasterTable` and `DetailTable`.

Relational Databases and Joins

Earlier in the chapter, you saw how to relate the `Customer`, `Orders`, `Items`, and `Parts` tables in a one-to-many relationship that is sometimes called a *master-detail relationship*. You relate all four tables in this section, but in a different kind of relationship: a *join*.

Here is a relatively lengthy query:

```
SELECT DISTINCT d.Company, d1.AmountPaid, d2.Qty,
               d3.Description, d3.Cost, d3.ListPrice
FROM "Customer.db" d, "Orders.db" d1,
     "Items.db" d2, "Parts.db" d3
WHERE (d1.CustNo = d.CustNo)
      AND (d2.OrderNo = d1.OrderNo)
      AND (d3.PartNo = d2.PartNo)
ORDER BY d.Company, d1.AmountPaid, d2.Qty,
         d3.Description, d3.Cost, d3.ListPrice
```

Though not horrendously complicated, the syntax is still ugly enough to give some people pause.

The basic principles involved in this kind of statement are simple enough to describe. All that's happening is that the Customer, Orders, Items, and Parts tables are being joined into one large table of the type you would have to create if you were trying to track all this information in a single flat-file database. The one proviso, of course, is that not all the fields from the four tables are being used; in fact, the only ones mentioned are as follows:

```
d.Company, d1.AmountPaid, d2.Qty,
d3.Description, d3.Cost, d3.ListPrice
```

Here the d, d1, d2, and d3 are described in the following From clause:,

```
"Customer.db" d, "Orders.db" d1,
"Items.db" d2, "Parts.db" d3
```

The Order By clause, of course, simply defines the sort order to be used on the table created by this join.

You can create a program that performs this join by dropping a TQuery, TDataSource, and TDBGrid on a form. Wire the objects together, wire the TQuery to the BCDEMOS database, and set its SQL property to the preceding query. A sample program called RelJoin demonstrates this process. The output from the program is shown in Figure 8.14.

FIGURE 8.14

The RelJoin program demonstrates a join on four tables.

Company	AmountPaid	Qty	Description	Cost	ListPrice
Action Club	$134.85	3	Krypton Flashlight	$20.68	$44.95
Action Club	$1,004.80	1	95.1 cu ft Tank	$130.00	$325.00
Action Club	$1,004.80	4	Flashlight (Rechargeable)	$50.99	$169.95
Action Club	$10,152.00	54	Depth/Pressure Gauge Console	$73.32	$188.00
Action Club	$20,108.00	8	Safety Knife	$13.12	$41.00
Action Club	$20,108.00	46	Regulator System	$154.80	$430.00
Action Diver Supply	$536.80	1	Second Stage Regulator	$95.79	$309.00
Action Diver Supply	$536.80	4	Medium Titanium Knife	$26.77	$56.95
Adventure Undersea	$0.00	1	Navigation Compass	$9.18	$19.95
Adventure Undersea	$0.00	2	Depth/Pressure Gauge	$48.30	$105.00
Adventure Undersea	$0.00	3	Electronic Console	$120.90	$390.00
Adventure Undersea	$0.00	3	Flashlight (Rechargeable)	$50.99	$169.95
Adventure Undersea	$0.00	3	Underwater Diver Vehicle	$504.00	$1,680.00
Adventure Undersea	$0.00	3	Welded Seam Stabilizing Vest	$109.20	$280.00
Adventure Undersea	$0.00	4	Depth/Pressure Gauge	$48.30	$105.00
Adventure Undersea	$0.00	5	Compass Console Mount	$10.15	$29.00
Adventure Undersea	$0.00	15	Flashlight	$29.25	$65.00
Adventure Undersea	$0.00	45	Depth/Pressure Gauge Console	$73.32	$188.00
Adventure Undersea	$2,195.00	5	Sonar System	$215.11	$439.00
Adventure Undersea	$3,117.00	3	60.6 cu ft Tank	$57.28	$179.00
Adventure Undersea	$3,117.00	6	Stabilizing Vest	$146.20	$430.00

If you are unfamiliar with this kind of join, you might want to bring up side by side the Relate and RelJoin programs from the CD-ROM that accompanies this book and compare them. Look, for instance, at the Action Club entries in the RelJoin program and trace them so that you see how they correspond to the entries in the Relate program.

Both programs describe an identical set of relationships; they just show the outcome in a different manner.

Notice that the AmountPaid column in the RelJoin program has the same number repeated twice in the Action Club section, as shown in Figure 8.14. In particular, the numbers $1,004.80 and $20,108.00 both appear twice because two different items are associated with these orders, as you can tell from glancing at the Parts table in the Relate program.

> **NOTE**
>
> Unless you are already familiar with this material, be sure to run the RelJoin and Relate programs and switch between them until you understand why the RelJoin program works as it does. I find it easy to understand the Relate program at a glance, but the RelJoin program is a bit more subtle.

Joins and Query By Example (QBE)

The RelJoin program is a good advertisement for the power of SQL. Putting the program together is simple after you compose the SQL statement. All the work is embodied in just a few lines of code, and constructing everything else is trivial. SQL can help concentrate the intelligence of a program in one small area—or at least it does in this example.

The sticking point, of course, is that not everyone is a whiz at composing SQL statements. Even if you understand SQL thoroughly, trying to string together all those related Select, Order By, From, and Where clauses can be confusing. What you need here is a way to automate this process.

Most of the versions of C++Builder ship with a useful tool that makes composing even relatively complex SQL statements easy. In particular, I'm talking about the QBE tool in the Database Desktop. You can use the SQL Builder instead, or some other third-party tool that you might favor. However, in this section of the book I concentrate on the QBE tool because it is available to nearly all readers.

Start the DBD and set the Working Directory to the BCDEMOS alias. Choose File, New, QBE Query. A dialog lists the tables in the BCDEMOS database; select the Customer table. Reopen the Select File dialog by clicking the Add Table icon in the toolbar. You can find the Add Table icon by holding the mouse cursor over each icon until the fly-by help comes up or until you see the hint on the status bar. You can also simply look for the icon with the plus sign on it. Continue until you have added the Orders, Items, and Parts tables to the query. You can resize the query window until all four tables are visible, as shown in Figure 8.15.

FIGURE 8.15

*Four tables used
in a single QBE
example.*

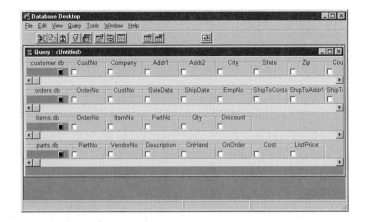

To join these tables, click the Join Tables icon (located just to the right of the lightning bolt) and then click the CustNo fields for the Customer and Orders tables. The word join1 appears in each field. Click the Join Tables icon again and link the Orders and Items tables on the OrderNo field. Join the Parts and Items tables on the PartNo field.

Select the fields you want to show after joining the tables; click in the check box associated with the fields you want to view. When you are done, the result should look like Figure 8.16.

FIGURE 8.16

*The complete QBE
query for joining
the* Customer,
Orders, Items, *and*
Parts *tables.*

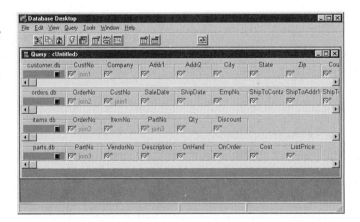

To test your work, click the lightning bolt icon. You should get a table that looks just like the one in the RelJoin program.

To translate the QBE statement into SQL, first close the result table so that you can view the query shown in Figure 8.16. Click the SQL icon to perform the translation. You can save this SQL to disk or block-copy and deposit it into the SQL property of a TQuery object.

On paper, this process takes a few minutes to explain. Once you understand the QBE tool, however, you can use it to relate multiple tables in just a few seconds. For most people, QBE is probably the simplest and fastest way to compose SQL Select statements. Don't neglect learning to use this simple, easy-to-use tool. It can save you hours of time.

That's it for the discussion of basic relational database principles. You've seen how to build master-detail relationships and how to construct joins. More important, you've seen how C++Builder encapsulates these key aspects of relational database design. The rest of this chapter digs in further and discusses other tools C++Builder uses to help you create client/server or standard database applications.

The Fields Editor

The Fields Editor enables you to associate custom objects with some or all of the fields from a table. By associating a custom object with a field, you can control the way a field displays, formats, validates, and inputs data. The Fields Editor also enables you to add new fields to a table at run time and to then calculate the values that will be shown in the new fields. When you are done, you will end up adding a *calculated field* to your table.

In this section and the next, you build a program called MASS, which illustrates both the Fields Editor and calculated fields. This program is important, so you should try to use your copy of C++Builder to follow the steps described.

You can access the Fields Editor from either a TTable or TQuery object. To get started, drop a TQuery object on a form, set up the BCDEMOS alias, enter the SQL statement **select * from animals**, and make the query active.

Bring down the Object Selector at the top of the Object Inspector. Notice that you currently have two components in use: Form1 and Query1.

Right-click the TQuery object and select the Fields Editor menu choice to bring up the Fields Editor. Right-click the Fields Editor and select Add Fields from the menu to bring up the Add Fields dialog, as shown in Figure 8.17.

FIGURE 8.17

The Add Fields dialog from the Fields Editor.

All the fields in the dialog are selected by default. Click the OK button to select all five fields and then close the Fields Editor.

Open the Object Selector a second time; notice that five new objects now appear on your form, as shown in Figure 8.18.

FIGURE 8.18

The Object Selector lists the objects created in the Fields Editor. You also can find this list in the TForm1 *class definition.*

These objects help you control your presentation of the Animals table.

Here's a complete list of the objects you just created:

```
TStringField *Query1NAME;
TSmallintField *Query1SIZE;
TSmallintField *Query1WEIGHT;
TStringField *Query1AREA;
TBlobField *Query1BMP;
```

I cut and pasted this list from the TForm1 class definition found in the editor window. The origins of the names shown here should be fairly obvious. The Query1 part comes from the default name for the TQuery object, and the second half of the name comes from the fields in the Animals table. If I had renamed the Query1 object to Animal, I would have produced names that looked like this:

```
AnimalNAME
AnimalSIZE
AnimalWEIGHT
```

This convention can be very useful if you are working with several tables and want to know, at a glance, which table and field are being referenced by a particular variable.

The names of the fields in the example shown here are capitalized only because the table in question is a dBASE table. dBASE tables automatically capitalize all letters in field names. If I had chosen to work with some other type of table, the capitalization of the letters in the field name would have followed the rules defined by the current database software.

Each of the objects created in the Fields Editor is a descendant of TField. The exact type of descendant depends on the type of data in a particular field. For instance, the Query1WEIGHT field is of type TSmallintField, whereas the Query1NAME field is of type TStringField. You will see these two field types most often. Other common types include TDateField and TCurrencyField, neither of which is used in this particular table. Remember that these types were selected to correspond with the field types in the table itself.

TStringField, TSmallintField, and the other objects shown here are all descendants of TField and share its traits. You can treat these objects exactly as you would the TField object. For instance, you can write this:

```
String S = Query1WEIGHT->AsString;
```

You can also write this:

```
String S = Query1WEIGHT->Name;
```

However, these TField descendants are smart objects and have several traits that go beyond the functionality of their common ancestor.

The most important property of TField is Value. You can access it like this:

```
void __fastcall TForm1::Button1Click(TObject *Sender)
{
  int i = Query1SIZE->Value;
  String S = Query1NAME->Value;
  i++;
  S = "Foo";
  Query1SIZE->Value = i;
  Query1NAME->Value = S;
}
```

The code shown here first assigns values to the variables i and S. The next two lines change these values, and the last two lines reassign the new values to the objects.

Writing code exactly like this in a program usually wouldn't make much sense, but it illustrates the syntax used by TField descendants.

The Value property always conforms to the type of field you have instantiated. For instance, TStringFields are AnsiStrings, whereas TCurrencyFields always return floating-point double values. However, if you show a TCurrencyField in a data-aware control, it returns a string that looks like this: "$5.00". The dollar sign and rounding to two decimal places are simply part and parcel of what a TCurrencyField is all about.

The preceding example might make you think that these variables are declared as Variants. The point here is that TCurrencyField::Value is declared as a double. If you tried to assign a string to it, you would get a type mismatch. Likewise, TIntegerField::Value is declared as an int, and so on. TSmallIntField and TWordField are both descendants of TIntegerField and inherit the Value declaration as an int. However, they have other internal code that has an effect on the Value field, just as the TCurrencyField rings some changes on its Value field to make it look like a monetary value. If you have the source, look up DBTABLES.PAS and DB.PAS to find the details of these constructions. The preceding code is an example of polymorphism; it is not an example of relaxed type-checking. The Value field has a specific type; it just undergoes polymorphic changes.

If you want the names of each field in the current dataset, you should reference the FieldName property through one of the following two methods:

```
S = Query1->Fields->Fields[0]->FieldName;
```

```
S = Query1NAME->FieldName;
```

If you want the name of an object associated with a field, you should use the Name property:

```
S = Query1->Fields->Fields[0]->Name;
```

```
S = Query1NAME->Name;
```

When you're using the Animals table, the first two examples shown here yield the string "NAME", whereas the second two lines yield "Query1NAME".

Special properties are associated with most of the major field types. For instance, TIntegerFields have DisplayFormat and DisplayEdit properties, as well as MinValue and MaxValue properties. TStringFields, on the other hand, have none of these properties, but they do have an EditMask property, which works just like the TEditMask component found on the Component Palette's Additional page. All these properties are used to control the way data is displayed to the user or the way input from the user should be handled.

Note

I don't want to get ahead of myself, but properties such as `MinValue` and `MaxValue` are also used in the Data Dictionary. This is explained later in this chapter. Changes made in the Data Dictionary will affect these values as seen in the Object Inspector, but changes in the Object Inspector will not affect the Data Dictionary. Don't worry if this information doesn't make the slightest bit of sense yet, as I will get to the Data Dictionary in this chapter.

You should be aware of one more thing about the Fields Editor. You can use this tool not only to build objects that encapsulate existing fields, but also to build objects that represent new fields. For instance, suppose you want to create a sixth field, `MASS`, which contains the product of the `SIZE` and `WEIGHT` fields in the `Animals` table.

To create the `MASS` field, open the Fields Editor again, right-click it, and select the New Field menu choice. Enter the word **MASS** in the top part of the New Field dialog. Now set its type to **Integer** and leave its field type set to `Calculated`, as shown in Figure 8.19.

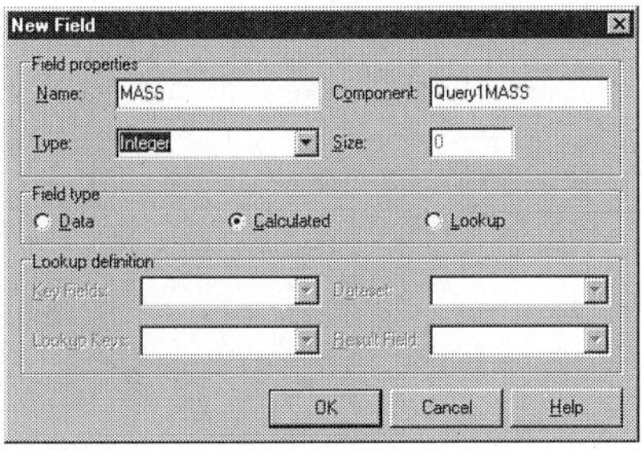

Figure 8.19

Creating the MASS *field in the Fields Editor.*

If you close the Fields Editor and add `TDataSource` and `TDBGrid` to your project, you will see that the `Animals` table now appears to have six fields, the last of which is called `MASS`.

Creating a field is one thing, of course, but filling it in at run time with an appropriate value is another. Placing a value in the new field you created involves calculated fields, which are addressed in the next section.

Calculated Fields

Calculated fields are one of the most valuable fruits of the Fields Editor. You can use these fields for several different purposes, but two stand out:

- If you need to perform calculations on two or more of the fields in a dataset and want to show the results of the calculations in a third field, you can use calculated fields. A scenario describing this type of situation was set up in the preceding section and is explained further in this section.

- If you are viewing one dataset and want to perform calculations or display data that involves lookups in at least one additional dataset, you can use the Fields Editor and calculated fields to show the results of these calculations in the first dataset's new field. You also can use a second, much better method for doing lookups. I will talk about that method later in this chapter. As a rule, you should perform calculations in calculated fields and lookups in lookup fields, although calculated fields are powerful enough to fill a number of roles in your programs.

The MASS program illustrates one example of the first of the two uses for calculated fields. You got this program started in the preceding section when you created the field called MASS and displayed it in a grid.

To continue working with the MASS program, highlight the Query1 object and set the Object Inspector to the Events page. Now create an OnCalcFields event that looks like this:

```
void __fastcall TForm1::Query1CalcFields(TDataSet *DataSet)
{
  Query1MASS->Value = Query1SIZE->Value * Query1WEIGHT->Value;
}
```

The code assigns the value of the Query1MASS object to the product of the Query1SIZE and Query1WEIGHT fields. This kind of multiplication is legal because all the fields are of the same type.

OnCalcFields methods get called each time a record is first displayed to the user. As a result, all the MASS fields displayed in the grid are properly filled in (see Figure 8.20).

FIGURE 8.20

The MASS *field contains the product of the* WEIGHT *and* SIZE *fields. A* TDBImage *control contains a bitmap from the table's* BMP *field.*

NAME	SIZE	WEIGHT	MASS	
Boa	10	8	80	
Critters	30	20	600	
House Cat	10	5	50	
Ocelot	40	35	1400	

To get the image shown in Figure 8.20, I opened the `Columns` property in the `TDBGrid` object and selected Add All Fields. I then deleted the `Area` and `BMP` fields and closed the `Columns` Property Editor. I will talk more about the grid object later in this chapter.

If you choose to never instantiate a particular field in the Fields Editor, that field is no longer contained in the current dataset; it can't be accessed programmatically or visually at run time. You usually want to achieve exactly this effect, so this trait can generally be perceived as a strong benefit. However, sometimes it might not serve your purposes; in those cases, you should either create an object for all the fields in a table or stay away from the Fields Editor altogether.

TDBGrid at Run Time

`DBGrids` can be completely reconfigured at run time. You can hide and show columns, and you can change the order, the color, and the width of columns.

The MOVEGRID program, depicted in Figure 8.21, shows how to take a `TDBGrid` through its paces at run time. Because of space considerations, I do not include the entire program as a listing in the text. Instead, the code for the MOVEGRID program is on this book's CD-ROM. The program is fairly straightforward except for two brief passages. The first passage involves creating check box controls on-the-fly, whereas the second shows how to change the order of items in a list box on-the-fly.

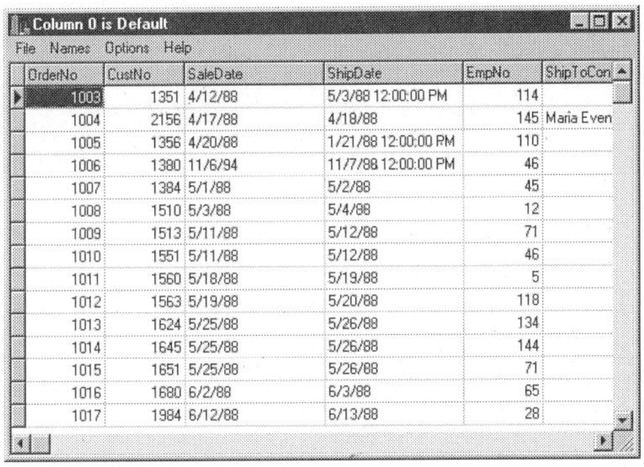

FIGURE 8.21

The main MOVEGRID program enables you to change the grid's run-time appearance.

When the user wants to decide which fields are visible, MOVEGRID brings up a second form and displays the names of all the fields from the `ORDERS` table in a series of check boxes. The user can then select the fields that he or she wants to make visible. The selected check boxes designate fields that are visible, whereas the unselected ones represent invisible fields. The program also enables you to set the order and width of fields, as well as hide and show the titles at the top of the grid.

The VisiForm unit, shown in Listings 8.1 and 8.2, displays a set of check boxes in which the user designates what fields are to be made visible.

LISTING 8.1   THE HEADER FOR THE VisiForm UNIT

```
#ifndef VisFormH
#define VisFormH

#include <Classes.hpp>
#include <Controls.hpp>
#include <StdCtrls.hpp>
#include <Forms.hpp>
#include <Db.hpp>

const int RadSize = 25;

class TVisiForm : public TForm
{
__published:    // IDE-managed Components
private:    // User declarations
  TCheckBox* R[26];
  void CreateRad(int Index, String Name, bool Visible);
public:        // User declarations
  __fastcall TVisiForm(TComponent* Owner);
  void ShowMe(TQuery* Query1);
};

extern PACKAGE TVisiForm *VisiForm;

#endif
```

LISTING 8.2   THE VisiForm UNIT

```
// Project Name: MOVEGRID

#include <vcl.h>
#pragma hdrstop

#include "VisForm.h"

#pragma package(smart_init)
#pragma resource "*.dfm"
TVisiForm *VisiForm;

__fastcall TVisiForm::TVisiForm(TComponent* Owner)
  : TForm(Owner)
{
}
```

```
void TVisiForm::CreateRad(int Index, String Name, bool Visible)
{
  R[Index] = new TCheckBox(this);
  R[Index]->Parent = VisiForm;
  R[Index]->Caption = Name;
  R[Index]->Left = 10;
  R[Index]->Top = Index * RadSize;
  R[Index]->Width = 200;
  R[Index]->Checked = Visible;
}

void TVisiForm::ShowMe(TQuery* Query1)
{
  int i;
  for (i=0;i<Query1->FieldCount;i++)
    CreateRad(i, Query1->Fields->Fields[i]->Name,
      Query1->Fields->Fields[i]->Visible);
  Height = (Query1->FieldCount - 1) * (RadSize + 5);
  ShowModal();
  for (int i=0;i<Query1->FieldCount;i++)
    Query1->Fields->Fields[i]->Visible = R[i]->Checked;
}
```

Listings 8.3 and 8.4 show the ShowOptions unit.

LISTING 8.3   THE HEADER FOR THE ShowOptions UNIT

```
#ifndef ShowOptions1H
#define ShowOptions1H

#include <Classes.hpp>
#include <Controls.hpp>
#include <StdCtrls.hpp>
#include <Forms.hpp>
#include <DBGrids.hpp>

class TShowOptionsForm : public TForm
{
__published:     // IDE-managed Components
  TCheckBox *CheckBox1;
  TCheckBox *CheckBox2;
  TCheckBox *CheckBox3;
  TCheckBox *CheckBox4;
  TCheckBox *CheckBox5;
  TCheckBox *CheckBox6;
  TCheckBox *CheckBox7;
  TCheckBox *CheckBox8;
  TCheckBox *CheckBox9;
  TCheckBox *CheckBox10;
```

continues

8

FIELDS AND
DATABASE TOOLS

LISTING 8.3   CONTINUED

```
  TCheckBox *CheckBox11;
  TCheckBox *CheckBox12;
  void __fastcall FormCreate(TObject *Sender);
private:      // User declarations
  TCheckBox* FCheckBox[12];
public:           // User declarations
  __fastcall TShowOptionsForm(TComponent* Owner);
  void ShowOptions(TDBGridOptions Options);
};

extern PACKAGE TShowOptionsForm *ShowOptionsForm;

#endif
```

LISTING 8.4   THE ShowOptions UNIT

```
#include <vcl.h>
#pragma hdrstop

#include "ShowOptions1.h"

#pragma package(smart_init)
#pragma resource "*.dfm"
TShowOptionsForm *ShowOptionsForm;

__fastcall TShowOptionsForm::TShowOptionsForm(TComponent* Owner)
  : TForm(Owner)
{
}

void __fastcall TShowOptionsForm::FormCreate(TObject *Sender)
{
  int j = 0;
  for (int i=0;i<ComponentCount;i++) {
    TCheckBox* cb = dynamic_cast<TCheckBox*>(Components[i]);
    if (cb) {
      FCheckBox[j] = cb;
      j++;
    }
  }
}

void TShowOptionsForm::ShowOptions(TDBGridOptions Options)
{
  for (int i=0;i<12;i++)
    if (Options.Contains((TDBGridOption)i))
      FCheckBox[i]->Checked = true;
    else
```

```
      FCheckBox[i]->Checked = false;
   ShowModal();
}
```

You will find descriptions of the key parts of the MOVEGRID program in the following sections. Understanding its constituent parts will help you take control over the grids you display in your programs.

Controlling the Options Property of a DBGrid at Run Time

You can use the Options field of a TDBGrid to change its appearance. The Options property has the following possible values:

dgEditing	Set to true by default, enables the user to edit a grid. You can also set the grid's ReadOnly property to true or false.
dgTitles	Designates whether titles can be seen.
dgIndicator	Determines whether to show the small icons on the left of the grid.
dgColumnResize	Designates whether the user can resize columns.
dgColLines	Determines whether to show the lines between columns.
dgRowLines	Designates whether to show the lines between rows.
dgTabs	Enables the user to press Tab and Shift+Tab between columns.
dgAlwaysShowEditor	Ensures that you are always in edit mode.
dgRowSelect	Can select rows; mutually exclusive with dgAlwaysShowEditor.
dgAlwaysShowSelection	Allows the selection to remain, even when the grid loses focus.
dgConfirmDelete	Shows a message box when a user presses Ctrl+Delete.
dgCancelOnExit	Cancels inserts on exit if no changes were made to row.
dgMultiSelect	Can select multiple contiguous or noncontiguous rows with Ctrl+click or Shift+click, and so on.

8

FIELDS AND
DATABASE TOOLS

The following is the declaration for the enumerated type where these values are declared:

```
enum TDBGridOption { dgEditing, dgAlwaysShowEditor, dgTitles, dgIndicator,
  dgColumnResize, dgColLines, dgRowLines, dgTabs, dgRowSelect,
  dgAlwaysShowSelection, dgConfirmDelete, dgCancelOnExit, dgMultiSelect };

typedef Set<TDBGridOption, dgEditing, dgMultiSelect>  TDBGridOptions;
```

For instance, you can set the options at run time by writing code that looks like this:

```
DBGrid1->Options = TDBGridOptions() << dgTitles;
```

The preceding code, in effect, turns all the options to `false` except `dgTitles`. More specifically, the code creates a temporary set of `TDBGridOptions`, adds the `dgTitles` value to the set, and then assigns the temporary set to the `Options` property.

You might wonder why it is necessary to create a temporary set. The C++ language doesn't have a `set` data type as does Object Pascal. Because sets are used heavily in the VCL, the C++Builder engineers developed the `Set` template to approximate an Object Pascal `set` type. The `Set` class works very well, but problems arise when modifying properties that are sets. For example, this code, while perfectly valid syntax, has no effect:

```
DBGrid1->Options << dgTitles;
```

This code has no effect because the `Options` property's write method is never called in this case. Why? Because a property's write method is only called on assignment and the insertion operator does not result in an explicit assignment. The trick, then, is to always make an explicit assignment when modifying a set property. Further, you should use direct assignment both when reading and when writing a set property. This assures that both the read and write methods for a property are called:

```
TDBGridOptions options = DBGrid1->Options;
DBGrid1->Options = options << dgTitles;
```

Getting back to the `TDBGrid::Options` property, the following code turns off all options except `dgTitles` and `dgIndicator`:

```
DBGrid1->Options = TDBGridOptions() << dgTitles << dgIndicator;
```

This code toggles `dgTitles` off and on each time it is called:

```
void __fastcall TForm1::ToggleTitles1Click(TObject *Sender)
{
  TDBGridOptions options = DBGrid1->Options;
  if (FShowTitles)
    DBGrid1->Options = options << dgTitles;
  else
    DBGrid1->Options = options>> dgTitles;
  FShowTitles = !FShowTitles;
}
```

The set insertion and extraction operators shown in `ToggleTitles1Click` move the `dgTitles` option in and out of the `Options` property.

The following code shows how to toggle back and forth between showing both indicators and titles and hiding both indicators and titles:

```
void __fastcall TForm1::ShowTitlesIndicator1Click(TObject *Sender)
{
  TDBGridOptions options = DBGrid1->Options;
  ShowTitlesIndicator1->Checked =
    !(options.Contains(dgIndicator)
      && options.Contains(dgTitles));
  if (ShowTitlesIndicator1->Checked)
    DBGrid1->Options = options << dgIndicator << dgTitles;
  else
    DBGrid1->Options = options>> dgIndicator>> dgTitles;
}
```

This code moves both the `dgIndicator` and `dgTitles` elements in and out of the `Options` set as needed. The << (insertion) operator adds elements to a set, and the >> (extraction) operator moves things out of the set.

In this section, you learned how to toggle the elements of the `Options` set back and forth at run time. Most of the code for this process is fairly simple, though you need to have a basic grasp of the C++Builder `Set` class and how it interacts with the VCL to understand how it works.

Displaying the `DBGrid` Options at Run Time

Now that you know how to toggle the `Options` of a `DBGrid`, spending a few moments learning how to display the `Options` to the user at run time might be worthwhile. As you can see in Figure 8.22, I use a set of 12 check boxes to depict the current state of the 12 `DBGrid` options. Next, I will explain how the code that drives this form works.

FIGURE 8.22

Using check boxes to depict the available DBGrid *options to the user at run time.*

The code for these operations appears in the `ShowOptions1` unit found in Listing 8.2. I declare an array of check boxes in the `TShowOptionsForm` class declaration:

```
TCheckBox* FCheckBox[12];
```

I initialize these check boxes in the OnCreate event handler for the ShowOptions form:

```
void __fastcall TShowOptionsForm::FormCreate(TObject *Sender)
{
  int j = 0;
  for (int i=0;i<ComponentCount;i++) {
    TCheckBox* cb = dynamic_cast<TCheckBox*>(Components[i]);
    if (cb) {
      FCheckBox[j] = cb;
      j++;
    }
  }
}
```

This code iterates over all the components on the form checking for those that are of type TCheckBox. When it finds one, it adds the component to the array of check boxes. The code uses the dynamic_cast operator to check whether each item in the components array is of type TCheckBox.

> **NOTE**
>
> A components array is implemented in TComponent and is maintained automatically for all components that descend from TComponent. The concept of *ownership* is what governs which items are put in the components array. All components that are owned by the form are automatically, and by definition, included in the components array for the form. In other words, if you drop a component on a form, it will be listed in the components array for the form. You can use the form's ComponentCount property to determine how many items are in the components array. Remember that it is not only forms that maintain components arrays; all components support the concept of components arrays.

After you fill in the array of check boxes, toggling the Checked property of each check box is a simple matter, depending on the current state of each DBGrid option:

```
void TShowOptionsForm::ShowOptions(TDBGridOptions Options)
{
  for (int i=0;i<12;i++)
    if (Options.Contains((TDBGridOption)i))
      FCheckBox[i]->Checked = true;
    else
      FCheckBox[i]->Checked = false;
  ShowModal();
}
```

This code calls the Set class's Contains() method to determine which items in the DBGridOptions set are turned on; it then toggles the appropriate check box. The code depends, of course, on the fact that the DBGridOptions set is a list of items with values ranging from 0 to 11. To understand this code, you must grasp that TDBGridOption is an enumerated type, as described earlier in this chapter.

Working with TDBGrid Columns

The following sections of the chapter cover changing the colors of the titles, columns, rows, and even individual cells in a TDBGrid. This type of change is not something you have to do very often, but the need is fairly pressing when it comes around. Furthermore, this code will help you learn enough about the grid object so that you can find your way around if you need to make other changes to its behavior. Be sure to run the MOVEGRID program before reading these sections; it will be hard to read the code without some understanding of what it does.

Changing the Titles in a TDBGrid Object

You can color the titles in a TDBGrid this way:

```
void TForm1::ColorTitles(bool UseDefaultColor)
{
  const TColor Colors[] =
    {clRed, clBlue, clGreen, clLime, clWhite, clFuchsia};
  for (int i=0;i<DBGrid1->Columns->Count;i++) {
    TColumn* Column = DBGrid1->Columns->Items[i];
    TColumnTitle* ColumnTitle = Column->Title;
    if (UseDefaultColor)
      ColumnTitle->Font->Color = FDefaultColor;
    else
      ColumnTitle->Font->Color = Colors[random(6)];
  }
}
```

This code first declares an array of colors. The constants seen here are predeclared colors of type TColor.

The actual number of colors in the ColorTitles method was chosen at random. I could have added or subtracted colors from the array without changing the rest of code in the routine, with the exception of the number 6, which is passed at random in the routine's last line of code.

The TColumn object defines how a column in a TDBGrid should look. That is, it defines the font, color, and width of the column. The Columns property of a TDBGrid is of type TDBGridColumns, which is a collection of TColumn objects. Each TColumn object has a title. This title is defined in an object of type TColumnTitle. Finally, a TColumnTitle has color, font, and caption properties:

```
TDBGrid Object
  Columns Property
    TColumn Object
      TColumnTitle Object
        Font, Color, Caption Objects
```

The preceding list is not an object hierarchy, but a way of illustrating the relationship between these different entities. In other words, the grid object contains a `Columns` property, the `Columns` property contains `TColumn` objects, and each `TColumn` object contains a `TColumnTitle`, which in turn contains a `Font`, `Color`, and `Caption`.

To get hold of a `TColumn` object, you can use the `Items` property of `TDBGridColumns`:

```
TColumn* Column = DBGrid1->Columns->Items[i];
```

You can use the `Title` property of a `TColumn` object to move from a `Column` object to a `TColumnTitle` object:

```
TColumnTitle* ColumnTitle = Column->Title;
```

After the preceding `ColorTitles` method has the `ColumnTitle` in its hands, it can set the `ColumnTitle` to whatever color it wants:

```
if (UseDefaultColor)
  ColumnTitle->Font->Color = FDefaultColor;
else
  ColumnTitle->Font->Color = Colors[random(6)];
```

The `FDefaultColor` variable is of type `TColor`. In the form's `OnCreate` event, I set it to the default color for the grid's font:

```
FDefaultColor = DBGrid1->Font->Color;
```

If you understand what has happened here, you will have no trouble with the next two sections, which cover changing the color of columns and rows in a grid.

Changing an Entire Column in a Grid

C++Builder makes changing the look of a single column easy. Writing this kind of code will enable you to emphasize a certain part of a dataset or to bring the user's eye to a certain part of your form.

This method changes the appearance of a column in a `TDBGrid`:

```
void __fastcall TForm1::MarkColumnClick(TObject *Sender)
{
  MarkColumn->Checked = !MarkColumn->Checked;
  TColumn* Column = DBGrid1->Columns->Items[DBGrid1->SelectedIndex];
  if (MarkColumn->Checked) {
```

```
      Column->Font->Color = NewColor;
      Column->Font->Style = TFontStyles() << fsBold;
      FTaggedColumns->Add(Column);
    } else {
      Column->Font->Color = FDefaultColor;
      Column->Font->Style.Clear();
      FTaggedColumns->Remove(Column);
    }
    HandleCaption();
}
```

This code first grabs hold of a selected column in a grid:

```
TColumn* Column = DBGrid1->Columns->Items[DBGrid1->SelectedIndex];
```

If the user has indicated that he or she wants this column to stand out, it is a simple matter to change its background color and set its font to bold:

```
Column->Font->Color = NewColor;
Column->Font->Style = TFontStyles() << fsBold;
```

I don't mention some parts of the code, such as MarkColumn and HandleCaption(), because they are merely part of this program's logic and are not germane to the subject of changing an individual column.

Changing the Color of a Row in a Grid

You worked with the TColumn object in the preceding two sections on columns and column titles. You can also change the color of the text in a TDBGrid by working with the font associated with the grid's TCanvas object:

```
void __fastcall TForm1::DBGrid1DrawColumnCell(TObject *Sender,
        const TRect &Rect, int DataCol, TColumn *Column,
        TGridDrawState State)
{
  if (IsTagged(Column)) {
    DBGrid1->Canvas->Brush->Color = clPurple;
    DBGrid1->Canvas->FillRect(Rect);
  }
  else if (ColorRows1->Checked) {
    if (DMod->Query1ItemsTotal->Value < 1000)
      DBGrid1->Canvas->Font->Color = clRed;
    else if (DMod->Query1ItemsTotal->Value < 10000)
      DBGrid1->Canvas->Font->Color = clBlue;
    else
      DBGrid1->Canvas->Font->Color = clGreen;
  }
  DBGrid1->DefaultDrawColumnCell(Rect, DataCol, Column, State);
}
```

8

FIELDS AND
DATABASE TOOLS

If you run the MOVEGRID program, you can see the effect of this code by choosing Color Rows from that program's Options menu. Be sure that none of the other special effects is turned on when you choose this option; they can interfere with your ability to see its results. Be sure to scroll the grid up and down after turning on the effect; the data at the top of the grid is homogenous.

The data shown in the grid is from the Orders table in the BCDEMOS database. The code shown here colors each row in the grid according to the amount of money reported in the ItemsTotal field of the Orders table. For instance, if the ItemsTotal field contains a sum less than $1,000, that row is painted Red:

```
DBGrid1->Canvas->Font->Color = clRed
```

Here the code sets the color of the TCanvas object font for the grid to clRed. Nothing could be simpler.

Changing the Width of a Column

The user can change the width of a column at run time by using the mouse. How can you do the same thing programmatically without any input from the user?

If you want to change the width of a column at run time, just change the DisplayWidth property of the appropriate TField object:

```
DBGrid1->SelectedField->DisplayWidth = 12;
```

The value 12 refers to the approximate number of characters that can be displayed in the control. Various factors, such as whether you are using a fixed-pitch font, affect the interpretation of this value. See the online help for additional information.

You can change the width of the column in the grid as follows without affecting the properties of the underlying field:

```
void __fastcall TForm1::ChangeWidthofField1Click(TObject *Sender)
{
  String S = "";
  TColumn* Column = DBGrid1->Columns->Items[DBGrid1->SelectedIndex];
  if (InputQuery("Data Needed", "New Width of Selected Field", S))
    Column->Width = S.ToInt();
}
```

This code asks the user for the width he or she wants to assign to the currently selected column. The code then makes the change by retrieving the column and changing its Width property.

Hiding or Moving Columns in a `TDBGrid`

The user can change the order of columns in a `TDBGrid` simply by clicking them and dragging them with a mouse. How do you proceed if you want to do the same thing at run time without the user's direct input?

If you want to hide a field at run time, you can set its `Visible` property to `false`:

```
DMod->Query1->FieldByName("CustNo")->Visible = false;
DMod->Query1CustNo->Visible = false;
```

Both lines of code perform identical tasks. To show the fields again, simply set `Visible` to `true`.

Alternatively, you can retrieve a `TColumn` object from the `Grid` and then hide it:

```
void __fastcall TForm1::HideCurrentColumn1Click(TObject *Sender)
{
  if (MessageBox(Handle, "Hide Column?",
       "Hide Info?", MB_YESNO | MB_ICONQUESTION) == ID_YES) {
    TColumn* Column = DBGrid1->Columns->Items[DBGrid1->SelectedIndex];
    Column->Visible = false;
  }
}
```

That'll do it! The column disappears from the grid. You can also set the width of a column to `0`, which makes the column itself go away, but not the lines between columns. These lines can, however, be toggled separately if you use the `Options` property.

Displaying a List of Visible Fields

To allow the user to decide which fields are visible, MOVEGRID brings up a second form with a series of check boxes on it, as shown in the `VisiForm` unit from Listings 8.1 and 8.2. The program actually creates each of these check boxes at run time. In other words, it doesn't just bring up a form with the correct number of check boxes on it, but instead iterates through the `Query1` object from the data module, finds out how many check boxes are needed, and then dynamically creates them at run time.

To perform these tasks, MOVEGRID calls on a form that is specially designed to display the check boxes:

```
void __fastcall TForm1::VisibleClick(TObject *Sender)
{
  VisiForm->ShowMe(DMod->Query1);
}
```

Before I discuss the `ShowMe()` method, I want to show you the code the `VisiForm` unit uses to initialize an array of check boxes. The `CreateRad()` method does the job by allocating memory for each member of the array of check boxes. The ShowMe() method, shown later in this section, iterates through the Query1 object and calls the CreateRad() function to assign one check box to each field. It also asks TQuery for the names of the fields and determines whether each field is currently hidden or visible. This code creates a check box on-the-fly:

```
void TVisiForm::CreateRad(int Index, String Name, bool Visible)
{
  R[Index] = new TCheckBox(this);
  R[Index]->Parent = VisiForm;
  R[Index]->Caption = Name;
  R[Index]->Left = 10;
  R[Index]->Top = Index * RadSize;
  R[Index]->Width = 200;
  R[Index]->Checked = Visible;
}
```

> **NOTE**
>
> C++Builder 3 and later support a control called TCheckListBox on the Component Palette's Additional page. This control allows you to work with lists of check boxes and would be a good alternative to the code shown here.

R is a simple array of check boxes:

```
TCheckBox* R[26];
```

Most of the code in this example performs relatively mundane tasks such as assigning names and locations to the check boxes. The following are the two key lines:

```
R[Index] = new TCheckBox(this);
R[Index]->Parent = VisiForm;
```

The first line actually creates the check box and gives it an owner. The second line assigns a parent to the check box. Assigning a parent is important; the check box will never show up on the form if you don't assign a parent.

> **NOTE**
>
> The difference between a parent and an owner can be confusing at times. A form is always the owner of the components that reside inside it. As such, it is responsible for allocating and deallocating memory for these components. A form might also be the parent of a particular component, which means that Windows will ensure that the component will be displayed directly on the form.

However, one component might also find that another component is its parent, even though both components are owned by the form. For instance, if you place a TPanel on a form and then two TButtons on the TPanel, the form owns all three components; however, the buttons will have the panel as a parent, whereas the TPanel will have the form as a parent. *Ownership* has to do with memory allocation. *Parenthood* usually describes what surface a component will be displayed on. Ownership is a C++Builder issue; parenthood is mostly a Windows API issue. In particular, Windows cares about parenting, and Windows handles the actual drawing of the controls. If you get confused about this issue while in the midst of a lengthy programming session, you can look it up in the VCL online help by searching on the topic "Parent."

The rest of the code in the CreateRad() method just gives each check box a caption derived from the name of the field it represents, and places the check box on the form in a location commensurate with the position of its field in the table.

The ShowMe() method of the VisiForm first calls CreateRad(), displays the form, and sets the state of the check boxes:

```cpp
void TVisiForm::ShowMe(TQuery* Query1)
{
  int i;
  for (i=0;i<Query1->FieldCount;i++)
    CreateRad(i, Query1->Fields->Fields[i]->Name,
      Query1->Fields->Fields[i]->Visible);
  Height = (Query1->FieldCount - 1) * (RadSize + 5);
  ShowModal();
  for (int i=0;i<Query1->FieldCount;i++)
    Query1->Fields->Fields[i]->Visible = R[i]->Checked;
}
```

Moving Columns at Run Time

To move the location of a column at run time, you can simply change its index, which is a zero-based number:

```cpp
DMod->Query1->FieldByName("CustNo")->Index = 0;
DMod->Query1CustNo->Index = 2;
```

By default, the CustNo field in the Orders table is at the second position, which means its index is 1. The code in the first example moves it to the first position, whereas the code that reads Query1CustNo->Index = 2; moves it to the third position. Remember, the Index field is zero-based, so moving a field to Index 1 moves it to the second field in a record.

When you change the index of a field, you do not need to worry about the indices of the other fields in a record; they are changed automatically at run time.

I've gone on at considerable length about DBGrid, but it is one of the tools that lie at the heart of many database programs.

NOTE

Now that you know what you can do with the VCL grid, some of you are likely to say, "Hey, that's all good and well, but I want even more power!" That's a reasonable request, so check out the InfoPower product by pointing your browser to http://www.woll2woll.com.

TurboPower also has a nice advanced grid; you can find it at http://www.turbopower.com.

Another is "Queen of Grids" at http://www.topsupport.com.

Finally, for a full listing of third-party components, visit the Inprise Web site at http://www.inprise.com.

The TDBGrid object features the capability to add combo boxes to the grid. This subject is covered in the next section on lookups.

Lookup Fields

You can use lookup fields to find a value in one table that you want to use in a second table. For instance, suppose you have two tables, one of which contains a list of books, the other of which contains a list of authors. It would be nice if you could automatically view a list of the existing authors whenever you need to add a new book to the Book table. That way, you could enter the book's name and then just look up the author in a drop-down list—presto, you would be done. The Book table would then automatically contain a reference to the appropriate author in the Author table. The author number from the Author table would automatically be inserted in the Book table.

I wouldn't go into all this detail unless C++Builder provided good support for using lookup fields. In particular, C++Builder allows you to perform automatic lookups inside grids, list boxes, and combo boxes. The Lookup program on the CD-ROM shows how to proceed. The code for this application is shown in Listings 8.5 through 8.7. In this case I don't show the headers for the units because they are entirely C++Builder generated and don't provide any meaningful information. The main form of the program is shown in Figure 8.23.

Figure 8.23

The AuthorLookup *field in the grid for the* Book *table is a lookup into the* Author *table.*

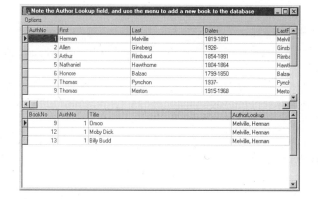

Listing 8.5   The Data Module for the Lookup Program

```cpp
#include <vcl.h>
#pragma hdrstop

#include "DMod.h"

#pragma package(smart_init)
#pragma resource "*.dfm"
TDMod1 *DMod1;

__fastcall TDMod1::TDMod1(TComponent* Owner)
  : TDataModule(Owner)
{
}

void __fastcall TDMod1::AuthorTableCalcFields(TDataSet *DataSet)
{
  AuthorTableLastFirst->Value =
    AuthorTableLast->Value + ", " + AuthorTableFirst->Value;
}

void __fastcall TDMod1::DMod1Create(TObject *Sender)
{
  AuthorTable->Open();
  BookLookupTable->Open();
  BookDetailTable->Open();
}

String __fastcall TDMod1::GetCurAuthor()
{
  return AuthorTable->FieldByName("FirstLast")->AsString;
}

String __fastcall TDMod1::GetCurBook()
```

continues

LISTING 8.5 CONTINUED

```
{
  return BookDetailTable->FieldByName("Title")->AsString;
}

void TDMod1::BookLookupCancel()
{
  if (BookLookupTable->State == dsEdit &&
      BookLookupTable->State == dsInsert)
    BookLookupTable->Cancel();
}

void TDMod1::BookLookupPost()
{
  if (((BookLookupTable->State == dsEdit) ||
       (BookLookupTable->State == dsInsert)))
    BookLookupTable->Post();
}

void TDMod1::FindAuthor(String S)
{
  AuthorTable->FindNearest(OPENARRAY(TVarRec, (S)));
}

void TDMod1::FindTitle(String S)
{
  String Temp = BookLookupTable->IndexName;
  BookLookupTable->IndexName = "idxTitle";
  BookLookupTable->FindNearest(OPENARRAY(TVarRec, (S)));
  BookLookupTable->IndexName = Temp;
}
```

LISTING 8.6 THE MAIN FORM FOR THE PROGRAM

```
/*

    This program shows how to use the lookup feature in BCB.
    The program allows you to type in the name of a new
    book, and then do a lookup into a list of
    authors in order to choose the author associated
    with the book.

    There is also a calculated field on the authors
    table, as well as a look up from the book table
    into the author table.
*/

#include <vcl.h>
#pragma hdrstop
```

```
#include "Main.h"
#include "DMod.h"
#include "FieldVew.h"

#pragma package(smart_init)
#pragma resource "*.dfm"
TForm1 *Form1;

__fastcall TForm1::TForm1(TComponent* Owner)
   : TForm(Owner)
{
}

void __fastcall TForm1::NewBook1Click(TObject *Sender)
{
  EntryForm->ShowInsert();
  DMod1->BookDetailTable->Refresh();
}

void __fastcall TForm1::EditBook1Click(TObject *Sender)
{
  EntryForm->ShowEdit(DMod1->CurBook);
  DMod1->BookDetailTable->Refresh();
}
```

LISTING 8.7   THE FieldVew UNIT SHOWS HOW TO USE A TDBLookupComboBox

```
#include <vcl.h>
#pragma hdrstop

#include "FieldVew.h"
#include "DMod.h"

#pragma package(smart_init)
#pragma resource "*.dfm"
TEntryForm *EntryForm;

__fastcall TEntryForm::TEntryForm(TComponent* Owner)
   : TForm(Owner)
{
}

void TEntryForm::ShowEdit(String S)
{
  DMod1->FindTitle(S);
  ShowModal();
  DMod1->BookLookupPost();
}
```

continues

LISTING 8.7 CONTINUED

```cpp
void TEntryForm::ShowInsert()
{
  DMod1->BookLookupTable->Insert();
  DMod1->BookLookupTableTitle->AsString = "My New Book";
  ShowModal();
  DMod1->BookLookupPost();
}

void __fastcall TEntryForm::CancelBtnClick(TObject *Sender)
{
  DMod1->BookLookupCancel();
}

void __fastcall TEntryForm::bbInsertClick(TObject *Sender)
{
  DMod1->BookLookupTable->Insert();
}

void __fastcall TEntryForm::DeleteBtnClick(TObject *Sender)
{
  if ((MessageBox(
    Handle, "Delete?" , "Delete Dialog", MB_YESNO) == ID_YES))
    DMod1->BookLookupTable->Delete();
}

void __fastcall TEntryForm::bbPostClick(TObject *Sender)
{
  DMod1->BookLookupTable->Post();
}
```

The Lookup program enables you to easily fill in the key fields of the Book table by looking them up in the Author table. To understand why this capability is important, notice that the only way to tell which author is associated with which book is by placing the appropriate author number in the Book table's AuthNo field. This approach is convenient from the point of view of the programmer who wants to construct a well-made relational database. In particular, it allows for saving space through the construction of one-to-many relationships. However, the user isn't going to want to have to remember that Herman Melville is associated with the number 1, Nathaniel Hawthorne with the number 5, and so on. The point of a lookup field is that it lets you look up a list of authors in the Author table; it then automatically assigns the chosen author number to the AuthNo field in the Book table.

This program uses two tables called, not surprisingly, AUTHOR.DB and BOOK.DB. Both of these tables are found on the CD-ROM that comes with this book. Tables 8.1 and 8.2 display the schema for both tables.

TABLE 8.1 AUTHOR.DB TABLE STRUCTURE

Name	Type	Keyed
AuthNo	AutoInc	Key
First	Character(25)	
Last	Character(25)	
Dates	Character(25)	
BirthPlace	Character(25)	

TABLE 8.2 BOOK.DB TABLE STRUCTURE

Name	Type	Keyed
BookNo	AutoInc	Key
AuthNo	LongInt	
Title	Character(35)	

Notice the use of the autoincrement fields in the table definitions shown in Tables 8.1 and 8.2. These fields are automatically filled in when the user adds a new record at run time. For instance, when you add the first record to the Book table, it will automatically be given a BookNo of 1. The second record is automatically given a BookNo of 2, and so on. Autoincrement fields are read-only, and they rarely need to be shown to the user at run time.

Little actual work is required to construct this program. In particular, look over the source code shown earlier; you will see that the only significant line of code in the whole program is the one for the OnCalcFields event. Other than that, it's just a matter of manipulating the visual tools.

To get started, create a new application and add a data module to it. Drag both the Author and Book tables out of the Explorer and onto the data module. Hook them up to two grids on the main form. Bring up the Fields Editor for both tables and create objects for all their fields. Give the tables and their data sources appropriate names, as shown in Figure 8.24.

FIGURE 8.24

The data module for the Lookup program.

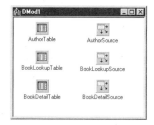

Create a calculated field called LastFirst inside the Author table. To create the calculated field, right-click the TTable object, right-click the Field's editor, and select New from the menu. Assign the following method to the OnCalcFields event after you create the calculated field:

```
void __fastcall TDMod1::AuthorTableCalcFields(TDataSet *DataSet)
{
  AuthorTableLastFirst->Value =
    AuthorTableLast->Value + ", " + AuthorTableFirst->Value;
}
```

This field will be the one that is looked up in the second table. The issue here is that just looking up the last name of an author is insufficient; you need to look up both first and last names to be sure you are finding a unique name for an author. Permanently adding a field to the table that combined the first and last names would be a waste of disk space, but you can create a temporary copy of that field with a calculated field.

Bring up the Fields Editor for the BookLookupTable table. Right-click it and create a new field called AuthorLookup. Set its Type to String and its Field Type to Lookup. The Key Fields should be set to AuthNo, the Dataset to AuthorTable, the Lookup Keys to AuthNo, and the Result field to LastFirst. Figure 8.25 shows how the New Field dialog should look when you are done. Notice that you can also fill in this same information in the Object Inspector if you first select the BookLookupTableAuthorLookup object. (In other words, you could create a new object and then close the Fields Editor without specifying any of its properties. Later, you could select the object and designate its type, its lookup fields, and so on.)

FIGURE 8.25

Filling in the New Field dialog.

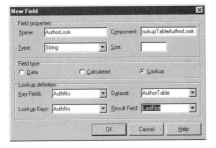

Go back to Form1; make sure the two DBGrids are arranged one above the other and are hooked up properly to the tables on the data module. Then run the application.

The AuthorLookup field in the DBGrid object associated with the BookAuthorLookup table is now a drop-down combo box that can be seen at run time. If you click it once and then bring down its list, you can then perform a lookup into the LastFirst field of the Author table. This lookup will automatically fill in the AuthNo field of the BookAuthorLookup table. You can use this lookup to insert a new author into a new record or to change the author of an existing record.

TIP

The ability to have a drop-down list in a grid object is included in C++Builder 4. Go back to design mode and open a grid object's Columns property. Add all the fields to the Columns list box. You can now select one of the fields, such as Title, and choose the PickList button to create a set of default values available for the field. The user can access these values at run time by clicking the field and dropping down the combo box, per the lookup example discussed previously.

Besides the TDBGrid object, two other controls in C++Builder understand lookup fields. The first is a TDBLookupComboBox, which is the default control you get if you drag and drop the AuthorLookup field from the Fields Editor onto a form. The control is hooked up automatically if you perform the drag-and-drop operation. If you want to hook it up manually, just connect its DataSource to the BookLookupSource object and its DataField to the AuthorLookup field. The TDBLookupListBox also works exactly the same way as the TDBLookupComboBox.

NOTE

Both the TDBLookupListBox and TDBLookupComboBox have fields that correspond to those you filled in with the New Field dialog shown in Figure 8.25. However, you don't need to fill in these fields a second time. Just hook up the DataSource and DataField properties, and you are ready to go.

Multirecord Objects

Another object that deserves mention is the DBCtrlGrid, shown in Figure 8.26 and on the CtrlGrid program from the CD-ROM that accompanies this book. You can use this object to view multiple records from a single table at one time without using the TDBGrid component. In other words, you can bring down TDBEdit controls onto a TDBCtrlGrid, and these edit controls will automatically be duplicated in a series of rows, where the first set of controls shows the first record; the second set, the second record; and so on. You have to bring down only one set of controls; the extra sets are duplicated for you automatically by the DBCtrlGrid, as shown in Figure 8.26.

FIGURE 8.26

The TDBCtrlGrid
*object on the form
of the* CtrlGrid
application.

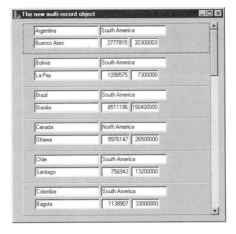

To begin this object, first start SQL Explorer by choosing Database, Explore from the
C++Builder main menu. Now drag and drop the Country table off the SQL Explorer and
onto the form. Delete the TDBGrid object and add the TDBCtrlGrid object off the
Component Palette's Data Controls page. Use the Fields Editor to drag and drop all the
fields from the Country table onto the top section of the DBCtrlGrid.

Notice that DBCtrlGrids have RowCount and ColCount properties, which enable you to
define the number of rows and columns in the object. In this case, I have set the
RowCount to 7.

The TDBCtrlGrid component doesn't bring any new functionality to C++Builder. It's
useful, however, as it eliminates the need to have the user slide the scrollbar back and
forth on a TDBGrid object.

Summary

In this chapter you learned some sophisticated methods for displaying the data from multiple tables. In particular, you saw how C++Builder handles the key features of a relational database.

The tools discussed in this chapter include the following:

- The Fields Editor
- The SQL Explorer
- The Database Desktop
- The Query by Example tool in the DBD

The components discussed in this chapter include the following:

- `TField` descendant objects
- The `TDBCtrlGrid`, `TDBLookupComboBox`, and `TDBLookupListBox` objects
- The `TDBGrid` component

The properties discussed in this chapter include the following:

- Calculated fields
- Lookup fields

Good database programmers will find that a considerable amount of power is hidden in the `TField` object and in the Fields Editor, as well as the other tools and components mentioned in this chapter. These database tools represent a very strong aspect of C++Builder, which is further expanded on by the work of third-party developers.

Flat-File
Real-World
Databases

by Charlie Calvert
and Kent Reisdorph

IN THIS CHAPTER

CHAPTER 9

This chapter is the first of a two-part series on constructing real-world databases. The goal is to move from the largely theoretical information you received in the preceding chapter into a few examples of how to make programs that someone could actually use for a practical purpose.

In several sections of this chapter, I go into considerable depth about design-related issues. One of the burdens of this chapter isn't merely to show how database code works, but to talk about how to create programs that have some viable use in the real world. Design-related issues are among the most important challenges that programmers face. Learning how to program is much easier than learning how to create programs that work.

Here is a quick look at the terrain covered in this chapter:

- Sorting data.
- Filtering data.
- Searching for data.
- Dynamically moving a table in and out of a read-only state.
- Forcing the user to select a field's value from a list of valid responses.
- Allowing the user to choose the colors of a form at run time.
- Saving information to the Registry. In particular, you see how to use the Registry to replace an INI file and how to save and restore information to and from the Registry at program startup.
- Using events that occur in a TDataModule inside the main form of your program. That is, the chapter shows how to respond to events specific to one form from inside a second form. More generally, it shows how to handle events manually rather than let C++Builder set up the event handler for you.

Be sure to read the readme files on the CD-ROM that accompanies this book for information about the alias used in the ADDRESS2 program and in other programs in this book. If you have trouble getting any of these programs running, check my Web site (http://users.aol.com/charliecal) for possible updates.

The key to getting the program up and running is to create a standard Paradox alias called BCB4UNLEASHED and point it to the directory where you have placed Address.db, Cats.db, and related files. These tables are stored by default in the Data directory on the CD-ROM that accompanies this book, and you should copy them onto your hard drive before you try to use them. As always, the best way to install the files is to use the installation program that comes with the CD-ROM. You can also copy the files over directly, but if you do, you should be sure they are not marked as read-only. You can remove the read-only attribute from a file using the Windows Explorer.

Overview of the Sample Program

In this chapter, you get a look at a simple, nearly pure, flat-file address book program called ADDRESS2. This program is designed to represent the simplest possible database program that is still usable in a real-world situation. The final product, though not quite up to professional standards, provides solutions to many of the major problems faced by programmers who want to create tools that can be used by the typical user.

I found, however, that it was simply impossible for me to create a completely flat-file database design. Thus, it does contain one small helper table that supports the database using relational database design principles. My inability to omit this table does more than anything else I can say to stress the weaknesses of the flat-file model, and to show why relational databases are essential.

In the next chapter, you will see a second database program with a powerful set of relational features that could, with the aid of a polished interface, stand up under the strain of heavy and complex demands. You could give this second program to a corporate secretary or executive, and that person could make some real use of it.

One of my primary goals in these two chapters is to lay out in the starkest possible terms the key differences between flat-file and relational databases. The point is for you to examine two database tools that perform the same task and see exactly what the relational tool brings to the table.

One of the points you shouldn't miss, however, is that the database from this chapter more than suits the needs of most people. A common mistake is to give people too many features, or to concentrate on the wrong set of features. Those of us who work in the industry forget how little experience most users have with computers. Even the simple database program outlined in this chapter might be too much for some people. Any attempt to sell them on the merits of the database from the next chapter would simply be an exercise in futility. They would never be willing to take the time to figure out what to do with it. As a result, I suggest that you not turn your nose up at the database shown in this chapter just because it isn't as powerful as the one in the next chapter. Simply because your typical Volkswagen isn't as powerful as an Alfa Romeo doesn't mean that the Volkswagen people are in a small business niche, or even that there is less money in VWs than in Alfa Romeos.

You will find that the program in this chapter is relatively long when compared to most of the programs you have seen so far in this book. The length of the program is a result of my aspiration to make it useful in a real-world setting, while providing at least a minimum degree of robustness. The act of adding a few niceties to the interface for a program gives you a chance to see how RAD and OOP programming can help solve some fairly difficult problems.

Designing an Application

Many books tell you to complete your plan before you begin programming. The only thing wrong with this theory is that I have never seen it work out as expected in practice.

Nearly all the real-world programs that I have seen, both my own and others, whether produced by individuals or huge companies, always seem to go through initial phases that are later abandoned in favor of more sophisticated designs.

Think hard about what you want to do. Then create a prototype. Critique it and rethink your design. Totally abandoning the first draft is rarely necessary, but you are almost certainly going to have to rewrite. For this reason, concentrating on details at first isn't a good idea. Get things up and running; then if they look okay, go back and optimize.

The process is iterative. You keep rewriting, over and over, the same way authors keep rewriting the chapters in their books. RAD programming tools help make this kind of cycle possible. The interesting thing about C++Builder is that the same tool that lets you prototype quickly is also the tool that lets you optimize down to the last clock cycle.

My experience leads me to believe that the practical plan that really works is iterative programming. Think for a little bit, and then write some code. Review it, then rewrite it, then review it, and then rewrite it, and so on. Another, somewhat more old-fashioned name for this process is simply: One heck of a lot of hard work!

When I first started programming, I lived under the glorious misconception that this job was mostly about writing code. The more programs I write, however, the more convinced I become that this job is really about designing applications.

In those days, when I found a bug in my program, I thought the solution was to open the debugger and start digging into my code to find out what went wrong. I still think that solution is sometimes the best. However, I'm increasingly finding the best way to resolve the bug is to shut down the compiler, bring out my design documents, and figure out how I got into such a mess. If I've designed my application correctly, most bugs seem to resolve themselves automatically. The program simply falls together, and I don't need to chase bugs all over the place.

In this portion of the chapter, I talk some about the task of designing an application. This description is hardly an exhaustive examination of the subject, but it at least opens the door a crack on this important subject.

Defining the Data

The first stage in designing a database is to decide what kind of data you need to capture. This decision can often be the most prolonged and difficult stage of the design process. However, this program has such a simple domain that it can be addressed fairly quickly.

When you're considering an address program, you can easily come up with a preliminary list of needed fields:

```
First Name
Last Name
Address
City
State
Zip
Phone
```

After making this list and contemplating it for a moment, you might ask the following questions:

- What about complex addresses that can't be written on one line?
- Is one phone number enough? What about times when I need a home phone and a work phone?
- Speaking of work, what about specifying the name of the company that employs someone on the list?
- What about faxes?
- This is the 1990s, so what about email addresses?
- What about generic information that doesn't fit into any of these categories?

This list of questions emerges only after a period of gestation. In a real-world situation, you might come up with a list of questions like this only after you talk with potential users of your program, after viewing similar programs that are on the market, or after experimenting with a prototype of the proposed program. Further information might be culled from your own experience using or writing similar programs. However you come up with the proper questions, the key point is that you spend the time to really think about the kind of data you need.

After considering the preceding questions, you might come up with a revised list of fields for your program:

```
First Name
Last Name
Company
Address1
Address2
City
State
Zip
Home Phone
Work Phone
Fax
EMail1
EMail2
Comment
```

This list might actually stand up to the needs of a real-world user. Certainly, it doesn't cover all possible situations, but it does represent a reasonable compromise between the desire to make the program easy to use and the desire to handle a variety of potential user demands.

At this stage, you might start thinking about some of the basic functionality you want to associate with the program. For example, you might decide that a user of the program should be able to search, sort, filter, and print the data. After stating these needs, you'll find that the user needs to break up the data into various categories so that it can be filtered. The question, of course, is how these categories can be defined.

After considering the matter for some time, you might decide that two more fields should be added to the list. The first field can be called `Category`; it holds a name that describes the type of record currently being viewed. For example, some entries in an address book might consist of family members, whereas other entries might reference friends, associates from work, companies where you shop, or other types of data. In this case, I declare the `Category` field as being of type `Long` and then do a lookup into a second table to a human-readable string I can show to the user. I discuss this process later in the chapter, in the section called "Working with Lookups and the `Category` Field." Besides the `Category` field, a second new field called `Marked` can be added; it designates whether a particular field is marked for some special processing.

Here is the revised list, with one additional field called `Category`, which is used to help the user filter the data he or she might be viewing, and a field called `Marked`:

```
First Name
Last Name
Company
Address1
Address2
City
State
Zip
Home Phone
Work Phone
Fax
EMail1
EMail2
Comment
Category
Marked
```

After you carefully consider the fields that might be used in the ADDRESS2 program, the next step is to decide how large and what type the fields should be. Table 9.1 shows proposed types and sizes.

TABLE 9.1 FIELDS USED BY THE ADDRESS2 PROGRAM

Name	Type	Size
FName	Character	40
LName	Character	40
Company	Character	40
Address1	Character	40
Address2	Character	40
City	Character	40
State	Character	5
Zip	Character	15
HPhone	Character	15
WPhone	Character	15
Fax	Character	15
EMail1	Character	45
EMail2	Character	45
Comment	Memo	20
Category	Long	
Marked	Logical	

As you can see, I prefer to give myself plenty of room in all the fields I declare. In particular, notice that I have opted for wide EMail fields to hold long Internet addresses, and I have decided to make the Comment field into a memo field so that it can contain long entries, if necessary. The names of some of the fields have also been altered so that they don't contain any spaces. This feature might prove useful if the data is ever ported to another database.

Considering Program Design

Now that you have decided on the basic structure of the table, the next task is to work out some of the major design issues. In particular, the following considerations are important:

- The program should run off local tables because this kind of tool is likely to be used on individual PCs rather than on a network. The choice of whether to use Paradox or dBASE tables is a toss-up, but I opt to use Paradox tables because they provide more features.

9

FLAT-FILE
REAL-WORLD
DATABASES

- The user should be able to sort the table on the FName, LName, and Company fields.
- Searching on the FName, LName, and Company fields should be possible.
- The user should be able to set up filters based on the Category field.
- The times when the table is editable should be absolutely clear, and the user should be able to easily move in and out of read-only mode.
- Printing the contents of the table based on the filters set up by the Category field should be possible.
- Choosing a set of colors that satisfies all tastes is very difficult, so the user should be able to set the colors of the main features in the program.

A brief consideration of the design decisions makes it clear that the table should have a primary index on the first three fields and secondary indices on the FName, LName, Company, and Category fields. The primary index can be used in place of a secondary index on the FName field, but the intent of the program's code will be clearer if a secondary index is used for this purpose. In other words, the code will be easier to read if it explicitly sets the IndexName to something called FNameIndex instead of simply defaulting to the primary index. Table 9.2 shows the final structure of the table. The three stars in the fourth column of the table show the fields that are part of the primary index. Table 9.3 shows the table used for the lookup into the Category field. I discuss that table in more depth later in the section called "Working with Lookups and the Category Field."

> **NOTE**
>
> This table doesn't have a code field—that is, it doesn't have a simple numerical number in the first field of the primary index. Most tables have such a value, but it isn't necessary here because this database is, at least in theory, a flat-file database. I say, "at least in theory," because I am going to make one small cheat in the structure of this database. In short, a second table will be involved simply because I could see no reasonable way to omit it from the design of this program.

TABLE 9.2 DETAILED LIST OF FIELDS USED BY THE ADDRESS2 PROGRAM

Name	Type	Size	PIdx	Index
FName	Character	40	*	FNameIndex
LName	Character	40	*	LNameIndex
Company	Character	40	*	CompanyIndex
Address1	Character	40		

Name	Type	Size	PIdx	Index
Address2	Character	40		
City	Character	40		
State	Character	5		
Zip	Character	15		
HPhone	Character	15		
WPhone	Character	15		
Fax	Character	15		
EMail1	Character	45		
EMail2	Character	45		
Comment	Memo	20		
Category	Long			CategoryIndex
Marked	Logical			

TABLE 9.3   THE Cats TABLE HOLDS THE VALUES DISPLAYED IN THE Category FIELD OF THE Address TABLE

Name	Type	Size	PIdx	Index
Code	AutoInc		*	
Category	Character	25		

Now that you have a clear picture of the types of tables that you need to create, you can open the Database Desktop and create them. Start with the Address table by creating its primary index and its four secondary indices. When you're done, the structure of the table should look like that in Figure 9.1. You can save the table under the name **ADDRESS.DB**.

FIGURE 9.1

Designing the main table for the ADDRESS2 program. Portions of the table are not visible in this figure.

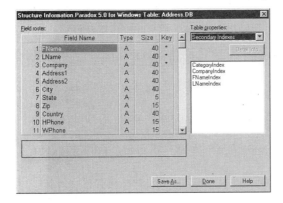

Here is another way of looking at the indices for this table:

```
Primary Index
LName
FName
Company

Category Index
Category

Company Index
Company
FName
LName

LName Index
LName
FName
Company

FName Index
FName
LName
Company
```

In this particular case, I actually end up using these fields and indices as designed. However, in an actual situation, you should expect to come up with a carefully thought-out draft like this, and then know in your heart that after you get the program up and running, some things will have to change. Don't tell someone, "Oh, I can complete this program in two weeks; this is going to be easy!" Instead, say, "In two weeks, I can get you a prototype, and then we can sit down and decide what changes need to be made."

You should, however, have some clearly defined boundaries. For example, this program is designed to be a flat-file database. If someone (yourself most especially included) tries to talk you into believing that this program should really be a relational database of the kind planned for the next chapter, you have to slam your foot down and say, "No way!" After you've started on a project, you should expect revisions, but you must not allow the goal of the project to be redefined. That method leads to madness.

Defining the Program's Appearance

Before beginning the real programming chores, you need to create a main form and at least one of the several utility forms that will be used by the program. You can let the Database Form Wizard perform at least part of this task for you, but I prefer to do the chore myself to give my program some individuality.

The main form of the ADDRESS2 program, shown in Figure 9.2, contains two panels. On the top panel are all the labels and data-aware controls necessary to handle basic input and output chores. All the main fields in the program can be encapsulated in `TDBEdit` controls, except for the `Comment` field, which needs a `TDBMemo`, and the `Category` field, which needs a `TDBLookupComboBox`. The names of the data-aware controls should match the field with which they are associated, so the first `TDBEdit` control is called `FNameEdit`; the second, `LNameEdit`; and so on. The `TDBLookupComboBox` is therefore called `CategoryCombo`; and the memo field, `CommentMemo`.

FIGURE 9.2

The main form for the ADDRESS2 program.

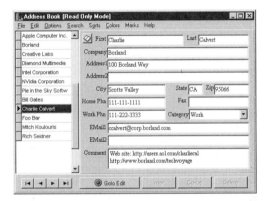

> **NOTE**
>
> If you find yourself chafing under the restraints of my naming conventions, you shouldn't hesitate to adopt the method you think best. For example, if you really prefer eFName or plain FName rather than FNameEdit as the name of a TDBEdit control, you should go with your gut instinct.
>
> My history in this regard is simple. I started out deploring Hungarian notation and then slowly inched over to the point at which I was reluctantly starting to use it in my programs. Then there came a day when I was squinting at some egregious variable name dreamed up by a Microsoft employee, and I just knew that I had had enough of abbreviations, and especially of prefixing them to a variable name that was itself abbreviated. For instance, I hate variable names that look like this: lpstrctr. Here, everything is abbreviated, and nothing is clear.
>
> After contemplating this situation for a while, I decided that the one thing I could bring to the table that I really cared about was clarity. As a result, I dropped Hungarian notation from all my new code and began using whole words whenever possible.

The bottom panel should contain four buttons for navigating through the table's records, as well as Edit, Insert, Cancel, and Delete buttons. A status bar at the bottom of the main form provides room for optionally reporting on the current status of the program.

The top of the program contains a menu with something like the following format:

```
Caption = "File"
  Caption = "Print Addresses"
  Caption = "Print Phone Only"
  Caption = "Print Everything"
  Caption = "Print By Group"
  Caption = "Print Forms"
  Caption = "------"
  Caption = "Exit"
Caption = "Edit"
  Caption = "Copy"
  Caption = "Cut"
  Caption = "Paste"
Caption = "Options"
  Caption = "Filter"
  Caption = "Edit Category"
  Caption = "Grid View"
Caption = "Search"
  Caption = "First Name"
  Caption = "Last Name"
  Caption = "Company"
Caption = "Sorts"
  Caption = "First Name"
  Caption = "Last Name"
  Caption = "Company"
Caption = "Colors"
  Caption = "Form"
  Caption = "Edits"
  Caption = "Edit Text"
  Caption = "Labels"
  Caption = "Panels"
  Caption = "------"
  Caption = "System Colors"
  Caption = "Default Colors"
  Caption = "The Blues"
  Caption = "The Greens"
  Caption = "------"
  Caption = "Save Custom"
  Caption = "Read Custom"
Caption = "Marks"
  Caption = "Mark All"
  Caption = "Clear All Marks"
  Caption = "Print Marked to File"
  Caption = "------"
  Caption = "Show Only Marked"
```

```
Caption = "Help"
   Caption = "Contents"
   Caption = "About"
```

Each line represents the caption for one entry in the program's main menu. The indented portions are the contents of the drop-down menus that appear when you select one of the menu items visible in Figure 9.2. After you create the program's menu, create a single alias called BCB4UNLEASHED that points to the tables that ship on the CD-ROM accompanying this book (if you haven't already done so). Take a look at the readme files on the CD-ROM for further information on aliases. Drop down a TTable and TDataSource on a data module, wire them up to ADDRESS.DB from the BCB4UNLEASHED alias, and hook up the fields to the appropriate data-aware control. Name the TTable object AddressTable and name the TDataSource object AddressSource.

Now switch back to the main form, choose File, Include Unit Hdr to connect the main form and the TDataModule, and hook up the data-aware controls shown in Figure 9.2 to the fields in the address table. The only tricky part of this process involves the Category field, which is connected to the TDBLookupComboBox. I explain how to use this field in the next section.

Working with Lookups and the Category Field

If you run the program you have created so far, you will find that the TDBLookupComboBox for the Category field doesn't contain any entries—that is, you can't drop down its list. The purpose of this control is to enable the user to select categories from a prepared list rather than force the user to make up categories on-the-fly. The list is needed to prevent users from accidentally creating a whole series of different names for the same general purpose.

Consider a case in which you want to set a filter for the program that shows only a list of your friends. To get started, you should create a category called Friend and assign it to all the rows of the Address table that fit that description. If you always choose this category from a drop-down list, it will presumably always be spelled the same. However, if you rely on users to type this word, you might get a series of related entries that looks like this:

```
Friend
Friends
Frends
Acquaintances
Buddies
Buds
```

```
Homies
HomeBoys
Amigos
Chums
Cronies
Companions
```

This mishmash of spellings and synonyms doesn't do you any good when you want to search for the group of records that fits into the category called Friend.

The simplest way to get control over your program's data is to use a TDBLookupCombo (found on the Component Palette's Win 3.1 tab) rather than a TDBLookupComboBox (on the Data Controls tab) To use this control, simply pop open the Property Editor for the Items property and type in a list of categories such as the following:

```
Home
Work
Family
Local Business
Friend
```

Now when you run the program and drop down the Category combo box, you will find that it contains your list.

The only problem with typing names directly into the Items property for the TDBLookupCombo is that changing this list at run time is impractical. To do away with this difficulty, the program stores the list in a separate table, called Cats.db. This table has two fields, an autoincrement code, and a single character field that is 25 characters wide. After creating the table in the Database Desktop, you can enter the following five strings into five separate records:

```
1          Home
2          Work
3          Family
4          Local Business
5          Friend
```

Now that you have two tables, it's best to switch away from the TDBLookupCombo and go instead with the TDBLookupComboBox. You make the basic connection to the TDBLookupComboBox by setting its DataSource property to AddressSource and its DataField to Category. Then, set the ListSource for the control to CatSource and set ListField and KeyField to Code.

To allow the user to change the contents of the `Cats` table, you can create a form like the one shown in Figure 9.3. This form needs only minimal functionality; discouraging the user from changing the list except when absolutely necessary is best. Note that you need to add the `CategoryDlg` module's header to the list of files included in the main form. You can do so simply by choosing File, Include Unit Hdr.

FIGURE 9.3

The Category form enables the user to alter the contents of Cats.db.

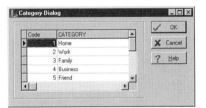

At program startup, the Category dialog—and the memory associated with it—doesn't need to be created and allocated. As a result, you should choose Project, Options, select the Forms page, and move the Category dialog into the Available Forms column. In response to a selection of the Edit Category menu item from the main form of the ADDRESS2 program, you can write the following code:

```
void __fastcall TForm1::CategoryClick(TObject *Sender)
{
  CatsDlg = new TCatsDlg(this);
  CatsDlg->ShowModal();
  delete CatsDlg;
}
```

This code creates the Category dialog, shows it to the user, and finally deallocates its memory after the user is done.

9

FLAT-FILE
REAL-WORLD
DATABASES

Setting Up the Command Structure for the Program

The skeletal structure of the ADDRESS2 program is starting to come together. However, you must complete one remaining task before the core of the program is complete. A number of basic commands are issued by the program, and they can be defined in a single enumerated type:

```
enum TCommandType { btClose, btInsert, btPrior,
                    btEdit, btNext, btCancel,
                    btPrint, btFirst, btLast,
                    btPrintPhone, btPrintAddress,
                    btPrintAll, btPrintGroup, btDelete,
                    btPrintMarked, btShowOnlyMarked };
```

This type enables you to associate each of the program's commands with the Tag field of the appropriate button or menu item, and then to associate all these buttons or menu items with a single method that looks like this:

```
void __fastcall TForm1::CommandClick(TObject *Sender)
{
  switch (TCommandType(dynamic_cast<TComponent*>(Sender)->Tag)) {
    case btClose: Close(); break;
    case btInsert: DMod->AddressTable->Insert(); break;
    case btEdit: HandleEditMode(); break;
    case btCancel: DMod->AddressTable->Cancel(); break;
    case btDelete: DMod->Delete(); break;

    case btPrint: PrintData(btPrint); break;
    case btPrintPhone: PrintData(btPrintPhone); break;
    case btPrintAddress: PrintData(btPrintAddress); break;
    case btPrintAll: PrintData(btPrintAll); break;
    case btPrintGroup: PrintData(btPrintGroup);
  }
}
```

This code performs a simple typecast to enable you to access the Tag field of the component that generated the command.

Many people might think that there is no reason why you can't have a different method associated with each of the buttons and menu items in the program. In such a scenario, the menu itself becomes the clearinghouse for commands, and you turn to it when you want an overview of the program's structure. However, handling traffic in the CommandClick method is arguably neater and simpler in that you have one central code-based clearinghouse for most of the activity in the program. This setup is particularly useful when you can handle most of the commands with a single line of code. Look at the `ctNext` and `ctCancel` portions of the `switch` statement in the `CommandClick` method. Certainly, you can find room for argument on either side, so you must choose the course of action you think best.

The key point here is to be sure that the `Tag` property of the appropriate control gets the correct value and that all the controls listed have the `OnClick` method manually set to the `CommandClick` method. I took all these steps while in Design mode, being careful to associate the proper value with the `Tag` property of each control.

Table 9.4 gives a brief summary of the commands passed to the `CommandClick` method.

TABLE 9.4 COMMANDS PASSED TO `CommandClick`

Command	Type	Name	Tag
Exit	TMenuItem	btClose	0
Insert	TButton	btInsert	1
Prior	TButton	btPrior	2
Edit	TButton	btEdit	3
Next	TButton	btNext	4
Cancel	TButton	btCancel	5
Print	TMenuItem	btPrint	6
First	TButton	btFirst	7
Last	TButton	btLast	8

All the code in this program compiles at this stage except for the references in CommandClick to `HandleEditMode` and `PrintData`. For now, you can simply create dummy `HandleEditMode` and `PrintData` private methods and leave their contents blank.

You can now run the ADDRESS2 program. When it's in memory, you can insert new data, iterate through the records you create, cancel accidental changes, and shut down the program from the menu. These capabilities create the bare functionality needed to run the program.

9

FLAT-FILE
REAL-WORLD
DATABASES

Examining the Rough Draft of an Application

The program as it exists now is what I mean by a "rough draft" of a program. A rough draft falls somewhere between a prototype and beta candidate. In other words, it contains more functionality than a prototype but is nowhere near a finished product. The rough draft gets the raw functionality of the program up and running with minimum fuss, and it lets you take a look at the program to see whether it passes muster. If you were working for a third-party client or a demanding boss, now would be the time to call the person or persons in question and have them critique your work. "Is this what you're looking for?" you might ask. "Do you think any fields need to be there that aren't yet visible? Do you feel that the project is headed in the right direction?"

Nine times out of ten, these people come back to you with a slew of suggestions, most of which have never occurred to you. If they have irreconcilable differences of opinion about the project, now is the time to find out. If they have some good ideas you never considered, now is the time to add them. This is also the time when you can critique your own work. Does this program really attain the goals I set for myself? Am I on track?

Now you also have your chance to let everyone know that, after this point, making major design changes might become impossible. Let everyone know that you're about to start doing the kind of detail work that is very hard to undo. If people need a day or two to think about your proposed design, give it to them. Making changes now, at the start, is better than after you have everything polished and spit-shined. By presenting people with a prototype, you give them a sense of participating in the project, which at least potentially puts them on your side when you turn in the finished project.

To help illustrate the purpose of this portion of the project development, I have waited until this time to point out that adding a grid to the program might be helpful so that the user can see a list of names from which to make a selection. This kind of option might make no sense if you're working with huge datasets, but if you have only a few hundred or a few thousand records, a grid can be useful. (The TDBGrid component is powerful enough to display huge datasets, but reasonable debate exists over whether grids are the right interface element for tables that contain thousands or millions of records.)

When using the grid, you have to choose which fields will be shown in it. If you choose the last name field, you have a problem for records that include only the company name, and if you use the company name, the reverse problem kicks in. To solve this dilemma, I create a calculated field called FirstLastCompany that looks like this:

```
void __fastcall TDMod::AddressTableCalcFields(TDataSet *DataSet)
{
  if (!AddressTableFName->IsNull || !AddressTableLName->IsNull)
    AddressTableFirstLast->Value = AddressTableFName->Value + " " +
      AddressTableLName->Value;
  else if (!AddressTableCompany->IsNull)
    AddressTableFirstLast->Value = AddressTableCompany->Value;
  else
    AddressTableFirstLast->Value = "Blank Record";
```

```
AddressTableCityStateZip->Value =
    AddressTableCity->Value + ", " + AddressTableState->Value + " " +
    AddressTableZip->Value;
}
```

The code specifies that if a first or last name appears in the record, that name should be used to fill in the value for the calculated field. However, if they are both blank, the program supplies the company name instead. As an afterthought, I decided that if all three fields are blank, the string "Blank Record" should appear in the calculated field.

I hope that you can now see why I feel that optimization issues should always be put off until the interface, design, and basic coding of the program are taken through at least one draft. You would be foolish to spend a lot of time optimizing routines that you or a client ultimately don't believe are necessary, or even want, in the final release version of the program. Get the program up and running, and then, if everyone agrees that it looks right, you can decide whether it needs to be optimized or whether you have time for optimization. Program development is usually an iterative process, with a heavy focus on design issues. I don't think working under the assumption that you'll get it right the first time is wise.

Creating Your Objects

Before you go too much further, you might start thinking about the basic objects needed to complete the program. This program is complex enough that I have tried to move most of the functionality out of Form1. In particular, I want Form1 to be little more than a clearinghouse for the routines conducted in this program.

As you will see when you view the finished program, I have created a unit called ColorClass1 that contains the following classes:

- TColorClass—A class that sets the colors for the various forms used in the project. All the details of specifying colors for panels, editor controls, forms, grids, and so on are delegated to this object.

- TMarks—The user of the database will be able to mark certain records and then perform operations on those marked records. All operations related to this process are handled in TMarks.

- TRegIniClass—The user can store default settings for the program in the Registry. This class handles talking to the Registry.

- TSearchSort—This class is designed to handle searching through the data in the program and also sorting the data.

The data module for the program, TDMod, is stored in a file called DMod1. It contains many of the routines involved with directly manipulating the Address and Cats tables.

Now that I have all these tasks out of the way, the main form for the program is primarily a clearinghouse designed to delegate events to the objects described in this section of the chapter. The only other tasks handled in the form itself are copy, cut, and paste operations, as well as filtering data. I could have handled the filtering in the TSearchSort object and created another object called TCopyCutPaste. I didn't take this approach, however, simply because I felt that the complexity of the TForm1 object was sufficiently reduced already and did not need any further attention.

Though I have been over this point before, I have to stress how much simpler I find it to write programs that delegate key functionality to small utility objects such as TColorClass or TMarks. If I tried to mix all this functionality into TForm1, the TForm1 object would be large, confusing, and hard to maintain. Breaking things out this way enables me to see easily how my program is constructed.

If I want to come back and improve some section of the program, this design will aid in the process. Suppose I wanted to improve the way the program handles marking records. This whole section of the program is now confined to a single object. I will have no trouble studying this object to see how this aspect of the program behaves at the current time. Expanding the marking functionality is now just a matter of adding methods to this one simple object.

If I didn't have the TMark object, I would have to sort through many different methods of TForm1, finding the ones that apply to marking records. Then I would have to keep all those methods in mind while I figured out how to expand their functionality. For most people, the task simply becomes too overwhelming, and as a result, the program never reaches its full potential.

Creating a Finished Program

The remaining portions of this chapter tackle the issues that improve this program to the point that it might be useful in a real-world situation. All but the most obvious or irrelevant portions of the code for the ADDRESS2 program are explained in detail in the remainder of this chapter.

Listings 9.1 through 9.7 show most of the code for the finished program. I discuss most of this code in one place or another in this chapter. The gap between the sketchy outline of a program, discussed earlier, and a product that is actually usable forms the heart of the discussion that follows. You have to know those raw tools to be able to write any kind of database program. However, they are not enough, and at some point, you have to start putting together something that might be useful to actual human beings. (Remember them?) That sticky issue of dealing with human beings, and their often indiscriminate foibles, forms the subtext for much of what is said in the rest of this chapter.

LISTING 9.1   THE HEADER FOR THE MAIN FORM OF THE ADDRESS2 PROGRAM

```cpp
#ifndef MainH
#define MainH

#include <Classes.hpp>
#include <Controls.hpp>
#include <StdCtrls.hpp>
#include <Forms.hpp>
#include <Buttons.hpp>
#include <DBCtrls.hpp>
#include <DBGrids.hpp>
#include <Dialogs.hpp>
#include <ExtCtrls.hpp>
#include <Grids.hpp>
#include <Mask.hpp>
#include <Menus.hpp>
#include <ClipBrd.hpp>
#include "ColorClass1.h"

const String ReadOnlyStr = " [Read Only Mode]";
const String EditModeStr = " [Edit Mode]";

enum TCommandType { btClose, btInsert, btPrior,
                    btEdit, btNext, btCancel,
                    btPrint, btFirst, btLast,
                    btPrintPhone, btPrintAddress,
                    btPrintAll, btPrintGroup, btDelete,
                    btPrintMarked, btShowOnlyMarked };

class TForm1 : public TForm
{
__published:     // IDE-managed Components
  TPanel *Panel1;
  TLabel *Label2;
  TLabel *Label3;
  TLabel *Address1;
  TLabel *Address2;
  TLabel *City;
  TLabel *State;
  TLabel *Zip;
  TLabel *Company;
  TLabel *HPhone;
  TLabel *WPhone;
```

continues

9

FLAT-FILE
REAL-WORLD
DATABASES

LISTING 9.1 CONTINUED

```
TLabel *Comment;
TLabel *EMail1;
TLabel *Category;
TLabel *EMail2;
TSpeedButton *SpeedButton1;
TLabel *FaxLabel;
TDBEdit *LNameEdit;
TDBEdit *FNameEdit;
TDBEdit *Address1Edit;
TDBEdit *Address2Edit;
TDBEdit *CityEdit;
TDBEdit *StateEdit;
TDBEdit *ZipEdit;
TDBEdit *CompanyEdit;
TDBEdit *HomePhoneEdit;
TDBEdit *WorkPhoneEdit;
TDBEdit *FaxEdit;
TDBEdit *EMail1Edit;
TDBEdit *EMail2Edit;
TDBMemo *CommentMemo;
TDBLookupComboBox *DBLookupComboBox1;
TDBGrid *DBGrid1;
TPanel *Panel3;
TButton *InsertBtn;
TButton *CancelBtn;
TDBNavigator *DBNavigator1;
TButton *DeleteBtn;
TBitBtn *GotoEditBtn;
TColorDialog *ColorDialog1;
TMainMenu *MainMenu1;
TMenuItem *File1;
TMenuItem *PrintAddresses1;
TMenuItem *PrintPhoneOnly1;
TMenuItem *PrintEverything1;
TMenuItem *PrintByGroup1;
TMenuItem *PrintForms1;
TMenuItem *N1;
TMenuItem *Exit1;
TMenuItem *Edit1;
TMenuItem *Copy1;
TMenuItem *Cut1;
TMenuItem *Paste1;
TMenuItem *Options1;
TMenuItem *Filter1;
TMenuItem *Category1;
TMenuItem *GridView1;
TMenuItem *Search1;
TMenuItem *FNameSearch;
TMenuItem *LNameSearch;
```

```
        TMenuItem *CompanySearch;
        TMenuItem *Sorts1;
        TMenuItem *FirstName1;
        TMenuItem *LastName1;
        TMenuItem *Company1;
        TMenuItem *Colors1;
        TMenuItem *FormColor1;
        TMenuItem *EditColor1;
        TMenuItem *EditText1;
        TMenuItem *Labels1;
        TMenuItem *Panels1;
        TMenuItem *N3;
        TMenuItem *System1;
        TMenuItem *Defaults1;
        TMenuItem *Blues1;
        TMenuItem *TheGreens1;
        TMenuItem *N4;
        TMenuItem *SaveCustom1;
        TMenuItem *ReadCustom1;
        TMenuItem *Marks1;
        TMenuItem *MarkAll1;
        TMenuItem *ClearAllMarks1;
        TMenuItem *PrintMarkedtoFile1;
        TMenuItem *N2;
        TMenuItem *ShowOnlyMarked1;
        TMenuItem *Help1;
        TMenuItem *Contents1;
        TMenuItem *About1;
        void __fastcall FormCreate(TObject *Sender);
        void __fastcall FormDestroy(TObject *Sender);
        void __fastcall About1Click(TObject *Sender);
        void __fastcall CommandClick(TObject *Sender);
        void __fastcall CategoryClick(TObject *Sender);
        void __fastcall ColorClick(TObject *Sender);
        void __fastcall Filter1Click(TObject *Sender);
        void __fastcall SortMenu(TObject *Sender);
        void __fastcall Search1Click(TObject *Sender);
        void __fastcall Marks1Click(TObject *Sender);
        void __fastcall SpeedButton1Click(TObject *Sender);
        void __fastcall Copy1Click(TObject *Sender);
        void __fastcall Paste1Click(TObject *Sender);
        void __fastcall Cut1Click(TObject *Sender);
        void __fastcall GridView1Click(TObject *Sender);
            void __fastcall Contents1Click(TObject *Sender);
private:    // User declarations
    String FCaptionStr;
    TColorClass* FColorClass;
    TSearchSort* FSearchSort;
    TMarks* FMarks;
    void HandleEditMode();
    void PrintData(TCommandType PrintType);
```

9

FLAT-FILE
REAL-WORLD
DATABASES

continues

LISTING 9.1   CONTINUED

```
public:            // User declarations
  __fastcall TForm1(TComponent* Owner);
  __property TSearchSort* SearchSort =
    { read = FSearchSort, write = FSearchSort };
  __property TColorClass* ColorClass =
    { read = FColorClass, write = FColorClass };
};

extern PACKAGE TForm1 *Form1;

#endif
```

LISTING 9.2   THE SOURCE CODE FOR THE MAIN FORM OF THE ADDRESS2 PROGRAM

```
#include <vcl.h>
#pragma hdrstop

#include "Main.h"
#include "DMod1.h"
#include "About.h"
#include "Cats.h"
#include "Search.h"
#include "Filter.h"
#include "GridVue1.h"
#include "qrAddress.h"
#include "qrAll.h"
#include "qrGroup.h"
#include "qrPhone.h"

#pragma package(smart_init)
#pragma resource "*.dfm"
TForm1 *Form1;

__fastcall TForm1::TForm1(TComponent* Owner)
  : TForm(Owner)
{
}

void __fastcall TForm1::FormCreate(TObject *Sender)
{
  FCaptionStr = Caption;
  Caption = FCaptionStr + ReadOnlyStr;
  FSearchSort = new TSearchSort;
  FMarks = new TMarks;
  FColorClass = new TColorClass(this);
  FColorClass->SetupColors();
}
```

```cpp
void __fastcall TForm1::FormDestroy(TObject *Sender)
{
  delete FColorClass;
  delete FSearchSort;
  delete FMarks;
}

void __fastcall TForm1::About1Click(TObject *Sender)
{
  AboutBox->Color = FColorClass->RegIniClass->GetIni(FormKey);
  AboutBox->ShowModal();
}

void __fastcall TForm1::CommandClick(TObject *Sender)
{
  switch (TCommandType(dynamic_cast<TComponent*>(Sender)->Tag)) {
    case btClose: Close(); break;
    case btInsert: DMod->AddressTable->Insert(); break;
    case btEdit: HandleEditMode(); break;
    case btCancel: DMod->AddressTable->Cancel(); break;
    case btDelete: DMod->Delete(); break;

    case btPrint: PrintData(btPrint); break;
    case btPrintPhone: PrintData(btPrintPhone); break;
    case btPrintAddress: PrintData(btPrintAddress); break;
    case btPrintAll: PrintData(btPrintAll); break;
    case btPrintGroup: PrintData(btPrintGroup);
  }
}

void __fastcall TForm1::CategoryClick(TObject *Sender)
{
  CatsDlg = new TCatsDlg(this);
  CatsDlg->ShowModal();
  delete CatsDlg;
}

void __fastcall TForm1::ColorClick(TObject *Sender)
{
  TColorType Code = TColorType(dynamic_cast<TMenuItem*>(Sender)->Tag);

  if (Code != ccBlue && Code != ccDefault &&
      Code != ccGreen && Code != ccSystem &&
      Code != ccReadRegistry && Code != ccWriteRegistry)
    if (!ColorDialog1->Execute())
      return;

  TColorClass* ColorClass = new TColorClass(this);
  switch (TColorType(Code)) {
    case ccForm: Color = ColorDialog1->Color; break;
    case ccEdit:
```

9

continues

LISTING 9.2   CONTINUED

```
      ColorClass->SetEdits(tcColor, ColorDialog1->Color); break;
    case ccEditText:
      ColorClass->SetEdits(tcFontColor, ColorDialog1->Color); break;
    case ccLabel: ColorClass->SetLabels(ColorDialog1->Color); break;
    case ccPanel: ColorClass->SetPanels(ColorDialog1->Color); break;
    case ccBlue: ColorClass->TheBlues(); break;
    case ccGreen: ColorClass->TheGreens(); break;
    case ccDefault: ColorClass->DefaultColors(); break;
    case ccSystem: ColorClass->SystemColors(); break;
    case ccWriteRegistry: ColorClass->RegIniClass->WriteRegistry(); break;
    case ccReadRegistry: ColorClass->RegIniClass->ReadRegistry(); break;
  }
  delete ColorClass;
}

void __fastcall TForm1::Filter1Click(TObject *Sender)
{
  if (Filter1->Caption == "Filter") {
    int Cat = FilterDlg->GetFilter();
    if (Cat == -1)
      return;
    Filter1->Caption = "Cancel Filter";
    DMod->AddressTable->IndexName = "CategoryIndex";
    DMod->AddressTable->SetRangeStart();
    DMod->AddressTable->FieldByName("Category")->AsInteger = Cat;
    DMod->AddressTable->SetRangeEnd();
    DMod->AddressTable->FieldByName("Category")->AsInteger = Cat;
    DMod->AddressTable->ApplyRange();
  } else {
    Filter1->Caption = "Filter";
    DMod->AddressTable->CancelRange();
  }
}

void __fastcall TForm1::SortMenu(TObject *Sender)
{
  SearchSort->Sort(TCCSortType(dynamic_cast<TComponent*>(Sender)->Tag));
}

void __fastcall TForm1::Search1Click(TObject *Sender)
{
  SearchSort->Search(TCCSortType(dynamic_cast<TComponent*>(Sender)->Tag));
}

void __fastcall TForm1::Marks1Click(TObject *Sender)
{
  switch (TCommandType(dynamic_cast<TMenuItem*>(Sender)->Tag)) {
    case btPrintMarked: FMarks->PrintMarks(); break;
    case btShowOnlyMarked: FMarks->ShowOnlyMarked();
```

```
    default:
      FMarks->SetClearMarks(dynamic_cast<TMenuItem*>(Sender)->Tag);
  }
}

void __fastcall TForm1::SpeedButton1Click(TObject *Sender)
{
  FMarks->ToggleBoolean();
}

void __fastcall TForm1::Copy1Click(TObject *Sender)
{
  TDBEdit* dbEdit = dynamic_cast<TDBEdit*>(ActiveControl);
  TDBMemo* dbMemo = dynamic_cast<TDBMemo*>(ActiveControl);
  TDBComboBox* dbCombo = dynamic_cast<TDBComboBox*>(ActiveControl);
  if (dbEdit)
    dbEdit->CopyToClipboard();
  else if (dbMemo)
    dbMemo->CopyToClipboard();
  else if (dbCombo)
    Clipboard()->AsText = DBLookupComboBox1->Text;
}

void __fastcall TForm1::Paste1Click(TObject *Sender)
{
  if (!DMod->AddressSource->AutoEdit) {
    ShowMessage("Must be in edit mode");
    return;
  }
  TDBEdit* dbEdit = dynamic_cast<TDBEdit*>(ActiveControl);
  TDBMemo* dbMemo = dynamic_cast<TDBMemo*>(ActiveControl);
  if (dbEdit)
    dbEdit->PasteFromClipboard();
  else if (dbMemo)
    dbMemo->PasteFromClipboard();
}

void __fastcall TForm1::Cut1Click(TObject *Sender)
{
  if (!DMod->AddressSource->AutoEdit) {
    ShowMessage("Must be in edit mode");
    return;
  }
  TDBEdit* dbEdit = dynamic_cast<TDBEdit*>(ActiveControl);
  TDBMemo* dbMemo = dynamic_cast<TDBMemo*>(ActiveControl);
  TDBComboBox* dbCombo = dynamic_cast<TDBComboBox*>(ActiveControl);
  if (dbEdit)
    dbEdit->CutToClipboard();
  else if (dbMemo)
    dbMemo->CutToClipboard();
  else if (dbCombo) {
```

9

FLAT-FILE
REAL-WORLD
DATABASES

continues

LISTING 9.2   CONTINUED

```cpp
//    cbCategory->Text = ClipBoard->AsText;
//   cbCategory->Text = "";
   }
}

void __fastcall TForm1::GridView1Click(TObject *Sender)
{
  GridView = new TGridView(this);
  GridView->ShowModal();
  delete GridView;
}

void TForm1::HandleEditMode()
{
  InsertBtn->Enabled = !DMod->AddressSource->AutoEdit;
  CancelBtn->Enabled = !DMod->AddressSource->AutoEdit;
  DeleteBtn->Enabled = !DMod->AddressSource->AutoEdit;
  if (!DMod->AddressSource->AutoEdit) {
    DMod->AddressSource->AutoEdit = true;
    GotoEditBtn->Caption = "Goto ReadOnly";
    Caption = FCaptionStr + EditModeStr;
  } else {
    if (DMod->AddressTable->State != dsBrowse)
      DMod->AddressTable->Post();
    DMod->AddressSource->AutoEdit = false;
    GotoEditBtn->Caption = "Goto Edit";
    Caption = FCaptionStr + ReadOnlyStr;
  }
}

void TForm1::PrintData(TCommandType PrintType)
{
  switch (PrintType) {
    case btPrintPhone: QuickPhone->QuickReport1->Preview(); break;
    case btPrintGroup: PrintGroup->QuickRep1->Preview(); break;
    case btPrintAddress: QuickAddress->QuickReport1->Preview(); break;
    // case btPrintAll: QuickAll->QuickReport->Preview;
  }
}

void __fastcall TForm1::Contents1Click(TObject *Sender)
{
  ShowMessage(HelpStr);
}
```

LISTING 9.3   THE HEADER FOR THE ADDRESS2 PROGRAM'S COLOR CLASS UNIT

```
#ifndef ColorClass1H
#define ColorClass1H

const int mfClearMarks  = 100;
const int mfMarkAll      = 101;
const String RegKey      = "SOFTWARE\\Charlie's Stuff\\CAddress2";
const String FormKey     = "Form";
const String PanelKey    = "Panels";
const String EditKey     = "Edits";
const String EditTextKey= "Edit Text";
const String LabelKey    = "Labels";

enum TColorType { ccForm, ccEdit,
    ccEditText, ccLabel, ccPanel, ccBlue,
    ccDefault, ccSystem, ccGreen, ccWriteRegistry,
    ccReadRegistry };
enum TChangeType  { tcColor, tcFontColor };
enum TCCSortType { stFirst, stLast, stCompany };

class TRegIniClass;

class TColorClass {
  private:
    TForm* FMainForm;
    TRegIniClass* FRegIniClass;
  public:
    TColorClass(TForm* AForm);
    ~TColorClass();
    void DefaultColors();
    void SetEdits(TChangeType TypeChange, TColor NewValue);
    void SetLabels(TColor C);
    void SetPanels(TColor C);
    void SetupColors();
    void SystemColors();
    void TheBlues();
    void TheGreens();
    __property TRegIniClass* RegIniClass =
      {read = FRegIniClass, write = FRegIniClass};
};

class TMarks {
  public:
    void PrintMarks();
    void SetClearMarks(int MarkType);
    void ShowOnlyMarked();
    void ToggleBoolean();
    void WriteRecord(TStringList* F);
};
```

continues

LISTING 9.3   CONTINUED

```
class TRegIniClass : public TObject {
  private:
    TColorClass* FColorClass;
  public:
    TRegIniClass(TColorClass* AColorClass);
    TColor GetIni(String CType);
    void ReadRegistry();
    void WriteRegistry();
};

class TSearchSort : public TObject {
  private:
    TCCSortType FSortType;
    void DoSearch(String S);
    void DoSort();
  public:
    void Sort(TCCSortType SortType);
    void Search(TCCSortType SortType);
};

#endif
```

LISTING 9.4   THE COLOR CLASS UNIT FOR THE **ADDRESS2** PROGRAM CONTAINS MOST OF THE CORE FUNCTIONALITY FOR THE PROGRAM

```
// Project Name: ADDRESS2

//   This is a relatively simple database program that
//   has enough error checking and safety features to
//   be useful in the real world. A practical example
//   of using a simple database structure to create
//   a useful program.

#include <vcl.h>
#include <db.hpp>
#include <registry.hpp>
#include <shellapi.h>
#pragma hdrstop

#include "ColorClass1.h"
#include "Main.h"
#include "DMod1.h"
#include "Search.h"

#pragma package(smart_init)
TColorClass::TColorClass(TForm* AForm)
{
```

```
    FMainForm = AForm;
    FRegIniClass = new TRegIniClass(this);
  }

TColorClass::~TColorClass()
{
    FRegIniClass->WriteRegistry();
    delete FRegIniClass;
}

void TColorClass::TheBlues()
{
    SetEdits(tcColor, TColor(0x00FF8080));
    SetEdits(tcFontColor, clBlack);
    SetLabels(clBlack);
    SetPanels(TColor(0x00FF0080));
    FMainForm->Color = TColor(0x00FF0080);
    dynamic_cast<TForm1*>(FMainForm)->DBGrid1->Color = TColor(0x00FF8080);
}

void TColorClass::DefaultColors()
{
    SetEdits(tcColor, clNavy);
    SetEdits(tcFontColor, clYellow);
    SetLabels(clBlack);
    SetPanels(clBtnFace);
    FMainForm->Color = clBtnFace;
    dynamic_cast<TForm1*>(FMainForm)->DBGrid1->Color = clNavy;
}

void TColorClass::TheGreens()
{
    SetEdits(tcColor, TColor(8454016));
    SetEdits(tcFontColor, TColor(8404992));
    SetLabels(TColor(0));
    SetPanels(TColor(32768));
    FMainForm->Color = clGreen;
}

void TColorClass::SetupColors()
{
    FRegIniClass->ReadRegistry();
}

void TColorClass::SetEdits(TChangeType TypeChange, TColor NewValue)
{
    for (int i=0;i<FMainForm->ComponentCount;i++) {
        TDBEdit* dbEdit = dynamic_cast<TDBEdit*>(FMainForm->Components[i]);
        if (dbEdit)
            switch (TypeChange) {
                case tcColor: dbEdit->Color = NewValue; break;
```

continues

LISTING 9.4   CONTINUED

```cpp
        case tcFontColor: dbEdit->Font->Color = NewValue;
    }
    TDBMemo* dbMemo = dynamic_cast<TDBMemo*>(FMainForm->Components[i]);
    if (dbMemo)
      switch (TypeChange) {
        case tcColor: dbMemo->Color = NewValue; break;
        case tcFontColor: dbMemo->Font->Color = NewValue;
    }
    TDBGrid* dbGrid = dynamic_cast<TDBGrid*>(FMainForm->Components[i]);
    if (dbGrid)
      switch (TypeChange) {
        case tcColor: dbGrid->Color = NewValue; break;
        case tcFontColor: dbGrid->Font->Color = NewValue;
    }
    TDBLookupComboBox* dbCombo =
      dynamic_cast<TDBLookupComboBox*>(FMainForm->Components[i]);
    if (dbCombo)
      switch (TypeChange) {
        case tcColor: dbCombo->Color = NewValue; break;
        case tcFontColor: dbCombo->Font->Color = NewValue;
    }
  }
}

void TColorClass::SetLabels(TColor C)
{
  for (int i=0;i<FMainForm->ComponentCount;i++) {
    TLabel* label = dynamic_cast<TLabel*>(FMainForm->Components[i]);
    if (label)
      label->Font->Color = C;
  }
}

void TColorClass::SetPanels(TColor C)
{
  for (int i=0;i<FMainForm->ComponentCount;i++) {
    TPanel* panel = dynamic_cast<TPanel*>(FMainForm->Components[i]);
    if (panel)
      panel->Color = C;
  }
}

void TColorClass::SystemColors()
{
  SetEdits(tcColor, clWindow);
  SetEdits(tcFontColor, clBlack);
  SetLabels(clBlack);
  SetPanels(clBtnFace);
  FMainForm->Color = clBtnFace;
```

```
}

// TRegIniClass

TRegIniClass::TRegIniClass(TColorClass* AColorClass)
{
  FColorClass = AColorClass;
}

TColor TRegIniClass::GetIni(String CType)
{
  TColor Color = TColor(RGB(127, 127, 127));
  TRegIniFile* RegFile = new TRegIniFile(RegKey);
  int result = RegFile->ReadInteger("Colors", CType, Color);
  delete RegFile;
  return TColor(result);
}

void TRegIniClass::ReadRegistry()
{
  TColor DefColor = TColor(GetSysColor(COLOR_BTNFACE));

  TRegIniFile* RegFile = new TRegIniFile(RegKey);

  Form1->Color =
    TColor(RegFile->ReadInteger("Colors", FormKey, DefColor));

  TColor Color =
    TColor(RegFile->ReadInteger("Colors", PanelKey, DefColor));
  FColorClass->SetPanels(Color);

  DefColor = TColor(RGB(255,255,0));
  Color = TColor(RegFile->ReadInteger("Colors", EditTextKey, DefColor));
  FColorClass->SetEdits(tcFontColor, Color);

  DefColor = TColor(RGB(0,0,0));
  Color = TColor(RegFile->ReadInteger("Colors", LabelKey, DefColor));
  FColorClass->SetLabels(Color);

  DefColor = TColor(RGB(0,0,127));
  Color = TColor(RegFile->ReadInteger("Colors", EditKey, DefColor));
  FColorClass->SetEdits(tcColor, Color);
  delete RegFile;
}

void TRegIniClass::WriteRegistry()
{
  TRegIniFile* RegFile = new TRegIniFile(RegKey);
  RegFile->WriteInteger("Colors", FormKey, Form1->Color);
  RegFile->WriteInteger(
    "Colors", EditTextKey, Form1->FNameEdit->Font->Color);
```

9

FLAT-FILE REAL-WORLD DATABASES

continues

LISTING 9.4   CONTINUED

```cpp
    RegFile->WriteInteger("Colors", PanelKey, Form1->Panel1->Color);
    RegFile->WriteInteger("Colors", LabelKey, Form1->Label2->Font->Color);
    RegFile->WriteInteger("Colors", EditKey, Form1->FNameEdit->Color);
    delete RegFile;
}

// TSearchSort

void TSearchSort::DoSearch(String S)
{
  DMod->AddressTable->SetKey();
  switch (FSortType) {
    case stFirst :
      DMod->AddressTable->FieldByName("FName")->AsString = S; break;
    case stLast :
      DMod->AddressTable->FieldByName("LName")->AsString = S; break;
    case stCompany :
      DMod->AddressTable->FieldByName("Company")->AsString = S;
  }
  DMod->AddressTable->GotoNearest();
}

void TSearchSort::DoSort()
{
  switch (FSortType) {
    case stFirst : DMod->AddressTable->IndexName = "FNameIndex"; break;
    case stLast : DMod->AddressTable->IndexName = "LNameIndex"; break;
    case stCompany: DMod->AddressTable->IndexName = "CompanyIndex";
  }
}

void TSearchSort::Search(TCCSortType SortType)
{
  FSortType = SortType;
  String S;
  if (!SearchDlg->GetSearchStr(SortType, S))
    return;
  DoSort();
  DoSearch(S);
}

void TSearchSort::Sort(TCCSortType SortType)
{
  FSortType = SortType;
  DoSort();
  DoSearch("A");
}

// TMarks
```

```
void TMarks::PrintMarks()
{
  String S = "";
  if (!InputQuery("File Name Dialog", "Enter File Name", S))
    return;
  TStringList* F = new TStringList;
  DMod->AddressTable->First();
  while (!DMod->AddressTable->Eof) {
    if (DMod->AddressTable->FieldByName("Marked")->AsBoolean)
      WriteRecord(F);
    DMod->AddressTable->Next();
  }
  F->SaveToFile(S);
  delete F;
  ShellExecute(0, "open", S.c_str(), 0, 0, SW_NORMAL);
}

void TMarks::SetClearMarks(int MarkType)
{
  String Value;
  switch (MarkType) {
    case mfMarkAll : Value = "T"; break;
    case mfClearMarks : Value = "F"; break;
    default :
      return;
  }
  DMod->AddressSource->Enabled = false;
  TBookmark B = DMod->AddressTable->GetBookmark();
  DMod->AddressTable->First();
  while (!DMod->AddressTable->Eof) {
    DMod->AddressTable->Edit();
    DMod->AddressTable->FieldByName("Marked")->AsString = Value;
    DMod->AddressTable->Next();
  }
  DMod->AddressTable->GotoBookmark(B);
  DMod->AddressTable->FreeBookmark(B);
  DMod->AddressSource->Enabled = true;
}

void TMarks::ShowOnlyMarked()
{
  Form1->ShowOnlyMarked1->Checked = !Form1->ShowOnlyMarked1->Checked;
  DMod->AddressTable->Filtered = Form1->ShowOnlyMarked1->Checked;
}

void TMarks::ToggleBoolean()
{
  DMod->AddressTable->Edit();
  DMod->AddressTable->FieldByName("Marked")->AsBoolean =
    !DMod->AddressTable->FieldByName("Marked")->AsBoolean;
  DMod->AddressTable->Post();
}
```

continues

LISTING 9.4   CONTINUED

```
void TMarks::WriteRecord(TStringList* F)
{
  F->Add(DMod->AddressTable->FieldByName("FName")->AsString + " "
    + DMod->AddressTable->FieldByName("LName")->AsString);
  if (DMod->AddressTable->FieldByName("Company")->AsString != "")
    F->Add(DMod->AddressTable->FieldByName("Company")->AsString);
  F->Add(DMod->AddressTable->FieldByName("Address1")->AsString);
  if (DMod->AddressTable->FieldByName("Address2")->AsString != "")
    F->Add(DMod->AddressTable->FieldByName("Address2")->AsString);
  F->Add(DMod->AddressTable->FieldByName("City")->AsString + " "
    + DMod->AddressTable->FieldByName("State")->AsString + " "
    + DMod->AddressTable->FieldByName("Zip")->AsString);
  F->Add("");
  F->Add("*************");
}
```

LISTING 9.5   THE HEADER FOR THE **ADDRESS2** PROGRAM'S DATA MODULE

```
#ifndef DMod1H
#define DMod1H

#include <Classes.hpp>
#include <Controls.hpp>
#include <StdCtrls.hpp>
#include <Forms.hpp>
#include <Db.hpp>
#include <DBTables.hpp>

class TDMod : public TDataModule
{
__published:     // IDE-managed Components
  TQuery *ChangeMarkedQuery;
  TDataSource *AddressSource;
  TDataSource *CatsSource;
  TTable *AddressTable;
  TStringField *AddressTableFName;
  TStringField *AddressTableLName;
  TStringField *AddressTableCompany;
  TStringField *AddressTableAddress1;
  TStringField *AddressTableAddress2;
  TStringField *AddressTableCity;
  TStringField *AddressTableState;
  TStringField *AddressTableZip;
  TStringField *AddressTableCountry;
  TStringField *AddressTableHPhone;
  TStringField *AddressTableWPhone;
  TStringField *AddressTableFax;
  TStringField *AddressTableEMail1;
```

```
      TStringField *AddressTableEMail2;
      TMemoField *AddressTableComment;
      TIntegerField *AddressTableCategory;
      TBooleanField *AddressTableMarked;
      TStringField *AddressTableFirstLast;
      TStringField *AddressTableCityStateZip;
      TStringField *AddressTableCatLookup;
      TTable *CatsTable;
      void __fastcall DModCreate(TObject *Sender);
      void __fastcall AddressTableCalcFields(TDataSet *DataSet);
      void __fastcall AddressSourceDataChange(TObject *Sender, TField *Field);
      void __fastcall AddressTableFilterRecord(TDataSet *DataSet,
            bool &Accept);
private:      // User declarations
      HBITMAP FBookOpen;
      HBITMAP FBookShut;
public:           // User declarations
      __fastcall TDMod(TComponent* Owner);
        void Delete();
        void ChangeMarked(bool NewValue);
};

extern PACKAGE TDMod *DMod;

#endif
```

LISTING 9.6   THE SOURCE CODE FOR THE ADDRESS2 PROGRAM'S DATA MODULE

```
#include <vcl.h>
#pragma hdrstop

#include "DMod1.h"
#include "Main.h"

#pragma package(smart_init)
#pragma resource "*.dfm"
TDMod *DMod;

__fastcall TDMod::TDMod(TComponent* Owner)
  : TDataModule(Owner)
{
}

void TDMod::Delete()
{
  if (MessageDlg("Are you sure you want to delete?", mtInformation,
      TMsgDlgButtons() << mbOK << mbCancel, 0) == IDOK)
    AddressTable->Delete();
}
```

continues

LISTING 9.6   CONTINUED

```cpp
void TDMod::ChangeMarked(bool NewValue)
{
  ChangeMarkedQuery->Close();
  if (NewValue)
    ChangeMarkedQuery->ParamByName("NewValue")->AsString = "T";
  else
    ChangeMarkedQuery->ParamByName("NewValue")->AsString = "F";
  ChangeMarkedQuery->ExecSQL();
  AddressTable->Refresh();
}

void __fastcall TDMod::DModCreate(TObject *Sender)
{
  AddressTable->Open();
  CatsTable->Open();
  AddressSource->AutoEdit = false;
}

void __fastcall TDMod::AddressTableCalcFields(TDataSet *DataSet)
{
  if (!AddressTableFName->IsNull || !AddressTableLName->IsNull)
    AddressTableFirstLast->Value = AddressTableFName->Value + " " +
      AddressTableLName->Value;
  else if (!AddressTableCompany->IsNull)
    AddressTableFirstLast->Value = AddressTableCompany->Value;
  else
    AddressTableFirstLast->Value = "Blank Record";

  AddressTableCityStateZip->Value =
    AddressTableCity->Value + ", " + AddressTableState->Value + " " +
    AddressTableZip->Value;
}

// C++Builder disposes of TBitMaps when the
// handle is assigned to a new value, so we have
// to keep reloading it. At least it's part of the
// executable this way, and not a separate file.
void __fastcall TDMod::AddressSourceDataChange(TObject *Sender,
    TField *Field)
{
  if (AddressTable->FieldByName("Marked")->AsBoolean) {
    FBookOpen = LoadBitmap(HInstance, "BookOpen");
    Form1->SpeedButton1->Glyph->Handle = FBookOpen;
  } else {
    FBookShut = LoadBitmap(HInstance, "BookShut");
    Form1->SpeedButton1->Glyph->Handle = FBookShut;
  }
}
```

```
void __fastcall TDMod::AddressTableFilterRecord(TDataSet *DataSet,
     bool &Accept)
{
  Accept = (AddressTableMarked->AsBoolean == true);
}
```

LISTING 9.7   THE `bits.rc` FILE CONTAINS SPECIAL RESOURCES USED BY THE PROGRAM

```
bookopen BITMAP "BOOKOPEN.BMP"
bookshut BITMAP "BOOKSHUT.BMP"
```

The ADDRESS2 program contains special forms not found in Listings 9.1 through 9.7. These forms include `FilterDlg` and `AboutBox`. You can readily grasp the concepts of these forms from just looking at the screen shots of them, shown in Figures 9.4 and 9.5.

FIGURE 9.4

The `FilterDlg` from the ADDRESS2 program.

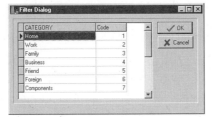

FIGURE 9.5

The `AboutBox` from the ADDRESS2 program.

The complete sample program, including all the forms, is included on the CD-ROM that accompanies this book. You will probably find it helpful to load that program into C++Builder and refer to it from time to time while reading the various technical discussions in the last half of this chapter.

Moving In and Out of Read-Only Mode

One of the most important single features of the ADDRESS2 program is its capability to move in and out of read-only mode. This capability is valuable because it enables the user to open the program and browse through data without ever having to worry about accidentally altering a record. In fact, when the user first opens the program, typing into any of the data-aware controls should be impossible. The only way for the program to get into Edit mode is for the user to click the Goto Edit button, which then automatically makes the data live.

When the program is in read-only mode, the Insert, Cancel, and Delete buttons are dimmed. When the user switches into Edit mode, all these controls become live, and the text in the Goto Edit button is changed so that it reads `"Goto ReadOnly"`. In other words, the caption for the Edit button says either `"Goto Edit"` or `"Goto ReadOnly"`, depending on whether you are in read-only mode. I also use red and green colored bitmaps to help emphasize the current mode and its capabilities, and list the mode in the caption at the top of the program. All these visual clues help make the current mode of the program obvious to the user.

The Edit button provides the user with a clue about the button's current function. In other words, the button doesn't report on the state of the program, but on the functionality associated with the button.

The functionality described is quite simple to implement. The key method to trace is called `HandleEditMode`.

The `HandleEditMode` routine is called from the `CommandClick` method described earlier:

```
void TForm1::HandleEditMode()
{
  InsertBtn->Enabled = !DMod->AddressSource->AutoEdit;
  CancelBtn->Enabled = !DMod->AddressSource->AutoEdit;
  DeleteBtn->Enabled = !DMod->AddressSource->AutoEdit;
  if (!DMod->AddressSource->AutoEdit) {
    DMod->AddressSource->AutoEdit = true;
    GotoEditBtn->Caption = "Goto ReadOnly";
    Caption = FCaptionStr + EditModeStr;
  } else {
    if (DMod->AddressTable->State != dsBrowse)
      DMod->AddressTable->Post();
    DMod->AddressSource->AutoEdit = false;
    GotoEditBtn->Caption = "Goto Edit";
    Caption = FCaptionStr + ReadOnlyStr;
  }
}
```

The primary purpose of this code is to ensure that the proper components are enabled or disabled, depending on the current state of the program.

The center around which this routine revolves is the AddressSource's AutoEdit property. When this property is set to false, all the data-aware controls on the form are disabled and the user cannot type in them. When the property is set to true, the data becomes live and the user can edit or insert records.

The purpose of the AutoEdit property is to determine whether a keystroke from the user can put a table directly into Edit mode. When AutoEdit is set to false, the user can't type information into a data-aware control. When AutoEdit is set to true, the user can switch the table into Edit mode simply by typing a letter in a control. Note that even when AutoEdit is set to false, you can set a table into Edit mode by calling the Edit or Insert methods. As a result, the technique shown here won't work unless you gray out the controls that give the user the power to set the table into Edit mode. You should also be sure to set the dgEditing element of the TDBGrid's Options property to false so that the user can never type anything in this control. The grid is simply not meant for enabling the user to modify records.

The HandleEditMode method is written so that the program is always moved into the opposite of its current state. At startup time, the table should be set to read-only mode (AutoEdit = false), and the appropriate controls should be disabled. Thereafter, every time you click the Goto Edit/Goto ReadOnly button, the program switches from its current state to the opposite state, from read-only mode to Edit mode and then back again.

In addition to the TDataSource AutoEdit property, there is another way you can take a table in and out of read-only mode. This second method is really more powerful than the first because it makes the table itself completely resistant to change. However, this second method is more costly in terms of time and system resources. The trick, naturally enough, is to change the ReadOnly property of a TTable component.

You cannot set a table in or out of read-only mode while it is open. Therefore, you have to close the table every time you change the ReadOnly property. Unfortunately, every time you close and open a table, you are moved back to the first record. As a result, you need to set a bookmark identifying your current location in the table, close the table, and then move the table in or out of read-only mode. When you are done, you can open the table and jet back to the bookmark. This process sounds like quite a bit of activity, but in fact it can usually be accomplished without the user being aware that anything untoward has occurred.

With the ADDRESS2 program, clearly the first technique for moving a program in and out of read-only mode is best. In other words, switching AddressSource in and out of

`AutoEdit` mode is much faster and much easier than switching `AddressTable` in and out of read-only mode.

On the whole, the act of moving ADDRESS2 in and out of read-only mode is fairly trivial. The key point to grasp is the power of the `TDataSource`'s `AutoEdit` method. If you understand how it works, you can provide this same functionality in all your programs.

Sorting Data

At various times, you might want the records stored in the program to be sorted by first name, last name, or company. These three possible options are encapsulated in the program's Sorts menu, which contains menu items called First Name, Last Name, and Company. These three sort categories are represented by an enumerated type declared in `ColorClass1.hpp`:

```
enum TCCSortType { stFirst, stLast, stCompany };
```

Note that this enumeration is named `TCCSortType` so that it doesn't conflict with the VCL's `TSortType` declared in `COMCTRLS.HPP`.

The `Tag` field from the Sorts drop-down menu makes it possible to detect which option the user wants to select:

```
void __fastcall TForm1::SortMenu(TObject *Sender)
{
  SearchSort->Sort(TCCSortType(dynamic_cast<TComponent*>(Sender)->Tag));
}

void TSearchSort::Sort(TCCSortType SortType)
{
  FSortType = SortType;
  DoSort();
  DoSearch("A");
}

void TSearchSort::DoSort()
{
  switch (FSortType) {
    case stFirst : DMod->AddressTable->IndexName = "FNameIndex"; break;
    case stLast : DMod->AddressTable->IndexName = "LNameIndex"; break;
    case stCompany: DMod->AddressTable->IndexName = "CompanyIndex";
  }
}
```

Note that I am showing you methods from two objects. The first method, which is part of `Form1`, acts only as a clearinghouse for the `TSearchSort` object. The actual work is done in the `Sort` and `DoSort()` methods of `TSearchSort`. In fact, the real burden of sorting is handled by the DoSort() method. If the user selects the menu option for sorting on the first name, the first element in the switch statement is selected; if the user opts to sort on the last name, the second element is selected; and so on.

If the Tag property for a menu item is 0, it gets translated into stFirst; if the property is 1, it goes to stLast; and 2 goes to stCompany. Everything depends on the order in which the elements of the enumerated type are declared in the declaration for TCCSortType. Of course, you must associate a different value between 0 and 2 for the Tag property.

After sorting, a group of blank records might appear at the beginning of the table. For example, if you choose to sort by the Company field, many of the records in the Address table are not likely to have anything in the Company field. As a result, several hundred, or even several thousand, records at the beginning of the table might be of no interest to someone who wants to view only companies. The solution, of course, is to search for the first record that doesn't have a blank value in the Company field. You can do so by using DoSearch() to search for the record that has a Company field that is nearest to matching the string "A". The actual details of searching for a record are covered in the next section. The downside of this process is that the cursor moves off the currently selected record whenever you sort.

Now you know all about sorting the records in the ADDRESS2 program. Clearly, this subject isn't difficult. The key point to grasp is that you must create secondary indices for all the fields on which you want to sort; then performing the sort becomes as simple as swapping indices.

Searching for Data

Searching for data in a table is a straightforward process. If you want to search on the Company field, simply declaring a secondary index called CompanyIndex isn't enough. To perform an actual search, you must make the CompanyIndex the active index and then perform the search. As a result, before you can make a search, you must do three things:

1. Ask the user for the string he or she wants to find.

2. Ask the user for the field where the string resides.

3. Set the index to the proper field.

Only after jumping through each of these hoops are you free to perform the actual search.

> **NOTE**
>
> Some databases don't force you to search only on actively keyed fields. Some SQL servers, for example, don't have this limitation. But local Paradox and dBASE tables are restricted in this manner, so you must use the techniques described here when searching for fields in these databases. If you chafe against these limitations, you can use the `OnFilterRecord()` process, in conjunction with `FindFirst()`, `FindNext()`, and so on. The `OnFilterRecord()` process plays a role later in this program when you need to filter on the marked field, which is of type `Boolean` and therefore cannot be indexed.

I use the same basic algorithm in the Search portion of the program as I do in the infrastructure for the sort procedure. The search method itself is simple enough, although once again it is divided over two objects:

```
void __fastcall TForm1::Search1Click(TObject *Sender)
{
  SearchSort->Search(TCCSortType(dynamic_cast<TComponent*>(Sender)->Tag));
}

void TSearchSort::Search(TCCSortType SortType)
{
  FSortType = SortType;
  String S;
  if (!SearchDlg->GetSearchStr(SortType, S))
    return;
  DoSort();
  DoSearch(S);
}

void TSearchSort::DoSearch(String S)
{
  DMod->AddressTable->SetKey();
  switch (FSortType) {
    case stFirst :
      DMod->AddressTable->FieldByName("FName")->AsString = S; break;
    case stLast :
      DMod->AddressTable->FieldByName("LName")->AsString = S; break;
    case stCompany :
      DMod->AddressTable->FieldByName("Company")->AsString = S;
  }
  DMod->AddressTable->GotoNearest();
}
```

This code retrieves the relevant string to search on from a simple dialog called SearchDlg. The code for the SearchDlg is so simple that I don't bother covering it here.

Suffice it to say that it allows the user to enter the string he or she wants to search on, as well as the name of the field on which to search.

After you get the search string from the user, the `DoSort()` method is called to set up the indices, and then the search is performed using `GotoNearest()`. The assumption, of course, is that the menu items appear in the same order as those for the sort process, and they have the same tags associated with them.

Once again, the actual code for searching for data is fairly straightforward. The key to making this process as simple as possible is setting up the `DoSort()` routine so that it can be used by both the Sorting and Searching portions of the program.

Filtering Data

The ADDRESS2 program performs two different filtering chores. The first involves enabling the user to see the set of records that fit in a particular category. For example, if you have set the `Category` field in 20 records to the string "Friend", you can reasonably expect to be able to filter out all other records that don't contain the word Friend in the `Category` field. After you have this process in place, you can ask the database to show you all the records that contain information about computers or work or local businesses, and so on.

The second technique for filtering in the ADDRESS2 program involves the `Marked` field. You might, for example, first use the Filter Category technique to show only the records of your friends. Let's posit that you're quite popular, so this list contains the names of 50 people. You can then use the `Marked` field to single out 10 of these records as containing the names of people you want to invite to a party. After marking the appropriate records, you can then filter on them so that the database contains only the names of your friends who have been "marked" as invited to the party.

In the next few paragraphs, I tackle the `Category` filter first and then explain how to filter on the `Marked` field.

Setting up a filter and performing a search are similar tasks. The first step is to find the category that the user wants to use as a filter. To do so, you can pop up a dialog that displays the `Cats` table to the user. The user can then select a category and click the OK button. You don't need to write any custom code for this dialog. Everything can be taken care of by the visual tools.

Here is how to handle the process back in the main form:

```
void __fastcall TForm1::Filter1Click(TObject *Sender)
{
  if (Filter1->Caption == "Filter") {
    int Cat = FilterDlg->GetFilter();
    if (Cat == -1)
```

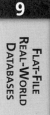

```
      return;
    Filter1->Caption = "Cancel Filter";
    DMod->AddressTable->IndexName = "CategoryIndex";
    DMod->AddressTable->SetRangeStart();
    DMod->AddressTable->FieldByName("Category")->AsInteger = Cat;
    DMod->AddressTable->SetRangeEnd();
    DMod->AddressTable->FieldByName("Category")->AsInteger = Cat;
    DMod->AddressTable->ApplyRange();
  } else {
    Filter1->Caption = "Filter";
    DMod->AddressTable->CancelRange();
  }
}
```

Alternatively, you can perform the same chore with the following code:

```
void __fastcall TForm1::Filter1Click(TObject *Sender)
{
  if (Filter1->Caption == "Filter") {
    int Cat = FilterDlg->GetFilter();
    if (Cat == -1)
      return;
    Filter1->Caption = "Cancel Filter";
    DMod->AddressTable->IndexName = "CategoryIndex";
    DMod->AddressTable->SetRange(
      OPENARRAY(TVarRec, (Cat)), OPENARRAY(TVarRec, (Cat)));
  } else {
    Filter1->Caption = "Filter";
    DMod->AddressTable->CancelRange();
  }
}
```

This code changes the Caption of the menu item associated with filtering the Category field. If the Address table isn't currently filtered, the menu reads "Filter". If the table is filtered, the menu reads "Cancel Filter". Therefore, the preceding code has two sections: one for starting the filter and the second for canceling the filter. The second part is too simple to merit further discussion, as you can see from a glance at the last two lines of written code in the method.

After enabling the user to select a category on which to search, the ADDRESS2 program sets up the CategoryIndex and then performs a normal filter operation:

```
DMod->AddressTable->IndexName = "CategoryIndex";
DMod->AddressTable->SetRange(
  OPENARRAY(TVarRec, (Cat)), OPENARRAY(TVarRec, (Cat)));
```

This simple process lets you narrow the number of records displayed at any one time. The key point to remember is that this whole process works only because the user enters data in the Category field by selecting strings from a drop-down combo box. Without the TDBComboLookupBox, the number of options in the Category field would likely become unmanageable.

Marking Files

The Marked field in this table is declared to be of type Boolean. (Remember that one of the fields of ADDRESS.DB is actually called Marked. In the first sentence, therefore, I'm not referring to an attribute of a field, but to its name.)

On the main form for the program is a TSpeedButton component that shows an open book glyph if a field is marked and a closed book if a field isn't marked. When the user scrolls up and down through the dataset, the light bulb switches on or off, depending on whether a field is marked. Here is a method for showing the user whether the Boolean Marked field is set to true or false:

```
void __fastcall TDMod::AddressSourceDataChange(TObject *Sender,
      TField *Field)
{
  if (AddressTable->FieldByName("Marked")->AsBoolean) {
    FBookOpen = LoadBitmap(HInstance, "BookOpen");
    Form1->SpeedButton1->Glyph->Handle = FBookOpen;
  } else {
    FBookShut = LoadBitmap(HInstance, "BookShut");
    Form1->SpeedButton1->Glyph->Handle = FBookShut;
  }
}
```

If the field is marked, a bitmap called BookOpen is loaded from one of the program's two resource files. This bitmap is then assigned to the Glyph field of a TSpeedButton. If the Marked field is set to false, a second bitmap is loaded and shown in the TSpeedButton. The bitmaps give a visual signal to the user as to whether the record is marked.

As I hinted in the preceding paragraph, the ADDRESS2 program has two resource files. The first is the standard resource file, which holds the program's icon. The second is a custom resource built from the RC file shown in Listing 9.7.

The AddressSourceDataChanged() method shown previously in this section is a delegated event handler for the AddressSource component in the data module. The interesting point here, of course, is that AddressSource is located in DMod.

Whenever the user toggles the TSpeedButton, the logical Marked field in the database is toggled:

```
void __fastcall TForm1::SpeedButton1Click(TObject *Sender)
{
  FMarks->ToggleBoolean();
}

void TMarks::ToggleBoolean()
{
```

9

FLAT-FILE
REAL-WORLD
DATABASES

```
DMod->AddressTable->Edit();
DMod->AddressTable->FieldByName("Marked")->AsBoolean =
  !DMod->AddressTable->FieldByName("Marked")->AsBoolean;
DMod->AddressTable->Post();
}
```

Note that this code never checks the value of the Marked field; it just sets that value to the opposite of its current state.

The program enables the user to show only the records that are currently marked. This filter can be applied on top of the Category filter or can be applied on a dataset that isn't filtered at all:

```
void TMarks::ShowOnlyMarked()
{
  Form1->ShowOnlyMarked1->Checked = !Form1->ShowOnlyMarked1->Checked;
  DMod->AddressTable->Filtered = Form1->ShowOnlyMarked1->Checked;
}
```

The preceding code sets the Address table into Filtered mode. The OnFilterRecord() event for the table, which is in the DMod unit, looks like this:

```
void __fastcall TDMod::AddressTableFilterRecord(TDataSet *DataSet,
      bool &Accept)
{
  Accept = (AddressTableMarked->AsBoolean == true);
}
```

Only the records that have the Marked field set to true pass through this filter. If the table is filtered, therefore, only those records that are marked are visible to the user.

If you give the user the ability to mark records, you also probably should give him or her the ability to clear all the marks in the program, or to mark all the records in the current dataset and then possibly unmark a few key records. For example, you might want to send a notice to all your friends, except those who live out of town. To do so, you can first mark the names of all your friends and then unmark the names of those who live in distant places.

You can set and clear the marks for all the rows in the database in two different ways. The following is one method:

```
void TMarks::SetClearMarks(int MarkType)
{
  String Value;
  switch (MarkType) {
    case mfMarkAll : Value = "T"; break;
    case mfClearMarks : Value = "F"; break;
    default :
      return;
```

```
  }
  DMod->AddressSource->Enabled = false;
  TBookmark B = DMod->AddressTable->GetBookmark();
  DMod->AddressTable->First();
  while (!DMod->AddressTable->Eof) {
    DMod->AddressTable->Edit();
    DMod->AddressTable->FieldByName("Marked")->AsString = Value;
    DMod->AddressTable->Next();
  }
  DMod->AddressTable->GotoBookmark(B);
  DMod->AddressTable->FreeBookmark(B);
  DMod->AddressSource->Enabled = true;
}
```

A second method is perhaps more efficient. The data module for the ADDRESS2 program contains a query with the following SQL statement:

```
Update Address
  Set Marked = :NewValue
```

This statement doesn't have a `where` clause to specify which records in the `Marked` field you want to toggle. As a result, the code changes all the records in the database with one stroke. Note how much more efficient this method is than iterating through all the records of a table with a `while (!Table1->Eof)` loop.

To use this SQL statement, you can write the following code:

```
void TDMod::ChangeMarked(bool NewValue)
{
  ChangeMarkedQuery->Close();
  if (NewValue)
    ChangeMarkedQuery->ParamByName("NewValue")->AsString = "T";
  else
    ChangeMarkedQuery->ParamByName("NewValue")->AsString = "F";
  ChangeMarkedQuery->ExecSQL();
  AddressTable->Refresh();
}
```

This method sets the `"NewValue"` field of the query to `T` or `F`, depending on how the method is called.

Using filters, like searching and sorting topics, is extremely easy to master. One of the points of this chapter is how easily you can harness the power of C++Builder to write great code that produces small, easy-to-use, robust applications.

Setting Colors

The ADDRESS2 program's Colors menu allows you to set the colors for most of the major objects in the program. The goal isn't to give the user complete control over every last detail in the program, but to let him or her customize the most important features. Even if you're not interested in giving the user the ability to customize colors in your application, you might still be interested in this section because I discuss Run Time Type Information (RTTI), as well as a method for iterating over all the components on a form.

The `ColorClick` method uses the time-honored method of declaring an enumerated type and then sets up the `Tag` property from a menu item to specify the selection of a particular option. The following is the enumerated type in question:

```
enum TColorType { ccForm, ccEdit,
    ccEditText, ccLabel, ccPanel, ccBlue,
    ccDefault, ccSystem, ccGreen, ccWriteRegistry,
    ccReadRegistry };
```

The routine begins by enabling the user to select a color from the Colors dialog and then assigns that color to the appropriate controls:

```
void __fastcall TForm1::ColorClick(TObject *Sender)
{
  TColorType Code = TColorType(dynamic_cast<TMenuItem*>(Sender)->Tag);

  if (Code != ccBlue && Code != ccDefault &&
      Code != ccGreen && Code != ccSystem &&
      Code != ccReadRegistry && Code != ccWriteRegistry)
    if (!ColorDialog1->Execute())
      return;

  TColorClass* ColorClass = new TColorClass(this);
  switch (TColorType(Code)) {
    case ccForm: Color = ColorDialog1->Color; break;
    case ccEdit:
        ColorClass->SetEdits(tcColor, ColorDialog1->Color); break;
    case ccEditText:
        ColorClass->SetEdits(tcFontColor, ColorDialog1->Color); break;
    case ccLabel: ColorClass->SetLabels(ColorDialog1->Color); break;
    case ccPanel: ColorClass->SetPanels(ColorDialog1->Color); break;
    case ccBlue: ColorClass->TheBlues(); break;
    case ccGreen: ColorClass->TheGreens(); break;
    case ccDefault: ColorClass->DefaultColors(); break;
    case ccSystem: ColorClass->SystemColors(); break;
    case ccWriteRegistry: ColorClass->RegIniClass->WriteRegistry(); break;
    case ccReadRegistry: ColorClass->RegIniClass->ReadRegistry(); break;
  }
  delete ColorClass;
}
```

If the user wants to change the form's color, the code to do so is simple enough:

```
case ccForm: Color = ColorDialog1->Color; break;
```

However, changing the color of all the data-aware controls is a more complicated process. To accomplish this goal, you must set the ColorClick() method to call the SetEdits() routine:

```
void TColorClass::SetEdits(TChangeType TypeChange, TColor NewValue)
{
  for (int i=0;i<FMainForm->ComponentCount;i++) {
    TDBEdit* dbEdit = dynamic_cast<TDBEdit*>(FMainForm->Components[i]);
    TDBMemo* dbMemo = dynamic_cast<TDBMemo*>(FMainForm->Components[i]);
    TDBGrid* dbGrid = dynamic_cast<TDBGrid*>(FMainForm->Components[i]);
    TDBLookupComboBox* dbCombo =
      dynamic_cast<TDBLookupComboBox*>(FMainForm->Components[i]);
    if (dbEdit)
      switch (TypeChange) {
        case tcColor: dbEdit->Color = NewValue; break;
        case tcFontColor: dbEdit->Font->Color = NewValue;
      }
    if (dbMemo)
      switch (TypeChange) {
        case tcColor: dbMemo->Color = NewValue; break;
        case tcFontColor: dbMemo->Font->Color = NewValue;
      }
    if (dbGrid)
      switch (TypeChange) {
        case tcColor: dbGrid->Color = NewValue; break;
        case tcFontColor: dbGrid->Font->Color = NewValue;
      }
    if (dbCombo)
      switch (TypeChange) {
        case tcColor: dbCombo->Color = NewValue; break;
        case tcFontColor: dbCombo->Font->Color = NewValue;
      }
  }
}
```

This code iterates through all the components belonging to the main form of the program and checks to see whether any of them are TDBEdits, TDBComboBoxes, TDBGrids, or TDBMemos. When it finds a hit, the code sets the component's color to the new value selected by the user.

Because this code searches for TDBEdits, TDBComboBoxes, TDBMemos, and TDBGrids, it very quickly changes all the data-aware controls on the form to a new color. Note that you need to use the dynamic_cast operator to check whether the cast will succeed before attempting to change the features of the controls.

The code for setting labels and panels works exactly the same way as the code for the data-aware controls. The only difference is that you don't need to worry about looking for multiple types of components:

9

FLAT-FILE
REAL-WORLD
DATABASES

```
void TColorClass::SetLabels(TColor C)
{
  for (int i=0;i<FMainForm->ComponentCount;i++) {
    TLabel* label = dynamic_cast<TLabel*>(FMainForm->Components[i]);
    if (label)
      label->Font->Color = C;
  }
}

void TColorClass::SetPanels(TColor C)
{
  for (int i=0;i<FMainForm->ComponentCount;i++) {
    TPanel* panel = dynamic_cast<TPanel*>(FMainForm->Components[i]);
    if (panel)
      panel->Color = C;
  }
}
```

After you devise a set of routines like this, you can write a few custom routines that quickly set all the colors in the program to certain predefined values:

```
void TColorClass::TheBlues()
{
  SetEdits(tcColor, TColor(0x00FF8080));
  SetEdits(tcFontColor, clBlack);
  SetLabels(clBlack);
  SetPanels(TColor(0x00FF0080));
  FMainForm->Color = TColor(0x00FF0080);
  dynamic_cast<TForm1*>(FMainForm)->DBGrid1->Color = TColor(0x00FF8080);
}

void TColorClass::DefaultColors()
{
  SetEdits(tcColor, clNavy);
  SetEdits(tcFontColor, clYellow);
  SetLabels(clBlack);
  SetPanels(clBtnFace);
  FMainForm->Color = clBtnFace;
  dynamic_cast<TForm1*>(FMainForm)->DBGrid1->Color = clNavy;
}

void TColorClass::TheGreens()
{
  SetEdits(tcColor, TColor(8454016));
  SetEdits(tcFontColor, TColor(8404992));
  SetLabels(TColor(0));
  SetPanels(TColor(32768));
  FMainForm->Color = clGreen;
}
```

```
void TColorClass::SystemColors()
{
  SetEdits(tcColor, clWindow);
  SetEdits(tcFontColor, clBlack);
  SetLabels(clBlack);
  SetPanels(clBtnFace);
  FMainForm->Color = clBtnFace;
}
```

The SystemColors() method sets all the colors to the default system colors as defined by the current user. The DefaultColors() method sets colors to values that I think most users will find appealing. The methods called TheBlues() and TheGreens() have a little fun by setting the colors of the form to something a bit unusual. The important point here is that the methods shown in this section of the chapter demonstrate how to perform global actions that affect all the controls on a form.

Clearly, taking control over the colors of the components on a form is a simple matter. Saving the settings between runs of the program is a bit more complicated. The following section, which deals with the Registry, focuses on how to create persistent data for the user-configurable parts of a program.

Working with the Registry

The simplest way to work with the Registry is to use the TRegIniFile class that ships with C++Builder. This object is a descendent of TRegistry. TRegistry is meant exclusively for use with the Windows Registry. TRegIniFile also works only with the Registry; however, it uses methods similar to those used with an INI file. In other words, TRegIniFile is designed to smooth the transition from INI files to the Registry and to make it easy to switch back if you want. Because TRegIniFile descends from TRegistry, it also provides all the functionality found in the TRegistry object.

I am not, however, interested in the capability of TRegIniFile to provide compatibility with INI files. This book works only with the Registry. I use TRegIniFile rather than TRegistry simply because the former object works at a higher level of abstraction than the latter object. Using TRegIniFile is easier than using TRegistry; therefore, I like it more. I can get my work done faster with it, and I am less likely to introduce a bug. The fact that knowing it well means that I also know how to work with INI files is just an added bonus, not a deciding factor.

> **CAUTION**
>
> When you're working with the Registry, damaging it is always possible. Of course, I don't think any of the code I show you in this book is likely to damage the Registry; it's just that being careful is always a good idea. Even if you're not writing code that alters the Registry, and even if you're not a programmer, you should still back up the Registry, just to be safe. I've never found a way to recover a badly damaged Registry. Whenever my Registry has been mangled by a program, I've always had to reinstall Windows from scratch.

Now that you have set up everything properly, you can start storing information in the Registry. In particular, your current goal is to save the colors for the key features of the ADDRESS2 program after the user has set them at run time. Back in the old days, when INI files were in fashion, you might have created an INI file with this information in it:

```
[Colors]
Form=8421440
Edits=8421376
EditText=0
Labels=0
Panels=12639424
```

This cryptic information might be stored in a text file called `Address2.ini` and read at run time by using calls such as `ReadPrivateProfileString()` or by using the `TIniFile` object that ships with C++Builder. This INI file has a single section called `Colors` in it, and under the `Colors` section are five entries specifying the colors for each of the major elements in the program. Translated into the language of the Registry, this same information looks like the RegEdit window shown in Figure 9.6.

FIGURE 9.6

The Registry set up to hold the key information for the current colors of the ADDRESS2 application.

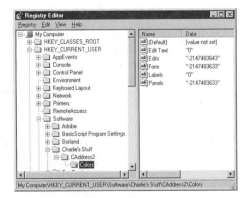

Using the TRegIniFile class, you can write code that enters the pertinent information into the Registry:

```
const String RegKey = "SOFTWARE\\Charlie's Stuff\\CAddress2";

void TRegIniClass::WriteRegistry()
{
  TRegIniFile* RegFile = new TRegIniFile(RegKey);
  RegFile->WriteInteger("Colors", FormKey, Form1->Color);
  RegFile->WriteInteger(
    "Colors", EditTextKey, Form1->FNameEdit->Font->Color);
  RegFile->WriteInteger("Colors", PanelKey, Form1->Panel1->Color);
  RegFile->WriteInteger("Colors", LabelKey, Form1->Label2->Font->Color);
  RegFile->WriteInteger("Colors", EditKey, Form1->FNameEdit->Color);
  delete RegFile;
}
```

The WriteInteger() method takes three parameters:

- The first is the name of the section (key) under which you want to enter information. I use the word *section* because it corresponds to the Colors section in the INI file shown right before Figure 9.6.

- The second is the key under which the information is stored. This parameter corresponds to the place where words such as "Form", "Edits", and so on were stored in the INI file.

- The third parameter is the actual value of the key that initially compelled you to store information in the Registry.

If the section or key that you want to use isn't already in the Registry, the preceding code creates the section automatically. If the section or key is already present, you can use the preceding code to update the values of the keys. In other words, you can use the same code to create or update the sections, keys, and values.

> **NOTE**
>
> Clearly, the TRegIniFile object makes it easy for you to begin adding entries to the Registry. If you know the bothersome Windows API code for doing the same thing, perhaps you can understand why I think TRegIniFile is a textbook case of how to use objects to hide complexity and promote code reuse. This object makes a difficult task easy to perform. Furthermore, now that you have written this object once correctly, you can use it over and over again to resolve Registry-related problems.

9

FLAT-FILE REAL-WORLD DATABASES

Before going any further with the discussion of the `TRegIniFile`, I should mention that after you are through with the object, you must deallocate the memory you created for it:

```
delete RegFile;
```

The `TRegIniFile` object enables you to both read and write values, and it enables you to work with a variety of types, including integers:

```
Form1->Color = TColor(RegFile->ReadInteger("Colors", FormKey, DefColor));
```

If the function fails to find the specified entry in the Registry, it returns the value specified in the third parameter; otherwise, it returns the item you sought. By the way, the cast to `TColor` is not strictly necessary but is added to avoid compiler warnings. The `Color` property is of type `TColor` but `ReadInteger()` returns an `int`. The cast keeps the compiler happy.

You're now at the end of the discussion of colors and the Registry. I've devoted considerable space to this subject because it is so important for developers who want to present finished applications to users. If you program for Windows 95/98 or Windows NT, you have to understand the Registry and how to get values in and out of it easily.

Using the Clipboard

Using C++Builder, you can easily cut information from a database to the Clipboard. The key point to understand here is that the currently selected control is always accessible from the `ActiveControl` property of the main form:

```
void __fastcall TForm1::Copy1Click(TObject *Sender)
{
  TDBEdit* dbEdit = dynamic_cast<TDBEdit*>(ActiveControl);
  TDBMemo* dbMemo = dynamic_cast<TDBMemo*>(ActiveControl);
  TDBComboBox* dbCombo = dynamic_cast<TDBComboBox*>(ActiveControl);
  if (dbEdit)
    dbEdit->CopyToClipboard();
  else if (dbMemo)
    dbMemo->CopyToClipboard();
  else if (dbCombo)
    Clipboard()->AsText = DBLookupComboBox1->Text;
}
```

This method is called when the user chooses Edit, Copy. The code first checks to see whether the currently selected control is one that contains data from the `Address` table—that is, the code checks to see if the control is a `TDBEdit`, `TDBMemo`, or `TDBLookupComboBox`. If it is, the control is typecast so that its properties and methods can be accessed.

The TDBEdit and TDBLookupComboBox controls have CopyToClipboard(), CutToClipboard(), and PasteFromClipboard() commands. Each of these commands simply copies, cuts, or pastes data from the live database control to the Clipboard or vice versa. The TDBLookupComboBox doesn't have quite as rich a set of built-in functions, so it is handled as a special case. In particular, note that you have to use the built-in Clipboard object, which can easily be a part of every C++Builder project. To access a fully allocated instance of this object, simply include the Clipbrd header unit in your current module:

```
#include <Clipbrd.hpp>
```

You can see that working with the Clipboard is a trivial operation in C++Builder. The Paste1Click() and Cut1Click() methods from the ADDRESS2 program demonstrate a specific technique you can use when pasting and cutting from or to the Clipboard.

Summary

In this chapter you looked at all the major portions of the ADDRESS2 program. The only items not mentioned in this chapter were the construction of the About dialog and few similarly trivial details.

I went into such detail about the ADDRESS2 program because it contains many of the features that need to be included in real-world programs. As I stated earlier, the ADDRESS2 program isn't quite up to the standards expected from a professional program, but it does answer some questions about how you can take the raw database tools described in the preceding chapters and use them to create a useful program.

An essentially flat-file database of the type shown in this chapter has a number of limitations in terms of its capabilities. The relational database shown in the next chapter is considerably more powerful, but also considerably more difficult for most users to master. In the future, it is likely that object-oriented databases will play an increasingly important role in programming, although at this time their use is still limited to only a few sites.

9

FLAT-FILE
REAL-WORLD
DATABASES

Relational Databases

*by Charlie Calvert
and Kent Reisdorph*

IN THIS CHAPTER

Now you can take a look at a real relational database in action. The preceding chapters have really been nothing but a long prelude to this chapter, where all the pieces finally come together.

This chapter features another address book program, which is this time based on a relational database. This second database allows you to add multiple street and email addresses and phone numbers to each name in the address book.

Subjects covered in this chapter include the following:

- Creating the tables for a relational database.
- Creating cascading deletes.
- Iterating through the controls on a form or a data module and performing certain actions on selected components at run time. (For instance, the code shows how to iterate through all the tables on a `TDataModule` to make sure that they are all posted.)
- Working with the `TPageControl` and `TTabSheet` objects.
- Working with `TTreeView`, `TImageList`, and `TTreeNode`.
- Retrieving error strings from a resource.
- Using the `TSession` object.

After you look at the address book program, I start a second program called KdAddExplore. You can find the program in the `Chap10/KdAddExplore` directory of the book's CD. This program looks and feels a lot like a miniature version of the SQL Explorer. You can use this program to explore the structure of the five tables used in the address book program found in the first half of this chapter.

The KdAddExplore program's main purpose is to let you see some of the functionality of the global `TSession` object that is automatically available in all C++Builder database applications. The `Session` object is created automatically at the startup of a database program.

The programs in this chapter use an alias called `BCB4UNLEASHED`, which points to the `Data` directory on the CD that accompanies this book. Remember that you must copy the data off the CD before you use it, and you must be sure the files are not marked read-only. I explain how to set up the `BCB4UNLEASHED` alias in Chapter 8, "Fields and Database Tools," in the "Creating an Alias" section.

Chapter 8 covers some of the theory behind relational databases. This chapter is about using that theory in practice. Unless you already understand relational databases, you should read Chapter 8 before reading this chapter. Furthermore, you will probably find a considerable difference between the theory of relational databases and what they start to look like in practice. In particular, the order of complexity increases almost geometrically as you add tables to a relational database. This chapter will introduce you to some of the principles you must master before you can create order out of that complexity.

Data in the Real World

The code in this chapter addresses the kinds of problems you find in real-world situations. In particular, I focus on the conflict between the rigid, inflexible nature of simple tables and the fluid, kaleidoscope-like nature of information in the real world.

When most people first try to build database programs, they tend to create one simple table, like the one shown in the ADDRESS2 program in the preceding chapter. The limitations of that kind of system might well emerge on the first day of use. For example, you might start transferring handwritten addresses into the database. Problems arise when you encounter entries in which one person has multiple phone numbers or multiple addresses. One person with three or more email addresses is not at all unusual. The ADDRESS2 program does not have a good solution for that kind of situation.

This problem can be multiplied many times in professional settings. For example, I need to track all the Inprise office locations throughout the world. Thus, I need numerous address entries under the name of a single company.

My job puts me in contact with a number of software vendors (ISVs) that use or create Inprise tools. Many of these people maintain offices both at home and at their businesses. Some of them frequent certain sites, and others have complex relationships with their companies that I can track in single table databases only via freehand notes.

As you can see, information in the real world is messy and complex. The ADDRESS2 program is simple and straightforward. Many people can make do with simple tools, but others need to have a more sophisticated system.

The KdAdd program found in this chapter is an attempt to resolve the kinds of problems you find in real-world situations. The form you see here is not quite as polished as the ADDRESS2 program. It is, however, much more sophisticated and much more powerful. With some work, it could easily form the basis for a professional-level database.

10

RELATIONAL DATABASES

Introducing the Relational Address Program

The KdAdd program uses five tables called `kdNames`, `kdAdds`, `kdPhone`, `kdMemo`, and `kdEmail`. The `kdNames` table is the master table that "owns" the other four tables. The other tables are detail tables. (As stated in an earlier chapter, this relationship is reflexive, but in this program, the `kdNames` table is always in charge.)

When the program first appears, it looks like the image shown in Figure 10.1. As you can see, the program uses a `TPageControl` with five pages, one for each of the tables. The `kdAdds` and `kdPhone` tables are also shown on the first page so that the user can see them easily. If you want to delete items from either an address or phone number, you should turn to the respective pages for those items.

FIGURE 10.1

The main screen for the KdAdd program.

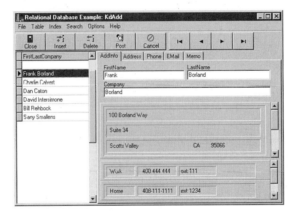

The data for the program is kept in the `Data` directory on the CD-ROM that comes with this book. The fields for the tables in the database are shown in Tables 10.1 through 10.5.

TABLE 10.1   THE STRUCTURE FOR THE kdName TABLE

Table Name	Type	Size	Primary Index
NameCode	+		*
FirstName	A	30	
LastName	A	30	
Company	A	30	

TABLE 10.2   THE STRUCTURE FOR THE kdAdds TABLE

Table Name	Type	Size	Primary Index
AddCode	+		*
Address1	A	30	
Address2	A	30	
City	A	30	
State	A	3	
Zip	A	10	
NameCode	I		

TABLE 10.3   THE STRUCTURE FOR THE kdPhone TABLE

Table Name	Type	Size	Primary Index
PhoneCode	+		*
Description	A	15	
Number	A	25	
Ext	A	5	
NameCode	I		

TABLE 10.4   THE STRUCTURE FOR THE kdEmail TABLE

Table Name	Type	Size	Primary Index
EMailCode	+		*
Address	A	50	
Description	A	65	
Service	A	25	
NameCode	I		

TABLE 10.5   THE STRUCTURE FOR THE kdMemo TABLE

Table Name	Type	Size	Primary Index
MemoCode	+		*
Description	A	25	
MemoData	M	15	
NameCode	I		

Four constraints are placed on the table in the form of foreign keys called NameCode. They are placed in each of the program's tables except for the master table. These constraints are shown in Figure 10.2.

FIGURE 10.2

You can see the foreign keys used by the database if you open the Referential Constraints section of kdNames *in the SQL Explorer.*

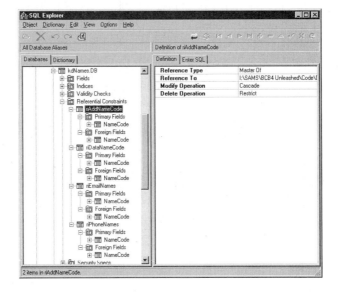

When you're viewing this information in the SQL Explorer, you should highlight the name of each constraint and then look at the definition page to read the Reference Type and Reference To fields. As you can see from Figure 10.2, these fields show which table the constraint references. The view shown here is of the kdNames table, and it is the master table in these relationships. The riAddNameCode constraint references the kdAdds table.

Table 10.6 shows another way to think about the referential integrity in this database.

TABLE 10.6 THE KEYS IN THE DATABASE

Table	Primary Key	Foreign Key
kdNames	NameCode	
KdAdds	AddCode	NameCode references kdNames->NameCode
kdPhone	PhoneCode	NameCode references kdNames->NameCode
kdEmail	EMailCode	NameCode references kdNames->NameCode
kdMemo	MemoCode	NameCode references kdNames->NameCode

As you can see, `kdAdds`, `kdPhone`, `kdEmail`, and `kdMemo` all have a single foreign key called `NameCode` that references the `NameCode` primary key in `kdNames`. The number in the foreign keys therefore must be a number found in the primary key of the `kdNames` table. Furthermore, you cannot delete a row from the `kdNames` table unless all its related fields in the other tables have been deleted first. You also cannot change the value in the `NameCode` field of `kdNames` if it will leave records in the other tables "stranded."

> **NOTE**
>
> If you are new to referential integrity, take the time to play with the database and test these constraints. Referential integrity exists to prevent the user from accidentally deleting needed data and from accidentally entering erroneous data. During the course of this chapter, you should test the restraints on this database so you can see how it establishes rules that help both the programmer and the user maintain a valid set of data.

The referential integrity relationships you see here represent the classic simplest case for constructing a real relational database. Most databases in the real world have more tables and more foreign keys. However, this one has all the elements of a real relational database, and the complexity level is sufficient for programmers who are new to this kind of programming.

Several secondary indices are used in this program, as shown in Tables 10.7 through 10.11. Most of these indices are the result of the foreign keys on the `NameCode` fields of `kdAdds`, `kdPhone`, `kdEmail`, and `kdMemo`. However, indices are also set up on the `Company`, `FirstName`, and `LastName` fields of the `kdNames` table. Note that `idxLastName` consists of both the last name and first name of each entry in the `kdNames` table. This convention is helpful when sorting lists wherein you have more than one entry with a particular last name. For instance, if you have two people with the last name of Jones, creating a key on the last and first names will ensure that Able Jones is listed before Betty Jones. If you further study the tables shown here, you will see that the `kdPhone` and `kdMemo` tables also have indices on their description fields.

TABLE 10.7   THE INDICES ON THE `kdNames` TABLE

Index	Index Fields
idxCompany	Company
idxFirstName	FirstName
idxLastName	LastName, FirstName

TABLE 10.8   THE INDEX ON THE kdAdds TABLE

Index	Index Fields
NameCode	NameCode

TABLE 10.9   THE INDICES ON THE kdPhone TABLE

Index	Index Fields
idxDescription	Description
NameCode	NameCode

TABLE 10.10   THE INDEX ON THE kdEmail TABLE

Index	Index Fields
NameCode	NameCode

TABLE 10.11   THE INDEX ON THE kdMemo TABLE

Index	Index Fields
NameCode	NameCode
idxDescription	Description

You now know all the core facts about the KdAdd program. After you have laid out the tables as shown here, all the really heavy work in constructing the program is completed. You still have considerable work to do in creating a front end for the program, but the core work for the project is done after you have created the tables and defined the ways they relate.

Analyzing the KdAdd Program

The code for the KdAdd program is shown in Listings 10.1 through 10.6. Notice the custom RC file and its include file for the project. These two tiny files store error strings. In later versions of the program, these files will become larger as more error strings are added to the code. For this release, all I have done is stub out these files so that they can easily be expanded later.

LISTING 10.1 THE HEADER FOR THE KDADD PROGRAM'S MAIN FORM

```
#ifndef MainH
#define MainH

#include <Classes.hpp>
#include <Controls.hpp>
#include <StdCtrls.hpp>
#include <Forms.hpp>
#include <ComCtrls.hpp>
#include <DBCGrids.hpp>
#include <DBCtrls.hpp>
#include <DBGrids.hpp>
#include <ExtCtrls.hpp>
#include <Grids.hpp>
#include <ImgList.hpp>
#include <Mask.hpp>
#include <Menus.hpp>
#include <ToolWin.hpp>

const int ERR_STRING_SIZE = 255;

class TForm1 : public TForm
{
__published:     // IDE-managed Components
  TDBGrid *FirstLastGrid;
  TPageControl *PageControl1;
  TTabSheet *AddInfo1;
  TLabel *Label15;
  TLabel *Label16;
  TLabel *Label17;
  TDBEdit *DBEdit13;
  TDBEdit *DBEdit14;
  TDBEdit *DBEdit15;
  TDBCtrlGrid *DBCtrlGrid4;
  TBevel *Bevel2;
  TBevel *Bevel1;
  TBevel *Bevel4;
  TBevel *Bevel3;
  TDBText *DBText1;
  TDBText *DBEdit17;
  TDBText *DBEdit18;
  TDBText *DBEdit19;
  TDBText *DBEdit20;
  TDBCtrlGrid *PhoneCtrlGrid;
  TBevel *Bevel7;
  TBevel *Bevel6;
  TBevel *A;
  TBevel *Bevel5;
```

continues

LISTING 10.1 CONTINUED

```
TDBText *DBEdit8;
TDBText *DBEdit7;
TDBText *DBEdit16;
TLabel *Label6;
TTabSheet *tsAddress;
TDBCtrlGrid *DBCtrlGrid2;
TLabel *Label1;
TLabel *Label2;
TLabel *Label3;
TLabel *Label4;
TLabel *Label5;
TDBEdit *DBEdit1;
TDBEdit *DBEdit2;
TDBEdit *City;
TDBEdit *DBEdit4;
TDBEdit *Zip;
TTabSheet *tsPhone;
TDBCtrlGrid *DBCtrlGrid5;
TLabel *Label23;
TLabel *Label24;
TLabel *Label25;
TDBEdit *DBEdit21;
TDBEdit *DBEdit22;
TDBEdit *DBEdit23;
TTabSheet *tsEMail;
TDBCtrlGrid *DBCtrlGrid3;
TLabel *Label12;
TLabel *Label13;
TLabel *Label14;
TDBEdit *DBEdit10;
TDBEdit *DBEdit11;
TDBEdit *DBEdit12;
TTabSheet *tsMemo;
TDBGrid *DBGrid2;
TDBMemo *DBMemo1;
TToolBar *ToolBar1;
TToolButton *CloseBtn;
TToolButton *InsertBtn2;
TToolButton *DeleteBtn2;
TToolButton *PostBtn2;
TToolButton *CancelBtn2;
TToolButton *ToolButton1;
TDBNavigator *DBNavigator1;
TMainMenu *MainMenu1;
TMenuItem *File1;
TMenuItem *Exit1;
TMenuItem *Table1;
TMenuItem *Insert1;
TMenuItem *Post1;
```

```
    TMenuItem *Delete1;
    TMenuItem *Cancel1;
    TMenuItem *Index1;
    TMenuItem *Last1;
    TMenuItem *First1;
    TMenuItem *Company1;
    TMenuItem *Seach1;
    TMenuItem *Last2;
    TMenuItem *First2;
    TMenuItem *Company2;
    TMenuItem *Options1;
    TMenuItem *Help1;
    TMenuItem *Contents1;
    TMenuItem *N1;
    TMenuItem *About1;
    TImageList *ImageList1;
    void __fastcall FormCreate(TObject *Sender);
    void __fastcall InsertBtn2Click(TObject *Sender);
    void __fastcall DeleteBtn2Click(TObject *Sender);
    void __fastcall PostBtn2Click(TObject *Sender);
    void __fastcall CancelBtn2Click(TObject *Sender);
    void __fastcall IndexClick(TObject *Sender);
    void __fastcall SearchClick(TObject *Sender);
    void __fastcall PageControl1Change(TObject *Sender);
    void __fastcall Exit1Click(TObject *Sender);
    void __fastcall DBText1Click(TObject *Sender);
private:
    String GetError(int ErrNo, String& S);      // User declarations
public:            // User declarations
    __fastcall TForm1(TComponent* Owner);
    void SetupIndex(TObject* Sender);
};

extern PACKAGE TForm1 *Form1;

#endif
```

LISTING 10.2 THE MAIN FORM FOR THE KDADD PROGRAM

```
////////////////////////////////////////
//    File: Main.cpp
// Project: KdAdd
//

#include <vcl.h>
#pragma hdrstop

#include "Main.h"
#include "DMod1.h"
```

10

RELATIONAL DATABASES

continues

LISTING 10.2   CONTINUED

```cpp
#pragma package(smart_init)
#pragma resource "*.dfm"
TForm1 *Form1;

__fastcall TForm1::TForm1(TComponent* Owner)
  : TForm(Owner)
{
}

void TForm1::SetupIndex(TObject* Sender)
{
  switch (dynamic_cast<TComponent*>(Sender)->Tag) {
    case 100: DMod->NamesTable->IndexName = "idxLastName"; break;
    case 101: DMod->NamesTable->IndexName = "idxFirstName"; break;
    case 102: DMod->NamesTable->IndexName = "idxCompany"; break;
    case 103: DMod->NamesTable->IndexName = "";
  }
}

void __fastcall TForm1::FormCreate(TObject *Sender)
{
  PageControl1->ActivePage = AddInfo1;
}

void __fastcall TForm1::InsertBtn2Click(TObject *Sender)
{
  switch (PageControl1->ActivePage->Tag) {
    case 1: DMod->NamesTable->Insert(); break;
    case 2: DMod->AddressTable->Insert(); break;
    case 3: DMod->PhoneTable->Insert(); break;
    case 4: DMod->EMailTable->Insert(); break;
    case 5: DMod->MemoTable->Insert();
  }
}

void __fastcall TForm1::CancelBtn2Click(TObject *Sender)
{
  switch (PageControl1->ActivePage->Tag) {
    case 1: DMod->NamesTable->Cancel(); break;
    case 2: DMod->AddressTable->Cancel(); break;
    case 3: DMod->PhoneTable->Cancel(); break;
    case 4: DMod->EMailTable->Cancel(); break;
    case 5: DMod->MemoTable->Cancel(); break;
    default : {
      String S;
      ShowMessage(GetError(1, S));
    }
  }
}
```

```
void __fastcall TForm1::DeleteBtn2Click(TObject *Sender)
{
  TMsgDlgButtons Btns;
  Btns << mbYes << mbNo;
  char* Msg = "Are you sure you want to delete\r\n%s?";
  String S;
  switch (PageControl1->ActivePage->Tag) {
    case 1: {
      S = S.sprintf(Msg,
        DMod->NamesTableFirstLastCompany->AsString.c_str());
      if ((MessageDlg(S, mtInformation, Btns, 0) == ID_YES))
        DMod->CascadingDelete();
      break;
    }

    case 2: {
      S = S.sprintf(Msg, DMod->Address.c_str());
      if ((MessageDlg(S, mtInformation, Btns, 0) == ID_YES))
        DMod->AddressTable->Delete();
      break;
    }

    case 3: {
      S = S.sprintf(Msg, DMod->Phone.c_str());
      if ((MessageDlg(S, mtInformation, Btns, 0) == ID_YES))
        DMod->PhoneTable->Delete();
      break;
    }

    case 4: {
      S = S.sprintf(Msg, DMod->EMail.c_str());
      if ((MessageDlg(S, mtInformation, Btns, 0) == ID_YES))
        DMod->EMailTable->Delete();
      break;
    }

    case 5: {
      S = S.sprintf(Msg, DMod->MemoTableDescription->AsString.c_str());
      if ((MessageDlg(S, mtInformation, Btns, 0) == ID_YES))
        DMod->MemoTable->Delete();
      break;
    }
    default: {
      String S;
      ShowMessage(GetError(1, S));
    }
  }
}
```

10

RELATIONAL DATABASES

continues

LISTING 10.2   CONTINUED

```cpp
void __fastcall TForm1::PostBtn2Click(TObject *Sender)
{
  DMod->PostAll();
}

void __fastcall TForm1::IndexClick(TObject *Sender)
{
  SetupIndex(Sender);
  DMod->NamesTable->FindNearest(OPENARRAY(TVarRec, ("AAAA")));
}

void __fastcall TForm1::SearchClick(TObject *Sender)
{
  String S = "";
  if ((InputQuery("Search for Name", "Enter Name: ", S))) {
    String IndexName = DMod->NamesTable->IndexName;
    SetupIndex(Sender);
    DMod->NamesTable->FindNearest(OPENARRAY(TVarRec, (S)));
    DMod->NamesTable->IndexName = IndexName;
  }
}

void __fastcall TForm1::PageControl1Change(TObject *Sender)
{
  DMod->PostAll();
  switch (PageControl1->ActivePage->Tag) {
    case 1: DBNavigator1->DataSource = DMod->dsNames; break;
    case 2: DBNavigator1->DataSource = DMod->dsAddress; break;
    case 3: DBNavigator1->DataSource = DMod->dsPhone; break;
    case 4: DBNavigator1->DataSource = DMod->dsEmail; break;
    case 5: DBNavigator1->DataSource = DMod->dsMemo;
  }
}

void __fastcall TForm1::Exit1Click(TObject *Sender)
{
  Close();
}

void __fastcall TForm1::DBText1Click(TObject *Sender)
{
  PageControl1->ActivePage = tsAddress;
}

String TForm1::GetError(int ErrNo, String& S)
{
  S.SetLength(ERR_STRING_SIZE);
  LoadString(HInstance, 1, S.c_str(), ERR_STRING_SIZE);
  return S;
}
```

LISTING 10.3 THE HEADER FOR THE KDADD PROGRAM'S DATA MODULE

```cpp
#ifndef DMod1H
#define DMod1H

#include <Classes.hpp>
#include <Controls.hpp>
#include <StdCtrls.hpp>
#include <Forms.hpp>
#include <Db.hpp>
#include <DBTables.hpp>

class TDMod : public TDataModule
{
__published:            // IDE-managed Components
  TTable *NamesTable;
  TAutoIncField *NamesTableNameCode;
  TStringField *NamesTableFirstName;
  TStringField *NamesTableLastName;
  TStringField *NamesTableCompany;
  TStringField *NamesTableFirstLastCompany;
  TDataSource *dsNames;
  TTable *AddressTable;
  TAutoIncField *AddressTableAddCode;
  TStringField *AddressTableAddress1;
  TStringField *AddressTableAddress2;
  TStringField *AddressTableCity;
  TStringField *AddressTableState;
  TStringField *AddressTableZip;
  TIntegerField *AddressTableNameCode;
  TTable *PhoneTable;
  TAutoIncField *PhoneTablePhoneCode;
  TStringField *PhoneTableDescription;
  TStringField *PhoneTableNumber;
  TStringField *PhoneTableExt;
  TIntegerField *PhoneTableNameCode;
  TTable *MemoTable;
  TAutoIncField *MemoTableMemoCode;
  TStringField *MemoTableDescription;
  TMemoField *MemoTableMemoData;
  TIntegerField *MemoTableNameCode;
  TDataSource *dsAddress;
  TDataSource *dsPhone;
  TDataSource *dsMemo;
  TTable *EMailTable;
  TAutoIncField *EMailTableEMailCode;
  TStringField *EMailTableAddress;
  TStringField *EMailTableDescription;
  TStringField *EMailTableService;
  TIntegerField *EMailTableNameCode;
```

continues

LISTING 10.3 CONTINUED

```
  TDataSource *dsEmail;
  TQuery *EMailDeleteQuery;
  TQuery *MemoDeleteQuery;
  TQuery *PhoneDeleteQuery;
  TQuery *AddressDeleteQuery;
  TQuery *NamesDeleteQuery;
  void __fastcall DModCreate(TObject *Sender);
  void __fastcall NamesTableCalcFields(TDataSet *DataSet);
private:
  String GetAddress();
  String GetPhone();
  String GetEMail();          // User declarations
public:                // User declarations
  __fastcall TDMod(TComponent* Owner);
  void CascadingDelete();
  void DoPost(TDataSet* Data);
  void PostAll();
  __property String Address  = { read = GetAddress };
  __property String Phone  = { read = GetPhone };
  __property String EMail  = { read = GetEMail };
};

extern PACKAGE TDMod *DMod;

#endif
```

LISTING 10.4 THE DATA MODULE FOR THE KDADD PROGRAM

```
/////////////////////////////////////
//    File: DMod1.cpp
// Project: KdAdd
//

#include <vcl.h>
#pragma hdrstop

#include "DMod1.h"

#pragma package(smart_init)
#pragma resource "*.dfm"
TDMod *DMod;
const char* CR = "\r\n";

__fastcall TDMod::TDMod(TComponent* Owner)
  : TDataModule(Owner)
{
}
```

```
void TDMod::CascadingDelete()
{
  EMailDeleteQuery->ParamByName("NameCode")->AsInteger =
    EMailTableNameCode->Value;
  EMailDeleteQuery->ExecSQL();

  MemoDeleteQuery->ParamByName("NameCode")->AsInteger =
    MemoTableNameCode->Value;
  MemoDeleteQuery->ExecSQL();

  PhoneDeleteQuery->ParamByName("NameCode")->AsInteger =
    PhoneTableNameCode->Value;
  PhoneDeleteQuery->ExecSQL();

  AddressDeleteQuery->ParamByName("NameCode")->AsInteger =
    AddressTableNameCode->Value;
  AddressDeleteQuery->ExecSQL();

  NamesDeleteQuery->ParamByName("NameCode")->AsInteger =
    NamesTableNameCode->Value;
  NamesDeleteQuery->ExecSQL();

  NamesTable->Refresh();
}

void TDMod::DoPost(TDataSet* Data)
{
  if (Data->State == dsInsert ¦¦ Data->State == dsEdit)
    Data->Post();
}

void TDMod::PostAll()
{
  for (int i=0;i<ComponentCount;i++) {
    TTable* table = dynamic_cast<TTable*>(Components[i]);
    if (table)
      DoPost(table);
  }
}

String TDMod::GetAddress()
{
  return DMod->AddressTableAddress1->AsString + CR +
    DMod->AddressTableAddress2->AsString + CR +
    DMod->AddressTableCity->AsString + CR +
    DMod->AddressTableState->AsString + CR +
    DMod->AddressTableZip->AsString;
}
```

continues

10

RELATIONAL
DATABASES

LISTING 10.4 CONTINUED

```
String TDMod::GetPhone()
{

  return DMod->PhoneTableDescription->AsString + CR +
    DMod->PhoneTableNumber->AsString + CR +
    DMod->PhoneTableExt->AsString;
}

String TDMod::GetEMail()
{
  return DMod->EMailTableAddress->AsString + CR +
    DMod->EMailTableDescription->AsString + CR +
    DMod->EMailTableService->AsString;
}

void __fastcall TDMod::DModCreate(TObject *Sender)
{
  NamesTable->Open();
  AddressTable->Open();
  PhoneTable->Open();
  MemoTable->Open();
  EMailTable->Open();
}

void __fastcall TDMod::NamesTableCalcFields(TDataSet *DataSet)
{
  String Temp =
    NamesTableFirstName->Value + " " + NamesTableLastName->Value;
  if (Temp == "")
    NamesTableFirstLastCompany->Value = NamesTableCompany->Value;
  else
    NamesTableFirstLastCompany->Value = Temp;
}
```

LISTING 10.5 THE CUSTOM RC FILE FOR THE PROJECT: A STUB TO BE FILLED OUT LATER

```
#include "kderrs.rh"
STRINGTABLE
{
  KDERR_CASESTATEMENT, "Command fell through case statement"
}
```

LISTING 10.6 THE INCLUDE FILE FOR THE RC FILE HAS ONLY ONE ENTRY: THIS IS A STUB TO BE FILLED OUT LATER

```
#define KDERR_CASESTATEMENT 1
```

The pages in the TPageControl are hidden from view in Figure 10.1. Figure 10.3 shows the Address page of the program's main window. I won't show the remaining pages of the page control as you can easily see what they do by compiling and running the program.

FIGURE 10.3

The tab sheet for the Address *table.*

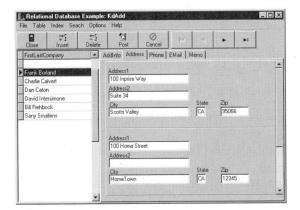

The KdAdd program has the minimal functionality needed to support the user's needs. For example, you can perform Insert, Post, Delete, and Cancel operations on all the tables. Access to these features is provided through both the menus and a toolbar. You can also set the index to the Company, First, or Last fields of the kdNames table. Finally, you can search on either the Company, First, or Last fields.

Setting Up the Index for KdAdd

The code that controls the index for the program forms one of the hubs around which the KdAdd program revolves. This code is called from several different places in the program. The obvious place to start studying it, however, is in the response method for the menu items that let the user change the index:

```
void TForm1::SetupIndex(TObject* Sender)
{
  switch (dynamic_cast<TComponent*>(Sender)->Tag) {
    case 100: DMod->NamesTable->IndexName = "idxLastName"; break;
    case 101: DMod->NamesTable->IndexName = "idxFirstName"; break;
    case 102: DMod->NamesTable->IndexName = "idxCompany"; break;
    case 103: DMod->NamesTable->IndexName = "";
  }
}

void __fastcall TForm1::IndexClick(TObject *Sender)
{
  SetupIndex(Sender);
  DMod->NamesTable->FindNearest(OPENARRAY(TVarRec, ("AAAA")));
}
```

The code has three menu choices for changing the index. The first lets the user set the index to the last name; the second, to the first name; and the third, to the company name. All three menu items are attached to the `IndexClick()` method shown here.

`IndexClick()` calls `SetupIndex()` to do the real work. You use the tag property of the `TMenuItem` that is clicked to decide which index to choose:

```
switch (dynamic_cast<TComponent*>(Sender)->Tag) {
```

Depending on the current value of the `Tag` property, you can choose which index to use.

This system is flexible enough to allow you to call the `SetupIndex()` method with just one parameter:

```
SetupIndex(Sender);
```

`SetupIndex()` then casts the `Sender` object so that it can get access to the `Tag` property.

After the index has been set up properly, you can search for the first relevant record in the database:

```
DMod->NamesTable->FindNearest(OPENARRAY(TVarRec, ("AAAA")));
```

The goal of this line is to skip over all the records that contain blanks in the field on which you're searching. For example, if you switch to the company index, you might find 20, 100, or even 5,000 records in the table that have no information in the `Company` field. To skip over these records, you can search for the first row that begins with the letter "A".

Searching for Records

The KdAdd program also uses the `SetupIndex()` method when it conducts searches. As stated previously, you can use one of three menu items to start a search. The first searches on last names; the second, on first names; and the third, on a company name. I have assigned the same values to the `Tag` properties of these `TMenuItems` that I did to the `Tag` properties of the `TMenuItems` concerned with switching indices. That way, I can set up the index properly with a simple call to `SetupIndex()`:

```
void __fastcall TForm1::SearchClick(TObject *Sender)
{
  String S = "";
  if ((InputQuery("Search for Name", "Enter Name: ", S))) {
    String IndexName = DMod->NamesTable->IndexName;
    SetupIndex(Sender);
    DMod->NamesTable->FindNearest(OPENARRAY(TVarRec, (S)));
    DMod->NamesTable->IndexName = IndexName;
  }
}
```

As you can see, the code also saves the current index so that the current state of the index can be restored after the search.

The point here is how easily you can take care of these chores by using the VCL. C++Builder makes database programming easy, even when you're working with a fairly complex program.

Inserting Data and Canceling Operations

Because this database has five tables, you have to devise a technique for specifying the name of the table on which you want to perform an insertion, deletion, or post. I use the TPageControl to handle these chores. In particular, I assume that the user wants to perform an action on the kdAdds table if he is looking at the Address page; if he is looking at the first page, I assume he wants to perform an operation on the kdNames table, and so on:

```
void __fastcall TForm1::InsertBtn2Click(TObject *Sender)
{
  switch (PageControl1->ActivePage->Tag) {
    case 1: DMod->NamesTable->Insert(); break;
    case 2: DMod->AddressTable->Insert(); break;
    case 3: DMod->PhoneTable->Insert(); break;
    case 4: DMod->EMailTable->Insert(); break;
    case 5: DMod->MemoTable->Insert();
  }
}
```

As you can see, I have set the Tag property for each of the pages to a unique value so that I can easily determine the current page:

```
switch (PageControl1->ActivePage->Tag) {
```

If the user makes a wrong decision, he can undo the most recent operation on the currently selected table by clicking Cancel:

```
void __fastcall TForm1::CancelBtn2Click(TObject *Sender)
{
  switch (PageControl1->ActivePage->Tag) {
    case 1: DMod->NamesTable->Cancel(); break;
    case 2: DMod->AddressTable->Cancel(); break;
    case 3: DMod->PhoneTable->Cancel(); break;
    case 4: DMod->EMailTable->Cancel(); break;
    case 5: DMod->MemoTable->Cancel(); break;
    default : {
      String S;
      ShowMessage(GetError(1, S));
    }
  }
}
```

This system is easy to implement, but it can be a bit confusing to the user when he or she is looking at the first page, which holds information about not only the kdNames table, but also the kdAdds and kdPhone tables. The issue here is that the database itself won't be much fun if you have to flip pages to get even the most basic information about a name. To remedy this problem, I put the Name, Address, and Phone information on the first page but I don't let the user edit it. If the user wants to edit a phone number or address, he has to turn to the appropriate page.

The program design helps the user by putting each table on a separate page. That way, the user can rely on the page metaphor when thinking about the underlying database structure. Providing metaphors for the user is a useful way to simplify an application's operation.

Working with the Data Module

The KdAdd program's data module is the central location for the program's database access code. I keep the code compartmentalized by putting all the database code in the data module. The main form doesn't need to contain any database-specific code, thereby making the program easier to maintain. Instead, the main form only calls specific functions in the data module to access the database. I describe the KdAdd program's database code in the following sections.

Deleting Data

The user can delete a record from the database by clicking the Delete button on the main form. The main form's DeleteBtn2Click() method contains code that deletes a record. It does this by calling the Delete() function of the appropriate table in the data module. Here is the DeleteBtn2Click() function:

```
void __fastcall TForm1::DeleteBtn2Click(TObject *Sender)
{
  TMsgDlgButtons Btns;
  Btns << mbYes << mbNo;
  char* Msg = "Are you sure you want to delete\r\n%s?";
  String S;
  switch (PageControl1->ActivePage->Tag) {
    case 1: {
      S = S.sprintf(Msg,
        DMod->NamesTableFirstLastCompany->AsString.c_str());
      if ((MessageDlg(S, mtInformation, Btns, 0) == ID_YES))
        DMod->CascadingDelete();
      break;
    }
```

```
case 2: {
  S = S.sprintf(Msg, DMod->Address.c_str());
  if ((MessageDlg(S, mtInformation, Btns, 0) == ID_YES))
    DMod->AddressTable->Delete();
  break;
}

case 3: {
  S = S.sprintf(Msg, DMod->Phone.c_str());
  if ((MessageDlg(S, mtInformation, Btns, 0) == ID_YES))
    DMod->PhoneTable->Delete();
  break;
}

case 4: {
  S = S.sprintf(Msg, DMod->EMail.c_str());
  if ((MessageDlg(S, mtInformation, Btns, 0) == ID_YES))
    DMod->EMailTable->Delete();
  break;
}

case 5: {
  S = S.sprintf(Msg, DMod->MemoTableDescription->AsString.c_str());
  if ((MessageDlg(S, mtInformation, Btns, 0) == ID_YES))
    DMod->MemoTable->Delete();
  break;
}
default: {
  String S;
  ShowMessage(GetError(1, S));
}
  }
 }
}
```

As you can see, this code uses the Tag property of the TTabSheet (obtained using PageControl1->ActivePage) to determine which table is focused.

The code then brings up a message box asking the user if he is sure about continuing with the deletion. In some cases, you can easily give the user an intelligent prompt about the contents of the current field:

```
S = S.sprintf(Msg, DMod->NamesTableFirstLastCompany->AsString.c_str());
```

In this case, the string garnered from one of the fields of the NamesTable provides all the information the user needs. In fact, the FirstLast field of the database is a calculated field. This calculated field consists of combined information from the First, Last, and Company fields of the kdNames. This combined information uniquely identifies a record so the user can feel secure when deleting it:

```
void __fastcall TDMod::NamesTableCalcFields(TDataSet *DataSet)
{
```

```
String Temp =
  NamesTableFirstName->Value + " " + NamesTableLastName->Value;
if (Temp == "")
  NamesTableFirstLastCompany->Value = NamesTableCompany->Value;
else
  NamesTableFirstLastCompany->Value = Temp;
}
```

As you can see, this code combines the first and last names into a single string. If the string is not empty, it is shown to the user as if it were a standard database field. If the current record has no information in either the first or last field, then the program assumes that the record must contain only company information:

```
NamesTableFirstLastCompany->Value = NamesTableCompany->Value;
```

The end result of this system is to show the user records that contain either someone's first or last name or just a company name. This way, you can ask the database to perform double duty as both a way of tracking company names and as a means of tracking the names of people.

This calculated field can be used not only to help with deletions, but also as an index appearing on the extreme left of the main form, as shown in Figure 10.1. The user will never edit this field directly but will use it as a guide to all the nearby records in the database. This kind of index is useful if you're searching for a particular name. For example, I use the database to track the members of my family. As a result, it has lots of Calverts in it. I can use the Last Name search to find the section where the Calverts are stored and then use the index to move back and forth between family members.

You actually have no guarantee that the string generated by this calculated field will be unique. The program is designed to make sure the `NameCode` in the `kdNames` table is unique, but nothing in the program prevents you from entering two identical names, addresses, phone numbers, and so on.

If the user wants to delete an address, you should show a confirmation dialog to ensure that the user actually wants to delete the record. You need to provide information from several different fields to uniquely identify a record in order to display a meaningful confirmation dialog to the user; Figure 10.4 illustrates.

FIGURE 10.4

A confirmation dialog that uniquely identifies the address shown in a particular row.

This time, I found it more convenient simply to add to the data module a method that would return a string uniquely identifying a record:

```
String TDMod::GetAddress()
{
  return DMod->AddressTableAddress1->AsString + CR +
    DMod->AddressTableAddress2->AsString + CR +
    DMod->AddressTableCity->AsString + CR +
    DMod->AddressTableState->AsString + CR +
    DMod->AddressTableZip->AsString;
}
```

I thought the most sensible approach was to add a read-only property to the data module to aid in retrieving this information:

```
__property String Address  = { read = GetAddress };
```

You can access this property by writing code that looks like this:

```
String S = DMod->Address;
```

In this particular case, it is arguable that the property doesn't do much for you other than cover the remote contingency that you might change the parameters of the `GetAddress()` method. On the other hand, the property doesn't cost you anything either; the compiler will obviously map any calls to the `Address` property directly to the `GetAddress()` method. In other words, this programming is very cautious because it is unlikely that the `GetAddress()` method will ever change its spots. However, being conservative when writing code is almost always best, as long as you're not doing serious damage to your program's performance.

It has taken me a long time to describe the various techniques I employ to prompt the user for the name of the record he is about to delete. However, after this process is taken care of, just one line is required to delete the record:

```
DMod->EMailTable->Delete();
```

I won't discuss any of the means for deleting from the other tables in this program, as they follow the pattern already established. The key point is that you have to show several fields to the user in order to identify a record uniquely. Furthermore, placing the burden of generating these strings on the program's data module is probably best. The reason for doing so is simply that the generation of these strings is dependent on the structure of the tables underlying the program. Isolating all code dependent on these structures inside one object is best. That way you won't have to hunt all over your program to find code that might need to be modified because of a change in the program's database.

Cascading Deletes

You have already seen that the data module contains special properties that retrieve strings uniquely identifying certain records. You have also seen the calculated field that generates a string "uniquely" identifying records from the kdNames table. You have yet to explore methods that aid in posting and deleting records.

The issue here is simply that the database contains a number of tables. If the user wants to delete a name from the database, he is really asking to not just delete the name, but also the other information associated with that name (addresses, phone numbers, and the like). This process is known as a *cascading delete*.

C++Builder provides support for cascading deletes via the referential integrity settings in SQL Explorer. You can see this option in Figure 10.5.

FIGURE 10.5

Choose Cascade or Restrict to get support for cascading deletes in databases that support this feature.

Many databases do not support cascading deletes, so you can implement it on the client side with just a few lines of code:

```
void TDMod::CascadingDelete()
{
  EMailDeleteQuery->ParamByName("NameCode")->AsInteger =
    EMailTableNameCode->Value;
  EMailDeleteQuery->ExecSQL();

  MemoDeleteQuery->ParamByName("NameCode")->AsInteger =
    MemoTableNameCode->Value;
  MemoDeleteQuery->ExecSQL();

  PhoneDeleteQuery->ParamByName("NameCode")->AsInteger =
    PhoneTableNameCode->Value;
  PhoneDeleteQuery->ExecSQL();
```

```
AddressDeleteQuery->ParamByName("NameCode")->AsInteger =
  AddressTableNameCode->Value;
AddressDeleteQuery->ExecSQL();

NamesDeleteQuery->ParamByName("NameCode")->AsInteger =
  NamesTableNameCode->Value;
NamesDeleteQuery->ExecSQL();

NamesTable->Refresh();
}
```

This code looks a bit complicated, in part because some of the lines are long and need to be wrapped. Underneath, however, its structure is very simple. I simply walk down the list of tables in the database, accessing the kdNames table last. I have created a SQL statement for each table that will delete all the records in the table that have a particular NameCode. For example, I use these SQL statements for deleting records in the kdNames or kdAdds tables:

```
Delete from kdNames where NameCode = :NameCode
Delete from kdAdds where NameCode = :NameCode
```

As I said, this technology is very simple, and the act of implementing cascading deletes in your application is trivial. The key to the whole process is recognizing that it's simplest to delegate the responsibility for deletions to the program's data module. You can then create a simple method in the data module to handle the logic of the operation; after about five minutes' work, you have a method that can be called from anywhere in your application with a single line of code. (You should, however, take more than five minutes to test your code against sample data to make sure that it is working properly.) Furthermore, you will find that many databases automatically support cascading deletes.

Mass Posts

The opposite problem from deleting records occurs when you have to post the data in your program. In these cases, you need to make sure that all the data in all the tables is posted. You wouldn't want to post just the data in the kdNames table and then leave updates to the kdAdds or kdPhones tables stranded.

The methods that handle posting the data look like this:

```
void TDMod::DoPost(TDataSet* Data)
{
  if (Data->State == dsInsert || Data->State == dsEdit)
    Data->Post();
}

void TDMod::PostAll()
{
```

10

RELATIONAL
DATABASES

```
for (int i=0;i<ComponentCount;i++) {
  TTable* table = dynamic_cast<TTable*>(Components[i]);
  if (table)
    DoPost(table);
}
}
```

This code iterates through all the components on the program's data module looking for
`TTable` objects. When the code finds one, it passes the object to a method called
`DoPost()`, which calls the `Post` method for the table. The code in `DoPost()` first checks
to make sure the table is in `dsInsert` or `dsEdit` mode, as it is an error to call post on a
table that is in `dsBrowse` or some other mode in which a post can't occur. You can alternatively check the value of `TTable::Modified` to discover a record's status.

Notice that I use the `ComponentCount` property of `TDataModule` to determine how many
components I need to check. I then use the `dynamic_cast` operator to determine whether
I can safely assume that the current component is a `TTable`.

As I have said, using a data module for all the KdAdd program's database operations
helps compartmentalize the code. Having the database code in one location makes the
main program code cleaner and helps in debugging as well. Next I discuss how the
KdAdd program uses string resources to display error messages to the user.

Putting Error Strings in String Resources

The other subject worth touching on briefly in regard to this program involves using
string resources to handle error strings. The program has a small string resource that contains only one string:

```
#include "kderrs.rh"
STRINGTABLE
{
  KDERR_CASESTATEMENT, "Command fell through case statement"
}
```

In a program used in the real world, you would probably want to generate many more
error strings.

The KdAdd program uses the `GetError()` method to retrieve error strings from the string
table which is linked to the program as a resource. Here is the `GetError()` method:

```
String TForm1::GetError(int ErrNo, String& S)
{
  S.SetLength(ERR_STRING_SIZE);
  LoadString(HInstance, 1, S.c_str(), ERR_STRING_SIZE);
  return S;
}
```

This code calls the Windows API routine called `LoadString()` to do the actual grunt work. Several built-in VCL routines also provide this same functionality. Notice that an include file defines the KDERR_CASESTATEMENT constant:

```
#define KDERR_CASESTATEMENT 1
```

You've come to the end of the KdAdd program discussion; the rest of the chapter consists of a discussion of KdAddExplore program. This program will show how to use the TSession object to explore the structure of the tables used in the KdAdd program. The next section begins an explanation of the TSession and TTreeView objects.

Using the KdAddExplore Program

The KdAddExplore program uses the TSession object to explore the tables used in the KdAdd program. The TSession object is often overlooked by VCL programmers because its operation is usually handled behind the scenes without need for intervention. If you want to explore the structure of a database at run time, this object is the one to use. In fact, this object might have been more usefully called the TDataExplorer object rather than TSession.

> **NOTE**
>
> An instance of TSession, called simply Session, is created automatically by an application on startup. If you're working inside a DLL or in a console mode application, then no default TApplication object exists to start a session. As a result, you might have to create your own TSession object or call a TApplication object's Initialize method. Otherwise, you cannot use databases inside your program.

Before you read the technical part of this section, spending a few moments running the KdAddExplore program found on the CD-ROM might be helpful. This program demonstrates techniques for examining an existing database's structure.

> **NOTE**
>
> The KdAddExplore program bears a close resemblance to a cut-down version of the SQL Explorer. Nothing about this similarity is coincidental. However, I have never seen the source to SQL Explorer nor discussed its structure with its author. My intention here is not to create a substitute for the SQL Explorer, but to
>
> *continues*

10

RELATIONAL
DATABASES

> provide a simple means of showing you how to explore database objects at run time.
>
> You can use this kind of information to provide utilities for your users or merely to extend your own knowledge of the BDE and VCL. The code also provides an example of how to use the `TTreeView` object.

Throughout the rest of this chapter, I use the global `TSession` object created automatically whenever you include database code in your programs. However, you also can drop a `TSession` component on your forms if you want to look at a visual object. I do not use it here because it would bring no additional functionality to my program. However, you might want to view the `TSession` component at least and take a look at its password-related properties.

Working with `TSession`

`TSession` is used to manage all the database connections within a session. It is a global object that wraps up not only `TTable` and `TQuery`, but also `TDatabase`. A single `TSession` object might manage many tables, queries, and databases.

The `TSession` object has two sets of methods. The first has to do with managing a session. The methods encompassing this set of functionality are shown in Table 10.12.

TABLE 10.12   THE SESSION MANAGEMENT ROUTINES FROM THE `TSession` OBJECT

Routine	Description
Close	Closes all databases
CloseDatabase	Closes a particular database
Open	Opens the session: `Active = true;`
OpenDatabase	Opens a specific database
AddPassword	Creates a password for the session
RemovePassword	Deletes a password
RemoveAllPasswords	Clears the password list
DropConnections	Closes all currently inactive databases and datasets

The second set of routines found in `TSession` includes the methods that are of interest in the current context of this book. These routines are shown in Table 10.13.

TABLE 10.13 ROUTINES FOR QUERYING A SESSION REGARDING THE AVAILABLE DATABASES, TABLES, DRIVERS, AND STORED PROCEDURES

Routine	Description
GetAliasNames	Gets the list of BDE aliases for a database
GetAliasParams	Gets the list of parameters for a BDE alias
GetAliasDriverName	Gets the BDE driver for an alias of a database
GetDatabaseNames	Gets a list of BDE aliases and TDatabase objects
GetDriverNames	Gets the names of installed BDE drivers
GetDriverParams	Gets parameters for a BDE driver
GetTableNames	Gets tables associated with a database
GetStoredProcNames	Gets stored procedures for a database

Routines such as GetDatabaseNames and GetTableNames can retrieve a list of all the available databases and tables on the current system. You can see this data on display inside the KdAddExplore program. For example, all the databases in my system at the time of this writing are visible in the main screen of the KdAddExplore program, as shown in Figure 10.6.

FIGURE 10.6

The KdAddExplore program displays all the available databases on my system.

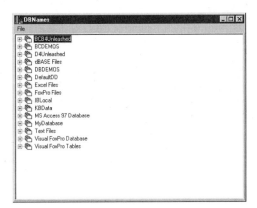

You can open the nodes of KdAddExplore to see a list of all the tables in a particular database, as shown in Figure 10.7. You can then drill down even further to the names of the fields and indices in a particular table. Finally, you can even see the names of the fields involved in a particular index, as shown in Figure 10.8.

FIGURE **10.7**
The tables in the
BCB4UNLEASHED
database that
holds most of the
data used in this
book.

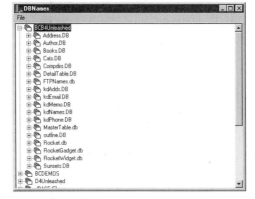

FIGURE **10.8**
The fields and
indices on the
kdNames *table.*
Notice that you
can drill down to
see the fields in
each index.

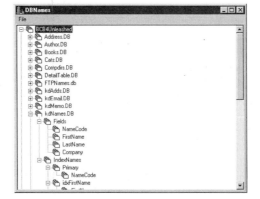

Another set of TSession functionality tapped into by the KdAddExplore program
involves looking at the alias found on a system. You can use this dialog to see the parameters passed to a particular alias, as shown in Figure 10.9.

FIGURE **10.9**
The KdAddExplore
program shows all
the aliases on the
system. The open
branch is from an
InterBase
database.

Analyzing the KdAddExplore Program

Most of the complexity in the KdAddExplore program comes from manipulating the TTreeView object. The code for querying the TSession object is fairly straightforward in most cases; the TTreeView makes the code a bit tricky in places. The source for this program is shown in Listings 10.7 through 10.11.

LISTING 10.7   THE HEADER FOR THE KDADDEXPLORE PROGRAM'S MAIN FORM

```cpp
#ifndef MainH
#define MainH

#include <Classes.hpp>
#include <Controls.hpp>
#include <StdCtrls.hpp>
#include <Forms.hpp>
#include <ComCtrls.hpp>
#include <ExtCtrls.hpp>
#include <ImgList.hpp>
#include <Menus.hpp>
#include <Db.hpp>
#include <DbTables.hpp>

class TDBNames : public TForm
{
__published:        // IDE-managed Components
  TPanel *Panel1;
  TTreeView *TView;
  TImageList *ImageList1;
  TMainMenu *MainMenu1;
  TMenuItem *File1;
  TMenuItem *AliasView1;
  TMenuItem *N1;
  TMenuItem *Exit1;
  void __fastcall FormShow(TObject *Sender);
  void __fastcall TViewExpanding(TObject *Sender, TTreeNode *Node,
        bool &AllowExpansion);
  void __fastcall Exit1Click(TObject *Sender);
  void __fastcall AliasView1Click(TObject *Sender);
private:
    void AddTables(TTreeNode* Node);         // User declarations
    void DeleteTemp(TTreeNode* Node);
    void FindFields(TTreeNode* Node, TTable* Table);
    void FindFieldsAndIndices(TTreeNode* Node);
    void FindIndices(TTreeNode* Node, TTable* Table);        // User
declarations
public:                     // User declarations
  __fastcall TDBNames(TComponent* Owner);
};

extern PACKAGE TDBNames *DBNames;

#endif
```

10
RELATIONAL DATABASES

LISTING 10.8 THE MAIN UNIT FOR THE KDADDEXPLORE PROGRAM

```cpp
/////////////////////////////////////
//    File: Main.cpp
// Project: KdAddExplore
//

#include <vcl.h>
#pragma hdrstop

#include "Main.h"
#include "AliasView1.h"
#include "DMod1.h"

#pragma package(smart_init)
#pragma resource "*.dfm"
TDBNames *DBNames;

__fastcall TDBNames::TDBNames(TComponent* Owner)
  : TForm(Owner)
{
}


//*************************************************************************
// AddTables
//
//    Delete child if (it's one of the "TEMP" placeholders.
//    Add all tables belonging to the database as children.
//
//    When calling GetTableNames, third parameter is set to
//    true, which means the extension of the table is also
//    retrieved. Without the extension, there can be trouble
//    exploring dBase files.
//*************************************************************************
void TDBNames::AddTables(TTreeNode* Node)
{
  String S = Node->Text;
  TStringList* List = new TStringList;

  DeleteTemp(Node);

  Session->GetTableNames(S, "*.*", true, false, List);
  for (int j=0;j<List->Count;j++) {
    TTreeNode* TempNode = TView->Items->AddChild(Node, List->Strings[j]);
    TTreeNode* ChildNode = TView->Items->AddChild(TempNode, "Fields");
    TView->Items->AddChild(ChildNode, "TEMP");
    ChildNode = TView->Items->AddChild(TempNode, "IndexNames");
    TView->Items->AddChild(ChildNode, "TEMP");
  }
  delete List;
}
```

```
//****************************************************************
// DeleteTemp
//
// Delete child if (it's one of the "TEMP" placeholders.
//****************************************************************
void TDBNames::DeleteTemp(TTreeNode* Node)
{
  if (Node->Count == 1) {
    TTreeNode* TempNode = Node->getFirstChild();
    if (TempNode->Text == "TEMP")
      TempNode->Delete();
  }
}

void TDBNames::FindFields(TTreeNode* Node, TTable* Table)
{
  for (int i=0;i<Table->FieldCount;i++)
    TView->Items->AddChild(Node, Table->Fields->Fields[i]->FieldName);
}

void TDBNames::FindFieldsAndIndices(TTreeNode* Node)
{
  TTable* Table = new TTable(this);

  Table->DatabaseName = Node->Parent->Parent->Text;
  Table->TableName = Node->Parent->Text;
  Table->Open();

  DeleteTemp(Node);

  if (Node->Count < 1)
    switch (Node->Index) {
      case 0: FindFields(Node, Table); break;
      case 1: FindIndices(Node, Table);
    }

  delete Table;
}

//  FindIndices
//
//  One way to get a list of the names of the Indices on a table
//  is through the GetIndexNames function:
//
//     TStringList *List = new TStringList;
//     Table->GetIndexNames(List);
//
//  However, here I need a bit more information, so I used the
```

continues

LISTING 10.8   CONTINUED

```
//  IndexDefs property instead. However, I still seem to need
//  to call GetIndexNames to prime the pump.
void TDBNames::FindIndices(TTreeNode* Node, TTable* Table)
{
  TStringList* List = new TStringList;
  Table->GetIndexNames(List);
  TIndexDefs* IndexDefs = Table->IndexDefs;
  for (int i=0;i<IndexDefs->Count;i++) {
    String S = IndexDefs->Items[i]->Name;
    if (S.Length() == 0)
      S = "Primary";
    TTreeNode* ChildNode = TView->Items->AddChild(Node, S);
    S = IndexDefs->Items[i]->Fields;
    TView->Items->AddChild(ChildNode, S);
  }
  delete List;
}

void __fastcall TDBNames::FormShow(TObject *Sender)
{
  TStringList* DBNamesList = new TStringList;
  ImageList1->ResourceLoad(rtBitmap, "FolderShut", clPurple);

  Session->GetDatabaseNames(DBNamesList);
  for (int i=0;i<DBNamesList->Count;i++) {
    String S = DBNamesList->Strings[i];
    TTreeNode* Node = TView->Items->Add(TView->Selected, S);
    TView->Items->AddChild(Node, "TEMP");
  }
  delete DBNamesList;
}

void __fastcall TDBNames::TViewExpanding(TObject *Sender, TTreeNode *Node,
      bool &AllowExpansion)
{
  switch (Node->Level) {
    case 0: if (Node->Count <= 1) AddTables(Node); break;
    case 2: FindFieldsAndIndices(Node);
  }
}

void __fastcall TDBNames::Exit1Click(TObject *Sender)
{
  Close();
}

void __fastcall TDBNames::AliasView1Click(TObject *Sender)
{
  AliasForm->Show();
}
```

LISTING 10.9   THE HEADER FOR THE Aliasview1 UNIT

```
#ifndef AliasView1H
#define AliasView1H

#include <Classes.hpp>
#include <Controls.hpp>
#include <StdCtrls.hpp>
#include <Forms.hpp>

class TAliasForm : public TForm
{
__published:    // IDE-managed Components
  TListBox *ListBox1;
  TMemo *Memo1;
  void __fastcall ListBox1Click(TObject *Sender);
  void __fastcall FormShow(TObject *Sender);
private:
public:          // User declarations
  __fastcall TAliasForm(TComponent* Owner);
};

extern PACKAGE TAliasForm *AliasForm;

#endif
```

LISTING 10.10   THE Aliasview1 UNIT ALLOWS YOU TO VIEW ALIASES AVAILABLE ON
YOUR SYSTEM

```
/////////////////////////////////////
//     File: AliasView1.cpp
// Project: KdAddExplore
//

#include <vcl.h>
#pragma hdrstop

#include "AliasView1.h"

#pragma package(smart_init)
#pragma resource "*.dfm"
TAliasForm *AliasForm;

__fastcall TAliasForm::TAliasForm(TComponent* Owner)
  : TForm(Owner)
{
}
```

continues

Listing **10.10** Continued

```
void __fastcall TAliasForm::ListBox1Click(TObject *Sender)
{
  String S = ListBox1->Items->Strings[ListBox1->ItemIndex];
  Session->GetAliasParams(S, Memo1->Lines);
}

void __fastcall TAliasForm::FormShow(TObject *Sender)
{
  Session->GetAliasNames(ListBox1->Items);
}
```

Listing **10.11** The Data Module for the Main Program Contains a TDatabase Object, but No Code

```
#ifndef DMod1H
#define DMod1H

#include <Classes.hpp>
#include <Controls.hpp>
#include <StdCtrls.hpp>
#include <Forms.hpp>
#include <DBTables.hpp>

class TDMod : public TDataModule
{
__published:    // IDE-managed Components
  TDatabase *Database1;
private:    // User declarations
public:        // User declarations
  __fastcall TDMod(TComponent* Owner);
};

extern PACKAGE TDMod *DMod;

#endif
```

Using a `TTreeView` to Display the Databases on a System

When the KdAddExplore program is launched, it first iterates through the available databases on the system and displays to the user in a TTreeView:

```
void __fastcall TDBNames::FormShow(TObject *Sender)
{
```

```
    TStringList* DBNamesList = new TStringList;
    ImageList1->ResourceLoad(rtBitmap, "FolderShut", clPurple);

    Session->GetDatabaseNames(DBNamesList);
    for (int i=0;i<DBNamesList->Count;i++) {
      String S = DBNamesList->Strings[i];
      TTreeNode* Node = TView->Items->Add(TView->Selected, S);
      TView->Items->AddChild(Node, "TEMP");
    }
    delete DBNamesList;
}
```

This code needs to have an icon that it can use to spruce up the `TTreeView` nodes. It stores that bitmap, called `FldrShut.bmp`, in an `ImageList` component. `FldrShut.bmp` is one of the files that ships in the `Images` subdirectory (beneath the Borland `Shared` directory) that is created when you install C++Builder or Delphi.

Because only one image appears in this image list, it is automatically associated with all the `TTreeView` object's nodes. In this particular case, that is a satisfactory solution to the problem of how to give some visual interest to the object.

After it sets up the icon, the program retrieves the list of available aliases from the `TSession` object and stores them inside a `TStringList`:

```
TStringList* DBNamesList = new TStringList;
Session->GetDatabaseNames(DBNamesList);
```

After you have the list of items, you can easily store each one inside a `TTreeNode` object that can be hung on the `TTreeView` for display to the user:

```
for (int i=0;i<DBNamesList->Count;i++) {
  String S = DBNamesList->Strings[i];
  TTreeNode* Node = TView->Items->Add(TView->Selected, S);
  TView->Items->AddChild(Node, "TEMP");
}
```

The `TTreeNode` object is clearly the key to working with a `TTreeView`. This object represents an individual node on a `TTreeView`. It encapsulates a bitmap and a caption and can be identified by a unique index number.

Notice that I call two methods of the `TTreeView` object's `Items` property, which in this program is called `TView`; it is not a type, but an abbreviation for `TreeView`. The first call adds the name of the database as a node. The next call adds a child to that database node containing a string consisting of the word "Temp". The temp node is never shown to the user but exists only to force the `TTreeView` to display a plus sign, which indicates to the user that the node can be expanded further. When it comes time to expand the node, I delete the word `Temp` and substitute a word that actually displays the name of one of the tables in the database.

The use of the temp node may seem like a nasty kluge at first. However, doing things this way is easier than forcing the user to sit still while I open all the databases, including those that might need a password, and find all the tables inside them. When you think of things from this perspective, adding a temporary node to each item in the tree suddenly seems very logical. If the user wants to expand a particular node, you can retrieve detailed information about that particular database. This approach is much better than trying to retrieve information about every table on the system in one long, time-consuming process.

Expanding the Nodes of the `TTreeView`

The program must respond appropriately when the user clicks a node of the `TTreeView` object. In particular, if the user is first opening a particular database node, the code needs to retrieve the list of tables in that database and display them to the user. If the user clicks one of the tables, a list of fields and indices must be retrieved, and so on.

An `OnExpanding` event gets called automatically when the user wants to open a node. The following is how the `KdAddExplore` program responds to this event:

```
void __fastcall TDBNames::TViewExpanding(TObject *Sender, TTreeNode *Node,
        bool &AllowExpansion)
{
  switch (Node->Level) {
    case 0: if (Node->Count <= 1) AddTables(Node); break;
    case 2: FindFieldsAndIndices(Node);
  }
}
```

As you can see, the program calls a method named `AddTables()` if the user is working at the first level of the tree, and it calls a method called `FindFieldsAndIndices()` if the user is working at the third level of the tree. (The second level contains the table names.) The level the user is currently exploring appears in the `Level` property of the `TTreeNode` passed to the `OnExpanding` event handler.

Before calling `AddTables()`, I check to see if more than one child node already appears on this particular node of the `TTreeView`. If more than one node exists, I assume that the database has already been explored and that the node can be opened without any further system querying. If only one node exists, I assume that this is the temp node created in the program's `OnShow` event, and I call `AddTables()` so that the node can be updated.

Adding a List of Available Tables to the `TTreeView`

The following code is called when it's time to explore the tables on the system:

```
void TForm1::DeleteTemp(TTreeNode* Node)
{
  if (Node->Count == 1) {
    TTreeNode* TempNode = Node->getFirstChild();
    if (TempNode->Text == "TEMP")
      TempNode->Delete();
  }
}

void TForm1::AddTables(TTreeNode* Node)
{
  String S = Node->Text;
  TStringList* List = new TStringList;

  DeleteTemp(Node);

  Session->GetTableNames(S, "*.*", true, false, List);
  for (int j=0;j<List->Count;j++) {
    TTreeNode* TempNode = TView->Items->AddChild(Node, List->Strings[j]);
    TTreeNode* ChildNode = TView->Items->AddChild(TempNode, "Fields");
    TView->Items->AddChild(ChildNode, "TEMP");
    ChildNode = TView->Items->AddChild(TempNode, "IndexNames");
    TView->Items->AddChild(ChildNode, "TEMP");
  }
  delete List;
}
```

The first method shown here, `DeleteTemp()`,deletes the temp nodes created in the `FormShow()` method. The code checks to make sure the string is actually set to "Temp" just to be sure that I haven't stumbled across a database that has only one table in it. The program would, of course, behave badly if it encountered a database with a single table called `Temp` in it!

The next step is for the program to retrieve the list of tables in a database from the `Session` object:

```
Session->GetTableNames(S, "*.*", true, false, List);
```

The code uses the string name from the node passed to the `OnExpanded` event to query `TSession` for the proper set of tables. You can look up `GetTableNames()` in the online help for detailed explanation of this call, but most readers should be able to figure out what is going on from this declaration:

```
void __fastcall GetTableNames(const System::AnsiString DatabaseName,
   const System::AnsiString Pattern, bool Extensions,
   bool SystemTables, Classes::TStrings* List);
```

Set `Extensions` to `true` if you want to retrieve the extension for a dBASE or Paradox table. Also set `Extensions` to `true` if you want to retrieve system tables for SQL databases such as InterBase.

The program is at last ready to add the tables to the `TTreeView`:

```
TTreeNode* TempNode = TView->Items->AddChild(Node, List->Strings[j]);
TTreeNode* ChildNode = TView->Items->AddChild(TempNode, "Fields");
TView->Items->AddChild(ChildNode, "TEMP");
ChildNode = TView->Items->AddChild(TempNode, "IndexNames");
TView->Items->AddChild(ChildNode, "TEMP");
```

This code first adds a table name to the `TTreeView`:

```
TempNode = TView->Items->AddChild(Node, List->Strings[j]);
```

It then adds two child nodes labeled `Fields` and `IndexNames` to the table name. Once again, I resort to the trick of placing a temp node under these two fields to indicate to the user that the nodes can be expanded further. However, I do not actually expand the nodes at this time because the user may not ever want to see the data in question.

Finding Out About Indices and Fields

To find out about indices and fields, I abandon the `TSession` object and instead create a `TTable` object. This object can give me the information I need:

```
void TForm1::FindFieldsAndIndices(TTreeNode* Node)
{
  TTable* Table = new TTable(this);

  Table->DatabaseName = Node->Parent->Parent->Text;
  Table->TableName = Node->Parent->Text;
  Table->Open();

  DeleteTemp(Node);

  if (Node->Count < 1)
    switch (Node->Index) {
      case 0: FindFields(Node, Table); break;
      case 1: FindIndices(Node, Table);
    }

  delete Table;
}
```

The program first queries `TTreeView` to retrieve the name of the database the user wants to explore and the name of the particular table under examination:

```
Table->DatabaseName = Node->Parent->Parent->Text;
Table->TableName = Node->Parent->Text;
```

The table is then opened, and the temp node associated with it is deleted:

```
Table->Open();
DeleteTemp(Node);
```

I hung the nodes with the labels `Fields` and `IndexNames` in a particular order, so I can use the `Index` property of the current `Node` to know when to retrieve information on fields and when to retrieve information on indices:

```
if (Node->Count < 1)
  switch (Node->Index) {
    case 0: FindFields(Node, Table); break;
    case 1: FindIndices(Node, Table);
  }
```

The `FindFields` method is very simple, in large part because it is a leaf node on the tree and does not need to be expanded further:

```
void TForm1::FindFields(TTreeNode* Node, TTable* Table)
{
  for (int i=0;i<Table->FieldCount;i++)
    TView->Items->AddChild(Node, Table->Fields->Fields[i]->FieldName);
}
```

I have to do a little coaxing to get the system to give up information on indices:

```
void TForm1::FindIndices(TTreeNode* Node, TTable* Table)
{
  TStringList* List = new TStringList;
  Table->GetIndexNames(List);
  TIndexDefs* IndexDefs = Table->IndexDefs;
  for (int i=0;i<IndexDefs->Count;i++) {
    String S = IndexDefs->Items[i]->Name;
    if (S.Length() == 0)
      S = "Primary";
    TTreeNode* ChildNode = TView->Items->AddChild(Node, S);
    S = IndexDefs->Items[i]->Fields;
    TView->Items->AddChild(ChildNode, S);
  }
  delete List;
}
```

I first get the list of index names from the `TTable` object and then retrieve the relevant `TIndexDefs` object. This object contains information on a particular index. I iterated through the `Items` in the `IndexDefs` and display the information to the user.

You might think that I need to have a second loop inside the first loop to handle a case in which an index consists of more than one field. However, a second loop is unnecessary because the list is sent to me in the form of a single string, with each index delimited by a semicolon. For example, the primary index of the Items table from BCDEMOS consists of two fields. This information is displayed by TIndexDefs as follows:

```
OrderNo;ItemNo
```

Displaying Aliases and Alias Parameters

After all the work involved with displaying information about databases, tables, indices, and fields, you will find that querying the system about aliases is relatively trivial. One of the main reasons this process is so much simpler is that I use list boxes rather than a TTreeView to display information. TTreeViews are great for the user, but not much fun for the programmer.

The following is the custom code from the unit that displays an alias to the user. All the other code in the unit is generated by the system.

```
void __fastcall TAliasForm::ListBox1Click(TObject *Sender)
{
  String S = ListBox1->Items->Strings[ListBox1->ItemIndex];
  Session->GetAliasParams(S, Memo1->Lines);
}

void __fastcall TAliasForm::FormShow(TObject *Sender)
{
  Session->GetAliasNames(ListBox1->Items);
}
```

The program opts to display this information in a separate form rather than overlay it on top of the information about databases. This form has two list boxes in it. The first list box holds the various aliases available on the system, and the second list box holds the parameters for the currently selected alias.

When the form is first shown, I call the GetAliasNames() method of the global Session object and then pass it the TStrings-based property of TListBox. That's all I need to do to show the user the aliases.

The ListBox1Click event handler is called if the user selects a particular item in the first list box. This code initializes a string to the name of the currently selected alias:

```
String S = ListBox1->Items->Strings[ListBox1->ItemIndex];
```

It then queries the Session object for the list of parameters associated with that object:

```
Session->GetAliasParams(S, Memo1->Lines);
```

As you can see, this second list is displayed in the list box on the right, as shown in Figure 10.9.

Summary

In this chapter you looked at relational databases. The core material was divided into two sections. The first section looked at a simple relational database program consisting of five interrelated tables. You saw how these tables are tied together and how to add, delete, insert, and edit records in these tables. Also included is a relatively lengthy discussion of the indices and keys in the table and why they were created. Other subjects included searching and storing strings in a string table.

The second half of the chapter was dedicated to an examination of the global TSession object that is created automatically whenever you use the BDE database tools in your program. You can use this object to query the system about aliases, databases, and tables. You also saw how to query a TTable object about its fields and indices.

Other information included in this chapter related mostly to using standard C++Builder components such as TTreeView. You saw that the powerful TTreeView object allows you to display information in a way that the user can easily comprehend. Several portions of the chapter focused on the TTreeNode object used to fill in the nodes of a TTreeView. In particular, you saw how to add child nodes to a TTreeView.

Working with the Local InterBase Server

*by Charlie Calvert
and Kent Reisdorph*

IN THIS CHAPTER

C++Builder ships with the Local InterBase Server, which is sometimes simply called *LIBS*. This tool provides all the capabilities of the full InterBase server, but it runs on a local machine. You do not need to be connected to a network to be able to run the Local InterBase Server.

The client software you get with C++Builder will talk to either LIBS or the standard version of the InterBase server. From your point of view as a programmer, you will find no difference between talking to LIBS and talking to an InterBase server across a network. The only way to tell which server you're connected to is by examining the path in your current alias. In short, LIBS is the perfect tool for practicing real client/server database programming even if you're not connected to a LAN.

This chapter's goal is to provide you with a useful introduction to LIBS and an overview of transactions. In particular, you will learn how to do the following:

- Connect to local InterBase tables
- Connect without having to specify a password
- Create databases
- Work with `TDatabase` objects
- Create tables
- Commit and roll back transactions in both local and InterBase tables
- Maintain the data you have created
- Work with cached updates
- Grant rights on a table
- Back up a database

Everything you read about the local InterBase in this chapter applies equally to the full-server version of InterBase. As a result, this chapter will also be of interest to people who use InterBase on a network.

If you work with another database (such as Oracle), you might still be interested in the material found in this chapter.

Databases and the Job Market

You probably work inside a corporation or at a small company. However, if you are a student or someone who wants to enter the computer programming world, you should pay special attention to the material in this and other chapters on InterBase.

Perhaps 80 percent of the applications built in America today use databases in one form or another. Indeed, most of these applications revolve around, and are focused on, manipulating databases. Furthermore, client/server databases such as InterBase, Oracle, and MS SQL Server form the core of this application development.

If you want to enter the programming world, getting a good knowledge of databases is one of the best ways to get started. Right now, there is virtually an endless need for good database programmers.

One note of caution should be added here. While I enjoy database programming, it is not the most romantic end of the computer business. If you're primarily interested in systems programming or game programming, then you should hold out for jobs in those fields rather than focus your career in an area of only minor interest to you.

Databases, however, offer the greatest opportunity for employment. In particular, client/server database programmers are almost always in demand. Because LIBS ships with your copy of C++Builder, you have a great chance to learn the ins and outs of this lucrative field.

Getting Started with InterBase

In particular, this chapter shows how you can use a local system to create a database that is fully compatible with the network version of InterBase. To convert a LIBS database to a real client/server application on a network, you just have to copy your database onto another machine:

```
copy MyDatabase.gdb p:\remote\nt\drive
```

You just copy the database file onto the network. No other steps are necessary, other than changing the path in your alias. Of course, you will also need a real copy of the InterBase server.

Note that the Enterprise version of C++Builder ships with five licenses for the full InterBase server. The real InterBase server runs on most platforms, including Windows 9x, Windows NT, and a wide range of UNIX platforms.

Many readers of this book will come from the world of "big iron," where the only kinds of databases that exist are servers such as Oracle, Sybase, InterBase, AS400, or DB2. Other readers come from the world of PCs, where tools such as dBASE, Paradox, Access, or FoxPro are considered the standard database tools. Overemphasizing the huge gap that exists between these two worlds is almost impossible.

Readers who are familiar with big iron and large network-based servers are likely to find the LIBS very familiar. Readers who come from the world of PCs are likely to find InterBase very strange indeed.

InterBase is meant to handle huge numbers of records, which are stored on servers. It does not come equipped with many of the amenities of a tool, such as dBASE or Paradox. In fact, InterBase supplies users with minimal interface and expects you to create programs with a client-side tool such as C++Builder. However, you will find that InterBase is not a particularly difficult challenge after you get some of the basics under your belt.

Setting Up the Local InterBase

Owners of C++Builder 4 Professional and Enterprise have the option to install LIBS when they install C++Builder. Enterprise users will also get a five-user license to a full-blown network-based version of the product. In most cases, InterBase will run smoothly without any need for you to worry about setup. However, you should take several key steps to ensure that all is as it should be.

If you have the Enterprise version of C++Builder, take a few moments to install the full network-based version of InterBase server, and use that instead of LIBS. As I stated, you will find no difference in the way LIBS works and the way the full InterBase server works; one just has more power than the other.

To install the InterBase server, click the InterBase 5.5 link on the C++Builder install launcher. When you install the true version of the InterBase server, you will find a file called SvrKey.txt in the IB5 directory on the C++Builder CD-ROM. This file contains the certificate information needed during the installation. Here is an example of the format of the registration keys:

```
Certificate ID:   XX-XX-ISC-XXXXX
Certificate Key:   XX-XX-XX-XX
```

The simplest way to enter these keys is to cut and paste between the list on the CD-ROM and the edit boxes in the InterBase install program.

Everything should work correctly after you install the full InterBase server and client. You can run the InterBase License Registration License Registration >utility if InterBase isn't installed correctly. To do so, choose Start, Programs, InterBase, License Registration Tool. After the License Registration application loads, enter all the keys you need, as defined in IBKey.txt from the CD-ROM.

Getting everything set up properly is very important. InterBase does not always give you sensible error messages when you don't have the keys installed properly. Instead, you might get an error message that leads you to look in some completely different area to fix the problem. You simply must have the product registered properly before you try to use it; otherwise, the product's behavior is completely undefined.

Working with the Local InterBase Server
CHAPTER 11

509

11

WORKING WITH
THE LOCAL
INTERBASE SERVER

> **CAUTION**
>
> You can drive yourself mad by having the product partially registered. For example, you might be able to get data from the product, update records, and so on, and think all is fine. Then you try to change some metadata. If the product is not registered to support this feature, your attempts will fail and the error messages you get back might not even hint at the fact that the product is not correctly registered. They might point you off in some other direction altogether. The simplest thing is to fully register the product right from the start and then run simple tests to ensure that it is working.

After you register the product, find out if LIBS or the real InterBase server is running. It will load into memory by default every time you boot up the system. If you're running Windows 9x, or NT 4, you should see the InterBase Guardian as a little splash of green on the system tray to the right of the toolbar. On Windows NT 3.51, an icon appears at the bottom of your screen. Click this green object, no matter what shape it takes, and you will see a report on the Local InterBase Server configuration.

The InterBase Guardian is actually a helper program designed to keep the server running. If for some reason your server is blown out of the water, the Guardian will start it again automatically. The Guardian will do nothing if you intentionally shut down the server. On NT, both the Guardian and the server are listed in the control panel's Services applet. You can read more about the Guardian in the operations guide for InterBase.

You must know where your copy of LIBS is installed. Most likely, it is in the `\Program Files\InterBase Corp\InterBase` subdirectory on the boot drive of your computer. Alternatively, it could be in the `\Program Files\Borland\IntrBase` subdirectory, which is where this file was put in previous versions of C++Builder. To find out where LIBS is installed for sure, right-click the InterBase icon on your taskbar and choose Properties; if you started InterBase as a service, examine the properties of your InterBase icons on the Windows Start menu.

To find this same information in the Registry, run `REGEDIT.EXE` and open `HKEY_LOCAL_MACHINE/Software/InterBase Corp/InterBase`.

Several nodes report on your server's location and other related information. (On Windows NT 3.51 machines, the program is called `REGEDIT32.EXE`.)

You should also be able to locate a copy of `GDS32.DLL` somewhere on your system, most likely in the `Windows\System` subdirectory or the `WinNT\System32` subdirectory, but possibly in either your `Bde` or `IntrBase` subdirectory.

A common problem occurs when InterBase users end up with more than one copy of GDS32.DLL. If you work with the networked version of InterBase, you probably already have a copy of the InterBase Client on your system. If this is the case, you should make sure that you don't have two sets of the file GDS32.DLL on your path. On my system, I use the copy of GDS32.DLL that comes with the InterBase server, instead of the one for LIBS. These tools communicate with both LIBS and the full networked version of InterBase. The point is not which version you use, but only that you know which version is on your path and that you have only one version on your system at a time.

Borland almost always puts the version number of a product as the time at which the files were modified. InterBase is on version 5.5 at the time of this writing. Therefore, your version of GDS32.DLL should be made at 6:50 a.m. or later, and should have a date of 10-18-98 or later. Make sure you are not running on an older version of GDS32.DLL, which could have gotten copied over with the new version installed by C++Builder.

To find out which version of InterBase you are currently using, run the InterBase Communication Diagnostic Tool that ships with C++Builder.

Use the Browse button to find the EMPLOYEE.GDB file, which is probably located in the \Program Files\InterBase Corp\InterBase\examples\database directory. Enter **SYSDBA**—all uppercase—as the username, and **masterkey**—all lowercase— as the password. (This example assumes that you have not changed the password from its default value.) You should get something similar to the following readout:

```
Path Name      = C:\WINNT\System32\gds32.dll
Size           = 335360 Bytes
File Time      = 06:50:00
File Date      = 10/18/1998
Version        = 5.5.0.742
This module has passed the version check.

Attempting to attach to D:\Program Files\
   InterBase Corp\InterBase\examples\database\Employee.gdb
      Attaching      ...Passed!
      Detaching      ...Passed!

InterBase versions for this connection:
InterBase/x86/Windows NT (access method), version "WI-V5.5.0.742"
on disk structure version 9.1

InterBase Communication Test Passed!
```

The key piece of information you're getting here is the location and version number of GDS32.DLL.

Here is how part of this output would look if you are connecting to the previous version of the server:

```
InterBase versions for this connection:
InterBase/x86/Windows NT (access method), version "WI-V4.2.1.328"
on disk structure version 8.0
```

This report comes from InterBase version 4.2, not from 5.5. If possible, you should make sure that your system is upgraded to version 5.5. Of course, you might have a later version of the product on your system. The point here is that you should be able to find a version number and be able to read it.

> **NOTE**
>
> If you want to connect to the full server version of InterBase, you will find that the procedure I have just outlined works fine, except that you must first have a network protocol such as TCP/IP loaded. This task is usually handled automatically by either Windows 9x or Windows NT. Setting up an InterBase connection is usually a fairly straightforward process when compared to setting up other servers.

The most obvious thing that can go wrong with an InterBase connection is it not starting automatically when you start Windows. If you are having trouble, try simply pointing the Explorer to the InterBase/bin subdirectory and clicking the IBServer.exe icon. The trouble could be that all is set up correctly, but for some reason the server is not currently running on your machine.

Setting Up an InterBase Alias

In the preceding section, you learned how to run a diagnostic tool to be sure that you are connected to InterBase. This section deals making sure that the BDE is able to connect to InterBase through the native SQL links driver. In other words, the previous section deals with making sure that InterBase runs correctly on your machine; this section deals with making sure C++Builder is connected to InterBase.

After you have InterBase set up, take a few minutes to make sure the connection to the BDE is working correctly. In particular, make sure an alias points to one of the sample tables that ships with LIBS. For example, after a normal full installation of C++Builder, you should have an alias called IBLocal that points to the EMPLOYEE.GDB file.

Next, you'll learn how to set up an alias identical to the IBLocal alias, except you can give it a different name. To begin, open the SQL Explorer and turn to the Databases page. Select the first node in the tree, the one that's called `Databases`. Choose Object, New, and then select `INTRBASE` as the Database Driver Name in the New Database Alias dialog. Click OK.

Name the new alias `TESTGDB` (or whatever name you prefer). The `ServerName` property for this alias should be set to `C:\Program Files\InterBase Corp\InterBase\Examples\Database\employee.gdb`. You can adjust the drive letter and path to reflect the way you have set up the files on your machine.

> **NOTE**
>
> When you are running against a server on a remote machine, you should reference that server in your server name:
>
> `\\Spider\c:\InterBase\Examples\Database\Employee.gdb`

Instead of trying to type this information directly, use the Browse button to search across your hard drive with the File Open dialog box. To get to this dialog box, look for the ellipsis (...) button on the far right of the editor control that lets you type in the server name.

Set the username to `SYSDBA`, and use the default password `masterkey`. (If someone has changed the password on your system, use the new password. You can change the default password in the InterBase Server Manager, as described later in this chapter's "Security and the InterBase Server Manager.") All the other settings in the SQL Explorer can have their default values, as shown in Figure 11.1. After you have everything set up correctly, choose Object, Apply. Click OK on the Save prompt.

FIGURE 11.1

A sample InterBase alias as it appears in the Database Explorer.

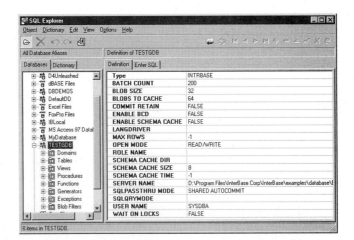

After you have set up and saved your alias, you can connect to the TESTGDB alias exactly as you would with any other set of data. From inside the SQL Explorer, just click the plus symbol before the TESTGDB node. A dialog box prompts you for a password. Make sure that the username is set to SYSDBA; enter **masterkey** as the password. Everything else will then be the same as when you're working with a Paradox table, except that you will find many new features, including stored procedures and triggers. Most of these new features are described in this chapter and the next.

To connect to the database from C++Builder, first drop a TTable component onto a form and set its DatabaseName property to **TESTGDB**. You are prompted for a password when you try to bring down the list of TableNames. Enter **masterkey** at this point, all in lower-case. Now bring down the list again and select a table. After taking these steps, you can set the Active property for Table1 to **true**. Everything is set up correctly if this call succeeds, and you can begin using the InterBase to create C++Builder database programs. If you can't set Active to true, go over the steps outlined previously and see if you can correct the problem.

> **NOTE**
>
> I usually use SYSDBA and masterkey as the username and password combination for the InterBase databases in this book. However, I sometimes work with USER1 and USER1 instead, simply because typing USER1 is easier than typing masterkey. One way to change the sign-on criteria for InterBase is via the InterBase Server Manager. The Server Manager is discussed later in "Security and the InterBase Server Manager."

In the preceding two sections you learned the basic facts about using LIBS. The next step is to learn how to create your own databases and tables.

Creating Databases

Unlike local Paradox or dBASE files, InterBase tables are not stored in separate files located within a directory. Instead, InterBase tables are stored in one large file called a *database*. Therefore, you must first go out and create a database; then you can create a series of tables inside this larger database.

> **NOTE**
>
> The single-file system is vastly superior to having a series of separate files. I'm sure you've noticed what happens after you have placed a few indexes on a typical Paradox table. The end result is that your table is associated with six or seven other files, some of which must be present if you want to get at your data. These files have names like Address.XG0 and Address.XG1. A big Paradox database might consist of a hundred or more files, all of which must be backed up, moved from place to place, and maintained. Life is much simpler when your whole database is stored in a single file!

The simplest way to create a database is with a third-party CASE tool such as SDesigner or Cadet. However, these tools do not ship with C++Builder, so you must instead choose from the Database Desktop (DBD), C++Builder itself, or the WISQL program that ships with the Local InterBase Server. WISQL stands for *Windows Interactive Structured Query Language*, or simply the *Interactive SQL tool*. Without a CASE tool, I find that my weapon of choice is WISQL, though this decision is certainly debatable. You can open this program by choosing Start, Programs, InterBase, InterBase Windows ISQL.

Using WISQL

WISQL is fundamentally a tool for entering SQL statements, with a few other simple features thrown in for good measure. One advantage of relying on WISQL is that it enables you to work directly in the mother tongue of databases, which is SQL. I find that defining databases directly in SQL helps me understand their structure, though there is little reason for resorting to these measures if you have a copy of SDesigner or ERWin available. (Cadet is a much less expensive tool that might still be available as shareware when you read this chapter.)

Also remember that WISQL bypasses the BDE altogether. You can therefore use it to test your connections to InterBase even if you are not sure whether you have the BDE set up correctly. For example, if you're having trouble connecting to InterBase and are not sure where the problem lies, start by trying to connect with WISQL. If that works, but you can't connect from inside C++Builder, the problem might lie not with your InterBase setup, but with the your BDE setup.

After you start WISQL, choose File, Create Database. A dialog like the one shown in Figure 11.2 appears. Set the Location Info to Local Engine because you are, in fact, working with Local InterBase. (Actually, I can't think of any reason why you must use Local InterBase rather than the full server version when you're working through these examples. However, I will reference LIBS throughout this chapter because it is the tool of choice for most readers.)

FIGURE 11.2

The dialog used to create databases inside WISQL.

In the Database field, enter the name of the database you want to create. If it is to be located inside a particular directory, include that directory in the database name. For practice, let's create a database called Info.gdb that is located in a subdirectory called Data.

First go to Windows Explorer and create the **Data** subdirectory (if it does not already exist on your system). After you set up the subdirectory, enter the following in the Database field:

D:\Data\Info.gdb

You can replace **D** with the appropriate drive on your system.

> **NOTE**
>
> The extension .gdb is traditional, though not mandatory. However, I suggest always using this extension so that you can recognize your databases instantly when you see them. Accidentally deleting even a recently backed up database can be a tragedy.

You can set the username to anything you want, although the traditional entry is SYSDBA and the traditional password is masterkey. When you start out with InterBase, sticking with this username and password combination is probably best. Even if you assign new passwords to your database, the SYSDBA/masterkey combination will work unless you explicitly remove it using the InterBase Server Manager (IBMGR32.EXE). Of course, you want to be more careful about how you set up your password when you have sensitive data to protect.

After you enter a username and password, you can create the database by clicking OK. If all goes well, you are then placed back inside WISQL. At this stage, you can either quit

WISQL or add a table to your database. An error message will appear if something goes wrong. Click the Details button on the Error dialog to try to track down the problem.

Creating a Table

Assuming all goes well, you can run the following SQL statement inside WISQL if you want to create a very simple table with two fields:

```
CREATE TABLE TEST1 (FIRST VARCHAR(20), LAST INTEGER);
```

Enter this line in the SQL Statement field at the top of WISQL and then click Run. (The Run button has a lightning bolt on it.) You can also select Query, Execute from the menu or press Ctrl+Enter to run the query. If all goes smoothly, your statement is echoed in the WISQL output window without being accompanied by an Error dialog. The lack of an Error dialog signals that the table has been created successfully.

The preceding CREATE TABLE command creates a table with two fields. The first is a character field that contains 20 characters, the second is an integer field. After you create a database and table, choose File, Commit Work. This command causes WISQL to actually carry out the commands you have issued; then choose File, Disconnect from Database.

The table-creation code shown here is used to describe or create a table in terms that WISQL understands. In fact, you can use this same code inside a TQuery object in a C++Builder program. Throughout most of this chapter and the next, I work with WISQL rather than with the DBD. In describing how to perform these actions in WISQL, I do not mean to imply that you can't use the Database Desktop to create or alter InterBase tables. In fact, the 32-bit version of DBD provides pretty good support for InterBase tables. Still, I have found WISQL considerably more powerful than I suspected when I began using it. Once again, I should add that neither of these tools is as easy to use as a good CASE tool.

In this section, you learned the basic steps required to use InterBase to create a database and table. The steps involved are not particularly complicated, although they can take a bit of getting used to if you're new to the world of SQL.

Exploring a Database with WISQL

WISQL provides several tools that can help you explore a database and its contents. In the preceding section you created a database with a single table. In this section you will learn how to connect to the database and table from inside WISQL. You also will see how to examine the main features of the entities you have created.

Working with the Local InterBase Server

CHAPTER 11

517

11

WORKING WITH
THE LOCAL
INTERBASE SERVER

Choose File, Connect to Database to connect to `Info.gdb`; the dialog shown in Figure 11.3 comes up. Enter the drive and the database as **D:\Data\Info.gdb**, where **D** represents the appropriate drive on your machine. Enter the user as **SYSDBA** and the password as **masterkey**. If all goes well, you should be able to connect to the database by clicking OK. Once again, success is signaled by the lack of an error message.

FIGURE 11.3

Connecting to the `Info.gdb` *database using WISQL.*

Choose Metadata, Show, and select Database from the options as shown in Figure 11.4. After you click OK, the information displayed in the WISQL output window should look something like this:

```
SHOW DB
Database: c:\data\info.gdb
        Owner: SYSDBA
PAGE_SIZE 1024
Number of DB pages allocated = 234
Sweep interval = 20000
```

FIGURE 11.4

Preparing to view information on the `Info.gdb` *database.*

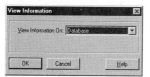

Choose Metadata, Show, Table to see the tables available in a database. You can leave the edit control labeled Object Name blank. If you fill it in with a table name, you will get detailed information on a specific table; you want general information on all tables in this case. Click OK and view the information, which should look like the following in the WISQL output window:

```
SHOW TABLES
    TEST1
```

Browse through the View Information dialog from the Metadata, Show menu choice; you can see that InterBase supports triggers, stored procedures, views, and a host of other advanced server features.

By choosing Metadata, Extract Database, you can find out more detailed information about the database and its tables. For example, if you choose Metadata, Extract Database, you get output similar to the following:

```
/* Extract Database d:\data\info.gdb */
CREATE DATABASE "d:\data\info.gdb" PAGE_SIZE 1024
;

/* Table: TEST1, Owner: SYSDBA */
CREATE TABLE TEST1 (FIRST VARCHAR(20),
        LAST INTEGER);

/* Grant permissions for this database */
```

If you choose Metadata, Extract Table, and select TEST1, you get the following output:

```
/* Extract Table TEST1 */

/* Table: TEST1, Owner: SYSDBA */
CREATE TABLE TEST1 (FIRST VARCHAR(20),
        LAST INTEGER);
```

Note that WISQL often asks whether you want to save the output from a command to a text file, and the File menu gives you some further options for saving information to files. You can take advantage of these options when necessary, but 90 percent of the time I pass them by with barely a nod. (Some CASE tools use the output from your choosing Metadata, Extract Database to reverse-engineer a database. If your CASE tool asks you for a script file, you can produce one this way.)

> **NOTE**
>
> The WISQL program accepts most SQL statements. For example, you can per-form `Insert`, `Select`, `Update`, and `Delete` statements from inside WISQL. Just enter the statement you want to perform in the SQL Statement area and then click Run.
>
> A book I have found useful for checking SQL syntax is called *The Practical SQL Handbook*, by Bowman, Emerson, and Darnovsky, Addison Wesley, ISBN 0-201-62623-3.

After reading the previous sections, you should have a fair understanding of how WISQL works and how you can use it to manage a database. The information provided in this chapter is simply an introduction to a complex and very sophisticated topic. However, you now know enough to begin using the Local InterBase. This accomplishment is not insignificant. Tools such as InterBase, Oracle, and Sybase lie at the heart of the client/server activity that is currently so volatile and lucrative. If you become proficient at talking to servers such as InterBase, you might find yourself at an important turning point in your career.

Manipulating Transactions

Now you can break out of the abstract theory rut and start writing some code that actually does something. You look at transactions in this section, followed by a discussion of cached updates. You see another real-world database in the next chapter, when you look at a sample program that tracks the albums, tapes, and CDs in a music collection.

The TRANSACT program, found on the CD-ROM that accompanies this book, gives a brief introduction to transactions. You must have a TDatabase component on your form in order to use transactions. Transactions work not only with real servers such as Sybase, Informix, InterBase, or the Local InterBase, but also with the 32-bit BDE drivers for Paradox or dBASE files. In other words, transactions can be part of most of the database work you will do with C++Builder. Using transactions is, however, a technique most frequently associated with client/server databases.

Creating the TRANSACT Program

To begin, drop a TDatabase component on a TDataModule. Name the TDatabase **TransDemo** and the TDataModule **DMod**, and save it in a file called **DMod1**, per the standards employed in this book. Set the AliasName property of the TDatabase object to a valid alias such as **IBLocal**. Create your own string, such as **TransactionDemo**, to fill in the DatabaseName property of the TDatabase object. In other words, when you're using a TDatabase component, you make up the DatabaseName rather than pick it from a list of available aliases.

Drop a TQuery object on the data module and hook it up to the EMPLOYEE.GDB file that ships with C++Builder. In particular, set the DatabaseName property of the TQuery object to **TransactionDemo**, not to IBLocal. In other words, set the DatabaseName property to the string you made up when filling in the DatabaseName property of the TDatabase component. You will find that TransactionDemo, or whatever string you chose, has been added to the list of aliases you can view from the property editor for the Query1 component's DatabaseName property. Now rename Query1 to **EmployeeQuery** and attach a

TDataSource object called `EmployeeSource` to it. Set the `EmployeeQuery` component's SQL property to the following string:

```
select * from employee
```

Set the `Active` property to **true** and set `RequestLive` to **true**.

Add a `TTable` object to the project, hook it up to the `SALARY_HISTORY` table, and call it **SalaryHistoryTable**. Set `Active` to **true**. Attach a data source called `SalaryHistorySource` to it. Relate the `SalaryHistoryTable` to the `EmployQuery` table via the `EMP_NO` fields of both tables. In particular, you should set the `MasterSource` property for the `SalaryHistoryTable` to **EmployeeSource**. Click the `MasterFields` property of the `TTable` object and relate the `EMP_NO` fields of both tables. This way you can establish a one-to-many relationship between the `EmployeeQuery` and the `SalaryHistoryTable`.

After you're connected to the database, you can add two grids to your main form so that you can view the data. Hook up one grid to one table via a `TDataSource` component and the second grid to the second table via a `TDataSource` component. Remember that you should choose File, Include Unit Hdr to link the `TDataModule` to the main form.

On the surface of the main form, add four buttons and give them the following captions:

```
Begin Transaction
Rollback
Commit
Refresh
```

The code associated with these buttons should look like this:

```cpp
void __fastcall TForm1::BeginTransactionClick(TObject *Sender)
{
  DMod->TransDemo->StartTransaction();
}

void __fastcall TForm1::RollbackClick(TObject *Sender)
{
  DMod->TransDemo->Rollback();
  RefreshClick(0);
}

void __fastcall TForm1::CommitClick(TObject *Sender)
{
  DMod->TransDemo->Commit();
}

// Because of the indexing, we can't call Refresh explicitly
```

```
void __fastcall TForm1::RefreshClick(TObject *Sender)
{
  TBookmark Bookmark = DMod->EmployeeQuery->GetBookmark();
  DMod->EmployeeQuery->Close();
  DMod->EmployeeQuery->Open();
  DMod->EmployeeQuery->GotoBookmark(Bookmark);
  DMod->EmployeeQuery->FreeBookmark(Bookmark);
}
```

Using the TRANSACT Program

At this point, run the program, click Begin Transaction, and edit a record of the
SalaryHistoryTable. When you do so, be sure to fill in all the table's fields except for
the first and last, which are called EMP_NO and NEW_SALARY. Be sure not to touch either of
those fields; they will be filled in for you automatically. In particular, you might enter the
following values:

```
CHANGE_DATE: 12/12/12
UPDATER_ID: admin2
OLD_SALARY: 105900
PERCENT_CHANGE:
```

These values are not randomly chosen. For example, you must enter **admin2**, or some
other valid UPDATER_ID, in the UPDATER_ID field. You can, of course, enter whatever values you want for the date, old salary, and percent change fields. Still, you must be careful
when working with the Employee tables. This database has referential integrity with a
vengeance.

After entering the preceding values, you can post the record by moving off it. When you
do, the NEW_SALARY field will be filled in automatically by something called a *trigger*. Go
ahead and experiment with these tables. For example, you might leave some of the fields
blank or enter invalid data in the UPDATER_ID field just to see how complex the rules that
govern this database are. This data is locked up tighter than Fort Knox, and you can't
change it unless you are very careful about what you're doing. (It's worth noting, however, that the developers of this database probably never planned to have anyone use these
two tables exactly as I do here. Defining rules that limit how you work with a database is
easy, but finding ways to break them is easier still. For all of its rigor, database programming is still not an exact science.)

If you started your session by clicking the Begin Transaction button, you can now click
RollBack and then Refresh. You will find that all your work is undone, as if none of the
editing occurred. If you edit three or four records and then click Commit, you will find
that your work is preserved.

> **NOTE**
>
> Although you are safe in this particular case, in some instances like this you can't call Refresh directly because the table you're using is not uniquely indexed. In lieu of this call, you can close the table and then reopen it. You could use bookmarks to preserve your location in the table during this operation, or if you're working with a relatively small dataset you can just let the user fend for himself or herself.

Note that you don't have to specify a password when you run the TRANSACT program included on the CD-ROM because the `TDatabase` object's `LoginPrompt` property is set to `false`, and the `Params` property contains the following string:

```
password=masterkey
```

Understanding Transactions

Now that you have seen transactions in action, you probably want a brief explanation of what they are all about. Here are some reasons to use transactions:

- *To ensure the integrity of your data.* Sometimes you must perform a transaction that affects several related tables. In these cases, altering two tables and then finding that the session is interrupted for some reason before you can alter the next two tables might not be a good idea. For example, you might find that a data entry clerk posts data to two records, but the system crashes before he can finish updating two more records in a different table. As a result, the data in your database might be out of sync. To avoid this situation, you can start a transaction, edit all the rows and tables that must be edited, and then commit the work in one swift movement. This way, an error is far less likely to occur because of a system crash or power failure.

- *To handle concurrency issues in which two or more people are accessing the same data at the same time.* You can use a transactions feature called `TransIsolation` levels to fine-tune exactly how and when updates are made. This way, you can decide how you will react if another user is updating records exactly on or near the record you're currently editing.

Now that you have read something about the theory behind transactions, you might want to think for a moment about the `TDatabase` object's `TransIsolation` property, which affects the way transactions are handled. Here are some quotes from the very important VCL online help entry called "TDatabase::TransIsolation":

- `tiDirtyRead`—Permits reading of uncommitted changes made to the database by other simultaneous transactions. Uncommitted changes are not permanent and can be rolled back (undone) at any time. At this level a transaction is least isolated from the effects of other transactions.
- `tiReadCommitted`—Permits reading of committed (permanent) changes made to the database by other simultaneous transactions. This is the default `TransIsolation` property value.
- `tiRepeatableRead`—Permits a single, one-time reading of the database. The transaction can't see any subsequent changes made by other simultaneous transactions. This isolation level guarantees that after a transaction reads a record, its view of that record does not change unless it makes a modification to the record itself. At this level, a transaction is most isolated from other transactions.

You can usually leave this field set to `tiReadCommitted`. However, you need to understand that you have several options regarding how the data in your database is affected by a transaction. The whole subject of how one database user might alter records in a table while they are being used by another user is quite complicated, and it poses several paradoxes for which no simple solution exists. The preceding `TransIsolation` levels enable you to choose your poison when dealing with this nasty subject.

You must consider other issues when you're working with transactions, but I have tried to cover some of the most important here. In general, I find that transactions are extremely easy to use. However, they become more complex when you consider the delicate subject of concurrency problems, which are frequently addressed through setting your transactions' `TransIsolation` levels.

Cached Updates

Cached updates are like the transactions just described, except that they enable you to edit a series of records without causing any network traffic. When you are ready to commit your work, cached updates enable you to do so on a record-by-record basis, where any records that violate system integrity can be repaired or rolled back on a case-by-case basis.

> **NOTE**
>
> Some users have reported remarkable increases in performance on some operations when they use cached updates.

The key feature of cached updates is that they let you work with data without allowing any network traffic to occur until you are ready for it to begin. A relatively complex mechanism also enables you to keep track of the status of each record on a field-by-field basis. In particular, when cached updates are turned on, you can query your records one at a time and ask them whether they have been updated. Furthermore, if they have been updated, you can ask the current value of each field in the updated record, and you can also retrieve the old or original value of the field.

You can do three things with the records in a dataset after the CachedUpdates property for the dataset has been set to true:

- You can call ApplyUpdates() on the dataset, which means that you will try to commit all the other records updated since CachedUpdates was set to true or since the last attempt to update the records. This is analogous to committing a transaction.
- You can call CancelUpdates(), which means that all the updates made so far will be canceled. This is analogous to rolling back a transaction.
- You can call RevertRecord(), which will roll back the current record but no other records in the dataset.

An excellent sample program in the C++Builder4\Examples\DBTasks\CachedUp subdirectory shows how to use cached updates. This program is a bit complex in its particulars, however, and can therefore be hard to understand. Instead of trying to go it one better, I will create a sample program that takes the basic elements of cached updates and presents them in the simplest possible terms.

The CacheUp program, shown in Figure 11.5, has one form. There is a copy of the Orders table on the form. Recall that the Orders table is related to both the Customer and the Items tables. As a result, changing either the OrderNo or CustNo fields without violating system integrity in one way or another is difficult. When working with this program, you should change these fields to values such as 1 or 2, which will almost surely be invalid. You can watch what happens when you try to commit the records you have changed.

The code for the CacheUp program is shown in Listings 11.1 and 11.2. Get this program running and then come back for a discussion of how it works. When you're implementing the code, the key point to remember is that none of it will work unless the CachedUpdates property of the OrdersTable is set to true.

FIGURE 11.5

The CacheUp program.

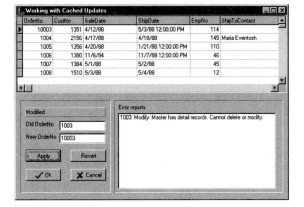

LISTING 11.1 THE HEADER FOR THE CACHEUP PROGRAM'S MAIN FORM

```cpp
#ifndef MainH
#define MainH

#include <Classes.hpp>
#include <Controls.hpp>
#include <StdCtrls.hpp>
#include <Forms.hpp>
#include <Buttons.hpp>
#include <Db.hpp>
#include <DBGrids.hpp>
#include <DBTables.hpp>
#include <ExtCtrls.hpp>
#include <Grids.hpp>

class TForm1 : public TForm
{
__published:    // IDE-managed Components
  TBevel *Bevel1;
  TLabel *Label1;
  TLabel *Label2;
  TLabel *Label3;
  TBevel *Bevel2;
  TDBGrid *DBGrid1;
  TBitBtn *bApply;
  TBitBtn *bRevert;
  TBitBtn *BitBtn1;
  TPanel *Panel1;
  TEdit *Edit1;
  TEdit *Edit2;
  TListBox *ListBox1;
  TBitBtn *BitBtn2;
  TTable *Table1;
```

continues

LISTING 11.1   CONTINUED

```
   TDataSource *DataSource1;
   void __fastcall bApplyClick(TObject *Sender);
   void __fastcall bRevertClick(TObject *Sender);
   void __fastcall Table1UpdateError(TDataSet *DataSet, EDatabaseError *E,
         TUpdateKind UpdateKind, TUpdateAction &UpdateAction);
   void __fastcall BitBtn1Click(TObject *Sender);
   void __fastcall DataSource1DataChange(TObject *Sender, TField *Field);
   void __fastcall BitBtn2Click(TObject *Sender);
private:    // User declarations
public:         // User declarations
   __fastcall TForm1(TComponent* Owner);
};

extern PACKAGE TForm1 *Form1;

#endif
```

LISTING 11.2   THE SOURCE FOR THE CACHEUP PROGRAM'S MAIN FORM

```
////////////////////////////////////
//    File: Main.cpp
// Project: CacheUp
//
//

// Working with cached updates.

// The simplest way to see the program in action is
// to change the OrderNo of several records to small
// integer values such as 1, 2, or 3. The press
// apply to see the errors this generates. The errors
// occur because these small integer values violate
// database integrity. To revert back to the old
// values press cancel. To change one value back at
// a time, first select the value,) press Revert.

#include <vcl.h>
#pragma hdrstop

#include <typinfo.hpp>
#include "Main.h"

#pragma package(smart_init)
#pragma resource "*.dfm"
TForm1 *Form1;

__fastcall TForm1::TForm1(TComponent* Owner)
  : TForm(Owner)
```

```
{
}

void __fastcall TForm1::bApplyClick(TObject *Sender)
{
  Table1->ApplyUpdates();
}

void __fastcall TForm1::bRevertClick(TObject *Sender)
{
  Table1->RevertRecord();
}

void __fastcall TForm1::Table1UpdateError(TDataSet *DataSet,
      EDatabaseError *E, TUpdateKind UpdateKind,
      TUpdateAction &UpdateAction)
{
  String S1;
  switch (UpdateKind) {
    case ukModify : S1 = "Modify: " + E->Message; break;
    case ukInsert : S1 = "Insert: " + E->Message; break;
    case ukDelete : S1 = "Delete: " + E->Message; break;
  }
  String S2 = DataSet->Fields->Fields[0]->OldValue;
  S2 = S2  + ": " + S1;
  ListBox1->Items->Add(S2);
  UpdateAction = uaSkip;
}

void __fastcall TForm1::BitBtn1Click(TObject *Sender)
{
  Table1->CancelUpdates();
}

void __fastcall TForm1::DataSource1DataChange(TObject *Sender,
      TField *Field)
{
  switch (Table1->UpdateStatus()) {
    case usUnmodified   : Panel1->Caption = "Unmodified"; break;
    case usModified   : Panel1->Caption = "Modified"; break;
    case usInserted   : Panel1->Caption = "Inserted"; break;
    case usDeleted  : Panel1->Caption = "Deleted"; break;
  }
  if (Table1->UpdateStatus() == usModified) {
    Edit1->Text = Table1->Fields->Fields[0]->OldValue;
    Edit2->Text = Table1->Fields->Fields[0]->NewValue;
  }
  else {
    Edit1->Text = "Unmodified";
    Edit2->Text = "Unmodified";
  }
```

continues

LISTING 11.2   CONTINUED

```
}

void __fastcall TForm1::BitBtn2Click(TObject *Sender)
{
  Close();
}
```

The first thing to notice about the CacheUp program is that it tracks which records have been modified. For example, change the OrderNo field of the first two records to the values 1 and 2. If you now select one of these records, you will see that the small panel in the lower-left corner of the screen gets set to Modified. This means that the update status for this field has been set to modified.

Here is the TUpdateStatus type:

```
enum TUpdateStatus { usUnmodified, usModified, usInserted, usDeleted };
```

Any particular record in a database is going to be set to one of these values.

Here is the code that sets the caption of the Panel component:

```
void __fastcall TForm1::DataSource1DataChange(TObject *Sender,
      TField *Field)
{
  switch (Table1->UpdateStatus()) {
    case usUnmodified   : Panel1->Caption = "Unmodified"; break;
    case usModified     : Panel1->Caption = "Modified"; break;
    case usInserted     : Panel1->Caption = "Inserted"; break;
    case usDeleted   : Panel1->Caption = "Deleted"; break;
  }
  if (Table1->UpdateStatus() == usModified) {
    Edit1->Text = Table1->Fields->Fields[0]->OldValue;
    Edit2->Text = Table1->Fields->Fields[0]->NewValue;
  }
  else {
    Edit1->Text = "Unmodified";
    Edit2->Text = "Unmodified";
  }
}
```

The relevant line in this case is the first in the body of the function. In particular, notice that it reports on the value of Table1->UpdateStatus(). This value will change to reflect the update status of the currently selected record.

At the same time the CacheUp program reports that a record has been modified, it also reports on the old and new value of the OrderNo field for that record. In particular, if you change the first record's OrderNo field to 1, it reports that the old value for the field was

Working with the Local InterBase Server

CHAPTER 11

529

11

WORKING WITH
THE LOCAL
INTERBASE SERVER

1003 and the new value is 1. (This assumes that you have the original data as it shipped with C++Builder. Remember that if you end up ruining one of these tables performing these kinds of experiments, you can always copy the table again from the CD-ROM. If you copy them directly using the Windows Explorer, remember that they will probably have the Read Only flag turned on. You can use the Windows Explorer to remove these flags.)

The following code reports on the old and new value of the OrderNo field:

```
Edit1->Text = Table1->Fields->Fields[0]->OldValue;
Edit2->Text = Table1->Fields->Fields[0]->NewValue;
```

As you can see, this information is easy enough to come by; you just have to know where to look.

If you enter the values 1 and 2 into the OrderNo fields for the first two records, you will encounter errors when you try to commit the data. In particular, if you try to apply the data, the built-in referential integrity will complain that you cannot link the Orders and Items tables on the new OrderNo you have created. As a result, committing the records is impossible. The code then rolls back the erroneous records to their original state.

When you are viewing these kinds of errors, choose Tools, Debugger Options and then turn off Integrated debugging. Alternatively, you can keep debugging on but let the user program handle Delphi exceptions. You can tell C++Builder to let the user program handle the exception by selecting the Debugger Options dialog's Language Exceptions page and then turning off the Stop on Delphi Exceptions option. The issue here is that you want the exception to occur, but you don't want to be taken to the line in your program where the exception surfaced. You don't need to view the actual source code because these exceptions are not the result of errors in your code. In fact, these exceptions are of the kind you want and must produce and which appear to the user in an orderly fashion via the program's list box.

> **NOTE**
>
> Referential integrity is a means of enforcing the rules in a database. Some tables must obey rules, and the BDE won't let users enter invalid data that violates these rules.

Here is the code that reports on the errors in the OrderNo field and rolls back the data to its original state:

```
void __fastcall TForm1::Table1UpdateError(TDataSet *DataSet,
    EDatabaseError *E, TUpdateKind UpdateKind,
```

```
      TUpdateAction &UpdateAction)
{
  String S1;
  switch (UpdateKind) {
    case ukModify : S1 = "Modify: " +  E->Message; break;
    case ukInsert : S1 = "Insert: " +  E->Message; break;
    case ukDelete : S1 = "Delete: " +  E->Message; break;
  }
  String S2 = DataSet->Fields->Fields[0]->OldValue;
  S2 = S2  + ": " + S1;
  ListBox1->Items->Add(S2);
  UpdateAction = uaSkip;
}
```

This particular routine is an event handler for the OnUpdateError event for the Table1 object. To create the routine, click the Table1 object, select its Events page in the Object Inspector, and then double-click the OnUpdateError entry.

The Table1UpdateError() method is called only if an error occurs in attempting to update records. It is called at the time the error is detected and before C++Builder tries to commit the next record.

Table1UpdateError() gets passed four parameters. The most important is the last, which is a TUpdateAction reference. You can set this parameter to one of the following values:

```
enum TUpdateAction { uaFail, uaAbort, uaSkip, uaRetry, uaApplied };
```

If you set the UpdateAction variable to uaAbort, the entire attempt to commit the updated data will be aborted. None of your changes will take place, and you will return to edit mode as if you had never attempted to commit the data. The changes you have made so far will not be undone, but neither will they be committed. You are aborting the attempt to commit the data, but you are not rolling the data back to its previous state.

If you choose uaSkip, the data for the whole table will still be committed, but the record that is currently in error will be left alone; it will be left at the invalid value assigned to it by the user.

If you set UpdateAction to uaRetry, that means you have attempted to update the information in the current record and that you want to retry committing it. The record you should update is the current record in the dataset passed as the first parameter to Table1UpdateError().

In the Table1UpdateError() method, I always choose uaSkip as the value to assign to UpdateAction. Of course, you could bring up a dialog and show the user the old and

Working with the Local InterBase Server

CHAPTER 11

531

11

WORKING WITH
THE LOCAL
INTERBASE SERVER

new values of the current record. The user would then have a chance to retry committing the data. Once again, you retrieve the data containing the current "problem child" record from the dataset passed in the first parameter of `Table1UpdateError()`. I show an example of accessing this data when I retrieve the old value of the `OrderNo` field for the record:

```
String S2 = DataSet->Fields->Fields[0]->OldValue;
S2 = S2  + ": " + S1;
ListBox1->Items->Add(S2);
```

The `OldValue` field is declared as a `Variant` in `DB.HPP`, which is the place where the `TDataSet` declaration is located:

```
Variant __fastcall GetOldValue();
__property Variant OldValue = {read=GetOldValue};
```

Two other values are passed to the `Table1UpdateError()` method. The first is an exception reporting on the current error, and the second is a variable of type `TUpdateKind`:

```
enum TUpdateKind { ukModify, ukInsert, ukDelete };
```

The variable of type `TUpdateKind` just tells you how the current record was changed. Was it updated, inserted, or deleted? The exception information is passed to you primarily so that you can get at the message associated with the current error:

```
S1 = "Modify: " +  E->Message;
```

If you handle the function by setting `UpdateAction` to a particular value, `uaSkip` for instance, C++Builder will not bring up a dialog reporting the error to the user. Instead, it assumes that you are handling the error explicitly and leaves it up to you to report the error as you see fit. In this case, I dump the error into the program's list box, along with some other information.

At this point, you should go back and run the Examples\DBTasks\CachedUp\Cache program that ships with C++Builder. It covers all the same ground covered in the preceding text, but it does so in a slightly different form. In particular, it shows how to bring up a dialog so that you can handle each `OnUpdateError` event in an intelligent and sensible manner.

In general, cached updates give you a great deal of power you can tap into when updating the data in a dataset. If necessary, go back and play with the CacheUp program until it starts to make sense to you. This subject isn't prohibitively difficult, but absorbing the basic principles involved takes some thought.

Security and the InterBase Server Manager

Before beginning the discussion of the Music program in the next chapter, it's a good idea to cover a few basic issues regarding security. The Music program tracks a CD and record collection. The program shows a good deal about working with relational databases in general and about working with InterBase in particular.

I included enough information so far to make any C++Builder programmer dangerous, so I might as well also equip you with some of the tools you need to defend your work against prying eyes. If you have the skill to create programs that others can use, then you also need to know how to manage those clients.

When you are working with passwords, making a distinction between user security for an entire server and access rights for a particular table is important. You will find buttons that let you add new users for the system if you open the InterBase Server Manager, log on, and select Tasks, User Security. By default, these users have access to very little. All you do is let them in the front door. You haven't yet given them a pass to visit any particular rooms in the house. As this discussion matures, I'll discuss how to grant particular rights to a user after he or she has been admitted.

If you are interested in setting up real security for your database, the first thing you should do is change the SYSDBA password. To change the password, sign on to the InterBase Server Manager as SYSDBA using the password masterkey. Select Tasks, User Security from the menu. Select the username SYSDBA and choose Modify User; enter a new password. After you do this, the system is truly under your control. No one else can get at your data unless you decide that user should have the right to do so. Even then, you can severely proscribe that user's activities with a remarkable degree of detail. After you establish your sovereignty, the next step is to go out and recruit the peons who will inhabit your domain. After you find a new user, select Tasks, User Security, Add User; give him or her a password. The person who creates users is the one who signs on as SYSDBA. SYSDBA has all power, which is the reason that changing the SYSDBA password is important if you are really serious about security.

If you create a new user, this newcomer has no rights on the system by default. To give a user rights, you must use the SQL grant command, which is discussed in the next section.

Defining Access Rights to a Table

After you create a user in the InterBase Server Manager, you grant him or her rights to access a table. To do so, open WISQL or the SQL Explorer and connect to the database

Working with the Local InterBase Server

CHAPTER 11

533

11

WORKING WITH
THE LOCAL
INTERBASE SERVER

you want to work with. To grant rights, you can enter SQL statements into WISQL and then execute them by pressing Ctrl+Enter. The actual statements you can use are discussed over the course of the next few paragraphs.

SQL databases give you extraordinary control over exactly how much access a user can have to a table. For example, you can give a user only the right to query one or more tables in your database:

```
grant select on Test1 to user1
```

Conversely, you may give a user complete control over a table, including the right to grant others access to the table:

```
grant all on album to Sue with grant option
```

The `with grant option` clause shown here specifies that Sue not only has her way with the `Album` table, but also can give others access to the table.

You can give a user six distinct types of privileges:

- `all`—Has select, delete, insert, update, and execute privileges
- `select`—Can view a table or portion of a table
- `delete`—Can delete from a table or view
- `insert`—Can add data to a table or view
- `update`—Can edit a table or view
- `execute`—Can execute a stored procedure

Using these keys to the kingdom, you can quickly start handing out passes to particular rooms in the palace. For example, you can write the following:

```
grant insert on Test1 to Sue
grant delete on Test1 to Mary with grant option
grant select on Test1 to Tom, Mary, Sue, User1
grant select, insert, delete, update on Test1 to Mary
grant delete, insert, update,
   references on country to public with grant option;
```

The last statement in this list comes from the `Employee.gdb` example that ships with C++Builder. Notice that it grants rights to the public, which means all users have absurdly liberal rights on the table.

The opposite of the `grant` command is `revoke`, which removes privileges given with `grant`. Here is an example :

```
revoke select on Test1 from Sue
```

This brief overview of the Server Manager and some related issues involving the `grant` command should give you a sense of how to limit access to your database. None of this material is particularly difficult, but SQL databases can be frustrating if you don't know how to control them.

Backing Up Tables with the Server Manager

Another important feature of the InterBase Server Manager is backing up tables. This task can be especially important if you must move a table from Windows 9x/NT to UNIX. The highly compressed backup format for InterBase tables is completely version independent, so you can back up an NT table and then restore it on a UNIX system.

To get started backing up a database, sign on to the InterBase Server Manager. To sign on, all you must do is specify the `masterkey` password; everything else is automatic when signing on to the local version of InterBase. Of course, if you changed the `SYSDBA` password from `masterkey` to something else, then you must use the new password you created.

Go to the Tasks menu and select Backup. Enter the path to the local database you want to back up. For example, you might type c:\data\info.gdb in the edit control labeled Database Path. This means you want to back up the database called `info.gdb`.

Enter the name of the backup table you want to create in the `Backup File` or `Device` field. For example, you might type c:\data\info.gbk. Use the `GDB` extension for live tables and `GBK` for backed-up tables. These are just conventions, but they are good ones.

Select Transportable Format from the Options group box and set any other flags you want to use. Click OK and then be prepared for a short delay while InterBase contemplates certain knotty passages from the works of the philosopher Immanuel Kant. If all goes well, the results of your work might look something like this:

```
Backup started on Sat Feb 06 11:17:22 1999...

gbak: gbak version WI-V5.5.0.742
gbak:    Version(s) for database "c:\Data\Info.gdb"
    InterBase/x86/Windows NT (access method), version "WI-V5.5.0.742"
    on disk structure version 9.1

Request completed on Sat Feb 06 11:17:23 1999
```

You can now close the InterBase Server Manager and copy your backed-up file to a floppy disk, zip drive, or other storage medium. Remember, the great thing about these files is that they are small, highly compressed, and can be moved from one operating system to another.

> **NOTE**
>
> InterBase runs on a wide variety of UNIX platforms, including Linux.

Summary

This chapter gives you a basic introduction to the Local InterBase and to several related subjects. In particular, you learned how to create and open InterBase databases, how to set up aliases, and how to perform fundamental database tasks such as transactions.

I should stress that InterBase is a very complex and powerful product, and what you read in this chapter should serve as little more than a brief introduction that will whet your appetite. In the next chapter you look at stored procedures, triggers, InterBase calls, and a few other tricks that should help you grasp the extent of the power in both the local and server-based versions of InterBase.

C++Builder protects you from the details of how a server handles basic database chores. However, C++Builder also enables you to tap into the power associated with a particular server. This was one of the most delicate balances that the developers had to consider when they created the VCL: How can you make a database tool as generic as possible without cutting off a programmer's access to a particular server's special capabilities? The same type of question drove the developers' successful quest to make VCL's language as simple and elegant as possible without cutting off access to the full power of the Windows API.

Now you can forage on to the next chapter. By this time, you are deep into the subject of databases. In fact, the stage is now set to open a view onto the most powerful tools in a database programmer's arsenal. After you master the stored procedures, generators, and triggers shown in the next chapter, you will be entering the world of real client/server programming as it is done on the professional level. These tools drive the big databases used by corporations, governments, and educational institutions around the world.

CHAPTER 12

InterBase Programming

*by Charlie Calvert
and Kent Reisdorph*

IN THIS CHAPTER

In this chapter you get a look at a fairly entertaining relational database and accompanying program called Music that tracks a CD and record collection. The program shows a good deal about working with relational databases in general and about working with InterBase in particular. The text and code are designed to advance your knowledge of SQL, database design, and client/server programming.

Important subjects covered in this chapter include

- Relational database design.
- Referential integrity.
- Stored procedures and the `TStoredProc` components.
- Triggers.
- Generators.
- Domains.
- Using SQL to extract facts from a database. How many of this type of item do I have? How can I write a stored procedure that retrieves information from several tables at once while still answering a real-world question about the amount of a particular kind of data?
- Placing forms on a TabControl. The kdAdd program had a huge number of fields in the main form for the application. In this chapter you see how to create separate forms for each page in a tabbed notebook. Each page exists inside its own discrete object, which helps you create well-organized, robust applications.
- Storing multiple types of data in a database and displaying it in a flexible manner. This database contains a table with information on books and another table with information on records. The TabControl technique described in the preceding bullet point allows you to seamlessly integrate different types of data in what appears to the user as one form. From the user's point of view, it seems that the program morphs to accommodate the type of data currently being displayed.
- Using SQL to alter a table.

The burden of the argument for this chapter is again carried by a sample database application. This one is designed to track household items such as books, CDs, or records. However, you can easily expand it to hold many different types of data. The core strength of this program is its flexible, extensible design.

By the time you finish this chapter, you should have a pretty good feel for how to tap into the power of InterBase. This chapter is not meant to appeal only to InterBase developers, however. It also contains many general comments about working with relational databases in general and SQL databases in particular. In other words, this chapter is about real client/server database programming.

Admittedly, database programming is not a particularly glamorous subject—but it does have its joys, and I hope that some of them become apparent while you are reading this chapter. The Music program digs far enough down into the guts of database design to let you have a little bit of fun. It's actually fairly interesting to see just how far you can go with a few tables and a couple of lines of SQL. By the time you are done, you should get the sense that you can ask this database just about anything about your record collection, and it will come back with all kinds of interesting bits of information.

About the Music Program

One of the interesting features of the Music database is the way it uses stored procedures to report on the information in the database. For instance, it lets you store CDs, tapes, and records and rate them according to four different, extensible criteria:

- What type of music is it? Classical? Jazz? Rock? Do you have categories of your own you want to add?
- How loud is the music? Is it peaceful, moderate, or raucous? You can add other categories if you want.
- How good is the music? On a scale of 1 to 10, how do you rate it?
- Finally, what medium is it on? CD? Tape? Record? DVD?

You can easily expand most of these lists to create as many categories as you want. Furthermore, you can query the database to ask questions such as

- How many records do I have?
- How many different artists are listed here?
- How many albums do I have that I rated in a certain range? For instance, which records did I rate as a complete 10? Which ones did I rate as only a 1 or 2?
- Which albums did I rate as loud?
- What albums are listed under the categories called Jazz or Folk?

The Music program uses several advanced Borland C++Builder 4 database features. For instance, you will find examples of data modules, lookups, filters, and searching a database with FindFirst() and FindNearest(). This program uses many other standard database techniques, such as calculated fields and working with ranges. You will also find numerous examples of how to use stored procedures and an example of how to search on records in the detail table of a master-detail relationship.

A complete copy of the Music database is available on the CD-ROM that accompanies this book. The first half of this chapter talks about the incremental steps involved in creating this database, but if you feel the need to see the complete database at any time, you can retrieve it from the CD-ROM in the file called `Music.gdb` in the `Data` directory.

To set up the alias for the database, choose Database, Explore to bring up the SQL Explorer. From the menu in the SQL Explorer, choose Object, New. Select `INTRBASE` as the type of alias you want to create and name the alias `MUSIC`. Set the User Name property to `SYSDBA` and the Server Name property so that it points to the place on your hard drive where you have installed the `MUSIC.GDB` file. Choose Object, Apply to save your work. Figure 12.1 shows how the alias should look when you are done.

FIGURE 12.1

The alias for `MUSIC.GDB` *as it appears in the SQL Explorer.*

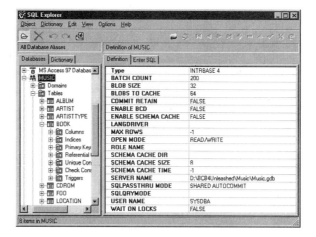

Music is a fairly complex program, but it gives you lots of hints on how to use a SQL database to your advantage. If you are having trouble with it, check my Web sites for tips or hints on using the program (`http://users.aol.com/charliecal`).

Overall, this chapter aims at taking the discussion of databases to a new level. After you read the text, you will be prepared to write professional-level client/server applications. All the information in this chapter applies to common professional database tasks such as creating an inventory system or even a point-of-sale application.

Designing the Music Program

It's now time to begin work on the Music program. This program enables you to keep track of CDs, records, tapes, and books. The main goal of the program is to enable you to enter the name of an artist (a musician or a writer) and add one or more titles associated with that artist.

NOTE

The main table of the Music program is called Artist for historical reasons. The database was originally intended to hold only CDs, records, and tapes. I expanded the program's scope later when I suddenly saw the way clear to add the Books table to the project.

The Music program uses eight tables, but three of them—Artist, Book, and Album—dominate the application. The Artist table is the master table; Book and Album are detail tables.

Besides the three main tables, several lookup tables are used to store the various lists of possible categories to which the albums and books can belong. Lookups are described in Chapter 8, "Fields and Database Tools," and Chapter 9, "Flat-File Real-World Databases." In this case, a lookup can allow you to convert a simple integer value into a string, by looking up the string associated with an integer. For instance, a record can be of type Jazz, Rock, Folk, Blues, and so on, and a book can be of type Fiction, Computer, Mystery, Science Fiction, Reference, and so on. These words are stored in lookup tables, while only a simple integer value is stored in the main table. This feature saves room in your database by allowing you to store a simple integer such as 1 or 2 in your main table and the string associated with that integer in a lookup table. Therefore, you store the string value only in one row rather than having to store it over and over again in multiple rows. You can store information used by both the Album and Book tables in one lookup table. You can then use a filter and the range of the table's primary key to distinguish between the different groups of information. You will read more about this technique later in the chapter.

Even with this relatively simple structure, however, you still have enough tables to provide some food for thought. In particular, how are these tables related, and how can you put constraints on them so that it's difficult for the user to accidentally break a dependency? For instance, if six albums are associated with an artist, a user should not be able to delete the artist without first deleting or reassigning the albums. How about generating the IDs for each artist and each album? This is not Paradox, so you won't find an autoincrement field. This means that you must create generators and employ some means of accessing the generators.

Clearly, there are enough questions to keep someone busy for an hour or two. The next few pages of this chapter provide answers for most of the questions I've been asking. In particular, you'll find that to resolve many of these issues, you need to generate a specific database schema.

12

INTERBASE PROGRAMMING

Creating the Database Schema

To get started with your database schema, it's probably best to start your work at the top with the `Artist` table. Start WISQL and type the following in the Query window:

```
/* Table: ARTIST, Owner: SYSDBA */
CREATE TABLE ARTIST (CODE CODE_DOM NOT NULL,
        LAST VARCHAR(30),
        FIRST VARCHAR(30),
        BORN DATE,
        DIED DATE,
        BIRTHPLACE VARCHAR(35),
        COMMENT BLOB SUB_TYPE TEXT SEGMENT SIZE 80,
        ARTISTTYPE INTEGER NOT NULL,
        PRIMARY KEY (CODE));
```

The definition for this table assumes the presence of a domain called `CODE_DOM`. You can create a domain in WISQL with the following code:

```
CREATE DOMAIN CODE_DOM AS INTEGER;
```

This code states that `CODE_DOM` is a domain of type `Integer`.

A *domain* is an alias for a type that is used more than once in the program. For instance, the `Code` field used in the `Album` table is referenced in the `Album` table in the `GroupCode` field:

```
CREATE TABLE ALBUM (CODE CODE_DOM NOT NULL,
        ALBUM VARCHAR(25) NOT NULL,
        TYPES SMALLINT,
        LOUDNESS SMALLINT,
        MEDIUM SMALLINT,
        RATING SMALLINT,
        GROUPCODE CODE_DOM NOT NULL,
        PRIMARY KEY (CODE));
```

The `GroupCode` field in the `Album` table is a foreign key. It references the group, or artist, associated with this particular album. For instance, if Bob Dylan's code is 57, and the name of the current album is *Blonde on Blonde*, the `GroupCode` field for the current record in the `Album` table is set to 57. This number ties the album *Blonde on Blonde* to the artist Bob Dylan.

Creating a domain called `CODE_DOM` allows you to easily assign the same type to the `Code` field in the `Artist` table and the `GroupCode` field in the `Album` table. It's not earth shattering in importance, but it can be helpful.

Altering Tables: To `Null` or Not to `Null`

Notice that the `Code` field is declared `NOT NULL`. This means that the user cannot leave this field blank, and any attempt to do so will raise an exception. This rule is implemented by the server and is enforced regardless of which front end you use to access the data. By definition, all primary keys must be declared `NOT NULL`.

The `ArtistType` field in the `Artist` table is declared as `NOT NULL`. All artists must be distinguished by type; that is, they have to be labeled as either Authors or Musicians. If they don't fit into one of these two categories, then they are never seen by the user because I set up a filter on this field, excluding all but the one type that the user currently wants to see. In short, the table is filtered to show either only musicians or only authors. If an entry in the `Artist` table does not fit into one of these two categories, then it is never seen by the user. As a result, I declare this field `NOT NULL` and then use a lookup table to give the user only two choices when filling it in. This way, I am sure that no records are lost.

Deciding which fields should get the value `NOT NULL` is one of the more difficult chores in creating a database. This is one of those decisions that I almost never get right in design mode. Instead, I am forced to go back and massage my data after creating a first draft of the data definition.

To change a table using WISQL, you must use a SQL command called `Alter Table`:

```
ALTER TABLE MYTABLE
    ADD NAME VARCHAR(25),
    DROP NAMES
```

This code adds a field called `NAME` to a table and drops a field called `NAMES`. You don't have to add and drop fields at the same time; for instance, you can write the following:

```
ALTER TABLE MYTABLE
    ADD NAME VARCHAR(25)
```

You can also write this:

```
ALTER TABLE MYTABLE
    DROP NAMES
```

Because you often alter the structure of an existing table, make sure you run many tests on your program before entrusting a large amount of data to your tables.

CAUTION

You should take extreme care whenever you alter a table. I suggest backing up the entire GDB file by copying it to a safe location. Alternatively, the InterBase Server Manger also provides a means for backing up tables.

In InterBase, you cannot alter a field that is part of a unique index, primary key, or foreign key, nor can you drop a unique index, primary key, or foreign key. You can, however, drop a standard index:

```
drop index myindex
```

When I say *standard index*, I am referring to an index that is not a unique index, is not a primary key, and is not a foreign key. Remember that a table may have many indexes, not just those required for maintaining relationships between tables.

Renaming a Field in an Existing Table

When you start altering tables, you soon need to transfer the values from one field to a new field. To show how to proceed, I will create a simple table that can serve as a scratch pad. All the work shown here was done with the WISQL utility that ships with InterBase in the BIN directory. I always keep WISQL on the Tools menu of my copy of C++Builder.

Consider the following SQL statements:

```
create table foo (sam Integer not null,
  Name VarChar(30), primary key (Sam));
insert into foo (Sam, Name) values (1, "Fred");
insert into foo (Sam, Name) values (2, "Sam");
insert into foo (Sam, Name) values (3, "Joe");
```

The four statements shown here create a table called Foo and place some simple values in it. Note that you can't run these statements as a batch; you must run them one at a time. WISQL lets you use the Previous query and Next query buttons so you can easily alter the insert command without retyping it each time.

After creating the table, I can easily test the data:

```
select * from foo
```

When this query executes, the WISQL Output window displays this:

```
select * from foo
        SAM NAME
=========== ===============================
          1 Fred
          2 Sam
          3 Joe
```

Suppose that I now decide I want to change the Name field to be NOT NULL and somewhat longer. How do I proceed?

The first step is to create a new field with all the traits in it that I want:

```
alter table foo
  add AName Varchar(50) NOT NULL;
```

Now the table has a field called ANname that is longer than the Name field and declared NOT NULL.

Issue the following command in WISQL to copy the data from the Name field to AName:

```
update foo
  set Aname = Name;
```

Here is how things stand at this point:

```
select * from Foo;
       SAM NAME                             ANAME
========== ============================= =========
         1 Fred                          Fred
         2 Sam                           Sam
         3 Joe                           Joe
```

Now you can simply delete the Name column:

```
alter table foo
  drop name;
```

Your efforts yield a table with the traits you sought:

```
select * from foo;
       SAM ANAME
========== ===================================================
         1 Fred
         2 Sam
         3 Joe
```

If necessary, you can then repeat the process to copy AName to a field called Name, or else you can just keep the new name for your table.

This whole technique is a bit laborious. However, if you play with WISQL for a while, all this work starts to become second nature. For instance, I can copy the AName field back to a new field called Name in well under a minute just by rapidly typing the following:

```
alter table foo add Name varchar(50) NOT NULL

update Foo
  set Name = AName

alter table foo drop Aname
```

You can execute these statements all at once if you create a SQL script file. (See the WISQL help file for information on creating a SQL script file.) In this case you will probably want to execute them one at a time simply because it is easier.

After you learn SQL, and assuming you can type well, you can usually invoke WISQL, enter the commands, and get out faster than you can load the weighty Database Desktop application. Certainly by the time I open Database Desktop, open the Restructure window, and start making changes, I've usually spent more time than it takes to do the whole procedure in WISQL. Another nice thing about WISQL is that it has a small footprint and can be left in memory without slowing down the system.

Creating Binary Large Object (BLOB) Fields

A *BLOB field* is a special database field used to store binary data. You can use BLOB fields to store bitmapped images, sounds, video segments, and text. InterBase has full support for BLOB fields.

After the discussion of Code field and the related NULL versus NOT NULL issues, the other fields in the Artist table are pretty straightforward:

```
CREATE TABLE ARTIST (CODE CODE_DOM NOT NULL,
        LAST VARCHAR(30),
        FIRST VARCHAR(30),
        BORN DATE,
        DIED DATE,
        BIRTHPLACE VARCHAR(35),
        COMMENT BLOB SUB_TYPE TEXT SEGMENT SIZE 80,
        ARTISTTYPE INTEGER NOT NULL,
        PRIMARY KEY (CODE));
```

The code for creating a BLOB field is a bit tricky, but fortunately, you can just block copy this code any time you need to create a text BLOB in InterBase. If you create a BLOB field as shown previously, then you can use it with the TDBMemo data-aware control that ships with C++Builder.

C++Builder offers two objects for working with BLOBS: TBlobField and TBlobStream. TBlobField has methods called LoadFromFile(), SaveToFile(), LoadFromStream(), and SaveToStream(). Use these methods to read and write BLOB data in and out of a database. You can also usually cut and paste data directly into a TDBMemo or TDBImage control by copying it to the Clipboard; paste it into the control by pressing Ctrl+V. To copy an image from a BLOB field to the Clipboard, press Ctrl+C or Ctrl+X. Alternatively, you can use the CopyToClipBoard() function of both TDBMemo or TDBImage.

Primary Keys and Foreign Keys

You were introduced to primary and foreign keys in Chapter 8. It's now time to put that theory into practice.

The final line in the definition for the Artist table defines the primary key:

```
PRIMARY KEY (CODE));
```

This line states that the primary key is the Code field. It's important that Code is a keyed field because it is referenced by a foreign key in the Album table. Furthermore, you want to be sure that no two rows have the same code in it, and the primary key syntax enforces this rule. Remember that all primary keys must be NOT NULL by definition.

Here, once again in slightly different form, is the definition for the Album table:

```
CREATE TABLE ALBUM (CODE CODE_DOM NOT NULL,
        ALBUM VARCHAR(25) NOT NULL,
        TYPES SMALLINT,
        LOUDNESS SMALLINT,
        MEDIUM SMALLINT,
        RATING SMALLINT,
        GROUPCODE CODE_DOM NOT NULL,
        PRIMARY KEY (CODE),
        FOREIGN KEY (TYPES) REFERENCES TYPES(CODE),
        FOREIGN KEY (LOUDNESS) REFERENCES LOUDNESS(CODE),
        FOREIGN KEY (MEDIUM) REFERENCES MEDIUM(CODE),
        FOREIGN KEY (GROUPCODE) REFERENCES ARTIST(CODE)
        );
```

As you can see, I modified the table to include foreign keys. These keys use the References syntax to show the dependencies that this table has on the fields of other tables.

The Code field contains a unique number for each new album entered by the user. A character field designates the name of the album or book, and the GroupCode field relates each record to the Artist table.

Notice that the GroupCode field is a foreign key referencing the Code field of the Artist table. A foreign key provides *referential integrity,* through the use of the References syntax. The foreign key asserts that

- Every GroupCode entry must have a corresponding Code field in the Artist table.
- You can't delete an Artist record if you have a corresponding record in the Album table with a GroupCode the same as the Code field of the record you want to delete.

These rules are enforced by the server, and they are implemented regardless of which front end attempts to alter the table. C++Builder will surface any violation of these rules as VCL exceptions.

You rarely should make a foreign key unique because the whole point of this exercise is to relate multiple albums with one artist.

To see referential integrity in action, run the Music program and try to delete one of the artist records that has an album associated with it. For instance, try to delete Bob Dylan,

Miles Davis, or Philip Glass. Your efforts are stymied because albums are associated with all these artists. In particular, you get a lovely message that reads something like the following:

```
General SQL Error: Violates FOREIGN KEY constraint
"INTEG_19" on table "Album"
```

You might as well savor this one because it is as close to poetry as you can get in the SQL database world.

Referential integrity is enforced automatically in C++Builder and the Database Desktop. To see how it works, go into the Database Desktop, enter a new album, and try to give it a GroupCode that does not have a corresponding entry in the Code field of the Artist table. The Database Desktop doesn't let you do it. (Note that other fields in this table have foreign keys, so you have to give valid values all the way around, or you aren't able to enter a record. You can, however, leave the other fields blank if you want.)

The Types, Loudness, Medium, and Rating fields are all integers. Types, Loudness, and Medium are all foreign keys that reference one of three small tables called, logically enough, Types, Loudness, and Medium:

```
/* Table: LOUDNESS, Owner: SYSDBA */
CREATE TABLE LOUDNESS (LOUDNESS VARCHAR(15) NOT NULL,
        CODE INTEGER NOT NULL,
        PRIMARY KEY (CODE));
/* Table: MEDIUM, Owner: SYSDBA */
CREATE TABLE MEDIUM (MEDIUM VARCHAR(15) NOT NULL,
        CODE INTEGER NOT NULL,
        PRIMARY KEY (CODE));
/* Table: TYPES, Owner: SYSDBA */
CREATE TABLE TYPES (TYPES VARCHAR(15) NOT NULL,
        CODE INTEGER NOT NULL,
        PRIMARY KEY (CODE));
```

The structure of these tables ought to be intuitively obvious. The Types table, for instance, is designed to hold the following records:

```
select * from types
TYPES                CODE
================ ===========
JAZZ                    1
ROCK                    2
CLASSICAL               3
NEW AGE                 4
FOLK                    5
BLUES                   6
COMPUTER             1000
FICTION              1001
SCIFI                1002
MYSTERY              1003
REFERENCE            1004
```

What you have here are six categories for albums and five categories for books. I separate the two types of categories by a large range so that you can add a virtually unlimited number of additional categories of either kind. If you want to work with more than 999 different types of music, then you have needs that cannot be met by this database in its current form.

Astute readers will probably notice that I designed the relationship between the Types field of the Album table and the Types table itself so that you can easily perform lookups on the Types table when necessary. You can refer to the discussion of lookup fields in Chapter 8 for more information.

Here is the definition for the Book table, which plays the same role in this program as the Album table:

```
CREATE TABLE BOOK (CODE CODE_DOM NOT NULL,
        ALBUM VARCHAR(25) NOT NULL,
        TYPES SMALLINT,
        MEDIUM SMALLINT,
        RATING SMALLINT,
        COMMENT BLOB SUB_TYPE TEXT SEGMENT SIZE 80,
        GROUPCODE CODE_DOM NOT NULL,
        PRIMARY KEY (CODE),
        Foreign key(GroupCode) references Artist(Code),
        Foreign key(Types) references Types(Code),
        Foreign key(Medium) references Medium(Code)
   );
```

Note that the two tables differ in several particulars. The interesting thing about the Music program is that it can handle both kinds of tables seamlessly. To the user, the forms involved with displaying this data just seem to morph as needed to accommodate the data.

Creating Indices on the Music Table

By now, you have seen most of the data definition for MUSIC.GDB. However, I want to discuss a few more details before moving on to take a look at the interface for the program.

The indices on the Music database provide fast access and automatic sorting of the data. If any of your searches takes too long, one of the best ways to address the problem is through enhancing your indices.

You need to see the difference between the primary and foreign keys that create referential integrity and add constraints to a table, and the ordinary indices, which speed up access to a particular record. A *primary key* is a type of super index. It gives you everything an index gives you and then a little more. When you create a primary key or foreign key in InterBase (or in Paradox), a unique index is automatically created on that key.

One simple way to view indices is to open the SQL Explorer and examine the indices listed under the `Album` or `Artist` table. The `Artist` table, for instance, has two indices. One is called `Artist_LastFirst_Ndx`, and I will describe it later in this section. The other index has the strange name `RDB$PRIMARY1`. This index was created when the code field was designated as a primary key. The name has that sibilant poetic ring to it that is so typical of automatically generated computer identifiers.

> **NOTE**
>
> You can add a primary or foreign key after a table is created, as long as doing so does not violate any other database rules. You should make sure that the tables involved are not in use by another program when you make these kinds of modifications.
>
> Here is an example of adding a primary key:
>
> ```
> ALTER TABLE FOO ADD PRIMARY KEY (Sam);
> ```
>
> Here is an example of adding a foreign key:
>
> ```
> ALTER TABLE FOO ADD FOREIGN KEY (Foreigner) REFERENCES Book(CODE);
> ```
>
> The foreign key example assumes that you added an `Integer` field called `Foreigner` to the `Foo` table.

Besides the primary keys and foreign keys, the following indices are also defined on the `Artist` and `Album` table:

```
CREATE INDEX GROUPALBUM_IDX ON ALBUM(GROUPCODE, ALBUM);
CREATE INDEX ARTIST_LASTFIRST_NDX ON ARTIST(LAST, FIRST);
```

If you want to create a new index in WISQL, you can do so with the SQL `Create Index` command, as shown in the preceding code. The command takes the name of the index, the name of the table on which the index is enforced, and finally, in parentheses, the names of the fields in the index. For more information on this and other commands, see the *InterBase 5 Server Language Reference*. Also helpful are third-party books such as the *Practical SQL Handbook* (ISBN: 0-201-62623-3).

I created these two indices for different reasons. The `Artist_LastFirst_Ndx` is meant primarily to speed up searches and sorts in the `Artist` table.

The GroupAlbum_Idx is created for a more specific reason. I need to create a new index that both relates the Album table to the Artist table, and also makes sure that the Album table is sorted correctly. The GroupAlbum_Idx serves this purpose. (I had a little trouble getting the GroupAlbum_Idx to work properly at first, but things cleared up when I closed the Album table and then reopened it.)

Generators, Triggers, and Stored Procedures

The next few sections of this chapter deal with triggers and generators. You will read a good deal about automatically generating values for primary keys and a little about the relative merits of triggers and generators.

Three generators provide unique numbers to use in the Code fields of the Artist, Book, and Album tables. Generators provide almost the same functionality in InterBase tables that autoincrement fields provide in Paradox tables. That is, they provide numbers to use in the keyed fields that bind tables together.

Autoincrement fields are filled in automatically at run time. Generators, however, are not directly tied to any field. They merely generate numbers in sequence, where the first number generated might be 1, the second 2, and so on. You can tell a generator to start generating numbers at a particular starting value, where the first number might be x, the next x + 1, and so on.

Here is how you create a generator in WISQL and set it to a particular value:

```
CREATE GENERATOR MUSIC_GEN;
SET GENERATOR MUSIC_GEN TO 300;
```

As a result of this code, the first number generated is 300, the next is 301, and so on.

I will now show how to write a trigger. The Music program uses triggers on the Artist table but not on the Album table. The reason for splitting things up this way is explained in this section and in the next section, "Don't Use Triggers on Active Indices."

Here is how you write a trigger that automatically puts a generated value into the Code field of the Artist table whenever an Insert occurs:

```
CREATE TRIGGER SETMUSICGEN FOR ARTIST
BEFORE INSERT AS
BEGIN
  NEW.CODE = GEN_ID(MUSIC_GEN, 1);
END
```

This code is stored and run on the server side. It's not C++Builder code. You enter it into WISQL exactly as shown. You never need to call this procedure explicitly. The whole point of triggers is that they run automatically when certain events occur. This one is designed to run right before an `Insert` occurs. In other words, the way to call this procedure from C++Builder is to perform an `Insert`.

The code states that you want to create a trigger called `SetMusicGen` to run on the `Artist` table. The generator is called before an `Insert` operation:

```
BEFORE INSERT AS
```

The actual body of the code is simple:

```
NEW.CODE = GEN_ID(MUSIC_GEN, 1);
```

The `NEW` statement says that you are going to define the new value for the `CODE` field of the record that is about to be inserted into a table. In this case, you reference the new value for the `CODE` field of the `Artist` table.

`GEN_ID`, which is a function built into InterBase, produces an integer value. It takes a generator as its first parameter and a step value as its second parameter. The step value increases or decreases the value produced by the generator. For instance, the preceding code increments the value by 1, which parallels the behavior of an autoincrement variable in Paradox.

Don't Use Triggers on Active Indices

You can get a generator to fill in a field automatically with the trigger shown in the preceding section. Unfortunately, C++Builder does not provide particularly good support for triggers on indexed or keyed fields.

One reason this weakness exists is that each server generates a different kind of trigger. The developers of the VCL didn't want to run around finding out how to handle triggers for 10 different kinds of servers and neither did the BDE developers.

In this case I need to be very explicit to make sure you are following my logic. It would be better if C++Builder had good support for triggers on keyed fields; it does not. In the two sections following this one, I will show you a workaround for this unfortunate weakness in C++Builder.

Some third-party solutions to this problem include a good one called the `IBEventAlerter`, which works with InterBase. This solution ships with C++Builder and is found on the Samples page of the Component Palette. However, its presence on the Samples page means it lives in a never-never land between the high-quality code made by the VCL team

and the sample code, written by me and many others like me, that appears in the
Examples/Controls/Source directory of a standard C++Builder installation.

In the example under discussion, C++Builder's poor support for triggers is not crucial
because the table is not sorted on the Code field, but on the Last and First fields. If it
were sorted on the Code field, this trigger might cause C++Builder to lose track of the
current record after the insert operation. C++Builder would not know that the Code value
was inserted because it would not know that the trigger fired. As a result, the current
record might be lost—not permanently lost, but removed from C++Builder's field of
sight. In other words, the index would cause the record to be moved to a particular place
in the dataset, but C++Builder would not know how to follow it.

> **NOTE**
>
> Here is another example of how to create a trigger using WISQL:
>
> ```
> CREATE TRIGGER SET_COMPANY_UPPER FOR COMPANY
> ACTIVE BEFORE INSERT POSITION 1
> AS
> BEGIN
>   NEW.COMPANY_UPPER = UPPER(NEW.COMPANY);
> END
> ```
>
> This code is called just before an insert operation on a table from another data-
> base called Company. This table contains a string field also called Company and a
> second field called Company_Upper. The second field is meant to mirror the
> Company field but have all its characters in uppercase letters. This second field
> takes up a lot of space, but it allows you to conduct searches and sorts on the
> Company field without taking into account character case. The goal of the trig-
> ger shown previously is to take the new value for the Company field and convert
> it into an uppercase version of the string for use in the Company_Upper field. The
> Upper macro shown here is built into InterBase.
>
> Notice the line that states when this trigger is fired:
>
> ```
> ACTIVE BEFORE INSERT POSITION 1
> ```
>
> C++Builder does not need to know that the Set_Company_Upper trigger
> occurred because the table is not sorted on the Company_Upper field.

You don't have any great need for alarm if you find yourself in a situation in which you
can't use a trigger. The absence of trigger support is not a big concern under most circumstances. Instead of using a trigger, you can use a stored procedure to retrieve the next
number from a generator. The next two sections show you how to proceed.

Working with Stored Procedures

In this section, you see a discussion of the stored procedures used by the Music program to enforce or support referential integrity. These simple stored procedures use a generator to fill in the value of a primary key. In other words, they solve the problem that triggers could not solve.

A *stored procedure* is simply a routine that is stored on the server side rather than listed in your source code. Like the language for writing triggers, there is a unique language for writing stored procedures that has nothing to do with C++ or SQL. In fact, you need to keep in mind that no particular relationship exists between C++Builder and InterBase. They are made by two different teams, using two different languages, with two different goals in mind.

One key difference between C++Builder code and InterBase code is that the language of stored procedures is completely platform independent. If you want to move your database back and forth between Windows and UNIX, you might find it helpful to create many stored procedures that handle the majority of work for your databases. You can then write very thin clients that simply ask the stored procedures to do all the work.

Stored procedures are not difficult to create. Here, for instance, is a stored procedure that returns the next number generated by the `Music_Gen` generator:

```
CREATE PROCEDURE GETMUSICGEN
RETURNS (NUM INTEGER)
AS
BEGIN
  NUM = GEN_ID(MUSIC_GEN, 1);
END
```

The first line tells WISQL that you are going to create a procedure called `GetMusicGen`. The next line states that it is going to return a value called `Num`, which is an integer. The `AS` statement tells InterBase that you are now ready to define the body of the procedure. The procedure itself appears between a `BEGIN..END` pair and consists of a call to the `GEN_ID` function, which returns the next number from the `MUSIC_GEN` generator. When it retrieves the number, it asks InterBase to increment its value by 1. You can increment by a larger number if you want.

Stored procedures are handled on the C++Builder end with either a `TStoredProc`component or by returning an answer set by way of a SQL statement. Here are some rules to guide you when deciding how to handle a stored procedure:

- In general, if the stored procedure returns several rows of data, you access it by way of a SQL statement in a `TQuery` component. The SQL statement to use in such a case is `Select * from GetAlbumGen`, where `GetAlbumGen` is the name of the procedure that returns one or more rows of data.

- If the stored procedure returns only a single item of data, you can call it with a `TStoredProc` component. Examples of both methods for calling stored procedures from C++Builder appear in the next section, in the form of excerpts from the Music program.

Stored Procedures in C++Builder

The `Album` and `Book` tables of the Music program use stored procedures to fill in their primary indices. Because both procedures are identical, I describe only the one for the `Album` table.

To get started, you need to be sure the stored procedure is set up on the server side. Here is the code you should enter into WISQL to create the procedure:

```
CREATE PROCEDURE GETALBUMGEN RETURNS (NUM INTEGER)
AS
BEGIN
  NUM = GEN_ID(ALBUM_GEN, 1);
END
```

As you can see, this simple stored procedure does nothing more than return a single value.

> **NOTE**
>
> You can start a new project, create a data module, and drop a `TDatabase` object on it. Connect it to the `Music` database that ships on the CD-ROM that accompanies this book. After you connect the `TDatabase` object to `MUSIC.GDB`, you can drop a `TStoredProc` on your data module and start working with it, as described in the rest of this section.
>
> Setting up the alias for the database is described in depth in the `readme` file from the CD-ROM. In general, follow the rules for creating aliases laid out in the preceding chapter. This time, though, create an alias called **Music** and point it to the `MUSIC.GDB` file.

To get started using a `TStoredProc`, drop it onto the `Album` page or onto a data module. Set the `StoredProcName` alias to the `GetAlbumGen` stored procedure.

After selecting the procedure to use with the `TStoredProc`, you can bring up the `Params` field to see the parameters passed to or returned by the function. In this case, only one parameter is returned as the result of the function.

12

INTERBASE PROGRAMMING

Whenever the user inserts a record into the `Album` table, the following procedure is called by the `AfterInsert` event of the `TTable` object:

```
void __fastcall TDMod::AlbumTableAfterInsert(TDataSet *DataSet)
{
  AlbumTableCODE->Value = 0;
  AlbumTableGROUPCODE->Value = 0;
}
```

It doesn't matter what value you assign to the `CODE` and `GROUPCODE` fields—just make sure they aren't set to `NOT NULL`. The correct value is filled in later by the `BeforePost` event of the `AlbumTable` object:

```
void __fastcall TDMod::AlbumTableBeforePost(TDataSet *DataSet)
{
  if (AlbumSource->State == dsInsert) {
    GetAlbumGen->Prepare();
    GetAlbumGen->ExecProc();
    AlbumTableCODE->AsInteger =
      GetAlbumGen->ParamByName("Num")->AsInteger;
    AlbumTable->FieldByName("GroupCode")->AsInteger =
      ArtistTableCODE->AsInteger;
  }
}
```

This code first executes the stored procedure and then snags its return value from the `Params` field of the `TStoredProc`. The `Params` field for stored procedures works the same way as the `Params` field for `TQuery` objects. Calling `Prepare()` can help optimize your code.

The rest of the object for updating the table occurs in the `AlbumForm`, where the user does his or her work:

```
void __fastcall TAlbumForm::sbInsertClick(TObject *Sender)
{
  String S = "";
  if (!InputQuery("Insert New Album Dialog", "Enter album name", S))
    return;
  DMod->AlbumTable->Insert();
  DMod->AlbumTable->FieldByName("Album")->AsString = S;
  DMod->AlbumTable->FieldByName("Types")->AsString = "";
  DMod->AlbumTable->FieldByName("Loudness")->AsString = "";
  DMod->AlbumTable->FieldByName("Medium")->AsString = "";
  DMod->PostAll();
  lcbType->SetFocus();
}
```

This code just makes sure that all the fields not handled by the stored procedure are filled in properly by the values the user entered. The call to `PostAll()` in this procedure causes `AlbumTableBeforePost()` to execute.

Following is the code for generating both the trigger and the stored procedure described previously. You should never include both the trigger and the stored procedure in the same database; you have to choose between the two techniques.

```
CREATE GENERATOR IMAGECODE;
CREATE PROCEDURE GETIMAGECODE RETURNS (NUM INTEGER)
AS
BEGIN
  NUM = GEN_ID(IMAGECODE, 1);
END

CREATE TRIGGER GENERATE_IMAGECODE FOR IMAGES
ACTIVE BEFORE INSERT POSITION 0
AS
BEGIN
  New.Code = Gen_ID(ImageCode, 1);
END
```

Server-Side Rules Versus Client-Side Rules

In many people's minds, the holy grail of contemporary client/server development is to place as many rules as possible on the server side of the equation. This means that the basic rules of the database are enforced no matter how the user accesses the data, and no matter how many front ends are written to access the data.

To avoid enforcing rules on the client side, you must create referential integrity on the server side using foreign keys or whatever tools are at your disposal. Furthermore, you should use triggers whenever possible to enforce additional rules. For instance, some people view it as an error to insert the Code field of the Album table using a stored procedure rather than a trigger; however, you might have no choice about how to proceed in some circumstances.

Even using triggers and referential integrity is not enough for many hard-core adherents of the server-side philosophy. This book, however, is written about a client-side tool, so I generally promote placing the referential integrity on the server side and then adding a few more triggers or stored procedures where necessary.

I find that many database chores are easier to perform on the C++Builder side. C++ is a powerful language with powerful debuggers to back it up. Most servers have neither a powerful language nor a powerful debugger. As a result, defining certain kinds of database logic in C++ is often wisest, as long as doing so does not exact a huge penalty in terms of performance. Obviously, if you need to fetch a lot of rows and then process them, doing that on the server side where the data itself is stored is best.

The emergence of Distributed OLE, CORBA, and other tools that support Remote Procedure Calls (RPC) is rapidly changing how databases are constructed. PC-based developers can now use Distributed COM or CORBA to place C++–based rules on middle-tier servers. I can therefore use C++Builder to enforce a bunch of rules and then encapsulate those rules in an object that resides on the same machine as the InterBase server, or on a middle-tier machine. This puts all my database logic on servers where they can be called from multiple clients. The goal is to provide a few entry points for my front-end program to call. That way, I keep the logic off the front end but still get to use a real language to define my business logic.

You will find out more regarding distributed architectures in Chapter 14, "Creating COM Automation Servers and Clients," and Chapter 19, "DCOM."

The Music Program Interface

The interface for the Music program presents the user with a main screen with three pages imbedded inside it. One page (shown in Figure 12.2) is meant only for performing searches. It gives you a view of both the Artist table and either the Book table or the Album table. You can't alter the Artist table from this screen, but you can change the Album or Book table.

FIGURE 12.2

The Index page from the Music program enables you to view artists and their related productions.

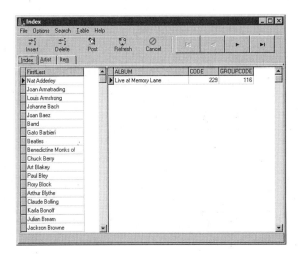

> **NOTE**
>
> I use the following code to prevent the user from using the Insert key to insert a record into either of the grids on the Index page:
>
> ```
> void __fastcall
> TIndexForm::ArtistGridKeyPress(TObject *Sender, char &Key)
> {
>   if (Key == VK_INSERT || Key == VK_DELETE)
>     Key = 0;
> }
> ```
>
> This code disarms Insert and Delete keystrokes. Users never know the method is called but find that they can't use those particular keys. The code is called in response to OnKeyPress events.

The second page in the Music program allows you to see one record from the Artist table, as shown in Figure 12.3.

FIGURE 12.3

The Artist page from the Music program.

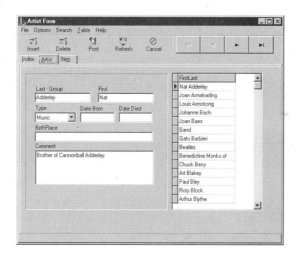

If users want to look at a particular record, they can switch to the Artist, Album, or Book pages. Figures 12.4 and 12.5 show the latter two.

FIGURE **12.4**
*The Album page
from the Music
program.*

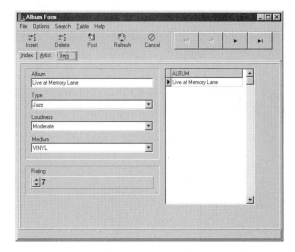

FIGURE **12.5**
*The Book page
from the Music
program.*

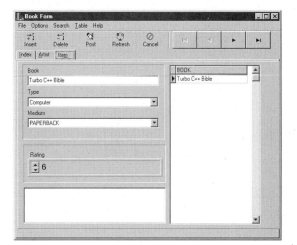

The Book or Album page is always the third page in the program. There is no fourth page. The Album form is shown if the current record is an album; the Book form is shown if it is a book.

Working with Child Forms

C++Builder provides a number of paged dialogs or notebooks that you can use to present data to the user. In this particular program, I use the TTabControl component in conjunction with a series of forms. My primary concern is allowing the programmer to place each major object in a separate unit rather than force the combination of various sets of functionality into one paged notebook. In other words, the Album page is a separate object, not a part of the `TTabControl` object.

The Music program has five major forms in it. The first supports the frame for the entire program, and the rest support the Index, Artist, Album, and Book pages. The next few paragraphs describe how to make a form become a child of a second form, which is what is really happening inside the Music program.

You need to convert the standard VCL pop-up form to a child form that has Form1 as its parent. Listings 12.1 and 12.2 show the header and source code for a child form that uses this technique.

LISTING 12.1   THE HEADER FOR THE POP-UP CHILD FORM

```
class TChildForm : public TForm
{
__published:     // IDE-managed Components
private:     // User declarations
public:         // User declarations
  __fastcall TChildForm(TComponent* Owner);
protected:
  void __fastcall Loaded();
  void __fastcall CreateParams(TCreateParams& Params);
};
```

LISTING 12.2   THE SOURCE CODE FOR THE POP-UP CHILD FORM

```
/////////////////////////////////////
// Purpose:
// Project: music2.BPR
//
#include <vcl.h>
#pragma hdrstop

#include "ChildForm1.h"

#pragma package(smart_init)
#pragma resource "*.dfm"
TChildForm *ChildForm;

__fastcall TChildForm::TChildForm(TComponent* Owner)
  : TForm(Owner)
{
}

void __fastcall TChildForm::Loaded()
{
  TForm::Loaded();
```

continues

LISTING 12.2 CONTINUED

```
   Visible = false;
   Position = poDefault;
   BorderIcons = TBorderIcons();
   BorderStyle = bsNone;
   HandleNeeded();
   SetBounds(0, 0, Width, Height);
}

void __fastcall TChildForm::CreateParams(TCreateParams& Params)
{
  TForm::CreateParams(Params);
  TForm* owner = dynamic_cast<TForm*>(Owner);
  Params.WndParent = owner->Handle;
  Params.Style = WS_CHILD | WS_CLIPSIBLINGS;
  Params.X = 0;
  Params.Y = 0;
}
```

The logic for the code shown here was based on work done by Pat Ritchey.

In the Music program, all the forms displayed within the tab control descend from
TChildForm shown previously. As a result, they inherit the capability to live as a child
form pasted on top of another form:

```
class TAlbumForm : public TChildForm
```

When using this technique, you want the parent form to explicitly create the child forms.
To do so, do not autocreate the forms; instead, choose Project, Options, Forms and move
the forms from the Auto-Create list box into the Available Forms list box. You can then
create the forms as needed inside Form1 with code that looks like this:

```
void __fastcall TForm1::FormCreate(TObject *Sender)
{
  IndexForm = new TIndexForm(this);
  AlbumForm = new TAlbumForm(this);
  ArtistForm = new TArtistForm(this);
  BookForm = new TBookForm(this);
  ChildForms[0] = IndexForm;
  ChildForms[1] = ArtistForm;
  ChildForms[2] = AlbumForm;
  ChildForms[3] = BookForm;
  for (int i=0;i<MaxForms + 1;i++)
    ChildForms[i]->Show();
}
```

To make sure the form adheres to the dimensions of its parent, you can respond to
OnResize events:

```
void __fastcall TForm1::FormResize(TObject *Sender)
{
  TRect R = TabControl1->DisplayRect;
  R.Top = R.Top + ToolBar1->Height;
  R.Bottom = R.Bottom - ToolBar1->Height;

  for (int i=0;i<MaxForms + 1;i++)
    MoveWindow(ChildForms[i]->Handle,
      R.Left, R.Top, R.Right, R.Bottom, true);
}
```

This code uses the `DisplayRect()` function call to get the size of the window to draw in, excluding the location where the tabs reside. It then resizes the child form so that it fits in this space.

Analyzing the Music Program

Now that you understand the Music program's basic structure, the next step is to take a look at the code and analyze any sections that need explanation. The code is too long to present in total. It is, of course, available in full on the CD-ROM that accompanies this book. The most important methods from the program are quoted in the body of the text itself.

When you study the Music program, note how you can make the tables in a relational database work together seamlessly toward a particular end. Because this program uses InterBase, you can use it in a rigorous multiuser environment without fear that it will collapse under the load. For instance, there is no reason this program cannot handle two or three hundred simultaneous users as is.

Suppressing the Password: The `TDatabase` Object

The `TDatabase` object on the main form has its `AliasName` property set to the `Music` alias. This alias was defined in the SQL Explorer (see Figure 12.1), and it points to the tables that make up the `Music` database.

The `DatabaseName` property of the `TDatabase` object is set to the string `MusicData`, which is the alias to which all the other `TTable`, `TStoredProc`, and `TQuery` objects in the program are attached. Remember: Only the `TDatabase` object attaches directly to the `Music` alias. This way, you can point the entire program to a second database by changing only one variable: the `AliasName` property. This feature can be handy if you need to experiment without touching your primary data.

The `Params` property for the `TDatabase` object contains the following information:

```
USER NAME=SYSDBA
PASSWORD=masterkey
```

The `LoginPrompt` property is then set to `false`, which enables you to launch the program without entering a password. This is a necessity during development, and it's a useful trait in a program such as this that probably has little fear of hostile attacks on its data.

The `FormCreate` Event

As you learned earlier, the constructor for the main form has to create the child windows that hold all the main controls used in the program:

```
void __fastcall TForm1::FormCreate(TObject *Sender)
{
  IndexForm = new TIndexForm(this);
  AlbumForm = new TAlbumForm(this);
  ArtistForm = new TArtistForm(this);
  BookForm = new TBookForm(this);
  ChildForms[0] = IndexForm;
  ChildForms[1] = ArtistForm;
  ChildForms[2] = AlbumForm;
  ChildForms[3] = BookForm;
  for (int i=0;i<MaxForms + 1;i++)
    ChildForms[i]->Show();
}
```

The first four lines of the routine create the forms. The next four lines assign them to an array of `TForm` pointers. You can then use this array to iterate through all the main forms for the program, as shown in the last two lines of the routine, and in the `OnResize` event handler shown previously.

As you can see, an ordinal value of `0` gives you immediate access to the `Index` form if you write code that looks like this:

```
ChildForms[0] = IndexForm;
```

One of the most important methods in the program is the `TabControl1Change()` event handler:

```
void __fastcall TForm1::TabControl1Change(TObject *Sender)
{
  DMod->PostAll();
  switch (TabControl1->TabIndex) {
    case 0 : {
      ChildForms[TabControl1->TabIndex]->BringToFront();
      Caption = "Index";
      DBNavigator1->DataSource = DMod->ArtistSource;
      DMod->TypesTable->Filtered = false;
```

```
      break;
    }

    case 1 : {
      ChildForms[TabControl1->TabIndex]->BringToFront();
      Caption = "Artist Form";
      DBNavigator1->DataSource = DMod->ArtistSource;
      InsertBtn->OnClick = ArtistForm->sbInsertClick;
      DeleteBtn->OnClick = ArtistForm->sbDeleteClick;
      PostBtn->OnClick = ArtistForm->PostBtnClick;
      CancelBtn->OnClick = ArtistForm->CancelBtnClick;
      break;
    }

    case 2 : {
      if (DMod->ArtistTable->FieldByName("ArtistType")->AsInteger == 1) {
        ChildForms[2]->BringToFront();
        Caption = "Album Form";
        DBNavigator1->DataSource = DMod->AlbumSource;
        InsertBtn->OnClick = AlbumForm->sbInsertClick;
        Insert1->OnClick = AlbumForm->sbInsertClick;
        DeleteBtn->OnClick = AlbumForm->sbDeleteClick;
        CancelBtn->OnClick = AlbumForm->CancelBtnClick;
        PostBtn->OnClick = AlbumForm->PostBtnClick;
        DMod->TypesTable->Filtered = false;
        DMod->MaxTypes = 999;
        DMod->MinTypes = 0;
        DMod->TypesTable->Filtered = true;
      }
      else  {
        ChildForms[3]->BringToFront();
        Caption = "Book Form";
        DBNavigator1->DataSource = DMod->BookSource;
        InsertBtn->OnClick = BookForm->sbInsertClick;
        Insert1->OnClick = InsertBtn->OnClick;

        DeleteBtn->OnClick = BookForm->sbDeleteClick;
        CancelBtn->OnClick = BookForm->CancelBtnClick;
        PostBtn->OnClick = BookForm->PostBtnClick;
        DMod->TypesTable->Filtered = false;
        DMod->MaxTypes = 1999;
        DMod->MinTypes = 1000;
        DMod->TypesTable->Filtered = true;
        BookForm->TypesCombo->Update();
      }
    }
  }
}
```

The primary burden of this code is to move the appropriate form to the front when requested by the user:

```
ChildForms[2]->BringToFront();
```

This code brings the AlbumForm to the front. To the user, this looks as though a hit on the TabControl caused the page to be "turned" inside the control. Of course, what really happens is that you simply push one form down in the Z order and bring another to the top. In short, you create your own page control out of separate forms. The beauty of this arrangement is that it ensures that each page of the TabControl exists as a separate object in its own module. This arrangement is much better than the system used in the kdAdd program.

Another key chore of the TabControl1Change() handler is to set the OnClick event for the buttons at the top of the form so that they reflect what happens inside the current page. For instance, if the BookForm is selected, a click on the Post button ought to call the Post() method of the Book table, not the Album or Artist table. To ensure that all works correctly, this method simply sets the OnClick event to the appropriate routine whenever the TabControl is changed:

```
InsertBtn->OnClick = AlbumForm->sbInsertClick;
DeleteBtn->OnClick = AlbumForm->sbDeleteClick;
CancelBtn->OnClick = AlbumForm->CancelBtnClick;
PostBtn->OnClick = AlbumForm->PostBtnClick;
```

In this case, the methods associated with the InsertBtn and so on are the methods from the AlbumForm. This technique helps you see how dynamic the delegation model can be if you need to push the envelope a bit.

I mentioned earlier that the Types table holds a series of types that can apply to either musical or written works. For instance, the table might look like this:

```
TYPES              CODE
================ ===========
JAZZ                  1
ROCK                  2
CLASSICAL             3
NEW AGE               4
FOLK                  5
BLUES                 6
COMPUTER           1000
FICTION            1001
SCIFI              1002
MYSTERY            1003
REFERENCE          1004
```

When the application is in Music mode, the first half of the table is used; otherwise, the second half of the table is used. Here is code from the TabControl1Change() handler that ensures that the proper part of the code is operative when the program is in Book mode:

```
DMod->TypesTable->Filtered = false;
DMod->MaxTypes = 1999;
```

```
DMod->MinTypes = 1000;
DMod->TypesTable->Filtered = true;
```

The following lines are executed when the user switches the program into Music mode:

```
DMod->TypesTable->Filtered = false;
DMod->MaxTypes = 999;
DMod->MinTypes = 0;
DMod->TypesTable->Filtered = true;
```

After you look at the code, you should not be surprised to learn that the Types table has an OnFilterRecord() event handler:

```
void __fastcall TDMod::TypesTableFilterRecord(TDataSet *DataSet,
     bool &Accept)
{
  Accept = (DMod->TypesTable->FieldByName("Code")->Value>= MinTypes) &&
     (DMod->TypesTable->FieldByName("Code")->Value <= MaxTypes);
}
```

After this method is defined, all you have to do is set the Types table's Filtered property to true, and only the selected half of the Types table is visible. By the time the Album or Book form gets at this table, it appears that it contains only values pertinent to the relevant form.

Of course, I defined a property so that the code in the main form never directly touches the privates of the TDataModule object:

```
__property int MaxTypes  = { read = FMaxTypes, write = FMaxTypes };
__property int MinTypes  = { read = FMinTypes, write = FMinTypes };
```

FMinTypes and FMaxTypes are private data for the program.

The following code from the main module of the program gets executed whenever the user switches between Music and Book mode:

```
void __fastcall TForm1::FilterOptionsClick(TObject *Sender)
{
  DMod->ArtistTable->Filtered = false;
  TComponent* c = dynamic_cast<TComponent*>(Sender);
  TFilterIndex fi = static_cast<TFilterIndex>(c->Tag);
  switch (fi) {
    case fiAlbumFilter : {
      IndexForm->BookGrid->Align = alNone;
      IndexForm->BookGrid->Visible = false;
      DMod->FilterType = (int)fiAlbumFilter;
      IndexForm->AlbumGrid->Align = alClient;
      IndexForm->AlbumGrid->Visible = true;
      break;
    }
```

```
   case fiBookFilter : {
     IndexForm->AlbumGrid->Align = alNone;
     IndexForm->AlbumGrid->Visible = false;
     DMod->FilterType = (int)fiBookFilter;
     IndexForm->BookGrid->Align = alClient;
     IndexForm->BookGrid->Visible = true;
     break;
   }
 }
 DMod->ArtistTable->Filtered = true;
}
```

The purpose of this code is to properly set up the two grids on the Index page. When the program is in Music mode, you want the right grid on the Music page to show the Music table, and you want it to show the Book table when you are in Book mode. I could have simply switched the DataSource for one form as needed, but that does not take care of the issue of defining the fields to be shown in the grid. Rather than try to create the columns on-the-fly, I decided instead to use the code shown here.

So far, most of the code you have analyzed from the Music program has been centered on the program's interface. Now it is time to move away from interface issues, and see something of code used to display and handle data. Subjects covered in this section include using lookups, using ranges, and asking the database a question.

The data for this program is quite complex, which you can see by looking at the data module for the program, shown in Figure 12.6.

FIGURE 12.6

The data for the Music program is fairly complex, as you can see from glancing at the TDataModule *object found in* DMod1.cpp.

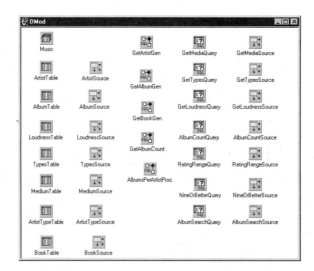

Using Lookups

This program uses a large number of lookups. All of them are defined on the TDataModule itself, although some are used in the grids on the Index form, others on the Book and Album pages, and some in both locations. In particular, when you enter a new album, you use lookups to specify whether the album is Loud, Medium, or Peaceful, and you use lookups to specify whether it is in a particular category such as Jazz, Folk, Rock, and so on.

The primary purpose of the lookups is to ensure that the user always chooses from preselected lists of values and does not start typing in his or her own values on-the-fly. For instance, you want the user to choose a type from the Types table, not to make up new types at random.

Because these lookups are so readily available, the user rarely has to type anything into a control. Instead, he or she can quickly select options from a lookup list. It is currently unavailable, but it is a nice gesture to the user to provide a means of editing the lookup tables, as shown in the Address program from Chapter 9.

Querying the Database

By this time, you know most of what you need to know to construct a reasonably powerful database. This feeling is good, and knowing that you can get this kind of control over an important domain of information is nice.

Despite this sense of accomplishment, you may have a nagging feeling that something is missing. After all, work is required to construct the database and to enter data into it, so where is the fun part? Where is the part that makes you say, in the cultured words of that dubious soul from Redmond, "Hey, that's cool!"

After you have a database up and running, the way to get joy from it is to ask it questions. At first, you might just want to ask simple questions. For instance, you might remember the beginning of the name of an album, but you can't remember the whole thing.

Suppose that you remember that an album name begins with the letter *L*. If you bring up WISQL, you can ask the following question:

```
select Album from album where album like "L%"
ALBUM
==========================
Letter From Home
La Mer
Life
Landing on Water
```

```
Live at the BBC
Longing in their Hearts
Live at the Royal Festival
Love Deluxe
Live at Memory Lane
Lookout Farm
Living
Lives in the Balance
Lawyers in Love
```

As you can see, the results returned from this question are names of the albums and books that start with the letter *L*.

This capability is fairly useful, but you really want to know not only the name of the album, but also the artist behind the album. You could, of course, ask the following question:

```
select Album, GroupCode from album where album like "L%"
ALBUM                        GROUPCODE
=========================== ===========
Letter From Home                  11
La Mer                            50
Life                               9
Landing on Water                   9
Live at the BBC                   13
Longing in their Hearts           28
Live at the Royal Festiva         92
Love Deluxe                       61
Live at Memory Lane              116
Lookout Farm                     130
Living                           161
Lives in the Balance             142
Lawyers in Love                  142
```

This question gives you the name of an album plus the `GroupCode` associated with the album. All you have to do then is run one more query to get the answer you need:

```
select First,Last from Artist where Code = 11
FIRST                            LAST
=========================== ================================
Pat                              Metheny
```

Of course, not having to ask this question in two stages would be nice. Instead, you might want to ask the following question, which performs a join between the `Album` and `Artist` tables:

```
select Artist.Last, Album.Album
  from  Album, Artist
where artist.code = album.groupcode and
Album.Album like "L%"
order by Artist.last
```

```
LAST                            ALBUM
==============================  ==========================
Adderley                        Live at Memory Lane
Beatles                         Live at the BBC
Browne                          Lawyers in Love
Browne                          Lives in the Balance
Collins                         Living
Debussy                         La Mer
Liebman                         Lookout Farm
McLaughlin                      Live at the Royal Festiva
Metheny                         Letter From Home
Raitt                           Longing in their Hearts
Sade                            Love Deluxe
Young                           Landing on Water
Young                           Life
```

Now you are starting to get somewhere. This information is fairly valuable to you. When composing the preceding query, you should be careful to include where clauses that both specify the letters you want to search on and the relationship between the Artist and Album tables:

```
where artist.code = album.groupcode
```

If you don't qualify the question in this way, you end up getting a much larger result set than you wanted. In particular, you indicate that the query shouldn't link the resulting albums to all the names in the Artist table but just link them to the names of the artists that have the same code as the groupcode of a particular album.

Now that you have seen this much, most people also want to get information about the rating for the album, as well as its type. One way to ask that question looks like this:

```
select Artist.Last, Album.Album, Album.Rating, Album.Types
  from  Album, Artist
  where artist.code = album.groupcode and
    Album.Album like "L%"
  order by Artist.last
```

```
LAST                            ALBUM                       RATING  TYPES
==============================  ==========================  ======  ======
Adderley                        Live at Memory Lane         7       1
Beatles                         Live at the BBC             6       2
Browne                          Lawyers in Love             6       2
Browne                          Lives in the Balance        6       2
Collins                         Living                      6       5
Debussy                         La Mer                      7       3
Liebman                         Lookout Farm                6       1
McLaughlin                      Live at the Royal Festiva   <null>  1
Metheny                         Letter From Home            9       1
Raitt                           Longing in their Hearts     <null>  <null>
Sade                            Love Deluxe                 8       1
Young                           Landing on Water            7       2
Young                           Life                        7       2
```

When you're reviewing this data, you may find it hard not to feel that something is missing from the `types` field. After all, what does the number 1 mean? What type is that?

Once again, you can get the question answered by going to the well a second time and querying the `Types` table. However, you should not be surprised to learn that a second solution is possible:

```
select Artist.Last, Album.Album, Album.Rating, Types.Types
  from  Album, Artist, Types
where artist.code = album.groupcode and
Album.Album like "L%" and
Types.Code = Album.Types
order by Artist.last
LAST                            ALBUM                            RATING TYPES
============================    ==========================       ====== =========
Adderley                        Live at Memory Lane                  7 JAZZ
Beatles                         Live at the BBC                      6 ROCK
Browne                          Lawyers in Love                      6 ROCK
Browne                          Lives in the Balance                 6 ROCK
Collins                         Living                               6 FOLK
Debussy                         La Mer                               7 CLASSICAL
Liebman                         Lookout Farm                         6 JAZZ
McLaughlin                      Live at the Royal Festiva      <null> JAZZ
Metheny                         Letter From Home                     9 JAZZ
Sade                            Love Deluxe                          8 JAZZ
Young                           Landing on Water                     7 ROCK
Young                           Life                                 7 ROCK
```

Here you broadened the question by specifying that you want to bring in the `Types` table:

```
from  Album, Artist, Types
```

Include one of its fields in the result set:

```
select Artist.Last, Album.Album, Album.Rating, Types.Types
```

Link the `Album` table and `Types` table on the primary and foreign keys of the two tables:

```
where ... Types.Code = Album.Types
```

As a developer you can run these queries from WISQL. A good application, however, must give the user an easy way of obtaining the data he or she seeks. You can take a number of courses at this point, but one of the best is to simply wrap your query in a stored procedure:

```
CREATE PROCEDURE ALBUMSEARCH (ANALBUMNAME VARCHAR(75))
RETURNS (ARTISTNAME VARCHAR(30),
ALBUMNAME VARCHAR(30),
RATINGVALUE VARCHAR(30),
TYPENAME VARCHAR(30),
MEDIUMNAME VARCHAR(30))
```

```
AS
begin
  for
    select Artist.Last, Album.Album,
      Album.Rating, Types.Types, Medium.Medium
    from Album, Artist, Types, Medium
    where artist.code = album.groupcode
      and Album.Album like :AnAlbumName
      and Types.Code = Album.Types and  Medium.Code = Album.Medium
    order by Artist.Last
    into :ArtistName, :AlbumName, :RatingValue, :TypeName, :MediumName
 do suspend;
end
```

You can break this procedure down into several sections to make some sense of it. First, notice the header:

```
CREATE PROCEDURE ALBUMSEARCH (ANALBUMNAME VARCHAR(75))
```

This header says that you are creating a stored procedure named `AlbumSearch` that takes a string as a parameter. You supply the name of the album you want to search in this string.

The next part of the procedure declares what is returned to the user:

```
RETURNS (ARTISTNAME VARCHAR(30),
ALBUMNAME VARCHAR(30),
RATINGVALUE VARCHAR(30),
TYPENAME VARCHAR(30),
MEDIUMNAME VARCHAR(30))
```

These rows set up what you want returned from the procedure. You state these names again at the very bottom of the procedure, saying that you want the query to be returned in these variables:

```
into :ArtistName, :AlbumName, :RatingValue, :TypeName, :MediumName
```

The query itself sits in between a `begin..end` pair, which nests around a `for...do` statement:

```
as
begin
  for
    // Query goes here
  do suspend;
end
```

If you forget to wrap your query in this faintly ridiculous-looking syntactical sugar, InterBase complains about a singleton query not being able to return multiple rows.

Now that you have your stored procedure all set up, the next thing to do is call it from C++Builder. The syntax for doing so could not be simpler:

```
select * from AlbumSearch(:SearchValue);
```

This simple SQL statement should reside inside the SQL property of a C++Builder TQuery component. You can then call this procedure with code that looks like this:

```
void TDMod::AlbumSearcher(String SearchValue)
{
  AlbumSearchQuery->Close();
  AlbumSearchQuery->ParamByName("SearchValue")->Value = SearchValue;
  AlbumSearchQuery->Open();
}
```

That's all there is to it. Now you can hook up a TDataSource to the TQuery and a TDBGrid to the TDataSource; you see the results of your query inside a C++Builder application after calling the AlbumSearch() function.

You can access a number of interesting stored procedures in this manner from the menus of the C++Builder program. Some of the most interesting ones involve asking about the ratings you assign to albums. For instance, you can ask to see all the albums that have a rating between 1 and 7 or a rating higher than 9. This set of queries is so important that I review them in the last section of this chapter, "Viewing a Range of Data."

Stored Procedures That Do Not Return Datasets

In the preceding section, you saw how to ask a question that returns a dataset. A different kind of stored procedure asks how to return a particular value such as a single number or string. For instance, you might want to ask the answer man how many albums are in the database:

```
select Count(*) from album;
      COUNT
===========
        288
```

To create a stored procedure that returns this kind of information, you should write the following:

```
CREATE PROCEDURE ALBUMCOUNT
RETURNS (NUM INTEGER)
AS
begin
  for
    select Count(*) from Album
    into :Num
  do exit;
end
```

This procedure doesn't take any parameters:

```
CREATE PROCEDURE ALBUMCOUNT
```

It does, however, return a value:

```
RETURNS (NUM INTEGER)
```

Because you ask for a single answer and not a series of rows, you can use exit instead of suspend:

```
for   // Query goes here
do exit;
```

After you compose the query, you can use a stored procedure on the C++Builder end to get data from it. To set up the stored procedure, all you have to do is drag it off the Component Palette, set its DataBaseName to the Music alias, and drop down the list from its StoredProcName property so you can choose the appropriate stored procedure.

The following code shows how to call the stored procedure from C++Builder:

```
int TDMod::GetTotalAlbumCount()
{
  GetAlbumCount->Prepare();
  GetAlbumCount->ExecProc();
  return GetAlbumCount->ParamByName("Num")->AsInteger;
}
```

This method returns an integer, which you can display to the user in any manner you think appropriate.

Viewing a Range of Data

Two interesting stored procedures allow you to ask questions such as, "What albums have a particular rating?" and "What albums have a rating of nine or better?" The following is the first of the two routines:

```
CREATE PROCEDURE NINEORBETTER
RETURNS (LAST VARCHAR(30),
ALBUM VARCHAR(30),
RATING INTEGER)
AS
begin
  for
    select Artist.Last, Album.Album, Album.Rating
    from Album, Artist
    where Album.GroupCode = Artist.Code
      and Album.Rating>= 9
    Order By Album.Rating Desc
    into :Last, :Album, :Rating
  do suspend;
end
```

The query at the heart of this procedure asks to see albums that have a rating higher than or equal to 9. To properly qualify the query, the code also asks to see only the entries from the Artist table that are associated with the albums that make it into the result set. The last line of the query asks to order the result set on the album.rating field with the highest ratings first.

The stored procedure shown here lets you ask for data from the table that falls into a particular range:

```
CREATE PROCEDURE RATINGRANGE (LOWRATING INTEGER,
HIGHRATING INTEGER)
RETURNS (LAST VARCHAR(30),
ALBUM VARCHAR(30),
RATING INTEGER)
AS
begin
  for
    select Artist.Last, Album.Album, Album.Rating
    from Album, Artist  where Album.GroupCode = Artist.Code
      and  Album.Rating>= :LowRating
      and  Album.Rating <= :HighRating
    Order By Album.Rating Desc
    into :Last, :Album, :Rating
  do suspend;
end
```

This procedure is very much like the previous one, but it takes parameters that allow you to specify the range you want to see, and it uses those parameters to customize the result set to your needs:

```
Album.Rating>= :LowRating and Album.Rating <= :HighRating
```

I've shown you several examples of stored procedures so that you might understand how much power exists in a simple query. To me, the most interesting thing about database programming is the ability to ask questions of the data you have collected. The key to that process is to write a query and then place it in a stored procedure so you can call it from your applications. You can also place the query directly in a TQuery component, but in that case the query takes longer to execute, and you have the bother of managing it on the client side. Everything is easier if you just leave the query on the server where it belongs. Either solution is reasonable in most cases.

Summary

I didn't mention a few lines of code in the Music program, but I reviewed most of the application in this chapter. This program contains code commonly used when constructing a relational database with C++Builder. The particular example shown is not robust enough to use in a professional setting, but it gives you a good feeling for how to proceed if you want to construct such an application.

In particular, you got a good look at the techniques used to create a powerful database with referential integrity. You also saw how to use generators, triggers, and stored procedures as well as how to perform filters and lookups on relational data. In general, this chapter sums up the core information necessary for you to produce a professional database program. If you understand all this material, you are not yet necessarily an expert, but you are ready to start building relational databases in a professional setting.

The Basics of COM and Type Libraries

by Charlie Calvert and Bruneau Babet

IN THIS CHAPTER

This chapter is about Component Object Model (COM) and the way it is implemented in C++Builder. The material in this chapter is vital to your understanding of much of the material presented in the rest of this book. By the time you are done with this chapter, you should understand the basic facts about how C++Builder implements COM. You should also learn a good deal about interfaces and see how they can be used in your programs, even if you are not particularly interested in COM. However, I should stress that this chapter is primarily theoretical in nature, and is designed to give you the background necessary to understand the other chapters on COM that are included in this book.

I am assuming that this chapter's readers have very little understanding of COM. This approach should be great for one set of readers, but a bit frustrating for people who know COM well and are trying to find out how C++Builder implements a technology they already understand. I ask this second group of readers to have patience. I know what it is you need to discover, and I will give you all the information you want; it's just unlikely that you will find the relevant materials presented quite as quickly, or exactly in the same order, as you might prefer.

General Introduction to COM

Few subjects in all programming are as large and as vast as COM. It is quite possible that COM is the single largest programming effort ever undertaken in the world of PC programming.

Despite its size and its sophistication, the first thing to understand about COM is that its architecture is not universally applauded. In fact, it's arguable that Microsoft could have come up with a better way to implement the lowest levels of COM, and in the future Microsoft may indeed improve its structure. Nevertheless, COM is currently what it is. Furthermore, the system undeniably works, and works well.

What Is COM?

COM stands for the Component Object Model. The theoretical purposes of COM are twofold:

- It provides a means of defining a specification for creating a set of non–language-specific standard objects.
- It provides a means of allowing you to implement objects that can be called between different processes, even if those processes are running on separate machines (DCOM).

In the concrete world of day-to-day practice, COM is most well known for bringing programmers the ability to do four things:

- Write code that can be used by multiple programming languages.
- Create ActiveX controls.
- Control other programs via OLE automation.
- Talk to objects or programs on other machines (DCOM).

When you take all these traits together, you end up with a very powerful solution to a wide range of problems. The solution is so powerful that Microsoft will increasingly be using COM as the primary interface into Windows.

COM and Windows

In the future, users will come to think of Windows as a set of COM interfaces that they can call when they need services. Even at this time, many services are already COM-based. For instance, the Windows Explorer is accessed primarily through COM. If you want to change features on the taskbar, you use COM. If you want to program some other feature of the basic Windows UI, you use a set of COM interfaces called the Shell API.

With Microsoft's rollout of Windows 2000, you will find that the entire operating system is increasingly revolving around COM. For instance, Word and Excel can be completely automated via COM. The same is true of the Internet Information Server, Internet Explorer, and many of the new features such as the Active Directory, DAO successors, the Microsoft Transaction Server, the Microsoft Message Queue, and innumerable other features.

13

THE BASICS OF
COM AND TYPE
LIBRARIES

Plug-and-Play Applications

There is no reason programmers can't make their programs out of a series of COM servers—at least in theory. These child programs could be plugged into a main program as needed. For instance, a debugger could be a standalone applet that is thoroughly integrated into an IDE via COM. It would sit unnoticed on the hard drive until the programmer needed it, and would pop up on demand, immediately integrating itself with the compiler. If you wanted to use another vendor's debugger, it too could support the same basic COM interfaces and therefore seamlessly plug itself into the current program.

Word and Excel (as well as the other Office applications) currently support applets of this type. For instance, Paint and the Equation editor can both be seamlessly integrated into Word as needed.

This kind of integration is often implemented through something called *in-place activation*. You can explore this technology by opening Word and choosing Insert, Object, Bitmap Image. This menu command should make a copy of Paint integrate into your version of Word as if they were one application. Of course, there is no reason another third-party application might not take the place of Paint on your system. In short, you can delete Paint from your system and use another third-party tool in its place. This second tool could also integrate itself into Word.

Programs such as Word and Paint follow the generic rules for integrating applications published in the OLE specification. This type of process falls under the general category of *object linking and embedding*, from which the acronym *OLE* is derived.

Technology that allows you to integrate one application into another is very flashy. However, that it is the most powerful part of COM.

COM's core is not ActiveX controls or in-place activation, but the relatively simple art of automation. The idea that you can use one program to control another program means that you can begin to view the entire system as nothing more than a suite of services that you can access as needed.

If you are writing a C++Builder program and need powerful word processing or spreadsheet functionality, one way to get it is to automate Word or Excel with COM. Let the user use these tools to develop or view documents. These same tools can be used to print or mail documents. In short, you can ask the VCL to do what it does best, which is work with databases, access system resources, and construct complex interfaces. If you need a spreadsheet, use COM as a conduit that allows you to call on Excel services. If you need a Word processor, you use COM to call on Word.

As systems become more distributed, COM steps in and allows you to reach out across the network to access services. Custom objects on the network might know how to access a particular database or how to run a particular query against your company's financial records. In a true distributed architecture, you would never have to open an Oracle database or write a complex query. Those chores would be handled by remote objects. Your job would be to simply call on the object to provide the service and then display the results to the user.

In the future, you may increasingly come to view your operating systems and the network as nothing more than a series of services that appear in the form of automated COM objects. Some developers will be creating these services, and others will be calling them. Behind them all will be COM automation and the very closely related field of Distributed COM.

Problems with COM

I have spent some time praising COM, but pointing out a few of its flaws is also worthwhile. The biggest problem with COM is that it is Windowscentric. As you will learn in the "COM on UNIX" section, there is a port of COM to UNIX. However, it is currently a new and untried technology. Certainly, most experts view Microsoft's primary goal as being the development of COM on the Windows platform with the intent of keeping its users locked into that operating system.

Another problem with COM is the fact that a plug-in or distributed architecture can be prone to bugs. These bugs often surface because of a lack of true compatibility between the different pieces of a program or integrated system.

If you integrated a program with Word via in-place activation and that program were buggy or misusing the OLE specification, then you could crash both Word and Windows. A crash can happen because of careless programming or a failure on Microsoft's part to clearly define the OLE specification. Another set of problems would arise if some portion of Microsoft's specification for OLE proved to be fundamentally flawed, which is not an unthinkable scenario.

Furthermore, software vendors in the current age are notably lacking in the sense of cooperation needed to gracefully succeed at something like this. For instance, it would be typical of today's software vendors to add custom interfaces that only they know about or that they fail to document properly. As a result, third parties would always struggle to keep up with a standard-setter who did not have their best interests at heart.

Despite the potential pitfalls, the idea of creating suites of relatively small standalone tools that work well together is very intriguing. COM can indeed help programmers achieve this goal.

COM on UNIX

The preceding section mentions that COM is now being ported to UNIX. The company that has done most of the work in this field is called Software AG, which you can find on the Web at `http://www.softwareag.com/corporat/solutions/entirex/entirex.htm`.

Software AG has already released the first commercial version of DCOM for UNIX. Apparently in the grip of an uncontrollable poetic frenzy, the people at Software AG decided to call their tool EntireX/DCOM. A version for Sun Microsystems' Solaris and OS/390 is available, as well as a version for Digital UNIX and Linux. The company says that additional releases, including one for IBM mainframes, will be coming down the pike in the next few months.

COM+ and the Future of COM

This section has a few words about the direction COM will likely move over the next few years. Several places reference specific technologies that will be explained immediately after this section, when I begin an examination of the technical side of COM.

Microsoft has decided to make major changes to COM. In truth, facets of the whole COM creation and object management scheme are perhaps less than optimal. Microsoft therefore plans to create something called COM+, which is an ongoing process that will take several years to complete.

One of the goals of COM+ is to promote the creation of type-rich objects that can be explored at run time just as a VCL class can be. COM+ will simplify some of the arcane and complex issues of COM. More specifically, COM+ will eliminate the programmer's need to focus on reference counting, `IUnknown`, `IClassFactory`, type libraries, and many other core COM-based technical schemes, most of which are discussed in the remainder of this chapter or in the next. Code that uses the old technologies should still be compatible with COM+, but new development will be done using COM+ itself.

For more information on COM+, go to the Microsoft Web site at `http://www.microsoft.com/com` and look for articles written by Mary Kirtland. The very useful COMSPEC is also available at the same site.

Creating and Using COM Interfaces

Now that you understand something of what COM is all about, it's time to see how to it is implemented inside both the operating system and in your C++Builder code. Interfaces are very much at the heart of this subject. When you thoroughly understand interfaces, you should be able to use COM and C++Builder to perform powerful feats that will greatly expand the reach of your programs.

C++Builder programmers can think of an interface as nothing more than a class with a set of pure virtual public methods. If you took a standard C++ object, stripped away the protected and private sections, removed all data members, and then declared all the remaining methods as pure virtual, you would have an interface.

Since its methods are specified as pure virtual, an interface simply defines a set of public methods for accessing the object, but it says nothing about the actual implementation of that object. In this sense, an interface is a pure virtual public interface to a standard C++ object.

The best way to fully understand this subject matter is to jump right in and see some code. C++Builder makes both COM and interfaces very easy to implement, so I'm going to show you how things work before I explain why they work that way, or even why they exist at all. After you see how easily you can create valid COM interfaces, I'll come back and explain what COM is and what you can do with it.

COM Interfaces Derive from `IUnknown`

First of all, all COM interfaces derive from the type `IUnknown`. In other words, `IUnknown` is a direct or indirect base class of all COM interfaces. To understand the reason for `IUnknown`, you need to understand the objective of COM. I mentioned earlier that COM interfaces are designed to be shared by applications written in different programming languages. If you've tried to share objects between applications or between dynamic link libraries and applications, you've undoubtedly encountered the problems that `IUnknown` addresses—memory management and object lifetime.

When sharing code, there must be an understanding about who allocates and who frees memory. Imagine the case in which a library creates an object and hands it to an application. The application can free the object when it no longer needs it but often there are memory manager conflicts: The application and the library have their own, distinct memory managers linked in.

To solve this problem, often the application asks the library to free the object it allocated. However, you then have a problem monitoring the object's lifetime. If the object is being shared, the library must keep track of the object's usage before really freeing it.

Now take that scenario one step further: What if that library is written in C++ but it exposes objects to be accessed from Delphi or Visual Basic applications? You have yet another problem—object indentity. How does a Visual Basic application specify to a C++ library that it wants an instance of the `TFooBar` object exposed by that library?

The problems with sharing objects are addressed by the three methods of the `IUnknown` interface. The following sections describe `IUnknown` from that point of view.

The Methods of `IUnknown`

The following shows a slightly edited prototype of the `IUnknown` interface taken from the standard header file `UNKNWN.H`:

```
MIDL_INTERFACE("00000000-0000-0000-C000-000000000046") IUnknown
{
public:
    virtual HRESULT   __stdcall QueryInterface(REFIID riid,➡
void** ppvObject) = 0;
    virtual ULONG     __stdcall AddRef( void) = 0;
    virtual ULONG     __stdcall Release( void) = 0;
};
```

In the context of the issues mentioned with sharing objects, the `QueryInterface()` method addresses the identify issue, while the other two methods, `AddRef()` and `Release()` solve the problem of the object's lifetime.

Interface Identify

Because COM is designed to be language-neutral, each COM interface must be identifiable in a language-neutral fashion. From a C++ point of view, your COM interface is a C++ class. For example, the following shows a COM interface of type `ICDPlayer`:

```
interface ICDPlayer : public IUnknown
{
  virtual void  Play()           = 0;
  virtual void  NextTrack()      = 0;
  virtual void  PreviousTrach()  = 0;
  virtual void  Stop()           = 0;
  virtual void  Eject()          = 0;
};
```

> **NOTE**
>
> It is customary to name interfaces with an *I* prefix. C++ Builder enforces this custom. When creating a new COM or automation object, C++Builder creates a new interface with the name `IYourSpecifiedClassName`.
>
> `interface` is not a true C++ language keyword. The header file `BASETYPS.H` contains a macro that maps the word `interface` to the `struct` keyword. As part of the COM+ effort, Microsoft has proposed that the keyword `interface` be recognized by C++ compilers. This change would allow the compiler to enforce the definition of an interface as well as eliminate the need to define the pure virtual specifiers on methods.

From a COM point of view, however, `ICDPlayer` is identified not by its C++ typename but rather by way of a GUID. Very briefly, a *GUID* is a 128-bit number that is guaranteed to be unique. The basic assumption is that only one instance of each GUID occurs in the entire world.

> **TIP**
>
> To generate a new GUID, Windows combines a unique number found on your network card with other information (such as the current date) to generate a number that is guaranteed to be unique. The algorithm for creating this number was created by the Open Software Foundation.
>
> To create your own GUIDs, you should first initialize COM by calling the Windows API function `CoInitialize`. You can then call `CoCreateGuid` to retrieve an instance of your unique GUID.

The utility GUIDGEN can also be used to create a new GUID. The source to GUID-GEN is included as part of the MFC examples shipping with C++Builder. For more information, look for the files in the EXAMPLES\MFC\UTILITY\GUIDGEN directory.

When an application wants to obtain a copy of the ICDPlayer interface exposed by your server, it turns to OLE and specifies that it is interested in an interface exposed by your server. OLE launches your server and returns an IUnknown to the application. (Remember, IUnknown is a base class of all interfaces.) That's where your interface's GUID and IUnknown's QueryInterface() method work together to get the application a copy of that specific interface. The client application invokes the QueryInterface() method that specifies your interface's GUID. The following pseudocode illustrates the process:

NOTE

In some cases throughout this chapter I use pseudocode to illustrate points rather than actual code or a full program listing. Please note that *psuedocode* is not actual code that can be compiled. It is a tool developers use to walk through the general logic of a program or algorithm. When I use psuedocode, I will note that in the text.

```
extern GUID IID_ICDPlayer;
// Call routine 'CallOleToGetUnknownOfServer' (not shown here) that
// utilizes OLE API to launch a server to obtain a copy to its interface.
IUnknown *pServerUnknown = CallOLEToGetIUnknownOfServer();ICDPlayer
➥*pCDPlayer;
pServerUnknown->QueryInterface(IID_ICDPlayer, (void**)&pCDPlayer);
```

For now, I'll skip the details of the CallOLEToGetIUnknownOfServer(). You've probably guessed that it's a little more complex than shown. However, I want to make sure that you understand the need for a language-neutral typing mechanism and the way IUnknown's QueryInterface works to retrieve a pointer to the interface whose GUID is specified as the first parameter.

NOTE

GUIDs are used to identify more than interfaces in the world of COM. For example, servers and type libraries are also identified. When a GUID identifies an interface, it is also known as an *IID (interface ID)*. The GUID is often defined as IID_IInterfaceName: IID_ICDPlayer, for example.

13

THE BASICS OF
COM AND TYPE
LIBRARIES

IUnknown, Memory Management, and Object Lifetime

In traditional C++ programming you create objects via the new operator; when you no longer need the object, you free it via a call to the delete operator. That mechanism works for objects within a single C++ application. As soon as you start sharing objects with other applications, you have the variance of memory managers to deal with. A new object in one C++Builder application should not be a delete object in another C++Builder application unless they share the same memory manager. Things get even more complicated when the object is shared with applications written in other languages.

To remedy these problems, COM specifies that an object's client handles no memory management. It obtains a pointer to the object by calling one or more OLE APIs. When the client no longer needs the object, it invokes the object's Release() method. If the client wants to make copies of the object, it invokes the AddRef() method of the object. For every AddRef() called, the client must invoke a corresponding Release(). The following pseudocode illustrates the concept:

```
void UseCDPlayerCOMServer()
{
  // Call OLE to obtain Server's IUnknown
  extern GUID IID_ICDPlayer;
  IUnknown *pServerUnknown = CallOLEToGetIUnknownOfServer();

  // Request specific ICDPlayer interface
  ICDPlayer *pCDPlayer;
  pServerUnknown->QueryInterface(IID_ICDPlayer, (void**)&pCDPlayer);

  // Release the IUnknown of the server
  pServerUnknown->Release();

  // Use CDPlayer interface
  pCDPlayer->Play();

  // Release CDPlayer interface
  pCDPlayer->Release();
}
```

The pseudocode illustrates the client's interface use. The server simply maintains a reference count for each interface it hands out. The count is incremented whenever AddRef() is invoked, and decreased when Release() is called. When the reference count reaches 0, the server is free to dispose of the interface.

There's more to IUnknown than mentioned so far. However, the details of IUnknown are automatically taken care of when you implement COM interfaces using C++Builder. C++Builder utilizes the Active Template Library (ATL) from Microsoft to handle the IUnknown details, as well as several other issues related to exposing COM interfaces.

Type Libraries

The methods of `IUnknown` and an IID overcome the generic issues of sharing objects across applications. However, in order for your object to be usable, client applications need to know about the object, the methods it supports, and the various parameters expected by each method.

Here's a C++ analogy: When you design a C++ class intended to be shared throughout your program, you typically declare the class in a header file. The latter is then included by all source modules that refer to that class. The class declaration in the header file describes your class' methods. Of course, a C++ header file is not useful to a Delphi or Visual Basic programmer. What you need is a language-neutral mechanism to describe interfaces, as well as their methods and parameters. That's exactly what a Type Library is all about.

A *Type Library* is simply a binary file that describes types. C++Builder automatically creates a Type Library for the OLE objects you create. You can also use C++Builder to view the Type Libraries of other COM servers. Simply select File, Open and select Type Library (*.tlb;*.dll;*.ocx;*.exe;*.olb) in the Files of Type drop-down list. The `STDVCL40.TLB` file included with your copy of C++Builder is a Type Library that describes some VCL types. The next chapter, "Creating COM Automation Servers and Clients," covers Type Libraries as well as the C++Builder Type Library Editor in greater detail.

Creating a COM Object

The following section takes you through the process of creating a COM object that exposes an interface that is accessible to other applications. You should note that there are various types of COM objects supported by C++Builder. Each COM object type supports varying numbers and types of COM interfaces. This section deals with a COM object that exposes a simple, user-defined COM interface, also known as a *custom interface*.

> **NOTE**
>
> Other types of COM objects supported by C++Builder include automation objects, ActiveX controls, property pages, and MTS objects. These objects implement specific sets of COM interfaces. A plain COM object, on the other hand, usually implements a simple user-defined interface.

Before you can expose a COM object, you must first create either an ActiveX library or an application in which to house the implementation of the object. In this example, I implement the object in a Dynamic Link Library. Here are the steps I follow:

1. Select File, New.

2. Turn to the ActiveX tab and select ActiveX Library. C++Builder creates a new project with two units named PROJECT1.CPP and PROJECT1_ATL.CPP. These files contain the basic infrastructure that allows your application to interact with the COM system.

3. Add a COM object to the project by choosing File, New, ActiveX, COM Object. When prompted for the CoClass name, enter **SimpleCOM**. Notice that the interface for that object is automatically named ISimpleCOM.

You may provide a description string in the appropriate field; then select the OK button. C++Builder takes you to the Type Library Editor as shown in Figure 13.1.

FIGURE 13.1

Setting up a COM application using the C++Builder 4 Type Library Editor.

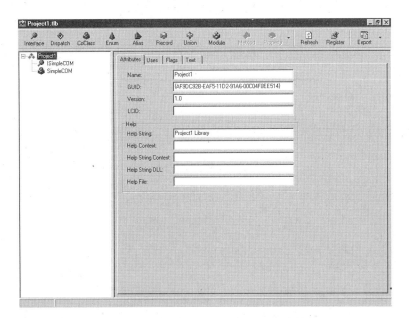

The addition of the COM object causes C++Builder to add two additional units to your project: The PROJECT1_TLB source and header files are a C++ translation of the types defined in your project's Type Library. The SimpleCOMImpl files contain the actual implementation of the new ISimpleCOM interface you are creating.

The bulk of designing COM interfaces in C++Builder involves the Type Library Editor. In standard C++ programming, you may be inclined to spend most of your design time in a header file editing class definitions. However, design work in COM programming is spent refining your interfaces' methods. Now add a method to your new interface.

Select the interface ISimpleCOM in the left pane of the Type Library Editor. Right click and select New, Method from the local menu; Method1() is added to the ISimpleCOM interface. Rename the method **ShowString()** and then turn to the Parameters tab and add a new parameter named **str** of type BSTR. Figure 13.2 shows the Type Library Editor with the new method.

FIGURE **13.2**

Adding a method to your COM application using the C++Builder 4 Type Library Editor.

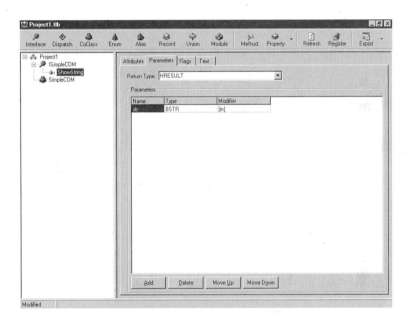

Once you've designed your interface methods, you must activate the Type Library Editor's Refresh button. This triggers C++Builder to update your project's files to reflect changes you made in the Type Library Editor. Pressing the Refresh button in this case regenerates the PROJECT1_TLB.H header file with an updated declaration of the ISimpleCOM interface. It also adds a ShowString() method to the SIMPLEIMPL.CPP file, where you can provide implementation for the new method of your interface (see Listing 13.1).

LISTING 13.1   THE SOURCE CODE IMPLEMENTING THE SimpleCOM SERVER METHODS

```
// SIMPLECOMIMPL : Implementation of TSimpleCOMImpl
//(CoClass: SimpleCOM, Interface: ISimpleCOM)

#include <vcl.h>
#pragma hdrstop

#include "SIMPLECOMIMPL.H"

/////////////////////////////////////////////////////////////////////////////
TSimpleCOMImpl

STDMETHODIMP TSimpleCOMImpl::ShowString(BSTR str)
{
  try
  {

  }
  catch(Exception &e)
  {
    return Error(e.Message.c_str(), IID_ISimpleCOM);
  }
  return S_OK;
};
```

You now have an ActiveX server that exposes an interface. This server is not very useful, but it does illustrate the concept of exposing a COM interface. The implementation of the ShowString() method can simply invoke the VCL ShowMessage() routine. To make your server accessible to client applications, you must register it; select Run, Register ActiveX Server to do so. Once successfully registered, your server is accessible to ActiveX client applications. Figure 13.3 shows a sample implementation of the ShowString() method and the result of registering the server.

FIGURE 13.3

You must register your server to make it accessible to client applications.

As you can imagine, there's quite a bit more going on under the hood that exposes an interface to other applications. However, leave the server's detail for now and look at what it takes for a client to access the COM object you've just created.

Using a COM Object

This section shows you three programs that invoke the ShowString() method of your COM server from C++, Visual Basic, and Delphi, respectively. As a C++ programmer, you may find interfaces, GUIDs, and Type Libraries unnecessary. As you've probably realized, however, C++Builder handles most of that madness for you. When you consider that your object is now accessible from a host of applications written in other languages—across machine boundaries and maybe even running on other platforms—COM becomes a very attractive approach.

A C++Builder COM Client

The SimpleClient program included on this book's CD-ROM contains an Edit field and a button. When the button is clicked, the text in the Edit field is passed to your server's ShowString() method (see Listing 13.2).

LISTING 13.2 THE SIMPLECLIENT PROGRAM'S SOURCE CODE

```
//------------------------------------------------
// MAINFORM.CPP
// MainForm source of SIMPLECLIENT application.
//------------------------------------------------
#include <vcl.h>
#pragma hdrstop

#include "MainForm.h"
#include "Project1_TLB.h"
//------------------------------------------------
#pragma package(smart_init)
#pragma resource "*.dfm"
TForm1 *Form1;
//------------------------------------------------
__fastcall TForm1::TForm1(TComponent* Owner)
        : TForm(Owner)
{
}
//------------------------------------------------
void __fastcall TForm1::Button1Click(TObject *Sender)
{
  TCOMISimpleCOM SimpleCOMServer = CoSimpleCOM::Create();
  SimpleCOMServer->ShowString(WideString(Edit1->Text));
}
//------------------------------------------------
```

When you run this program, you see a form with a button and an Edit control on it. If you click the button on the form, the text in the Edit field is passed to the ShowString() method of the SimpleCOM server, as shown in Figure 13.4.

FIGURE 13.4

The COM client application invoking the COM server.

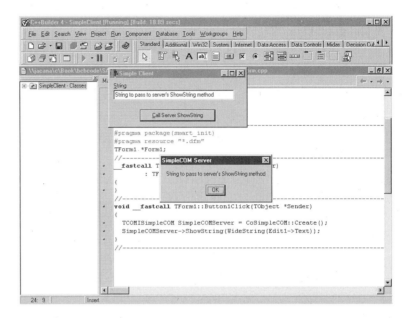

The main form's `Button1Click` method is the key to understanding the SimpleClient program:

```
void __fastcall TForm1::Button1Click(TObject *Sender)
{
  TCOMISimpleCOM SimpleCOMServer = CoSimpleCOM::Create();
  SimpleCOMServer->ShowString(WideString(Edit1->Text));
}
```

The program takes advantages of classes declared in the server's `Project1_TLB` files to create the server and invoke the methods of its interface. You can use raw OLE API calls to launch an OLE server and to obtain a pointer to an interface it exposes. However, if your client application is written in C++, it's much easier to simply add the server's `xxxx_TLB` source and header files to your project and use the client wrappers provided in that file.

A Visual Basic COM Client

The Visual Basic client is very similar to the one in C++. To make the `SimpleCOM` object accessible in Visual Basic, you must first enable the Project1 Type Library in VB's References dialog. Figure 13.5 shows the `SimpleCOM` object within the Visual Basic v6.0 object browser.

FIGURE **13.5**

Browsing the CBuilder COM server in Visual Basic.

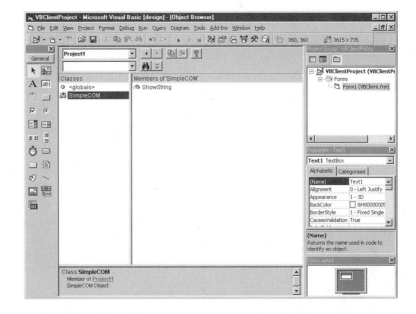

13

THE BASICS OF
COM AND TYPE
LIBRARIES

> **NOTE**
>
> Because both Visual Basic and C++Builder default to the name Project1 for a project, you need to rename your Visual Basic project before you enable the SimpleCOM's Project1 Library in Visual Basic's References dialog.

The VBClientProject sample application included in the SimpleClient directory invokes your server's ShowString() method. Figure 13.6 shows that Visual Basic application.

A Delphi COM Client

Of course, your server is also accessible from within a Delphi application. Like C++Builder, Delphi exposes an Import Type Library menu item from the Project menu. You can use that option to have Delphi automatically create a Project1_TLB.pas file for your server. This file is the Pascal equivalent of the C++ Project1_TLB header and source files. Listing 13.3 shows a sample Delphi routine that accesses your COM server.

FIGURE 13.6

Invoking the CBuilder COM server from Visual Basic.

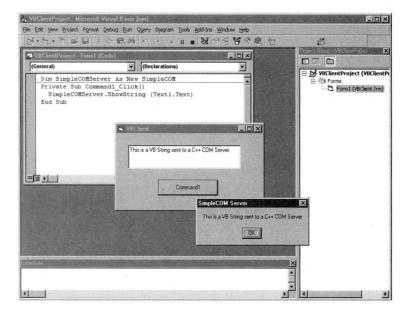

LISTING 13.3   THE SOURCE OF A DELPHI APPLICATION THAT ACCESSES YOUR SIMPLECOM SERVER

```
unit Unit1;

interface

uses
  Windows, Messages, SysUtils, Classes, Graphics, Controls, Forms,
  Dialogs, StdCtrls;
type
  TForm1 = class(TForm)
    Button1: TButton;
    Edit1: TEdit;
    procedure Button1Click(Sender: TObject);
  private
    { Private declarations }
  public
    { Public declarations }
  end;

var
  Form1: TForm1;

implementation

uses Project1_TLB;
```

```
{$R *.DFM}

procedure TForm1.Button1Click(Sender: TObject);
var
  SimpleCOMServer: ISimpleCOM;
begin
  SimpleCOMServer := CoSimpleCOM.Create();
  SimpleCOMServer.ShowString(Edit1.Text);
end;

end.
```

Dissecting a C++Builder ActiveX Server

Now that you've seen a sample ActiveX Server built with C++Builder and various client applications, it's time to dig down into the makeup of such a server. The goal here is to provide information that allows you to customize your server. I also point out how the code generated by C++Builder relates to general COM concepts. Because C++Builder uses the Active Template Library for its servers, you'll be better poised to take full advantage of C++Builder's ActiveX Server support if you have an understanding of the ATL basics. From a client point of view, C++Builder's bulk support comes from templates declared in the files INCLUDE\VCL\UTILCLS.H and INCLUDE\VCL\SAFEARRY.H. You may find it useful to familiarize yourself with the classes in these headers.

13

THE BASICS OF COM AND TYPE LIBRARIES

The ActiveX Server's Project File

Listing 13.4 shows your SimpleCOM server's Project file. SimpleCOM is an *inproc server*—it is implemented in a Dynamic Link Library. You can also create ActiveX servers that are standalone executables. These servers are commonly referred to as *local servers*. A local server's Project file is slightly different from that of an inproc server. Listing 13.5 shows a local server's Project file.

LISTING 13.4   THE SIMPLECOM SERVER'S PROJECT SOURCE

```
#include <vcl.h>
#pragma hdrstop
#include <atl\atlvcl.h>

#include "SimpleCOMImpl.h"
#pragma package(smart_init)
USERES("Project1.res");
```

continues

LISTING 13.4   CONTINUED

```
USEUNIT("Project1_ATL.cpp");
USETLB("Project1.tlb");
USEUNIT("Project1_TLB.cpp");
USEUNIT("SimpleCOMImpl.cpp"); /* SimpleCOM: CoClass */
//————————————————————————————————————.
TComModule  Project1Module;
TComModule & _Module = Project1Module;

// The ATL Object map holds an array of _ATL_OBJMAP_ENTRY structures
// that described the objects of your OLE server. The MAP is handed
// to your project's CComModule-derived _Module object via the Init
// method.
//
BEGIN_OBJECT_MAP(ObjectMap)
  OBJECT_ENTRY(CLSID_SimpleCOM, TSimpleCOMImpl)
END_OBJECT_MAP()

// Entry point of your Server invoked by Windows for processes or
// threads are initialized or terminated.
//
int WINAPI DllEntryPoint(HINSTANCE hinst, unsigned long reason, void*)
{
    if (reason == DLL_PROCESS_ATTACH)
    {
        _Module.Init(ObjectMap, hinst);
        DisableThreadLibraryCalls(hinst);
    }
    return TRUE;
}


// _Module.Term is typically invoked from the DLL_PROCESS_DETACH of
// your DllEntryPoint. However, this may result in an incorrect
// shutdown sequence.
// Instead an Exit routine is setup to invoke the cleanup routine
// CComModule::Term.
//
void ModuleTerm(void)
{
    _Module.Term();
}
#pragma exit ModuleTerm 63

// Entry point of your Server invoked to inquire whether the DLL is no
// longer in use and should be unloaded.
//
STDAPI __export DllCanUnloadNow(void)
{
    return (_Module.GetLockCount()==0) ? S_OK : S_FALSE;
}
```

```
// Entry point of your Server allowing OLE to retrieve a class object
// from your Server
//
STDAPI __export DllGetClassObject(REFCLSID rclsid, REFIID riid,
                                  LPVOID* ppv)
{
    return _Module.GetClassObject(rclsid, riid, ppv);
}

// Entry point of your Server invoked to instruct the server to
// create registry entries for all classes supported by the module
//
STDAPI __export DllRegisterServer(void)
{
    return _Module.RegisterServer(TRUE);
}

// Entry point of your Server invoked to instruct the server to remove
// all registry entries created through DllRegisterServer.
//
STDAPI __export DllUnregisterServer(void)
{
    return _Module.UnregisterServer();
}
//---------------------------------------------
```

LISTING 13.5   A C++BUILDER LOCAL SERVER'S PROJECT SOURCE

```
//---------------------------------------------
#include <vcl.h>
#pragma hdrstop
#include <atl\atlmod.h>
#include "MyCOMObjectImpl.h"
USERES("Project1.res");
USEFORM("Unit1.cpp", Form1);
USETLB("Project1.tlb");
USEUNIT("Project1_TLB.cpp");
USEUNIT("MyCOMObjectImpl.cpp"); /* MyCOMObject: CoClass */
USEUNIT("Project1_ATL.cpp");
//---------------------------------------------
TComModule _ProjectModule(0 /*InitATLServer*/);
TComModule &_Module = _ProjectModule;

// The ATL Object map holds an array of _ATL_OBJMAP_ENTRY structures
// that described the objects of your OLE server. The MAP is handed to
// your project's CComModule-derived _Module object via the Init method
//
BEGIN_OBJECT_MAP(ObjectMap)
  OBJECT_ENTRY(CLSID_MyCOMObject, TMyCOMObjectImpl)
END_OBJECT_MAP()
```

continues

13

THE BASICS OF COM AND TYPE LIBRARIES

LISTING 13.5   CONTINUED

```
//--------------------------------------.
WINAPI WinMain(HINSTANCE, HINSTANCE, LPSTR, int)
{
        try
        {
                Application->Initialize();
                Application->CreateForm(__classid(TForm1), &Form1);
                Application->Run();
        }
        catch (Exception &exception)
        {
                Application->ShowException(&exception);
        }
        return 0;
}
//--------------------------------------.
```

A C++Builder ActiveX server's project source contains more than what is initially obvious. The following describes various interesting sections of the project source file:

- Like all C++Builder project files, an ActiveX server's project source informs the IDE of the files used by your project.

- The `USETLB("Project1.tlb");` statement informs the IDE's linker to bind the server's Type Library as a resource to the server's link library or executable.

- The USEUNIT("Project1_TLB.cpp"); macro instructs the Project Manager to compile and link the source code that contains C++ declarations of the types defined in your server's Type Library. This file contains only the GUIDs defined by your server.

- `USEUNIT(ProjectName_ATL.CPP)` instructs the Project Manager to compile the `ProjectName_ATL.CPP` source file. This file simply pulls in various ATL headers and source files.

- Statements of the format `USEUNIT("MyCOMObjectImpl.cpp"); /* MyCOMObject: CoClass */` instruct the Project Manager to compile and link the source code. The comment following the macro informs the IDE's Code Manager that this file implements the methods of the CoClass `MyCOMObject`. If you ever notice that the IDE is no longer providing empty implementation bodies for the methods of an interface of your CoClass, it could be that this comment was accidentally modified or removed.

- The `TComModule` type is a template that extends ATL's own `CComModule` class. It performs various tasks, specifically in the case of VCL local servers. It takes care of initializing OLE by virtual of its `TInitOle` data member. It allows OLE initialization in VCL applications. It registers the objects exposed by the server and detects various registration options passed on the command line. It also warns the user if the latter attempts to terminate a server with outstanding objects owned by one or more clients.

- The object map defined with the BEGIN_OBJECT_MAP and END_OBJECT_MAP macros lists the objects exposed by your server and the C++ class that implements each object's interfaces.

C++Builder inproc servers expose various entry points in their project source. These are the standard entry points of DLL servers. The DLL_PROCESS_ATTACH section of the DllEntryPoint function initializes the TComModule instance by passing it a pointer to the server's Object table. There's no special code that performs any cleanup in the DLL_PROCESS_DETACH section as you would expect. Instead, a #pragma exit routine is set up to handle this chore. This was necessary to work around problems related to the order in which global and static objects are cleaned up.

The Project file of local servers, on the other hand, don't seem to perform any initialization related to COM. The WinMain routine is identical to that of a non-ActiveX server. The answer to this mystery lies in the TComModule constructor. Local servers use the constructor that takes an additional parameter:

```
TComModule _ProjectModule(0 /*InitATLServer*/);
```

A quick check in the ATLMOD.H header reveals that this constructor inserts a special function—InitATLServer—in the initialization system of VCL applications. This allows ActiveX server executables to perform all setup tasks without interfering with the normal flow of VCL applications.

A Server's Object Implementation File

C++Builder creates an IMPL (implementation) source and header file pair for each object or CoClass exposed by your ActiveX server. By default, the files are named after the CoClass with the Impl suffix added. For example, the files SimpleCOMImpl.h and SimpleCOMImpl.cpp contain the implementation of the SimpleCOM object. Listing 13.6 shows the implementation header file of the SimpleCOM server. The following section examines the contents of that file.

LISTING 13.6 THE IMPLEMENTATION HEADER OF THE SIMPLECOM SERVER

```
// SIMPLECOMIMPL.H : Declaration of the TSimpleCOMImpl

#ifndef __SIMPLECOMIMPL_H_
#define __SIMPLECOMIMPL_H_
```

continues

LISTING 13.6   CONTINUED

```
#include "Project1_TLB.H"


//////////////////////////////////////////////////////////////////
// TSimpleCOMImpl      Implements ISimpleCOM, default interface of
//                     SimpleCOM
// ThreadingModel : Apartment
// Dual Interface : FALSE
// Event Support  : FALSE
// Default ProgID : Project1.SimpleCOM
// Description    :
//////////////////////////////////////////////////////////////////
class ATL_NO_VTABLE TSimpleCOMImpl :
  public CComObjectRootEx<CComSingleThreadModel>,
  public CComCoClass<TSimpleCOMImpl, &CLSID_SimpleCOM>,
  public ISimpleCOM
{
public:
  TSimpleCOMImpl()
  {
  }

  // Data used when registering Object
  //
  DECLARE_THREADING_MODEL(otApartment);
  DECLARE_PROGID("Project1.SimpleCOM");
  DECLARE_DESCRIPTION("");

  // Function invoked to (un)register object
  //
  static HRESULT WINAPI UpdateRegistry(BOOL bRegister)
  {
    TTypedComServerRegistrarT<TSimpleCOMImpl>
    regObj(GetObjectCLSID(), GetProgID(), GetDescription());
    return regObj.UpdateRegistry(bRegister);
  }


BEGIN_COM_MAP(TSimpleCOMImpl)
  COM_INTERFACE_ENTRY(ISimpleCOM)
END_COM_MAP()

// ISimpleCOM
public:

  STDMETHOD(ShowString(BSTR str));
};

#endif //__SIMPLECOMIMPL_H_
```

Base Classes of a COM Object

The `TSimpleCOMImpl` class implements the interfaces of the `SimpleCOM` CoClass. It derives from three classes:

- `CComObjectRootEx` is an ATL template that provides a standard implementation of `IUnknown`.

- `CComCoClass` is another ATL template. It provides various methods to retrieve your object's CLSID and several overloaded `Error` methods.

- The `TSimpleCOMImpl` class derives from the `ISimpleCOM` interface since that is the default interface created by C++Builder for your COM object.

> **NOTE**
>
> Which base classes your server's C++ class derives from depends upon the type of COM object the class implements. Automation objects, for example, derive from the ATL template `IDispatchImpl`, while Remote Data Module objects derive from the `IDataBrokerImpl` template. It's very enlightening to use C++Builder's class browser and scan through the various base classes used by your COM object.

Server Registration Macros

Your objects must be registered with COM in order to be available to clients. In other words, there must be some information about your object stored in the system Registry. This information allows COM to know about your object, the interfaces it supports, and the location of the server that implements the object.

When you create a COM object in C++Builder, the wizard allows you to customize various options that are eventually used when the object is registered. For example, you can provide a description string that C++Builder then uses during the registration process. You can, however, leave these options at their default settings and customize them later. The most important ones are exposed as macros right within your class' declaration:

- The DECLARE_THREADING_MODEL macro selects your object's threading model. The macro expects a member of the `ObjectThreadingModel` enumeration defined in `ATLMOD.H`:

```
enum ObjectThreadingModel
{
  otSingle,
  otApartment,
```

```
otFree,
otBoth,
otAmbientThreadModel
};
```

The first members correspond to the COM threading models `Single`, `Apartment`, `Free`, and `Both`. The last member, `otAmbientThreadModel`, is actually for compatibility with previous versions of C++Builder in which the _ATL_*xxxx*_INSTANC-ING macros determined the threading models of all objects exposed by a server. For newly created objects, you should select the member that corresponds to the threading model matching the concurrency requirements of your object. If you are unaware of any concurrency requirements, the default setting, `Apartment`, is probably fine for your object.

- DECLARE_PROGID declares your object's programmatic identifier (progid). A *progid* is a string that can be used to identify your COM object when using its CLSID would be inconvenient. For example, progids are the preferred way to refer to COM objects in scripting environments. By default, C++Builder assigns your object the progid `ServerName.CoClassName`. Therefore, your server's `SimpleCOM` object has the progid `Project1.SimpleCOM`.

- DECLARE_DESCRIPTION provides a description of your object used by C++Builder when registering the object with COM.

Besides the registration macros, your class will also contain a static method—`UpdateRegistry`—which is invoked to register or unregister your object. This function utilizes information provided by the macros just mentioned. You can modify or expand this function as you need to register additional information about your objects. For example, if your object support certain component categories, you can add the appropriate calls to register these in the `UpdateRegistry` function.

> **NOTE**
>
> The Active Template Library provides a sophisticated `registrar` object to perform Registry-related chores. It is implemented in the file ATL.DLL. C++Builder, however, does not utilize the `registrar` object in order to avoid the need to redistribute ATL.DLL with your COM server. Instead, C++Builder servers use a combination of registration macros and various registrar templates defined in the file ATLMOD.H.

The implementation source file of each COM object exposed by your server is very simple: It merely contains empty implementations of the methods of the object's interface. Listing 13.1 shows the content of the implementation source file for the SimpleCOM object. C++Builder provides a fair amount of automatic code management for keep your server's implementation in sync with the definition of the interface it implements. If you add a new method or modify an existing interface method, the IDE will attempt to detect the appropriate modifications required to the implementation header and source files.

ATL Options Page

Additional settings for your ActiveX server can be found on the ATL page, which is accessible from the Project, Options menu item. Figure 13.7 shows the ATL options page.

FIGURE 13.7

The CBuilder's ATL Options page.

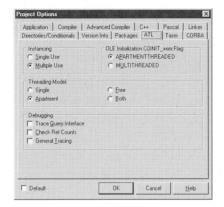

Unfortunately, the C++Builder help documentation about this page is somewhat erroneous. The following information provides a quick description of each setting:

- The Instancing setting allows you to control whether your server's object is visible to only one or to multiple clients. This setting is only relevant for objects exposed in a local server. Select Single Use if you want only one client to be able to access each instance of your server's object. The default setting, Multiple Use, allows more than one application to connect to your server's object.

- The OLE Initialization COINIT_xxxx Flag option allows you to determine whether OLE should be initialized with the COINIT_APARTMENTTHREADED or COINIT_MULTITHREADED flag. The parameter is passed to the OLE API CoInitializeEx. Select MULTITHREADED if your object is free-threaded. This informs OLE that there is no need to serialize calls to your object. While this option provides the best performance, it also requires that you code your object to handle the resulting concurrency issues. Unless you are familiar with the various COM concurrency models, I suggest that you stick to the default APARTMENT-THREADED setting.

- The Threading Model option is related to the OLE Initialization COINIT_xxxx Flag. However, it's only applicable to ActiveX servers created with previous versions of C++Builder. With C++Builder 4, each object exposes its threading model via the DECLARE_THREADING_MODEL registration macro. You can most likely ignore this setting.

- The Debugging option defines debugging various macros exposed by ATL. When enabled, these macros trigger the generation of trace message about QueryInterface calls, reference count changes, and general diagnostic messages. You can view these message in the C++Builder IDE's Event Log while debugging your ActiveX server.

More About GUIDs and the Registry

COM objects must be registered. This chapter also mentioned that COM objects are identified by a GUID, commonly referred to as a CLSID. A COM object implements one or more COM interfaces. Each COM interface is uniquely identified by a GUID, commonly referred to as an IID. When a client application wants to access a particular interface, it invokes some OLE API specifying the COM object's CLSID and the IID of the interface it wants to obtain. Given this scenario, it makes sense that the Registry must contain information about servers, as well as COM objects and interfaces.

When it comes to COM objects, the Registry can be viewed as a simple database that has one primary task: associating a server with each COM object available on the system. This definition of the Registry is incomplete, but it's sufficient for now.

To work with the Registry, open REGEDIT.EXE. You will see something that looks like Figure 13.8.

Open the tree called HKEY_CLASSES_ROOT. Scroll down the list of entries until you come to one called CLSID. Open the CLSID tree (see Figure 13.9) and scroll down the entries.

FIGURE 13.8

The Registry Editor displays this screen when it first opens.

FIGURE 13.9

The CLSID *section of* HKEY _CLASSES_ROOT *in the RegEdit program. The CLSIDs are on the left; the associated program, class, or file type is on the right.*

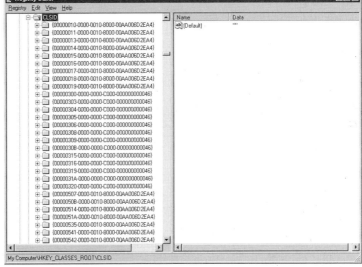

You might notice that various familiar names appear on the right side of the RegEdit screen. For instance, CLSID //0003000C-0000-0000-C000-000000000046} is associated with the Package program. Scroll down even further in HKEY_CLASSES_ROOT and you come to an entry on the left side that reads Package. If you open the tree for the Package entry, as shown in Figure 13.10, you see a CLSID entry identical to the one you found earlier. Depending on the version of your operating system, you may have more (or fewer) registration entries under the Package entry.

FIGURE **13.10**

The Package *tree
entry.*

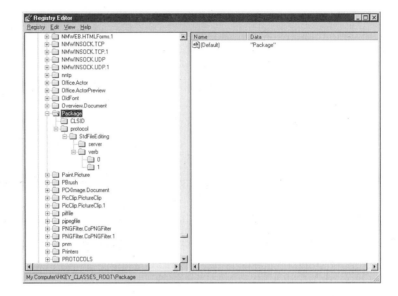

The Package entry in REGEDIT.EXE has leaves called CLSID, protocol, server, and verb. The point here is that you can find the CLSID of the Package program by looking up the program's name in the Registry. Conversely, if you have an object's CLSID, you can find its name. Figure 13.10 suggests that other important pieces of information are also stored in RegEdit and associated with the Package program. For now all you need to know is that it's a place to store CLSIDs.

If you want to insert an entry or set of entries in the Registry, you can often let C++Builder perform the task for you. You can also call certain Windows API functions such as RegCreateKey or RegCreateKeyEx. Alternatively, you can register a GUID by preparing text such as the SIMPLECOM.REG file. Consider the following entry in that file:

```
HKEY_CLASSES_ROOT\Project1.SimpleCOM\CLSID =
➡{AF9DC92E-EAF5-11D2-91A6-00C04F8EE514}
```

I divided this entry into two lines because of space considerations. You, however, should type it as a single line. The code shown in Listing 13.7 tells the Registry to create an entry called SimpleCOM\CLSID and to associate a particular CLSID with that entry.

LISTING 13.7   THE REGISTRATION FILE FOR THE SimpleCOM OBJECT

```
REGEDIT
HKEY_CLASSES_ROOT\Project1.SimpleCOM = SimpleCOM Object
HKEY_CLASSES_ROOT\Project1.SimpleCOM\CLSID =
➥{AF9DC92E-EAF5-11D2-91A6-00C04F8EE514}
HKEY_CLASSES_ROOT\CLSID\{AF9DC92E-EAF5-11D2-91A6-00C04F8EE514}
➥= SimpleCOM Object
HKEY_CLASSES_ROOT\CLSID\{AF9DC92E-EAF5-11D2-91A6-00C04F8EE514}\
➥InprocServer32 = "c:\Book\bcbcode\SAMS\BCB4UNLE\CODE\chap13\
➥SimpleCOM\Project1.dll"
HKEY_CLASSES_ROOT\CLSID\{AF9DC92E-EAF5-11D2-91A6-00C04F8EE514}\ProgID
➥= Project1.SimpleCOM
HKEY_CLASSES_ROOT\CLSID\{AF9DC92E-EAF5-11D2-91A6-00C04F8EE514}\
➥Version=1.0
```

In order to print this file in the book, I have had to break lines at some unusual locations. As a result, you might want to reference the source on the CD-ROM that accompanies this book.

Besides associating a CLSID with a name and a name with a CLSID, the Registry also associates a CLSID with a path to an executable or DLL:

```
HKEY_CLASSES_ROOT\CLSID\{AF9DC92E-EAF5-11D2-91A6-00C04F8EE514}\
➥InprocServer32 ="c:\Book\bcbcode\SAMS\BCB4UNLE\CODE\chap13\
➥SimpleCOM\Project1.dll"
```

Given an entry like this in the Registry database, you can easily see how you can give the COM services a CLSID and then have COM load a DLL or executable that is associated with the CLSID. The fact that you can easily create an error condition by specifying the wrong path in your REG file should be obvious. If you are having trouble launching an ActiveX server, it's often useful to peek at the information stored in the Registry.

The Registry will come up again frequently in the remaining chapters of this book, but it is no longer focused on here. The key point to remember is that the Registry is just a database. This database serves a wide range of purposes, but one of the most important is that it associates CLSIDs with the names of programs and with other associated bits of information, such as version numbers and the location at which binaries are stored. The next chapter gives explicit examples of how C++Builder automatically registers an object for you.

The _TLB Files

For each Type Library associated with a project, C++Builder maintains a corresponding source and header file pair typically named ProjectName_TLB.CPP/H. From a server's point of view, this file provides a C++ definition of the interfaces implemented by the server. It also defines the GUID of the server's COM object and COM interfaces. The file also contains C++ definitions for all other types defined in that type library. For example, a complex server may define various structures, interfaces, and unions to be used as parameter types of its interface. Understanding the contents of the _TLB file is fairly important. The following section examines the content of your SimpleCOM object's _TLB file. The contents of the header file are shown in Listing 13.8.

LISTING **13.8**   THE SimpleCOM OBJECT'S _TLB HEADER FILE

```
// C++ TLBWRTR : $Revision:    1.96.1.27   $
// File generated on 4/10/99 2:24:13 PM from Type Library below.


// ********************************************************************
// Type Lib: I:\SAMS\BCB4UNLE\CODE\chap13\SimpleCOM\Project1.tlb
// IID\LCID: {AF9DC92B-EAF5-11D2-91A6-00C04F8EE514}\0
// Helpfile:
// DepndLst:
//    (1) v2.0 stdole, (C:\WINNT\System32\STDOLE2.TLB)
//    (2) v4.0 StdVCL, (C:\WINNT\System32\STDVCL40.DLL)
// ********************************************************************
#ifndef   __Project1_TLB_h__
#define   __Project1_TLB_h__

#pragma option push -b -w-inl

#include <vcl/utilcls.h>
#if !defined(__UTILCLS_H_VERSION) || (__UTILCLS_H_VERSION < 0x0101)
#error "This file requires a newer version of the file UTILCLS.H"
#endif

#include <olectl.h>
#include <ocidl.h>
#if defined(USING_ATLVCL) || defined(USING_ATL)
#if !defined(__TLB_NO_EVENT_WRAPPERS)
#include <atl/atlmod.h>
#endif
#endif


namespace Stdvcl {class IStrings; class IStringsDisp;}
using namespace Stdvcl;

namespace Project1_tlb
{

// ********************************************************************
// HelpString: Project1 Library
// Version:    1.0
// ********************************************************************
```

```
// *********************************************************************
// GUIDS declared in the TypeLibrary. Following prefixes are used:
//    Type Libraries     : LIBID_xxxx
//    CoClasses          : CLSID_xxxx
//    DISPInterfaces     : DIID_xxxx
//    Non-DISP interfaces: IID_xxxx
// *********************************************************************
DEFINE_GUID(LIBID_Project1, 0xAF9DC92B, 0xEAF5, 0x11D2, 0x91, 0xA6, \
0x00, 0xC0, 0x4F, 0x8E, 0xE5, 0x14);
DEFINE_GUID(IID_ISimpleCOM, 0xAF9DC92C, 0xEAF5, 0x11D2, 0x91, 0xA6, \
0x00, 0xC0, 0x4F, 0x8E, 0xE5, 0x14);
DEFINE_GUID(CLSID_SimpleCOM, 0xAF9DC92E, 0xEAF5, 0x11D2, 0x91, 0xA6, \
0x00, 0xC0, 0x4F, 0x8E, 0xE5, 0x14);

// *********************************************************************
// Forward declaration of types defined in TypeLibrary
// *********************************************************************
interface DECLSPEC_UUID("{AF9DC92C-EAF5-11D2-91A6-00C04F8EE514}")
ISimpleCOM;

// *********************************************************************
// Declaration of CoClasses defined in Type Library
// (NOTE: Here we map each CoClass to its Default Interface)
//
// *********************************************************************
typedef ISimpleCOM SimpleCOM;

#define LIBID_OF_SimpleCOM (&LIBID_Project1)
// *********************************************************************
// Interface: ISimpleCOM
// Flags:     (0)
// GUID:      {AF9DC92C-EAF5-11D2-91A6-00C04F8EE514}
// *********************************************************************
interface ISimpleCOM : public IUnknown
{
public:
  virtual HRESULT STDMETHODCALLTYPE ShowString(BSTR str/*[in]*/) = 0;

#if !defined(__TLB_NO_INTERFACE_WRAPPERS)



#endif //    __TLB_NO_INTERFACE_WRAPPERS

};

#if !defined(__TLB_NO_INTERFACE_WRAPPERS)
// *********************************************************************
// SmartIntf: TCOMISimpleCOM
```

continues

LISTING 13.8   CONTINUED

```
// Interface: ISimpleCOM
// ************************************************************************
template <class T /* ISimpleCOM */>
class TCOMISimpleCOMT : public TComInterface<ISimpleCOM>,
                       public TComInterfaceBase<IUnknown>
{
public:
  TCOMISimpleCOMT() {}
  TCOMISimpleCOMT(ISimpleCOM *intf, bool addRef = false) :
              TComInterface<ISimpleCOM>(intf, addRef) {}
  TCOMISimpleCOMT(const TCOMISimpleCOMT& src) :
              TComInterface<ISimpleCOM>(src) {}
  TCOMISimpleCOMT& operator=(const TCOMISimpleCOMT& src)
              { Bind(src, true); return *this;}

  HRESULT          __fastcall ShowString(BSTR str/*[in]*/);

};
typedef TCOMISimpleCOMT<ISimpleCOM> TCOMISimpleCOM;


// ************************************************************************
// SmartIntf: TCOMISimpleCOM
// Interface: ISimpleCOM
// ************************************************************************
template <class T> HRESULT __fastcall
TCOMISimpleCOMT<T>::ShowString(BSTR str/*[in]*/)
{
  return (*this)->ShowString(str);
}


// ************************************************************************
// The following typedefs expose classes (named CoCoClassName) that
// provide static Create() and CreateRemote(LPWSTR machineName) methods
// for creating an instance of an exposed object. These functions can
// be used by client wishing to automate CoClasses exposed by this
// typelibrary.
// ************************************************************************


// ************************************************************************
// COCLASS DEFAULT INTERFACE CREATOR
// CoClass  : SimpleCOM
// Interface: TCOMISimpleCOM
// ************************************************************************
typedef TCoClassCreatorT<TCOMISimpleCOM, ISimpleCOM, &CLSID_SimpleCOM,
                        &IID_ISimpleCOM> CoSimpleCOM;
#endif //    __TLB_NO_INTERFACE_WRAPPERS


};     // namespace Project1_tlb
```

```
#if !defined(NO_IMPLICIT_NAMESPACE_USE)
using  namespace Project1_tlb;
#endif

#pragma option pop

#endif // __Project1_TLB_h__
```

The very first item in a _TLB file is a warning about the fact that this file is automatically regenerated by the C++Builder IDE. This can be rather annoying, especially when you want to make an innocuous change to the file. Unfortunately, C++Builder regenerates the content of that file when the underlying Type Library changes, when the project is saved, or simply when the weather is fair in California. Bottom line: Don't rely on your changes to this file unless you're working outside of the C++Builder IDE environment.

The contents of the _TLB file can be divided into two categories: part of the file is used by the server implementing the CoClasses defined in the Type Library; the rest of the file is for C++ clients accessing the CoClasses of these servers. The following section approaches the _TLB file from that angle.

Server Declarations in the _TLB File

After displaying some information about the Type Library and including headers that define types typically used in Type Libraries, the TLB header file declares the GUIDs of objects defined in the Type Library. The very first GUID is that of the Type Library itself. Then follows that of the CoClasses and interfaces defined in the Type library. As mentioned in the comment line (Listing 13.8) preceding the declaration of the GUIDs, each type of object uses a particular prefix for its GUID declaration.

The _TLB file uses a `typedef` statement to map each CoClass name to that of its default interface:

```
typedef ISimpleCOM SimpleCOM;
```

This is a very important step. A CoClass or COM object is an abstract concept of a class that exposes one or more interfaces. You don't obtain a pointer to a CoClass; instead, you obtain a pointer to an interface it implements. A interface, for example, can refer to a CoClass as the type of a method parameter. In essence, the parameter refers to the default interface of that CoClass. The mapping of a CoClass name to that of its default interface represents this notion.

The definitions of interfaces defined in the Type Library follow:

```
interface ISimpleCOM : public IUnknown
{
public:
  virtual HRESULT STDMETHODCALLTYPE ShowString(BSTR str/*[in]*/) = 0;
};
```

These interface definitions are used by the server's IMPL file. Whenever appropriate, the interface definition also contains additional non-virtual methods that are designed to simplify access to the interface. These are defined at the end of the interface definition and are mainly for the use of C++ clients using the interface. The following section looks at these and other client-related declarations.

Client Declarations in the _TLB File

Although most of the types declared in the _TLB file are for the Server's use, C++Builder client applications do need access to the definition of interfaces and GUIDs exposed by the server. There is also a group of functions generated exclusively for these client applications. The functions are sandwiched between preprocessor checks for the __TLB_NO_INTERFACE_WRAPPERS macro:

```
#if !defined(__TLB_NO_INTERFACE_WRAPPERS)
// Client types/declarations here
#endif //    __TLB_NO_INTERFACE_WRAPPERS
```

Client Declarations in Interfaces

The Type Library Editor will generate various client-specific additions to an interface declaration. The following listing illustrates a sample interface:

```
interface IMyAutoObject : public IDispatch
{
public:
  virtual HRESULT STDMETHODCALLTYPE
          get_Caption(BSTR* Value/*[out,retval]*/) = 0;
  virtual HRESULT STDMETHODCALLTYPE
          set_Caption(BSTR Value/*[in]*/) = 0;

#if !defined(__TLB_NO_INTERFACE_WRAPPERS)

  BSTR __fastcall get_Caption(void)
  {
    BSTR Value= 0;
    OLECHECK(this->get_Caption(&Value));
    return Value;
  }
```

```
    __property  BSTR  Caption = {read = get_Caption, write = set_Caption};

#endif //    __TLB_NO_INTERFACE_WRAPPERS

};
```

The interface proper only exposes two virtual methods: get_Caption and set_Caption. The first addition is an overloaded version of get_Caption. This flavor of the routine aims at providing a routine that hides the fact that interface methods return HRESULTs. The new version frees client applications from having to deal with reference return parameters. This feature is referred to as the *safecall calling convention* in Delphi. Visual C++ users often refer to it as HRESULT *hiding*.

The interface also exposes a __property declaration that encapsulates the setter and getter pair of virtual functions. This allows client applications to write code as simple as:

```
    Edit1->Text = AutoObjectIntf->Caption;
```

Class Wrapper for Default Interfaces

The _TLB file also contains a C++ wrapper class for the default interface of every CoClass defined in the Type Library:

```
// ******************************************************************
// SmartIntf: TCOMISimpleCOM
// Interface: ISimpleCOM
// ******************************************************************
template <class T /* ISimpleCOM */>
class TCOMISimpleCOMT : public TComInterface<ISimpleCOM>,
                        public TComInterfaceBase<IUnknown>
{
public:
  TCOMISimpleCOMT() {}
  TCOMISimpleCOMT(ISimpleCOM *intf, bool addRef = false) :
                        TComInterface<ISimpleCOM>(intf, addRef) {}
  TCOMISimpleCOMT(const TCOMISimpleCOMT& src) :
                        TComInterface<ISimpleCOM>(src) {}
  TCOMISimpleCOMT& operator=(const TCOMISimpleCOMT& src)
                        { Bind(src, true); return *this;}

  HRESULT        __fastcall ShowString(BSTR str/*[in]*/);

};
typedef TCOMISimpleCOMT<ISimpleCOM> TCOMISimpleCOM;

// ******************************************************************
// SmartIntf: TCOMISimpleCOM
// Interface: ISimpleCOM
// ******************************************************************
```

```
template <class T> HRESULT __fastcall
TCOMISimpleCOMT<T>::ShowString(BSTR str/*[in]*/)
{
  return (*this)->ShowString(str);
}
```

This class' purpose is to provide a smart interface wrapper. In other words, if used properly, this class can eliminate the chores of AddRef and Release calls expected of a client. The class also redefines the methods of the interface. This allows you to invoke these methods using a . (dot) operator instead of the -> (arrow) operator:

```
void InvokeServer(TCOMISimpleCOM server)
{
  server.ShowString(WideString("This is a test"));
  server->ShowString(WideString("This also works"));
}
```

> **NOTE**
>
> I recommend that you stick to the -> (arrow) operator when using the smart interface wrappers. It's more consistent with the way VCL components are accessed. It will also make your code consistent in the way you use other interfaces; the _TLB file provides a wrapper only for the default interface of CoClasses, not for every interface.

Creator Classes for Default Interfaces

The least obvious but most important client-specific declarations in the _TLB file are the CoClass creator types. They allow clients to easily request a pointer to the default interface of a COM object defined in the Type Library. The following shows the CoClass creator declaration for the SimpleCOM object:

```
typedef TCoClassCreatorT<TCOMISimpleCOM, ISimpleCOM,
                    &CLSID_SimpleCOM, &IID_ISimpleCOM> CoSimpleCOM;
```

A C++ client application that wants to obtain a pointer to the SimpleCOM object can simply invoke the Create method of the type declared earlier:

```
TCOMISimpleCOM SimpleCOMServer = CoSimpleCOM::Create();
SimpleCOMServer->ShowString(WideString(Edit1->Text));
```

The _TLB file will contain more declarations that those listed here. For example, if your COM object is an automation object, the _TLB file will contain a wrapper to invoke it methods via the traditional dispatch mechanism. Similarly, if your COM object exposes an event interface, the _TLB file will contain various event wrappers used by your server to fire events. However, the preceding code gives you an overview of the type of information you can expect in the file.

Virtual Method Tables

You have read through a rather long description of COM and interfaces without ever once seeing any mention of vtables. vtables play a key role in the implementation of interface technology, so I will say a few words about them before closing this chapter.

A *virtual method table* is sometimes called a vtable, and programmers occasionally abbreviate it as *vtbl*. A *vtable* is what you get when you declare an interface. In short, you have created a virtual method table if you declare a class (or struct) with all of its methods declared as purely virtual. A slightly different take on the subject would define a virtual method table as a structure whose members are all method pointers.

Earlier in this chapter you learned that an interface is similar to a class declared as a set of public pure virtual methods. All interfaces, whether declared in Delphi or the Microsoft or Borland versions of C++, are laid out with exactly the same binary layout—there's an absolute one-to-one correspondence between the elements of each construct. In a computer's memory, they look identical.

When you invoke virtual methods of a C++ class, the methods are called according to the order in which they are declared, not according to the names of the actual methods involved. That's how COM achieves binary compatibility across languages: All languages that support COM use the same vtable layout. The interface can therefore be defined in any language and accessed from any other language.

Summary

In this chapter you learned about the basics of COM and interfaces. You saw how to implement a COM object with a single interface and how to access that implementation from various clients. You also learned about the various files that make up a C++Builder ActiveX server.

This chapter also discussed COM in general terms, describing some of the benefits that can be derived from this technology. A number of those benefits involve some pretty fancy concepts such as ActiveX controls and DCOM, where the latter technology allows you to call an object's methods remotely from another machine and get function results or parameters sent back to you over the network. It seems like a long leap from the topics discussed in this chapter to something such as an ActiveX control or to DCOM. However, many of the most complicated subjects involved with this technology are already in your ken. In fact, before the next chapter is over, you will start to see how you can put these things to use in your own programs.

13

THE BASICS OF COM AND TYPE LIBRARIES

I should add that you can get up to speed on ActiveX controls and perhaps even DCOM without understanding all the material in this chapter. However, having this knowledge under your belt will enable you to get a much deeper and much more useful understanding of all C++Builder's COM-related technologies. Having a good base to build on is often the key to creating a robust infrastructure. You should be ready to set forth on a productive career as a COM programmer.

CHAPTER 14

Creating COM Automation Servers and Clients

by Charlie Calvert and Bruneau Babet

IN THIS CHAPTER

In this chapter, you learn about OLE automation—that is, you learn how to create OLE Automation servers and clients. This material is closely related to important topics covered later in the book, such as using MIDAS, using DCOM, and automating Word and Excel.

More particularly, in this chapter, you learn the following:

- Why OLE automation exists and what it does
- How to create simple clients and servers
- What type libraries are and how to work with them
- How the two types of automation interfaces work
- How to work with `Variants`

A great deal of material is presented in this chapter. Most of it is not particularly difficult to understand, but it takes awhile to absorb. If you are new to this subject, I suggest you read this chapter in its entirety. Sometimes I introduce a topic, tell you enough about it to allow you to get some work done, and then put the topic aside until later. This means you won't know all you need to learn about some topics until you have read the entire chapter.

In general, however, OLE automation is not a particularly difficult subject. You just need to understand a little theory and get acquainted with a few tools, and in no time you will be up and running.

Understanding OLE Automation Clients and Servers

Together, simple COM clients and servers of the type shown in this chapter are, in my opinion, one of the most important developments in contemporary programming. We already have multitasking operating systems that allow us to smoothly and easily run multiple programs at the same time. What COM brings to the picture is the ability to get these programs working together in a single, concerted effort.

Often programmers build large monolithic programs that could easily be broken up into a series of smaller COM objects. These smaller programs are easier to debug, easier to understand, and easier to maintain. Any shared code that needs to be used by all the applications in a project can be placed in DLLs, preferably COM-based DLLs.

Programmers might object to this kind of architecture for one reason or another, but one thing you don't need to worry about is the possibility that the COM subsystem will let you down. OLE automation has always worked for me. I've never asked a local COM server to do something and have it fail to respond or fail to work because of some innate shortcoming in the COM subsystems. OLE automation is very reliable. I regard it as reliable in the same sense I think of a DOS batch file as reliable—it always works.

> **NOTE**
>
> Do not be tempted to use DDE instead of COM. DDE, in my opinion and the opinion of many others, was simply a failed first attempt at automation. Its primary value stems from the lessons Microsoft engineers learned in this, their first attempt at interprocess communication. In particular, I think DDE is overly complex and fraught with hard-to-track-down bugs that Microsoft never satisfactorily resolved. It is also a dead-end technology that is no longer evolving. COM, on the other hand, is a clean technology that is continually evolving, and it is the focus of a great deal of effort at Redmond.

Another reason to embrace OLE automation is simply because it's the polite thing to do. I'm reaching the point where I find it very annoying to discover applications that don't let me use their resources via automation. As a programmer, I get frustrated paying money for a product only to find that I can't script it with OLE automation. Here is this great tool sitting on my system that can perhaps solve all kinds of problems for me, but I always have to use it through a slow, clunky, menu-based interface. Why don't the developers let me take full advantage of their tool?

Viewing this situation from the opposite perspective, many programmers might find new audiences for their tools by providing automation interfaces. Suddenly, their programs might sell not only to end users, but also to programmers who might want to distribute the application widely to use its services.

The final vision that OLE automation brings to mind is a version of the distributed programming model discussed later in this book. In this vision, small automation objects are distributed widely across one or more machines and are available on most systems for a variety of purposes. In this world of distributed automation objects, programmers rarely write low-level code. Instead, they simply call the various COM objects and automation services available on a particular system. This distributed computing model might seem far-fetched to some people, but it is becoming more of a reality almost daily.

I think wise programmers will begin to think in terms of creating systems of related COM and automation objects. Then they can call on these services from a variety of locations and use them for whatever purpose they see fit. The technology to do so reliably is totally in place; the difficulty is in learning to redesign and rethink our applications so that they fit into this model.

14

CREATING COM
AUTOMATION
SERVERS/CLIENTS

Building a Simple COM Server and Client

In this section, you see how to create a simple automation server and client. Later in the chapter, after I discuss more about the theory behind COM, I return to this subject and show how to create more complex automation servers.

This section of the chapter is built around two sample programs: one a client and the other a server. You can find both examples of SimpleAutoServer on the CD-ROM that accompanies the book.

Building a Simple Server

To create a new automation object, open an existing project that you want to turn into a server or create a new project. In this particular case, starting with a new project is best, but in your own work, you should be aware that you can sometimes begin with an existing program that you want to offer as a service to others. When you are ready to go, you should proceed as follows:

1. Select File, New Application.

2. Select File, New and choose the ActiveX page from the New Items dialog.

3. Click the icon labeled Automation Object. The Automation Object Wizard appears and prompts you for a CoClass name. Type a reasonable name, such as `MethodObject`. Select the OK button. You are taken immediately to the Type Library Editor.

4. Save your project via the File Save All menu option, saving `MethodObjectImpl.cpp`, renaming `Unit1.cpp` to `MainServer.cpp`, and renaming `Project1.bpr` to `SimpleAutoServer.bpr`.

These steps are the only ones necessary to create an automation server. At this point in your project development, you have a main program, an attached module for defining your automation object, and a type library. In short, you have a complete automation server that doesn't yet do anything useful.

I have a fairly simple convention for naming clients and servers. In a classic situation, I name the file that implements my server *XXX*IMPL.cpp (C++Builder automatically assigns the name `CoClassNameIMPL.CPP` to the file implementing the server object), the main form for the project `MainServer.cpp`, and the server itself *XXX*Server.bpr. The main form of the client is usually called `MainClient`, and the project source is named *XXX*Client.bpr. I often save the client into a directory called `Client` and the server into a directory called `Server`.

> **TIP**
>
> If you want to convert a standard application to an automation server, you should leave the body of your application unchanged. Simply add one or more automation objects to your application and have these objects expose the functionality of your main application. In other words, don't try to integrate the automation objects into the source for your application. Instead, simply wrap your main objects inside an automation object.

Adding Methods to Your Server

Take a moment to consider the steps necessary to create a method in the Type Library Editor. This method can be called from a client program, and it can add real-world functionality to your program. (If you are having trouble reaching the Type Library Editor, chose View, Type Library from the C++Builder menu. If this option is grayed out, you are not working with a valid automation server. Review the steps in the preceding section to fix this problem.)

Here are the steps you take in the Type Library Editor to add a method to your interface:

1. Select the interface you want to work with (see Figure 14.1). In this case, it is called `IMethodObject`.

FIGURE 14.1

A type library, as it should appear just before you start to insert methods or properties.

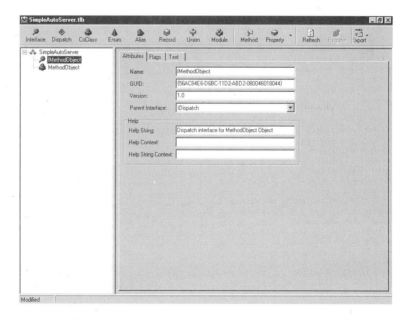

2. Select the Method button from the toolbar at the top of the editor. (If your toolbar buttons do not display accompanying Text Labels, right-click the Toolbar and select Text Labels to view the Labels. If the Method button is grayed, make sure that the IMethodObject interface is selected in the left pane of the Type Library Editor.)

3. Type the name of your method in the Name field of the Attributes page (see Figure 14.2). In this case, you should type **GetName**.

FIGURE 14.2

Giving your method a name.

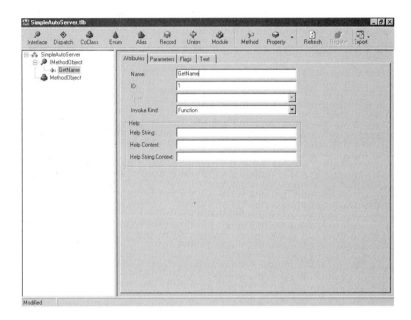

4. Turn to the Parameters page and add a parameter of the type BSTR* using the following steps: Select the Add button. Edit the Param1 field to read **Name**. Change the Type from long to BSTR*. Specify that the parameter is the return value of the method by selecting the Modifier field and clicking the button to the right. This brings up the Parameters Flag dialog. Enable the out and retval flags. Figure 14.3 shows the Parameters page of our new method.

5. Turn to the Text page to check the code generated for your method:

```
[id(0x00000001)]
HRESULT _stdcall GetName([out, retval] BSTR * Name );
```

6. Click the Refresh button at the right of the toolbar at the top of the Type Library Editor. (Saving your project performs an automatic refresh.)

FIGURE **14.3**

Parameters page of new method returning a string.

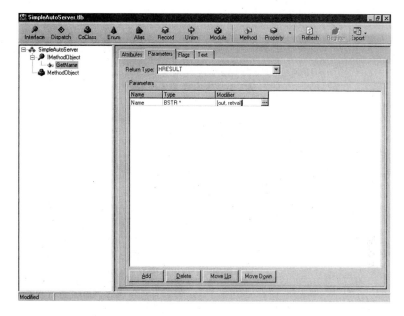

At this stage, you are free to leave the Type Library Editor, as your work there is completed. If you want to return to it at any time, you can select View, Type Library.

Several files were created while you were in the Type Library Editor, as shown in Table 14.1 (the default filenames shown here might be different in your project). Some of these files, particularly the TLB file, might not be fully generated until you click the Refresh button. Furthermore, you might need to go to the View, Units menu item to actually view the file. However, by the time you save and compile the files, you should be able to find them in complete form.

TABLE **14.1**   FILES CREATED IN THE TYPE LIBRARY EDITOR

Filename	Description
SimpleAutoServer_TLB.cpp/.h	These files contain the declarations for your interfaces and classes. They describe the ActiveX objects exposed by your server via C++ classes. You should never edit these files by hand, but you should look at them carefully so you understand what they do. If you want to make changes to these files, select View, Type Library and make changes through the editor. I explain more about the code in these files later in this chapter.

continues

TABLE 14.1   CONTINUED

Filename	Description
MethodObjectIMPL.cpp/.h	Here, you can find the implementation of the automation object exposed by your application. In the .cpp file, you can add code that makes your object do what you want it to do. Most of the time, you can ignore the TLB file and focus your attention primarily on this one. Programmers often save this file with a name that ends in IMPL because it is the place where you *implement* your objects.

I discuss the Type Library Editor in much more depth later in this chapter, in the section called "Type Libraries," and in the subsections that immediately follow it.

Viewing the Generated Source Code

In your MethodObjectImpl.h source code, you should now find the following object declaration:

```
///////////////////////////////////////////////////////////////////////
// TMethodObjectImpl Implements IMethodObject, interface of MethodObject
// ThreadingModel : Apartment
// Dual Interface : TRUE
// Event Support  : FALSE
// Default ProgID : Project1.MethodObject
// Description    :
///////////////////////////////////////////////////////////////////////
class ATL_NO_VTABLE TMethodObjectImpl :
  public CComObjectRootEx<CComSingleThreadModel>,
  public CComCoClass<TMethodObjectImpl, &CLSID_MethodObject>,
  public IDispatchImpl<IMethodObject, &IID_IMethodObject,
                                     &LIBID_SimpleAutoServer>
{
public:
  TMethodObjectImpl()
  {
  }

  // Data used when registering Object
  //
  DECLARE_THREADING_MODEL(otApartment);
  DECLARE_PROGID("SimpleAutoServer.MethodObject");
  DECLARE_DESCRIPTION("");

  // Function invoked to (un)register object
  //
  static HRESULT WINAPI UpdateRegistry(BOOL bRegister)
  {
```

```
    TTypedComServerRegistrarT<TMethodObjectImpl>
    regObj(GetObjectCLSID(), GetProgID(), GetDescription());
    return regObj.UpdateRegistry(bRegister);
  }


BEGIN_COM_MAP(TMethodObjectImpl)
  COM_INTERFACE_ENTRY(IMethodObject)
  COM_INTERFACE_ENTRY(IDispatch)
END_COM_MAP()

// IMethodObject
public:

  STDMETHOD(GetName(BSTR* Name));
};
```

An empty implementation for your object is shown in the CPP file for your custom object:

```
STDMETHODIMP TMethodObjectImpl::GetName(BSTR* Name)
{
}
```

You should leave the format of this code alone, doing nothing more than adding your implementation:

```
STDMETHODIMP TMethodObjectImpl::GetName(BSTR* Name)
{
  *Name = WideString(TimeToStr(Now())).Detach();
  return S_OK;
}
```

At this point, you can save and compile your application server. Be sure to run it once so that it is registered with the system. To check that you server is registered, open RegEdit.exe, a utility that comes with Windows, and look for your server by its application name in the HKEY_CLASSES_ROOT section. Note that this section begins with a bunch of extensions, all of which begin with a period. You should be looking for a listing that reads SimpleAutoServer.MethodObject.

Adding Properties to Interfaces

This sample program doesn't provide a property, but if you want to create a new one, click the Property button on the toolbar of the Type Library Editor. On the Attributes page, you can rename the property and give it a type. You can also add parameters to a property or fine-tune its features on the Flags page. However, I do not use either of these options in this book, as they are beyond the scope of the current work. For more information on types that automation objects use, see the "Valid Automation Types" section in this chapter.

Building a Simple Client

Your client program is going to access the automation objects that reside in your server. A description of those objects is stored in both SimpleAutoServer_TLB and in the server's type library. The type library was created automatically when you were in the Type Library Editor. You can recognize this file on disk by its .tlb extension.

On the client side, you can now do one of two things:

1. Add SimpleAutoServer_TLB.cpp to the Project of your client.

2. Go to the C++Builder menu and choose Project, Import Type Library. Doing so automatically causes the recreation of SimpleAutoServer_TLB.cpp and adds the file to your project.

At this stage, I don't want to talk too much about type libraries, as that is a subject I explore in depth later in this chapter, in a section called "Type Libraries." All you really have to see right now is that as long as you have a binary automation object and its type library, you can automatically generate the .h and .cpp file pair that declares the object's types and gives you access to the object itself.

Now take a look at SimpleAutoServer_TLB.h, shown in Listing 14.1, and try to understand why it exists and what it can do for you.

LISTING 14.1   SimpleAutoServer_TLB.h CONTAINS THE DECLARATIONS FOR THE OBJECTS IN YOUR SERVER

```
// C++ TLBWRTR : $Revision:   1.96.1.27  $
// File generated on 3/10/99 8:23:03 AM from Type Library below.

// ********************************************************************.
// Type Lib:
// D:\Program Files\Borland\CBuilder4\Projects\SimpleAutoServer.tlb
// IID\LCID: {56AC64E5-D6BC-11D2-ABD2-080046018044}\0
// Helpfile:
// DepndLst:
//   (1) v2.0 stdole, (C:\WINDOWS\SYSTEM\STDOLE2.TLB)
//   (2) v4.0 StdVCL, (C:\WINDOWS\SYSTEM\STDVCL40.DLL)
// ********************************************************************
#ifndef   __SimpleAutoServer_TLB_h__
#define   __SimpleAutoServer_TLB_h__

#pragma option push -b -w-inl

#include <vcl/utilcls.h>
#if !defined(__UTILCLS_H_VERSION) || (__UTILCLS_H_VERSION < 0x0101)
#error "This file requires an newer version of the file UTILCLS.H"
#endif
```

```
#include <olectl.h>
#include <ocidl.h>
#if defined(USING_ATLVCL) || defined(USING_ATL)
#if !defined(__TLB_NO_EVENT_WRAPPERS)
#include <atl/atlmod.h>
#endif
#endif


namespace Stdvcl {class IStrings; class IStringsDisp;}
using namespace Stdvcl;

namespace Simpleautoserver_tlb
{

// *********************************************************************
// HelpString: Project1 Library
// Version:    1.0
// *********************************************************************


// *********************************************************************
// GUIDS declared in the TypeLibrary. Following prefixes are used:
//    Type Libraries     : LIBID_xxxx
//    CoClasses          : CLSID_xxxx
//    DISPInterfaces     : DIID_xxxx
//    Non-DISP interfaces: IID_xxxx
// *********************************************************************
DEFINE_GUID(LIBID_SimpleAutoServer, 0x56AC64E5, 0xD6BC, 0x11D2, 0xAB, \
                     0xD2, 0x08, 0x00, 0x46, 0x01, 0x80, 0x44);
DEFINE_GUID(IID_IMethodObject, 0x56AC64E6, 0xD6BC, 0x11D2, 0xAB, 0xD2, \
                     0x08, 0x00, 0x46, 0x01, 0x80, 0x44);
DEFINE_GUID(CLSID_MethodObject, 0x56AC64E8, 0xD6BC, 0x11D2, 0xAB, \
                     0xD2, 0x08, 0x00, 0x46, 0x01, 0x80, 0x44);

// *********************************************************************
// Forward declaration of types defined in TypeLibrary
// *********************************************************************
interface DECLSPEC_UUID("{56AC64E6-D6BC-11D2-ABD2-080046018044}")
            IMethodObject;

// *********************************************************************
// Declaration of CoClasses defined in Type Library
// (NOTE: Here we map each CoClass to its Default Interface)
// *********************************************************************
typedef IMethodObject MethodObject;

#define LIBID_OF_MethodObject (&LIBID_SimpleAutoServer)
// *********************************************************************
```

continues

LISTING 14.1   CONTINUED

```
// Interface: IMethodObject
// Flags:     (4416) Dual OleAutomation Dispatchable
// GUID:      {56AC64E6-D6BC-11D2-ABD2-080046018044}
// ********************************************************************
interface IMethodObject : public IDispatch
{
public:
  virtual HRESULT STDMETHODCALLTYPE
               GetName(BSTR* Name/*[out,retval]*/) = 0;

#if !defined(__TLB_NO_INTERFACE_WRAPPERS)

  BSTR __fastcall GetName(void)
  {
    BSTR Name= 0;
    OLECHECK(this->GetName(&Name));
    return Name;
  }



#endif //    __TLB_NO_INTERFACE_WRAPPERS

};

#if !defined(__TLB_NO_INTERFACE_WRAPPERS)
// ********************************************************************
// SmartIntf: TCOMIMethodObject
// Interface: IMethodObject
// ********************************************************************
template <class T /* IMethodObject */>
class TCOMIMethodObjectT : public TComInterface<IMethodObject>,
                      public TComInterfaceBase<IUnknown>
{
public:
  TCOMIMethodObjectT() {}
  TCOMIMethodObjectT(IMethodObject *intf, bool addRef = false) :
            TComInterface<IMethodObject>(intf, addRef) {}
  TCOMIMethodObjectT(const TCOMIMethodObjectT& src) :
            TComInterface<IMethodObject>(src) {}
  TCOMIMethodObjectT& operator=(const TCOMIMethodObjectT& src)
            { Bind(src, true); return *this;}

  HRESULT         __fastcall GetName(BSTR* Name/*[out,retval]*/);
  BSTR            __fastcall GetName(void);

};
typedef TCOMIMethodObjectT<IMethodObject> TCOMIMethodObject;
```

```
// *********************************************************************
// DispIntf:  IMethodObject
// Flags:     (4416) Dual OleAutomation Dispatchable
// GUID:      {56AC64E6-D6BC-11D2-ABD2-080046018044}
// *********************************************************************
template<class T>
class IMethodObjectDispT : public TAutoDriver<IMethodObject>
{
public:
  IMethodObjectDispT(){}

  IMethodObjectDispT(IMethodObject *pintf)
  {
    TAutoDriver<IMethodObject>::Bind(pintf);
  }

  IMethodObjectDispT& operator=(IMethodObject *pintf)
  {
    TAutoDriver<IMethodObject>::Bind(pintf);
    return *this;
  }

  HRESULT BindDefault(/*Binds to new instance of CoClass MethodObject*/)
  {
    return OLECHECK(Bind(CLSID_MethodObject));
  }

  HRESULT BindRunning(
        /*Binds to a running instance of CoClass MethodObject*/)
  {
    return BindToActive(CLSID_MethodObject);
  }

  HRESULT        __fastcall GetName(BSTR* Name/*[out,retval]*/);
  BSTR           __fastcall GetName(void);

};
typedef IMethodObjectDispT<IMethodObject> IMethodObjectDisp;

// *********************************************************************
// SmartIntf: TCOMIMethodObject
// Interface: IMethodObject
// *********************************************************************
template <class T> HRESULT __fastcall
TCOMIMethodObjectT<T>::GetName(BSTR* Name/*[out,retval]*/)
{
  return (*this)->GetName(Name);
}
```

continues

LISTING 14.1   CONTINUED

```cpp
template <class T> BSTR __fastcall
TCOMIMethodObjectT<T>::GetName(void)
{
  BSTR Name= 0;
  OLECHECK(this->GetName(&Name));
  return Name;
}

// **********************************************************************
// DispIntf:   IMethodObject
// Flags:      (4416) Dual OleAutomation Dispatchable
// GUID:       {56AC64E6-D6BC-11D2-ABD2-080046018044}
// **********************************************************************
template <class T> HRESULT __fastcall
IMethodObjectDispT<T>::GetName(BSTR* Name/*[out,retval]*/)
{
  static _TDispID _dispid(*this, OLETEXT("GetName"), DISPID(1));
  TAutoArgs<0> _args;
  return OutRetValSetterPtr(Name /*[VT_BSTR:1]*/, _args,
                     OleFunction(_dispid, _args));
}

template <class T> BSTR __fastcall
IMethodObjectDispT<T>::GetName(void)
{
  BSTR Name;
  this->GetName(&Name);
  return Name;
}

// **********************************************************************
// The following typedefs expose classes (named CoCoClassName) that
// provide static Create() and CreateRemote(LPWSTR machineName) methods
// for creating an instance of an exposed object. These functions can
// be used by client wishing to automate CoClasses exposed by this
// typelibrary.
// **********************************************************************

// **********************************************************************
// COCLASS DEFAULT INTERFACE CREATOR
// CoClass   : MethodObject
// Interface: TCOMIMethodObject
// **********************************************************************
typedef TCoClassCreatorT<TCOMIMethodObject, IMethodObject,
                    &CLSID_MethodObject,
                    &IID_IMethodObject> CoMethodObject;
#endif  //    __TLB_NO_INTERFACE_WRAPPERS
```

```
};      // namespace Simpleautoserver_tlb

#if !defined(NO_IMPLICIT_NAMESPACE_USE)
using  namespace Simpleautoserver_tlb;
#endif

#pragma option pop

#endif // __SimpleAutoServer_TLB_h__
```

The following section describes the main objects declared inside
SimpleAutoServer_TLB:

- IMethodObject—This class is the primary interface of the object exposed by your automation server. It implements the IDispatch interface, which makes it callable from languages such as VB and other applications with scripting support. You can access the methods of this class via direct calls in C++ You might notice that the class also provides overloaded versions of some methods wherever they ease C++ applications access. For example, the GetName() method is overloaded to return a BSTR parameter so you don't have to pass the return parameter by reference.

- TCOMIMethodObject—This class gives you an easy means of directly calling the methods and properties exposed by the IMethodObject interface. The main purpose of this class is to encapsulate the IMethodObject interface. It handles reference counting for you and also allows you to use the object.method() syntax instead of the more awkward object->method(). An instance of this class is created for you if your client creates the server using the CoMethodObject class.

- CoMethodObject—Use this class to automatically create instances of your object. This class is a typed version of the TCoClassCreatorT template. It exposes static functions Create and CreateRemote to allow you to create instances of your server. CoMethodObject exists because the standard means of creating a COM class involves calling a somewhat complicated function named CoCreateInstance. The call to this function can be confusing to neophytes and annoying to sophisticates, so CoMethodObject can be used to call the function for you automatically. I do, however, show you how to call CoCreateInstance at the end of this chapter.

- IMethodObjectDisp—Use this class if you want to automate an instance of your server via the IDispatch.Invoke call. You probably will never use this class because talking to a server via Invoke involves additional overhead that is best avoided. However, there are a few special cases where you can use this class instead of TCOMIMethodObject. Notice that this class exposes a BindDefault function to launch a new instance of your server. It also provides a BindRunning method that allows you to talk to an already-running instance of the server.

Calling Methods via `TCOMInterface`

As described in the previous section, you can access the methods of an automation object from a remote program in several different ways. One method allows you to access the methods by direct calls, and a second lets you get at them via something called a `IDispatch.Invoke`. A third technology involves the use of the `OleProcedure`, `OleFunction`, `OlePropertyGet`, and `OlePropertySet` functions of the `Variant` class. See the file SYSVARI.H for more information. Examples of the first two technologies are shown in Listing 14.2.

LISTING 14.2   THE MAIN FORM FROM THE SIMPLEAUTOCLIENT PROJECT

```
//////////////////////////////////
// MAINCLIENT.H
// Purpose: Call SimpleAutoServer
// Project: SimpleAutoClient
//

//-------------------------------------------------------------
#ifndef MainClientH
#define MainClientH
//-------------------------------------------------------------
#include <Classes.hpp>
#include <Controls.hpp>
#include <StdCtrls.hpp>
#include <Forms.hpp>
#include <ExtCtrls.hpp>
#include "SimpleAutoServer_TLB.h"
//-------------------------------------------------------------
class TForm1 : public TForm
{
__published:    // IDE-managed Components
        TButton *AutomateVTable;
        TButton *AutomateDispatch;
        TButton *CloseServer;
        TEdit *Edit1;
        TLabel *Label1;
        TBevel *Bevel1;
        void __fastcall AutomateVTableClick(TObject *Sender);
        void __fastcall CloseServerClick(TObject *Sender);
private:        // User declarations
        TCOMIMethodObject SimpleServerObj;
public:         // User declarations
        __fastcall TForm1(TComponent* Owner);
};
//-------------------------------------------------------------
extern PACKAGE TForm1 *Form1;
//-------------------------------------------------------------
#endif
```

```
/////////////////////////////////
// MAINCLIENT.CPP
// Purpose: Call SimpleAutoServer
// Project: SimpleAutoClient
//

//---------------------------------------------------------------
#include <vcl.h>
#pragma hdrstop

#include "MainClient.h"
#include "SimpleAutoServer_TLB.h"
//---------------------------------------------------------------
#pragma package(smart_init)
#pragma resource "*.dfm"
TForm1 *Form1;
//---------------------------------------------------------------
__fastcall TForm1::TForm1(TComponent* Owner)
        : TForm(Owner)
{
}

void __fastcall TForm1::AutomateVTableClick(TObject *Sender)
{
  if (!SimpleServerObj)
    SimpleServerObj = CoMethodObject::Create();
  Edit1->Text = SimpleServerObj->GetName();
}
//---------------------------------------------------------------

void __fastcall TForm1::CloseServerClick(TObject *Sender)
{
  if (SimpleServerObj)
    SimpleServerObj.Unbind();
}
//---------------------------------------------------------------

void __fastcall TForm1::AutomateDispatchClick(TObject *Sender)
{
  IMethodObjectDisp dispServer;
  dispServer.BindDefault();
  Edit1->Text = dispServer.GetName();
}
//---------------------------------------------------------------
---
```

When you run this program, you can see that the interface contains three buttons and an edit control. If you click the button labeled AutomateServerVTable, the server is called, and the GetName method on the server returns a string that is displayed in the client's edit control. The outcome is shown in Figure 14.4. This application has its `FormStyle` set to `fsStayOnTop`. I use this setting to ensure that the server does not cover up the client, thereby hiding the client's interface from you.

FIGURE 14.4

The string retrieved by calling GetName() *is visible in the client's edit control.*

Here is a method that uses `CoMethodObject` to create an instance of your server and then calls the exposed methods:

```
class TForm1 : public TForm
{
        ...
_       void __fastcall AutomateVTableClick(TObject *Sender);
        ...
 private:      // User declarations
        TCOMIMethodObject SimpleServerObj;
        ...
};

void __fastcall TForm1::AutomateVTableClick(TObject *Sender)
{
  if (!SimpleServerObj)
    SimpleServerObj = CoMethodObject::Create();
  Edit1->Text = SimpleServerObj->GetName();
}
```

`CoMethodObj.Create` is declared the file `UTILCLS.H`. See the template `TCoClassCreator` for more information. `CoMethodObj` is a specialized type of that template declared in `SimpleAutoServer_TLB`. To truly understand the OLE automation support of C++Builder, you must spend a considerable amount of time with this file that was auto-generated by the Type Library Editor. Note that you need to add `SimpleAutoServer_TLB.h` to the list of header files to be included by your client header file.

This code uses the `CoMethodObject` object to return an instance of your object. If you look beneath the hood, you can see that `CoMethodObject.Create` just calls `CoCreateInstance`, as explained in the preceding section of this chapter. `CoCreateInstance` is the standard Microsoft OLE technology for creating an instance of an object. Here is the declaration of the `TCoClassCreatorT` template:

```
// Template used to expose 'factory-like' Create/CreateRemote
// routines for Clients
//
template <class TOBJ, class INTF, const CLSID* clsid, const IID* iid>
class TCoClassCreatorT : public CoClassCreator
{
public:
  static TOBJ    Create();
  static HRESULT Create(TOBJ& intfObj);
  static HRESULT Create(INTF** ppintf);

  static TOBJ    CreateRemote(LPCWSTR machineName);
  static HRESULT CreateRemote(LPCWSTR machineName, TOBJ& intfObj);
  static HRESULT CreateRemote(LPCWSTR machineName, INTF** ppIntf);
};
```

This declaration provides two groups of methods: one for creating a remote object and one for creating a local object. In this chapter, I use the local routine (see Chapter 19, "DCOM," to learn about creating remote objects):

```
SimpleServerObj = CoMethodObject::Create();
```

After you have the object back, you can call its methods directly. Note that your calls do not go through `IDispatch.Invoke`. You are actually making a direct call into the object's VMT. However, the call must still be marshaled across the boundary between your client application and the server. This marshaling is handled automatically by Windows, and neither you nor the C++Builder developers have to do anything special to make it happen.

When you're examining this call, note the use of the BSTR type. BSTRs are BASIC strings that have two bytes per character. It is the type used to pass string data in COM. I talk more about both marshaling and BSTRs later in this chapter. For now, all you really need to know is that whenever you want to pass string data in COM, you must use a BSTR or a class that encapsulates BSTR such as the `WideString` class. Note that you can easily convert between C++Builder `AnsiStrings` and `WideString` or BSTR types.

Before closing this section, I should perhaps make a few other points. The first is that you should never close a server manually if it was launched via automation. Instead, simply let the variable that points at it in your client go out of scope, or set it to 0:

```
void __fastcall TForm1::CloseServerClick(TObject *Sender)
{
  if (SimpleServerObj)
    SimpleServerObj = 0;
}
```

The code shown here closes the server. You can also call the Unbind method to disconnect from the server. You can legally launch and close the server as many times as you
want during the run of the client. If you want, you can even write code like this:

```
void __fastcall TForm1::AutomateVTableClick(TObject *Sender)
{
  TCOMIMethodObject SimpleServerObj = CoMethodObject::Create();
  Edit1->Text = SimpleServerObj->GetName();
}
```

This code hangs onto the server just long enough to call GetName. Then, the moment
SimpleServerObj goes out of scope, the server disappears.

That covers this simple example. In the next section, I talk a little about using dispinterfaces.

Calling Methods via a Dispinterface

Ninety-nine percent of the time, you want to make your calls to a server using standard
interfaces as shown in the preceding section. However, some servers might only expose a
dispinterface requiring that you automate the server via IDispatch.Invoke calls. As a
result, C++Builder supports dispinterface wrapper classes in the TLB file.

Here is an example of how to get to an object using the dispinterface wrapper class:

```
void __fastcall TForm1::AutomateDispatchClick(TObject *Sender)
{
  IMethodObjectDisp dispServer;
  dispServer.BindDefault();
  Edit1->Text = dispServer.GetName();
}
```

If you look in the header for the SimpleAutoServer_TLB file, you can find the following
method of the IMethodObjDisp class:

```
template <class T> HRESULT __fastcall
IMethodObjectDispT<T>::GetName(BSTR* Name/*[out,retval]*/)
{
  static _TDispID _dispid(*this, OLETEXT("GetName"), DISPID(1));
  TAutoArgs<0> _args;
  return OutRetValSetterPtr(Name /*[VT_BSTR:1]*/, _
      _args, OleFunction(_dispid, _args));
}
```

This code is generated for you automatically by the Type Library Editor. It calls the
method of the object you want to access, using the dispatch identifier of the method. In
this particular case, we're calling the method GetName() whose dispatch identifier is 1.
The call to OleFunction ultimately resolves into a call to IDispatch.Invoke.

To understand all this information better, you should look at the UTILCLS.H header from the C++Builder include\vcl directory. You can also step through your call to GetName() with the debugger. You see the various structures that need to be initialized before the final call. Whenever possible, you should attempt to step through the code generated by the Type Library Editor to better understand the underpinnings of each class.

Calling Methods off a Variant

Finally, if you don't have access to the requisite headers or to a type library, you can still call the methods of an object off the IDispatch interface. If you want, you can call methods of IDispatch directly. A simpler way to access the same technology is provided by automation methods of the Variant class:

```
void __fastcall TForm1::AutomateDispatchClick(TObject *Sender)
{
  Variant server = CreateOleObject("SimpleAutoServer.MethodObject");
  server.OleFunction("GetName");
}
```

> **NOTE**
>
> Due to a bug in the shipping version of C++Builder 4, this code will compile, but not work properly: OleFunction fails to returns the result of a call. The bug is fixed in the C++Builder 4 update available from Borland's Web site at www.borland.com.

In the technology shown here, you can create an instance of an object by calling the VCL routine CreateOleObject. Simply pass in the ProgID of the object you want to retrieve, and you receive in return a Variant that wraps an instance of IDispatch. The ProgID is a string made up of the name of your server, a period, and the name of your automation object.

If you are unclear as to what the ProgID for your class might be, simply open RegEdit.exe. Look in the HKEY_CLASSES_ROOT section for the alphabetically arranged listings of all the automation servers on your system. At the start, extensions are listed, each beginning with a period. Obviously, they are listed before the servers, which are listed by name, where the name in question is the name of your server, plus your automation class. So skip over the extensions and look for SimpleAutoServer.MethodObject. (You can figure out the ProgID for yourself, but if you do get confused, you can always look up the name in the Registry.)

The `Variant` type has a number of automation methods that work by calling methods of the `IDispatch` interface. These methods are cumbersome and involve quite a bit of overhead. However, `Variants` do have the major advantage of allowing you to work in the absence of type libraries or interface declarations or when you're just in too much of a hurry to want to mess with either of those tools. For more information, see the `OleFunction`, `OleProcedure`, `OlePropertyGet`, and `OlePropertySet` methods of `Variant`.

When you call automation routines of the `Variant` class, such as `OleFunction`, the code ends up calling two methods of `IDispatch`: `GetIDsOfNames` and `Invoke`. This approach involves a lot of overhead. Whenever possible, use the classes generated in the TLB files when importing a server. Use the automation methods of the `Variant` class if you do not have a type library for the server you want to automate.

This is the end of my description of a simple automation client and server. At this stage, you should begin to have some sense of how automation is put together, but you might still have a number of unanswered questions. To help you better understand how automation works, I'm going to back away from the hands-on material found in this section and talk a little bit more about the theory behind this technology.

IDispatch, Dual Interfaces, and Dispinterfaces

`IDispatch` is an important interface that plays a big role in OLE automation. This interface is meant primarily for Visual Basic users, although C++ and C++ programmers can also access it. `IDispatch` is useful to tools that allow users to run scripts. The script engine can expose automation objects to script writers. The engine converts calls to these objects into `IDispatch.GetIDsOfNames` and `IDispatch.Invoke` calls. Applications such as Microsoft Word and Microsoft Excel expose automation objects in this fashion.

> **NOTE**
>
> `IDispatch` is typically slower than other interfaces. However, COM interfaces accessed across program or network boundaries are always quite slow compared to calls into your current program or into a DLL. It's arguable that these cross-boundary calls are so slow that the additional overhead of `IDispatch` isn't particularly significant.

You might find IDispatch useful under two circumstances:

- When you want to find a quick and dirty way to get to an automation object.

- When you want to make sure that the objects you create can be used by third-party developers. In particular, you might want your code callable from languages that do not support true objects.

Interfaces that support both IDispatch and direct calls are known as dual interfaces. C++Builder automation objects expose dual interfaces. Therefore, the objects you create can be accessed via IDispatch from Word, or the same object can be accessed directly from C++ or Delphi. (When I say you can access the object directly, I mean you can access it the same way you would access standard, non-COM objects via C++ or Delphi.)

The following section discusses the use of virtual function tables.

Calling the `SimpleAutoServer` from Word

Calling your C++Builder automation server from Word is extremely simple. To get started, create a new blank document in Microsoft Word. This example uses Word 97 but should also work with earlier versions that support COM.

In the document, enter some text that says "Press button to call C++Builder Server." In Word, choose View, Toolbar and pop up the Control Toolbox dialog. Drop a button on your document from the Control Toolbox. You are automatically placed in design mode when you drop buttons. Double-click the button, and Visual Basic for Word comes up automatically.

Enter the following method into Visual Basic:

```
Private Sub CommandButton1_Click()
  Dim CppBuilderObject As Object
  Set CppBuilderObject = CreateObject("SimpleAutoServer.MethodObject")
  ActiveDocument.Paragraphs(1).Range.InsertAfter
            (CppBuilderObject.GetName)
End Sub
```

Save your work. When you click the button on your document, the C++Builder server is called, and the text retrieved from the server is displayed in your document.

> **CAUTION**
>
> If you make a typo entering the ProgID of your server, you have to wait for the operation to time out. This process can take quite a while, perhaps several minutes. In the meantime, Word and Visual Basic for Word do not respond at all.

For the sake of clarity, I should add that a special edition of Visual Basic comes with each copy of Word 97. It is not the standard version of Visual Basic, but it is powerful enough for you to do fairly serious programming inside it, assuming that you are willing to live within the constraints of the BASIC language. Chapter 21, "ActiveForms," discusses this version of Visual Basic in greater detail and shows how to embed an entire C++Builder form inside a Microsoft Word or Microsoft Excel document.

You can find an example of the code discussed in this section of the chapter in the Word 97 document named `CallC++BuilderObjectFromWord.doc` on the CD-ROM that accompanies this book. To get to the code stored in the document, load the document into Word and select Tools, Macro, Visual Basic Editor.

As a final note to this section: I am as concerned as anyone I know about the degree to which Microsoft has come to dominate the desktop. Nevertheless, the fact that Word and Excel come with built-in versions of Visual Basic that are automation-aware is an extremely significant fact from the point of view of many developers. This incredibly powerful technology significantly changes the range of things you can easily do with a copy of C++Builder.

vtables and Dual Interfaces

By now, you should have some sense of the importance of `IDispatch` and dispinterfaces. However useful they might be for Word, Excel, and Visual Basic developers, though, C++Builder programmers still rely primarily on standard interfaces and their vtables. If you are not clear on what a vtable is, refer to Chapter 13, "The Basics of COM and Type Libraries," for more information.

Obviously, a conflict of interest exists between the needs of Word, Excel, and VB and the needs of C++Builder programmers. One group of people likes `IDispatch` and dispinterfaces, whereas the second group likes straight vtables. The solution to this problem is provided by C++Builder with something called a dual interface.

A dual interface is an interface that lets the easy languages such as VB or Excel call COM objects via `IDispatch`. At the same time, C++ programmers can call the object's methods via a virtual function table.

C++Builder automation servers expose dual interfaces, which means that in this one case, you can have your cake and eat it, too, and still have something left over for late-night snacks. That is, you can create one object that supports both VB and C++ by exposing the IDispatch interface and direct calls via virtual function tables.

Dual interfaces are not nearly as complicated as they might sound. They are simply objects that have virtual function tables that include all the methods from `IDispatch` plus any functions you want to tack on to the end. If you want to call your custom methods, you can simply jump to the point in the vtable where your method pointers are found. It's simply not important to C++ programmers that your interface also support `IDispatch.Invoke` and the rest of the `IDispatch` interface. In particular, `IDispatch` has four methods that would appear in your object in addition to the three from `IUnknown` and any that you might declare. Here is the `IDispatch` interface as it appears in `OAIDL.H`:

```
MIDL_INTERFACE("00020400-0000-0000-C000-000000000046")
    IDispatch : public IUnknown
    {
    public:
        virtual HRESULT STDMETHODCALLTYPE GetTypeInfoCount(
            /* [out] */ UINT __RPC_FAR *pctinfo) = 0;

        virtual HRESULT STDMETHODCALLTYPE GetTypeInfo(
            /* [in] */ UINT iTInfo,
            /* [in] */ LCID lcid,
            /* [out] */ ITypeInfo __RPC_FAR *__RPC_FAR *ppTInfo) = 0;

        virtual HRESULT STDMETHODCALLTYPE GetIDsOfNames(
            /* [in] */ REFIID riid,
            /* [size_is][in] */ LPOLESTR __RPC_FAR *rgszNames,
            /* [in] */ UINT cNames,
            /* [in] */ LCID lcid,
            /* [size_is][out] */ DISPID __RPC_FAR *rgDispId) = 0;

        virtual /* [local] */ HRESULT STDMETHODCALLTYPE Invoke(
            /* [in] */ DISPID dispIdMember,
            /* [in] */ REFIID riid,
            /* [in] */ LCID lcid,
            /* [in] */ WORD wFlags,
            /* [out][in] */ DISPPARAMS __RPC_FAR *pDispParams,
            /* [out] */ VARIANT __RPC_FAR *pVarResult,
            /* [out] */ EXCEPINFO __RPC_FAR *pExcepInfo,
            /* [out] */ UINT __RPC_FAR *puArgErr) = 0;

    };
```

In effect, when you create a dual interface in the `SimpleAutoServer` object, you end up with a declaration that looks like this:

```
interface IMethodObject : public IUnknown
    {
    public:
        virtual HRESULT STDMETHODCALLTYPE GetTypeInfoCount(
            /* [out] */ UINT __RPC_FAR *pctinfo) = 0;

        virtual HRESULT STDMETHODCALLTYPE GetTypeInfo(
            /* [in] */ UINT iTInfo,
            /* [in] */ LCID lcid,
```

14

```
      /* [out]- */ ITypeInfo __RPC_FAR *__RPC_FAR *ppTInfo) = 0;

   virtual HRESULT STDMETHODCALLTYPE GetIDsOfNames(
      /* [in] */ REFIID riid,
      /* [size_is][in] */ LPOLESTR __RPC_FAR *rgszNames,
      /* [in] */ UINT cNames,
      /* [in] */ LCID lcid,
      /* [size_is][out] */ DISPID __RPC_FAR *rgDispId) = 0;

   virtual /* [local] */ HRESULT STDMETHODCALLTYPE Invoke(
      /* [in] */ DISPID dispIdMember,
      /* [in] */ REFIID riid,
      /* [in] */ LCID lcid,
      /* [in] */ WORD wFlags,
      /* [out][in] */ DISPPARAMS __RPC_FAR *pDispParams,
      /* [out] */ VARIANT __RPC_FAR *pVarResult,
      /* [out] */ EXCEPINFO __RPC_FAR *pExcepInfo,
      /* [out] */ UINT __RPC_FAR *puArgErr) = 0;

   virtual HRESULT STDMETHODCALLTYPE
           GetName(BSTR* Name/*[out,retval]*/) = 0;

};
```

This object has all the methods of IDispatch in it, plus your method called GetName(). Additional methods can be tacked on to the end of this object, just as GetName() has already been added to the object.

Having waxed so poetic in my explanation of the virtues of virtual function tables, I'll now turn around and speak a few closing words in defense of IDispatch. The great thing about IDispatch is that it lets you call the methods of an object without having complete knowledge of the object's full structure. In other words, you can call its methods without ever having to see, or declare, its interface. Even though calls of this type take longer than standard C++ method calls, the innate human propensity toward laziness finds a certain attraction in this arrangement. (And, of course, C++ purists throw up their hands in horror at the very thought of such an arrangement!)

Of course, C++ programmers always have ways of overcoming adversity. A binary construct called a type library can contain a copy of the interface for an object. If you talk to this library politely, it gives you a premade copy of the interface for an object. In other words, it generates the header file for that object automatically.

C++Builder has technology that allows you to automatically generate and read type libraries for COM objects. I discuss this extremely important technology in the next section, "Type Libraries."

Before closing this section, however, I ought to say a few words about which technology you should use when building COM objects. There is some virtue in simply creating objects that derive directly from IUnknown—that is, that don't implement IDispatch. However, dual interfaces give you most of the advantages of code that descends directly from IUnknown, and yet classes of this type are still available to other programming languages because they implement IDispatch. IDispatch is a small class and does not add much code to your programs. Therefore, if you are in doubt, always use dual interfaces that implement IDispatch. Advanced programmers find reasons for taking another approach, but this default is good if you are unsure what to do.

Type Libraries

This section explains what a type library is and how you work with the C++Builder Type Library Editor. You got a brief introduction to this material in the section "Building a Simple COM Server and Client." The subject comes up again in several other places in this chapter, notably the section "Getting Two or More Interfaces from One CoClass."

What Is a Type Library?

If the only people who used COM objects were C++ programmers, I could pass around a C++Builder interface definition to define the proper way to access an interface. However, COM needs to be available to a wide range of programmers using a diverse set of tools.

Fortunately, the declarations for COM objects can be stored in something called a type library. Type libraries contain code that can be called to describe the structure of a particular object, including its names, methods, the parameters passed to the methods, and some of the types used by the object.

In short, a type library is just a C++Builder interface declaration packaged so multiple languages can use it. A type library defines the types found in a particular interface or set of interfaces. If you build an ActiveX control, it should have a type library defining all the interfaces and types supported by that object. Each language—VB, Delphi, C++Builder, and so on—can open a type library, read its contents, and generate code or other symbols of use to programmers accessing that object from a particular language or tool.

Besides using a type library for defining interfaces, you can use it for defining enumerated types and structures. A few other options are also available, but they are used infrequently, so I consider them beyond the scope of this book.

14

CREATING COM
AUTOMATION
SERVERS/CLIENTS

Creating Type Libraries

The most basic fact you need to know is how to create a type library. The most common way to build such a library is to let one of the wizards do it for you. For instance, if you turn to the ActiveX page in the Object Repository, most of the options you select result in the creation of a type library. For instance, creating an automation object, as explained earlier in this chapter, causes a type library to be created automatically. To view that library while you are working on your project, choose View, Type library from the C++Builder menu.

When you are looking at a type library, as shown in Figure 14.5, you see a toolbar along the top of the object. At the bottom of the window is a status bar. On the left is the object list pane. On the right are several pages of type information.

FIGURE 14.5

The Type Library Editor with the toolbar, status bar, object list pane, and type information.

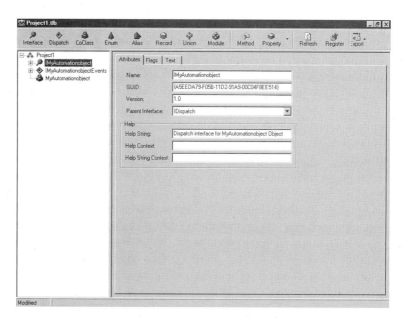

When you want to get help on the type library, you can usually press F1 to bring up the help page called the Type Library Editor. At the bottom of the Type Library Editor page in the help is a link called *type information*. This link leads to a description of the various types found on the toolbar. In fact, this help page is the key to getting the scoop on most of the top-level functions of the Type Library Editor.

If you right-click the Type Library Editor, you can open a small window that shows any errors in the library you are creating. This window is similar to the messages window commonly displayed at the bottom of the IDE.

As is often the case with this sort of thing, the people who created the specification for type libraries did not consider the development of a clean, easy-to-understand, easy-to-use, well-defined graphical user interface as one of their highest priorities. As a result, the science of creating type libraries is a black art.

Before C++Builder 3, programmers who created type libraries usually first defined their objects in a language called Interface Definition Language (IDL). The programmers' newly minted IDL script was then passed to a compiler of some sort—the most common being a Microsoft tool called MIDL. The output from this compiler is a binary type library with a TLB extension. In C++Builder 3.0, however, Borland introduced a graphical type library editor, which made the use of MIDL unnecessary.

You can extract the types defined in a type library by using a tool such as C++Builder's TLIBIMP. The tool then generates a declaration of the objects found in that type library in the current language, such as Delphi or C++. (In C++Builder, you can pass a library this way by choosing Project, Import Type Library.)

IDL is an industry-wide standard also used to define CORBA objects. As a result, many people have gone to the trouble to learn IDL, and understanding the basics of this language is a valuable asset for most programmers. Therefore, IDL plays a role in C++Builder development, but it is not necessarily the primary means of creating a type library. If you select the appropriate button in the Type Library Editor, you can convert your interfaces into raw IDL. You can choose to generate either COM or CORBA IDL, where COM IDL follows Microsoft's standards and CORBA IDL follows the OMG's standards. For more information on CORBA and the OMG, read Chapter 22, "CORBA."

You can also usually see the IDL you are generating by selecting the Text page in the Type Library Editor. If you are looking at an individual method property, the Text page shows you an IDL declaration for that method or property. However, if you are looking at an interface, CoClass, or the entire type library, the Text page shows you the underlying COM-based IDL.

14

CREATING COM
AUTOMATION
SERVERS/CLIENTS

> **NOTE**
>
> The purpose of IDL is simply to provide a language-neutral way to define an interface. Like a type library, IDL is meant to be usable by a wide range of programmers working in a wide range of languages. The Type Library Editor exists solely so that you do not have to wrestle with the vagaries of the IDL specification.

By using the Type Library Editor, you can define a COM interface by using an intuitive and easy-to-understand technology. If your goal is to go the other way around, from existing type library to code, a built-in solution also is available: Simply go to the C++Builder menu, choose Project, Import Type Library, and select a type library that will be automatically converted into a set of C++ declarations.

Valid Automation Types

You can pass any of the following types back and forth in an automation server. In particular, any of these types are marshaled for you automatically:

BYTE (unsigned char)	CY (Currency)
float	double
(unsigned) long	(unsigned) short
BSTR (widestring)	WideString
DATE (TDateTime)	VARIANT (Variant)
bool (OLE_BOOL)	WordBool
All interface types	

In addition, pointers to all of the valid automation types will be automatically marshaled. Knowing the valid automation types is important because the Type Library Editor does not enforce parameter types.

Registration Issues

Before going further, I want to mention a few issues about CLSIDs and the Registry. If you already understand the Registry, you can skip this section.

The Registry is a place where information can be stored. It's a database. GUIDs are statistically unique numbers that can be used by the operating system or a programmer to reference an OLE object. A CLSID is a GUID that references a COM object that contains one or more interfaces. You declare a COM object inside a CoClass. For instance, here is the CoClass from the SimpleAutoServer example shown earlier in this chapter:

```
coclass MethodObject
//
  [default] interface IMethodObject;
};
```

CLSIDs are stored in the Registry. In this case, visiting the actual perpetrator in its native habitat is probably best. In the example explained here, I'm assuming that you have a copy of Word loaded on your system.

To get started, use the Run menu on the Windows taskbar to launch the RegEdit program that ships with Windows NT or Windows 9x. To start the program, just type **RegEdit** in the Run box and click OK. The program is on your path.

After the program is open, search through HKEY_CLASSES_ROOT for the Word.Basic entry, as shown in Figure 14.6. (If you don't have Word, you can look instead for one of the following entries: InternetExplorer.Application, Paint.Picture, or Wordpad.Document.1) When you find Word.Basic, you can see that it's associated with the following CLSID:

//000209FE-0000-0000-C000-000000000046

FIGURE 14.6

If you run the Windows program Regedit.exe, *you can see the registration database entry for* Word.Basic *appears under* HKEY_CLASSES_ ROOT.

This unique class ID is inserted into the Registry of all machines that contain a valid and properly installed copy of Word for Windows. The only application that uses this ID is Word for Windows. It belongs uniquely to that application.

Now go further up HKEY_CLASSES_ROOT and look for the CLSID branch. Open it and search for the CLSID shown previously. When you find it, you can see two entries associated with it: one is called LocalServer, or LocalServer32, and the other is called ProgID. The ProgID is set to Word.Basic. The LocalServer32 entry looks something like this:

```
C:\WINWORD\WINWORD.EXE /Automation
```

If you look at this command, you can begin to grasp how Windows can translate the CLSID passed to `CoCreateInstance` or `CoGetClassObject` into the name of an executable. In particular, Windows looks up the CLSID in the Registry and then uses the `LocalServer32` entry to find the directory and name of the executable or DLL you want to launch. You are loading the DLL or executable so that you can access the COM objects that reside inside it.

Having these kinds of entries in the registration database does not mean that the applications in question are necessarily automation servers. For example, many applications with `LocalServer` and `ProgID` entries are not automation servers. However, all automation servers do have these two entries. Note that this example is a reference to the automation server in Word, not a reference to Word as a generic application. It references an automation object inside Word, not Word itself. (The automation object is an instance of `IDispatch`. It was not created with the C++Builder ActiveX Wizard, but it has all the same attributes. Many, but not all, of the Word interfaces support dual interfaces.)

The same basic scenario outlined here takes place when you call `CoGetClassObject` or `CoCreateInstanceEx` and specify the CLSID of an object on another machine. In particular, Windows contacts the specified machine, asks it to look up the CLSID in the Registry, and then marshals information back and forth between the two machines. You learn much more about this subject in the next chapter.

CLSIDs are said to be statistically unique. You can create a new CLSID by calling `CoCreateGuid`. The following code shows one way to make this call:

```
#include <ole2.h>

::CoInitialize(0);

  GUID newguid;
  ::CoCreateGuid(&newguid);

// eventually you should call CoUninitialize;
```

The code shown here begins by calling `CoInitialize`, which is usually unnecessary in C++Builder ActiveX projects because these projects typically initialize OLE via an instance of the `TInitOle` class (see `UTILCLS.H` for more information).

`CoCreateGuid` is the call that retrieves the new CLSID from the system. This ID is guaranteed to be unique as long as you have a network card on your system. Each network card has a unique number on it, and this card number is combined with the date and time and other random bits of information to create a unique number that could only be generated on a machine with your network card at a particular date and time. Rumors that the phase of the moon and current ages of Bill Gates's children are also factored in are probably not true. At any rate, the result is a number that is guaranteed to be statistically unique, within the tolerance levels for your definition of that word given your faith in mathematicians in general and Microsoft-based mathematicians in particular. (Actually, the algorithm used here was developed by the Open Software Foundation.)

The `StringFromCLSID` routine converts a CLSID into a string. Seen in its raw form, a CLSID looks like this:

```
//FC41CC90-C01D-11CF-8CCD-0080C80CF1D2
```

These numbers can be converted into a structure of type `GUID` that can be used in a C++Builder. The `GUID` type is defined in `BASETYPS.H` as follows:

```
typedef struct _GUID
{
    unsigned long Data1;
    unsigned short Data2;
    unsigned short Data3;
    unsigned char Data4[8];
} GUID;
```

This subject can appear a bit tricky at first, but ultimately it is not really as tough as you might think. The truth is that I found out a lot about GUIDs simply by wandering around in the Registry, poking my nose into this and that. The Registry is a dry and dusty place, but it can develop a certain elusive charm if you come to see it in the right light. Of course, you have to keep this kind of interest to yourself, as nothing is more apt to destroy your popularity at a cocktail party than a reference to a personal hobby that involves exploring the more obscure nodes of the Windows system Registry.

Marshaling Data Automatically

Marshaling is a term for the technique used to transfer data or function calls back and forth between two applications that reside in separate processes. For example, if you pass a parameter to a function across application boundaries, you have to be sure that it is treated properly by both applications. If you declare the parameter as an `int` in C++, that means you're passing a four-byte ordinal value. You might also describe that as a `long`. But how do you describe it in Visual Basic? How can you find a common language that defines the object once and for all in a wide range of languages? The answers to these questions are expressed in COM by a complex interface called `IMarshal`, which is beyond the scope of this chapter. Indeed, `IMarshal` is notorious for being difficult to implement.

Here is how the Microsoft documentation, in a rare moment of clarity, defines `IMarshal`: "'Marshaling' is the process of packaging data into packets for transmission to a different process or machine. 'Unmarshaling' is the process of recovering that data at the receiving end. In any given call, method arguments are marshaled and unmarshaled in one direction, while return values are marshaled and unmarshaled in the other." This is all good and well. Unfortunately, as I stated earlier, the IMarshal interface is very hard to implement.

It happens that if you're using a standard COM object, you don't have to implement IMarshal because these interfaces are marshaled for you automatically by the system. In other words, if you're implementing an instance of IDispatch, IUnknown, IClassFactory, IOleContainer, or any other predefined COM class, you don't have to worry about marshaling. Microsoft takes care of this job for you. If you're creating a custom object of your own, you need to implement IMarshal unless you stick with the safe parameter types listed in the section "Valid Automation Types."

You can use techniques involving SAFEARRAYs to marshal complex custom types such as records or arrays. Chapter 13 describes this terminology.

Getting Two or More Interfaces from One CoClass

In most cases, you want to store multiple automation interfaces inside a single library. The sample program shown in this section of the chapter demonstrates how to store these interfaces. In particular, you see how to export three interfaces from one server, and one of the interfaces you create is descended from one of the other interfaces.

To get started, create a new program and save it in its own directory. Choose File, New and turn to the ActiveX page. Create a new automation object and call it TwoFaceServer. At this stage, you have a CoClass and one interface with no methods in it. To enrich the object somewhat, give it a single method called GetNameOne that takes a pointer to a BSTR as a parameter:

```
[id(0x00000001)]
HRESULT _stdcall GetNameOne([out, retval] BSTR * Name );
```

Now create a second interface by choosing the Interface button on the far left of the toolbar at the top of the Type Library Editor. Rename the interface **IFaceTwo**. Create a single method for this interface called **GetNameTwo**:

```
[id(0x00000001)]
HRESULT _stdcall GetNameTwo([out, retval] BSTR * Name );
```

> **NOTE**
>
> If you have more than one interface in a CoClass, all those methods are implemented by a single C++ class. In other words, one class that appears in your *XXX*_IMPL file contains all the methods from the different interfaces in one CoClass.
>
> If you insert more than one CoClass into a single type library, the second CoClass does not automatically get an *XXX*_IMPL file associated with it. Instead, you have to create the *XXX*_IMPL file by hand.

Highlight the CoClass, which might be called TwoFaceObject but can have whatever name you choose. Flip to the Implements page, right-click the center of the white area, and select Insert Interface from the pop-up menu. You see a list of available interfaces, one of which is called IFaceTwo. Select this interface. (The Implements page doesn't show up unless you have first directly clicked the CoClass.)

To check how you are doing, continue to highlight the CoClass and turn to the Text page, where you can see the IDL that is being generated (see Listing 14.3). You should see both your interfaces listed in the CoClass. Listing 14.4 shows the code that wraps the type library and other key units in this example. Listing 14.5 shows the implementation files.

LISTING 14.3   THE IDL FOR THE TwoFaceServer COCLASS

```
[
  uuid(0FCEDDC3-DBD8-11D2-AE5D-00D54CC10000),
  version(1.0),
  helpstring("TwoFaceServer Object")
]
coclass TwoFaceServer
{
  [default] interface ITwoFaceServer;
  interface IFaceTwo;
};
```

LISTING 14.4   THE TwoMoonServer_TLB FILE IS CREATED AUTOMATICALLY BY THE TYPE LIBRARY EDITOR

```
// C++ TLBWRTR : $Revision:   1.96.1.27  $
// File generated on 3/16/99 7:55:11 PM from Type Library described below.
```

continues

14

CREATING COM
AUTOMATION
SERVERS/CLIENTS

Listing 14.4   Continued

```
// ************************************************************************
// Type Lib:
// C:\Program Files\Borland\CBuilder4\Projects\TwoMoonServer.tlb
// IID\LCID: {0FCEDDC0-DBD8-11D2-AE5D-00D54CC10000}\0
// Helpfile:
// DepndLst:
//    (1) v2.0 stdole, (C:\WINDOWS\SYSTEM\STDOLE2.TLB)
//    (2) v4.0 StdVCL, (C:\WINDOWS\SYSTEM\STDVCL40.DLL)
// ************************************************************************
#ifndef   __TwoMoonServer_TLB_h__
#define   __TwoMoonServer_TLB_h__

#pragma option push -b -w-inl

#include <vcl/utilcls.h>
#if !defined(__UTILCLS_H_VERSION) || (__UTILCLS_H_VERSION < 0x0101)
#error "This file requires an newer version of the file UTILCLS.H"
#endif

#include <olectl.h>
#include <ocidl.h>
#if defined(USING_ATLVCL) || defined(USING_ATL)
#if !defined(__TLB_NO_EVENT_WRAPPERS)
#include <atl/atlmod.h>
#endif
#endif


// ************************************************************************
// Forward reference of some VCL types (to avoid including STDVCL.HPP)
// ************************************************************************
namespace Stdvcl {class IStrings; class IStringsDisp;}
using namespace Stdvcl;

namespace Project1_tlb
{

// ************************************************************************
// HelpString: Project1 Library
// Version:    1.0
// ************************************************************************


// ************************************************************************
// GUIDS declared in the TypeLibrary. Following prefixes are used:
//    Type Libraries     : LIBID_xxxx
//    CoClasses          : CLSID_xxxx
//    DISPInterfaces     : DIID_xxxx
//    Non-DISP interfaces: IID_xxxx
```

```
// **********************************************************************
DEFINE_GUID(LIBID_TwoMoonServer, 0x0FCEDDC0, 0xDBD8, 0x11D2, 0xAE, \
                       0 x5D, 0x00, 0xD5, 0x4C, 0xC1, 0x00, 0x00);
DEFINE_GUID(IID_ITwoFaceServer, 0x0FCEDDC1, 0xDBD8, 0x11D2, 0xAE, 0x5D,\
                        0x00, 0xD5, 0x4C, 0xC1, 0x00, 0x00);
DEFINE_GUID(IID_IFaceTwo, 0x0FCEDDC5, 0xDBD8, 0x11D2, 0xAE, 0x5D, 0x00,\
                        0xD5, 0x4C, 0xC1, 0x00, 0x00);
DEFINE_GUID(CLSID_TwoFaceServer, 0x0FCEDDC3, 0xDBD8, 0x11D2, 0xAE,\
                        0x5D, 0x00, 0xD5, 0x4C, 0xC1, 0x00, 0x00);

// **********************************************************************
// Forward declaration of types defined in TypeLibrary
// **********************************************************************
interface DECLSPEC_UUID("{0FCEDDC1-DBD8-11D2-AE5D-00D54CC10000}")
                        ITwoFaceServer;
interface DECLSPEC_UUID("{0FCEDDC5-DBD8-11D2-AE5D-00D54CC10000}")
                        IFaceTwo;

// **********************************************************************
// Declaration of CoClasses defined in Type Library
// (NOTE: Here we map each CoClass to its Default Interface)
// **********************************************************************
typedef ITwoFaceServer TwoFaceServer;

#define LIBID_OF_TwoFaceServer (&LIBID_TwoMoonServer)
// **********************************************************************
// Interface: ITwoFaceServer
// Flags:     (4416) Dual OleAutomation Dispatchable
// GUID:      {0FCEDDC1-DBD8-11D2-AE5D-00D54CC10000}
// **********************************************************************
interface ITwoFaceServer : public IDispatch
{
public:
  virtual HRESULT STDMETHODCALLTYPE
               GetNameOne(BSTR* Name/*[out,retval]*/) = 0;

#if !defined(__TLB_NO_INTERFACE_WRAPPERS)

  BSTR __fastcall GetNameOne(void)
  {
    BSTR Name= 0;
    OLECHECK(this->GetNameOne(&Name));
    return Name;
  }


#endif //    __TLB_NO_INTERFACE_WRAPPERS
```

continues

LISTING 14.4   CONTINUED

```
};

// **********************************************************************
// Interface: IFaceTwo
// Flags:     (4416) Dual OleAutomation Dispatchable
// GUID:      {0FCEDDC5-DBD8-11D2-AE5D-00D54CC10000}
// **********************************************************************
interface IFaceTwo : public IDispatch
{
public:
  virtual HRESULT STDMETHODCALLTYPE
              GetNameTwo(BSTR* Name/*[out,retval]*/) = 0; // [1]

#if !defined(__TLB_NO_INTERFACE_WRAPPERS)

  BSTR __fastcall GetNameTwo(void)
  {
    BSTR Name= 0;
    OLECHECK(this->GetNameTwo(&Name));
    return Name;
  }



#endif //    __TLB_NO_INTERFACE_WRAPPERS

};

#if !defined(__TLB_NO_INTERFACE_WRAPPERS)
// **********************************************************************
// SmartIntf: TCOMITwoFaceServer
// Interface: ITwoFaceServer
// **********************************************************************
template <class T /* ITwoFaceServer */>
class TCOMITwoFaceServerT : public TComInterface<ITwoFaceServer>,
                        public TComInterfaceBase<IUnknown>
{
public:
  TCOMITwoFaceServerT() {}
  TCOMITwoFaceServerT(ITwoFaceServer *intf, bool addRef = false) :
                    TComInterface<ITwoFaceServer>(intf, addRef) {}
  TCOMITwoFaceServerT(const TCOMITwoFaceServerT& src) :
                    TComInterface<ITwoFaceServer>(src) {}
  TCOMITwoFaceServerT& operator=(const TCOMITwoFaceServerT& src)
                    { Bind(src, true); return *this;}

  HRESULT          __fastcall GetNameOne(BSTR* Name/*[out,retval]*/);
  BSTR             __fastcall GetNameOne(void);
```

```
};
typedef TCOMITwoFaceServerT<ITwoFaceServer> TCOMITwoFaceServer;

// ********************************************************************
// DispIntf:  ITwoFaceServer
// Flags:     (4416) Dual OleAutomation Dispatchable
// GUID:      {0FCEDDC1-DBD8-11D2-AE5D-00D54CC10000}
// ********************************************************************
template<class T>
class ITwoFaceServerDispT : public TAutoDriver<ITwoFaceServer>
{
public:
  ITwoFaceServerDispT(){}

  ITwoFaceServerDispT(ITwoFaceServer *pintf)
  {
    TAutoDriver<ITwoFaceServer>::Bind(pintf);
  }

  ITwoFaceServerDispT& operator=(ITwoFaceServer *pintf)
  {
    TAutoDriver<ITwoFaceServer>::Bind(pintf);
    return *this;
  }

  HRESULT BindDefault(/*Binds to new instance of
                        CoClass TwoFaceServer*/)
  {
    return OLECHECK(Bind(CLSID_TwoFaceServer));
  }

  HRESULT BindRunning(/*Binds to a running instance of
                        CoClass TwoFaceServer*/)
  {
    return BindToActive(CLSID_TwoFaceServer);
  }

  HRESULT          __fastcall GetNameOne(BSTR* Name/*[out,retval]*/);
  BSTR             __fastcall GetNameOne(void);

};
typedef ITwoFaceServerDispT<ITwoFaceServer> ITwoFaceServerDisp;

typedef TComInterface<IFaceTwo>   TCOMIFaceTwo;

// ********************************************************************
// DispIntf:  IFaceTwo
// Flags:     (4416) Dual OleAutomation Dispatchable
// GUID:      {0FCEDDC5-DBD8-11D2-AE5D-00D54CC10000}
```

14

CREATING COM
AUTOMATION
SERVERS/CLIENTS

continues

LISTING 14.4   CONTINUED

```cpp
// ********************************************************************
template<class T>
class IFaceTwoDispT : public TAutoDriver<IFaceTwo>
{
public:
  IFaceTwoDispT(){}

  IFaceTwoDispT(IFaceTwo *pintf)
  {
    TAutoDriver<IFaceTwo>::Bind(pintf);
  }

  IFaceTwoDispT& operator=(IFaceTwo *pintf)
  {
    TAutoDriver<IFaceTwo>::Bind(pintf);
    return *this;
  }

  HRESULT          __fastcall GetNameTwo(BSTR* Name/*[out,retval]*/);
  BSTR             __fastcall GetNameTwo(void);

};
typedef IFaceTwoDispT<IFaceTwo> IFaceTwoDisp;

// ********************************************************************
// SmartIntf: TCOMITwoFaceServer
// Interface: ITwoFaceServer
// ********************************************************************
template <class T> HRESULT __fastcall
TCOMITwoFaceServerT<T>::GetNameOne(BSTR* Name/*[out,retval]*/)
{
  return (*this)->GetNameOne(Name);
}

template <class T> BSTR __fastcall
TCOMITwoFaceServerT<T>::GetNameOne(void)
{
  BSTR Name= 0;
  OLECHECK(this->GetNameOne(&Name));
  return Name;
}

// ********************************************************************
// DispIntf:  ITwoFaceServer
// Flags:     (4416) Dual OleAutomation Dispatchable
// GUID:      {0FCEDDC1-DBD8-11D2-AE5D-00D54CC10000}
// ********************************************************************
template <class T> HRESULT __fastcall
ITwoFaceServerDispT<T>::GetNameOne(BSTR* Name/*[out,retval]*/)
```

```
{
  static _TDispID _dispid(*this, OLETEXT("GetNameOne"), DISPID(1));
  TAutoArgs<0> _args;
  return OutRetValSetterPtr(Name /*[VT_BSTR:1]*/, _args,
                       OleFunction(_dispid, _args));
}

template <class T> BSTR __fastcall
ITwoFaceServerDispT<T>::GetNameOne(void)
{
  BSTR Name;
  this->GetNameOne(&Name);
  return Name;
}

// *********************************************************************
// DispIntf:  IFaceTwo
// Flags:     (4416) Dual OleAutomation Dispatchable
// GUID:      {0FCEDDC5-DBD8-11D2-AE5D-00D54CC10000}
// *********************************************************************
template <class T> HRESULT __fastcall
IFaceTwoDispT<T>::GetNameTwo(BSTR* Name/*[out,retval]*/)
{
  static _TDispID _dispid(*this, OLETEXT("GetNameTwo"), DISPID(1));
  TAutoArgs<0> _args;
  return OutRetValSetterPtr(Name /*[VT_BSTR:1]*/, _args,
                       OleFunction(_dispid, _args));
}

template <class T> BSTR __fastcall
IFaceTwoDispT<T>::GetNameTwo(void)
{
  BSTR Name;
  this->GetNameTwo(&Name);
  return Name;
}

// *********************************************************************
// The following typedefs expose classes (named CoCoClassName) that
// provide static Create() and CreateRemote(LPWSTR machineName) methods
// for creating an instance of an exposed object. These functions can
// be used by client wishing to automate CoClasses exposed by this
// typelibrary.
// *********************************************************************

// *********************************************************************
// COCLASS DEFAULT INTERFACE CREATOR
// CoClass   : TwoFaceServer
// Interface: TCOMITwoFaceServer
```

continues

LISTING 14.4 CONTINUED

```
// **********************************************************************//
typedef TCoClassCreatorT<TCOMITwoFaceServer, ITwoFaceServer,
                         &CLSID_TwoFaceServer,
                         &IID_ITwoFaceServer> CoTwoFaceServer;
#endif  //   __TLB_NO_INTERFACE_WRAPPERS


};     // namespace Project1_tlb

#if !defined(NO_IMPLICIT_NAMESPACE_USE)
using  namespace Project1_tlb;
#endif

#pragma option pop

#endif // __TwoMoonServer_TLB_h__



// C++ TLBWRTR : $Revision:   1.96.1.27  $
// File generated on 3/16/99 7:55:11 PM from Type Library below.

// **********************************************************************
// Type Lib:
// C:\Program Files\Borland\CBuilder4\Projects\TwoMoonServer.tlb
// IID\LCID: {0FCEDDC0-DBD8-11D2-AE5D-00D54CC10000}\0
// Helpfile:
// DepndLst:
//   (1) v2.0 stdole, (C:\WINDOWS\SYSTEM\STDOLE2.TLB)
//   (2) v4.0 StdVCL, (C:\WINDOWS\SYSTEM\STDVCL40.DLL)
// **********************************************************************

#include <vcl.h>
#pragma hdrstop

#include "TwoMoonServer_TLB.h"

#if !defined(__PRAGMA_PACKAGE_SMART_INIT)
#define     __PRAGMA_PACKAGE_SMART_INIT
#pragma package(smart_init)
#endif

namespace Project1_tlb
{


// **********************************************************************
// GUIDS declared in the TypeLibrary
```

```
// ********************************************************************
extern "C" const GUID LIBID_TwoMoonServer = {0x0FCEDDC0, 0xDBD8, 0x11D2,
                { 0xAE, 0x5D, 0x00, 0xD5, 0x4C, 0xC1, 0x00, 0x00} };
extern "C" const GUID IID_ITwoFaceServer = {0x0FCEDDC1, 0xDBD8, 0x11D2,
                { 0xAE, 0x5D, 0x00, 0xD5, 0x4C, 0xC1, 0x00, 0x00} };
extern "C" const GUID CLSID_TwoFaceServer = {0x0FCEDDC3, 0xDBD8, 0x11D2,
                { 0xAE, 0x5D, 0x00, 0xD5, 0x4C, 0xC1, 0x00, 0x00} };
extern "C" const GUID IID_IFaceTwo = {0x0FCEDDC5, 0xDBD8, 0x11D2,
                { 0xAE, 0x5D, 0x00, 0xD5, 0x4C, 0xC1, 0x00, 0x00} };
};      // namespace Project1_tlb
```

LISTING 14.5   THE IMPLEMENTATION FOR THE TwoMoon SERVER

```
// TWOFACESERVERIMPL.H : Declaration of the TTwoFaceServerImpl

#ifndef __TWOFACESERVERIMPL_H_
#define __TWOFACESERVERIMPL_H_

#include "TwoMoonServer_TLB.h"


//////////////////////////////////////////////////////////////////////
// TTwoFaceServerImpl     Implements ITwoFaceServer,
//                        default interface of TwoFaceServer
// ThreadingModel : Apartment
// Dual Interface : TRUE
// Event Support  : FALSE
// Default ProgID : Project1.TwoFaceServer
// Description    :
//////////////////////////////////////////////////////////////////////
class ATL_NO_VTABLE TTwoFaceServerImpl :
  public CComObjectRootEx<CComSingleThreadModel>,
  public CComCoClass<TTwoFaceServerImpl, &CLSID_TwoFaceServer>,
  public IDispatchImpl<ITwoFaceServer,
                    &IID_ITwoFaceServer,
                    &LIBID_TwoMoonServer>,
  DUALINTERFACE_IMPL(TwoFaceServer, IFaceTwo)
{
public:
  TTwoFaceServerImpl()
  {
  }

  // Data used when registering Object
  //
  DECLARE_THREADING_MODEL(otApartment);
  DECLARE_PROGID("TwoMoonServer.TwoFaceServer");
  DECLARE_DESCRIPTION("");
```

continues

LISTING 14.5   CONTINUED

```cpp
// Function invoked to (un)register object
//
static HRESULT WINAPI UpdateRegistry(BOOL bRegister)
{
  TTypedComServerRegistrarT<TTwoFaceServerImpl>
  regObj(GetObjectCLSID(), GetProgID(), GetDescription());
  return regObj.UpdateRegistry(bRegister);
}


BEGIN_COM_MAP(TTwoFaceServerImpl)
  COM_INTERFACE_ENTRY(ITwoFaceServer)
  COM_INTERFACE_ENTRY2(IDispatch, ITwoFaceServer)
  DUALINTERFACE_ENTRY(IFaceTwo)
END_COM_MAP()

// ITwoFaceServer
public:

  STDMETHOD(GetNameOne(BSTR* Name));
  STDMETHOD(GetNameTwo(BSTR* Name));
};

#endif //__TWOFACESERVERIMPL_H_



// TWOFACESERVERIMPL : Implementation of TTwoFaceServerImpl
//                 (CoClass: TwoFaceServer, Interface: ITwoFaceServer)

#include <vcl.h>
#pragma hdrstop

#include "TWOFACESERVERIMPL.H"

//////////////////////////////////////////////////////////////////////
// TTwoFaceServerImpl

STDMETHODIMP TTwoFaceServerImpl::GetNameOne(BSTR* Name)
{
  *Name = WideString("ITwoFaceServer::GetNameOne").Detach();
  return S_OK;
}


STDMETHODIMP TTwoFaceServerImpl::GetNameTwo(BSTR* Name)
{
  *Name = WideString("IFaceTwo::GetNameTwo").Detach();
  return S_OK;
}
```

The purpose of the TwoMoonServer program is to show how you can support more than one interface on a single automation object, or more specifically, on a single CoClass. This subject is very important because you want to create automation servers that support a wide range of capabilities and some very complex class structures. The program shows you how to get started.

When you are looking at an IDL file like this one, a good place to begin is in the CoClass statement:

```
[
  uuid(0FCEDDC3-DBD8-11D2-AE5D-00D54CC10000),
  version(1.0),
  helpstring("TwoFaceServer Object")
]
coclass TwoFaceServer
{
  [default] interface ITwoFaceServer;
  interface IFaceTwo;
};
```

Here you can see the two interfaces that are exported from this file.

To find out about these interfaces, you need to go to the `TwoFaceServer_TLB.h` file. In it, you find the `IDispatch` interface for both objects.

Note, however, that the `Class Creator` returns only the first interface:

```
// ********************************************************************
// COCLASS DEFAULT INTERFACE CREATOR
// CoClass  : TwoFaceServer
// Interface: TCOMITwoFaceServer
// ********************************************************************
typedef TCoClassCreatorT<TCOMITwoFaceServer, ITwoFaceServer,
                         &CLSID_TwoFaceServer,
&IID_ITwoFaceServer> CoTwoFaceServer;
```

As previously shown, the `CoTwoFaceServer` template provides an easy way to obtain a pointer to `ITwoFaceServer`, the first interface (default interface) of the server. But how does one obtain a pointer to the second interface of the server? Listing 14.6 illustrates the solution. After the listing, I describe the technique in detail.

LISTING 14.6   THE MAIN FORM FOR THE TWOCLIENT PROGRAM

```
////////////////////////////////////////////////////////////////////
// TWOFACECLIENTFORM.H
//
// Form of Client which automates the TwoFace Automation Server
```

continues

LISTING **14.6**   CONTINUED

```cpp
//////////////////////////////////////////////////////////////////
//-----------------------------------------------------------------
#ifndef TwoFaceClientFormH
#define TwoFaceClientFormH
//-----------------------------------------------------------------
#include <Classes.hpp>
#include <Controls.hpp>
#include <StdCtrls.hpp>
#include <Forms.hpp>
#include "TwoMoonServer_TLB.h"
//-----------------------------------------------------------------
class TForm1 : public TForm
{
__published:    // IDE-managed Components
        TEdit *Edit1;
        TEdit *Edit2;
        TButton *Button1;
        TButton *Button2;
        TButton *Button3;
        void __fastcall Button1Click(TObject *Sender);
        void __fastcall Button3Click(TObject *Sender);
        void __fastcall Button2Click(TObject *Sender);
private:        // User declarations
        ITwoFaceServerDisp server;
        IFaceTwoDisp otherInterface;
public:         // User declarations
        __fastcall TForm1(TComponent* Owner);
};
//-----------------------------------------------------------------
extern PACKAGE TForm1 *Form1;
//-----------------------------------------------------------------
#endif




//////////////////////////////////////////////////////////////////
// TWOFACECLIENTFORM.CPP
//
// Form of Client which automates the TwoFace Automation Server
//////////////////////////////////////////////////////////////////
#include <vcl.h>
#pragma hdrstop

#include "TwoFaceClientForm.h"

//-----------------------------------------------------------------
#pragma package(smart_init)
#pragma resource "*.dfm"
TForm1 *Form1;
```

```
//------------------------------------------------------------------
__fastcall TForm1::TForm1(TComponent* Owner)
        : TForm(Owner)
{
}
//------------------------------------------------------------------
// Button handling 'Invoke TwoFace Server' command
void __fastcall TForm1::Button1Click(TObject *Sender)
{
  // Verify that we're already bound to server
  if (!server)
  {
    // Launch new copy of server and bind to it
    server.BindDefault();

    // Invoke method of first (default) interface
    Edit1->Text = server.GetNameOne();

    // Get pointer to other interface from server
    IFaceTwo* secondInterface = 0;
    server->QueryInterface(IID_IFaceTwo, (LPVOID*)&secondInterface);
    otherInterface.Bind(secondInterface);

    // Invoke method of second interface
    Edit2->Text = otherInterface.GetNameTwo();
  }
  else
    ShowMessage("Server is already running. Choose Shutdown first!");
}
//------------------------------------------------------------------
// Button handling 'Shutdown Server' command
void __fastcall TForm1::Button3Click(TObject *Sender)
{
  // Verify that we're bound to Server
  if (server)
  {
    server = 0;                // Release default interface
    otherInterface = 0;        // Release other interface

    Edit1->Text = "";          // Clear Edit1 data
    Edit2->Text = "";          // Clear Edit2 data
  }
  else
    ShowMessage("Not connected! Select 'Invoke' button first!");
}
//------------------------------------------------------------------
// Button handling 'Use CoCreateInstance' command
void __fastcall TForm1::Button2Click(TObject *Sender)
{
```

continues

14

CREATING COM
AUTOMATION
SERVERS/CLIENTS

LISTING 14.6   CONTINUED

```
    // Verify that we're not bound to server already
    if (!server)
    {
      // Create new instance of server requesting default interface
      ITwoFaceServer *twoFaceServerIntf = 0;
      ::CoCreateInstance(CLSID_TwoFaceServer, 0, CLSCTX_SERVER,
                         IID_ITwoFaceServer, (LPVOID*)&twoFaceServerIntf);
      server = twoFaceServerIntf;

      // Invoke method of first interface
      Edit1->Text = server.GetNameOne();

      // Get pointer to other interface from server
      IFaceTwo* secondInterface = 0;
      server->QueryInterface(IID_IFaceTwo, (LPVOID*)&secondInterface);
      otherInterface.Bind(secondInterface);

      // Invoke method of second interface
      Edit2->Text = otherInterface.GetNameTwo();
    }
    else
      ShowMessage("Already connected. Select 'Shutdown Server' first!");
}
//------------------------------------------------------------------
```

In the `Button1Click()` method, I create an instance of the `TwoMoonServer` by using a standard `BindDefault()` method provided by C++Builder's `ITwoFaceServerDisp` dispinterface wrapper in the *xxxx*_TLB.H file:

```
// Launch new copy of server and bind to it
    server.BindDefault();

    // Invoke method of first (default) interface
    Edit1->Text = server.GetNameOne();
```

Here everything is more or less as you would expect. I bind to a new copy of the server, call one of its methods, and show the results to the user in an edit control.

When it comes time to get the second interface, I use the `QueryInterface()` method:

```
    // Get pointer to other interface from server
    IFaceTwo* secondInterface = 0;
    server->QueryInterface(IID_IFaceTwo, (LPVOID*)&secondInterface);
    otherInterface.Bind(secondInterface);

    // Invoke method of second interface
    Edit2->Text = otherInterface.GetNameTwo();
```

After you have back the `IFaceTwo` interface from `QueryInterface()`, I bind the interface to an instance of `IFaceTwoDisp`, a dispinterface wrapper defined in the *xxxx*`_TLB` file. This wrapper exposes the methods of the `IFaceTwo` interface. You can invoke the `GetNameTwo()` method via the wrapper.

Calling `CoCreateInstance`

This section explains how to call `CoCreateInstance` directly rather than having C++Builder call it for you. The following method shows you how to proceed:

```
// Create new instance of server requesting default interface
ITwoFaceServer *twoFaceServerIntf = 0;
::CoCreateInstance(CLSID_TwoFaceServer, 0, CLSCTX_SERVER,
         IID_ITwoFaceServer, (LPVOID*)&twoFaceServerIntf);
server = twoFaceServerIntf;

// Invoke method of first interface
Edit1->Text = server.GetNameOne();
```

`CoCreateInstance` takes five parameters:

```
WINOLEAPI CoCreateInstance(REFCLSID rclsid, LPUNKNOWN pUnkOuter,
              DWORD dwClsContext, REFIID riid, LPVOID FAR* ppv);
```

Here is a detailed explanation of each parameter:

- `rclsid`—The first parameter is the CLSID for the CoClass you want to create.

- `pUnkOuter`—The second can always be 0, as it is used only by aggregation, which is an advanced technique not relevant to this chapter.

- `dwClsContext`—The third parameter is a constant designating the kind of server you want to access. The possible values are declared as follows:

```
typedef
enum tagCLSCTX
   {       CLSCTX_INPROC_SERVER = 0x1,
     CLSCTX_INPROC_HANDLER = 0x2,
     CLSCTX_LOCAL_SERVER    = 0x4,
     CLSCTX_INPROC_SERVER16     = 0x8,
     CLSCTX_REMOTE_SERVER  = 0x10,
     CLSCTX_INPROC_HANDLER16        = 0x20,
     CLSCTX_INPROC_SERVERX86        = 0x40,
     CLSCTX_INPROC_HANDLERX86       = 0x80,
     CLSCTX_ESERVER_HANDLER     = 0x100
   }       CLSCTX;
```

  In this case, of course, you can pass in `CLSCTX_LOCAL_SERVER`.
  `CLSCTX_INPROC_SERVER` is for DLLs loaded into your program's address space, and

the other commonly used option is CLSCTX_REMOTE_SERVER. Remote applications are discussed in the next chapter.

- riid—The fourth parameter is the GUID of the interface that you want to retrieve.
- ppv—The final parameter is a pointer to a pointer to the interface that you want to retrieve from the COM server.

CoCreateInstance returns an HRESULT, and you can pass it through the SUCCEEDED macro to see whether everything worked out as you had planned. If it did not, you can call the VCL routine OleCheck to see what went wrong. OleCheck does not report on all possible OLE errors, but it catches a lot of the big ones. If you want, you can just wrap each of the COM calls inside a call to OleCheck:

```
OleCheck(CoCreateInstance(...));
```

This syntax ensures that any call that fails is reported to you immediately. If you ever end up doing any serious COM programming, not checking the value of every single HRESULT returned to and by your program is absolute folly.

After calling CoCreateInstance, I then call QueryInterface to retrieve the second interface:

```
// Get pointer to other interface from server
    IFaceTwo* secondInterface = 0;
    server->QueryInterface(IID_IFaceTwo, (LPVOID*)&secondInterface);
```

QueryInterface is part of IUnknown, so it is part of all COM objects. After you have some interfaces from a CoClass, you should always be able to call QueryInterface to retrieve an instance of some other interface of the CoClass. In this case, I call QueryInterface on the TwoMoon interface and ask for a pointer to the IFaceTwo interface.

The value that is returned from QueryInterface in its second parameter is a pointer to the object you requested. Although you can use that interface directly, it's easier to bind it to a wrapper class provided by the *xxxx*_TLB class first. You can then use the wrapper to invoke methods exposed by the interface. And, more importantly, you don't have to worry about releasing the interface.

Summary

In this chapter, you learned some of the basic facts about OLE automation. As we move into a world based on distributed architectures that consist of suites of applications, COM will become central to our vision of computer programming on the Windows platform.

In particular, this chapter covered creating COM servers and clients, working with type libraries, interfaces and CoClass, and also calling core COM functions such as `CoCreateInstance` and `QueryInterface`.

If you are thinking of moving to Java or to CORBA, much of the information presented in this chapter is still germane. Java is even more applet- and control-centric than Windows. The whole idea of presenting interfaces defined by a language like IDL is central to the very idea of CORBA programming. In short, distributed architectures built on top of COM, or something like COM, are almost certain to be part of any conceivable programming future.

In Chapter 19, "DCOM," you see how to take the principles learned in this chapter and move them onto the network. You find that almost everything you learned in this chapter applies to DCOM programming. So gather your wits about you and prepare to journey into the future of computer programming.

14

CREATING COM
AUTOMATION
SERVERS/CLIENTS

Using C++Builder to Automate Word and Excel

by Charlie Calvert and Bruneau Babet

IN THIS CHAPTER

The goal of this chapter is to get you up to speed automating Excel and Word from a C++Builder application. Most of the text will focus on Excel, but you will find that if you understand Excel automation, you need only a few hints to get started automating Word. If you are primarily interested in Word, I ask you to patiently read through the material on Excel, as almost all of it applies to Word.

You can use C++Builder to fully control virtually all the features of Excel and Word. You can do very little from inside Excel or Word that you cannot also automate from outside. In other words, both Excel and Word can be fully controlled from C++Builder applications using OLE automation.

For the most part, the act of controlling Excel or Word from a C++Builder application is not terribly challenging. Whatever difficulty you experience comes not from C++Builder's side of the equation, but from the innate complexity of the Excel and Word object hierarchies. Not that I find the hierarchies unreasonable, but they do encapsulate sufficient complexity to require a significant period of study. In particular, these automation classes give you rather detailed control over all the features of Word and Excel that you can access through those program's menus. Because they are complex applications, the interface to them also needs to be complex. The purpose of this chapter is to unscramble that hierarchy and show its underlying structure.

This chapter shows automating Word and Excel using methods of the `Variant` class and the `IDispatch` mechanism as well as through direct calls via dual interfaces exposed by these servers. All these technologies are closely related. However, you will find two significant differences between them:

- Using `Variant`s is usually the easiest, the most terse, but also the slowest way to get things done in terms of performance.
- Using COM interfaces is usually a little more difficult but also yields the highest performance.

I'm aiming this material primarily at intermediate or experienced programmers, but I hope it is accessible to anyone who has a basic understanding of how to use C++Builder, Word, and Excel. Though you should not need a high level of expertise to understand this chapter, I am trying to cover the subject in some depth. For many people, a more high-level, abstract view might be more appropriate. But I believe some people also have a need for a more-detailed look at this subject, which is why I have written this chapter.

System Requirements for Automating Office Applications

This chapter assumes the use of Microsoft Office 97. Portions of the chapter also work with Office 95, but the sections on interfaces, in particular, require that you use Office 97.

> **NOTE**
>
> Each version of Office exposes slightly different objects with different methods and properties. This chapter deals with Office 97. The code presented here has not been tested with Office 2000.

To perform automation successfully with Excel or Word, you need a fairly powerful system with lots of RAM. I've been automating Excel for at least four years. When I first started, I considered the technology a bit suspect simply because it was terribly slow. Now, however, machines are powerful enough to take Excel through its paces in a few short moments. In particular, if you have a Pentium 120 class machine or above, and at least 48MB of RAM, this technology works well for many types of projects. Excel or Word will load quite quickly, and you can open and insert data into them in the blink of an eye. However, if you want to iterate over lots of data inside a Word or Excel document, that process can be time-consuming when compared to performing similar tasks inside a C++Builder database application.

The bottom line here is that if you know Excel can do something well, and you know your target machines are powerful and will have Excel loaded on them, you don't need to search for third-party components to perform spreadsheet-related functions. Instead, you can just automate Excel from inside a C++Builder application and get your work done professionally in just a few short hours. The icing on the cake is that you can then use MAPI to mail the results of your work to anyone who has a mail system and the ability to read Excel files. Or, if you want, you can simply print the document using the printing facilities built into Word or Excel. Other options include faxing the document and saving it in HTML format. The point is that the recipient of your work need not actually have a copy of your C++Builder application running when viewing the output from your program. Instead, you can just send the recipient the results in an Excel or Word document. Word document viewers can be downloaded for free from Microsoft's Web site at www.microsoft.com.

15

AUTOMATING
WORD AND EXCEL

Getting Started with C++Builder and Excel

You can run OLE automation from inside C++Builder in two different ways. One involves using interfaces, and the second involves using IDispatch along with a C++Builder type called a Variant. Interfaces give you the advantage of type-checking your code on the client side, as well as providing relatively high performance. (For more information on interfaces and IDispatch, see Chapter 13, "The Basics of COM and Type Libraries.")

Initially, this chapter discusses the somewhat easier-to-understand IDispatch and Variants technology and then moves on to cover interfaces after all the basics are clearly established. Do not worry if you don't yet understand the differences between the two techniques, as this subject will be cleared up over the course of the chapter. At this stage, you just need to be aware that you can use at least two ways to access OLE automation objects from C++Builder, and that I am going to start out by showing you one that uses IDispatch and Variants.

Launching Excel

Listings 15.1 and 15.2 show a bare-bones example of a C++Builder application that launches Excel. Just skim over the code for now, as I will spend the rest of this section explaining how it works.

LISTING 15.1   THE HEADER FOR THE EXCEL1 PROGRAM'S MAIN UNIT

```
//-------------------------------------------------------------
#ifndef MainH
#define MainH
//-------------------------------------------------------------
#include <Classes.hpp>
#include <Controls.hpp>
#include <StdCtrls.hpp>
#include <Forms.hpp>
#include <Buttons.hpp>
//-------------------------------------------------------------
class TForm1 : public TForm
{
__published:    // IDE-managed Components
  TBitBtn *Button1;
  void __fastcall Button1Click(TObject *Sender);
  void __fastcall FormDestroy(TObject *Sender);
```

```
private:      // User declarations
  Variant V;
public:          // User declarations
  __fastcall TForm1(TComponent* Owner);
};
//---------------------------------------------------------------
extern PACKAGE TForm1 *Form1;
//---------------------------------------------------------------
#endif
```

LISTING 15.2 THE SOURCE CODE FOR THE EXCEL1 PROGRAM'S MAIN UNIT

```
//---------------------------------------------------------------
#include <vcl.h>
#pragma hdrstop
#include <utilcls.h>
#include <comobj.hpp>
#include "Main.h"
//---------------------------------------------------------------
#pragma package(smart_init)
#pragma resource "*.dfm"
TForm1 *Form1;
//---------------------------------------------------------------
__fastcall TForm1::TForm1(TComponent* Owner)
  : TForm(Owner)
{
}
//---------------------------------------------------------------
void __fastcall TForm1::Button1Click(TObject *Sender)
{
  V = CreateOleObject("Excel.Application");
  V.OlePropertySet("Visible", true);
}
//---------------------------------------------------------------
void __fastcall TForm1::FormDestroy(TObject *Sender)
{
  if (!V.IsEmpty())
    V.OleFunction("Quit");
}
```

You can find this example in the program called Excel1 on the CD-ROM that accompanies this book. The code does nothing more than create an instance of Excel, make it visible, and then close it down when the user exits the C++Builder application. The code does not check to make sure the user is not creating multiple instances of the application, but it does close down a single copy of Excel when the user exits.

15
AUTOMATING
WORD AND EXCEL

Using `COMObj`

The `COMObj` unit contains routines for launching OLE automation objects. The UTILCLS.H header provides various OLE helper classes. For example, there's a class to simplify the initialization and shutdown of OLE. So you should always start your automation client applications by including `COMObj.hpp` and `UtilCls.h`:

```
#include <utilcls.h>
#include <comobj.hpp>
```

To launch an Automation server, you can use the `CreateOleObject()` function. Behind the scenes, C++Builder uses the `CoCreateInstance` routine to create the object. `CreateOleObject()` returns the automation object in a `Variant` class. The `Variant` class exposes routines that allow you to invoke methods and properties exposed by an automation object. I will give you more information on these routines later. For now, let's take a look at the relevant lines of the example that illustrate how to launch a server and invoke one property.

These simple lines of code launch Excel from inside C++Builder:

```
V = CreateOleObject("Excel.Application");
V.OlePropertySet("Visible", true);
```

The first line of code launches Excel. The background behind the call to `CreateOleObject()` is relatively complex, so I will explain it in the section "Understanding `CreateOleObject()`."

After executing the first line, Excel comes up in the background, entirely offscreen, invisible to the user. This effect may, in fact, be what you want to achieve. However, when you first start programming Excel, and whenever you are debugging your Excel automation application, you probably want to be able to see what is going on inside Excel. Therefore, I set the `Visible` property of the Excel `Application` object equal to `true`. This setting ensures that you can see what is actually happening on the Excel server. If you have thoroughly debugged your application, you might want to skip this step, but I will include it in all the examples I cover in this chapter.

Understanding Simple Automation of Excel

I haven't told you enough yet to make the code shown in the preceding sections entirely comprehensible. What is the purpose, for instance, of the variable `V`? What does `CreateOleObject()` actually do?

As it turns out, the answers to these questions are nontrivial. The variable `V` is a `Variant`, and `CreateOleObject()` creates an instance of a COM object called `IDispatch` and returns it to you inside a `Variant`. But saying as much doesn't help if you don't understand COM, `IDispatch`, and `Variants`. Therefore, I strongly recommend you read (if you haven't yet) Chapter 13, "The Basics of COM and Type Libraries," and Chapter 14, "Creating COM Automation Servers and Clients."

Comparing Interfaces and `Variants`

One of the key differences between using interfaces and using `Variants` is that interfaces allow you to call COM objects using the much faster dispatching technologies native to C++. The *xxxx*_TLB file generated when importing a type library also provides dispinterface wrappers typically named `IInterfaceNameDisp`. These classes offer a middle path between the `Variant` methods and direct interface calls.

`Variants` get their name because they can provide a wide *variety* of functions, depending on the circumstances. For instance, they can contain a string, an integer, or, in special cases, a COM object. In other words, the type of variable held in a `Variant` *varies* from one occasion to the next. That's why they're called `Variants`. (For more information, look up "Variant" in the C++Builder online help.)

> **NOTE**
>
> There has been considerable confusion about the fact that C++Builder supports a total of four different `Variant` data types, which can be used more or less interchangeably. A complete explanation of why there are four different types and how they have evolved would be beyond the scope of this book. However, it is worth taking a moment to explain what they are and how they are different.
>
> `VARIANT` is a native windows structure that can hold any element that is of an automation-compatible type. (For more information about automation-compatible types, see Chapter 13.) It must be allocated, deleted, and interpreted using special API calls provided by Microsoft for that purpose.
>
> `Variant` is a VCL-native wrapper of the `VARIANT` type; it takes care of all the low-level system work for you; you simply create the object like any other VCL object, and the system calls are hidden. Because it is a native VCL type used internally by Delphi and C++Builder, however, it can hold types that are not automation compatible.
>
> `OleVariant` is a specialized version of `Variant` that can hold only automation-compatible types.
>
> *continues*

15

AUTOMATING WORD AND EXCEL

TVariant (or VARIANTOBJ) is a C++ wrapper of the VARIANT data type. It was designed to provide more natural C++ semantics than were possible with the Variant type.

Most code that is automatically generated by C++Builder uses the TVariant type; all VCL functions expect the Variant type. Converting between them is relatively easy, as the Variant type provides a C++[nd]style copy constructor and equality operator for the TVariant type. That is, code like the following compiles seamlessly:

```
Variant foo;
TVariant bar;
foo = bar;
```

However, going the other way is a little bit more complicated because the TVariant type does not provide copy semantics for the Variant type. Thus, you need to explicitly typecast the TVariant first:

```
Variant foo;
TVariant bar;
bar = (TVariant)foo;
```

Understanding `CreateOleObject()`

CreateOleObject() calls a number of internal system OLE functions. The end result of these series of calls is that the function returns a COM object containing an interface on the object you want to call. In particular, you get back a Variant that is wrapped around the IDispatch interface. By using a combination of the IDispatch methods and various C++Builder technologies covered later in this chapter, you can call the methods of the object you requested.

With all this information in mind, let's go back and view the two lines of code that retrieve the Excel object:

```
V = CreateOleObject("Excel.Application");
V.OlePropertySet("Visible", true);
```

The first line of code asks for an object called Application that resides inside Excel. CreateOleObject() retrieves an instance of the object in the form of an IDispatch interface encapsulated inside a Variant called V. This Variant is valuable to you because it allows you to call the methods and properties of the Excel object using a simple syntax. For instance, you can access the Visible property of the object by writing V.OlePropertySet("Visible", true).

You would be mistaken, however, if you were to assume that the line of code containing the Visible property is doing the same thing as a standard C++Builder line of code that looks like this:

```
Form1->Visible = true;
```

If you call the Visible property of a C++Builder form object, the property is changed almost instantly. Calling the Visible property of an OLE automation Variant sets off a series of internal events that result in a change to the Visible property of an object inside Excel, but many steps occur along the way. In particular, several methods of IDispatch such as GetIDsOfNames() and Invoke() must be called behind the scenes before the call is complete.

This chapter is not designed to cover the mechanisms used in dispatching a call on a Variant-encapsulated COM object, nor do you need to understand how it works to use this technology. The key point to grasp is merely that things aren't quite as simple as they at first appear. Having said all that, I will now show you how to get into this subject a bit deeper if you so desire, and if you have the C++Builder RTL and VCL source on your machine.

To get started, invoke the Project Options dialog and select the Linker page. Turn on the Use Debug Libraries option and rebuild the application. Next, put a breakpoint on the line:

```
V.OlePropertySet("Visible", true);
```

Then run the program. When you get to the breakpoint, press F7 to step into the code. After a brief detour through one of the AnsiString constructors, you are taken to the Variant class' OlePropertySet() function:

```
void Variant::OlePropertySet(const String& name, P1 p1)
{
  TAutoArgs<1> args;
  args[1] = p1;
  OlePropertySet(name, static_cast<TAutoArgsBase&>(args));
}
```

Press F8 until you get to the last line in this function, and then press F7 to step into yet another OlePropertySet() function (the Variant class has many overloaded OlePropertySet() functions).

Eventually, you will get to a call to GetIDsOfNames() and finally to Invoke(). Behind the scenes, C++Builder is calling the appropriate methods of the IDispatch interface to "invoke" your call to Excel.

One of the lessons to be learned from this example is that, at bottom, not such a big difference exists between the interface technology shown in the second part of this chapter and the Variant-based technology I am discussing here. For instance, IDispatch is an interface, and ultimately this interface must be called for the Variant-based technology to work. Only C++Builder is able to hide the interface complexity from you, so you do not need to understand it at all to use Variants to call automation objects. (Once again, I need to emphasize that I am not giving a full explanation of this technology in this chapter.)

> **NOTE**
>
> Calling a method off IDispatch is usually a two-step process. First, you call IDispatch::GetIDsOfNames() to get an ID or code for the method you call. You pass in the name of the method you want to call, and GetIDsOfNames() returns some numerical values that will help you make the call. Second, you call IDispatch::Invoke(), passing in the IDs returned to you by GetIDsOfNames(). This two-step process allows you to invoke a method off an instance of IDispatch. This process is handled automatically for you behind the scenes in C++Builder.

Variants and Types

One of the biggest consequences of calling the methods of an object off a Variant is that C++Builder cannot type-check your code at compile time. In other words, C++Builder does not really know whether the Excel Application object has a property called Visible. It takes you at your word when you claim this is true. In this case, this approach proves to be the correct thing to do. However, it would also compile the following code without error:

```
V.OleFunction("TransferMoney",
  "From = Bill Gates", "To = Charlie Calvert", 100000);
```

This code is certainly intriguing, but the Excel Application object unfortunately does not support it. Therefore, a program containing it will compile and load without error, but a call to the TransferMoney() function at run time will raise an exception. Both C++Builder and Excel are able to handle this exception flawlessly, without destabilizing the system in any way. It is nice, however, if you can type-check at compile time rather than having to wait until run time to see whether all is set up correctly. The interface and dispinterface technologies covered in the second part of this chapter show how to get compile-time type-checking of OLE objects.

`IDispatch` and `Variants` are important subjects, but you need not understand them in depth to use this technology. If all is not clear to you yet, you can continue without fear.

After you create an Excel `Application` object, you need some way to close it down. You can do so by calling its `Quit()` method:

```
if (!V.IsEmpty())
  V.OleFunction("Quit");
```

This code checks to make sure that the `Variant` `V` refers to something, and then it attempts to call the `Quit()` method of the Excel `Application` object. If `V` is indeed a valid pointer to such an object, then Excel will close. This code is not perfect in all cases because `V` could contain a reference to something other than an Excel `Application` object, thereby allowing `IsEmpty()` to return `true`, even though the call to `Quit()` would fail. For instance, I could write

```
V = 10;
```

After making this call, `IsEmpty()` would return `false`, but the call to `Quit()` would obviously fail. However, in the `Excel1` application, found in Listing 15.1, `V` usually is either empty or points to a COM object. Therefore, the code is reasonably robust. The key point, at any rate, is that you don't want to fail to call `Quit()` for the `Application` object; otherwise you can end up cluttering memory with multiple instances of Excel. Remember that Excel owns the `Application` object, and it will not necessarily be removed from memory just because you close your C++Builder application. In other words, you should definitely call `Application` `Quit()`, or else repeated calls to Excel from a C++Builder application will bog down your machine by draining system resources.

Creating Excel Automation Objects

Now that you have been introduced to the topic of automating Excel, the next step is to learn something about what creating an OLE automation object means.

The call to `CreateOleObject()` returns a COM object called `IDispatch` housed inside a `Variant`. You can pass a string to `CreateOleObject()` specifying the name of the COM object you want to retrieve. In this case, I have retrieved the main Excel automation object by passing in the string `Excel.Application`. You can find this string in the Registry and can trace that reference to the CLSID associated with the Local Server that returns the object. If you don't know anything about CLSIDs or about Local Servers, don't be too concerned. The point is simply that `CreateOleObject()` returns a COM object of your choice if you pass in the correct string. In particular, it looks up your string in the Registry, finds the CLSID associated with the string, looks up the CLSID, and finds the Local Server associated with that CLSID. The Local Server will be a string pointing to the application that contains the object you want to retrieve. For instance, in this case, on my system, the Local Server string looks like this:

```
C:\Program Files\Microsoft Office\Office\excel.exe /automation
```

This string is copied directly from the REGEDIT.EXE application. I found it in HKEY_CLASSES_ROOT\CLSID, under the GUID listed next to Excel.Application. GUIDs are 16-byte numbers designed to uniquely identify an object.

TIP

The strings you pass into CreateOleObject() are called ProgIDs. The ProgIDs valid on your system are listed in the Registry under the section HKEY_CLASSES_ROOT. The C++Builder documentation is not the place to turn to find the ProgIDs you pass in to the various COM servers available on your system. Instead, you should turn to the documentation for the application you want to control. For instance, Excel has extensive COM documentation in an online help file called VBAXL8.HLP that ships with Microsoft Office If you are doing a lot of OLE automation with Excel, you should add this file to C++Builder's Tools menu so that you can get to it easily. For information on retrieving objects, use the Index feature in the Excel help to look up "OLE programmatic identifiers."

In the Excel online help, you will find that this spreadsheet application has three main objects you can retrieve by using CreateOleObject():

```
CreateOleObject("Excel.Application");
CreateOleObject("Excel.Sheet");
CreateOleObject("Excel.Chart");
```

These strings, and slight variations on these strings, are the only valid parameters to pass to CreateOleObject() if you want to talk to Excel via COM. Many more objects are available inside Excel. However, these three are the only ones you can retrieve from outside Excel by using the CreateOleObject() function. After you retrieve one of these objects, you can use it as your access to all the other objects in the Excel hierarchy. Getting at these objects is a bit like unwinding a ball of thread. You first need a handle to the ball of thread, which you get by calling CreateOleObject(). After you have a handle, you can use it to get to all the different objects inside Excel. Just keep pulling at the thread you get back from CreateOleObject(), and all the rest of the objects will come unraveled. This subject is explained in more depth in the next section.

Understanding Excel Automation Objects

If you are an experienced C++Builder programmer, you might find Excel's objects a bit confusing at first. Like standard C++ objects, they exist inside a hierarchy, but that hierarchy, at least as it is presented to the public, is not based on inheritance. Instead, the main glue that holds the hierarchy together is the fact that you can access one particular object from another particular object.

For instance, the top member of the Excel hierarchy is called Application. Beneath it is the Workbooks object, and beneath that are the Worksheets and Charts objects:

```
1) Application:
  A) Workbooks
    i) Worksheets
    ii) Charts
```

Accessing Objects Within the Application Object

If you want to get to the Workbooks object, you can access it from the Application object:

```
Variant MyWorkbooks = V.OlePropertyGet("Workbooks");
```

As you can see, MyWorkbooks is declared as a Variant. In all cases, during this first part of this chapter, I am using Variants to access the underlying Excel objects. Given the previous code, you can now create a new workbook with code like this:

```
MyWorkbooks.OleFunction("Add");
```

If you want to get to the Worksheets object, you can access it from the Workbooks object, and so on.

If you saw this hierarchy in a C++Builder application, you would assume that Workbooks is a descendant of Application, and Worksheets a descendant of Workbooks. That kind of thinking is completely off center when it comes to OLE automation. The standard OOP hierarchy found in C++ and Pascal has nothing to do with OLE automation. Here you find a totally different kind of hierarchy intended only to express which objects can be accessed from another object. As you will see in the second part of this chapter, it may also be true that a valid OOP inheritance-based hierarchy is simultaneously implemented on these objects. However, that hierarchy is not the main one to focus on when using automation, and I think it is easiest at first to pretend that it does not exist at all.

If you want to talk about all the `Worksheets` and `Charts` in a `Workbook`, you use the `Sheets` object. When thinking about the `Sheets` object, you could rewrite the preceding hierarchy as follows:

```
1) Application
   A) Workbooks
      i) Sheets
      ii) Worksheets
      iii) Charts
```

The point is that this hierarchy is meant to denote the order in which you access objects, and as such it has a somewhat more slippery structure than you would find in a typical inheritance hierarchy. In fact, it seems that you can get to most any object from any one point in the hierarchy, so the actual structure of the hierarchy is a little dependent on your current position inside it.

You get to the `Workbooks` object from the `Application` object. You get to the `Sheets`, `Worksheets`, and `Charts` objects from the `Workbooks` object.

Saying that the `Application` object is synonymous with the binary file `Excel.exe` would be untrue, but it does have some things in common with this executable. For instance, the `Application` object is the most abstracted, the most generalized way that you have of referring to the set of available Excel automation objects. If you open Excel and have no documents loaded, then you are looking at a visual representation of the `Application` object. It is not the same thing as the `Application` object, but it can serve as a metaphor for what the object does. It is analogous to it. It is the highest level container for accessing all the functionality available from Excel. However, it is so generalized that it can't do much that is useful without help from other objects. But you get to those other objects by starting with the `Application` object. All this is equally true of `Excel.exe`. If you open `Excel.exe` with no documents in it, then it has little use on its own, but it is still the gateway you would use to access all these documents.

The `Workbooks` object contains a collection of `Worksheets` and `Charts`. A `Worksheet` is a standard page from a spreadsheet, and a `Chart` is a graph. The `Sheets` object contains both `Worksheets` and `Charts`, whereas the `Worksheets` and `Charts` objects contain only `Worksheets` or `Charts`. Your job as an Excel automation programmer is to start learning how to make statements like these. In other words, this kind of logic underlies the Excel hierarchy of objects. As an automation programmer, your job is to figure out how to get to one object from another object and to understand what each object does.

Here is another way to think about what you are really trying to do. Most computer users understand how to use Excel. Using the automation objects discussed in this chapter, you can write code that manipulates Excel just as you would manipulate Excel with a mouse.

You probably already know how to open a spreadsheet, enter data, perform calculations, and chart data. Your goal as an automation programmer is to find out how to do the same things in code. You just need to know which object refers to which sets of tools inside Excel. Figure that out and figure out how to get to each of these objects given the existence of an `Application` object, and you are ready to roll.

Using Automation

The program in Listings 15.3 and 15.4 shows an application that provides a summary of the major points made here. Glance over it once and then read on to find an explanation of how it works.

LISTING 15.3   THE HEADER FOR THE EXCEL2 PROGRAM'S MAIN UNIT

```
//------------------------------------------------------------
#ifndef MainH
#define MainH
//------------------------------------------------------------
#include <Classes.hpp>
#include <Controls.hpp>
#include <StdCtrls.hpp>
#include <Forms.hpp>
//------------------------------------------------------------
class TForm1 : public TForm
{
__published:    // IDE-managed Components
  TButton *Button1;
  TListBox *ListBox1;
  void __fastcall Button1Click(TObject *Sender);
  void __fastcall FormDestroy(TObject *Sender);
private:    // User declarations
  Variant XLApplication;
public:        // User declarations
  __fastcall TForm1(TComponent* Owner);
};
//------------------------------------------------------------
extern PACKAGE TForm1 *Form1;
//------------------------------------------------------------
#endif
```

LISTING 15.4   THE SOURCE CODE FOR THE EXCEL2 PROGRAM'S MAIN UNIT

```
//------------------------------------------------------------
#include <vcl.h>
#pragma hdrstop
```

continues

15

AUTOMATING WORD AND EXCEL

LISTING 15.4 CONTINUED

```cpp
#include <utilcls.h>
#include <comobj.hpp>

#include "Main.h"
//---------------------------------------------------------------
#pragma package(smart_init)
#pragma resource "*.dfm"
TForm1 *Form1;
//---------------------------------------------------------------
__fastcall TForm1::TForm1(TComponent* Owner)
  : TForm(Owner)
{
}
//---------------------------------------------------------------
void __fastcall TForm1::Button1Click(TObject *Sender)
{
  // XlWBATemplate
  const int xlWBatChart = -4109;
  const int xlWBatWorksheet = -4167;

  XLApplication = CreateOleObject("Excel.Application");
  XLApplication.OlePropertySet("Visible", true);
  Variant XLWorkbooks = XLApplication.OlePropertyGet("Workbooks");
  XLWorkbooks.OleFunction("Add");
  XLWorkbooks.OleFunction("Add", xlWBatChart);
  XLWorkbooks.OleFunction("Add", xlWBatWorksheet);
  Variant XLBook = XLWorkbooks.OlePropertyGet("Item", 2);
  Variant XLChart = XLBook.OlePropertyGet("Charts");
  XLChart.OleFunction("Add");
  XLBook = XLWorkbooks.OlePropertyGet("Item", 3);
  Variant XLSheet = XLBook.OlePropertyGet("Sheets");
  XLSheet.OleFunction("Add");
  int count = XLWorkbooks.OlePropertyGet("Count");
  for (int i=0;i<count;i++) {
    XLBook = XLWorkbooks.OlePropertyGet("Item", i + 1);
    ListBox1->Items->Add(XLBook.OlePropertyGet("Name"));
    Variant XLSheets = XLBook.OlePropertyGet("Sheets");
    int sheetCount = XLSheets.OlePropertyGet("Count");
    for (int j=0;j<sheetCount;j++) {
      Variant XLSheet = XLSheets.OlePropertyGet("Item", j + 1);
      ListBox1->Items->Add("     " + XLSheet.OlePropertyGet("Name"));
    }
  }
}
//---------------------------------------------------------------
void __fastcall TForm1::FormDestroy(TObject *Sender)
{
  if (!XLApplication.IsEmpty()) {
    // Discard unsaved files....
```

```
        XLApplication.OlePropertySet("DisplayAlerts", false);
        XLApplication.OleFunction("Quit");
    }
}
```

This application starts an instance of Excel and then populates it with three workbooks. One of the workbooks contains a default number of worksheets, a second contains a user-defined number of worksheets, and a third contains some charts. The following paragraphs explain how this example works.

Take a moment to study the core of the `Button1Click()` method:

```
void __fastcall TForm1::Button1Click(TObject *Sender)
{
  // XlWBATemplate
  const int xlWBatChart = -4109;
  const int xlWBatWorksheet = -4167;

  XLApplication = CreateOleObject("Excel.Application");
  XLApplication.OlePropertySet("Visible", true);
  Variant XLWorkbooks = XLApplication.OlePropertyGet("Workbooks");
  XLWorkbooks.OleFunction("Add");
  XLWorkbooks.OleFunction("Add", xlWBatChart);
  XLWorkbooks.OleFunction("Add", xlWBatWorksheet);
  Variant XLBook = XLWorkbooks.OlePropertyGet("Item", 2);
  Variant XLChart = XLBook.OlePropertyGet("Charts");
  XLChart.OleFunction("Add");
  XLBook = XLWorkbooks.OlePropertyGet("Item", 3);
  Variant XLSheet = XLBook.OlePropertyGet("Sheets");
  XLSheet.OleFunction("Add");
  int count = XLWorkbooks.OlePropertyGet("Count");
  for (int i=0;i<count;i++) {
    XLBook = XLWorkbooks.OlePropertyGet("Item", i + 1);
    ListBox1->Items->Add(XLBook.OlePropertyGet("Name"));
    Variant XLSheets = XLBook.OlePropertyGet("Sheets");
    int sheetCount = XLSheets.OlePropertyGet("Count");
    for (int j=0;j<sheetCount;j++) {
      Variant XLSheet = XLSheets.OlePropertyGet("Item", j + 1);
      ListBox1->Items->Add("     " + XLSheet.OlePropertyGet("Name"));
    }
  }
}
```

`XLApplication` is a `Variant` that contains an instance of `IDispatch` used for accessing the Excel `Application` object. As you know, `Application` contains a property called `Visible`. If you set it to `true`, Excel will appear on your screen. Once again, this is not the time or place to explore the subject, but COM objects support the notion of properties. These properties are very different internally from C++Builder properties, but they behave more or less the same.

Workbooks is a collection object. It contains a collection of workbooks. This pattern is followed over and over in Excel. The Sheets object contains a collection of sheets. The Worksheets object contains a collection of worksheets. The Charts object contains a collection of charts. Inside Word, the Paragraphs object contains a collection of paragraphs. The Words object contains a collection of words. The Tables object contains a collection of tables and so on.

You get to members of a collection through this syntax:

```
Variant XLBook = XLWorkbooks.OlePropertyGet("Item", 1);
```

You need to be conscious of the difference between a collection object and a normal object. For instance, to understand a Worksheets object, you should look up both Worksheets and Worksheet in the Excel help; to understand the Tables object, you should look up both Tables and Table in the Word help.

Workbooks contains a method called Add(), which you use to add a workbook to a workbooks collection. COM objects support the idea of variable parameter lists. You therefore can simply skip passing in parameters to a method if you want. In this case, if you call Workbooks::Add() with no parameters, you will create a workbook with some predefined number of worksheets in it. The default number is three, but you can change the number from inside Excel if you prefer. When you are working with interfaces rather than Variants, you cannot omit parameters (unless the interface declaration provided in the *xxxx*_TLB file provides default arguments for optional parameters).

If you want to create a new Workbook with exactly one Worksheet in it, then you call Add() and pass in the constant xlWBatWorksheet. Declare this constant explicitly inside this program. In the next section, I will tell you how to get a complete list of all the Excel and Word constants.

If you want to create a new workbook with exactly one chart in it, you call Add() and pass in the constant xlWBatChart.

If you then want to add one worksheet to the second workbook you created, you would write the following code:

```
XLBook = XLWorkbooks.OlePropertyGet("Item", 3);
Variant XLSheet = XLBook.OlePropertyGet("Sheets");
XLSheet.OleFunction("Add");
```

Here is how to create a new chart:

```
Variant XLBook = XLWorkbooks.OlePropertyGet("Item", 2);
Variant XLChart = XLBook.OlePropertyGet("Charts");
XLChart.OleFunction("Add");
```

The `for` loop at the bottom of the sample method iterates through each of the work-groups, finds the names of each of the sheets available in each workbook, and then adds them to the list box. In short, the code shows how to retrieve the names of the members of a series of workbooks, while simultaneously showing how to iterate over all their members.

Here is how to reference the number of workbooks in the application:

```
int count = XLWorkbooks.OlePropertyGet("Count");
for (int i=0;i<count;i++) {
```

Here is how to count the number of sheets in a `Workbook`:

```
Variant XLSheets = XLBook.OlePropertyGet("Sheets");
int sheetCount = XLSheets.OlePropertyGet("Count");
for (int j=0;j<sheetCount;j++) {
```

Here is how to find the name of a particular worksheet or chart in `Workbook`:

```
Variant XLSheet = XLSheets.OlePropertyGet("Item", j + 1);
ListBox1->Items->Add("     " + XLSheet.OlePropertyGet("Name"));
```

If you spend a little while contemplating the `Button1Click()` method, the logic behind the objects in Microsoft Excel should become clear to you (as clear as mud, I should say). Of course, I have additional matters to cover, such as entering data and creating graphs. But, as you will see, most of that material is relatively straightforward after you understand the way the Excel object hierarchy works.

As always, you should be particularly aware of saving clock cycles when you are inside a loop. A call that takes one second to execute is easy for the user to bear if it occurs once. But put it in a loop, execute it 2,000 times, and the user will hate you. A general rule of thumb is that the user should never have to wait for anything, that everything should happen in real time. If that is not possible, you might be comforted to know that most users will happily wait up to two seconds for you to do most chores. Longer than that, and they get impatient. Two seconds is several eons in computer time, so normally you don't have to fret about optimization issues. The C++Builder team already did all the sweating for you. But when automating Excel or Word, you can get in trouble fairly quickly, so you might need to think about optimization in places where you wouldn't worry about it in a normal C++Builder application. Remember that Excel automation is called "Visual Basic for Applications." As you will see later, these Excel classes are actually real objects, so clearly this subject doesn't have much to do with Visual Basic, but the mere presence of the word *Basic* costs you, by default, thousands of clock cycles.

Finding the Constants Used in Excel

You can determine all the constants used by Excel by reading its type library. You can read a type library in at least two simple ways:

- You can read the type library with a third-party tool, such as the OleView application that ships with the Microsoft SDK.

- You can ask C++Builder to read the library for you and to translate the information stored in the library into C++. Obviously, this is the preferred technique.

I have included the translations of the Excel and Word type libraries with this chapter on the CD-ROM. However, if you want to create your own versions of these libraries, you can select Project, Import Type Library from the C++Builder menu, and then select the appropriate type library. A C++Builder translation of the type library will be created automatically. (You should be aware, however, that the process of generating the file is extremely resource-intensive and might take up to several minutes on a normal machine.)

The files you want to import usually have a `.tlb`, `.dll`, or `.exe` extension. When working with Office 97, however, you want one with an `.olb` extension. The file to use with Word is `MSWORD8.OLB`, and the one to use with Excel is `EXCEL8.OLB`. On my system, I found these entries in the `...\Microsoft Office\Office` directory.

After you import the OLB file, a new file called `Excel_TLB.h` is created in the `C++Builder4\Imports` directory. In this file, you will find declarations for all the constants used by Excel 97.

The C++ translations of the interfaces to all the objects used in Excel or Word are found in the files created by importing `EXCEL8.OLB` and `MSWORD8.OLB`. Until now, I have ignored these interfaces and shown you how to work directly with `Variant` objects. Word and Excel interfaces are defined in the `EXCEL_TLB.H` and `WORD_TLB.H` header files generated by importing the type libraries.

> **NOTE**
>
> The following samples rely on a patch to the code that generates *xxxx*_TLB.*
> files that was released by Borland in May 1999. If you have the shipping version
> of C++Builder, download the patch from the Borland Web site. To confirm
> whether you have the patch applied, you can compare the WORD_TLB.H and
> EXCEL_TLB.H files you generate with the ones included on the CD-ROM accom-
> panying this book.

Storing and Accessing Data in an Excel Worksheet

Throughout the next few sections, I will be working with a sample program called Excel3. The header for the main form of this program is shown in Listing 15.5, and the source for the main form is shown in Listing 15.6. Just take a quick look at the code for now, and then read on to get an explanation of how it works.

LISTING 15.5   THE HEADER FOR THE MAIN FORM OF THE EXCEL3 PROGRAM

```
//----------------------------------------------------------------
#ifndef MainH
#define MainH
//----------------------------------------------------------------
#include <Classes.hpp>
#include <Controls.hpp>
#include <StdCtrls.hpp>
#include <Forms.hpp>
//----------------------------------------------------------------
class TForm1 : public TForm
{
__published:    // IDE-managed Components
        TButton *Button1;
        void __fastcall Button1Click(TObject *Sender);
        void __fastcall FormDestroy(TObject *Sender);
private:    // User declarations
        TCOM_Application m_XLApp;     // Excel's Application Object
        WorksheetPtr    m_Worksheet;  // A Worksheet object
        RangePtr        m_Cells;      // A Range object of Cells
        RangePtr        m_Columns;    // A Range object of Columns

        void    InsertData();
        void    ChangeColumns();
        void    HandleRange();
public:        // User declarations
        __fastcall TForm1(TComponent* Owner);
};
//----------------------------------------------------------------
extern PACKAGE TForm1 *Form1;
//----------------------------------------------------------------
#endif
```

LISTING 15.6   THE SOURCE FOR THE MAIN FORM OF THE EXCEL3 PROGRAM

```
//----------------------------------------------------------------
#include <vcl.h>
#include "Excel_TLB.h"
#pragma hdrstop
```

continues

LISTING 15.6   CONTINUED

```cpp
#include "main.h"
#include <graphics.hpp>

//----------------------------------------------------------------
#pragma package(smart_init)
#pragma resource "*.dfm"
TForm1 *Form1;
//----------------------------------------------------------------
__fastcall TForm1::TForm1(TComponent* Owner)
        : TForm(Owner)
{
}
//----------------------------------------------------------------
void __fastcall TForm1::Button1Click(TObject *Sender)
{
  // Create/Launch EXCEL
  if (!m_XLApp)
    m_XLApp = CoApplication_::Create();
  // Make EXCEL visible
  m_XLApp->set_Visible(0, true);
  // Add a Worksheet
  m_XLApp->Workbooks->Add(xlWBATWorksheet);
  // Get the newly added Worksheet object
  m_Worksheet = m_XLApp->Workbooks->get_Item(1)->Worksheets->get_Item(1);
  // Set its name to "C++Builder Data";
m_Worksheet->Name = WideString("C++Builder Data");
  // Call routines to insert Data
  InsertData();
  HandleRange();
  ChangeColumns();
}
//----------------------------------------------------------------
void __fastcall TForm1::FormDestroy(TObject *Sender)
{
  if (m_XLApp)
  {
    m_XLApp->set_DisplayAlerts(0, false);
    m_XLApp->Quit();
  }
}
//----------------------------------------------------------------
void TForm1::InsertData()
{
  int i;
  for (i=1; i<=10; i++)
    m_Worksheet->Cells->set__Default(i, 1, i);
  m_Worksheet->Cells->set__Default(i, 1, "=SUM(A1:A10)");
}
```

```cpp
void TForm1::HandleRange()
{
  RangePtr range = m_Worksheet->get_Range("C1:F25");
  range->Formula = "=RAND()";
  range->Columns->Interior->ColorIndex = 3;
  range->Borders->LineStyle = xlContinuous;
}

void TForm1::ChangeColumns()
{
  // Get interface to first column
  RangePtr firstCol = m_Worksheet->Columns->get__Default(1);
  firstCol->ColumnWidth = 20;              // Set width
  firstCol->Font->Bold = true;             // Set BOLD font
  firstCol->Font->Italic = true;           // Enable Italic
  firstCol->Font->Color = clBlue;          // Tweak color
}
```

As shown here, you can easily insert data in a spreadsheet. In fact, the technique involved is similar to what you would use to put data into a TStringGrid control in C++Builder.

To get started, open Excel and create a new spreadsheet:

```cpp
void __fastcall TForm1::Button1Click(TObject *Sender)
{
  // Create/Launch EXCEL
  if (!m_XLApp)
    m_XLApp = CoApplication_::Create();
  // Make EXCEL visible
  m_XLApp->set_Visible(0, true);
  // Add a Worksheet
  m_XLApp->Workbooks->Add(xlWBATWorksheet);
  // Get the newly added Worksheet object
  m_Worksheet = m_XLApp->Workbooks->get_Item(1)->Worksheets->get_Item(1);
  // Set its name to "C++Builder Data";
m_Worksheet->Name = WideString("C++Builder Data");
  // Call routines to insert Data
  InsertData();
  HandleRange();
  ChangeColumns();
}
```

As you can see, I create a single workbook with one worksheet in it. The code then names the worksheet C++Builder Data. The InsertData, HandleRange, and ChangeColumns calls are custom routines that I will now describe.

To insert data into the spreadsheet, execute the following function:

```
void TForm1::InsertData()
{
  int i;
  for (i=1; i<=10; i++)
    m_Worksheet->Cells->set__Default(i, 1, i);
  m_Worksheet->Cells->set__Default(i, 1, "=SUM(A1:A10)");
}
```

The code inserts 10 integers into the sheet. The set__Default member of the object returned by the Cells property works exactly as you would expect, except that Excel puts the Row first and the Column second (followed by the data Value).

After the numbers are inserted in the worksheet, the final stage is to insert a formula and add the column of numbers. To do so, you simply insert the formula much as you would if you were in Excel itself. In particular, you store the formula in a string and then insert it into the appropriate cell:

```
m_Worksheet->Cells->set__Default(i, 1, "=SUM(A1:A10)");
```

Working with Columns and Range Attributes

Sometimes you might want to perform an operation on a range of data in the spreadsheet. To do so, you use the Excel Range object:

```
RangePtr range = m_Worksheet->get_Range("C1:F25");
range->Formula = "=RAND()";
```

You can insert this code into the bottom of the InsertData method. It fills all the cells between C1 and F25 with random numbers between 0 and 1.

One of the key objects in both Excel and Word is the Range object. It allows you to work with a range of cells or columns at one time. In either Word or Excel, you generally enter or read data by using the Range object. In short, if you want to insert text into a Word document, you generally use the Range object.

> **NOTE**
>
> With Word, you also can insert data via a considerably simpler method. For instance, the following procedure enters data at the current insertion point into an open document in Microsoft Word:
>
> ```
> void TForm1::Button1Click(TObject* Sender)
> {
>   Variant V;
> ```

```
    V = GetActiveOleObject("Word.Basic");
    V.OleFunction("Insert", "Sam");
}
```

In this case, I have chosen not to open a new version of Word, but instead to call GetActiveOleObject to get a handle to a document in an instance of Word that is already running. This kind of technology is very easy to use and is perfect for some projects. It doesn't, however, have the power of the technology I am showing you in this chapter.

To access a Range object in Excel, simply specify the range with which you want to work:

```
RangePtr range = m_Worksheet->get_Range("C1:F25");
```

In this case, the code defines a range from cell C1 to cell F25. Any operations performed on the returned Range object will affect all the cells in that range.

This simple function shows how to change the values and appearance of a range of cells:

```
void TForm1::HandleRange()
{
  RangePtr range = m_Worksheet->get_Range("C1:F25");
  range->Formula = "=RAND()";
  range->Columns->Interior->ColorIndex = 3;
  range->Borders->LineStyle = xlContinuous;
}
```

The first line of code in the body of the method returns a pointer to the range you want to manipulate. The second line fills all the values in the range C1:F25 with random numbers between 0 and 1, as explained earlier.

The next-to-last line of code in the body of the method changes the color of the entire block of cells to red. You can use the Excel online help to see the values in the ColorIndex, but the first few default values are as follows: black, white, red, green, blue, yellow, purple, cyan. Red is the third item in the list, so setting the ColorIndex to 3 makes the selected range of cells red.

At the same time that you change the color, you also lose your borders. This loss is a peculiarity of Excel, but you can work around it by resetting the LineStyle of the selected cells as shown in the last line of code in the procedure. Once again, when you are working with constants like this, you can find them in the EXCEL_TLB.H file included with the sample programs found on the CD-ROM that accompanies this book, or you can retrieve them from the type library as explained earlier.

15

AUTOMATING WORD AND EXCEL

If you are interested, this line of code changes the background of a range:

```
Range->Columns->Interior->Pattern = xlPatternCrissCross;
```

The following function changes the width and font of a column:

```
void TForm1::ChangeColumns()
{
  // Get interface to first column
  RangePtr firstCol = m_Worksheet->Columns->get__Default(1);
  firstCol->ColumnWidth = 20;            // Set width
  firstCol->Font->Bold = true;           // Set BOLD font
  firstCol->Font->Italic = true;         // Enable Italic
  firstCol->Font->Color = clBlue;        // Tweak color
}
```

As you can see, when you want to work with the columns in a worksheet, you can access them from a Range object. In particular, the Range object contains a collection of columns that you can access using array notation. The preceding code retrieves the range for the first column.

To change the width of a column, use the ColumnWidth property, and to change the font, use the Font property. Going into much more detail would be pointless because this code is easy to write.

Sharing a Chart Between Excel and Word

Creating and working with a chart are just as easy as doing everything else in Excel automation. In the example shown in this section, refer to the program called Excel4.bpr. This program is shown in Listings 15.7 and 15.8. I include the listing here so that you can take a quick glance through it and then refer to it during the discussion of its inner workings that follows. In other words, I don't expect you to understand the program completely at a single glance but will instead spend the remainder of this section discussing it in some depth.

LISTING 15.7   THE HEADER OF THE EXCEL4 PROGRAM

```
//------------------------------------------------------------------
#ifndef MAINH
#define MAINH
//------------------------------------------------------------------
#include <Classes.hpp>
#include <Controls.hpp>
#include <StdCtrls.hpp>
```

```
#include <Forms.hpp>
//---------------------------------------------------------------
class TForm1 : public TForm
{
__published:    // IDE-managed Components
        TButton *Button1;
        TButton *Button2;
        void __fastcall Button1Click(TObject *Sender);
        void __fastcall FormDestroy(TObject *Sender);
private:    // User declarations
        Excel_tlb::TCOM_Application      m_XLApp;
        WorksheetPtr                     m_Worksheet;
        Excel_tlb::RangePtr              m_SheetRange;
        ChartPtr                         m_Chart;

        Word_tlb::TCOM_Application       m_WordApp;

        void    InitWorksheetData();
        void    InitChartData();

        void    CopyCellsToWord();
        void    CopyChartToWord();
public:         // User declarations
        __fastcall TForm1(TComponent* Owner);
};
//---------------------------------------------------------------
extern PACKAGE TForm1 *Form1;
//---------------------------------------------------------------
#endif
```

LISTING 15.8   THE SOURCE OF THE EXCEL4 PROGRAM

```
//---------------------------------------------------------------
#include <vcl.h>
#include "Excel_TLB.h"
#include "Word_TLB.h"
#pragma hdrstop

#include "MAIN.h"
#include <safearry.h>
//---------------------------------------------------------------
#pragma package(smart_init)
#pragma resource "*.dfm"
TForm1 *Form1;
//---------------------------------------------------------------
__fastcall TForm1::TForm1(TComponent* Owner)
        : TForm(Owner)
{
```

continues

LISTING 15.8   CONTINUED

```cpp
}
//-----------------------------------------------------------------
void __fastcall TForm1::Button1Click(TObject *Sender)
{
  if (!m_XLApp)
    m_XLApp = Excel_tlb::CoApplication_::Create();

  m_XLApp->set_Visible(0, true);
  m_XLApp->Workbooks->Add(xlWBATWorksheet);
  m_Worksheet =
          m_XLApp->Workbooks->get_Item(1)->Worksheets->get_Item(1);
  m_Worksheet->Name = WideString("C++Builder Data");

  InitWorksheetData();
  InitChartData();

  // Launch Word, if necessary
  if (!m_WordApp)
    m_WordApp = Word_tlb::CoApplication_::Create();

  // Make Word visible and add a document
  m_WordApp->Visible = true;
  m_WordApp->Documents->Add();

  // Copy Excel data to Word
  CopyCellsToWord();
  CopyChartToWord();

  Button2->Enabled = true;
}
//-----------------------------------------------------------------
void    TForm1::InitWorksheetData()
{
  // Set some data on some cells
  for (int i=1; i<=10; i++)
    m_Worksheet->Cells->set__Default(i, 1, i);
  // Get a range object pointing to these cells
  m_SheetRange = m_Worksheet->get_Range("A1:A10");
}

void    TForm1::InitChartData()
{
  // Create a chart
  ChartPtr chart1 = m_XLApp->Workbooks->get_Item(1)->Sheets->Add(
                            TNoParam(), TNoParam(), 1, xlChart);
  chart1->ChartType = xl3DPie;
```

```cpp
  // Get series object of chart, set its values to the range
  // of our sheet and enable Datalabels
  SeriesCollectionPtr series = chart1->SeriesCollection();
  series->Item(1)->Values = LPDISPATCH(m_SheetRange);
  series->Item(1)->HasDataLabels = true;

  // Create another chart
  ChartPtr chart2 = m_XLApp->Workbooks->get_Item(1)->Sheets->Add(
                          TNoParam(), TNoParam(), 1, xlChart);
  chart2->ChartType = xl3DColumn;

  // Get its series and set the values to the same sheet range
series = chart2->SeriesCollection();
  series->Item(1)->Values = LPDISPATCH(m_SheetRange);

  // Create a safe array with some values
  TSafeArrayDim1 dim(10);
  TSafeArrayInt1 sa(dim);
  for (int i=0; i<10; i++)
    sa[i] = i;

  // Create a new series and set it Values to the data in the SAFEARRAY
series->NewSeries()->Values = sa.Detach();
}

void    TForm1::CopyCellsToWord()
{
  // Activate Excel's worksheet, select the range and
  // copy it to the clipboard
  m_Worksheet->Activate();
  m_SheetRange->Select();
  m_Worksheet->get_UsedRange()->Copy();

  // Set some text in the active document
  Word_tlb::RangePtr range = m_WordApp->ActiveDocument->Range();
  range->Text = WideString("This is a column from a spreadsheet:");

  // Add 3 paragraphs
  for (int i=1; i<3; i++)
    m_WordApp->ActiveDocument->Paragraphs->Add();

  // Paste the worksheet to the 2nd paragraph
int startRange =
    m_WordApp->ActiveDocument->Paragraphs->Item(2)->Range->Start;
  range = m_WordApp->ActiveDocument->Range(&TVariant(startRange));
  range->Paste();
}

void    TForm1::CopyChartToWord()
{
```

continues

15
AUTOMATING
WORD AND EXCEL

LISTING 15.8   CONTINUED

```cpp
  // Add a new paragraph
  ParagraphPtr para = m_WordApp->ActiveDocument->Paragraphs->Add();

  // Get range of new paragraph and set some text
  Word_tlb::RangePtr range = para->Range;
  range->Text = WideString("This is a graph: ");

  // Add a few more paragraphs
  for (int i=0; i<2; i++)
    m_WordApp->ActiveDocument->Paragraphs->Add();

  // Copy the Excel chart to the clipboard
  ChartPtr chart = m_XLApp->Sheets->get_Item("Chart1");
  chart->Select();
  chart->Copy();

  // Add one more and paste the chart
  range = m_WordApp->ActiveDocument->Paragraphs->Add()->Range;
  range->Paste();
}

void __fastcall TForm1::FormDestroy(TObject *Sender)
{
  if (m_XLApp)
  {
    m_XLApp->set_DisplayAlerts(0, false);
    m_XLApp->Quit();
  }
  if (m_WordApp)
  {
    m_WordApp->ActiveDocument->Close(wdDoNotSaveChanges);
    m_WordApp->Quit();
  }
}
//--------------------------------------------------------------------
```

This code opens a copy of Excel, inserts some data into it, and creates two graphs of the data. Then it opens a copy of Word, copies the cells from the worksheet to a new Word document, and then copies one of the charts into the same document. When you are through, you have a Word document containing some spreadsheet cells with C++Builder data in them, and below these cells, a graph. You might not see the graph at first when looking at your copy of Word. To find the graph, scroll down the document a bit. By default, a fairly large margin appears at the top of a graph, so you might need to scroll down farther than you think. After you create the Word document, you have a chance to mail it via Microsoft Mail.

The following section examines the individual operations performed on Word and Excel in the EXCEL4 sample program.

Creating a Spreadsheet

The `Button1Click()` method drives the entire application:

```
void __fastcall TForm1::Button1Click(TObject *Sender)
{
  if (!m_XLApp)
    m_XLApp = Excel_tlb::CoApplication_::Create();

  m_XLApp->set_Visible(0, true);
  m_XLApp->Workbooks->Add(xlWBATWorksheet);
  m_Worksheet = m_XLApp->Workbooks->get_Item(1)->Worksheets->get_Item(1);
  m_Worksheet->Name = WideString("C++Builder Data");

  InitWorksheetData();
  InitChartData();

  // Launch Word, if necessary
  if (!m_WordApp)
    m_WordApp = Word_tlb::CoApplication_::Create();

  // Make Word visible and add a document
  m_WordApp->Visible = true;
  m_WordApp->Documents->Add();

  // Copy Excel data to Word
  CopyCellsToWord();
  CopyChartToWord();

  Button2->Enabled = true;
}
```

This method starts by creating an Excel `Application` object, setting the `Visible` property of the object to `true`, adding a new workbook, and stuffing a single worksheet into it. The C++Builder application then calls my custom `InitWorksheetData` and `InitChartData` methods to insert data into the spreadsheet:

```
void    TForm1::InitWorksheetData()
{
  // Set some data on some cells
  for (int i=1; i<=10; i++)
    m_Worksheet->Cells->set__Default(i, 1, i);
  // Get a range object pointing to these cells
  m_SheetRange = m_Worksheet->get_Range("A1:A10");
}
```

The code found in the `InitWorksheetData` method is rather simple. Ten cells are assigned the values of 1 through 10. Then the `Range` variable `m_SheetRange` is made to point to the range of these cells. You'll see next how that next `Range` object is assigned to a chart triggering the latter to plot the values of the range.

Creating a Chart

Now that you have a worksheet and some data, it's time to create a graph. The following procedure from the Excel4 program should get you started working with charts:

```
void    TForm1::InitChartData()
{
  // Create a chart
  ChartPtr chart1 = m_XLApp->Workbooks->get_Item(1)->Sheets->Add(
                              TNoParam(), TNoParam(), 1, xlChart);
  chart1->ChartType = xl3DPie;

  // Get series object of chart, set its values to the
  // range of our sheet and enable Datalabels
  SeriesCollectionPtr series = chart1->SeriesCollection();
  series->Item(1)->Values = LPDISPATCH(m_SheetRange);
  series->Item(1)->HasDataLabels = true;

  // Create another chart
  ChartPtr chart2 = m_XLApp->Workbooks->get_Item(1)->Sheets->Add(
                              TNoParam(), TNoParam(), 1, xlChart);
  chart2->ChartType = xl3DColumn;

  // Get its series and set the values to the same sheet range
series = chart2->SeriesCollection();
  series->Item(1)->Values = LPDISPATCH(m_SheetRange);

  // Create a safe array with some values
  TSafeArrayDim1 dim(10);
  TSafeArrayInt1 sa(dim);
  for (int i=0; i<10; i++)
    sa[i] = i;

  // Create a new series and set its Values to the data in the SAFEARRAY
series->NewSeries()->Values = sa.Detach();
}
```

This function creates two different charts. I've arranged things this way so that you can get a look at some of the different techniques needed to create charts.

The code starts by adding a single chart to a `Sheets` object in a `Workbook`:

```
// Create a chart
ChartPtr chart1 = m_XLApp->Workbooks->get_Item(1)->Sheets->Add(
                        TNoParam(), TNoParam(), 1, xlChart);
```

As you can see, I just ignore the first two parameters by specifying instances of the `TNoParam` class. The third and fourth parameters specify that I want to insert one sheet of the type `xlChart`.

A lot of the trick to working with Excel is to find the right object to work with. The `Sheets` object provides a simple and convenient way to create a chart, but it is not the only way of doing so. Remember that the `Sheets` object contains both the `Worksheets` and `Charts` objects inside a `Workbook`, so you can use it to add either worksheets or charts.

You should further understand that I am talking about adding `Charts` to a `Sheets` object, which is different from adding `ChartObjects` to a worksheet. In other words, you can insert a graph into a worksheet, but that operation is different from the one shown here. The key to embedding a chart into a worksheet is the Excel `ChartObjects` collection, which is not discussed further in this chapter.

After the chart has been created, the code sets the `SeriesCollection` of the `Chart` object to the range of the worksheet. In this particular example, the range is the same used in the Excel3 application, when I inserted 10 numbers into the A column and then supplied a formula to add them.

```
// Get series object of chart, set its values to the range of our
➥ sheet and enable Datalabels
   SeriesCollectionPtr series = chart1->SeriesCollection();
   series->Item(1)->Values = LPDISPATCH(m_SheetRange);
```

That is all you need to do to graph a range of data. As I will explain later in this chapter, you might want to manipulate the chart further, but just doing what I have done here is enough to start charting data.

Using the `SeriesCollection` Object

Stepping back and looking at the `SeriesCollection` object to see what it represents might be worthwhile. To get started, you need to understand that a `Series` is simply a range of data that you want to graph. A `SeriesCollection` is a collection of ranges of data; that is, it is a collection of `Series`.

15

AUTOMATING
WORD AND EXCEL

If you have several Series together in one place, you would have a SeriesCollection.

To see a SeriesCollection on the Excel side, load an Excel chart, right-click it, select the Source Data item from the menu, and turn to the Series page, as shown in Figure 15.1.

FIGURE 15.1

Showing a Series *inside Excel.*

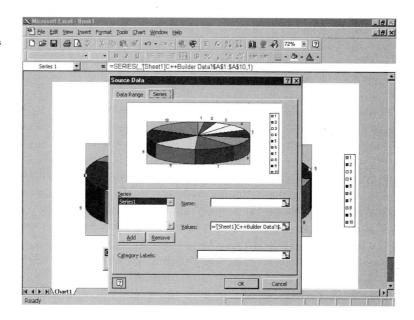

This Series is created for the first graph made by the Excel4 program. As you can see, the Series is described with a single cryptic line:

```
="C++Builder Data"!$A$1:$A$10
```

If you think about this line for a second, you can see how it corresponds to the code you wrote in C++Builder. To help you see the relationship, let's look at code that highlights the relationship:

```
SeriesCollectionPtr series = chart1->SeriesCollection();
series->Item(1)->Values = LPDISPATCH(m_SheetRange);
```

When you create a new chart, one Series is made for you automatically. By default, it charts whatever value is in cell A1 of a particular worksheet. In this case, I have changed that Series to point to a new range of data. In other words, I have changed the Values associated with the Series. As you will soon see, you can add additional Series.

The code goes on to specify that the chart has a Series of data labels:

```
series->Item(1)->HasDataLabels = true;
```

Now you're ready to look at the second chart created by the `ChartData` method:

```
// Create another chart
ChartPtr chart2 = m_XLApp->Workbooks->get_Item(1)->Sheets->Add(
                         TNoParam(), TNoParam(), 1, xlChart);
chart2->ChartType = xl3DColumn;

// Get its series and set the values to the same sheet range
series = chart2->SeriesCollection();
  series->Item(1)->Values = LPDISPATCH(m_SheetRange);

Sheets->Item["Chart2"]->SeriesCollection->Add(ARange);

// Create a safe array with some values
TSafeArrayDim1 dim(10);
TSafeArrayInt1 sa(dim);
for (int i=0; i<10; i++)
  sa[i] = i;

// Create a new series and set its Values to the data in the SAFEARRAY
series->NewSeries()->Values = sa.Detach();
```

This chart graphs a `SeriesCollection` that contains not one, but two `Series`. The first `Series` is identical to the `Series` graphed by the first chart, but the second `Series` is slightly different, in that its values come not from an Excel worksheet, but from a range of data directly specified inside C++Builder.

Take a moment to consider what is happening here. The first set of data graphed is specified exactly as in the previous example:

```
// Get its series and set the values to the same sheet range
series = chart2->SeriesCollection();
  series->Item(1)->Values = LPDISPATCH(m_SheetRange);
```

Adding a new range specifies the next `Series`:

```
Sheets->Item["Chart2"]->SeriesCollection->Add(ARange);
```

Then the code creates a `SAFEARRAY` with predetermined data:

```
// Create a safe array with some values
  TSafeArrayDim1 dim(10);
  TSafeArrayInt1 sa(dim);
  for (int i=0; i<10; i++)
    sa[i] = i;
```

The program then creates a new `Series` and sets its `Values` to the data in the `SAFEARRAY`:

```
// Create a new series and set its Values to the data in the SAFEARRAY
  series->NewSeries()->Values = sa.Detach();
```

The `Series` created by this code is shown on the Excel side in Figure 15.2.

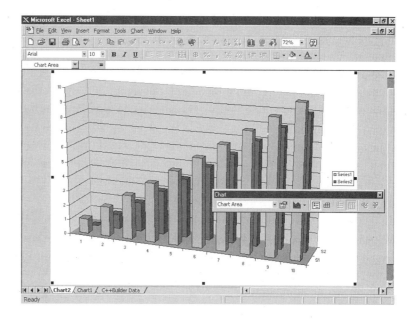

FIGURE 15.2

A SAFEARRAY created in C++Builder as it is depicted in Excel.

You are at last ready to copy the worksheet and two charts that you have created from Excel into Word. This operation is relatively complex, so I will discuss it in the next few sections.

Copying the Data from Excel to Word

The process of copying data from Excel to Word has two parts. The first part involves copying the data to the Clipboard, and the second part involves pasting the data into the Word document. In other words, you need to have both Excel and Word open to make this process work. Furthermore, the tricky part is not so much copying the data from Excel, but inserting it correctly into Word.

The following method copies the data from Excel to the Clipboard. Note that I have created two methods called `CopyCellsToWord` and `CopyChartToWord`.

To copy data from a range in a worksheet to the Clipboard, I first activate the `Worksheet` object, select `SheetRange` and then copy the data to the Clipboard:

```
// Activate Excel's worksheet, select the range and
// copy it to the clipboard
  m_Worksheet->Activate();
  m_SheetRange->Select();
  m_Worksheet->get_UsedRange()->Copy();
```

In this process, I essentially mirror the actions I would take when doing this process manually. In other words, I first click the worksheet I want to use; that is, I activate it. I then select a range of data from it, and finally I press Ctrl+C to copy it to the Clipboard. Of course, I'm not really doing these things, but I'm executing in code the steps necessary to duplicate these actions as follows:

1. Call `Activate`—Click the page using the mouse.
2. Call `Select`—Select data using the mouse.
3. Call `Copy`—Press Ctrl+C or pull down the Edit menu and choose Copy.

After the program copies a range of cells to memory, the next step is to copy the cells to Word. In this explanation, however, I will temporarily pass over the act of copying the data to Word, and instead show you how to copy the Chart to memory. Note, however, that you obviously must do these things one at a time because the Clipboard can hold only one object in memory at a time. In short, you can't copy both the worksheet and the chart to two separate places in the Clipboard and then copy them both to Word in one motion. The problem, of course, is that the Clipboard has only one area available in memory at this time.

Here is how to copy a chart to the Clipboard:

```
// Copy the Excel chart to the clipboard
  ChartPtr chart = m_XLApp->Sheets->get_Item("Chart1");
  chart->Select();
  chart->Copy();
```

This code first selects `Chart1` and then copies it to the Clipboard. Again, I am mirroring the actions I would take if I were performing these steps manually. That is, I first select the object and then "press Ctrl+C" to copy it. Once again, I don't explicitly press Ctrl+C, but instead perform the steps in code that duplicate this action.

Creating a Word Document

Before you can copy the Excel data that we've put in the clipboard, you need to launch Word and create a Word document. The following code snippet illustrates how to launch Word and set up a document to receive the Excel data.

```
// Launch Word, if necessary
  if (!m_WordApp)
    m_WordApp = Word_tlb::CoApplication_::Create();

  // Make Word visible and add a document
  m_WordApp->Visible = true;
  m_WordApp->Documents->Add();
```

To get started in Word, you follow more or less the same steps you would in Excel. The code creates a Word Application object, sets the Visible property of the object to true, and adds a single document to it.

To add text to the document, execute the following code:

```
// Set some text in the active document
Word_tlb::RangePtr range = m_WordApp->ActiveDocument->Range();
range->Text = WideString("This is a column from a spreadsheet:");
```

In this case, the code retrieves a Range object representing the entire document, which, of course, starts out completely empty. To place text in the document, you can use the Text property of the range.

You could simply paste the data from Excel directly into your document. However, you want to be able to have some control over the location where the cells are placed. To have this control, you need some whitespace in the document; that is, you need a series of carriage returns through which you can iterate:

```
// Add 3 paragraphs
for (int i=1; i<3; i++)
  m_WordApp->ActiveDocument->Paragraphs->Add();
```

You can now use the Goto method of the Range or Document object to move back and forth across this range of paragraphs. Or, if you want, you can select a new range, and then paste your Excel data into that range. In my experience, this second method is the easiest means of moving through a document. Here is the code for selecting a Range covering the second paragraph of a document:

```
int startRange =
    m_WordApp->ActiveDocument->Paragraphs->Item(2)->Range->Start;
range = m_WordApp->ActiveDocument->Range(&TVariant(startRange));
```

This code states that I want to define a range on the second paragraph of the document. I explicitly state that the range starts at the beginning of the paragraph, but I do not define the end of the range. I can now paste in the Excel code with a single, easy-to-write line:

```
range->Paste();
```

After pasting in this range of cells, I find that several new paragraphs have been added to my document. There is no specific way for me to be sure how many because the number of cells I paste in may vary with different versions of my program. So when I get ready to paste in the chart from Excel, I start by adding a brand new paragraph:

```
void    TForm1::CopyChartToWord()
{
  // Add a new paragraph
  ParagraphPtr para = m_WordApp->ActiveDocument->Paragraphs->Add();

  // Get range of new paragraph and set some text
  Word_tlb::RangePtr range = para->Range;
  range->Text = WideString("This is a graph: ");

  // Add a few more paragraphs
  for (int i=0; i<2; i++)
    m_WordApp->ActiveDocument->Paragraphs->Add();

  // Copy the Excel chart to the clipboard
  ChartPtr chart = m_XLApp->Sheets->get_Item("Chart1");
  chart->Select();
  chart->Copy();

  // Add one more and paste the chart
  range = m_WordApp->ActiveDocument->Paragraphs->Add()->Range;
  range->Paste();
}
```

The next step is to enter a single, descriptive line of text, followed by a few additional paragraphs:

```
  // Get range of new paragraph and set some text
  Word_tlb::RangePtr range = para->Range;
  range->Text = WideString("This is a graph: ");

  // Add a few more paragraphs
  for (int i=0; i<2; i++)
    m_WordApp->ActiveDocument->Paragraphs->Add();
```

Then I copy the `Chart` to the Clipboard, create another paragraph in the Word document, and position myself at that location:

```
// Add one more and paste the chart
  range = m_WordApp->ActiveDocument->Paragraphs->Add()->Range;
```

To paste the `Chart`, I simply invoke the `Paste` method of the `Range` object:

```
range->Paste();
```

Figure 15.3 shows some Excel data pasted in a Word document. You also can invoke the `PasteSpecial` method instead of `Paste`. The former takes several optional parameters. You can look them up in the Word VBA documentation.

FIGURE **15.3**
Copying Excel data to a Word document via OLE automation.

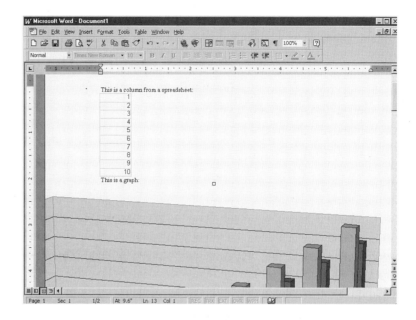

> **NOTE**
>
> Remember that the Word VBA help file is not installed by default, so you might need to run the Word installation and explicitly ask for the file, or else copy it off the CD-ROM manually.

Mailing a Document

The Documents object also has Save, SaveAs, and Open methods you can use when opening or saving a document. In fact, many methods and properties are associated with most of the objects discussed in this chapter. The only way to get to know them all is to open the Word or Excel help and start browsing through it. This chapter is meant to give you a conceptual overview of how to use Word and Excel automation objects; it is not a complete examination of the subject.

You can save the current Word document as follows:

```
m_WordApp->ActiveDocument->SaveAs(&TVariant("\\foo.doc"));
```

The following code allows you to send a mail message:

```
void __fastcall TForm1::Button2Click(TObject *Sender)
{
  m_WordApp->ActiveDocument->SaveAs(&TVariant("\\foo.doc"));
  m_WordApp->Options->SendMailAttach = true;
  m_WordApp->ActiveDocument->SendMail();
}
```

If you have a MAPI client set up on your computer, you can send a document to another user directly from Excel using the preceding code to do so. This code will automatically open the mail services, allowing you to pick a user and send the document. The document you created will be attached to your message. If you don't have mail set up on your machine, this code obviously won't work.

Summary

This chapter covers only the basic steps involved with automating Excel and Word from C++Builder. This subject is obviously large, and I could say much more about it. However, the information you read here should open up the topic sufficiently to allow you to perform most tasks.

By now, it should be obvious to you that the automation objects in Excel and Word are extremely powerful. If you were creating an actual word processor, you couldn't ask for much more in terms of functionality, but, of course, you would look for a little better performance.

Internet Connection with C++Builder

by Kent Reisdorph

IN THIS CHAPTER

Internet programming is becoming increasingly prevalent. It could be that today you don't care about Internet programming and you don't think it is important. Tomorrow, though, a customer, a co-worker, or your boss may ask you to write an application that requires Internet programming.

Internet programming means different things to different people. To some, it means writing CGI or WebBroker utilities for Web servers. To others, Internet programming means writing an application that sends or receives email, transfers files to and from an FTP server, or implements a Web browser. To still others, it means writing a multitiered database application that includes a thin client application, a middle-tier application server, and a main server, all running on different machines. The world of Internet programming runs the gamut from simple client applications to huge application suites that can be incredibly complex.

> **NOTE**
>
> When I talk about Internet programming I am including network programming as well. Some of your applications will reach around the world to access remote machines. Others may connect to a remote machine just a few feet away. The principles are, for the most part, the same whether you are doing Internet programming or network programming.

Internet programming can be broken down into two primary, broad-based categories:

- Client applications
- Server applications

The bulk of you will probably write client applications. For example, say that you are tasked with writing an application that scans your company's newsgroups in order to compile information on newsgroup participants, message volume, and so on. You don't have to worry about writing a news server because that part is presumably already done. You will write a client application that accesses the news server. Any application you write that accesses a server—a Web server, FTP server, news server, mail server, and so on—is a client application. For the most part, writing client applications is not terribly complex, at least when compared with writing server-side Internet applications.

A few lucky souls among you will be tasked with writing server applications. Writing server applications requires more work, especially if the server must handle multiple client requests. Any server that handles multiple client requests is generally a multi-threaded application.

This chapter explains some of the programming tasks you will have to consider when writing client-side Internet applications. A fair amount of the chapter deals with Microsoft's Remote Access Services (RAS) API. RAS is the Windows service that handles dial-up connections on Win9x/NT systems. If you are writing applications for users with a permanent Internet connection, then the sections on RAS may not apply to you. The first part of the chapter deals with setting up TCP/IP on your system. Following that is a section on detecting an Internet connection.

Installing TCP/IP

This section briefly discusses the process of setting up TCP/IP on a Windows 95/98 machine. The process is nearly identical on a Windows NT 4 machine, though the dialogs may have a slightly different name or appearance.

TCP/IP is the protocol of choice when you're working over the Internet. In fact, it is the backbone on which the Internet is built. The TCP/IP protocol ships automatically with 32-bit Windows products. To see whether TCP/IP is installed on your system, open the Control Panel and launch the Network applet. If you have TCP/IP installed, it will show up on the Configuration page of this applet. (On NT, it's the Protocols page.)

If TCP/IP is not installed, you should click the Add button on the Configuration page to bring up the Select Network Component Type dialog. Select Protocol from the list of drivers and again choose the Add button. In the Select Network Protocol dialog, choose Microsoft in the left list box and TCP/IP in the right list box. Windows will then install the necessary software, which may require the use of your Windows install CD-ROM.

You will probably also have to specify an IP address, subnet mask, gateway, and DNS server. This information can be garnered from your network administrator. If you are working on a small local network with Windows machines that you have set up in your office or home, you can ignore the DNS server and make up your own IP address, subnet mask, and gateway. For instance, the following numbers would do, as long as you are not connected to the real Internet and are talking only to the machines in your home or office:

```
IP Address: 192.168.0.2
Subnet mask: 255.255.255.0
Gateway: 192.168.0.1
```

The other machines on your network should have the same subnet and gateway, but the IP address should be unique. For instance, the next machine should have an IP address of 192.168.0.3; the next, 192.168.0.4; and so on. Remember, don't make up your own numbers if you are connected to the Internet. (Most ISPs assign you a dynamic IP address each time you connect to their server.) The range of IP address shown here (those beginning with 192) has been set aside for people who do not want to communicate with the Internet. If you have an Internet connection, contact your network administrator or Internet service provider (ISP) for more information. Your network administrator should be completely familiar with this subject because it is as central to network computing as the idea of a method or function is to programming.

To check whether you are connected properly, open a DOS window and try to ping one of the machines in your network. You can do this with Windows' PING utility. PING is a built-in application that ships with Windows 9x/NT. If you installed TCP/IP as explained previously, PING will be set up on your machine.

To get started, you can try to ping your own machine:

```
ping 192.168.0.2
```

The following is a built-in address for referencing your own machine:

```
ping 127.0.0.1
```

This number is aliased as localhost, so you can also type the following:

```
ping localhost
```

Alternatively, you can try to ping one of the other machines in your network:

```
ping 192.168.0.3
```

Here is the result of a successful ping:

```
ping 143.186.186.2
Pinging 143.186.186.2 with 32 bytes of data:
Reply from 143.186.186.2: bytes=32 time=55ms TTL=32
Reply from 143.186.186.2: bytes=32 time=1ms TTL=32
Reply from 143.186.186.2: bytes=32 time=1ms TTL=32
Reply from 143.186.186.2: bytes=32 time=1ms TTL=32
```

Here is the result of a failed ping:

```
ping 143.186.186.3
Pinging 143.186.186.3 with 32 bytes of data:
Request timed out.
Request timed out.
Request timed out.
Request timed out.
```

Failed sessions usually occur because your machine is not configured properly, the server is busy, or the wires connecting you to the network are not set up correctly. (For instance, you might have forgotten to plug into the network.)

If you are attached to the Internet and have a DNS server, you can try to ping one of the big servers on the Net:

```
ping borland.com
```

Pinging `borland.com` is the same thing as pinging `207.105.83.51`. In fact, it's the job of the DNS server (the Domain Name Server) to resolve a human-readable name such as `borland.com` into an IP address.

Now that you have TCP/IP set up properly, we can move on to a discussion of how to ping remote machines within your C++Builder applications.

Using PING to Detect an Internet Connection

If you are writing Internet client applications, you need to know whether your users are connected to the Internet before attempting to connect to a server. For users with a permanent Internet connection, this isn't generally a problem. For users configured for dial-up networking, though, you will have to dial the modem in order to establish a connection to the Internet.

There are a number of ways your users may connect to the Internet:

- Through phone lines using a conventional modem
- Through cable television systems that support Internet access and a cable modem
- Through Integrated Services Digital Network (ISDN) and an ISDN modem
- Through Digital Subscriber Line (DSL) and a DSL modem
- Through a dedicated connection, such as a T1 or T3 line

This is by no means a complete list of ways to connect to the Internet. There are no doubt other technologies that I am not aware of and additional technologies are almost certainly on the horizon.

Most Windows 9x systems are configured to auto-dial when a connection is required. Windows NT has auto-dial capability, but it doesn't work very well; I always disable the Remote Access Autodial Manager service on my home system. In either case, I don't like depending on the operating system to establish a connection. I'd rather be in control of the dialing process so that my software works in a wide variety of user configurations. In this section I discuss how to ping a remote machine in order to determine if a connection to the Internet exists. Later, beginning with the section "Connecting to the Internet with RAS," I explain how to use RAS to establish a connection to a remote machine.

Some of the ways you can detect whether the user is connected to the Internet (listed from easiest to most complex) are

- Try to connect using one of the C++Builder Internet components and catch any resulting exceptions
- Using a `ping` component
- Using WinInet's `InternetCheckConnection()` function
- Using Microsoft's `ICMP.DLL`
- Using Winsock and raw sockets

I'll discuss each of these methods in the following sections. Because the first three methods listed are fairly simple, I cover them in a single section.

Ping the Easy Way

Using the Internet components to determine whether the user is connected to the Internet is certainly easy, but there are problems with this approach. First let me show you how the code might look:

```
try {
  FTP->Connect();
}
catch (ESockError&) {
  // connection failed
  return;
}
// connection succeeded
```

This example assumes that you have a `TNMFTP` component on your form, that you have set its `Host` property to point to a known FTP server, and that you have set the `UserID` and `Password` properties as required for the FTP server to which you are attempting to connect.

I don't particularly like this approach for a number of reasons. For one thing, this code attempts to connect to a specific FTP server. It is certainly possible that the user is connected to the Internet, that the machine on which the server resides is up and running, but that the FTP server itself is down. You could use any of the Internet components (`TNMSMTP`, `TNMHTTP`, `TNMNNTP`, and so on) if you choose this approach, but all suffer from the same limitations.

This approach feels like a hack to me. Your intent is to detect whether the user is connected to the Internet, not necessarily to connect to an FTP server (unless that is your ultimate goal, of course). Finally, consider what happens if this code fails. Once in the `catch` block, you still don't know the cause of the failure; you'll have to either bail out entirely or perform some other tests to determine the cause of the failure. Clearly, this isn't the best approach.

If you are looking for a ready-made solution to pinging a server, using a `ping` component is a good way to go. There are several freeware `ping` components on the Web, but the one I see recommended most often is François Piette's TPing component. TPing is part of François' Internet Component Suite (ICS). You can download the ICS from François' Web site at `http://www.rtfm.be/fpiette/icsuk.htm`.

Pinging a machine with TPing is a trivial task. Just set the `Address` property to a known IP address or host name and then write code like this:

```
bool goodPing = Ping1->Ping();
if (goodPing)
  // connected
else
  // not connected
```

If the `Ping()` method returns `false`, you still aren't guaranteed that the user isn't connected to the Internet. It could be that the particular machine you are pinging is down.

NetMasters also has a `ping` component, but it doesn't ship with C++Builder 4. Check the NetMasters Web site at `http://www.netmastersllc.com` for updates.

Pinging a server with a third-party `ping` component is an easy and—depending on how the component writer implemented the ping—effective solution for detecting an Internet connection. For those who want to maintain independence from third-party component writers, you can easily implement your own ping routine as discussed in the next section.

Another way to ping a server is by using WinInet's `InternetCheckConnection()` function. (WinInet is described in Chapter 18, "WinInet and FTP.") I tried to use the `InternetCheckConnection()` function in a quick test application and couldn't get it to work reliably. Later I was reading an MSDN article and the author of that article commented on the unreliability of WinInet's Internet connection functions. I mention `InternetCheckConnection()` because you should be aware of its existence.

Ping Using `ICMP.DLL`

I believe in using existing components whenever and wherever possible. On the other hand, I sometimes have a compulsion to get down to the API level to learn more about how certain aspects of Windows works. This was the case when I set out to find a way of pinging a machine. I found that the easiest way to do this was with the functions found in Windows `ICMP.DLL`. Until recently, the functions in this DLL were not very well documented (and still aren't, for the most part). The `ICMP` functions are now part of the Windows CE API, and as such are documented in MSDN and on the Microsoft Web site. Microsoft documentation (aside from the CE documentation) warns that `ICMP.DLL` may eventually be removed from Windows. I suspect that this warning was issued several years ago and that Microsoft has had a change of mind regarding `ICMP.DLL`. It's my belief that `ICMP.DLL` won't be going away anytime soon. Still, if you are paranoid about the Microsoft warning regarding `ICMP.DLL`, you may want to use one of the other methods of pinging a server. The ICS `TPing` component mentioned earlier uses `ICMP.DLL` to perform a ping, so keep that in mind if you decide to use `TPing`.

The SimplePing example, shown in Listings 16.1 and 16.2, displays the most basic method of implementing a ping. Figure 16.1 shows the SimplePing program running. Before you can use `ICMP.DLL` in your programs, you need to create an import library file for the DLL. I used the IMPLIB utility that ships with C++Builder to create an import library called `ICMP.LIB`. I then added this LIB file to the SimplePing project.

FIGURE 16.1

The SimplePing program allows you to ping a machine on the network or across the Internet.

LISTING 16.1   THE HEADER FOR THE SIMPLEPING PROGRAM

```
#ifndef SimplePingUH
#define SimplePingUH

#include <Classes.hpp>
#include <Controls.hpp>
#include <StdCtrls.hpp>
#include <Forms.hpp>

class TMainForm : public TForm
{
__published:    // IDE-managed Components
  TEdit *IPEdit;
```

Internet Connection with C++Builder

CHAPTER 16

721

16

INTERNET
CONNECTION WITH
C++ BUILDER

```cpp
   TLabel *Label1;
   TButton *PingBtn;
   void __fastcall PingBtnClick(TObject *Sender);
private:
   // User declarations
   bool Ping(int addr);
   int MakeIPAddress(String AddressString, int& ErrCode);
public:          // User declarations
   __fastcall TMainForm(TComponent* Owner);
};

extern PACKAGE TMainForm *MainForm;

#endif
```

LISTING 16.2   THE SOURCE CODE FOR THE SIMPLEPING PROGRAM

```cpp
#include <vcl.h>
#pragma hdrstop

#include "SimplePingU.h"
#include "winsock.h"
extern "C" {
#include "ipexport.h""
#include "icmpapi.h"
}

#pragma package(smart_init)
#pragma resource "*.dfm"
TMainForm *MainForm;

__fastcall TMainForm::TMainForm(TComponent* Owner)
   : TForm(Owner)
{
}

void __fastcall TMainForm::PingBtnClick(TObject *Sender)
{
   int errorCode;
   int addr = MakeIPAddress(IPEdit->Text, errorCode);
   if (!addr) {
     String S = String().sprintf("Winsock error: %d", errorCode);
     ShowMessage(S);
     return;
   }
   if (Ping(addr))
     ShowMessage("Ping successful!");
   else
     ShowMessage("Ping failed.");
```

continues

LISTING 16.2   CONTINUED

```cpp
}

bool TMainForm::Ping(int addr)
{
  bool result = true;
  HANDLE hIcmp = IcmpCreateFile();
  if (!hIcmp) {
    ShowMessage("Unable to load ICMP.DLL.");
    return false;
  }
  int size = sizeof(icmp_echo_reply) + 8;
  char* buff = new char[size];
  DWORD res = IcmpSendEcho(hIcmp, addr, 0, 0, 0, buff, size, 1000);
  if (!res)
    // timed out
    result = false;
  else {
    icmp_echo_reply reply;
    memcpy(&reply, buff, sizeof(reply));
    delete[] buff;
    if (reply.Status> 0)
      // error
      result = false;
  }
  IcmpCloseHandle(hIcmp);
  return result;
}

int TMainForm::MakeIPAddress(String AddressString, int& ErrCode)
{
  // Intialize Winsock.dll
  WSADATA wsaData;
  memset(&wsaData, 0, sizeof(WSADATA));
  #pragma warn -prc
  Word lowVersion = MAKEWORD(2, 0);
  int res = WSAStartup(lowVersion, &wsaData);
  if (res) {
    ErrCode = res;
    return 0;
  }
  // Strip spaces from the AddressString text
  for (int i=AddressString.Length();i>0;i—) {
    if (AddressString[i] == ' ')
      AddressString.Delete(i, 1);
  }
  // Is the address in IP format?
  int addr = inet_addr(AddressString.c_str());
  if (addr == -1) {
    // Is the address a host name?
```

```
    hostent* he = gethostbyname(AddressString.c_str());
    if (!he) {
      ErrCode = WSAGetLastError();
      return 0;
    }
    else
      memcpy(&addr, he->h_addr_list[0], sizeof(int));
  }
  WSACleanup();
  return addr;
}
```

This program allows you to enter an IP address in an edit control on the main form. The IP address can be specified in either IP dot notation (165.212.210.12, for example) or by host name (www.turbopower.com). When you click the Ping button, the program performs a ping and displays the results in a message box.

Notice that the code in Listing 16.2 includes two headers called IPEXPORT.H and ICMPAPI.H. These two headers are required for the ICMP.DLL functions. I had a bit of a time hunting these headers down. ICMPAPI.H is included in the Win32 SDK, so finding it wasn't too much trouble. (You can get it from MSDN and from Microsoft's Web site, as well as the Win32 SDK.) IPEXPORT.H proved a little more difficult. I eventually found IPEXPORT.H on the Web. I searched for "ICMP," "ICMP.DLL," and "IcmpSendEcho." I eventually arrived at a site that contained the Microsoft headers. The action starts when the Ping button on the form is clicked. Here's the code for the Ping button's OnClick event handler:

```
void __fastcall TMainForm::PingBtnClick(TObject *Sender)
{
  int errorCode;
  int addr = MakeIPAddress(IPEdit->Text, errorCode);
  if (!addr) {
    String S = String().sprintf("Winsock error: %d", errorCode);
    ShowMessage(S);
    return;
  }
  if (Ping(addr))
    ShowMessage("Ping successful!");
  else
    ShowMessage("Ping failed.");
}
```

The first few lines of code convert the text in the form's edit control to a 32-bit IP address. All the work is done in the form's MakeIPAddress() function. I'm going to detour from the main topic for a moment and explain what this function does.

The SimplePing program allows you to specify the IP address either in dot notation or by host name. The `MakeIPAddress()` function first assumes that the IP address string is an IP address in dot notation. It attempts to convert that string to a 32-bit IP address value. If that conversion fails, it is assumed that the IP address was expressed as a domain name, and the function again attempts to convert the string to an IP address value using a different method. Here's the code for the `MakeIPAddress()` function:

```
int TMainForm::MakeIPAddress(String AddressString, int& ErrCode)
{
  // Intialize Winsock.dll
  WSADATA wsaData;
  memset(&wsaData, 0, sizeof(WSADATA));
  #pragma warn -prc
  Word lowVersion = MAKEWORD(2, 0);
  int res = WSAStartup(lowVersion, &wsaData);
  if (res) {
    ErrCode = res;
    return 0;
  }
  // Strip spaces from the AddressString text
  for (int i=AddressString.Length();i>0;i—) {
    if (AddressString[i] == ' ')
      AddressString.Delete(i, 1);
  }
  // Is the address in IP format?
  int addr = inet_addr(AddressString.c_str());
  if (addr == -1) {
    // Is the address a host name?
    hostent* he = gethostbyname(AddressString.c_str());
    if (!he) {
      ErrCode = WSAGetLastError();
      return 0;
    }
    else
      memcpy(&addr, he->h_addr_list[0], sizeof(int));
  }
  WSACleanup();
  return addr;
}
```

The first few lines in this function initialize WinSock. (It probably goes without saying, but if you didn't know, WinSock is Microsoft's implementation of TCP/IP sockets.)

```
WSADATA wsaData;
memset(&wsaData, 0, sizeof(WSADATA));
#pragma warn -prc
Word lowVersion = MAKEWORD(2, 0);
int res = WSAStartup(lowVersion, &wsaData);
```

Internet Connection with C++Builder
CHAPTER 16

725

16

INTERNET
CONNECTION WITH
C++ BUILDER

```
if (res) {
  ErrCode = res;
  return 0;
}
```

This code initializes WinSock, telling Windows that we will be using WinSock version 2.0. We are safe using version 2.0 because Win9x/NT use WinSock 2.0 or later. If the call to WSAStartup() succeeds, Winsock is initialized and we can convert the IP address string to a 32-bit IP address value.

The next section of code strips any blanks from the IP address string:

```
for (int i=AddressString.Length();i>0;i—) {
  if (AddressString[i] == ' ')
    AddressString.Delete(i, 1);
}
```

It is important that an IP address specified in IP dot notation doesn't contain any blanks. If the IP address contains blanks, the IP address will be improperly interpreted when WinSock converts the string to a 32-bit IP address value. I prefer to avoid the issue entirely by stripping the blanks from the IP address.

CAUTION

Another interesting aspect of IP addresses is that a leading zero in any of the sections of an IP address string will cause the value to be interpreted as an octal value. Take this IP address, for example:

165.212.210.012

Note the leading 0 in the final section. When WinSock converts this IP address string, it generates a 32-bit value representing this IP address:

165.212.210.10

Obviously, these two IP addresses are not the same. Be sure you don't put any leading 0s in your IP address strings unless you intend for the IP address to be interpreted as an octal value.

The next line of code attempts to convert the IP address to a string using WinSock's inet_addr() function:

```
int addr = inet_addr(AddressString.c_str());
```

The `inet_addr()` function returns a 32-bit IP address on success, `-1` on failure. This function will succeed if the text passed to `inet_addr()` contains an IP address expressed in IP dot notation. If the call succeeds, I have a valid IP address value that I can use to perform the ping. If the call to `inet_addr()` fails, I assume that the IP address was expressed as a host name. This section of code converts a host name to an IP address:

```
if (addr == -1) {
  // Is the address a host name?
  hostent* he = gethostbyname(AddressString.c_str());
  if (!he) {
    ErrCode = WSAGetLastError();
    return 0;
  }
  else
    memcpy(&addr, he->h_addr_list[0], sizeof(int));
}
```

This code passes the IP address string to WinSock's `gethostbyname()` function. This function returns a pointer to a `hostent` structure. If the call to `gethostbyname()` fails, the IP address string could not be converted to an IP address value.

> **NOTE**
>
> `gethostbyname()` uses a Domain Name Service (DNS) to convert the domain name to an IP address value. Nearly all ISPs and networks have a DNS server running to perform host name lookups. If for some reason you don't have access to a DNS server, the call to `gethostbyname()` will fail. This is not something you have to give much thought to, but understand that it is possible that a DNS server will be available in all circumstances. For this reason it is usually best to specify the IP address in IP dot notation.
>
> The fact that `gethostbyname()` uses DNS to perform the host name lookup has implications if you are trying to ping a server *silently* (without the user being aware of it). The primary implication is that on Win9x machines, calling `gethostbyname()` may result in the Windows auto dialer kicking in. If you want to ping silently, use a known IP address instead of a host name lookup.

If `gethostbyname()` returns successfully, you can copy the first 4 bytes of the `hostent` structure's `h_addr_list` member to a variable that holds the 32-bit IP address:

```
memcpy(&addr, he->h_addr_list[0], sizeof(int));
```

At the end of this process, I notify WinSock that I don't need its services anymore and return the 32-bit IP address I have obtained:

Internet Connection with C++Builder

CHAPTER 16

727

16

INTERNET
CONNECTION WITH
C++ BUILDER

```
WSACleanup();
return addr;
```

Now let's get back to the actual ping operation. The ping is performed by calling the SimplePing program's `Ping()` method:

```cpp
bool TMainForm::Ping(int addr)
{
  bool result = true;
  HANDLE hIcmp = IcmpCreateFile();
  if (!hIcmp) {
    ShowMessage("Unable to load ICMP.DLL.");
    return false;
  }
  int size = sizeof(icmp_echo_reply) + 8;
  char* buff = new char[size];
  DWORD res = IcmpSendEcho(hIcmp, addr, 0, 0, 0, buff, size, 1000);
  if (!res)
    // timed out
    result = false;
  else {
    icmp_echo_reply reply;
    memcpy(&reply, buff, sizeof(reply));
    delete[] buff;
    if (reply.Status> 0)
      // error
      result = false;
  }
  IcmpCloseHandle(hIcmp);
  return result;
}
```

As you can see, there isn't a lot of code in this function. The first line declares a `bool` variable that will contain the status of the ping (success or failure). The next few lines call `IcmpCreateFile()` to get an ICMP handle (required later) and determine whether a valid handle was returned:

```cpp
HANDLE hIcmp = IcmpCreateFile();
if (!hIcmp) {
  ShowMessage("Unable to load ICMP.DLL.");
  return false;
}
```

After that I set up a buffer that will receive the reply information from the server:

```cpp
int size = sizeof(icmp_echo_reply) + 8;
char* buff = new char[size];
```

This is the minimum buffer size required to perform a ping. It allocates the size of an `icmp_echo_reply` structure, plus eight bytes of overhead space. Now I can call `IcmpSendEcho()` to ping the server:

```cpp
DWORD res = IcmpSendEcho(hIcmp, addr, 0, 0, 0, buff, size, 1000);
```

The first parameter to `IcmpSendEcho()` is the ICMP handle returned from the earlier call to `IcmpCreateFile()`. The second parameter is the 32-bit IP address of the server to ping. The value I pass for this parameter was obtained when I called `MakeIPAddress()` as discussed earlier. The next three parameters are not used when performing a simple ping. If you were performing a complex ping (such as a trace route), you would use these parameters to provide additional request information. The sixth parameter is the address of the buffer that will receive the reply information from the server, and the seventh parameter is the buffer 's size. If `IcmpSendEcho()` returns successfully, this buffer will hold the reply information. The last parameter is the timeout value. If the server doesn't respond within the number of milliseconds specified in the timeout value, the call to `IcmpSendEcho()` will fail.

The return value of `IcmpSendEcho()` is the number of echo replies stored in the reply buffer. There will only be one echo reply in the case of a simple ping. If `IcmpSendEcho()` returns 0, the operation timed out and you can assume that the ping failed. In the case of the `Ping()` method, I simply return `false` if the return value from `IcmpSendEcho()` is 0:

```
if (!res)
  // timed out
  result = false;
```

If `IcmpSendEcho()` returns a non-zero value, you can't necessarily assume that the ping succeeded. The operation may not have timed out, but may have encountered some other error. A common error condition is "destination net unreachable." (If you have used the Windows pinging to any extent, you have no doubt seen this message.)

If `IcmpSendEcho()` returns successfully, you must still check the ping status to see if an error occurred. To detect ping status errors, you must first copy the data in the reply buffer to an instance of the `icmp_echo_reply` structure and then check the value of its `Status` member. Here's the code:

```
else {
  icmp_echo_reply reply;
  memcpy(&reply, buff, sizeof(reply));
  if (reply.Status> 0)
    // error
    result = false;
}
```

First, I declare an instance of the `icmp_echo_reply` structure. Second, I copy the first few bytes of the reply buffer to the address of the `icmp_echo_reply` instance. I can then check the value of the `icmp_echo_reply` structure's `Status` member. Some sort of error occurred if this value is greater than 0. The value of the `Status` member will be one of the error values defined in `IPEXPORT.H`:

Internet Connection with C++Builder

Chapter 16

729

16

INTERNET
CONNECTION WITH
C++ BUILDER

```
#define IP_STATUS_BASE                11000
#define IP_BUF_TOO_SMALL             (IP_STATUS_BASE + 1)
#define IP_DEST_NET_UNREACHABLE      (IP_STATUS_BASE + 2)
#define IP_DEST_HOST_UNREACHABLE     (IP_STATUS_BASE + 3)
#define IP_DEST_PROT_UNREACHABLE     (IP_STATUS_BASE + 4)
#define IP_DEST_PORT_UNREACHABLE     (IP_STATUS_BASE + 5)
#define IP_NO_RESOURCES              (IP_STATUS_BASE + 6)
#define IP_BAD_OPTION                (IP_STATUS_BASE + 7)
#define IP_HW_ERROR                  (IP_STATUS_BASE + 8)
#define IP_PACKET_TOO_BIG            (IP_STATUS_BASE + 9)
#define IP_REQ_TIMED_OUT             (IP_STATUS_BASE + 10)
#define IP_BAD_REQ                   (IP_STATUS_BASE + 11)
#define IP_BAD_ROUTE                 (IP_STATUS_BASE + 12)
#define IP_TTL_EXPIRED_TRANSIT       (IP_STATUS_BASE + 13)
#define IP_TTL_EXPIRED_REASSEM       (IP_STATUS_BASE + 14)
#define IP_PARAM_PROBLEM             (IP_STATUS_BASE + 15)
#define IP_SOURCE_QUENCH             (IP_STATUS_BASE + 16)
#define IP_OPTION_TOO_BIG            (IP_STATUS_BASE + 17)
#define IP_BAD_DESTINATION           (IP_STATUS_BASE + 18)
#define IP_GENERAL_FAILURE           (IP_STATUS_BASE + 50)
```

In the case of the SimplePing program I am not specifically concerned with what the Status value contains, only if it is 0 (success) or a value greater than 0 (failure). I don't particularly care why the ping failed, so I simply return false if the Status member is a value greater than 0.

If the Status member of the icmp_echo_reply structure is 0, I have a good ping. I set the value of the result variable to true at the top of the Ping() method. If all went well, the value of result is still true when the function ends.

Before returning from the Ping() function, I call IcmpCloseHandle() to close the handle obtained earlier. After that I return the result of the ping:

```
IcmpCloseHandle(hIcmp);
return result;
```

This ping routine is short enough that I prefer to use it in my applications rather than a ping component. I'd rather have a single short routine of my own creation than worry about installing additional components and their related packages.

Obtaining More Ping Information

The SimplePing program in the preceding section is fine for checking to see if the user is connected to the Internet. At times, however, you may want to perform a ping similar to what the Windows PING utility provides. For example, you may want to check the speed of the connection to determine whether your applications will work properly. In that case you need to extract the desired information from the echo reply data.

The example for this section is called Ping2. It roughly emulates what the Windows PING utility does: pings a remote machine and displays the return echo time and the packet's time to live (TTL). Figure 16.2 shows the Ping2 program running.

FIGURE 16.2

The Ping2 program pings a server and displays portions of the echo reply.

I won't show the entire code listing for the Ping2 program because much of it is the same as the SimplePing program. Instead, I'll discuss the sections of code that show how to extract the echo reply information. The complete project can be found in the code for this chapter on the book's CD-ROM.

Earlier I discussed the icmp_echo_reply structure. The declaration for this structure looks like this:

```
struct icmp_echo_reply {
  IPAddr Address;                       // Replying address
  unsigned long Status;                 // Reply IP_STATUS
  unsigned long RoundTripTime;          // RTT in milliseconds
  unsigned short DataSize;              // Reply data size in bytes
  unsigned short Reserved;              // Reserved for system use
  void FAR *Data;                       // Pointer to the reply data
  struct ip_option_information Options; // Reply options
};
```

The comments after each data member in the structure explain what each is for. The Address member contains the address of the replying server. In most cases this address is the same one you sent when you performed the ping. In some cases it might be a different address (if the original address was redirected, for example). As you saw in the SimplePing example, the Status member contains status information. The RoundTripTime is the amount of time that has elapsed between the time the echo request was sent and the reply received. The Data and DataSize members are used when performing complex pings, such as a trace route. I am not using extra data in this and in the SimplePing examples. The Options member contains additional information in the form of an ip_option_information structure. That structure is declared as follows:

```
struct ip_option_information {
  unsigned char Ttl;                    // Time To Live
  unsigned char Tos;                    // Type Of Service
  unsigned char Flags;                  // IP header flags
```

```
unsigned char OptionsSize;        // Size in bytes of options data
unsigned char FAR *OptionsData;   // Pointer to options data
};
```

The only data member I use in the Ping2 program is the `Ttl` member.

As I have said, most of the code in the Ping2 program is identical to the SimplePing program. In the Ping2 program I set up a loop to ping the server three times:

```
for (int i=0;i<3;i++) {
  Application->ProcessMessages();
  // Call IcmpSendEcho().
  DWORD res = IcmpSendEcho(hIcmp,
    addr, 0, 0, 0, buff, size, 1500);
  if (!res) {
    Memo1->Lines->Add("Request timed out.");
    Sleep(1000);
    continue;
  }
  // code omitted
}
```

If `IcmpSendEcho()` returns 0, I add a status message to the main form's `Memo` component, indicating that the ping request timed out. I sleep for a second and then continue the loop. If `IcmpSendEcho()` returns a non-zero value, I check the value of the `Status` member of the `icmp_echo_reply` structure.

```
icmp_echo_reply reply;
memcpy(&reply, buff, sizeof(reply));
if (reply.Status> 0)
  Memo1->Lines->Add(
    ErrorStrings[reply.Status - 11000]);
```

I had previously declared an array of strings that correspond to the ping error codes:

```
String ErrorStrings[] = {
  "Error Base",
  "Buffer too small.",
  "Destination net unreachable.",
  "Destination host unreachable.",
  "Destination protocol unreachable.",
  "Destination port unreachable.",
  "Out of resources.",
  "Bad option.",
  "Hardware error.",
  "Packet too large.",
  "Request timed out.",
  "Bad request.",
```

```
    "Bad route.",
    "TTL expired in transit.",
    "TTL expired REASSEM.",
    "Param problem.",
    "Source quench.",
    "Option too large.",
    "Bad destination.",
    "Address deleted.",
    "Spec MNU change.",
    "MTU change.",
    "Unload"
};
```

This list of error strings corresponds directly to the list of error codes discussed in the previous section. The error values start at 11,000, so I subtract 11,000 from the Status value in order to get the corresponding string from the error message array.

If the Status value is 0, I extract the round trip time (RTT) and TTL values, build a string containing the information I want to display, and add it to the memo. After that, I sleep for a second and then continue the loop. Here's the code that performs those steps:

```
else {
  String rtt = reply.RoundTripTime;
  String ttl = reply.Options.Ttl;
  String S = "Reply from " + IPEdit->Text +
    " time=" + rtt + "ms TTL=" + ttl + "ms";
  Memo1->Lines->Add(S);
}
  Sleep(1000);
}
```

When this code executes, a text message is displayed in the Memo as shown in Figure 16.2.

For my money, performing a ping with ICMP.DLL is the way to go. Once you understand the basics of the ICMP functions, it takes very little code to ping a remote machine using ICMP.

Pinging with Raw Sockets

Probably the "safest" way to perform a ping is using WinSock and raw sockets. The reason pinging with raw sockets might be preferred over IcmpSendEcho() is due to the fact that ICMP.DLL might not be included with future versions of Windows. The drawback to using raw sockets is that it requires quite a bit more code. I won't explain how to ping using raw sockets because it is beyond the scope of this book. Instead, I'll refer you to a Microsoft example project called PING.C. If you have MSDN, search for *Ping: SOCK_RAW in WinSock 2.0*. If you don't have MSDN, search the Microsoft Web site for the same topic.

Connecting to the Internet with RAS

Most of the documentation you read on client-side Internet programming seems to assume that all users have T1 connections. Rarely is there any information on establishing a connection to the Internet on machines that use dial-up networking. The remainder of this chapter shows you how to use Microsoft's Remote Access Services (RAS) to establish a dial-up connection to the Internet.

RAS is the Windows service that handles Dial-Up Networking connections. On the client side, the primary task of RAS is to establish a connection to a remote machine, usually through a modem. Typically this means that RAS is dealing with a single connection (the modem). On the server side, RAS can be used to write a remote access server. A remote access server would be able to accept incoming calls, authenticate users, perform *callbacks* (where the server authenticates the user, hangs up, and calls the client machine back), and so on. A remote access server typically handles multiple connections through special multi-port or multi-modem hardware.

> **NOTE**
>
> The term *modem* is an acronym for modulator/demodulator, the process by which analog signals are converted to digital data (A/D) and back again (D/A). I use the term *modem* to refer to any device that is used to establish a connection to a remote machine. In this day and age, there are a host of digital devices that are called modems but don't perform modulation/demodulation. For example, an ISDN modem isn't really a modem at all since it deals only with digital signals. The same goes for cable modems, DSL modems, and similar devices. I will refer to both analog and digital devices with the term *modem*.

How you implement RAS depends on what your application does. Because most of you will write client-side applications, this chapter will focus on the client-side aspects of RAS. Writing a RAS server is not something you are likely to undertake and, as such, I don't cover the server-side capabilities of RAS.

Using RAS in Your Applications

The primary RAS API functions are located in Windows `RASAPI32.DLL`. When you build a C++Builder application that uses RAS, C++Builder will link the RAS library functions to your application. Due to the fact that static linking is involved, the application will load `RASAPI32.DLL` during application startup. That might sound good at first, but understand that your application will fail on startup when run on machines that don't have RAS installed. Consider this scenario: You have created an application that uses RAS to establish a dial-up connection. You have tested your application thoroughly on your development machine, on your co-workers' machines, and have conducted a beta test, all without incident. You deploy your application to the world, and suddenly you are getting reports from users that your application won't even start on a particular machine. What went wrong? You failed to consider that RAS is not installed on every Windows machine, even though those machines are fully Internet-enabled.

RAS is installed by default on most Win9x machines. RAS is not installed on NT machines, however, until you add a modem device to the system configuration. On my work machine, for example, I don't have RAS installed; I have a permanent Internet connection and have no need for Dial-Up Networking. Any application that statically links the RAS functions will fail to run on my machine.

If you absolutely, positively know that your application will only run on machines with Dial-Up Networking installed, you can take the easy road and simply allow C++Builder to statically link the RAS DLL. If there is any chance that your application might be run on machines that don't have RAS installed, you should opt for dynamic loading of the RAS DLLs. That means using `LoadLibrary()` to load the RAS DLLs, and getting `GetProcAddress()` to obtain function pointers to the RAS functions. I'll explain how to do this later in the sections that show you actual code. The point I want to drive home is that you should never assume that RAS is installed on all machines.

Another important aspect of RAS that you should be aware of is that Windows NT has many more RAS functions than do either Win95 or Win98. Further, Windows 2000 will provide more RAS functions than does Windows NT 4.0. At the time of this writing, Windows 2000 is still in beta (and will be for quite some time), so I won't attempt to cover the RAS functions specific to that operating system. The point is that you need to be aware of your target platform and program accordingly. The Win32 help file clearly states the operating systems that a particular RAS function supports. As you read this chapter you can assume that the functions I am discussing in a given section are for both WinNT and Win9x unless otherwise specifically stated.

> **CAUTION**
>
> The RAS headers that C++Builder provides include future support for Windows 2000. This is accomplished by use of the WINVER macro. In C++Builder 3, WINVER was defined as `0x400`. In C++Builder 4, however, WINVER is defined as `0x500`. Unless you are targeting Windows 2000 specifically, you will need to redefine the WINVER macro in order to avoid run-time errors. An example follows:
>
> ```
> #pragma warn -dup
> #define WINVER 0x400
> #include <ras.h>
> #define WINVER 0x500
> ```
>
> The first line in this code snippet suppresses the warning the compiler will issue when you redefine WINVER. The second line redefines WINVER to `0x400`. This will allow your C++Builder programs to work correctly on either WinNT or Win9x. The third line, naturally, includes the `RAS.H` header. The last line sets WINVER to its original value of `0x500`.

You need a bit more theory before I get into the sections that show you RAS code. Part of that theory deals with phonebooks and how RAS uses them.

Using Phonebooks

Windows uses phonebooks to store Dial-Up Networking information. A phonebook entry contains the parameters needed to establish a dial-up connection to a server. That information includes, but is not limited to, the following:

- The phonebook entry name
- The area code and phone number of the server to dial
- The country code of your current location
- The modem to use to dial
- The dial-up server type
- Scripting information
- Advanced configuration settings

Each of the individual 32-bit operating systems vary slightly in the connection information that phonebook entries contain. Windows NT, for example, allows you to specify the network protocols that the connection will support. NT also lets you specify a list of phone numbers to dial, whereas Win9x only lets you specify a single phone number.

Many users have only one phonebook entry, and that phonebook entry is typically the connection to their ISP. Other users will have multiple phonebook entries. For example, a user might have phonebook entries representing his ISP, his office network, CompuServe, AOL, and MSN. Full-featured RAS applications should allow the user to select the connection he or she wants to use when dialing. If your application connects to a dedicated server, then you may have to add a phonebook entry to represent that connection.

One other major difference exists regarding phonebooks in WinNT versus Win9x: Win9x contains a single phonebook, which is stored in the Registry, while Windows NT allows multiple phonebooks, which are stored in files. Phonebook files end with an extension of .PBK. The default system phonebook is called RASPHONE.PBK and is located in the WinNT\System32\ras subdirectory. (If you are interested, an NT phonebook file is nothing more than a text file in INI file format.) It is unlikely that you will have to deal with multiple phonebooks in your applications, but you need to know that the possibility exists that NT users may have more than one phonebook.

Your applications can manipulate phonebook entries in a variety of ways. One way is to display a dialog to the user and let him create, edit, or delete an entry. Windows has built-in dialogs you can invoke for this purpose. Figure 16.3 shows the Windows NT Dial-Up Networking configuration dialog.

FIGURE 16.3

Your applications can display a dialog allowing the user to change Dial-Up Networking settings.

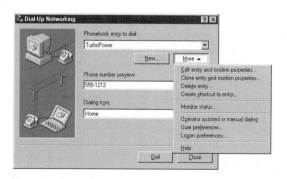

Applications written for all versions of Windows can call the RasCreatePhonebookEntry() function to allow the user to create a new phonebook entry. (If you are specifically targeting Windows NT, you should call RasEntryDlg() instead.) Calling RasCreatePhonebookEntry() under Windows Win9x will invoke the Make New Connection Wizard. Under Windows NT, calling RasCreatePhonebookEntry() will display the NT New Phonebook Entry dialog. The call to RasCreatePhonebookEntry() is trivial:

```
RasCreatePhonebookEntry(Handle, 0);
```

Internet Connection with C++Builder

CHAPTER 16

737

16

INTERNET
CONNECTION WITH
C++ BUILDER

The first parameter to this function is the handle of the Window that will act as the parent for the dialog. The second parameter is used to specify the phonebook to use. This parameter is ignored under Win9x because there is only one phonebook. Passing 0 for this parameter causes the default phonebook to be used on Windows NT systems.

Similarly, you can allow the user to edit a phonebook entry by calling the `RasEditPhonebookEntry()` function:

```
RasEditPhonebookEntry(Handle, 0, "TurboPower Local");
```

When this code executes, Windows displays a dialog allowing the user to change phonebook entry parameters. The name of the phonebook entry is passed in the last parameter to `RasEditPhonebookEntry()`. The string passed for this parameter must be the name of an existing phonebook entry. If the entry cannot be found, `RasEditPhonebookEntry()`returns `ERROR_CANNOT_FIND_PHONEBOOK_ENTRY`. Figure 16.4 shows the dialog displayed in Windows 95 when `RasEditPhonebookEntry()` is called.

FIGURE 16.4

Windows 95 users can edit a phonebook entry's properties.

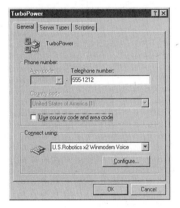

Windows NT allows you to create a phonebook entry without user intervention through the `RasSetEntryProperties()` function. If you want to add a phonebook entry silently in Win9x, you need to manually manipulate the Registry.

You can delete phonebook entries with the `RasDeleteEntry()` function and rename phonebook entries with the `RasRenameEntry()` function. You can change one or more phonebook entry parameters using the `RasSetEntryProperties()` >and `RasSetEntryDialParams()` functions. I don't anticipate these functions being widely used in your programs; I won't go into detail on their use.

The book's CD-ROM includes a program called RasPhonebook. This example allows you to create, edit, and delete phonebook entries. You can use the RasPhonebook program to see how the various RAS phonebook functions are used.

Dialing with RAS

Dialing the modem with RAS is relatively simple. Getting to the point where you are ready to dial, however, is where the real work comes in. An application that uses Dial-Up Networking properly should perform the following steps:

1. Determine whether the user is currently connected.

2. If the user is not connected, present a choice of phonebook entries the user wants to use to dial.

3. Dial the modem.

This section explains how to perform each of these steps. The example program I use is called RasDial. The program connects to the Internet via Dial-Up Networking and, optionally, downloads a file from the TurboPower Software FTP site. Status information is shown in a memo on the main form. The program has a second form that gets the phonebook entry from the user. Figure 16.5 shows the RasDial main form and Figure 16.6 shows the phonebook entry form.

FIGURE 16.5

The RasDial example program allows the user to connect to the Internet via Dial-Up Networking.

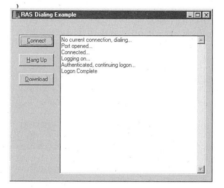

FIGURE 16.6

The PBEntries form allows the user to choose the phonebook entry used to establish a connection.

Internet Connection with C++Builder

CHAPTER 16

739

16

INTERNET
CONNECTION WITH
C++ BUILDER

First look at the code and then I'll explain how the code works. The main unit for the RasDial program is shown in Listings 16.3 and 16.4. I don't show the source or header for the PBEntries form because it contains no code other than what C++Builder generates. I don't discuss the code that downloads the file via FTP because it is standard code for using the TNMFTP component and doesn't require further explanation.

LISTING 16.3 THE HEADER FOR THE RASDIAL PROGRAM'S MAIN UNIT

```
#ifndef RasDialUH
#define RasDialUH

#include <Classes.hpp>
#include <Controls.hpp>
#include <StdCtrls.hpp>
#include <Forms.hpp>
#include <NMFtp.hpp>
#include <Psock.hpp>
#pragma warn -dup
#define WINVER 0x400
#include <ras.h>
#include <raserror.h>
#define WINVER 0x500

class TMainForm : public TForm
{
__published:      // IDE-managed Components
  TButton *ConnectBtn;
  TMemo *Memo1;
  TButton *HangUpBtn;
  TNMFTP *FTP;
  TButton *DownloadBtn;
  void __fastcall ConnectBtnClick(TObject *Sender);
  void __fastcall HangUpBtnClick(TObject *Sender);
  void __fastcall DownloadBtnClick(TObject *Sender);
  void __fastcall FTPConnect(TObject *Sender);
  void __fastcall FTPSuccess(TCmdType Trans_Type);
  void __fastcall FormCreate(TObject *Sender);
  void __fastcall FormDestroy(TObject *Sender);
private:      // User declarations
  HRASCONN hRas;
  bool AlreadyConnected;
  HRASCONN CheckForConnections();
  String GetPhoneBookEntry();
  void CheckRnaApp();
public:          // User declarations
  __fastcall TMainForm(TComponent* Owner);
};

extern PACKAGE TMainForm *MainForm;

#endif
```

LISTING 16.4   THE SOURCE CODE FOR THE RASDIAL PROGRAM'S MAIN UNIT

```cpp
#include <vcl.h>
#pragma hdrstop

#include "RasDialU.h"
#include "RasEntriesU.h"

#pragma resource "*.dfm"
TMainForm *MainForm;

typedef DWORD (__stdcall *pRasGetErrorString)(UINT, LPTSTR, DWORD);
typedef DWORD (__stdcall *pRasDial)(LPRASDIALEXTENSIONS, LPTSTR,
  LPRASDIALPARAMS, DWORD, LPVOID, LPHRASCONN);
typedef DWORD (__stdcall *pRasEnumConnections)
  (LPRASCONN, LPDWORD, LPDWORD);
typedef DWORD (__stdcall *pRasGetConnectStatus)
  (HRASCONN, LPRASCONNSTATUS);
typedef DWORD (__stdcall *pRasEnumEntries)(LPTSTR, LPTSTR,
  LPRASENTRYNAME, LPDWORD, LPDWORD);
typedef DWORD (__stdcall *pRasHangUp)(HRASCONN);


pRasGetErrorString fRasGetErrorString;
pRasDial fRasDial;
pRasEnumConnections fRasEnumConnections;
pRasGetConnectStatus fRasGetConnectStatus;
pRasEnumEntries fRasEnumEntries;
pRasHangUp fRasHangUp;
HINSTANCE hRasInstance;

VOID WINAPI RasCallback(HRASCONN hrasconn, UINT unMsg,
  RASCONNSTATE rascs, DWORD dwError, DWORD dwExtendedError)
{
  String S = "";
  if (dwError) {
    // Error occurred, show the error string.
    char buff[256];
    fRasGetErrorString(dwError, buff, sizeof(buff));
    MainForm->Memo1->Lines->Add(buff);
    return;
  }
  switch (rascs) {
    // Build a status string based on the
    // status message.
    case RASCS_PortOpened :
      S = "Port opened..."; break;
    case RASCS_DeviceConnected :
      S = "Connected..."; break;
    case RASCS_Authenticate :
      S = "Logging on..."; break;
    case RASCS_Authenticated :
```

```cpp
          S = "Authenticated, continuing logon..."; break;
      case RASCS_Connected : {
        S = "Logon Complete";
        MainForm->DownloadBtn->Enabled = true;
        break;
      }
      case RASCS_Disconnected :
        S = "Disconnected"; break;
    }
    // Show the status message in the memo.
    if (S != "")
      MainForm->Memo1->Lines->Add(S);
}

__fastcall TMainForm::TMainForm(TComponent* Owner)
  : TForm(Owner)
{
}

void __fastcall TMainForm::FormCreate(TObject *Sender)
{
  hRas = 0;
  hRasInstance = LoadLibrary("RASAPI32.DLL");
  if (!hRasInstance) {
    ShowMessage("Unable to load RAS DLL.");
    return;
  }
  fRasGetErrorString = (pRasGetErrorString)
    GetProcAddress(hRasInstance, "RasGetErrorStringA");
  fRasDial = (pRasDial)
    GetProcAddress(hRasInstance, "RasDialA");
  fRasEnumConnections = (pRasEnumConnections)
    GetProcAddress(hRasInstance, "RasEnumConnectionsA");
  fRasGetConnectStatus = (pRasGetConnectStatus)
    GetProcAddress(hRasInstance, "RasGetConnectStatusA");
  fRasEnumEntries = (pRasEnumEntries)
    GetProcAddress(hRasInstance, "RasEnumEntriesA");
  fRasHangUp = (pRasHangUp)
    GetProcAddress(hRasInstance, "RasHangUpA");
  if (!fRasGetErrorString || !fRasDial || !fRasEnumConnections ||
      !fRasGetConnectStatus || !fRasEnumEntries || !fRasHangUp) {
    ShowMessage("Error loading RAS functions");
  }
}

void __fastcall TMainForm::FormDestroy(TObject *Sender)
{
  // Terminate the connection if necessary
```

continues

LISTING 16.4   CONTINUED

```
  if (hRas && !AlreadyConnected)
    HangUpBtnClick(this);
  FreeLibrary(hRasInstance);
}

void __fastcall TMainForm::ConnectBtnClick(TObject *Sender)
{
  Memo1->Lines->Clear();
  // Check for existing connections.
  hRas = CheckForConnections();
  String PBEntry;
  if (hRas) {
    Memo1->Lines->Add("\r\nUsing existing connection...");
    Memo1->Lines->Add("\r\nClick the Download button to transfer files.");
    DownloadBtn->Enabled = true;
    AlreadyConnected = true;
    // No need to call RasDial for an existing connection.
    return;
  }
  else {
    // Get the phonebook entry to use to dial.
    PBEntry = GetPhoneBookEntry();
    if (PBEntry == "") {
      Memo1->Lines->Add("Dialing aborted\r\n");
      return;
    }
  }

  Memo1->Lines->Add("No current connection, dialing...");
  // Check for RNAAPP running in Win9x.
  CheckRnaApp();
  // Set up the connection params.
  RASDIALPARAMS params;
  params.dwSize = sizeof(params);
  strcpy(params.szEntryName, PBEntry.c_str());
  strcpy(params.szPhoneNumber, "");
  strcpy(params.szCallbackNumber, "");
  strcpy(params.szUserName, "");
  strcpy(params.szPassword, "");
  strcpy(params.szDomain, "*");
  // Dial.
  DWORD res = fRasDial(0, 0, &params, 1, RasCallback, &hRas);
  if (res) {
    char buff[256];
    fRasGetErrorString(res, buff, sizeof(buff));
    Memo1->Lines->Add(buff);
  }
  else
    HangUpBtn->Enabled = true;
```

Internet Connection with C++Builder

CHAPTER 16

743

16

INTERNET
CONNECTION WITH
C++ BUILDER

```
}

HRASCONN TMainForm::CheckForConnections()
{
  char buff[256];
  RASCONN rc;
  rc.dwSize = sizeof(RASCONN);
  DWORD numConns;
  DWORD size = rc.dwSize;
  // Enumerate the connections.
  DWORD res = fRasEnumConnections(&rc, &size, &numConns);
  if (!res && numConns == 0)
    // No connections, return 0.
    return 0;
  if (res) {
    // Error. Report it.
    fRasGetErrorString(res, buff, sizeof(buff));
    Memo1->Lines->Add(buff);
  } else {
    // Get the connection status.
    RASCONNSTATUS status;
    status.dwSize = sizeof(status);
    res = fRasGetConnectStatus(rc.hrasconn, &status);
    if (res) {
      // Error. Report it.
      fRasGetErrorString(res, buff, sizeof(buff));
      Memo1->Lines->Add(buff);
      return 0;
    } else {
      // Found connection, show details.
      if (status.rasconnstate == RASCS_Connected) {
        Memo1->Lines->Add("Existing connection found:");
        Memo1->Lines->Add("     Device type: " +
          String(rc.szDeviceType));
        Memo1->Lines->Add("     Device name: " +
          String(rc.szDeviceName));
        Memo1->Lines->Add("     Connected to: " +
          String(rc.szEntryName));
        return rc.hrasconn;
      } else {
        // A connection was detected but its
        // status is RASCS_Disconnected.
        Memo1->Lines->Add("Connection Error");
        return 0;
      }
    }
  }
  return 0;
}
```

continues

LISTING 16.4   CONTINUED

```cpp
String TMainForm::GetPhoneBookEntry()
{
  RASENTRYNAME* entries = new RASENTRYNAME;
  entries->dwSize = sizeof(RASENTRYNAME);
  DWORD numEntries;
  DWORD size = entries->dwSize;
  DWORD res = fRasEnumEntries(0, 0, entries, &size, &numEntries);
  if (numEntries == 1) {
    String entryName = entries->szEntryName;
    delete entries;
    return entryName;
  }

  if (res == ERROR_BUFFER_TOO_SMALL) {
    // allocate enough memory to get all the phonebook entries
    delete entries;
    entries = new RASENTRYNAME[numEntries];
    entries[0].dwSize = sizeof(RASENTRYNAME);
    res = fRasEnumEntries(0, 0, entries, &size, &numEntries);
    if (res) {
      char buff[256];
      fRasGetErrorString(res, buff, sizeof(buff));
      ShowMessage(buff);
    }
  }
  TPBEntriesForm* form = new TPBEntriesForm(this);
  for (int i=0;i<(int)numEntries;i++)
    form->EntriesCb->Items->Add(entries[i].szEntryName);
  form->EntriesCb->ItemIndex = 0;
  String S;
  if (form->ShowModal() == mrCancel)
    S = "";
  else
    S = form->EntriesCb->Text;
  delete form;
  delete[] entries;
  return S;
}

void __fastcall TMainForm::HangUpBtnClick(TObject *Sender)
{
  Memo1->Lines->Add("\r\nHanging up...");
  if (!hRas)
    return;
  // Hang up.
  fRasHangUp(hRas);
  // Be sure the RAS state machine has cleared.
  DWORD res = 0;
```

Internet Connection with C++Builder

CHAPTER 16

745

16

INTERNET
CONNECTION WITH
C++ BUILDER

```cpp
    while (res != ERROR_INVALID_HANDLE) {
      RASCONNSTATUS status;
      status.dwSize = sizeof(status);
      res = fRasGetConnectStatus(hRas, &status);
      Sleep(0);
    }
    AlreadyConnected = false;
    hRas = 0;
    Memo1->Lines->Add("\r\nDisconnected");
    DownloadBtn->Enabled = false;
    HangUpBtn->Enabled = false;
}

void __fastcall TMainForm::DownloadBtnClick(TObject *Sender)
{
  FTP->Connect();
}

void __fastcall TMainForm::FTPConnect(TObject *Sender)
{
  Memo1->Lines->Add("Connected to TurboPower FTP Site");
  FTP->ChangeDir("pub");
}

void __fastcall TMainForm::FTPSuccess(TCmdType Trans_Type)
{
  switch (Trans_Type) {
    case cmdChangeDir : {
      Memo1->Lines->Add("Changed directory");
      FTP->Download("00index.txt", "00index.txt");
      break;
    }
    case cmdDownload : {
      Memo1->Lines->Add("File downloaded!");
      break;
    }
  }
}

void TMainForm::CheckRnaApp()
{
  if (Win32Platform == VER_PLATFORM_WIN32_NT)
    // RNAAPP is only Win9x
    return;
  HWND hWnd = FindWindow("RnaEngClass", 0);
  if (hWnd) {
    // Found it, kill it.
    PostMessage(hWnd, WM_CLOSE, 0, 0);
    // Delay a bit for good measure.
    Sleep(2000);
  }
}
```

In the following sections I explain how various RAS operations work and show the code that pertains to those operations. (I don't show all of the error-handling code from Listing 16.2 because it complicates the code examples and the corresponding text.)

Dynamically Loading the RAS DLL

You should load the RAS DLL dynamically in order to avoid problems when your application is run on machines that don't have RAS installed. The code at the top of the main form's source in Listing 16.4 sets up function pointers for the functions that RasDial uses. For example, here is the typedef and function pointer declaration for the RasDial() function:

```
typedef DWORD (__stdcall *pRasDial)(LPRASDIALEXTENSIONS, LPTSTR,
  LPRASDIALPARAMS,  DWORD, LPVOID, LPHRASCONN);
```

This code sets up a typedef to represent the RasDial() function. The name of the type is pRasDial. Later, I declare a variable called fRasDial of type pRasDial:

```
pRasDial fRasDial;
```

I do the same for each of the RAS functions the program uses. In the FormCreate() method I load the RAS DLL and assign values to the function pointers. Here's the code that loads RASAPI32.DLL:

```
hRasInstance = LoadLibrary("RASAPI32.DLL");
if (!hRasInstance) {
  ShowMessage("Unable to load RAS DLL.");
  return;
}
```

The call to LoadLibrary() loads the RAS DLL and assigns its HINSTANCE to the form's hRasInstance variable. If the call to LoadLibrary() fails, I display a message to the user and return. At this point I might as well close the program because none of the rest of the program will work if RAS is not installed. Remember, your own Internet client programs may still work if RAS is not installed because the user may have a permanent Internet connection.

If the call to LoadLibrary() succeeds, I can then use GetProcAddress() to get the addresses of the RAS functions I intend to call. For example

```
fRasDial = (pRasDial)
  GetProcAddress(hRasInstance, "RasDialA");
```

This code gets the address of the RasDialA() function in RASAPI32.DLL and stores it in the fRasDial variable. Later I will use the fRasDial variable to call the RasDial() function.

NOTE

You might be wondering why I am getting the address of the function called RasDialA() rather than RasDial(). Technically, there is no function called RasDial() in RASAPI32.DLL. Instead, there are two functions: RasDialA() and RasDialW(). This is standard Windows fare for dealing with single-byte and multi-byte installations of Windows. The RasDialA() function is used for Windows installations that use single-byte character sets and RasDialW() is used for multi-byte operating systems. You will find the following somewhere in RAS.H:

```
#ifdef UNICODE
#define RasDial RasDialW
// other defines omitted
#else
#define RasDial RasDialA
```

If UNICODE is defined (for multi-byte character sets), then the RasDial macro is set to RasDialW, otherwise it is set to RasDialA. As you can see, RasDial is simply a macro and not a real function at all. If you are writing programs for multi-byte versions of Windows, you will want to load RasDialW() instead of RasDialA().

In the form's OnDestroy event handler I unload RASAPI32.DLL with a call to FreeLibrary():

```
FreeLibrary(hRasInstance);
```

I'll admit that all this messing around with function pointers—LoadLibrary(), GetProcAddress(), and FreeLibrary()—is a bit cumbersome. You will have to take this approach if you are going to write applications that will work on all machines.

NOTE

The RasDial example shows you how to dial with RAS. It does not, however, illustrate how to write an Internet client that handles both dial-up and permanent Internet connections. Your applications should detect whether the user has a permanent connection or is using Dial-Up Networking and automatically handle the connection based on the connection type.

Detecting a Connection

The next step is to detect whether the user is currently connected to the Internet via Dial-Up Networking. If the user is already connected to the Internet, you don't need to dial the modem. For example, I typically connect to the Internet and then use any of several Internet-enabled applications such as my email client, a Web browser, or a newsreader. An Internet-enabled application should be prepared to use an existing connection if one exists.

The RasDial program's `ConnectBtnClick()` method performs the following:

1. Checks for an existing connection and uses the connection if it exists.
2. Gets a phonebook entry from the user if no connection exists.
3. Dials the modem using the phonebook entry selected by the user.

The following is an abridged version of the `ConnectBtnClick()` method:

```
void __fastcall TMainForm::ConnectBtnClick(TObject *Sender)
{
  hRas = CheckForConnections();
  String PBEntry;
  if (hRas) {
    // No need to call RasDial for an existing connection.
    return;
  }
  else {
    // Get the phonebook entry to use to dial.
    PBEntry = GetPhoneBookEntry();
  }
  // Dial
  DWORD res = fRasDial(0, 0, &params, 1, RasCallback, &hRas);
}
```

The code that is pertinent to this section is the call to the form's `CheckForConnections()` method:

```
hRas = CheckForConnections();
```

This function returns the handle to an existing connection; it returns 0 if no connection is detected. The rest of the code in this section is from the RasDial program's `CheckForConnections()` method.

You check for existing connections using the `RasEnumConnections()` function:

```
RASCONN rc;
rc.dwSize = sizeof(RASCONN);
DWORD numConns;
DWORD size = rc.dwSize;
DWORD res = fRasEnumConnections(&rc, &size, &numConns);
```

Internet Connection with C++Builder

CHAPTER 16

749

16

INTERNET
CONNECTION WITH
C++ BUILDER

First I declare an instance of the RASCONN structure and set its dwSize member to the size of a RASCONN structure. This is standard Windows modus operandi. Setting the dwSize member allows Windows to perform a version check, ensuring that the structure being passed to RasEnumConnections() is the correct size. Next, I declare a variable called numConns. This variable will contain the number of active connections when RasEnumConnections() returns. I also declare a variable called size and set it to the size of a RASCONN structure. Finally, I call RasEnumConnections(), passing the address of the RASCONN structure in the first parameter, the address of the size variable in the second parameter, and the address of the numConns variable in the final parameter. (Remember, the fRasEnumConnections variable is a pointer to the RasEnumConnections() function in the RAS DLL.) If RasEnumConnections() returns 0, the function call succeeded. The rc variable will contain the connection information and the numConns variable will contain the number of active connections.

RasEnumConnections() might fail for any number of reasons, but the most common is that the buffer passed in the first parameter is too small. Let me explain, since understanding how RAS deals with multiple connections will have benefit later on.

A particular machine may be capable of maintaining multiple connections. For example, a user may have a cable modem connection and may also be connected via a conventional modem. If RasEnumConnections() returns ERROR_BUFFER_TOO_SMALL (decimal 603), then there are likely multiple connections and RAS could not return all of the data for the connections in the single instance of the RASCONN structure passed in. If that happens, the size variable passed to RasEnumConnections() will contain the required buffer size, and the numConns variable will contain the number of active connections. You must allocate a new buffer of the required size and call RasEnumConnections() again. The RasDial program does not account for multiple connections. If it did, the code would look like this:

```
if (res == ERROR_BUFFER_TOO_SMALL) {
  RASCONN* rc = new RASCONN[numConns];
  rc[0].dwSize = sizeof(RASCONN);
  size = sizeof(RASCONN) * numConns;
  res = fRasEnumConnections(rc, &size, &numConns);
  // decide what connection to use
  delete[] rc;
}
```

This code simply allocates an array of RASCONN structures, based on the number of connections detected. It then sets the dwSize member of the first structure in the array to the size of a RASCONN structure. You are required to set the dwSize member of the first structure in the array, but not for every structure in the array. It then sets the size variable to

the new buffer size and calls `RasEnumConnections()` again. When
`RasEnumConnections()` returns, the array of structures will be filled with the connection
information for each active connection. This scenario is very common in Windows API
programming. It's as if Windows is saying, "Try to call the function. I'll let you know if
you need to allocate more memory. Once you have allocated more memory, call the
function again."

Now let's get back to the `CheckForConnections()` function. If the `numConns` variable
contains 0 after calling `RasEnumConnections()`, there are no active connections. I
return 0:

```
if (!res && numConns == 0)
  // No connections, return 0.
  return 0;
```

I know I have an active connection if `numConns` is not 0. I then check the connection state
by calling the `RasGetConnectStatus()` function:

```
// Get the connection status.
RASCONNSTATUS status;
status.dwSize = sizeof(status);
res = fRasGetConnectStatus(rc.hrasconn, &status);
```

First I declare an instance of the `RASCONNSTATUS` structure and, as always, set its `dwSize`
member. I then call `RasGetConnectionStatus()`, passing the `hrasconn` member of the
`RASCONN` structure in the first parameter. This is the handle to the connection detected by
the earlier call to `RasEnumConnections()`. The second parameter of
`RasGetConnnectionStatus()` is the address of the `RASCONNSTATUS` structure.

If `RasGetConnectionStatus()` returns successfully, I check the value of the `RAS-CONNSTATUS` structure's `rasconnstate` member to determine the connection state:

```
if (status.rasconnstate == RASCS_Connected) {
```

If the connection is active, the connection state will be `RASCS_Connected`. If the connection status is not `RASCS_Connected`, the connection could be inactive (the user just disconnected) or the connection could be in one of the various stages of logging onto the
remote machine.

If the connection status is `RASCS_Connected`, I extract connection information from the `RAS-CONN` structure's various members and display that information in the main form's memo:

```
Memo1->Lines->Add("Existing connection found:");
Memo1->Lines->Add("    Device type: " +
 String(rc.szDeviceType));
Memo1->Lines->Add("    Device name: " +
  String(rc.szDeviceName));
```

Internet Connection with C++Builder

CHAPTER **16**

751

16

INTERNET
CONNECTION WITH
C++ BUILDER

```
Memo1->Lines->Add("      Connected to: " +
  String(rc.szEntryName));
```

I then return the handle to the connection:

```
return rc.hrasconn;
```

The `ConnectBtnClick()` method that calls `CheckForConnections()` takes appropriate action based on whether a valid connection handle was returned or whether 0 was returned. If no existing connection was detected, the RasDial program displays a list of phonebook entries to the user so that a dial-up connection can be established.

Enumerating Phonebook Entries

A well-designed, Internet-enabled application gives the user a choice of phonebook entries used to dial the modem. That means that you must enumerate the phonebook entries and present the list of entries to the user. When the user has selected a phonebook entry, you can use that entry to dial the modem.

The function in the RasDial program that enumerates entries in the phonebook is called `GetPhoneBookEntry()`. The function returns a string containing the name of the phonebook entry. It enumerates entries using the `RasEnumEntries()` function. In one regard, this function works in much the same way as the `RasEnumConnections()` function—you try to call the function and see if you have allocated enough memory to hold all the phonebook entries. If you haven't allocated enough memory, allocate more memory and call the function again. First look at the code that calls `RasEnumEntries()` on the initial attempt:

```
RASENTRYNAME* entries = new RASENTRYNAME;
entries->dwSize = sizeof(RASENTRYNAME);
DWORD numEntries;
DWORD size = entries->dwSize;
DWORD res = fRasEnumEntries(0, 0, entries, &size, &numEntries);
```

The initial attempt at getting the phonebook entries assumes that there is only one entry and that a single `RASENTRYNAME` structure will be enough to hold the entry. The parameters passed to `RasEnumEntries()` are nearly identical to those passed to `RasEnumConnections()` discussed earlier. The first parameter is reserved and must be set to 0. The second parameter is used to specify the phonebook and is usually 0 (the default phonebook). The third parameter is a pointer to the buffer that will contain the entry information when `RasEnumEntries()` returns. The fourth parameter is used to specify the size of the buffer. If `RasEnumEntries()` fails with an `ERROR_BUFFER_TOO_SMALL` error, the size variable will contain the number of bytes RAS requires to enumerate all entries. The final parameter is a pointer to a `DWORD` value that will contain the number of entries in the phonebook when `RasEnumEntries()` returns.

If the initial call to `RasEnumEntries()` succeeds, there is either a single entry in the phonebook or no entry at all. The name of the phonebook entry is returned from the `GetPhonebookEntry()` function if the `numEntries` variable is 1:

```
if (numEntries == 1) {
  String entryName = entries->szEntryName;
  delete entries;
  return entryName;
}
```

If there is only one phonebook entry, the RasDial program uses that entry to dial the modem without further intervention by the user. (The form enumerating the phonebook entries is never shown.) If more than one phonebook entry is found, a dialog is displayed to the user so that he or she can select the phonebook entry used to dial.

> **TIP**
>
> When experimenting with the RasDial program, you may want to add a few extra phonebook entries to your system. That will allow you to test the code that enumerates multiple phonebook entries.

If the initial call to `RasEnumEntries()` fails with an error code of `ERROR_BUFFER_TOO_SMALL`, there are multiple phonebook entries. In that case, I allocate more memory based on the number of entries (as indicated by the `numEntries` variable). This is another one of those cases of, "Oops, the buffer isn't big enough. Try again." Here's the code that reallocates memory and then calls `RasEnumEntries()` again:

```
if (res == ERROR_BUFFER_TOO_SMALL) {
  // allocate enough memory to get all the phonebook entries
  delete entries;
  entries = new RASENTRYNAME[numEntries];
  entries[0].dwSize = sizeof(RASENTRYNAME);
  res = fRasEnumEntries(0, 0, entries, &size, &numEntries);
}
```

Note that I set the `dwSize` member of the first structure in the array to the size of a `RASENTRYNAME` structure. I then call `RasEnumEntries()` again.

You might think that in order to avoid allocating, freeing, and reallocating memory you could initially create an array of `RASENTRYNAME` structures large enough to hold all the entries the first time you call `RasEnumEntries()`. What is large enough? You might think that allocating space for five phonebook entries is enough; then you run into a user who has six phonebook entries and your application breaks. You could create an array of 256

Internet Connection with C++Builder

CHAPTER 16

753

16

INTERNET
CONNECTION WITH
C++ BUILDER

phonebook entries, but that would be gross memory misuse. The code presented here is robust enough to handle any number of phonebook entries without risking run-time errors and never allocates any more memory than necessary.

If `RasEnumEntries()` succeeds on the second attempt, you have a list of phonebook entries from which the user can select. In the case of the RasDial program, I decided to show a dialog with a combo box containing the phonebook entries. The entry selection form contains no code because all the work is done from the `GetPhonebookEntry()` function. Here's how the code looks:

```
TPBEntriesForm* form = new TPBEntriesForm(this);
for (int i=0;i<(int)numEntries;i++)
  form->EntriesCb->Items->Add(entries[i].szEntryName);
form->EntriesCb->ItemIndex = 0;
String S;
if (form->ShowModal() == mrCancel)
  S = "";
else
  S = form->EntriesCb->Text;
```

For the RasDial program, I chose not to auto-create the PBEntries form. Instead, I create it only when necessary and delete it immediately after I am done with it. After I have created the form, I execute a loop to run through the array of `RASENTRYNAME` structures. I add the value of the `szEntryName` member of each structure in the array to the combo box on the PBEntries form. (A `RASENTRYNAME` structure contains the `szEntryName` and the ever-present `dwSize` member.) I then show the PBEntries form by calling its `ShowModal()` method. If the user presses the Cancel button on the form, I set the temporary variable S to an empty string. If the user presses the OK button, I set the variable S to the combo box's `Text` property. Windows gave me the names of the phonebook entries when I enumerated the entries, so I know that the combo box's `Text` property contains a valid phonebook entry name. All that's left to do at this point is clean up and return the phonebook entry string:

```
delete form;
delete[] entries;
return S;
```

Now we can get back to the `ConnectBtnClick()` method and the act of dialing the modem.

Dialing the Modem

At this point in the RasDial program I have established that the user is not connected and I have obtained a phonebook entry name and am ready to dial the modem. Before I explain the code used to dial the modem, I want to explain how the `RasDial()` function works.

RasDial() can be called either synchronously or asynchronously. If RasDial() is called *synchronously*, control will not be returned to the calling application until after the connection is fully established. If RasDial() is called *asynchronously*, control returns immediately to the calling program while dialing is taking place. The connection mode (synchronous or asynchronous) is determined by the fifth parameter of RasDial(). First, look at the declaration for RasDial():

```
DWORD RasDial(
  LPRASDIALEXTENSIONS lpRasDialExtensions,
  LPTSTR lpszPhonebook,
  LPRASDIALPARAMS lpRasDialParams,
  DWORD dwNotifierType,
  LPVOID lpvNotifier,
  LPHRASCONN lphRasConn
);
```

The first two parameters of RasDial() are specific to NT and should be set to 0 unless you are explicitly targeting NT. The third parameter is a pointer to a RASDIALPARAM structure (which I will explain in just a bit).

The fourth and fifth parameters are used to specify the type and the address of a RAS callback function. The callback function is called periodically as RAS carries out the dialing operation. RasDial() executes synchronously if this parameter is 0; no callback function is specified. If a callback function is provided, RasDial() executes asynchronously. I will explain the use of the callback function in the next section. The last parameter is used to return the RAS connection handle when RasDial() returns successfully. This handle is used in subsequent RAS calls.

Now look at how I initiate a connection in the ConnectBtnClick() method. Before I call RasDial(), I declare an instance of the RASDIALPARAMS structure and fill in its members:

```
RASDIALPARAMS params;
params.dwSize = sizeof(params);
strcpy(params.szEntryName, PBEntry.c_str());
strcpy(params.szPhoneNumber, "");
strcpy(params.szCallbackNumber, "");
strcpy(params.szUserName, "");
strcpy(params.szPassword, "");
strcpy(params.szDomain, "*");
```

Some explanation of each of the members of the RASDIALPARAMS structure is required. As you can deduce from this code, each of the members of this structure are character arrays (other than the dwSize member, of course). These are not char pointers, but char arrays ranging in size from 128 to 256 bytes (with the exception of the szDomain member, which has a size of 16 bytes). Because the members are character arrays, I use strcpy() to assign values to them.

The szEntryName member is a text string containing the phonebook entry that will be dialed. This entry was obtained in the previous call to GetPhonebookEntry(). If this parameter is an empty string, RAS will perform a simple dial on the first available port. You won't have Dial-Up Networking at that point, just a connection to a modem on the other end.

The szPhoneNumber parameter is set to an empty string with the exception of two cases. The first case is when you are performing a simple dial as explained in the previous paragraph. If the szEntryName parameter is an empty string, you must specify the phone number to dial in the szPhoneNumber parameter. The second case is when you want to override the phone number in the phonebook entry. If szPhoneNumber is empty, the phonebook entry's phone number will be used.

The szCallbackNumber parameter is used in cases where the RAS server (on the remote machine) hangs up and calls the client machine back. Callback only works if the RAS server has set callback permissions for the client machine.

The szUserName and szPassword are the username and password used to log onto the remote machine. If you want to specifically set the username and password, you can do so by filling in these members of the RASDIALPARAMS structure before calling RasDial(). You can specify the username, the password, or both. Either szUserName or szPassword can contain empty strings. How RAS operates in this case depends on whether the client machine is a Windows NT machine or a Win9x machine. If the client machine is running Windows NT, RAS sends the currently logged-on user's username and password to the RAS server. If the client machine is Windows 95 or 98, a dialog with prompts for the username, the password, or both is displayed to the user.

Finally, we get to the point where we can actually dial the modem. This is done with the RasDial() function:

```
DWORD res = fRasDial(0, 0, &params, 1, RasCallback, &hRas);
```

I pass 0 for the first two parameters because they are NT–specific. The third parameter is the address of the RASDIALPARAMS structure. The fourth parameter is the type of callback function I am using, and the fifth parameter is a pointer to the callback function. For the sixth and final parameter, I pass the address of the variable that will receive the RAS handle if RasDial() returns successfully.

Because I am using a callback function, RasDial() executes asynchronously and Windows returns control to my application immediately after RAS starts the dialing operation. That leads us to the next subject: dealing with the callback function.

Using the RAS Callback Function

RAS provides three types of callback functions. The basic RAS callback, called a
RasDialFunc() callback, is declared as follows:

```
VOID WINAPI RasDialFunc(
  UINT unMsg, RASCONNSTATE rasconnstate, DWORD dwError);
```

The unMsg parameter indicates the RAS message being sent to the callback. At this time,
the only RAS message Windows sends is WM_RASDIALEVENT, so you won't have any reason to check the value of this parameter in the current incarnations of Windows. The
rasconnstate parameter is one of the RASCS_ connection state values. The connection
state parameters you are most likely to be interested in are RASCS_Connected,
RASCS_Disconnected, RASCS_DeviceConnected, RASCS_PortOpened,
RASCS_Authenticate, and RASCS_Authenticated. See RAS.H for a complete list of the
possible connection state values. The dwError parameter indicates success or failure of a
particular RAS state. If dwError is 0, no error occurred. If dwError is a non-zero value,
an error occurred during a particular state.

The second type of RAS callback, RasDialFunc1(), is declared like this:

```
VOID WINAPI RasDialFunc1(HRASCONN hrasconn, UINT unMsg,
  RASCONNSTATE rascs, DWORD dwError, DWORD dwExtendedError);
```

As you can see, this type of callback provides you with more information than does the
first callback type discussed. The additional parameters in a RasDialFunc1() callback
are the handle to the RAS connection (hrasconn) as returned by RasDial(), and the
extended error information (dwExtendedError).

The third callback type is called RasDialFunc2(). Here is that declaration:

```
DWORD WINAPI RasDialFunc2(
  DWORD dwCallbackId, DWORD dwSubEntry, HRASCONN hrasconn,
  UINT unMsg, RASCONNSTATE rascs, DWORD dwError, DWORD dwExtendedError);
```

The RasDialFunc2() callback is only used with Windows NT, so I won't discuss its
specifics.

I decided to use a RasDialFunc1() callback for the RasDial program. As it turns out, I
could have used a RasDialFunc() because the only parameters I am using are the rascs
parameter and the dwError parameter. Here is the RasDial program's RAS callback function:

```
VOID WINAPI RasCallback(HRASCONN hrasconn, UINT unMsg,
  RASCONNSTATE rascs, DWORD dwError, DWORD dwExtendedError)
{
```

Internet Connection with C++Builder

CHAPTER 16

757

16

INTERNET
CONNECTION WITH
C++ BUILDER

```
String S = "";
if (dwError) {
  // Error occurred, show the error string.
  char buff[256];
  fRasGetErrorString(dwError, buff, sizeof(buff));
  MainForm->Memo1->Lines->Add(buff);
  return;
}
switch (rascs) {
  // Build a status string based on the
  // status message.
  case RASCS_PortOpened :
    S = "Port opened..."; break;
  case RASCS_DeviceConnected :
    S = "Connected..."; break;
  case RASCS_Authenticate :
    S = "Logging on..."; break;
  case RASCS_Authenticated :
    S = "Authenticated, continuing logon..."; break;
  case RASCS_Connected : {
    S = "Logon Complete";
    MainForm->DownloadBtn->Enabled = true;
    break;
  }
  case RASCS_Disconnected :
    S = "Disconnected"; break;
}
// Show the status message in the memo.
if (S != "")
  MainForm->Memo1->Lines->Add(S);
}
```

There's not much point explaining this code because the code mostly adds a status string
to the memo on the main form based on the connection state. Note that the RAS callback
must be a standalone function; it cannot be a member of the form's class. As such, I have
to specifically reference the memo through the main form's pointer:

```
MainForm->Memo1->Lines->Add(S);
```

For the RasDial program, I chose to use a memo to display the status information. In a
real-world application I would probably show status information in a dialog or in the status bar.

Terminating the Connection

The only aspect of the RasDial program left to discuss is the act of hanging up the
modem. This is accomplished by calling the RasHangUp() function, passing the handle to
the RAS connection:

```
fRasHangUp(hRas);
```

Remember, the RAS handle might have been obtained as a result of enumerating active connections, or might have been returned as a result of calling `RasDial()`.

RAS takes a few milliseconds to terminate the dial-up connection. After you call `RasHangUp()`, you should enter a loop that checks to see if the connection was actually terminated before your application continues:

```
DWORD res = 0;
while (res != ERROR_INVALID_HANDLE) {
  RASCONNSTATUS status;
  status.dwSize = sizeof(status);
  res = fRasGetConnectStatus(hRas, &status);
  Sleep(0);
}
```

This code isn't particularly smart in that it doesn't completely eliminate the possibility that the application could hang in this loop. Its purpose, though, is to show you how to ensure that the RAS state machine has cleared before continuing with your application.

Microsoft documentation on `RasHangup()` indicates that it may take from one to two seconds for the RAS state machine to clear after calling `RasHangup()`. A quick and dirty solution would be to simply call the following after calling `RasHangup()`:

```
Sleep(3000);
```

Dealing with `RNAAPP.EXE` in Win9x

You should be aware of one other aspect of establishing a dial-up connection under Win9x systems: Windows connections are managed by an application called `RNAAPP.EXE`. When you establish a Dial-Up Networking connection, `RNAAPP` is loaded into memory. When you terminate a dial-up connection, `RNAAPP` is not immediately unloaded from memory. Windows keeps it around in case another dial-up connection is needed. Windows will eventually unload `RNAAPP` from memory, but there's no telling when that will occur.

In some cases, initiating a dial-up connection with RAS results in an error, indicating that the port is in use. This is because Windows has `RNAAPP` open and it is in a questionable state. The solution is to terminate `RNAAPP` programmatically before dialing with RAS. This is much less a problem when dialing with RAS as it is when dialing directly through the modem using the Windows API. Still, it can happen.

Internet Connection with C++Builder

CHAPTER 16

759

16

INTERNET
CONNECTION WITH
C++ BUILDER

The RasDial program has a routine called `CheckRnaApp()`. This function checks for the existence of RNAAPP and, if found, terminates it. Here's the `CheckRnaApp()` function:

```
void TMainForm::CheckRnaApp()
{
  if (Win32Platform == VER_PLATFORM_WIN32_NT)
    // RNAAPP is only Win9x
    return;
  HWND hWnd = FindWindow("RnaEngClass", 0);
  if (hWnd) {
    // Found it, kill it.
    PostMessage(hWnd, WM_CLOSE, 0, 0);
    // Delay a bit for good measure.
    Sleep(2000);
  }
}
```

The first few lines check to see if the operating system is Windows NT using the VCL `Win32Platform` global variable. If the OS is Windows NT, then the function returns without doing anything further. If the OS is Win9x, I call `FindWindow()` passing the class name for RNAAPP.EXE, which is `RnaEngClass`. If `FindWindow()` returns a window handle, I send the window a `WM_CLOSE` message to terminate RNAAPP. `CheckRnaApp()` is a simple function, but one that I have found useful. I'd rather not depend on Windows to do the right thing, so I typically kill RNAAPP prior to dialing the modem.

Summary

This chapter covers some of the aspects of Internet programming that you must understand before you can deploy your Internet-enabled applications. Detecting a connection to the Internet is the first step. That is why understanding how to ping a remote machine is important. If no connection exists, you must know how to connect to the Internet using Dial-Up Networking through RAS. Some Windows systems have auto-dial enabled, but you can't count on that to be the case for every one of your users. Don't assume that your users are all using Win9x with auto-dial enabled. Further, never count on the operating system to do your work for you. A robust Internet client application will try to account for all possible user configurations and know how to handle each gracefully.

The WebBroker: CGI and ISAPI

by Bob Swart (aka Dr. Bob)

IN THIS CHAPTER

The C++Builder 4 WebBroker Technology consists of a Web Server Application Wizard and Database Web Application Wizard, together with the TWebModule, TWebDispatcher, TWebRequest, TWebResponse, TPageProducer, TDataSetPageProducer, TDataSetTableProducer, and TQueryTableProducer components.

The two WebBroker wizards and components are found in C++Builder 4 Enterprise. At this time, they will not become available as separate add-on packages for C++Builder 4 Professional users.

In this chapter you'll find that the terms *WebBroker* and *Web module* are used to refer to the same thing. Actually, the WebBroker could be seen as a part of the entire Web module (the Action Dispatcher, to be precise), but for the purpose of this chapter you can assume that both terms refer to the entire collection of wizards, components, and support classes.

The WebBroker technology allows you to build ISAPI/NSAPI, CGI, or WinCGI Web server applications without having to worry about too many low-level details. In fact, to the developer, the development of the Web module application is virtually the same no matter what kind of Web server application is being developed (you can even change from one type to another during development, as you'll see later on).

Specifically, the Web Bridge allows developers to use a single API for both Microsoft ISAPI (all versions) and Netscape NSAPI (up to version 3), so you don't have to concern yourself with the differences between these APIs. Moreover, Web server applications are non-visual applications (that is, they run on the Web server, but the user interface is represented by the client using a Web browser), and yet the Web module wizards and components offer us design-time support, compared to writing non-visual C++ code.

Starting the Web Server Application Wizard

The basic Web Server Application Wizard can be found in the Repository, ready to be selected after you choose File, New, as shown in Figure 17.1.

If you start the Web Server Application Wizard, you can specify what kind of Web server application you need: CGI, WinCGI, or the default choice, ISAPI/NSAPI (see Figure 17.2).

FIGURE 17.1

You can find the Web Server Application Wizard in the Object Repository (New Items) window.

FIGURE 17.2

You can specify what kind of Web server application you need from the New Web Server Application dialog.

Let's briefly examine the three different types of Web Server application options and compare them.

ISAPI/NSAPI

ISAPI (Microsoft IIS) or NSAPI (Netscape) Web server extension DLLs are just like WinCGI/CGI applications, with the important difference that the DLL stays loaded after the first request. This means that subsequent requests are executed faster (no loading/unloading).

> **NOTE**
>
> Netscape will also support the ISAPI protocol in the future. Since you can use a "translation" DLL to map ISAPI calls to NSAPI (when using an older Netscape Web Server), I'll use the term *ISAPI* in the remainder of this chapter when in fact I'm talking about both ISAPI and NSAPI.

CGI

A Common Gateway Interface (CGI) Web server application is a console application, loaded by the Web server for each request and unloaded directly after completing the request. Client input is received on the standard input, and the resulting output (usually HTML) is sent back to the standard output. The application object is of type `TCGIApplication`.

WinCGI

WinCGI is a Windows-specific implementation of the CGI protocol. Instead of standard input and standard output, an `.INI` file is used to send information back and forth. The application object is again of type `TCGIApplication`. The only programming difference with a standard (console) CGI application is that a WinCGI application is now a GUI application, albeit still an invisible one, of course.

Comparing Web Server Application Options

The generated source code for CGI and WinCGI Web module applications is almost identical. And although an ISAPI/NSAPI DLL has a somewhat different main section (it's a DLL, not an executable), the Web module itself is exactly the same for all three. Hence, if you want to produce a CGI application but want to test it as an ISAPI DLL first (because you can debug ISAPI DLLs from within the C++Builder IDE itself), you should just create three project targets (one each for CGI, WinCGI, and ISAPI/NSAPI) that all share the same WebBroker unit.

Personally, I always start by developing an ISAPI Web server extension DLL. Even if you actually want to develop a CGI application, it's easier to start with an ISAPI DLL and change the main project file from ISAPI to CGI after you're done.

The main disadvantages of the different approaches are that CGI is slower compared to ISAPI (the CGI application needs to be loaded and unloaded for every request), while the ISAPI DLL is less robust because a rogue DLL could potentially crash the entire Web server. The latter is a good reason to make sure an ISAPI DLL is 100% error-proof. It's important to test and debug your Web server application before deployment. This is maybe even more important than making sure your regular applications are error-proof.

WebBroker Components

After you've made a choice in the New Web Server Application dialog, C++Builder generates a new WebBroker project and an empty Web module unit. Save this new project under the name **Unleashed**, and save the generated unit under the name **WebMod** to be used for the entire chapter.

The Web module is the place to drop the special WebBroker components, such as the `PageProducers` and `TableProducers`. The WebBroker components can be found on the Internet tab of the C++Builder 4 Component Palette, as shown in Figure 17.3. (Note that I've removed most of the icons from this Internet tab in order to focus only on the WebBroker-specific components.)

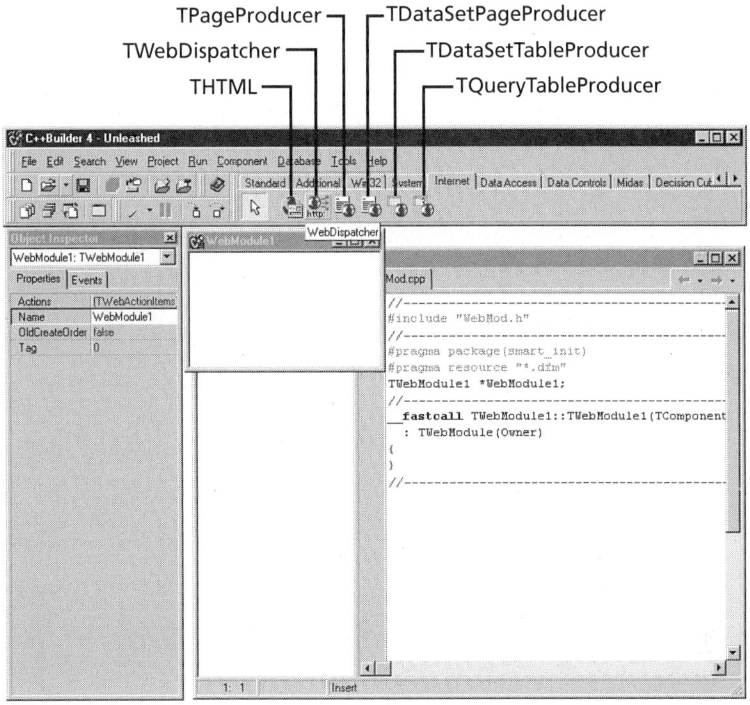

FIGURE 17.3

WebBroker components are on the Internet tab of the C++Builder 4 Component Palette.

The WebBroker components are THTML (not a WebBroker component), TWebDispatcher, TPageProducer, TDataSetPageProducer, TDataSetTableProducer, and TQueryTableProducer. The THTML ActiveX component is not one of the WebBroker components, but it is used to implement the IntraBob host application with which you can debug Web module applications from within the C++Builder IDE itself.

In addition to the components on the Component Palette, we'll also take a closer look at the TWebModule component and the TWebRequest and TWebResponse support classes.

TWebDispatcher

The TWebDispatcher component is one that you'll seldom need to drop on a Web module. In fact, this component is already built into the Web module itself, and is merely available to transform an existing data module into a Web module (that is: TDataModule plus TWebDispatcher equals TWebModule).

TWebModule

The most important property of the Web module is the `Actions` property of type `TWebActionItems`. You can start the Action Editor for these `TWebActionItems` in a number of ways. First, you can go to the Object Inspector and click the ellipsis next to the `(TWebActionItems)` value of the `Action` property. You can also right-click the Web module (see Figure 17.4) and select the Action Editor to specify the different requests to which the Web module will respond.

Inside the Action Editor, you can define a number of Web action items. Each of these items can be distinguished from the others by the `PathInfo` property. This contains extra information added to the request, right before the `Query` fields. This means that a single Web server application can respond to different Web action items, as we'll see several times in this chapter.

For the examples used in this chapter, you can define nine different `TWebActionItems`, which will be used to illustrate the different uses and abilities of the Web module components.

Note that the first item has no `PathInfo` specified and is the only default Web action item. This means that it's the `TWebActionItem` that will be selected when no `PathInfo` is given, or when no other `PathInfo` matches the given `PathInfo` (that is, when the default action is needed). In this chapter, the `TWebActionItem` will mostly be used to demonstrate a certain feature or effect. The other eight `PathInfo` values are `/hello`, `/alias`, `/table`, `/fields`, `/connect`, `/browse`, `/image` and `/query`, and they will be used for bigger examples throughout the chapter.

In order to write an event handler for the default `TWebActionItem`, select the `WebActionItem1` in the Action Editor (see Figure 17.5), go to the Events tab of the Object Inspector, and double-click the `OnAction` event.

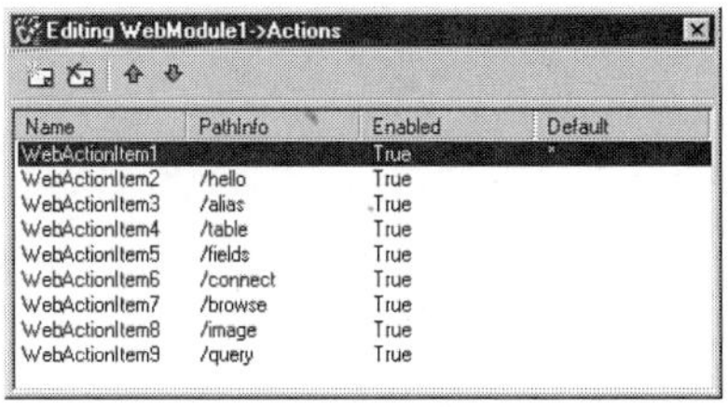

Figure 17.5

From the Action Editor, you can define a number of Web action items.

This will take you to the code editor, where you'll see the following code:

```
void __fastcall TWebModule1::WebModule1WebActionItem1Action(
    TObject *Sender, TWebRequest *Request, TWebResponse *Response,
    bool &Handled)
{

}
```

Before you write any event handling code here, you should first learn the specifics of the `Request` and `Response` parameters.

TWebResponse

`Response` (of type `TWebResponse`) has a number of properties to specify the generated output. The most important property is `Content`, a string in which you can put any HTML code that should be returned to the client. For example, the following code will produce "Hello, world!":

```
void __fastcall TWebModule1::WebModule1WebActionItem1Action(
    TObject *Sender, TWebRequest *Request, TWebResponse *Response,
    bool &Handled)
{
  Response->Content = "<H1>Hello, world!</H1>";
}
```

Of course, you can assign anything to the `Response->Content` property. Usually, it will be of type `text/html`, which is the default value of the `Response->ContentType` property. In case you want to return anything else, you need to set the `Response->ContentType` to the correct type. Binary output (such as images) cannot be returned directly using the `Response->Content`; you must use the `Response->ContentStream` property instead.

TWebRequest

`Request` (of type `TWebRequest`) contains a number of useful properties and methods that hold the input query. Based on the method used to send the query (`GET` or `POST`), the input data can be found in the `QueryFields` or the `ContentFields`. In code, you can determine this as follows:

```
void __fastcall TWebModule1::WebModule1WebActionItem1Action(
     TObject *Sender, TWebRequest *Request, TWebResponse *Response,
     bool &Handled)
{
  Response->Content = "<H1>Hello, world!</H1>";
  if (Request->Method == "GET")
    Response->Content = Response->Content + "<B>GET</B>" +
      "<BR>Query: " + Request->Query;
  else
    if (Request->Method == "POST")
      Response->Content = Response->Content + "<B>POST</B>" +
        "<BR>Content: " + Request->Content;
}
```

GET Versus POST

There are a number of differences between the `GET` and `POST` protocols that are important to know. When you're using the `GET` protocol, the query fields are passed on the URL. This is fast, but it limits the amount of data that can be sent (a few KB at most, enough for most cases). A less visible way to pass data is by using the `POST` protocol, where content fields are passed using standard input/output techniques (or a Windows `.INI` file for WinCGI). This is slower, but is limited only to the amount of free disk space. Besides, when you're using `POST`, you cannot see the data being sent on the URL itself, so there's no way of accidentally tampering with it and getting incorrect results.

I prefer to use the `POST` protocol (clean URLs, no limit on the amount of data, but slightly slower) and only use the `GET` protocol when I have a good reason to.

IntraBob

It's time to test the first Web module application. But since it's a DLL, you cannot just press the Run button. In fact, you actually need a Web server to test the Web module application. This means that you should first deploy the application to your remote Web server or test it with a Personal Web Server.

> **TIP**
>
> Before going on, I should mention that Microsoft distributes a free Web server called the *Personal Web Server*. This tool allows you to test Web server applications inside a Web browser. The Personal Web Server ships with FrontPage, some versions of Internet Explorer, and other Microsoft products such as the MSDN, and is usually available for free download from www.microsoft.com.

Chapter 28 of the *Borland C++Builder 4 Developer's Guide* (one of the manuals that came with your copy of C++Builder 4) contains clear instructions on how to set up your Personal Web Server in order to test and debug ISAPI DLLs or CGI applications. However, for simple cases, you can get a helping hand from IntraBob v3.02, my personal ISAPI Debugger host that replaces the Personal Web Server with a local Web server application host. The advantage of IntraBob is that you don't need to upload your applications to the Web server, nor do you need to start/stop the Web server when you want to debug your Web server applications. The downside of IntraBob is that it's limited to only one CGI HTML Form at a time. (It cannot distinguish between multiple Submit buttons, as you'll see later in this chapter.)

To use IntraBob, just put a copy of IntraBob.exe (available on the CD-ROM or from my Web site at http://www.drbob42.com/tools) in the same directory as your ISAPI project source code, and enter the location of IntraBob as "Host Application" in the Run, Run Parametersdialog, as shown in Figure 17.6.

FIGURE 17.6

Using IntraBob as a Web module host application.

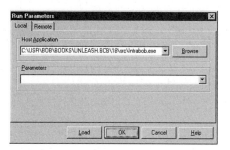

When you execute the ISAPI DLL, the host application IntraBob (or your Web server) is executed instead. And the best thing is that you can now use the C++Builder integrated debugger to set breakpoints in the source code. For example, set a breakpoint at the first line that checks the Request->Method and you'll see that the C++Builder IDE will break here as soon as you run the Web module application.

In order to actually start the ISAPI DLL, you must write a Web page containing an HTML form that will load the Web module application. If you uploaded the ISAPI DLL called `Unleashed.dll` to the `cgi-bin` directory on my Web server at `http://www.drbob42.com`, you'd need an action with the value `"http://www.drbob42.com/cgi-bin/Unleashed.dll"`, as seen in the following HTML form code:

```
<HTML>
<BODY>
<H1>WebBroker HTML Form</H1>
<HR>
<FORM ACTION="http://www.drbob42.com/cgi-bin/Unleashed.dll" METHOD=POST>
Name: <INPUT TYPE=EDIT NAME=Name><P>
<INPUT TYPE=SUBMIT>
</FORM>
</BODY>
</HTML>
```

When you load this Web page in IntraBob, you'll see the WebBroker HTML Form Web page. Fill in a value, and then click the Submit button to load and start your first Web module application, as shown in Figure 17.7.

FIGURE 17.7

Using IntraBob to load and start your first Web module application.

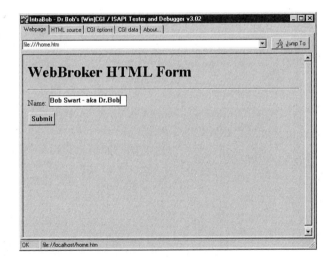

IntraBob parses the HTML form and automatically fills in the CGI Options tab with the value of the remote CGI (or ISAPI) application, the name of the local executable (or DLL), and the `PathInfo`, if specified. You can also go to the CGI Options tab, shown in Figure 17.8, and set these options manually. (This is an easy way to change the value of `PathInfo` and fire another `WebActionItem`.)

FIGURE 17.8

Using IntraBob CGI Options tab to set options manually.

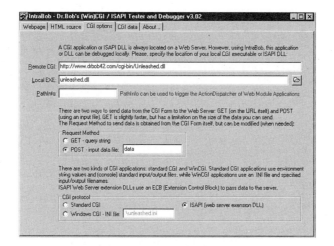

Remember the breakpoint you set on the first line that checked the `Request->Method` value? Well, as soon as you click the Submit button, the default `WebActionItem` will be fired, meaning this breakpoint will be triggered and you end up in the C++Builder Integrated Debugger. As you can see in figure 17.9, you can use Tooltip Expression Evaluation to check the value of `Request->Method` or `Request->Content` directly.

FIGURE 17.9

Viewing a Web module breakpoint in C++Builder IDE.

```
WebMod.cpp
WebMod.cpp | Unleashed.cpp |
  #pragma package(smart_init)
  #pragma resource "*.dfm"
  TWebModule1 *WebModule1;
  //-----------------------------------------
  __fastcall TWebModule1::TWebModule1(TComponent* Owner)
    : TWebModule(Owner)
  {
  }
  //-----------------------------------------
  void __fastcall TWebModule1::WebModule1WebActionItem1Action(
      TObject *Sender, TWebRequest *Request, TWebResponse *Response,
      bool &Handled)
  {
    Response->Content = "<H1>Hello, world!</H1>";
    if (Request->Method == "GET")
      Response->Content = Response->Content + "<B>GET</B>" +
        "<BR>Query: " + Request->Query;
    else
      if (Request->Method == "POST")
        Response->Content = Response->Content + "<B>POST</B>" +
          "<BR>Content: " + Request->Content;
  }
                          Request->Content = { Data:"Name=Bob+Swart+-+aka+Dr.Bob" }
  18   1         Insert
```

If you press F9, you see the final result in IntraBob, as shown in Figure 17.10.

FIGURE 17.10

*Displaying Web
module results
using IntraBob.*

> ## CAUTION
>
> A Delphi exception is raised with the following text: `Project Intrabob.exe`
> `raised exception class Exception with message 'Only one data module`
> `per application'. Process Stopped. Use Step or Run to continue.`
>
> One way to get rid of this exception is to clear the Stop on Delphi Exceptions
> option in the Language Exceptions tab of the Tools, Debugger Options dialog.

Viola is an HTML form debugger that will return what you've specified as input fields.
This can be quite helpful when a certain `WebActionItem` doesn't seem to work and you
need to check if it received the input data in good order. Note that spaces are replaced by
plus signs (+), and you'll find all special characters replaced by a % followed by the hexa-
decimal value of the character itself.

Another way to see the (unencoded) CGI data is by looking at the CGI data tab of
IntraBob.

TPageProducer

You can put anything in the `Response->Content` string variable, even whole Web pages.
Sometimes you'll want to return HTML strings based on a template, where only certain

fields need to be filled in (with a name and a date, for example, or specific fields from a record in a table). In those cases, you should use a TPageProducer component (see Figure 17.11).

FIGURE 17.11

Web module with
PageProducer
component.

TPageProducer has two properties to specify predefined content. HTMLFile points to an external HTML file, which is useful if you want to be able to change your Web page template without having to recompile the application itself. The HTMLDoc property, on the other hand, is of type TStrings and contains the HTML text (hardcoded in the .DFM file).

The predefined content of a TPageProducer component can contain any HTML code as well as special #-tags. These #-tags are invalid HTML tags, so they will be ignored by Web browsers but not by the OnHTMLTag event of TPageProducer. Inside this event, you can change an encountered TagString and replace it with ReplaceText. For more flexibility, #-tags can also contain parameters, right after the name itself.

As an example, let's fill the HTMLDoc property with the following content:

```
<H1>TPageProducer</H1>
<HR>
<#Greeting> <#Name>,
<P>
It's now <#Time> and we're playing with the PageProducers...
```

You see three #-tags that will fire the OnHTMLTag event of the TPageProducer. The following code for the OnHTMLTag event shows how to replace each tag with a sensible text value:

```
void __fastcall TWebModule1::PageProducer1HTMLTag(TObject *Sender,
    TTag Tag, const AnsiString TagString, TStrings *TagParams,
    AnsiString &ReplaceText)
{
  if (TagString == "Name")
    ReplaceText = "Bob"; // hardcoded name...
  else
  if (TagString == "Time")
```

```
      ReplaceText = DateTimeToStr(Now());
  else // TagString == "Greeting"
    if ((double)Time() < 0.5)
      ReplaceText = "Good Morning";
    else
      if ((double)Time()> 0.7)
        ReplaceText = "Good Evening";
      else
        ReplaceText = "Good Afternoon";
}
```

Note that you have to use an explicit (double) cast for the call to Time(), since it would otherwise introduce an ambiguity between the double and int results of TDateTime.

Using a ReplaceText with a fixed value of "Bob" feels a bit awkward, especially since the HTML form specifically asks the user to enter a name. Can't you just use that value here instead by using the QueryFields or the ContentFields? Well, you'd love to, of course, but you're inside the OnHTMLTag event of the TPageProducer and not in the OnAction event where you can directly access the Request object. Fortunately, you can access the Request property of the TWebModule, which is always assigned to the Request property of the current Action. The same holds for the Response property, by the way.

This effectively changes the code for the OnHTMLTag event as follows:

```
void __fastcall TWebModule1::PageProducer1HTMLTag(TObject *Sender,
      TTag Tag, const AnsiString TagString, TStrings *TagParams,
      AnsiString &ReplaceText)
{
  if (TagString == "Name")
  {
    if (Request->Method == "POST")
      ReplaceText = Request->ContentFields->Values["Name"];
    else
      ReplaceText = Request->QueryFields->Values["Name"];
  }
  else
  if (TagString == "Time")
    ReplaceText = DateTimeToStr(Now());
  else // TagString == "Greeting"
    if ((double)Time() < 0.5)
      ReplaceText = "Good Morning";
    else
      if ((double)Time()> 0.7)
        ReplaceText = "Good Evening";
      else
        ReplaceText = "Good Afternoon";
}
```

This will be the last time that you explicitly check the Request->Method field. From now on, assume a POST method at all times (but you can still support GET as well as POST by using the technique outlined previously).

Before you can finally test this code, you need to write the code for the `/hello` `OnAction` event to connect the `TPageProducer` output to the `Response` argument:

```
void __fastcall TWebModule1::WebModule1WebActionItem2Action(
     TObject *Sender, TWebRequest *Request, TWebResponse *Response,
     bool &Handled)
{
  Response->Content = PageProducer1->Content();
}
```

In order to activate this specific `WebActionItem`, be sure to pass the `/hello` `PathInfo` to the Web module, either by specifying it in the `PathInfo` edit box of IntraBob (see Figure 17.8) or by including the `PathInfo` string in the `ACTION` value:

```
<FORM ACTION=http://www.drbob42.com/cgi-bin/Unleashed.dll/hello

 METHOD=POST>
```

If you load the HTML form in IntraBob, fill in the name **Bob Swart** again, and click the Submit button, you'll get the output shown in Figure 17.12.

FIGURE 17.12

Displaying an HTML page with `TPageProducer`.

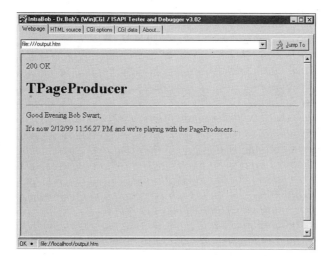

TDataSetPageProducer

The `TDataSetPageProducer` component is derived from the `TPageProducer`. Instead of just replacing #-tags with regular values, the `TDataSetPageProducer` has a new `DataSet` property and will try to match the name of the #-tag with a field name from the `DataSet` property and replace the #-tag with the actual value of that field.

To illustrate the use of this component, drop a TDataSetPageProducer component and a TTable component on the Web module. Rename the TTable component **Master**, assign the DatabaseName to BCDEMOS and the TableName to BIOLIFE.DB, and set the Active property of the Master table to true (so you don't have to open the table yourself). Next, connect the DataSet property of the TDataSetPageProducer component to the Master table and put the following lines in the HTMLDoc property:

```
<H1>BIOLIFE Info</H1>
<HR>
<BR><B>Category:</B> <#Category>
<BR><B>Common_Name:</B> <#Common_Name>
<BR><B>Species Name:</B> <#Species Name>
<BR><B>Notes:</B> <#Notes>
```

These special HTML #-tag codes indicate that you want to see four specific fields from the BIOLIFE table. The TDataSetPageProducer will automatically replace the #-tags with the actual values of these fields, so the only code you need to write is for the TWebActionItem event handler. Let's use the default TWebActionItem again without a specific PathInfo. Start the Action Editor, click the first ActionItem, go to the events tab of the Object Inspector, and double-click the OnAction event to write the following code. You can remove the existing code from the first example.

```
void __fastcall TWebModule1::WebModule1WebActionItem1Action(
        TObject *Sender, TWebRequest *Request, TWebResponse *Response,
        bool &Handled)
{
  Response->Content = DataSetPageProducer1->Content();
}
```

You also need to change the ACTION= value of the HTML form back to start the default TWebActionItem again, as follows:

```
<FORM ACTION="http://www.drbob42.com/cgi-bin/Unleashed.dll" METHOD=POST>
```

The result of running the Web module with this request is shown in Figure 17.13.

There are two things here that should strike you as incorrect. First of all, you see "(MEMO)" instead of the actual contents of this Notes field, and second, you don't get the value of the Species Name field.

You can solve the first problem by making use of the fact that the TDataSetPageProducer is derived from the TPageProducer, so for every #-tag the OnHTMLTag event is still fired. Inside this event handler, you can check the value of the ReplaceText argument to see if it has been set to "(MEMO)", in which case you should change it to the real contents. This can be done by using the AsString property of the field:

```
void __fastcall TWebModule1::DataSetPageProducer1HTMLTag(TObject *Sender,
     TTag Tag, const AnsiString TagString, TStrings *TagParams,
     AnsiString &ReplaceText)
{
  if (ReplaceText == "(MEMO)")
    ReplaceText = Master->FieldByName(TagString)->AsString;
}
```

FIGURE 17.13

Displaying field values on a Web page using TDataSetPage Producer.

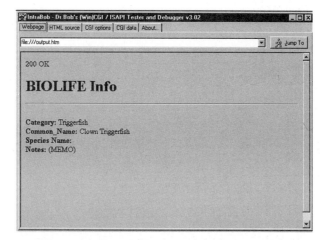

NOTE

Sometimes you get (Memo) instead of (MEMO) as the value for TMemoFields. The difference is simple: (Memo) indicates an empty memo field, whereas (MEMO) indicates a memo field with some content—and hence some content that has to be processed by your OnHTMLTag event handler.

The second problem can be explained by the fact that the Species Name field contains a space, and spaces are used as terminators for the #-tag names. Therefore, the TDataSetPageProducer would have been looking for a field named Species instead of the field Species Name.

Personally, I consider it bad database design to specify fields with spaces inside their names. Nevertheless, you may encounter this from time to time, in which case the easiest solution is to fall back to the OnHTMLTag event handler again, but this time to replace the #Species TagString with the content of the actual field Species Name. In order to do so, you need to modify the OnHTMLTag event handler as follows:

```
void __fastcall TWebModule1::DataSetPageProducer1HTMLTag(TObject *Sender,
     TTag Tag, const AnsiString TagString, TStrings *TagParams,
     AnsiString &ReplaceText)
```

```
{
  if (TagString == "Species") // Species Name
    ReplaceText = Master->FieldByName("Species Name")->AsString;
  else
    if (ReplaceText == "(MEMO)") // Notes
      ReplaceText = Master->FieldByName(TagString)->AsString;
}
```

Using these changes in the source code, the final result as you'd like to see it is in Figure 17.14.

FIGURE 17.14

When you use a special event handler with TDataSetPage Producer, *field values for Species and Notes are displayed.*

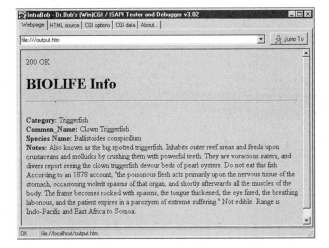

Browsing State

Seeing a single record from a table in a Web browser is fine, but you'd like to see the next record as well, and the next, and the last, and back to the first again. In short, you want the ability to browse through the records in the table. To do so, you need to use the TDataSetPageProducer and code you've written so far, but extend it just a little bit to support browsing.

The main problem you have to solve when it comes to moving from one record to another is maintaining state information: which record number are you currently looking at? HTTP itself is a stateless protocol, so you must find a way to store this information yourself.

Saving state information can be done in three different ways: fat URLs, cookies, or hidden fields.

Fat URLs

A common way to retain state information is by adding form variables with their values to the URL itself. Adding the RecNo property of the Master table, for example, could lead to the following ACTION URL:

```
<FORM ACTION=http://www.drbob42.com/cgi-bin/Unleashed.dll?RecNo=1

METHOD=POST>
```

Note that the general method to send form variables is still POST, although the state (RecNo) variable is passed using the GET protocol. This means you'll see the RecNo and its value appear on the URL, which is something that can be experienced with some search engines on the Web as well.

Personally, I believe that any information sent on the URL is error-prone, so I generally try to avoid it. (Although using the POST method to send regular form fields and the GET method to send state fields is actually a nice way to separate the two kinds of fields.)

Cookies

Cookies are sent by the server to the browser. The initiative is with the Web server but the client can deny or disable a cookie. Sometimes, servers even send cookies when you don't ask for them, which is one reason why some people don't like cookies (like me, for example).

Cookies can be set as part of the Response, using the SetCookieField method. Like CGI values, a cookie is of the form "NAME=VALUE", so you can put a "RecNo=value" in there as follows:

```
TStringList* Cookies = new TStringList();
Cookies->Add("RecNo="+IntToStr(Master->RecNo));
Response->SetCookieField(Cookies,NULL,NULL,Now()+1,False);
Cookies->Free();
```

Note that you're using a TStringList to set up a list of cookie values (as the first parameter). Each list of cookies can have an associated Domain and Path to indicate to which URL the cookie should be sent. You can pass NULL, so the cookie will always be included. The fourth parameter specifies the expiration date of the cookie, which is set to Now()+1 day, so the next time the user is back the cookie should have expired. The final argument specifies if the cookie is used over a secured connection.

Now, assuming the user accepts the cookie, having set the cookie is still only half the work. In a follow-up OnAction event, you need to read the value of the cookie to determine how far to step within the `Master` table to show the next record. In this case, cookies are part of the `Request` class, just like the `ContentFields`, and they can be queried using the `CookieFields` property:

```
int RecNo = StrToInt(Request->CookieFields->Values["RecNo"]);
```

Other than that, cookies work just like any CGI content field. Just remember that while a content field is part of your request (and is always up-to-date), a cookie may have been rejected, resulting in a possible older value (which was still on your disk) or no value at all. This will result in an exception thrown by `StrToInt` in the preceding line of code.

Hidden Fields

Using hidden fields is the third and, in my book, most flexible way to maintain state information. To implement hidden fields, you first need to write an HTML form, specifying the default `WebActionItem` and using four different Submit buttons, each with a different value as a caption. You also need to make sure the current record number is stored in the generated HTML form, which you can do by embedding a special #-tag with the `RecNo` name inside. In the `OnHTMLTag` event handler, this tag will be replaced by the current record number of the table:

```
<FORM ACTION="http://www.drbob42.com/cgi-bin/Unleashed.dll" METHOD=POST>
<H1>BIOLIFE Info</H1><HR>
<INPUT TYPE=SUBMIT NAME=SUBMIT VALUE="First">
<INPUT TYPE=SUBMIT NAME=SUBMIT VALUE="Prior">
<INPUT TYPE=SUBMIT NAME=SUBMIT VALUE="Next">
<INPUT TYPE=SUBMIT NAME=SUBMIT VALUE="Last">
<#RecNo>
<BR><B>Category:</B> <#Category>
<BR><B>Common_Name:</B> <#Common_Name>
<BR><B>Species Name:</B> <#Species Name>
<BR><B>Notes:</B> <#Notes>
</FORM>
```

In order to replace the #RecNo tag with the current record number, you use the HTML syntax for hidden fields, which is as follows:

```
<INPUT TYPE=HIDDEN NAME=RecNo VALUE=1>
```

This indicates that the hidden field named `RecNo` has a value of 1. Hidden fields are invisible to the end user, but the names and values are sent back to the Web server and Web module application as soon as the user clicks any of the four Submit buttons. Apart from the hidden field, you can also display some visual information, like the current record number and the total number of records in the table:

```
void __fastcall TWebModule1::DataSetPageProducer1HTMLTag(TObject *Sender,
    TTag Tag, const AnsiString TagString, TStrings *TagParams,
```

```
      AnsiString &ReplaceText)
{
  if (TagString == "RecNo")
    ReplaceText =
      "<INPUT TYPE=HIDDEN NAME=RecNo VALUE=" +
        IntToStr(Master->RecNo) + // current record number
      "> " + IntToStr(Master->RecNo) +"/"+
            IntToStr(Master->RecordCount) + "<P>";
  else
    if (TagString == "Species") // Species Name
      ReplaceText = Master->FieldByName("Species Name")->AsString;
    else
      if (ReplaceText == "(MEMO)") // Notes
        ReplaceText = Master->FieldByName(TagString)->AsString;
}
```

Now all you need to do is specify the action the `WebActionItem` has to perform for each of the Submit buttons. You could have split this up into four different Web action items themselves, but then you'd have to use four forms, meaning four copies of the hidden field and any other information necessary (and this gets worse, as the next example will show you). For now, the default `WebActionItem` event handler just needs to obtain the value of the hidden `RecNo` field and the value of the Submit button with the specific action to be taken:

```
void __fastcall TWebModule1::WebModule1WebActionItem1Action(
      TObject *Sender, TWebRequest *Request, TWebResponse *Response,
      bool &Handled)
{
  DataSetPageProducer1->DataSet->Open(); // In case it isn't open, yet!
  int RecNr = 0;
  AnsiString Str = Request->ContentFields->Values["RecNo"];
  if (Str != "") RecNr = StrToInt(Str);
  Str = Request->ContentFields->Values["SUBMIT"];
  if (Str == "First") RecNr = 1;
  else
    if (Str == "Prior") RecNr—;
    else
      if (Str == "Last") RecNr =
        DataSetPageProducer1->DataSet->RecordCount;
      else // if Str = 'Next' then { default }
        RecNr++;
  if (RecNr> DataSetPageProducer1->DataSet->RecordCount)
    RecNr = DataSetPageProducer1->DataSet->RecordCount;
  if (RecNr < 1) RecNr = 1;
  if (RecNr != DataSetPageProducer1->DataSet->RecNo)
    DataSetPageProducer1->DataSet->MoveBy(
      RecNr - DataSetPageProducer1->DataSet->RecNo);
  Response->Content = DataSetPageProducer1->Content();
}
```

The result is the display you saw in Figure 17.14, but this time with four buttons that enable you to go to the first, prior, next, or last record of the BIOLIFE table. (Note that in Figure 17.15, I've pressed the Next button three times already).

FIGURE 17.15

Using special fields and TDataSetPage Producer *to handle browser state.*

There's one problem when you're testing the preceding technique with IntraBob: you use the fact that each Submit button can have a special value (such as the captions of the four buttons in Figure 17.15). However, the THTML component, which is the basis for IntraBob, can't "capture" the value of the Submit buttons, so for IntraBob there's no difference between any of these buttons. Any Submit button triggers the "Next" action, so at least you can test that. For a fully functional test, you need a real Personal Web Server.

The techniques shown here to keep state information and use it to browse through a table can be used in other places as well, of course. Note that while you used RecNo to retain the current record number, you could also pass the current (unique) key values and use them to search for the current record instead (especially when browsing a dynamic table where lots of users are adding new records while you're browsing it).

Advanced Page Producing

You saw what the individual page producers can do. However, it gets really interesting once you combine these components and connect the output of one to the input of another. The example you're going to build at this time is a table viewer like the BIOLIFE example you just saw, but with the ability to dynamically specify the DatabaseName (alias), TableName, and FieldNames. This is the purpose of the WebActionItems with the /alias, /table, and /fields PathInfo.

First, drop a `TSession` component on the Web module and set the `AutoSessionName` property to `true`. Then, select the third `ActionItem` (with the `/alias` PathInfo), and write the following code in the `OnAction` event handler; calling the `Session->GetAliasNames()` method to obtain a list of known aliases:

```
void __fastcall TWebModule1::WebModule1WebActionItem3Action(
      TObject *Sender, TWebRequest *Request, TWebResponse *Response,
      bool &Handled)
{
  Response->Content = "<H1>Alias Selection</H1><HR><P>";
  TStringList* AliasNames = new TStringList();
  AliasNames->Sorted = True;
  try {
    Session1->Active = True;
    Session1->GetAliasNames(AliasNames);
    Session1->Active = False;
    Response->Content = Response->Content +
      "Please select a database alias." +
      "<FORM ACTION=\"Unleashed.dll/table\" METHOD=POST>" +
      "Alias: <SELECT NAME=\"alias\">";
    for (int i=0; i < AliasNames->Count; i++)
      Response->Content = Response->Content +
        "<OPTION VALUE=\"" + AliasNames->Strings[i] + "\">" +
      AliasNames->Strings[i];
    Response->Content = Response->Content +
      "<SELECT>" +
      "<P>" +
      "<INPUT TYPE=RESET> <INPUT TYPE=SUBMIT>" +
      "</FORM>";
  }
  __finally
  {
    AliasNames->Free();
    Session1->Active = false;
  }
}
```

Note that the `ACTION` part of the generated HTML form is just `Unleashed.dll/table`. This means that the name of the ISAPI DLL and the `PathInfo` are specified correctly, but not the exact location on the actual Web server. This works fine in combination with IntraBob (which is a local ISAPI DLL debugger host), but you need to specify the full `ACTION` path when deploying and testing using your real Personal Web Server.

Running this action will return the output shown in Figure 17.16. (Remember to set the value of `PathInfo` to `/alias`.)

FIGURE **17.16**

Alias selection.

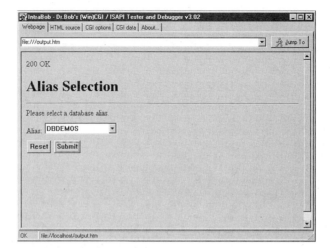

Select the BCDEMOS alias. The /table WebActionItem's OnAction event will be executed when you click the Submit button.

The next step consists of generating a list of TableNames for the alias that you selected in the previous step. This can again be done by using the TSession component, this time by calling the GetTableNames method:

```
void __fastcall TWebModule1::WebModule1WebActionItem4Action(
      TObject *Sender, TWebRequest *Request, TWebResponse *Response,
      bool &Handled)
{
  Response->Content = "<H1>Table Selection</H1><HR><P>";
  TStringList* TableNames = new TStringList();
  TableNames->Sorted = true;
  try {
    Session1->Active = true;
    Session1->GetTableNames(Request->ContentFields->Values["alias"],
                            "",true,false,TableNames);
    Session1->Active = false;
    Response->Content = Response->Content +
      "Please select a database table." +
      "<FORM ACTION=\"Unleashed.dll/fields\" METHOD=POST>" +
      "<INPUT TYPE=HIDDEN NAME=\"alias\" VALUE=\"" +
        Request->ContentFields->Values["alias"] + "\">" +
      "<TABLE>";
    Response->Content = Response->Content +
      "<TR><TD ALIGN=RIGHT>Master: </TD><TD><SELECT NAME=\"table\">";
    for (int i=0; i < TableNames->Count; i++)
      Response->Content = Response->Content +
        "<OPTION VALUE=\"" + TableNames->Strings[i]+"\">" +
        TableNames->Strings[i];
```

```
Response->Content = Response->Content +
    "</SELECT></TD></TR>";
  Response->Content = Response->Content +
    "</TABLE><P>" +
    "<INPUT TYPE=RESET> <INPUT TYPE=SUBMIT>" +
    "</FORM>";
  }
  __finally
  {
    TableNames->Free();
    Session1->Active = false;
  }
}
```

Note that you need to pass the Alias field with the previously selected value to the next Web page as well, so you can use it to combine with the selected TableName. This is done by passing a hidden field with the "alias" name.

Running this WebActionItem results in an HTML form with the new /fields PathInfo. The output seen inside IntraBob is shown in Figure 17.17.

FIGURE 17.17

Selecting Tablename *based on* Alias.

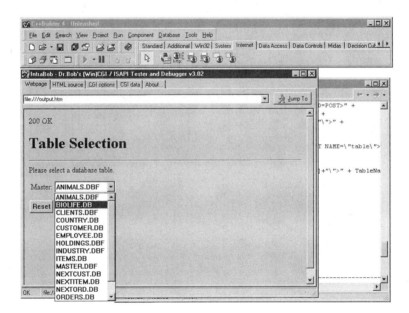

After you select a TableName and click the Submit button, the /fields WebItemAction is executed, which is implemented as follows:

```
void __fastcall TWebModule1::WebModule1WebActionItem5Action(
    TObject *Sender, TWebRequest *Request, TWebResponse *Response,
    bool &Handled)
```

```
{
  Response->Content = Response->Content +
      "<H1>Table Fields</H1><HR><P>" +
      "<FORM ACTION=\"Unleashed.dll/browse\" METHOD=POST>" +
      "<INPUT TYPE=HIDDEN NAME=\"alias\" VALUE=\"" +
        Request->ContentFields->Values["alias"] + "\">" +
      "<INPUT TYPE=HIDDEN NAME=\"table\" VALUE=\"" +
        Request->ContentFields->Values["table"] + "\">";
  Session1->Active = true;
  Master->DatabaseName = Request->ContentFields->Values["alias"];
  Master->TableName = Request->ContentFields->Values["table"];
  Master->FieldDefs->Update(); // no need to actually Open the Table
  Response->Content = Response->Content +
    "<TABLE><TR><TD WIDTH=200 BGCOLOR=FFFF00> <B>Table: </B>" +
      Master->TableName + " </TD>" +
    "<TR><TD BGCOLOR=CCCCCC VALIGN=TOP>";
    for (int i=0; i < Master->FieldDefs->Count; i++)
      Response->Content = Response->Content +
        "<INPUT TYPE=\"checkbox\" CHECKED NAME=\"M" +
          Master->FieldDefs->Items[i]->DisplayName + "\" VALUE=\"on\"> " +
          Master->FieldDefs->Items[i]->DisplayName + "<BR>";
  Response->Content = Response->Content +
    "</TD></TR></TABLE><P>" +
    "<INPUT TYPE=RESET> <INPUT TYPE=SUBMIT>" +
    "</FORM>";
  Session1->Active = false;
}
```

Note that you now need to pass both the Alias field and the Table field with the previously selected values to the next Web page, so you can use them to combine with the selected FieldNames. This is done by passing two hidden fields.

Executing this OnAction event finally results in a form with the /browse PathInfo, where you can select the fields from the table you've selected in the previous step. Note that field names with spaces can be a problem here because they may not be converted correctly by the TDataSetPageProducer component.

Figure 17.18 shows the /fields action seen in IntraBob.

FIGURE 17.18

Specifying table fields.

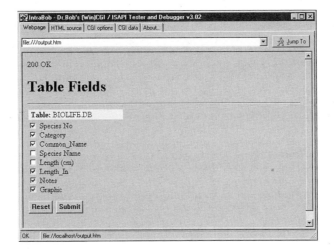

After you select some of the fields, as seen in Figure 17.18, and click the Submit button, the final /browse TWebItemAction is executed, which is implemented as follows:

```
void __fastcall TWebModule1::WebModule1WebActionItem7Action(
    TObject *Sender, TWebRequest *Request, TWebResponse *Response,
    bool &Handled)
{
  Response->Content = Response->Content +
    "<H1>Table Contents</H1><HR><P>" +
    "<FORM ACTION=\"Unleashed.dll/browse\" METHOD=POST>" +
    "<INPUT TYPE=HIDDEN NAME=\"alias\" VALUE=\"" +
      Request->ContentFields->Values["alias"] + "\">" +
    "<INPUT TYPE=HIDDEN NAME=\"table\" VALUE=\"" +
      Request->ContentFields->Values["table"] + "\">" +
    "<INPUT TYPE=SUBMIT NAME=SUBMIT VALUE=\"First\"> " +
    "<INPUT TYPE=SUBMIT NAME=SUBMIT VALUE=\"Prior\"> " +
    "<INPUT TYPE=SUBMIT NAME=SUBMIT VALUE=\"Next\"> " +
    "<INPUT TYPE=SUBMIT NAME=SUBMIT VALUE=\"Last\"> " +
    "<#RecNo>";
  Session1->Active = true;
  try {
    Master->DatabaseName = Request->ContentFields->Values["alias"];
    Master->TableName = Request->ContentFields->Values["table"];
    Master->Open();
```

```
    for (int i=0; i < Master->Fields->Count; i++)
      if (Request->ContentFields->Values["M"+
        Master->Fields->Fields[i]->FieldName] == "on")
        Response->Content = Response->Content +
          "<INPUT TYPE=HIDDEN NAME=\"M" +
          Master->Fields->Fields[i]->FieldName + "\" VALUE=\"on\">";
    // locate correct record
    int RecNr = 0;
    AnsiString Str = Request->ContentFields->Values["RecNo"];
    if (Str != "") RecNr = StrToInt(Str);
    Str = Request->ContentFields->Values["SUBMIT"];
    if (Str == "First") RecNr = 1;
    else
      if (Str == "Prior") RecNr—;
      else
        if (Str == "Last") RecNr = Master->RecordCount;
        else // if Str = "Next" then { default }
          RecNr++;
    if (RecNr> Master->RecordCount) RecNr = Master->RecordCount;
    if (RecNr < 1) RecNr = 1;
    if (RecNr != Master->RecNo)
      Master->MoveBy(RecNr - Master->RecNo);
    // display fields
    Response->Content = Response->Content + "<TABLE CELLSPACING=4>";
    for (int i=0; i < Master->Fields->Count; i++)
      if (Request->ContentFields->Values["M"+
        Master->Fields->Fields[i]->FieldName] == "on")
        Response->Content = Response->Content +
            "<TR><TD VALIGN=TOP ALIGN=RIGHT><B>" +
            Master->Fields->Fields[i]->FieldName + ":</B> </TD><TD>" +
          "<#" + Master->Fields->Fields[i]->FieldName + "></TD></TR>";
      else
        Response->Content = Response->Content + "-";
    Response->Content = Response->Content + "</TABLE>";
    DataSetPageProducer1->HTMLDoc->Clear();
    DataSetPageProducer1->HTMLDoc->Add(Response->Content);
    Response->Content = DataSetPageProducer1->Content();
  }
  __finally
  {
    Master->Close();
    Session1->Active = false;
  }
}
```

Note that since you want to browse through the result, you need to keep the value of the Alias and the Table, as well as all selected FieldNames. These are all passed as hidden fields in the HTML CGI form.

The final output, in which you can browse through the BIOLIFE table, showing all the fields you've selected, is shown in Figure 17.19. (Note that I did not select any fields with spaces in their names.)

FIGURE 17.19

TDataSetPage
Producer *browsing
selected fields in*
BIOLIFE.DB.

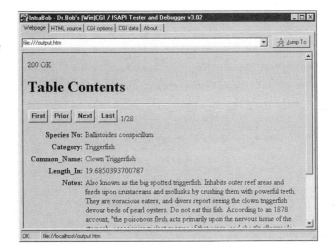

All selected fields are shown as you want them to be, and the Memo fields are nicely expanded too. Note that there is one kind of field that hasn't been covered yet: Graphics fields.

Like Memo fields, Graphics fields return (Graphic) if their content is empty, so you should focus only on (GRAPHIC). In that particular case, you need to return an image from the database table, which cannot be done directly. This should be done indirectly using another call to the same ISAPI DLL with the /image action. You can make the call in the OnHTMLTag event handler of the TDataSetPageProducer component:

```
void __fastcall TWebModule1::DataSetPageProducer1HTMLTag(TObject *Sender,
    TTag Tag, const AnsiString TagString, TStrings *TagParams,
    AnsiString &ReplaceText)
{
  if (TagString == "RecNo")
    ReplaceText =
      "<INPUT TYPE=HIDDEN NAME=RecNo VALUE=" +
        IntToStr(Master->RecNo) + // current record number
      "> " + IntToStr(Master->RecNo) +"/"+
          IntToStr(Master->RecordCount) + "<P>";
  else
    if (TagString == "Species") // Species Name
      ReplaceText = Master->FieldByName("Species Name")->AsString;
    else
      if (ReplaceText == "(MEMO)") // Notes
        ReplaceText = Master->FieldByName(TagString)->AsString;
      else
        if (ReplaceText == "(GRAPHIC)") // Image
          ReplaceText =
            "<IMG SRC=\"Unleashed.dll/image?RecNo=" +
              IntToStr(Master->RecNo) + "\" ALT=\"Image: " +
              IntToStr(Master->RecNo) + "\">";
}
```

The call to the /image action is accompanied by a GET input parameter RecNo, which holds the current record number for that particular image. Note that you don't pass the actual field name or field number. So this trick only works with tables that have only one Graphic field because the /image action event handler is implemented as follows (unfortunately, IntraBob currently cannot handle these indirect calls inside image HTML tags):

```
void __fastcall TWebModule1::WebModule1WebActionItem8Action(
      TObject *Sender, TWebRequest *Request, TWebResponse *Response,
      bool &Handled)
{
  int RecNo = StrToInt(Request->QueryFields->Values["RecNo"]);
  Master->Open();
  for (int i=0; i < RecNo; i++) Master->Next();
  for (int i=0; i < Master->Fields->Count; i++)
  {
    if (Master->Fields->Fields[i]->DataType == ftBlob)
    {
      TMemoryStream* ImageStream = new TMemoryStream();
   ((TBlobField*)Master->Fields->Fields[i])->SaveToStream(ImageStream);
      Response->ContentStream = ImageStream;
      Response->ContentType = "image/jpg"; // assume JPG format
      i = Master->Fields->Count; // break
    }
  }
}
```

Note that the preceding code will result in a correct image only if the image in the table is indeed stored in JPEG format. In all other cases, you should convert the image to JPEG first.

Finally, you can even turn this into a master-detail output. However, you need the TDataSetTableProducer component, which is covered in the next section.

TDataSetTableProducer

The TDataSetTableProducer component also uses a DataSet property, just like TDataSetPageProducer. This time, however, you get more than one record and the output is formatted in a grid-like table.

Drop a second TTable component on the Web module and call it Detail (to prepare for the master-detail relationship you're going to build in a little while). Set the DatabaseName (alias) to BCDEMOS again, set the TableName to CUSTOMER.DB, and open the table by setting Active to true.

Now, drop a TDataSetTableProducer on the Web module and set the DataSet property to the Detail table. The TDataSetTableProducer has a number of properties that are used to control the HTML code being generated. First of all, you have the Header and Footer properties, which hold the lines of text that precede and follow the table output. Then you have the TableAttributes and RowAttributes properties, which can be used to define the layout (Alignment, Color, and so on) of the table itself and of the rows. You can experience a more visual approach to specifying what the table should look like by using the Column property, and especially the Column property editor. From the Object Inspector, start the Columns property editor by clicking on the ellipsis next to the Columns property (THTMLTableColumns) value. This brings up the DataSetTableProducer1->Columns editor, as shown in Figure 17.20.

FIGURE 17.20

The DataSetTable Producer *columns editor.*

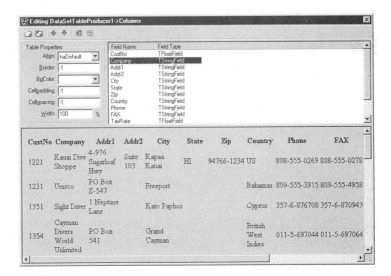

Since you opened the Detail table, you immediately see all fields in the Columns editor. Initially, you cannot delete any fields from this view, nor can you move them. This may feel like a bug, but it can be explained by the fact that you haven't explicitly specified which fields you would like to see in the output table. The reason that you see all fields at this time is because that's the default behavior of the TTable component—if you don't specify which fields you want, you get them all.

However, in order to delete fields from the complete list or change the order in which the fields appear, you need to add a physical list of fields. Right-click the list of field names and pick the Add All Fields option. You'll see no apparent change right now. However, the default list of all fields has suddenly become an actual list of all fields, and now you can delete fields or move them around in the list.

You can also set the output table options, like Border=1 to get a border, specifying a value for the BgColor property to get a background color, and so on. Note that individual field (= column) settings have to be done by selecting a field and going to the Object Inspector to set the BgColor, Align (left, center, right), and VAlign (top, middle, bottom, baseline) properties. To change the captions of the fields, you can modify the Title property, again in the Object Inspector. The Title property consists of subproperties like Align (this time for the title only, not the entire column) and Caption. Hence, to change the title of the Addr1 field to Address, you only need to change the Title->Caption property of the Addr1 field in the Object Inspector, as shown in Figure 17.21.

FIGURE 17.21

Changing field properties in the Object Inspector.

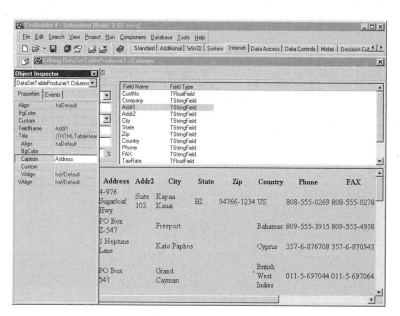

The latter changes will automatically be reflected back in the Columns editor, so after a little playing around with these properties, your output preview may look like the one shown in Figure 17.22 (depending on your taste for colors, that is).

That concludes the design-time tweaking of the TDataSetTableProducer output. Note that you haven't written a single line of code for the TDataSetTableProducer example yet. Of course, you need to hook it up to a WebActionItem OnAction event handler, and you can use the default WebActionItem again (removing the existing lines of code) as follows:

```
void __fastcall TWebModule1::WebModule1WebActionItem1Action(
     TObject *Sender, TWebRequest *Request, TWebResponse *Response,
     bool &Handled)
{
  Response->Content = DataSetTableProducer1->Content();
}
```

FIGURE 17.22

The DataSetTable
Producer *columns
editor (with
changes applied).*

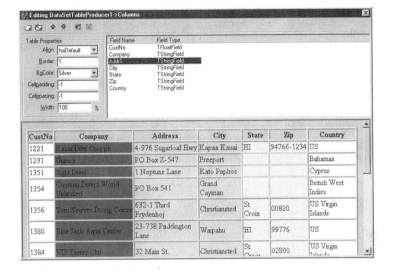

There are a few more ways you can tweak and customize the output a little further. First
of all, you may want to flag certain countries with a special color, like the U.S., for
which shipping can be done over land instead of by sea or by air. Or you may want to
display fields with no contents (like making the state and zip code for non-U.S. addresses
silver so they don't stand out too much). Both of these changes can be done in the
OnFormatCell event of the TDataSetTableProducer component. All you need to do is
check if the CellData is empty and then assign Silver to the BgColor. Or, if the
CellData contains US and the CellColumn equals 6, you should change the BgColor to
Red, for example:

```
void __fastcall TWebModule1::DataSetTableProducer1FormatCell(
      TObject *Sender, int CellRow, int CellColumn, THTMLBgColor &BgColor,
      THTMLAlign &Align, THTMLVAlign &VAlign, AnsiString &CustomAttrs,
      AnsiString &CellData)
{
  if (CellData == "") BgColor = "Silver";
  else
    if ((CellColumn == 6) && (CellData.Pos("US")> 0))
      BgColor = "Red";
}
```

Executing this code produces the output shown in Figure 17.23.

FIGURE 17.23

Using the `OnFormatCell` *event in* `DataSetTable Producer`.

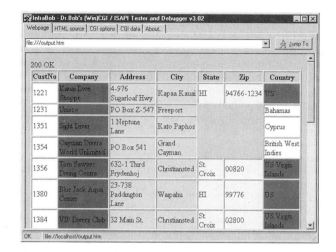

As a last enhancement, you may want to see the orders for a specific customer in a follow-up window. Orders are linked to the `CustNo` identifier, so you could change that one to a link that would start another Web module request to dynamically generate HTML output, with an overview of the orders for the given customer. Let's put that one on hold for now, since you can use the final component—the `TQueryTableProducer`—to assist in solving this request.

Database Web Application Wizard

Before you continue with the last component from the WebBroker toolset, quickly check out a wizard related to `TDataSetTableProducer`.

Compared to C++Builder 3 client/server, the Database Web Application Wizard, which is found on the Business tab in the Object Repository, is an addition to the WebBroker set of components and wizards. However, a long name is not enough to impress me. If you check out this DB Web Application Wizard in action, you'll find that all it does is allow you to specify a database alias, a table name, some field names, and a few properties for the `TDataSetTableProducer`. All it generates is a new Web module application, with a `TWebModule`, a `TSession` (`AutoSessionName = true`), a `TTable`, and a `TDataSetTableProducer`. That's it. You could drop these components and set their properties in the same time it takes to fill in the wizard, but maybe the wizard is helpful for developers who are just beginning with the WebBroker technology.

TQueryTableProducer

The `TQueryTableProducer` component produces output similar to
`TDataSetTableProducer`. The difference is not that you can only connect a `TQuery` component to the `TQueryTableProducer` (after all, you can connect any `TDataSet` or derived component, including `TTables` and `TQueries`, to the `TDataSetTableProducer`), but that the `TQueryTableProducer` has special support for filling in the parameters of a parameterized `TQuery`.

Drop a `TQueryTableProducer` component and a `TQuery` component on the Web module. Set the `DatabaseName` (alias) of the `TQuery` component to `BCDEMOS` and write the following code in the `SQL` property:

```
SELECT * FROM ORDERS.DB AS O
WHERE (O.CustNo = :CustNo)
```

This is a `SQL` query with one parameter. You now need to specify the type of the parameter in the `Parameter` Property Editor of the `TQuery` component. Click the ellipsis next to the `Params` property in the Object Inspector to get the Tquery Params Editor, as shown in Figure 17.24.

FIGURE 17.24

Specifying the type of parameter in the Parameter *Property Editor of the* TQuery *component.*

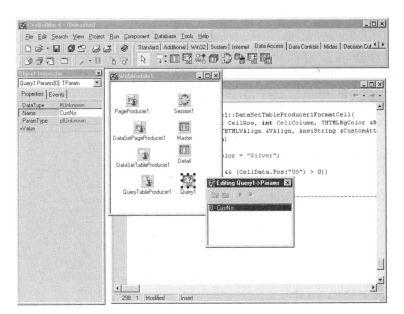

Note that the Params property editor changed from C++Builder 3 to C++Builder 4. Select the CustNo parameter, and then go to the Object Inspector to set the DataType to ftInteger, the ParamType to ptInput, and the Value to a default value of 0 (so you can activate the query at design time).

You can open the TQuery component (set Active to true) to check if you made any typing mistakes. Now click the TQueryTableProducer and assign the Query property to the TQuery component. Note that the TQueryTableProducer contains the same properties to customize its output as the TDataSetTableProducer (see previous section). In fact, TQueryTableProducer and TDataSetTableProducer are both derived from TDSTableProducer, and TQueryTableProducer adds only the Query Parameter Handling to its special behavior.

The TQueryTableProducer works by looking for the parameter name (CustNo in this case) among the ContentFields (or QueryFields, if you're using the GET method), and filling in the value of the field as the value for the parameter. In this case, it means you need a sample HTML startup file defined as follows:

```
<HTML>
<BODY>
<H1>WebBroker HTML Form</H1>
<HR>
<FORM ACTION=http://www.drbob42.com/cgi-bin/Unleashed.dll/query
  METHOD=POST>
CustNo: <INPUT TYPE=EDIT NAME=CustNo>
<P>
<INPUT TYPE=SUBMIT>
</FORM>
</BODY>
</HTML>
```

Note that the name of the input field is CustNo, which is the name of the Query parameter. If you fill in a value, like 1221 (see Figure 17.23), you should get all orders for this particular customer. As long as you set the MaxRows property to a really high value (99,999 will do fine), you're pretty sure to see all detail records.

Note that setting the MaxRows property to a high value (especially for the TDataSetTableProducer) results in more records being shown, and slower output. The latter is not only caused by the fact that the output is simply bigger and has to be transferred over the network, but also by the fact that an HTML table doesn't show itself until the closing </TABLE> tag is reached. This means that for a really big table with 99,999 rows, you may actually see a blank browser window for a while until suddenly the table is drawn.

To finish this example, you only need to write one line of code in the `OnAction` event handler for the `/query` WebActionItem:

```
void __fastcall TWebModule1::WebModule1WebActionItem9Action(
      TObject *Sender, TWebRequest *Request, TWebResponse *Response,
      bool &Handled)
{
  Response->Content = QueryTableProducer1->Content();
}
```

Running the `WebActionItem` with the `/query` PathInfo and entering 1221 in the `CustNo` editbox, you get the result shown in Figure 17.25.

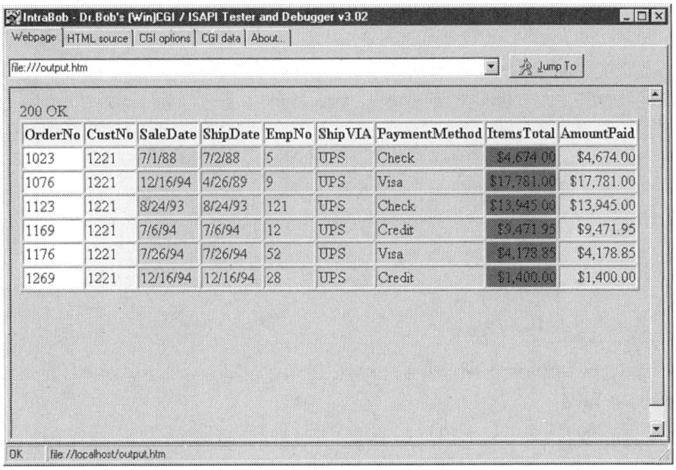

FIGURE 17.25

*TQueryTable
Producer-
generated HTML
output for /query
action shown in
IntraBob.*

Now, this just screams to be used together with the previous `TDataSetTableProducer` on the `Customer` table, so you can drill-down to the detail records in a single click. And in fact, you can do this by extending the `OnFormatCell` event handler from the `TDataSetTableProducer` to generate a request to the `/query` WebActionItem, accompanied by a hidden field (with the name `CustNo`) that holds the value of `CustNo` that you're interested in. Basically, for the first column (where `CellColumn` has the value 0), you can change the actual `CellData` into a hyperlink to the `/query` WebActionItem, with the current `CellData` (the `CustNo`) as the value of a field named `CustNo`, all passed on the URL—thus using the `GET` protocol in a useful way again.

Alternately, you can change each `CustNo` value to a new form with the `/query` action and a hidden field with the `CustNo` name and specific `CustNo` value. Both options are implemented in the following extended `OnFormatCell` event handler code (you can switch between options by using `#define LINK`):

```
void __fastcall TWebModule1::DataSetTableProducer1FormatCell(
   TObject *Sender, int CellRow, int CellColumn, THTMLBgColor &BgColor,
THTMLAlign &Align, THTMLVAlign &VAlign, AnsiString &CustomAttrs,
      AnsiString &CellData)
{
  if ((CellColumn == 0) && (CellRow> 0)) // first Column - CustNo
    CellData =
#ifdef LINK
 "<A HREF=\"http://www.drbob42.com/cgi-bin/Unleashed.dll/query?CustNo=" +
CellData + ">" + CellData + "</A>";
#else
      (AnsiString)"<FORM ACTION=\"Unleashed.dll/query\" METHOD=POST>" +
      "<INPUT TYPE=HIDDEN NAME=CustNo VALUE=" + CellData + ">" +
      "<INPUT TYPE=SUBMIT VALUE=" + CellData + ">" +
      "</FORM>";
#endif
  else
  if (CellData == "") BgColor = "Silver";
  else
    if ((CellColumn == 6) && (CellData.Pos("US")> 0))
      BgColor = "Red";
};
```

Since IntraBob can only be used to test and debug ISAPI requests that are started by an HTML form, you cannot test the hyperlink option (but you can test and deploy that option using your Personal Web Server). Instead, you can test the Form option, which generates the output shown in Figure 17.26 for the TDataSetTableProducer on the CUSTOMER table.

FIGURE 17.26

TableProducer-generated output for MASTER *table in IntraBob.*

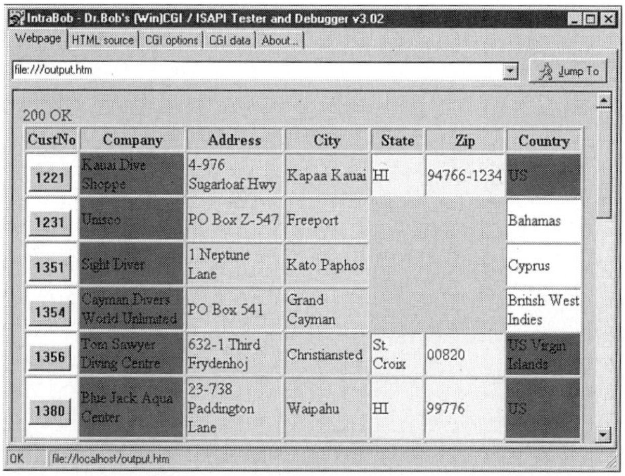

It should be clear from this figure what will happen as soon as you click one of these CustNo buttons. For example, if you click the 1231 button to see which orders are placed for this company in the Bahamas, you get the output shown in Figure 17.27.

OrderNo	CustNo	SaleDate	ShipDate	EmpNo	ShipVIA	PaymentMethod	ItemsTotal	AmountPaid
1060	1231	2/28/89	3/1/89	94	US Mail	Check	$15,355.00	$15,355.00
1073	1231	4/15/89	4/16/89	2	US Mail	MC	$19,414.00	$19,414.00
1102	1231	6/6/92	6/6/92	105	UPS	Credit	$2,844.00	$2,844.00
1160	1231	6/1/94	6/1/94	110	US Mail	Check	$2,206.85	$2,206.85
1173	1231	7/16/94	7/16/94	127	US Mail	MC	$54.00	$54.00
1178	1231	8/2/94	8/2/94	24	DHL	Credit	$5,511.75	$5,511.75
1202	1231	10/6/94	10/6/94	145	UPS	Credit	$4,205.00	$4,205.00
1278	1231	12/23/94	12/23/94	71	DHL	Credit	$11,568.00	$11,568.00
1302	1231	1/16/95	1/16/95	52	UPS	Credit	$24,485.00	$24,485.00

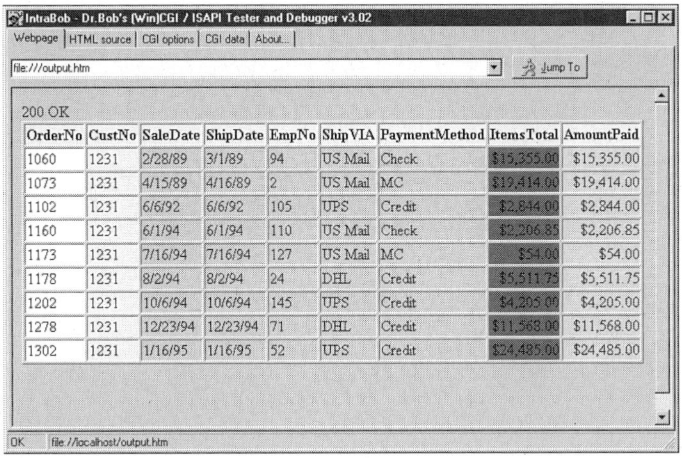

FIGURE 17.27
Detailed `QueryTableProducer` *outputfor* `MASTER` *table shown in IntraBob.*

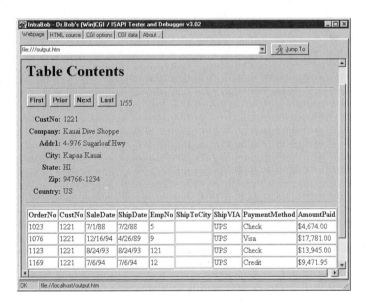

If that doesn't smell like a master-detail overview, I don't know what does. Okay, I know what does: let's backtrack to the dynamic table browser in Figure 17.19. Wouldn't it be nice to connect this `TDataSetPageProducer` (with the master record) with the output of a `TDataSetTableProducer` (with the detail records), but this time all in one page?

Just in case you can't imagine how it would look, see figure 17.28.

OrderNo	CustNo	SaleDate	ShipDate	EmpNo	ShipToCity	ShipVIA	PaymentMethod	AmountPaid
1023	1221	7/1/88	7/2/88	5		UPS	Check	$4,674.00
1076	1221	12/16/94	4/26/89	9		UPS	Visa	$17,781.00
1123	1221	8/24/93	8/24/93	121		UPS	Check	$13,945.00
1169	1221	7/6/94	7/6/94	12		UPS	Credit	$9,471.95

FIGURE 17.28
Output generated by the PageProducer Master-detail relationship is shown in IntraBob.

It takes a few pages to explain the steps in detail, but basically it's nothing more than you've done before. I'll leave it as an exercise to the reader. (You can find a detailed paper about this final example on my Web site at `http://www.drbob42.com/CBuilder`.)

The output should be worth it: a dynamic master-detail relationship where you can specify both the master and detail, their fields, and the master-detail connection all at run time. This is truly any data, any time, anywhere.

Summary

You've seen it all: Web modules, Web action items, page producers, and table producers, for CGI and ISAPI. You've encountered problems and solved them or produced workarounds. You produced some pretty useful and powerful example programs along the way.

All in all, I have shown that the C++Builder 4 WebBroker technology is a powerful set of tools for Internet server-side application development.

WinInet and FTP

by Charlie Calvert
and Kent Reisdorph

IN THIS CHAPTER

In this chapter you will look at techniques for building File Transfer Protocol (FTP) clients. Most of the chapter is dedicated to a discussion of WinInet, which is a relatively simple Windows API for creating FTP, Gopher, and Hypertext Transfer Protocol (HTTP) applications. This API is especially appealing because it is built into the operating system, ships with all versions of Windows starting with Windows NT 4, and enables you to create small, fast applications. If you don't have WININET.DLL on your system, you can download it free from Microsoft's Web site. It works with all 32-bit versions of Windows and ships with Windows NT 4 and Windows 98.

A class wrapped around WinInet's FTP services is this chapter's focus. Another topic I touch on in this chapter is how to use the TListView control. This subject comes up in the course of creating an application that can display the files shown in an FTP directory search.

Understanding WinInet and FTP

The next few sections provide general information about WinInet and the services upon which it relies. Most people will want to read the first section called "Required Files." The section on setting up FTP may not be interesting to experienced Internet users. As soon as this introductory material is covered, I begin an explanation of the technical aspects of WinInet and its FTP services.

Required Files

C++Builder Professional and Enterprise versions ship with two sets of files for WinInet access. One set of files is the VCL implementation of WinInet. It includes WININET.PAS, WININET.HPP, and WININET.DCU. This set of files is of primary interest to Delphi programmers and is included as part of the base VCL units. The second set of files isn't a set at all, but rather a single file called WININET.H. This is the Windows header for the functions found in WININET.DLL. C++Builder programmers can ignore the VCL files regarding WinInet and use the Windows header directly. Microsoft's WININET.DLL is freely distributable and is available from Microsoft if it is not already installed in your Windows/System or Winnt/System32 directory. As stated earlier, Windows NT 4 ships with WININET.DLL, as does Windows 98. WININET.DLL also runs fine on Windows 95 and is installed on some Win95 systems (those that have Internet Explorer 3 and later installed).

One of the best places to get help on the subject of WinInet is in the ActiveX SDK that ships as part of the MSDN and that has frequently been available for downloading from www.microsoft.com. Search the Microsoft Web site for "wininet" and you will find many topics on the subject. If you want a list of WinInet functions, search for the topic "WinInet API."

Another important link for this type of programming is `http://www.microsoft.com/workshop/`.

You can use public FTP server sites such as `ftp.microsoft.com` or `ftp.borland.com` to test against. However, you will be better off if you have an FTP server of your own. Windows NT 4 Server comes with the excellent Internet Information Server (IIS), or you can usually download the Personal Web Server from the Microsoft Web site or get it with a copy of FrontPage. Personal Web Server supports FTP, and it runs on Windows 95, Windows 98, or Windows NT. I have heard a few complaints about the Personal Web Server's robustness in commercial settings. These complaints might or might not be well founded, but the usefulness of the tool cannot be denied when you are developing an application. If need be, you can copy your finished files to a more robust server after you complete the development cycle.

Making Sure That FTP Is Working on Your System

FTP's sole purpose is to transfer files between computers using TCP/IP services. If you're connected to the Internet, even just over a modem, you should be able to FTP into various sites to see the contents of directories and to transfer files. For example, to connect to the `borland.com` FTP site, type the following at the command prompt:

```
ftp ftp.borland.com
```

When the system asks for a username, type **anonymous**. When it requests a password, type your email address. Figure 18.1 shows a screen shot of a typical old-fashioned, command-line–based FTP session.

To exit FTP and return to a regular command prompt, type **bye** at the FTP command prompt.

If you can't FTP into `borland.com`, `microsoft.com`, `ftp.download.com`, or some site on the Internet, something is wrong with your Windows setup. You should clear up that problem before tackling the material in this chapter. In particular, make sure that TCP/IP is set up properly on your system. Setting up TCP/IP is discussed in the "Installing TCP/IP" section of Chapter 16, "Internet Connection with C++Builder."

Figure 18.2 shows the program developed in this chapter, which works from inside Windows. The program, called FTP Pipeline, allows you to use standard Windows controls to make and maintain your connections. FTP Pipeline has provisions for copying multiple files from and to FTP sites, for deleting files and creating directories, and for using the mouse to navigate through directories.

Figure 18.1

FTP from the command line.

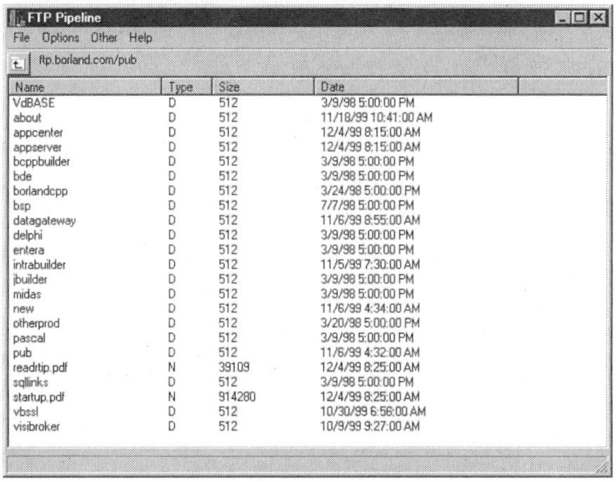

Figure 18.2

The main form for the FTP Pipeline program shows a connection to ftp.borland.com, *in the* pub *directory.*

FTP Using WinInet

Now you're ready to look at the code needed to use the WinInet DLL in an FTP session. This study will not be exhaustive, but it should help get you up and running.

The first fact you must know about this technology is that some of the WinInet functions return a pointer variable declared to be of type HINTERNET. This pointer acts as a handle to the various Internet services you employ. After retrieving the handle, you will pass it in as the first parameter to many of the other WinInet functions you call throughout the life of a single session.

You must remember to return the handle to the system when you're finished using it, usually by calling the WinInet function InternetCloseHandle(). Just hearing this much information should tip you off to the fact that you should make use of OOP when using WinInet and should consider creating a component. The tip-off here is the need to perform housekeeping chores with pointers.

Objects and components are the tools you can use to make C++ safe. If you build an object properly, it will always take care of chores such as allocating and deallocating memory for you. Get the job done right once, or find someone who has done it right once, and you can reuse the object without concern for petty housekeeping chores. In particular, a good practice is to allocate memory in the constructor and deallocate memory in the destructor. I like to vary from this approach only when I allocate and deallocate memory inside the span of a single method.

What causes trouble is allocating memory in one routine other than the constructor and then planning to deallocate it in a routine other than the destructor. The problem isn't so much that you are unlikely to remember to deallocate the memory, but that it is very hard to figure out what has gone wrong or even to know that something is wrong if you do make a mistake. On the other hand, if you follow the methodical scheme laid out in the beginning of this chapter, you can double-check your work relatively easily and make sure you got it right. On occasions when you can't allocate memory in the constructor, try to provide a second routine with an obvious name such as Initialize() for allocating memory. If at all possible, deallocate the memory in the destructor. The most important goal is to be able to look in one place, the destructor, to make sure all your pointers are freed.

The key point to absorb is that some developers, myself included, believe that almost any moderately complicated chore that involves allocating and deallocating memory is a strong candidate for wrapping in an object. Even better, put the code in a component; there is then almost no chance you will misuse it.

In the next few pages, I will show you a class that wraps the FTP calls found in WinInet. I will present the WinInet calls to you at the same time I slowly construct the pieces of a class called TUnlFTP. The listing for the class is too long to include in the book, but you can find it on the CD-ROM that accompanies this book. The filename is UNLFTP.CPP. All the key methods from the control are quoted in full in the text.

> **NOTE**
>
> The TUnlFTP class was originally a component written by Charlie. For this version of the book, I decided to use a class rather than a component so that you could compile and run the example program without the need to install a component into C++Builder. A component is almost always easier to use than a class. The point of TUnlFTP, however, is to show you how to perform FTP operations through WinInet, and a class serves that purpose just as well as a component. TUnlFTP can easily be turned into a component by deriving from TComponent rather than TObject and by moving its properties and events to the __published section rather than the public section where they reside now.

Before explaining the WinInet-specific code in this class, I want to take one moment to glance at the constructor:

```
__fastcall TUnlFTP::TUnlFTP() : TObject()
{
  FCurFiles = new TStringList;
  FFileList = new TList;
  Instance = this;
}
```

The constructor allocates memory for a TStringList and a TList. I then deallocate the memory in the destructor. These lists are used to hold the names of the files in the directories visited by the FTP session. The record stored in the TList looks like this:

```
struct TFileInfo {
  TFileInfo() {
    Attribute = 0;
    FileName = 0;
  }
  char* Attribute;
  char* FileName;
  __int64 FileSize;
  TDateTime FileTime;
};
```

The TStringList version of the files in a directory is very easy to use because you can just assign it to a TListBox::Items field. The list box will then contain a series of strings, each one showing the names of the files, their sizes, dates, and types.

The TList version is more flexible than the TStringList version because it gives you separate fields for each of a file's attributes. You might want to use this kind of structure if you are working with a TListView or TTreeView component. It is, however, harder to use than the TStringList version.

The `Instance` variable shown in the last line of the constructor is used in the callback function that I will explain in the section "Creating a Callback." Callbacks can be useful when you want the system to report back to you on the progress it is making while completing a potentially time-consuming process.

Using `InternetOpen()`

Call `InternetOpen()` to get a WinInet session started. Here is the declaration for `InternetOpen()`:

```
HINTERNET InternetOpen(
  IN LPCSTR lpszAgent,       // Name of app opening the session
  IN DWORD dwAccessType,     // The access type, usually set to 0
  IN LPCSTR lpszProxyName,   // For use in specifying a proxy, pass 0
  IN LPCSTR lpszProxyBypass, // For use in specifying a proxy, pass NULL
  IN DWORD dwFlags           // You can set up a callback here.
);
```

As shown in my brief comments, the first parameter is the name of the application opening the session. You can pass in any string you want in this parameter. For what it's worth, the Microsoft documentation states, "This name is used as the user agent in the HTTP protocol." The remaining parameters can be set to 0 or NULL.

The following are some options for use in the `dwAccessType` parameter:

LOCAL_INTERNET_ACCESS	Connects only to local Internet sites
GATEWAY_INTERNET_ACCESS	Allows connections to any site on the Web
CERN_PROXY_INTERNET_ACCESS	Uses a CERN proxy to access the Web

The options appear like this in `WININET.HPP`:

```
// use registry configuration
#define INTERNET_OPEN_TYPE_PRECONFIG                     0
// direct to net
#define INTERNET_OPEN_TYPE_DIRECT                        1
// via named proxy
#define INTERNET_OPEN_TYPE_PROXY                         3
// prevent using java/script/INS
#define INTERNET_OPEN_TYPE_PRECONFIG_WITH_NO_AUTOPROXY   4

// old names for access types

#define PRE_CONFIG_INTERNET_ACCESS   INTERNET_OPEN_TYPE_PRECONFIG
#define LOCAL_INTERNET_ACCESS        INTERNET_OPEN_TYPE_DIRECT
#define CERN_PROXY_INTERNET_ACCESS   INTERNET_OPEN_TYPE_PROXY
```

As you can see, passing in 0 means that you will use information already stored in the Registry.

The next two parameters for `InternetOpen()` are involved with setting up a proxy server, a subject not covered in this book. The last parameter has only one possible flag:

```
INTERNET_FLAG_ASYNC
```

This chapter is not meant to be an exhaustive reference to WinInet, so I'm going to ask you to refer to the Microsoft documentation for additional information on the `InternetOpen()` function.

The following is an example of a typical call to `InternetOpen()`:

```
FINet = InternetOpen("Pipeline", 0, 0, 0, 0);
```

Using `InternetConnect`

After you open the session, the next step is to connect to the server using `InternetConnect()`, which is declared as follows:

```
HINTERNET InternetConnect(         // Handle from InternetOpen
   IN HINTERNET hInternetSession,  // Server: e.g., www.borland.com
   IN LPCSTR lpszServerName,       // Usually 0
   IN INTERNET_PORT nServerPort,   // Usually anonymous
   IN LPCSTR lpszUsername,         // Usually your email address
   IN LPCSTR lpszPassword,         // FTP, HTTP, ¦¦ Gopher?
   IN DWORD dwService,             // Usually 0
   IN DWORD dwFlags,               // User-defined context number
   IN DWORD dwContext              // for a callback
);
```

If you have made it this far in the chapter, you should have no trouble understanding the first five parameters to this function. All you need to do is read my short comments on each field. The main purpose of the first five parameters is to give you a chance to explain what server, password, and username you want to use.

These three self-explanatory and mutually exclusive flags can be passed in the `dwService` parameter:

```
INTERNET_SERVICE_FTP
INTERNET_SERVICE_GOPHER
INTERNET_SERVICE_HTTP
```

The following is the option for the `dwFlags` parameter:

```
INTERNET_CONNECT_FLAG_PASSIVE
```

This option is valid only if you passed `INTERNET_SERVICE_FTP` in the previous parameter. At this time, no other flags are valid for this parameter.

If the session succeeds, `InternetOpen()` returns a valid pointer; otherwise, it returns 0. Remember that you will have to deallocate the return value later. I do so in the object's destructor.

My use of the `InternetConnect()` method provides code that brings up a message explaining exactly what might have gone wrong in case of an error:

```
void TUnlFTP::Connect(String AppName)
{
  FINet = InternetOpen(AppName.c_str(), 0, 0, 0, 0);
  FFtpHandle = InternetConnect(FINet, FServer.c_str(), 0,
    FUserID.c_str(), FPassword.c_str(),
    INTERNET_SERVICE_FTP, 0, ContextNum);
  if (FFtpHandle == 0) {
    String S = "Connection failed\r\n"
      "Server: " + FServer + "\r\n" +
      "UserID: " + FUserID + "\r\n" +
      "Password: " + FPassword;
    throw new FtpException(S);
  }
  else {
    SetUpNewDir();
  }
}
```

This function throws an exception in case of an error. As a result, it does not return a value. You don't have to concern yourself with whether the function succeeds because none of the code after the exception is thrown will be executed. Your program itself won't end, but you will automatically be popped out of the current process and sent back to the message loop if something goes wrong. The only way to stop that process is to catch the exception. It is usually best not to try to handle the exception in a `try/catch` block, but instead to let the exception-handling process resolve the problem for you automatically.

Notice that I have created an exception class called `FtpException`. Here is the entire declaration for the object:

```
class FtpException : public Exception {
  public:
    virtual __fastcall FtpException(String Msg) :
      Exception(Msg) {}
};
```

I create this object only so you can know where the error came from. In other words, you can see that the type of the exception is `FtpException` and know immediately that it must have originated in the `UNLFTP.CPP` unit.

After the object is complete, you can start a session by simply calling the `Connect()` method and passing in the name of your application as a parameter:

```
void __fastcall TForm1::Connect1Click(TObject *Sender)
{
  UnlFTP->Connect("Pipeline");
}
```

Getting the Current Directory

After you are connected, you can call `GetCurrentDirectory()` to retrieve the name of the current directory:

```
String TUnlFTP::GetCurrentDirectory()
{
  DWORD Len = MAX_PATH;
  char buff[MAX_PATH];
  FtpGetCurrentDirectory(FFtpHandle, buff, &Len);
  return String(buff);
}
```

This function calls `FtpGetCurrentDirectory()`, which is declared as follows:

```
BOOL FtpGetCurrentDirectory(          // handle from InternetConnect
  IN HINTERNET hFtpSession,           // directory returned here
  OUT LPSTR lpszCurrentDirectory,     // buf size of 2nd parameter
  IN OUT LPDWORD lpdwCurrentDirectory // true on success
);
```

I have included my own comments on the value of each field here.

If you set the last parameter to `0`, WinInet will use this parameter to return the length of the directory string. You can then allocate memory for your string and call the function a second time to retrieve the directory name. The documentation states that you can use a buffer of size `MAX_PATH` when calling `FtpGetCurrentDirectory()`. That notwithstanding, you may opt to let WinInet tell you how large the buffer should be and dynamically allocate the buffer at that time.

Finding Files in a Directory: The `FindFiles()` Function

The following function returns the currently available files in a particular directory:

```
TStringList* TUnlFTP::FindFiles()
{
  FCurFiles->Clear();
  WIN32_FIND_DATA FindData;
  HINTERNET FindHandle =
    FtpFindFirstFile(FFtpHandle, "*.*", &FindData, 0, 0);
```

```
  if (FindHandle) {
    FCurFiles->Add(GetFindDataStr(FindData));
    while (InternetFindNextFile(FindHandle, &FindData))
      FCurFiles->Add(GetFindDataStr(FindData));
    InternetCloseHandle(FindHandle);
    GetCurrentDirectory();
  }
    return FCurFiles;
}
```

The key WinInet functions to notice here are `FtpFindFirstFile()`, `InternetFindNextFile()`, and `InternetCloseHandle()`. You use these functions in a manner similar to that employed when calling the VCL functions `FindFirst()`, `FindNext()`, and `FindClose()`. In particular, you use `FtpFindFirstFile()` to get the first file in a directory. You then call `InternetFindNextFile()` repeatedly until the function returns `false`. After you finish the session, call `InternetCloseHandle()` to inform the operating system that it can deallocate the memory associated with this process. Calling `InternetCloseHandle()` is by no means optional, and in fact, forgetting to call it constitutes a fairly serious error.

The `FindFiles()` method uses an instance of the `WIN32_FIND_DATA` structure. `WIN32_FIND_DATA` is declared like this in the Windows headers:

```
typedef struct _WIN32_FIND_DATAA {
  DWORD dwFileAttributes;
  FILETIME ftCreationTime;
  FILETIME ftLastAccessTime;
  FILETIME ftLastWriteTime;
  DWORD nFileSizeHigh;
  DWORD nFileSizeLow;
  DWORD dwReserved0;
  DWORD dwReserved1;
  CHAR   cFileName[ MAX_PATH ];
  CHAR   cAlternateFileName[ 14 ];
};
```

This structure is designed to hold information about a file, such as its size, date and time of creation, date and time of last access, and so on. Notes in the WinInet help file state that not all the date and time fields will necessarily be filled out correctly by WinInet routines. This is particularly true if you are accessing a UNIX box via FTP. I discuss the `nFileSizeHigh` and `nFileSizeLow` fields in the next section.

`FindFiles()` stores all information in a string list called `FCurFiles`. You can access the `FCurFiles` list through the `TUnlFTP` property called `CurFiles`. In your main program, you can simply assign it to the items property of a list box. `FCurFiles` is created in the object's constructor and destroyed in the destructor.

The following function returns a simple string designating what type of file is retrieved by a call to `FtpFindFirstFile()` or `InternetFindNextFile()`:

```
String TUnlFTP::GetFindDataStr(WIN32_FIND_DATA FindData)
{
  String S;
  switch (FindData.dwFileAttributes) {
    case FILE_ATTRIBUTE_ARCHIVE: S = "A"; break;
    case FILE_ATTRIBUTE_COMPRESSED: S = "C"; break;
    case FILE_ATTRIBUTE_DIRECTORY: S = "D"; break;
    case FILE_ATTRIBUTE_HIDDEN: S = "H"; break;
    case FILE_ATTRIBUTE_NORMAL: S = "N"; break;
    case FILE_ATTRIBUTE_READONLY: S = "R"; break;
    case FILE_ATTRIBUTE_SYSTEM: S = "S"; break;
    case FILE_ATTRIBUTE_TEMPORARY: S = "T"; break;
    default : S = IntToStr(FindData.dwFileAttributes);
  }
  S = S + "     " + FindData.cFileName;
  String Temp;
  Temp.StringOfChar(' ', 75 - S.Length());
  S = S + Temp;
  FILETIME LocalFileTime;
  __int64 FileSize =
      MAKEDWORDLONG(FindData.nFileSizeLow, FindData.nFileSizeHigh);
  S.Insert(FileSize, 25);
  FileTimeToLocalFileTime(&FindData.ftLastWriteTime, &LocalFileTime);
  Word DosDate;
  Word DosTime;
  FileTimeToDosDateTime(&LocalFileTime, &DosDate, &DosTime);
  TDateTime DateTime = FileDateToDateTime(MAKELONG(DosTime, DosDate));
  S.Insert(DateTimeToStr(DateTime), 45);
  return S;
}
```

I use this information to create a simple string I can show to the user explaining the type of file currently under examination. For example, the string might look like this if I find a directory:

```
D WINDOWS 0 4/01/98 19:38:00
```

The string might look like this if I find a file:

```
F AUTOEXEC.BAT 706 7/22/98 15:48:00
```

The most difficult part of writing this function was converting the `WIN32_FIND_DATA` date and time information into something that C++Builder can use. To accomplish this feat, I used the Windows API functions `FileTimeToLocalFileTime()` and `FileTimeToDosDateTime()`.

> **NOTE**
>
> The GetFindDataStr() method takes some special steps to handle a case in which a file is larger than 4 billion bytes. I explain this issue in the next section, where I show you a second version of the routine.

Storing Files in a List

Retrieving the information about a directory as a string provides a simple method for getting up and running, but it is probably not the right solution for a more professional program. Aiming a little higher, I rewrote the routines shown in the preceding section for those people who have the time to create a more polished program.

As mentioned earlier, the key step was to store the information not in a single string, but in a TFileInfo record. I stored these records on a TList object as follows:

```
TList* TUnlFTP::FindFileRecs()
{
  WIN32_FIND_DATA FindData;
  HINTERNET FindHandle =
    FtpFindFirstFile(FFtpHandle, "*.*", &FindData, 0, 0);
  EmptyList(FFileList);
  if (FindHandle) {
    FFileList->Add(GetFindDataRec(FindData));
    while (InternetFindNextFile(FindHandle, &FindData))
      FFileList->Add(GetFindDataRec(FindData));
    InternetCloseHandle(FindHandle);
    GetCurrentDirectory();
  }
  return FFileList;
}
```

This is the same routine as the FindFile() method in the preceding section, except that this time I store the information in a TFileInfo record:

```
TFileInfo* TUnlFTP::GetFindDataRec(WIN32_FIND_DATA FindData)
{
  TFileInfo* FileInfo = new TFileInfo;
  String S;
  switch (FindData.dwFileAttributes) {
    case FILE_ATTRIBUTE_ARCHIVE: S = "A"; break;
    case FILE_ATTRIBUTE_COMPRESSED: S = "C"; break;
    case FILE_ATTRIBUTE_DIRECTORY: S = "D"; break;
    case FILE_ATTRIBUTE_HIDDEN: S = "H"; break;
    case FILE_ATTRIBUTE_NORMAL: S = "N"; break;
    case FILE_ATTRIBUTE_READONLY: S = "R"; break;
    case FILE_ATTRIBUTE_SYSTEM: S = "S"; break;
```

```
      case FILE_ATTRIBUTE_TEMPORARY: S = "T"; break;
      default : S = FindData.dwFileAttributes;
   }

   FileInfo->Attribute = new char[S.Length() + 1];
   strcpy(FileInfo->Attribute, S.c_str());
   FileInfo->FileName = new char[strlen(FindData.cFileName) + 1];
   strcpy(FileInfo->FileName, FindData.cFileName);
   FileInfo->FileSize = MAKEDWORDLONG(
     FindData.nFileSizeLow, FindData.nFileSizeHigh);

   FILETIME LocalFileTime;
   Word DosDate;
   Word DosTime;
   if (FileTimeToLocalFileTime(&FindData.ftLastWriteTime, &LocalFileTime))
     FileTimeToDosDateTime(&LocalFileTime, &DosDate, &DosTime);
   FileInfo->FileTime = FileDateToDateTime(MAKELONG(DosTime, DosDate));
   return FileInfo;
}
```

Again, you can see that I carefully tucked away key information about the filename, file size, and so on. Notice that the size of the file is stored in two fields: `nFileSizeLow` and `nFileSizeHigh`. Each is declared to be of type `DWORD`, an unsigned 32-bit value.

To convert two `DWORD`s into a single 64-bit value, I use Windows' MAKEWORDLONG macro:

```
FileInfo->FileSize = MAKEDWORDLONG(
  FindData.nFileSizeLow, FindData.nFileSizeHigh);
```

I assume that Windows returns these values in two `DWORD`s because either no such thing as a 64-bit integer value existed when the Win32 API was created or because the Microsoft developers were afraid that most compilers could not handle a 64-bit type. At any rate, that restriction has disappeared over the years, and this code now exists only for historical reasons.

Retrieving a File: The `FtpGetFile()` Function

You can use the `FtpGetFile()` function to retrieve a file via FTP. Here is that function's declaration:

```
BOOL FtpGetFile(
   IN HINTERNET hFtpSession,          // Returned by InternetConnect
   IN LPCSTR lpszRemoteFile,          // File to get
   IN LPCSTR lpszNewFile,             // Where to put it on your PC
   IN BOOL fFailIfExists,             // Overwrite existing files?
```

```
  IN DWORD dwLocalFlagsAndAttributes,   // File attribute-See CreateFile
  IN DWORD dwInternetFlags,             // Binary or ASCII transfer
  IN DWORD dwContext                    // Usually zero
);                                      // returns true on success
```

The following is an example of how to use this call:

```
bool TUnlFTP::GetFile1(String FTPFile, String NewFile)
{
  HINTERNET H = InternetSetStatusCallback(FFtpHandle, MyCallback);
  if (H == INTERNET_INVALID_STATUS_CALLBACK)
    ShowMessage("No callback");

  bool Result = FtpGetFile(FFtpHandle, FTPFile.c_str(), NewFile.c_str(),
    false, FILE_ATTRIBUTE_NORMAL, FTP_TRANSFER_TYPE_BINARY, ContextNum);
  if (!Result)
    throw new FtpException("Copy Failed: " + FTPFile);

  InternetSetStatusCallback(FFtpHandle, 0);
  return Result;
}
```

The `FtpGetFile()` function takes the handle to your session in the first parameter. The second and third parameters contain the local and remote versions of the name of the file you want to call. The next parameter defines whether you want to automatically overwrite existing copies of the file.

The following are the possible file attributes:

```
FILE_ATTRIBUTE_NORMAL
FILE_ATTRIBUTE_ARCHIVE
FILE_ATTRIBUTE_COMPRESSED
FILE_ATTRIBUTE_HIDDEN
FILE_ATTRIBUTE_NORMAL
FILE_ATTRIBUTE_OFFLINE
FILE_ATTRIBUTE_READONLY
FILE_ATTRIBUTE_SYSTEM
FILE_ATTRIBUTE_TEMPORARY
```

I retrieved these values by looking up `CreateFile()` in the Windows API help file. The `dwFlags` parameter can be set to either `FTP_TRANSFER_TYPE_BINARY` or `FTP_TRANSFER_TYPE_ASCII`.

The `FtpGetFile()` method transfers a file for you in one fell swoop, as if it were a bird carrying something in its beak between point A and point B. This process is a bit like going to the DOS prompt and typing the following:

```
copy a:\FileA.Txt c:\FileA.txt
```

18

WinInet and FTP

The copy takes places simply and easily, but you get no feedback on what is happening. Because file transfers can take a long time, I try to give the user some feedback on what is happening by setting up a callback. I will discuss the callback in the next section.

The following is an example of how to call the `GetFile1()` method:

```
void __fastcall TForm1::GetFile1Click(TObject *Sender)
{
  TListItem* Item = ListView1->Selected;
  if (!Item)
    return;
  String S = Item->Caption;
  OpenDialog1->FileName = S;
  if (OpenDialog1->Execute())
    UnlFTP->GetFile1(S, OpenDialog1->FileName);
}
```

This method retrieves the name of the file to copy from a list view. I will explain how to set up the list view at the end of this chapter, when I discuss the code for the Pipeline program. The `GetFile1Click()` method gets the name of the file to write from a `TOpenDialog`. It then copies the file using the `TUnlFTP` class and its `GetFile1()` method.

Creating a Callback

As I'm sure you noticed, the `TUnlFTP::GetFile1()` method begins and ends by setting up a callback. This callback receives notice when the handle for the transfer is created and destroyed, and it receives notices of progress at regular intervals during the actual file transfer.

The first thing you need to do is set up the callback function:

```
void WINAPI MyCallback(HINTERNET Handle, DWORD Context,
  DWORD Status, void* Info, DWORD StatLen)
{
  String S;
  switch (Status) {
    case INTERNET_STATUS_RESOLVING_NAME: S = "Resolving"; break;
    case INTERNET_STATUS_NAME_RESOLVED: S = "Resolved"; break;
    case INTERNET_STATUS_CONNECTING_TO_SERVER:
      S = "Connecting to server"; break;
    case INTERNET_STATUS_CONNECTED_TO_SERVER: S = "Connected"; break;
    case INTERNET_STATUS_SENDING_REQUEST: S = "Sending Request"; break;
    case INTERNET_STATUS_REQUEST_SENT: S = "Request sent"; break;
    case INTERNET_STATUS_RECEIVING_RESPONSE:
      S = "Receiving response"; break;
    case INTERNET_STATUS_RESPONSE_RECEIVED:
      S = "Response received"; break;
    case INTERNET_STATUS_CTL_RESPONSE_RECEIVED:
      S = "CTL Response received"; break;
```

```
      case INTERNET_STATUS_PREFETCH: S = "Prefetch"; break;
      case INTERNET_STATUS_CLOSING_CONNECTION:
        S = "Closing connection"; break;
      case INTERNET_STATUS_CONNECTION_CLOSED:
        S = "Connection closed"; break;
      case INTERNET_STATUS_HANDLE_CREATED: S = "Handle created"; break;
      case INTERNET_STATUS_HANDLE_CLOSING: S = "Handle closing"; break;
      case INTERNET_STATUS_REQUEST_COMPLETE:
        S = "Request complete"; break;
      case INTERNET_STATUS_REDIRECT: S = "Status redirect"; break;
      case INTERNET_STATUS_INTERMEDIATE_RESPONSE:
        S = "Intermediate response"; break;
      case INTERNET_STATUS_STATE_CHANGE: S = "State change"; break;
      default : S = "Unknown status";
  }
  if (Instance)
    if (Instance->OnStatus)
      Instance->OnStatus(Instance, Context, S, Info, StatLen);
}
```

The `MyCallback()` function is of type `INTERNET_STATUS_CALLBACK`, which is declared in
`WININET.H`. Note that the callback function invokes the `TUn1FTP` class's `OnStatus` event
through the `Instance` variable. The declaration for the event handler is as follows:

```
typedef void __fastcall (__closure *TStatusEvent)
  (System::TObject* Sender, DWORD Context, String Status,
   void* Info, DWORD StatLen);
```

> **NOTE**
>
> C++Builder programmers don't typically use events in their classes. There's no
> reason you can't use events in C++ classes, provided the class is derived from
> `TObject` or one of its derived classes. The `TUn1FTP` class provides an example of
> using events in a C++ class.

The last three lines of `MyCallback()` check to see whether the user has assigned an event
handler to the `OnStatus` event:

```
if (Instance)
  if (Instance->OnStatus)
    Instance->OnStatus(Instance, Context, S, Info, StatLen);
```

The first `if` statement just checks to see whether the `Instance` variable is `0`. The
`Instance` variable is a pointer to the `TUn1FTP` class, and it is created explicitly so that this
method can get at the fields of the `TUn1FTP` object. In particular, note that `MyCallback()`
is not a class member, but a standalone function. I want it to have access to `TUn1FTP`, so I

assign the variable `Instance` to `this` during the constructor of `TUnlFTP`, as described earlier in this chapter.

The event handler for the `OnStatus` event is going to be called when the handle for the file transfer is created and at various other times during the file transfer. In particular, it appears to be called after each 4,096 bytes of the file are successfully transferred. Though I looked rather assiduously, I could not find any specification defining exactly when and how my callback was going to be called. The best I can do for you here is inform you of the results I received.

The following is an event handler for the `OnStatus` event:

```
void __fastcall TForm1::UnlFTPStatus(System::TObject* Sender,
  DWORD Context, String Status, void* Info, DWORD StatLen)
{
  StatusBar1->SimpleText = Status;
}
```

This method writes the current status of the transfer to the program's status bar.

> **NOTE**
>
> I'm showing you two techniques for transferring files, but I do not mean to imply that I favor one technology over the other. I wish the callbacks for the `FtpGetFile()` function were more clearly documented, but certainly the function is very easy to use, and with a little testing, you could confirm the validity of the technique I describe here for tracking the progress of the file transfer.
>
> The `FtpGetFile()` method ensures that the whole transfer is handled by the system. I hope that this means it is handled in the most reliable manner possible. The technique I show you in the next section is easy to implement but possibly not quite as robust, depending a little on how the boys and girls in Redmond actually implemented `FtpGetFile()`. I have to confess, however, that you could probably feel pretty safe putting your money on the Redmondites in this matter.

After you have set up the callback function, you need to tell the system to call it. To do so, call `InternetSetStatusCallback()`:

```
bool TUnlFTP::GetFile1(String FTPFile, String NewFile)
{
  HINTERNET H = InternetSetStatusCallback(FFtpHandle, MyCallback);
  if (H == INTERNET_INVALID_STATUS_CALLBACK)
    ShowMessage("No callback");
```

```
bool Result = FtpGetFile(FFtpHandle, FTPFile.c_str(), NewFile.c_str(),
  false, FILE_ATTRIBUTE_NORMAL, FTP_TRANSFER_TYPE_BINARY, ContextNum);
if (!Result)
  throw new FtpException("Copy Failed: " + FTPFile);

InternetSetStatusCallback(FFtpHandle, 0);
return Result;
}
```

I pass the handle to the session and the address of the callback to
`InternetSetStatusCallback()`. The callback is then made active. To deactivate it, I
pass in the handle to the session and 0.

Setting up the callback for each step you take in the process of working with an FTP session is very important. In other words, you might be inclined to set up the callback during the constructor of the program and to set it back to 0 in the destructor. However, this approach would cause a series of errors to occur. Rather than trying for one global callback, you need to set up a "new" callback for each step of the FTP session that you undertake. For instance, here I set up the callback for a file transfer. If I wanted to then get the current directory, I would have to set up the callback again. If I didn't, I would risk getting a series of nasty access violations.

The final, key point you need to grasp about callbacks is that they require you to specify the context for your session. In this control, I declare a global constant called
`ContextNum` and set it to 255. I pass this number into the initialization of the entire session in the last parameter of `InternetConnect()`:

```
FFtpHandle = InternetConnect(FINet, FServer.c_str(), 0,
  FUserID.c_str(), FPassword.c_str(),
  INTERNET_SERVICE_FTP, 0, ContextNum);
```

When you call `FtpGetFile()`, you need to pass this number in again as the last parameter. Otherwise, your callback will not be called.

```
bool Result = FtpGetFile(FFtpHandle, FTPFile.c_str(), NewFile.c_str(),
  false, FILE_ATTRIBUTE_NORMAL, FTP_TRANSFER_TYPE_BINARY, ContextNum);
```

This whole process of setting up and handling a callback is not difficult, but it is a bit involved and takes time to set up correctly. However, taking the time to create callbacks for all the key steps in this process will enable you to create a very professional-looking program that handles FTP file transfers gracefully.

Retrieving a File: The `GetFile2()` Method

WinInet provides a function called `InternetReadFile()` that lets you transfer a file back and forth *X* number of bytes at a time. It enables you to tell the user exactly how many

18

WinInet AND
FTP

bytes you have transferred so far and how many more need to be transferred. In other words, it provides a 100 percent reliable means of obtaining the information you need to set up a progress bar. It is slightly more difficult to call than `FtpGetFile()`, but it saves you the hassle of having to set up a callback, thereby making the method a bit easier to use than `FtpGetFile()`.

The following method shows how to call `InternetReadFile()`:

```
bool TUnlFTP::GetFile2(String FTPFile, String NewFile)
{
  const int BufSize = FileChunkSize;
  __int64 TotalSent = 0;
  TFileStream* FileStream = new TFileStream(NewFile, fmCreate);
  HINTERNET FHandle =
    FtpOpenFile(FFtpHandle, FTPFile.c_str(),
      GENERIC_READ, FTP_TRANSFER_TYPE_BINARY, 0);
  char* Buffer = new char[BufSize];
  DWORD NumRead;
  if (FHandle) {
    do {
      InternetReadFile(FHandle, Buffer, BufSize, &NumRead);
      if (NumRead > 0)
        FileStream->Write(Buffer, NumRead);
      if (FOnTransfer) {
        TotalSent = TotalSent + NumRead;
        FOnTransfer(this, NumRead, TotalSent);
      }
    } while (NumRead >= BufSize);
  } else
    ShowMessage("Failed");
  InternetCloseHandle(FHandle);
  delete[] Buffer;
  delete FileStream;
  return true;
}
```

A call to `InternetReadFile()` begins by first opening the file using `FtpOpenFile()`. The declaration for `FtpOpenFile()` looks like this:

```
HINTERNET FtpOpenFile(
  IN HINTERNET hFtpSession,  // Handle to the ftp session
  IN LPCSTR lpszFileName,    // File to open
  IN DWORD fdwAccess,        // GENERIC_READ or GENERIC_WRITE
  IN DWORD dwFlags,          // FTP_TRANSFER_TYPE_ASCII or
                             // FTP_TRANSFER_TYPE_BINARY
  IN DWORD dwContext         // The context used for callbacks
);
```

This method returns a handle to your file transfer session. You need this handle to call `InternetReadFile()`. The `FtpOpenFile()` method itself is straightforward, providing a means to specify the file you want to transfer, whether you want to read or write it, and whether you want to use ASCII or binary transfer. You can set up a callback if you want to trace the progress of opening the file.

The following is the declaration for `InternetReadFile()`, along with my comments on each field:

```
BOOL InternetReadFile(
   IN HINTERNET hFile,                 // Handle FtpOpenFile
   IN LPVOID lpBuffer,                 // Pointer to buffer
   IN DWORD dwNumberOfBytesToRead,     // Size of buffer
   OUT LPDWORD lpNumberOfBytesRead     // Returns number of bytes read
);                                     // Returns failure or success
```

Again, this method is very straightforward. You just pass in the handle you got from `FtpOpenFile()` and then a buffer that can hold a few bytes. Add information on the size of your buffer or on the amount of the buffer that you want to use. Because you normally want to use the whole buffer, this third parameter usually boils down to just being a report on the size of the buffer you created. The fourth parameter tells you how many bytes were actually read.

My implementation of this method works with a standard VCL file stream to write the bytes to disk on the client machine. Look at this paired-down version of the transfer method that focuses on the parts that use the `TFileStream` object:

```
TFileStream* FileStream = new TFileStream(NewFile, fmCreate);
do {
  InternetReadFile(FHandle, Buffer, BufSize, &NumRead);
  if (NumRead > 0)
    FileStream->Write(Buffer, NumRead);
} while (NumRead >= BufSize);
delete FileStream;
```

This method is straightforward because all the program needs to do is create the stream, call its `Write()` method, and close the stream when done.

Once again, I have created an event handler that a program can subscribe to if it wants to trace the progress of the file transfer:

```
if (FOnTransfer) {
  TotalSent = TotalSent + NumRead;
  FOnTransfer(this, NumRead, TotalSent);
}
```

The following is the declaration for the `OnTransfer` method type:

```
typedef void __fastcall (__closure *TTransferEvent)
  (System::TObject* Sender, int BytesSent, __int64 TotalSent);
```

Each time the method is called, the client program is notified of how many bytes were sent in the last transfer and how many bytes have been sent total.

It seems unlikely that anything would ever go wrong using the techniques outlined in this section. However, as mentioned earlier, `FtpGetFile()` allows the system to handle all the details. All you have to do is set up the callback, do some mind reading to figure out how the callback is called, and wait while the transfer occurs. If you use `InternetReadFile()`, you are involved in more of the nitty-gritty; therefore, you have to handle things such as full disks or writes to bad sectors, and so on.

Sometimes you will want complete control over a file transfer, so `InternetReadFile()` might be your only choice in those cases. In particular, I believe I will have to use `InternetReadFile()` when I add the ability to cancel a file transfer to this program.

Sending Files to the Server (Simple Method)

When you're sending files to an NT site, remember that you probably don't have rights in the default FTP directory. Instead, you should change to another directory where your user has rights. You can usually configure what rights a particular user has on a server through the server-side tools provided for administrating user accounts.

This function copies a file to a server:

```
bool TUnlFTP::SendFile1(String FTPFile, String NewFile)
{
  DWORD Size= 3000;
  bool Transfer = FtpPutFile(FFtpHandle, FTPFile.c_str(),
    NewFile.c_str(), FTP_TRANSFER_TYPE_BINARY, 0);

  if (!Transfer) {
    DWORD Error = GetLastError();
    ShowMessage(String().sprintf(
      "Error Number: %d. Hex: %x", Error, Error));
    char* buff = new char[Size];
    if (!InternetGetLastResponseInfo(&Error, buff, &Size)) {
      Error = GetLastError();
      ShowMessage(String().sprintf(
        "Error Number: %d. Hex: %x", Error, Error));
    }
    ShowMessage(String().sprintf("Error Number: %d. Hex: %x Info: %s",
      Error, Error, buff));
  } else
    ShowMessage("Success");
  return Transfer;
}
```

The core function looks like this:

```
bool Transfer = FtpPutFile(FFtpHandle, FTPFile.c_str(),
  NewFile.c_str(), FTP_TRANSFER_TYPE_BINARY, 0);
```

FtpPutFile() takes the following parameters respectively:

- The session handle
- The file to copy from your hard drive
- The filename as it will be on the server
- Whether to conduct a binary or ASCII transfer
- Information about the context of the transfer (usually set to 0)

The rest of the code in the SendFile1() function is dedicated to error handling. Call GetLastError() to retrieve the error code and call InternetGetLastResponseInfo() to retrieve a human-readable description of the error.

You can set up a callback for this function as described in the analysis of the FtpGetFile() function. Furthermore, the TUnlFTP class shows a second method for sending files that uses InternetReadFile(). However, this second method— SendFile2()—is nearly identical to GetFile2(). I will not describe it here.

Deleting Files

The act of deleting a file on a server is extremely simple:

```
void TUnlFTP::DeleteFile(String S)
{
  if (!FtpDeleteFile(FFtpHandle, S.c_str()))
    throw new FtpException("Could not delete file");
}
```

FtpDeleteFile() takes a handle to the current FTP session in the first parameter and a string specifying the file to delete in the second parameter. The call could not be much simpler.

Creating and Removing Directories

WinInet makes the process of creating and deleting directories trivial. One function is used for each task, and each takes the connection handle for your connection in the first parameter and the name of the directory you want to create or destroy in the second parameter. Here are the declarations for the `FtpCreateDirectory()` and `FtpRemoveDirectory()` functions:

```
BOOL FtpCreateDirectory(
    IN HINTERNET hFtpSession, // Handle to session
    IN LPCSTR lpszDirectory    // Name of directory
);

BOOL FtpRemoveDirectory(
    IN HINTERNET hFtpSession, // Handle to session
    IN LPCSTR lpszDirectory    // Name of directory
);
```

The following two simple functions demonstrate how to use the routines:

```
void TUnlFTP::CreateDirectory(String S)
{
  if (!FtpCreateDirectory(FFtpHandle, S.c_str()))
    throw new FtpException("Could not create directory");
}

void TUnlFTP::DeleteDirectory(String S)
{
  if (!FtpRemoveDirectory(FFtpHandle, S.c_str()))
    throw new FtpException("Could not remove directory");
}
```

Assuming the presence of these routines, you can then write a function like the following to provide an interface with which the user can interact:

```
void __fastcall TForm1::DeleteDirectory1Click(TObject *Sender)
{
  TListItem* ListItem = ListView1->Selected;
  String S = ListItem->Caption;
  if (InputQuery("Remove Directory", "Directory Name", S)) {
    UnlFTP->DeleteDirectory(S);
    UnlFTPNewDir(0);
  }
}
```

This routine first retrieves the name of the directory you want to delete from a list view. The `InputQuery()` function is then used to check with the user to be sure that this action is really what he or she wants to do. If the user replies in the affirmative, the directory is deleted and the user is shown the directory's new state. I explain the `InputQuery()` routine at the end of this section.

Here is a similar function used to create a directory:

```
void __fastcall TForm1::CreateDirectory1Click(TObject *Sender)
{
  String S = "";
```

```
    if (InputQuery("Create Directory", "Directory Name", S)) {
      UnlFTP->CreateDirectory(S);
      UnlFTPNewDir(0);
    }
}
```

In this case, the VCL InputQuery() dialog box is invoked. This function takes a title in the first parameter, a prompt in the second parameter, and the string you want the user to enter or edit in the third parameter. If the user clicks OK in the dialog box, the directory is created and the user's view of the directory is refreshed by a call to UnlFTPNewDir().

Using the FTP Class in a Program

The FtpPipieline program uses the TUnlFTP class. To start, you create an instance of the class and assign values to the RemoteServer, UserID, and Password properties. The class automatically returns the contents of the current remote directory in either a TStringList or a TList object. It enables you to perform file transfers, delete files, create and delete directories, and navigate through directories. You need to add a function to the program to let you enter in the name of a directory so that you can switch to directories that cannot be immediately browsed.

In Listings 18.1 and 18.2 you find the header and main form of the program called FtpPipeline. Listings 18.3 and 18.4 contain a dialog used to report the status of the program when transferring a file. Additional dialogs and forms are included with the complete source for the program found on the CD-ROM that comes with this book.

The program's main screen is shown earlier in this chapter in Figure 18.2. A form in which users can select FTP connections is shown in Figure 18.3, and a form for transferring multiple files is shown in Figure 18.4.

18

WinINet AND
FTP

FIGURE 18.3

A form used by the FTP Pipeline program to allow users to select an FTP connection from a table.

FIGURE 18.4

The file transfer form download-ing several files from a remote site.

LISTING 18.1   THE HEADER FOR THE FTPPIPELINE PROGRAM'S MAIN UNIT

```
#ifndef MainH
#define MainH

#include <Classes.hpp>
#include <Controls.hpp>
#include <StdCtrls.hpp>
#include <Forms.hpp>
#include <ComCtrls.hpp>
#include <Dialogs.hpp>
#include <ExtCtrls.hpp>
#include <ImgList.hpp>
#include <Menus.hpp>
#include <ToolWin.hpp>
#include "UnlFtp.h"

enum TFtpMode {ftpCopy, ftpSend};

class TForm1 : public TForm
{
__published:    // IDE-managed Components
  TSplitter *Splitter1;
  TListView *ListView1;
  TStatusBar *StatusBar1;
  TMainMenu *MainMenu1;
  TMenuItem *File1;
  TMenuItem *Connect1;
  TMenuItem *N1;
  TMenuItem *Exit1;
  TMenuItem *Options1;
  TMenuItem *Back1;
  TMenuItem *N2;
  TMenuItem *Copy1;
  TMenuItem *Send1;
  TMenuItem *N3;
  TMenuItem *DeleteFile1;
```

```cpp
    TMenuItem *CreateDirectory1;
    TMenuItem *DeleteDirectory1;
    TMenuItem *N4;
    TMenuItem *Refresh1;
    TMenuItem *Other1;
    TMenuItem *GetFile1;
    TMenuItem *Help1;
    TMenuItem *Contents1;
    TMenuItem *MyWebSite1;
    TMenuItem *N5;
    TMenuItem *About1;
    TSaveDialog *SaveDialog1;
    TOpenDialog *OpenDialog1;
    TToolBar *ToolBar1;
    TToolButton *ToolButton1;
    TImageList *ImageList;
    TLabel *Label1;
    TToolButton *ToolButton2;
    void __fastcall About1Click(TObject *Sender);
    void __fastcall Back1Click(TObject *Sender);
    void __fastcall Connect1Click(TObject *Sender);
    void __fastcall Copy1Click(TObject *Sender);
    void __fastcall DeleteFile1Click(TObject *Sender);
    void __fastcall CreateDirectory1Click(TObject *Sender);
    void __fastcall DeleteDirectory1Click(TObject *Sender);
    void __fastcall FormShow(TObject *Sender);
    void __fastcall GetFile1Click(TObject *Sender);
    void __fastcall ListView1DblClick(TObject *Sender);
    void __fastcall Send1Click(TObject *Sender);
    void __fastcall FormCreate(TObject *Sender);
    void __fastcall FormDestroy(TObject *Sender);
private:        // User declarations
    TFtpMode FTPMode;
    Graphics::TBitmap* FFolderBitmap;
    Graphics::TBitmap* FFileBitmap;
    void __fastcall UnlFTPStatus(System::TObject* Sender,
      DWORD Context, String Status, void* Info, DWORD StatLen);
    void __fastcall UnlFTPTransfer(
      System::TObject* Sender, int BytesSent, __int64 TotalSent);
    void __fastcall UnlFTPNewDir(TObject* Sender);
public:         // User declarations
    __fastcall TForm1(TComponent* Owner);
    TUnlFTP* UnlFTP;
};

extern PACKAGE TForm1 *Form1;

#endif
```

LISTING 18.2   THE SOURCE CODE FOR THE FTPPIPELINE PROGRAM'S MAIN UNIT

```cpp
#include <vcl.h>
#pragma hdrstop

#include "Main.h"
#include "AboutBox1.h"
#include "ProgressDlg1.h"
#include "SendDlg1.h"
#include "FtpNames1.h"

#pragma package(smart_init)
#pragma resource "*.dfm"
TForm1 *Form1;

__fastcall TForm1::TForm1(TComponent* Owner)
  : TForm(Owner)
{
}

void __fastcall TForm1::About1Click(TObject *Sender)
{
  AboutBox->ShowModal();
}

void __fastcall TForm1::Back1Click(TObject *Sender)
{
  UnlFTP->BackOneDir();
}

void __fastcall TForm1::UnlFTPStatus(System::TObject* Sender,
  DWORD Context, String Status, void* Info, DWORD StatLen)
{
  StatusBar1->SimpleText = Status;
}

void __fastcall TForm1::UnlFTPTransfer(
  System::TObject* Sender, int BytesSent, __int64 TotalSent)
{
  if (FTPMode == ftpCopy)
    ProgressDlg->ProgressBar->Position = TotalSent;
  else
    SendDlg->ProgressBar->Position = TotalSent;
  Application->ProcessMessages();
}

void __fastcall TForm1::UnlFTPNewDir(TObject* Sender)
{
  TList* L = UnlFTP->FindFileRecs();
  ListView1->Items->Clear();
  for (int i=0;i<L->Count;i++) {
```

```
      TListItem* ListItem = ListView1->Items->Add();
      TFileInfo* FileInfo = (TFileInfo*)L->Items[i];
      ListItem->Caption = FileInfo->FileName;
      ListItem->SubItems->Add(FileInfo->Attribute);
      ListItem->SubItems->Add(IntToStr(FileInfo->FileSize));
      ListItem->SubItems->Add(DateTimeToStr(FileInfo->FileTime));
    }
  Label1->Caption = FtpNames->Server + UnlFTP->CurDir;
}

void __fastcall TForm1::Connect1Click(TObject *Sender)
{
  if (FtpNames->GetConnectionData()) {
    Application->ProcessMessages();
    Screen->Cursor = crHourGlass;
    UnlFTP->Server = FtpNames->Server;
    UnlFTP->UserID = FtpNames->UserID;
    UnlFTP->Password = FtpNames->Password;
    UnlFTP->Connect("Pipeline");
    Screen->Cursor = crDefault;
  }
}

void __fastcall TForm1::Copy1Click(TObject *Sender)
{
  String S;
  if (ListView1->Selected == 0)
    ShowMessage("Select a file first");
  else if (InputQuery(
    "Select Directory", "Directory Name", S)) {
    FTPMode = ftpCopy;
    ProgressDlg->Run(ListView1, S, UnlFTP->CurDir);
  }
}

void __fastcall TForm1::DeleteFile1Click(TObject *Sender)
{
  TListItem* ListItem = ListView1->Selected;
  if (MessageBox(Handle, "Delete selected files?",
    "Delete File Dialog", MB_ICONQUESTION | MB_YESNOCANCEL) == IDYES) {
    UnlFTP->DeleteFile(ListItem->Caption);
    for (int i=0;i<ListView1->SelCount;i++) {
      ListItem =  ListView1->GetNextItem(
        ListItem, sdAll, TItemStates() << isSelected);
      UnlFTP->DeleteFile(ListItem->Caption);
    }
    UnlFTPNewDir(0);
  }
}
```

18

WININET AND FTP

continues

LISTING 18.2 CONTINUED

```cpp
void __fastcall TForm1::CreateDirectory1Click(TObject *Sender)
{
  String S = "";
  if (InputQuery("Create Directory", "Directory Name", S)) {
    UnlFTP->CreateDirectory(S);
    UnlFTPNewDir(0);
  }
}

void __fastcall TForm1::DeleteDirectory1Click(TObject *Sender)
{
  TListItem* ListItem = ListView1->Selected;
  String S = ListItem->Caption;
  if (InputQuery("Remove Directory", "Directory Name", S)) {
    UnlFTP->DeleteDirectory(S);
    UnlFTPNewDir(0);
  }
}

void __fastcall TForm1::FormShow(TObject *Sender)
{
  Label1->Caption = "Not connected.";
}

void __fastcall TForm1::GetFile1Click(TObject *Sender)
{
  TListItem* Item = ListView1->Selected;
  if (!Item)
    return;
  String S = Item->Caption;
  OpenDialog1->FileName = S;
  if (OpenDialog1->Execute())
    UnlFTP->GetFile1(S, OpenDialog1->FileName);
}

void __fastcall TForm1::ListView1DblClick(TObject *Sender)
{
  TListItem* ListItem = ListView1->Selected;
  Screen->Cursor = crHourGlass;
  UnlFTP->ChangeDirExact(ListItem->Caption);
  Screen->Cursor = crDefault;
}

void __fastcall TForm1::Send1Click(TObject *Sender)
{
  if (OpenDialog1->Execute()) {
    FTPMode = ftpSend;
    SendDlg->Run(OpenDialog1, UnlFTP->CurDir);
  }
```

```
    UnlFTPNewDir(0);
}

void __fastcall TForm1::FormCreate(TObject *Sender)
{
  UnlFTP = new TUnlFTP;
  UnlFTP->Server = "ftp.microsoft.com";
  UnlFTP->UserID = "myname@mycompany.com";
  UnlFTP->Password = "anonymous";
  UnlFTP->OnStatus = UnlFTPStatus;
  UnlFTP->OnTransfer = UnlFTPTransfer;
  UnlFTP->OnNewDir = UnlFTPNewDir;
}

void __fastcall TForm1::FormDestroy(TObject *Sender)
{
  delete UnlFTP;
}
```

LISTING 18.3 THE HEADER FOR THE FTPPIPELINE PROGRAM'S SendDlg1 UNIT

```
#ifndef SendDlg1H
#define SendDlg1H

#include <Classes.hpp>
#include <Controls.hpp>
#include <StdCtrls.hpp>
#include <Forms.hpp>
#include <Buttons.hpp>
#include <ComCtrls.hpp>
#include <ExtCtrls.hpp>

class TSendDlg : public TForm
{
__published:    // IDE-managed Components
  TBevel *Bevel2;
  TBitBtn *CancelBtn;
  TBitBtn *CopyBtn;
  TListBox *ListBox1;
  TBevel *Bevel1;
  TEdit *CopyFromEdit;
  TLabel *Label1;
  TLabel *Label2;
  TEdit *CopyToEdit;
  TProgressBar *ProgressBar;
  void __fastcall CopyBtnClick(TObject *Sender);
  void __fastcall FormShow(TObject *Sender);
private:        // User declarations
  String FCurDir;
```

continues

LISTING 18.3   CONTINUED

```cpp
  TOpenDialog* FOpenDialog;
  void SendMultipleFiles();
  __int64 BigFileSize(String FileName);
public:          // User declarations
  __fastcall TSendDlg(TComponent* Owner);
  void Run(TOpenDialog* OpenDialog, String CurDir);
};

extern PACKAGE TSendDlg *SendDlg;

#endif
```

LISTING 18.4   THE SOURCE CODE FOR THE FTPPIPELINE PROGRAM'S SendDlg1 UNIT

```cpp
#include <vcl.h>
#pragma hdrstop

#include "SendDlg1.h"
#include "Main.h"

#pragma package(smart_init)
#pragma resource "*.dfm"
#pragma warn -osh
TSendDlg *SendDlg;

__fastcall TSendDlg::TSendDlg(TComponent* Owner)
  : TForm(Owner)
{
}

void TSendDlg::SendMultipleFiles()
{
  ListBox1->ItemIndex = 0;
  ListBox1->Update();
  for (int i=0;i<ListBox1->Items->Count;i++) {
    ListBox1->ItemIndex = i;
    __int64 Size = BigFileSize(ListBox1->Items->Strings[i]);
    ProgressBar->Max = Size;
    ProgressBar->Position = 0;
    ProgressBar->Update();
    CopyFromEdit->Text = ListBox1->Items->Strings[i];
    CopyToEdit->Text =
      FCurDir + ExtractFileName(ListBox1->Items->Strings[i]);
    Form1->UnlFTP->SendFile2(
      ExtractFileName(ListBox1->Items->Strings[i]),
      ListBox1->Items->Strings[i]);
  }
}
```

```cpp
void TSendDlg::Run(TOpenDialog* OpenDialog, String CurDir)
{
  FOpenDialog = OpenDialog;
  Caption = "Remote Directory: " + CurDir;
  FCurDir = CurDir;
  ShowModal();
}

void __fastcall TSendDlg::CopyBtnClick(TObject *Sender)
{
  SendMultipleFiles();
  ShowMessage("Success!");
  Close();
}

void __fastcall TSendDlg::FormShow(TObject *Sender)
{
  ListBox1->Clear();
  for (int i=0;i<FOpenDialog->Files->Count;i++)
    ListBox1->Items->Add(FOpenDialog->Files->Strings[i]);
}

__int64 TSendDlg::BigFileSize(String FileName)
{
  if (FileName.Length() == 0)
    return 0;

  HANDLE hFile = CreateFile(FileName.c_str(), GENERIC_READ,
    FILE_SHARE_READ, 0, OPEN_EXISTING, FILE_FLAG_SEQUENTIAL_SCAN, 0);

  if (!hFile)
    return 0;

  DWORD LoSize, HighSize;
  LoSize = GetFileSize(hFile, &HighSize);
  CloseHandle(hFile);
  return MAKEDWORDLONG(LoSize, HighSize);
}
```

Connecting to the Server

When FtpPipeline calls the TUnlFTP::Connect() function, it does so in a function that looks like this:

```cpp
void __fastcall TForm1::Connect1Click(TObject *Sender)
{
  if (FtpNames->GetConnectionData()) {
    Application->ProcessMessages();
    Screen->Cursor = crHourGlass;
    UnlFTP->Server = FtpNames->Server;
```

```
    UnlFTP->UserID = FtpNames->UserID;
    UnlFTP->Password = FtpNames->Password;
    UnlFTP->Connect("Pipeline");
    Screen->Cursor = crDefault;
  }
}
```

The GetConnectionData() function makes sure that the Server, UserID, and Password properties are filled in correctly. It does so by calling the FtpNames form's GetConnectionData() method:

```
bool TFtpNames::GetConnectionData()
{
  if (ShowModal() == mrOk) {
    FServer = FTPTableServer->Value;
    FUserID = FTPTableUserID->Value;
    FPassword = FTPTablePassword->Value;
    return true;
  }
  else
    return false;
}
```

The program stores a list of previously used FTP sessions in a database table. This table ensures that you don't have to retype the user ID, password, and server name for sites that you have already visited.

Notice that the Connect() function sets the program's icon to an hourglass and calls the following:

```
Application->ProcessMessages();
```

The program takes this step to be sure that the screen is properly redrawn before handing control over to the system. Especially if something goes wrong, the system could take a minute or more to return from a call to InternetConnect(). Two things should occur while you're waiting for the system to either time out or resolve the call: the screen should look right and you should tell users that all is well and that they should sit tight.

Responding to OnNewDir Events

If you respond to the TUnlFTP class's OnNewDir event, you can get a directory listing for the current FTP site mirrored in a ListView by writing the following lines of code:

```
void __fastcall TForm1::UnlFTPNewDir(TObject* Sender)
{
  TList* L = UnlFTP->FindFileRecs();
  ListView1->Items->Clear();
  for (int i=0;i<L->Count;i++) {
```

```
    TListItem* ListItem = ListView1->Items->Add();
    TFileInfo* FileInfo = (TFileInfo*)L->Items[i];
    ListItem->Caption = FileInfo->FileName;
    ListItem->SubItems->Add(FileInfo->Attribute);
    ListItem->SubItems->Add(IntToStr(FileInfo->FileSize));
    ListItem->SubItems->Add(DateTimeToStr(FileInfo->FileTime));
  }
  Label1->Caption = FtpNames->Server + UnlFTP->CurDir;
}
```

The majority of the code in the UnlFTPNewDir() method just iterates through the files
available in a directory and puts them in a list view.

To work with a list view, first drop a TListView component on a form; then use the
Columns property in the Object Inspector to give the list view four columns called Name,
Type, Size, and Date. Finally, set the ViewStyle property of the TListView to vsReport.

To add items to the list in code, call the Items->Add() method of a TListView control.
Give the node a caption by writing the following:

```
TListItem* ListItem = ListView1->Items->Add();
ListItem->Caption = FileInfo->FileName;
```

You can then call the SubItems->Add() method to fill in additional nodes on the item:

```
ListItem->SubItems->Add(FileInfo->Attribute);
ListItem->SubItems->Add(IntToStr(FileInfo->FileSize));
ListItem->SubItems->Add(DateTimeToStr(FileInfo->FileTime));
```

Changing Directories

After you have displayed a directory of files, the program still must provide a technique
for letting the user change directories. One simple method is to respond to double-clicks
on a directory name by changing into the selected directory:

```
void __fastcall TForm1::ListView1DblClick(TObject *Sender)
{
  TListItem* ListItem = ListView1->Selected;
  Screen->Cursor = crHourGlass;
  UnlFTP->ChangeDirExact(ListItem->Caption);
  Screen->Cursor = crDefault;
}
```

Notice that this code sets the program's cursor to an hourglass so that the user feels comfortable while waiting for the operation to complete.

The following is the code for ChangeDirExact() from TUnlFTP class:

```
bool TUnlFTP::ChangeDirExact(String S)
{
```

```
if (S != "")
  FtpSetCurrentDirectory(FFtpHandle, S.c_str());
FindFiles();
SetUpNewDir();
return true;
}
```

This code calls the self-explanatory FtpSetCurrentDirectory() method and then updates the file list to automatically show the contents of the new directory.

Techniques similar to this are used for creating directories, deleting directories, and for deleting files. However, the code is too trivial to explain in this text.

Tracking a File Transfer

When the user wants to copy or send files, the program provides the opportunity to transfer multiple files at one time. This capability allows you to update or download the contents of an entire directory with a single command.

To allow a user to select multiple files in a TListView control, set its MultiSelect property to true. To do the same thing in a TOpenDialog, set the Options property's ofMultiSelect set element to true.

I set up a separate dialog for both sending and receiving files. I do this in part to create a clean interface and in part because I can bring it up as a modal dialog, thereby ensuring that the user does not try to do anything else while the transfer is occurring.

The following is the code to set up the SendDlg form used to send files:

```
void __fastcall TForm1::Send1Click(TObject *Sender)
{
  if (OpenDialog1->Execute()) {
    FTPMode = ftpSend;
    SendDlg->Run(OpenDialog1, UnlFTP->CurDir);
  }
  UnlFTPNewDir(0);
}
```

As you can see, I have opted to simply pass in the TOpenDialog object itself and leave it up to the SendDlg object to parse the user's selections:

```
void __fastcall TSendDlg::FormShow(TObject *Sender)
{
  ListBox1->Clear();
  for (int i=0;i<FOpenDialog->Files->Count;i++)
    ListBox1->Items->Add(FOpenDialog->Files->Strings[i]);
}
```

```
void TSendDlg::SendMultipleFiles()
{
  ListBox1->ItemIndex = 0;
  ListBox1->Update();
  for (int i=0;i<ListBox1->Items->Count;i++) {
    ListBox1->ItemIndex = i;
    __int64 Size = BigFileSize(ListBox1->Items->Strings[i]);
    ProgressBar->Max = Size;
    ProgressBar->Position = 0;
    ProgressBar->Update();
    CopyFromEdit->Text = ListBox1->Items->Strings[i];
    CopyToEdit->Text =
      FCurDir + ExtractFileName(ListBox1->Items->Strings[i]);
    Form1->UnlFTP->SendFile2(
      ExtractFileName(ListBox1->Items->Strings[i]),
      ListBox1->Items->Strings[i]);
  }
}
```

In the `FormShow()` method, I iterate the selected items in the `OpenDialog`, transferring their names to a list box. I do so just to give the user a second chance to be sure he or she has picked the files correctly. Also, I can point at each of the files in turn in the list box, helping the user see which file is currently being transferred and how many more files need to be sent. The program could be improved by displaying the size of the files in the list box.

I actually do retrieve the size of each file so that I can accurately gauge the progress of the file transfer. To get information on the size of the file, I can't call the VCL `FileSize()` routine because it returns a 32-bit integer. Instead, I call a custom function called `BigFileSize()`:

```
__int64 TSendDlg::BigFileSize(String FileName)
{
  if (FileName.Length() == 0)
    return 0;

  HANDLE hFile = CreateFile(FileName.c_str(), GENERIC_READ,
    FILE_SHARE_READ, 0, OPEN_EXISTING, FILE_FLAG_SEQUENTIAL_SCAN, 0);

  if (!hFile)
    return 0;

  DWORD LoSize, HighSize;
  LoSize = GetFileSize(hFile, &HighSize);
  CloseHandle(hFile);
  return MAKEDWORDLONG(LoSize, HighSize);
}
```

This function calls the Windows API `CreateFile()` routine to open the file. It then uses the Windows API `GetFileSize()` routine to return the size of the file. Finally, the routine closes the file and returns its size with the help of the MAKEWORDLONG macro, as described earlier in the chapter.

The `SendDlg` object contains a `TProgressBar` control from the Win32 page of the Component Palette. With each iteration of the loop, I set the maximum value of the gauge to the file's size and its current position to 0:

```
__int64 Size = BigFileSize(ListBox1->Items->Strings[i]);
ProgressBar->Max = Size;
ProgressBar->Position = 0;
ProgressBar->Update();
```

I then inform the user explicitly where the file is being copied from and to:

```
CopyFromEdit->Text = ListBox1->Items->Strings[i];
CopyToEdit->Text =
  FCurDir + ExtractFileName(ListBox1->Items->Strings[i]);
```

Finally, I send the file itself using the `SendFile2()` routine from the `TUnlFTP` class:

```
Form1->UnlFTP->SendFile2(
  ExtractFileName(ListBox1->Items->Strings[i]),
  ListBox1->Items->Strings[i]);
```

While the file is being transferred, status messages are being sent to the main form of the program by the `TUnlFTP` class. The following routine handles the message after it is sent to the main form:

```
void __fastcall TForm1::UnlFTPTransfer(
  System::TObject* Sender, int BytesSent, __int64 TotalSent)
{
  if (FTPMode == ftpCopy)
    ProgressDlg->ProgressBar->Position = TotalSent;
  else
    SendDlg->ProgressBar->Position = TotalSent;
  Application->ProcessMessages();
}
```

As you can see, this trivial code first checks to see whether the user is in the `ProgressDlg` for copying files or the `SendDlg` for sending files. It then updates the gauge in the appropriate dialog. Because the range of the gauge has already been set, nothing else needs to be done, and the program only needs to pause to update the screen before exiting the method.

In this section, you have followed the whole process of sending a series of files to a remote server. I'm not going to take you through the same process for copying files from the server because it differs in only minor ways from the process shown here.

Summary

In general, the Pipeline program provides a fairly robust means of transferring files to and from a server via FTP. I developed the program because I needed a way to help maintain my AOL Web site. However, I use it for a wide range of purposes. As a rule, this kind of tool is now meant mostly for programmers and IS employees, as the hoi polloi now use Web browsers to initiate FTP transfers.

Someday I would like to create a second chapter or article showing how to use the HTTP services that are also part of WinInet. As you have seen, WinInet is a very elegantly designed interface and is extremely easy to use. Taking advantage of its HTTP services by wrapping them in a component would be a useful service for many programming shops.

This chapter focuses on WinInet and FTP. WinInet turns out to be a fairly simple API to use. It provides a great means for creating small, powerful objects that enable you to access the key features of the Internet. You should visit Microsoft's Web site to download additional information about WinInet. Remember that the DLL that makes this all possible is called, naturally enough, `WININET.DLL`. Starting with Windows NT 4, it ships with all versions of Windows and is freely available for distribution with your applications. It works fine on Windows 95 and ships with Windows 98.

DCOM

19

by Charlie Calvert and Bruneau Babet

IN THIS CHAPTER

This chapter is about distributed computing. I want to show you how to build Distributed Component Object Model (DCOM) applications so that you can call objects that reside on other machines. I also want to show you how to use DCOM to create a lightweight, no-cost technology for distributing your databases across the network.

You will find a number of sample programs in the current chapter. The included code shows server applications running on remote machines and client applications that invoke the methods and properties of these servers.

COM and Distributed Architectures

Let's see how DCOM actually performs its magic. I will begin by discussing exactly what the technology does and then describe how to use it on both Windows NT and Windows 9x.

The true power of COM is revealed when you remove it from the context of a single machine and spawn it on a network. Distributed COM, or DCOM, is possibly the strongest and most mature of the available tools in this field, but it has historically been hampered by the fact that it worked primarily on 32-bit Windows operating systems. However, ports of COM to UNIX are available, as discussed in the "COM on UNIX" section of Chapter 13, "The Basics of COM and Type Libraries."

DCOM is important because it allows applications to talk to one another across a network. In particular, it allows you to share objects that reside on two separate machines. This means you can create an object in one application or DLL and then call the methods of that object from an application that resides on a different computer. When you are making these calls, the application server is loaded in the address space of the server machine and does not consume resources on the client. In particular, DCOM maps method calls down to standard RPC calls and then marshals the data passed as parameters between machines.

If you already understand COM, then you will find learning about DCOM trivial. DCOM works on the same principles as COM. Through the use of the DComCnfg.exe utility, you can convert existing COM objects into DCOM objects with no change to your code. Even without DComCnfg.exe, you should not have to change your server at all. Changes to your client involve adding only one or two lines of code.

Running DCOM Servers on Windows 9x/NT

The hard part of using DCOM is setting up your system correctly. After you get over the setup issues, everything else should be easy.

You can set up DCOM networks in three ways:

1. DCOM servers and clients work very well between two Windows NT machines.
2. If you are using Windows 98 as the client, then all works well as long as the server is running on an NT machine.
3. You also can use a Windows 98 machine as a server, but the results are a bit more problematic, particularly when you consider the all-important matter of security.

On the Windows NT side, you should install at least Service Pack 3 on a Windows NT 4 Server. Windows NT 5 (Windows 2000) is in beta as I write this chapter, so I will not comment on its impact on this issue at all. I have used DCOM on Windows 95 and 98, and all of what I describe in this chapter works fine on both of those operating systems.

DCOM is built into Windows 98 and NT, but as it ships, DCOM is not built into Windows 95. As a result, Windows 95 users should download DCOM95 from the following site: `http://www.microsoft.com/com/dcom/dcom1_2/dcom1_2.asp`.

If you have trouble reaching this site, try removing the `dcom1_2.asp` part of the URL.

> **Note**
>
> In this chapter, if I describe Windows 98 directly, what I write is also true of Windows 95, unless I explicitly indicate otherwise.

Your Windows 98 machine should probably be switched from the default share-level to user-level access. You can do so via the Network applet found in the Control Panel.

User-level sharing requires that an NT Domain Server or some other source of user access lists be available on your network. With user-level access, administrators of a server grant each user certain rights. In particular, the user can be granted the right to run one or more DCOM programs. If you give the user rights to run all DCOM programs on your server, you are in effect giving the user the right to do whatever he or she wants on the server. A clever user who can run any DCOM server on your machine can probably figure out how to give himself or herself the right to do just about anything.

To help configure your server and its DCOM security levels, you can use the DComCnfg.exe application, shown in Figure 19.1. It comes with Windows 98 and Windows NT and is freely available from Microsoft's Web server at the same site as DCOM95. Note that after installing DCOM95 version 1.2, you will find a set of notes on using this tool in a subdirectory called DCOM95 beneath your Windows/System directory.

FIGURE 19.1

You can use the
DComCnfg.exe *utility to make remote servers appear as local servers so that you can call them with*
CreateOleObject.

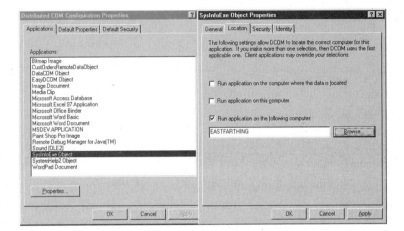

NOTE

As I stated earlier, you can connect to a DCOM server on a Windows NT machine without switching to user access, but you will probably lose some security options when taking that route. I have been able to consistently connect to any Windows NT DCOM server, regardless of how the NT and 98 machines are configured, just by signing on to both my Windows 98 client and my Windows NT machine with the same username and password. Under those circumstances, I don't have to make any other changes to either Windows 9x or Windows NT, other than ensuring that DCOM is installed on Windows 95. In particular, you don't need a domain set up to run this way.

You should keep these points in mind:

- To convert a standard Windows NT 4 server to a domain server requires a complete reinstallation.

- You cannot remotely launch an automation server that resides on a Windows 98 machine. The process must be in memory before you can call it. This is not true of

NT machines, which can automatically launch a server if it is not already in memory.

- On a Windows NT 4 machine, `DComCnfg.exe` is found by default in the `WinNt/System32` directory, whereas on a Windows 98 machine, it is found in the `Windows/System` directory. It is also installed to the `Windows/System` directory when you download and install DCOMCNFG95.

Using Windows 98 as a DCOM Server

A Windows 98 box is crippled as a server. I prefer to have an NT machine act as my DCOM server and to let Windows 98 machines act only as clients. However, if you are determined to use a Windows 98 machine as a server, check out the following article, which describes in more depth how to set up a Windows 98 machine as a DCOM server:
`http://support.microsoft.com/support/kb/articles/q165/1/01.asp`.

If you have trouble reaching this link, look for Microsoft Article ID: Q165101, titled "HOWTO: Use Win95 or Windows 98 as a DCOM Server." You can find additional related information at the following URLs:
`http://support.microsoft.com/support/kb/articles/q182/2/48.asp`
`http://support.microsoft.com/support/kb/articles/q165/3/00.asp`

If you have trouble reaching these links, look for Microsoft Article ID: Q165300, titled "BUG: Remote COM Calls Fail Because RPCSS Is Not Started."

The inestimable Dan Miser maintains a page that focuses on Windows 98 DCOM users:
`http://www.execpc.com/~dmiser/dcom95.htm`.

Dan is one of the foremost experts in this field, and his many articles on the subject are worth seeking out. He is also one of those sainted individuals who contribute frequently to the Borland newsgroups, and going to the multitier forums at `http://www.borland.com/newsgroups` to get his opinion on various DCOM and distributed computing related questions is worthwhile. If you are using DCOM on Windows 98, you should definitely check out Dan's page.

Much of the information regarding Windows 98 DCOM servers in the previously mentioned articles can be rather sketchily summarized as follows:

You might have to manually launch a program called `RPCSS.EXE` on Windows 98 machines that are acting as servers.

19

DCOM

Change the following key in the Windows 98 Registry:

```
HKEY_LOCAL_MACHINE\Software\Microsoft\OLE\EnableRemoteConnect
```

When you are done, the value of the key should be set to Y. Failure to set this key results in the following error on the client:

```
Run-time error "429": ActiveX component can"t create object
```

Dan Miser also suggests setting the following value in the same part of the Registry:

```
LegacyAuthenticationLevel == 1.
```

If all this information seems a bit confusing, it can be summarized even more succinctly: Microsoft apparently wants you to buy its server product if you want to use DCOM. As a result, any attempts to use Windows 98 machines as servers will prove to be little more than hacks. What the situation will be like under Windows 2000 is not clear at the time of this writing, but you can check my Web sites (`http://users.aol.com/charliecal` and `http://www.borland.com/techvoyage`) for possible updates on this matter.

You might be a bit overwhelmed with DCOM at first. The key point to grasp is that DCOM is really nothing more than a new capability added to the already existing COM technology. If you have working COM objects, then upgrading them to work with DCOM is trivial.

The following sections describe how to create DCOM clients and servers using C++Builder. As you are about to see, most of the material relevant to automation servers and clients (see Chapter 14, "Creating COM Automation Servers and Clients,") apply to Distributed servers and clients.

A Simple DCOM Client and Server

In Chapter 14 you learned about the basics of the IDispatch interface. IDispatch is the COM object that makes OLE automation possible from many programming environments. This section shows how to implement OLE automation that works not only between two applications, but between two applications that reside on separate machines.

You will find that the server part of the client/server pair shown in the first simple example is just a standard automation server like the one you created in Chapter 14. As a result, my examination of it will be short.

Building the Server

To get started creating the server, you do the same things you do when creating a simple automation server. A C++Builder automation server is no different from a DCOM server.

In particular, go to the File menu in C++Builder and choose New, ActiveX, Automation Object, as shown in Figure 19.2.

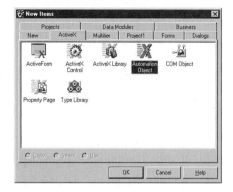

After selecting the automation object icon, you are presented with a dialog requesting the CoClass name of your server. In this case, you might call it EasyDCOM. Leave everything else at the default value and click the OK button.

You should now save your work. I suggest keeping the default EasyDCOMImpl.cpp for the automation object implementation and renaming the main form (unit1.cpp) to MainServer.cpp. You can save the project itself as EasyDCOMServer.bpr.

If the Type Library Editor is not already visible, bring it up by choosing View, Type Library from the C++Builder menu. Use the editor to create two methods: GetName() and Square(). GetName() returns BSTR* (as a reference, [out, retval] parameter), and Square() takes a long and a long* as parameters. The first parameter, a long, is called InX, and the second, a long*, is an out, retval parameter called OutX.

You now have a simple automation server that exposes two methods. The steps to create this server were not different from those to create nondistributed automation server. The magic to make your server accessible from another machine is built into COM. The bulk of that support has to do with transporting parameters across machine boundaries, also known as *parameter marshaling*. The next section looks at the marshaling support provided by COM.

Marshaling Data Between Machines

The TEasyDCOMImpl class exposes two methods whose data is automatically marshaled for you across application or machine boundaries. Remember that there are limits to the types that can be automatically marshaled. They are the same types mentioned as valid automation types. The following is a short list of commonly passed types, as discussed in Chapter 14:

char	unsigned char
short	unsigned short
long	unsigned long
float	double
CY(Currency)	BSTR(WideString)
DATE(TDateTime)	VARIANT(TVariant)
SAFEARRAY(TSafeArray<>)	All interface types
BOOL(TOLEBOOL)	

In addition, pointers to the types listed are also marshaled by the COM for you.

The complete source for a simple EasyDCOMServer is shown in Listing 19.1 through Listing 19.3. You can also find the program on the CD-ROM that accompanies this book.

LISTING 19.1   THE HEADER FILE FOR THE EasyDCOMServer OBJECT

```
// EASYDCOMIMPL.H : Declaration of the TEasyDCOMImpl

#ifndef __EASYDCOMIMPL_H_
#define __EASYDCOMIMPL_H_

#include "EasyDCOMServer_TLB.h"


/////////////////////////////////////////////////////////////////////////////
// TEasyDCOMImpl    Implements IEasyDCOM, default interface of EasyDCOM
// ThreadingModel : Apartment
// Dual Interface : TRUE
// Event Support  : FALSE
// Default ProgID : Project1.EasyDCOM
// Description    :
/////////////////////////////////////////////////////////////////////////////
class ATL_NO_VTABLE TEasyDCOMImpl :
  public CComObjectRootEx<CComSingleThreadModel>,
  public CComCoClass<TEasyDCOMImpl, &CLSID_EasyDCOM>,
  public IDispatchImpl<IEasyDCOM,
                       &IID_IEasyDCOM,
                       &LIBID_EasyDCOMServer>
{
public:
  TEasyDCOMImpl()
  {
  }
```

```
    // Data used when registering Object
    //
    DECLARE_THREADING_MODEL(otApartment);
    DECLARE_PROGID("EasyDCOMServer.EasyDCOM");
    DECLARE_DESCRIPTION("");

    // Function invoked to (un)register object
    //
    static HRESULT WINAPI UpdateRegistry(BOOL bRegister)
    {
      TTypedComServerRegistrarT<TEasyDCOMImpl>
      regObj(GetObjectCLSID(), GetProgID(), GetDescription());
      return regObj.UpdateRegistry(bRegister);
    }


BEGIN_COM_MAP(TEasyDCOMImpl)
  COM_INTERFACE_ENTRY(IEasyDCOM)
  COM_INTERFACE_ENTRY(IDispatch)
END_COM_MAP()

// IEasyDCOM
public:

  STDMETHOD(GetName(BSTR* Value));
  STDMETHOD(Square(long InX, long* OutX));
};

#endif //__EASYDCOMIMPL_H_
```

LISTING 19.2   THE SOURCE FILE FOR THE EasyDCOMServer OBJECT

```
// EASYDCOMIMPL : Implementation of TEasyDCOMImpl
// (CoClass: EasyDCOM, Interface: IEasyDCOM)

#include <vcl.h>
#pragma hdrstop

#include "EASYDCOMIMPL.H"

//////////////////////////////////////////////////////////////////
// TEasyDCOMImpl

STDMETHODIMP TEasyDCOMImpl::GetName(BSTR* Value)
{
  *Value = WideString("TEasyDCOM").Detach();
  return S_OK;
```

19

DCOM

continues

LISTING 19.2   CONTINUED

```
}


STDMETHODIMP TEasyDCOMImpl::Square(long InX, long* OutX)
{
  *OutX = InX * InX;
  return S_OK;
}
```

LISTING 19.3   THE _TLB HEADER FILE FOR THE EasyDCOMServer OBJECT

```
// C++ TLBWRTR : $Revision:   1.96.1.27  $
// File generated on 3/31/99 7:28:42 PM from Type Library described below.

// ************************************************************************
// Type Lib:  \BCB4UNLE\CODE\chap19\EasyDCOM\server\EasyDCOMServer.tlb
// IID\LCID: {71FAE7C8-E7E0-11D2-91A4-00C04F8EE514}\0
// Helpfile:
// DepndLst:
//    (1) v2.0 stdole, (C:\typelib\STDOLE2.tlb)
//    (2) v4.0 StdVCL, (C:\WINNT\System32\STDVCL40.DLL)
// ************************************************************************
#ifndef    __EasyDCOMServer_TLB_h__
#define    __EasyDCOMServer_TLB_h__

#pragma option push -b -w-inl

#include <vcl/utilcls.h>
#if !defined(__UTILCLS_H_VERSION) || (__UTILCLS_H_VERSION < 0x0101)
#error "This file requires an newer version of the file UTILCLS.H"
#endif

#include <olectl.h>
#include <ocidl.h>
#if defined(USING_ATLVCL) || defined(USING_ATL)
#if !defined(__TLB_NO_EVENT_WRAPPERS)
#include <atl/atlmod.h>
#endif
#endif


namespace Stdvcl {class IStrings; class IStringsDisp;}
using namespace Stdvcl;

namespace Easydcomserver_tlb
{
```

```
// ********************************************************************
// HelpString: Project1 Library
// Version:    1.0
// ********************************************************************


// ********************************************************************
// GUIDS declared in the TypeLibrary. Following prefixes are used:
//    Type Libraries     : LIBID_xxxx
//    CoClasses          : CLSID_xxxx
//    DISPInterfaces     : DIID_xxxx
//    Non-DISP interfaces: IID_xxxx
// ********************************************************************
DEFINE_GUID(LIBID_EasyDCOMServer, 0x71FAE7C8, 0xE7E0, 0x11D2, 0x91,\
               0xA4, 0x00, 0xC0, 0x4F, 0x8E, 0xE5, 0x14);
DEFINE_GUID(IID_IEasyDCOM, 0x71FAE7C9, 0xE7E0, 0x11D2, 0x91, 0xA4, \
             0x00, 0xC0, 0x4F, 0x8E, 0xE5, 0x14);
DEFINE_GUID(CLSID_EasyDCOM, 0x71FAE7CB, 0xE7E0, 0x11D2, 0x91, 0xA4,\
               0x00, 0xC0, 0x4F, 0x8E, 0xE5, 0x14);

// ********************************************************************
// Forward declaration of types defined in TypeLibrary
// ********************************************************************
interface DECLSPEC_UUID("{71FAE7C9-E7E0-11D2-91A4-00C04F8EE514}")
                                                         IEasyDCOM;


// ********************************************************************
// Declaration of CoClasses defined in Type Library
// (NOTE: Here we map each CoClass to its Default Interface)
// ********************************************************************
typedef IEasyDCOM EasyDCOM;

#define LIBID_OF_EasyDCOM (&LIBID_EasyDCOMServer)
// ********************************************************************
// Interface: IEasyDCOM
// Flags:     (4416) Dual OleAutomation Dispatchable
// GUID:      {71FAE7C9-E7E0-11D2-91A4-00C04F8EE514}
// ********************************************************************
interface IEasyDCOM : public IDispatch
{
public:
  virtual HRESULT STDMETHODCALLTYPE
             GetName(BSTR* Value/*[out,retval]*/) = 0; // [1]
  virtual HRESULT STDMETHODCALLTYPE
             Square(long InX/*[in]*/, long* OutX/*[out,retval]*/)
             ➡= 0; // [2]

#if !defined(__TLB_NO_INTERFACE_WRAPPERS)
```

19

DCOM

continues

LISTING 19.3   CONTINUED

```
BSTR __fastcall GetName(void)
{
  BSTR Value= 0;
  OLECHECK(this->GetName(&Value));
  return Value;
}

long __fastcall Square(long InX/*[in]*/)
{
  long OutX;
  OLECHECK(this->Square(InX, &OutX));
  return OutX;
}



#endif //    __TLB_NO_INTERFACE_WRAPPERS

};

#if !defined(__TLB_NO_INTERFACE_WRAPPERS)
// ********************************************************************
// SmartIntf: TCOMIEasyDCOM
// Interface: IEasyDCOM
// ********************************************************************
template <class T /* IEasyDCOM */ >
class TCOMIEasyDCOMT : public TComInterface<IEasyDCOM>,
                       public TComInterfaceBase<IUnknown>
{
public:
  TCOMIEasyDCOMT() {}
  TCOMIEasyDCOMT(IEasyDCOM *intf, bool addRef = false) :
             TComInterface<IEasyDCOM>(intf, addRef) {}
  TCOMIEasyDCOMT(const TCOMIEasyDCOMT& src) :
             TComInterface<IEasyDCOM>(src) {}
  TCOMIEasyDCOMT& operator=(const TCOMIEasyDCOMT& src)
             { Bind(src, true); return *this;}

  HRESULT fastcall GetName(BSTR* Value/*[out,retval]*/);
  BSTR    fastcall GetName(void);
  HRESULT fastcall Square(long InX/*[in]*/, long* OutX/*[out,retval]*/);
  long    fastcall Square(long InX/*[in]*/);

};
typedef TCOMIEasyDCOMT<IEasyDCOM> TCOMIEasyDCOM;

// ********************************************************************
// DispIntf:  IEasyDCOM
// Flags:     (4416) Dual OleAutomation Dispatchable
```

```
// GUID:        {71FAE7C9-E7E0-11D2-91A4-00C04F8EE514}
// ****************************************************************
template<class T>
class IEasyDCOMDispT : public TAutoDriver<IEasyDCOM>
{
public:
  IEasyDCOMDispT(){}

  IEasyDCOMDispT(IEasyDCOM *pintf)
  {
    TAutoDriver<IEasyDCOM>::Bind(pintf);
  }

  IEasyDCOMDispT& operator=(IEasyDCOM *pintf)
  {
    TAutoDriver<IEasyDCOM>::Bind(pintf);
    return *this;
  }

  HRESULT BindDefault(/*Binds to new instance of CoClass EasyDCOM*/)
  {
    return OLECHECK(Bind(CLSID_EasyDCOM));
  }

  HRESULT BindRunning(/*Binds to a running instance of CoClass EasyDCOM*/)
  {
    return BindToActive(CLSID_EasyDCOM);
  }

  HRESULT fastcall GetName(BSTR* Value/*[out,retval]*/);
  BSTR     fastcall GetName(void);
  HRESULT fastcall Square(long InX/*[in]*/, long* OutX/*[out,retval]*/);
  long     fastcall Square(long InX/*[in]*/);

};
typedef IEasyDCOMDispT<IEasyDCOM> IEasyDCOMDisp;

// ****************************************************************
// SmartIntf: TCOMIEasyDCOM
// Interface: IEasyDCOM
// ****************************************************************
template <class T> HRESULT __fastcall
TCOMIEasyDCOMT<T>::GetName(BSTR* Value/*[out,retval]*/)
{
  return (*this)->GetName(Value);
}

template <class T> BSTR __fastcall
TCOMIEasyDCOMT<T>::GetName(void)
```

continues

Listing 19.3   Continued

```
{
  BSTR Value= 0;
  OLECHECK(this->GetName(&Value));
  return Value;
}

template <class T> HRESULT __fastcall
TCOMIEasyDCOMT<T>::Square(long InX/*[in]*/, long* OutX/*[out,retval]*/)
{
  return (*this)->Square(InX, OutX);
}

template <class T> long __fastcall
TCOMIEasyDCOMT<T>::Square(long InX/*[in]*/)
{
  long OutX;
  OLECHECK(this->Square(InX, &OutX));
  return OutX;
}


// ************************************************************************
// DispIntf:  IEasyDCOM
// Flags:     (4416) Dual OleAutomation Dispatchable
// GUID:      {71FAE7C9-E7E0-11D2-91A4-00C04F8EE514}
// ************************************************************************
template <class T> HRESULT __fastcall
IEasyDCOMDispT<T>::GetName(BSTR* Value/*[out,retval]*/)
{
  static _TDispID _dispid(*this, OLETEXT("GetName"), DISPID(1));
  TAutoArgs<0> _args;
  return OutRetValSetterPtr(Value /*[VT_BSTR:1]*/, _args,
                            OleFunction(_dispid, _args));
}

template <class T> BSTR __fastcall
IEasyDCOMDispT<T>::GetName(void)
{
  BSTR Value;
  this->GetName(&Value);
  return Value;
}

template <class T> HRESULT __fastcall
IEasyDCOMDispT<T>::Square(long InX/*[in]*/, long* OutX/*[out,retval]*/)
{
  static _TDispID _dispid(*this, OLETEXT("Square"), DISPID(2));
```

```
    TAutoArgs<1> _args;
    _args[1] = InX /*[VT_I4:0]*/;
    return OutRetValSetterPtr(OutX /*[VT_I4:1]*/, _args,
                             OleFunction(_dispid, _args));
}

template <class T> long __fastcall
IEasyDCOMDispT<T>::Square(long InX/*[in]*/)
{
    long OutX;
    this->Square(InX, &OutX);
    return OutX;
}

// *******************************************************************
// The following typedefs expose classes (named CoCoClassName) that
// provide static Create() and CreateRemote(LPWSTR machineName) methods
// for creating an instance of an exposed object. These functions can
// be used by client wishing to automate CoClasses exposed by this
// typelibrary.
// *******************************************************************

// *******************************************************************
// COCLASS DEFAULT INTERFACE CREATOR
// CoClass  : EasyDCOM
// Interface: TCOMIEasyDCOM
// *******************************************************************
typedef TCoClassCreatorT<TCOMIEasyDCOM, IEasyDCOM,
                         &CLSID_EasyDCOM,
                         &IID_IEasyDCOM> CoEasyDCOM;
#endif  //    __TLB_NO_INTERFACE_WRAPPERS


};      // namespace Easydcomserver_tlb

#if !defined(NO_IMPLICIT_NAMESPACE_USE)
using  namespace Easydcomserver_tlb;
#endif

#pragma option pop

#endif // __EasyDCOMServer_TLB_h__
```

This program is meant to be run from a client. As such, it has no controls on it and no public interface other than the OLE object itself. I do, however, give the main form a distinctive look, as you can see in Figure 19.3.

FIGURE 19.3

*The main form
for the
EasyDCOMServer
program.*

Of course, there is no reason that a single program could not simultaneously have an OLE server interface and a set of standard controls. For instance, Word and Excel are OLE servers, but they are also standard applications run through a set of menus and other controls. It is not unusual for the same application to work as a server, a standard application, and as a client. In fact, many programmers will want to extend standard applications so that they also work as servers.

> **NOTE**
>
> After you have created the server, don't forget to register it by running it once. You must register the server, or the client will not be able to access it.
>
> C++Builder automation objects are registered repeatedly, whenever you run the program. If you move the application to a new location, you can register this change with the system by running it once. By doing so, you guarantee that the old information associated with your CLSID will be erased, and new information will be entered automatically. Registering a class ID multiple times does not mean that you will end up with multiple items in the Registry because each registration of a CLSID will overwrite the previous registration. All OLE servers worth their salt provide this service.

Remember that this code does not work unless you first register the IEasyDCOM object with the system by running the server once.

Creating the DCOM Client

You can access the EasyDCOMServer with the EasyDCOMClient program found on the CD-ROM that accompanies this book. EasyDCOMClient automatically launches the server program and then calls its GetName and Square functions. This client program is much like the type of application you write in a standard C++Builder automation program. However, I'm going to cover key aspects of its creation, emphasizing the parts of the program used to retrieve an object remotely rather than locally.

If you look at the main form for the program, as shown in Figure 19.4, you can see that it has several buttons. One is for launching the server remotely, and another is for launching it locally. In this chapter, I'm going to make short shrift of the techniques used to call the program locally and will focus instead on remote invocation of the server.

FIGURE 19.4

The main form for the EasyDCOMClient application.

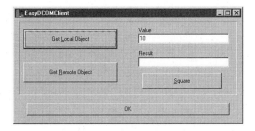

The source for the EasyDCOMClient program is shown in Listings 19.4 and 19.5. Note that it makes use of the `EasyDCOMServer_TLB` files from the server. You can bring this file into your program in two ways:

- Add the file to your client project, thereby linking it into your program directly from the directory where the server resides.

- Recreate the file by choosing Project, Import Type Library and importing the TLB file from your server. This approach causes a copy of the file to be placed in the \imports directory and automatically adds it to your project.

LISTING 19.4 THE HEADER FILE OF THE MAIN FORM FOR THE EASYDCOMCLIENT OLE CLIENT APPLICATION

```
//--------------------------------------------------------------------
#ifndef MainClientH
#define MainClientH
//--------------------------------------------------------------------
#include <Classes.hpp>
#include <Controls.hpp>
#include <StdCtrls.hpp>
#include <Forms.hpp>
#include <ExtCtrls.hpp>
//--------------------------------------------------------------------
class TForm1 : public TForm
{
__published:    // IDE-managed Components
```

continues

19

DCOM

LISTING 19.4   CONTINUED

```
        TButton *LocalBtn;
        TButton *RemoteBtn;
        TButton *OKButton;
        TEdit *ValueEdit;
        TEdit *ResultEdit;
        TLabel *Label1;
        TLabel *Label2;
        TPanel *Panel1;
        TButton *SquareBtn;
        TLabel *Label3;
        TLabel *Label4;
        void __fastcall OKButtonClick(TObject *Sender);
        void __fastcall LocalBtnClick(TObject *Sender);
        void __fastcall RemoteBtnClick(TObject *Sender);
        void __fastcall SquareBtnClick(TObject *Sender);
private:    // User declarations
        TCOMIEasyDCOM   Server;
public:         // User declarations
        __fastcall TForm1(TComponent* Owner);
};
//----------------------------------------------------------------
extern PACKAGE TForm1 *Form1;
//----------------------------------------------------------------
#endif
```

LISTING 19.5   THE SOURCE FILE OF THE MAIN FORM FOR THE EASYDCOMCLIENT OLE
CLIENT APPLICATION

```
//----------------------------------------------------------------
#include <vcl.h>
#pragma hdrstop

#include "EasyDCOMServer_TLB.h"
#include "MainClient.h"


//----------------------------------------------------------------
#pragma package(smart_init)
#pragma resource "*.dfm"
TForm1 *Form1;
//----------------------------------------------------------------
__fastcall TForm1::TForm1(TComponent* Owner)
        : TForm(Owner)
{
}
//----------------------------------------------------------------
```

```
void __fastcall TForm1::OKButtonClick(TObject *Sender)
{
  Close();
}
//-------------------------------------------------------------

void __fastcall TForm1::LocalBtnClick(TObject *Sender)
{
  Server = CoEasyDCOM::Create();
  WideString name = Server->GetName();
  Caption = AnsiString(Sysutils::Now()) + ":Connected, Name: " + name;
}
//-------------------------------------------------------------

void __fastcall TForm1::RemoteBtnClick(TObject *Sender)
{
  AnsiString MachineName;
  if (Dialogs::InputQuery("Enter Machine Name", "Machine Name:",
                          MachineName))
  {
        Screen->Cursor = crHourGlass;
        Server = CoEasyDCOM::CreateRemote(WideString(MachineName));
        Screen->Cursor = crDefault;
        WideString name= Server->GetName();
        Caption = AnsiString(Sysutils::Now())   +
                ":Connected to " + MachineName +
                ", Name: " + name;
  }
}
//-------------------------------------------------------------


void __fastcall TForm1::SquareBtnClick(TObject *Sender)
{
  if (Server)
  {
    int val = StrToInt(ValueEdit->Text);
    ResultEdit->Text = IntToStr((int)Server->Square(val));
  }
  else
    ShowMessage(
            "Not currently connected to Server. Please connect first!");
}
//-------------------------------------------------------------
```

19

DCOM

When you run this program, you get the option of using two different methods for accessing the server. The first lets you access the object locally, and the second lets you access it remotely.

If you want to create an instance of the object locally, just call the predeclared
CoEasyDCOM constructor from the EasyDCOMServer_TLB file:

```
void __fastcall TForm1::LocalBtnClick(TObject *Sender)
{
  Server = CoEasyDCOM::Create();
  WideString name = Server->GetName();
  Caption = AnsiString(Sysutils::Now()) + ":Connected, Name: " + name;
}
```

This technology is covered in Chapter 14.

> ### TIP
>
> By using DComCnfg.exe, you can configure your machine so that it will launch a
> remote program using the same commands that you use to launch a local pro-
> gram. In particular, you can use Dcomcnfg.exe to insert certain symbols in the
> Registry that will cause Windows to look for a program not on the local
> machine, but on a remote machine.
>
> To get started, launch DComCnfg.exe. Select the program you want to run. If it
> does not appear in the list on the Applications page, then run the server once
> on your current machine so that it is registered. Double-click the application
> when you find it on the Applications page. Turn to the Location page, select
> Run Application on the Following Computer, and enter the name of the com-
> puter. Now the program will be launched on that remote computer even if you
> use the standard COM calls for launching it locally.

The following method illustrates how to create the object remotely:

```
void __fastcall TForm1::RemoteBtnClick(TObject *Sender)
{
  AnsiString MachineName;
  if (Dialogs::InputQuery("Enter Machine Name", "Machine Name:",
                                                MachineName))
  {
        Screen->Cursor = crHourGlass;
        Server = CoEasyDCOM::CreateRemote(WideString(MachineName));
        Screen->Cursor = crDefault;
        WideString name= Server->GetName();
        Caption = AnsiString(Sysutils::Now())   +
                ":Connected to " + MachineName +
                ", Name: " + name;
  }
}
```

In this case, you are once again calling one of the class methods from the premade proxy objects in the EasyDCOMServer_TLB file. These classes are very easy to use, but you should step through them at least once to see how they work. Now, I'm going to describe the CreateRemote() method.

When you call CreateRemote, you are mapped to the following function in the UTILCLS.H file in the include\vcl directory:

```
template <class TOBJ, class INTF, const CLSID* clsid, const IID* iid>
HRESULT
TCoClassCreatorT<TOBJ, INTF,
                clsid, iid>::CreateRemote(LPCWSTR machineName,
                                          INTF **ppIntf)
{
  static TInitOle initOle;
  COSERVERINFO serverInfo = {0, const_cast<LPWSTR>(machineName), 0, 0};
  MULTI_QI    mqi      = {iid, 0, 0};
  HRESULT hr = ::CoCreateInstanceEx(*clsid, 0,
                                    CLSCTX_REMOTE_SERVER,
                                    &serverInfo, 1, &mqi);
  if (SUCCEEDED(hr))
    *ppIntf = (INTF*)mqi.pItf;
  return hr;
}
```

CoCreateInstanceEx is a Windows API routine similar to the CoCreateInstance function, discussed at the end of Chapter 14:

```
WINOLEAPI CoCreateInstanceEx(
    REFCLSID                Clsid,
    IUnknown     *          punkOuter, // only relevant locally
    DWORD                   dwClsCtx,
    COSERVERINFO *          pServerInfo,
    DWORD                   dwCount,
    MULTI_QI          *     pResults );
```

The last three parameters differ from CoCreateInstance. They allow you to specify a machine name and provide a way for you to retrieve more than one interface with a single call.

You don't really have to understand CoCreateInstanceEx to create an instance of a remote server. You can stick with the CreateRemote routine provided in the xxxx_TLB.h file generated when importing a server. However, it helps to understand what's happening under the hood.

Using a Remote Object

The hard part about using remote objects is accessing them. Using the server after you have such an object is trivial:

```cpp
void __fastcall TForm1::SquareBtnClick(TObject *Sender)
{
  if (Server)
  {
    int val = StrToInt(ValueEdit->Text);
    ResultEdit->Text = IntToStr((int)Server->Square(val));
  }
  else
    ShowMessage(
        "Not currently connected to Server. Please connect first!");
}
```

I've put some window dressing on the call, but all I'm really doing here is calling the `Square()` method directly off the `Server` object. At this stage, you should start to have a feeling for how DCOM programs are put together. There's nothing special about the server. In fact, you could remotely access the automation servers built in Chapter 15, "Using C++Builder to Automate Word and Excel." The big difference is the way that client applications connect to the servers. Once connected to the server, clients access the server the same way they access servers running on the same machine. The next section illustrates a remote automation server that provides information about the machine on which it is running.

The SystemInformation Program

Listings 19.6 shows some helper functions used by the SystemInformation program. Since the program displays information about the machine it's running on, Listing 19.6 contains routines to retrieve a computer's name and some information about the drives available on the computer.

LISTING 19.6   HELPER ROUTINES USED BY SYSTEMINFORMATION SERVER

```cpp
//---------------------------------------------------------------
#include <vcl.h>
#pragma hdrstop

#include "SysInfoCore.h"

//---------------------------------------------------------------
#pragma package(smart_init)

// Returns computer name in a WideString
```

```
// (Upon failure, string is empty)
WideString GetComputerName()
{
  WideString computerName;
  TCHAR name[MAX_COMPUTERNAME_LENGTH+1];
  DWORD size = sizeof(name);
  if (::GetComputerName(name, &size) != 0)
    computerName = name;
  return computerName;
}

// Gets logical drive strings; also returns count of strings
//
int GetDriveStringsAndCount(TCHAR *buffer, int len)
{
  int count = 0;
  if (::GetLogicalDriveStrings(len, buffer) != 0)
  {
    LPCTSTR p = buffer;
    while (*p)
    {
      count++;
      while (*p++)
        ;
    }
  }
  return count;
}

// Gets information about the specified drive
//
BOOL GetDiskInfo(LPCTSTR rootPath, TDriveInfoStruct& di)
{
  // Clear structure
  ZeroMemory(&di, sizeof(TDriveInfoStruct));
  // Update the root path name
  lstrcpy(di.m_RootPathName, rootPath);
  // Get disk space information
  if (::GetDiskFreeSpace(rootPath,
                         &di.m_SectorsPerCluster,
                         &di.m_BytesPerSector,
                         &di.m_NumberOfFreeClusters,
                         &di.m_TotalNumberOfClusters) == 0)
    return FALSE;
  // Get the drive type
  di.m_DriveType = ::GetDriveType(rootPath);
  return TRUE;
}
```

continues

LISTING 19.6   CONTINUED

```cpp
// Returns a string representing the specified DriveType
//
WideString DriveTypeToString(UINT drvType)
{
  WideString drvTypeStr;
  switch (drvType)
  {
  case  DRIVE_UNKNOWN:      drvTypeStr = "Unknown"; break;
  case  DRIVE_NO_ROOT_DIR:  drvTypeStr = "Not a root drive"; break;
  case  DRIVE_REMOVABLE:    drvTypeStr = "Removable"; break;
  case  DRIVE_FIXED:        drvTypeStr = "Fixed"; break;
  case  DRIVE_REMOTE:       drvTypeStr = "Remote"; break;
  case  DRIVE_CDROM:        drvTypeStr = "CDROM"; break;
  case  DRIVE_RAMDISK:      drvTypeStr = "RAMDisk"; break;
  default:
        drvTypeStr = "Error!!";
        break;
  };
  return drvTypeStr;
}
```

Listings 19.7 and 19.8 are the core files of the SystemInformation program and a client application that exercises the server. In the sections following these listings, I analyze the key portions of the server and client applications.

LISTING 19.7   THE IMPLEMENTATION FOR THE **DCOM** SERVER

```cpp
// SYSINFOIMPL : Implementation of TSysInfoImpl
// (CoClass: SysInfo, Interface: ISysInfo)

#include <vcl.h>
#pragma hdrstop

#include "SYSINFOIMPL.H"
#include "sysinfocore.h"
#include <safearry.h>

///////////////////////////////////////////////////////////////////
// TSysInfoImpl

STDMETHODIMP TSysInfoImpl::get_ComputerName(BSTR* Value)
{
  *Value = GetComputerName().Detach();
  return S_OK;
};
```

```
STDMETHODIMP TSysInfoImpl::get_DriveCount(long* Value)
{
  // Retrieve Drives information, if this is first call
  if (!m_DrivesCount)
    GetDrivesInformation();
  // Return count
  *Value = m_DrivesCount;
  // Flag coast's clear
  return S_OK;
};


void TSysInfoImpl::GetDrivesInformation()
{
  // Clear previously cached information
  m_DrivesInfo = 0;

  // Retrieve the logical drive strings
  TCHAR drvStrings[_MAX_DRIVE*26 + _MAX_PATH/*Some padding*/];
  m_DrivesCount = GetDriveStringsAndCount(drvStrings,
                                          sizeof(drvStrings));

  // If there are valid drives, grab some information about the drives
  if (m_DrivesCount)
  {
    // Allocate structures to hold drive information
    m_DrivesInfo = new TDriveInfoStruct[m_DrivesCount];

    // Point to beginning of logical drive strings
    LPCTSTR pDrv = drvStrings;

    // Iterate through drives
    for (int i=0; i<m_DrivesCount; i++)
    {
      // Retrieve drive information
GetDiskInfo(pDrv, m_DrivesInfo[i]);

      // Skip past current drive string
      while (*pDrv++)
        ;

      // Abort if we encounter the double nuls
      if (!*pDrv)
        break;
    }
  }
}
```

continues

19

DCOM

LISTING 19.7   CONTINUED

```
STDMETHODIMP TSysInfoImpl::GetDriveInfo(long DriveIndex,
  TVariant* DriveInfo)
{
  // Get Drives information
  if (!m_DrivesCount)
    GetDrivesInformation();

  if (DriveIndex < 0 || DriveIndex >= m_DrivesCount)
    return E_INVALIDARG;

  // Now allocate a SAFEARRAY to put all that drive information in
  TSafeArrayDim1 dim(sizeof(TDriveInfoStruct));
  TSafeArrayChar1 sa(dim);

  // Copy over data (Faster to lock array but
  //                 illustrating accessing array here!)
  // (NOTE: We treat the TDriveInfoStruct as a flat character array!!)
  for (int i=0; i<sizeof(TDriveInfoStruct); i++)
    sa[i] = ((char*)(&m_DrivesInfo[DriveIndex]))[i];

  // Return the SAFEARRAY in the Variant
  *DriveInfo = sa.Detach();

  // Signal all's fine
  return S_OK;
}
```

LISTING 19.8   THE MAIN FORM FOR THE CLIENT PROGRAM

```
//-------------------------------------------------------------------
#include <vcl.h>
#pragma hdrstop

#include "SysInfoServer_TLB.h"
#include "MainClient.h"
#include "..\server\sysinfocore.h"
#include <safearry.h>

//-------------------------------------------------------------------
#pragma package(smart_init)
#pragma resource "*.dfm"
TForm1 *Form1;
//-------------------------------------------------------------------
__fastcall TForm1::TForm1(TComponent* Owner)
        : TForm(Owner)
{
}
//-------------------------------------------------------------------
```

```
void __fastcall TForm1::OKClick(TObject *Sender)
{
  Close();
}
//-------------------------------------------------------------------
void __fastcall TForm1::DisconnectBtnClick(TObject *Sender)
{
  SysInfoServer = 0;
  ComputerName->Text = "Not Connected";
  DrvInfoMemo->Clear();
  DriveCountLabel->Caption = "";
}
//-------------------------------------------------------------------
void __fastcall TForm1::ConnectBtnClick(TObject *Sender)
{
  // Connect to Server, if necessary
  if (!SysInfoServer)
  {
    AnsiString machineName;
    if (Dialogs::InputQuery("Enter Machine Name", "Machine Name:",
                            machineName))
    {
      Screen->Cursor = crHourGlass;
      SysInfoServer  = CoSysInfo::CreateRemote(WideString(machineName));
      Screen->Cursor = crDefault;
    };
  };

  if (!SysInfoServer)
  {
    ShowMessage("Unable to connect to server!");
    ComputerName->Text = "Not Connected";
  }
  else
  {
    // Get the computer name
    ComputerName->Text = SysInfoServer->ComputerName;
    // Get the count of drives
    long DriveCount = SysInfoServer->DriveCount;
    DriveCountLabel->Caption = IntToStr(int(DriveCount));

    // Clear list of drives, info. etc.
    DrvInfoMemo->Clear();

    // Get some information about each drive
    for (int i=0; i<DriveCount; i++)
    {
      TVariant drvInfo = SysInfoServer->GetDriveInfo(i);
      // Access raw data sent as SAFEARRAY
```

19

DCOM

continues

LISTING 19.8   CONTINUED

```
    TSafeArrayChar1 sa = LPSAFEARRAY(drvInfo);
    // Convert raw info. into what we know it is
    TDriveInfoStruct di;
    for (int j=0; j<sizeof(TDriveInfoStruct); j++)
      ((char*)(&di))[j] = sa[j];

    // Add information to driveInfo Memo
    DrvInfoMemo->Lines->Append(AnsiString(di.m_RootPathName) + "\t" +
                             DriveTypeToString(di.m_DriveType));
    }
  }
}
//- - - - - - - - - - - - - - - - - - - - - - - - - - - - - - - - - - - - - - - - - - -
```

This program is interesting because it illustrates the fact that a DCOM server is running on the remote machine, not in the address space of the client. When you launch this server, it explores the hard drive and some other aspects of the machine on which it is running. It sends that information back to the client, where it is displayed for the user. Thus, if the client is on machine A, and the server is on machine B, the client program run on machine A reports on the status of the program on machine B.

The fact that the server runs in a separate address space from the client is important for two reasons:

- The server does not take up address space, clock cycles, or hard drive space on the client, thus leaving the client machine free to handle other chores.
- If the server is much more powerful than the client, the client program can delegate tasks to the server that the client machine cannot handle.

Understanding the Server

This program separates the main functionality of the server from the implementation of the DCOM object. In the file called SYSINFOCORE.H, I create a structure that looks like this:

```
struct TDriveInfoStruct
{
  TCHAR       m_RootPathName[_MAX_DRIVE+1];
  DWORD       m_SectorsPerCluster;
  DWORD       m_BytesPerSector;
  DWORD       m_NumberOfFreeClusters;
  DWORD       m_TotalNumberOfClusters;
  UINT        m_DriveType;
};
```

This structure stores information about a disk. The `m_RootPathName` member contains a string that specifies the root directory of the disk. The other members are self-descriptive. They contain information about the number of clusters, sectors, and free space on the drive. The `m_DriveType` member contains a value that specifies the type of the drive. For more information about these members, you can consult any Windows API documentation about the `GetDiskFreeSpace` and `GetDriveType` functions.

The `SYSINFOCORE` files also provide a few basic routines to retrieve the computer's name and the count, root directories, and size of the drives available on the machine:

```
WideString GetComputerName();
WideString DriveTypeToString(UINT drvType);
int        GetDriveStringsAndCount(TCHAR *buffer, int len);
BOOL       GetDiskInfo(LPCTSTR rootPath, TDriveInfoStruct& di);
```

What is important here is the separation of the engine code from the DCOM server implementation. Constructing an application this way is good because it allows you to easily reuse the core functionality of the program in multiple settings. For instance, you could create a standalone EXE with this functionality, a DLL with this functionality, and, as I have done here, a DCOM server with this same functionality. My DCOM object is simply a wrapper around the core functions provided by the `SYSINFOCORE` files. For example, the server exposes a `ComputerName` property. Its implementation simply delegates to the function implemented in `SYSINFOCORE`:

```
STDMETHODIMP TSysInfoImpl::get_ComputerName(BSTR* Value)
{
  *Value = GetComputerName().Detach();
  return S_OK;
};
```

Similarly, the server exposes a `DriveCount` property, which uses the functions provided by `SYSINFOCORE`. This server illustrates a few concepts worth exploring further. Notably, it illustrates how to pass structure parameters via a `SAFEARRAY`.

The `SYSINFOSERVER` exposes a `DriveCount` property. After a client has obtained the `DriveCount`, it can invoke the GetDriveInfo method exposed by the server, passing in the index of the drive. The server returns a `TDriveInfoStruct` packet of data describing the drive. However, if you recall, `TDriveInfoStruct` is not one of the types allowed in automation. To work around this limitation, our server embeds the structure in a `SAFEARRAY`.

First, the server allocates a `SAFEARRAY` of `CHAR` set to the size of a `TDriveInfoStruct` structure using the `TSafeArray` template defined in the `SAFEARRY.H` header file:

```
TSafeArrayDim1 dim(sizeof(TDriveInfoStruct));
TSafeArrayChar1 sa(dim);
```

19

DCOM

Next, the information in the TDriveInfoStruct is copied over to the SAFEARRAY:

```
for (int i=0; i<sizeof(TDriveInfoStruct); i++)
    sa[i] = ((char*)(&m_DrivesInfo[DriveIndex]))[i];
```

Finally, the underlying SAFEARRAY is detached from the TSafeArray template and returned via a VARIANT parameter:

```
*DriveInfo = sa.Detach();
return S_OK;
```

> **NOTE**
>
> Using SAFEARRAYs is not always the best method of passing chunks of data via automation. Often the structure being passed back is best exposed as another automation object. For example, our server could define a second automation object with properties corresponding to the members of the TDriveInfoStruct type. The GetDriveInfo member would return an instance of that object instead of passing back a SAFEARRAY.
>
> You can design the Object Model of your automation server in many ways. How you expose information will often be determined by the clients you are targeting and the performance requirements of your server.

The SYSINFO Client

The core sections of the SYSINFO client application are similar to those of other automation clients. The connection to the server is initiated via a call to the CreateRemote routine provided by the CoCoClassName template of the server's _TLB.H header file:

```
SysInfoServer = CoSysInfo::CreateRemote(WideString(machineName));
```

After the connection has been established, the client simply invokes the methods and properties exposed by the server:

```
// Get the computer name
    ComputerName->Text = SysInfoServer->ComputerName;
    // Get the count of drives
    long DriveCount = SysInfoServer->DriveCount;
    DriveCountLabel->Caption = IntToStr(int(DriveCount));

    // Clear list of drives, info. etc.
    DrvInfoMemo->Clear();
```

```
// Get some information about each drive
for (int i=0; i<DriveCount; i++)
{
  TVariant drvInfo = SysInfoServer->GetDriveInfo(i);
  // Access raw data sent as SAFEARRAY
  TSafeArrayChar1 sa = LPSAFEARRAY(drvInfo);
  // Convert raw info. into what we know it is
  TDriveInfoStruct di;
  for (int j=0; j<sizeof(TDriveInfoStruct); j++)
    ((char*)(&di))[j] = sa[j];

  // Add information to driveInfo Memo
  DrvInfoMemo->Lines->Append(AnsiString(di.m_RootPathName) + "\t" +
                             DriveTypeToString(di.m_DriveType));
}
```

Particularly interesting is the way the client decodes the SAFEARRAY data sent back via the GetDriveInfo call. The return result is stored in a local VARIANT object:

```
TVariant drvInfo = SysInfoServer->GetDriveInfo(i);
```

The SAFEARRAY is then extracted from the VARIANT and stored in a TSafeArray instance to facilitate its manipulation. Each byte of the SAFEARRAY is copied over to a TDriveInfoStruct local variable:

```
TSafeArrayChar1 sa = LPSAFEARRAY(drvInfo);
TDriveInfoStruct di;
for (int j=0; j<sizeof(TDriveInfoStruct); j++)
  ((char*)(&di))[j] = sa[j];
```

After the information has been restored to a TDriveInfoStruct format, the client simply proceeds to display the information stored in the members of the structure.

NOTE

Notice that the client application relies on the server's SYSINFOCORE header file for the definition of the TDriveInfoStruct type. It would have been better for the server to define this structure in its type library. Doing so would have removed the current dependencies between the server and client source code. A more flexible approach would have been to expose the information in the TDriveInfoStruct as another automation object. However, I chose to use SAFEARRAYs to illustrate their usage in cases where you want to pass chunks of information via automation.

19

DCOM

Testing the Remote Debugging System

If you are working on an NT machine, you can debug both the client and server parts of a client/server application at the same time. That is, you can run both from inside the IDE and step through the code of both applications.

Using the client/server version of C++Builder, you can debug applications remotely. You might want to use this feature when a program runs okay on your development machine but does not run correctly on a second machine. It is also a way to test client/server programs and to debug DirectX exclusive mode applications.

The purpose of this brief section is to describe how to debug an application remotely. Get started with remote debugging on the remote machine by going to the `c:\program files\borland\cbuilder4\bin` directory and typing the following:

```
borrdbg41 -listen
```

This line starts the Borland Remote Debugger Server on the remote machine. On an NT machine, you can just run this executable as a service that you set from the Services applet in the Control Panel. You'll notice that the Remote Debugger Server inserts a small icon illustrating a green critter on the tray of your computer's taskbar.

On the client machine, create a new application, put a single button on it, and write the following code in response to a click on the button:

```
void __fastcall TForm1::Button1Click(TObject *Sender)
{
  Caption = "Foo";
}
```

Select Project, Options and turn to the Directories Conditional page. There you can set the output directory to some location you have mapped to on the remote machine. For instance, set it to `h:\temp`, where `h:` refers to a physical drive on the remote machine. Obviously, you can get the application you want to debug onto the remote machine in many other ways, but this method will do for testing purposes. Click OK to close the dialog.

Choose Run, Parameters. Turn to the Remote page in the Run Parameters dialog and type the local path for the remote location of your executable. For instance, if you are going to place the application on the C: drive off the remote machine, type the following:

```
C:\temp\project1.exe
```

Notice that I have included the full path on the remote machine, as well as the executable name that you are going to run. If you are mapped to the C: drive on the remote machine, do not type in the drive letter you have mapped to. For instance, if the C: drive of the remote machine is mapped to your H: drive, do not type the following:

```
H:\temp\project1.exe;
```

Type the name of the actual drive on the remote machine, as shown in the first of these two examples—not the logical drive. Type the IP address or the name of your remote server in the Remote Host field. While you are in the Run Parameters dialog, make sure the Debug Project on Remote Machine option is checked. Click OK to close the Run Parameters dialog.

At this stage, you are ready to run. Set a breakpoint on the sole line of code in your program and run the application. The program should start visibly on the remote machine. Click the button on the form of the program on the remote machine. You should be taken back to the breakpoint you set in your source code on the local machine. You can now step through your code as if you were on your local machine.

Summary

In this chapter you learned how to use C++Builder to build applications that take advantage of the Distributed Component Object Model. You have seen that combining C++Builder, DCOM, and OLE automation provides a simple method for allowing one application to control or use another application that resides on a second machine.

As you've seen, the bulk of Distributed COM is handled by the COM binaries. A DCOM server is no different from a local automation server.

There are various other technologies for accessing applications remotely. Borland's Entera and CORBA Technologies offer alternative approaches to DCOM. However, C++Builder greatly eases the use of DCOM. The ability to step from a client to a server application while debugging is a new C++Builder 4 feature. Similarly, the various wrapper classes provided in the _TLB file make it very easy for a client to connect to a remote server.

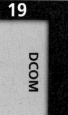

Because DCOM is so simple to use, distributing the workload of a particular application across multiple machines is now easy. My guess is that distributing computing will prove to be one of the most important fields of computer science over the next 5 to 10 years.

MIDAS

CHAPTER 20

by Charlie Calvert and Bob Swart

In this chapter you learn about multitier database computing as implemented in a C++Builder-hosted technology called MIDAS. Multitier database computing allows you to partition applications so you can access data on a second machine without having a full set of database tools on your local machine, or use a middle machine to take care of load-balancing issues on the data machine. It also allows you to centralize business rules and processes and to distribute the processing load throughout the network.

This chapter focuses on database computing while the preceding chapter, "DCOM," concentrated on distributed objects. One example in that chapter worked with databases, but it merely showed one custom and rather limited way to marshal data between machines without using MIDAS. This chapter uses MIDAS in all its examples, which means it features a more general-purpose and robust technology. It also means that you must have a copy of the Enterprise edition of C++Builder to run the programs in this chapter. (The examples in the preceding chapter, however, did not require the Enterprise edition of the product.)

This chapter is divided into three parts:

- An introduction to multitier database computing
- An overview of Borland's MIDAS Technology
- A detailed look at creating MIDAS servers and clients

Throughout this chapter, I use the terms *multitier computing*, *distributed datasets*, *remote datasets*, and *MIDAS* as approximate synonyms. In the next section of the chapter, you find some comments on terminology that should help you to understand the significance of these words.

An Overview of Multitier Computing

In this section, I make a few broad statements about multitier database computing. My goal is to give a general definition of the technology, particularly for the sake of users who are new to the subject. In later portions of the chapter, the discussion is increasingly technical and specific.

Borland supports a three-tier technology, which in its classic form consists of the following:

- A database server on one machine
- An application server on a second machine
- A thin client on a third machine

In this classic form, the server is a tool such as InterBase, Oracle, Sybase, MS SQL server, and so on. The application server and the thin client are built in C++Builder. The application server contains the business rules and the tools for manipulating the data. The client does nothing more than present the data to the user for viewing and editing.

In most scenarios, the database access software (for example, BDE, SQL*NET, and so on) runs on the same machine as the application server. Remember that this is simply the classic case, and many other configurations are possible.

n-tier computing refers to the fact that all these tiers can be spread out across multiple machines. For instance, you might have the employee server on one machine and the payroll server on another machine. One of these application servers might access Oracle data from machine C, and the other server might access InterBase data from machine D. Hence, you have not three tiers, but n-tiers.

> **NOTE**
>
> The term *n-tier* can be considered a bit misleading, at least from some perspectives. No matter how you break up your database servers, application servers, and clients, you still end up with three tiers of computing. Just because you have the middle tier spread out over 10 machines doesn't really change the fact that all 10 machines are involved in middle-tier computing.

The C++Builder team refers to its specific tools for implementing this technology as distributed datasets or MIDAS. C++Builder implements a multitier technology via a set of components, and our documents refer to the technology supported by these components as distributed datasets. *MIDAS* is the term the marketing team uses to refer to this same technology.

If the definition of distributed technology given here seems a bit abstract to you, it might help to consider the fact that the Web is a classic distributed technology. In particular, a person working on the Web can use a browser to view a dataset on a remote machine without having any database tools on the client. Quite frequently the database server does not run on the same machine as the Web server. As a result, you again end up with three tiers: the browser on the client, the Web server on the middle tier, and the database server on the third tier. The same basic format is found on Borland's multitier implementation of distributed datasets.

20

MIDAS

Unlike MIDAS, browsers are limited in terms of functionality and performance. For instance, on the Web it is difficult to enforce constraints; to program a browser to perform a join; to create a fancy, modern, high-performance interface; or to set up tables in a one-to-many relationship. These chores are simple to execute inside a C++Builder multitier application. C++Builder's high-performance compiled applications are much faster and more responsive than HTML-based applications. (However, you can put MIDAS in an ActiveForm and show that over the Web if your clients support ActiveX—that is, if your clients are using Internet Explorer.)

What Is MIDAS?

MIDAS is based on technology that allows you to package datasets in a `Variant` and send them across the network as parameters to remote method calls. It includes technology for converting a dataset into a `Variant` on the server side, and unbundling the dataset on the client and displaying it to the user in a grid via the aid of the `TClientDataSet` component.

Seen from a slightly different angle, MIDAS is a technology for moving a dataset from a `TTable` or `TQuery` object on a server to a `TClientDataSet` object on a client. `TClientDataSet` looks, acts, and feels exactly like a `TTable` or `TQuery` component, except that it doesn't have to be attached to the BDE. In this particular case, the `TClientDataSet` gets its data from unpacking the variant that it retrieves from the server.

MIDAS allows you to use all the standard C++Builder components including database tools in your client-side applications, but the client side does not have to include the Borland Database Engine, ODBC, or any client database libraries (for example, Oracle SQL*NET, Sybase CT-Lib, and so on). Somewhere on the network, the BDE or a similar engine needs to exist, but you don't need to have it on the client side. In short, you now need only one set of server-side database tools, whereas before you needed database tools on each client machine. A small (about 211KB) file called `DBCLIENT.DLL` is needed on the client side, but that is very little when compared with the many megabytes of files required by the BDE or other database middle-ware.

> **NOTE**
>
> I should make a few brief comments about the word behind the technology. Midas was a mythical king of Greece who received from Dionysus a gift enabling him to turn all he touched into gold. After a period in which all his food and key members of his family were turned into gold, Midas grew weary of the gift and was released from it by washing his hands in a river. The sands of that river were then turned into golden-colored sand, a fact to which contemporary visitors of Greece can still attest today.

The two different layers of the MIDAS technology are as follows:

- The components found on the Component Palette and built in to the VCL.
- The protocol used to send messages over the Internet. This layer might be DCOM, OLEnterprise, CORBA, or just plain old TCP/IP (sockets).

The built-in C++Builder components enable you to easily connect two machines and pass datasets back and forth between them. In the simplest scenarios, they make it possible for you to build middle-tier and client applications with just a few clicks of the mouse.

Goals of Distributed Computing

One of the big goals of distributed computing is to create servers that contain all the rules and logic for accessing data. In a typical example, you might have one or more large NT servers hosting a series of MIDAS application servers built in C++Builder. These servers can serve up data to their clients. All the logic and intelligence is in the server, and the client is just a thin shell that enables the user to view and edit the data.

You can create a whole complex of servers working together to represent complex entities such as a company or department. One server might represent the payroll department, another the human resources department, and a third might keep track of inventory. Or, you could even break up the model into more fine-tuned entities, such as one server that represents an employee object, one that represents a widget, and a third that represents the company calendar.

As you can tell from the examples listed in the preceding two paragraphs, a clear parallel exists between distributed computing and OOP. Just as each entity in a program should have its own object, each entity, or perhaps each related group of entities, should have its own MIDAS application server.

This approach to distributed technology turns a network into a resource full of intelligent objects that can represent the entire structure of your company. The idea is to keep the clients simple and to put the intelligence in the middle tier. Over time, the middle tier should become so intelligent that it appears to represent its own powerful force in the computing world. To a large degree, the Web has already achieved this goal. Furthermore, the claim of one bold company that the "network is the computer" very closely reflects the idea behind distributed computing.

Distributed datasets are one means of cutting down on network traffic. After you download data from the server, you can manipulate it on the client side, without initiating any more network traffic until you are ready to update the server. This means you can edit, insert, and delete multiple records without causing network traffic. When you're ready to update the server, you can send multiple data packets over the network at one specific, prechosen time.

Access to database constraints are another important aspect of the MIDAS technology. When you download data from the server, you can simultaneously download a set of constraints that can be automatically enforced. The constraints can help programmers ensure that the user enters only valid data. When you are reconnected to the network, your data can be updated without mishap.

If perchance an error does occur while you are updating the dataset, built-in mechanisms can aid the programmer in reporting and handling the error. For instance, if a second user has updated a record that you are trying to update, that fact can be surfaced, and the user can be given a choice of options on how to proceed. A prebuilt form that ships in the C++Builder Object Repository makes it simple to implement error handling in your application.

Yet another important feature of Borland's multitier computing includes distributing the load borne by a database over multiple servers, as well as providing fail-over capabilities in case of an error.

An Overview of the Briefcase Model

Using what is called the *briefcase model*, you can disconnect the client from the network and still access the data. Here's how it works:

- Save a remote dataset to disk, shut down your machine, and disconnect from the network. You can then boot up again and edit your data without connecting to the network.
- When you get back to the network, you can reconnect and update the database. A mechanism is provided for being notified about database errors and resolving any conflicts that might occur. For instance, if two people edit the same record, you are notified of the fact and given options to resolve the problem. All this occurs without the presence of large database tools on the client machine.

The point is that you don't have to actually be able to reach the server at all times to be able to work with your data. This capability is ideal for laptop users or for sites where you want to keep database traffic to a minimum.

Terminology

I want to spend a few paragraphs on terminology because the technology is new and is being interpreted in various ways by different companies. This chapter is about something called, at various times, the following:

- Distributed computing
- Client/server computing

- Multitier computing
- n-tiered computing
- Remote datasets
- Distributed datasets

A host of other terms are also used, many of which are often cited out of context or in a very loosely defined manner. In general, I find this field of computing to be overrun with marketing propaganda. To get anything done, you have to understand the technology itself. You should work hard to avoid being sucked in by a lot of fancy word slingers who don't know a curly brace from a {..} pair, a LongInt from a LongWord, an integer from an interface, a not from a null, a variable from a reference, a buffer from a debugger, a substring from a subtype, a callback from a rollback, or a module from a mutex.

Finding a Broker

C++Builder and MIDAS provide access to several different brokers. You can access world-class brokers like those you find in CORBA and Entera and smaller, more modest brokers such as C++Builder's OLEnterprise and TSimpleObjectBroker. In between, you find MTS, which is a growing technology with a future that is not yet clearly defined.

OLEnterprise provides an alternative to DCOM, which can, under some circumstances, simplify the task of connecting two machines and particularly of connecting two Windows 95/98 machines. OLEnterprise comes from Borland's purchase of the Open Environment Corporation. The purchase of OEC also gave Borland access to an Object Broker that allows you to randomly distribute the load of a task across several servers. In particular, you can load your server tools on several machines; then the broker chooses one of these machines each time you make a connection. For example, if you have 100 clients and three servers, the Object Broker randomly divides the load across the three servers so that each has (approximately) 33 clients.

The broker also provides support for those occasions when a server is forced to shut down unexpectedly. By writing a few lines of code, you can provide fail-over services that switch clients of a downed server over to a running server. Furthermore, the broker never attempts to connect a new client to a server that has gone down but instead automatically connects the client to one of the servers that is still running. I include a short sample procedure later in this chapter that demonstrates how to implement this fail-over process in the section "Using OLEnterprise."

If you don't want to use OLEnterprise, fail-over and load distribution are also provided by the TSimpleObjectBroker component. This component serves up a computer name from a list of computer names, and then you can ask that computer for the interface you

20

MIDAS

want. In C++Builder 4, TSimpleObjectBroker does not know anything about interfaces. It only serves up a list of computer names, but it gives you the list in random order, thereby providing you with load balancing and support for fail-over. Over time, the TSimpleObjectBroker technology can be improved and expanded, so if you are reading this book some months or years after C++Builder 4 shipped, you might want to look for updates that expand the object's functionality.

Neither OLEnterprise nor the TSimpleObjectBroker provides the same level of service that you get from a CORBA or Entera broker. Both CORBA and Entera are designed to provide true load balancing and fail-over, and they are sophisticated enough to keep a mission-critical application server running 24 hours a day, seven days a week.

MTS provides a level of support somewhere between that provided by OLEnterprise and that provided by a technology such as CORBA. You can use MIDAS with either CORBA or MTS. MIDAS is somewhat harder to use on MTS, however, because MTS prefers that its objects not maintain state.

Technology Details: Using Distributed Datasets

It is now time to start analyzing the technology involved in C++Builder's distributed datasets. In other words, the chapter now switches from theory to practice. This section gives an overview of the components involved in this technology, and the next section begins a detailed examination of the components.

Four key C++Builder tools make distributed datasets possible. The first two appear on the server side:

- *Remote data modules* are just like standard data modules, except that they help you broadcast data not to your current application, but to locations on the network. In particular, they turn a simple data module into a COM object, thereby allowing you to access the data module from a remote server via DCOM.

- The TProvider component resides on remote data modules just as a TTable object can reside on a standard data module. The difference is that a TProvider broadcasts a table across the network. Provider objects are also included in the TTable and TQuery objects as properties. However, if you access them as standalone components, you have more flexibility and power. In particular, you hook up a TProvider component to a TTable or TQuery so that other programs on the network can access the data from the `TTable` or `TQuery` via DCOM. The job of the remote data module is to give clients access to the specific providers available on a server. The client first connects to the remote data module and then queries the remote data module for a list of available providers on its server.

On the client side, you use two components to access the data supplied by the server:

- The `TRemoteServer` component gives the client the capability to connect to the server. More specifically, it connects to the COM interface supported by the remote data module. Despite the implication inherent in its name, `TRemoteServers` exist on the client side, not on the server side. `TRemoteServer` is the component that knows how to browse the Registry in search of available servers. After the server is found, the `TRemoteServer` connects to it.

- The `TClientDataSet` component hooks up to the `TRemoteServer` component and then attaches to a specific provider on the server. They give the data sources on the client application something to plug into when they want to connect to a remote dataset. In short, the `TClientDataSet` plays the same role as a `TQuery` or `TTable`, except that it serves up data from a remote site. Imagine the traditional `TDatabase`, `TTable`, `TDataSource`, `TDBGrid` configuration seen in many standard C++Builder applications. In a remote dataset, you make a slight change to these configurations by using `TRemoteServer`, `TClientDataSet`, `TDataSource`, and `TDBGrid`. In this new scenario, `TRemoteServer` plays a role roughly parallel to `TDatabase`, and `TClientDataSet` plays a role fairly similar to that traditionally played by `TTable` or `TQuery`. I don't mean to imply a one-to-one correspondence between `TDatabase` and `TRemoteServer`, but a rough similarity can be seen between the roles played by the two components.

The diagram shown in Figure 20.1 depicts the architecture of a remote dataset application. On the top of half is the server side of the equation, which consists of a remote data module, three tables, and three providers. On the client side, you find a `TRemoteServer` and three `TClientDatasets`. Attached to the client dataset, you could have a series of data sources and visual controls. Notice that you need one provider and one client dataset for each table you want to broadcast. You could have varying numbers of tables, as well as many other objects, forms, and so on, on each side of the equation. My goal here is to focus on only the core elements in a proposed three-table scenario that must be present to make the concept of remote datasets work.

FIGURE 20.1

*The architecture
of a remote
dataset.*

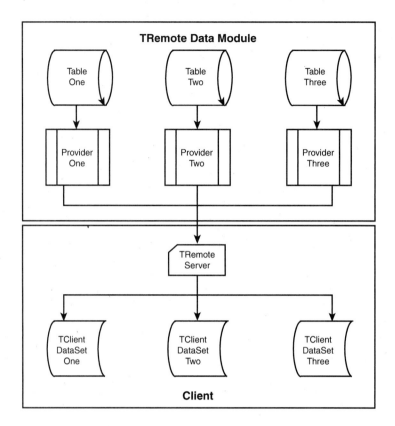

Building a Simple MIDAS Application

In this section, I describe one possible technique for building a server for a remote
dataset. Here is a quick overview of the steps involved:

1. Start a new application, hook it up to some data as you would in any other
   C++Builder application, and save it to disk.

2. Choose File, New, MultiTier, Remote Data Module to create a remote data module.

3. Place one or more TTable and TProvider components on the remote data module.

4. Hook up the TProvider to the TTable or TQuery object.

5. Right-click the TProvider to create interface methods for accessing the provider
   on a remote machine.

6. Save your work and register the server.

On the disk that comes with this book you find a sample program called SimpleMidas. It
represents the simplest possible MIDAS application that you can build. You can see the
key files in the client and server for this application in Listings 20.1 through 20.3.

LISTING 20.1   THE `MainImpl.cpp` FILE CONTAINS THE IMPLEMENTATION OF THE
SIMPLEMIDAS SERVER

```cpp
#include <vcl.h>
#pragma hdrstop

#include "MainImpl.h"

#if !defined(__PRAGMA_SMART_INIT_DEFINED)
#define __PRAGMA_SMART_INIT_DEFINED
#pragma package(smart_init)
#endif

#pragma resource "*.dfm"


///////////////////////////////////////////////////////////////////////
// Global instance of TSimpleMidasImpl
///////////////////////////////////////////////////////////////////////
TSimpleMidas *SimpleMidas;


///////////////////////////////////////////////////////////////////////
// TSimpleMidas::TSimpleMidas
///////////////////////////////////////////////////////////////////////
__fastcall TSimpleMidas::TSimpleMidas(TComponent* Owner) : TDataModule
➥(Owner)
{
}


STDMETHODIMP TSimpleMidasImpl::get_CountryProvider(IProvider** Value)
{
  try
  {
  _di_IProvider IProv = m_DataModule->CountryProvider->Provider;
  IProv->AddRef();
  *Value = IProv;
  }
  catch(Exception &e)
  {
    return Error(e.Message.c_str(), IID_ISimpleMidas);
  }
  return S_OK;
};
```

LISTING 20.2   THE LIBRARY (HEADER) FILE FOR THE SimpleMidas SERVER

```
// ********************************************************************* //
// WARNING                                                             //
// -------                                                             //
// The types declared in this file were generated from data read from a //
// Type Library. If this type library is explicitly or indirectly (via //
// another type library referring to this type library) re-imported, or //
// the 'Refresh' command of the Type Library Editor activated while    //
// editing the Type Library, the contents of this file will be         //
// regenerated and all manual modifications will be lost.              //
// ********************************************************************* //

// C++ TLBWRTR : $Revision:   1.96.1.27  $
// File generated 4/2/99 10:14:23 AM from Type Library described below.


// ********************************************************************* //
// Type Lib: D:\USR\BOB\BOOKS\UNLEASH.BCB\20\SRC\SERVER\SimpleMidasServer
➡.tlb
// IID\LCID: {9CAE8DAF-E8BE-11D2-92DA-0080C7C19BE0}\0
// Helpfile:
// DepndLst:
//   (1) v2.0 stdole, (C:\WINNT\System32\STDOLE2.TLB)
//   (2) v4.0 StdVCL, (C:\WINNT\System32\STDVCL40.DLL)
// ********************************************************************* //
#ifndef    __SimpleMidasServer_TLB_h__
#define    __SimpleMidasServer_TLB_h__

#pragma option push -b -w-inl

#include <vcl/utilcls.h>
#if !defined(__UTILCLS_H_VERSION) || (__UTILCLS_H_VERSION < 0x0101)
#error "This file requires an newer version of the header file UTILCLS.H"
#endif


#include <olectl.h>
#include <ocidl.h>
#if defined(USING_ATLVCL) || defined(USING_ATL)
#if !defined(__TLB_NO_EVENT_WRAPPERS)
#include <atl/atlmod.h>
#endif
#endif


#include "databkr.hpp"

// *********************************************************************//
// Forward reference of some VCL types (to avoid including STDVCL.HPP) //
// *********************************************************************//
namespace Stdvcl {class IStrings; class IStringsDisp;}
using namespace Stdvcl;
```

```
namespace Simplemidasserver_tlb
{

// *********************************************************************//
// HelpString: SimpleMidasServer Library
// Version:    1.0
// *********************************************************************//


// *********************************************************************//
// GUIDS declared in the TypeLibrary. Following prefixes are used:    //
//    Type Libraries     : LIBID_xxxx                                 //
//    CoClasses          : CLSID_xxxx                                 //
//    DISPInterfaces     : DIID_xxxx                                  //
//    Non-DISP interfaces: IID_xxxx                                   //
// *********************************************************************//
DEFINE_GUID(LIBID_SimpleMidasServer, 0x9CAE8DAF, 0xE8BE, 0x11D2, 0x92, 0x
➥DA, 0x00, 0x80, 0xC7, 0xC1, 0x9B, 0xE0);
DEFINE_GUID(IID_ISimpleMidas, 0x9CAE8DB0, 0xE8BE, 0x11D2, 0x92, 0xDA, 0x0
➥0, 0x80, 0xC7, 0xC1, 0x9B, 0xE0);
DEFINE_GUID(CLSID_SimpleMidas, 0x9CAE8DB2, 0xE8BE, 0x11D2, 0x92, 0xDA, 0x
➥00, 0x80, 0xC7, 0xC1, 0x9B, 0xE0);

// *********************************************************************//
// Forward declaration of types defined in TypeLibrary                //
// *********************************************************************//
interface DECLSPEC_UUID("{9CAE8DB0-E8BE-11D2-92DA-0080C7C19BE0}") Isimple
➥Midas;

// *********************************************************************//
// Declaration of CoClasses defined in Type Library                   //
// (NOTE: Here we map each CoClass to its Default Interface)           //
//                                                                     //
// The LIBID_OF_ macro(s) map a LIBID_OF_CoClassName to the GUID of this//
// TypeLibrary. It simplifies the updating of macros when CoClass name //
// change.                                                             //
// *********************************************************************//

#define LIBID_OF_SimpleMidas (&LIBID_SimpleMidasServer)
// *********************************************************************//
// Interface: ISimpleMidas
// Flags:     (4416) Dual OleAutomation Dispatchable
// GUID:      {9CAE8DB0-E8BE-11D2-92DA-0080C7C19BE0}
// *********************************************************************//
interface ISimpleMidas : public IDataBroker
{
public:
  virtual HRESULT STDMETHODCALLTYPE get_CountryProvider(IProvider** Value
➥/*[out,retval]*/) = 0; // [1]
```

continues

20

MIDAS

LISTING 20.2   CONTINUED

```cpp
#if !defined(__TLB_NO_INTERFACE_WRAPPERS)

  IProvider* __fastcall get_CountryProvider(void)
  {
    IProvider* Value= 0;
    OLECHECK(this->get_CountryProvider(&Value));
    return Value;
  }


  __property  IProvider*    CountryProvider =
➥{read = get_CountryProvider};

#endif //    __TLB_NO_INTERFACE_WRAPPERS

};

#if !defined(__TLB_NO_INTERFACE_WRAPPERS)
// ************************************************************************//
// SmartIntf: TCOMISimpleMidas
// Interface: ISimpleMidas
// ************************************************************************//
template <class T /* ISimpleMidas */>
class TCOMISimpleMidasT : public TComInterface<ISimpleMidas>, public Tcom
➥InterfaceBase<IUnknown>
{
public:
  TCOMISimpleMidasT() {}
  TCOMISimpleMidasT(ISimpleMidas *intf, bool addRef = false) :
➥TcomInterface<ISimpleMidas>(intf, addRef) {}
  TCOMISimpleMidasT(const TCOMISimpleMidasT& src) : TComInterface<Isimple
➥Midas>(src) {}
  TCOMISimpleMidasT& operator=(const TCOMISimpleMidasT& src) { Bind(src,
➥true); return *this;}

  HRESULT        __fastcall get_CountryProvider(IProvider** Value/*[out,
➥retval]*/);
  IProvider*     __fastcall get_CountryProvider(void);

  __property  IProvider*    CountryProvider =
➥{read = get_CountryProvider};
};
typedef TCOMISimpleMidasT<ISimpleMidas> TCOMISimpleMidas;

// ************************************************************************//
// DispIntf:  ISimpleMidas
// Flags:     (4416) Dual OleAutomation Dispatchable
// GUID:      {9CAE8DB0-E8BE-11D2-92DA-0080C7C19BE0}
// ************************************************************************//
```

```
template<class T>
class ISimpleMidasDispT : public TAutoDriver<ISimpleMidas>
{
public:
  ISimpleMidasDispT(){}

  ISimpleMidasDispT(ISimpleMidas *pintf)
  {
    TAutoDriver<ISimpleMidas>::Bind(pintf);
  }

  ISimpleMidasDispT& operator=(ISimpleMidas *pintf)
  {
    TAutoDriver<ISimpleMidas>::Bind(pintf);
    return *this;
  }

  HRESULT BindDefault(/*Binds to new instance of CoClass SimpleMidas*/)
  {
    return OLECHECK(Bind(CLSID_SimpleMidas));
  }

  HRESULT BindRunning(/*Binds to a running instance of CoClass
➥SimpleMidas*/)
  {
    return BindToActive(CLSID_SimpleMidas);
  }

  HRESULT        __fastcall get_CountryProvider(IProvider** Value/*[out,
➥retval]*/);
  IProvider*     __fastcall get_CountryProvider(void);
  HRESULT        __fastcall GetProviderNames(TVariant* Value/*[out,
➥retval]*/);
  TVariant       __fastcall GetProviderNames(void);

  __property  IProvider*     CountryProvider =
➥{read = get_CountryProvider};

};
typedef ISimpleMidasDispT<ISimpleMidas> ISimpleMidasDisp;

// **********************************************************************//
// SmartIntf: TCOMISimpleMidas
// Interface: ISimpleMidas
// **********************************************************************//
template <class T> HRESULT __fastcall
TCOMISimpleMidasT<T>::get_CountryProvider(IProvider** Value/*[out,
➥retval]*/)
```

continues

LISTING 20.2   CONTINUED

```
{
  return (*this)->get_CountryProvider(Value);
}

template <class T> IProvider* __fastcall
TCOMISimpleMidasT<T>::get_CountryProvider(void)
{
  IProvider* Value= 0;
  OLECHECK(this->get_CountryProvider(&Value));
  return Value;
}

// **********************************************************************//
// DispIntf:  ISimpleMidas
// Flags:     (4416) Dual OleAutomation Dispatchable
// GUID:      {9CAE8DB0-E8BE-11D2-92DA-0080C7C19BE0}
// **********************************************************************//
template <class T> HRESULT __fastcall
ISimpleMidasDispT<T>::get_CountryProvider(IProvider** Value/*[out,
➥retval]*/)
{
  static _TDispID _dispid(*this, OLETEXT("CountryProvider"), DISPID(1));
  TAutoArgs<0> _args;
  return OutRetValSetterPtr((LPDISPATCH*)Value /*[VT_USERDEFINED:2]*/,
➥ _args, OlePropertyGet(_dispid, _args));
}

template <class T> IProvider* __fastcall
ISimpleMidasDispT<T>::get_CountryProvider(void)
{
  IProvider* Value;
  this->get_CountryProvider(&Value);
  return Value;
}

template <class T> HRESULT __fastcall
ISimpleMidasDispT<T>::GetProviderNames(TVariant* Value/*[out,retval]*/)
{
  static _TDispID _dispid(*this, OLETEXT("GetProviderNames"), DISPID
➥(22929905));
  TAutoArgs<0> _args;
  return OutRetValSetterPtr(Value /*[VT_VARIANT:1]*/, _args, OleFunction
➥(_dispid, _args));
}
```

```
template <class T> TVariant __fastcall
ISimpleMidasDispT<T>::GetProviderNames(void)
{
  TVariant Value;
  this->GetProviderNames(&Value);
  return Value;
}

// **********************************************************************//
// The following typedefs expose classes (named CoCoClassName) that    //
// provide static Create() and CreateRemote(LPWSTR machineName) methods //
// for creating an instance of an exposed object. These functions can   //
// be used by client wishing to automate CoClasses exposed by this      //
// typelibrary.                                                          //
// **********************************************************************//

// **********************************************************************//
// COCLASS DEFAULT INTERFACE CREATOR
// CoClass   : SimpleMidas
// Interface: TCOMISimpleMidas
// **********************************************************************//
typedef TCoClassCreatorT<TCOMISimpleMidas, ISimpleMidas,
➡&CLSID_SimpleMidas, &IID_ISimpleMidas> CoSimpleMidas;
#endif  //    __TLB_NO_INTERFACE_WRAPPERS


};      // namespace Simplemidasserver_tlb

#if !defined(NO_IMPLICIT_NAMESPACE_USE)
using  namespace Simplemidasserver_tlb;
#endif

#pragma option pop

#endif // __SimpleMidasServer_TLB_h__
```

LISTING 20.3 THE SOURCE FOR THE MAIN FORM OF THE SIMPLEMIDASCLIENT
APPLICATION

```
//------------------------------------------------------------------
#include <vcl.h>
#pragma hdrstop

#include "MainClient.h"
//------------------------------------------------------------------
#pragma package(smart_init)
```

continues

20

MIDAS

LISTING 20.3   CONTINUED

```cpp
#pragma resource "*.dfm"
TForm1 *Form1;
//-----------------------------------------------------------------
__fastcall TForm1::TForm1(TComponent* Owner)
        : TForm(Owner)
{
}
//-----------------------------------------------------------------
void __fastcall TForm1::Connect1Click(TObject *Sender)
{
  AnsiString S;
  if (InputQuery("Enter Machine Name:", "Machine Name", S))
  {
    DCOMConnection1->ComputerName = S;
//  DCOMConnection1->Connected = true;
    ClientDataSet1->Active = true;
  }
}
//-----------------------------------------------------------------

void __fastcall TForm1::ConnectTCPIP1Click(TObject *Sender)
{
  AnsiString S;
  if (InputQuery("Enter Machine Name (or IP Address):", "Machine Name/IP
➤Address", S))
  {
    SocketConnection1->Address = S;
//  SocketConnection1->Connected = true;
    ClientDataSet1->RemoteServer = SocketConnection1;
    ClientDataSet1->Active = true;
  }
}
//-----------------------------------------------------------------
```

This application and client pair display the Country table of the BCDEMOS database. The client side of the equation has a simple grid on it displaying the contents of the Country table, as shown in Figure 20.2. The server side has no interface, so I simply put a nice picture of C++Builder 4 on it, as shown in Figure 20.3. If the server appears in front of the client when run, simply minimize its form to view the data behind it.

Name	Capital	Continent	Area	Population
Argentina	Buenos Aires	South America	2777815	32300003
Bolivia	La Paz	South America	1098575	7300000
Brazil	Brasilia	South America	8511196	150400000
Canada	Ottawa	North America	9976147	26500000
Chile	Santiago	South America	756943	13200000
Colombia	Bagota	South America	1138907	33000000
Cuba	Havana	North America	114524	10600000
Ecuador	Quito	South America	455502	10600000
El Salvador	San Salvador	North America	20865	5300000
Guyana	Georgetown	South America	214969	800000
Jamaica	Kingston	North America	11424	2500000
Mexico	Mexico City	North America	1967180	88600000
Nicaragua	Managua	North America	139000	3900000
Paraguay	Asuncion	South America	406576	4660000
Peru	Lima	South America	1285215	21600000
United States of America	Washington	North America	9363130	249200000
Uruguay	Montevideo	South America	176140	3002000
Venezuela	Caracas	South America	912047	19700000

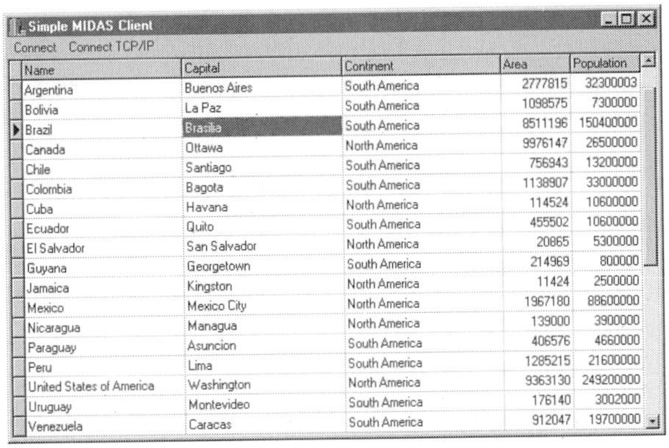

FIGURE 20.2
The main form of the SimpleMidasClient displays the `Country` *table in a standard C++Builder grid.*

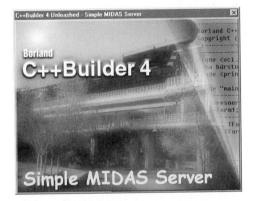

FIGURE 20.3
The main form of the SimpleMidasServer has no interface to speak of, so I display a picture on its surface.

Now that you've seen the end result, it's time to get to work and recreate the MIDAS server and client yourself. Believe me, this is the best way to experience how easy it is to create multitier applications.

Creating the SimpleMidasServer

To begin recreating the SimpleMidasServer, you should start a C++Builder application and save it to disk. When I made the program, I created a single directory called `SimpleMidas` and beneath it two directories called `Server` and `Client`. I saved the main form of the server as `MainServer.cpp` and the project file itself as `SimpleMidasServer.bpr`.

NOTE

You might find me uncharacteristically dogmatic about the names I suggest you give the components and examples shown in this chapter. Of course, you are free to name your controls whatever you want, and ultimately I naturally expect and want you to give them your own names. The somewhat claustrophobic dogmatism that I exhibit in this chapter occurs because the names you give to various controls come into play several times in ways that are not immediately evident at first.

For instance, when you are creating the client/server pairs for the examples in this chapter, you probably end up opening the Project Manager and displaying both the client and the server at the same time in a single group. If you call the main form of each program `Main.cpp`, you create two legal programs, but you end up with two files called `Main.cpp` open in the IDE. Having two such files is not an error, but it can waste your time, as you can find yourself pressing Ctrl+Tab to the wrong page on an annoyingly frequent basis. As a result, I suggest naming the server's main form `MainServer` and the client's main form `MainClient`. If you follow this convention, you always know which form is which.

Another example occurs later in the chapter when you drop down a control called `TProvider`. I again ask you to give this control a specific name. The reason for using this naming convention is that you can access this name from the client program. If you do not give the control a reasonable name, you might not know what you are looking at when you are in your client program.

In short, I believe that naming conventions are very important in this type of program. After you grasp the reasoning behind my suggested names, you can develop your own conventions—or not—depending on your own inclinations.

Choose File, New, MultiTier and elect to create a new Remote Data Module. Set the `ClassName` field to `SimpleMidas` and leave everything else at the default value. By accepting the default threading (and instance) model, you automatically create a server that has the correct threading model to handle multiple clients at the same time. Click OK and save your work as `MainIMPL.cpp`.

Drop a `TTable` object on the remote data module and rename it `CountryTable`. Hook it up to the `Country` table from the `BCDEMOS` database. Drop down a `TProvider` component and rename it `CountryProvider`. Attach its `DataSet` field to the `TTable` object. Right-click it and choose Export Country Provider from Data Module from the menu. Save your work and run the application once to register it.

That is all you need to do to create a MIDAS server. If you get good at it, you should be able to finish all these steps in fewer than five minutes. That's not instantaneous, but it is an improvement over the time required by most other distributed database development platforms in the same way that taking a jet airplane from Washington, D.C., to San Francisco is an improvement over walking. Of course, you would learn a lot if you walked from the Washington monument to the Golden Gate Bridge, but perhaps this is not entirely the right time in your life to undertake such an adventure.

Understanding the Server

As simple as it is to build the server, you still need to understand a bit more of what goes on beneath the covers.

The following are the two main classes (TSimpleMidas and TSimpleMidasImpl) in your header file:

```
class TSimpleMidas : public TDataModule
{
__published:  // IDE-managed Components
        TTable *CountryTable;
        TProvider *CountryProvider;
private:        // User declarations
public:         // User declarations
   __fastcall TSimpleMidas(TComponent* Owner);

__published:
};


//////////////////////////////////////////////////////////////////////
//////////////////////////////////////////////////////////////////////
extern PACKAGE TSimpleMidas *SimpleMidas;


//////////////////////////////////////////////////////////////////////
// TSimpleMidasImpl     Implements ISimpleMidas, default interface of
➥SimpleMidas
// ThreadingModel : Apartment
// Dual Interface : TRUE
// Event Support  : FALSE
// Default ProgID : SimpleMidasServer.SimpleMidas
// Description    :
//////////////////////////////////////////////////////////////////////
class ATL_NO_VTABLE TSimpleMidasImpl: REMOTEDATAMODULE_IMPL
➥(TsimpleMidasImpl, SimpleMidas, TSimpleMidas, ISimpleMidas)
```

```
{
public:

BEGIN_COM_MAP(TSimpleMidasImpl)
  AUTOOBJECT_COM_INTERFACE_ENTRIES(ISimpleMidas)
END_COM_MAP()

  // Data used when registering Object
  //
  DECLARE_THREADING_MODEL(otApartment);
  DECLARE_PROGID("SimpleMidasServer.SimpleMidas");
  DECLARE_DESCRIPTION("");

  // Function invoked to (un)register object
  //
  static HRESULT WINAPI UpdateRegistry(BOOL bRegister)
  {
    TRemoteDataModuleRegistrar regObj(GetObjectCLSID(), GetProgID(),
➡GetDescription());
    return regObj.UpdateRegistry(bRegister);
  }


// ISimpleMidas
protected:
  STDMETHOD(get_CountryProvider(IProvider** Value));
};
}
```

Class declarations of this type provide an implementation for a COM object. The COM interface in question is called ISimpleMidas. You should note that ISimpleMidas is a dual-interfaced COM object, which means that it supports both IDispatch and ISimpleMidas. It can be accessed from other applications via OLE automation and from remote machines via distributed COM. ISimpleMidas has an accompanying type library, described in a separate unit shown in Listing 20.2. (If you are having trouble understanding terms such as *COM object* or *type library*, you can go back and read Chapter 13, "The Basics of COM and Type Libraries.")

Even if it didn't have any methods, you could access the TSimpleMidas object from a second application or second machine. Under such circumstances, you could do nothing more than launch the server. It would have no functionality.

To make the server useful, you have to provide a mechanism that allows the client to get at the TProvider object you dropped on the remote data module. More particularly, you need to access the IProvider interface supported by the TProvider component. To give clients access to a provider, you need to add properties to the ISimpleMidas COM object. This process is simple, but you can do it in several different ways, which I describe in the following section.

Exporting the `IProvider` Interface

There are three ways to add a property to a Remote Data Module that automatically export the provider interface:

- As you have seen, you can right-click a `TProvider` object and select Export *XXX* from Data Module, where *XXX* is the name of your `TProvider` component. The code produced by this action is explained later. If you right-click the provider component and don't see this option, that means it has already been selected. In other words, the option is removed from the menu after you select it once.

- You also have the option to export the provider interface directly from a `TTable` or `TQuery` object placed on a remote data module. Each `TTable` or `TQuery` object has a provider interface built in to it. Most programmers probably use this `IProvider` interface rather than the one from the `TProvider` object. I like to use a separate `TProvider` object because it makes my program easier to understand and provides me with a more flexible structure. In particular, I could point the standalone `TProvider` component to a different table and yield different results. You should also note the events associated with the `TProvider` component. These events are not available if you access this interface directly from a `TTable` or `TQuery`. Regardless of my preferences, your code will work perfectly well if you never drop a `TProvider` component on a remote data module but instead use the `IProvider` interface on the `TTable` or `TQuery` object.

- Another alternative is to use the Type Library Editor, which you can reach from the View menu or by hitting F12 when the TLB.h file is open in the IDE. You can then create a property called `CountryProvider` that returns an `IProvider` interface. In short, you can use this tool to add a property to the COM object that is being created behind the scenes.

Of these methods, a right-click action on the `TProvider`, `TQuery`, or `TTable` object is the simplest to perform, so they are the default techniques you should employ. As you know, I prefer to use a `TProvider` component, but in simple programs like this, my preference is merely a matter of taste.

Whatever technique you choose, you should end up with a method that looks like this:

```
STDMETHODIMP TSimpleMidasImpl::get_CountryProvider(IProvider** Value)
{
  try
  {
  _di_IProvider IProv = m_DataModule->CountryProvider->Provider;
  IProv->AddRef();
  *Value = IProv;
  }
```

```
catch(Exception &e)
{
  return Error(e.Message.c_str(), IID_ISimpleMidas);
}
return S_OK;
};
```

The declaration and statements for this method are created automatically by the IDE. If you use the Type Library Editor to create the method, you need to write the three lines of code (between the try-catch pair) that return the IProvider interface from the CountryProvider object. This task is taken care of for you automatically if you just right-click the component and select Export *XXX* from Data Module from the menu.

When you're using type libraries directly to create this method, you might notice that along with these Get methods, a Set method is also produced for the property. You can leave it blank or use the Type Library Editor to remove it. In other words, having an almost empty method in your TCustOrdersRemoteData object that looks like this is not an error:

```
STDMETHODIMP TSimpleMidasImpl::get_CountryProvider(IProvider** Value)
{
  try
  {

  }
  catch(Exception &e)
  {
    return Error(e.Message.c_str(), IID_ISimpleMidas);
  }
  return S_OK;
};
```

Preparing the Server for the Client Program

Save your work and run the program once with the parameter /RegServer to register it with the system, you create a remote data server. You now have the choice of accessing the server locally or placing this object on a remote NT server, as described later in the chapter.

The following is a summary of the steps outlined in the sections on building a server:

1. Create a standard C++Builder application.

2. Add a remote data module and drop down a TTable and a TProvider object on it.

3. Use the DataSet property of the TProvider to connect to the TTable object.

4. Right-click the TProvider to create a method that retrieves the appropriate provider interface.

5. Compile the application and run it once on the client with the command line parameter /RegServer. You can now test your application. If you want to move the server to a remote machine, run it once on the client and once on the remote machine, again with the /RegServer parameter.

As you can see, building an application server in C++Builder is simple. I have gone into such detail when explaining the process so that you can become familiar with the theory behind the process, thereby understanding not only how to build the server, but why it is architected in this particular manner.

Creating a Simple MIDAS Client

Creating a MIDAS client that talks to the SimpleMidasServer is extremely simple. At this stage, you should not be trying to run the client and the server on separate machines. Instead, get everything up and running on one machine and later you can distribute the application on the network.

This brief tutorial shows how to create the client:

1. Create a new application and save it into the Client directory right next to your Server directory. Save the main form as MainClient.cpp and save the server as SimpleMidasClient.bpr.

2. Drop down a TDCOMConnnection component from the Midas page and set its ServerName property to the ProgID SimpleMidasServer.SimpleMidas. You should be able to pick this ProgID from a drop-down list in the TDCOMConnection editor. If you can't find the server in this list, the server is not properly registered on your system. All you need to do to register the server is run it once with the /RegServer parameter. Assuming everything is set up correctly, you should now be able to automatically launch the server by setting the DComConnection1.Connected property to true. You don't need to start the server first, as setting Connected to true should launch the server and make it visible on your screen.

> **NOTE**
>
> Although this will always work when the server and client are on the same machine, it may not always work when they are on different machines. This depends on the DCOM security settings on the server machine.

3. Drop down a TClientDataSet component from the Midas page and set its RemoteServer property to TDCOMConnection1 and its ProviderName property to CountryProvider. Again, you should be able to pick CountryProvider from a drop-down list. If you can't, then either your server is not set up correctly, or else you do not have the TDCOMConnection properly attached to your server. Common problems at this stage occur because you might not have properly hooked up the TProvider component to the TTable component or because you have not properly exported the Get_CountryProvider method from the server. In particular, check your type library in the server and make sure it lists the CountryProvider property as type ISimpleMidas. If all is set up correctly, you should be able to set the ClientDataSet.Active property to true and connect to the data on your server.

4. At this stage, you can simply drop down a TDataSource, connect it to the TClientDataSet, and then add a grid and view your data. (Hint: Set the TClientDataSet.Active property to true to see the data at design time.)

As a final step, I like to turn the TClientDataSet.Active property to false and do the same with the Connected property of the TDComconnection. Now drop down a menu, add a menu item called Connected, and associate the following method with its OnClick event:

```
void __fastcall TForm1::Connect1Click(TObject *Sender)
{
  DCOMConnection1->Connected = true;
  ClientDataSet1->Active = true;
}
```

Actually, only the last statement is needed, because the ClientDataSet forces a connection to be made if one is not already in place (so you can leave the first line out, if you want).

This method is helpful because you don't want to close the client project when it is still hooked up to the server. If you leave it connected, you can have trouble if you come back some months later and load the client application into the IDE when the server is not registered. In particular, the client tries to connect to the server, fails to do so, and leaves the whole IDE seemingly locked up during the several minutes that it takes for the operation to time out.

Before closing this section, I want to add that you can perform the same operation shown in this section with either the TDCOMConnection, the TMidasConnection, or the TRemoteServer. For all intents and purposes, these three components perform the same tasks.

Understanding the Simple MIDAS Client

Building a MIDAS client is clearly very simple. However, you should consider several points so that you can better understand not only what to do, but why you are doing it.

First, you need to be sure you understand how the client is connecting to the server. In this case, you are using the TDCOMConnection component. Because both the server and the client are on the same machine, you are really just using simple automation to attach the server and client. So in this one case, it's really a TCOMConnection component rather than a TDCOMConnection component.

When you set TDCOMConnection.Connected to true, you cause CoCreateInstanceEx to be called somewhere in the bowels of VCL. In other words, you are using the same technology that has been outlined in previous chapters that discussed COM, DCOM, or OLE automation.

MIDAS happens to work just as well if you are using other technologies such as OLEnterprise, TCP/IP, or even CORBA. This flexibility comes about because the core of the technology is the capability to wrap a dataset in an OleVariant (or a CORBA Any). The transport that is used to talk across the network is not really very important.

Having said this, I have to point out that the MIDAS technology is based on the COM programming model. When MIDAS uses TCP/IP, it goes to considerable lengths to make TCP/IP look and feel like COM. In fact, even a TCP/IP-based version of IDispatch is built in to the TCP/IP code that MIDAS uses. Even CORBA programs in C++Builder 4 are forced to go through a COM layer before information is sent to or from a server.

20

MIDAS

The actual technology used to marshal the data back and forth across the network is encapsulated in a class called TDataPacketWriter found in the file Provider.cpp. This object has methods called PutField, PutArrayField, PutBlobField, AddColumn, and so on, all of which are clearly designed to allow you to wrap a standard dataset in a Variant.

On the other end, the TClientDataSet is smart enough to unpack this data and make it available to the standard methods of a TDataSource component. In particular, you can set the TClientDataSet.Data property equal to a variant that contains a dataset, and the TClientDataSet automatically unpacks it and makes it available to a TDataSource. You have several chances to see this being done in later chapters.

Accessing the Server Remotely

At this stage, you should have a pretty good feel for how the SimpleMidasServer and its client work. The final stage is to make the connection not just locally, but also remotely.

The details of setting up DCOM were covered in Chapter 19, "DCOM." In that chapter, you learned that it is best to set up the server half of the DCOM program on a machine that's running as a Windows NT domain server. In particular, you don't want to run the server on a Windows 95 or Windows 98 machine, and it is best if the server machine is a domain server and the client machines are all part of this domain or on good terms with it. If you don't have an NT domain server available, you probably should set up your client and server machine to have the same logon and the same password, at least during the initial stages of testing. Windows 98 ships with DCOM as part of the system, whereas Windows 95 machines need to have DCOM added to the system. You can download the DLLs necessary to implement DCOM on a Windows 95 machine from the Microsoft Web site.

You must have the server registered on both the client and the server machines. The client program could still locate and launch the server if you failed to register it, but COM could not marshal data back and forth if the type library for the server is not registered on the client machine. You can do so by running the server once on both machines, or just run it once on the server and then register the TLB file on the client using TRegSvr.exe. In this case, the TLB file is called SimpleMidasServer.tlb. This file was generated automatically when you created the server.

When you access this server remotely from a client machine, you need to install the single C++Builder client executable on the client side only. No database tools are needed, other than the 211KB DBClient.dll file. On the server side, you should include STDVCL40.DLL. It is installed automatically if C++Builder is on the server.

MIDAS
CHAPTER 20
903

Assuming you have everything set up correctly, all you have to do to connect the client to the server is fill in the `ComputerName` property of the `TDCOMConnection` component. Letting the user fill in this property at run time is often simplest:

```
void __fastcall TForm1::Connect1Click(TObject *Sender)
{
  AnsiString S;
  if (InputQuery("Enter Machine Name:", "Machine Name", S))
  {
    DCOMConnection1->ComputerName = S;
//  DCOMConnection1->Connected = true;
    ClientDataSet1->Active = true;
  }
}
```

When the dialog pops up asking for the name of the machine that hosts the server, you can type in either a human-readable machine name or an IP address. You can find the name of your Windows 95 or 98 machine by choosing Start, Settings, Control Panel, Network, Identification from the Explorer menu; you can also use a fully qualified domain name or IP address.

If you don't want to prompt the user for the name of the server machine, you can hard-code the information into the client using the `ComputerName` property in the Object Inspector. Or, you can store the information in the Registry or tuck it away in an INI file. Whatever technique you use, DCOM can take your machine name or IP address and use it to connect you to the server. After the connection is made, data can be marshaled over the network and displayed for the user.

> **NOTE**
>
> If you want, you can use `DComCfg.exe` to point DCOM to the remote machine when running your server, as explained in Chapter 19, or you can use `OLEnterprise` to do the same thing. In short, you have lots of different options, and the techniques I mention here are only suggestions.

Using TCP/IP Rather Than DCOM

If you don't have an NT domain server available on your network, you should probably not try to use DCOM at all and instead use TCP/IP. A socket connection works even if no NT server is in the equation, and it is usually much easier to set up than a DCOM connection. However, security is much more difficult to enforce on a socket connection.

20

MIDAS

You can easily convert SimpleMidasClient into a TCP/IP program. You don't need to make any changes to your server to make it work. Of course, your code will not be any good to you if you do not have TCP/IP set up correctly, as described in Chapter 18, "WinINet and FTP."

To get started building your socket-based MIDAS program, run the ScktSrvr.exe program found in the `CBuilder4/Bin` directory on the server machine. This program must be running on the server, or this system will not work.

Drop down a `TSocketConnection` component from the Midas page of the Component Palette on the main form of the client program. Set its `Address` property to the IP address of the machine where the server resides. It can be a remote machine or your current machine (for example, "localhost"). Fill in the `ServerName` property, just as you did in the DCOM example. You should now be able to test your connection by setting the `Connected` property to `true`. As explained earlier, you should not leave the `Connected` property set to `true`.

Assuming you have dropped down a `TSocketConnection` component on the form and set its `ServerName` property correctly, you can simply add the following method to your `SimpleMidasClient` program to convert it into a single server that supports both DCOM and sockets:

```
void __fastcall TForm1::ConnectTCPIP1Click(TObject *Sender)
{
  AnsiString S;
  if (InputQuery("Enter Machine Name (or IP Address):",
    "Machine Name/IP Address", S))
  {
    SocketConnection1->Address = S;
//  SocketConnection1->Connected = true;
    ClientDataSet1->RemoteServer = SocketConnection1;
    ClientDataSet1->Active = true;
  }
}
```

This method should be called in response to a click of a menu item or button. In particular, you might add a second menu item that reads `Connect TCP/IP` to your program. When the user clicks that button, he is prompted for the IP address of the machine where the server resides. Assuming your system is set up correctly, you can also pass in the human-readable equivalent of that IP address.

The code sets the `SocketConnection1.Address` property to the address supplied by the user. It then changes the `ClientDataSet1.RemoteServer` property so that it points not at the `TDCOMConnection` component, but at that `TSocketConnection` component. Finally, it sets the `Active` property of the `TClientDataSet` to `true`. Setting the `Active` property to `true` automatically causes the `TSocketConnection.Connected` property to be set to `true`.

At this stage, you should be fully connected to your server and viewing your data. This approach works equally well whether the server is on the same machine or on a remote machine. Furthermore, you don't need an NT Domain server or even an NT Server, although I recommend that you use one.

Finally, I should add that I do not think the `TSocketConnection` component plays second fiddle to the `TDCOMConnection` component. If security is not a big issue to you, sockets can be an excellent solution and one that can prove to be quite robust. The `TSocketConnection` component even has threading support built in to it.

Building a One-to-Many Server

Next, I show how to build a program featuring a master/detail relationship using MIDAS. The client portion of this program is shown in Figure 20.4. I am showing you this program to drive home the point that you can do all the things in a MIDAS application that you can do in a standard C++Builder database application. All the same controls still work, and by and large, the same rules still apply. In the course of exploring this subject, I also bring out a number of other interesting aspects of MIDAS programming.

FIGURE 20.4

The interface for a simple client MIDAS application showing a one-to-many relationship between the Customer *and* Order *tables from the* BCDEMOS *database.*

Creating the One-to-Many Server

To start building the server, create a new directory called CustOrders and beneath it create two directories called Client and Server. Construct a standard C++Builder application and save it to disk in the Server directory. You can now choose File, New to create a remote data module. You are prompted to supply a class name. I recommend giving this remote data module a descriptive name such as CustOrdersRemoteData. Remember that the remote data module is just like a standard data module, except that it has a COM interface on it. Accept the defaults for all other options.

Drop two TTable objects on the remote date module and connect one to the Customer and the other to the Orders table from the BCDEMOS alias. Create sensible names for the components you use. For instance, I call the table that points to the Customer table CustomerTable. The detail table is called OrdersTable.

In this example, do not create the one-to-many relationship on the server; instead, do so on the client. In the NestedDataSet example, discussed later in this chapter, I use the opposite approach. In the section of this chapter called "Server-Side Logic Versus Client-Side Logic," I explain the relative merits of each approach.

Continue your construction of the program by dropping down two TProvider controls from the Midas page of the Component Palette on the CustOrdersRemoteData module. Name the provider that is hooked up to the Customer table the CustomerProvider and the other control the OrdersProvider.

Right-click both the CustomerProvider and the OrdersProvider and export them from the data module. When you are done, you should end up with two methods that look like this:

```
STDMETHODIMP TCustOrdersRemoteDataImpl::get_CustomerProvider(
  IProvider** Value)
{
  try
  {
  _di_IProvider IProv = m_DataModule->CustomerProvider->Provider;
  IProv->AddRef();
  *Value = IProv;
  }
  catch(Exception &e)
  {
    return Error(e.Message.c_str(), IID_ICustOrdersRemoteData);
  }
  return S_OK;
};
```

```
STDMETHODIMP TCustOrdersRemoteDataImpl::get_OrdersProvider(
  IProvider** Value)
{
  try
  {
  _di_IProvider IProv = m_DataModule->OrdersProvider->Provider;
  IProv->AddRef();
  *Value = IProv;
  }
  catch(Exception &e)
  {
    return Error(e.Message.c_str(), IID_ICustOrdersRemoteData);
  }
  return S_OK;
};
```

You can add a picture or some text (like "CustOrders MIDAS Server") to the main form of the application. At this point, save your work and run the application once to register it.

The act of running the server with the /RegServer parameter places an entry in the Windows Registry. To see the entry, run the Windows utility RegEdit.exe from the Run menu item on the Start menu. Open HKEY_CLASSES_ROOT and search for the name of the executable that contains the server. For instance, the key to search for in this case is called CustOrdersServer.CustOrdersRemoteData, which is also known as the Prog ID for the server. The first half of this key is from the executable name of the server, and the second half is from the name you gave to the remote data module, which is also, by default, the name of the exported COM interface.

When you find the entry for this Prog ID in the Registry, you see that a Class ID is associated with it. Move up the Registry a short way from the CustOrdersServer entry until you find the section called Class ID. Open this key and browse for the Class ID of your component. It should have a LocalServer32 key that points to CustOrdersServer.exe, and it should have another key called the Borland DataBroker. The C++Builder IDE references this second key when it is deciding which servers should be shown in the drop-down list for the DCOMConnection.ServerName property on your client.

Now that you've finished the Remote Data Server, it's time to start working on the client.

20

MIDAS

Building a Remote Data Client Application

Now that you have the server set up, the next thing to do is set up the client. In this example, I assume you are running both the server and the client on the same machine. After the design phase is over, you can move the server to a remote machine, as discussed earlier in the chapter.

Here is quick overview of the steps involved in creating the client:

1. Drop down a TDCOMConnection and use its ServerName property to connect it to the CustOrdersServer. The Prog ID for this server should be listed in a drop-down combo box in the editor for the ServerName property. You should now be able to set the Connected property to true. If you cannot perform this last step, make sure you have run the server once on your current machine so that it is properly registered.

2. Drop down a TClientDataSet control and set its RemoteServer property to the TDCOMConnection component you just wired up. Set the ProviderName property to the name of the CustomerProvider from the server. The provider name should be listed in a drop-down combo. After you have everything set up properly, rename the control **CustomerClientDataSet**. Drop down a second TClientDataSet and wire it up to the OrdersProvider on the server. Rename this second client dataset OrdersClientDataSet. Set the Active property to true for both client datasets. If you are having trouble completing these steps, refer to the notes on this subject in the previous example in this chapter.

3. Hook up database controls to the TClientDataSet just as you would if you were using a TTable or TQuery. That is, you should drop down two TDataSources and two TDBGrids, and hook one pair up to the Customer table and the other to the Orders table.

4. Arrange the two TClientDataSets in a one-to-many relationship. To do so, connect the MasterSource property of the OrdersClientDataSet to the data source for the CustomerClientDataSet. Click the MasterFields property of the OrdersDataSet and set up a relationship between the tables based on the CustNo key, as shown in Figure 20.5.

FIGURE 20.5

*Establishing a
one-to-many rela-
tionship in the*
MasterFields
property of the
OrdersClientData
Set *component.*

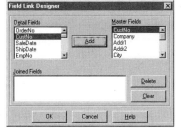

5. Run your application. The code for the main form of the client is shown in Listing 20.4. (Note that some code from this listing hasn't been written, yet.)

LISTING 20.4   THE CODE FOR THE MAIN FORM OF THE CUSTORDERSCLIENT PROGRAM

```
//------------------------------------------------------------------
#include <vcl.h>
#pragma hdrstop

#include "MainClient.h"
#include "ReconcileErrorDialog.h"
//------------------------------------------------------------------
#pragma package(smart_init)
#pragma resource "*.dfm"

#define CustomerFile "Customer.cds"
#define OrdersFile   "Orders.cds"

TForm1 *Form1;
//------------------------------------------------------------------
__fastcall TForm1::TForm1(TComponent* Owner)
        : TForm(Owner)
{
}
//------------------------------------------------------------------
void __fastcall TForm1::Connect1Click(TObject *Sender)
{
//DCOMConnection1->Connected = true;
  CustomerClientDataSet->Active = true;
  OrdersClientDataSet->Active = true;
}
//------------------------------------------------------------------
void __fastcall TForm1::BriefcaseSave1Click(TObject *Sender)
{
  CustomerClientDataSet->SaveToFile(CustomerFile);
  OrdersClientDataSet->SaveToFile(OrdersFile);
}
```

continues

20

MIDAS

LISTING 20.4   CONTINUED

```cpp
//-------------------------------------------------------------------------
void __fastcall TForm1::BriefcaseLoad1Click(TObject *Sender)
{
  CustomerClientDataSet->LoadFromFile(CustomerFile);
  OrdersClientDataSet->LoadFromFile(OrdersFile);
}
//-------------------------------------------------------------------------
void __fastcall TForm1::ApplyUpdates1Click(TObject *Sender)
{
  CustomerClientDataSet->ApplyUpdates(-1);
}
//-------------------------------------------------------------------------
void __fastcall TForm1::Refresh1Click(TObject *Sender)
{
  if (CustomerClientDataSet->ApplyUpdates(-1) == 0)
    CustomerClientDataSet->Refresh();
  if (OrdersClientDataSet->ApplyUpdates(-1) == 0)
    OrdersClientDataSet->Refresh();
}
//-------------------------------------------------------------------------
void __fastcall TForm1::Exit1Click(TObject *Sender)
{
  Close();
}
//-------------------------------------------------------------------------
void __fastcall TForm1::CustomerClientDataSetReconcileError(
      TClientDataSet *DataSet, EReconcileError *E, TUpdateKind
➥UpdateKind,
      TReconcileAction &Action)
{
  HandleReconcileError(this, DataSet, UpdateKind, E);
}
//-------------------------------------------------------------------------
void __fastcall TForm1::OpenDataSetsAlternativeWay1Click(TObject *Sender)
{
  int RecsOut;
  OleVariant V;
  CustomerClientDataSet->Provider->GetRecords(-1, RecsOut,V);
  CustomerEdit->Text = IntToStr(RecsOut);
  CustomerClientDataSet->AppendData(V, true);
  OrdersClientDataSet->Provider->GetRecords(-1, RecsOut,V);
  OrdersEdit->Text = IntToStr(RecsOut);
  OrdersClientDataSet->AppendData(V, true);
}
//-------------------------------------------------------------------------
```

Perhaps the most interesting aspect of the CustOrders sample program is its capability to use the `MasterSource` and `MasterFields` property of the `TClientDataSet` control to establish a one-to-many relationship. The point is that C++Builder enables you to enforce rules and use visual controls in distributed programs much as you would in a local database program. This kind of power and flexibility lies very much at the heart of what's best in the MIDAS technology.

Updating and Refreshing Data

In this section, I briefly cover the simple subject of updating the server after you have edited records on the client. To the degree that it was possible, the C++Builder team tried to make this process entirely transparent to you. However, you need to learn a few simple rules.

If you have edited one or more records and want to make the changes permanent, you should call `ApplyUpdates`:

```
CustomerClientDataSet->ApplyUpdates(-1);
```

This method takes a single parameter called `MaxErrors`. Passing `-1` to this method means that you want the update process to stop when an error occurs. If this happens, no changes occur to the server-side version of the data. The client-side log where C++Builder tracks the changes you made to the dataset also remains unchanged. You are informed that the error occurred and told its exact nature.

If you set `MaxErrors` to a positive number, the update process continues until it encounters the number of errors you specified in this parameter. If that happens, no changes occur to either the server-side data or your change log. If fewer than `MaxErrors` occur, all the successfully changed records are updated and removed from the change log. `ApplyUpdates` returns the number of errors it encountered.

To understand what is happening here, you have to know that C++Builder caches all the changes you make to a dataset. In other words, it keeps both the original record and the updated record. When you call `ApplyUpdates`, errors can be reported, and you have the chance to revert to the original record or to attempt to push your changes through. Error handling is explained in the section "Error Handling."

If you have successfully updated the server, you probably also want to refresh your dataset with any changes made by other users. To do so, call `Refresh`. The following typical example shows how the whole process might look in action:

```
if (CustomerClientDataSet->ApplyUpdates(-1) == 0)
  CustomerClientDataSet->Refresh();
if (OrdersClientDataSet->ApplyUpdates(-1) == 0)
  OrdersClientDataSet->Refresh();
```

A quick glance at this code shows that it might be a bit difficult to understand, but it certainly is easy to implement; a Refresh is needed to cause new data to be retrieved only if the ApplyUpdates succeeds. Otherwise, you don't perform the Refresh (which would overwrite your data), but must perform some error handling (see the section "Error Handling").

The Briefcase Model

In this section, I talk about the briefcase model, which is one of the more interesting and useful aspects of this technology. It is particularly valuable for users who have laptops; but on other occasions, you might want to use it in standard MIDAS applications.

As described earlier, the briefcase model allows you to load or save the contents of a client dataset to disk. It depends on two methods of TClientDataSet called LoadFromFile and SaveToFile:

```
CustomerClientDataSet->SaveToFile("Customer.cds");
CustomerClientDataSet->LoadFromFile("Customer.cds");
```

Clearly, these simple methods take nothing more than the name of the file where the dataset is stored. By convention, this file has a .cds extension, where CDS stands for client dataset. After you have created one of these files, any TClientDataSet object can read its contents.

In some applications, if you want to save two tables linked in a master-detail relationship, you should save and read them both to separate files:

```
#define CustomerFile "Customer.cds"
#define OrdersFile   "Orders.cds"

TForm1 *Form1;
//--------------------------------------------------------------------
void __fastcall TForm1::BriefcaseSave1Click(TObject *Sender)
{
  CustomerClientDataSet->SaveToFile(CustomerFile);
  OrdersClientDataSet->SaveToFile(OrdersFile);
}
//--------------------------------------------------------------------
void __fastcall TForm1::BriefcaseLoad1Click(TObject *Sender)
{
  CustomerClientDataSet->LoadFromFile(CustomerFile);
  OrdersClientDataSet->LoadFromFile(OrdersFile);
}
//--------------------------------------------------------------------
```

Saving the two files separately like this is not necessary if you are working with nested datasets. A nested dataset is automatically saved when you save its parent.

After you have executed the Save portion of this equation, you can disconnect from the server and still access the data by simply calling the Load method. For instance, if you are using a laptop, you can connect once to your server and then save the information you retrieve to disk. Now you can shut down your laptop and take it home with you. At home or on the road, you can boot it up and edit your database to your heart's content. When you get back to the shop and reconnect to the server, you can update the files by calling ApplyUpdates. Errors and conflicts are handled for you automatically, as explained in the section called "Error Handling."

Clearly, the act of saving and reading files from disk is trivial in the extreme. However, you need to take some additional points into consideration to use the briefcase model properly. Most of these points are covered in the next section on PacketRecords.

> **NOTE**
>
> The briefcase model can even be applied to applications that do not use MIDAS. If you drop a TTable and TClientDataSet on a form, you can, while still in Design mode, connect the TClientDataSet directly to the TTable and then save the resulting dataset to disk. To do so, just hook the TTable object to a table using the BDE; then right-click the TClientDataSet to draw the data from the TTable and save it to disk.
>
> After you save the table to disk, you can delete the TTable object from your form and move your program on to a machine that does not contain the BDE. Now just call ClientDataSet1->LoadFromFile to load the data from disk. This free technology does not cost you the usual fees associated with MIDAS. In my opinion, it is one of the more outstanding features of the C++Builder database technology. Read the section "Required DLLs" later in this chapter so that you know the small support files needed on your new, BDE-free machine.

PacketRecords

The important PacketRecords property of TClientDataSet is one you need to spend some time contemplating. In the next few paragraphs, I discuss it from several angles. In particular, I make several references to its importance when using the briefcase model.

20

MIDAS

To make the briefcase model work correctly, you sometimes need to make sure the files on the server are not arranged in a one-to-many relationship and that you have set the `PacketRecords` property on both the `ClientDataSets` to `-1`. Setting `PacketRecords` to `0` brings down the metadata, setting it to `-1` brings down all the data, and setting it to some positive number *n* brings down *n* records per request.

If you have already gotten the metadata for a dataset, setting `PacketRecords` to `-1` or to some positive number other than zero retrieves only data. However, if you have not gotten the metadata, setting `PacketRecords` to `-1` or to some positive number other than zero retrieves both the metadata and the records.

> **TIP**
>
> When using distributed datasets, you don't want to bring down the whole of a large dataset onto the client. This is simply not the right model for this kind of computing. At most, you probably want to bring down a few thousand records at one time, and I heartily recommend working with even smaller datasets. For some programmers, using small datasets might appear to be a severe limitation, but the user really does not want to see 10,000 or 20,000 records at one time. Find ways to filter your data with queries, or else set `PacketRecords` to some small number so you get a reasonable number of records for the user to peruse. C++Builder automatically maintains state for you, so subsequent requests get the next *n* number of records that you request rather than bringing down the same *n* records you retrieved the first time. In saying this, I'm not implying that C++Builder or your network can't bring down huge datasets at one time, only that you strain the patience of both C++Builder and your network, potentially inciting their ire.
>
> By the way, I use `TTable` objects in this chapter mostly because I want to create the simplest possible examples. In most cases, I assume programmers working in corporate settings need to use queries to manipulate their data. That, however, is another subject altogether, and in this chapter, I am focusing on MIDAS.

If you want to use the briefcase model, you usually should bring down the whole dataset, which means you want to set `PacketRecords` to `-1`. (Of course, a query on a server could already filter a large portion of a table for you, but you still want to set `PacketRecords` to `-1` to retrieve all the records from the query.)

If you just want to establish a one-to-many relationship and don't care about the briefcase model, you probably want to set `PacketRecords` to zero on the detail table and to `-1` on the master table. These settings retrieve all the records from the master table but only the metadata for the detail table. Then internally, C++Builder calls `TClientDataSet->AppendData` to bring down just those detail records that are needed when you're viewing one particular master record. This capability is great for many situations, but it is probably not what you want if you are using the briefcase model. When using the briefcase model, you usually set `PacketRecords` to `-1`, and the master detail is still done, but the whole detail dataset is available on the server at all times. Having the whole dataset available is obviously impractical when you're working with very large datasets.

Because this issue is so important, I am going to show you how to write some code that allows you to fine-tune this process. The following code represents a nonsensical case in which you first retrieve the metadata and then retrieve the records. I say this example is nonsensical because the metadata is retrieved automatically the first time you access the data. However, assuming you had some reason to get the metadata first and then get all the records, you could write code that looks like this:

```
{
  ClientDataSet1->Close();
  ClientDataSet1->PacketRecords = 0;
  ClientDataSet1->Open();
  ClientDataSet1->PacketRecords = -1;
  ClientDataSet1->GetNextPacket();
}
```

If you want to be very fancy, you can study this code from MIDAS guru Josh Dahlby:

```
{
  int RecsOut;
  OleVariant V;
  CustomerClientDataSet->Close();
  CustomerClientDataSet->Provider->GetMetaData(V);
  CustomerClientDataSet->AppendData(V, false)
  CustomerClientDataSet->Provider->GetRecords(-1,RecsOut,V);
  CustomerClientDataSet->AppendData(V, true);
}
```

In this case, you first close the client dataset and then use the `GetMetaData` function to retrieve the metadata inside an `OleVariant`. At this time, you can pass the result of this function directly to `AppendData`, which adds the records you just retrieved to any that might currently be in the dataset.

`AppendData` takes two parameters. The first is the data retrieved from the server; the second is whether you hit EOF when retrieving the data. Remember that you don't have to use either `GetRecords` or `AppendData`; you should normally use `GetNextPacket`. Furthermore, the simplest way to perform this operation is simply to call `Open` or to set `Active` to `true`. I've shown you `GetNextPacket` and `AppendData` simply so you can have more control over the process if you happen to need it. Remember that you have the `TPacketWriter` code in `Provider.cpp` if you want to create your own packets.

20

MIDAS

This method provides an alternative way to connect to the data on your server:

```
void __fastcall TForm1::OpenDataSetsAlternativeWay1Click(TObject *Sender)
{
  int RecsOut;
  OleVariant V;
  CustomerClientDataSet->Provider->GetRecords(-1, RecsOut,V);
  CustomerEdit->Text = IntToStr(RecsOut);
  CustomerClientDataSet->AppendData(V, true);
  OrdersClientDataSet->Provider->GetRecords(-1, RecsOut,V);
  OrdersEdit->Text = IntToStr(RecsOut);
  OrdersClientDataSet->AppendData(V, true);
}
```

I've designed this method to report the number of rows in the Customer and Orders tables. There is no need to retrieve this information—I'm just showing you so that you can get at it if you are interested in seeing it.

The OpenDataSetsAlternativeWay1Click() method also works in cases where you get an EOleException with message *Field 'CustNo' is not indexed and cannot be modified.*, which typically is caused by having a value of 0 assigned to the PacketRecords property of the OrdersClientDataSet. (I don't know how or what, but on two separate occasions, I got this exception and know for a fact that I didn't assign 0 to the PacketRecords property myself.)

A related subject that I do not cover in depth in this chapter is constraints. Just as you can automatically download the metadata for your application, you can also download the constraints. To do so, set the Constraints field of the IProvider interface to true. When you do, the constraints set up on your server are automatically enforced on your client.

Error Handling

When you're working with remote datasets, errors occur on some occasions. For instance, if two users are accessing a table at the same time, they might both want to change the same record. In this case, the person who first performed the update succeeds in changing the record, and the second person gets an error.

Errors are passed back to a TClientDataSet and can be handled by responding to the OnReconcileErrorEvent. A detailed explanation of responding to errors would take up almost as many pages as I've written so far . However, I can cover a simple solution to this whole problem in just a few paragraphs.

The trick to handling errors returned from an application server is to use a form stored in the C++Builder Object Repository. To find the form in question, select File, New, turn to the Dialogs page, and opt to Copy the Reconcile Error Dialog. Save the dialog in the same directory as your current project and remove it from the files that are automatically created at startup. To do so, choose Project, Options, Forms from the C++Builder menu.

Include the header file of the Reconcile Error dialog in the appropriate form in your project (using File, Include Unit Hdr). In many cases, it is the main form for your project. Now add the following in response to the OnReconcileError events of the ClientDataSets:

```
void __fastcall TForm1::CustomerClientDataSetReconcileError(
      TClientDataSet *DataSet, EReconcileError *E, TUpdateKind UpdateKind,
      TReconcileAction &Action)
{
  HandleReconcileError(DataSet, UpdateKind, E);
}
```

This one-line function launches the dialog you found in the Object Repository and enables the user to handle any errors, as shown in Figure 20.6.

FIGURE 20.6

The ReconcileError dialog from the C++Builder Object Repository as it appears at run time.

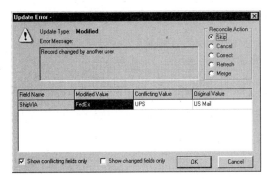

The grid in the center of the form tells the name of the field on which the error occurred. The Modified Value is the value the client application wanted to insert into the record. The Conflicting Value is the value the "other guy" who beat you to the update inserted into the record. The Original Value is the value the record had before either update was made. As you can see, the user has the option to Skip, Cancel, Correct, Refresh, or Merge the data.

You can make all these changes and access all these options by writing your own code. However, it probably makes more sense just to use this dialog or to use the dialog as the basis for your own code.

20

MIDAS

Server-Side Logic Versus Client-Side Logic

You naturally have a choice as to how much logic you put on the middle tier—that is, the server—of your applications. For instance, you decide whether to arrange the tables in a one-to-many relationship on the server.

Under certain circumstances, if you arrange the tables this way, when you query the server from the client, you get from the detail table only the records that are currently visible on the server. This result might, in fact, be exactly what you want, particularly if the detail table is large.

However, if both the master and detail tables are small, you might prefer to access all records from both tables. On this book's CD-ROM, you find an example program, NestedDataSet, that creates the one-to-many logic on the server side but brings the whole dataset over at once. In addition, the program allows you to work with nested datasets, where the detail table is literally embedded in one of the fields of the master table.

To create this program, start as you normally would, creating a directory called NestedDataSet and putting Client and Server directories beneath. Start your server application and save it as NestedServer.bpr. Add a remote data module to this program and save it as NestedDataImpl.cpp. Call the interface for the data module INestedData or some other name of your choosing.

Drop down two tables on the remote data module and hook them up to the Customer and the Orders tables. Drop down a TDataSource and hook it up to the Customer tables. Create a one-to-many between the Customer and Orders tables, with the Customer table being the master, using the same techniques described in the CustOrdersClient program.

At this stage, instead of dropping down two TProvider components, one for each table, you need drop down only one. When you query this object from the client, it automatically contains both the complete Customer table and the Orders table nested inside it, as shown in Figure 20.7.

FIGURE 20.7

You can see the DataSet *field of the* Customer *table and the floating grid object that appears when you double-click the* DataSet *field.*

On the client side, the TDBGrid object you connected to the TClientDataSet automatically has a new field appended to the end of each record. This field is, by default, called (DataSet). To see the field, you have to scroll all the way over to the far right of the DBGrid object.

If you click the DataSet field, you see that it has an ellipses button on its far right. If you click this button, a second dataset appears showing the detail records for the currently selected record in the Customer table. Alternatively, you can just double-click the DataSet field, and the detail grid pops up automatically.

As you can probably imagine, you don't need to do any special work on the client side to make all this happen. All you need to do is create a standard C++Builder MIDAS client, dropping down a TDCOMConnection, TClientDataSet connection, a TDataSource, and TDBGrid. Hook them up following the same pattern laid out in the two previous programs from this chapter and, voilà, you have a nested dataset with the logic all done on the server side.

The next section of this chapter covers the very important subject of required DLLs for MIDAS applications.

Required DLLs

When you are installing your MIDAS applications, several files are needed on both sides. Server-side files include the following:

- A complete installation of the BDE
- DBCLIENT.DLL
- IDPROV40.DLL
- STDVCL40.DLL

DBCLIENT and IDPROV40 are included only in the Enterprise edition of C++Builder. To get them on your system, you need to answer Yes to the license agreement screen in the installation.

DBCLIENT and STDVCL40 need to be registered—that is, entered in the Registry of the server. You can register them by using REGSVR32.EXE from Microsoft or the TRegServ C++Builder program from the Bin directory.

DBCLIENT.DLL is the only DLL needed on the client side. STDVCL40.DLL is not required, but you almost certainly need it. It is the type library for IProvider and IDataBroker, and because all MIDAS applications use IProvider, you had better include it. DBCLIENT needs to be registered on the client. If it is on the path, it is registered automatically when your application loads.

Using OLEnterprise

OLEnterprise is an alternative to DCOM. If you use OLEnterprise, you do not need to have DCOM on your system. Although I personally do not believe OLEnterprise is the future of distributed computing here on planet Earth, nevertheless, it has several advantages over DCOM, such as the following:

- It allows you to make connections between two Windows 95 machines, even if no NT server is available. Connections without an NT server are all but impossible under DCOM, as explained in Chapter 19. Connections between two Windows 95 machines, even when a server is present, are either impossible or extremely problematic under DCOM. You can reliably connect from a Windows 95/98 machine to an NT machine with DCOM, but not vice versa, nor can you reliably connect between two Windows 95/98 machines.

- OLEnterprise has an Object Broker that allows you to distribute the load of connections over multiple machines. In particular, each time a new user signs on to a database, he can be randomly routed to an available server, thereby distributing the load over multiple servers. The act of replicating the data between servers is, quite naturally, not supported by OLEnterprise but is instead the responsibility of the server itself.

- OLEnterprise has fail-over capability, which is available if you write a few lines of code.

This fail-over example was provided by the good graces of the indefatigable Mike Destein:

```
void TForm1::ButtonClick(Sender: TObject);
{
  try
  {
    ClientDataSet1->ApplyUpdates(-1);
  }
  catch (EOleException &eOle)
  {
    if (eOle.ErrorCode == -2147023169) // I dont know the const name
    {
      // Handle RPC failure by resetting server
      RemoteServer1->Connected = false;
      RemoteServer1->Connected = TRUE;
      ClientDataSet1->ApplyUpdates(-1);
    }
    else ShowMessage(IntToStr(eOle.ErrorCode));
  }
}
```

(Some users have reported having trouble using this code with some versions of OLEnterprise.)

Installing and Understanding OLEnterprise

When you're installing OLEnterprise on a Windows 95/98 machine, do not install into the default directory; instead, install off your root and try to avoid long filenames in the directory path. Any problems with OLEnterprise and long filenames on Windows 95 machines will be corrected in future releases of the product.

The four key pieces in the OLEnterprise toolset are as follows:

- The Object Broker, called Broker.exe. It should be run on the server machine before loading the Object Factory. If you start it with a -D option, it spews out debug information that can help you understand your program and help you confirm that connections are occurring in the correct order and at the correct time.

- The OLEnterprise Configuration utility, called OLECFG.exe. This utility is used to specify whether you are using an Object Broker and what machine the Object Broker is running on. Remember that the broker's job is to distribute connections randomly; as such, it is not needed to make the connection. It is a helpful utility, but not a necessity. Therefore, the configuration gives you the option of turning it off. You should run the configuration utility on both the client and the server.

- The Object Factory, called ObjFact.exe. This utility is the core of the system, and you must run it on the server, or OLEnterprise does not work. However, you do not need to have this utility running on the client to make a connection.

- The Object Explorer, called OLEntExp.exe. This program plays a similar role to DCOMCFG.exe. It allows you to browse the objects available on your system, export objects from a server, and import objects from a remote system. You should remember that the Explorer uses the Registry as the main repository of information about the objects on a system. If you have run a server once on a machine, the Explorer finds the object in the Registry, and you can then use the menu to export or import the object. If you are on a client machine and are using the Explorer to search for programs on remote machines, you must be sure that you have used the OLEnterprise Configuration utility to specify where the Object Broker you are currently using is running. If you launch the Explorer, and it takes a very long time to come up, or it appears to hang at times, it is likely that the machine is searching for the Broker but cannot find it. The program can take several minutes before it allows the search to time out and return control to the user. The same thing happens if you click on the Object Broker option in the program's left panel. One click and a search for the Broker begins. If the Broker is not found, use the configuration utility to specify its location, or else go to the remote machine and make sure the Broker is running. If you start the Broker with the -D option, you should see output from it when you start an Object Factory on the same machine or when you try to connect to it from a remote machine.

When using the Explorer, you need to learn how to import and export objects. This intuitive process is accomplished by manipulating the menus or by right-clicking items in the main panels of the application. You should probably spend some time using the default sample programs shipping with the product to make sure you understand importing and exporting objects. In particular, go to etc\samples\auto\memoedit to find a good prebuilt sample program.

OLEnterprise was an extremely valuable tool before Windows supported DCOM. At this time, I still regard it as a useful tool, but have to confess that it is not a particular favorite of mine.

Summary

In this chapter you looked at Borland's multitier technology. In particular, you saw how to create servers and clients and how to use DCOM and OLEnterprise to connect to a remote server.

This technology is important for several reasons:

- It provides a means of creating thin clients that make few demands on the client system.
- It simplifies—in fact, nearly eliminates—the need to configure the client machine.
- It allows you to partition applications in logical compartments. If you want, each of these compartments can be run on a separate machine, thereby distributing the load of the application.
- It provides a means for distributing a load over several server machines or for routing the load to a specific machine with the power to handle heavy demands.
- It provides a robust architecture for handling and reporting errors, particularly in a multiuser environment. It also allows you to automatically download metadata and constraints onto your thin client, thereby enabling you to build robust applications with sophisticated interfaces and feedback for the user.
- It allows you to use a briefcase technology that stores files locally and then allows you to reload them when it is time to update the server. This capability is ideal for laptop users who spend a lot of time on the road.

For many users, this technology is so compelling that it entirely replaces the standard client/server database architectures. These users are attracted to the ability to partition the applications into logical pieces, even if the entire application is being run on a single machine. However, the biggest benefits achieved by this architecture become apparent when you bring multiple machines, and even multiple servers, into play.

Personally, I have no question but that distributed computing is going to become one of the most important fields in all of computer science. The materials shown in this chapter should get you started using some of the more sophisticated aspects of this technology. There will come a time when nearly every computer in the world will be continually connected to nearly every other computer, and when that occurs, distributed computing will become one of the most essential fields of study in computer programming.

20

MIDAS

ActiveForms

by Charlie Calvert (with Bob Swart)

In this chapter you learn how to create ActiveForms that can be displayed in a Web browser. You also see how to convert a C++Builder form into a component that can be displayed on any Windows-based machine equipped with Internet Explorer or any other ActiveX-aware HTML browser. For good measure, at least one of the forms shown in this chapter will contain the thin client portion of a multitier application.

Introduction to ActiveForms

One of C++Builder's most powerful features is the capability to wrap an entire form inside an ActiveX control and publish it on the Web or insert it into another application such as VB or Word. You should read the following sections on ActiveForms even if you think you understand this technology from experience with C++Builder 3.

> **NOTE**
>
> It would appear that Microsoft likes giving new names to existing technologies. ActiveX controls started life under the name OCX. (In fact, most ActiveX controls have an .ocx extension.) Somewhere along the way the term *ActiveX* was proffered and became the new industry buzzword.

An ActiveForm is, in the end, a regular C++Builder form wrapped as an ActiveX control. I will refer to ActiveForms as both ActiveX and ActiveForms in this chapter.

You can do several different things with an ActiveForm. For instance, you can deploy it in another ActiveX-aware program such as Visual Basic, Word, or Excel. Most users find this technology easy to use, but I will step you through the process of using an ActiveForm inside Word as an example. Those interested in this subject should read the bits on the Internet Explorer anyway, as they will find important points about distributing ActiveForms that they need to understand.

You can also deploy ActiveForms on a Web page. This process is a bit tricky at times, so I cover it in some depth. This technology is particularly important, however, because it can be an excellent way to create a distributed application.

In theory, you should be able to put an ActiveForm in any tool that can act as an ActiveX container. However, ActiveX technology is not well documented. As a result, many containers—even some from Microsoft—do not properly implement aspects of the specification. As a result, problems can occur. You should have no trouble running C++Builder ActiveForms in VB, Word, Excel, or Internet Explorer.

The old joke about this technology involves the confusion fulminated in shops where management makes some brain-dead declaration such as "We support only Microsoft standards, so all applications must be built in VB." The solution to this form of madness is to build forms in C++Builder and then drop them into VB applications as ActiveX controls. Management personnel get their VB app and you get to write your application in C++Builder. If people get really insistent upon asking why your applications are so much faster and robust than the other applications turned out in the shop, you can tell them what you are really doing. Be careful, though. Anyone irrational enough to insist that you use VB is, by definition, capable of doing almost anything.

> **TIP**
>
> Before going on, I should mention that Microsoft distributes a free Web server called the *Personal Web Server*. This great tool allows you to test your ActiveForms inside Internet Explorer. The Personal Web Server probably could not stand the strain of thousands of simultaneous users, but it is ideal for testing your controls or for use with small networks that have only a few users. It ships with FrontPage, some versions of Internet Explorer, and other Microsoft products such as the MSDN, and is usually available for free download from `www.microsoft.com`.

Building an ActiveForm

You can begin building an ActiveForm two ways. One is to build the program from scratch; the other is to borrow an existing form from another application. I start by building an ActiveForm from scratch. The program I build is called EasyActiveForm, and you can find the source on the CD-ROM that accompanies this book. The "Using Templates with ActiveForms" section describes how to reuse a form from another application in an ActiveForm.

To build a form from scratch, choose File, New, ActiveX, Active Form. The ActiveForm Wizard appears and prompts you for a project name. You can use the default name or choose a new name. You need to fill out three edit controls at this point, but you can usually get away with just changing the first one, New ActiveX Name. If you change the New ActiveX Name, the names in the other fields change automatically. For this example, name your project `EasyActiveForm`.

When you click OK in the ActiveForm Wizard, you will probably be told that you cannot add an ActiveX control to the current project because it is not an ActiveX library. (Of course, you won't get this message if you have already started an ActiveX library.) If you get the message, just click OK to start a DLL that can host an ActiveX control. To avoid this message, close all projects before creating the new ActiveForm.

Note that the DLL should get the `.ocx` extension, which is specified automatically for an ActiveX library. (See the Application tab of the Project Options dialog and the PROJECT rule in the Project Makefile.)

Invoke the Project Options dialog, select the Linker page, and turn off the Dynamic RTL option. Switch to the Packages page and turn off the Build with Runtime Packages options. The issue here is that the RTL DLL and run-time packages have to be included with your ActiveForm if you elect to use them in your project. Distributing these packages with your project should not be difficult, as C++Builder can handle that chore automatically. Nonetheless, you don't want to worry about that kind of thing when you are starting out.

For this first form, keeping everything as simple as possible is best. As a result, drop a single button on the form and associate it with the following function:

```
void __fastcall TEasyActiveForm::Button1Click(TObject *Sender)
{
  ShowMessage("Hello from C++Builder 4");
}
```

Now save your project to disk. At this stage, you have completed the construction of your ActiveForm.

Deploying an ActiveForm for Use in Internet Explorer

The next step is to deploy your ActiveForm. In this case, the goal is to have it appear inside Internet Explorer; you will not be able to proceed unless you have IE 3.X or later.

If you are deploying onto the Web, start by choosing Web Deployment Options from the Project menu. A dialog like the one shown in Figure 21.1 comes up. Your project must be compiled and linked before this dialog appears, so you may experience a delay while your files are processed.

FIGURE 21.1

The Web Deployment Options dialog as it appears when you first open it.

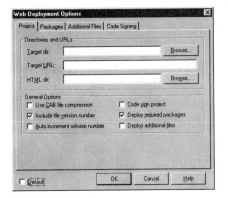

Setting Options for an ActiveForm

There are three controls at the top of the Deployment Options dialog:

- `Target dir`
- `Target URL`
- `HTML dir`

In the `Target dir` field, you list where you want to deploy your ActiveForm and any related binary files. These files can be distributed to anyone who attaches to your machine over the Web. If you have a Web server available, you typically should deploy these files in your `wwwroot` directory or in some directory beneath this location. For instance, you might place them in `c:\webshare\wwwroot`, `c:\inetpub\wwwroot`, or `c:\inetpub\wwwroot\MyActiveForms`.

The `Target URL` you specify is used by the HTML or INF file that launches your ActiveForm. The string you enter in this field should point to the directory where your ActiveForm is located when it is ready to be deployed. Usually, you should specify this directory as an URL. For instance, you might write `http://ccalvertpc3/MyActiveForms`, but you can also specify a relative URL such as `./` to specify the fact that the ActiveForm and the HTML and/or INF file reside in the same directory on the Web server.

The subject of Deployment is complicated enough that I want to explain it in more depth. Furthermore, this explanation is enhanced by numerous examples later in the chapter.

C++Builder creates sample HTML and INF files for your project by default. The HTML file can be loaded into a browser and used to launch your ActiveForm. Most of the time, however, you will copy the HTML code out of the file that C++Builder creates and paste it into your "real" HTML file. The key section of code is the `OBJECT` tag. If your project deploys multiple files, the HTML file will reference a second file with an `.inf` extension. The INF file will contain the URL where your ActiveForm resides, as well as any helper files needed by your project such as packages or the run-time library. If your project doesn't use packages or the run-time library, no INF file is created. In short, the `Target URL` either points directly to your ActiveForm or directly to an INF file that, in turn, points to your ActiveForm, as well as any packages or related files you might be using.

If you are deploying your control on a Web server located on a machine called `ccalvertpc3`, and you deploy your ActiveForm in the `wwwroot` directory, then you should type `http://ccalvertpc3` as the `Target URL`. This URL points, by default, to the `wwwroot` directory on your server machine. If you do not have a Web server available while you are testing, simply hard-code in the name of the directory that you specified in the `Target dir`, such as `c:\webshare\wwwroot\`. Of course, if you don't have a server, you can access the object only from the same machine or from a machine that has a mapped drive to your server.

`HTML dir` indicates where the sample HTML and INF files that C++Builder generates will be placed. Typically, this location is the same directory you specified in the `Target dir`, which is another reason to specify `./` as `Target URL`.

When you are done filling out these fields, make sure the Auto Increment Release Number check box is checked. Now close the Web Deployment Options dialog and choose Web Deploy from the Project menu. Your project will be copied automatically into the directories you specified in the Web Deployment Options dialog.

> **NOTE**
>
> This last step is not nearly so simple if you are using packages. In that case, you need to go through several more steps on different pages of the Web Deployment Options dialog before you're done. The steps aren't hard to complete, but they can test your patience. The "Working with CAB Files and Packages" section of this chapter explains these steps.

Connecting to an ActiveForm

At this point, you are ready to connect from another machine, download the ActiveForm onto that second machine, and view it in a browser. To understand how this procedure works, consider the HTML generated by C++Builder:

```
<HTML>
<H1> C++Builder 4 ActiveX Test Page </H1><p>
You should see your C++Builder 4 forms or controls embedded in the form
```

```
➡ below.
<HR><center><P>
<OBJECT
  classid="clsid:E224D1C0-AC19-11D2-8244-0040052A83C4"
  codebase=" http://ccalvertpc3/activestuff/
    EasyActiveFormProj1.ocx#version=1,0,0,0"
  width=480
  height=252
  align=center
  hspace=0
  vspace=0
>
</OBJECT>
</HTML>
```

The CLSID shown here specifies the GUID associated with your object. The line labeled `codebase` points to the place on your system where the ActiveForm resides. You specified a portion of the contents of this line in the `Target URL` field of the Web Deployment Options dialog. If you are running on a single machine that does not feature a Web server, then this should be a DOS path rather than an URL. For instance, it might read as follows:

```
c:\webshare\wwwroot\activestuff\easyformproj1.ocx#version=1,0,0,0
```

What if you place the ActiveForms in the same directory with the HTML or INF file (and hence `Target URL` is set to `./`)? The codebase will be as follows:

```
./easyformproj1.ocx#version=1,0,0,0
```

In this example I have actually deployed my ActiveX control in a directory called `ActiveStuff` beneath `wwwroot`. This is just a matter of housekeeping, however, and you can feel free to put your ActiveForm in `wwwroot` or in some other location if you prefer. However, you almost certainly will be unable to run the version on the CD-ROM that accompanies this book unless you first change this line. You can now bring up a browser on your own machine or on a remote machine, and point it to the place where your HTML file is stored:

```
http://ccalvertpc3/activestuff/EasyFormProj1.htm
```

Of course, the specific place where your file is stored may differ, depending on the machine you are using and the way you have set up your paths.

The ActiveX should now appear in your browser. If it does not, consider the following checklist:

- Are you using IE 3.X or later? If not, ActiveX controls may not be supported on your browser.

- If you are using IE 3.X, choose View, Options in the IE menu system and turn to the Security page. Choose Safety Level and set it to Medium. Set it to Low if you are using IE 4 or 4.1. In general, you should give yourself as much security as possible, while still being able to use the ActiveX control.

- Make sure that you turned off the Runtime Packages and Dynamic RTL options when you built your control.

When you are launching the control in the browser, you will probably see some security dialogs that ask questions about code signing. Just click Yes to all questions so that you can download your ActiveForm. If you want to get involved in code-signing your ActiveForms, go to www.microsoft.com and check out the articles on Authenticode and Security.

Understanding the OCCACHE

After you deploy an ActiveForm, you will almost certainly see some changes that you want to make to it.

After an ActiveX control is loaded into memory on Windows 9x, the only way you can be sure it is unloaded is to reboot Windows. In other words, when you try to redeploy the ActiveX, you may keep getting the same ActiveX in your client application because the old DLL may not have been unloaded from memory. Although Windows officially lets go of a DLL when finished with it, Windows does not provide a practical way to definitively unload a DLL from memory.

> **NOTE**
>
> Some people use DLL unloaders in these cases, and I have heard of others performing a LoadLibrary once on the recalcitrant DLL, then making two calls to FreeLibrary.

Furthermore, the ActiveXs that you download onto a machine are often stored in a directory called OCCACHE, which is just below the Windows or Winnt directory on Windows 95 and Windows NT 4 machines. (Windows 98 and those 95 machines with IE4 installed have a similar directory called Downloaded Files or Downloaded Program Files.) Sometimes you will find further directories called conflict.1, conflict.2, and so on, beneath the OCCACHE directory.

If you are developing a program and want to be sure that you are starting with a clean client machine, you should be sure to not only reboot the system, but also to delete suspect files from all cache directories. Furthermore, you may find that other files are

installed in the Windows\System or Winnt\System32 directories, as explained in the section called "Working with CAB Files and Packages." If necessary, you may have to hunt these files out and then unregister and delete them before you create a truly clean machine on which to run tests. In particular, packages usually get installed in these directories (but beware that you don't accidentally delete any run-time packages that are needed by C++Builder itself).

I can't emphasize enough the extreme importance of testing your ActiveForms on clean machines before you attempt to distribute them to an unsuspecting public.

Consider what happens if your code uses packages that were installed by default on your test machine, but that will not be available on prospective customers' machines. For instance, some poor ActiveX vendor somewhere in the world is undoubtedly distributing sample versions of his wares that do not install properly because of a missing DLL or package. As a result, everyone who tries this hapless vendor's code finds that it doesn't work and immediately abandons that product and searches out some other tool that will do the job correctly. Don't let this scenario happen to you. Understand what files are distributed with your ActiveForm and test to be sure they are distributed correctly.

If at all possible, try installing your ActiveForm on a completely clean machine that has nothing on it but a copy of Windows. It is what software developers call a *Test Bed Box*. Neglecting to take this step is the rough equivalent of taking off in a jet airplane without checking to make sure someone closed the door. You might be okay, but the odds are you are going to have trouble.

Working with CAB Files and Packages

A *CAB file* is a kind of compressed file that Windows understands and automatically decompresses. C++Builder will automatically package your ActiveForm and any additional files in CAB files if you check the Use CAB File Compression option in the Web Deployment Options dialog. CAB files transfer to a client machine faster than normal files because they are compressed. (I've seen CAB files half the size of the original file, and hence twice as fast when downloading.)

You can find a second ActiveForm example in the SimpleActiveForm directory on the CD-ROM that accompanies this book. In that example, I use packages and CAB files. Using both packages and CAB files may sound like a bit much, but may be the way you want to distribute the actual ActiveForms you create. This method is preferred if your users are a known group, such as a group of employees accessing your ActiveForm via an intranet. After downloading the first ActiveForm with its required packages and DLLs, subsequent ActiveForms won't need to include these files. The advantage is that it keeps the size of your ActiveForms to a minimum. It makes sense particularly if you are distributing multiple ActiveForms to the same system or set of systems. If your ActiveForm is expected to be used by the general public, you may want to build your ActiveForm without packages, and the dynamic RTL as the size of the overall file to download will almost certainly be smaller. For example, the C++Builder RTL DLL (CP3245MT.DLL) is more than 900KB in size (and needs BORLNDMM.DLL at an additional 24KB), and the VCL40.BPL package is around 1.8MB. That's a lot of additional over-head, especially if users are downloading your ActiveForm via dial-up at a connection speed of 28.8. Note that you don't have to build your ActiveForm to use both the dynamic RTL and packages, but one usually goes with the other.

> **NOTE**
>
> Packages save memory because they place commonly used code in a special DLL called a *package*. For instance, the database tools take up somewhere between 100–200KB in even a very simple database program. If you don't use packages and you deploy six database applications, you will have that 200KB repeated in each executable. If you use packages and deploy six database applications, you have to deploy the database code only once. During the deployment of six database applications, putting the database code in a package may save you approximately 1MB of disk space.

In this example you create an ActiveForm called **SimpleFormProj1.ocx**. Fill out the ActiveX Wizard appropriately so that you get this filename for your control. This time, be sure that your project will use packages. This setting is the default for C++Builder, so you probably don't have to do anything further.

Add a TImage control from the Additional page of the Component Palette and a TToolBar control and TImageList control from the Win32 page of the Component Palette to your project's main form. Double-click the ImageList control to invoke the ImageList Editor and browse to the Program Files\Common Files\Borland Shared\Images\Buttons directory to add a few buttons to this control. Pick those that strike your fancy. Now link the toolbar to the TImageList control via the toolbar's ImageList property. Add a few buttons to the toolbar and hook them up to the proper offsets of some images in the image list. (The toolbar buttons automatically have their ImageIndex properties set, so this step is not absolutely necessary.) Finally, browse your hard drive to find an image to insert into the TImage control on the form. Some pictures in the `Images\Splash` directory were created when you installed C++Builder, so you can use one of those. When you are done, you might have a form that looks something like the image in Figure 21.2.

Figure 21.2

The form for the `SimpleFormProj1` *ActiveForm control.*

Give the `Target dir`, `Target URL`, and `HTML dir` fields the appropriate values for your Web server. In the Web Deployment Options dialog, check Use CAB File Compression.

> **Note**
>
> When you are working in the Web Deployment Options dialog, you might notice that a Default check box appears at the bottom of a number of these pages. If you check this option, the current choices in your dialog—including the paths and directories—will be copied to the Registry and reused automatically the next time you open the project. This feature can be a big help if you always deploy controls to the same directories with the same options.

At this point you are ready to close the Web Deployment Options dialog and deploy your ActiveForm. Choose Project, Web Deploy to start the process. This process could take several minutes, as a CAB file needs to be created before it can be copied to your wwwroot directory or some other directory of your choosing.

Note that in the Web Deployment Options dialog you had the option of either placing all your files in one big CAB file or of working with a set of distinct CAB files. I choose to put each control or package in a separate CAB file, mostly because doing so simulates a fairly complex installation that really puts the system through its paces.

You can now move to your client machine, type in the URL where you stored the HTML file generated by C++Builder, and watch while each CAB file is copied over and automatically installed. For instance, you might type the following:

```
http://ccalvertpc3/activestuff/SimpleFormProj1.htm
```

When you are finished, the ActiveForm and INF files should be in the OCCACHE directory, and the package files with .bpl extensions should be in the System or System32 directory of your client machine. This is assuming you are working with Windows 95 or Windows NT 4. I do not know where these files will be put on Windows NT 5, though it would be reasonable to assume that at least the System and System32 directories will remain constant. On Windows 98, you might check the c:\Windows\Downloaded Program Files directory for the ActiveForm and INF files. If that fails, open RegEdit and look up downloaded controls in the Registry.

You will also find a program called SimpleActiveForm2 on the CD-ROM that accompanies this book. This program is similar to the SimpleFormProj1 program, but instead of using CAB files, I deploy the ActiveForm and related packages separately. Deploying this way can be tricky because you have to be sure the package or packages you use are deployed to the right place. To get started, repeat all the steps for building the SimpleFormProj1 program, but turn off CAB files and turn on the Deploy Required Packages option. Now turn to the Packages page and make sure all packages are being deployed to the correct location. (In this program, you should need only VCL40.BPL, CP3245MT.DLL, and BORLNDMM.DLL; you might need many more packages in other programs.) Don't assume that the packages will go to the right place; click each one in the list box and make sure it is going where you want it to go. In particular, make sure the package is deployed to the right directory and has the URL you specified in the Target URL entry on the first page of the Web Deployment Options dialog. Click each file you are going to deploy and make sure its settings are correct. Don't just click the top file; click each one in turn. (In this case, you have only two, but in other cases, you will have to set the path and target URL multiple times, once for each file.)

If you are having trouble getting a control to appear, don't panic! Remember, the ActiveX technology itself is solid. You don't have to worry about whether the control is built correctly. The likely problem is that you are not deploying the proper set of packages or additional files on which your ActiveForm is dependent. This is happening because you aren't specifying the correct deployment directory or URL, not because C++Builder is too dumb to know which files need to be deployed.

Now, go open the INF file for your control and see whether everything you would expect to find is in there. Are the proper CAB or DLL files available in the wwwroot or related directories? Did they all get copied over to the client as expected? Can you find them on the client? This isn't black magic. The controls have to be somewhere on the client machine's hard drive. If they aren't there, then they probably aren't being copied over properly.

IE's complete lack of error messages can be a bit disconcerting; if something goes wrong, you need to have some way of focusing your mind on the likely causes of the problem.

> **NOTE**
>
> I assume IE emits no error messages because it doesn't want a user to be troubled with these messages when loading a Web page. Broken links aren't the user's fault, so perhaps it is logical that she shouldn't be bothered with error messages if problems occur.

Understanding INF Files

You can see the INF file for SimpleFormProj in Listing 21.1. Get used to reading these INF files. They are the road map to distributing an ActiveX control.

LISTING 21.1 THE INF FILE FOR THE SIMPLEFORMPROJ SAMPLE PROGRAM

```
;C++Builder-generated INF file for SimpleFormProj1.ocx
[Add.Code]
SimpleFormProj1.ocx=SimpleFormProj1.ocx
cp3245mt.dll=cp3245mt.dll
borlndmm.dll=borlndmm.dll
Vcl40.bpl=Vcl40.bpl

[SimpleFormProj1.ocx]
file=http://ccalvertpc3/activeStuff/SimpleFormProj1.ocx
clsid={1703C666-AC20-11D2-8244-0040052A83C4}
RegisterServer=yes
FileVersion=1,0,0,0

[cp3245mt.dll]
file=http://ccalvertpc3/activeStuff/cp3245mt.dll
FileVersion=4,80,0,0

[borlndmm.dll]
file=http://ccalvertpc3/activeStuff/borlndmm.dll
FileVersion=4,0,14,4
DestDir=11

[Vcl40.bpl]
file=http://ccalvertpc3/activeStuff/Vcl40.bpl
FileVersion=4,0,5,108
DestDir=11
```

Check each of the CAB files listed in this INF source. Note the URL associated with the control. The client machine is going to use this URL when it tries to load the CAB file in question. If the URL doesn't make sense to you, then it won't make sense to the client machine. If you are having troubles, take a look at these URLs and make sure they say something sensible. If you are unsure which controls go in which package, choose Component, Install Packages, and then browse through the available packages. If you click the Components button when any one package is selected, you can see the controls found in that package.

Here are some other entries that might show up in a database application distributed over the Web:

```
[ibsmp40.bpl]file=http://ccalvertpc3/activeStuff/ibevnt40.cab
DestDir=11

[vcldb40.bpl]
file=http://ccalvertpc3/activeStuff/vcldb40.cab
FileVersion=4,0,3;58
DestDir=11
```

> **NOTE**
>
> The `DestDir` value of 11 specifies the `System` or `System32` directory.

Get to know these different packages so you can understand which ones you need in a particular project.

Overall, the Web deployment options for a form are not particularly difficult. However, they can be a bit tricky if you don't understand the issues involved. Take the time to make sure you understand the issues addressed in this section. If you know how to deploy your ActiveX control correctly, that knowledge will almost certainly save you time and heartache later in the development process.

Licensing Issues

You can build ActiveX controls that work only at design time, only at run time, or that work in either situation. If you are distributing a control with one of your applications, you probably want it to work only at run time so that it aids your application but can't be used by other developers. Conversely, if you want to sell a component to someone, you might like to give that person a sample control that he can use at design time but that can't be used at run time. Conversely, perhaps you want to release your control for everyone's use, in which case you don't need a license.

IE gets the run-time licensing information for licensed components using LPK files. They are built with a utility named `LPKTOOL.EXE`, which resides on the server. IE knows about it via the `LPKPath PARAM` tag. Here's an example:

```
<OBJECT
    CLASSID="clsid:5220cb21-c88d-11cf-b347-00aa00a28331">
    <PARAM NAME="LPKPath" VALUE="MyCompnt.LPK">
</OBJECT>
```

The following URL is a good introduction to LPK files: `http://msdn.microsoft.com/msdn-online/workshop/components/activex/licensing.asp`.

Links on the Internet can change over time. If this one fails, you might try searching for the subject on `http://msdn.microsoft.com/default.asp`.

Running an ActiveForm in Word

If you want to show your form in VB or some other standard application, such as Word, all you have to do is compile and link it; then make sure it is registered. In other words, you don't have to deploy the form to be able to use it in VB or Word, though you can do so if you want.

You can register an application or DLL from inside the C++Builder Type Library Editor. At the top of the editor is a small icon like the one associated with the standard Windows application called RegEdit. This icon is located second from the right; click it to register your form. Your form can also be registered automatically when you deploy it. You can also register your DLL with either the standard Microsoft application called `RegSvr32.exe` or with a Borland application called `TRegSvr.exe`. To register an ActiveX named `Sam.ocx`, you would type either `Regsvr32 Sam.ocx` or `TRegSvr Sam.ocx`. For additional help running either application, just type its name at the command prompt with no parameters.

To run the `EasyActiveForm` ActiveX in Word, you first need to learn a few basic facts about how Word Basic is put together. This example refers to Word 97.

Word comes with a fairly complete version of Visual Basic built into it. You can reach this application by selecting Tools, Macro, Visual Basic Editor from the Word menu.

Using the Visual Basic Editor

New projects in the Visual Basic Editor aren't started the same way you start a new project in C++Builder or the standard version of Visual Basic. Instead, you get a new embedded "project" for each new document you start in Word.

If you open Word and then create a single document, or just work with the default document, the Visual Basic Editor will normally have two projects open inside. The first project, usually called Normal, is associated with your current template. The second project, usually called Document1, is associated with your current default document. If you open or create additional documents, projects will also be associated with each of these documents.

To see a project in Visual Basic, go to the View menu and choose Project Explorer. Now you should be able to see a list of the currently open projects, as shown in Figure 21.3.

FIGURE 21.3

The Word Visual Basic Editor with the Project Explorer open on its left side.

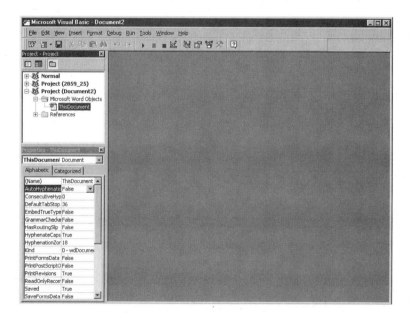

Adding Controls to a Document

You are given the choice of inserting a user form or a module when you right-click the project associated with your document. In this case, you might choose to insert a user form, which brings up a form similar to one you would see in C++Builder. Associated with the form is a toolbox with several basic controls on it. Right-click a blank area in this toolbox; you get an option to bring up the Additional Controls dialog.

The Additional Controls dialog lists all the currently registered ActiveX controls on your system. Scroll around a bit; you should be able to find and select the EasyActiveForm control, as shown in Figure 21.4.

FIGURE 21.4

Selecting the
EasyActiveForm
control from the
Additional
Controls dialog.

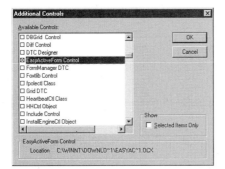

After you select the EasyActiveForm control, the control appears as an icon in the toolbox associated with your form. Select this icon and then click your Visual Basic form to place the control, as shown in Figure 21.5.

FIGURE 21.5

A C++Builder
form in the com-
pany of a Visual
Basic form.

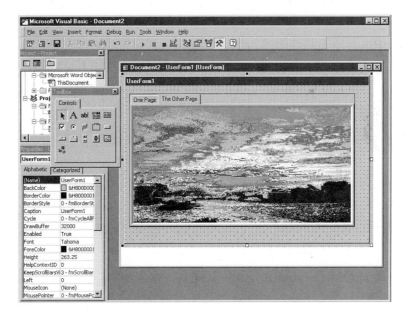

Now you can save your work and return to Word. Go to the Word menu and select View, Toolbars, Control Toolbox. Doing so brings up a dialog or floating toolbar similar to the toolbox you saw in Word Visual Basic. Select the Command Button tool from the toolbox and drop it on your Word document. Double-click the button and create a routine associated with it that looks something like the following:

```
Private Sub CommandButton1_Click()
  UserForm1.Show
End Sub
```

This code brings up the contents of UserForm1. Assuming that UserForm1 contains your ActiveX control, this is the key to displaying a sophisticated C++Builder control in the midst of a Word document via the good graces of a lowly Visual Basic form. Note that you may have to close the Word document and reload it in order for the button to function. If you have trouble getting this project together, you will find a sample Word document in the directory called EasyActiveForm on the CD-ROM that accompanies this book. The document is called ShowEasyForm.doc, and it contains the code necessary to bring up the EasyActiveForm ActiveX as long as the ActiveX is available and registered on your system.

I really like this technology. Being able to embed C++Builder forms in the midst of a Word document is great. In fact, if we can ever get past the roadblocks that prevent making easy sales from the Web, releasing books directly in Word documents that you can interact with in a manner similar to the one discussed in this section would be possible.

Using Templates with ActiveForms

You might want to create an ActiveForm from an existing application. C++Builder makes this process simple. The key to grabbing a form from a second application is to save it as an active template. In particular, if you bring up the form in the IDE, you can use the mouse to select all the components on the form. Now go to the Component menu and choose Create Component Template. A new template is saved, replete with all the controls and their associated code from your form.

At this point, you can go to the menu and choose File, New, ActiveX, Active Form. The IDE will probably prompt you to create a new library; click Yes. Go to the Component Palette's Templates page and select the new template you just finished making. Drop it on the ActiveForm. You can now save your project and compile it. That's all there is to building an ActiveForm that encapsulates an existing form in one of your projects.

NOTE

Component templates have a limitation. When you create a component template, all of the event-handling code associated with the controls in the template is saved. What is not saved, however, are any user-defined methods that the templates call. Assume that the `OnClick` event handler for a button calls a method of the form called `Go` to do some processing. The `OnClick` handler itself will be saved with the component template, but the `Go` function will not. The net result is that this component template will not function properly (and likely won't even compile) when you place it on your ActiveForm. All the code for a component template must be contained within the components' event handlers.

There are a number of form events that do not reappear as ActiveForm events. Most notably, these include `OnShow`, `OnHide`, `OnClose`, `OnCloseQuery`, `OnResize`, `OnCanResize`, `OnDock`, and `OnMouseWheel`. Code for these event handlers should be placed elsewhere in your ActiveForm.

At this point you've learned all about creating ActiveX controls for distribution over the Web or in Word, VB, or other third-party tools. You should understand most of the issues involved and feel comfortable creating ActiveForms.

The only subject not covered in-depth was code-signing your forms. To do that, you should go to the Microsoft Web site and read up on the subject. The point here is that Inprise is not authorized to create valid code-signing documents for you. As a result, you should use the system that Microsoft has set up for this process. My understanding is that Microsoft will point you to a third-party vender (`www.verisign.com`) that will arrange to code-sign your controls. That's how the security system works for ActiveX controls.

In the following section you read how to combine the ActiveForm technology with the MIDAS sockets technology. This can give you the ability to create code that takes browsers into a new and fairly powerful realm.

Sockets and ActiveForms

This section gives you an overview of sockets and shows another way you can use ActiveForms. The program in this section combines Borland's MIDAS technology with Microsoft's ActiveForm technology to create a Web-based distributed application running inside a true C++Builder binary. This technology will work using IE 3.X or higher only. It will not work with Netscape's technology unless you are using some form of plug-in that supports ActiveX controls. (For example, you can try ScriptActive from NCompass, available at `www.ncompasslabs.com`.)

You will take a standard sockets-based MIDAS application and place it on an ActiveForm. The Windows user who connects to your server can then download this form and attach to a database on your system using the MIDAS sockets technology. No database tools are needed on the client side.

Some of the technologies shown in this section, such as that in Chapter 20, "MIDAS," are covered elsewhere in this book. As a result, I will give only a brief look and then move quickly to show how this technology works in the current context. Be aware that the MIDAS components only ship with the Enterprise version of C++Builder.

A Brief Overview of Sockets

Windows sockets provide connections based on the TCP/IP protocol. They also allow connections that use the Xerox Network System (XNS), Digital's DECnet protocol, or Novell's IPX/SPX family.

Sockets give you some of the power of DCOM without loading you down with concerns regarding connectivity, security, and Windows NT domains. The disadvantage of sockets is that they lack the backing of a full object-oriented scheme such as you find in COM.

Technically, sockets are very easy to use. Two sets of controls wrap this technology. One is the MIDAS controls on the Component Palette's Midas tab, and the other is the `TServerSocket` and `TClientSocket` controls from the Internet page. Both sets of controls are easy to use. The only catch is that you have to remember to first load the `ScktSrvr.exe` program found in the `CBuilder4\Bin` directory. However, `ScktSrvc.exe` is also new to C++Builder 4; it is a service that can be run under Windows NT to alleviate having to remember to run `ScktSrvr.exe`. Keep this information in mind if you are developing under NT. Almost all the troubles I've had with sockets boiled down to my foolishly forgetting to load `ScktSrvr.exe`.

For many developers, the easy-to-use and flexible socket technology will be the ideal solution when building distributed applications. Because it is built on TCP/IP, this technology should be especially appealing to people who want to work across very large distances using the Internet.

Building the MIDAS ActiveForm with Sockets Support

Most distributed architectures are actually easy to build. Developing the infrastructure for a distributed application might be difficult, but that's not the responsibility of most programmers. Most developers simply use the infrastructure; they don't have to create it.

The average developer is going to build applications on top of TCP/IP, ActiveX, CORBA, RMI, or DCOM. Most developers aren't responsible for creating a distributed architecture any more than they are responsible for writing an operating system, compiler, or Web server. Everyone knows that writing a compiler is a tricky job, but it isn't difficult to use one—at least it shouldn't be. The same is true of building MIDAS-based ActiveForms. Some tricky technology is involved, but most programmers are just using the technology; they aren't actually developing it.

To build this distributed ActiveForm application, you have to start by creating an application server. This server will be a typical MIDAS application that exports a simple database containing pictures and text. The tables for the database are in a folder called Data on the CD-ROM that accompanies this book. The code for the examples in this section are found in the ActiveSocketForm directory. (Its subdirectories are called SunsetServer and SunsetClient. SunsetServer contains an application called ActiveSocketForm, while SunsetClient contains an application called SunsetActiveFormProj1.)

The actual database contains some pictures of a sunset that I took recently, along with some poems that William Shakespeare wrote about 400 years ago. You should copy this data from the CD-ROM and create a Standard Paradox alias called SunsetData that points to it; alternatively you can use the BCB4UNLEASHED alias, which you probably created while reading an earlier part of this book.

Start a new application and turn it into a distributed database application by choosing File, New, Remote Data Module from the C++Builder menu. This option takes a standard data module and wraps it inside a COM object. This COM object will be used to export an object called a Provider. A Provider is so called because it provides information about your data set to remote clients. In other words, the Provider object is the DCOM automation object that lets the client application talk to the server. They talk about the contents of a data set; that is, they talk about the pictures and poems in the Sunset database. More explicitly, the Provider marshals the data from the Sunset database between the client and the server.

When you are creating the remote data module, you are prompted for a name. In this sample project, I called my remote data module SocketObject. A remote data module looks just like a standard data module when displayed in the IDE.

In the Project Options dialog, turn off the Dynamic RTL and Build with Runtime Packages options. You should now save all your work into a unique directory. Your application server will reside in this directory, so put some thought into where you put it. Windows can always find the directory because a reference to it will be stored in the Registry. You want the directory somewhere on your hard drive that makes sense to you. I named the module where the data will reside SocketFormImpl.cpp, the main form Main.cpp, and the project source ActiveSocketForm.bpr.

The next stage in developing the project involves dropping a TTable object on the remote data module and hooking it up to the Sunset table. You don't need to activate the table, as that is done automatically when a client connects to your server.

Drop a TProvider component from the Component Palette's MIDAS page on the SocketObject form (the same form where you placed the TTable object). Use the Object Inspector to hook up the TProvider's DataSet property to the TTable object. Right-click TProvider and choose Export Provider1 from Data Module. This action produces the following lines of code:

```
STDMETHODIMP TSocketObjectImpl::get_Provider1(IProvider** Value)
{
  try
  {
  _di_IProvider IProv = m_DataModule->Provider1->Provider;
  IProv->AddRef();
  *Value = IProv;
  }
  catch(Exception &e)
  {
    return Error(e.Message.c_str(), IID_ISocketObject);
  }
  return S_OK;
}
```

The client will call this method when it wants to retrieve the Provider object. The Provider object is the one that knows how to marshal data back and forth between the client and the server. You can add something to the main form to make it recognizable when you see it again. I have added another piece of disparate art, this time in the form of a picture I took during a blurry, vaguely remembered vacation in the Loire valley.

At this point, you have finished creating your application server. Run it once to register it; then sit back and admire your work.

When all is said and done, nothing could be much simpler than this task. Again, building a distributed application is not a particularly difficult endeavor. If you have questions about this process, go to Chapter 20, "MIDAS," and read what I have to say there about creating automation objects.

Creating the MIDAS-Based ActiveForm

Now you create an ActiveForm that will serve as the client for the server you created in the preceding section. You can then embed this form in a Web page and display your data across a network using a true, distributed architecture. In other words, you will be able to have one database, residing on one machine, and have your clients reside on any Windows machine that is running Internet Explorer 3 or later.

Create a new ActiveForm project and provide a name for the ActiveForm. In the sample program for this section of the chapter, I call the SocketForm program. This example is available in the ActiveSocketForm directory on this book's CD-ROM. The actual ActiveForm that lives in this directory is called SunsetActiveFormProj1.

You should create a standard MIDAS client on the form that you created. Start by dropping a TSocketConnection component on the form. Now is a good time to go to the CBuilder4\Bin directory and make sure that the ScktSrvr.exe application is running on your server machine. You won't be able to connect to your client unless the socket server application is running. Remember, IE won't give you any error messages if the connection fails. If you forgot to launch ScktSrvr.exe, nobody's going to be helpful enough to actually tell you what you did wrong.

Click the Address property of the TSocketConnection and enter the name or the IP address of the machine where you created your application server. In most standard development situations, it will be the same machine on which you are building your client. Typically, you create the server and client on one machine, test them, and then move one or the other to a remote machine. (If you move the server, you need to change the name or number you put in the Address property.)

Drop down the ServerName property of the TSocketConnection; you should now be able to pick the name of your application server from a drop-down list. If something goes wrong, the two most obvious problems are that you didn't run your server and it is therefore not registered, or else you forgot to run the ScktSrvr.exe application.

Drop a TClientDataSet component on the form and hook its RemoteServer property to the TSocketConnection component. Drop down the ProviderName property of the TClientDataSet and choose the provider you created, which is probably Provider1. If this field is blank, the problem is likely that you are no longer connected to the server. Alternatively, you may have forgotten to right-click the Provider component back on the server so that you could choose the menu option that would write the code for exporting your provider.

After you connect the TClientDataSet to the Provider, you are home free. Now you can set the control's Active property to true. The application server should now load into memory.

Drop a TDataSource on the form and connect it to the TClientDataSet. Add a TDBImage and TDBMemo control to your form and hook them up to the Picture and Description fields. You should now be able to see one of the pictures of the California sunset and some labyrinthine words from the holy blissful bard.

Your ActiveForm is complete at this point. The only change you might want to make involves giving the user the option to connect to the data after the form has loaded. This option is helpful because it separates the act of loading the form from the act of connecting to the database. As you know, the form will rely on several different packages. Just getting them loaded properly is enough for one operation. It's best if you let that task stand on its own and then check to make sure you can come up with a connection.

Troubleshooting the Form

You should note that these the only things likely to go wrong when loading the form:

- You somehow forgot to send one of the needed packages with the form. I am not using packages in this case, so this should not be a problem.

- Perhaps you are experiencing some kind of versioning mismatch with one of the supporting files.

On the database side, the following errors might occur:

- You forgot to start the ScktSrvr.exe file on the server. I dwell on this possibility so frequently in the vague hope that multiple reminders will spare you the suffering of spending hours tracking down a bug that turns out to be nothing more than a simple failure to load ScktSrvr.exe. In particular, note that if you reboot your server frequently, you might want to put ScktSrvr.exe in the Start Up folder; use the ScktSrvc.exe NT service if you are running Windows NT.

- You forgot to point the client to the machine specified in the Address property.

Neither problem should be hard to solve. However, it helps if you know which problem you are wrestling with at the time it arises. If the form doesn't load, then it's a DLL or package problem. If the form loads okay but you can't connect, then it's either a SckSrvr.exe problem or a simple problem with an alias.

Testing the Form

To let the user connect to the database at run time, first be sure that both the Active property of the TClientDataSet and the Connected property of the TSocketConnection component are set to false. Drop a button on the form and label it **Connect**. Associate the following method with the button:

```
void __fastcall TSunsetActiveFormX::ConnectClick(TObject *Sender)
{
  ClientDataSet1->Active = true;
}
```

This code will set both the `TSocketConnection::Connected` and the `TClientDataSet::Active` property to `true`. When you are done with your form, it might look something like the image shown in Figure 21.6.

FIGURE 21.6

The ActiveForm for the SunsetActiveForm -Proj1 sample program.

When working with this application, you should note that I have designed it so that all the poems and pictures come down the wire at once when you connect to the database. This design will work with a relatively small chunk of data like the one shown here, especially if you are on a local network. However, you will have performance problems if you move on to a 28.8Kbps modem connection or let the database grow much larger. The solution might be to eliminate the pictures or to use SQL to request one row of data at a time.

If you need to pass a SQL statement back to the server, you can do so in a number of ways. One of the simplest is to add new methods to the object that exports your provider interface. You could then call that method as needed to send data back to the server.

I should perhaps expend a few more words talking about deploying your form on the Web. I spent considerable time on this subject earlier in this discussion on ActiveForms. As a result, I won't go into much depth.

The choices you make when distributing the ActiveForm are yours, but you probably want to build with packages. Next, you will probably want to wrap all the pieces of the application in CAB files and then deploy them to your wwwroot directory or some other place where the controls can be available to users.

Now you can go to a client machine and access the ActiveForm. For maximum effect, you should go to a machine that doesn't have C++Builder on it and that doesn't have any database tools on it. When you attach to the URL where you stored your controls, the ActiveForm will be downloaded and the user can access the database running on your server. This is a classic thin client application. The great advantage here is that the code executing inside the Web browser is built entirely in C++Builder and has very high performance characteristics not found in the slow Java- or HTML-bound Web-based world. Of course, unlike Java, this is a Windows-only solution. However, it is indeed a very powerful solution, and one that works on the platform supported by 90% of the computers in the world.

Summary

You learned about ActiveForms in this chapter. You also saw how to move a multitiered database into the Web browser arena using an ActiveX form and the MIDAS sockets technology.

If you are interested in this field, you should look at Inprise's Entera and OLE Enterprise products, as well as the CORBA technology discussed in this book. You should also consider the native Java technology called RMI.

You were exposed to the building blocks of multitiered database projects. The DirectX material found elsewhere in this book is arguably more fun, but probably no other material in this book is as important nor as innately interesting as what you saw in this chapter. We are entering the age when PCs are at last moving onto a great global network. This chapter introduced you to the information needed to program for the Internet.

CORBA

CHAPTER 22

*by Charlie Calvert
and Dana Scott Kaufman*

IN THIS CHAPTER

This chapter is about using CORBA in C++Builder 4 Enterprise. In particular, you will see

- How to use the basic tools of CORBA such as the ORB, the BOA, and the Smart Agent
- How to create a simple CORBA server and client
- How to call a CORBA object using dynamic invocation
- How to use the Interface Repository

The struggle to get all programs on all systems talking to each other, regardless of which language they are written in, is one of the grandest quests yet undertaken by programmers. Certainly, DCOM shares in this quest, but for now it is more limited than CORBA because it lacks CORBA's cross-platform agenda. Of course, DCOM has the advantage of riding the crest of Windows development, and it does not come with a forbidding price tag that limits a technology's usefulness. Despite this, it is CORBA that has the grandest agenda, and everyone who works with this technology should feel something of the excitement inherent in the endeavor.

Understanding CORBA

C++Builder 4 Enterprise provides a comprehensive set of tools for developing complete CORBA solutions. It is the easiest way to develop full-scale C++ CORBA servers and clients. C++Builder 4 Enterprise's CORBA integration makes it easy for you to create CORBA objects and connect to them using either static or dynamic invocation. Dynamic invocation is a technology discussed in some depth later in this chapter. Components and wizards are available and allow you to create and access CORBA objects from C++Builder with very little effort on your part. The C++Builder CORBA support is very robust, allowing C++Builder applications to access advanced CORBA services such as the naming service, location service, and so on. Objects you access can be written in any CORBA-compliant language, and the objects you create can be accessed using traditional CORBA programming techniques from any other CORBA-aware language such as Java or Delphi Pascal.

In the next few pages, I will explain what CORBA is and how it works. After this brief introduction to the subject, I will show you several hands-on examples. In particular, the next few introductory sections will cover the following topics:

- What is CORBA?
- What is an ORB?
- What is the Smart Agent?

- What is the BOA?
- What are proxies, stubs, and skeletons?

What Is CORBA?

This chapter is designed to get you up to speed with CORBA and C++Builder Enterprise. CORBA development continues to grow in popularity. There are many sources for more information. A good place to start is `http://www.omg.org/corba/beginners.html`, where you can find many articles on CORBA development. A key book on this subject is *Client Server Programming with Java and CORBA*, by Robert Orfali and Dan Harkey. It is sometimes also called the "Martian book" because of the pictures of Martians used throughout the text.

CORBA is an acronym standing for the Common Object Request Broker Architecture. If the acronym had been chosen more for its usefulness than its marketing value, it might have been called OMDC, or the Object Model for Distributed Computing.

CORBA was created by the OMG, or Object Management Group. Its Web site is `http://www.omg.org`, and anyone interested in this technology should visit that URL regularly. The OMG has many contributing members, and many of them are large companies:

Microsoft	Iona
Netscape	Hewlett-Packard
Sun Microsystems	Computer Associates
Oracle	Anderson Consulting
Novell	Fujitsu
Micro Focus	Platinum
Lockheed Martin	Rational Software
IBM	Rogue Wave
Inprise	Sybase
Informix	Xerox

Many others also are auditing or influencing the process.

The primary goal of the OMG is to create an OOP-based, cross-platform, distributed architecture that can host a large number of servers and clients and that scales well, even under extremely heavy pressure. In particular, the developers of CORBA design their specification to support millions of servers and tens of thousands of simultaneous users. CORBA has an extremely robust architecture that meets the needs of large corporations.

The OMG drew up the specification for CORBA. Companies such as Visigenic and IONA actually implement the specification. As you might know, Visigenic was acquired by Inprise during the spring of 1998, which means that Inprise is now in control of a commonly used CORBA implementation.

Throughout this chapter you can assume that I am talking about the Inprise/Visigenic version of CORBA unless I specifically say otherwise. The name for Inprise's implementation of CORBA is the VisiBroker.

Not all the things I say apply to CORBA as a whole, as you can take certain shortcuts when using the Visigenic ORB that are not specifically mentioned in the CORBA specification. These shortcuts make your life easier, and they are built on top of a fully correct implementation of the OMG 2.1 standard for CORBA. In other words, the presence of these extensions does not imply that the Visigenic ORB is not fully compliant with the CORBA 2.1 standard.

Comparing DCOM and CORBA

If you come from Windows, you might be wondering what the difference is between CORBA and DCOM. In many ways, the technologies parallel each other, and indeed they perform very similar tasks.

Both COM and CORBA provide a means of creating distributed, object-oriented architectures. In other words, they both provide means of calling an object residing in a binary executable on another machine.

Both COM and CORBA have various utilities that support them, such as MTS, ITS, brokers, registries, and so on. Each architecture has specific advantages.

COM, being a Microsoft and Windows-based technology, has the advantage of being integrated into 90% of the desktop machines in the world. It is free and has excellent support from a wide range of vendors.

CORBA is probably somewhat better at this time at providing true 24-hour-a-day, 7-day-a-week support. For instance, it probably has better support for fail-over and load distribution than COM does, though this balance of power is changing even as this book is written. For instance, C++Builder now provides the TSimpleObjectBroker MIDAS component to provide load balancing and fail-over for DCOM objects. *Fail-over* refers to the functionality of being able to automatically find another server should a problem arise with the currently accessed server. Certainly, CORBA has much better support for a wide range of operating systems than does COM.

Finally, both architectures are similar in the fanaticism of their adherents. I've heard people from both sides of this ongoing battle claim that they have complete dominance of the distributed architecture playing field. The truth of the matter is that this is very much an ongoing battle. COM is widespread, but CORBA has important friends in big companies such as Sun, Netscape, and IBM.

The truth is that no one knows who is going to win this battle, just as people once didn't know if OS2 or Windows was going to win, or if Apple or Microsoft was going to win. In this unfolding story, the only serious mistake you can make is taking at face value the occasionally absurd claims and accusations made by both sides of this argument. For instance, COM programmers sometimes claim that COM works well on a range of operating systems or will soon work well on a range of operating systems. Such statements should be taken with a grain of salt. Likewise, I find suspect CORBA adherents' claims of "transparent" interoperability between different ORBs and different operating systems. CORBA's pretty good, but not quite that good.

The only way to know which side is really going to win is to wait and watch, always taking into account the possibility that both technologies will exist into the indefinite future.

What Is an ORB?

An ORB, or Object Request Broker, is often spoken of as merely the generic name for the set of services used to connect a client and a server and to pass method calls and information back and forth between a client and a server. As such, it is not so much a specific entity as it is a concept.

However, the ORB has to be implemented somewhere. In Windows, it is made manifest by a series of DLLs designed to help you link objects across the network or across process boundaries. These DLLs have names such as `ORB_BR.DLL` and they are installed by default in the `C:\Program Files\Borland\VBroker\Bin` directory. Because the ORB is implemented in DLLs, they reside in process with your server and client implementations. Because you do not have to call across process boundaries to access their methods, in-process DLLs are fast.

These DLLs total several megabytes in size, and they need to be installed on all client and server machines that use CORBA. You are unlikely to ever have occasion to call specific functions in these DLLs, but you will be using them continually without ever directly referencing them. In other words, you call routines or objects that reside inside these DLLs, but you do not need to know what functions or methods reside in which DLLs, or even that the functions or methods are in fact stored in DLLs. The VCL takes care of those kinds of details for you.

You need to understand that the ORB DLLs are merely artifacts of Visigenic's implementation of the CORBA standard. The standard itself does not say anything about these DLLs, but Visigenic created them to implement the requirements laid down in the specification. In other words, the DLLs were one logical and robust way to create an implementation of the specification.

By now, you probably sense the extreme importance placed on the specification developed by the OMG. This specification is the CORBA standard, and if CORBA is not centered on standards, then it has almost no meaning. The whole point of CORBA is that it is a cross-platform standard for building distributed object architectures. If the standard is violated, then the various pieces might not work together; the whole system is then useless.

To sum up from the C++Builder programmer's point of view, an ORB is a set of DLLs residing in the `VBroker\Bin` directory. However, you should remember that this is just one way to implement a set of functionality described by the OMG in their specification. More important than the specific implementation are the things that an ORB does for a programmer. These things are perhaps best understood by looking at the Smart Agent.

What Is the Smart Agent?

The Smart Agent is a directory service that helps your client automatically locate a server. When you start a client, it will automatically ask the Smart Agent to look up your server in its directory. It does so and helps the two applications establish a relationship. (Needless to say, you can expect the relationship to be warm and fuzzy and very tasteful!)

Starting the Smart Agent

Like the ORB DLLs, the Smart Agent is not part of the CORBA specification. It is merely a means of obtaining an end. However, it is one of the most important parts of the VisiBroker.

If you are on an NT system, the Smart Agent is a service that you can access by starting the Control Panel, loading the Services applet, and then scrolling toward the bottom of the list until you find the Visigenic services. There is no concept of a service if you are on Windows 9x, and the Smart Agent cannot be started automatically. Instead, you should run `OSAgent.exe`, which is located in the `VisiBroker\Bin` directory. (`OSAgent` is also the name of the file that is run as a service on an NT box.)

C++Builder 4 Enterprise also has the capability of starting the Smart Agent through the IDE. In the Tools menu, there is a VisiBroker SmartAgent menu item. Clicking this starts the Smart Agent. If there is a checkmark to the left of the menu item, the Smart Agent is already running.

22

> **NOTE**
>
> Whether you are running on Windows 9x or Windows NT, you must make sure the Smart Agent is running. If it is not, you will be unable to do any CORBA programming with the VisiBroker ORB.

You don't need to run the Smart Agent on every machine, but one version of the Smart Agent should be running on each local area network that supports CORBA. During development, it is simplest to run the Smart Agent on your current machine and to save until later the task of deciding how to set up your local area network.

Understanding the Smart Agent

The Smart Agent's purpose is to help clients connect to servers and to perform other important tasks such as load balancing and restarting crashed objects. When a client is launched, it uses the ORB to talk to the Smart Agent, and the Smart Agent connects the client program to a server. In other words, the Smart Agent contains directory services that track the location of objects and connect clients to them.

> **NOTE**
>
> As far as the Smart Agent is concerned, all objects that it knows about are already running. It doesn't know how to start a service automatically. There is, however, a second service; the OAD will fool the Smart Agent into thinking that a service is running. The Smart Agent relays object requests to the OAD and the OAD starts the object.
>
> This system is quite different from the one used by COM and DCOM. DCOM clients can never access their server unless the server is actually registered in the Registry. It can be started automatically if it is registered. CORBA servers, on the other hand, can be accessed without being officially registered. However, this process won't work if they're not already running. If you want a CORBA object to behave like a DCOM object, you have to first learn about the OAD. The OAD is not discussed in this book. For more info on OAD and other Visibroker features, see Inprise's Visibroker Web site at
> `http://www.inprise.com/visibroker`.

A client or server program does not need to know where its copy of the Smart Agent is located. The ORB sends out broadcast messages searching for the Smart Agent the moment the ORB is loaded into memory by a client or server. Once it finds the agent, it will communicate with it using UDP.

Be sure to note that the ORB finds a Smart Agent automatically, without having to be told its location. This point is important because it allows the client to be set up without any configuration other than installing the ORB DLLs. In particular, the files ORB_BR.dll, CP3245MT.dll, and BORLNDMM.dll should both be on the path. ORB_BR.dll is a threaded version of ORB_B.dll.

Normally, you will want to start multiple Smart Agents on a single local area network. That way, if one of the Smart Agents goes down, others can step in to take its place. The details of ensuring that all Smart Agents know about all the objects on the system are automatically taken care of for you. In other words, you just start the Smart Agent; it in turn will automatically discover all the servers running on your LAN.

> **NOTE**
>
> You also need to be careful not to start too many Smart Agents on each local area network. Multiple agents are good for redundancy and fail-over, but remember that the agents also need to communicate with each other. Too many agents can add unnecessary overhead. Two agents on each local area network should be fine for most applications.

You can have more than one domain of servers on a single LAN, and obviously you can get Smart Agents on different LANs to talk to one another. In particular, you do so by creating an agentaddr file which is kept in a directory specified by the VBROKER_ADM environment variable. For more information on this topic, see the *VisiBroker Programmer's Guide* (vbcpgmr.pdf), available on the VisiBroker Web site at http://www.inprise.com.

Starting the Smart Agent from within C++Builder is extremely easy. Simply select VisiBroker Smart Agent from the C++Builder's Tools menu. The Smart Agent can also be started as an NT service or manually by running OsAgent.exe in c:\Program Files\Borland\Vbroker. When running the Smart Agent manually, it can be run as a console application by passing it the -C option.

You can ensure that a particular CORBA server will not go down by starting more than one instance of the server on a LAN. If one instance goes down at that point, the Smart

Agent automatically connects the client to the second instance of the object. This fail-over technology works best if your object is stateless, but reconnecting to an object that maintains state is possible if you perform extra work. Again, you should read the *VisiBroker Programmer's Guide* for more details.

The Smart Agent is actually an extension of the Basic Object Adaptor (BOA) standard. This standard is discussed in the next section of this chapter. You should note, however, that in many cases a close relationship exists between the BOA and the Smart Agent. The BOA is part of the CORBA standard, whereas the Smart Agent is a VisiBroker–specific extension to the standard designed to make your life easier. (In the future, something called the POA will replace the BOA. The POA is discussed briefly later in this chapter.)

In C++Builder, the ORB is encapsulated inside a class and is available to you automatically by including the header file `corba.h`. You can find the `corba.h` and the rest of the CORBA header files in the `vbroker\include` directory. The ORB class is actually defined in the header file `orb.h`. This brings up an interesting point, the ORB will automatically go out on the network and find an instance of the requested object. Microsoft Distributed COM (DCOM) architecture requires the naming of a specific server where the object is located in order to use a remote object. This is one of the major differences between DCOM and CORBA. Later in the chapter I will describe what you can do with an ORB object.

What Is the BOA?

The Basic Object Adaptor (BOA) allows a server to register itself. When a server is launched, one of the first things it does is initialize the ORB; the second thing it does is get a copy of the BOA from the ORB. CORBA 2 specifies that all ORBs should support a BOA. (As mentioned earlier, the OMG does not say that all ORBs should support a Smart Agent. The Smart Agent is something like a super BOA, designed to make it easy for you to connect with servers, to perform load balancing, and automatically support fail-over.)

> **NOTE**
>
> Even standard C++Builder MIDAS applications now support load balancing and fail-over via the `TSimpleObjectBroker` component.

The client never has anything to do with the BOA, and indeed the client does not need to know that the BOA even exists. Only the server deals with the BOA. Most, but by no means all, of the BOA's activities occur automatically without server intervention.

22

CORBA

I'm going to write some pseudocode that shows what happens when a server registers itself at load time:

```
Orb = Orb->Create(Params);
BOA = Orb->InitializeBOA();
MyCorbaObject = TmyCorbaObject->Create();
BOA->ObjectIsReady(MyCorbaObject);
BOA->ImplementationIsReady();
```

Before going any further, let me emphasize that you will not find code like this anywhere in the C++Builder source code nor will you find any such thing as a method called InitializeBOA, ObjectIsReady, or ImplementationIsReady. However, similar methods are being called behind the scenes, and similar code is called in standard Java or Pascal programs. Nevertheless, this example is pseudocode and is designed only to give you some sense of what happens behind the scenes when you launch a server.

The key points to note when you're studying this pseudocode are that the BOA is retrieved from the ORB and that CORBA makes a distinction between registering an object (ObjectIsReady) and announcing that a server is usable (ImplementationIsReady). In particular, an individual server might call ObjectIsReady many times, one for each of its objects. It would then call ImplementationIsReady once to announce that it has initialized all its objects and is ready to go. (I use the term ImplementationIsReady because it closely follows the language used by CORBA venders. If I were using my own terms, I would say ServerIsReady.)

In other words, these calls are made when a server is launched, and the end result is that the Smart Agent knows about your object. In the case of the VisiBroker, the Smart Agent automatically implements the BOA for you. In a sense, the Smart Agent is the BOA, except that it is really a kind of super BOA because it does more than the BOA specification ever declares necessary.

> **NOTE**
>
> Having said all this, I confess that I find the BOA a somewhat nebulous entity whose precise lineaments appear lost in the thick, swirling fog that lingers around the Smart Agent's actual implementation. Perhaps this is due to some shortcoming on my part, but I think it may be also due to the fact that the OMG did not properly define the BOA when the specification was first drawn up. As a result, each vendor had to come up with its own solution to certain poorly defined aspects of the specification.
>
> In the future, the BOA will probably be replaced with the POA, or Portable Object Adaptor. The POA, which is a more completely fleshed-out specification,

should prove easier to understand. A huge amount of code is already implemented on top of the BOA at this stage, so the change to the POA will probably not occur overnight. (I assume it is called the Portable Object Adaptor because it is meant to be portable between vender implementations.)

Understanding IDL

The Interface Definition Language (IDL) is used to define the object interfaces that client programs may use to interact with a CORBA server. IDL compilers are used to convert the IDL in language-specific implementations. The IDL2CPP compiler uses your interface definition to generate C++ code. When developing Java clients or servers, the IDL can be processed through the IDL2JAVA compiler, which will generate Java code.

The interface definition defines the name of the object as well as all of the methods the object offers. Each method specifies the parameters that will be passed to the method, their type, and whether they are for input or output. The listing shows an IDL specification for an object named `account`. The example object has only one method, `calcInterest`:

```
interface account{
  float calcInterest(in float rate);
};
```

This code is admirably clean and succinct. It looks vaguely like C++, but remember that it is meant to be language-neutral. In other words, Inprise tools can convert an interface like this into C++ objects or Java objects. Over time, tools should be available for converting an interface like this in Object Pascal.

What Are Proxies, Stubs, and Skeletons?

The client cannot talk directly to a server in a distributed application, and a server cannot talk directly to a client. Instead, function calls and their parameters have to be marshaled across the network from one application to the other. Programmers don't usually care how this marshaling takes place any more than they care exactly how a compiler turns their C++ code into machine code. I'm not saying that it might not be helpful to have an intimate knowledge of such matters, but it is not something most programmers concern themselves with on a day-to-day basis.

It is clear that information about function calls and their parameters flows back and forth between the client and the server over some unspecified protocol such as TCP/IP, or in the case of CORBA, over a TCP/IP derivative called IIOP(Internet Inter-ORB Protocol). IIOP is an object-oriented protocol developed by the OMG that makes it possible for distributed programs written in different programming languages to communicate. A proxy must be established on both the client and the server side in order to make this architecture work.

The proxy on the client side is called a *stub*, and the proxy on the server side is called a *skeleton*. Together, this pair of conspirators trick the client into believing that it is talking directly to the server. In other words, the client has faux methods that make it think it is talking directly to the server as if it were just another object inside the client application. On the server side, a second proxy is established to relay the client's calls directly to real methods in the server. A schematic overview of the Smart Agent and the rest of the CORBA architecture is shown in Figure 22.1.

FIGURE 22.1

A CORBA client and server use proxies to talk to the ORB, BOA, and Smart Agent.

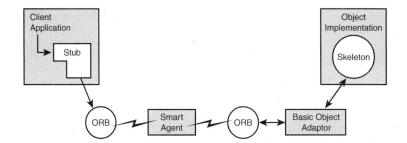

> **NOTE**
>
> In law, a proxy is someone who stands in for another person. In other words, if one person cannot represent himself in court, a proxy might be appointed to represent and speak for him. A proxy is a person who represents another person, much as a publicity agent might represent a client. In the same way, the *proxy stub* in a client represents the server, even though the server cannot be there "in person." Conversely, the *proxy skeleton* represents the client for the server, even though the client can't be there "in person" to talk to the server.

Consider the following pseudocode representing a proxy stub method for the client:

```
function Integer MyRemoteStub::Square(int I)
{
  MarshalDataToServer("Square", I);  // Call the real square method
  return UnMarshalDataFromServer();  // Get the result from the server
}
```

If a method like this existed on a client, then the client could call this function as if it were a real routine that actually returned an integer's square. However, a pseudo-function called MarshalDataToServer is actually called. MarshalDataToServer is designed to invoke a remote call across a network and to marshal parameters over the network to the remote routine. In other words, MarshalDataToServer knows all about IIOP and the ORB, and it can use that technology to make remote procedure calls.

After the call to the server is completed, the method can then ask for the return value to the remote procedure call. This return value is then passed on to the user as the result of the MyRemoteStub::Square method call.

As far as the client application is concerned, it just made a simple call into a local method called Square. Something much more complicated occurred underneath the covers. The client didn't have to know about any of those details because the proxy stub method surreptitiously took care of all the hard work. These types of methods are generically known as proxies; they are known inside CORBA as stubs on the client and skeletons on the server.

On the opposite side of the equation, the server has its own set of proxy methods called a skeleton. Pseudocode for a typical skeleton looks like this:

```
void MySkeleton::Square;
{
  int I;
  UnMarshalDataFromClient(I);    // Get the parameter from the client
  I = MyObject->Square(I);       // Call the real square method
  SendDataBackToClientStack(I);  // Send the result back to the client
}
```

This method is called automatically when word is sent over the network to the server that the client has called the Square method. The exact method used to invoke the Square method is again not relevant to this discussion any more than the exact method Windows uses to write a message box to the screen is not relevant to most discussions of Windows API programming. Clearly, the client passed a string to the server saying that it wanted to call the Square method, and somehow the server resolved that string into a real call to the MyObject->Square method. The details are not important, nor are they necessarily made known to the programmer.

After MySkeleton->Square is invoked, the first task is to marshal the data across from the client. Again, a custom method is called to perform this low-level task. The real Square method on the server is then invoked, and the result is returned in a local variable called I. Finally, the result of the function call is sent back to the client, where it waits in a queue for the client stub function to retrieve it.

The programmer doesn't have to write the stub and skeleton methods that marshal functions and parameters back and forth between the client and the server. Instead, this process is taken care of automatically by the IDL2CPP compiler. As you will see later in the chapter, the actual stub and skeleton objects are placed in the files created by IDL2CPP after processing an IDL file. The stubs are placed in files that end in `_c.cpp` and the skeletons in files that end in `_s.cpp`. You don't ever actually have to look at these methods, but I think you will find it helpful if I point them out to you. If you look at the actual methods, you will see that they are similar to the pseudocode written here. A more in-depth discussion of stubs and skeletons occurs later in this chapter; check out "Understanding the Stub" and "Understanding the Skeleton."

Understanding C++Builder and CORBA

By this time, you should have a fairly good understanding of how CORBA works and what kinds of things you can do with it. As you have seen, it does more or less the same things DCOM does, except that it will work cross platform. To wind up this overview of CORBA, I'm going to spend a few more paragraphs discussing C++Builder Enterprise's implementation of CORBA.

C++Builder Enterprise contains the most complete environment for developing CORBA applications. The integration of the CORBA tools within the C++Builder IDE is very good. C++Builder Enterprise ships with VisiBroker for C++, including the IDL2CPP compiler for turning IDL into C++ code. C++Builder recognizes files with `.IDL` extensions that are added to a C++Builder project as IDL and will automatically call the IDL2CPP compiler to generate the stubs and skeletons.

Because of the IDL compiler support, C++Builder applications can leverage other CORBA services, including the naming and location services, among others. This allows the creation of very robust multitier applications. In addition, several wizards are included to aid in the creation of CORBA servers and clients. These make CORBA development much simpler and are discussed later. C++Builder Enterprise makes CORBA programming easy, and that is no easy accomplishment.

Two Important CORBA Repositories

This brief section quickly introduces you to the concept of an Interface and Implementation Repository. These important services are provided by CORBA. C++Builder provides a wizard to automate the registration of your objects with the Interface Repository. This makes dealing with the Interface Repository much easier.

What Is the Interface Repository?

The *Interface Repository* is a place where you can store the details about your objects, such as their methods and the parameters passed to them. This repository serves three purposes:

- It provides a place where users can look up relatively detailed information about the objects available on the network or on their own system.
- It provides a mechanism that allows CORBA to perform type checking on method calls.
- It also allows you to make dynamic calls to an object at run time rather than forcing you to statically prepare the call at compile time. In other words, it lets you do the equivalent in CORBA to calling a COM object off a variant.

The Interface Repository can be started directly from within the C++Builder if it is not already running. The following steps show how this is done:

1. Select IDL Repository from C++Builder's Tools menu. This will display a dialog stating that no interface repositories have been found and asking if it is okay to start one.
2. Press the Yes button to display the Start Interface Repository dialog. The dialog allows you to enter several options.
3. You first enter a repository name, which is a name chosen to distinguish one instance of the repository from another.
4. The next field is the `Storage File`, which is the initial file to load into the Interface Repository. If left blank, you can add files later from the command line or through the Update IDL Repository dialog discussed later.
5. Lastly, the Console checkbox is used to specify whether the Interface Repository should start up as a console or as a windows application.

The Start Interface Repository dialog is shown in Figure 22.2.

FIGURE 22.2

The Start Interface Repository dialog is set to start a new Interface Repository with the name
`CorbaTestServer1.`

Once the Interface Repository is started, the Update IDL Repository dialog is shown. This dialog is also displayed when you select the Tools, IDL Repository menu item and the Interface Repository is already started. The dialog is used to add new interfaces to the Interface Repository. The following steps will add a new interface into the repository:

1. Select the repository to register your interface with by selecting the Repository Name from a drop-down list. If you would like to start a new repository with a different name press the Add IRep button to display the Start IRep dialog.

2. Select the IDL files to place in the repository by selecting the check box next to the filenames in the IDL Files listbox. All IDL files in the current C++Builder project will be listed. IDL files not automatically listed can be added using the Add File button. These IDL files contain the definitions of the interfaces that are stored in the repository. I explain this topic in more depth later in the chapter.

3. Click the Replace Definitions button to indicate that any interfaces already registered with the Interface Repository that have the same names as the interfaces in your selected IDL files should be replaced by the interfaces in your IDL files.

The Update IDL Repository dialog is shown in Figure 22.3.

FIGURE 22.3

The Update IDL Repository dialog.

Alternatively, the Interface Repository can be started manually by typing `irep.exe MyRepository` at the command line, where `MyRepository` is a randomly chosen name that distinguishes one instance of the repository from another. After loading the repository, you can use a utility called `IDL2IR.exe` to load IDL files into the repository; alternatively, you can use the IREP GUI. These IDL files contain the definitions of the interfaces that are stored in the repository. I explain this topic in more depth later in the chapter.

You can see the Interface Repository started as a Windows application in Figure 22.4.

FIGURE 22.4

The Interface Repository showing the interface to a simple CORBA object.

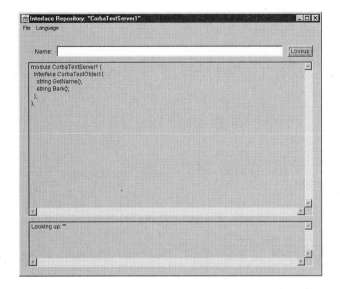

What Is the Implementation Repository?

The Implementation Repository is used to store information about servers so that the Smart Agent can automatically start a server. In particular, the Implementation Repository contains information on the name of servers and on the path to the directory where their executables can be found.

When a CORBA service referred to as the OAD (Object Activation Daemon) needs to start a server, OAD can locate the server by looking it up in the Implementation Repository and then executing the file listed there. When you register a DCOM server, you are asking the Windows Registry to play more or less the same role that the Implementation Repository plays in CORBA development. In other words, the Implementation Repository is just a place to store the path and executable name for a server, along with some other related information. The Smart Agent asks the OAD to start the server if the server is not running and if it is registered in the Implementation Repository. The OAD can also be used to restart a server that has crashed.

By default, you can find the actual files used to define the implementation repository in the VBroker\Adm directory or in a subdirectory immediately beneath it. You can use an environment variable to point to the VBroker\Adm directory.

Simple CORBA Objects

It is now time to dig into the code for creating a CORBA application. C++Builder Enterprise makes this process very simple. A CORBA project is usually started by writing one or more IDL files. The IDL describes the CORBA objects to be created and implemented within the project. On most CORBA projects, a good deal of time is spent up front identifying distributed objects and defining them into IDL definitions.

The Server

Here you can see exactly how to create a simple CORBA application that contains no database tools:

1. Choose File, New. Turn to the multitier page, select CORBA Server and click OK. Choose the Windows Application radio button and select the Add New IDL File checkbox. Press the OK button. This creates a windowed CORBA server application and a new IDL file. Save the application into its own directory. I like to create one directory named after the server application I want to create; beneath that directory I create two additional subdirectories, one named `Client` and the second named `Server`. Needless to say, I usually put the client application in the `Client` directory and server application in the `Server` directory.

2. Add the following text to the IDL file and save it:

```
module CorbaTestServer1 {
  interface CorbaTestObject {
    string GetName();
    string Bark();
  };
};
```

3. Choose File, New. Turn to the multitier page and select CORBA Object Implementation. This starts the IDL2CPP compiler on the IDL file and displays the Corba Object Implementation Wizard. Select CorbaTestServer1::CorbaTestObject from the Interface Name drop-down listbox. The `Unit Name`, `Class Name`, and `Object Name` fields are automatically filled in. Make sure the In WinMain() checkbox is selected and press the OK button. The stub and skeleton file are added to your project. An object implementation .cpp file is also add to the project. This is where the code is added and gives your object some functionality.

4. Fill in the implementation for the `GetName()` method so that it returns a string containing the name of your object. The implementation should be in a file called `CorbaTestObjectServer.cpp`. You can also add code to the `Bark()` method to give it functionality. In the sample code each of these methods tracks the number of times they are called and displays the count on the server's main form.

5. Save your work. Run the application once. At this stage, the application must be running first; otherwise, your client won't be able to access it.

The CORBA Object Implementation Wizard is shown in Figure 22.5.

FIGURE 22.5

The CORBA Object Implementation Wizard.

If you are working in Windows NT, you will be able to run both the client and server application from the C++Builder IDE. If you are working in Windows 9x, you will have to run the server from the Windows Explorer and the client from inside the IDE, or vice versa.

In Listings 22.1 through 22.5, you will find the code for the Simple CORBA server object you created in the steps listed previously. You can find this program in the `CorbaTest1` directory on the CD-ROM that comes with this book. The server project is called `CorbaTestServer1.bpr`. Following is a list of the files contained in the example project and a description of what they are used for:

Filename	Description
`Main.cpp`	Servers main form.
`CorbaTestObjectServer.cpp`	Implementation of the CORBA object. This is where you make the CORBA object do something.
`CorbaTestServer1.cpp`	Contains `WinMain()` code, which is executed on startup.
`CorbaTestServer1.idl`	IDL file.
`CorbaTestServer1_c.cpp`	Stub file used when creating CORBA clients, this file is automatically generated by the IDL2CPP compiler.
`CorbaTestServer1_s.cpp`	Skeleton file used when creating CORBA servers, this file is automatically generated by the IDL2CPP compiler.

LISTING 22.1   THE MAIN FORM FOR A SIMPLE CORBA OBJECT SERVER

```cpp
//////////////////////////////////////////
// Purpose: Main.cpp is the main form file for the project
// Project: CorbaTestServer1.bpr
//
//-------------------------------------------------------------------
#include <vcl.h>
#pragma hdrstop

#include "Main.h"
//-------------------------------------------------------------------
#pragma package(smart_init)
#pragma resource "*.dfm"
/*-----------------------------------------------------------------
   Each time a server method is invoked, it calls the main form a which
   displays how many calls have been made.
   ---------------------------------------------------------------*/
TForm1 *Form1;
//-------------------------------------------------------------------
__fastcall TForm1::TForm1(TComponent* Owner)
        : TForm(Owner)
{
  //Initialize counts
  barkCount=0;
  nameCount=0;
}
//-------------------------------------------------------------------
void TForm1::UpdateNameCount()
{
  nameCount++;
  UpdateCountDisplay();
}
//-------------------------------------------------------------------
void TForm1::UpdateBarkCount()
{
  barkCount++;
  UpdateCountDisplay();
}
//-------------------------------------------------------------------
---
void TForm1::UpdateCountDisplay()
{
  Panel1->Caption="BarkCount=" + IntToStr(barkCount) + " NameCount="+
    IntToStr(nameCount);
}
//-------------------------------------------------------------------
```

LISTING 22.2   THE SIMPLE CORBA OBJECT SERVER'S WinMain()

```cpp
/////////////////////////////////////
// Purpose: Show simple CORBA server.
// Project: CorbaTestServer.dpr
//
//-------------------------------------------------------------------------
#include <vcl.h>
#pragma hdrstop
#include "CorbaTestObjectServer.h"

#include <corba.h>
USERES("CorbaTestServer1.res");
USEIDL("CorbaTestServer1.idl");
USEFORM("Main.cpp", Form1);
USEUNIT("CorbaTestServer1_c.cpp");
USEUNIT("CorbaTestServer1_s.cpp");
/* CorbaTestServer1.idl: CORBAIdlFile */
USEUNIT("CorbaTestObjectServer.cpp");
//-------------------------------------------------------------------------
WINAPI WinMain(HINSTANCE, HINSTANCE, LPSTR, int)
{
        try
        {
          Application->Initialize();
          // Initialize the ORB and BOA
          CORBA::ORB_var orb = CORBA::ORB_init(__argc, __argv);
          CORBA::BOA_var boa = orb->BOA_init(__argc, __argv);
          CorbaTestObjectImpl
          corbaTestObject_CorbaTestObjectObject("CorbaTestObjectObject");
          boa->obj_is_ready(&corbaTestObject_CorbaTestObjectObject);
          Application->CreateForm(__classid(TForm1), &Form1);
          Application->Run();
        }
        catch (Exception &exception)
        {
          Application->ShowException(&exception);
        }
        return 0;
}
//-------------------------------------------------------------------------
```

22

CORBA

LISTING 22.3   THE IMPLEMENTATION FOR A CORBA OBJECT

```
/////////////////////////////////////
// Purpose: Show simple CORBA server.
// Project: CorbaTestServer.bpr
//
//------------------------------------------------------------------
#include <vcl.h>
#pragma hdrstop

#include <corba.h>
#include "CorbaTestObjectServer.h"
#include "main.h"


//------------------------------------------------------------------
#pragma package(smart_init)


/*------------------------------------------------------------------
  This simple CORBA server will track the number of client method calls.
  Other than that, it's just meant to be a minimal example to show how
  to create a CORBA server.

  It has a dog-oriented theme because the main form has a picture of a
  dog on it.
  -----------------------------------------------------------------*/

CorbaTestObjectImpl::CorbaTestObjectImpl(const char *object_name):
        _sk_CorbaTestServer1::_sk_CorbaTestObject(object_name)
{
}

char* CorbaTestObjectImpl::Bark()
{
  Form1->UpdateBarkCount();
  AnsiString msg;
  msg="Bow Wow!";
  return CORBA::string_dup(msg.c_str());
}

char* CorbaTestObjectImpl::GetName()
{
  Form1->UpdateNameCount();
  AnsiString msg("CorbaTestObject: " + DateTimeToStr(Now()));
  return CORBA::string_dup(msg.c_str());
}
```

LISTING 22.4 THE IDL FOR A SIMPLE CORBA OBJECT

```
module CorbaTestServer1 {
  interface CorbaTestObject {
    string GetName();
    string Bark();
  };
};
```

LISTING 22.5 THE SIMPLE CORBA OBJECT'S SKELETON CorbaTestServer1_s.cpp

```
/**

***********************************************************************
*                       -- DO NOT MODIFY --                          *
*  This file is automatically generated by the VisiBroker IDL compiler. *
*  Generated code conforms to OMG's IDL-to-C++ 1.1 mapping as specified *
*  in OMG Document Number: 96-01-13                                   *
*                                                                     *
*  VisiBroker is copyrighted by Visigenic Software, Inc.              *
***********************************************************************
 */

#include <corbapch.h>
#pragma hdrstop
#include "CorbaTestServer1_s.hh"

static CORBA::MethodDescription
  __sk_CorbaTestServer1_CorbaTestObject_methods[] = {
    {"GetName", &_sk_CorbaTestServer1::_sk_CorbaTestObject::_GetName},
    {"Bark", &_sk_CorbaTestServer1::_sk_CorbaTestObject::_Bark}
};

const CORBA::TypeInfo
  _sk_CorbaTestServer1::_sk_CorbaTestObject::_skel_info(
    "CorbaTestServer1::CorbaTestObject",
    (CORBA::ULong)2,
    __sk_CorbaTestServer1_CorbaTestObject_methods);

_sk_CorbaTestServer1::_sk_CorbaTestObject::_sk_CorbaTestObject(
  const char *_obj_name) {
    _object_name(_obj_name);
}

_sk_CorbaTestServer1::_sk_CorbaTestObject::_sk_CorbaTestObject(
    const char *_serv_name,
    const CORBA::ReferenceData& _id) {
```

continues

LISTING 22.5   CONTINUED

```
    _service(_serv_name, _id);
}

void _sk_CorbaTestServer1::_sk_CorbaTestObject::___noop() {}
void _sk_CorbaTestServer1::_sk_CorbaTestObject::_GetName(
    void *_obj,
    CORBA::MarshalInBuffer &_istrm,
    CORBA::Principal_ptr _principal,
    const char *_oper,
    void *_priv_data) {
  VISistream& _vistrm = _istrm;
  CorbaTestServer1::CorbaTestObject *_impl =
    (CorbaTestServer1::CorbaTestObject *)_obj;

  CORBA::String_var _ret = _impl->GetName(
      );

  VISostream& _ostrm = *(VISostream *)
    (CORBA::MarshalOutBuffer*)_impl->_prepare_reply(_priv_data);
  _ostrm << _ret;
}

void _sk_CorbaTestServer1::_sk_CorbaTestObject::_Bark(
    void *_obj,
    CORBA::MarshalInBuffer &_istrm,
    CORBA::Principal_ptr _principal,
    const char *_oper,
    void *_priv_data) {
  VISistream& _vistrm = _istrm;
  CorbaTestServer1::CorbaTestObject *_impl =
    (CorbaTestServer1::CorbaTestObject *)_obj;

  CORBA::String_var _ret = _impl->Bark(
      );

  VISostream& _ostrm = *(VISostream *)
    (CORBA::MarshalOutBuffer*)_impl->_prepare_reply(_priv_data);
  _ostrm << _ret;
}
```

To run this program, you must start OSAgent.exe on Windows 9x, or start the Smart
Agent service on Windows NT. After doing that, you should be able to successfully compile and run the program.

This server has no interface to speak of. I put a picture of a dog on the front of its form, but that is only a conceit and adds no functionality to the program. For all intents and purposes, the server is useless without a client. Therefore, you build a client application before this application is discussed in any depth.

The Client

It is now time to see how to create a client application that can access the CORBA server. This chore is not particularly difficult. The IDL2CPP compiler generates client stubs, which makes the creation of CORBA clients fairly straightforward. This, coupled with the CORBA Client Wizard, greatly simplifies the client development.

Complete the following steps to build your client:

1. Choose File, New. Turn to the multitier page and select CORBA Client. Select the Windows Application radio button and uncheck the BOA Init check box. Because you are writing a client, you don't need a BOA. Press the Add button and select the same IDL file that was created previously for the Simple Corba Server. Press the OK button.

2. Choose Edit, Use CORBA Object from the main menu. Select the `CorbaTestServer1::CorbaTestObject` interface from the Interface Name drop-down box. Press the OK button.

3. Write code to call methods off the CORBA object instance. The Use Corba Object Wizard makes this easy by creating a property on the form that holds the object reference. Make the method calls to that object.

4. Make sure that the Smart Agent is started and then launch your server and client application. Call into the methods defined on your server. (Remember that unless you are using OAD, you must explicitly start your server. It won't start automatically.)

The Use CORBA Object Wizard is shown in Figure 22.6.

In Listings 22.6 through 22.9 you find the source to a simple CORBA client application. Take a look at the code and then read on to learn some of the details of how this application is put together.

FIGURE 22.6

*The Use CORBA
Object Wizard.*

LISTING 22.6   THE MAIN FORM FOR A SIMPLE CORBA CLIENT

```
/////////////////////////////////////
// Purpose: Client to the CorbaTestServer1 server
// Project: CorbaTestClient.dpr
//
//-----------------------------------------------------------------------
#include <vcl.h>
#pragma hdrstop

#include <corba.h>
#include "MainClient.h"
//-----------------------------------------------------------------------
#pragma package(smart_init)
#pragma resource "*.dfm"
TForm1 *Form1;
//-----------------------------------------------------------------------
__fastcall TForm1::TForm1(TComponent* Owner)
        : TForm(Owner)
{
}
//-----------------------------------------------------------------------


CorbaTestServer1::CorbaTestObject_ptr __fastcall
  TForm1::GetcorbaTestObject(void)
{
        if (FcorbaTestObject == NULL)
        {
                FcorbaTestObject =
                    CorbaTestServer1::CorbaTestObject::_bind();
        }
```

```
          return FcorbaTestObject;
}

void __fastcall
  TForm1::SetcorbaTestObject(CorbaTestServer1::CorbaTestObject_ptr _ptr)
{
        FcorbaTestObject = _ptr;
}
void __fastcall TForm1::BitBtn1Click(TObject *Sender)
{
  Edit1->Text=corbaTestObject->Bark();
}
//-----------------------------------------------------------------
void __fastcall TForm1::BitBtn2Click(TObject *Sender)
{
  Edit1->Text=corbaTestObject->GetName();
}
//-----------------------------------------------------------------
```

LISTING 22.7 THE HEADER FILE FOR A SIMPLE CORBA CLIENT'S MAIN FORM

```
//-----------------------------------------------------------------
#ifndef MainClientH
#define MainClientH
//-----------------------------------------------------------------
#include <Classes.hpp>
#include <Controls.hpp>
#include <StdCtrls.hpp>
#include <Forms.hpp>
#include <Buttons.hpp>
#include "CorbaTestServer1_c.hh"
//-----------------------------------------------------------------
class TForm1 : public TForm
{
__published:   // IDE-managed Components
    TEdit *Edit1;
    TBitBtn *BitBtn1;
    TBitBtn *BitBtn2;
    void __fastcall BitBtn1Click(TObject *Sender);
    void __fastcall BitBtn2Click(TObject *Sender);
private:        // User declarations
    CorbaTestServer1::CorbaTestObject_ptr __fastcall
      GetcorbaTestObject();
```

continues

LISTING 22.7   CONTINUED

```
    CorbaTestServer1::CorbaTestObject_var FcorbaTestObject;
    void __fastcall
      SetcorbaTestObject(CorbaTestServer1::CorbaTestObject_ptr _ptr);
public:          // User declarations
    __fastcall TForm1(TComponent* Owner);
    __property CorbaTestServer1::CorbaTestObject_ptr
      corbaTestObject = {read=GetcorbaTestObject,
        write=SetcorbaTestObject};
};
//-------------------------------------------------------------
extern PACKAGE TForm1 *Form1;
//-------------------------------------------------------------
#endif
```

LISTING 22.8   THE WinMain() FOR A SIMPLE **CORBA** CLIENT

```
//-------------------------------------------------------------
#include <vcl.h>
#pragma hdrstop
#include <corba.h>
USERES("CorbaTestClient.res");
USEFORM("MainClient.cpp", Form1);
USEIDL("..\Server\CorbaTestServer1.idl");
USEUNIT("..\Server\CorbaTestServer1_c.cpp");
USEUNIT("..\Server\CorbaTestServer1_s.cpp");
//-------------------------------------------------------------
WINAPI WinMain(HINSTANCE, HINSTANCE, LPSTR, int)
{
        try
        {
                Application->Initialize();
                // Initialize the ORB
                CORBA::ORB_var orb = CORBA::ORB_init(__argc, __argv);
                Application->CreateForm(__classid(TForm1), &Form1);
                Application->Run();
        }
        catch (Exception &exception)
        {
                Application->ShowException(&exception);
        }
        return 0;
}
//-------------------------------------------------------------
```

LISTING 22.9   THE SIMPLE CORBA CLIENT STUB

```
/**

*************************************************************************
*                                                                       *
*                    -- DO NOT MODIFY --                                *
*  This file is automatically generated by the VisiBroker IDL compiler. *
*  Generated code conforms to OMG's IDL-to-C++ 1.1 mapping as specified *
*  in OMG Document Number: 96-01-13                                     *
*                                                                       *
*  VisiBroker is copyrighted by Visigenic Software, Inc.                *
*************************************************************************
 */

#include <corbapch.h>
#pragma hdrstop
#include "CorbaTestServer1_c.hh"

CorbaTestServer1::CorbaTestObject_ptr
  CorbaTestServer1::CorbaTestObject_var::_duplicate
    (CorbaTestServer1::CorbaTestObject_ptr _p)
{ return CorbaTestServer1::CorbaTestObject::_duplicate(_p); }
void CorbaTestServer1::CorbaTestObject_var::_release
    (CorbaTestServer1::CorbaTestObject_ptr _p) { CORBA::release(_p); }

CorbaTestServer1::CorbaTestObject_var::CorbaTestObject_var() :
  _ptr(CorbaTestServer1::CorbaTestObject::_nil()) {}

CorbaTestServer1::CorbaTestObject_var::CorbaTestObject_var
  (CorbaTestServer1::CorbaTestObject_ptr _p) : _ptr(_p) {}

CorbaTestServer1::CorbaTestObject_var::CorbaTestObject_var
  (const CorbaTestServer1::CorbaTestObject_var& _var) :
   _ptr(CorbaTestServer1::CorbaTestObject::_duplicate
    ((CorbaTestServer1::CorbaTestObject_ptr)_var)) {}

CorbaTestServer1::CorbaTestObject_var::~CorbaTestObject_var()
  { CORBA::release(_ptr); }

CorbaTestServer1::CorbaTestObject_var&
  CorbaTestServer1::CorbaTestObject_var::operator=
    (CorbaTestServer1::CorbaTestObject_ptr _p) {
  CORBA::release(_ptr);
  _ptr = _p;
  return *this;
}
```

continues

22

CORBA

LISTING 22.9   CONTINUED

```
CorbaTestServer1::CorbaTestObject_ptr&
  CorbaTestServer1::CorbaTestObject_var::out() {
  CORBA::release(_ptr);
  _ptr = (CorbaTestServer1::CorbaTestObject_ptr)NULL;
  return _ptr;
}

VISistream& operator>>(VISistream& _strm,
                       CorbaTestServer1::CorbaTestObject_var& _var) {
  _strm>> _var._ptr;
  return _strm;
}

VISostream& operator<<(VISostream& _strm,
                       const CorbaTestServer1::CorbaTestObject_var& _var) {
  _strm << _var._ptr;
  return _strm;
}

Istream& operator>>(Istream& _strm,
                    CorbaTestServer1::CorbaTestObject_var& _var) {
  VISistream _istrm(_strm);
  _istrm>> _var._ptr;
  return _strm;
}

Ostream& operator<<(Ostream& _strm,
                    const CorbaTestServer1::CorbaTestObject_var& _var) {
  _strm << (CORBA::Object_ptr)_var._ptr;
  return _strm;
}

const CORBA::TypeInfo CorbaTestServer1::CorbaTestObject::_class_info(
  "CorbaTestServer1::CorbaTestObject",
  "IDL:CorbaTestServer1/CorbaTestObject:1.0",
  NULL,
  &CorbaTestServer1::CorbaTestObject::_factory,
  NULL, 0,
  NULL, 0,
  CORBA::Object::_desc(),
  0);

VISistream& operator>>(VISistream& _strm,
                       CorbaTestServer1::CorbaTestObject_ptr& _obj) {
  CORBA::Object_var _var_obj(_obj);
  _var_obj =
    CORBA::Object::_read(_strm,
CorbaTestServer1::CorbaTestObject::_desc());
  _obj = CorbaTestServer1::CorbaTestObject::_narrow(_var_obj);
```

```
      return _strm;
}

VISostream& operator<<(VISostream& _strm,
                       const CorbaTestServer1::CorbaTestObject_ptr _obj) {
  _strm << (CORBA_Object_ptr)_obj;
  return _strm;
}


const CORBA::TypeInfo *CorbaTestServer1::CorbaTestObject::_desc()
{ return &_class_info; }

const CORBA::TypeInfo *CorbaTestServer1::CorbaTestObject::_type_info()
  const { return &_class_info; }

void *CorbaTestServer1::CorbaTestObject::_safe_narrow(
                                const CORBA::TypeInfo& _info) const {
  if ( _info == _class_info)
    return (void *)this;
  return CORBA_Object::_safe_narrow(_info);
}

CORBA::Object *CorbaTestServer1::CorbaTestObject::_factory() {
  return new CorbaTestServer1::CorbaTestObject;
}

CorbaTestServer1::CorbaTestObject_ptr
  CorbaTestServer1::CorbaTestObject::_this() {
    return CorbaTestServer1::CorbaTestObject::_duplicate(___root);
}

CorbaTestServer1::CorbaTestObject_ptr
  CorbaTestServer1::CorbaTestObject::_narrow(CORBA::Object *_obj) {
  if ( _obj == CORBA::Object::_nil() )
    return CorbaTestObject::_nil();
  else
    return CorbaTestObject::_duplicate(
      (CorbaTestObject_ptr)_obj->_safe_narrow(_class_info));
}

CorbaTestServer1::CorbaTestObject
  *CorbaTestServer1::CorbaTestObject::_bind(
    const char *_object_name,
    const char *_host_name,
    const CORBA::BindOptions *_opt,
    CORBA::ORB_ptr _orb) {
  CORBA::Object_var _obj= CORBA::Object::_bind_to_object(
      "IDL:CorbaTestServer1/CorbaTestObject:1.0",
```

continues

LISTING 22.9   CONTINUED

```
      _object_name, _host_name, _opt, _orb);
  return CorbaTestObject::_narrow(_obj);
}

char* CorbaTestServer1::CorbaTestObject::GetName(
    ) {

  char* _ret = (char*)0;
  CORBA_MarshalInBuffer_var _ibuf;
  CORBA::MarshalOutBuffer_var _obuf;

  while( 1 ) {
    _obuf = ___root->_create_request(
        "GetName",
        1,
        6507);


    try {
      _ibuf = ___root->_invoke(_obuf);
    } catch (const CORBA::TRANSIENT& ) {
      continue;
    }
    break;
  }
  VISistream& _vistrm = *(CORBA::MarshalInBuffer *)_ibuf;
  _vistrm>> _ret;
  return _ret;
}

char* CorbaTestServer1::CorbaTestObject::Bark(
    ) {

  char* _ret = (char*)0;
  CORBA_MarshalInBuffer_var _ibuf;
  CORBA::MarshalOutBuffer_var _obuf;

  while( 1 ) {
    _obuf = ___root->_create_request(
        "Bark",
        1,
        795);
```

```
  try {
    _ibuf = ___root->_invoke(_obuf);
  } catch (const CORBA::TRANSIENT& ) {
    continue;
  }
  break;
}
VISistream& _vistrm = *(CORBA::MarshalInBuffer *)_ibuf;
_vistrm>> _ret;
return _ret;
}
```

To run this extremely simple program, first compile and launch the server. Then compile and launch the client and click one of the buttons on the main form of the client. A message is retrieved from the server and shown in an edit control, as depicted in Figure 22.7.

FIGURE 22.7

The CorbaTestObject client and server programs in action.

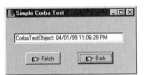

If you are using Windows NT, you can run both the server and the client from inside the IDE. To do so, choose Project, Build All; select View, Project Manager. Focus the server application and then run it. Now use the Project Manager to focus the client application and run it. The key to this process is making sure that both applications are fully built before running either of them. Building the applications first is necessary because building or making a C++Builder project is impossible while one or more applications are being run from the IDE.

Understanding the Server

The server application is very simple. The first thing to look at is the server registration code. In this example the registration occurs in the `WinMain()` method. The code is exactly like the psuedocode you saw earlier. Here is the C++Builder–generated code from the `CorbaTestServer1.cpp` file that creates a reference to the ORB and registers the simple CORBA object:

```
CORBA::ORB_var orb = CORBA::ORB_init(__argc, __argv);
CORBA::BOA_var boa = orb->BOA_init(__argc, __argv);
MyCorbaObjectImpl myCorbaObject_CorbaObjectObject("CorbaObjectObject");
boa->obj_is_ready(&myCorbaObject_CorbaObjectObject);
boa->impl_is_ready();
```

First you create a reference to the ORB, passing any command line arguments that might have been passed to the server for use in configuration of the ORB. A reference to the BOA is retrieved next. The actual object to be exposed by the server is then instantiated. You then register the newly created object with the ORB through the BOA. Lastly, call the BOA's `impl_is_ready`, which enters the server into a loop waiting to handle client requests.

The server object is implemented in `CorbaTestObjectServer.cpp`. The server implements the skeleton `_sk_CorbaTestServer1::_sk_CorbaTestObject`, which was generated by the IDL2CPP compiler. All you need to do is fill in the code in the server methods. These methods are automatically called when the client invokes the methods. The C++Builder Use CORBA Object Wizard generates the empty methods and you just fill in the functionality. Here is the `GetName()` method implementation:

```
char* CorbaTestObjectImpl::GetName()
{
  Form1->UpdateNameCount();
  AnsiString msg("CorbaTestObject: " + DateTimeToStr(Now()));
  return CORBA::string_dup(msg.c_str());
}
```

The last line is the important one. After you determine which string should be sent back to the client, it must be duplicated in order to be sent back. Because strings in C++ are usually `char *`, they are really pointers to memory. In order for the string to be returned to the client, a copy of it must be made. For `char *` string copying, the method `CORBA::string_dup` is included.

The server code is fairly straightforward. The skeleton discussion is picked up in more detail later.

Understanding the Client

The client application consists of a simple form. After launching the application, you can click a button on the form. If the server and the Smart Agent are running, the click connects you with the server and allows you to call the `GetName()` method. The value returned from the `GetName()` method is shown in a message box.

What makes the client simple is the `corbaTestObject` property that was generated by the Use CORBA Object Wizard. The code connects to the CORBA server and gets a reference to the `CorbaTestObject` object the first time this property is accessed. The property code is shown here:

```
CorbaTestServer1::CorbaTestObject_ptr __fastcall
  TForm1::GetcorbaTestObject(void)
{
        if (FcorbaTestObject == NULL)
        {
                FcorbaTestObject =
                    CorbaTestServer1::CorbaTestObject::_bind();
        }
        return FcorbaTestObject;
}

void __fastcall
  TForm1::SetcorbaTestObject(CorbaTestServer1::CorbaTestObject_ptr _ptr)
{
        FcorbaTestObject = _ptr;
}
```

The bind method comes from the C++ code in the client stub:

```
CorbaTestServer1::CorbaTestObject
  *CorbaTestServer1::CorbaTestObject::_bind(
    const char *_object_name,
    const char *_host_name,
    const CORBA::BindOptions *_opt,
    CORBA::ORB_ptr _orb) {
  CORBA::Object_var _obj= CORBA::Object::_bind_to_object(
      "IDL:CorbaTestServer1/CorbaTestObject:1.0",
      _object_name, _host_name, _opt, _orb);
  return CorbaTestObject::_narrow(_obj);
}
```

This code is auto-generated by the IDLCPP compiler. Its purpose is to bind you to an instance of your server. Note that this is a *static method*, which means you can call it without first creating an instance of the `CorbaTestObject` object.

Because the stub code is auto-generated, you should never have to modify it. The stub takes care of the details of invoking calls on the CORBA server and retrieving results. It is a good idea to study the stub and skeleton code when you start developing CORBA applications to get a feel for what goes on under the covers.

One significant part of the code shown here is the bit that specifies the Factory Repository ID: `IDL:CorbaTestServer1/CorbaTestObject:1.0`. This string uniquely identifies the object that implements the `CorbaTestObject` interface.

22

CORBA

The result of the bind operation is the fruit of your endeavor—the interface itself. After you have an instance of the CORBA object, you are then free to call its methods. For instance, you could write either of the following two lines:

```
Edit1->Text=corbaTestObject->GetName();
```

```
Edit1->Text=corbaTestObject->Bark();
```

Remember that even simple examples such as this capture the very essence of this technology. The whole point here is to make function calls between methods on separate machines. This technology makes porous the barrier that separates one machine from another, one binary entity from another. The goal is to achieve a technology that flows back and forth across the network, that connects the machines on the Internet, and the people who run them, each to each.

If you want to run this program so that it works across the network, just keep the OSAgent and server running somewhere on the LAN and copy your client out to another machine that has an ORB installed on it; now run the client. It will find the server automatically and connect to it. I have better luck running the server on NT than I do running the server on Windows 9x. The client can be on either a Windows 9x machine or on an NT machine.

Understanding the CORBA Stub

Taking a moment to consider the proxies that play such a key role in binding a client to its server is worthwhile. This code is also generated for you automatically by IDL2CPP, but taking a few moments to penetrate its mysteries will behoove you.

The following is an actual client stub method from the `CorbaTestServer1_c.cpp` file rather than the pseudocode you saw earlier:

```
char* CorbaTestServer1::CorbaTestObject::GetName(
    ) {

  char* _ret = (char*)0;
  CORBA_MarshalInBuffer_var _ibuf;
  CORBA::MarshalOutBuffer_var _obuf;

  while( 1 ) {
    _obuf = ___root->_create_request(
        "GetName",
        1,
        6507);


    try {
      _ibuf = ___root->_invoke(_obuf);
```

```
    } catch (const CORBA::TRANSIENT& ) {
      continue;
    }
    break;
  }
  VISistream& _vistrm = *(CORBA::MarshalInBuffer *)_ibuf;
  _vistrm>> _ret;
  return _ret;
}
```

As you recall, this is a really faux method designed to fool the client into thinking it is talking directly to the server, as if the server were merely another object inside the client.

The ___root is of type `CorbaTestObject_ptr`, which is a reference to the `CorbaTestObject`. The `root->_create_request` method binds the name of the function you want to call in a variable of type `CORBA::MarshalOutBuffer_var`, which can be sent across the network. After the package is constructed, you call `_invoke` to send the message to the server and to retrieve a response from that same server. The `_ibuf` variable, of type `CORBA_MarshalInBuffer_var`, contains the response. The buffer contents can then be converted to the proper type and you can taste the fruits of your labors.

As you can see, the calls inside the client stub are not difficult to understand. This elegant system was designed to speed your messages back and forth across the network. You can create your own stubs if you prefer, but letting IDL2CPP do the job for you is much simpler.

Understanding the CORBA Skeleton

The skeleton is no more complicated than the stub. Remember that its purpose is simply to receive the message sent by the stub's call to `_invoke`. After it receives the message, it calls the real `GetName()` method and then bundles up the result and whisks it back to the client:

```
void _sk_CorbaTestServer1::_sk_CorbaTestObject::_GetName(
    void *_obj,
    CORBA::MarshalInBuffer &_istrm,
    CORBA::Principal_ptr _principal,
    const char *_oper,
    void *_priv_data) {
  VISistream& _vistrm = _istrm;
  CorbaTestServer1::CorbaTestObject *_impl =
    (CorbaTestServer1::CorbaTestObject *)_obj;

  CORBA::String_var _ret = _impl->GetName(
      );

  VISostream& _ostrm = *(VISostream *)
```

```
    (CORBA::MarshalOutBuffer*)_impl->_prepare_reply(_priv_data);
  _ostrm << _ret;
}
```

The first step is to call GetName off the internal _obj variable that is passed into the method. _obj is merely a variable pointing to your object's real interface. Because you are now inside the server itself, this is a real pointer to the actual object you created; this call executes your code and returns the value you assign to the function result.

The next step is to bundle up the function result and send it back to the client. You do so through a call to prepare_reply and placing the result in a VISostream. As you can see, the skeleton is very simple but elegant. It makes interaction with the client extremely easy.

Simple CORBA Dynamic Project

The next thing to explore is how to call a CORBA server using dynamic invocation. This technology closely parallels calling a COM server off a variant. In particular, CORBA has a type called Any, which plays roughly the same role in CORBA that a variant plays in COM. In other words, this CORBA technology is like the COM technology shown in earlier chapters.

Dynamic invocation is used to connect directly to a server and start calling its methods dynamically. You will have success at run time if you call them correctly. If you make a mistake, CORBA will tell you that you have a parameter mismatch at run time or that you tried to call a method that does not exist. Checking your calls at compile time is impossible under such circumstances.

To make a dynamic call, you have to load the IDL for your server into an Interface Repository. As explained previously, you can start the Interface Repository by using the Start Interface Repository dialog from the Tools menu or manually by typing **irep MyName** at the command prompt, where irep is the name of a utility, and MyName is the name you give to a particular instance of the Interface Repository.

After you start the Interface Repository, you can use the Update IDL Repository dialog to add interfaces to the repository. In addition, you can use the Interface Repository GUI menu to browse across your hard drive and locate an IDL file. When you choose the file, the Repository reads it in and keeps a record of its contents. The ORB can then check this record when you make a dynamic call. You must load the IDL for your server in the Interface Repository, or your client application will be unable to determine what the interface looks like dynamically and thus will not be able to make calls to those objects.

The Interface Repository can also serve as a single place where you can reference the objects available on your system. If you load two or more objects into the repository, then you can save them to disk by using the program's interface. The next time you load the Interface Repository, you can then read these two interfaces back in with a single gesture by simply loading the file you saved to disk.

After you have the Interface Repository set up, you can call the methods on your server with a few lines of code. Here, for example, you can see how to call a C++ server:

```
//--------------------------------------------------------------
__fastcall TForm1::TForm1(TComponent* Owner)
        : TForm(Owner)
{
  orb = CORBA::ORB_init(__argc, __argv);
}
//--------------------------------------------------------------
void __fastcall TForm1::Button1Click(TObject *Sender)
{
  CORBA::Object_var diiObj;

  try
  {
    diiObj = orb->bind("IDL:CorbaTestServer1/CorbaTestObject:1.0");
  } catch (const CORBA::Exception& E)
  {
    ShowMessage("Error binding to client!");
    return;
  }
  CORBA::Request_var req = diiObj->_request("GetName");

  // Set result
  req->set_return_type(CORBA::_tc_string);
  req->invoke();

  //Check if call was sucessful
  if (req->env()->exception()){
    ShowMessage("Got an error!!");
    Return;
  }
  else
  {
      char * val;

      CORBA::Any& result = req->return_value();
      result>>= val;

      ShowMessage(val);
  }
}
```

You need to initialize the ORB before connecting to a remote object. This is the same line of code used in the static client except that this line has been moved from the `WinMain()` method to the form's constructor. You need a reference to the ORB so that you can make `bind` calls against it. Now focus on the `Button1Click` code. The first method binds you to the server. This call will not succeed if you do not pass in the correct Repository ID. You can usually retrieve the Repository ID from the server code or the client stub; you can also reassemble it from the bits and pieces in the Interface Repository. This chapter later tells you how you can find the Repository ID for an application using something called the VisiBroker Manager.

The `bind` call returns `CORBA::Object_var`, which is a reference to the CORBA object on the server. This call should be wrapped in a `trycatch` block to ensure that your `bind` call succeeded. The `_request` method is called on the CORBA object to get a reference to the `GetName()`. The reference is returned as a `CORBA::Request_var`. Before you can call the server method, the `Request` object needs to be informed of what type of result will be returned. This is done by calling the request object's `set_return_type` method. In this case you are expecting a string.

Now you are ready to execute the function on the server by calling the `invoke` method. The request object's `env()->exception()` method is then called to see if the invocation was successful.

As you can see, dynamic invocation is easy to use. It can help to make CORBA programming in C++Builder a relatively simple and enjoyable process. If the call is successful, the result can be retrieved from the request's `return_value` function. The result is placed in a `CORBA::Any` variable. This is then converted to the appropriate type of the return value. In this case it's converted to a string and then displayed in a dialog.

> **NOTE**
>
> The preceding example is a very simple client using dynamic invocation. In this case the method name and return type were known ahead of time. If you know this information ahead of time, it is impractical to use dynamic invocation because of the complexity of the needed code and the extra overhead of making several method calls in order to make a single method invocation on the server. The stub is preferred.

Dynamic invocation is very useful for developing generic clients who will not know what the server objects will look like. There are many methods available for object discovery through the Dynamic Invocation Interface (DII). With these methods, the client can determine method names, parameters, and return types at run time. See the *VisiBroker for C++ Programmer's Guide* for more information.

Listings 22.10 through 22.12 show how to create a simple C++ server in which the client uses dynamic binding to call the simple CORBA server created previously.

LISTING 22.10   THE CLIENT SHOWING HOW TO DYNAMICALLY CALL A CORBA OBJECT

```
/////////////////////////////////////
// Purpose: Client showing dynamic corba invocation
// Project: DynamicCorbaTestClient
//
//-----------------------------------------------------------------
#include <vcl.h>
#pragma hdrstop
#include <corba.h>

#include "MainClient.h"
//-----------------------------------------------------------------
#pragma package(smart_init)
#pragma resource "*.dfm"
TForm1 *Form1;
//-----------------------------------------------------------------
__fastcall TForm1::TForm1(TComponent* Owner)
        : TForm(Owner)
{
  orb = CORBA::ORB_init(__argc, __argv);
}
//-----------------------------------------------------------------
void __fastcall TForm1::Button1Click(TObject *Sender)
{
  CORBA::Object_var diiObj;

  try
  {
    diiObj = orb->bind("IDL:CorbaTestServer1/CorbaTestObject:1.0");
  } catch (const CORBA::Exception& E)
```

continues

LISTING 22.10   CONTINUED

```
  {
    ShowMessage("Error binding to client!");
    return;
  }
  CORBA::Request_var req = diiObj->_request("GetName");

  // Set result
  req->set_return_type(CORBA::_tc_string);
  req->invoke();

  //Check if call was sucessful
  if (req->env()->exception()){
    ShowMessage("Got an error!!");
    return;
  }
  else
  {
      char * val;

      CORBA::Any& result = req->return_value();
      result>>= val;

      ShowMessage(val);
  }
}
```

LISTING 22.11   THE HEADER FILE FOR THE DYNAMIC CLIENT

```
////////////////////////////////////
// Purpose: Client showing dynamic corba invocation
// Project: DynamicCorbaTestClient
//
//-------------------------------------------------------------
#ifndef MainClientH
#define MainClientH
//-------------------------------------------------------------
#include <Classes.hpp>
#include <Controls.hpp>
#include <StdCtrls.hpp>
#include <Forms.hpp>
#include "CorbaTestServer1_c.hh"
//-------------------------------------------------------------
class TForm1 : public TForm
{
```

```
__published:    // IDE-managed Components
        TButton *Button1;
        void __fastcall Button1Click(TObject *Sender);
private:        // User declarations
          // Initialize the ORB and BOA
          CORBA::ORB_var orb;
public:         // User declarations
        __fastcall TForm1(TComponent* Owner);
};
//--------------------------------------------------------------
extern PACKAGE TForm1 *Form1;
//--------------------------------------------------------------
#endif
```

LISTING 22.12   THE WinMain() FOR THE DYNAMIC CLIENT

```
/////////////////////////////////////////
// Purpose: Client showing dynamic corba invocation
// Project: DynamicCorbaTestClient
//
//--------------------------------------------------------------
#include <vcl.h>
#pragma hdrstop
#include <corba.h>
#include "MainClient.h"
USERES("DynamicCorbaTestClient.res");
USEFORM("MainClient.cpp", Form1);
//--------------------------------------------------------------
WINAPI WinMain(HINSTANCE, HINSTANCE, LPSTR, int)
{
        try
        {
          Application->Initialize();
          Application->CreateForm(__classid(TForm1), &Form1);
          Application->Run();
        }
        catch (Exception &exception)
        {
          Application->ShowException(&exception);
        }
        return 0;
}
//--------------------------------------------------------------
```

As usual, you should first check to make sure the OSAgent is running as a program or service; then go ahead and launch the server. When you run the client, you should be able to call the methods on the server without having the stub compiled into the client.

Working with the VisiBroker Manager and `OSFind`

Two tools can help you when working with CORBA programming. One is a VisiBroker add-on called the VisiBroker Manager. A trial version of this tool can be downloaded from the Inprise Web site. The second is a command-line utility called `OSFind`.

The VisiBroker Manager is called `VBM.exe`. Before you run it, you must first make sure the OSAgent is running, and you must load the location server, which is a separate executable that comes with the VisiBroker Manager.

The VisiBroker Manager uses a tabbed notebook metaphor. On the first page is a list of services and servers running on the current LAN. You can use this list to find a server's correct Repository ID. You can also see what other servers might be running on your system or on your LAN, as shown in Figure 22.8.

FIGURE 22.8

Browsing CORBA objects in the VisiBroker Manager.

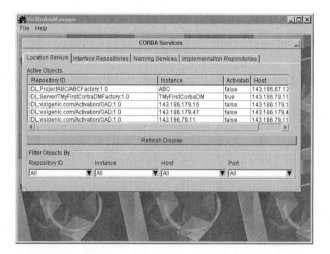

The second page of the VisiBroker Manager lets you explore any Interface Repositories that might be loaded. You can drill down in this dialog, seeing the individual methods in an interface and even checking the parameters passed to them. I use this tool primarily to be sure the IR contains the correct values for my current server. In other words, it helps me debug my CORBA servers.

You can explore the other pages in the VisiBroker Manager at your own leisure. The most important of these helps you work with the OAD, which is a service for starting servers automatically. If you don't want to use the VisiBroker Manager, you have a good built-in alternative in the command-line–based OSFind utility. To use this program, go to a command window and type **OSFIND**. The following is standard output from an OSFind session:

```
osfind: Found one agent at port 14000
HOST: ccalvertpc7

osfind: There are no OADs running on in your domain.

osfind: There are no Object Implementations registered with OADs.

osfind: Following are the list of Implementations started manually.
        HOST: PONGO

REPOSITORY ID: IDL:visigenic.com/tools/ir/RepositoryManager:1.0
    OBJECT NAME: Rep1

    REPOSITORY ID: IDL:CorbaDataTestServer2/CorbaDataObject2Factory:1.0
        OBJECT NAME: CorbaDataObject2

    REPOSITORY ID: IDL:visigenic.com/irtx/Repository:1.0
        OBJECT NAME: Rep1
```

The output shown here says the Smart Agent is running at port 14000 on PONGO. No OADs or object implementations are available. An Interface Repository named Rep1 and one object named CorbaDataObject2 are loaded.

Summary

In this chapter you looked at CORBA programming with C++Builder. You started out with the CORBA basics including the ORB, Smart Agents, and BOA. You learned about IDL and how the IDL2CPP compiler generates stubs and skeletons for use in your CORBA projects. You saw how to create simple CORBA servers and clients and learned how to handle dynamic invocation. Other subjects covered in this chapter included the VisiBroker Manager and OSFind.

In the next chapter you will see how to call C++Builder CORBA applications from Delphi and Java and how to call Delphi and Java CORBA servers from C++Builder. By the time you are through, you will have had a fairly in-depth introduction to the basics of CORBA programming.

22

CORBA

C++Builder, Java, and Delphi

by Charlie Calvert
and Dana Scott Kaufman

CHAPTER 23

In this chapter you will learn how to use CORBA to share objects among C++Builder, JBuilder, and Delphi. The chapter takes you through several examples and allows you to create servers and clients in C++Builder, JBuilder, and Delphi.

The examples shown here are simpler than those you are likely to encounter in your work. They focus, however, on the interaction between C++Builder and other languages such as Delphi Pascal and Java. This kind of multilanguage interaction is exactly what many CORBA programmers are likely to encounter.

The code in this chapter is designed to run with GUI programs produced by Delphi and JBuilder. As such, they have Delphi– and JBuilder–specific features and are not necessarily portable across a wide variety of platforms. (The Java code will port, of course, but you would need to bring your JBCL packages with you.) Furthermore, my client programs buck the trend of CORBA examples, which are usually command-line–based. My desire is to show you how to create programs that users would actually understand and be comfortable using.

I'm going to assume you have an understanding of JBuilder 2 and Delphi 4. If you need more information on JBuilder, I recommend *Sams Teach Yourself Borland JBuilder in 21 Days*, by Donald Doherty and Michelle Manning (Sams Publishing) and *JBuilder Essentials*, by Carey Jensen (Osborne/McGraw Hill). If you need information on Delphi, I recommend *Sams Teach Yourself Delphi in 21 Days*, by Kent Reisdorph (Sams Publishing).

If you have no interest in either of these environments, then the JBuilder code I am writing is still standard Java source, so I'm sure you can adopt it to work in your tool of choice. I'm going to confine all my examples to Windows applications, but there is no reason the same type of code shouldn't work from a UNIX box or on any operating system that supports CORBA and Java.

Using CORBA with C++Builder and Java

This section shows you two sets of client/server programs that link C++Builder and Java using CORBA. As you can guess, one pair of programs will be a Java client talking to a C++Builder server, and the other will be a C++Builder client talking to a Java server.

Creating a Java Client for Your C++Builder Server

The first example I want to show you calls a C++Builder server from a Java client. The server in this case is the one found in the `CorbaTest1/Server` directory from Chapter 22, "CORBA." The important part is the use of the server IDL to build the client.

To get started creating this example, you need to bring up JBuilder and start a new project. Don't add a program to it; just start the project. Now add the CORBA IDL file `CorbaTestServer1.idl` from the C++ server into your JBuilder project. Right-click the IDL file inside JBuilder and choose Make. When you do so, a set of classes designed to help you access your object is automatically generated. In particular, you will find a set of files generated in a directory called `..\myclasses\Generated Source`. The files in this directory are read-only, and they do not ship on the CD-ROM that accompanies this book. This means that you must right-click the IDL file and generate these files by running Make even if you are running the example that ships with the CD-ROM.

> **NOTE**
>
> When you right-click the IDL and choose Make, JBuilder runs `IDL2Java.exe`. This file comes with the VisiBroker, but not necessarily with the C++Builder or Delphi versions of the VisiBroker. The same files referenced in the preceding paragraph are generated for you automatically when you run `IDL2Java` yourself from the command line. In other words, you don't need JBuilder to do this exercise—you just need VisiBroker for Java and a valid Java compiler.
>
> I find the generated files extremely hard to read because of the way the code is formatted. One thing you can do to help is turn off the option that generates comments. To turn off comments, right-click the IDL file and choose IDL Properties from the menu. The code generated inside the IDE when you run `IDL2Java` is read-only. As a result, you cannot reformat it.

Listings 23.1 through 23.3 contain the source for some of the key files in this project. I do not include all the source files in these listings, but you can find them in the `JavaClient` directory on the CD-ROM accompanying this book; you can also auto-generate them.

LISTING 23.1 THE SOURCE FOR THE MAIN FRAME FROM THE JAVA PROGRAM THAT CALLS YOUR DELPHI SERVER

```java
package CorbaTestJava;

// See CorbaTestJava.html for a description of the project.

import java.awt.*;
import java.awt.event.*;
import borland.jbcl.control.*;
import borland.jbcl.layout.*;

public class Frame1 extends DecoratedFrame
{
  //Construct the frame
  BorderLayout borderLayout1 = new BorderLayout();
  XYLayout xYLayout2 = new XYLayout();
  BevelPanel bevelPanel1 = new BevelPanel();
  ButtonControl buttonControl1 = new ButtonControl();
  TextFieldControl textFieldControl1 = new TextFieldControl();

  public Frame1()
  {
    try
    {
      jbInit();
    }
    catch (Exception e)
    {
      e.printStackTrace();
    }
  }
//Component initialization

  private void jbInit() throws Exception
  {
    this.setLayout(borderLayout1);
    this.setSize(new Dimension(400, 300));
    this.setTitle("Frame Title");
    buttonControl1.setLabel("buttonControl1");
    buttonControl1.addActionListener(new java.awt.event.ActionListener()
    {
      public void actionPerformed(ActionEvent e)
      {
        buttonControl1_actionPerformed(e);
      }
    });
    textFieldControl1.setText("textFieldControl1");
    bevelPanel1.setLayout(xYLayout2);
    this.add(bevelPanel1, BorderLayout.CENTER);
    bevelPanel1.add(buttonControl1,
```

```
→new XYConstraints(117, 125, 152, 76));
    bevelPanel1.add(textFieldControl1,
    →new XYConstraints(84, 32, 209, 26));
  }


/***********************************************************************
 *  Attach to the orb.
 *  Get a copy of the CorbaTestObject.
 *  Call the methods of your object.
 ***********************************************************************/
  void buttonControl1_actionPerformed(ActionEvent e)
  {
    String[] args = {};

    org.omg.CORBA.ORB orb = org.omg.CORBA.ORB.init(args,null);

    CorbaTestServer1.CorbaTestObject TestObject =
      CorbaTestServer1.CorbaTestObjectHelper.bind(orb,
        "");

    String AName = TestObject.GetName();

    textFieldControl1.setText(AName);
  }
}
```

LISTING 23.2 THE SOURCE TO THE AUTOMATICALLY GENERATED JAVA DEFINITION FOR YOUR INTERFACE: CORBATESTOBJECT.JAVA

```
package CorbaTestServer1;
public interface CorbaTestObject extends org.omg.CORBA.Object {
  public java.lang.String GetName();
  public java.lang.String Bark();
}
```

LISTING 23.3 THE SOURCE TO THE AUTOMATICALLY GENERATED JAVA DEFINITION FOR THE CORBATESTOBJECT HELPER CLASS

```
package CorbaTestServer1;
abstract public class CorbaTestObjectHelper {
  public static  CorbaTestServer1.CorbaTestObject
    narrow(org.omg.CORBA.Object object) {
    return narrow(object, false);
  }
  private static
    CorbaTestServer1.CorbaTestObject
```

continues

LISTING 23.3   CONTINUED

```
    narrow(org.omg.CORBA.Object object, boolean is_a) {
  if(object == null) {
    return null;
  }
  if(object instanceof CorbaTestServer1.CorbaTestObject) {
    return (CorbaTestServer1.CorbaTestObject) object;
  }
  if(is_a || object._is_a(id())) {
    CorbaTestServer1._st_CorbaTestObject result =
      (CorbaTestServer1._st_CorbaTestObject)new
        CorbaTestServer1._st_CorbaTestObject();
    ((org.omg.CORBA.portable.ObjectImpl) result)._set_delegate
      (((org.omg.CORBA.portable.ObjectImpl) object)._get_delegate());
    ((org.omg.CORBA.portable.ObjectImpl) result._this())._set_delegate
      (((org.omg.CORBA.portable.ObjectImpl) object)._get_delegate());
    return (CorbaTestServer1.CorbaTestObject) result._this();
  }
  return null;
}
public static CorbaTestServer1.CorbaTestObject
  bind(org.omg.CORBA.ORB orb) {
  return bind(orb, null, null, null);
}
public static CorbaTestServer1.CorbaTestObject
  bind(org.omg.CORBA.ORB orb, java.lang.String name) {
  return bind(orb, name, null, null);
}
public static CorbaTestServer1.CorbaTestObject
  bind(org.omg.CORBA.ORB orb, java.lang.String name,
      java.lang.String host,
        org.omg.CORBA.BindOptions options) {
  return narrow(orb.bind(id(), name, host, options), true);
}
private static org.omg.CORBA.ORB _orb() {
  return org.omg.CORBA.ORB.init();
}
public static CorbaTestServer1.CorbaTestObject
  read(org.omg.CORBA.portable.InputStream _input) {
  return CorbaTestServer1.CorbaTestObjectHelper.narrow(_
    input.read_Object(), true);
}
public static void write(org.omg.CORBA.portable.OutputStream _output,
                         CorbaTestServer1.CorbaTestObject value) {
  _output.write_Object(value);
}
public static void insert(org.omg.CORBA.Any any,
                          CorbaTestServer1.CorbaTestObject value) {
```

```
    org.omg.CORBA.portable.OutputStream output =
      any.create_output_stream();
    write(output, value);
    any.read_value(output.create_input_stream(), type());
  }
  public static CorbaTestServer1.CorbaTestObject
    extract(org.omg.CORBA.Any any) {
    if(!any.type().equal(type())) {
      throw new org.omg.CORBA.BAD_TYPECODE();
    }
    return read(any.create_input_stream());
  }
  private static org.omg.CORBA.TypeCode _type;
  public static org.omg.CORBA.TypeCode type() {
    if(_type == null) {
      _type = _orb().create_interface_tc(id(), "CorbaTestObject");
    }
    return _type;
  }
  public static java.lang.String id() {
    return "IDL:CorbaTestServer1/CorbaTestObject:1.0";
  }
}
```

You should make sure that you have launched your C++Builder server before you run this program. If you are running on Windows NT, make sure that the Smart Agent service is running. If you are running on Windows 95/98, make sure that OSAGENT.exe is running.

Run the Java client application and click the button on the form. The server will be contacted; a string is returned and displayed in the client's text control, as shown in Figure 23.1.

FIGURE 23.1

The Java client application retrieves a string from the barking C++Builder dog server.

You don't need to understand all the code I have shown here, though much of it is very simple. For instance, Listings 23.2 and 23.3 are the auto-generated interfaces to the CorbaTestObject. Here, for instance, is the CorbaTestObject interface:

```
package CorbaTestServer1;

public interface ICorbaTestObject extends org.omg.CORBA.Object
{
  public java.lang.String GetName();
  public java.lang.String Bark();
}
```

The first line states that this is a package. A *package* is the Java equivalent of a unit. The next line declares the interface for the object, just like an interface declaration in Delphi. The last two lines declare the methods supported by the interface, along with their function return types. In this case, both methods return a string.

As you can see, mixing languages and CORBA is very easy. Because this translation would be impossible without the IDL, the code shown here should help drive home the key role that IDL plays in this technology.

Implementing the Java Client

After you have generated the Java helper classes produced by IDL2Java, the next step is to create a client program that can converse with your server. To do so, choose File, New from the JBuilder menu and create a new application. Drop a button and a textFieldControl control on your new frame and then associate the following code with the button click:

```
void buttonControl1_actionPerformed(ActionEvent e)
{
String[] args = {};

    org.omg.CORBA.ORB orb = org.omg.CORBA.ORB.init(args,null);

    CorbaTestServer1.CorbaTestObject TestObject =
      CorbaTestServer1.CorbaTestObjectHelper.bind(orb,
        "");

    String AName = TestObject.GetName();

    textFieldControl1.setText(AName);
}
```

This code first ensures that the ORB is loaded. It then creates an instance of the CorbaTestObject object by calling a method in the

CorbaTestObjectHelper.java file. CorbaTestObjectHelper.java was auto-generated when you right-clicked the IDL file and chose Make; it was also auto-generated when you ran IDL2Java from the command line.

After you have an instance of CorbaTestObject, you are set up and can begin calling C++Builder methods from inside a Java program to your heart's content.

The code on the button response method calls the bind method in the auto-generated CorbaTestObjectHelper. The relevant code in that auto-generated file looks like this:

```
public static CorbaTestServer1.CorbaTestObject bind(org.omg.CORBA.ORB orb,
➥ java.lang.String name) {
    return bind(orb, name, null, null);
  }
```

This example is one of several overloaded bind methods, each distinguished by the parameters it takes. For instance, this one takes two parameters and sets the remaining parameters of the real bind method to null. The other versions of the bind method take more or fewer parameters and set some corresponding number of the parameters to null.

When you call bind, the code you use looks like this:

```
org.omg.CORBA.ORB orb = org.omg.CORBA.ORB.init(args,null);

    CorbaTestServer1.CorbaTestObject TestObject =
      CorbaTestServer1.CorbaTestObjectHelper.bind(orb,
        " CorbaTestObjectObject");
```

The first line initializes the ORB and the second line passes in the ORB to the bind method. You also pass in the name of the object to which you want to connect. You can find this name in the C++Builder server when you create the CORBA object's implementation, in the parameter passed to the CorbaTestObjectImpl constructor:

```
WINAPI WinMain(HINSTANCE, HINSTANCE, LPSTR, int)
{
        try
        {
                Application->Initialize();
                // Initialize the ORB and BOA
                CORBA::ORB_var orb = CORBA::ORB_init(__argc, __argv);
                CORBA::BOA_var boa = orb->BOA_init(__argc, __argv);
                CorbaTestObjectImpl corbaTestObject_CorbaTestObjectObject
➥("CorbaTestObjectObject");
                boa>obj_is_ready(&corbaTestObject_CorbaTestObjectObject);
                Application->CreateForm(__classid(TForm1), &Form1);
                Application->Run();
        }
        catch (Exception &exception)
```

```
        {
                Application->ShowException(&exception);
        }
        return 0;
}
```

After you've written the few lines discussed here, you can run the Smart Agent, start the C++Builder server, and call it with this C++Builder program. This system will work equally well if all the programs are on one machine or if they are spread out across a LAN.

> **NOTE**
>
> Consult the VisiBroker documentation when your CORBA objects are on differ-ent domains (subnets) because they won't work out-of-the-box in that state; they will need some additional configuration. You may want to test that config-uration with some of the sample CORBA objects supplied with the product before attempting to work with programs you develop yourself.
>
> If you are very new to working with networks, don't let this note confuse you. For instance, you can ignore this note if you are working on a simple Windows network at home. It applies only to people who have complex network setups.

Writing this code is quite simple, though I do find the numerous files produced by IDL2Java a bit confusing. However, the level of complexity is relatively mild, and you should soon be able to start cranking out programs of this type in fairly short order.

Calling a Java Server from C++Builder

The technique involved in calling a Java server is exactly what you saw in the preceding chapter when working with a C++Builder server. The Java sample server used in this section is found in the Chap23/JavaServer directory. Beneath that directory you will find a directory called BCBClient; it holds the client program that calls the Java server.

This is a C++Builder book, but I talk briefly here about building a server in Java. The code for the key modules in the Java server appears in Listings 23.4 through 23.6. Listings 23.7 and 23.8 show the C++Builder client that talks to the server.

LISTING 23.4   THE IDL THAT DEFINES THE INTERFACE FOR THE OBJECT SUPPORTED BY THE
JAVA SERVER

```
module BCBCORBA
{
  interface BCBServer
  {
    string GetName();
  };
};
```

LISTING 23.5   THE CODE FOR THE INTERFACE OF THE OBJECT IN THE JAVA SERVER

```
package JavaServer;

public class BCBServer extends BCBCORBA._BCBServerImplBase
{
  String FName;

  public BCBServer(java.lang.String name)
  {
    super(name);
    FName = name + " calling from Java";
  }

  public BCBServer()
  {
    super();
    FName = "BCBServer calling from Java";
  }

  public java.lang.String GetName()
  {
    return FName;
  }
}
```

LISTING 23.6   THE CODE THAT BINDS THE JAVA SERVER TO THE ORB

```
package JavaServer;

import java.util.*;

public class JavaBCBServer {
```

continues

LISTING 23.6   CONTINUED

```
  public static void main(String[] args) {
    try {
      org.omg.CORBA.ORB orb = org.omg.CORBA.ORB.init();
      org.omg.CORBA.BOA boa = orb.BOA_init();
      BCBCORBA.BCBServer implObject = new BCBServer("BCBServer");
      boa.obj_is_ready(implObject);
      System.out.println(implObject+ " is ready.");
      boa.impl_is_ready();
    }
    catch (Exception e) {
      e.printStackTrace();
    }
  }
}
```

LISTING 23.7   THE C++BUILDER CLIENT WINMAIN() THAT CALLS THE SERVER

```
//-------------------------------------------------------------------
#include <vcl.h>
#pragma hdrstop
#include <corba.h>
USERES("BCBClient.res");
USEFORM("MainClient.cpp", Form1);
USEIDL("JavaServerForBCB.idl");
USEUNIT("JavaServerForBCB_c.cpp");
USEUNIT("JavaServerForBCB_s.cpp");
//-------------------------------------------------------------------
WINAPI WinMain(HINSTANCE, HINSTANCE, LPSTR, int)
{
        try
        {
                Application->Initialize();
                // Initialize the ORB
                CORBA::ORB_var orb = CORBA::ORB_init(__argc, __argv);
                Application->CreateForm(__classid(TForm1), &Form1);
                Application->Run();
        }
        catch (Exception &exception)
        {
                Application->ShowException(&exception);
        }
        return 0;
}
//-------------------------------------------------------------------
```

LISTING 23.8 THE C++BUILDER CLIENT FORM THAT CALLS THE SERVER

```
//--------------------------------------------------------------
#include <vcl.h>
#pragma hdrstop

#include <corba.h>
#include "MainClient.h"
//--------------------------------------------------------------
#pragma package(smart_init)
#pragma resource "*.dfm"
TForm1 *Form1;
//--------------------------------------------------------------
__fastcall TForm1::TForm1(TComponent* Owner)
        : TForm(Owner)
{
}
//--------------------------------------------------------------

BCBCORBA::BCBServer_ptr __fastcall TForm1::GetbCBServer(void)
{
        if (FbCBServer == NULL)
        {
                FbCBServer = BCBCORBA::BCBServer::_bind();
        }
        return FbCBServer;
}

void __fastcall TForm1::SetbCBServer(BCBCORBA::BCBServer_ptr _ptr)
{
        FbCBServer = _ptr;
}
void __fastcall TForm1::Button1Click(TObject *Sender)
{
  Edit1->Text = bCBServer->GetName();
}
//--------------------------------------------------------------
```

The Java server shows up in a simple command-line window. It contains nothing more to see than a few simple lines of text, as shown in Figure 23.2. To access the server, you use a very simple C++Builder client, as shown in Figure 23.3.

FIGURE **23.2**

The Java server appears in a text window.

FIGURE **23.3**

The C++Builder client has a button and an edit control. The program retrieves a string from the server.

The IDL for the server describes a single simple interface with a method called GetName in it:

```
module BCBCORBA
{
  interface BCBServer
  {
    string GetName();
  };
};
```

You should do the same thing with this IDL file that you did with the C++Builder–generated IDL in the previous example. That is, add it to a new JBuilder project, right-click it, and choose Make to auto-generate a number of Java source files.

One of the files you create will be a sample implementation of your server called _example_BCBServer.java. If this file is not created automatically, right-click the IDL file inside JBuilder, choose IDL Properties from the menu, and make sure the Generate Sample Implementation option is checked.

The _example_BCBServer file is read-only, so you can't edit it. Instead, copy it to the Clipboard and create a new file called **BCBServer.java** based on this example. The file you want to create is shown in Listing 23.5. Notice in particular that I have changed the name of the class that was auto-generated and that I wrote a few lines of code to properly implement my methods.

> **NOTE**
>
> I have heard some users say that they like to have the IDL2JAVA compiler generate the sample files, copy them to a separate directory, delete the generated files, and then rerun the IDL compiler without having it generate the examples. These users say this helps them avoid naming conflicts and makes it easier to cut and paste without the need to modify names.
>
> The main point here is not which specific technique you use, but only that you understand what needs to be done and that you find some way to do it.

BCBServer.java has two key methods in it. The first is the constructor, which assigns a string to an internal data member:

```
public BCBServer()
{
  super();
  FName = "BCBServer calling from Java";
}
```

This is the second method is the implementation of the GetName routine:

```
public java.lang.String GetName()
{
  return FName;
}
```

As you can see, this method does nothing more than return the string you initialized in the constructor.

After you have declared the implementation for your server object, JBuilder will automatically wrap it in a server object for you. To accomplish this goal, choose File, New, VisiBroker, Corba Server from the JBuilder menu. A dialog, as shown in Figure 23.4, will appear with a default name for your server. I ended up saving this file, shown in Listing 23.6, under the name JavaBCBServer.java.

FIGURE 23.4

*The JBuilder
dialog shows the
user when it is
about to auto-
generate the code
for a CORBA
server.*

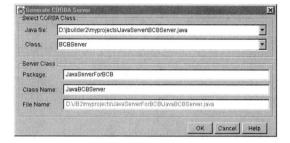

The code in `JavaBCBServer.java` is designed to register the server with the ORB when the server gets loaded into memory. This code accomplishes the task:

```
org.omg.CORBA.ORB orb = org.omg.CORBA.ORB.init();
org.omg.CORBA.BOA boa = orb.BOA_init();
BCBCORBA.BCBServer implObject = new BCBServer("BCBServer");
boa.obj_is_ready(implObject);
System.out.println(implObject+ " is ready.");
boa.impl_is_ready();
```

The first line of code initializes the ORB. The second retrieves an instance of the BOA from the ORB. The third line creates an instance of the server. The fourth line tells the ORB that the interface supported by the `BCBServer` object is ready to use. The final line in the program starts a loop that repeats until your server is taken out of memory.

The server is built at this stage, and you can simply launch it from the JBuilder IDE. It creates a text window stating that the server is ready. The VisiBroker server then goes into a loop waiting for a client to call on it.

Writing a simple C++Builder method on the client that will call the server is extremely easy. First, the ORB is initialized in `WinMain()`:

```
// Initialize the ORB
CORBA::ORB_var orb = CORBA::ORB_init(__argc, __argv);
```

Now you create a property to hold the CORBA object to which you want to make calls. The Use CORBA Object Wizard can generate the code automatically in C++Builder:

```
BCBCORBA::BCBServer_ptr __fastcall TForm1::GetbCBServer(void)
{
        if (FbCBServer == NULL)
        {
                FbCBServer = BCBCORBA::BCBServer::_bind();
        }
        return FbCBServer;
}
```

```
void __fastcall TForm1::SetbCBServer(BCBCORBA::BCBServer_ptr _ptr)
{
        FbCBServer = _ptr;
}
```

If the CORBA object `FbCBServer` has not been initialized, the `bind` method is called to get a valid reference to the server object. This is returned as the `bCBServer` property. The stub generated by the IDL2CPP compiler makes getting instances of CORBA objects easy. You can now make calls on the property. In this case the result of the `GetName` method is displayed in a `TEditBox`:

```
Edit1->Text = bCBServer->GetName();
```

Remember that none of this works unless you have the Smart Agent running and you have properly set up the Interface Repository.

The next section shows you the same type of code, though this time with Delphi.

Calling a C++Builder CORBA Server from Delphi

Building CORBA clients/servers in Delphi is a little different than using C++Builder or Java. In particular, no tight binding existed between the Pascal language and CORBA at the time Delphi Client/Server was created. Other languages, such as C++ and Java, could easily call and create CORBA servers because the VisiBroker had already laid the groundwork. In the future, the same should be true of Object Pascal. At the time I am writing, there is no easy way for a Pascal programmer to call or create CORBA servers using standard CORBA techniques such as calling `IDL2JAVA` or `IDL2CPP`. In other words, no `IDL2DELPHI` utility is available.

Delphi Client/Server provides a solution to this problem. Many of the details of how this solution works are wrapped up in `ORBPAS.DLL`, which ships with each copy of Delphi Client/Server. The source for this DLL is unfortunately not available. As a result, the actual details of how Delphi allows you to call and create CORBA servers are shrouded in mystery.

Programmers naturally don't like black boxes, but I should point out that distributed architectures always include black boxes. The way functions get called and parameters get marshaled is never explained in CORBA, DCOM, Entera, or in any other distributed architecture that I have used. Delphi has its own black box, but there is nothing unusual about that.

A more serious issue in Delphi Client/Server is the fact that you use COM IDL to define your object's interface. This means that certain types commonly used in CORBA IDL cannot be properly defined in Delphi because of limitations in the structure of COM IDL. Furthermore, you cannot easily convert standard CORBA IDL into Object Pascal. As a result, using static binding is difficult when you're connecting a Delphi client to a CORBA server written in some other language. The solution to this problem is to use dynamic binding, which Delphi does support. The concepts of dynamic binding are discussed in detail in Chapter 22.

Overall, there is no denying that you are limited in what you can do with Delphi Client/Server and CORBA. However, the technology does make it very easy for you to create CORBA servers. Furthermore, you can use dynamic binding to talk to CORBA objects that are made by other compilers and that might be running on other, non-Windows–based platforms. Finally, I should point out that although CORBA programming in Delphi is not as feature-complete as other CORBA implementations, it is much easier than traditional CORBA programming in Java or in C++.

Dynamic invocation is important in Delphi Client/Server because no IDL2PAS.exe utility is available with the product. Because you cannot automatically create a Delphi client for a C++ or Java server, the simplest approach is to connect directly to a server and start calling its methods dynamically. You will have success at run time if you call them correctly. If you make a mistake, CORBA at run time tells you that you have a parameter mismatch or that you tried to call a nonexistent method. Under such circumstances, checking your calls at compile time is impossible.

To make a dynamic call, you have to load the IDL for your server into an Interface Repository. The process of starting the Interface Repository and loading an IDL was covered in Chapter 22. You must load the IDL for your server in the Interface Repository—your dynamic calls from Delphi will otherwise not succeed.

After you have the Interface Repository set up, you can call the methods on your server with a few simple lines of code. Here, for example, you can see how to call a C++Builder server:

```
procedure TForm1.Button1Click(Sender: TObject);
var
  DynamicObject: TAny;
begin
  DynamicObject :=
    Orb.Bind('IDL:CorbaTestServer1/CorbaTestObject:1.0');
  Edit1.Text := DynamicObject.GetName;
end;
```

The first method binds you to the server. You do not need to do anything to prepare the ORB variable other than include `CorbObj` in your `uses` clause. This call will not succeed if you do not pass in the correct Repository ID. You can usually retrieve the Repository ID from the C++ server's skeleton code.

In Delphi 4, you can tell whether your `bind` call succeeded by checking the value of the `TAny` variable it returns. A `TAny` in Delphi is defined as a variant, and it allows you to work with the CORBA `Any` type. Your call succeeded if the `TAny` `DynamicFactory` variable is set to `Unknown`. If it is set to `Unassigned`, then the call failed. (I'm not sure the significance of these return values are stated so explicitly anywhere in the documentation, but they are the values I get upon success or failure.)

If the `bind` call is successful, you are free to make calls directly off the return value of `Orb.Bind`. As you can see, dynamic invocation is easy to use. It can help make CORBA programming in Delphi a relatively simple and enjoyable process.

Listings 23.9 show how to create a simple Delphi server and client, where the client uses dynamic binding to call the server. The Delphi example shown here is again running against the C++Builder `CorbaTestObject` program created in the preceding chapter and is found in the `CorbaTest1/Server` directory.

LISTING 23.9 THE DELPHI DYNAMIC CLIENT FORM THAT CALLS THE C++BUILDER SERVER

```
/////////////////////////////////////////
// File: MainForm.pas
// Description: Example Dynamic Client in Delphi
//
unit MainForm;

interface

uses
  Windows, Messages, SysUtils, Classes, Graphics, Controls,
  Forms, Dialogs, StdCtrls;

type
  TForm1 = class(TForm)
    Button1: TButton;
    Edit1: TEdit;
    procedure Button1Click(Sender: TObject);
  private
    { Private declarations }
  public
    { Public declarations }
  end;
```

continues

23

C++BUILDER, JAVA, AND DELPHI

LISTING 23.9 CONTINUED

```
var
  Form1: TForm1;

implementation

uses CorbaObj;

{$R *.DFM}

procedure TForm1.Button1Click(Sender: TObject);
var
  DynamicObject: TAny;
begin
  DynamicObject :=
    Orb.Bind('IDL:CorbaTestServer1/CorbaTestObject:1.0');
  Edit1.Text := DynamicObject.GetName;
end;
end.
```

As you can see, creating Delphi CORBA clients is very easy. Remember that Delphi clients require the use of the Interface Repository when accessing non-Delphi CORBA servers because there is no IDL2PAS compiler. Figure 23.5 shows the Delphi client and C++Builder CORBA server.

FIGURE 23.5

The Delphi client accessing a C++Builder CORBA server.

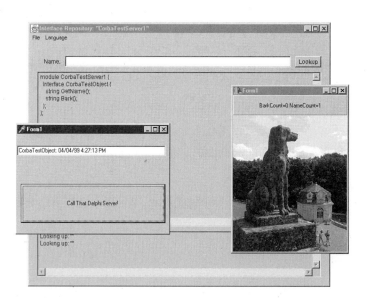

Now look at the reverse—using a C++Builder client and a Delphi server.

Building a CORBA Server in Delphi and Calling It from C++Builder

Delphi Client/Server makes CORBA programming simple, and that is no easy accomplishment. In fact, distinguishing between creating a standard Delphi COM object or MIDAS application and creating a Delphi\CORBA application is difficult.

The similarity between Delphi MIDAS and CORBA applications gives you the advantage of being able to write one set of code that works in either environment. However, you should not be misled into thinking that these two technologies are truly similar.

You can automatically convert an OLE automation server into a CORBA server by right-clicking the code for your server. An item called Expose as CORBA Object will appear in the local menu. Choosing this option automatically makes it possible for you to call your COM object from CORBA.

The following steps will create a new Delphi server:

1. Start a new Delphi application by selecting File, New Application.
2. Create a new CORBA object by selecting File, New and choosing the CORBA object from the Multitier tab of the New Items dialog.
3. The Corba Object Wizard comes up. The name of the new CORBA object can be specified here. In this example it's `DelphiCorbaObject`. Pressing OK creates the new CORBA object and places you in the Delphi editor.
4. Select Type Library from the View menu. This displays the Type Library in which you can add a method to the interface that is generated by Delphi. In this case you add the `GetName` that returns a `WideString` to the `IDelphiCorbaObject` interface.
5. Save all of the files in the project.

The Delphi sample server created in this example is found in the `Chap23/DelphiCorbaServer` directory.

Notice how similar this is to creating a COM object in C++Builder. Delphi creates a stub automatically in a Pascal unit and adds it to the project. This example's unit is named `DelphiCorbaObject_IMPL.pas`. A `GetName` method has been created in that file. Add code to send a string back to the client.

Also notice the code at the bottom of the file. Code has been added in the `initialization` section in order to automatically create and register a factory called `DelphiCorbaObjectFactory`. *Factories* are a common part of CORBA development and many projects use them. You simply hook to the factory object from a CORBA client and call its `CreateInstance` method. This method returns a reference to the actual object you are looking for.

Every Delphi CORBA server requires the use of a factory. This is due to the close relationship between COM and CORBA in Delphi. Borland was able to quickly add CORBA support to Delphi by leveraging the existing COM technology already included within Delphi. The Delphi/CORBA object factory mechanism is nothing more than a thinly veiled COM class factory and is required as a side effect of the way Delphi's CORBA implementation is based on COM. In addition, using factories allows Delphi to keep track of object resources. A `Factory` object should always be used to get an instance of a CORBA object from a Delphi CORBA server.

One last thing: You need an IDL file in order for clients other than Delphi to access this server. To generate the IDL, go into the Type Library Editor and choose the icon on the far right of the toolbar (at the top of the editor); select Export to CORBA IDL. (If you don't see any toolbar at all, right-click the editor and select the Toolbar option.) Save the IDL file for use in the client. Listings 23.10 through 23.13 show the code for the Delphi server.

LISTING 23.10 THE MAIN FORM FOR THE DELPHI CORBA SERVER

```
/////////////////////////////////////////
//          File: MainForm.pas
// Description: DelphiCorbaServer1.dpr
//
unit MainForm;

interface

uses
  Windows, Messages, SysUtils, Classes, Graphics, Controls, Forms,
Dialogs,
➡ DelphiCorbaObject_IMPL,
  StdCtrls, jpeg, ExtCtrls;

type
  TForm1 = class(TForm)
    Label1: TLabel;
    Image1: TImage;
  private
    { Private declarations }
```

```
public
  { Public declarations }
end;

var
  Form1: TForm1;

implementation

{$R *.DFM}

end.
```

LISTING 23.11 THE DELPHICORBAOBJECT IMPLEMENTATION

```
/////////////////////////////////////
//          File: DelphiCorbaObject_IMPL.pas
// Description: DelphiCorbaServer1.dpr
//
unit DelphiCorbaObject_IMPL;

interface

uses
  Windows, Messages, SysUtils, Classes, Graphics, Controls, ComObj,
➡StdVcl,
  CorbaObj, DelphiCorbaServer1_TLB;

type

  TDelphiCorbaObject = class(TCorbaImplementation, IDelphiCorbaObject)
  private
    { Private declarations }
  public
    { Public declarations }
  protected
    function GetName: WideString; safecall;
  end;

implementation

uses CorbInit;

function TDelphiCorbaObject.GetName: WideString;
begin
  Result:='Simple Delphi Corba Server, '+DateTimeToStr(Now);
end;
```

continues

LISTING 23.11   CONTINUED

```
initialization
  TCorbaObjectFactory.Create('DelphiCorbaObjectFactory',
'DelphiCorbaObject',
➥ 'IDL:DelphiCorbaServer1/DelphiCorbaObjectFactory:1.0',
➥ IDelphiCorbaObject,
    TDelphiCorbaObject, iMultiInstance, tmSingleThread);
end.
```

LISTING 23.12   THE DELPHI–GENERATED TYPE LIBRARY FILE

```
unit DelphiCorbaServer1_TLB;

// ****************************************************************//
// WARNING                                                        //
//                                                                //
// -------                                                        //
//                                                                //
// The types declared in this file were generated from data read from a //
// Type Library. If this type library is explicitly or indirectly (via  //
// another type library referring to this type library) re-imported, or //
// the 'Refresh' command of the Type Library Editor activated while     //
// editing the Type Library, the contents of this file will be          //
// regenerated and all manual modifications will be lost.               //
// ****************************************************************//

// PASTLWTR : $Revision:   1.11.1.75  $
// File generated on 04/04/99 1:46:46 PM from Type Library described below.

// ****************************************************************//
// Type Lib: D:\Apps\SAMS\BCB4Unleashed\Code\Chap23\DelphiCorbaServer\
➥DelphiCorbaServer1.tlb
// IID\LCID: {A9BD4A96-EAB3-11D2-BFCE-006008240ECC}\0
// Helpfile:
// HelpString: DelphiCorbaServer1 Library
// Version:    1.0
// ****************************************************************//
```

```
interface

uses Windows, ActiveX, Classes, Graphics, OleCtrls, StdVCL, SysUtils,
➡ CORBAObj, OrbPas, CorbaStd;

// ****************************************************************//
// GUIDS declared in the TypeLibrary. Following prefixes are used: //
//   Type Libraries    : LIBID_xxxx                                //
//   CoClasses         : CLASS_xxxx                                //
//   DISPInterfaces    : DIID_xxxx                                 //
//   Non-DISP interfaces: IID_xxxx                                 //
// ****************************************************************//
const
  LIBID_DelphiCorbaServer1: TGUID = '{A9BD4A96-EAB3-11D2-BFCE-
➡006008240ECC}';
  IID_IDelphiCorbaObject: TGUID = '{A9BD4A97-EAB3-11D2-BFCE-
➡006008240ECC}';
  CLASS_DelphiCorbaObject: TGUID = '{A9BD4A99-EAB3-11D2-BFCE-
➡006008240ECC}';
type

// ****************************************************************//
// Forward declaration of interfaces defined in Type Library      //
// ****************************************************************//
  IDelphiCorbaObject = interface;
  IDelphiCorbaObjectDisp = dispinterface;

// ****************************************************************//
// Declaration of CoClasses defined in Type Library               //
// (NOTE: Here we map each CoClass to its Default Interface)       //
// ****************************************************************//
  DelphiCorbaObject = IDelphiCorbaObject;


// ****************************************************************//
// Interface: IDelphiCorbaObject                                  //
// Flags:     (4416) Dual OleAutomation Dispatchable              //
// GUID:      {A9BD4A97-EAB3-11D2-BFCE-006008240ECC}              //
// ****************************************************************//
  IDelphiCorbaObject = interface(IDispatch)
    ['{A9BD4A97-EAB3-11D2-BFCE-006008240ECC}']
    function GetName: WideString; safecall;
  end;
```

continues

LISTING 23.12 CONTINUED

```
// ****************************************************************//
// DispIntf:  IDelphiCorbaObjectDisp
// Flags:     (4416) Dual OleAutomation Dispatchable
// GUID:      {A9BD4A97-EAB3-11D2-BFCE-006008240ECC}
// ****************************************************************//
  IDelphiCorbaObjectDisp = dispinterface
    ['{A9BD4A97-EAB3-11D2-BFCE-006008240ECC}']
    function GetName: WideString; dispid 1;
  end;

  TDelphiCorbaObjectStub = class(TCorbaDispatchStub, IDelphiCorbaObject)
  public
    function GetName: WideString; safecall;
  end;

  TDelphiCorbaObjectSkeleton = class(TCorbaSkeleton)
  private
    FIntf: IDelphiCorbaObject;
  public
    constructor Create(const InstanceName: string; const Impl:
➡ IUnknown); override;
    procedure GetImplementation(out Impl: IUnknown); override; stdcall;
  published
    procedure GetName(const InBuf: IMarshalInBuffer; Cookie: Pointer);
  end;

  CoDelphiCorbaObject = class
    class function Create: IDelphiCorbaObject;
    class function CreateRemote(const MachineName: string):
➡ IDelphiCorbaObject;
  end;

  TDelphiCorbaObjectCorbaFactory = class
    class function CreateInstance(const InstanceName: string):
➡ IDelphiCorbaObject;
  end;

implementation

uses ComObj;

{ TDelphiCorbaObjectStub }

function TDelphiCorbaObjectStub.GetName: WideString;
var
  OutBuf: IMarshalOutBuffer;
  InBuf: IMarshalInBuffer;
begin
  FStub.CreateRequest('GetName', True, OutBuf);
  FStub.Invoke(OutBuf, InBuf);
```

```
  Result := UnmarshalWideText(InBuf);
end;

{ TDelphiCorbaObjectSkeleton }

constructor TDelphiCorbaObjectSkeleton.Create(const InstanceName: string;
➡ const Impl: IUnknown);
begin
  inherited;
  inherited InitSkeleton('DelphiCorbaObject', InstanceName,
➡ 'IDL:DelphiCorbaServer1/IDelphiCorbaObject:1.0',
➡ tmMultiThreaded, True);
  FIntf := Impl as IDelphiCorbaObject;
end;

procedure TDelphiCorbaObjectSkeleton.GetImplementation(out Impl: IUnknown);
begin
  Impl := FIntf;
end;

procedure TDelphiCorbaObjectSkeleton.GetName(const InBuf:
➡ IMarshalInBuffer; Cookie: Pointer);
var
  OutBuf: IMarshalOutBuffer;
  Retval: WideString;
begin
  Retval := FIntf.GetName;
  FSkeleton.GetReplyBuffer(Cookie, OutBuf);
  OutBuf.PutWideText(PWideChar(Pointer(Retval)));
end;

class function CoDelphiCorbaObject.Create: IDelphiCorbaObject;
begin
  Result := CreateComObject(CLASS_DelphiCorbaObject) as IDelphiCorbaObject;
end;

class function CoDelphiCorbaObject.CreateRemote(const MachineName: string):
➡ IDelphiCorbaObject;
begin
  Result := CreateRemoteComObject(MachineName, CLASS_DelphiCorbaObject) as
➡ IDelphiCorbaObject;
end;

class function TDelphiCorbaObjectCorbaFactory.CreateInstance
➡(const InstanceName: string): IDelphiCorbaObject;
```

continues

LISTING 23.12   CONTINUED

```
begin
  Result := CorbaFactoryCreateStub('IDL:DelphiCorbaServer1/
➥DelphiCorbaObjectFactory:1.0', 'DelphiCorbaObject',
    InstanceName, '', IDelphiCorbaObject) as IDelphiCorbaObject;
end;

initialization
  CorbaStubManager.RegisterStub(IDelphiCorbaObject,
➥TDelphiCorbaObjectStub);
  CorbaInterfaceIDManager.RegisterInterface(IDelphiCorbaObject,
'IDL:DelphiCorbaServer1/IDelphiCorbaObject:1.0');
  CorbaSkeletonManager.RegisterSkeleton(IDelphiCorbaObject,
➥ TDelphiCorbaObjectSkeleton);

end.
```

LISTING 23.13   THE DELPHI–GENERATED CORBA IDL

```
unit DelphiCorbaServer1_TLB;
module DelphiCorbaServer1
{
  interface IDelphiCorbaObject;

  interface IDelphiCorbaObject
  {
    wstring GetName();
  };

  interface DelphiCorbaObjectFactory
  {
    IDelphiCorbaObject CreateInstance(in string InstanceName);
  };

};
```

Creating a client in C++Builder for the Delphi server is easy. Delphi generated the IDL, so you simply need to include it in the C++Builder client project. Follow the steps for creating a C++Builder client that are given in the Java example. The BCBClient program has a simple form with one button and one edit control on it, as shown in Figure 23.6. When you click the button, a string is retrieved from the server and displayed in the edit control. The program will not work unless you run the server first and unless you have the OSAgent loaded as a service on NT or as a program on Windows 9x.

This server has no GUI interface to speak of. I put a picture of a dog on the front of its form, but that is only a conceit and adds no functionality to the program. For all intents and purposes, the server is useless without a client. Therefore, it will be helpful if you build a client application before reading about this application in any depth.

FIGURE 23.6

The DelphiCorba Server1 and the C++Builder client program as they appear at run time.

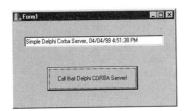

The C++Builder client is straightforward except for one small twist. Because Delphi servers require the use of a factory to get a reference to the object you actually want, the C++Builder code must first connect to the factory object and then call its `CreateInstance` method. Listings 23.14 and 23.15 show the client code for calling the Delphi server.

LISTING 23.14 THE C++BUILDER MAINFORM HEADER FILE

```
///////////////////////////////////////
//          File: MainClient.h
// Description: BCBClient.bpr
//
//----------------------------------------------------------------
#ifndef MainClientH
#define MainClientH
//----------------------------------------------------------------
#include <Classes.hpp>
#include <Controls.hpp>
#include <StdCtrls.hpp>
#include <Forms.hpp>
#include "DelphiCorbaServer1_c.hh"
//----------------------------------------------------------------
class TForm1 : public TForm
{
__published:    // IDE-managed Components
        TButton *Button1;
        TEdit *Edit1;
```

continues

23

C++BUILDER,
JAVA, AND DELPHI

LISTING 23.14   CONTINUED

```
        void __fastcall Button1Click(TObject *Sender);
private:        // User declarations
        DelphiCorbaServer1::DelphiCorbaObjectFactory_ptr __fastcall
➡ GetdelphiCorbaObjectFactory();
        DelphiCorbaServer1::DelphiCorbaObjectFactory_var
➡ FdelphiCorbaObjectFactory;
        void __fastcall SetdelphiCorbaObjectFactory(DelphiCorbaServer1::
➡DelphiCorbaObjectFactory_ptr _ptr);
public:         // User declarations
        __fastcall TForm1(TComponent* Owner);
        __property DelphiCorbaServer1::
➡DelphiCorbaObjectFactory_ptr delphiCorbaObjectFactory =
➡ {read=GetdelphiCorbaObjectFactory, write=
➡SetdelphiCorbaObjectFactory};
};
//-------------------------------------------------------------
extern PACKAGE TForm1 *Form1;
//-------------------------------------------------------------
#endif
```

LISTING 23.15   THE C++BUILDER MAINFORM THAT CALLS THE DELPHI **CORBA** SERVER

```
/////////////////////////////////////////
//        File: MainClient.cpp
// Description: BCBClient.bpr
//
//-------------------------------------------------------------
#include <vcl.h>
#pragma hdrstop

#include <corba.h>
#include "MainClient.h"
//-------------------------------------------------------------
#pragma package(smart_init)
#pragma resource "*.dfm"
TForm1 *Form1;
//-------------------------------------------------------------
__fastcall TForm1::TForm1(TComponent* Owner)
        : TForm(Owner)
{
}
```

```
//-------------------------------------------------------------------

DelphiCorbaServer1::DelphiCorbaObjectFactory_ptr __fastcall TForm1::
➥GetdelphiCorbaObjectFactory(void)
{
        if (FdelphiCorbaObjectFactory == NULL)
        {
                FdelphiCorbaObjectFactory = DelphiCorbaServer1::
➥DelphiCorbaObjectFactory::_bind();
        }
        return FdelphiCorbaObjectFactory;
}

void __fastcall TForm1::SetdelphiCorbaObjectFactory(DelphiCorbaServer1::
➥DelphiCorbaObjectFactory_ptr _ptr)
{
        FdelphiCorbaObjectFactory = _ptr;
}
void __fastcall TForm1::Button1Click(TObject *Sender)
{
    DelphiCorbaServer1::IDelphiCorbaObject_ptr Foo =
➥ delphiCorbaObjectFactory->CreateInstance("CorbaTest");
    Edit1->Text = Foo->GetName();

}
//-------------------------------------------------------------------
```

The C++Builder client was created in exactly the same way previous clients were created with one small exception: Because of the way CORBA is implemented in Delphi, the CORBA object is retrieved from the Delphi server using the factory and not directly. Select the `DelphiCorbaServer1::DelphiCorbaObjectFactory` interface from the Use CORBA Object Wizard; do not choose the interface of the object you really want. C++Builder generates a property on the main form for the factory. The following code retrieves the object you really want from the factory:

```
DelphiCorbaServer1::IDelphiCorbaObject_ptr Foo =
➥delphiCorbaObjectFactory->CreateInstance("CorbaTest");
Edit1->Text = Foo->GetName();
```

The factory itself is a CORBA object, so call its `CreateInstance` method; a `DelphiCorbaServer1::IdelphiCorbaObject_ptr` is returned. You can call server methods directly on the returned object.

Summary

In this chapter you learned how to get C++Builder, Delphi, and Java all working together by creating a series of CORBA servers and clients. Because C++ and Java both have access to IDL compiler, clients and servers written in these languages can easily interchange. You can write the same type of code shown in all the C++Builder client programs to talk to C++ or Java servers running on UNIX, the Macintosh, or on any other operating system that supports CORBA.

Delphi also has good CORBA support despite not having an IDL2PAS compiler. C++Builder can be used to create both clients and servers that communicate with Delphi via CORBA. In particular, the dynamic CORBA capabilities of Delphi allow it to communicate with C++Builder servers.

With the new CORBA features in C++Builder 4 Enterprise, C++Builder is rapidly becoming the easiest way to build CORBA applications. The integration of the IDL2CPP compiler, as well as many wizards and utilities, into the C++Builder IDE makes CORBA development a breeze.

In this and the preceding chapter you looked at C++Builder's support for CORBA. At this time, CORBA is the only major cross-platform solution for creating distributed objects. CORBA is, however, in direct competition with DCOM, which is the tool of choice when creating distributed objects on the Windows platform. Watching what happens over the next few years will be interesting as these two technologies struggle for dominance in a marketplace hungry for cross-platform distributed programming solutions.

VCL Graphics Classes

CHAPTER 24

by Jeff Cottingham

IN THIS CHAPTER

Many programmers find graphics development to be the most enjoyable type of programming. In fact, I like to say that we are all just frustrated artists at heart. Developing graphics is your chance to exercise your artistic skills inside your own programs and also to have some fun.

Graphics give an application the capability to draw itself on the screen. They can also be used to make an application stand out. For example, if an application takes a long time to initially load, having a splash screen to look at is much nicer than just the Windows desktop.

When I buy a new programming book, the first section I turn to is the one covering graphics. I want to see whether it has any new methods, tips, or tricks that I haven't seen before. In this chapter, which covers Visual Component Library (VCL) graphics classes, I'm going to focus on the following:

- The GDI
- TCanvas
- Brushes
- Pens
- Fonts
- Palettes
- Bitmaps
- Metafiles

By the time you are done with this chapter, you should know how to draw directly on the surface of a form or other component. This knowledge will allow you to create flexible, interesting applications. It will also lay the foundation for more advanced work in graphics.

The Windows Graphics Device Interface (GDI)

In the next few sections, I will introduce you to graphics programming using C++Builder. In particular, I will focus on the technology used to draw to the screen in Windows. Windows presents this technology to you in a system called the Graphics Device Interface (GDI). It is presented to you by the VCL in an object called TCanvas and in all the supporting classes of TCanvas. TCanvas wraps the GDI and makes it much easier to use.

The GDI is the key to standard graphics programming in Windows. Like any artist, you need to have something to draw, scribble, or paint on. In straight Windows API programming, this surface is the window itself. You access the surface of that window through the GDI. Everything you need to draw on this window must be accessed through a device context (DC).

The GDI function group contains all the necessary functions to allow you to draw on the surface of a window. These functions allow you to draw text, shapes, and bitmaps to the screen. They provide complete control over fonts, colors, line thickness, shading, scaling, orientation, and many other related matters. However, you must do several things before you start drawing.

First, you must get the device context of the window you want to draw on. After that you do your painting or drawing. Finally, you release the device context. This last step is very important because if you don't release the DC, at the very least, you will have a resource leak in your program. At the very worst, you could experience what we at Inprise like to call "the blue screen of death," or in layman's terms, a system crash. The code that follows shows how to use the GDI to change a pixel at screen coordinate 10,10 to pure red:

```
HDC hDC = GetDC(Handle);
SetPixel(hDC, 10, 10, RGB(255, 0, 0));
ReleaseDC(Handle, hDC);
```

The first call in this three-step process is GetDC, which returns a device context. This function takes one parameter, which is the handle of the window on which you want to draw. Now you are ready to write to the screen. Every time you draw to the screen you must use the device context. In this case I pass the DC as the first parameter of SetPixel.

The next two parameters of SetPixel specify the x and y coordinates of the pixel to be drawn. The last parameter specifies the color. The final call in this example releases the device context. Most GDI functions take a device context in the first parameter. That's the signature of a GDI function.

The VCL TCanvas Class

The VCL provides you with the TCanvas object, which is a wrapper around the GDI. The TCanvas object handles the DC and its resource management for you behind the scenes. Granted, TCanvas relieves you from the burden of knowing everything there is to know about the GDI. It does not, however, make the DC inaccessible. If you need to get at the device context, it is always available through the Handle property of the TCanvas object.

24

VCL GRAPHICS
CLASSES

This property is, in reality, just the handle to the device context of the object's canvas. You access it as shown in the following line of code:

```
HDC hDC = MyCanvas->Handle;
```

A VCL example of the code snippet from the previous section would be as follows:

```
Canvas->Pixels[10][10] = clRed;
```

In this code, you are accessing the Canvas property of the main form. In particular, you are accessing the Pixels property of the TCanvas object. Later in the chapter, I will explain the Pixels property in depth, but for now, you can see that it provides an easy way to draw to the screen without having to worry about device contexts. It lets you concentrate on the task at hand. Also, using the VCL classes, the amount of code you have to write is diminished. In the preceding example, three lines of code are boiled down to one. This difference might not seem like much, but as your application grows, you will appreciate the terseness of the VCL.

The following sections describe the basic GDI objects: brushes, pens, and fonts.

Using Brushes

A *brush*, encapsulated by the VCL TBrush object, is a graphics tool that an application uses to paint the interior of polygons and ellipses, or the background of a window or windowed control. For example, by setting Canvas's brush color to white, I can set the entire background of a form so that the form is white and not the default color, clBtnFace. To achieve this effect, I simply set the Color property of the form in the Object Inspector to clWhite. This setting changes the form's brush color to white and paints the background white instead of gray.

In this section, you will get a look at the TBrush object. In particular, I will show you four of its most important methods or properties: Color, Style, Assign(), and Bitmap.

Color. When drawing objects on a canvas, you need to specify what color to use to paint or "fill" the canvas or shape. You do so with a brush, or more specifically with a TBrush object. You don't need to create a brush, since the VCL has already created one for you to use.

A more in-depth discussion of colors and palettes follows in this chapter. For now, I use some of the predefined Windows colors. Here is a partial list of predefined colors that you can use:

clBlack	clPurple	clLime
clMaroon	clTeal	clBlue
clGreen	clGray	clFuchsia
clOlive	clSilver	clAqua
clNavy	clRed	clWhite

To set the brush's color to one of your own choosing, use the brush's `Color` property as shown here:

```
Canvas->Brush->Color = clRed;
```

`Style`. The `Style` property is the pattern the brush uses when it paints. Table 24.1 shows the predefined patterns that are available to you and can be assigned to the `Canvas`'s brush.

TABLE 24.1 TBrush Style Types

Value	Description
bsSolid	A solid color
bsCross	Intersecting vertical and horizontal lines
bsClear	Transparent
bsDiagCross	Intersecting diagonal lines in both directions
bsBDiagonal	Backward diagonal lines
bsHorizontal	Horizontal lines
bsFDiagonal	Forward diagonal lines
bsVertical	Vertical lines

You set the pattern or style of the brush as shown:

```
Canvas->Brush->Style = bsCross;
```

24

VCL Graphics Classes

In Figure 24.1 you can see one example of the different types of pattern brushes that are available using the Brush sample program. The radio buttons you see on the form in Figure 24.1 correspond to the constants in Table 24.1. By selecting one of the radio buttons, you can see the effect of a particular brush style applied.

FIGURE 24.1

An example of using the pattern brush style bsVertical *to paint the background of an* Image *component.*

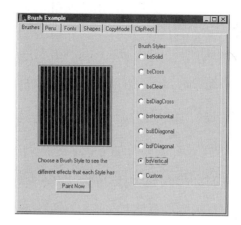

Bitmap. In addition to these predefined patterns, you can also create your own custom patterns stored in bitmap format or use pre-existing bitmaps. These custom bitmaps are loaded through the Bitmap property of the brush. Custom bitmaps are handled differently on Windows 95 than they are on Windows NT and Windows 98. On Windows 95, the bitmap that the brush uses is limited to eight pixels by eight pixels in size. If the image is larger than this, only the top-left eight-by-eight region is used. Windows NT and Windows 98 can use bitmap patterns of any size. Another thing to remember is that if you do use a custom pattern, it will override whatever style you have set. After you're done with the custom pattern, you have to do your own cleanup because the brush will not do it for you.

The following code snippets show you how to set the brush to a bitmap. The first thing you have to do is declare a variable of type Graphics::TBitmap* and create an instance of this type:

```
Graphics::TBitmap* MyCustomBrush = new Graphics::TBitmap;
```

Next, load a bitmap into the object and then make the assignment to the brush's Bitmap property:

```
MyCustomBrush->LoadFromFile("MyPattern.bmp");
Canvas->Brush->Bitmap = MyCustomBrush;
```

Always remember to reset this property to 0 and free the bitmap when you are done with it. Failure to delete the bitmap will result in a memory leak in your program. Here's the code that frees the memory for the bitmap and sets the `Bitmap` property to 0:

```
Canvas->Brush->Bitmap = 0;
delete MyCustomBrush;
```

Figure 24.2 shows an example of setting the brush to a custom image component using the preceding code.

FIGURE 24.2

A custom or bitmapped brush is used to paint the background of an Image *component.*

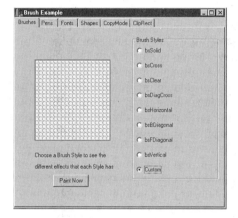

`Assign()`.This rather handy method allows you to copy one brush's contents to another `TBrush` instance. You can create several custom brushes and work with them at the same time simply by switching brushes. The following example copies the current brush into `myBrush`:

```
TBrush* myBrush = new TBrush;
myBrush->Assign(Image1->Canvas->Brush);
```

Now `myBrush` has all the attributes of the canvas's current brush.

Using Pens

The `TPen` object specifies the pen the canvas uses for drawing lines and outlining shapes. The pen has several properties and methods in common with the brush. Both the `Color` and `Style` properties and the `Assign()` method function the same way for both the pen and the brush. In this section, I will discuss the properties that are different, including `Style`, `Width`, and `Mode`.

`Style`. Like a brush, a pen has a `Style` property. The two property names are the same, but I want to explain the difference because a pen and a brush are obviously different

GDI elements. In the case of a pen, the pen style indicates how a line on the screen will be drawn. Table 24.2 shows the different styles that the pen can assume.

TABLE 24.2 PEN STYLE TYPES

Pen Style	Description
psSolid	A solid line
psDash	A dashed line
psDot	A dotted line
psDashDot	A line consisting of dashes and dots
psDashDotDot	A line consisting of one dash and two dots
psClear	A transparent line
psInsideFrame	A solid line, but one that can use a dithered color if the width is greater than one pixel

The pen styles shown in Table 24.2, with the exception of psSolid, have an effect only when the pen's Width property is set to one pixel. If the width is greater than one, this property is ignored.

Width. The Width property allows you to change the width, in pixels, of a Pen object at run time. Here's how:

```
Canvas->Pen->Width = 5;
```

This example sets the form's pen width to five pixels. So now every time you draw a line on the form's canvas, the pen width will be five pixels wide.

Mode. The Mode property dictates how the color of the pen interacts with the color of the Canvas. Three factors are taken into consideration when a line is drawn on the canvas:

- The pen color
- The destination color
- The pen mode

The pen mode is known as a ROP (Raster Operation). Table 24.3 describes the different available pen modes. The "Boolean Operation" column uses bitwise operator syntax to show how the pen and surface colors are combined. (P is the pen color and D is the destination on the canvas.)

TABLE 24.3   PEN MODES

TPenMode	Description	Boolean Operation
pmBlack	Always black	0
pmWhite	Always white	1
pmNop	Unchanged	D
pmNot	Inverse of canvas background color	notD
pmCopy	Pen color specified in Color property	P
pmNotCopy	Inverse of pen color	notP
pmMergePenNot	Combination of pen color and inverse of canvas background	P ¦¦ notD
pmMaskPenNot	Combination of colors common to both pen and inverse of canvas background	P && notD
pmMergeNotPen	Combination of canvas background color and inverse of pen color	notP ¦¦ D
pmMaskNotPen	Combination of colors common to both canvas background and inverse of pen	notP && D
pmMerge	Combination of pen color and canvas background color	P ¦¦ D
pmNotMerge	Inverse of pmMerge: combination of pen color and canvas background color	not(P ¦¦ D)
pmMask	Combination of colors common to both pen and canvas background	P && D
pmNotMask	Inverse of pmMask: combination of colors common to both pen and canvas background	not(P && D)
pmXor	Combination of colors in either pen or canvas background, but not both	P xor D_
pmNotXor	Inverse of pmXor: combination of colors in either pen or canvas background, but not both	not(P xor D)

24

VCL GRAPHICS CLASSES

The following code, which demonstrates pmMergePenNot, is in effect for Figure 24.3:

```
Canvas->Pen->Mode = pmMergePenNot;
Canvas->Pen->Color = clRed;
Canvas->Pen->Width = 5;
```

FIGURE 24.3

An example of pen mode pmMergePenNot *with a pen color of* clRed.

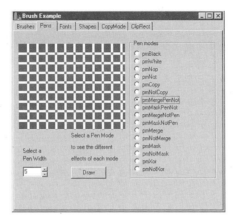

It's difficult to tell from a grayscale figure, but the result of the intersecting line is the pen drawing the inverse of the merging operation with the pen and the surface color. Assume you have a red pen color and are drawing on a red surface. The result of red merging (applying a logical and) with red is red. The pmMergePenNot pen mode takes the inverse of the merge operation by applying a logical not to the result of the merge. If you run the Brush program, you can see the effects that the different pen modes have. You might also try setting the pen's color to different colors and observing the effects.

> **NOTE**
>
> The easiest way that I know to learn the effects of the pen mode is to just use them. You can also use a calculator in binary mode to calculate the results that you want and pick the mode that applies.

Using Fonts

Just like pens and brushes, fonts are just another type of drawing you can do on the canvas. Fonts are the way you present text on the screen. Fonts are represented in the VCL via the TFont object and are surfaced for your use through the Font property. Font properties of interest include Height, Size, Name, and Style.

Height. The Height of a font is simply the height of the font without the internal leading that appears at the top of the font. The Height of a font is measured in pixels. C++Builder determines the value of the Height property using this formula:

```
Font->Height = -Font->Size * Font->PixelsPerInch / 72;
```

Therefore, whenever you enter a positive value for the `Height` property, the font's `Size` property value changes to a negative number. Conversely, if you enter a negative value for the `Size` property, the font's `Height` property changes to a positive number. A positive `Height` value includes the internal leading, and a negative value excludes it.

`Size`. The `Size` property is relational with the `Height` and should be something that you are familiar with if you have ever used a word processor. A font's size is its point size. An example would be 10-point Arial, where 10 is the font's `Size` property. C++Builder calculates size using this formula:

```
Font->Size = -Font->Height * 72 / Font->PixelsPerInch;
```

Therefore, whenever you enter a point size in the `Size` property, you'll notice the `Height` property changes to a negative value. Conversely, if you enter a positive `Height` value, the `Size` property value changes to a negative value. When the font size includes internal leading, the `Size` or the `Height` property is expressed as a negative value. Figure 24.4 breaks down just how a font is put together in Windows.

FIGURE 24.4

Many elements are used to specify a font.

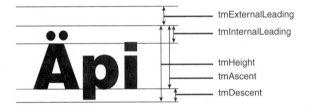

`Name`. The `Name` property defines the font that is to be used, such as Arial, Times New Roman, or Wingdings. You can use any installed font on the system, or you can create your own custom font. I have found many interesting fonts on the Internet. My favorite one is an Elven font created from the writings of J.R.R. Tolkien. In C++Builder, you can set the `Name` property of a font like this:

```
Canvas->Font->Name = "Arial";
```

As you can see, there isn't much to setting the `Name` property. Simply assign a text string containing the typeface name to the `Name` property—Windows does the rest.

`Style`. To conclude the discussion of the `TFont` object, you need to visit the `Style` property. Unlike the `Style` property of pens and brushes, which are enumerated data types, the `Style` property of the `TFont` object is a set. By having this property as a set, you can

24

VCL GRAPHICS CLASSES

have one or more in effect at any given time. You access this property through the `TFontStyles` data type. These font styles are defined:

- `fsBold`
- `fsItalic`
- `fsUnderline`
- `fsStrikeOut`

The following example shows how to set the font style for the form's canvas:

```
TFontStyles style;
style << fsBold << fsUnderline;
Canvas->Font->Style = style;
```

If you do not understand what a set is, you can find a good explanation in the C++Builder online help files, or you can view the source. An important thing to remember is that Search, Find in Files is your best friend when coding. My favorite saying is, "Use the Source, Luke. Use the Source."

Additional `TCanvas` Properties

As you've seen, many VCL components have a `Canvas` property. This property provides a surface on which to paint. Because you must learn to walk before you can run, I've focused on the basics of the `TCanvas` class. The `TCanvas` object uses aggregation to encompass a number of graphics-related VCL classes. Now look at a few additional useful properties, namely `PenPos`, `ClipRect`, `CopyMode`, and `Pixels`. Unless otherwise noted, all the following code uses the form's canvas.

`PenPos`. This is a very simple property. `PenPos` is just a placeholder for the current position of the active pen on the canvas or drawing surface. The pen position is stored in a point structure and can be accessed by the following means:

```
int xPos = Canvas->PenPos.x;
int yPos = Canvas->PenPos.y;
```

This is the starting point of a line drawn by the `LineTo` method. You can also write to `PenPos`, as shown in the following code:

```
Canvas->PenPos.x = x;
Canvas->PenPos.y = y;
```

Setting the `PenPos` property is equivalent to calling the `MoveTo` method. Like I said, `PenPos` is a very simple property.

`ClipRect`. The `ClipRect` property defines a specific rectangular region that you want to draw in. If you specify a clipping rectangle, no drawing is done outside this region even if the image or shape is larger than the `ClipRect`. An example would be to define a rectangular region on a canvas that is smaller than the canvas itself and try to draw a larger shape on the canvas that intersects the clipping rectangle. Figure 24.5 provides an example. The code for this program sets the clipping rectangle and then draws an ellipse that is slightly larger than the clipping rectangle. It does this three times, each time in a different location on the canvas. Notice that only the portion of the ellipse that falls within the clipping rectangle is drawn; everything outside this `ClipRect` is not drawn.

FIGURE 24.5

An example of creating different clipping regions on the canvas.

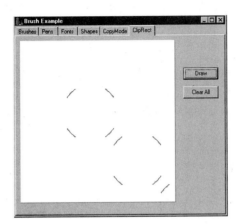

CopyMode. The `CopyMode` property is similar to the pen's `Mode` property. It determines how an image is copied from one canvas to another. Set `CopyMode` to affect the way graphical images are drawn onto the canvas. You use the `CopyMode` when copying an image from another canvas using the `CopyRect` method. You can create many different effects by using the `CopyMode` property, including special effects such as merging images and making parts of a bitmap transparent by combining multiple images with different `CopyModes`. To see the effects of `CopyMode`, run the Brush program, which you can find on the accompanying CD-ROM, and choose the Copy Mode tab. Playing with this program to see what it is all about is worthwhile. Table 24.4 shows the different modes that are available.

TABLE 24.4   TCanvas COPY MODES

CopyMode	Description
cmBlackness	Fills the destination rectangle on the canvas with black.
cmDstInvert	Inverts the image on the canvas and ignores the source.
cmMergeCopy	Combines the image on the canvas and the source bitmap by using the Boolean AND operator.

continues

TABLE 24.4 CONTINUED

CopyMode	Description
cmMergePaint	Combines the inverted source bitmap with the image on the canvas by using the Boolean OR operator.
cmNotSrcCopy	Copies the inverted source bitmap to the canvas.
cmNotSrcErase	Combines the image on the canvas and the source bitmap by using the Boolean OR operator, and inverts the result.
cmPatCopy	Copies the source pattern to the canvas.
cmPatInvert	Combines the source pattern with the image on the canvas using the Boolean XOR operator.
cmPatPaint	Combines the inverted source bitmap with the source pattern by using the Boolean OR operator. Combines the result of this operation with the image on the canvas by using the Boolean OR operator.
cmSrcAnd	Combines the image on the canvas and source bitmap by using the Boolean AND operator.
cmSrcCopy	Copies the source bitmap to the canvas.
cmSrcErase	Inverts the image on the canvas and combines the result with the source bitmap by using the Boolean AND operator.
cmSrcInvert	Combines the image on the canvas and the source bitmap by using the Boolean XOR operator.
cmSrcPaint	Combines the image on the canvas and the source bitmap by using the Boolean OR operator.
cmWhiteness	Fills the destination rectangle on the canvas with white.

Pixels. The Pixels property allows you either to read the color of the pixel at a specified location inside a clipping rectangle or to change the color of that pixel. You set the pixel at coordinate 10,10 to the color red like this:

```
Canvas->Pixels[10][10] = clRed;
```

TCanvas Methods

Table 24.5 shows the key methods of TCanvas and provides a short description of each. The sample programs in this chapter show how to implement and use some of these drawing functions.

TABLE 24.5 THE TCanvas METHODS

Method	Description	Function Call
Arc()	Renders an arc.	Arc(X1,Y1,X2,Y2,X3,Y3,X4,Y4)
Chord()	Renders an arc with a line that joins the endpoints of the arc.	Chord(X1,Y1,X2,Y2, X3,Y3,X4,Y4)
CopyRect()	Transfers part of the image on another of the TCanvas object. canvas to the image	CopyRect(Dest, Canvas, Source)
Draw()	Draws a graphical image on the canvas.	Draw(X,Y,Graphic)
Ellipse()	Renders an ellipse.	Ellipse(X1,Y1,X2, Y2)
FillRect()	Fills a rectangle.	FillRect(Rect)
FloodFill()	Fills an enclosed area.	FloodFill(X,Y,Color, FillStyle)
FrameRect()	Draws a border around a rectangle.	FrameRect(Rect)
LineTo()	Renders a line.	LineTo(x,y)
MoveTo()	Renders a line.	MoveTo(x,y)
Pie()	Renders a pie-shaped area.	Pie(X1,Y1,X2,Y2,X3,Y3, X4,Y4)
Polygon()	Renders a many-sided shape.	Polygon(points, numPoints - 1)
PolyLine()	Connects a series of points on a canvas.	Polyline(points,numPoints - 1)
Rectangle()	Renders a rectangle.	Rectangle(X1,Y1,X2,Y2)
RoundRect()	Renders a rectangle with rounded corners.	RoundRect(X1,Y1,X2,Y2, X3,Y3)
StretchDraw()	Fits the graphical image to the size of the canvas.	StretchDraw(Rect, Graphic)
TextHeight()	Determines the height a string will occupy in the image.	TextHeight(AString)
TextOut()	Writes a string onto the canvas.	TextOut(X,Y,Text)
TextRect()	Writes a string within a limited rectangular region	TextRect(Rect,X,Y,Text)
TextWidth()	Determines the length a string will occupy in the image.	TextWidth(Text)

24

VCL GRAPHICS CLASSES

The Brush Example Program

You haven't seen much code, but that is about to change. You needed to get a good understanding of the tools you will be using before you started using them. The following sections show just how these tools do what you want them to do by putting them to practice. Listings 24.1 and 24.2 show the code for the Brush program. Take a moment to familiarize yourself with the code; I dissect the major functions of this program.

LISTING 24.1   THE HEADER FOR THE BRUSH PROGRAM'S MAIN UNIT

```
#ifndef BrushMainH
#define BrushMainH

#include <Classes.hpp>
#include <Controls.hpp>
#include <StdCtrls.hpp>
#include <Forms.hpp>
#include <Buttons.hpp>
#include <ComCtrls.hpp>
#include <ExtCtrls.hpp>

enum TEnum { dsLine,dsRectangle,dsEllipse };

class TForm1 : public TForm
{
__published:      // IDE-managed Components
  TPageControl *PageControl1;
  TTabSheet *TabSheet1;
  TImage *Image1;
  TLabel *Label1;
  TLabel *Label2;
  TRadioGroup *RadioGroup1;
  TButton *Button2;
  TTabSheet *TabSheet2;
  TImage *Image2;
  TLabel *Label3;
  TLabel *Label4;
  TLabel *Label5;
  TLabel *Label6;
  TLabel *Label7;
  TRadioGroup *RadioGroup2;
  TUpDown *UpDown1;
  TEdit *Edit1;
  TButton *Button1;
  TTabSheet *TabSheet3;
  TImage *Image3;
  TLabel *Label8;
  TLabel *Label9;
```

```
TImage *Image4;
TLabel *Label10;
TLabel *Label11;
TGroupBox *GroupBox1;
TCheckBox *CheckBox1;
TCheckBox *CheckBox2;
TCheckBox *CheckBox3;
TCheckBox *CheckBox4;
TEdit *Edit2;
TCheckBox *CheckBox5;
TTabSheet *TabSheet4;
TLabel *Label12;
TLabel *Label13;
TPanel *Panel1;
TImage *Image5;
TPanel *Panel2;
TSpeedButton *SpeedButton1;
TSpeedButton *SpeedButton2;
TSpeedButton *SpeedButton3;
TSpeedButton *SpeedButton4;
TSpeedButton *SpeedButton5;
TTabSheet *TabSheet5;
TPanel *Panel3;
TImage *Image6;
TRadioGroup *RadioGroup3;
TPanel *Panel4;
TImage *Image7;
TBitBtn *BitBtn1;
TBitBtn *BitBtn2;
TBitBtn *BitBtn3;
TTabSheet *TabSheet6;
TPanel *Panel5;
TImage *Image8;
TButton *Button3;
TButton *Button4;
void __fastcall RadioGroup1Click(TObject *Sender);
void __fastcall RadioGroup2Click(TObject *Sender);
void __fastcall Button1Click(TObject *Sender);
void __fastcall Button2Click(TObject *Sender);
void __fastcall FormShow(TObject *Sender);
void __fastcall Edit2Change(TObject *Sender);
void __fastcall CheckBox1Click(TObject *Sender);
void __fastcall FormCreate(TObject *Sender);
void __fastcall Image5MouseDown(TObject *Sender, TMouseButton Button,
        TShiftState Shift, int X, int Y);
void __fastcall Image5MouseUp(TObject *Sender, TMouseButton Button,
        TShiftState Shift, int X, int Y);
void __fastcall Image5MouseMove(TObject *Sender, TShiftState Shift,
        int X, int Y);
```

continues

LISTING 24.1 CONTINUED

```cpp
    void __fastcall SpeedButton2Click(TObject *Sender);
    void __fastcall SpeedButton4Click(TObject *Sender);
    void __fastcall SpeedButton1Click(TObject *Sender);
    void __fastcall SpeedButton3Click(TObject *Sender);
    void __fastcall RadioGroup3Click(TObject *Sender);
    void __fastcall BitBtn1Click(TObject *Sender);
    void __fastcall BitBtn2Click(TObject *Sender);
    void __fastcall BitBtn3Click(TObject *Sender);
    void __fastcall Button3Click(TObject *Sender);
    void __fastcall Button4Click(TObject *Sender);
private:
    bool Check, Rendering, CanRender;
    TBrushStyle  myBrushStyle;
    TPenMode  myMode;
    TFontStyles oldStyle;
    TFontStyles myStyle;
    int TFontHeight;
    TPoint Point1, Point2;
    TEnum dsCurrentShape;
    int TCopyMode;
    void DrawShape(int w, int x, int y, int z);
    void Render(int x, int y);      // User declarations
public:              // User declarations
    __fastcall TForm1(TComponent* Owner);
};

extern PACKAGE TForm1 *Form1;

#endif
```

LISTING 24.2 THE SOURCE CODE FOR THE BRUSH PROGRAM'S MAIN UNIT

```cpp
#include <vcl.h>
#pragma hdrstop

#include "BrushMain.h"

#pragma package(smart_init)
#pragma resource "*.dfm"
TForm1 *Form1;

__fastcall TForm1::TForm1(TComponent* Owner)
    : TForm(Owner)
{
}

void TForm1::DrawShape(int w, int x, int y, int z)
{
```

```
  switch (dsCurrentShape) {
    case dsEllipse : Image5->Canvas->Ellipse(w,x,y,z); break;
    case dsRectangle : Image5->Canvas->Rectangle(w,x,y,z); break;
    case dsLine :
    {
      Image5->Canvas->MoveTo(w,x);
      Image5->Canvas->LineTo(y,z);
      break;
    }
  }
}

void TForm1::Render(int x, int y)
{
  if (CanRender && Rendering && !SpeedButton4->Down)
  {
    Image5->Canvas->Brush->Style = bsClear;
    Image5->Canvas->Pen->Mode = pmNotXor;
    Image5->Canvas->Pen->Style = psDot;
    DrawShape(Point1.x,Point1.y,Point2.x,Point2.y);
    Point2.x = x;
    Point2.y = y;
    DrawShape(Point1.x,Point1.y,Point2.x,Point2.y);
  } else
    Rendering = false;
}

void __fastcall TForm1::RadioGroup1Click(TObject *Sender)
{
  switch (RadioGroup1->ItemIndex) {
    case 8 : Check = true;
    case 7 : myBrushStyle = bsVertical; break;
    case 6 : myBrushStyle = bsFDiagonal; break;
    case 5 : myBrushStyle = bsBDiagonal; break;
    case 4 : myBrushStyle = bsHorizontal; break;
    case 3 : myBrushStyle = bsDiagCross; break;
    case 2 : myBrushStyle = bsClear; break;
    case 1 : myBrushStyle = bsCross; break;
    case 0 : myBrushStyle = bsSolid; break;
  }
  Button2Click(0);
}

void __fastcall TForm1::RadioGroup2Click(TObject *Sender)
{
  switch (RadioGroup2->ItemIndex) {
    case 15 : myMode = pmNotXor; break;
    case 14 : myMode = pmXor; break;
    case 13 : myMode = pmNotMask; break;
```

24

VCL GRAPHICS CLASSES

continues

LISTING 24.2   CONTINUED

```cpp
    case 12 : myMode = pmMask; break;
    case 11 : myMode = pmNotMerge; break;
    case 10 : myMode = pmMerge; break;
    case  9 : myMode = pmMaskNotPen; break;
    case  8 : myMode = pmMergeNotPen; break;
    case  7 : myMode = pmMaskPenNot; break;
    case  6 : myMode = pmMergePenNot; break;
    case  5 : myMode = pmNotCopy; break;
    case  4 : myMode = pmCopy; break;
    case  3 : myMode = pmNot; break;
    case  2 : myMode = pmNop; break;
    case  1 : myMode = pmWhite; break;
    case  0 : myMode = pmBlack; break;
  }
  Button1Click(0);
}

void __fastcall TForm1::Button1Click(TObject *Sender)
{
  int y = 20;
  int x = 20;
  Image2->Canvas->Pen->Mode = myMode;
  Image2->Canvas->Pen->Width = Edit1->Text.ToInt();

  for (int i=0;i<10;i++) {
    Image2->Canvas->MoveTo(0,y);
    Image2->Canvas->LineTo(Image2->Width,y);
    y += 20;
  }

  for (int i=0;i<13;i++) {
    Image2->Canvas->MoveTo(x,0);
    Image2->Canvas->LineTo(x,Image2->Height);
    x += 20;
  }
}

void __fastcall TForm1::Button2Click(TObject *Sender)
{
  if (Check) {
    Graphics::TBitmap* CustomBrush = new Graphics::TBitmap;
    try {
      CustomBrush->LoadFromFile("Custom.bmp");
      Image1->Canvas->Brush->Bitmap = CustomBrush;
      Image1->Canvas->FillRect(
        Rect(3,3,Image1->Width - 3, Image1->Height - 3));
    }
    __finally {
      Image1->Canvas->Brush->Bitmap = 0;
```

```
      delete CustomBrush;
    }
    Check = false;
  } else {
    Image1->Canvas->Brush->Style = myBrushStyle;
    Image1->Canvas->FillRect(
      Rect(3,3,Image1->Width - 3, Image1->Height - 3));
  }
}

void __fastcall TForm1::FormShow(TObject *Sender)
{
  Image1->Canvas->Rectangle(0,0,Image1->Width,Image1->Height);
  Image2->Canvas->FillRect(Image2->Canvas->ClipRect);
  Image3->Canvas->FillRect(Image3->Canvas->ClipRect);
  Image4->Canvas->FillRect(Image4->Canvas->ClipRect);
  Image5->Canvas->FillRect(Image5->Canvas->ClipRect);
  Image6->Canvas->FillRect(Image6->Canvas->ClipRect);
  Image7->Canvas->FillRect(Image7->Canvas->ClipRect);
  Image8->Canvas->FillRect(Image8->Canvas->ClipRect);
}

void __fastcall TForm1::Edit2Change(TObject *Sender)
{
  myStyle = oldStyle;

  Image3->Canvas->Font = Edit2->Font;
  Image4->Canvas->Font = Edit2->Font;
  Image3->Canvas->Font->Style = myStyle;

  if (CheckBox1->Checked)
  {
    myStyle = myStyle << fsBold;
    Image3->Canvas->Font->Style = myStyle;
  }
  if (CheckBox2->Checked)
  {
    myStyle = myStyle << fsItalic;
    Image3->Canvas->Font->Style = myStyle;
  }
  if (CheckBox3->Checked)
  {
    myStyle = myStyle << fsUnderline;
    Image3->Canvas->Font->Style = myStyle;
  }
  if (CheckBox4->Checked)
  {
    myStyle = myStyle << fsStrikeOut;
    Image3->Canvas->Font->Style = myStyle;
```

24

VCL GRAPHICS
CLASSES

continues

LISTING 24.2   CONTINUED

```
  }
  if (CheckBox5->Checked)
    Image3->Canvas->Font->Height = TFontHeight - 10;
  else {
    Image3->Canvas->Font->Height = TFontHeight;
    Image3->Canvas->Font->Size = 20;
  }

  Image3->Canvas->FillRect(Image3->ClientRect);
  Image3->Canvas->TextOut(10,20,Edit2->Text.c_str());

  Image4->Canvas->FillRect(Image4->ClientRect);
  Image4->Canvas->TextOut(10,20,Edit2->Text.c_str());
}

void __fastcall TForm1::CheckBox1Click(TObject *Sender)
{
  Edit2->SetFocus();
  Edit2->SelStart = Edit2->SelLength;
}

void __fastcall TForm1::FormCreate(TObject *Sender)
{
  Image1->Canvas->Pen->Width = 3;
  Image1->Canvas->Pen->Color = clRed;

  Image2->Canvas->Brush->Style = bsSolid;
  Image2->Canvas->Brush->Color = clBlue;
  Image2->Canvas->Pen->Color = clRed;

  Image3->Canvas->Font->Size = 20;
  TFontHeight = Image3->Canvas->Font->Height;
  oldStyle = Image3->Canvas->Font->Style;

  Image4->Canvas->Font->Size = 20;
}

void __fastcall TForm1::Image5MouseDown(TObject *Sender,
      TMouseButton Button, TShiftState Shift, int X, int Y)
{
  Point1.x = X;
  Point1.y = Y;
  Point2.x = X;
  Point2.y = Y;
  Rendering = true;
}

void __fastcall TForm1::Image5MouseUp(TObject *Sender,
  TMouseButton Button, TShiftState Shift, int X, int Y)
```

```
{
  Rendering = false;
  Image5->Canvas->Pen->Style = psSolid;
  Image5->Canvas->Pen->Mode = pmCopy;
  if (CanRender && !Rendering)
    DrawShape(Point1.x,Point1.y,X,Y);
  if (SpeedButton5->Down)
  {
    Image5->Canvas->Brush->Color = clRed;
    Image5->Canvas->FloodFill(X,Y,clBlack,fsBorder);
    Image5->Canvas->Brush->Color = clWhite;
  }
}

void __fastcall TForm1::Image5MouseMove(
  TObject *Sender, TShiftState Shift, int X, int Y)
{
  if (CanRender)
    Render(X,Y);
}

void __fastcall TForm1::SpeedButton2Click(TObject *Sender)
{
  CanRender = true;
  dsCurrentShape = dsEllipse;
}

void __fastcall TForm1::SpeedButton4Click(TObject *Sender)
{                 CanRender = false;
  Rendering = false;
  Image5->Canvas->Brush->Style = bsSolid;
  Image5->Canvas->FillRect(Image5->ClientRect);
}

void __fastcall TForm1::SpeedButton1Click(TObject *Sender)
{
  CanRender = true;
  dsCurrentShape = dsLine;
}

void __fastcall TForm1::SpeedButton3Click(TObject *Sender)
{
  CanRender = true;
  dsCurrentShape = dsRectangle;
}

void __fastcall TForm1::RadioGroup3Click(TObject *Sender)
{
  switch (RadioGroup3->ItemIndex) {
```

continues

24

VCL GRAPHICS
CLASSES

LISTING 24.2   CONTINUED

```
      case 14 : TCopyMode = cmWhiteness; break;
      case 13 : TCopyMode = cmSrcPaint; break;
      case 12 : TCopyMode = cmSrcInvert; break;
      case 11 : TCopyMode = cmSrcErase; break;
      case 10 : TCopyMode = cmSrcCopy; break;
      case  9 : TCopyMode = cmSrcAnd; break;
      case  8 : TCopyMode = cmPatPaint; break;
      case  7 : TCopyMode = cmPatInvert; break;
      case  6 : TCopyMode = cmPatCopy; break;
      case  5 : TCopyMode = cmNotSrcErase; break;
      case  4 : TCopyMode = cmNotSrcCopy; break;
      case  3 : TCopyMode = cmMergePaint; break;
      case  2 : TCopyMode = cmMergeCopy; break;
      case  1 : TCopyMode = cmDstInvert; break;
      case  0 : TCopyMode = cmBlackness; break;
   }
}

void __fastcall TForm1::BitBtn1Click(TObject *Sender)
{
  Image6->Canvas->Brush->Color = clWhite;
  Image6->Canvas->Brush->Style = bsSolid;
  Image6->Canvas->FillRect(Image6->Canvas->ClipRect);
  Image6->Canvas->Brush->Color = clGreen;
  Image6->Canvas->Rectangle(25,25,140,140);
}

void __fastcall TForm1::BitBtn2Click(TObject *Sender)
{
  Image7->Canvas->Brush->Color = clWhite;
  Image7->Canvas->Brush->Style = bsSolid;
  Image7->Canvas->FillRect(Image7->Canvas->ClipRect);
  Image7->Canvas->Brush->Color = clBlue;
  Image7->Canvas->Rectangle(60,60,190,190);
}

void __fastcall TForm1::BitBtn3Click(TObject *Sender)
{
  Image7->Canvas->CopyMode = TCopyMode;
  Image7->Canvas->CopyRect(Image7->Canvas->ClipRect,
    Image6->Canvas, Image6->Canvas->ClipRect);
}

void __fastcall TForm1::Button3Click(TObject *Sender)
{
  HRGN MyRgn = CreateRectRgn(100,100,200,200);
  SelectClipRgn(Image8->Canvas->Handle,MyRgn);
  Ellipse(Image8->Canvas->Handle,90,90,210,210);
```

```
    Image8->Invalidate();
    SelectClipRgn(Image8->Canvas->Handle,0);
    DeleteObject(MyRgn);

    MyRgn = CreateRectRgn(200,200,300,300);
    SelectClipRgn(Image8->Canvas->Handle,MyRgn);
    Ellipse(Image8->Canvas->Handle,190,190,310,310);
    Image8->Invalidate();
    SelectClipRgn(Image8->Canvas->Handle,0);
    DeleteObject(MyRgn);

    MyRgn = CreateRectRgn(300,300,400,400);
    SelectClipRgn(Image8->Canvas->Handle,MyRgn);
    Ellipse(Image8->Canvas->Handle,290,290,410,410);
    Image8->Invalidate();
    SelectClipRgn(Image8->Canvas->Handle,0);
    DeleteObject(MyRgn);
}

void __fastcall TForm1::Button4Click(TObject *Sender)
{
    Image8->Canvas->FillRect(Image8->Canvas->ClipRect);
}
```

If you run the Brush program, you can see that you have the beginnings of a fairly simple Paint program. So let's get started looking at Listing 24.2 piece by piece.

The OnCreate Event

Begin by looking at the Brush program's OnCreate event:

```
void __fastcall TForm1::FormCreate(TObject *Sender)
{
    Image1->Canvas->Pen->Width = 3;
    Image1->Canvas->Pen->Color = clRed;

    Image2->Canvas->Brush->Style = bsSolid;
    Image2->Canvas->Brush->Color = clBlue;
    Image2->Canvas->Pen->Color = clRed;

    Image3->Canvas->Font->Size = 20;
    TFontHeight = Image3->Canvas->Font->Height;
    oldStyle = Image3->Canvas->Font->Style;

    Image4->Canvas->Font->Size = 20;
}
```

As you can see, I am assigning various values to the Pen, Font, and Brush objects that I am going to use when the form first paints itself. They can always be changed later at run time, as you will see later in this chapter. You don't need to do this if you are going to use the default values that are set when each object is created.

> **TIP**
>
> I find it is easier to group relevant lines of code together and separate them with a space. Grouping makes the code a lot more readable, but it is based on my own coding style and is a matter of personal preference.

The `FormShow()` Method

Now that the values are set, I need to address any drawing that I want done when the form first shows itself. I do so in the form's `FormShow()` method:

```
void __fastcall TForm1::FormShow(TObject *Sender)
{
  Image1->Canvas->Rectangle(0,0,Image1->Width,Image1->Height);
  Image2->Canvas->FillRect(Image2->Canvas->ClipRect);
  Image3->Canvas->FillRect(Image3->Canvas->ClipRect);
  Image4->Canvas->FillRect(Image4->Canvas->ClipRect);
  Image5->Canvas->FillRect(Image5->Canvas->ClipRect);
  Image6->Canvas->FillRect(Image6->Canvas->ClipRect);
  Image7->Canvas->FillRect(Image7->Canvas->ClipRect);
  Image8->Canvas->FillRect(Image8->Canvas->ClipRect);
}
```

Because all the images' canvases have not been drawn on, I need to initialize them so the `Canvas`'s brush paints them white when the form is shown. Notice that I am using the rectangle function for `Image1`. The result is the three-pixel wide red border drawn around the canvas. This was done for demonstration purposes; this way you can see how the canvas uses the pen to draw the shapes' borders. As for the rest of the images, I am filling the `ClipRect`, which is the largest rectangle that can be drawn on the canvas. You will see later in the code how to adjust the `ClipRect` to fit your needs.

Now look at the code that demonstrates setting the `Brush` styles:

```
void __fastcall TForm1::RadioGroup1Click(TObject *Sender)
{
  switch (RadioGroup1->ItemIndex) {
    case 8 : Check = true;
    case 7 : myBrushStyle = bsVertical; break;
    case 6 : myBrushStyle = bsFDiagonal; break;
    case 5 : myBrushStyle = bsBDiagonal; break;
    case 4 : myBrushStyle = bsHorizontal; break;
```

```
    case 3 : myBrushStyle = bsDiagCross; break;
    case 2 : myBrushStyle = bsClear; break;
    case 1 : myBrushStyle = bsCross; break;
    case 0 : myBrushStyle = bsSolid; break;
  }
  Button2Click(0);
}
```

In this method I set a brush style into the variable `myBrushStyle` and call `Button2Click()` so that the effects of the style can immediately be seen. Here's the `Button2Click()` method:

```
void __fastcall TForm1::Button2Click(TObject *Sender)
{
  if (Check) {
    Graphics::TBitmap* CustomBrush = new Graphics::TBitmap;
    try {
      CustomBrush->LoadFromFile("Custom.bmp");
      Image1->Canvas->Brush->Bitmap = CustomBrush;
      Image1->Canvas->FillRect(
        Rect(3,3,Image1->Width - 3, Image1->Height - 3));
    }
    __finally {
      Image1->Canvas->Brush->Bitmap = 0;
      delete CustomBrush;
    }
    Check = false;
  } else {
    Image1->Canvas->Brush->Style = myBrushStyle;
    Image1->Canvas->FillRect(
      Rect(3,3,Image1->Width - 3, Image1->Height - 3));
  }
}
```

This method sets the brush's style on the Brushes tab of the program. In this method, I am using either one of the stock brush styles or a custom bitmap for the brush. Notice that I wrap the code for using the custom brush in a `try`/`__finally` block. I use this block so the application will not cause an access violation if the `LoadFromFile()` function call fails. I simply catch the exception and handle it. You can put a `MessageBox()` in the `__finally` block to let the user know if the application could not load the bitmap. You would probably combine the preceding methods in your own code. I coded them this way for demonstration purposes only. If you combine these two methods into one, you can eliminate the two class member variables, `Check` and `myBrushStyle`, and make them local to the method. This is good coding style; you should use class member variables only when really necessary. As said earlier, when using a custom brush you need to set the brush's bitmap property to `0` when you finished.

Setting the Pen Mode

Now look at the code that handles the OnClick event for the Pens page of the Brush program:

```
void __fastcall TForm1::RadioGroup2Click(TObject *Sender)
{
  switch (RadioGroup2->ItemIndex) {
    case 15 : myMode = pmNotXor; break;
    case 14 : myMode = pmXor; break;
    case 13 : myMode = pmNotMask; break;
    case 12 : myMode = pmMask; break;
    case 11 : myMode = pmNotMerge; break;
    case 10 : myMode = pmMerge; break;
    case  9 : myMode = pmMaskNotPen; break;
    case  8 : myMode = pmMergeNotPen; break;
    case  7 : myMode = pmMaskPenNot; break;
    case  6 : myMode = pmMergePenNot; break;
    case  5 : myMode = pmNotCopy; break;
    case  4 : myMode = pmCopy; break;
    case  3 : myMode = pmNot; break;
    case  2 : myMode = pmNop; break;
    case  1 : myMode = pmWhite; break;
    case  0 : myMode = pmBlack; break;
  }
  Button1Click(0);
}
```

This method is the same as the brush's style except that I am setting the pen mode in the myMode variable and then calling the Button1Click() method:

```
void __fastcall TForm1::Button1Click(TObject *Sender)
{
  int y = 20;
  int x = 20;
  Image2->Canvas->Pen->Mode = myMode;
  Image2->Canvas->Pen->Width = Edit1->Text.ToInt();

  for (int i=0;i<10;i++) {
    Image2->Canvas->MoveTo(0,y);
    Image2->Canvas->LineTo(Image2->Width,y);
    y += 20;
  }

  for (int i=0;i<13;i++) {
    Image2->Canvas->MoveTo(x,0);
    Image2->Canvas->LineTo(x,Image2->Height);
    x += 20;
  }
}
```

Again, you would likely combine these methods into a single method in your own code. The preceding code allows this application's user to set the width of the pen through the spin edit control. I used this method to introduce you to the `MoveTo()` and `LineTo()` methods. The first `for` loop draws the horizontal lines, and the next `for` loop draws the vertical lines.

Working with Fonts

Now look at the code for the program's Fonts tab. Here, you will see the use of the different font properties and methods:

```
void __fastcall TForm1::Edit2Change(TObject *Sender)
{
  myStyle = oldStyle;

  Image3->Canvas->Font = Edit2->Font;
  Image4->Canvas->Font = Edit2->Font;
  Image3->Canvas->Font->Style = myStyle;

  if (CheckBox1->Checked)
  {
    myStyle = myStyle << fsBold;
    Image3->Canvas->Font->Style = myStyle;
  }
  if (CheckBox2->Checked)
  {
    myStyle = myStyle << fsItalic;
    Image3->Canvas->Font->Style = myStyle;
  }
  if (CheckBox3->Checked)
  {
    myStyle = myStyle << fsUnderline;
    Image3->Canvas->Font->Style = myStyle;
  }
  if (CheckBox4->Checked)
  {
    myStyle = myStyle << fsStrikeOut;
    Image3->Canvas->Font->Style = myStyle;
  }
  if (CheckBox5->Checked)
    Image3->Canvas->Font->Height = TFontHeight - 10;
  else {
    Image3->Canvas->Font->Height = TFontHeight;
    Image3->Canvas->Font->Size = 20;
  }

  Image3->Canvas->FillRect(Image3->ClientRect);
  Image3->Canvas->TextOut(10,20,Edit2->Text.c_str());
```

```
   Image4->Canvas->FillRect(Image4->ClientRect);
   Image4->Canvas->TextOut(10,20,Edit2->Text.c_str());
}
```

This method is interesting in that it covers a lot of ground and demonstrates many concepts previously discussed. The first line of code simply clears all styles that have been previously set in the `myStyle` variable; it also returns the style to the default values, which I saved in the `OnCreate` event; I assign this variable to the canvas's `Font::Style` property. The next four `if` statements add a style to the set if the check box is selected. This is done with the `<<` operator. Remember that with font styles, you are dealing with a set, as discussed earlier. The next `if` statement simply plays around with the size and height properties to show you how this works. The last four lines are kind of interesting. I am allowing any changes made to the style to show up as the user types in characters in the edit box, making the changes in real time. The `FillRect()` call repaints the image box, and `TextOut()` puts the new string on the image's canvas with all the changes in effect.

Drawing Shapes on the Canvas

Next, look at the code that drives the Brush program's Shapes page. A lot is going on in this section, so you will spend a fair amount of time here. The first method I would like to discuss is `DrawShape()`:

```
void TForm1::DrawShape(int w, int x, int y, int z)
{
  switch (dsCurrentShape) {
    case dsEllipse : Image5->Canvas->Ellipse(w,x,y,z); break;
    case dsRectangle : Image5->Canvas->Rectangle(w,x,y,z); break;
    case dsLine :
    {
      Image5->Canvas->MoveTo(w,x);
      Image5->Canvas->LineTo(y,z);
      break;
    }
  }
}
```

The whole purpose of `DrawShape()` is to draw the shape that the user has selected on the canvas via the `dsCurrentShape` variable. You also need it to do your cleanup, as you will see when looking at the `Render()` function. Before I describe that process, look at the functions that determine what to draw, as well as when to and when not to draw:

```
procedure TForm1::SpeedButton1Click(Sender: TObject);
{
  CanRender = true;
  dsCurrentShape = dsLine;
```

```
}

void __fastcall TForm1::SpeedButton2Click(TObject *Sender)
{
  CanRender = true;
  dsCurrentShape = dsEllipse;
}

void __fastcall TForm1::SpeedButton3Click(TObject *Sender)
{
  CanRender = true;
  dsCurrentShape = dsRectangle;
}
```

Each preceding method sets two variables. CanRender is a bool flag set to true when a valid shape has been chosen for drawing. dsCurrentShape is a variable that holds the type of shape the user has selected and that I am going to draw. Each shape has its own Click() method. However, you can combine all the methods into one common method, as shown here:

```
void __fastcall TForm1::SpeedButtonClick(TObject *Sender)
{
  TSpeedButton* button = dynamic_cast<TSpeedButton*>(Sender);
  if (button->Down)
    CanRender = true;
  if (button->Name == "SpeedButton1")
    dsCurrentShape = dsLine;
  else if(button->Name == "SpeedButton2")
    dsCurrentShape = dsEllipse;
  else if (button->Name == "SpeedButton3")
    dsCurrentShape = dsRectangle;
}
```

Either way is valid; however, if you have a lot of different shape values that dsCurrentShape can assume, writing a method for each is better. This approach is better because you will encounter a performance hit due to the fact that each value must be evaluated until a match is encountered.

After the user has chosen a valid shape, I must draw it where he or she wants it to be drawn. I will use the MouseDown event to set some further needed values:

```
void __fastcall TForm1::Image5MouseDown(TObject *Sender,
     TMouseButton Button, TShiftState Shift, int X, int Y)
{
  Point1.x = X;
  Point1.y = Y;
  Point2.x = X;
  Point2.y = Y;
  Rendering = true;
}
```

Here, I have two point structures and a Boolean. The `Point1` variable memorizes the starting or *anchor* point of the shape I am going to draw. `Point2` holds the current mouse position. The `Rendering` variable lets the application know that I can start drawing. I must start drawing when the user begins moving the mouse. To that end, I use the `MouseMove` event as follows:

```
void __fastcall TForm1::Image5MouseMove(
  TObject *Sender, TShiftState Shift, int X, int Y)
{
  if (CanRender)
    Render(X,Y);
}
```

If a valid shape is chosen, I call the `Render()` function and pass the current mouse position. The `Render()` function does all the work:

```
void TForm1::Render(int x, int y)
{
  if (CanRender && Rendering && !SpeedButton4->Down) {
    Image5->Canvas->Brush->Style = bsClear;
    Image5->Canvas->Pen->Mode = pmNotXor;
    Image5->Canvas->Pen->Style = psDot;
    DrawShape(Point1.x,Point1.y,Point2.x,Point2.y);
    Point2.x = x;
    Point2.y = y;
    DrawShape(Point1.x,Point1.y,Point2.x,Point2.y);
  } else
    Rendering = false;
}
```

The first thing I do here is check to see whether I can draw. `CanRender` and `Rendering` work in tandem to determine when I can do something and when I cannot. Without this check, I could be drawing when the user doesn't want to. Next, I set the brush style to `bsClear` so I do not erase the background. I then set the pen mode to `pmNotXor`. This combination results in what is known as *rubber banding*. Notice that `DrawShape()` is called twice. The first call will erase the old image because of the pen mode `pmNotXor` at the previous location. I then assign the new cursor position to `Point2` and call `Render()` again to draw the shape using the current coordinates. This cycle goes on erasing and redrawing until the user releases the mouse button.

The `OnMouseUp` event handler ends the rubber banding and draws the shape:

```
void __fastcall TForm1::Image5MouseUp(TObject *Sender,
  TMouseButton Button, TShiftState Shift, int X, int Y)
{
  Rendering = false;
  Image5->Canvas->Pen->Style = psSolid;
  Image5->Canvas->Pen->Mode = pmCopy;
```

```
if (CanRender && !Rendering)
  DrawShape(Point1.x,Point1.y,X,Y);
if (SpeedButton5->Down)
{
  Image5->Canvas->Brush->Color = clRed;
  Image5->Canvas->FloodFill(X,Y,clBlack,fsBorder);
  Image5->Canvas->Brush->Color = clWhite;
}
}
```

In this function, I draw the final shape. I set Rendering to false so that I won't do any inadvertent drawing, reset the pen to draw the final shape, and draw it at the current position by calling DrawShape() one last time. I also check to see whether the user wants to fill a selected area by checking the value of SpeedButton5->Down. If the Down property is true, I fill it, in this particular case, with the red brush. I reset the brush color, and I am done.

Using CopyModes

Heading for the home stretch, we come to the Brush program's CopyMode tab. The code for this page is so similar to the pen's and brush's sheets that I don't need to discuss all the methods here. The only method that I need to discuss is the following:

```
void __fastcall TForm1::BitBtn3Click(TObject *Sender)
{
  Image7->Canvas->CopyMode = TCopyMode;
  Image7->Canvas->CopyRect(Image7->Canvas->ClipRect,
    Image6->Canvas, Image6->Canvas->ClipRect);
}
```

I just set CopyMode to the one that the user has chosen and then copy the rectangle on Image6's canvas to Image7's canvas.

Modifying the ClipRect

Last is the example program's ClipRect page. It is interesting because I need to combine Win32 API calls with VCL code:

```
void __fastcall TForm1::Button3Click(TObject *Sender)
{
  HRGN MyRgn = CreateRectRgn(100,100,200,200);
  SelectClipRgn(Image8->Canvas->Handle,MyRgn);
  Ellipse(Image8->Canvas->Handle,90,90,210,210);
  Image8->Invalidate();
  SelectClipRgn(Image8->Canvas->Handle,0);
  DeleteObject(MyRgn);
```

24

VCL GRAPHICS
CLASSES

```
    MyRgn = CreateRectRgn(200,200,300,300);
    SelectClipRgn(Image8->Canvas->Handle,MyRgn);
    Ellipse(Image8->Canvas->Handle,190,190,310,310);
    Image8->Invalidate();
    SelectClipRgn(Image8->Canvas->Handle,0);
    DeleteObject(MyRgn);

    MyRgn = CreateRectRgn(300,300,400,400);
    SelectClipRgn(Image8->Canvas->Handle,MyRgn);
    Ellipse(Image8->Canvas->Handle,290,290,410,410);
    Image8->Invalidate();
    SelectClipRgn(Image8->Canvas->Handle,0);
    DeleteObject(MyRgn);
}
```

In this method, I am changing the clipping region from the VCL default rectangle (the whole canvas) to one of my own definition. Because the `ClipRect` property is read-only, I can't set it directly. I must do some behind-the-scenes work and then let the VCL do its work. First, I need to define a region. I do so with the API call `CreateRectRgn()` and pass it the region I want to create. In the first case, I am creating a 100×100-pixel region anchored at 100,100 on the canvas. Next, I select this region as the clipping `Rect` by using `SelectClipRgn()`. This function takes two parameters: a DC, which in this case is `Image8->Canvas->Handle`, and the region I want to select. Next, I draw my ellipse immediately followed by a call to the `Invalidate()` method. This method causes a `WM_PAINT` message to be dispatched, which causes the image to be redrawn. VCL reads the `ClipRect`, which is now the region that I defined, and does the drawing accordingly. A second call to `SelectClipRgn()` passes 0 as the second parameter. This code reselects the clipping region I had prior to my redefining it. Last, I need to do my own cleanup, so I make the call to `DeleteObject()` to release the region. This is a good example of mixing VCL code with straight Windows API code.

Finally, you can see that `ClipRect` has indeed been reset to the default value:

```
void __fastcall TForm1::Button4Click(TObject *Sender)
{
    Image8->Canvas->FillRect(Image8->Canvas->ClipRect);
}
```

This function call repaints the whole canvas, proving that the `ClipRect` is back to normal.

Creating Custom Pen Lines

Until now, I have used the pen to draw lines. The `Width` property was the only property you could manipulate that would affect how that line was drawn on the canvas. You could alter how wide the line was drawn but little else. Granted, if the width were one pixel, you could draw dots and dashes—but what if you want to have a custom line, a line, for example, that looks as if it were drawn by a calligraphy pen? The fact is, you can draw just about any type of line you want. The only catch is that it will not be a line at all. Drawing a line that is not a line? You can create such a line by drawing a series of shapes that are connected so that they appear to be a line. To draw a line that appears and acts like one drawn by a calligraphy pen is quite simple. You use the canvas method `Polygon` to draw what are called *parallelograms*. Figure 24.6 demonstrates what this looks like.

FIGURE 24.6

This view shows a series of interconnected polygons.

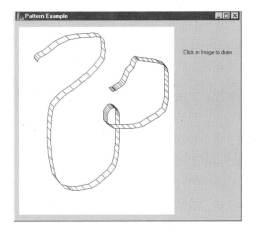

Remember that a shape method, when called, draws the outline of the shape with the current pen; that shape is filled with the current brush. If you set both the pen and brush to the same color, you get what appears to be your custom "line," as shown in Figure 24.7.

FIGURE 24.7

This view shows the custom line.

The Pattern program, shown in Listings 24.3 and 24.4, will draw calligraphy pen-type lines.

LISTING 24.3   THE HEADER FOR THE PATTERN PROGRAM

```cpp
#ifndef PatternMainH
#define PatternMainH

#include <Classes.hpp>
#include <Controls.hpp>
#include <StdCtrls.hpp>
#include <Forms.hpp>
#include <ExtCtrls.hpp>

class TForm1 : public TForm
{
__published:      // IDE-managed Components
  TImage *Image1;
  TLabel *Label1;
  void __fastcall Image1MouseDown(TObject *Sender, TMouseButton Button,
          TShiftState Shift, int X, int Y);
  void __fastcall Image1MouseMove(TObject *Sender, TShiftState Shift,
          int X, int Y);
  void __fastcall Image1MouseUp(TObject *Sender, TMouseButton Button,
          TShiftState Shift, int X, int Y);
  void __fastcall FormCreate(TObject *Sender);
private:      // User declarations
  bool FRendering;
  TPoint org, next1;
public:            // User declarations
  __fastcall TForm1(TComponent* Owner);
};

extern PACKAGE TForm1 *Form1;

#endif
```

LISTING 24.4   THE MAIN UNIT FOR THE PATTERN PROGRAM

```cpp
////////////////////////////////////////////////////////////////////////
//  PatternMain.cpp                                                    //
//  Project: Pattern                                                   //
////////////////////////////////////////////////////////////////////////
#include <vcl.h>
#pragma hdrstop

#include "PatternMain.h"

#pragma package(smart_init)
```

```
#pragma resource "*.dfm"
TForm1 *Form1;

__fastcall TForm1::TForm1(TComponent* Owner)
    : TForm(Owner)
{
}

void __fastcall TForm1::Image1MouseDown(TObject *Sender,
        TMouseButton Button, TShiftState Shift, int X, int Y)
{
  FRendering = true;
  org = Point(X,Y);
  next1 = Point(X,Y);
}

void __fastcall TForm1::Image1MouseMove(
  TObject *Sender, TShiftState Shift, int X, int Y)
{
  TPoint points[4];
  if (FRendering) {
    next1 = Point(X,Y);
    points[0] = org;
    points[1] = next1;
    points[2] = Point(next1.x + 8,next1.y + 8);
    points[3] = Point(org.x + 8,org.y + 8);
    Image1->Canvas->Polygon(points, 3);
    org = Point(X ,Y );
  }
}

void __fastcall TForm1::Image1MouseUp(TObject *Sender,
  TMouseButton Button, TShiftState Shift, int X, int Y)
{
  FRendering = false;
}

void __fastcall TForm1::FormCreate(TObject *Sender)
{
  Image1->Canvas->Brush->Color = clRed;
  Image1->Canvas->Pen->Color = clRed;
}
```

In the FormCreate() method, I assign the same color to the pen and brush. In the Image1MouseDown() method, I get the points at which to begin drawing. The real work is done with the Image1MouseMove() method:

```
void __fastcall TForm1::Image1MouseMove(
  TObject *Sender, TShiftState Shift, int X, int Y)
```

24

VCL GRAPHICS CLASSES

```
{
  TPoint points[4];
  if (FRendering) {
    next1 = Point(X,Y);
    points[0] = org;
    points[1] = next1;
    points[2] = Point(next1.x + 8,next1.y + 8);
    points[3] = Point(org.x + 8,org.y + 8);
    Image1->Canvas->Polygon(points, 3);
    org = Point(X ,Y );
  }
}
```

In this method, while the mouse is moving and the rendering flag is `true`, I am drawing a polygon using the ending points of the last polygon as the starting points of the next one.

By using your imagination, you can now draw any line style by simply using different shapes, combinations of shapes, pen and brush colors, and pen width. You can even use bitmap brushes to fill the shapes. You are probably beginning to see that just about anything is possible with the VCL graphics operations.

Looking Deeper into the VCL

In this section, I drill down a little bit further into the VCL and look at some of the basics that all graphical programming is built upon.

From there, I move on to discuss some of the higher-level VCL graphical container classes. Finally, I show you some sample code that manipulates bitmaps.

The `TColor` Data Type

`TColor` is one of the most basic VCL types. Colors in Windows programming are defined as RGB values. This means that you have three base colors—red, green, and blue—each with a value from `0` to `255`. These values make up all the different colors that you see on your screen.

The lower three bytes of a `TColor` value represent RGB color intensities for blue, green, and red, respectively. The value `0x00FF0000` represents pure, full-intensity blue;

0x0000FF00 is pure green; 0x000000FF is pure red. 0x00000000 is black and 0x00FFFFFF is white.

The high-order byte of a TColor value contains palette information. If the highest-order byte is zero (00), the color obtained is the closest matching color in the system palette. If the highest-order byte is one (01), the color obtained is the closest matching color in the currently realized palette. If the highest-order byte is two (02), the value is matched with the nearest color in the logical palette of the current device context.

The VCL header that describes the VCL graphics classes is Graphics.hpp. Among other things, it contains definitions of useful constants for TColor. For example, some of the definitions include clBlue, clGreen, and clRed. These constants map either directly to the closest matching color in the system palette (for example, clBlue maps to blue) or to the corresponding system screen element color defined in the Appearance section of the Windows control panel icon display. For example, clBtnFace maps to the system color for button faces.

The built-in color constants provide easy access to the most commonly used colors. At times, however, you need to use a custom color. For those times you can assign a hexa-decimal value to any component's Color property:

```
Form1->Color = (TColor)0x00C700;  // a shade of green
```

The cast to TColor is necessary to avoid a compiler warning. You can also make a direct assignment into the Color property of an object in the Object Inspector, as shown in Figure 24.8.

FIGURE 24.8

Making a direct color assignment in the Object Inspector.

The constants that map to the closest matching system colors are as follows:

clAqua	clGreen	clPurple
clBlack	clLime	clRed
clBlue	clLtGray	clSilver
clDkGray	clMaroon	clTeal
clFuchsia	clNavy	clWhite
clGray	clOlive	clYellow

The constants that map to the system screen element colors are as follows:

clActiveBorder	clHighlightText
clActiveCaption	clInactiveBorder
clAppWorkSpace	clInactiveCaption
clBackground	clInactiveCaptionText
clBtnFace	
clBtnHighlight	clMenu
clBtnShadow	clMenuText
clBtnText	clScrollBar
clCaptionText	clWindow
clGrayText	clWindowFrame
clHighlight	clWindowText

If you search in the C++Builder help file for `TColor`, you will find a full explanation of these color constants and how they relate to real-world colors.

> **NOTE**
>
> Be careful with the use of color in your applications—especially colors used for controls such as buttons, edit controls, list boxes, and so on. What appeals to you as a programmer may not appeal to your users. Use the system color constants (`clBtnFace`, `clWindow`, `clWindowText`, and so on) whenever possible. These constants will map to the color scheme on each user's machine, thereby making your application look the way the user wants.

The Colors Sample Project

When I began programming for Windows I used straight Windows API calls. This Colors sample project is one of the first I wrote to start understanding how Windows graphics worked. At that time, the program took about five pages of code. The brevity of this code says a lot about the power and eloquence of the VCL and C++Builder. Listings 24.5 and 24.6 illustrate how to manipulate colors in a program.

LISTING 24.5   THE HEADER FOR THE COLORS PROGRAM

```
#ifndef ColorMainH
#define ColorMainH

#include <Classes.hpp>
#include <Controls.hpp>
#include <StdCtrls.hpp>
#include <Forms.hpp>
#include <ComCtrls.hpp>
#include <ExtCtrls.hpp>

class TForm1 : public TForm
{
__published:      // IDE-managed Components
  TLabel *Label1;
  TLabel *Label2;
  TLabel *Label3;
  TLabel *Label4;
  TLabel *Label5;
  TLabel *Label6;
  TLabel *Label7;
  TTrackBar *TrackBar1;
```

24

VCL GRAPHICS
CLASSES

continues

Listing 24.5   Continued

```
    TTrackBar *TrackBar2;
    TTrackBar *TrackBar3;
    TPanel *Panel1;
    TPaintBox *PaintBox1;
    TEdit *Edit1;
    TEdit *Edit2;
    TEdit *Edit3;
    TEdit *Edit4;
    void __fastcall TrackBar1Change(TObject *Sender);
    void __fastcall PaintBox1Paint(TObject *Sender);
private:      // User declarations
public:           // User declarations
    __fastcall TForm1(TComponent* Owner);
};

extern PACKAGE TForm1 *Form1;

#endif
```

Listing 24.6   The Colors Program's Main Unit

```
///////////////////////////////////////////////////////////////////
//   ColorMain.cpp                                                 //
//   Project: Colors                                               //
///////////////////////////////////////////////////////////////////
#include <vcl.h>
#pragma hdrstop

#include "ColorMain.h"

#pragma package(smart_init)
#pragma resource "*.dfm"
TForm1 *Form1;

__fastcall TForm1::TForm1(TComponent* Owner)
    : TForm(Owner)
{
}

void __fastcall TForm1::TrackBar1Change(TObject *Sender)
{
   PaintBox1->Canvas->Brush->Color = (TColor)RGB(
     TrackBar1->Position, TrackBar2->Position, TrackBar3->Position);

   Edit1->Text = TrackBar1->Position;
   Edit2->Text = TrackBar2->Position;
   Edit3->Text = TrackBar3->Position;
   Edit4->Text = IntToHex(PaintBox1->Canvas->Brush->Color,8);
```

```
  PaintBox1->Canvas->FillRect(PaintBox1->ClientRect);
}

void __fastcall TForm1::PaintBox1Paint(TObject *Sender)
{
  PaintBox1->Color = (TColor)RGB(TrackBar1->Position,
    TrackBar2->Position, TrackBar3->Position);
  PaintBox1->Canvas->FillRect(PaintBox1->Canvas->ClipRect);
}
```

The OnChange Event Handler

ColorMain has only two methods: an OnChange event handler for TrackBar and an OnPaint event handler for PaintBox. I discuss only the OnChange event handler here and reserve the OnPaint event handler discussion for when I talk about the PaintBox component.

```
void __fastcall TForm1::TrackBar1Change(TObject *Sender)
{
  PaintBox1->Canvas->Brush->Color = (TColor)RGB(
    TrackBar1->Position, TrackBar2->Position, TrackBar3->Position);

  Edit1->Text = TrackBar1->Position;
  Edit2->Text = TrackBar2->Position;
  Edit3->Text = TrackBar3->Position;
  Edit4->Text = IntToHex(PaintBox1->Canvas->Brush->Color,8);

  PaintBox1->Canvas->FillRect(PaintBox1->ClientRect);
}
```

Although TrackBar1Change() is a very simple method, a lot is going on here. On the surface, I am only using the value of each TrackBar's current position to set the red, green, and blue values of the color. I can do a direct read of this value because I gave the TrackBar a range from 0 to 255. I then complete the following steps:

1. Use the RGB Windows API macro, which takes the three Trackbar values and converts them to a COLORREF data type.

2. Display the values and fill the PaintBox with the new color whenever a change occurs in any of the three values using the FillRect() method of the PaintBox's canvas.

When your computer has its display mode set to anything greater than 256 colors, everything looks normal and great. Figure 24.9 shows how a pure color looks in 24-bit color. If you are running in 256-color mode, you might get a screen that looks like the one in Figure 24.10.

24

VCL GRAPHICS CLASSES

Figure 24.9

A view of a pure color.

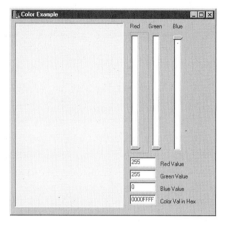

Figure 24.10

A view of a dithered color in 256-color mode.

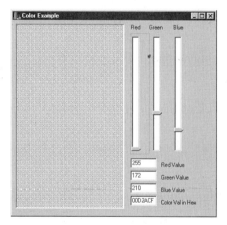

As computers become more and more powerful, having differing color modes is not a factor; most new computers can display true color. Despite this, it is still worth discussion. What you see in Figure 26.10 is an effect called *dithering*. In 256-color mode, only 236 colors are available for use at any given time; Windows uses the other 20 colors for itself. The question is this: "What about all the other colors that I might want to use—the rest of the rainbow, so to speak?" Windows uses dithering to display these colors. Windows creates a custom brush composed of a pixel pattern that combines pixels of different pure colors to fool your eyes into seeing the color you request. Windows can display about 262,144 dithered colors in 256-color mode. If you play with the Colors program in 256-color mode, you will see what I am talking about.

Working with Palettes

Now I will break away from colors and give a brief overview of palettes. In 16- or 256-color mode—the only modes that support palettes—a *palette* is just a collection of colors stored in a Windows LOGPALETTE structure. Palettes are used by controls and graphical images to store information about the specific colors that they will need when they are drawn on the screen. Windows refers to this process as *realizing palettes*. Realizing palettes ensures that the topmost window uses its full palette and that windows in the background use as much of their palettes as possible. Windows then maps any other colors to the closest available colors in the "real" palette. As windows move in front of one another, Windows continually realizes the palettes. The VCL provides no specific support for creating or maintaining palettes, other than in bitmaps.

If you want to explore how to work with palettes in Windows, you might want to start by looking at the palette functions in the Win32 API. Here's a list of some of the palette functions:

AnimatePalette()	RealizePalette()
CreateHalftonePalette()	ResizePalette()
CreatePalette()	SelectPalette()
GetColorAdjustment()	SetColorAdjustment()
GetNearestColor()	SetPaletteEntries()
GetNearestPalette()	SetSystemPaletteUse()
IndexGetPaletteEntries()	UnrealizeObject()
GetSystemPaletteEntries()	UpdateColors()
GetSystemPaletteUse()	

The following are the color structures used by Windows for palette operations:

COLORREF
LOGPALETTE
PALETTEENTRY

Image File Formats in Windows

Earlier in the chapter I gave a very short bitmap definition. It allowed you to do what you needed, but now it's time to revisit bitmaps and other Windows image file formats. The revisit will give you a greater understanding of the files that you will be working with.

Bitmaps and DIBs

You already know that a bitmap is a binary representation of an image, but what does this really mean? A *bitmap* consists of two distinct parts. The first part is a BITMAPINFO structure describing the dimensions of the bitmap and color palette that Windows will use when the image is displayed. If this structure does not contain any color palette information, Windows uses the system palette when the image is displayed. You refer to this type of bitmap as a *device-dependent bitmap*, or *DDB*.

If the bitmap does contain color palette information, it is a *device-independent bitmap*, or *DIB*. The second part of the file contains the array of bytes defining the bitmap's pixels. After the image is stored in memory, however, there is no difference between the two. A BMP image might vary slightly when displayed on machines that have different video hardware installed, whereas a DIB will always look the same because it contains its own palette information. Both types of bitmaps are identified by the .bmp file extension.

Icons

Icons typically have the file extension .ico. Like any other Windows resource, they can also be stored in a resource file that an application then uses. Icons typically come in large and small sizes. Windows uses the large icon to represent the application on the desktop; it is 32×32 pixels. The small icon is displayed in the upper-left corner of a window; it is 16×16 pixels. Figure 24.11 shows an icon during the design or drawing phase. When you create an icon using the Image Editor that ships with C++Builder, a second image or mask is also created for you. Figure 24.12 shows the icon and the mask. This mask causes a certain color in the icon to be transparent. You can almost always use the mask if you do not want the icon's background to be displayed. If your application uses a large number of icons, you should use an ImageList component to manage these icons for you. Icons are represented in C++Builder as TIcon objects.

FIGURE 24.11
Designing an icon in the Image Editor.

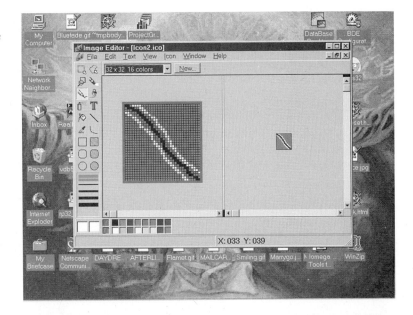

FIGURE 24.12
An icon and its mask in the Image Editor.

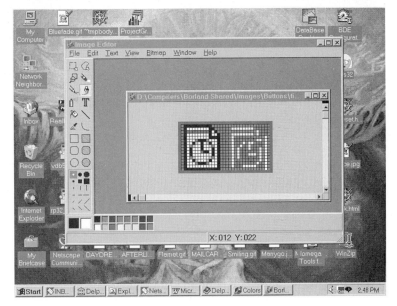

Metafiles

Metafiles are different from other image formats in that they are not graphical images, but a series of GDI functions that represent how an image is drawn. If you have ever written a keystroke macro, you already have a basic understanding of how a metafile works. You record a drawing routine and then play it to display the image. The following sample code is a text representation of how a metafile can look:

```
Rectangle(hdcmeta,0,0,100,100);
Rectangle(hdcmeta,20,20,120,120);
Rectangle(hdcmeta,40,40,140,140);
```

This example will draw three overlapping rectangles when played onto an `Image` canvas. Figure 24.13 displays a metafile after it has been played to the screen.

FIGURE 24.13

A displayed metafile.

Using this type of image format poses advantages and disadvantages. One of the major advantages is the file's size. Because a metafile does not have to store information about each pixel to be drawn, only how to draw the overall image, the actual file size can be dramatically reduced. Another advantage of using metafiles is the capability to precisely edit the picture's contents. You get this advantage because metafiles are just a series of shapes that can be edited separately through the shape's function call. Finally, due to their nature, metafiles are much better at scaling than are bitmaps. This is particularly important if you have to stretch an image.

The major disadvantage is that you cannot easily store a scanned image in this format. This is because a metafile is just a series of drawing calls.

Metafiles come in two flavors: 16-bit .WMF (Windows metafile) files and 32-bit .EMF (enhanced metafile). The EMF files are far more powerful than the WMF files. The code shown in Listings 24.7 and 24.8 makes use of this type of graphic file.

LISTING 24.7   THE HEADER FOR THE METAFILE PROGRAM

```
#ifndef MetaMainH
#define MetaMainH

#include <Classes.hpp>
#include <Controls.hpp>
#include <StdCtrls.hpp>
#include <Forms.hpp>
#include <ExtCtrls.hpp>

class TForm1 : public TForm
{
__published:     // IDE-managed Components
  TImage *Image1;
  TButton *Button1;
  TButton *Button2;
  TButton *Button3;
  TButton *Button4;
  TButton *Button5;
  void __fastcall Button1Click(TObject *Sender);
  void __fastcall Button2Click(TObject *Sender);
  void __fastcall Button3Click(TObject *Sender);
  void __fastcall FormCreate(TObject *Sender);
  void __fastcall Button5Click(TObject *Sender);
  void __fastcall Button4Click(TObject *Sender);
private:     // User declarations
  TMetafile* pMetafile;
  TMetafileCanvas* pCanvas;
public:          // User declarations
  __fastcall TForm1(TComponent* Owner);
};

extern PACKAGE TForm1 *Form1;

#endif
```

24

VCL GRAPHICS CLASSES

LISTING 24.8   THE METAFILE PROGRAM'S MAIN UNIT

```
///////////////////////////////////////////////////////////////
//  MetaMain.cpp                                              //
//  Project: Metafile                                         //
///////////////////////////////////////////////////////////////
```

continues

LISTING 24.8   CONTINUED

```cpp
#include <vcl.h>
#pragma hdrstop

#include "MetaMain.h"

#pragma package(smart_init)
#pragma resource "*.dfm"
TForm1 *Form1;

__fastcall TForm1::TForm1(TComponent* Owner)
  : TForm(Owner)
{
}

void __fastcall TForm1::Button1Click(TObject *Sender)
{
  try {
    pMetafile->LoadFromFile("enhanced.emf");
    Image1->Canvas->Draw(0,0,pMetafile);
  }
  catch (...) {
    Application->MessageBox("Could not load Metafile.", 0, MB_OK);
  }
}

void __fastcall TForm1::Button2Click(TObject *Sender)
{
  try {
    pCanvas = new TMetafileCanvas(pMetafile, 0);
    pCanvas->Draw(0,0,pMetafile);
    pCanvas->Brush->Color = clYellow;
    pCanvas->Ellipse(100,100,200,200);
  }
  __finally {
    delete pCanvas;
    pCanvas = 0;
  }
  Image1->Canvas->Draw(0,0,pMetafile);
}

void __fastcall TForm1::Button3Click(TObject *Sender)
{
  pMetafile->SaveToFile("modified.emf");
}

void __fastcall TForm1::FormCreate(TObject *Sender)
{
  pMetafile = new TMetafile;
}
```

```
void __fastcall TForm1::Button5Click(TObject *Sender)
{
  Image1->Canvas->Brush->Color = clWhite;
  Image1->Canvas->FillRect(Image1->Canvas->ClipRect);
}

void __fastcall TForm1::Button4Click(TObject *Sender)
{
  try {
    pMetafile->LoadFromFile("modified.emf");
    Image1->Canvas->Draw(0,0,pMetafile);
  }
  catch (...) {
    Application->MessageBox("Could not load Metafile.", 0, MB_OK);
  }
}
```

Now examine the important parts of the code in Listing 24.8. The first method you need to look at is `FormCreate()`:

```
void __fastcall TForm1::FormCreate(TObject *Sender)
{
  pMetafile = new TMetafile;
}

void __fastcall TForm1::Button5Click(TObject *Sender)
{
  Image1->Canvas->Brush->Color = clWhite;
  Image1->Canvas->FillRect(Image1->Canvas->ClipRect);
}
```

I am simply creating a new metafile object for my use.

Now look at `Button1Click()`:

```
void __fastcall TForm1::Button1Click(TObject *Sender)
{
  try {
    pMetafile->LoadFromFile("enhanced.emf");
    Image1->Canvas->Draw(0,0,pMetafile);
  }
  catch (...) {
    Application->MessageBox("Could not load Metafile.", 0, MB_OK);
  }
}
```

I am loading a metafile from a file on disk and playing it onto the canvas of `Image1`. I also could have loaded it directly into the `Picture` property and let the VCL do all the drawing:

```
Image1->Picture->LoadFromFile("enhanced.emf");
```

This method will not let you do any further drawing on it. If you just want to display a metafile, this method is the proper way to do it.

Here's the meat of the program:

```
void __fastcall TForm1::Button2Click(TObject *Sender)
{
  try {
    pCanvas = new TMetafileCanvas(pMetafile, 0);
    pCanvas->Draw(0,0,pMetafile);
    pCanvas->Brush->Color = clYellow;
    pCanvas->Ellipse(100,100,200,200);
  }
  __finally {
    delete pCanvas;
    pCanvas = 0;
  }
  Image1->Canvas->Draw(0,0,pMetafile);
}
```

I am creating a `MetafileCanvas`. Each `MetafileCanvas` is associated with a particular metafile. The next step is important but a little confusing. You need to create a `MetafileCanvas` before you can record or modify a metafile. You are free to modify it after creating it. Here is the confusing part: You must first delete `MetafileCanvas` before you can play it. You can think in terms of using a tape recorder: You must record something before you can play it. When you delete the `MetafileCanvas`, this action is the same as pushing the Stop button and then pushing Rewind. After you do so, you are ready to play what you recorded. The other functions arc fairly self-explanatory.

TPaintBox and TImage

You have used both the `TPaintBox` and `TImage` components, though I have yet to talk about them. These components may appear to be interchangeable because they have many properties in common. They have some major but subtle differences that are worth talking about.

`TPaintBox` requires you to draw directly on a canvas. Because no mechanism is in place for a `PaintBox` to remember what was drawn on the canvas at any given time, you must do all the redrawing yourself when its canvas is invalidated. Another window passing in front of your window is an example. Nothing will be redrawn if you do not override the `OnPaint` event handler. Figure 24.14 shows what happens if you do not override the Colors program's `OnPaint` method.

FIGURE 24.14

If the paint method is not overridden, the form is not repainted properly.

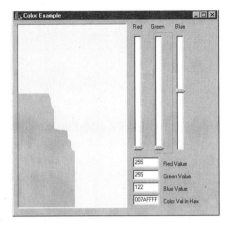

The following code is from the Colors example:

```
void __fastcall TForm1::PaintBox1Paint(TObject *Sender)
{
  PaintBox1->Color = (TColor)RGB(TrackBar1->Position,
    TrackBar2->Position, TrackBar3->Position);
  PaintBox1->Canvas->FillRect(PaintBox1->Canvas->ClipRect);
}
```

I am overriding the OnPaint() method with this code in place, and my program properly repaints itself when the need arises.

As you might have guessed, TPaintBox is sometimes not the right tool for a particular job. When this is the case, you have the TImage component to fall back on. TImage displays an image that is stored in a bitmap, an icon, or a metafile. It also maintains an in-memory internal bitmap that you can draw on. Thus, when its canvas is invalidated, it has the mechanism to know and remember how to repaint itself. When it needs to repaint itself, it simply copies the current state of this bitmap onto the canvas. TImage does not have an OnPaint() method, as it handles all the repainting internally; you do not have to concern yourself with it.

Optimizing Graphics Programs

I need to say a few words about graphics programming in general before proceeding. Generally speaking, in graphics programming you are concerned with speed and how fast you can get your drawing algorithm to draw. Sometimes, this means rolling some of your code out to assembly so that you control how it behaves rather than depending on the compiler. Other times, this means simply thinking about what you want to do and doing it in the most efficient way possible. None of the code in this section has been optimized for speed; it is there to give you a starting place to write truly fast code using the VCL. I will touch on some areas to make the code faster when the need arises. Whole books are written on the art of code optimization if you want to explore this part of programming.

You have learned how to load a bitmap, display it, and draw on its canvas. What if you want to directly manipulate the image or copy it to another bitmap in an altered state and display the altered image? A good example is to *invert* an image (draw it upside down). You could use the Pixels property to copy each pixel in the original bitmap to the location you choose on the destination bitmap. This process would be very inefficient. Luckily, C++Builder gives you a TBitmap property to make your job easier, not to mention faster. ScanLine allows you to get an entire row of pixels at once that can be addressed like an array. Instead of having to do a read for each pixel in the bitmap, you can do a read for each line. Reading a bitmap this way speeds your drawing routines immensely.

Displaying Motion

The SlideEffects program, shown in Listings 24.9 and 24.10, combines two bitmaps to make a third image that is displayed. Take a look at the following code before examining how it works. Hazard a guess at what it does.

LISTING 24.9 THE HEADER FOR THE SLIDEEFFECTS PROGRAM

```
#ifndef MainH
#define MainH

#include <Classes.hpp>
#include <Controls.hpp>
#include <StdCtrls.hpp>
#include <Forms.hpp>
#include <ExtCtrls.hpp>
#include <Menus.hpp>

class TForm1 : public TForm
{
__published:      // IDE-managed Components
  TImage *Image1;
  TMainMenu *MainMenu1;
  TMenuItem *File1;
  TMenuItem *Exit1;
  TMenuItem *Effect1;
  TMenuItem *SlideFromLeft1;
  TMenuItem *SlideFromRight1;
  TMenuItem *ShutterHorizontal1;
```

```
     TMenuItem *ShutterVertical1;
     TMenuItem *Unroll1;
     void __fastcall FormCreate(TObject *Sender);
     void __fastcall SlideFromLeft1Click(TObject *Sender);
     void __fastcall SlideFromRight1Click(TObject *Sender);
     void __fastcall ShutterHorizontal1Click(TObject *Sender);
     void __fastcall ShutterVertical1Click(TObject *Sender);
     void __fastcall Unroll1Click(TObject *Sender);
     void __fastcall FormDestroy(TObject *Sender);
     void __fastcall Exit1Click(TObject *Sender);
private:        // User declarations
   Graphics::TBitmap* Bitmap1;
   Graphics::TBitmap* Bitmap2;
   Graphics::TBitmap* Bitmap3;
   bool Image1Loaded, Image2Loaded;
public:              // User declarations
     __fastcall TForm1(TComponent* Owner);
};

extern PACKAGE TForm1 *Form1;

#endif
```

LISTING 24.10 THE MAIN UNIT FOR THE SLIDEEFFECTS PROGRAM

```
//////////////////////////////////////////////////////////////
//  Main.cpp                                                  //
//  Project: SlideEffects                                     //
//////////////////////////////////////////////////////////////

#include <vcl.h>
#pragma hdrstop

#include "Main.h"

#pragma package(smart_init)
#pragma resource "*.dfm"
TForm1 *Form1;

__fastcall TForm1::TForm1(TComponent* Owner)
  : TForm(Owner)
{
}

void __fastcall TForm1::FormCreate(TObject *Sender)
{
  Bitmap1 = new Graphics::TBitmap;
  Bitmap2 = new Graphics::TBitmap;
```

continues

24

VCL GRAPHICS
CLASSES

LISTING 24.10   CONTINUED

```cpp
    Bitmap3 = new Graphics::TBitmap;
    Bitmap1->PixelFormat = pf8bit;
    Bitmap2->PixelFormat = pf8bit;
    Bitmap3->PixelFormat = pf8bit;

    try {
      Bitmap1->LoadFromFile("factory.bmp");
      Bitmap2->LoadFromFile("handshak.bmp");
      Image1Loaded = true;
      Image2Loaded = true;
      Bitmap3->Palette = Bitmap1->Palette;
      Bitmap3->Height = Bitmap1->Height;
      Bitmap3->Width = Bitmap1->Width;
    }
    catch (...) {
      Image1Loaded = false;
      Image2Loaded = false;
    }
}

void __fastcall TForm1::SlideFromLeft1Click(TObject *Sender)
{
  if (!Image1Loaded)
   ShowMessage("Bitmap1 not loaded");
  if (!Image2Loaded)
   ShowMessage("Bitmap2 not loaded");
  if (Image1Loaded && Image2Loaded) {
    for (int i=0;i<Bitmap1->Width;i++) {
      for (int y=0;y<Bitmap1->Height;y++) {
        char* Current = (char*)Bitmap1->ScanLine[y];
        char* Next = (char*)Bitmap2->ScanLine[y];
        char* ToDisplay = (char*)Bitmap3->ScanLine[y];
        for (int z=0;z<i;z++)
            ToDisplay[z] = Next[z];
        for (int j=i;j<Bitmap1->Width;j++)
            ToDisplay[j] = Current[j];
      }
      Image1->Canvas->Draw(0,0,Bitmap3);
      Application->ProcessMessages();
    }
  }
}

void __fastcall TForm1::SlideFromRight1Click(TObject *Sender)
{
  if (!Image1Loaded)
   ShowMessage("Bitmap1 not loaded");
  if (!Image2Loaded)
   ShowMessage("Bitmap2 not loaded");
```

```
    if (Image1Loaded && Image2Loaded) {
      for (int i=0;i<Bitmap1->Width;i++) {
        for (int y=0;y<Bitmap1->Height;y++) {
          char* Current = (char*)Bitmap1->ScanLine[y];
          char* Next = (char*)Bitmap2->ScanLine[y];
          char* ToDisplay = (char*)Bitmap3->ScanLine[y];
          for (int z=0;z<Bitmap1->Width;z++)
            ToDisplay[z] = Current[z];
          for (int j=Bitmap1->Width-i;j<Bitmap1->Width;j++)
            ToDisplay[j] = Next[j];
        }
        Image1->Canvas->Draw(0,0,Bitmap3);
        Application->ProcessMessages();
      }
    }
  }
}

void __fastcall TForm1::ShutterHorizontal1Click(TObject *Sender)
{
  int FY = 0;
  if (!Image1Loaded)
   ShowMessage("Bitmap1 not loaded");
  if (!Image2Loaded)
   ShowMessage("Bitmap2 not loaded");
  if (Image1Loaded && Image2Loaded) {
    Bitmap3->Canvas->CopyRect(Rect(0,0,Bitmap3->Width,Bitmap3->Height),
      Bitmap1->Canvas,Rect(0,0,Bitmap1->Width, Bitmap1->Height));
    for (int i=0;i<30;i++) {
       while (FY < Bitmap1->Height) {
          char* Next = (char*)Bitmap2->ScanLine[FY + i];
          char* ToDisplay = (char*)Bitmap3->ScanLine[FY + i];
          for (int x=0;x<Bitmap3->Width;x++)
             ToDisplay[x] = Next[x];
          FY = FY + 30;
       }
       Image1->Canvas->Draw(0,0,Bitmap3);
       Application->ProcessMessages();
       Sleep(40);
       FY = 0;
    }
  }
}

void __fastcall TForm1::ShutterVertical1Click(TObject *Sender)
{
  if (!Image1Loaded)
   ShowMessage("Bitmap1 not loaded");
  if (!Image2Loaded)
   ShowMessage("Bitmap2 not loaded");
```

24

VCL GRAPHICS
CLASSES

continues

LISTING 24.10   CONTINUED

```cpp
    if (Image1Loaded && Image2Loaded) {
      Bitmap3->Canvas->CopyRect(Rect(0,0,Bitmap3->Width,Bitmap3->Height),
                               Bitmap1->Canvas,Rect(0,0,Bitmap1->Width,
                               Bitmap1->Height));
      int FX = 0;
      for (int i=0;i<30;i++) {
        for (int y=0;y<Bitmap1->Height;y++) {
          char* ToDisplay = (char*)Bitmap3->ScanLine[y];
          while (FX < Bitmap3->Width - 1) {
            char* Next = (char*)Bitmap2->ScanLine[y];
            ToDisplay[FX + i] = Next[FX + i];
            FX = FX + 30;
          }
          FX = 0;
        }
        Image1->Canvas->Draw(0,0,Bitmap3);
        Application->ProcessMessages();
        Sleep(40);
      }
    }
}

void __fastcall TForm1::Unroll1Click(TObject *Sender)
{
  if (!Image1Loaded)
   ShowMessage("Bitmap1 not loaded");
  if (!Image2Loaded)
   ShowMessage("Bitmap2 not loaded");

  if (Image1Loaded && Image2Loaded) {
    Bitmap3->Canvas->CopyRect(Rect(0,0,Bitmap3->Width,Bitmap3->Height),
                             Bitmap1->Canvas,Rect(0,0,Bitmap1->Width,
                             Bitmap1->Height));
    for (int i=0;i<Bitmap1->Width;i++) {
      for (int y=0;y<Bitmap1->Height;y++) {
        char* Next = (char*)Bitmap2->ScanLine[y];
        char* ToDisplay = (char*)Bitmap3->ScanLine[y];
        if(i < Bitmap1->Width - 15) {
          for (int j=1;j<15;j++)
            if(y == 0 || y == Bitmap1->Height - 1)
              ToDisplay[i+j] = clBlack;
            else
              ToDisplay[i+j] = Next[i+10-j];
        }
        ToDisplay[i] = Next[i];
      }
      Sleep(10);
      Image1->Canvas->Draw(0,0,Bitmap3);
      Application->ProcessMessages();
```

```
      }
    }
  }

void __fastcall TForm1::FormDestroy(TObject *Sender)
{
  delete Bitmap1;
  delete Bitmap2;
  delete Bitmap3;
}

void __fastcall TForm1::Exit1Click(TObject *Sender)
{
  Close();
}
```

Did you hazard a guess as to what this program does? One image slides on top of the other (among other things). Take a closer look at what is going on. I use three bitmaps instead of two in the FormCreate() method. Look at what happens when I load the first image:

```
void __fastcall TForm1::FormCreate(TObject *Sender)
{
  Bitmap1 = new Graphics::TBitmap;
  Bitmap2 = new Graphics::TBitmap;
  Bitmap3 = new Graphics::TBitmap;
  Bitmap1->PixelFormat = pf8bit;
  Bitmap2->PixelFormat = pf8bit;
  Bitmap3->PixelFormat = pf8bit;

  try {
    Bitmap1->LoadFromFile("factory.bmp");
    Bitmap2->LoadFromFile("handshak.bmp");
    Image1Loaded = true;
    Image2Loaded = true;
    Bitmap3->Palette = Bitmap1->Palette;
    Bitmap3->Height = Bitmap1->Height;
    Bitmap3->Width = Bitmap1->Width;
  }
  catch (...) {
    Image1Loaded = false;
    Image2Loaded = false;
  }
}
```

I could not assign the Bitmap3 size or palette until I loaded the first bitmap. I need to know the properties of the first bitmap so that I can assign them to the third one, my work area. I am also setting an ImageLoaded Boolean flag. This flag is used in later functions.

Look at the methods that do all the work. Because the algorithm is basically the same for `SlideFromLeft1Click` and `SlideFromRight1Click`, you need to examine only one to understand how the other works:

```
void __fastcall TForm1::SlideFromLeft1Click(TObject *Sender)
{
  if (!Image1Loaded)
   ShowMessage("Bitmap1 not loaded");
  if (!Image2Loaded)
   ShowMessage("Bitmap2 not loaded");
  if (Image1Loaded && Image2Loaded) {
    for (int i=0;i<Bitmap1->Width;i++) {
      for (int y=0;y<Bitmap1->Height;y++) {
        char* Current = (char*)Bitmap1->ScanLine[y];
        char* Next = (char*)Bitmap2->ScanLine[y];
        char* ToDisplay = (char*)Bitmap3->ScanLine[y];
        for (int z=0;z<i;z++)
           ToDisplay[z] = Next[z];
        for (int j=i;j<Bitmap1->Width;j++)
           ToDisplay[j] = Current[j];
      }
      Image1->Canvas->Draw(0,0,Bitmap3);
      Application->ProcessMessages();
    }
  }
}
```

First, I check to see if I have valid bitmaps loaded into the two source bitmaps. If I have two valid images, I do the slide. The slide is done with my loop logic. The outer loop is the most interesting, so I examine it first. This loop controls the actual drawing of the changed image on the screen:

```
Image1->Canvas->Draw(0,0,Bitmap3);
Application->ProcessMessages();
```

The first line draws the image. The second lets the application actually draw it on the screen. You must give the application time to draw the bitmap to the screen, and you do so with `ProcessMessages()`. The outer loop is going to send 240 separate paint messages, one for each time through the loop. Sending this many paint messages will make for very smooth drawing, but is very slow. To speed this portion of the loop, you might want to do the draw only every second or third pixel. The overall effect will hardly be noticeable to the eye, but the slide will be a lot faster. The two inner loops are also interesting:

```
for (int z=0;z<i;z++)
  ToDisplay[z] = Next[z];
for (int j=i;j<Bitmap1->Width;j++)
  ToDisplay[j] = Current[j];
```

I am copying only the part of each bitmap that I want displayed to the work area. Here is one place you could speed things dramatically. If you do not want to preserve the original image, you can draw the second image onto the first and gain a great deal of speed.

The other effects are variations on the preceding algorithm. Let me add an interesting note: I wrote this code while working in a demo booth at SDWest98 (Software Developer Conference West). Until I had the loop logic dialed in, there was an access violation every time I ran the application. This problem occurred in front of a lot of people, so do not get discouraged if you get a few violations while coding. As an old support engineer used to say, "If it doesn't break every so often while you are writing it, you're not doing anything worthwhile anyway."

Summary

This chapter covered the center point of VCL graphics programming and the tools it uses. This center point is the TCanvas object. I have also covered most of the building blocks that you need to get started. I suggest that you play with the different pen modes, brush styles, and copy modes to fully understand what effects each one has. You saw how to create a custom line that shows a little imagination; you also learned about one of the most basic of the VCL graphics types—TColor. You then worked through palettes and into the different Windows graphical file formats. You took a brief stop to see how metafiles work. You got a good look at the components that are used to display these files. Finally, you saw how to manipulate bitmaps and display them on the screen. You should now have a very good understanding of basic graphics programming using the VCL.

24

VCL GRAPHICS
CLASSES

CHAPTER 25

Graphics Programming with DirectDraw

*by Charlie Calvert
and Kent Reisdorph*

IN THIS CHAPTER

This chapter is about DirectDraw programming. This technology is designed to allow you to create high-performance graphics applications. DirectDraw is a Component Object Model (COM) interface that gives you direct access to the hardware on Windows 9x/NT machines. With DirectDraw, you can create applications that run as fast as DOS applications that have complete control over the hardware on a machine.

By the time you complete this chapter, you will understand how to do the following:

- Initialize DirectDraw
- Run DirectDraw in Exclusive mode
- Run DirectDraw in Windowed mode
- Animate objects using DirectDraw
- Manipulate palettes using DirectDraw

This subject is moderately demanding, but with a little bit of work, you should have no trouble mastering this material.

Understanding DirectDraw

The next few sections of the chapter describe DirectDraw programming. In particular, they cover the following topics:

- What is DirectDraw?
- How do I initialize DirectDraw?
- What is a `DirectDrawSurface`?

DirectDraw is part of a complex set of tools called DirectX, which consists of several different technologies such as DirectDraw, Direct3D, DirectSound, DirectPlay, DirectInput, and DirectSetup. Each of these technologies focuses on a different type of multimedia or gaming technology, such as sound, 3D graphics, network play, hardware devices such as mice or force feedback, and so on. This chapter zeroes in exclusively on DirectDraw—a subject that is easily big enough to fill up this chapter and several more. I know this topic pretty well by this time, and I can get you up and running in short order and leave you with plenty of other resources with which you can follow up on for further study.

DirectDraw programs require that you have the DirectDraw run-time DLLs on your system. The run-time files, which are just a set of DLLs, are available from Microsoft's Web site. Many machines, however, have DirectX installed already, as it ships with a wide variety of products, including games, Windows 98, and the future operating system Windows 2000 (formerly known as Windows NT 5). If you are using NT 4, you should upgrade to at least Service Pack 3 so that you can have access to DirectDraw 3, which is part of that Service Pack. Windows 2000 should have support for DirectX 6. Don't try to install the DirectDraw run time on a Windows NT 4 system. The run time installation is meant only for Windows 95 or 98. One way to tell whether you have DirectDraw on your system is to look in the `Windows/System` directory or `Winnt/System32` directory for the files `DDRAW.DLL` and `DSOUND.DLL`. If you have those files, DirectDraw is installed on your system.

If at all possible, you should try to acquire the DirectDraw SDK from Microsoft. This SDK can usually be downloaded from Microsoft's Web site, but beware—it is at least 30MB. If you install the SDK, it creates a directory called `DXSDK` on your hard drive. Beneath this directory is the `SDK` directory, which contains various documents, sample files in C/C++, and help files. You may also be able to obtain the SDK on CD directly from Microsoft. In particular, it may be shipped as part of the MSDN. The book *Inside DirectX*, from Microsoft Press, also contains the DirectX SDK.

For best results, you should have at least 2MB of memory on your video card. For information beyond that supplied in this chapter, go to the DirectDraw area on Microsoft's Web site at `http://www.microsoft.com/directx/default.asp` or visit my Web site at `http://users.aol.com/charliecal`, where you will find links to various DirectX programmers' sites.

What Is DirectDraw?

DirectDraw is an interface that gives you access to the video hardware on your system. Having immediate access to hardware allows you to create fast, colorful displays that catch the users' eyes and hold their attention. It can also allow you to create advanced games with the most cutting-edge performance characteristics.

As I stated earlier in the book, programs are fast enough when they don't force the users to wait for something to happen. Most of the time, the standard Windows Graphics Device Interface (GDI) will allow you to create programs that run fast enough to satisfy most users. This is true even of the interface for many traditional animated games.

Many programmers have failed to notice that as computers improved, so have the performance of standard graphics routines. Contemplate the evolution from 486s, to Pentium 90s and 120s, then on to 150s and 166s, and on yet further to 200s and 266s, the 300 series, and now, finally, to the world of 450MHz machines and beyond. A lot has changed during this evolutionary process, and of course, by the time you read this, even faster processors will come out that will dwarf the performance of the fastest machines mentioned here. The video cards we now use are highly optimized for standard Windows video routines. As a result, the standard Windows GDI has become an increasingly viable tool for creating animations. I will prove this point in the last chapter of this book, when I show you code that performs well in both DirectDraw and in Windows GDI versions.

Nevertheless, sometimes you want to extract the last bits of performance out of your machine. To do so, you should use DirectDraw.

Every time you write to the screen in standard Windows programming, you must do so without directly accessing the hardware. Instead, you request that a set of drivers built by third parties perform the actions you want to carry out. This process is a bit like asking a robot to perform actions for you. The robot is very efficient and very reliable, but it is not much help when certain kinds of speed and dexterity are required. Think, for instance, of the robots in *Star Wars*. They did certain things very well, but it is hard to imagine them performing magic tricks as well as a sleight-of-hand artist. Traditional Windows video drivers have the same characteristics: They give you remarkable device independence, but usually sacrifice speed in the process.

Windows forces you to access video memory through a set of drivers for two reasons:

- The drivers are designed so that you can issue one set of commands that will work equally well on a wide range of hardware. For instance, under Windows GDI, you don't have to create new versions of your program when a new video card comes out.

- Windows is a protected mode operating system that protects you and other system users from careless programmers who can accidentally crash the system by making mistakes when writing directly to hardware. To prevent a situation like this from happening, the Windows GDI will not let you write directly to hardware devices such as video cards. These restrictions make the system safer, but graphics programmers are thereby prevented from directly manipulating the memory they most want to access.

DirectDraw's main purpose is to allow you to write directly to video memory if you want. It will also allow you to easily manipulate offscreen buffers that can be quickly flipped on to visible video memory. This way, you can create smooth animations through a technique called *double buffering*, which I will explain later in this chapter.

DirectDraw is also designed to automatically give you access to the latest features of video cards, even if you are unaware that those features exist. In other words, the DirectX team is working full time to give you access to the latest features. In particular, the team builds those features into DirectX, so you get access to them without having to even be conscious of their existence. For instance, if a new video card supports manipulating rectangles in an extremely optimized way, or stretching a graphic in a fast, powerful manner, DirectDraw will automatically take advantage of that capability when you draw rectangles to the screen. A specific example was the MMX technology that Intel introduced some time ago. Even if you wrote your DirectX game before MMX was created, you will get access to MMX functionality automatically because the latest DirectDraw drivers take advantage of it.

Another DirectDraw feature is that it allows you to set your program's screen resolution and bit depth. In other words, you can take over the whole screen, switch to 300×200 mode, and set the bit depth to 256 colors if you so choose. Likewise, you can switch to very high resolutions and get whatever color depth you want. The decision is up to you.

To a large degree, DirectDraw removes the shackles that inhibit fast video output in Windows. However, DirectDraw still does everything it can to ensure that you will not accidentally crash Windows. For instance, it provides you with a preallocated pointer that gives you direct access to video memory. This capability is different from allowing you to write to a specific video address. In particular, it ensures the buffer you are writing to is valid video memory, and it will swap you out into main memory automatically if you need more room for your images, text, or animations.

DirectDraw is not the API you should use to create 3D graphics. The technology is sufficiently powerful to allow you to create powerful, high-performance 3D games on the order of Doom or Quake, but the amount of work involved would be prohibitive. Use Direct3D, described in Chapter 26, "More DirectX Technologies," if you want to create 3D games. Direct3D provides the primitives you need to quickly create 3D games or graphics.

A Few Thoughts on Double Buffering

Before I get into much depth regarding the way this code works, I need to spend a few minutes talking about *double buffering*. The idea behind this technology is to emulate as closely as possible the frame-based techniques used in celluloid-based movies. Double buffering simply shows the users a series of still pictures at a rate sufficiently hurried as to give the illusion of fluid motion or animation.

In particular, what you do is compose a frame offscreen and then flip it in front of the viewers. While the viewers are absorbing this information, you compose another scene and then flip it to the screen. For instance, you might start out with the first frame showing a ball at the far left of the screen; you can move the ball from left to right a few pixels each frame to create the illusion of movement. With each slight change of position, you flip a new picture in front of the users. You are showing a series of static pictures of a ball, but the users perceive this as animated motion.

The average movie flips the screen at a rate of approximately 25 frames per second. These kinds of rates are so rapid that the human eye never detects the presence of individual frames but instead sees a convincing illusion of true motion. If you move a ball across the screen at rates close to 25 frames per second, users will think they are seeing not a series of still pictures of a ball, but an actual movie of a ball moving through space. Depending on the quality of your code, DirectX is capable of performing at rates much higher than 25 frames per second. Although 24 frames per second is adequate, higher rates result in even smoother animation.

> **NOTE**
>
> When I first started creating animations, I believed it was foolish to compose an entire buffer and flip it to the screen. This seemed wasteful to me, and I was determined to make all my changes directly on the screen. It turned out that my approach was entirely wrong. I found it very hard to hide the changes you make directly on the screen. This kind of sleight of hand should almost always be done on a back buffer, out of the user's sight. When you flip the picture to the screen, the user sees only a fully composed image.
>
> Recall what I said earlier about the DirectDraw subsystem guaranteeing that page flips will occur in sync with a screen refresh. I've never met anyone who could see a 72MHz screen refresh actually taking place. If a picture is refreshed at that rate, the user will be unable to consciously detect the instant when you blit an image to the screen. Some readers will be determined to try to make changes to the area of the screen the user is actually looking at. Although there are a few occasions when this is appropriate, the vast majority of the time, you want to compose your images offscreen and then flip them in front of the user. If you try doing things that way and get frustrated, come back and try double buffering. You'll be amazed at how quickly it solves seemingly intractable problems.

DirectDraw allows you to create a back buffer, draw to it, and then flip it to the visible area in your video memory. Assuming that you are in Exclusive mode and have enough video memory to keep both your primary surface and back surface in video RAM, then the flip operation is not a copy procedure. Instead, the flip operation simply changes the address of the block of memory referenced by the visible area of your video card's memory. In other words, only four bytes of memory need to change when you perform page flips; everything else can stay where it is. The only thing that changes is the four bytes of memory that point to the currently active video page. Therefore, the operation is very fast; furthermore, it is guaranteed to happen in sync with the refresh operations on your monitor. As a result, you can use DirectDraw to perform very smooth animations.

Hardware Versus Emulation

DirectDraw and other DirectX technologies do the best they can to provide you with a sophisticated set of video routines. For instance, the 3D routines attempt to use the hardware to perform super-fast operations. However, many video cards or other hardware devices do not provide all the functionality you might desire. In these cases, DirectX will attempt to emulate the missing hardware functionality via software.

The whole question of which kinds of functionality are provided in software and which are provided in hardware is an extremely technical subject, well beyond the scope of this book. However, you can keep tabs on the status of DirectDraw on your particular system by running the DirectX Viewer that comes with the Microsoft SDK. This viewer exercises a series of DirectX capability routines that report on the status of various types of multimedia hardware on a particular system. You can also query these subsystems yourself at run time, but that is a subject only tangentially covered in this book.

For now, all you really need to know is that some DirectX functionality is executed in hardware, and other parts are emulated. The emulated functions are, perhaps somewhat whimsically, handled by the HEL (Hardware Emulation Layer). The nonemulated parts of your program are handled by a second subsystem with yet another rather whimsical name, the HAL (Hardware Abstraction Layer). Either the HEL or the HAL handle all your DirectDraw operations. These drivers make DirectDraw possible.

> **NOTE**
>
> You can initialize DirectDraw to use either the HEL or the HAL exclusively. However, this is a rather advanced feature, and one that you are unlikely to need to call on in the course of even rather rigorous performance tests.

A Simple DirectDraw Program

Now that you have some idea what DirectDraw is all about, the next step is to start learning how it all works. DirectDraw is not a simple API, but neither is it enormously complex. One of the difficulties of the technology is that a lot of the most complex code needs to be mastered up front, before you can start programming. Even relatively difficult tasks are much easier to master if you can get up and running quickly, and then

25

DIRECTDRAW

master the details one step at a time. Unfortunately, in this case, a considerable amount of complexity must be mastered up front, and then you can get a chance to play with the technology.

In such situations, people want to have complex technology wrapped up in components that help simplify the programmer's task. (Check the various C++Builder and Delphi Web sites for components that wrap DirectX.) However, I strongly suggest that you understand the basics of DirectDraw programming before using such a library.

To get you started with DirectDraw, I have created the DirectDraw1 program, which allows you to see all the basic functionality needed in a DirectDraw program. Listings 25.1 and 25.2 show the source code for this program.

LISTING 25.1 THE HEADER FOR THE DIRECTDRAW1 PROGRAM

```cpp
#ifndef MainH
#define MainH

#include <Classes.hpp>
#include <Controls.hpp>
#include <StdCtrls.hpp>
#include <Forms.hpp>
#include <ExtCtrls.hpp>

const String AFileName = "c:\\debug.txt";

class TForm1 : public TForm
{
__published:     // IDE-managed Components
  TTimer *Timer1;
  void __fastcall FormCreate(TObject *Sender);
  void __fastcall FormDestroy(TObject *Sender);
  void __fastcall FormKeyDown(TObject *Sender, WORD &Key,
        TShiftState Shift);
  void __fastcall FormPaint(TObject *Sender);
  void __fastcall Timer1Timer(TObject *Sender);
private:     // User declarations
  LPDIRECTDRAW FDirectDraw;              // DirectDraw object
  LPDIRECTDRAWSURFACE FPrimarySurface; // DirectDraw primary surface
  LPDIRECTDRAWSURFACE FBackSurface;     // DirectDraw back surface
  bool FActive;                         // is application active?
  char FPhase;
  String FFrontMsg;
  String FBackMsg;
  TStringList* DebugFile;
  void Start();
public:          // User declarations
  __fastcall TForm1(TComponent* Owner);
```

```
};

extern PACKAGE TForm1 *Form1;

#endif
```

LISTING 25.2   THE MAIN UNIT FOR THE DIRECTDRAW1 PROGRAM

```cpp
///////////////////////////////////////
// Purpose:
// Project: DirectDraw1.bpr
//
#include <vcl.h>
#include <ddraw.h>
#pragma hdrstop

#include "Main.h"

#pragma package(smart_init)
#pragma resource "*.dfm"
TForm1 *Form1;

__fastcall TForm1::TForm1(TComponent* Owner)
  : TForm(Owner)
{
}

void __fastcall TForm1::FormCreate(TObject *Sender)
{
  Width = 640;
  Height = 480;
  FDirectDraw = 0;
  FPhase = 0;
  FActive = false;
  FFrontMsg = "Front buffer (F12 or Esc to quit)";
  FBackMsg = "Back buffer (F12 or Esc to quit)";
  DebugFile = new TStringList;
}

void __fastcall TForm1::FormDestroy(TObject *Sender)
{
  if (FDirectDraw != 0) {
    FDirectDraw->FlipToGDISurface();
    FDirectDraw->SetCooperativeLevel(Handle, DDSCL_NORMAL);
    if (FPrimarySurface != 0) {
      FPrimarySurface->Release();
      FPrimarySurface = 0;
    }
```

continues

25

DIRECTDRAW

LISTING 25.2   CONTINUED

```
    FDirectDraw->Release();
    FDirectDraw = 0;
  }
  DebugFile->SaveToFile(AFileName);
  delete DebugFile;
}

void TForm1::Start()
{
  DDSURFACEDESC SurfaceDesc;
  HRESULT hr = DirectDrawCreate(0, &FDirectDraw, 0);
  if (hr == DD_OK) {
    // Get exclusive mode
    hr = FDirectDraw->SetCooperativeLevel(
      Handle, DDSCL_EXCLUSIVE | DDSCL_FULLSCREEN);
    if (hr == DD_OK) {
      hr = FDirectDraw->SetDisplayMode(640, 480, 8);
      if (hr == DD_OK) {
        // Create the primary surface with 1 back buffer
        DDSCAPS DDSCaps;
        SurfaceDesc.dwSize = sizeof(SurfaceDesc);
        SurfaceDesc.dwFlags = DDSD_CAPS | DDSD_BACKBUFFERCOUNT;
        SurfaceDesc.ddsCaps.dwCaps =
          DDSCAPS_PRIMARYSURFACE | DDSCAPS_FLIP | DDSCAPS_COMPLEX;
        SurfaceDesc.dwBackBufferCount = 1;
        hr = FDirectDraw->CreateSurface(
          &SurfaceDesc, &FPrimarySurface, 0);
        if (hr == DD_OK) {
          // Get a pointer to the back buffer
          DDSCaps.dwCaps = DDSCAPS_BACKBUFFER;
          hr = FPrimarySurface->
            GetAttachedSurface(&DDSCaps, &FBackSurface);
          if (hr == DD_OK) {
            // draw some text.
            HDC DC;
            if (FPrimarySurface->GetDC(&DC) == DD_OK) {
              SetBkColor(DC, RGB(0, 0, 255));
              SetTextColor(DC, RGB(255, 255, 0));
              TextOut(DC, 0, 0, FFrontMsg.c_str(), FFrontMsg.Length());
              FPrimarySurface->ReleaseDC(DC);
            }

            if (FBackSurface->GetDC(&DC) == DD_OK) {
              SetBkColor(DC, RGB(0, 0, 255));
              SetTextColor(DC, RGB(255, 255, 0));
              TextOut(DC, 0, 0, FBackMsg.c_str(), FBackMsg.Length());
              FBackSurface->ReleaseDC(DC);
            }
```

```
            // Create a timer to flip the pages
            FActive = true;
            Timer1->Enabled = true;
            return;
          }
        }
      }
    }
  }
  String S;
  S.sprintf("Direct Draw Init Failed %x", hr);
  MessageBox(Handle, S.c_str(), "ERROR", MB_OK);
  Close();
}

void __fastcall TForm1::FormKeyDown(TObject *Sender, WORD &Key,
      TShiftState Shift)
{
   switch (Key) {
     case VK_F3: Start(); break;
     case VK_ESCAPE :
     case VK_F12: {
       Timer1->Enabled = false;
       Close();
     }
   }
}

void __fastcall TForm1::FormPaint(TObject *Sender)
{
  const char* Msg =
    "Page Flipping Test: Press F3 to start, F12 or Esc to exit";
  if (!FActive) {
    HDC DC = GetDC(Handle);
    TRect rc = GetClientRect();
    DebugFile->Add("Left: " + String(rc.Left) +
      " Top: " + String(rc.Top) +
      " Right: " + String(rc.Right) +
      " Bottom: " + String(rc.Bottom));
    TSize size;
    GetTextExtentPoint(DC, Msg, strlen(Msg), &size);
    SetBkColor(DC, RGB(0, 0, 0));
    SetTextColor(DC, RGB(255, 255, 0));
    TextOut(DC, (rc.Right - size.cx) / 2,
      (rc.Bottom - size.cy) / 2, Msg, strlen(Msg));
    ReleaseDC(Handle, DC);
  }
}
```

continues

25

DirectDraw

LISTING 25.2   CONTINUED

```cpp
void __fastcall TForm1::Timer1Timer(TObject *Sender)
{
  HDC DC;
  if (FBackSurface->GetDC(&DC) == DD_OK) {
    if (FPhase != 0) {
      SetBkColor(DC, RGB(0, 0, 255));
      SetTextColor(DC, RGB(255, 255, 0));
      TextOut(DC, 0, 0, FFrontMsg.c_str(), FFrontMsg.Length());
      FPhase = 0;
    } else {
      SetBkColor(DC, RGB(0, 0, 255));
      SetTextColor(DC, RGB(0, 255, 255));
      TextOut(DC, 0, 0, FBackMsg.c_str(), FBackMsg.Length());
      FPhase = 1;
    }
    FBackSurface->ReleaseDC(DC);
  }

  while (true) {
    HRESULT hr = FPrimarySurface->Flip(0, 0);

    if (hr == DD_OK)
      break;

    if (hr == DDERR_SURFACELOST) {
      hr = FPrimarySurface->Restore();
      if (hr != DD_OK)
        break;
    }

    if (hr != DDERR_WASSTILLDRAWING)
      break;
  }
}
```

The code shown here is the simplest possible DirectDraw program. It is modeled closely after the DDX1 C++ example that ships with Microsoft's DirectDraw SDK. I've simply taken that program and rewritten it to compile under a form-based environment. In particular, the code uses a TTimer object rather than calling SetTimer, and it responds to events such as OnKeyDown rather than directly handling WM_KEYDOWN messages. The conversion to a form-based paradigm makes the code easier to read but doesn't change its underlying structure.

The code in this project has six methods:

- FormCreate()—Performs trivial initialization of variables.
- FormDestroy()—Destroys the DirectDraw surfaces created in the Start method.

- Start()—Calls DirectDrawCreate(), which initializes DirectDraw and returns a pointer to a DirectDraw object. Calls SetCooperativeLevel() to switch into Exclusive mode. Calls SetDisplayMode() to switch to 640×480 8-bit resolution. Calls CreateSurface() to create a primary surface. Calls GetAttachedSurface() to get a pointer to the back surface. Paints the front and back surface to black, and paints text to each so you can recognize them when they are flipped to the screen. Enables the timer.

- FormKeyDown()—Responds to key presses designating the user's desire to switch into Exclusive mode and begin the demo. Responds to the F12 or Esc keys by shutting down the application.

- FormPaint()—Paints some simple instructions for the user in the middle of the screen. This method is not called while the program is in Exclusive mode. In other words, it tells the user how to activate DirectX and begin the demo proper.

- Timer1Timer()—Flips between the primary and back surfaces. This is the key method in this demo, as it shows how to swap two different surfaces, which is what you want to do in an animated graphics program. This method is somewhat misleading, though, because most of the time you will want to swap at the fastest rate possible rather than wait for the timer to call your program and ask you to swap. For instance, a smooth animation should have a frame rate of at least 25 frames per second, a rate that is not practical to achieve using the standard Windows timer. I want you to be conscious of each page flipping, so I slow things down to the point where you can see it happen.

A few of the steps outlined here require more detailed examination. In particular, I want to describe the code that initializes DirectDraw, the code that flips between the front and back surface, and the code that deallocates memory for the object.

Initializing DirectDraw

To create a DirectDraw object, you call DirectDrawCreate():

```
HRESULT hr = DirectDrawCreate(0, &FDirectDraw, 0);
```

This function is part of the Windows DirectDraw API. To use any of the DirectDraw functions you must include DDRAW.H in your program:

```
#include <ddraw.h>
```

DirectDrawCreate() is declared like this:

```
HRESULT WINAPI DirectDrawCreate(
  GUID FAR *lpGUID,
  LPDIRECTDRAW FAR *lplpDD,
  IUnknown FAR *pUnkOuter );
```

25

DIRECTDRAW

In almost all cases, you can set the first and third parameters to 0. In fact, I have never seen a case in which anyone has done otherwise. In the second parameter, you should pass in the variable that has been declared as LPDIRECTDRAW.

Here is the rundown on the parameters you can pass to DirectDrawCreate():

- The first parameter to DirectDraw should be 0 unless you want to force DirectDraw to always use hardware-specific code (the HAL) or to always use emulation (the HEL). Passing 0 tells DirectDraw to use the active display driver. Pass in DDCREATE_HARDWAREONLY to use hardware only and pass in DDCREATE_EMULATIONONLY if you want to always use the HEL regardless of your current system's capabilities. If you choose the first option, any calls that cannot be executed in hardware will fail with a return value of DDERR_UNSUPPORTED.

- The second parameter you pass in will return a fully initialized instance of the IDirectDraw object. I will discuss this object in more depth later in this chapter's "Setting Exclusive Mode and Screen Resolution" section.

- The final parameter is currently unsupported but may be used in the future to support COM aggregation. For now, Microsoft regards it as an error to pass in anything but 0 in this parameter.

If DirectDrawCreate() fails, it will return one of the following self-explanatory values:

```
DDERR_DIRECTDRAWALREADYCREATED
DDERR_GENERIC
DDERR_INVALIDDIRECTDRAWGUID
DDERR_INVALIDPARAMS
DDERR_NODIRECTDRAWHW
DDERR_OUTOFMEMORY
```

The only identifier requiring explanation here is DDERR_NODIRECTDRAWHW, which means you have attempted to create a hardware-only instance of DirectDraw on a system that has no DirectDraw hardware.

By now, you know more about DirectDrawCreate() than you probably ever wanted to know or imagined necessary. Nevertheless, I'm not quite done with this little fellow. It happens that using it in a component that runs on NT causes C++Builder to have trouble loading packages. As even the Microsoft DirectX team will admit, this difficulty is due to some peculiarities in the way the DirectDrawCreate() function is designed and has nothing to do with C++Builder packages.

Fortunately, you can use a simple workaround for those cases when you don't want to call DirectDrawCreate() directly:

```
CoInitialize(0);
HRESULT hr = CoCreateInstance(CLSID_DirectDraw,
```

```
    0, CLSCTX_ALL, IID_IDirectDraw, (void**)&FDirectDraw);
FDirectDraw->Initialize(0);
```

These three calls use standard COM calls to create the DirectDraw object. The first is a call to `CoInitialize()`, which initializes COM. Next is a call to `CoCreateInstance()`, the standard COM routine for creating a COM object. The third call ensures that DirectDraw is properly initialized. You do not need to call `Initialize()` if you use `DirectDrawCreate()`.

Deallocating Interfaces

You must deallocate DirectDraw objects when you are done with them. This is done by calling `Release()`:

```
if (FDirectDraw != 0) {
  if (FPrimarySurface != 0) {
    FPrimarySurface->Release();
    FPrimarySurface = 0;
  }
  FDirectDraw->Release();
  FDirectDraw = 0;
}
```

Failing to call `Release()` for the objects you use will result in an application that leaks memory.

> **NOTE**
>
> The `Release()` function will return an `Integer` value stating the number of counts against a particular object. For instance, if you have allocated memory for an interface twice, the method will return 1 the first time you call `Release()`, and it will return 0 if you call it a second time. This knowledge can sometimes help you debug an application.

Setting Exclusive Mode and Screen Resolution

After you initialize an instance of DirectDraw, the next step is to set the cooperative level:

```
hr = FDirectDraw->SetCooperativeLevel(
  Handle, DDSCL_EXCLUSIVE | DDSCL_FULLSCREEN);
```

The code shown here sets the `CooperativeLevel` to full-screen Exclusive mode. As a result, your program will take up the whole screen and no other windows will be allowed

25

DIRECTDRAW

to overlap it unless you explicitly switch away from your program by pressing Alt+Tab. You can also initialize the cooperative level to DDSCL_NORMAL, which is a Windowed mode. For now, I'm going to ignore that setting; in some ways it is considerably more complicated than Exclusive mode.

You have the choice of setting the resolution and bit depth of your program if you are in Exclusive mode. You can proceed as follows:

```
hr = FDirectDraw->SetDisplayMode(640, 480, 8);
```

This code sets the screen resolution to 640×480 and gives you a bit depth of 8, which means you can show a maximum of 256 colors.

Until quite recently, picking a resolution and bit depth any greater than this was fruitless. About 300KB is required to hold a single copy of a 640×480 screen, which means you need at least 600KB to hold one screen and back buffer. That was about the maximum you could expect to get from most systems, so trying a higher resolution was fruitless. Now some video cards give decent performance if you go to a higher resolution, but it is still not something you can count on. As a result, I usually stick with this relatively simple resolution, though it does mean that I have to learn to cope with palettes.

What Is a DirectDraw Surface?

After you set the cooperative level and screen resolution, the next step is to get the two surfaces that you will flip between. In other words, you have to create a pointer to the video memory that the user looks at and to a back buffer that you can use for double buffering (page flipping). You can proceed like this:

```
DDSURFACEDESC SurfaceDesc;
DDSCAPS DDSCaps;
SurfaceDesc.dwSize = sizeof(SurfaceDesc);
SurfaceDesc.dwFlags = DDSD_CAPS | DDSD_BACKBUFFERCOUNT;
SurfaceDesc.ddsCaps.dwCaps =
   DDSCAPS_PRIMARYSURFACE | DDSCAPS_FLIP | DDSCAPS_COMPLEX;
SurfaceDesc.dwBackBufferCount = 1;
hr = FDirectDraw->CreateSurface(&SurfaceDesc, &FPrimarySurface, 0);
DDSCaps.dwCaps = DDSCAPS_BACKBUFFER;
hr = FPrimarySurface->GetAttachedSurface(&DDSCaps, &FBackSurface);
```

This admittedly rather convoluted chunk of code creates both your primary surface and the back surface. The primary surface is what the user sees, and the back surface is what will be flipped onto the primary surface when you call the DirectDraw Flip() function to implement double buffering.

Here is the declaration for the DDSCAPS structure:

```
typedef struct _DDSCAPS
{
   DWORD dwCaps;  // capabilities of surface wanted
} DDSCAPS;
```

This structure may appear fairly simple at first glance, but a little exploration will prove that it is indeed quite complex. In fact, both the DDSCAPS and the DDSURFACEDESC structures are almost hopelessly complex structures that handle a painfully large number of constants. Rather than drive you mad trying to describe them, I will tell you that you simply have to get the DirectX SDK to look up these parameters in the online help. For instance, the sole field of the DDSCAPS structure, dwCaps, takes 30 possible constants, many of which are quite complicated to explain. Here, however, is a list of a few of the most important ones:

```
DDSCAPS_3D                  0x00000001
DDSCAPS_ALPHA               0x00000002
DDSCAPS_BACKBUFFER          0x00000004
DDSCAPS_COMPLEX             0x00000008
DDSCAPS_FLIP                0x00000010
DDSCAPS_FRONTBUFFER         0x00000020
DDSCAPS_OFFSCREENPLAIN      0x00000040
DDSCAPS_OVERLAY             0x00000080
DDSCAPS_PALETTE             0x00000100
DDSCAPS_PRIMARYSURFACE      0x00000200
DDSCAPS_PRIMARYSURFACELEFT  0x00000400
DDSCAPS_SYSTEMMEMORY        0x00000800
DDSCAPS_TEXTURE             0x00001000
DDSCAPS_3DDEVICE            0x00002000
DDSCAPS_VIDEOMEMORY         0x00004000
DDSCAPS_VISIBLE             0x00008000
DDSCAPS_WRITEONLY           0x00010000
DDSCAPS_ZBUFFER             0x00020000
DDSCAPS_OWNDC               0x00040000
DDSCAPS_LIVEVIDEO           0x00080000
DDSCAPS_HWCODEC             0x00100000
DDSCAPS_MODEX               0x00200000
DDSCAPS_MIPMAP              0x00400000
DDSCAPS_ALLOCONLOAD         0x04000000
```

Here is the declaration for the DDSURFACEDESC structure:

```
typedef struct _DDSURFACEDESC
{
   DWORD dwSize;    // size of the DDSURFACEDESC structure
   DWORD dwFlags;   // determines what fields are valid
   DWORD dwHeight;  // height of surface to be created
   DWORD dwWidth;   // width of input surface
   union
```

25

DIRECTDRAW

```
   {
      LONG  lPitch; // distance to start of next line (return value only)
      DWORD dwLinearSize; // Formless late-allocated optimized surface size
   };
   DWORD dwBackBufferCount;  // number of back buffers requested
   union
   {
      DWORD dwMipMapCount;       // number of mip-map levels requested
      DWORD dwZBufferBitDepth; // depth of Z buffer requested
      DWORD dwRefreshRate;
          // refresh rate (used when display mode is described)
   };
   DWORD dwAlphaBitDepth;         // depth of alpha buffer requested
   DWORD dwReserved;              // reserved
   LPVOID lpSurface;             // pointer to the associated surface memory
   DDCOLORKEY ddckCKDestOverlay;  // color key for destination overlay use
   DDCOLORKEY ddckCKDestBlt;      // color key for destination blt use
   DDCOLORKEY ddckCKSrcOverlay;   // color key for source overlay use
   DDCOLORKEY ddckCKSrcBlt;       // color key for source blt use
   DDPIXELFORMAT ddpfPixelFormat; // pixel format description of surface
   DDSCAPS ddsCaps;               // direct draw surface capabilities
} DDSURFACEDESC;
```

The complexity of this structure is enough to make a grown man cry; or at any rate, it is enough to drive an author to utter distraction. Rather than take you through this monstrosity field by field, I will instead point out that this structure can be used to retrieve the size, height, width, pixel depth, and a pointer to the actual bytes that describe a surface. One of the more tricky fields here is called Pitch, which describes the distance to the start of the next line of a surface. This is not necessarily the width of your surface, so you need to make a special call to retrieve the real width. Pay close attention to the pitch when you are directly manipulating the bytes (or bits) of a DirectDraw surface.

After you create the primary surface, you can easily get to the premade back surface that you use for page flipping:

```
DDSCaps.dwCaps = DDSCAPS_BACKBUFFER;
hr = FPrimarySurface->GetAttachedSurface(&DDSCaps, &FBackSurface);
```

This simple code retrieves the back surface. I always maintain a pointer to the back surface so I can access it when I need it. In this example the pointer is called FBackSurface.

Chapter 26 shows that you often should create a third surface or even multiple additional surfaces. When I work with DirectDraw, I use the DirectDraw CreateSurface() routine to create a third surface that I call the WorkSurface. I then paint my images onto this surface, blit it to the back surface, and then flip the back surface so that the user can see it. I have come to doubt the usefulness of my WorkSurface object, but there are certainly times when you want to work with more than just the back surface. This topic will come up again later in this chapter.

Writing Text to the Screen

Now that you have the primary and the back surfaces, you can draw something to the
back surface and show it to the user by performing a page flip. Here is how to get
started:

```
if (FBackSurface->GetDC(&DC) == DD_OK) {
  SetBkColor(DC, RGB(0, 0, 255));
  SetTextColor(DC, RGB(255, 255, 0));
  TextOut(DC, 0, 0, FBackMsg.c_str(), FBackMsg.Length());
  FBackSurface->ReleaseDC(DC);
}
```

In this code, I call the GetDC() method of the back surface to retrieve a device context. I
then write some text to the back buffer, using standard Windows calls. I should point out
that most of the time you are actually working with bitmaps rather than standard GDI
calls like those shown here. Custom DirectDraw functions are available for working with
bitmaps, but the technology also supports standard GDI code.

You might find yourself wondering why I make GDI calls after going to such lengths to
explain that GDI is inherently inferior to DirectDraw when it comes to performance. It is
true that the GDI is slower, and the calls shown here take a ridiculously long time to execute. On the other hand, one of the DirectDraw's goals is to allow you to use existing
Windows technology. In this case, I do want to use that existing technology; DirectDraw
lets me do so, even if some of the DirectX developers wince to see me do it. Later in the
book I will show you how to use a C++Builder TCanvas object in conjunction with a
DirectDraw surface.

You can also use VCL's TCanvas to perform this step. Since TCanvas does not directly
support SetBkColor(), the code ends up being a mix of VCL and API calls:

```
if (FBackSurface->GetDC(&DC) == DD_OK) {
  TCanvas* C = new TCanvas;
  C->Handle = DC;
  SetBkColor(C->Handle, RGB(0, 0, 255));
  C->Font->Color = TColor(RGB(0, 255, 255));
  C->TextOut(0, 0, FBackMsg);
  FBackSurface->ReleaseDC(C->Handle);
  delete C;
}
```

In this case the VCL doesn't offer much in the way of simplicity when compared to
using the API directly. In addition, this code will execute ever so slightly slower than the
straight GDI code presented earlier. Ultimately, it's up to you to decide whether to use
the VCL, the GDI, or the DirectDraw routines to write to a DirectDraw surface.

Flipping Surfaces

So now, at long last, you are ready to show the user something. The following code will let the user see what you have been up to:

```
while (true) {
  HRESULT hr = FPrimarySurface->Flip(0, 0);

  if (hr == DD_OK)
    break;

  if (hr == DDERR_SURFACELOST) {
    hr = FPrimarySurface->Restore();
    if (hr != DD_OK)
      break;
  }

  if (hr != DDERR_WASSTILLDRAWING)
    break;
}
```

The key line of code here is the call to `Flip()`. This method will swap the primary buffer and the back buffer so that the primary buffer becomes the back buffer and the back buffer becomes the primary buffer. (Remember that you got the back buffer from the primary buffer by calling `GetAttachedSurface()`. The two surfaces are linked in the mind of DirectDraw, so this kind of thing comes to you for free.)

If all goes well, you can immediately break out of the `while` statement that encapsulates the call to `Flip()`. However, the call sometimes fails, usually for one of two reasons:

1. The surface was lost. This failure occurs when you press Alt+Tab to move away from a DirectDraw application and then press Alt+Tab to move back. When you press Alt+Tab to move back, the surface you were working with needs to be restored before it can be used. The following code performs that function:

    ```
    if (hr == DDERR_SURFACELOST) {
      hr = FPrimarySurface->Restore();
      if (hr != DD_OK))
        break;
    }
    ```

2. The previous flip operation has not yet completed, or you are still busy drawing something to the back surface. In that case, you need to cycle through the `while` loop one or more times, waiting for the surfaces to become free so they can be flipped. The extremely simple code for handling this situation is shown at the end of the `while` loop.

That's all there is to page flipping, or double buffering, as it's commonly called. This relatively simple process of swapping the primary and back buffers is probably the single most important piece of technology in the entire DirectX API. This is what makes DirectX so fast, and this is the technology you need to master if you want to get good at this stuff.

> **NOTE**
>
> You can call Flip() only when you are in full-screen Exclusive mode. You can't use this technology when you are in Windowed mode. However, I'm not saying that DirectDraw can be of no significant help to you in Windowed mode. The concept of surfaces is still available to you in Windowed mode, which means you have an offscreen buffer you can write to. Furthermore, DirectDraw provides functions that allow you to speedily blit one surface onto another. As a result, you can quickly blit your secondary surface onto the primary surface, thereby showing it to the user. This technology is not as good as true flipping, but it is sufficient to handle most situations.

Deallocating Memory

This code cleans up the surfaces when you are ready to exit the program:

```
void __fastcall TForm1::FormDestroy(TObject *Sender)
{
  if (FDirectDraw != 0) {
    FDirectDraw->FlipToGDISurface();
    FDirectDraw->SetCooperativeLevel(Handle, DDSCL_NORMAL);
    if (FPrimarySurface != 0) {
      FPrimarySurface->Release();
      FPrimarySurface = 0;
    }
    FDirectDraw->Release();
    FDirectDraw = 0;
  }
}
```

The first significant step in this method is to call FlipToGDISurface(). You need to make this call if you want to show a dialog or other standard Windows window to the user. I then get out of Exclusive mode, which ensures that standard windowing behavior will be available on the desktop. Finally, I call Release() on my surfaces by setting them equal to 0. You may have noticed that I don't call Release() on the back surface. This is because the back surface is owned by the primary surface and will be deallocated automatically when the primary surface is freed.

All this work might seem a bit like overkill to some users. I am being so cautious before deallocating my surfaces because raising an exception while you are in Exclusive mode

25

DIRECTDRAW

is not a good idea. If an exception is raised, the user is shown a dialog. You completely own the desktop if you are in Exclusive mode, which means that Windows will not be able to display a dialog where the user can see it. Unfortunately, Windows will show the dialog behind the scenes. You won't be able to see it and therefore won't know where to click to shut it down. Furthermore, if C++Builder tries to take you to the line of code where the exception occurred, C++Builder also won't be able to show you what it is doing. The end result is a situation in which your machine appears to be locked up, even though you really are probably doing little more than handling a simple exception.

These kinds of problems do have solutions. They involve catching exceptions before they are shown to the user and then flipping to the GDI surface so that you can inform the user about what has happened.

NOTE

If you are in Exclusive mode and want to raise an exception, you should first make a call to `FlipToGDISurface()`. In fact, you can make this call whenever you want to show a message box or C++Builder form to the user.

The following two methods (from the SimpleHermes2 program found on the CD-ROM that accompanies this book) shows one generic solution to handling exceptions:

```
void __fastcall TForm1::FormCreate(TObject* Sender)
{
  Width = 640;
  Height = 480;
  Application->OnCatchException = FormCatchException;
}


void __fastcall TForm1::FormCatchException(TObject* Sender,
Exception* E)
{
  DirectDraw->FlipToGDISurface();
  ShowMessage(E->Message);
}
```

This code ensures that all the exceptions you don't explicitly handle will be passed on to a method called `FormCatchException()`. This method first calls `FlipToGDISurface()` and then calls `ShowMessage()`. If you do explicitly handle an exception someplace else in your code, you should call `FlipToGDISurface()` before showing your message. After calling `FlipToGDISurface()` you can show a C++Builder form or a `MessageBox` until you restore the DirectDraw surface. The next time you call `Flip()` in your code, you need to restore the DirectDraw surface. The code I'm showing you usually does that automatically.

Smooth Animation

You will find several more examples of relatively simple DirectDraw programs on the CD-ROM that accompanies this book. Most of them come with explanations of what is happening in the code. You should run these programs and study them to learn how they work. In particular, take a look at the DirectDraw3 program, which animates a series of color shapes, as shown in Figure 25.1.

FIGURE 25.1

The DirectDraw3 program shows that you can smoothly animate multiple shapes in C++Builder DirectDraw application.

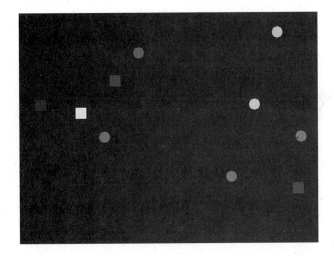

To create smooth animation, you need to respond to the OnIdle event of the Application object. This event can be initialized in your program's constructor:

```
Application->OnIdle = IdleEvent;
```

The actual IdleEvent method looks like this:

```
void __fastcall TForm1::IdleEvent(TObject* Sender, bool& Done)
{
  Done = false;

  if (!FActive)
    return;

  PerformAction();

  while (true) {
    HRESULT hr = FPrimarySurface->Flip(0, 0);
    if (hr == DD_OK)
      break;

    if (hr == DDERR_SURFACELOST) {
```

25

DIRECTDRAW

```
      hr = FPrimarySurface->Restore();
      if (hr != DD_OK)
        break;
    }

    if (hr != DDERR_WASSTILLDRAWING)
      break;
  }
}
```

This code sets the Done variable passed to the IdleEvent to false. This means that you want C++Builder to call the IdleEvent again as soon as possible. The OnIdle event will be called the next time your application is idle.

As you can see, the main code in the IdleEvent does little more than prepare the back surface by calling PerformAction and then flip the back and primary surfaces. The whole point here is that the IdleEvent method will be called at every possible opportunity, and that you will prepare the back buffer and then perform a page flip when it is called. As a result, you get the fastest possible frame rate and therefore the smoothest possible animation.

Listings 25.3 and 25.4 show the complete code for the DirectDraw3 program. You should study this code to get some sense of how the flow of events is channeled in a DirectDraw program that has a small degree of complexity in it.

LISTING 25.3   THE HEADER FOR THE DIRECTDRAW3 PROGRAM

```
#ifndef MainH
#define MainH

#include <Classes.hpp>
#include <Controls.hpp>
#include <StdCtrls.hpp>
#include <Forms.hpp>
#include <ddraw.h>

const int CIRCLETYPE = 0;
const int RECTTYPE = 1;
const String AFileName = "c:\\debug.txt";

class TDrawShape {
  private:
    int FMoveValX;
    int FMoveValY;
    TRect FPrevRect;
    TRect FPrevRect2;
    int FX;
    int FY;
    int FX1;
```

```
      int FY1;
      TRect FShapeRect;
      int FShapeType;
      TColor FColor;
      void SetRect(TRect R);
      TRect GetRect();
  public:
      TDrawShape(int ValX, int ValY,
        int X, int Y, int AType, TColor AColor);
      TDrawShape(int ValX, int ValY);
      void Move();
      void Draw(HDC& DC);
      __property TRect ShapeRect  =
        { read = GetRect, write = SetRect };
      __property int ShapeType  =
        { read = FShapeType, write = FShapeType };
      __property TColor Color  =
        { read = FColor, write = FColor };
};

class TForm1 : public TForm
{
__published:    // IDE-managed Components
  void __fastcall FormCreate(TObject *Sender);
  void __fastcall FormDestroy(TObject *Sender);
  void __fastcall FormKeyDown(TObject *Sender, WORD &Key,
        TShiftState Shift);
  void __fastcall FormPaint(TObject *Sender);
private:        // User declarations
  LPDIRECTDRAW2 FDirectDraw;            // DirectDraw2 object
  LPDIRECTDRAWSURFACE FPrimarySurface; // DirectDraw primary surface
  LPDIRECTDRAWSURFACE FBackSurface;    // DirectDraw back surface
  bool FActive;                        // is application active?
  char FPhase;
  String FFrontMsg;
  String FBackMsg;
  int FValueAdd;
  TRect FShapeRect;
  TList* FShapeList;
  void DrawShape(HDC DC);
  void __fastcall IdleEvent(TObject* Sender, bool& Done);
  void PaintSurfaces();
  void Start();
  void BuildList();
  void PerformAction();
public:         // User declarations
  __fastcall TForm1(TComponent* Owner);
};

extern PACKAGE TForm1 *Form1;

#endif
```

25

DIRECTDRAW

LISTING 25.4   THE DIRECTDRAW3 PROGRAM AUTOMATES SEVERAL SMOOTHLY SCROLLING SHAPES

```cpp
/////////////////////////////////////
// Purpose:
// Project: DirectDraw3.bpr
//
#include <vcl.h>
#pragma hdrstop

#include "Main.h"

#pragma package(smart_init)
#pragma resource "*.dfm"
TForm1 *Form1;
TStringList* DebugFile;

__fastcall TForm1::TForm1(TComponent* Owner)
  : TForm(Owner)
{
}


//-----------------------------------------------------------------
// --- TDrawShape -------------------------------------------------
//-----------------------------------------------------------------
TDrawShape::TDrawShape(int ValX, int ValY,
  int X, int Y, int AType, TColor AColor)
{
  FMoveValX = ValX;
  FMoveValY = ValY;
  ShapeRect = Rect(X, Y, X+25, Y+25);
  ShapeType = AType;
  Color = AColor;
}

TDrawShape::TDrawShape(int ValX, int ValY)
{
  FMoveValX = ValX;
  FMoveValY = ValY;
}

void TDrawShape::SetRect(TRect R)
{
  FX = R.Left;
  FY = R.Top;
  FX1 = R.Right;
  FY1 = R.Bottom;
}

TRect TDrawShape::GetRect()
{
```

```
    return Rect(FX,FY,FX1,FY1);
}

void TDrawShape::Move()
{
  FPrevRect2 = Rect(FPrevRect.Left,
    FPrevRect.Top, FPrevRect.Right, FPrevRect.Bottom);
  FPrevRect = Rect(FX, FY, FX1, FY1);
  FX = FX + FMoveValX;
  FY = FY + FMoveValY;
  FX1 = FX1 + FMoveValX;
  FY1 = FY1 + FMoveValY;
  if (FX1 > 637)
    FMoveValX = -2;
  if (FX < 3)
    FMoveValX = 2;
  if (FY1 > 477)
    FMoveValY = - 2;
  if (FY < 3)
    FMoveValY = 2;
}

void TDrawShape::Draw(HDC& DC)
{
  HBRUSH Brush = CreateSolidBrush(RGB(0, 0, 0));
  HBRUSH OldBrush = SelectObject(DC, Brush);
  if (FShapeType == CIRCLETYPE)
    Ellipse(DC, FPrevRect2.Left-1,
      FPrevRect2.Top-1, FPrevRect2.Right+1, FPrevRect2.Bottom+1);
  else if (FShapeType == RECTTYPE)
    Rectangle(DC, FPrevRect2.Left-1,
      FPrevRect2.Top-1, FPrevRect2.Right+1, FPrevRect2.Bottom+1);

  SelectObject(DC, OldBrush);
  DeleteObject(Brush);

  Move();

  Brush = CreateSolidBrush(FColor);
  OldBrush = SelectObject(DC, Brush);

  if (FShapeType == CIRCLETYPE)
    Ellipse(DC, FX, FY, FX1, FY1);
  else if (FShapeType == RECTTYPE)
    Rectangle(DC, FX, FY, FX1, FY1);

  SelectObject(DC, OldBrush);
  DeleteObject(Brush);
```

continues

25

DIRECTDRAW

LISTING 25.4   CONTINUED

```cpp
    DebugFile->Add("Draw");
}

//------------------------------------------------------------------
// --- TForm1 ------------------------------------------------------
//------------------------------------------------------------------
void __fastcall TForm1::FormCreate(TObject *Sender)
{
  Width = 640;
  Height = 480;
  FDirectDraw = 0;
  FPhase = 0;
  FActive = false;
  FFrontMsg = "Front buffer (F12 or Esc to quit)";
  FBackMsg = "Back buffer (F12 or Esc to quit)";
  FShapeRect = Rect(25, 25, 50, 50);
  Application->OnIdle = IdleEvent;
  FValueAdd = 2;
  DebugFile = new TStringList;
  BuildList();
}

void __fastcall TForm1::FormDestroy(TObject *Sender)
{
  if (FShapeList) {
    for (int i=0;i<FShapeList->Count;i++) {
      TDrawShape* Shape =
        static_cast<TDrawShape*>(FShapeList->Items[i]);
      delete Shape;
    }
    delete FShapeList;
  }
  if (FDirectDraw != 0) {
    FDirectDraw->FlipToGDISurface();
    FDirectDraw->SetCooperativeLevel(Handle, DDSCL_NORMAL);
    if (FPrimarySurface != 0) {
      FPrimarySurface->Release();
      FPrimarySurface = 0;
    }
    FDirectDraw->Release();
    FDirectDraw = 0;
  }
  DebugFile->SaveToFile(AFileName);
  delete DebugFile;
}

void __fastcall TForm1::IdleEvent(TObject* Sender, bool& Done)
{
  Done = false;
```

```
    if (!FActive)
      return;

    PerformAction();

    while (true) {
      HRESULT hr = FPrimarySurface->Flip(0, 0);
      if (hr == DD_OK)
        break;

      if (hr == DDERR_SURFACELOST) {
        hr = FPrimarySurface->Restore();
        if (hr != DD_OK)
          break;
      }

      if (hr != DDERR_WASSTILLDRAWING)
        break;
    }
}

void TForm1::DrawShape(HDC DC)
{
  DebugFile->Add("Count: " + String(FShapeList->Count));
  for (int i=0;i<FShapeList->Count;i++) {
    TDrawShape* Shape = static_cast<TDrawShape*>(FShapeList->Items[i]);
    Shape->Draw(DC);
  }
}

void TForm1::PaintSurfaces()
{
  HDC DC;
  if (FPrimarySurface->GetDC(&DC) == DD_OK) {
    SetBkColor(DC, RGB(0, 0, 255));
    SetTextColor(DC, RGB(255, 255, 0));
    TextOut(DC, 0, 0, FFrontMsg.c_str(), FFrontMsg.Length());
    FPrimarySurface->ReleaseDC(DC);
  }

  if (FBackSurface->GetDC(&DC) == DD_OK) {
    HBRUSH Brush = CreateSolidBrush(RGB(0, 0, 0));
    HBRUSH OldBrush = SelectObject(DC, Brush);
    SetBkColor(DC, RGB(0, 0, 0));
    SetTextColor(DC, RGB(255, 255, 0));
    TextOut(DC, 0, 0, FBackMsg.c_str(), FBackMsg.Length());
    Rectangle(DC, 0, 0, 640, 480);
    SelectObject(DC, OldBrush);
    DeleteObject(Brush);
    FBackSurface->ReleaseDC(DC);
```

continues

25

DIRECTDRAW

LISTING 25.4   CONTINUED

```cpp
    }
}

void TForm1::Start()
{
  DDSURFACEDESC SurfaceDesc;
  LPDIRECTDRAW ADirectDraw;
  HRESULT hr = DirectDrawCreate(0, &ADirectDraw, 0);
  if (hr == DD_OK) {
    ADirectDraw->QueryInterface(IID_IDirectDraw2, (void**)&FDirectDraw);
    // Free DirectDraw One.
    ADirectDraw->Release();
    ADirectDraw = 0;
    // Get exclusive mode
    hr = FDirectDraw->SetCooperativeLevel(Handle, // DDSCL_NORMAL);
      DDSCL_EXCLUSIVE | DDSCL_FULLSCREEN);
    if (hr == DD_OK) {
      hr = FDirectDraw->SetDisplayMode(640, 480, 8, 0, 0);
      if (hr == DD_OK) {
        // Create the primary surface with 1 back buffer
        DDSCAPS DDSCaps;
        SurfaceDesc.dwSize = sizeof(SurfaceDesc);
        SurfaceDesc.dwFlags = DDSD_CAPS | DDSD_BACKBUFFERCOUNT;
        SurfaceDesc.ddsCaps.dwCaps =
          DDSCAPS_PRIMARYSURFACE | DDSCAPS_FLIP | DDSCAPS_COMPLEX;
        SurfaceDesc.dwBackBufferCount = 1;
        hr = FDirectDraw->CreateSurface(
          &SurfaceDesc, &FPrimarySurface, 0);
        if (hr == DD_OK) {
          // Get a pointer to the back buffer
          DDSCaps.dwCaps = DDSCAPS_BACKBUFFER;
          hr = FPrimarySurface->
            GetAttachedSurface(&DDSCaps, &FBackSurface);
          if (hr == DD_OK) {
            PaintSurfaces();
            return;
          }
        }
      }
    }
  }
  String S;
  S.sprintf("Direct Draw Init Failed %x", hr);
  MessageBox(Handle, S.c_str(), "ERROR", MB_OK);
  Close();
}

void TForm1::BuildList()
{
```

```
    FShapeList = new TList;

    FShapeList->Add(new TDrawShape(-2, 2, 175, 175, CIRCLETYPE, clLime));
    FShapeList->Add(new TDrawShape(2, 2, 125, 125, RECTTYPE, clBlue));
    FShapeList->Add(new TDrawShape(2, -2, 200, 200, RECTTYPE, clYellow));
    FShapeList->Add(new TDrawShape(2, -2, 75, 75, CIRCLETYPE, clRed));
    FShapeList->Add(new TDrawShape(-2, 2, 325, 350, RECTTYPE, clPurple));
    FShapeList->Add(new TDrawShape(-2, -2, 275, 250, CIRCLETYPE,
➥clFuchsia));
    FShapeList->Add(new TDrawShape(-2, 2, 125, 325, CIRCLETYPE, clTeal));
    FShapeList->Add(new TDrawShape(2, 2, 350, 175, RECTTYPE, clNavy));
    FShapeList->Add(new TDrawShape(2, -2, 150, 250, CIRCLETYPE, clOlive));
    FShapeList->Add(new TDrawShape(-2, 2, 225, 25, CIRCLETYPE, clSilver));
}

void TForm1::PerformAction()
{
    // Don't step through code that has lock on it!
    // Getting a DC may put a lock on video memory.
    HDC DC;
    if (FBackSurface->GetDC(&DC) == DD_OK) {
        DrawShape(DC);
        FBackSurface->ReleaseDC(DC);
    }
}

void __fastcall TForm1::FormKeyDown(TObject *Sender, WORD &Key,
        TShiftState Shift)
{
    switch (Key) {
        case VK_F3: {
            FActive = true;
            Start();
            break;
        }
        case VK_ESCAPE :
        case VK_F12: {
            Close();
        }
    }
}

void __fastcall TForm1::FormPaint(TObject *Sender)
{
    const char* Msg =
        "Page Flipping Test: Press F3 to start, F12 or Esc to exit";
    if (!FActive) {
        HDC DC = GetDC(Handle);
        TRect rc = GetClientRect();
```

continues

LISTING 25.4 CONTINUED

```
    DebugFile->Add("Left: " + String(rc.Left) +
      " Top: " + String(rc.Top) +
      " Right: " + String(rc.Right) +
      " Bottom: " + String(rc.Bottom));
    TSize size;
    GetTextExtentPoint(DC, Msg, strlen(Msg), &size);
    SetBkColor(DC, RGB(0, 0, 0));
    SetTextColor(DC, RGB(255, 255, 0));
    TextOut(DC, (rc.Right - size.cx) / 2,
      (rc.Bottom - size.cy) / 2, Msg, strlen(Msg));
    ReleaseDC(Handle, DC);
  }
}
```

When you run this program, a series of colored shapes appear on the screen. As you watch, they smoothly scroll back and forth.

The following code updates the back surface of the application whenever the `IdleEvent` is called:

```
void TForm1::PerformAction()
{
  // Don't step through code that has lock on it!
  // Getting a DC may put a lock on video memory.
  HDC DC;
  if (FBackSurface->GetDC(&DC) == DD_OK) {
    DrawShape(DC);
    FBackSurface->ReleaseDC(DC);
  }
}

void TForm1::DrawShape(HDC DC)
{
  DebugFile->Add("Count: " + String(FShapeList->Count));
  for (int i=0;i<FShapeList->Count;i++) {
    TDrawShape* Shape = static_cast<TDrawShape*>(FShapeList->Items[i]);
    Shape->Draw(DC);
  }
}
```

Notice that the first method shown here warns you not to step through code that has a DC in it taken from a `DirectDrawSurface`. If you do attempt to step through this code, you will almost certainly lock up the system about as hard and as finally as you could ever imagine.

The DrawShape() method works with a list containing a series of colored shapes. You can retrieve these shapes from the program and then use simple polymorphism to paint them to the screen. This process is really very simple. The only hard part is initializing DirectDraw and understanding how to flip back and forth between surfaces. After you master these technologies, you can do quite a bit in DirectDraw without exerting any undo effort.

DirectDraw is not entirely simple, but the amount of complexity you find here is manageable. Furthermore, most of the code you have seen is boilerplate. You can write it once and then use it over and over again. However, you need to understand it if you are going to work with DirectDraw.

Working with Bitmaps

Before closing this chapter, I want to show you how to work with bitmaps in a DirectDraw application. The program shown in Listings 25.5 and 25.6 is the simplest I could devise that would still allow you to see how to use a bitmap in a DirectDraw program.

The DirectDrawPicture2 program, shown in Figure 25.2, is a more interesting example of what you can do with bitmaps in DirectDraw. However, the core issue you need to master is that of simply loading a bitmap into a DirectDraw program and then showing it to the user. The DirectDrawPicture1 program is designed to show you that process in the clearest and most uncluttered way possible.

FIGURE 25.2

The DirectDraw-Picture2 program shows how to work with sprites and how to create transparent areas.

```cpp
#ifndef MainH
#define MainH

#include <Classes.hpp>
#include <Controls.hpp>
#include <StdCtrls.hpp>
#include <Forms.hpp>
#include <ExtCtrls.hpp>
#include <ddraw.h>
#include "ddutil.h"

const char* Background = "BACK";
const String AFileName = "c:\\debug.txt";

class TForm1 : public TForm
{
__published:    // IDE-managed Components
  TTimer *Timer1;
  void __fastcall FormCreate(TObject *Sender);
  void __fastcall FormDestroy(TObject *Sender);
  void __fastcall FormKeyDown(TObject *Sender, WORD &Key,
          TShiftState Shift);
  void __fastcall FormPaint(TObject *Sender);
  void __fastcall Timer1Timer(TObject *Sender);
private:        // User declarations
  LPDIRECTDRAW FDirectDraw;              // DirectDraw2 object
  LPDIRECTDRAWSURFACE FPrimarySurface; // DirectDraw primary surface
  LPDIRECTDRAWSURFACE FBackSurface;    // DirectDraw back surface
  LPDIRECTDRAWPALETTE FDirectDrawPalette; // DirectDraw palette
  bool FActive;                          // is application active?
  char FPhase;
  String FFrontMsg;
  String FBackMsg;
  TStringList* DebugFile;
  void PaintSurfaces();
  void Start();
  void GetPicture();
public:         // User declarations
  __fastcall TForm1(TComponent* Owner);
};

extern PACKAGE TForm1 *Form1;

#endif
```

LISTING 25.6 THE DIRECTDRAWPICTURE1 PROGRAM SHOWS HOW TO WORK WITH
BITMAPS

```
/////////////////////////////////////
// Purpose:
// Project: DirectDrawPicture1.bpr
//
#include <vcl.h>
#pragma hdrstop

#include "Main.h"

#pragma package(smart_init)
#pragma resource "*.dfm"
TForm1 *Form1;

__fastcall TForm1::TForm1(TComponent* Owner)
  : TForm(Owner)
{
}

void __fastcall TForm1::FormCreate(TObject *Sender)
{
  Width = 640;
  Height = 480;
  FDirectDraw = 0;
  FPhase = 0;
  FActive = false;
  FFrontMsg = "Front buffer (F12 or Esc to quit)";
  FBackMsg = "Back buffer (F12 or Esc to quit)";
  DebugFile = new TStringList;
}

void __fastcall TForm1::FormDestroy(TObject *Sender)
{
  if (FDirectDraw != 0) {
    FDirectDraw->FlipToGDISurface();
    FDirectDraw->SetCooperativeLevel(Handle, DDSCL_NORMAL);
    if (FDirectDrawPalette != 0) {
      FDirectDrawPalette->Release();
      FDirectDrawPalette = 0;
    }
    if (FPrimarySurface != 0) {
      FPrimarySurface->Release();
      FPrimarySurface = 0;
    }
    FDirectDraw->Release();
    FDirectDraw = 0;
```

continues

25

DIRECTDRAW

LISTING 25.6   CONTINUED

```cpp
  }
  DebugFile->SaveToFile(AFileName);
  delete DebugFile;
}

void __fastcall TForm1::FormKeyDown(TObject *Sender, WORD &Key,
      TShiftState Shift)
{
   switch (Key) {
     case VK_F3: {
       Start();
       break;
     }
     case VK_ESCAPE :
     case VK_F12: {
       Timer1->Enabled = false;
       Close();
     }
   }
}

void TForm1::PaintSurfaces()
{
  HDC DC;
  if (FPrimarySurface->GetDC(&DC) == DD_OK) {
    SetBkColor(DC, RGB(0, 0, 255));
    SetTextColor(DC, RGB(255, 255, 0));
    TextOut(DC, 0, 0, FFrontMsg.c_str(), FFrontMsg.Length());
    FPrimarySurface->ReleaseDC(DC);
  }

  if (FBackSurface->GetDC(&DC) == DD_OK) {
    SetBkColor(DC, RGB(0, 0, 255));
    SetTextColor(DC, RGB(255, 255, 0));
    TextOut(DC, 0, 0, FBackMsg.c_str(), FBackMsg.Length());
    FBackSurface->ReleaseDC(DC);
  }
}

void TForm1::Start()
{
  DDSURFACEDESC SurfaceDesc;
  HRESULT hr = DirectDrawCreate(0, &FDirectDraw, 0);
  if (hr == DD_OK) {
    // Get exclusive mode
    hr = FDirectDraw->SetCooperativeLevel(Handle, // DDSCL_NORMAL);
      DDSCL_EXCLUSIVE | DDSCL_FULLSCREEN);
    if (hr == DD_OK) {
      hr = FDirectDraw->SetDisplayMode(640, 480, 8);
```

```
      if (hr == DD_OK) {
        // Create the primary surface with 1 back buffer
        DDSCAPS DDSCaps;
        SurfaceDesc.dwSize = sizeof(SurfaceDesc);
        SurfaceDesc.dwFlags = DDSD_CAPS | DDSD_BACKBUFFERCOUNT;
        SurfaceDesc.ddsCaps.dwCaps =
          DDSCAPS_PRIMARYSURFACE | DDSCAPS_FLIP | DDSCAPS_COMPLEX;
        SurfaceDesc.dwBackBufferCount = 1;
        hr = FDirectDraw->CreateSurface(
          &SurfaceDesc, &FPrimarySurface, 0);
        if (hr == DD_OK) {
          // Get a pointer to the back buffer
          DDSCaps.dwCaps = DDSCAPS_BACKBUFFER;
          hr = FPrimarySurface->
            GetAttachedSurface(&DDSCaps, &FBackSurface);
          if (hr == DD_OK) {
            PaintSurfaces();
            GetPicture();
            Timer1->Enabled = true;
            FActive = true;
            return;
          }
        }
      }
    }
  }
  String S;
  S.sprintf("Direct Draw Init Failed %x", hr);
  MessageBox(Handle, S.c_str(), "ERROR", MB_OK);
  Close();
}

void TForm1::GetPicture()
{
  FDirectDrawPalette = DDLoadPalette(FDirectDraw, Background);
  if (FDirectDrawPalette) {
    HRESULT hr = FPrimarySurface->SetPalette(FDirectDrawPalette);
    if (hr == DD_OK) {
      DDReLoadBitmap(FBackSurface, Background);
    }
  }
}

void __fastcall TForm1::FormPaint(TObject *Sender)
{
  const char* Msg =
    "Page Flipping Test: Press F3 to start, F12 or Esc to exit";
  if (!FActive) {
    HDC DC = GetDC(Handle);
```

continues

LISTING 25.6   CONTINUED

```
    TRect rc = GetClientRect();
    DebugFile->Add("Left: " + String(rc.Left) +
      " Top: " + String(rc.Top) +
      " Right: " + String(rc.Right) +
      " Bottom: " + String(rc.Bottom));
    TSize size;
    GetTextExtentPoint(DC, Msg, strlen(Msg), &size);
    SetBkColor(DC, RGB(0, 0, 0));
    SetTextColor(DC, RGB(255, 255, 0));
    TextOut(DC, (rc.Right - size.cx) / 2,
      (rc.Bottom - size.cy) / 2, Msg, strlen(Msg));
    ReleaseDC(Handle, DC);
  }
}

void __fastcall TForm1::Timer1Timer(TObject *Sender)
{
  GetPicture();
  HDC DC;
  if (FBackSurface->GetDC(&DC) == DD_OK) {
    if (FPhase) {
      SetBkColor(DC, RGB(0, 0, 255));
      SetTextColor(DC, RGB(255, 255, 0));
      TextOut(DC, 0, 0, FFrontMsg.c_str(), FFrontMsg.Length());
      FPhase = 0;
    } else {
      SetBkColor(DC, RGB(0, 0, 255));
      SetTextColor(DC, RGB(0, 255, 255));
      TextOut(DC, 0, 0, FBackMsg.c_str(), FBackMsg.Length());
      FPhase = 1;
    }
    FBackSurface->ReleaseDC(DC);
  }

  while (true) {
    HRESULT hr = FPrimarySurface->Flip(0, 0);

    if (hr == DD_OK)
      break;

    if (hr == DDERR_SURFACELOST) {
      hr = FPrimarySurface->Restore();
      if (hr != DD_OK)
        break;
    }
```

```
      if (hr != DDERR_WASSTILLDRAWING)
        break;
    }
}
```

This code works with the Background variable, which can be used to reference a bitmap stored in a resource linked with the program's executable. In other words, the executable has a bitmap bound to it, and I can access that bitmap just by passing DirectDraw the name of the resource I want to use. The Background variable is a string listing that resource's name.

The core routines here are called DDLoadPalette() and DDReLoadBitmap(). The first of these routines opens a bitmap and discovers its palette. After you have a handle to the palette, you can use the SetPalette() routine to inform DirectDraw of the palette you want to use.

The next step is to load the bitmap you want to use and to blit it into the back surface. I end up calling this method right before I call Flip(). Therefore, it will first be loaded into the original back surface and then loaded into the original primary surface. As a result, it is part of both surfaces and is shown continuously to the user.

DDLoadPalette() and DDReLoadBitmap() are utility routines that ship with the DirectX SDK. As of this writing, the utility routines are expected to ship with C++Builder 4. You should find them in the CBuilder4\Examples\DDraw\Utils directory in the file called DDUTIL.CPP. Add this file to your DirectDraw projects that require bitmap and palette support.

Game Resources

Game programming is more complicated than most standard Windows programming tasks for many reasons. The root of this complexity is the need to use special graphics tools such as DirectX. Many first-time game programmers underestimate the complexity of creating art.

Many books are available on game programming and on producing art for games. I have found two useful:

- *Tricks of the Game Programming Gurus.* LaMothe, Ratcliff, et al., Sams Publishing.
- *The Ultimate Game Developers Sourcebook.* Ben Sawyer, Coriolis Group Books.

You also need a paint program. I find that the inexpensive shareware program called Paint Shop Pro (www.jasc.com) meets most of my needs, although many other powerful programs such as Fractal Paint (`www.fractal.com`) are available. Here's the contact information for Paint Shop Pro:

> JASC, Inc.
> P.O. Box 44997
> Eden Prairie, MN 55344
> 930-9171
> `www.jasc.com`

Other key paint programs that I use often include TrueSpace (`www.caligari.com`) and VistaPro from Virtual Reality Laboratories. TrueSpace allows you to create three-dimensional objects, and VistaPro allows you to create landscapes. I use VistaPro to create background scenes that show rolling hills, mountains, and trees. Here is the contact information:

> Virtual Reality Laboratories
> San Luis Obisbo, CA
> 805-545-8515
> `VRLI@aol.com`
> `http://www.romt.com`

You might find additional game components, links, or code available at these sites:

- `http://www.spinlogic.com/GameDev/`
- `http://www.geocities.com/SiliconValley/Way/3390/`
- `http://users.aol.com/charliecal/`
- `http://www.microsoft.com/directx/default.asp`

Many other Web sites are of interest to game developers, but you can find links to most of them from the sites listed here. On CompuServe, type `GO GAMEDEV` to find the game developers' forum.

As stated previously, game programming is an extremely complex undertaking. The biggest mistake you can make is to try to create tools from scratch. Use the tools included with this book to get some sense of what you can gain from a graphics engine and a set of gaming tools, then go out and search the Web and your local bookstores for ready-made graphics and game engines. Build your games using these tools; don't try to create your own tools from scratch unless you're sure, double-sure, and then triple-sure you know what you're doing and why.

If you have never built a game before, then don't even consider building one from scratch. Build your first game with someone else's engine. Then, after you understand something about the tools that are available, you might finally be in a position to consider creating some of your own tools. Even then, however, I still recommend using someone else's tools rather than trying to create your own. The *Ultimate Game Developers*

Sourcebook, mentioned previously, offers a great deal of information on finding third-party game engines.

Summary

You had a look at DirectDraw technology in this chapter. In particular, you saw how to

- Initialize DirectDraw
- Flip between surfaces
- Use DirectDraw and the GDI at the same time
- Load and blit bitmaps to the screen

You have considerably more to learn about DirectDraw. However, by now, you should have the basics under your belt. You will have the opportunity to study this subject in more depth while reading the next chapter.

CHAPTER 26

More DirectX Technologies

*by Charlie Calvert
and Kent Reisdorph*

IN THIS CHAPTER

This chapter contains samples of DirectSound and Direct3D code. It also features a reasonably enjoyable game called BCBMan, which is very loosely based on the old Pacman arcade game. BCBMan takes advantage of both DirectDraw and DirectSound technologies.

The DirectSound and BCBMan parts of the chapter use a set of components called Artemis that allow you to manipulate DirectSound and DirectDraw with relative ease. They are not professional-level components, but if you are willing to baby them, they allow you to create games in a fairly short period of time.

Any one of the subjects covered in this chapter could easily fill several hundred pages of text. Unfortunately, I do not have the room available to explore these subjects in such depth. As a result, you will find that the material presented here is a bit cursory in nature and that I have not included full listings for the projects in this chapter. However, I will tell you enough to get you up and running using the code that I provide, and the full source is available on the CD-ROM.

Using DirectSound

DirectSound has two primary benefits:

- It allows you to play a sound at a particular instant. Consider the case in which you are creating a game and need to play a sound the moment two sprites come in contact. It won't do if the sound is played a few seconds after the user sees the sprites collide. The collision and the sound must occur at the same instant. DirectSound is designed to allow you to play a sound the instant you request that the sound be played.

- DirectSound allows you to play two or more sounds at the same time.

The DirectSound technology that I show you comes in a component called TZounds. TZounds relies on a binary file called SoundLib.dll, which must be on your path; otherwise, the component will not work. The source for SoundLib is provided on the CD-ROM that accompanies this book. The code kept in the DLL is boilerplate code meant for reading and writing WAV files from disk.

I will not show you the code from SoundLib, as it is uninteresting. However, the class declaration for the TZounds component is shown in Listing 26.1. The entire component is available on the CD-ROM, but I have not included it all here because of space restrictions. Much of the code that I do not include in the listings is found in the analysis of the object that follows these listings.

LISTING 26.1 THE TZounds COMPONENT ALLOWS YOU TO USE DIRECTSOUND IN YOUR PROGRAMS

```
class PACKAGE TZounds : public TComponent
{
private:
  LPDIRECTSOUND DirectSound;
  TBufferInfo BufferInfo[MAXSOUNDBUFFERS];
  BOOL AppCreateBasicBuffer(
    LPDIRECTSOUND lpDirectSound, LPDIRECTSOUNDBUFFER *DSBuffer,
    int FileSize, LPWAVEFORMATEX WaveFormatInfo);
  BOOL AppWriteDataToBuffer(LPDIRECTSOUNDBUFFER lpDsb,
    DWORD dwOffset, LPBYTE lpbSoundData, DWORD dwSoundBytes);
  void OpenWaveFile(char *pszFileName,  HMMIO *phmmioIn,
    WAVEFORMATEX **ppwfxInfo, MMCKINFO *pckInRIFF);
  void LoadWaveFile(char *pszFileName, UINT *cbSize,
    DWORD *pcSamples, WAVEFORMATEX **ppwfxInfo, BYTE **ppbData);
  void CloseWaveFile(HMMIO *phmmio, WAVEFORMATEX **ppwfxSrc);
  void ReadWaveFile(HMMIO hmmioIn, UINT cbRead, BYTE *pbDest,
    MMCKINFO *pckIn, UINT *cbActualRead);
  void StartWaveRead(HMMIO *phmmioIn,
    MMCKINFO *pckIn, MMCKINFO *pckInRIFF);
  BOOL IsValidWave(LPSTR pszFileName);
  void CleanBufferInfo(int Buffer);
  void CleanBuffers();
public:
  virtual __fastcall TZounds(TComponent *AOwner);
  virtual __fastcall ~TZounds();
  void Create();
  BOOL EnumerateDrivers(TStrings *List);
  void inline LoadFromFile(AnsiString &S, int Buffer)
  {
    OpenFile(S, Buffer);
  }
  void OpenFile(AnsiString &S, int Buffer);
  void Play(int Buffer, bool Loop);
  long GetVolume(int Buffer);
  long GetFrequency(int Buffer);
};
```

The TZounds component allows you to work with two WAV files at the same time. DirectSound will allow you to work with many more files, but I have only taken the component to this stage at the current time. The DirectSoundTest example, found on the CD-ROM that comes with this book and shown in Figure 26.1, provides a simple method for using the component in a non-visual context:

```
void __fastcall TForm1::Button1Click(TObject *Sender)
{
  if (!Z)
```

```
    Z = new TZounds(this);
  Z->EnumerateDrivers(ListBox1->Items);
  if (OpenDialog1->Execute()) {
    Z->OpenFile(OpenDialog1->FileName, 1);
    Z->Play(1, false);
  }
}
```

FIGURE 26.1

The
DirectSoundTest
*plays a WAV file
and shows the
available drivers
on the system.*

The Button1Click() method first creates an instance of the object if it has not already been created; it then shows the available drivers on the system to the user. You need not iterate through the drivers, but the option is there if you want it. Finally, the code calls the OpenFile() and Play() methods. All four calls—to Create(), EnumerateDrivers(), OpenFile(), and Play()—are discussed over the course of the next few pages of this chapter.

Initializing `DirectSound`

This section discusses the code necessary to initialize an instance of the DirectSound object.

The field of the TZounds component called DirectSound is of type LPDIRECTSOUND, a pointer to an IDirectSound interface. This interface plays the same role in DirectSound that the IDirectDraw interface does in DirectDraw. TZounds initializes its instance of IDirectSound in the Create() method, called when the user first opens a file:

```
void TZounds::Create()
{
  HRESULT        hr;

  if (DirectSound != NULL)
    return;

  hr = DirectSoundCreate(NULL, &DirectSound, NULL);
  if(hr != 0)
    throw Exception("DirectSoundCreate failed");

  hr = DirectSound->Initialize(NULL);
```

```
    if(SUCCEEDED(hr) ¦¦ (hr == DSERR_ALREADYINITIALIZED ))
    {
      HWND Handle = Application->MainForm->Handle;
      hr = DirectSound->SetCooperativeLevel(Handle, DSSCL_PRIORITY);
      if(hr != 0)
        throw Exception("SetCooperativeLevel failed");
    }
}
```

This code exits immediately if the DirectSound object is already initialized. If it's not, DirectSoundCreate() is called. Here is the declaration for DirectSoundCreate():

```
HRESULT WINAPI DirectSoundCreate(
  LPGUID lpGuid,
  LPDIRECTSOUND * ppDS,
  IUnknown FAR * pUnkOuter
)
```

The first parameter of DirectSoundCreate() can be one of the GUIDs returned when you enumerate the available drivers on the system, as described later in this section. If you just want the default driver, pass in 0. The second parameter is a pointer to an IDirectSound interface. When DirectSoundCreate() returns, the variable passed in this parameter can be used to manipulate the DirectSound object. The last parameter of DirectSoundCreate() is reserved and must always be 0.

You should call SetCooperativeLevel() after you have created the DirectSoundObject. Here's that declaration:

```
HRESULT SetCooperativeLevel(
  HWND hwnd,
  DWORD dwLevel
);
```

The first parameter of this function is the handle of your application's main window. The second parameter can take one of the following flags:

- DSSCL_EXCLUSIVE—If you use this flag, your application has exclusive access at the moment your application is granted access to the sound card.
- DSSCL_NORMAL—Your application will share the sound card with other applications if you use this flag. This choice is probably the best for most applications, and my component would be better if it gave the user the option of using this flag.
- DSSCL_PRIORITY—This flag allows you to call SetFormat() and Compact(). (The SetFormat() function allows you to specify the WAV file format, and the Compact() function places all WAV data into a single, contiguous block of memory.)
- DSSCL_WRITEPRIMARY—This flag, which sets the highest priority, gives you access to primary sound buffers, which are the buffers the user is currently hearing.

Enumerating the Sound Drivers

You can use the TZounds::EnumerateDrivers() method to enumerate the sound drivers on the system:

```
bool TZounds::EnumerateDrivers(TStrings *List)
{
  if (DirectSoundEnumerate((LPDSENUMCALLBACK)DSEnumProc, List) != DS_OK)
  {
    ShowMessage("No Enumeration");
    return false;
  }
  return true;
}
```

This method sets up a standard Windows callback. The enumeration function, DSEnumProc(), looks like this:

```
bool CALLBACK DSEnumProc(LPGUID lpGUID, LPCTSTR lpszDesc,
  LPCTSTR lpszDrvName, LPVOID lpContext)
{
  TStrings *List = (TStrings*)lpContext;
  List->Add(lpszDesc);
  return true;
}
```

When you call DirectSoundEnumerate(), you are telling Windows that you want to be told about the drivers on the system. Windows does so by calling the callback function repeatedly, once for each driver on the system. The parameters passed to the callback function describe each driver in turn. The callback function must have a particular signature:

```
BOOL DSEnumCallback(
  LPGUID lpGuid,
  LPCSTR lpcstrDescription,
  LPCSTR lpcstrModule,
  LPVOID lpContext
);
```

The first parameter is the GUID for the sound driver. It can be passed to DirectSoundCreate() if you want to specify a particular driver to use. The second parameter describes the driver and the third lists the device driver (VXD). For instance, the driver for my AWE32 card is SB16.VXD.

The last parameter is a pointer to any kind of user-defined data you might want to set up. Most Windows callbacks have a user data parameter. You can define this data when you first call DirectSoundEnumerate(). In my case, I use this parameter to pass a pointer to a list box's Items property:

```
bool TZounds::EnumerateDrivers(TStrings *List)
{
  if (DirectSoundEnumerate((LPDSENUMCALLBACK)DSEnumProc, List) != DS_OK)
  {
    ShowMessage("No Enumeration");
    return False;
  }
  return true;
}
```

This `TStrings` object is then passed to the Windows callback and I can use it as I see fit:

```
TStrings *List = (TStrings*)lpContext;
List->Add(lpszDesc);
```

Here, you can see that I typecast the user-defined data as a `TStrings` object. I use a C-style cast here because I know the pointer passed in will be a valid `TStrings` pointer. I then add the driver name (the value of the `lpszDesc` parameter) to the list box through the pointer I specified in the user data parameter.

You will probably want to handle this situation somewhat differently. My point is not that you should follow this specific example, but that you be aware that the sparameter is available if you need it.

Working with a `DirectSoundBuffer`

Besides the `IDirectSound` object itself, perhaps the single most important part of the DirectSound API is the `IDirectSoundBuffer` interface. `IDirectSoundBuffer` is a DirectX interface designed to encapsulate and manipulate a WAV file. For instance, after you have initialized an instance of this interface, you can call its `Play()` method to play a WAV file:

```
DirectSoundBuffer->Play(0,0,Flags);
```

The `Play()` method is dicussed in more depth later in the chapter. Here you're simply getting a sense of the importance of this interface.

When you first create the `TZounds` component, the following code is called:

```
inline __fastcall TZounds::TZounds(TComponent *AOwner)
 : TComponent(AOwner)
{
  DirectSound = NULL;
  for (int i = 0; i < MAXSOUNDBUFFERS; i++)
    BufferInfo[i].DirectSoundBuffer = NULL;
}
```

Note that I set each instance of the `DirectSoundBuffer` to `0`, which is my way of telling the component that the buffer is currently uninitialized. The constructor method works with a custom array of records of type `TBufferInfo`:

```
struct TBufferInfo
{
  LPDIRECTSOUNDBUFFER DirectSoundBuffer;
  WAVEFORMATEX *WaveFormatInfo;
  BYTE *Data;
};
```

The other fields of the `TBufferInfo` record are used to initialize the `DirectSoundBuffer`. This method actually initializes the buffer:

```
bool TZounds::AppCreateBasicBuffer(LPDIRECTSOUND lpDirectSound,
  LPDIRECTSOUNDBUFFER *DSBuffer,
  int FileSize, LPWAVEFORMATEX WaveFormatInfo)
{
  WAVEFORMATEX WaveFormat;
  DSBUFFERDESC BufferDesc;
  HRESULT hr;

  // Set up wave format structure.
  memset(&WaveFormat, 0, sizeof(WAVEFORMATEX));
  WaveFormat.wFormatTag = WAVE_FORMAT_PCM;
  WaveFormat.nChannels = 2;
  WaveFormat.nSamplesPerSec = 22050;
  WaveFormat.nBlockAlign = 4;
  WaveFormat.nAvgBytesPerSec =
    WaveFormat.nSamplesPerSec * WaveFormat.nBlockAlign;
  WaveFormat.wBitsPerSample = 16;
  WaveFormat.cbSize = 0;

  // Set up DSBUFFERDESC structure.
  memset(&BufferDesc, 0, sizeof(DSBUFFERDESC)); // Zero it out.
  BufferDesc.dwSize = sizeof(DSBUFFERDESC);
  // Need default controls (pan, volume, frequency).
  BufferDesc.dwFlags =
    DSBCAPS_CTRLDEFAULT | DSBCAPS_STATIC | DSBCAPS_GETCURRENTPOSITION2;

  // 3-second buffer.
  BufferDesc.dwBufferBytes = FileSize; //9 * WaveFormat.nAvgBytesPerSec;
  BufferDesc.lpwfxFormat = (LPWAVEFORMATEX)WaveFormatInfo;

  // Create buffer.
  hr = lpDirectSound->CreateSoundBuffer(&BufferDesc, DSBuffer, NULL);
  if(DS_OK == hr)
  { // Succeeded. Valid interface is in *DSBuffer.
    return true;
  } else
```

```
    {  // Failed.
      *DSBuffer = NULL;
      return FALSE;
    }
}
```

You can call the method this way:

```
AppCreateBasicBuffer(DirectSound, &BufferInfo[Buffer].DirectSoundBuffer,
   Size, BufferInfo[Buffer].WaveFormatInfo);
```

As you can see, the call into the object uses the `BufferInfo` structure's field. By the time you make this call, the `BufferInfo::WaveFormatInfo` structure is filled out in another procedure that gets the information it needs from reading in the WAV file itself.

The `AppCreateBasicBuffer()` method fills out a DirectSound buffer description record and then passes it to the `CreateSoundBuffer()` method of the `IDirectSound` interface. The result is a valid instance of an `IDirectSoundBuffer` interface that is designed to handle a particular WAV file.

Opening a WAV File

The `TZounds` component's `OpenFile()` method loads a WAV file for later playback. It looks like this:

```
void TZounds::OpenFile(AnsiString &S, int Buffer)
{
  UINT Size;
  DWord Samples;

  Buffer--;
  if ((Buffer>= MAXSOUNDBUFFERS) || (Buffer < 0))
    throw Exception("OpenFile: Buffer number error!");

  if (!DirectSound)
    Create();

  if(BufferInfo[Buffer].DirectSoundBuffer)
    CleanBufferInfo(Buffer);

  if(!IsValidWave(S.c_str()))
  {
    ShowMessage("Wave File Invalid");
    return;
  }

  LoadWaveFile(S.c_str(), &Size, &Samples,
    &BufferInfo[Buffer].WaveFormatInfo, &BufferInfo[Buffer].Data);
```

```
if(AppCreateBasicBuffer(DirectSound,
    &BufferInfo[Buffer].DirectSoundBuffer,
    Size, BufferInfo[Buffer].WaveFormatInfo))
{
  AppWriteDataToBuffer(BufferInfo[Buffer].DirectSoundBuffer,
    0, BufferInfo[Buffer].Data, Size);
}
}
```

This function takes two parameters. The first is the name of the WAV that you want to
load, and the second is the buffer number you want to assign to the file. This buffer number, which is 1-based, is stored in an internal variable kept by the TZounds component.
This version of the component supports only two buffers, so the only valid values to pass
in this parameter are 1 and 2.

> **NOTE**
>
> I have never made any attempt to increase the number of buffers that this com-
> ponent will handle. When I wrote the component, I tried to set things up so
> that the program could handle a variable number of buffers. In theory, you can
> simply increase the MAXSOUNDBUFFERS constant declared in ZOUNDS.H if you want
> to work with more than two sound files at a time. I have never tested that fea-
> ture, so some experimentation might be required if you decide to try it.

The code in the open file method first decrements the buffer count the user passed to the
procedure. This operation is necessary because I want the user to work with a 1-based set
of numbers, but the internal data of the component is 0-based. After decrementing the
count, I determine that the number passed in is within a valid range. If the
DirectSoundObject is not yet initialized, I initialize it as explained earlier in this chapter. If this is not the first time the buffer has been used, I dispose of all the old data in the
current BufferInfo record:

```
void TZounds::CleanBufferInfo(int Buffer)
{
  if (BufferInfo[Buffer].DirectSoundBuffer)
  {
    BufferInfo[Buffer].DirectSoundBuffer->Release();
    BufferInfo[Buffer].DirectSoundBuffer = NULL;
  }

  if(BufferInfo[Buffer].WaveFormatInfo)
  {
    GlobalFree(BufferInfo[Buffer].WaveFormatInfo);
    BufferInfo[Buffer].WaveFormatInfo = NULL;
```

```
    }

    if (BufferInfo[Buffer].Data)
    {
        GlobalFree(BufferInfo[Buffer].Data);
        BufferInfo[Buffer].Data = NULL;
    }
}
```

This code is shown so you can see how to free the memory associated with a sound buffer. To free the DirectSoundBuffer, which is a COM object, you call Release() on the object and then set the object's pointer to 0 (NULL).

The other portions of the TBufferInfo record were allocated either in the SoundLib.dll or in other portions of the component by calling GlobalAlloc(). This means you need to call GlobalFree() when you deallocate them. If the result of this operation is 0, you know it was successful; otherwise, the system could not deallocate the memory.

Now that you see how to clean up the TBufferInfo record, I need to turn my attention back to the OpenFile() method, which is still not quite fully explained. The next step in the OpenFile() method's long journey is to determine whether the file you want to open is valid. It does this by calling the IsValidWave() function of the TZounds object:

```
bool TZounds::IsValidWave(LPSTR pszFileName)
{
    bool           Result = False;
    HMMIO          hmmio;
    MMCKINFO       mmck;
    WAVEFORMATEX   *pwfx;

    OpenWaveFile(pszFileName, &hmmio, &pwfx, &mmck);

    if (pwfx->wFormatTag == WAVE_FORMAT_PCM)
    {
        Result = true;
    }

    CloseWaveFile(&hmmio, &pwfx);

    return Result;
}
```

OpenWaveFile() is in SoundLib.dll, but you don't need to understand how it works. It just opens a WAV file and returns a description of some of its features. After you have the file open, you get back a variable of type WAVEFORMATEX, which contains a field called wFormatTag. If this field in the returned structure is not WAVE_FORMAT_PCM, the other methods used by the TZounds component will not work correctly. Most—but by no means all—WAV files use this format.

> **NOTE**
>
> You should not use this code for creating a generic WAV player; the routines shown here work with most, but not all, WAV files. However, it should work fine for most games and custom applications; you can control the format of WAV files that are being played in those situations.
>
> If you are desperate to use a WAV file that is not handled by these routines, you might want to try converting the file into a standard format. For instance, I have used the WaveStudio utility that comes with my AWE64 card to convert between a nonstandard and a standard WAV format. Most other sound cards have similar utilities, and various utilities of this type are available on the Internet.

The last lines of the OpenFile() routine call LoadWaveFile() and AppCreateBasicBuffer(). The first routine loads a WAV file, and the second creates an IDirectSoundBuffer that wraps the file, as shown earlier in this chapter.

Playing a Sound File

After you finally have a DirectSoundBuffer initialized, using it is extremely easy:

```
void TZounds::Play(int Buffer, bool Loop)
{
  int Flags = 0;

  Buffer--;
  if (Loop)
    Flags = DSBPLAY_LOOPING;

  if (BufferInfo[Buffer].DirectSoundBuffer)
    BufferInfo[Buffer].DirectSoundBuffer->Play(0,0,Flags);
}
```

This routine takes the number of the buffer you want to play in its first parameter. This number was assigned to the buffer when you called OpenFile(). The second parameter specifies whether you want to play the file once or whether you want to have the buffer played in a loop. If a loop is requested, the second parameter to the DirectSoundBuffer's Play() method should be set to true:

```
DirectSoundBuffer->Play(0, true);
```

If you don't want the sound to loop, pass in false for the second parameter.

Playing Large Files

The TZounds component reads in an entire WAV file at a time. Playing entire files works fine for short sound effects in a game. However, if you want to work with very large files, you don't want to read them all in at once. Instead, you would create a buffer, one end of which is continually being played by DirectSound, and the other end of which you are continually feeding from an open file stream. Nothing inherent in the routines I have provided would keep you from playing files this way, but you would need to tweak my code in several different places to implement it.

Playing Two WAV Files at Once

On the CD-ROM that accompanies this book is a program called DirectSoundTwo; it uses the TZounds component. The program allows you to load a WAV file into each of the component's two buffers and to play them back at the same time. To help emphasize the fact that both files are being played at once, I loop the first file you elect to play and then let you select a menu item to play the second file.

The following code loads the files the user selects:

```
void __fastcall TForm1::Buffer11Click(TObject *Sender)
{
  if (OpenDialog1->Execute())
    Zounds1->OpenFile(OpenDialog1->FileName, 1);
}

void __fastcall TForm1::Buffer21Click(TObject *Sender)
{
  if (OpenDialog1->Execute())
    Zounds1->OpenFile(OpenDialog1->FileName, 2);
}
```

Notice that I pass the first filename to buffer 1 of the TZounds component and the second filename to buffer 2.

The following code plays the files:

```
void __fastcall TForm1::PlayBufferOne1Click(TObject *Sender)
{
  Zounds1->Play(1, true);
}

void __fastcall TForm1::PlayBufferTwo1Click(TObject *Sender)
{
  Zounds1->Play(2, false);
}
```

Notice that the first routine loops through the first buffer, whereas the second routine plays the second buffer only once. This way, you can keep a continuously playing file in the background and play the second buffer on top of it. I found it fun to work the sounds from the Windows Jungle sound scheme when testing this program. For instance, you can pass in the sound of a frog croaking in the first buffer so that it is repeated continuously in the background as if you were near a pond on a summer's evening. On top of this sound you can have lions roar, monkeys howl, or any other sound that might create a nice effect.

This introduction has given you enough information to begin using the technology in your own programs. The TZounds component is certainly easy to use, and you should feel free to drop it into your own programs whenever you need it.

Creating a DirectX Game

This section shows you how to build a simple arcade game using a set of DirectX components. The components I have created are stored in a package called Artemis20, which is shown in Listing 26.2.

LISTING 26.2   THE PACKAGE FOR A SET OF DIRECTX COMPONENTS

```
#include <vcl.h>
#pragma hdrstop
USERES("Artemis20.res");
USEUNIT("Artemis.CPP");
USERES("Artemis.dcr");
USEUNIT("Errors1.cpp");
USEFORM("ArtemisEditor1.cpp", SceneEditorDlg);
USEUNIT("zounds.cpp");
USEPACKAGE("vcl40.bpi");

#pragma package(smart_init)

//   Package source.

int WINAPI DllEntryPoint(HINSTANCE hinst, unsigned long reason, void*)
{
  return 1;
}
```

This package must be compiled with WIN32 defined. I have defined this symbol in the Conditional defines field on the Conditionals/Defines page of the Project Options dialog.

You end up with five key components when you compile this package and install it:

- `THermes`—This component is a wrapper around the `IDirectDraw` object. It allows you to go into windowed or exclusive mode and to choose from a few simple resolutions. A `THermes` object is useless unless you attach its `Scene` property to either a `TScene` or `TspriteScene` object. In a sense, the relationship between the `THermes` component and the `TScene` component is roughly similar to the relationship between a `TTable` component and a `TDataSource` component. In particular, the `THermes` component needs to be linked to a `TScene` component before it can be used to display graphics to the user.

- `TScene`—This object automatically creates a primary surface, a back surface, and a work surface. You can add a bitmap to the work surface and display it to the user, or you can simply blank the surface and draw on it. You should always add at least one small bitmap to the `TScene` object, even if you don't want to display it. Don't ever use a bitmap that is larger than the resolution that you choose. For instance, if you go into 640×480 exclusive mode, don't try to display a picture larger than 640×480. You can load pictures into this control either directly from disk or by first placing them inside a resource file that is part of a DLL.

- `TSpriteScene` and `TSprite`—Use these objects if you want to have a background picture and then one or more sprites that you display on top of it. These controls, rather than `TScene`, are the ones I use in the BCBMan game that will be developed in this chapter.

- `TZounds`—This DirectSound component is explored in the first section of this chapter.

I do not spend much time discussing these components, as they are really nothing more than wrappers around the functionality described in the preceding chapter. In other words, they are designed to automatically call `DirectDrawCreate()` (or `CoCreateInstance()`), `SetCooperativeLevel()`, `SetDisplayMode()`), and to create the surfaces you need. I have tested these components extensively under Windows 95/98 and under Windows NT 4.

The only tricky parts involved in using the objects can be covered by the following points:

- Be sure to use the Object Inspector to assign the `Scene` property of the `THermes` object to a `TScene` or `TSpriteScene` object. As mentioned earlier, this process is a bit like connecting a `TTable` object and a `TDataSource` object.

- Set the `ShowBitmap` and `BlankScene` properties of the `TScene` and `TSpriteScene` objects to their appropriate values. If you are in 256-color mode, you can define a

transparent color for a sprite by selecting its palette offset with the
`TransparentColor` property of `TSprite`.

- Setting up the sprite objects takes a single line per object. These simple lines of
  code assign a sprite to a `TSpriteScene` object just as you must assign a `TScene`
  object to a `THermes` object. The following code sets up seven sprite objects that are
  owned by a single `TSpriteScene` object:

```
void __fastcall TForm1::SpriteScene1SetupSurfaces(TObject *Sender)
{
  SpriteScene1->AddSprite(DotSprite);
  SpriteScene1->AddSprite(BlankSprite);
  SpriteScene1->AddSprite(VertSprite);
  SpriteScene1->AddSprite(ManSprite);
  SpriteScene1->AddSprite(BadSprite1);
  SpriteScene1->AddSprite(BadSprite2);
  SpriteScene1->AddSprite(BadSprite3);
}
```

- When you are ready to run the components you have set up, call the `Run()` method:

```
Hermes1->Run();
```

You will find three programs—SimpleHermesSprite, SimpleHermes2, and
SimpleHermesDraw—on the CD-ROM that comes with this book. These programs are
designed to show the minimal settings for using these components in their various
modes. For instance, SimpleHermes2 shows the simplest possible program that uses
`THermes` and `TScene` to display a bitmap. SimpleHermesSprite shows the simplest possible program that displays a background bitmap with one sprite on it. SimpleHermesDraw
loads a tiny bitmap that is never displayed and then draws animated pictures on the surfaces provided by these components.

> **NOTE**
>
> My code simply won't work correctly without a bitmap because several of my
> methods assume that there is one. The component would be better if I didn't
> make this assumption. You will find that there is custom code in the compo-
> nents that create DirectDraw surfaces that don't rely on bitmaps, but I have not
> yet incorporated that code into all the necessary routines.

Because of space considerations, I will not discuss these programs in depth. They are
available for you to study so that you can learn the basics of how to use my components.
The BCBMan program provides a more in-depth look at how to work with these components.

Creating the BCBMan Program

BCBMan uses the THermes, TSpriteScene, TSprite, and TZounds components to create a Pacman-like game, as shown in Figure 26.2. The game allows you to move through a succession of four different mazes, each one more complex than the one that precedes it. To move from one maze to the next, you must make the character eat all the dots in the maze.

FIGURE 26.2

The BCBMan game allows you to run around a maze eating dots while being chased by brightly colored, highly voracious beasts of prey.

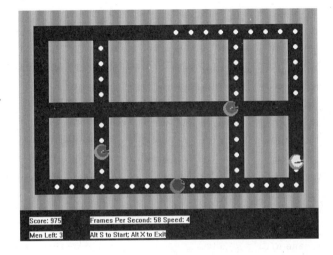

The beasts that chase you do not explicitly follow you but instead pursue entirely random patterns that are likely to put you in their way. You lose the game if you get eaten by the beasts four times. If you make it past all the beasts and eat all the dots, you proceed to the next level. If you eat the dots in all four levels, you win the game.

The game can be played in exclusive mode, as shown in Figure 26.2, or in windowed mode, as shown in Figure 26.3. When you start the game, you are presented with a simple dialog that lets you choose the mode you want. The dialog is shown in Figure 26.4.

When you run BCBMan, a small display at the bottom of the screen shows how many frames are being displayed per second. On my 266 machine with an NVIDIA card, this number is usually around 59 or 60 in exclusive mode. On my old 133 with a 512K video card, the game runs about 35 frames per second in exclusive mode and about 22 frames per second in windowed mode. Going much slower than 22 frames per second would probably take most of the fun out of the game. To help compensate for slower machines, I give you the option of running the game in fast mode, which means that the sprites move four pixels rather than two each time the surfaces are flipped.

FIGURE 26.3

The BCBMan program running in windowed mode, displaying the last and most complicated maze.

FIGURE 26.4

The dialog that allows you to set the game's operation mode.

This game is designed to run in 640×480 mode. If you run in windowed mode, you must use that size; if you are in exclusive mode, you should also select that size—otherwise the game won't look quite right. The components I have created support either 16-bit or 8-bit color, but the bitmaps in the shipping version of the game are designed for a 256-color 8-bit palette.

Even without including the source for the THermes, TSpriteScene, and TScene components, the listings for this game are quite long. As a result, I have cut them down to the bare minimum, showing only the class declarations from most of the units. The header for the program's main unit is shown in Listing 26.3. Listings 26.4 through 26.6 show the headers for the other supporting units. You can find the full code for the program on the CD-ROM that accompanies this book.

LISTING 26.3 THE HEADER FOR THE BCBMAN PROGRAM'S MAIN UNIT

```cpp
#ifndef MainH
#define MainH

#include <Classes.hpp>
#include <Controls.hpp>
#include <StdCtrls.hpp>
#include <Forms.hpp>
#include "Artemis.h"
#include "zounds.h"
#include "Robots2.h"

#define MaxBadMen 3
#define WM_STARTALL WM_USER

class TForm1 : public TForm
{
__published:    // IDE-managed Components
  TZounds *Zounds1;
  THermes *Hermes1;
  TSpriteScene *SpriteScene1;
  TSprite *DotSprite;
  TSprite *BlankSprite;
  TSprite *VertSprite;
  TSprite *ManSprite;
  TSprite *BadSprite1;
  TSprite *BadSprite2;
  TSprite *BadSprite3;
  void __fastcall SpriteScene1SetupSurfaces(TObject *Sender);
  void __fastcall SpriteScene1DrawScene(TObject *Sender,
          IDirectDrawSurface *Surface);
  void __fastcall FormCreate(TObject *Sender);
  void __fastcall FormDestroy(TObject *Sender);
  void __fastcall FormKeyDown(TObject *Sender, WORD &Key,
          TShiftState Shift);
  void __fastcall FormShow(TObject *Sender);
  void __fastcall FormClose(TObject *Sender, TCloseAction &Action);
private:
  TBadMan *FBadMen[MaxBadMen];
  long FFrameRate;
  long FFrameCount;
  long FFrameCount0;
  long FFrameTime;
  long FFrameTime0;
  TGameScore *FGameScore;
  TMainMan *FMainMan;
  void BlankDot();
  void CheckFrameCount();
  void CheckGameStatus();
  Boolean Collision();
```

continues

LISTING 26.3   CONTINUED

```
    void DrawBackground();
    void DrawBadGuy(int Value);
    void DrawMan();
    void DrawStats();
    void GameOver();
    Boolean HasWon();
    void __fastcall IdleProc(TObject *Sender, bool &Done);
    void Move();
    void ResetAll();
    void SetupBadMen();
    MESSAGE void WMStartAll(TMessage &Msg);

public:
    __fastcall TForm1(TComponent* Owner);
    void CheckError(HRESULT hr);
    __property TGameScore* GameScore={read=FGameScore,write=FGameScore};
BEGIN_MESSAGE_MAP
    MESSAGE_HANDLER(WM_STARTALL, TMessage, WMStartAll);
END_MESSAGE_MAP(TForm);
};

extern PACKAGE TForm1 *Form1;
```

LISTING 26.4   THE HEADER FOR THE Robots2 UNIT, WHICH HANDLES THE LOGIC FOR THE CHARACTERS THAT MOVE IN THE MAZE

```
#ifndef Robots2H
#define Robots2H

#include "globals.h"
#include "grid2.h"
#include "GameScore2.h"

typedef enum {tdNone = 0, tdRight, tdLeft, tdUp, tdDown} TDirection;

    class TRobot: public TBCBManBase
    {
      friend class TMainMan;
    private:
      int FXPos;
      int FYPos;
      int FGridX;
      int FGridY;
      TDirection FDirection;
      TDirection FRequestDir;
      TSprite *FSprite;
      void CheckRequest(TBoard *Board);
```

```
      void SetDirection(TDirection Value);
      void SetGridX(int Value);
      void SetGridY(int Value);
      void SetRequestDir(TDirection Value);
      void SetXPos(int Value);
      void SetYPos(int Value);
   public:
      TRobot();
      void Draw(THermes *Hermes1, TSprite *Sprite);
      void virtual Move(TGameScore *GameScore);
      __property TDirection Direction=
        {read=FDirection, write=SetDirection};
      __property int GridX={read=FGridX, write=SetGridX};
      __property int GridY={read=FGridY, write=SetGridY};
      __property TDirection RequestDir=
        {read=FRequestDir, write=SetRequestDir};
      __property TSprite *Sprite={read=FSprite, write=FSprite};
      __property int XPos={read=FXPos, write=SetXPos};
      __property int YPos={read=FYPos, write=SetYPos};
   };

   class TBadMan: public TRobot
   {
   public:
      void virtual Move(TGameScore *GameScore);
   };

   class TMainMan: public TRobot
   {
   private:
   public:
      TMainMan();
      void Home();
      void virtual Move(TGameScore * GameScore);
   };

#endif
```

LISTING 26.5 THE HEADER FOR THE Grid2 UNIT, WHICH HANDLES THE VARIOUS MAZES
DISPLAYED BY THE GAME

```
#ifndef Grid2H
#define Grid2H

#include "Artemis.h"
#include "globals.h"

#define DibSize 32
#define MaxLevels 4
```

continues

LISTING 26.5 CONTINUED

```
#define MaxY 13
#define MaxX 20
#define svBlank 2
#define svDot 0
#define svVert 1

typedef int TGrid[MaxY][MaxX];
typedef TSprite* TSpriteAry[3];

  class TBoard: public TBCBManBase
  {
  private:
    int FCurLevel;
    int FLevel;
    int FNumLevels;
  public:
    TBoard();
    void Draw(THermes *Hermes1, TSpriteAry Sprites);
    void SetDataXY(int X, int Y, int Value);
    int GetDataXY(int X, int Y);
    Boolean GotoNextLevel();
    __property int Level={read=FLevel};
  };

#endif
```

LISTING 26.6 THE HEADER FOR THE GameScore2 UNIT

```
#ifndef GameScore2H
#define GameScore2H

#include "globals.h"
#include "grid2.h"

typedef enum {gsPaused = 0, gsStopped, gsRunning,
  gsGameOverWon, gsGameOverLost, gsLevelOver} TGameStatus;

  class TGameScore: public TBCBManBase
  {
  private:
    TBoard *FBoard;
    int FMenLeft;
    long FPoints;
    TGameStatus FStatus;
    int FSpeed;
    void SetMenLeft(int Value);
    void SetPoints(long Value);
    void SetStatus(TGameStatus Value);
```

```
    void SetBoard(TBoard *Value);
  public:
    TGameScore();
    virtual ~TGameScore();
    void Faster();
    void Slower();
    __property TBoard *Board={read=FBoard, write=SetBoard};
    __property int MenLeft={read=FMenLeft, write=SetMenLeft};
    __property long Points={read=FPoints, write=SetPoints};
    __property int Speed={read=FSpeed};
    __property TGameStatus Status={read=FStatus, write=SetStatus};
  };
```

As I explained in Chapter 1, "Program Design Basics," the key to writing a robust OOP-based program is discovering the objects of which it consists. The objects I found in the BCBMan program look like this:

- TForm1—This is the main form that controls all the core objects in the program.

- TRobot, TBadMan, and TMainMan—These characters run through the maze. TRobot defines the default behavior for a character, and TBadMan is a descendant of TRobot that defines additional behavior for the vicious creatures that inhabit the maze. TMainMan, another descendant of TRobot, is the sprite the user controls while playing the game.

- TBoard—This board object is used to draw and define the maze through which the characters run.

- TGameScore—This simple object owns the TBoard object and also tracks basic facts about the game such as the score, the speed the characters move, and the number of bad guys on the board.

Each of these objects was quite easy to create. Building the maze that the characters run in was simple, as was building each of the characters and keeping track of the score. The only slightly tricky part was teaching the bad guys to roam about in a truly random fashion, but even that was not particularly difficult.

If you take all these different factors and put them together inside the context of a single program, the sheer number of details begins to add up. This is the problem I discussed in this book's first chapter. Each step in creating a computer program is usually very simple. What's difficult is managing the enormous volume of individual steps.

In this case, I managed complexity by creating simple objects, each entirely discrete, each with its own manageable problem domain. At the top level, I could then call on these objects to perform their assigned task. For instance, when it comes time to move the characters on the board, I just call this simple method:

```
void TForm1::Move()
{
  int i;

  FMainMan->Move(FGameScore);
  for (i = 0; i < MaxBadMen; i++)
  {
    FBadMen[i]->Move(FGameScore);
  }
}
```

All the logic for moving the characters is buried in the TMainMan and TBadMan objects. Taken on a character-by-character basis, this logic is pretty simple. If I had tried to include it in the program's main form, it would have soon become unmanageable. I avoid that quagmire by simply delegating the logic to a secondary object.

Likewise, I write the following code when it comes time to actually draw the new state of the board:

```
void TForm1::DrawBackground()
{
  TSpriteAry Sprites;

  Sprites[svDot] = DotSprite;
  Sprites[svVert] = VertSprite;
  Sprites[svBlank] = BlankSprite;

  FGameScore->Board->Draw(Hermes1, Sprites);
}

void TForm1::DrawBadGuy(int Value)
{
  FBadMen[Value]->Draw(Hermes1, FBadMen[Value]->Sprite);
}

void TForm1::DrawMan()
{
  FMainMan->Draw(Hermes1, ManSprite);
}
```

Except for a little setup in the DrawBackground() method, the act of drawing a character to the screen consists of nothing more than calling its Draw() method. When I call the Draw() method, I pass in entire objects as parameters. This approach could be a way to get myself in trouble, particularly if I started letting these objects access one another's private data. I don't do that; instead, I carefully force each object to access other objects through a defined interface.

The act of sharing data between two components creates two components that are bound together in an unnatural way. To understand how I use data hiding to avoid cross-linking objects, you might want to consider the way the `TBoard` object from the `Grid1` unit is defined. Each individual maze is defined as a two-dimensional array of `int`s:

```
typedef int TGrid[MaxY][MaxX];

TGrid Data1 =
    {{1, 1, 1, 1, 1, 1, 1, 1, 1, 1, 1, 1, 1, 1, 1, 1, 1, 1, 1},
     {1, 0, 0, 0, 0, 0, 0, 0, 0, 0, 0, 0, 0, 0, 0, 0, 0, 0, 1},
     {1, 0, 1, 1, 1, 0, 1, 1, 1, 1, 1, 1, 1, 1, 0, 1, 1, 1, 0, 1},
     {1, 0, 1, 1, 1, 0, 1, 1, 1, 1, 1, 1, 1, 1, 0, 1, 1, 1, 0, 1},
     {1, 0, 1, 1, 1, 0, 1, 1, 1, 1, 1, 1, 1, 1, 0, 1, 1, 1, 0, 1},
     {1, 0, 1, 1, 1, 0, 1, 1, 1, 1, 1, 1, 1, 1, 0, 1, 1, 1, 0, 1},
     {1, 0, 0, 0, 0, 0, 0, 0, 0, 0, 0, 0, 0, 0, 0, 0, 0, 0, 1},
     {1, 0, 1, 1, 1, 0, 1, 1, 1, 1, 1, 1, 1, 1, 0, 1, 1, 1, 0, 1},
     {1, 0, 1, 1, 1, 0, 1, 1, 1, 1, 1, 1, 1, 1, 0, 1, 1, 1, 0, 1},
     {1, 0, 1, 1, 1, 0, 1, 1, 1, 1, 1, 1, 1, 1, 0, 1, 1, 1, 0, 1},
     {1, 0, 1, 1, 1, 0, 1, 1, 1, 1, 1, 1, 1, 1, 0, 1, 1, 1, 0, 1},
     {1, 0, 0, 0, 0, 0, 0, 0, 0, 0, 0, 0, 0, 0, 0, 0, 0, 0, 1},
     {1, 1, 1, 1, 1, 1, 1, 1, 1, 1, 1, 1, 1, 1, 1, 1, 1, 1, 1}};
```

Every time I list the number 1, I want to draw a wall in the maze, and when I list the number 0, I am defining part of the hallway. The `TBoard` object has four `TGrid` objects.

The rubber meets the road at this point. I could have set up an array of `TGrid` objects. A `TGrid` array is easy to work with, and just giving other objects direct access to this array of data is supremely tempting. For example, I could have created a `Data` property with `read` and `write` methods called `GetData()` and `SetData()`. In this case, the `GetData()` and `SetData()` methods would give you direct access to the currently selected maze in the array.

The problem with using this approach is that it gives other objects direct access to the underlying data structures upon which the mazes are built. If you do so, a number of things can start going wrong:

- You are locked into this one data format. If you ever want to change the format, you would have to rewrite not only this object, but any object that is using its data.

- The other objects would have to deal with the quirks of the way this data is stored, which could lead to errors. For instance, the `TGrid` object stores points in Y-X order rather than X-Y order: `MyMazePoint = Grid[Y][X]`. Here, the rows are stored before the columns, which is the opposite order from which PC programmers generally work. As a result, you can accidentally write `MyMazePoint = Grid[X][Y]`, thereby introducing a bug.

- After you give a second object a piece of data, the object might start doing things with the data that are not properly part of its domain. For instance, if a secondary object wanted to zero out the dots in a grid, it might be tempted to perform that task itself because it already has direct access to the grid. A task like that should be taken care of by the TBoard object itself via a method with a name such as TBoard::ClearDots(). By not sharing data with other objects, you can help remind the other objects not to overstep their bounds; in the process, you remind yourself to add methods such as ClearDots() to the proper object.

Instead of giving other objects direct access to the underlying grid, I provide a set of access methods:

```
void SetDataXY(int X, int Y, int Value);
int GetDataXY(int X, int Y);
```

If another object wants to know what's going on at a particular point in the grid, it can use these methods. Notice that the parameters to the methods are declared in X-Y order, so they follow the conventions of traditional PC programming. The SetDataXY() and GetDataXY() methods perform the translation from X-Y to Y-X.

This technique is slower from a performance perspective than giving other objects direct access to internal data. If I had completed the project and decided that performance was a problem, I might have revisited this issue. This program runs at 59 frames per second on my mid-range 266MHz computer with a 4MB video card; running 59 frames a second is pretty darn fast. You also need to consider that 8MB and 12MB video cards are becoming standard, and 500MHz and even 1,000MHz machines are just around the corner. Furthermore, if I did allow these objects to share data, this sharing would probably not affect the frame rate at all; I am almost certain that it would not raise the rate more than one or two frames per second. In other words, I doubt that this part of the program is a good candidate for optimizations because these optimizations are unlikely to significantly improve overall performance.

NOTE

One extremely interesting footnote to this matter is the fact that on my STB NVIDIA card, my program runs much faster in windowed mode than it does in exclusive mode. I am seeing rates of 131 frames per second when I go into windowed mode on this machine, which is blindingly fast. On all other machines, exclusive mode is nearly twice as fast as windowed mode. Things go the opposite way on this particular machine, which is a somewhat mind-boggling fact.

Running 131 frames per second is too fast for this program.

Notes on Implementing the BCBMan Program

By this time, you should understand the main objects from which the BCBMan program is made. I will now add a short overview of the program's structure so that you can easily begin working with it and learn the details of its construction.

The program starts by creating the main objects needed during a run of the game:

```
void __fastcall TForm1::FormCreate(TObject *Sender)
{
  FMainMan = new TMainMan();
  FGameScore = new TGameScore();
  SetupBadMen();

  ClientHeight = 480;
  ClientWidth = 640;
  Application->OnIdle = IdleProc;
}
```

Here, I create the MainMan object and call SetupBadMen() to create the three vicious characters that roam the maze:

```
void TForm1::SetupBadMen()
{
  int i;
  for (i = 0; i <  MaxBadMen; i++)
  {
    FBadMen[i] = new TBadMan();
    FBadMen[i]->GridX = 18;
    FBadMen[i]->GridY = 11;
    FBadMen[i]->XPos = FBadMen[i]->GridX * DibSize;
    FBadMen[i]->YPos = FBadMen[i]->GridY * DibSize;
    FBadMen[i]->RequestDir = tdUp;
    FBadMen[i]->Sprite = (TSprite *)
      (FindComponent("BadSprite" + IntToStr(i + 1)));
  }
}
```

This code simply defines the startup position for each of the bad guys, tells them the direction they should move when the game starts, and assigns them a TSprite object. Each of the sprites is represented by a TSprite component on the program's main form.

The FormCreate() method also creates an instance of the TGameScore object, which in turn instantiates an instance of the TBoard object. The code also ensures that the main form is 640×480 in size, has an active OnIdle event, and that the TZounds component has a sound it can play when the main man eats a dot.

The following code is executed when the OnShow event for the game form is fired:

```
void __fastcall TForm1::FormShow(TObject *Sender)
```

```
{
  AnsiString S = "Temp1.wav";
  Zounds1->OpenFile(S, 1);
  Hermes1->Run();
  PostMessage(Handle, WM_STARTALL, 0, 0);
}
```

After opening the TEMP1.WAV sound file, this code initializes the Artemis components by calling Run(). The Run() method ensures that CoCreateInstance() is called to create the DirectDraw interface, that the DirectDraw surfaces are set up properly, and that the video screen is set to the right mode.

After setting up the components, I post a WM_STARTALL message to the main form. WM_STARTALL is a custom message designed for use in this one program:

```
#define WM_STARTALL WM_USER
```

The message handler for the message looks like this:

```
void TForm1::WMStartAll(TMessage &Msg)
{
  DrawBackground();
  Hermes1->Flip();
  Hermes1->Flip();
  Hermes1->Active = False;
}
```

WMStartAll() is called after the form has been shown to the user. If I called it from the OnShow event handler, the form would not have been drawn to the screen and DirectX might not handle the drawing correctly in windowed mode. The job of the WMStartAll() method is to simply paint the maze to the screen and then set the Hermes1 component in the inactive state so that no animation occurs before the user is ready to begin the game.

When the user is ready to start playing, she presses Alt+S, which is handled by the FormKeyDown() method:

```
void __fastcall TForm1::FormKeyDown(TObject *Sender, WORD &Key,
    TShiftState Shift)
{
  if (Key == VK_ESCAPE)
  {
    Close();
    return;
  }

  if (Shift.Contains(ssAlt))
  {
    switch (Char(Key))
    {
```

```
    case 'X':
    {
      Close();
      Form2->Close();
      return;
    }
    case 'S': {
      FGameScore->Status = gsRunning;
      Hermes1->Active = true;
    }
  }
}
switch (Key)
{
  case VK_LEFT: FMainMan->RequestDir = tdLeft; break;
  case VK_RIGHT: FMainMan->RequestDir = tdRight; break;
  case VK_DOWN: FMainMan->RequestDir = tdDown; break;
  case VK_UP: FMainMan->RequestDir = tdUp; break;
}
}
```

FormKeyDown() closes the game form if the user presses Esc or Alt+X. It also notifies the main man sprite if the user wants to move in a new direction. The most important role it has is to set Hermes1->Active to true if the user is ready to play.

If Active is true, then the IdleProc() method can be used as an engine to drive the program's animation:

```
void __fastcall TForm1::IdleProc(TObject *Sender, bool &Done)
{
  Done = false;
  if (Hermes1->Active)
  {
    Move();
    Hermes1->Flip();
    CheckGameStatus();
    CheckFrameCount();
  }
}
```

The idle loop sets the Done parameter to false, which ensures that C++Builder will call the method again the moment it is free to do so. The code then calls the Move() method, which calculates the next position for the bad guys and the main man. I then flip the surfaces, which draws the characters to the screen.

Each time the THermes object's Flip() method is called, a method called SpriteScene1DrawScene() gets called. This method is the event handler for the TSpriteScene's OnDrawScene event. Here's how it looks:

```
void __fastcall TForm1::SpriteScene1DrawScene(TObject *Sender,
    IDirectDrawSurface *Surface)
{
  int i;
  if (Hermes1->DrawState == tsDrawAll)
    DrawBackground();
  DrawMan();
  for (i = 0; i < MaxBadMen; i++)
    DrawBadGuy(i);
  DrawStats();
}
```

This event is set up to give the developer a chance to do any custom drawing to the screen just before the surfaces are flipped. Here, for instance, is the code that ends up drawing the bad guy or main man sprite to the screen:

```
void TRobot::Draw(THermes *Hermes1, TSprite *Sprite)
{
  HRESULT hr;

  RECT R = Sprite->SpriteBounds;

  hr = Hermes1->BackSurface->BltFast(XPos, YPos,
    Sprite->Surface, &R,
    DDBLTFAST_WAIT | DDBLTFAST_SRCCOLORKEY);
  if ((FAILED(hr)) && (hr != DDERR_SURFACELOST))
    Hermes1->Active = false;
}
```

`BltFast()` is a method of the `IDirectDrawSurface` object that paints a bitmap on a surface with the fastest methods available on any particular system. Notice that I perform the bit blit from the `Sprite` surface object to the `BackSurface` object. After this method executes, `THermes` calls `IDirectDraw::Flip()`, which flips the back surface and the primary surface and shows the user the new state of affairs.

Controlling the Robots

The characters that move in the maze always have momentum that carries them in a particular direction. The momentum is implemented using the same techniques shown for animating the objects in the preceding chapter.

Each time one of the bad guys reaches a turning point in the maze, it has a 50-50 chance of taking the turn or of continuing on in the same direction. I use the `random()` function to calculate the odds of one of the bad guys making a turn in a new direction.

The user controls the main man. As you saw in the `FormKeyDown()` method, the main man has a `RequestDir` property, which stores the direction the user wants the main man to move. Whenever the main man reaches a turning point in the maze, it checks the

RequestDir property; if it specifies a direction to take, then the main man heads off in that new direction. For instance, the following code is executed if the user wants to turn to the right:

```
switch (RequestDir)
{
  case tdRight:
  {
    Data = Board->GetDataXY(GridX + 1, GridY);
    if (((YPos % DibSize) == 0) && (DataIsDotOrBlank(Data)))
      Direction = tdRight;
    break;
  }
  // Code for turning in other directions omitted...
}
```

If you can evenly divide (using the modulus operator) the current Y position by the size of the character's bitmap, the character might be lined up along one of the empty hallways in the maze. To confirm this fact, I check the current tile in the maze that is immediately to the character's right. The character is free to turn to the right if it is a dot or a blank; I set the character's new direction to tdRight. If it is not a dot or a blank, then the position next to the main character is either a bad guy or a wall of the maze. In either case, he can't turn and will continue in the current direction. He is probably about to be eaten if the character next to him is a bad guy, but I don't try to confirm that logic in this method. Instead, I let a different custom routine handle that situation.

Considerably more code is used to control the movements of the characters. However, most of it is similar to what I have shown you here, so I do not bother to discuss it in this text, though you may want to pursue the subject with the BCBMan source code and with the aid of the debugger.

Summarizing the BCBMan Program

I showed you how to put together a game using C++Builder and DirectX. If you are interested in this technology, I'm sure you will want to dig into this code a little more deeply than I have in this book. You do have the outline for how to proceed and an example of how to start creating your own interactive games.

A Brief Look at Direct3D

You will find two programs on the CD-ROM that accompanies this book—Direct3DView and Room3D—that show you how to use the Direct3D API in a C++Builder program. Unfortunately, this subject is much too complicated to explain in this chapter. I will give a brief overview of the subject so that you have a place to start when you begin examining the programs on your own.

The Direct3DView program is part of a Direct3D program written by the highly talented John Thomas. When the program starts, you are given the chance of selecting a file with an .x extension (an X file); such are a Microsoft format for describing three-dimensional objects. For instance, if you want to draw a cube to the screen, you can define it as a series of points and lines in space. The points define the four corners of the cube, and the lines define the edges of the cube. You can also store color and shading information in an X file. I have included a few X files on the CD-ROM that accompanies this book, and you can get many more from the Microsoft DirectX Web site and from the Microsoft DirectX Development Kit. Microsoft offers utilities that convert 3DS files from 3D Studio format to X files.

After you have loaded a mesh from an X file, the next step is to select a texture that will be painted on the mesh. When you are playing Wolfenstein, Doom, or Quake, the walls and buildings you see are not just simple line drawings; they appear to be made of brick, stone, wood, or some other real-world substance. These materials are actually just bitmaps painted on top of the points and lines that form the framework for a scene. These bitmaps are called *textures*, and they are a key ingredient in most of the 3D code you see in contemporary games.

When the Direct3DView program loads, it gives you a chance to select not only a mesh, but a texture that can be painted on top of the mesh. Combining these two objects allows you to view a rotatable 3D object like the one shown in Figure 26.5.

FIGURE 26.5

The Direct3DView program allows you to manipulate 3D objects such as this spaceship.

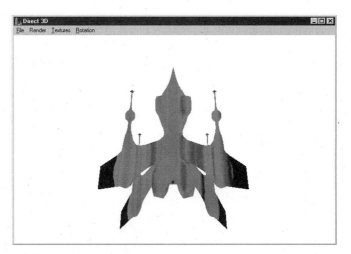

Now that the basics of Direct3D have been covered, take a look at some other Direct3D technologies.

Key 3D Technologies

Direct3D programmers have a choice between two different technologies: immediate mode and retained mode. Immediate mode is very low level and difficult to use. It is also very fast. Retained mode is based on a series of relatively high-level functions for manipulating 3D objects. The code used in the Direct3DView and Room3D programs is all retained mode code. One of the great benefits of using retained mode is that it lets you work directly with X files rather than having to individually define all the nodes and polygons in your objects. A third, non–DirectX technology is called OpenGL. It is similar to Direct3D immediate mode, but it is not covered in this book.

You need a way to describe 3D spaces when working with Direct3D. The keystone for describing a 3D space is the origin. The *origin* is the base point from which all other points in the scene are defined. The origin is usually defined as resting at point 0, 0, 0.

Three-dimensional space has three axes: X, Y, and Z. A *point* is an infinitely small area in space described by three values, one for each axis. A *vector* is a line between two points. *Planes* are flat surfaces that extend infinitely in two directions. A *vertex* is a point used to describe the corners of a face. In Direct3D, a *face* is a triangular area on a plane.

You can describe 3D shapes with a mesh, usually built in a third-party tool and stored in an X file. A *mesh* is made up of a series of faces. *Normals* are vectors used to describe the colors of the faces in a mesh. You control a mesh with the `IDirect3DRMMesh` or `IDirect3DRMMeshBuilder` interfaces. The `IDirect3DRMMeshBuilder` interface is easier to use, but it is slower. (3DRM stands for 3D retained mode.)

The act of moving a 3D object through space in Direct3D is called a *translation*. If you change the size of a 3D object, then you are *scaling* it. To turn an object in Direct3D, you *rotate* it. You can move objects in several ways in a Direct3D program, but you often use the `IDirect3DRMMeshBuilder` or `IDirect3DRMMeshBuilderFrame` interfaces.

Textures and materials are bitmaps painted on a mesh. Textures are what Wolfenstein, Doom, and Quake are all about. You can scale, wrap, and animate textures by using the `IDirect3DRMTexture` and the `IDirect3DRmTextureWrap` interfaces.

A material controls whether an object is shiny, dull, or appears to emit light. Use the `IDirect3DRMMaterial` interface to control this feature.

Lights in Direct3D can be colored, or they can be just plain white ramp lights. *Ambient lights* illuminate an entire scene, whereas a point light emanates in all directions from one location. *Directional lights* come from one direction but have no particular origin. *Spot lights* produce light in a cone shape. You can manipulate lights in Direct3D with the `Direct3DRMLight` interface, which is created by the `CreateLight()` and

CreateLightRGB() functions. You can use the AddLight() method of the IDirect3DRMFrame interface to attach lights to a frame.

Z Buffering is a technique that ensures that time is not wasted drawing surfaces that are never shown to the user. Rendering is performed in front to back order, so hidden surfaces are never drawn. A program running in 800×600 16-bit mode requires a megabyte of memory to render a single frame.

You can render a scene in several ways. WireFrame mode draws only the edges of a face. Unlit scenes render quickly, but objects appear flat and lifeless. Flat mode renders a mesh with each face completely flat; it uses face normals. Gouraud shading uses vertex normals, and light intensities are averaged over the face to create realistic effects. Phong shading uses vertex normals and calculates light intensities over the face to create very smooth, pleasing shapes that look like real-world objects.

Animating an object in Direct3D is fairly easy. Motion attributes will allow you to translate, rotate, or scale an object. Key-framing technologies allow you to declare a path's starting and ending points. The computer then moves the object from point A to point B over a vector or spline path. You can do so by using the IDirect3DRMAnimation interface.

This brief overview of Direct3D should give you a starting point when you begin digging into the sample programs on the CD-ROM. A considerable amount of additional information is available in the Microsoft DirectX SDK.

> **NOTE**
>
> Before I call any Direct3D methods, I pass a constant to the C++Builder Set8087CW() method:
>
> ```
> Set8087CW(0x133f);
> ```
>
> This code disables all floating-point exceptions, which makes the Borland compiler compatible with Microsoft's floating-point routines. Additional information is available on the Intel Web site, where you can see how to handle floating-point code.

Summary

Material covered in this chapter includes a discussion of DirectSound, an overview of a set of components that can be used to help you add RAD technology to your game development, and a brief look at Direct3D. Perhaps the most interesting portions of the chapter show how to put together a Pacman-like game in which a good guy runs through a perilous maze while being pursued by fiendish monsters.

Some day I would like to write an entire book on game and multimedia development. *C++Builder 4 Unleashed*, however, wasn't the place to go into these subjects in depth. Instead, I showed you a few simple DirectX technologies that you can use in your own programs. This code should be enough to show you how to get started using the powerful DirectX code bases in your own programs.

You should be aware that I have only touched the surface of DirectX technologies. The new DirectMusic code in DirectX 6 provides a rich playing field for professional musicians who want to work with Windows. DirectInput helps you work with mice and joysticks. Other important DirectX topics include network support, DirectAnimation, and DirectMovie.

C++Builder is a great platform for game development, and I hope the last two chapters of this book have provided you with enough information to get started using DirectX to create games of simulations. Of course, I also hope that you have had some fun playing with this great technology, and that it has perhaps given you a little spark of enthusiasm that will help you derive more pleasure from your career or hobby as a programmer.

Finally, I want to close this chapter and the book with a prediction that the DirectX API will prove to be much more important in the computer world than some might suspect. Over the next few years, we are going to get machines that will run Windows the same way our current machines run DOS. In other words, they will whiz through standard Windows code in no time, leaving developers free to add new features to those programs. My bet is that sound 3D graphics and real-world simulations will take up a lot of those free clock cycles.

DirectDraw, DirectSound, and Direct3D are likely to start playing very important roles in standard programming technology when people decide to start building programs that simulate real-world scenes. After all, why provide a database that lets you look up volumes in a library if you can create an actual library simulation that lets you browse the shelves of a set of virtual stacks? Why have people learn how to use a database when you can create a 3D simulation that looks and feels like a real filing cabinet or that lets you walk down the corridors of a real building? These possibilities sound like science fiction to us now, but almost everything covered in this book would have sounded like science fiction 20 years ago.

INDEX

SYMBOLS

+ (plus) sign, 363
-> (arrow) operator, 616
. (dot) operators, 616
3D graphics
Direct3D, see Direct3D
DirectDraw, 1095
4GB address space, 182

A

Abort parameter, 67
abort variable, 66
About property editors,
92-94
AboutBox form (ADDRESS2
program example), 439
AbuseAFoo( ) function, 158
access
Fields Editor, 369
rights (InterBase server),
532-534
threads, 199-200
critical sections, 200-206
mutexes, 206-211
AComponent parameter, 109
Action Editor, 766-767
Actions property, 766
Active property, 947
Active Template Library
(ATL), 138, 604
ActiveControl property, 456
ActiveForm wizard, 927-928
ActiveForms, 926-927
CAB files, 933-937
connecting to, 930-932
creating, 927-928
deployment, 928-929, 932
OCCACHE directory,
932-933
redeployment, 932
setting up, 929-930
INF files, 937-938
licensing, 938-939

MIDAS
creating, 946-948
sockets, 943-944
testing, 948-950
troubleshooting, 948
naming, 927
packages, 933-934
sockets, 943-946
templates, 942-943
testing, 933
Word (Microsoft), 939-942
ActiveX controls, 926
ActiveForms, *see* ActiveForms
SDK (WinInet), 802
Server, *see* ActiveX Server
ActiveX Server, 597
ATL options page, 605-606
COM (Component Object
Model), 597
implementation files,
601-602
project file, 597-601
Add Fields dialog,
369-370
Add Property dialog, 32
Add( ) method, 304
AddCode key, 464
AddIcon( ) function, 274-275
AddLight( ) method, 1166
AddPassword method, 488
AddRef( ) method, 585, 588
address books (KdAdd pro-
gram), 462-466
cascading deletes, 484-485
data module, 473-476, 480
deleting data, 480-483
header, 466, 468-469
indexes, 465-466, 477-478
inserting data, 479
keys, 464-465
NameCode, 464
posting data, 485-486
referential integrity, 465
searches, 478-479
source code, 469-472
string resources, 486-487

tab sheets, 477
undoing errors, 479-480
Address property, 483,
947-948
address spaces (processes),
181-183
ADDRESS2 program example,
403, 461
AboutBox form, 439
application design, 404
bits.rc file, 439
Clipboard, 456-457
Color Class Unit, 430-436
Colors menu, 449-453
command designs, 416-417
data module, 436-439
database design, 404-407
FilterDlg form, 439
filtering, 445-446
header, 421-424
main form, 410-413, 424-430
marking files, 447-449
object design, 419-420
program design, 407-410
Read-Only mode, 440-442
Registry, 453-456
rough draft, 417-419
searches, 443-445
sorting, 442-443
TDBLookupCombo control,
413-415
AddressSourceDataChanged( )
method, 447
AddTables( ) method, 498
AfterInstall event (TService
class), 244
AfterUninstall event
(TService class), 244
agentaddr file, 958
aggregation (components),
43-47
window handles, 47-49
AlbumTableBeforePost( )
function, 556
algorithms, STL (Standard
Template Library), 168
find, 168-169
max( ), 169

H

X-Y-Z

C++Builder Resources

Following is a list of resources for C++Builder programmers. The list includes books, periodicals, and Internet resources. In particular, be sure to check out the Internet resources as a source of good, free information regarding C++Builder programming.

Books

Sams Teach Yourself C++Builder 3 in 21 Days by Kent Reisdorph; Sams Publishing

Borland C++Builder How-To by John Miano, Harold Howe, and Tom Cabanski; Waite Group Press

Developing Custom Delphi Components by Ray Konopka; The Coriolis Group

Delphi Component Design by Danny Thorpe; Addison Wesley

Internet Resources

The Bits: `http://www.richplum.co.uk/cbuilder`

BCBDEV.COM: `http://www.bcbdev.com`

Dr. Bob's C++Builder, Gate: `http://www.drbob42.com/cbuilder`

Robert Dunn's RichEdit Site: `http://home.att.net/~robertdunn/Yacs.html`

Reisdorph Publishing: `http://www.reisdorph.com/bcb`

borland.com: `http://www.borland.com`

Inprise: `http://www.inprise.com`

Borland Newsgroups: point your newsreader to `forums.borland.com` or `forums.inprise.com`

Periodicals

C++Builder Developer's Journal. Reisdorph Publishing; `http://www.reisdorph.com`

Visual Developer Magazine. The Coriolis Group; `http://www.visual-developer.com`

What's on the Disc

The companion CD-ROM contains all of the authors' source code and samples from the book and some third-party software products.

Windows 95, Windows 98, and Windows NT 4 Installation Instructions

1. Insert the CD-ROM disc into your CD-ROM drive.
2. From the desktop, double-click on the My Computer icon.
3. Double-click on the icon representing your CD-ROM drive.
4. Double-click on the icon titled START.EXE to run the installation program.
5. Follow the onscreen instructions to finish the installation.

NOTE

If Windows 95, Windows 98, or Windows NT 4 is installed on your computer, and you have the AutoPlay feature enabled, the START.EXE program starts automatically whenever you insert the disc into your CD-ROM drive.